Queensland

Hugh Finlay
Andrew Humphreys
Mark Armstrong

Queensland

2nd edition

Published by
Lonely Planet Publications ABN 36 005 607 983
90 Maribyrnong St, Footscray Victoria 3011, Australia

Head Office:	Locked Bag 1, Footscray, Victoria 3011, Australia
Branches:	150 Linden Street, Oakland CA 94607, USA
	10a Spring Place, London NW5 3BH, UK
	1 rue du Dahomey, 75011 Paris, France

Printed by
The Bookmaker International Ltd
Printed in China

Photographs by

David Andrew	Rob Drummond	Chris Klep	David Sherman
Mark Armstrong	Gadi Farfour	Holger Leue	Tony Wheeler
Michael Aw	Simon Foale	R & V Moon	Steve Womersley
Robert Charleton	Healesville Sanctuary	Richard Nebesky	
David Curl	Richard I'Anson	Queensland Tourist &	
Sally Dillon	IndyCar Australia	Travel Corporation	

Front cover: Wanggodba Creek, Fraser Island (Richard I'Anson, Lonely Planet Images)

First Published
January 1996

This Edition
January 1999

Although the authors and publisher have tried to make the information as accurate as possible, they accept no responsibility for any loss, injury or inconvenience sustained by any person using this book.

National Library of Australia Cataloguing in Publication Data

Finlay, Hugh
Queensland.

2nd ed.
Includes index.
ISBN 0 86442 590 2.

I. Queensland - Description and travel - 1990- .
2. Queensland - Guidebooks. I. Humphreys, Andrew, 1965- .
II. Armstrong, Mark, 1961- . III. Title

919.430466

Hugh Finlay

Deciding there must be more to life than civil engineering, Hugh took off around Australia in the mid-70s, working at everything from spray painting to diamond prospecting before hitting the overland trail. He joined Lonely Planet in 1985 and has written *Jordan & Syria* and *Northern Territory*, co-authored *Kenya* and *Morocco, Algeria & Tunisia*, and updated *Nepal* and the Queensland chapter of *Australia*. He lives in central Victoria with his partner, Linda, and daughters Ella and Vera.

Andrew Humphreys

Andrew is a big fan of rugby league, cold Castlemaine XXXX and hot sun. He's far too widely travelled to even think about listing the countries here and he's worked in journalism since 1991. This book included, he's authored, co-authored or updated some ten titles for Lonely Planet, although under pressure he'll admit that none of it would have been possible without the assistance of his wife Gadi. She also sat next to him in a lot of buses and cars in Queensland.

Mark Armstrong

Mark was born in Melbourne and completed his tertiary studies at the University of Melbourne. Among other things, he has worked in computer sales and marketing, as a restorer of old houses, as a fencing contractor and in the hospitality industry. He has lived in Barcelona for a while and has travelled in South-East Asia, Europe and north America. Since 1992 he has worked on several LP guides, including *Victoria, Australia, Islands of Australia's Great Barrier Reef, Melbourne* and *Spain*.

From the Authors

Hugh Many thanks to all the people who gave their time, energy and hospitality. In particular, thanks to Brits:Australia for their assistance.

Andrew Many people gave up their time to help me in my research without any money ever changing hands – some of them even bought *me* drinks. I'm extremely grateful to far too many people to mention here, but some of those who must be singled out for thanks and praise include Nick Earls (buy his books, they'll make you laugh), Davi Gibson, Brisbane historian and the best ma to ride a City Cat with, Mark the singin ranger of Fraser Island, Dominique Whit of the QTTC, Casey O'Hare of Brisban Tourism, Denis J Casey of Queensland Rai Gerard Ross of the Queensland Writers' As sociation and Brett Murray of IndyCa Australia.

Extra special thanks go to Jeff, Aliso and Callum for their reckless loan of house, car and computer. The BBQs an Westcoasters were much appreciated too.

This Book

The 1st edition of *Queensland* was researched and written by Mark Armstrong. This 2nd edition was updated by Hugh Finlay (northern Queensland) and Andrew Humphreys (southern Queensland).

From the Publisher

This edition was produced at Lonely Planet Melbourne. Thanks to David Andrew, Clay Lucas, Chris Wyness and Ada Cheung for editing and proofing; Anne Mulvaney for proofing; and Mary Neighbour and Ada Cheung for indexing. Thanks to Louise Klep for layout, design and her unerring attention to detail; Lisa Borg, Tony Fankhauser, Chris Lee Ack and Piotr Czajkowski for extra mapping; Margie Jung for the cover design; Mick Weldon for the cartoon; and Tim Uden for all his help.

Warning & Request

Things change - prices go up, schedules change, good places go bad and bad places go bankrupt — nothing stays the same. So, if you find things better or worse, recently opened or long since closed, please tell us and help make the next edition even more accurate and useful.

We value all of the feedback we receive from travellers. Julie Young coordinates a team who read and acknowledge every letter, postcard and email, and ensure that every morsel of information finds its way to the appropriate authors, editors and publishers.

Everyone who writes to us will find their name in the next edition of the appropriate guide, and will also receive a free subscription to our quarterly newsletter, *Planet Talk*. The very best contributions will be rewarded with a free Lonely Planet guide.

Excerpts from your correspondence may appear in new editions of this guide; in our newsletter, *Planet Talk*; or in updates on our Web site — so please let us know if you don't want your letter published or your name acknowledged.

Thanks

Many thanks to the travellers who used the last edition and wrote to us with helpful hints, useful advice and interesting anecdotes. Your names follow:

Bernadette & Warren, Richard Adams, Fiona Allan, Rachel Askham, John Atwood, Eva Bach-Moore, James Bain, Bill & Marian Barnes, Asat Begerano, Chris Bentley, Din Bhumgara, Nina Beynon, Shelly Blackmore, Edgar Boniface, Alex Bortoli, Pat Botham, Dr SJ Bourne, Philip Britton, Suzanne Brown, Caroline Buchanan, Meike Buhlmann, Kevin Burke, Beverley Burns, Karen Burt, Belinda Callow, Michael Cave, Zelmer Chessen, Robert Colman, Jill Colquhoun, Val Coombe, Karen Cooper, Gil Debeze, Dr Monica Dematte, Helen de Roo, G & J Dobson, Joshua A Drew, Jane Dunn, Lesley Durn, Marc Dyer, Lyn Eather, Anne Eddison, Jean-Paul & Elsbeth Fahrner, Craig Farr, Janet Ferguson, Sheryl Fever, Tom Fisher, Anna Foares, Antonella Gallo, Ed Griffin, Cheryl Haisch, Hanno Haisch, R Hall, K Hanks, Isabel Hay, Susanne Heckeroth, Clotilde Henriot, Steve Hill, Bill Hines, Rachel Hirschfeld, Witold Horbowski, Jean Jacques, Franki Jay, Karen Jensen, Helen Jonas, Barnie Jones, Alistair Kelly, Dave Kelly, Meaghan Keppie, V Kerin, Claudia Klaassen, Anke Kotte, Eric Kuttunen, Harriet Lammin, Vicki McDonald, Angela McKay, Nina McKenna, Keren McSweeney, Jaylean Mead, Deena Miller, Dr Simon Modi, Sue Mooney, Lillian Moore, Alan Morris, Reiner Parzefall, M & M Paterson, Monica Pokorny, Di Pollard, Darren Poulianakis, Barry & Victoria Price, Morna Prince, Iain & Sue Ralston, J Randall, Jenny Rankin, Peter Reeve, Sue Rolfe, Darren Rose, Cathleen Rusden, Simone Rutishauser, Rosa Salinas, Andres Schwerdtle, Eric Scott, Wendy Shallard, Holly Sherman, Cliona Sherwin, R Shoesmith, Rogier Souverein, Shirley Stockdale, Paul Storm, Nicolas Stricher, M B Such, Lucy Sweetman, Richard Tan, Garry Telford, Deon Tucker, John-Paul Vass, Mr & Mrs Keith Walker, Roxanne Winkler, Ian Woolfenden, Hilary Wunsch

Contents

NORTH COAST **351**

FAR NORTH QUEENSLAND **398**

CAPE YORK PENINSULA **478**

GULF SAVANNAH **508**

OUTBACK QUEENSLAND 525

GLOSSARY 564

INDEX 568

Map Legend

BOUNDARIES

------- .... State Boundary

— — — — — — — — — .... Marine Park

ROUTES

============== .... Major Road

============== .... Minor Road

============== .... City Road

============== .... City Street

============== .... City Lane

├─┼─┼─┼──●──┼─┤ .... Train Route, with Station

╫─╫─╫─╫─╫─╫─╫─╫ .... Cable Car

- - - - - - - - - .... Ferry Route

— — — — — — — — .... Walking Track

AREA FEATURES

.... Beach

.... Building

.... National Park

+ + + + + + + + ... Cemetery (Christian)

✿ .... Park, Gardens

.... Reef

HYDROGRAPHIC FEATURES

.... Coastline

.... Creek, River

.... Lake

)) .... Waterfalls

.... Swamp

SYMBOLS

◉	CAPITAL	.... State Capital
●	CITY	.... City
●	Town	.... Town
●	Village	.... Village
■		.... Place to Stay
▼		.... Place to Eat
✚		.... Airfield
✈		.... Airport
❸		.... Bank
⬈		.... Beach
⚑		.... Camping Ground
ⱪ		.... Caravan Park

▦	.... Cathedral
⊞	.... Church
♿	.... Disabled Access
◥	.... Dive Site
⚐	.... Golf Course
✛	.... Hospital
❶	.... Information
☀	.... Lookout
⚰	.... Monument
▲	.... Mountain or Hill
⌒⌒	.... Mountain Range
🏛	.... Museum
⚑	.... National Park
Ⓟ	.... Parking

◖	.... Petrol Station
★	.... Police Station
○	.... Point of Interest
✉	.... Post Office
⚐	.... Pub or Bar
∴	.... Ruins
⚓	.... Shipwreck
❖	.... Shopping Centre
▣	.... Snorkelling
🏛	.... Stately Home
▭	.... Swimming Pool
■	.... Temple
⬤	.... Transport
➤	.... Zoo

Note: not all symbols displayed above appear in this book

Map Index

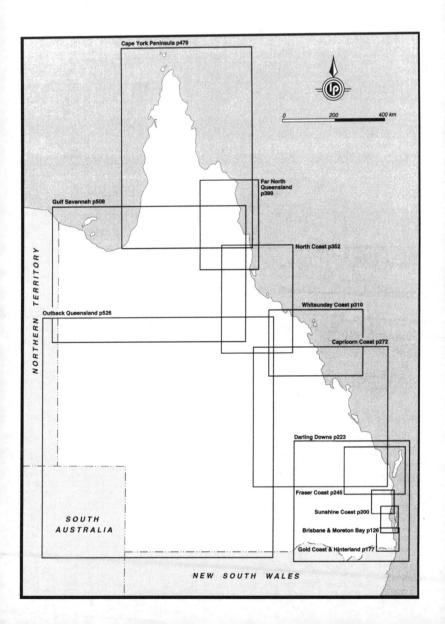

Cape York Peninsula p479

Far North Queensland p399

Gulf Savannah p508

North Coast p352

NORTHERN TERRITORY

Whitsunday Coast p310

Outback Queensland p526

Capricorn Coast p272

Darling Downs p223

Fraser Coast p245

SOUTH AUSTRALIA

Sunshine Coast p200

Brisbane & Moreton Bay p126

Gold Coast & Hinterland p177

NEW SOUTH WALES

0   200   400 km

Introduction

Queensland is a vast and often surprising place that is widely known as the 'Sunshine State' – an alluring land of blue skies, holidays and brighter tomorrows.

Queensland's popularity as a tourism destination is easily understood. Apart from the fact that the sun (almost) always shines, the state is blessed with an abundance of natural riches. Three areas – the Great Barrier Reef, the majestic Fraser Island and the Wet Tropics rainforests of the Far North – have been inscribed on the World Heritage List. In addition, there are dozens of stunning national parks which encompass a tremendous diversity of landscapes – from the red-sand wilds of the Simpson Desert to the dense greenery of the coastal forests, and from the oasis-like beauty of the Carnarvon Gorge to the ancient volcanic lava tubes at Undara.

The major resorts are sprinkled all the way up the east coast, and travellers have a choice between the hustle and bustle of places like the Gold Coast and Cairns and the smaller and more sophisticated 'boutique style' towns like Port Douglas and Noosa Heads. These developed resort towns contrast dramatically with Queensland's magnificent wilderness areas, which include places like the Cape York Peninsula, the Gulf Savannah, Hinchinbrook Island, and the vast and empty expanses of the mystical outback.

The Great Barrier Reef is sprinkled with coral cays and continental islands, and it isn't too difficult to find an island to suit

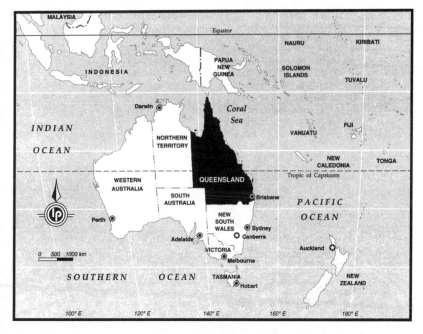

your particular fantasy, whether you want to string a tent between two palm trees on a deserted island or indulge yourself in a luxurious island resort. Or if you'd rather stay on the mainland, there's a veritable armada of operators offering trips out to the reef and its islands from the coastal towns.

Plenty of people head for Queensland wanting nothing more than a banana lounge and a beach, but if you're into outdoor activity you can choose from white-water rafting, scuba-diving and snorkelling on the Barrier Reef, bushwalking, rock climbing, horse riding, surfing and swimming, bungee jumping, skydiving, abseiling, birdwatching and more.

While there is a not-entirely-inaccurate perception that Queensland has laid itself bare at the altar of packaged tourism, the Sunshine State still has plenty to offer independent travellers who want to get off the beaten track. We're all looking for something different, so whether you just want to recline by the pool in the shade of a palm tree while sipping on multi-coloured cocktails or strap on a backpack and discover the undiscovered side of Queensland, this book should help point you in the right direction.

Facts about Queensland

HISTORY
Aborigines

It is believed that the ancestors of the Aborigines journeyed from South-East Asia to the Australian mainland at least 40,000 years ago, possibly much earlier. During the last Ice Age, land bridges connected Malaysia to Indonesia and Australia to New Guinea, but watercraft would still have been needed to reach Australia. These people may have made the perilous 120km sea journey across the Timor Sea to Australia, or they may have island-hopped across to Papua New Guinea and travelled overland into Australia. Either way, northern Queensland would have been their main entry point.

Although much of Australia is today arid, the first migrants found a much wetter continent, with large forests and many inland lakes teeming with fish. The fauna included giant marsupials such as 3m-tall kangaroos, giant koalas and wombats, and huge, flightless birds. The environment was relatively non-threatening – only a few carnivorous predators existed.

Archaeological evidence suggests that, with such favourable conditions, the descendants of these first settlers colonised the whole of the continent within a few thousand years.

As the last Ice Age ended around 15,000 to 10,000 years ago, sea levels rose and the Aborigines were isolated on the continent. Many of the inland lakes dried up and vast deserts formed, and the majority of the inhabitants lived in coastal areas.

By the time the Europeans arrived, it's estimated there were at least 300,000 Aborigines living in Australia and around 250 different languages spoken, many of them mutually unintelligible. Queensland was the most densely populated area, supporting as many as 100,000 to 120,000 people in about 200 tribal groups of between 500 and 1500 people each. The Cape York Peninsula alone may have supported up to 30,000 people.

Early European settlers considered the Aborigines to be a backward race. This assumption was based on the definition of civilisation being the progression from a hunter-gatherer society to an agricultural one. Failure to cultivate plants and crops and domesticate animals was seen as a failure to progress, but these theories have since been dismissed on the basis that the Aboriginal people had no need for agriculture. The land they lived in supplied them in abundance, and their survival and prosperity were a result of their deep understanding of a rich environment. In his book *Triumph of the Nomads*, Geoffrey Blainey writes that the average Aborigine, as far as food, health, warmth and shelter are concerned, probably enjoyed as good a standard of living as the average European in 1800.

Their semi-nomadic existence was a defining feature of their adaptation to the Australian landscape. This is amply evidenced by the fact that they were able to survive in areas Europeans would later consider to be uninhabitable.

Before his disappearance, the explorer Ludwig Leichhardt would write of the Aborigines:

They seem to have tasted everything from the highest top of the bunya tree and the seaforthia and cabbage palm, to the grub which lies in the rotten tree of the bush.

Coastal tribes lived on an amazingly wide variety of plants and vegetables, supplementing their diet with fish, turtles and dugong from the sea. Shellfish were collected and eaten on the beaches; evidence of these feasts in the form of huge shell middens have been found all along the Queensland coast, at places like Weipa, Fraser Island and Double Island Point.

Inland tribes were expert game hunters,

using nets to catch kangaroos, spears to kill emus and boomerangs to bring down birds. They also built stone dams in rivers to trap fish. In the arid north-west, the Kalkadoons dug wells up to 10m deep to supply themselves with water. The rainforests supplied wild berries and other plants, and the coastal mangroves provided them with food such as water-lily tubers and seeds, mangrove pods, crabs and shellfish.

They also had inter-tribal barter systems and well-developed trading routes which followed the major river systems in what is now Queensland. Cape York tribes were in regular contact with Torres Strait Islanders.

Ross Fitzgerald noted in his *History of Queensland* that the European settlers brought with them a notion of progress which upset the equilibrium between humans and nature, and which in turn ushered in the destruction of Aboriginal culture.

Because of the fragmented nature of Aboriginal society, which was based on family groups with an egalitarian political structure, a coordinated response to the European colonisers was not possible. Despite the presence of the Aborigines, the newly arrived Europeans considered the new continent to be *terra nullius* – a land belonging to no-one. Conveniently, they saw no recognisable system of government, no commerce or permanent settlements and no evidence of land ownership. Thus, when Governor Phillip raised the Union Jack at Sydney Cove in 1788, the laws of England became the laws governing all Aborigines on the Australian continent. All land in Australia was from that moment the property of the British Crown.

If the Aborigines had had a readily recognisable political system and had resisted colonisation by organised force, the English might have been forced to recognise a prior title to the land and therefore legitimise their colonisation by entering into a treaty with the Aboriginal landowners.

At a local level, individuals resisted the encroachment of settlers. Warriors including Pemulwy, Yagan, Dundalli, Pigeon and Nemarluk were, for a time, feared by the colonists in their areas. But, although some settlements had to be abandoned, the effect of such resistance was only to temporarily postpone the inevitable.

Without any legal right to the lands they once lived on, some Aborigines were driven from their lands by force, and some succumbed to exotic diseases. Other Aborigines voluntarily left their lands to travel to the fringes of settled areas to obtain new commodities such as steel and cloth, and experience hitherto unknown drugs such as tea, tobacco, alcohol and narcotics.

By the early 1900s legislation designed to segregate and 'protect' Aboriginal people was passed in all states. The legislation imposed restrictions on the Aborigines' right to own property and seek employment, and the Aboriginals' Ordinance of 1918 even allowed the state to remove children from Aboriginal mothers if it was suspected that the father was non-Aboriginal. In these cases the parents were considered to have no rights over the children, who were placed in foster homes or childcare institutions. Often referred to as the 'Stolen Generation', many are still understandably bitter about being separated from their families and made to grow up apart from their people. An advantage of the Ordinance was that it gave a degree of protection for 'full-blood' Aborigines living on reserves, as non-Aborigines could enter only with a permit, and mineral exploration was forbidden.

The process of social change was accelerated by WWII, and 'assimilation' became the stated aim of post-war governments. To this end, the rights of Aborigines were subjugated even further – the government had control over everything, from where Aborigines could live to whom they could marry. Many people were forcibly moved to townships, the idea being that they would adapt to the European culture, which would in turn aid their economic development. The policy was a dismal failure.

In the 1960s the assimilation policy came under a great deal of scrutiny, and white

MARK ARMSTRONG

DAVID SHERMAN

QUEENSLAND TOURIST AND TRAVEL CORPORATION

Top: Cattlegrid on the long dusty road to Birdsville in the south-west of the state.
Middle: Lush subtropical rainforest in Lamington National Park, south-east Queensland –
    a popular place for hikers, campers, birdwatchers and nature lovers.
Bottom: Point Lookout, North Stradbroke Island, is popular with day trippers from Brisbane.

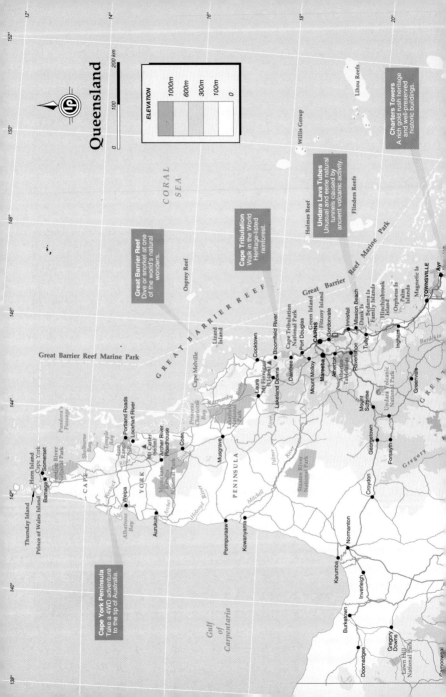

Queensland

ELEVATION

1000m
600m
300m
100m
0

0   100   200 km

Cape York Peninsula
Take a 4WD adventure to the tip of Australia.

Great Barrier Reef
Dive or snorkel at one of the world's natural wonders.

Cape Tribulation
Walk in the World Heritage-listed rainforest.

Undara Lava Tubes
Unusual and eerie natural tunnels caused by ancient volcanic activity.

Charters Towers
A rich gold-rush heritage and well-preserved historic buildings.

CORAL SEA

GREAT BARRIER REEF

Great Barrier Reef Marine Park

Great Barrier Reef Marine Park

Willis Group

Lihou Reefs

Osprey Reef

Holmes Reef

Flinders Reefs

Gulf of Carpentaria

CAPE YORK PENINSULA

Thursday Island
Prince of Wales Island
Horn Island
Cape York
Somerset
Bamaga
Jardine River National Park

Weipa
Aurukun

Pandora's Passage

Shelburne Bay

Temple Bay

Portland Roads
Lockhart River

Iron Range National Park

Mt Carter (665m)
Archer River Roadhouse
Coen

Princess Charlotte Bay

Lakefield National Park

Cape Melville

Lizard Island

Cooktown
Bloomfield River
Daintree
Mount Molloy
Cape Tribulation National Park
Port Douglas
Green Island
Fitzroy Island
CAIRNS
Gordonvale
Mareeba
Atherton
Tablelands
Ravenshoe
Innisfail
Mission Beach
Dunk Is
Bedarra Is
Family Islands
Tully
Hinchinbrook Island

Laura
Mt Finnigan (1165m)
Lakeland Downs

Musgrave

Staaten River National Park

Pormpuraaw
Kowanyama

Normanton
Croydon
Georgetown
Forsayth
Mount Surprise
Undara Volcanic National Park
Greenvale
Ingham
Orpheus Is
Palm Islands
Magnetic Is
TOWNSVILLE
Ayr

Karumba
Burketown
Doomadgee
Inverleigh
Gregory Downs
Lawn Hill National Park

Burdekin

GREAT

Eungella National Park
Spy on the elusive platypus in a magnificent rainforest setting

Fraser Island
Crystal clear freshwater lakes and towering forests on the world's largest sand island

Noosa
Indulge in Queensland's best restaurants

Gold Coast
Nightlife and surf beaches – be prepared to play hard in this glitzy city.

Lamington National Park
Walk along many trails through subtropical rainforest, teeming with birdlife.

Birdsville
The outback town that comes alive once a year for a horse race.

MICHAEL AW

Green Island, a coral cay on the Great Barrier Reef 27km north-east of Cairns, is easily reached for a day trip or overnight stay. Surrounded by accessible coral and safe waters, Green Island makes a great introduction to the reef's colourful and diverse marine life.

Australians became increasingly aware of the inequity of their treatment of Aborigines. In 1967 non-Aboriginal Australians voted to give Aborigines and Torres Strait Islanders the status of citizens, and gave the federal government power to legislate for them in all states. The states had to provide them with the same services that were available to other citizens, and the federal government set up the Department of Aboriginal Affairs to identify the special needs of Aborigines and legislate for them.

The assimilation policy was finally dumped in 1972, to be replaced by the government's policy of self-determination, which for the first time enabled Aborigines to participate in decision-making processes.

In 1976 the Aboriginal Land Rights (Northern Territory) Act gave Aborigines in that region indisputable title to all Aboriginal reserves (about 20% of the Territory) and a means for claiming other Crown land. It also provided for mineral royalties to be paid to Aboriginal communities. This legislation was supposed to be extended to cover all of Australia, but the removal of the reformist Labor government in 1975 put paid to that prospect.

Mabo & the Native Title Act Only very recently has the non-Aboriginal community begun to come to grips with the fact that a meaningful conciliation between white Australia and its indigenous population was vital to the psychological well-being of all Australians.

In May 1982, five Torres Strait Islanders led by Eddie Mabo began an action for a declaration of native title over Queensland's Murray Islands. They argued that the legal principle of *terra nullius* had wrongfully usurped their title to land, as for thousands of years Murray Islanders had enjoyed a relationship with the land that included a notion of ownership. In June 1992 the High Court of Australia rejected *terra nullius* and the myth that Australia had been unoccupied. In doing this, it recognised that a principle of native title existed before the arrival of the British.

The High Court's judgment became known as the Mabo decision, one of the most controversial decisions ever handed down by an Australian court. It was ambiguous, as it didn't outline the extent to which native title existed in mainland Australia. It received a hostile reaction from the mining and other industries, and resulted in some hysterical responses from non-Aborigines who feared their back yards were suddenly going to be subject to Aboriginal land claims. However, the decision was hailed by Aborigines and then-Prime Minister Paul Keating as an opportunity to create a basis for reconciliation between Aboriginal and non-Aboriginal Australians.

To define the principle of native title, the federal parliament passed the Native Title Act in December 1993. Despite protest from the mining industry, the act gives Australian Aboriginal people very few new rights. It limits the application of native title to land which no-one else owns or leases, and also to land with which Aboriginal people have continued to have a physical association. The act states that existing ownership or leases extinguish native title, although native title may be revived after mining leases have expired. If land is successfully claimed by Aboriginal people under the act, they will have no veto over developments, including mining.

The Wik Decision Several months before the Native Title Act becoming law, the Wik and Thayorre peoples had made a claim for native title in the Federal Court to land on Cape York Peninsula. The area claimed included two pastoral leases. Neither had ever been permanently occupied for that purpose, but the Wik and Thayorre peoples had been in continuous occupation of them. They argued that native title coexisted with the pastoral leases.

In January 1996 the Federal Court decided the claim could not succeed because the granting of pastoral leases under Queensland law extinguished any native title rights. The Wik people appealed that decision in the High Court, where it was subsequently overturned.

The High Court determined that, under the law that created pastoral leases in Queensland, native title to the leases in question had not been extinguished. Further, it said that native title rights could continue at the same time that land was under lease, and that pastoralists did not have exclusive right of possession to their leases. Importantly, it also ruled that where the two were in conflict, the rights of the pastoralists would prevail.

Despite the fact that lease tenure was not threatened, the Wik decision brought a hue and cry from pastoral lessees across Australia, who demanded that the federal government step in to protect them by legislating to limit native title rights, as was intended in the original act. Aboriginal leaders were equally adamant that native title must be preserved.

In late 1997 the government responded with its so-called 10 Point Plan, a raft of proposed legislative amendments to the Native Title Act which would further entrench the pastoralists' position and effectively extinguish native title – something the Wik judgement does not do. The proposed legislation was not passed by parliament, and was rejected a second time in early 1998. Whatever the outcome of the federal government's response to Wik, it's obvious that failure to resolve the native title issue will put new and extravagant meaning into 'lawyers' picnic', and will make reconciliation less rather than more likely.

European Exploration

Historians believe that Portuguese sailors were the first Europeans to sight the Australian coast early in the 16th century, although because of the secrecy that shrouded maritime discoveries of that time there are no records of these voyages.

In 1606 the Spaniard Torres is known to have sailed through the strait between Cape York and New Guinea that still bears his name, although there's no record of his actually sighting the Australian continent. During the same year the Dutch explorer Willem Jansz sailed the *Duyfken* into the Gulf of Carpentaria, charting part of the Queensland coastline. In 1623 another Dutchman, Jan Carstensz, landed at Cape York and explored a little, but like Janz before him, he considered the land inhospitable and unsuitable for settlement.

This apparently dismal continent was forgotten until 1768, when the British Admiralty instructed Captain James Cook to lead a scientific expedition to Tahiti, to observe the transit of Venus across the Sun, and then begin a search for the Great South Land. On board his ship *Endeavour* were also several scientists, including an astronomer and a group of naturalists and artists led by Joseph Banks.

On 19 April 1770 the extreme southeastern tip of the continent was sighted and named Point Hicks, and Cook turned north to follow the coast and search for a suitable landfall. It was nine days before an opening in the cliffs was sighted and the ship and crew found sheltered anchorage in a harbour they named Botany Bay.

After leaving Botany Bay, Cook continued north, charting the coastline and noting that the fertile east coast was a different story from the inhospitable land the earlier explorers had seen to the west. He named a number of places as he sailed up the coast of what is now Queensland, including Moreton Bay, the Whitsundays and Cape Tribulation. On 11 June 1770 the *Endeavour* struck a reef off Cape Tribulation and was badly damaged.

After heaving various heavy items overboard, including an anchor and six cannons, the *Endeavour* was freed from the reef. The ship limped up the coast to the Endeavour River, landing at the site of present-day Cooktown. It took six weeks to repair the ship, during which time Cook and the scientists investigated their surroundings further, this time making contact with the local Aborigines.

Cook was quite taken with the indigenous people and wrote:

They may appear to some to be the most wretched people upon the earth: but in reality they are far happier than we Europeans ... They live in a tranquillity which is not disturbed by the inequality of condition ... they seem to set no value upon anything we gave them, nor would they ever part with anything of their own ...

After repairing the *Endeavour*, navigating the Great Barrier Reef and rounding Cape York, Cook put ashore at Possession Island to raise the Union Jack, rename the continent New South Wales and claim it for the British in the name of King George III.

Convicts & European Settlement

Following the American Revolution, Britain was no longer able to transport convicts to North America. With jails and prison hulks already overcrowded, it was essential that an alternative be found quickly. In 1779 Joseph Banks suggested New South Wales as a fine site for a colony of thieves, and in 1786 Lord Sydney announced that the king had decided on Botany Bay as a place for convicts under sentence of transportation.

Less than two years later, in January 1788, the First Fleet sailed into Botany Bay. The Second Fleet arrived in 1790 with more convicts and some supplies, and a year later, following the landing of the Third Fleet, the population had increased to 4000.

Little of the country was explored during those first years. Then a great period of white discovery started as the vast inland was gradually explored and the coastline extensively charted. In 1799 Matthew Flinders left Sydney in the *Norfolk* to explore the northern coast and search for useful ports and rivers; he landed at Bribie Island north of Moreton Bay and sailed as far north as Fraser Island before returning to Sydney.

Moreton Bay Penal Colony

By 1822 the penal colonies at Norfolk Island and Port Jackson were overcrowded, and it was suggested that a new settlement be established for the more recalcitrant convicts. John Oxley, the surveyor general of New South Wales, was sent north to investigate the Moreton Bay area as a prospective site. On his return he recommended Redcliffe Point as the site for the new colony. Oxley returned in 1824 with a settlement party of about 35 convicts and a regiment led by Lieutenant Henry Miller.

The new settlement only lasted several months at Redcliffe Point. The site was soon considered unsuitable, owing to a combination of factors including the lack of a safe anchorage and fresh water, swampy land and trouble with local tribes. In May 1825 the settlement was moved up the Brisbane River to the site of present-day Brisbane, which offered a safe harbour, fertile land and fresh water from a string of water holes. The colony was never really a success; being so far from Sydney it was very difficult to administer, and it never accommodated more than about 1100 convicts.

Gradually, explorers ventured west from Moreton Bay into the hinterland. Coal and limestone deposits were found in the vicinity of present-day Ipswich, and in 1827 Allan Cunningham discovered the vast, grassy plains of the Darling Downs. The following year he returned and found the gap through the mountains of the Great Dividing Range which now bears his name. Patrick Leslie and his brothers became the first permanent settlers on the Darling Downs when they arrived in 1840. Within another couple of years the entire district had been taken up by free settlers.

British authorities gradually lost interest in the penal system and Brisbane's convict era ended in 1839. Three years later the Moreton Bay area was opened up to free settlers, and the fertile lands around the Brisbane River were also quickly taken up for farming.

Exploration of Queensland

By the 1840s most of Queensland's vast interior was still unexplored, but a dramatic series of expeditions – some ill-fated – gradually opened it up.

Ludwig Leichhardt In 1843 the enigmatic Prussian explorer Ludwig Leichhardt arrived in Brisbane after trekking overland from Sydney, and soon announced plans to continue his overland trek to the newly established outpost of Port Essington, 3000km away near present-day Darwin. Despite his eccentricities and notorious incompetence as an explorer, Leichhardt and his party completed the journey – in 15 months, twice as long as planned.

Leichhardt returned to Sydney in 1846 as a hero. Almost immediately, he mounted another expedition, this time to cross the continent from east to west, but the party turned back after only six months. Undeterred, Leichhardt mounted yet another expedition and recruited six new men, all of whom were inexperienced in outback travel. The party set out from the Darling Downs in April 1848 and were never seen again. Their disappearance remains one of the great mysteries of Australian exploration.

Eccentric explorer Ludwig Leichhardt vanished without trace in the Queensland outback.

Edmund Kennedy In 1848 assistant surveyor Edmund Kennedy was given what turned out to be an impossible mission, that of trekking overland from Rockingham Bay (south of present-day Cairns) to the top of the Cape York Peninsula.

The ship HMS *Rattlesnake*, which was to explore the coast and meet Kennedy at the top of the Cape, dropped his party at Tam O'Shanter Point (at present-day Mission Beach). The expedition almost immediately struck trouble when their heavy supply carts could not be dragged through the swampy ground around Tully.

The rugged land, harsh climate, lack of supplies, hostile Aborigines and missed supply drops all took their toll and nine of the party of 13 died. Kennedy himself was speared to death in an attack by Aborigines when he was only 30km from the end of the fearsome trek. His Aboriginal servant, Jacky Jacky, was the only expedition member to finally reach the supply ship.

Burke & Wills In 1860 the stage was set for the greatest act in the exploration of Australia. Some would say today that it was the greatest folly, but the Burke and Wills expedition was the largest, most lavish and best equipped expedition that set out to solve the riddle of inland Australia.

With much fanfare Robert O'Hara Burke led an expedition north out of Melbourne on 20 August 1860. Chosen by a committee of the Royal Society, Burke was neither an explorer nor a surveyor, had no scientific training, had never led an expedition of any kind, had not set foot out of Victoria since arriving there just a few years previously, and was considered to be, if anything, a very poor bushman. He also ignored the advice of earlier explorers to enlist the help of Aboriginal guides.

Leaving most of his group at Menindee (New South Wales), Burke and his second-in-command, William John Wills, pushed north to Cooper Creek where they set up a depot. From there Burke chose Wills, Charles Grey and John King to accompany him to the Gulf of Carpentaria, leaving the

Perhaps the two most infamous explorers in Australian history, Robert O'Hara Burke (left) and William John Wills (right) perished after an epic journey to the Gulf of Carpentaria ... on foot.

depot and the remainder of the expedition on 16 December 1860. At the height of summer, these men set out to walk 1100km through central Australia to the sea! It says something of their fortitude and sheer guts that they made it, reaching the mangroves that barred their view of the Gulf of Carpentaria on 11 February 1861. Camp No 119, near present-day Normanton, was their northernmost camp and can be visited today.

Turning their backs on the sea, the rush south became a life-or-death stagger with Grey dying at a place later called Lake Massacre, just west of the Cooper Creek depot. When Burke, Wills and King arrived at the depot they were astonished to find that the men there had retreated to Menindee that very morning! The famous 'Dig Tree', arguably the most historic site in inland Australia, still stands on the banks of Cooper Creek in Queensland, near the border with South Australia. Trapped at Cooper Creek the explorers wasted away, dying on the banks of this desert oasis. Only King, who had been befriended by some Aborigines, was alive when the first of the rescue parties arrived in September 1861.

These rescue expeditions really opened up the interior, with groups from Queensland, South Australia and Victoria crisscrossing the continent in search of Burke and Wills. Howitt, McKinlay, Landsborough and Walker were not only better explorers than Burke, but experienced bushmen who proved that Europeans, cattle and sheep could survive in these regions.

William Landsborough Landsborough, a successful stockman, gold miner and pastoralist, was chosen by the Victorian government to lead one of the expeditions that went in search of Burke and Wills.

Landsborough travelled south from the Gulf of Carpentaria along the Gregory River as far as the Barkly Tableland before returning to his depot on the Gulf, then followed the Flinders River south to the site of present-day Hughenden. At a station further south, he heard that Burke and Wills had perished, and he continued south all the way to Melbourne.

Ironically, Landsborough's party became the first to cross Australia from north to south. In his search, Landsborough had discovered Queensland's rich inland grazing areas. His reports of the country as being the finest pastoral land he had ever seen were responsible for a minor rush to settle the area.

The Jardines In 1863 John Jardine was made the first government magistrate of the settlement of Somerset on the tip of the Cape York Peninsula. He considered the Cape to be commercially viable cattle country, and commissioned his sons, Frank and Alick, both then aged in their 20s, to overland a mob of cattle from Rockhampton to the new settlement.

Their epic journey took 10 months, and they arrived at Somerset in March 1865. Along the way they overcame lack of water, skirmishes with Aborigines, flooded rivers and a maze of swamps and waterways.

Frank Jardine later took over from his father as government magistrate at Somerset, where he died in 1919 after building an empire of cattle farming and pearl fishing.

Other Explorers Many other explorers were responsible for opening up Queensland's vast interior to settlement. They included George Elphingstone Dalrymple, who in 1859 led an expedition inland from Rockhampton and discovered the rich pastoral districts of the Burdekin Valley. In 1872 William Hann spent five months exploring the Cape York Peninsula and named many of the Cape's major rivers. Hann found traces of gold in the Palmer River, leading to a major gold rush to the area in 1873.

In 1855-56 Augustus Gregory led an expedition from the Victoria River, near the border of Western Australia and the Northern Territory, across the top of the continent and down through Queensland's coastal hinterland to Moreton Bay.

Separation & Growth
At the end of 1859 Queensland finally won separation from New South Wales, with Brisbane as the capital of the new colony. At this time there were only about 28,000 Europeans in the colony, but separation

ushered in one of Queensland's major periods of growth and prosperity.

Initially, this growth was based on the steady development of the pastoral industry. Landholdings grew larger, and small-scale settlers found it increasingly hard to compete with huge pastoral companies, such as the Northern Australian Pastoral Company, many of which were backed by foreign funds. The number of sheep grazing in Queensland went from eight million in 1870 to more than 20 million in the 1890s; the number of cattle rose from one million in 1870 to over six million by the 1920s.

By the 1860s Brisbane had shed its convict background and developed into a handsome provincial centre, although it wasn't until the 1880s that the central business district was transformed by the construction of many fine public and commercial buildings.

The rapid growth of the colony came at a hefty price to both the landscape and the indigenous people who had lived in it for thousands of years. The early white settlers saw the land and its resources as theirs to be exploited as quickly as possible. The pastoral industry quickly exhausted vast areas of natural grasslands; wholesale clearing of the forests followed, and cut timber was either burnt or left to rot. Sawmilling operations cut huge swathes through the forests, supplying the timber-hungry building, mining and railway industries. As early as the 1880s, many of the cedar and pine species in Queensland's coastal ranges were almost exhausted.

The Aborigines were looked upon as little more than animals and ruthlessly pushed off their lands as settlers continued to take up land for farming, and later mining. Tribal boundaries, hunting rights and sacred grounds were all ignored in the land grab. Particularly in northern Queensland, many tribes resisted forcefully, and a virtual frontier war was waged for years.

Although some settlers tried to maintain friendly relations with the tribes, others hunted Aborigines for sport or killed them with gifts of flour laced with arsenic. Many

Europeans were themselves killed in this guerrilla war, but the Aborigines ultimately lost almost every battle, and every white death was followed by brutal reprisals. Estimates suggest that while four to five hundred Europeans were killed in the struggle, Aboriginal losses were anywhere from five to fifteen thousand.

The notorious Native Mounted Police force was responsible for some of the bloodiest massacres in Australian history. Made up of Aborigines from disrupted tribes, they were a virtual paramilitary force of black troopers who were used against their own people. With their skills in tracking and bushcraft combined with the use of European weaponry, they were a terrifyingly effective force against Queensland's Aborigines until they were abolished in 1900.

One of the most infamous episodes of the time was the Hornet Bank Massacre in 1857. Led by two deserters from the Native Mounted Police, a group of Aborigines from the local Jiman tribe attacked a remote station on the Dawson River, killing a widow, seven of her children and three shepherds. A revenge 'posse' was made up of squatters and members of the Native Mounted Police. The reprisals that followed continued for six weeks, at the end of which not one Jiman was left in the Dawson valley.

Gold & Mining

The discovery of gold in Queensland in the 1860s and 70s brought about the most significant social and economic changes. The first major find was at Gympie in 1867; more than 15,000 diggers rushed the site. In 1872 the rich Charters Towers goldfields were discovered; the town grew so quickly and so dominated life in northern Queensland that it came to be known as 'The World'. Mt Morgan, which became the richest of Queensland's mines, was discovered near Rockhampton in 1882.

In 1873 the legendary Palmer River gold rush began. William Hann found traces of gold there in 1872, and a party of diggers led by James Venture Mulligan travelled to the river soon after. Their reports of a rich

The Chinese in Queensland

During the gold-rush era Chinese prospectors poured into Queensland in their thousands. At one stage of the Palmer River gold rush, there were 11,000 Chinese miners and only 1500 Europeans. The Chinese were diligent workers, but kept largely to themselves and were strongly resented by the Europeans. They were stereotyped as immoral and diseased heathens, and subjected to racist attacks. Leading prospector James Venture Mulligan expressed his anti-Chinese feelings in a letter to the *Queenslander* in 1874:

'They follow up in swarms with odious filth, get the best gold, never give the miner the opening and chance to fall back on old ground where a man could get a little if he did not succeed in other directions.'

Workers also came to resent the presence of the Chinese, especially during the recession of the 1890s when they were blamed for taking the jobs of others and lowering wages by working cheaply. Anti-Chinese leagues were formed; the government was eventually pressured into placing restrictions on the economic activities of the Chinese and, finally, restricting further migration. In the 1870s the Chinese made up almost 6% of Queensland's population. But as the gold ran out and they were continually hounded and repressed by racist policies, many left during the 1880s and 90s, and by the turn of the century they made up less than 2% of the population. Of those who remained, the majority worked in rural industries such as sugar cane production and banana plantations, and came to be valued as workers.

alluvial field prompted a major rush, despite the inhospitality of the region.

Many of these early mining towns were frenetic, chaotic places, filled with larrikin diggers who drank and gambled in wild frenzies. They were also places of great contrasts: between those lucky few who struck it rich and the battlers, many of whom ended up broke, or worse still, dead. Accidents and disease claimed a heavy toll.

Between 1860 and 1915 more than £81 million worth of gold was recorded to have been won in Queensland, reaching a peak of £2.8 million in 1900.

Gold wasn't the only mineral to feed the Queensland economy. Extensive deposits of tin were found at places like Stanthorpe, Herberton and Irvinebank. Rich copper deposits were discovered at Cloncurry, Chillagoe, Mt Garnet and Mt Molloy, and coal-mining provided the main source of energy for the railways, mines and factories.

Sugar & the Plantation Economy

After early experiments with cotton plantations, sugar cane production quickly became the colony's major industry. The first plantation was established at Moreton Bay in 1864, and over the next decade cane plantations spread like wildfire up the fertile coastal belt. By the late 1860s the plantations had reached the Mackay district, and then spread further north to the delta of the Burdekin River, to Bowen, and to the Mulgrave and Johnstone rivers. A feature of Queensland's early sugar cane industry was its use and exploitation of cheap imported labour.

Labour vs Capital

The last part of the 19th century was a time of social upheaval in Queensland, characterised by a series of clashes between labour and capital which at times bordered on civil war, but which would eventually lead to the election of the world's first (albeit brief) Labor government.

By the 1880s many of the goldfields had been exhausted and the labour markets were flooded with diggers. Wages dropped and working conditions were tightened, and a world-wide recession led to the collapse of the Queensland economy.

In this climate, a number of radical weekly newspapers emerged, including the *Boomerang* and the *Worker*. These papers had wide appeal to their working-class audiences and featured articles and stories which began to espouse alternative theories of social organisation. At the same time the labour movement initiated the formation of craft and labour unions to represent seamen, factory workers, miners and shearers.

The first major battlefront was in the Darling Downs. In an attempt to break the hold of the shearers' unions, the newly formed Darling Downs Pastoralists' Association employed non-union labour at Jondaryan Station. During the subsequent strike, the Queensland Shearers' Union appealed to the waterside workers and seamen's unions for support, and the refusal of the maritime workers to handle the Jondaryan wool won a settlement in favour of the shearers. However, the maritime strike eventually ended in October 1890 with the defeat of maritime workers' unions all along the east coast.

Further major confrontations took place in 1891 and 1894 on the immense pastoral stations of central and western Queensland. During the famous shearers' strike near Barcaldine in 1891, the strikers responded to the use of non-union labour by forming themselves into armed camps, rioting and sabotaging property belonging to the pastoralists. The government supported the pastoralists and sent in more than 1400 soldiers armed with machine guns and field artillery to confront the strikers. Twelve of the strike leaders were arrested without warrants, and 10 of them were later convicted of conspiracy and sentenced to three years' jail with hard labour. The strike was ended a couple of weeks later, defeated by the close relationship between the government and the pastoralists, a lack of funds and the massive supply of unemployed labour that was willing to take the strikers' places.

The Kanakas

Based on the convenient 19th century concept that Europeans were inherently unsuited to work in the tropics, Queensland's early squatters used Indian and Chinese labourers and German contract workers to do much of the hard work on the land. As the sugar industry grew, these cheap labour sources came into short supply, and a new source of labour had to be found. Robert Towns, the founder of Townsville, had previously been a South Seas trader and had the idea to import Islanders to work on his cotton plantation south of Brisbane. In 1863, his ship the *Don Juan* returned from the Solomons with 67 Islanders, who were employed for either six or 12 months at 10 shillings a month. These men were the first of Queensland's Kanakas.

Desperate for labourers, Queensland's sugar pioneers followed Towns' lead, and soon found that Islander labour was easy to import, cheap and reliable. Initial workers were contracted for three years and paid £6 a year, with full board and a return passage. As the demand for labourers grew, a fleet of 'recruiting' boats operated between the islands and the mainland. Not all of these recruiters operated scrupulously, and the process of collecting and delivering them came to be known as 'blackbirding' – a euphemism for kidnapping.

The term 'kanaka' was derived from a Hawaiian word for 'man', but its use to describe these Islanders came to be contemptuous and condescending. The Kanakas were 'recruited' from various Melanesian islands, including the Solomons, New Guinea, the New Hebrides and the Torres Strait Islands. Voluntary workers or not, the Kanakas worked long hours in sometimes appalling conditions, and their mortality rate was up to five times higher than for Europeans. By the late 1860s those who recognised the immorality of exploiting the Islanders began to voice their criticism, but mainly because of Queensland's growing economic reliance on the sugar industry, the practice continued.

In 1868 the Queensland government responded to pressure by passing the Polynesian Labourers Act (the act was incorrectly named; the Kanakas were Melanesian, not Polynesian). The act required all employers to register their recruits and guarantee to return them within three years, and led to the placement of government agents on all recruiting vessels.

Despite these changes, pressure to abolish the practice grew. The missionary William Gray travelled to Queensland to inspect the plantations, and later wrote: '... I went to Queensland determined to keep my mind open ... I would now say what I would not have said before I went ... that the Kanaka Labour Traffic is veiled slavery'. The British government denounced the practice, as did the *Sydney Morning Herald*. Yet Queensland's politicians refused to bow to the pressure, and the large plantation owners of the north were increasingly compared to those of the American South during the slave-owning days.

By the 1880s there were about 14,000 Kanakas working in Queensland. Despite the harsh conditions, some of the Islanders adapted to life in Queensland. Many learned English and developed basic skills; some were converted to Christianity, but others were more captivated by the evils of alcohol. Settlers began to complain of 'social problems', and a growing anti-Kanaka movement developed in the Labor movement as workers began to resent the exclusive use of Islander labour by many plantation owners.

Restrictions on recruiting vessels were tightened after 1884 by Samuel Griffith's government, which had campaigned on a platform of abolishing Kanaka labour. A number of recruiters were later charged with kidnapping and murder, but ruled by internal economic pressures, Griffith never upheld his campaign policy. It wasn't until Federation in 1901 that the Federal government passed the Pacific Island Labourers Act and terminated the use of Islander labour; by this time more than 60,000 Islanders had worked in the canefields of Queensland. As a result of the racist White Australia policy, only about 1600 Kanakas were allowed to remain in Queensland after 1906.

Support for the parliamentary Labor Party, which had been formed in 1890, continued to grow throughout the 1890s. In the elections of 1899, disputes between Queensland's governing Liberal and Conservative factions allowed the Labor Party, led by Andrew Dawson, to form the world's first Labor government. Dawson's government lasted only six days – he was defeated after the Liberals and Conservatives managed to reconcile their differences.

The 20th Century

Federation to WWII Queensland voted to join the other states and became part of the Commonwealth of Australia on 1 January 1901. In 1901 the Immigration Restriction Bill, known as the White Australia policy, was passed by the federal parliament to prevent the immigration of Asians and Pacific Islanders. Prospective immigrants were required to pass a dictation test in a European language. The language in which the test was given could be as obscure a tongue as the authorities wished. The dictation test was not abolished until 1958.

Like the rest of Australia, Queensland greeted the outbreak of WWI with naive enthusiasm; Queensland-born Prime Minister Andrew Fisher pledged that 'Australians will stand beside our own to help and defend her (England) to the last man and our last shilling'.

While support for Australia's involvement in the war remained strong, efforts to introduce conscription led to bitter argument, both in parliament and on the streets. In Queensland, the radical Labor Party (led by the brilliant barrister TJ Ryan) won government in 1915 with a platform of anti-conscription policies.

Labor went on to dominate Queensland politics for the next 42 years. Ryan remained as premier until 1919, introducing a series of social and industrial reforms including compulsory voting, improved safety and working conditions, workers' compensation and an Arbitration Court. Ryan resigned in 1919 to enter federal politics.

The aviation era of the 1920s brought a number of significant changes to Queensland. Qantas was formed in 1920 to provide the first air transport service for the outback. John Flynn, a minister from the Australian Inland Mission, established the first Flying Doctor Service base at Cloncurry, and, in conjunction with Alfred Traeger's pedal wireless, gave the stations of the remote outback access to medical services.

There was great economic expansion in the 1920s and in 1923 incredibly rich copper, lead, silver and zinc deposits were discovered at Mt Isa, leading to a new phase in Queensland's resource boom.

All this came to a halt with the Great Depression, which hit Australia hard. In 1931 almost a third of breadwinners were unemployed and poverty was widespread. Swagmen became a familiar sight once more, as thousands of men took to the 'wallaby track' in search of work in the country. By 1932, however, Australia's economy was starting to recover, a result of rises in wool prices and a rapid revival of manufacturing.

WWII & the Post-War Years In the years before WWII, Australia became increasingly fearful of Japan. When war did break out, Australian troops fought beside the British in Europe, but after the Japanese bombed Pearl Harbor, Australia's own national security finally began to take priority.

Singapore fell, the northern Australian towns of Darwin and Broome and the New Guinean town of Port Moresby were bombed, the Japanese advanced southward, and still Britain called for more Australian troops. This time the Australian prime minister, John Curtin, refused. Australian soldiers were needed to fight the Japanese advancing over the mountainous Kokoda Trail towards Port Moresby.

During the war, large areas of Queensland were transformed into military camps, and a string of air bases built all the way from Brisbane to the top of Cape York. Thousands of American troops were garrisoned in various places in Queensland, including Cape York, the Atherton Tableland and Townsville, and the United States Navy established a base in the Coral Sea. Townsville was damaged by bombs from Japanese flying boats, and attempts were made to bomb Cairns.

Ultimately it was the USA, not Britain, that helped protect Australia from the Japanese, defeating them in the Battle of the Coral Sea. This event was to mark the beginning of a profound shift in Australia's allegiance away from Britain and towards the USA. Although Australia continued to support Britain in the war in Europe, its appreciation of its own vulnerability had been sharpened immeasurably by the Japanese advance.

One result of this was the post-war immigration program, which offered assisted passage not only to Britons but also to refugees from eastern Europe in the hope that the increase in population would strengthen Australia's economy and contribute to its ability to defend itself. 'Populate or Perish' became the catch phrase. Between 1947 and 1968 more than 800,000 non-British migrants came to live in Australia, although Queensland received a smaller proportion of migrants than other states.

The post-war years also saw Queensland begin its shift from a rural to an industrial economy as the state's vast resources of raw materials were increasingly exploited. Labor's long rule came to an end in 1957 when internal conflict led to the formation of the breakaway Queensland Labor Party by then-premier Vincent Gair. Divided, Labor was defeated by the Country and Liberal parties who formed a coalition and pooled their votes. They ruled until 1983 when the National Party won government in its own right. (Before the 1974 elections, the Country Party had changed its name to the National Party.)

The Country/Liberal Party's first premier, George Nicklin, ruled from 1957 to 1968. He was succeeded by Jack Pizzey, who died soon after taking over, opening the way for the Country Party's charismatic Sir Johannes Bjelke-Petersen (universally known as Joh) to become premier. Aided by a gerrymandered electoral system, Joh went on to become Queensland's longest serving premier, ruling the state with his 'progress'-oriented policies for 19 years. Economically, his policies were a huge success, attracting overseas investment to fund a major mining and industrial boom.

Recent Developments Joh and his right-wing Nationals were also Australia's most controversial state government. Whether it was views on rainforests, Aboriginal land rights, the public's right to hold demonstrations or even whether condom machines should be allowed in universities, you could count on the Queensland government to take the opposite stand to just about everybody else.

Under the Nationals, the state also had more than its fair share of corruption scandals. In 1987 Joh's own party decided he was a liability and replaced him. Since the defeat of the Nationals in the 1989 state election, it seems everyone from the former commissioner of Queensland police to Joh himself has appeared in court on charges relating to some sort of shady deal.

Queensland's rapid economic growth, its favourable climate and Joh's 1977 decision to abolish death duties have all been factors in attracting a massive wave of internal migration. Since 1980 over half a million Australians from other states have packed up and moved to Queensland.

Australia found itself in recession again in the early 1990s, although Queensland wasn't as hard hit as the southern states. It continues to grow faster than other states, and the economic future looks bright.

A state election held in July 1995 saw the incumbent Labor government, led by Wayne Goss, scrape home with a one-seat majority. The surprise swing against the government was in part a swing back to Queensland's conservative past, and in part a backlash against the Goss government's failure to deliver on promised reforms.

The Politics of Resentment

Pauline Hanson and her One Nation party have exposed a simmering resentment in some sections of the Australian community. Anger at rising unemployment, increased economic uncertainty and a rapidly changing lifestyle is finding a release in her calls to end Asian immigration and multiculturalism, abolish Aboriginal land rights and reintroduce protectionist trade policies.

Pauline Hanson, a fish and chip shop owner until her election as an independent to the federal seat of Oxley, in Queensland, in 1996, has brought far right politics into the public arena, in a guise acceptable to some of the population, most of whom feel jaded by traditional politicians. As leader of new party One Nation she has masqueraded as a 'battler', an anti-politician. She has directed her resentment at those groups she perceives are getting something more than her: Aborigines, migrants (especially Asians), the unemployed – while drawing a parliamentary salary of over $80,000 on top of income from investment properties and a $400,000 cattle stud.

One Nation plays on people's legitimate concerns about their declining quality of life amid rising economic uncertainty. However, the party offers simple solutions to complex problems: if the country's foreign debt increases, print more money; if there are too many unemployed, halt immigration; and if crime soars, loosen gun control laws so people can protect their homes.

The party's simple promises saw One Nation win 11 seats and 23% of the vote at the June 1998 Queensland election. The party is confident of continuing its winning streak in a federal election. The rise of One Nation is often dismissed as an aberration: a typical result from Queensland with its large rural population and right-wing political history. However, the party's success shows parallels with the rise of far right movements in many other countries experiencing a surge of ultra-nationalism, including France, India, and the UK.

Sally Dillon

What followed was extraordinary: Labor held a seat in Townsville, Mundingburra, by only 16 votes, but in early 1996 the count was ruled invalid. The resulting by-election saw the seat go to the Liberals, the Goss government thrown out on its ear and the conservatives returned.

The most recent state elections were held in May 1998, and the outcome was another surprise – not only was the conservative government under Rob Borbidge tipped out, but the controversial One Nation party, led by federal independent MP Pauline Hanson, gained more than 25% of the vote (see the boxed text). The Labor party just failed to get a majority, but managed to form a government thanks to the support of an independent member.

GEOGRAPHY

Australia is the world's sixth largest country. Its area is 7,682,300 sq km, about the same size as the 48 mainland states of the USA and half as large again as Europe, excluding the former USSR. It is approximately 5% of the world's land surface. Lying between the Indian and Pacific oceans, Australia is about 4000km from east to west and 3200km from north to south, with a coastline 36,735km long.

Queensland, Australia's second-largest state, has an area of 1,727,200 sq km, making up about 22% of the Australian continent; at its widest point, it is about 1500km from west to east, and stretches for over 2000km from north to south, with a coastline 5208km long.

Queensland has a series of distinct regions. The Great Dividing Range, the mountain range which continues down through New South Wales and Victoria, runs generally parallel with the coastline of the Coral Sea. The coastal strip between the mountains and the sea is the basis for Queensland's booming tourist trade, with its beaches, bays, islands and, of course, the Great Barrier Reef. Much of the coastal region is green and productive with lush rainforests, endless fields of sugar cane and stunning national parks.

The Great Dividing Range is most spectacular in the Far North – at several places, the mountains actually run right down to the coastline, and the Bellenden Ker Range, which is south of Cairns, has Queensland's highest mountain, Mt Bartle Frere (1657m). The McPherson Ranges, in the south-east corner, contain some of the state's most spectacular areas, including the pleasant and mountainous Lamington and Springbrook national parks.

Running to the west of the mountain range are the tablelands – vast areas of flat agricultural land with rich volcanic soils. These areas, which include the Darling Downs in the south and the Atherton Tablelands in the Far North, are some of Australia's most fertile and productive.

Finally, there's the vast inland area, the barren outback, which fades into the Northern Territory further west. Rain can temporarily make this arid area bloom, but it's a place of sparse population, long, empty roads and tiny, distant settlements.

The Great Artesian Basin lies under much of this region. Water from the Great Dividing Range takes about 2.5 million years to seep westwards to any one of the 7500 artesian wells that provide some of the only sources of water for the area's huge sheep and cattle stations.

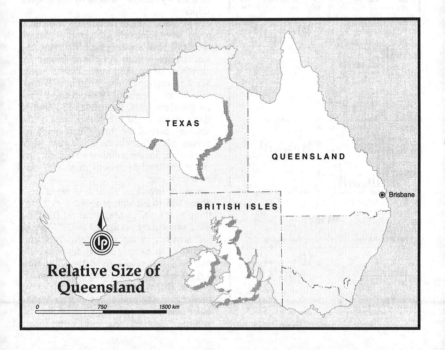

Relative Size of Queensland

TEXAS

QUEENSLAND

BRITISH ISLES

Brisbane

0   750   1500 km

There are a couple of variations from these basic divisions. In the far northern Gulf Savannah and Cape York Peninsula there are huge, empty regions cut by countless dry riverbeds which can become swollen torrents in the wet season. At such times the whole area becomes covered by a network of waterways, which sometimes brings road transport to a complete halt.

CLIMATE

Australian seasons are the opposite of those in Europe and North America, so that January is the height of summer and July the depths of winter.

The Queensland seasons are more a case of hotter and wetter, or cooler and drier,

than of summer or winter. The Tropic of Capricorn crosses Queensland about a third of the way up, running through the major city of Rockhampton and the outback town of Longreach. The northern two-thirds of the state is within the tropics, but only the extreme north lies within the monsoon belt. Although the annual rainfall there looks adequate on paper, it comes in more or less one short, sharp burst. This has prevented the Top End from becoming seriously productive agriculturally.

November-December to April-May is the wetter, hotter half of the year, while the real Wet, particularly affecting northern coastal areas, is January to March. Cairns usually gets about 1300mm of rain in these three months; Tully, 100km south of Cairns, is the wettest place in Australia, with a drenching 4400mm of rain each year!

Summer is also the season for cyclones, and if one hits, the main road north (the Bruce Hwy) can be blocked by the ensuing floods.

By comparison, the south-east and inland areas have relatively little rain – though they still have a wet season. Brisbane and Rockhampton both get about 450mm of rain from January to March. Further north, Mackay receives about 1250mm, Townsville 850mm, Innisfail 1800mm and Weipa, on the Cape York Peninsula, 1300mm in these months. Just halfway across the southern part of the state, Cunnamulla receives only 400mm in the whole year, while Birdsville, in the south-west corner, receives the least amount of rain, with only 150mm a year.

Except inland or upland at night from about May to September, it rarely gets anything like cold. Temperatures in Brisbane peak somewhere in the 20 to 29°C range just about every day of the year. In Cairns the daily maximum is usually between 25°C and 32°C whereas around the Gulf, few days in the year fail to break the 30°C mark. Over at Birdsville you can expect 33°C or more every day from November to March, but rarely more than 20°C from June to August.

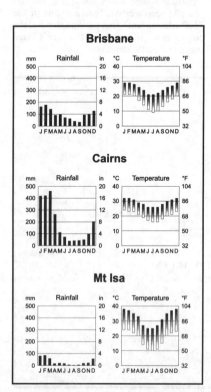

Fauna & Flora of Queensland

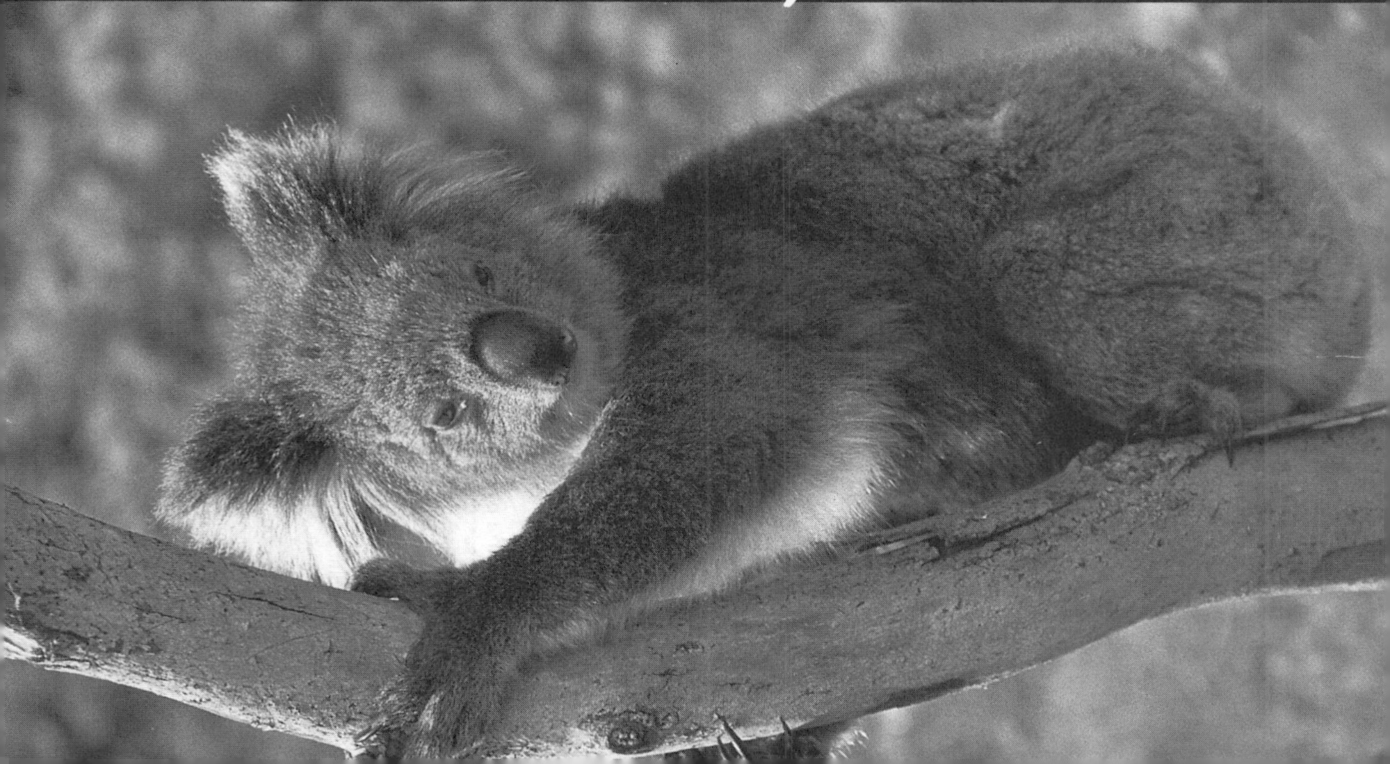

The Australian land mass broke from the southern supercontinent of Gondwanaland more than 50 million years ago and drifted north to warmer climes. Since then the continent has suffered no major climatic upheavals, and its rich and varied indigenous wildlife has had an unusually long period in which to evolve in isolation. In particular the marsupials, an early evolutionary branch of mammals, have evolved to fill nearly every ecological niche.

Australia's distinctive vegetation began to take shape about 55 million years ago. At the time it was completely covered by cool-climate rainforest, but with the gradual drying of the continent, rainforests retreated, plants such as eucalypts (gum trees) and acacias (wattles) took over and grasslands expanded. Over a vast period of time eucalypts and acacias adapted to the increased natural occurrence of fire and its later use for hunting and other purposes by Aborigines. Now many species benefit from fire and even rely on it to crack open their tough seed casings.

Climatic changes and Aborigines were responsible for a gradual process of vegetation change and wildlife extinction, but this process was accelerated with the arrival of Europeans: in the past 200 years some 17 species of mammals have become extinct. Perhaps the greatest change was instigated by the introduction of livestock, whose hooves cut the ancient friable soils and caused massive erosion. Further threats are posed by feral predators such as foxes, and hardy descendants of domestic goats and pigs, which cause drastic environmental damage. Perhaps the best known of Queensland's introduced pests is the cane toad, a voracious predator which breeds prolifically and will eat any animal small enough to swallow whole.

FAUNA

Australia's unique wildlife is famous the world over. Although environmental changes have taken their toll, much is still common and easy to see in its wild state. Queensland has the greatest diversity of wildlife in Australia and many forms are found only in this state; the Wet Tropics in particular host many unique forms, from rainforest possums and birds to frogs and an abundance of insects.

Mammals

Australia's unique and bizarre mammals have caused comment and speculation since their discovery by science. Two groups in particular, the marsupials and monotremes, are remnants of an ancient evolutionary line that have their stronghold in Australia; a high percentage of these are found in Queensland. Most mammals are nocturnal and difficult to see, but several species of kangaroos and wallabies are common and can be seen in any sizeable patch of bush.

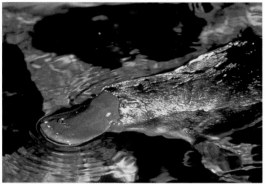

HEALESVILLE SANCTUARY

The platypus is so unusual that its unlikely combination of webbed feet, duck-like bill and soft fur were once thought to be an elaborate hoax. The platypus is quite common in unpolluted water-ways of eastern Australia, although it is extremely shy and not usually active during the day. It preys on worms, yabbies and other aquatic life which it finds with its sensitive bill.

DAVID CURL

The sugar glider is common in forests, where it is strictly nocturnal and lives high in the trees. Gliders have a flap of loose skin between their front and back legs and move by gliding from high in one tree to the trunk of another, then scampering up the trunk to repeat the process.

CHRIS KLEP

Also known as the spiny anteater, the echidna lives entirely on ants. It is a common animal of woodlands and forests, and is often seen ambling about in broad daylight. Like the platypus, the echidna lays eggs, even though the female produces milk to feed her young. Echidnas are unique to Australia and New Guinea.

ROB DRUMMOND

The galah is a common member of the cockatoo family. Galahs nest in hollows in tree trunks or branches and feed mainly on seeds. They have adapted to eat grain and thrive in agricultural areas, where they sometimes incur the wrath of farmers.

CHRIS KLEP

Although comical and awkward on land, the Australian pelican is graceful in flight. This striking bird inhabits coastal and inland waterways, where it scoops up fish in its massive bill.

QUEENSLAND TOURIST & TRAVEL CORPORATION

The striking Ulysses butterfly is a fast and high flying inhabitant of coastal forests in Queensland.

DAVID CURL

Queensland has dozens of species of frogs, many of which are attractively coloured. They reach their greatest diversity in the tropics, although several species are now seriously endangered.

RICHARD I'ANSON

The saltwater or estuarine crocodile is increasing in numbers and becoming common in parts of tropical Queensland.

RICHARD I'ANSON

Eucalypts – better known as gum trees – are probably the most famous Australian plants. Hundreds of species are known, and many produce masses of blossoms which attract birds, insects and nectar-feeding mammals.

RICHARD NEBESKY

Everlastings are part of the widespread daisy family. Daisies may form carpets across suitable habitat, especially in the drier parts of the state.

DAVID ANDREW

Unique to Australia, banksias can grow to 10m high and form dense forests in sandy areas such as Fraser Island. Banksia seeds are very hard and rely on the heat of bushfires to crack open and start germination.

Kangaroos & Wallabies Perhaps the most famous inhabitants of the bush are the large marsupials known as kangaroos. But the family also includes many smaller species such as wallabies and even some adapted to life in the treetops – the tree-kangaroos.

In all there are about 50 species; two of the most commonly encountered in Queensland are the eastern grey kangaroo and agile wallaby. The former is a large species found mainly in woodlands; the latter lives in tropical savannah. The tree-kangaroos are an unusual group adapted to life in tropical forests. Two species are found only in north Queensland, Lumholtz's and Bennet's tree-kangaroos, although they are nocturnal and difficult to see. Both are agile climbers that feed on leaves, fruits and even small animals in the canopy.

Kangaroos have an extraordinary breeding cycle that is well adapted to Australia's harsh, often unpredictable environment. The young kangaroo, or joey, just millimetres long at birth, claws its way unaided to the mother's pouch where it attaches itself to a nipple that expands inside its mouth. A day or two later the mother mates again, but the new embryo does not begin to develop until the first joey has left the pouch permanently. At this point the mother produces two types of milk – one formula to feed the joey at heel, the other for the baby in her pouch. If environmental conditions are right, the mother will then mate again. If food or water is scarce, however, the breeding cycle will be interrupted until conditions improve.

There are now more kangaroos in Australia than there were when Europeans arrived, a result of the better availability of water and the creation of grasslands for sheep and cattle. About three million kangaroos are culled legally each year in Australia, but probably as many more are killed for sport or by farmers who believe the cull is insufficient to protect their paddocks from overgrazing.

Possums & Gliders Australian possums share a distant ancestry with the marsupial opossums of the Americas – to which they owe their common name. Although found throughout the whole of Australia they reach their evolutionary peak in the Queensland rainforests.

Brush-tailed and **ring-tailed possums** can be found even in the heart of big cities, where they have learned to scavenge for household scraps. The **striped possum**, unique to the Wet Tropics, is boldly striped in black and white, and has an elongated finger for digging into rotten wood for grubs.

Gliders have a membrane stretching between their front and hind legs that acts as a parachute as they jump between trees. Several species are common in woodlands and forests.

Wombat Slow, solid and powerfully built, wombats are marsupials adapted to a burrowing life. They dig extensive tunnels with powerful limbs and the female has a backward-facing pouch so she doesn't shovel dirt over her young.

Wombats eat roots, grasses and the inner bark of trees. They are mainly nocturnal, sleeping during the day in burrows.

Koalas are common in eastern Queensland, although their habit of sleeping in treetops during the day can make them difficult to spot.

Koala Probably the most endearing and recognisable of Australia's marsupials, the koala is adapted to life in trees, where it feeds exclusively on eucalyptus leaves. The female carries her young in her pouch until it is old enough to cling to her back. Although once hunted for its fur and threatened by habitat destruction, it is still common along the eastern seaboard. Koalas are not always active during the day and can be overlooked as they sleep in the treetops. Their cuddly appearance belies an irritable nature, and koalas will scratch and bite if provoked.

Platypus & Echidna The platypus and echidna are the only living representatives of the most primitive group of mammals, the monotremes. Both lay eggs, as reptiles do, but suckle their young on milk secreted directly through the skin from mammary glands. The **platypus**' duck-like bill, webbed feet and sleek fur are superb adaptations to its aquatic lifestyle. Although shy and rarely seen by the casual observer, it is widespread in rivers, streams and lakes of eastern Australia. One of the best places to look for it is in the forest pools at Eungella National Park (see the Whitsunday Coast chapter).

The **echidna** lives exclusively on ants, which it sucks through its tube-like mouth with the aid of its long, sticky tongue. Also known as the spiny anteater, it is protected by stout spines and hides from predators by digging into the ground or by rolling itself into a bristling ball.

Dingo Australia's wild dog was domesticated by Aborigines and is thought to have arrived with them 40,000 years ago. Dingoes are not marsupials, and probably competed with, and indirectly hastened the extinction of, large marsupial predators on the mainland. Dingoes can become quite tame around campgrounds, particularly on Fraser Island.

Whales, Dolphins & Dugong See the Fraser Coast chapter for details on whale-watching off the Queensland coast. Dolphins of several species are common in Queensland waters. The dugong, also known as the sea cow, is an odd marine mammal that grazes on sea grass meadows. Good areas to see dugongs include the shallow waters of Moreton Bay and Torres Strait. Take care when boating in these areas – dugongs are slow moving and can be injured by propellors.

Birds

With a total topping 600 species, Queensland can boast a greater variety of birds than any other Australian state. A number are unique to Queensland and a few are found elsewhere only in New Guinea. The majority can be seen in eastern Queensland, particularly in the tropics, and avid birdwatchers will find an excellent variety of bird habitats within a 100km radius of Cairns.

Emu & Cassowary These huge, flightless birds are related to the ostrich of Africa. The **emu** has loose, shaggy feathers and inhabits woodlands and grasslands west of the Great Dividing Range. The **cassowary** is adapted for life in dense rainforests, where it feeds on fallen fruit. Both are also unusual because only the males incubate the eggs and care for the young.

Brush Turkey & Scrubfowl The **brush turkey** has all-black feathers but a bald neck and head, which are coloured red and yellow; the **scrubfowl** is soberly coloured apart from bright orange legs. These primitive birds of the rainforest make huge mounds of earth and rotting leaves in which the female lays her eggs. The eggs are incubated by the heat of the mound, which the parents regulate by adding or removing material.

Waterbirds This broad category includes a great variety, such as ducks and geese, herons and egrets, and smaller species that inhabit the margins of waterways. The best places to see a good variety are the tropical lagoons of the far north, especially as the dry season wears on and wildlife starts to congregate near permanent water.

Several species of **herons** and **egrets** feed side by side, spearing fish and frogs; one of the most attractive is the little **pied heron** of tropical lagoons. Two tiny ducks known as **pygmy-geese** feed and shelter among water lilies and the large **magpie goose** congregates in flocks around drying waterholes. The **black-necked stork** – popularly known as jabiru – is a striking iridescent black and white bird that grows to 1.2m tall. Most people assume jabiru is its Aboriginal name, but it is actually a Portuguese name for a South American stork.

The **comb-crested jacana** goes by a number of names, including lilytrotter and Jesus Christ bird, because it walks across floating vegetation on its enormously long, splayed toes. Jacanas are common on still waters. A bird you'll often see in rural Queensland is the stately **brolga** – a member of the crane family that feeds on frogs, insects and small reptiles. Brolgas are usually found near wetlands although it's not unusual to see them wandering around small outback towns like Normanton. Brolgas perform graceful courtship displays which have been absorbed into Aboriginal legends and ceremonies.

Birds of Prey Various birds of prey, including eagles, hawks and kites, are commonly seen perched along roadsides. The largest of all is the **wedge-tailed eagle**, which often feeds on road kills. The 'wedgie' is a massive bird; with a wingspan approaching 3m it soars on thermals while scanning the ground for prey such as rabbits and young kangaroos. Smaller species include the attractive **nankeen kestrel**, which hovers

Emus are common birds on the plains of outback Queensland. The cute, downy young are striped fawn and brown, and follow the male around in little groups.

over paddocks looking for mice and lizards, and the delicate **black-shouldered kite**. On the coast watch for fish-eating species such as the **osprey** and **white-bellied sea-eagle**.

Waders Every year vast flocks of small migratory birds arrive on Queensland's mudflats and waterways. These long-distance champions have flown from as far away as Siberia and run the gauntlet of hunters in South-East Asia before reaching protected shores in Australia. There are many species, including **sandpipers**, **plovers**, **curlew**, **stints** and **shanks**; all arrive in their nondescript non-breeding plumage of greys and browns which can make identification difficult. One of the best places to watch waders is on the Esplanade at Cairns, where high tide pushes them to within a few metres of the shore.

Parrots & Cockatoos Queensland has all bar a few of Australia's 53 species of parrots. Noisy, garrulous and colourful, most are also very common and a visitor will have little trouble seeing a few species anywhere in the state. Nor are the best restricted to the tropics: the **rainbow lorikeet** must be among the most gorgeous of all birds, yet it is extremely common along the east coast. Cockatoos have their stronghold in Australia and several species are very common indeed: the **galah** is an attractive pink and grey bird that can be seen in any rural area and the **sulphur-crested cockatoo** is a striking white bird that makes an appalling racket.

Queensland holds the dubious distinction of being the former home of Australia's only extinct bird. The **paradise parrot** once lived in the open woodlands west of the Great Dividing Range, but it was last seen in the 1920s and habitat destruction by cattle is thought to have contributed to its demise.

Kookaburras & Kingfishers The kookaburra's raucous laughter is one of the most distinctive sounds of the bush. Two species of these large kingfishers are found in Queensland – the widespread **laughing kookaburra** and the **blue-winged kookaburra**, which is found mainly in the tropics. Laughing kookaburras can become quite tame in campgrounds.

Smaller but more colourful kingfishers include the **sacred** and **forest kingfishers**, both of which are live mainly in forest, and the blue and orange **azure kingfisher**, which is always found near water. During the Wet the rainforests of north Queensland host the magnificent **buff-breasted paradise-kingfisher**, which nests in termite mounds on the forest floor. Julatten (see the Far North Queensland chapter) is a good place to see this beautiful bird.

The laughing kookaburra is a large and common member of the kingfisher family that feeds on lizards, small snakes and large insects.

Bowerbirds Unique to Australia and New Guinea, the bowerbirds have some of the most remarkable behaviour of any birds. The male constructs a bower of vegetation and decorates it with leaves, flowers and pebbles to attract a mate. The male **satin bowerbird** is a shimmering blue bird that even uses artificial blue objects, such as pen tops, drinking straws and clothes pegs, to decorate its bower. Two species – the **golden** and **tooth-billed bowerbirds** – are unique to the Wet Tropics, and the stunning **regent bowerbird** is found in the rainforests of south-east Queensland.

Birds of Paradise Although their stronghold is New Guinea, three species of this incredible group are found in the rainforests of Queensland. All are known as **riflebirds** and are quite common, although more often heard than seen. The male has glossy black plumage and an iridescent gorget which he shows off in a mesmeric display from a tree stump.

Magpie & Currawong The **Australian magpie** is a bold, common bird that is often seen around cities and towns. It has a distinctive and beautiful warbling call. Its relatives the **currawongs** are more common in forests. Currawongs are large black and white birds, with beady yellow eyes, that prey on small animals and nestlings. Their ringing calls are one of the most haunting sounds of the forest.

The Australian magpie can be aggressive in defence of its nest, swooping to drive off any intruder.

Reptiles & Frogs

As with so much of Australia's wildlife, reptiles reach their greatest number and diversity in Queensland. Many have a fearsome reputation, but the vast majority are harmless. All reptiles are protected in this state.

Turtles Sea turtles are found in tropical waters the world over, and are sometimes encountered by divers around islands of the Great Barrier Reef. **Sea turtles** live to a great age and spend all of their lives at sea, except when the females come ashore to lay their eggs. This spectacle can be seen at Mon Repos Beach near Bundaberg (see the Sunshine Coast chapter). A number of freshwater turtles – popularly called tortoises – live in inland rivers and creeks. A common species is the **snake-necked tortoise**, which draws its long neck sideways into its shell when threatened.

Snakes Many of Queensland's snakes are strikingly beautiful, although the chances of encountering one are not high. **Pythons** are subtly patterned and some species reach a great size. Pythons are harmless to humans and feed on small mammals which they crush to death before swallowing whole. The **green tree snake** is a slender, attractive snake common in rainforests. In arid areas, the **brown snake** is a common venomous species.

Treat all snakes with caution if you are unsure of their identification. Very few are aggressive and they'll usually get out of your way before you even realise they're there. See the Dangers & Annoyances section of the Facts for the Visitor chapter for ways of avoiding snakebite.

Once hunted almost to extinction, saltwater crocodiles are now protected and increasing in numbers. All crocodiles should be treated with caution.

Lizards There is a wide variety of lizards, from tiny **skinks** to prehistoric-looking **goannas** that can grow up to 2.5m long. Goannas can run very fast and when threatened will use their big claws to climb the nearest tree – or leg! Goannas can usually be seen around the park entrance at Noosa National Park (see the Sunshine Coast chapter). The slow-moving **bluetongue lizard** is sometimes kept as a pet by children; its even slower relation, the **shingleback**, is common in the outback. **Geckoes** are commonly seen in the tropics around lights at night, scaling walls and ceilings after small insects. The **leaf-tailed gecko** of rainforests grows up to 30cm in length and is superbly camouflaged to resemble bark and lichen.

Crocodiles Both Australia's species of crocodiles are found in Queensland: the large **saltwater** or **estuarine crocodile** and the smaller **freshwater** variety. 'Salties' are found in coastal areas north of Mackay, though there have been occasional sightings further south. Salties aren't confined to saltwater: they inhabit estuaries and after floods may be found many kilometres from the coast. They may even be found in permanent freshwater more than 100km inland. A large saltie – they can grow to 7m in length – can attack and kill a person.

'Freshies' are smaller than salties – anything over 4m should be regarded as a saltie. Freshies can be identified by their narrower snouts and smaller teeth that suit their fish diet. Though generally harmless to humans, freshies have been known to bite in defence of their nests, and children in particular should be kept away from them.

Very few tourists have been killed by salties and attacks still make headlines, but all crocodiles should be treated with extreme caution. To avoid the possibility of attack stay out of the water whenever you're in croc territory. Observe the guidelines contained in park brochures and you'll be quite safe.

Frogs Queensland has an astonishing diversity of frogs, from tiny froglets of marshes to the large tree frogs of the tropical rainforests. All frogs are totally inoffensive. The green tree frog is a large, bright green species that commonly inhabits outhouses and laundries; one can be found in virtually any caravan park in the state. By walking through rainforest at night with a torch (flashlight) you should be able to pick out the eyeshine of several other species of frogs.

Other wildlife

Queensland has an incredibly rich and diverse fauna of which, not surprisingly, smaller animals such as insects make up the vast majority of species. A dazzling variety of creatures – too many to describe in this space – inhabits the warm waters of the Great Barrier Reef (see the Capricorn Coast chapter for a brief introduction to the reef's amazing fauna).

Anglers will find good pickings virtually anywhere along the coast. The famous **barramundi** is a highly prized sports fish found in tropical coastal and estuarine waters. The bizarre **lungfish** is a rare prehistoric relic found only in a handful of Queensland rivers. It lives in fresh water and normally breathes through its gills, but if the water is stagnant and the level of oxygen in the water drops too low, it can surface and breath air through its lung. It can also survive out of water for a couple of days in a damp environment.

Mention should be made of the host of **butterflies** to be found in Queensland, particularly in the tropics. Many large and beautiful species are common, particularly on the edge of rainforests. The **birdwing** is aptly named as its 20cm wingspan and flight pattern give it a bird-like appearance from a distance. The male is boldly marked in green and black. The **Ulysses butterfly** is a large, electric blue species that flies high and fast. It has been adopted as the logo for Dunk Island (see the North Coast chapter).

FLORA

Queensland's diverse landforms support an incredible variety of plants, from the arid lands of the vast outback that burst into bloom after rains, to forests dominated by eucalypts and dense rainforests which support complex plant communities.

Good collections of native plants are grown at Brisbane's Mt Coot-tha Botanic Gardens, which features arid-zone plants; Flecker Botanic Gardens in Cairns, which has an interesting Aboriginal plant use area; and Townsville's Anderson Park, which features rainforest plants and palms from Cape York Peninsula and the tropical north.

Eucalypts Trees of the genus *Eucalyptus* dominate much of the Australian landscape; better known as gum trees, or eucalypts, they include about 560 species. Gums have tough, leathery leaves and periodically flower in profusion. Some species grow into huge trees and form extensive forests; others may be stunted by low rainfall or other climatic factors. They have adapted perfectly to the ancient cycles of drought, fire and flood, and old specimens play an important ecological role by providing nesting hollows for birds and mammals.

River red gums are generally confined to watercourses where their roots can tap a reliable supply of moisture. They have a dangerous habit of dropping large limbs, so while they may be good shade trees it is not wise to camp under one. The **ghost gum** is a striking tree of the outback, with glossy white bark and bright green leaves. These often majestic, spreading trees are common in tropical northern Australia. Common along watercourses and flood plains right through the outback's drier areas is the **coolabah**. All eucalypts are hardwoods and the coolabah is said to have the hardest timber of all: it is very strong and termite-resistant and became

Crush a eucalyptus leaf next time you're in the bush, and savour the refreshing aroma released. Eucalypts dominate the landscape over much of Queensland.

Acacias make up a huge group of trees better known as wattles. Most wattles are fast-growing and germinate quickly after fires.

sought after for building fences and stockyards before steel became readily available.

Eucalyptus oil is used for pharmaceuticals and perfumed products; their flowers are valued in honey production; and the gum tree features in folklore, art and literature. The smell of burning eucalyptus leaves and twigs is guaranteed to make any expatriate Aussie homesick.

Acacias These widespread plants go by many common names around the globe and are perhaps best known as the trees which dominate the savannahs of Africa. Many of the 660 species found in Australia are known as wattles. They tend to be fast-growing and short-lived, and come in many forms – from tall, weeping trees to prickly shrubs. Despite their many differences, all wattles have furry yellow flowers shaped like either a spike or a ball.

Mulga is a common acacia which occurs over vast tracts of the outback. Mulga sometimes forms dense thickets (the explorer John McDouall Stuart complained how the scrub near Alice Springs tore his clothes and pack saddles to bits) but usually grows as open woodland. Mulga leaves are very resistant to water loss, and the tree's shape directs any rain down to the base of the trunk where roots are densest. With these attributes mulga is a great drought survivor, but being good fodder for stock puts it at risk from overgrazing.

Mangroves Once considered to be swampy wastelands, mangrove forests are now recognised as an essential part of coastal ecosystems. Mangroves grow in dense stands along parts of Queensland's coast and tidal estuaries, where they help to stabilise the shoreline and provide habitat for a huge range of fish, birds, crabs, prawns and other wildlife.

Mangroves are uniquely adapted to survive inundation in saltwater: excess salt is expelled through their leaves; their tangled root systems enable them to 'breathe' when exposed at low tide; and they can store oxygen in spongy tissues for use during high tides. Mangroves are fascinating areas to explore, particularly at low tide, although they can also support huge populations of mosquitoes and sandflies. Mangroves are a favourite haunt of crocodiles.

Rainforest Almost all of the remnants of the tropical rainforest which once covered the Australian continent are found in north Queensland. While early settlers cleared most of these forests for farming and timber milling, they ignored some of the less accessible areas of the coastal mountains and ranges. These tropical forests provide a fascinating insight into a rich ecosystem of plants and animals, and are one of the major drawcards for visitors to the state. The **Moreton Bay fig** is one of many species of figs that are an integral part of rainforest ecology. They can grow to an enormous size, with broad, buttressed trunks and a dense canopy that can spread to cover an area the size of a small house. Their purple-green fruits are extremely attractive to birds and fruit bats. These majestic evergreen trees have been planted throughout Australia in avenues, parks and other public places.

Boab Trees Also known as bottle trees, these trees are similar in appearance to the African baobab tree, with their small bushy heads and swollen, pregnant-looking bases. They are widely found in the semi-arid areas of central Queensland and have been planted in avenues in quite a few outback towns (especially Roma). Boab trees can tolerate long periods of drought, and although it's a myth that their base contains drinkable water, their fibrous interior pith absorbs and stores moisture. During severe drought, pastoralists have been known to cut down bottle trees and feed this pith to cattle.

Spinifex One of the hardiest and most common desert plants is spinifex, the dense, dome-shaped masses of long, needle-like grass that grow on sandy soils and rocky hills. There are many species of spinifex, but most share an important characteristic: in dry times their leaves roll into tight cylinders to reduce the number of pores exposed to the sun and wind. This keeps water loss through evaporation to a minimum, but even so, most plants will succumb during a prolonged drought. Spinifex grasslands are very difficult to walk through – the explorer Ernest Giles called the prickly spinifex 'that abominable vegetable production'. They cover vast areas of the outback, and harbour rich populations of reptiles, rodents and other small animals.

Saltbush Millions of sheep and cattle living in the arid zone owe their survival to dry shrubby plants called saltbush, which get their name from their tolerance to saline conditions. Saltbush – there are 30 species – is extremely widespread and can be the dominant vegetation over vast areas.

Wildflowers After good autumn rains the normally arid inland explodes in a multicoloured carpet of wildflowers. The most common of these ephemerals, or short-lived plants, are the numerous species of daisy. Others include docks (which came to Australia in camel-saddle stuffing last century), parakelias, pussy tails and pea flowers. The seeds of desert ephemerals can lie dormant in sand for years until the right combination of temperature and moisture triggers germination. When this happens, life in the desert moves into top gear as the ephemerals hurry to complete their brief life cycles and woody plants burst into bloom. Sandhills, plains and rocky ridges come alive with nectar-feeding birds and insects, which adds up to a bumper harvest for predators. For nature lovers this is definitely the best time to tour the outback.

The boab tree's unusual shape has earned it the popular name 'bottle tree'. Boabs grow in outback Queensland but only in the tropics.

Cane Toads

One of the most enduring aural memories of the thousands of kilometres I drove through Queensland was the regular 'crunch-squelch' as I ran over yet another cane toad. That may sound sadistic but these gruesome, horny toads are everywhere, and constantly swerving to avoid them would be impossible, not to mention dangerous. Besides, I figured I was making a small contribution to the Queensland environment by running a few of the bastards over.

Ironically, cane toads were deliberately imported into Queensland from South America in 1935 in an attempt to combat the sugar-cane beetle, whose larvae had devastated Queensland's sugar industry. The experiment was an ecological disaster. The cane toads were supposed to be a predator of the beetles, but they soon realised it was much easier to dine on native insects, frogs and other unsuspecting goodies than worry about trying to catch flying beetles. And when they weren't gorging themselves, the toads spent their time having sex. They are prolific breeders, with the females laying up to 35,000 eggs in a single spawn. Before too long they had spread throughout Queensland in plague proportions, and in recent years have moved into parts of northern New South Wales. The toads have had a devastating effect on native animals – they have a poisonous gland on their shoulders, and their venom kills most of the birds, snakes and mammals that eat them.

Despite the toads' ugliness and ecological impact, Queenslanders have developed an almost grudging respect for them and their survival instinct. Cane toad races are a feature at quite a few pubs throughout Queensland – definitely one of the weirdest forms of gambling you'll come across.

There has even been a film made about them. If you want to learn more, hire the video *Cane Toads – An Unnatural History*, an offbeat and comical 1988 documentary that takes an in-depth look at the plague upon Queensland.

Mark Armstrong

ECOLOGY & ENVIRONMENT

While humans have been living in, and changing, the physical environment in Australia for at least 50,000 years, it is in the 200 years since European settlement that dramatic – and often harmful – change has taken place.

With the spread of settlement and the increase in pastoral use came clearing of native bush. The last 200 years have seen the loss or severe altering of 70% of all native vegetation, including the total loss of 40% of total forest area and 75% of rainforests. Land clearing continues today at the alarming rate of 600,000 hectares annually. Not only is marginal land being cleared for even more marginal farming, but old growth forests are logged for timber products.

Development, often in the name of tourism, has been the cause of numerous battles between developers and environmentalists in Queensland. Foremost among these was the furore which erupted when the then National government decided to bulldoze a road through the (now World

Heritage-listed) rainforest in the Daintree area of the far north. Most recently the Port Hinchinbrook development near Cardwell has been in the spotlight. The development work on the coast is on the edge of a World Heritage-listed area, and dredging work of the Hinchinbrook Channel has led to concern about the well-being of the local (and endangered) dugong population.

See the Useful Organisations section of the Facts for the Visitor chapter for details of environmental groups.

NATIONAL PARKS & STATE FORESTS
Queensland has an excellent system of national parks and other reserves, preserving unique flora, fauna and landscapes, areas of outstanding natural beauty and popular recreational areas such as islands of the Great Barrier Reef.

National Parks
Queensland has 212 national parks – protected wilderness areas of environmental or natural importance. While some cover just a single hill or lake, others are large wilderness areas. Many islands and stretches of the coast are national parks, including Fraser Island, Hinchinbrook Island, Moreton Island, Lizard Island, and most of the Whitsundays group.

Cape York Peninsula contains some of the state's best and most remote parks, including the Lakefield and Mungkan Kaanju national parks. And inland, some of the most spectacular parks are Lamington, on the forested rim of an ancient volcano on the New South Wales border; Carnarvon, with its 30km gorge south-west of Rockhampton; Lawn Hill, an oasis-like river gorge in the remote north-west corner; and rainforested Eungella, near Mackay, which is swarming with wildlife.

The international World Heritage List, which includes the Taj Mahal, the Pyramids and the Grand Canyon, currently includes four of Queensland's most significant areas: the Great Barrier Reef, the Wet Tropics areas of the coastal north, Fraser Island and the Riversleigh fossil fields at Lawn Hill. In recent years, various bodies have lobbied to have the Cape York Peninsula included on the list.

Queensland's national parks are managed by the Department of Environment. The Department operates the following main regional information centres:

Naturally Queensland Information Centre (the national parks head office)
   (☎ 3227 8185), 160 Ann St, Brisbane
South-West/Central Regional Office
   (☎ 4639 4599), 158 Hume St, Toowoomba
Central Coast Regional Office
   (☎ 4936 0511), corner of Yeppoon and Norman Sts, North Rockhampton
North Queensland Regional Office
   (☎ 4721 2399), Great Barrier Reef Wonderland, Townsville
Far North Regional Office
   (☎ 4052 3096), 10 McLeod St, Cairns

Another major office is the Whitsundays Regional Office (☎ 4946 7022), Shute Harbour Rd, Airlie Beach. It's worth calling at one of these to find out what's where, and to get the rundown on camping in the national parks.

There are also information centres and/or ranger stations in many of the parks, as well as Department of Environment offices in many towns. The park rangers themselves are often the best sources of info – they usually know their parks like the backs of their hands, and can tell you which are the best walking areas, which camping grounds are crowded, what birds and wildlife to look out for etc.

Public access to the parks is encouraged, so long as safety and conservation regulations are observed. Many parks have camping grounds with water, toilets and showers, and there are often privately run camping grounds, motels or lodges on the park fringes. Sizeable parks usually have a network of walking tracks, ranging from short discovery strolls to longer treks such as the three to five-day walk on Hinchinbrook Island.

To camp in a national park – whether in a camping ground or in the bush – you need a permit which you can either get in advance (by writing or calling in at the appropriate Department of Environment office) or from the ranger at the park itself. Many camping grounds also have self-registration booths, so if the rangers aren't around you can fill in a registration form and leave your permit fee in an envelope.

With the exception of Moreton and Fraser islands, camping fees at all national park sites are $3.50 per night per person for anyone over the age of four. Some of the more popular camping grounds fill up at holiday times, so you may need to book well ahead. Lists of camping grounds are available from Department of Environment offices.

The Department publishes a series of handy booklets called *Discover National Parks*, which have useful information about Queensland's national parks and state forests, including brief descriptions of the parks, suggestions for things to do, camping details and how to get to the parks. They cost $3 each and are available from bookshops and Department of Environment offices. Another booklet, *Camping in Queensland* ($5), contains useful info on more than 100 national parks, state forests and lakeside reserves with camping facilities throughout the state, including rates.

The Department of Environment publishes *Shades of Green: Exploring Queensland's Rainforests*, an excellent large-format paperback with colour photos and brief notes on the state's rainforest national parks and state forests.

State Forests

Queensland also has a large number of state forests – timber reserves which are selectively logged – and public reserves around reservoirs and water-catchment areas. These areas can be just as scenic and wild as national parks, depending of course on how recently the area has been logged. There are plenty of opportunities for recreation in the reserves – scenic drives, camping (free), bushwalking, trail-bike riding, 4WDing etc.

You can get information on state forest camping sites and facilities from tourist offices or from the Forest Services section of the Department of Primary Industry (☎ 3234 0158), on the 5th floor at 160 Mary St, Brisbane. Other forestry offices are at Fraser Rd, Two Mile, near Gympie; 52 McIllwraith St, Ingham; Gregory St, Cardwell; and also at 83 Main St, Atherton.

GOVERNMENT & POLITICS
Australian Government

Australia is a federation of six states and two territories, and has a parliamentary system of government based on the Westminster model. There are three tiers of government: federal, state and local. Under the Constitution, which came into force on 1 January 1901 when the colonies joined to form the Commonwealth of Australia, the federal government is mainly responsible for the national economy and Reserve Bank, customs and excise, immigration, defence, foreign policy, and post and telecommunications. The state governments are chiefly responsible for health, education, housing, transport and justice. There are both federal and state police forces.

In the federal parliament, the lower house is the House of Representatives, the upper house the Senate, and the government is led by a prime minister. Elections for the lower house are held at least every three years; senators serve six-year terms, with elections for half of them every three years.

Australia is currently a constitutional monarchy. The head of state is the governor general, and each state also has its own governor. Technically, the governor general and governors are the representatives of the British monarch – while the respective governments appoint them, these decisions must be ratified by the monarch. The issue of Australia becoming a republic is one of the hot topics of the late 90s (the boxed text gives more details).

Queensland Government

Queensland's state government is based in Brisbane. Queensland is the only state

Which Way an Australian Republic?

With the turn of the millennium looming, and with it the Sydney 2000 Olympic Games, followed closely by the centenary anniversary of Australian federation, the debate about Australia's national identity has become one of the major issues of the day. At the core of the debate is the current constitution, which sees Britain's Queen Elizabeth as the Australian head of state. On one side are the republicans, who want an Australian as head of state, on the other side the monarchists, who favour the status quo.

In a nutshell, the republican argument is that Australia over the past 40 years has become a multicultural society, with immigrants from at least 100 countries, a far cry from the Anglo-Celtic dominated population of a century ago. To republicans, the current constitutional set-up is an anachronism. Against this, monarchists argue that the current system of government has served Australia well – if it ain't broke, they say, why fix it?

The republic issue has been simmering since the mid-90s when it became a hobby horse of the then-prime minister, Paul Keating. It seemed back then that a republic was a sure bet, and that it was just a matter of time, and probably sooner rather than later. With the victory of John Howard, an avowed monarchist, in the 1996 election, however, the process slowed.

In 1997 Howard grudgingly set up a constitutional convention for early 1998, but put the onus on the 152 delegates at the convention to come up with a 'workable' model for an Australian republic. If they were able to do this, and the model was passed by a referendum to be held in 1999, Australia would become a republic on 1 January 2001, exactly 100 years after the current constitution, which saw the federation of the six colonies come into being.

The constitutional convention saw a frenzy of activity which eventually led to the adoption of a republic model. This model allowed for an Australian president chosen by the prime minister from a list prepared by a 15-member committee from public nominations, and the choice agreed to by the Opposition leader and a two-thirds majority of parliament.

While this model is not the one favoured by the majority of the roughly 60% of Australians who want a republic (they would prefer to see a president directly elected by popular vote), it is the one which will be put to the referendum vote in 1999. Changes to the constitution don't come easily, and it remains to be seen whether Australians are willing to accept the compromise model, cut ties with Britain and move into the next century as a republic.

without an upper house – it was abolished in 1922. Instead, the decisions of the Legislative Assembly (the lower house) are ratified by the Executive Council, which comprises the cabinet ministers and the governor. Elections for the lower house are held at least every three years; voting is by secret ballot and is compulsory for everyone 18 years of age and over.

Queensland's four main political parties are the Liberal Party, the Australian Labor Party (ALP), the National Party, and the new kid on the block, Pauline Hanson's One Nation Party. The Liberal Party is tra-

ditionally conservative, representing the interests of free enterprise, law and order and family values; the Australian Labor Party is traditionally socialist, having grown out of the workers' disputes and shearers' strikes of the 1890s; and the National Party is traditionally the party of rural interests, having originally formed to represent conservative farmers' unions.

One Nation is a new party which has struck a chord with many people disenchanted with what they see as the failure of the major parties to deliver, especially in 'the bush'. Ms Hanson's anti-immigration, anti-Asian, anti-tariff policies are seen to be simplistic, economically unsustainable and even downright racist, but they do have appeal to people who feel the major parties aren't listening to them. Her highly reported anti-immigration and anti-Asian sentiments have certainly done nothing to help Australia's image in Asia. It remains to be seen whether One Nation's support flows on to the next federal election (see also 'The Politics of Resentment' boxed text).

ECONOMY
Queensland is richly endowed with natural resources. Until the mining boom of the 1960s, Queenslanders were largely dependent on agricultural and pastoral production for most of their wealth.

Agriculture still plays a major economic role, employing around 10% of the state's workforce. Sugar cane is the major crop; Queensland produces about 95% of Australia's 35 million tonne sugar crop and exports nearly 4 million tonnes of raw sugar annually. Other major crops include wheat, sorghum, maize, barley and sunflower seed. A thriving fruit industry supplies most of Australia's tropical fruits, such as mangoes, bananas, pineapples and pawpaws, as well as producing many other fruits, such as apples, pears peaches, apricots etc.

The pastoral industry has always been one of the state's economic mainstays, and raising beef cattle for meat is the largest rural industry. Wool growing is also important, although less so in recent years.

Since the 1960s the mining sector has been at the forefront of the Queensland economy. Coal from the huge open-cut mines of central Queensland is the state's major export, with international shipping facilities at Hay Point (near Mackay), Abbot Point (near Bowen), and Gladstone. North-west Queensland is mineral-rich, and the copper, zinc, silver and lead mine at Mt Isa is one of the world's largest underground mines. On the Cape York Peninsula, Weipa has the world's largest bauxite mine. Goldmining has also undergone a resurgence in recent years. The Kidston mine in

north Queensland is the state's richest, and old mines at places like Charters Towers, Ravenswood and Mt Morgan are being reworked successfully.

Nowadays the manufacturing sector is playing an increasingly important economic role. The area around Brisbane is the main industrial centre, with textile, metal, food processing, car assembly and many other industries.

Other major industrial centres include Ipswich, Townsville and Gladstone, and sugar refineries are found throughout the north.

As this book indicates, Queensland is also incredibly rich in natural 'tourism' resources. In recent decades tourism has been the fastest growing sector of the economy and is now one of the state's major sources of income.

POPULATION & PEOPLE
Queensland has a population of more than 3.4 million, making up about 19% of the total Australian population. It's growth rate of 2.4% is double the national average. Around 80% of people live in urban areas, and the majority of Queenslanders live along the fertile coastal strip between Brisbane and Cairns. The other parts of the state are sparsely populated.

Queensland is notable for being the Australian mainland state with the largest proportion of its people living outside its capital city. The south-east corner of the state is Queensland's most crowded region, and more than 60% of the total population live within 150km of Brisbane. Brisbane has more than 1.5 million residents; the Gold Coast, Toowoomba and the Sunshine Coast are the south-east's other major population centres.

Of the string of cities along the east coast, Maryborough, Hervey Bay, Bundaberg, Gladstone, Rockhampton, Mackay, Townsville and Cairns have populations of more than 20,000. In contrast, the mining town of Mt Isa is the only place in the interior to top this figure.

In a 1996 census, around 95,500 people

stated they were of indigenous origin: Aborigines and Torres Strait Islanders, most of whom live in the north of the state or on the islands between Cape York and Papua New Guinea.

The first European settlers to arrive were predominantly of English, Scottish or Irish descent. At first, these settlers had access to convict labour, but with the closure of the Moreton Bay penal colony in 1842 they were forced to find alternative sources of labour. The solution was to begin importing cheap labour from other countries – Indian and Chinese coolies, Melanesians (known as Kanakas), and German contract workers – to work the land, a pattern which continued until WWI.

From the mid-1800s, a series of large-scale migration programs and promotional campaigns were instigated to boost Queensland's white population, which by 1861 numbered a mere 30,000. Britons and Germans were the main targets of these programs, but many Irish, Scandinavians and Italians packed up and moved to Queensland, lured by incentives including sponsored passage or free land on arrival.

The discovery of gold in Queensland provided an even greater incentive, and people from all around the world poured into Queensland during the 1870s, including thousands of Chinese miners. By 1876, the Chinese comprised 6% of Queensland's population, but far from being welcomed into the young colony, the Chinese were vilified and portrayed as immoral heathens. Hounded by racist attitudes and policies, the majority of them left in the 1880s.

By 1891 the state's population had risen to 394,000; by 1921 it was 756,000. At this stage, the majority of Queenslanders were still of English, Scottish and Irish descent, although a significant number of Italians were working in the sugar industry of north Queensland. Germans, Scandinavians, Russians, and Spaniards comprised the other significant minority groups.

Throughout these growth periods, Queensland's immigration policies led to ongoing racial tensions, with xenophobic Anglo

workers resenting having to compete with cheap imported labour. As a result, Queensland's Labor government developed policies biased towards Anglo-Celtic migrants.

After WWII Australia's mass migration policies transformed the country from a predominantly Anglo-Celtic culture into the multi-cultural society it is today.

Thousands of Jewish survivors of the Holocaust came to Australia, along with people from Italy, Greece, Turkey, Lebanon and Yugoslavia. More recently there have been large influxes of Asians, particularly Vietnamese after the Vietnam War.

Queensland, however, received only about 8% of new immigrants after WWII, with the state government actively discouraging immigrants from moving to urban centres and 'cluttering up the labour market'. As a result, Queensland has a less diverse cultural mix than other states.

In recent years, Queensland's major source of human resources has been internal migration. Since 1980, more than half a million Australians have moved to Queensland from other states, seeking a new life in the land of sunshine and dreams.

ARTS & CULTURE

In the epilogue to his 1982 *A History of Queensland*, local historian Ross Fitzgerald lamented 'the cultural wasteland that is Queensland'. Fitzgerald thought the blame for Queensland's cultural malaise lay with a range of factors, including the authoritarianism and anti-intellectualism of the then National/Liberal Party government, the historically low value that had been placed on education in Queensland, and the low levels of overseas migration that meant that 'Queenslanders have been less exposed than other Australians to the clash and challenge of new and heterodox ideas'.

Times have changed somewhat. The National Party finally fell from grace, and with them went much of the repressiveness and intolerance that characterised their reign.

The former state Labor government restored the civil liberties which were taken away by the former Bjelke-Petersen government, such as the right to assembly, and did much to stimulate and encourage artistic and cultural developments. Never-the-less, it has to be said that Queensland retains strong elements of its conservative past, and that in many ways it is still well and truly entrenched in the cultural main-stream.

Painting

Most of the major developments in the world of Australian visual arts since settlement have taken place in Sydney and Melbourne. Queensland has played only a minor role, although there are a number of excellent galleries which exhibit the works of Australian artists. In particular, the Queensland Art Gallery in Brisbane is well worth visiting and has an excellent Australian collection.

Lloyd Rees is probably the best-known artist to have come out of Queensland and has an international reputation. Others include Ian Fairweather, Godfrey Rivers, Davida Allen (famous for her obsessive portraits of the actor Sam Neill) and Bill Robinson, who won the 1995 Archibald Prize for portraiture with his quirky *Portrait of the Artist With Stunned Mullet*.

Queensland is a rich centre of traditional and contemporary Aboriginal art. Judy Watson and Gordon Bennett have both won the Moët & Chandon Prize for contemporary artists.

Although Tracey Moffatt is now based in Sydney, her work is also worth looking out for. See the Brisbane chapter for details of galleries featuring Australian art.

Literature

Two of the most widely acclaimed early Australian writers were AB ('Banjo') Paterson and Henry Lawson. Paterson's classics include *Clancy of the Overflow* and *The Man from Snowy River*. Henry Lawson's greatest legacy are his short stories of life in the bush – *The Drover's Wife* and *A Day on a Selection* are good examples. Lawson published a number of short story collections, including *While the*

Billy Boils (1896) and *Joe Wilson and His Mates* (1901).

Steele Rudd, a contemporary of Paterson and Lawson's, was born in Toowoomba in 1868. With his classic sketches of the hardships of early Queensland life and the enduring characters he created like 'Dad & Dave' and 'Mother & Sal', Rudd became one of the country's best loved comic writers.

Rolf Boldrewood's classic *Robbery Under Arms* tells the tale of Captain Starlight, Queensland's most notorious bushranger and cattle thief. Neville Shute's famous novel *A Town Like Alice* is partly set in Burketown, in the Gulf Savannah.

The prolific Ion Idriess was one of Australia's most popular early writers, and most of his stories were set in the outback. They include *Flynn of the Inland*, the story of the man who created the Flying Doctor Service; *The Cattle King*, a portrayal of the life of wealthy pastoralist Sydney Kidman; and *Nemarluk: King of the Wilds*, about an Aboriginal resistance fighter in the Top End.

Ray Lawler's play *Summer of the Seventeenth Doll*, about two north Queensland cane cutters and their girlfriends, was first performed back in 1955. With its portrayal of mateship and the ethos of the stereotypical bushmen, 'The Doll' is considered to be a watershed in Australian drama.

Queensland has produced plenty of outstanding writers of its own. In particular, Brisbane's University of Queensland has for many years been one of Australia's richest literary breeding grounds.

David Malouf is one of Queensland's most internationally recognised writers. Born in Brisbane to Lebanese immigrants, his novels include the evocative *Johnno* and *12 Edmondstone Street*, tales of an Australian boyhood set in the Brisbane of the 1940s and 1950s. Malouf's other works include *The Great World* (perhaps his best), *Fly Away Peter* and *An Imaginary Life*.

Australia's best-known Aboriginal poet and writer, Oodgeroo Noonuccal (Kath Walker) was born on North Stradbroke Island in 1920, and buried there in September 1993. Her 1964 book *We Are Going* was the first published work by an Aboriginal woman; her other works include *My People*.

Thea Astley's 11 published novels include *Hunting the Wild Pineapple*, set in the rainforests of north Queensland, and *It's Raining in Mango*, a historical saga which traces the fortunes and failures of one pioneer family from the 1860s to the 1980s.

Expatriate writer Janet Turner Hospital was born in Melbourne but moved to Brisbane aged seven, and attended school and university there. Her works include *The Ivory Swing*, *The Tiger in the Tiger Pit*, *Charade* and the wonderful *The Last Magician*, parts of which are set in the rainforests of Queensland.

Ipswich-born Thomas Shapcott is an editor and one of Australia's most prolific writers. His recent books include *The White Stag of Exile*, set in Brisbane and Budapest around the turn of the century.

Rodney Hall, who attended school in Brisbane but now lives in NSW, is another major Australian literary figure and his masterpiece, the *Yandilla Trilogy*, is one of the great epics of Australia's colonial era. It comprises the novels *Captivity Captive*, *The Second Bridegroom* and *The Grisly Wife*.

Nancy Cato writes popular historical and romantic works which include *All the Rivers Run*, which was made into a TV series. Another of Cato's works, *Brown Sugar*, is billed as 'a story of love and inter-racial passions set against the backdrop of the Queensland sugar industry'. Hmmm.

Journalist Hugh Lunn has written a number of popular books on and about Queensland. They include his humorous two-part autobiography *Over the Top With Jim* and *Head Over Heels*.

In recent years, Brisbane has produced a new wave of promising young writers. Andrew McGahan, a university dropout, wrote his controversial first novel *Praise* in about two months – it shows, but he won the prestigious Australian Vogel Literary Award. Set in the seedy underbelly of Brisbane's Fortitude Valley, *Praise* is a tale of

sex, unemployment, sex, drugs and more sex. Verano Armanno's *Romeo of the Underworld* is another contemporary novel set in the Valley. Another prominent young writer is Matthew Condon, whose novels include *The Motorcycle Cafe* and *Usher*. Helen Darville gained notoriety for her novel *The Hand That Signed the Paper*, which won the Miles Franklin Award.

Architecture

Queensland's architectural beginnings were of the humblest kind. Many of the first settlers to arrive in the colony lived itinerant lives, and their homes reflected this. Canvas tents and tarpaulins, slab-timber cabins and bark huts were the most common types of early dwelling, and even by the time of the first census in 1861, more than 50% of housing was classified as 'temporary'.

As the colony became more established, towns grew and settlers settled, and temporary dwellings were gradually replaced by more permanent structures, the majority of which were built from locally sawn timber. Brick was used in a handful of areas which had local clay deposits, but timber was by far the most common building material. Early houses were even roofed with shingles or bark sheets, although galvanised iron soon took over and became the ubiquitous roofing material.

These early squatters' houses built from timber and iron became the model for the classic 'Queenslanders', the distinctive buildings which you'll still see throughout the state. Queenslanders (we're talking houses, not people ...) are generally square in shape and raised off the ground by stumps or poles, with a high-pitched iron roof and broad, shady verandahs on at least two, and often four sides. There are various advantages to having the houses raised off the ground: the under-house ventilation keeps them cooler and reduces humidity; pests such as termites can be controlled by protecting the stumps with tar or creosote; and using stumps of varying heights allows the houses to be built on hillsides.

Queenslanders are found in all parts of

the state, and while the designs vary idiosyncratically from place to place, the general format remains the same. From the lonely houses surrounded by cane fields in the north, to the clusters of timber houses in Brisbane's hill suburbs, these buildings remain an enduring image of Queensland for most travellers.

On the other hand, for a time many locals grew to be less than enchanted with them as homes, and considered them to be ugly, pest-ridden woodpiles that were hard to keep clean. In recent years there has been something of a turnaround in attitudes, and Queenslanders are now widely appreciated as a unique part of the state's architectural heritage. These days many people renovate and restore their old homes instead of tearing them down and replacing them with modern, functional and dull brick blocks.

Apart from lots of old Queenslanders, almost every town in Queensland has a number of impressive public buildings. First and foremost would have to be the country pub, perhaps the most important of all public facilities and traditionally the town's social focus. Town halls, railway stations, courthouses, post offices, banks and masonic lodges are also worth looking out for – you can read much about each town's history from a study of its public buildings.

Most of Queensland's more impressive public buildings date back to the boom years of the mid to late-1800s (the height of the Victorian era), or to the period between the turn of the century and WWI (the Federation era). Some of the state's finest Victorian architecture is found in the old gold-mining towns, places like Charters Towers, Ravenswood, Cooktown, Gympie and Mt Morgan, while the immense pastoral wealth of the Darling Downs built towns like Roma, Toowoomba and Warwick. Brisbane, as the capital, seat of government and economic centre, also has its fair share of prominent Victorian-era buildings.

By the 1890s many of the goldfields had begun to decline, and a world-wide recession had brought Queensland's economy to its knees; together, these factors brought Queensland's first construction boom to a grinding halt.

As the turn of the century and Australia's pending federation approached, a new style of architecture known as Federation began to evolve. It featured simplicity of design and less ornamentation, and produced buildings more suited to the Australian climate and environment.

Much of Queensland's modern architecture is less noteworthy. Rabid developers and a short-sighted obsession with 'progress' have produced such architectural eyesores as the high-rise concrete jungles that engulf the Gold Coast and parts of the Sunshine Coast, and several other booming tourist centres are in danger of following suit.

On a more positive note, Queensland's growing ecotourism industry has led to a trend in resort developments that attempt to blend in with their environment and achieve a degree of stylistic integrity – see the Far North Queensland chapter for examples.

Music

Queensland is the birthplace of Australia's most famous song. Banjo Patterson wrote the lyrics to *Waltzing Matilda*, Australia's unofficial national anthem, early in 1895 while he was visiting his fiancée at an outback station near Winton in central Queensland.

Queensland hosts a wide range of music festivals throughout the year, featuring everything from jazz and blues to chamber music and alternative rock. Two of the best known music events are the legendary Woodford Folk Festival, held annually between Christmas and New Year, and the Brisbane Biennial International Music Festival, held every odd year from late May to early June.

Plenty of towns in Queensland host regular bush dances featuring folk and country bands – bush dances are great fun, and an excellent way to meet the locals and gain an insight into Australian music.

Country and western line dancing has also become incredibly popular in recent years.

Indigenous music is one of the Australian music industry's great success stories of recent years. Yothu Yindi, with their land rights anthem *Treaty*, is the country's best known Aboriginal band, but Queensland has produced some outstanding indigenous musicians of its own. Christine Anu is a Torres Strait Islander who was born in Cairns. Her debut CD *Stylin' Up* blends Creole-style rap, Islander chants and traditional languages with English – highly recommended listening.

Brisbane's pub-rock scene may not have produced the same wealth of bands that have come out of Sydney and Melbourne, but a couple of Australia's all-time greatest bands had their beginnings in the Sunshine State. The Go Betweens started out in Queensland, and many of their songs like *Cattle & Cane* evoke a strong sense of place. Their best albums include *Tallulah* and *Before Hollywood* – great driving music while you're travelling around Queensland.

The Saints, considered by many people to be one of the seminal punk bands, started out in Brisbane in the mid-1970s before moving onto bigger things in Sydney, and later London.

More recently, Brisbane bands like Custard and Regurgitator have shot to prominence in Australia's alternative music scene.

Cinema

Queensland has a growing film industry based around the Warner-Roadshow studios at Movie World on the Gold Coast, and has also become a popular location for foreign productions, although none has so far done much at the box office.

Films which have been made or shot in Queensland recently include *Streetfighter*, based on a popular martial arts video game, starring Kylie Minogue and Jean-Claude Van Damme; *Escape from Absalom*, a futuristic action-adventure set on a prison island, starring Ray Liotta; *Rough Diamonds*, in which an ex-pop star and her 13-year-old daughter leave Brisbane and travel to the outback where they meet a singing cattle breeder (Jason Donovan); *Travelling North*, based on a play by David Williamson and starring Leo McKern and Julia Blake; *The Fringe Dwellers*, based on the novel of the same name by Nene Gare; *Broken Highway*, made by writer-director Laurie McGuinness and starring Claudia Karvan and Aden Young; *The Island of Dr Moreau*; and *The Phantom*.

Parts of the hit films *Muriel's Wedding* and *Crocodile Dundee I* were also shot on location in Queensland.

Alternative Lifestyles

Under the National Party, Queensland considered itself to be one of Australia's great bastions of conservatism. The leader of the Nationals, Sir Joh Bjelke-Petersen, had a reputation as a wowser, and considered all that hippie nonsense that went on down in the southern states to be totally unsuitable for Queenslanders. The notorious 1976 raid on the 'hippie commune' at Cedar Bay, in the rainforests north of Cape Tribulation, was one of many examples of Joh's refusal to accept anyone or anything beyond the mainstream.

Attitudes have changed substantially since then, although Queensland still has nothing to compare to the alternative lifestyle communities that have flourished in northern New South Wales since the late 1960s. There are several alternative lifestyle towns in the Sunshine Coast hinterland, such as Maleny, Mooloolah and Eumundi, and several of Brisbane's inner suburbs have a distinctly alternative flavour. The mountain village of Kuranda near Cairns has always attracted its share of hippies, but in recent years Kuranda has been turned into a mainstream tourist attraction based on its 'alternative charm and character' – most of which has been destroyed by the flood of commercial tourism.

The rainforests of Far North Queensland are home to the state's best known communities of alternative lifestylers – the Ferals.

Environmental as Anything

Ferals, the alternative lifestylers who live deep in the dark rainforests of Far North Queensland, are the hippies of the 1990s – with a couple of fundamental differences. The long hair, flares, tie-dyed clothes and peace signs of the 1960s and 70s have been replaced by shaven or dreadlocked hair, ragged rainbow-coloured clothes, bare feet or heavy work boots, and pierced noses, ears and belly-buttons. And instead of peace, love and understanding, ferals espouse radical environmentalism.

Ideologically, ferals reject contemporary culture and see city life as the ultimate urban nightmare. They consider the mass-production, mass-consumption doctrines that drive modern society to be totally unsustainable in the long term. Rather than seeing themselves as dropouts, ferals consider their lifestyle to be the way of the future, and believe that their rejection of materialism is the only way modern society will ever progress to a point where life on earth is sustainable.

Ferals live in communal, semi-nomadic tribal groups. Most of them are vegetarians who live off unemployment benefits and avoid using mass produced goods or fossil fuels; they see themselves at the protectors of the forests they live in. You'll often see them wandering barefoot around places like Cairns and Mossman, where they come to collect supplies and their unemployment benefits.

RELIGION

A shrinking majority of people in Queensland are at least nominally Christian. Most Protestant churches have merged to become the Uniting Church, although the Church of England has remained separate. The Catholic Church is popular, with the original Irish adherents now joined by large numbers of Mediterranean immigrants.

Non-Christian minorities abound, the main ones being Buddhist, Jewish or Muslim. Almost 20% of the population describe themselves in the 1996 census as having no religion.

ABORIGINAL CULTURE
Aboriginal Religion

Traditional Aboriginal cultures are either irreligious or are nothing but religion, depending on how you look at it. Is a belief system which views every event, no matter how trifling, in a non-material context a religion? The early Christian missionaries certainly didn't think so. For them a belief in a deity was an essential part of a religion, and anything else was mere superstition.

Sacred Sites

Aboriginal sacred sites are a perennial topic of discussion. Their presence can lead to headline-grabbing controversy when they stand in the way of developments such as roads, mines and dams. This is because most other Australians still have difficulty understanding the Aborigines' deep spiritual bond with the land.

Aboriginal religious beliefs centre on the continuing existence of spirit beings that lived on Earth during the Dreamtime, which occurred before the arrival of humans. These beings created all the features of the natural world and were the ancestors of all living things. They took different forms but behaved as people do, and as they travelled about they left signs to show where they passed. Most Australians have heard of rainbow serpents carving out rivers as they slithered from A to B. On a smaller scale you can have a pile of rocks marking the spot where an ancestor defecated, or a tree that sprang from a thrown spear.

Despite being supernatural, the ancestors were subject to ageing and eventually they returned to the sleep from which they'd awoken at the dawn of time. Some sank back into the ground while others changed into physical features including the moon and stars. Here their spirits remain as eternal forces that breathe life into the newborn and influence natural events. Each ancestor's spiritual energy flows along the path it travelled during the Dreamtime and is strongest at the points where it left physical evidence of its activities, such as a tree, hill or claypan. These features are sacred sites.

The ancestors left strict laws that determine the behaviour of people and animals, the growth of plants, and natural events such as rain and the change of seasons. Although all living things are considered to be conscious beings with their own language and way of life, they are still required to live in accordance with their ancestors' laws.

Every person, animal and plant is believed to have two souls – one mortal and one immortal. The latter is part of a particular ancestral spirit and returns to the sacred sites of that ancestor after death, while the mortal soul simply fades into oblivion. Each person is spiritually bound to the sacred sites that mark the land associated with his or her ancestor. It is the individual's obligation to help care for these sites by performing the necessary rituals and singing the songs that tell of the ancestor's deeds. By doing this, the order created by that ancestor is maintained.

However, the ancestors are extremely powerful and restless spirits and require the most careful treatment. Calamity can befall those who fail to care for their sites in the proper manner. As there is nowhere beyond the influence of an angry ancestor, the unpleasant consequences of either disrespect or neglect at a single site may stretch far and wide.

Some of the sacred sites are believed to be dangerous and entry is prohibited under traditional Aboriginal law. These restrictions often have a pragmatic origin. One site in northern Australia was believed to cause sores to break out all over the body of anyone visiting the area. Subsequently, the area was found to have a dangerously high level of radiation from naturally occurring radon gas. In another instance, fishing from a certain reef was traditionally prohibited. This restriction was scoffed at by local Europeans until it was discovered that fish from this area had a high incidence of ciguatera, which renders fish poisonous if eaten by humans.

Unfortunately, Aboriginal sacred sites are not like Christian churches, which can be desanctified before the bulldozers move in. Neither can they be bought, sold or transferred. Other Australians find this difficult to accept because they regard land as belonging to the individual, whereas in Aboriginal society the reverse applies. In a nutshell, Aborigines believe that to destroy or damage a sacred site threatens not only the living but also the spirit inhabitants of the land. It is a distressing and dangerous act, and one that no responsible person would condone.

Throughout much of Australia when pastoralists were breaking the Aborigines' subsistence link to the land, many Aborigines sought refuge on missions and became Christians. However, becoming Christians has not, for most Aborigines, meant renouncing their traditional religion. Many senior Aboriginal law men are also devout Christians, and in many cases ministers.

Aboriginal Language

At the time of contact there were around 250 separate Australian languages spoken by the 600 to 700 Aboriginal 'tribes', and many of these languages were as distinct from each other as English and French. Often three or four adjacent tribes would speak what amounted to dialects of the same language, but another adjacent tribe might speak a completely different language.

It is believed that all the languages evolved from a single language family as the Aborigines gradually moved out over the entire continent and split into new groups. There are a number of words that occur right across the continent, such as

Traditional Aboriginal Culture

Early European settlers and explorers usually dismissed the entire Aboriginal population as 'savages' and 'barbarians', and it was some time before the Aborigines' deep spiritual bond with the land, and their relationship to it, was understood by non-indigenous Australians.

Society & Lifestyle Traditionally, the Aborigines were tribal people living in extended family groups or clans, with clan members descending from a common ancestral being. Tradition, rituals and laws linked the people of each clan to the land they occupied. Each clan had various sites of spiritual significance on their land and places to which their spirits would return when they died. Clan members came together to perform rituals to honour their ancestral spirits and the creators of the Dreaming. These traditional religious beliefs were the basis of the Aborigines' ties to the land they lived and thrived on for thousands of years before the coming of Europeans.

It was the responsibility of the clan, or particular members of it, to correctly maintain and protect the sites so that the ancestral beings were not offended and would continue to protect the clan. Traditional punishments for those who neglected these responsibilities was often severe, as their actions could easily affect the well-being of the whole clan – food and water shortages, natural disasters or mysterious illnesses could all be attributed to disgruntled or offended ancestral beings.

Many Aboriginal communities were almost nomadic, others sedentary, one of the deciding factors being the availability of food. Where food and water were readily available the people tended to remain in a limited area. When they did wander, however, it was to visit sacred places to carry out rituals, or to take advantage of seasonal foods available elsewhere. They did not, as is still widely believed, roam aimlessly and desperately in search for food and water.

The traditional role of the men was that of hunter, tool-maker and custodian of male law; the women reared the children, and gathered and prepared food. There was also female law and ritual for which the women were responsible.

Environmental Awareness Wisdom and skills obtained over millennia enabled Aborigines to use their environment to the maximum. An intimate knowledge of the behaviour of animals and the correct time to harvest the many plants they utilised ensured that food shortages were rare. They never hunted an animal species or harvested a plant species to the point where it was threatened with extinction. Like other hunter-gatherer peoples of the world, the Aborigines were true ecologists.

Although Aborigines in northern Australia had been in regular contact with the farming peoples of Indonesia for at least 1000 years, the farming of crops and the domestication of

jina (foot) and *mala* (hand), and similarities also exist in the often complex grammatical structures.

Following European contact the number of Aboriginal languages was drastically reduced. At least eight separate languages were spoken in Tasmania alone, but none of these was recorded before the native speak-

ers either died or were killed. Of the original 250 or so languages, only around 30 are today spoken on a regular basis and are taught to children.

Aboriginal Kriol is a new language which has developed since European arrival in Australia. It is spoken across northern Australia and has become the 'native' lan-

livestock held no appeal. The only major modification of the landscape practised by the Aborigines was the selective burning of undergrowth in forests and dead grass on the plains. This encouraged new growth, which in turn attracted game animals to the area. It also prevented the build-up of combustible material in the forests, making hunting easier and reducing the possibility of major bush fires. Dingoes were domesticated to assist in the hunt and to guard the camp from intruders.

Hunting & Trading Similar technology – for example the boomerang and spear – was used throughout the continent, but techniques were adapted to the environment and the species being hunted. In the wetlands of northern Australia, fish traps hundreds of metres long made of bamboo and cord were built to catch fish at the end of the wet season. In the area now known as Victoria, permanent stone weirs many kilometres long were used to trap eels, while in the tablelands of Queensland finely woven nets were used to snare mobs of wallabies and kangaroos.

The Aborigines were also traders. Trade routes crisscrossed the country, dispersing goods and a variety of produced items along their way. Many of the items traded, such as certain types of stone or shell, were rare and had great ritual significance. Boomerangs and ochre were other important trade items. Along the trading networks which developed, large numbers of people would often meet for 'exchange ceremonies', where not only goods but also songs and dances were passed on.

Cultural Life The simplicity of the Aborigines' technology contrasts with the sophistication of their cultural life. Religion, history, law and art are integrated in complex ceremonies which depict the activities of their ancestral beings, and prescribe codes of behaviour and responsibilities for looking after the land and all living things. The link between the Aborigines and the ancestral beings are totems, each person having their own totem, or Dreaming. These totems take many forms, such as caterpillars, snakes, fish and magpies. Songs explain how the landscape contains these powerful creator ancestors, who can exert either a benign or a malevolent influence. They tell of the best places and the best times to hunt, and where to find water in drought years. They can also specify kinship relations and marriage partners.

guage of many young Aborigines. It contains many English words, but the pronunciation and grammar are along Aboriginal lines, the meaning is often different, and the spelling is phonetic. For example, the sentence in English 'He was amazed' becomes 'I bin luk kwesjinmak' in Kriol.

There are a number of generic terms which Aborigines use to describe themselves, and these vary according to the region. The most common of these is Koori, used for the people of south-east Australia; Murri is used to refer to the people of Queensland.

Facts for the Visitor

HIGHLIGHTS

Mention Queensland and most people immediately think of endless sunshine and blue skies, the wonders of the Great Barrier Reef, island resorts and beaches, and the rainforests of North Queensland. Well, there's all of that, and much more ...

Taking it from the top, the **Cape York Peninsula** is one of Australia's last great adventure trips. All the roads through the Cape are dirt and there are numerous river crossings, so you need a 4WD to get all the way to the top. The diversity of landscapes on the Cape is amazing. It's one of the last frontiers, a rugged place of crocodiles and barramundi, remote national parks, rainforested mountains, tropical savannah, Aboriginal rock art and lonely roadhouses.

The **Gulf Savannah**, in the northwestern corner of Queensland, is also largely the domain of the adventure traveller. It's a remote, hot, tough and sparsely populated region, and most visitors come for the fishing (sensational!) or are 4WD travellers on their way somewhere. The Gulf also has two of Queensland's most spectacular natural attractions – the **Lawn Hill National Park**, an oasis-like river gorge with the superb Riversleigh fossil field in the north-west; and the **Undara Lava Tubes**, a series of ancient and enormous volcanic tubes about 260km southwest of Cairns.

Far North Queensland is a relatively small area, but it's jam-packed with tourist drawcards. Centred around **Cairns**, this area has it all – the reef and islands, the rainforests, **Cape Tribulation** and the **Daintree**, the **Atherton Tablelands** – and you don't have to travel far inland to sample the outback. North of Cairns, **Port Douglas** is one of the state's most fashionable resort towns. Further north again is **Cooktown**, on the fringe of Cape York and a great place to visit if you want to sample

what Far North Queensland was like pretourism.

On the **North Coast** between Cairns and Townsville, **Hinchinbrook Island** is a majestic island national park and unspoiled wilderness. The Thorsborne Trail, a 32km walking track along the island's east coast, takes a memorable three to five days. Townsville has the **Great Barrier Reef Wonderland** with its excellent aquarium, and inland from Townsville you can visit the old **gold-mining centres** of Charters Towers and Ravenswood. There are some great little national parks along the coast between Townsville and Mission Beach, including Paluma Range. Bedarra Island, offshore from Mission Beach, is perhaps the best and most exclusive of the **island resorts** along the coast, and if you can afford the $1000-plus a night don't miss it.

The continental islands of the **Whitsundays** contrast idyllically with the deep blue-green waters which surround them, and the Whitsundays is one of the best areas for pleasure boating. There are some great resorts out on the islands, ranging from simple backpackers' cabins on Hook Island to the indulgence of five-star luxury on Hayman Island. **Eungella National Park**, inland from Mackay, is one of the best places to see platypus in the wild – it's also a great spot for bushwalks, camping and hang-gliding.

On the **Capricorn Coast**, north-east of Rockhampton, **Great Keppel Island** is one of the most attractive and popular islands along the coast. There's a resort, plus a few more affordable options, and Keppel's beaches are just great. Further south are the Southern Reef Islands – Lady Elliot and Heron islands offer some of the best diving along the reef. Inland from Rockhampton is the spectacular **Blackdown Tableland National Park**, and the rugged gemfields around Sapphire and Rubyvale are also well worth a visit. A couple of hundred km south of Sapphire is the **Carnarvon National Park**, another oasis-like gorge and a wonderful place for bushwalking.

Back on the coast is **Fraser Island**, the world's largest sand island and one of the state's true gems. Fraser is simply stunning. Between August and mid-October, you can join one of the many **whale-watching** tours which operate out of nearby **Hervey Bay**.

The south-east corner of Queensland is the state's most densely populated area, and a popular one for tourism. **Brisbane** is often overlooked by travellers, but it's a surprisingly cosmopolitan city with a lively inner-city area, and there's an amazing diversity of attractions within a couple of hours' drive of the state capital. One hour north of Brisbane is the **Sunshine Coast**, with a string of busy resort towns along the coast (including trendy Noosa Heads), and an attractive hinterland packed with surprises.

The **Gold Coast** is the most heavily developed tourist area in Queensland – it might not be to everybody's taste, but its beaches, restaurants, nightclubs and theme parks attract millions of visitors every year. A short drive inland from the Gold Coast are the wonderful **Springbrook** and **Lamington national parks** – great places for bushwalking, camping and generally communing with nature. The **Darling Downs**, south-west of Brisbane, also has some great national parks. The area around Stanthorpe is one of the only places in Queensland where it really does get cold – they celebrate winter by holding the Brass Monkey Festival! Stanthorpe is also the centre of the state's only winery district. Warwick and Toowoomba are both attractive cities, with plenty of historic buildings.

Queensland's vast **outback** offers a completely different experience to the hedonistic pleasures of the coast. The outback towns all have their own particular character – places like **Birdsville**, with its famous pub and annual race meeting; Longreach, with the **Stockman's Hall of Fame**; **Mt Isa**, with its enormous mine brooding

darkly over the town; and the dozens of little places, like Stonehenge, where you can meet the entire population while you're sitting on a bar stool. And between the towns? Endless wide open spaces, the monotony of the lonely roads, huge road trains spewing trails of dust, slow-moving cattle and sheep, graceful emus and brolgas ...

PLANNING
When to Go

The winter months are Queensland's busiest time for tourism – it's the place the Mexicans (a banana-bender's term for anyone from south of the border) head for to escape the cold southern winters. The main tourist season stretches from April to November, and the official high-season is from June to September. As with elsewhere in the country, the Easter and Christmas breaks are also considered to be high-season.

Queensland doesn't really have what most of us would call a winter. Even in mid-July, when people in the southern states are snuggling up in front of open fires and heading for the ski slopes, you'll find people swimming at Queensland's beaches. Winter is the perfect time to visit – the extreme heat and stifling humidity of summer have been replaced by warm sunny days and surprisingly cool, even cold, nights. The cooler weather also deters the bushflies, sandflies and mosquitoes, which in the warmer months can be an absolute nightmare. In particular, the April to November period is the best time for visits to Far North Queensland, the outback and the Top End.

In the Far North, summer is the wet season and the heat and humidity can make life pretty uncomfortable. Once the monsoonal rains of the Wet arrive, most parts of the Cape York Peninsula and the Gulf of Carpentaria, and much of the outback, are often inaccessible except by light aircraft. To make matters worse, swimming in the sea is not possible anywhere north of Rockhampton due to the deadly 'stingers' (box jellyfish) which frequent the waters at this time (see the Dangers & Annoyances section later in this chapter). On the other hand, if you want to see the Top End green and free of dust, be treated to some spectacular electrical storms and enjoy the best of the barramundi fishing while all the other tourists are down south, this is the time to do it. See the Activities section of this chapter for details on the closed season for barra fishing.

Of course, Queensland covers a huge and diverse area, and as you would expect the climate varies significantly from one end to the other. For more specific information, see the Climate section in the Facts about Queensland chapter.

Apart from the climate, the other major factor you'll need to take into consideration is the school holidays. Australian families take to the road (and air) en masse at these times and a significant proportion of them head for the Sunshine State, which means many places are booked out, prices rise and things generally get a bit crazy.

School holidays vary somewhat from state to state, and from year to year. The Australian school year is divided into four terms; the main holiday period is the Christmas break, which lasts from mid-December until late January. The Christmas holidays are definitely the high-season in Queens-land, particularly in southern Queensland and on the Barrier Reef islands. The other two-week breaks are roughly from early to late April (depending on when Easter falls), from late June to mid-July and from late September to early October.

Maps

The Royal Automobile Club of Queensland (RACQ) publishes a good series of regional road maps which show almost every driveable road in the state – these are free to RACQ members, and to members of affiliated motoring organisations. There are also plenty of road maps published by the various oil companies, and these are available from service stations.

Queensland's Department of Lands produces the Sunmap Tourist Maps which, together with commercial maps by companies including Hema, Gregory's and UBD, are available from most newsagents and many bookshops in Queensland. World Wide Maps & Guides (☎ 3221 4330), on the corner of George and Adelaide Sts in Brisbane, has one of the best selections of maps in the state.

For bushwalking and other activities which require large-scale maps, the topographic sheets put out by the Australian

---

Life Is Great In The Sunshine State

Some days it seems like you've more chance of spotting a tap-dancing koala troupe than you have of meeting a native Queenslander. While out on the coast researching, it seemed that almost every motel and hostel we checked into was run by a transplanted Victorian or a couple from New South Wales. Why? Well, one clue is that Channel Nine's 'Money' program recently awarded Queensland its gold medal as the best state in which to live.

According to a report in Brisbane's Sunday Mail, while interstate migration into Queensland peaked in the early 1990s, thousands are still relocating here every year; 26,500 southerners switched states to Queensland in 1996-97.

The most commonly cited reasons for relocating are the safety and sense of community offered by Queensland's towns and cities; the lack of traffic, even in Brisbane; and affordable housing and a low cost of living. That's not to mention the climate, widely accepted as being Australia's best. As one guesthouse owner we spoke to on the Capricorn Coast said: 'Queensland's too good to leave to the Queenslanders.'

Surveying & Land Information Group (AUSLIG) are the ones to get. Many of the more popular sheets are available over the counter at shops which sell specialist bushwalking gear and outdoor equipment. AUSLIG also has special-interest maps showing various types of land use, population densities and Aboriginal land. For more information, or a catalogue, contact AUSLIG (☎ 3233 7600 or toll-free on 1800 800 173) at Level 6, 313 Adelaide St, Brisbane, Qld 4000.

What to Bring

With its tropical climate and relaxed attitudes, Queensland's unwritten dress code is 'cool and casual'. Apart from swimwear, the most useful items of clothing are shorts and T-shirts, cotton dresses and tops, perhaps a sarong – in general, light and loose-fitting clothing. Most people dress informally – even businesspeople seldom wear suits and ties – although many resorts, pubs and restaurants specify shirts for men and ban bare feet and thongs, especially in their dining areas. The only places where you'll need a jacket for dinner are at the fancier restaurants at places like Hayman Island and in Brisbane's five-star hotels.

You are unlikely to need anything warmer than a long-sleeved shirt, although if you're visiting southern Queensland or you're there during the winter months, it's worth bringing a light jacket or a jumper (sweater, pullover) for the occasional chilly evening. Wet weather gear – an umbrella or perhaps a waterproof poncho – will prove handy for the tropical downpours which are regular occurrences during the summer months and in the rainforests of the Far North.

You need to be aware of the dangers of UV radiation in Queensland. Partially due to a hole in the ozone layer, Australians have the highest incidence of skin cancer in the world. A broad-brimmed sunhat, good sunglasses and effective sunscreen are all essential, especially for fair-skinned folks from cooler climates. Snorkelling without wearing a T-shirt and sunscreen is an especially good way to get sunstroke. Like safe sex, safe sun is an important health consideration – in both cases, use protection.

Another important item is insect repellent. In tropical Queensland, it sometimes seems like the mosquitoes, sandflies and various other insects are queuing up to bite you – a good repellent will usually (but not always) help alleviate the problem. Antihistamine tablets (preferably the kind that don't make you drowsy) are the most effective way to relieve insect bites, particularly those of sandflies.

When it comes to footwear, 'reef sandals' are all the go in Queensland. Reef sandals are sturdy rubber-soled sandals with Velcro straps. Cooler than shoes and with good grip, you can wear them just about anywhere – on the beach (hot sand is a summer hazard), in most pubs and clubs, and on boat trips. While sandals are OK for shorter walks, if you're planning to do any serious bushwalking a pair of strong and comfortable walking shoes or boots is essential.

TOURIST OFFICES

There are a number of information sources for visitors to Queensland and you can easily drown yourself in brochures and booklets, maps and leaflets.

Local Tourist Offices

There are plenty of places throughout Queensland willing to provide tourists with information, although it's worth noting that most of these places aren't strictly independent.

There are 14 major regional tourist associations in Queensland, each with their own tourist information centre. These offices are generally extremely helpful and can provide a good range of information on their respective regions, although they will generally only provide you with information on businesses that are paid-up members of the association. Offices are found in the following cities: Brisbane, Surfers Paradise (Gold Coast), Maroochydore (Sunshine Coast), Toowoomba and Warwick (Darling Downs), Maryborough (Fraser Coast),

Gladstone, Blackall (Outback Queensland), Rockhampton (Capricorn Coast), Bundaberg, Mackay, Airlie Beach (Whitsundays), Townsville (North Coast) and Cairns (Far North Queensland). See the information sections under individual towns for addresses, phone numbers and opening hours.

There are also hundreds of privately run 'tourist information centres' which are basically booking agents. These places can also be helpful, but bear in mind that they make a commission on whatever tours or accommodation they book for you.

RACQ offices are another very helpful source of information about road and weather conditions, and they can also book accommodation and tours. For information on national and state parks, contact one of the Department of Environment offices. See the Useful Organisations section later in this chapter for more details on both of these groups.

Interstate Tourist Offices

The Queensland Tourist & Travel Corporation is the government-run body responsible for promoting Queensland interstate and overseas. Their offices act primarily as promotional and booking offices, not information centres, but are worth contacting when you're planning a trip to Queensland.

The central contact number for all Australian offices is ☎ 13 1801; visit them on the Net at www.qttc.com.au or email them at qldtravl@ozemail.com.au. There are Queensland Government Travel Centres in the following places:

Australian Capital Territory
(☎ (02) 6248 8411) 25 Garema Place, Canberra 2601
New South Wales
(☎ (02) 9209 8600) 75 Castlereagh St, Sydney 2000
(☎ (02) 9200 8888) Shop 2, 376 Victoria Ave, Chatswood 2067
(☎ (02) 9865 8400) Shop 2158, Westfield Shoppingtown, Parramatta 2150
(☎ (02) 4926 2800) 97 Hunter St, Newcastle 2300

Queensland
(☎ 3874 2800) Corner of Adelaide and Edward Sts, Brisbane 4000
South Australia
(☎ (08) 8401 3100) 10 Grenfell St, Adelaide 5000
Victoria
(☎ (03) 9206 4500) 257 Collins St, Melbourne 3000
Western Australia
(☎ (08 9322 1777) Shop 6, 777 Hay St, Perth 6000

Overseas Representatives

Australian Tourist Commission The Australian Tourist Commission (ATC) is the government body intended to inform potential visitors about the country. There's a very definite split between promotion outside and inside Australia. The Australian Tourist Commission is strictly an external operator; it does minimal promotion within the country and has little contact with visitors to Australia. Within the country, tourist promotion is handled by state or local tourist offices.

The Australian Tourist Commission maintains a good Web site at www.aussie .net.au/pl/atc:1.

The ATC also maintains a number of Helplines (often toll-free), which independent travellers can ring or fax to get specific information about Australia. All requests for information should be directed through these numbers:

France
☎ toll-free 0591 5626
Germany
☎ toll-free 0130 825 182
Hong Kong
☎ 2802 7817, fax 2802 8211
Japan
☎/fax (03) 5229 0021
New Zealand
☎ toll-free 0800 650 303
Singapore
☎ 250 6277, fax 253 8431
UK
☎ 0990 022 000
USA
☎ (847) 296 4900, fax 635 3718

QTTC The Queensland Tourist & Travel Corporation (QTTC) also has its own overseas representatives, so for information specifically about Queensland, contact one of the following offices:

Europe
 (☎ (089) 2317 7177) Neuhauserstrasse 27, 4th Floor, 80331 Munich
Hong Kong
 (☎ 2827 4322) Room 2209, 22nd Floor, Harbour Centre, 25 Harbour Rd, Wanchai
Japan
 (☎ (03) 3214 4931) Suite 1301, Yurakucho Denki Building North Wing, 7-1 Yurakucho 1 Chome, Chiyoda-ku, Tokyo 100
Korea
 (☎ 756 9011) Suite 301B, Hotel President 188-3, Ulchiro 1-Ka, Chung-Ku, Seoul 100-191
New Zealand
 (☎ (09) 377 9053) 9th Floor, Quay Tower, 29 Customs St West, Auckland
Singapore
 (☎ 253 2811) 101 Thompson Rd, No 07-04, United Square, Singapore 307591
Taiwan
 (☎ (02) 2723 0656) Suite 2601, 26th Floor, International Trade Building, 333 Keelung Rd, Section 1, Taipei 10548
UK
 (☎ (0181) 780 2227) Queensland House, 392/3 The Strand, London WC2R OLZ
USA
 (☎ (310) 788 0997) Northrop Plaza, Suite 330, 1800 Century Park East, Los Angeles, CA 90067

VISAS & DOCUMENTS
Visas
All visitors to Australia need a visa. Only New Zealand nationals are exempt, and even they receive a 'special category' visa on arrival.

Visa application forms are available from Australian diplomatic missions overseas and travel agents, and you can apply by mail or in person. There are several different types of visas, depending on the reason for your visit.

Tourist Visas Tourist visas are issued by Australian consular offices abroad; they are the most common visa and are generally valid for a stay of either three or six months. The three-month visas are free; for the six-month visa there is a $35 fee.

The visa is valid for use within 12 months of the date of issue and can be used to enter and leave Australia several times within that 12 months.

When you apply for a visa, you need to present your passport and a passport photo, as well as signing an undertaking that you have an onward or return ticket and 'sufficient funds' – the latter is obviously open to interpretation.

You can also apply for a long-stay visa, which is a multiple-entry, four-year visa allowing for stays of up to six months on each visit. These also cost $35.

Electronic Travel Authority (ETA) Visitors who require a tourist visa of three months or less can make the application through an IATA-registered travel agent (no form required), who can then make the application direct and issue the traveller with an ETA, which replaces the usual visa stamped in your passport. This system was only introduced in late 1997, and the nationalities to which it is available is so far limited, but includes passport holders of the UK, the USA, most European and Scandinavian countries, Malaysia and Singapore, and the list is likely to grow rapidly.

Working Holiday Visas Young, single visitors from the UK, Canada, Korea, the Netherlands and Japan may be eligible for a 'working holiday' visa. 'Young' is fairly loosely interpreted as around 18 to 25, although exceptions are made and people up to 30, and young married couples without children, may be given a working holiday visa, but it's far from guaranteed.

A working holiday visa allows for a stay of up to 12 months, but the emphasis is supposed to be on casual employment rather than a full-time job. For this reason you are only supposed to work for one employer for three months, but there's nothing to stop you from working for more than one employer in the 12 months. This visa can only be applied for from outside Australia (preferably but not necessarily in your country of citizenship), and you can't change from a tourist visa to a working holiday visa.

You can apply for a working holiday visa up to 12 months in advance, and it's a good idea to do so as early as possible as there is a limit on the number issued each year. Conditions attached to a working holiday visa include having sufficient funds for a ticket out, and taking out private medical insurance; a fee of $145 is payable when you apply for the visa.

See the section on Work later in this chapter for details of what sort of work is available and where.

Travel Insurance

A travel insurance policy to cover theft, loss and medical problems is a good idea. The policies handled by STA Travel and other student travel organisations are usually good value. Some policies offer lower and higher medical-expense options; the higher ones are chiefly for countries such as the USA which have extremely high medical costs. There is a wide variety of policies available so check the small print.

Some policies specifically exclude 'dangerous activities', which can include scuba diving, motorcycling and even trekking. A locally acquired motorcycle licence is not valid under some policies.

You may prefer a policy which pays doctors or hospitals direct rather than you having to pay on the spot and claim later. If you have to claim later make sure you keep all documentation. Some policies ask you to call back (reverse charges) to a centre in your home country where an immediate assessment of your problem is made.

Check that the policy covers ambulances or an emergency flight home.

Visa Extensions The maximum stay allowed to visitors is one year, including extensions.

Visa extensions are made through Department of Immigration & Ethnic Affairs offices in Australia and, as the process takes some time, it's best to apply about a month before your visa expires. There is an application fee of $145 – and even if they turn down your application they can still keep your money. To qualify for an extension you are required to take out private medical insurance to cover the period of the extension, and have a ticket out of the country.

If you're trying to stay for longer in Australia the books *Temporary to Permanent Resident in Australia* and *Practical Guide to Obtaining Permanent Residence in Australia*, both published by Longman Cheshire, might be useful.

Medicare Card

Under reciprocal arrangements, residents of the UK, New Zealand, the Netherlands, Finland, Malta and Italy are entitled to free or subsidised medical treatment under Medicare, Australia's compulsory national health insurance scheme. To enrol you need to show your passport and health care card or certificate from your own country, and you are then given a Medicare card.

Once you have a card you can get free necessary hospital treatment (provided you are not treated as a private patient), and visits to a private doctor's practice are also claimable under Medicare, although depending on the claim method used by the doctor you may have to pay the bill first and then make a claim yourself from Medicare. You also need to find out how much the doctor's consultation fee is, as Medicare only covers you for a certain amount and you will need to pay the balance. Clinics which advertise 'bulk billing' are the easiest to use as they charge Medicare direct and you don't have to pay up front.

For more information phone Medicare on ☎ 13 2011.

Driving Licence

You can use your own foreign driving licence in Australia, as long as it is in English (if it's not, a translation must be carried). As an International Licence cannot be used alone and must be supported by your home licence, there seems little point in getting one.

EMBASSIES
Australian Embassies Abroad

Australian consular offices overseas include:

Canada
(☎ (613) 783 7619, fax 236 4376) Suite 710, 50 O'Connor St, Ottawa, Ontario K1P 6L2
also in Vancouver

China
(☎ (10) 6532 2331, fax 6532 4349) 21 Dongzhimenwai Dajie, Sanlitun, Beijing 100600
(☎ 2827 8881, fax 2585 4459) 24th Floor, Harbour Centre, 25 Harbour Rd, Wanchai, Hong Kong
also in Guangzhou and Shanghai

France
(☎ (01) 40 59 33 06, fax 40 59 35 38) 4 Rue Jean Rey, 75724 Cedex 15, Paris

Germany
(☎ (0228) 81 030, fax 373 145) Godesberger-allee 107, Bonn 53175

Greece
(☎ (01) 644 7303, fax 646 6595) 37 Dimitriou Soutsou, Ambelokipi, Athens 115-21

India
(☎ (011) 688 8223, fax 688 7536) 1/50-G Shantipath, Chanakyapuri, New Delhi 110021
also in Mumbai (Bombay)

Indonesia
(☎ (021) 522 7111, fax 522 7110) Jalan HR Rasuna Said Kav C15-16, Kuningan, Jakarta Selatan 12940
(☎ (0361) 23 5002, fax 23 1990) Jalan Prof Moh Yamin 4, Renon, Denpasar, Bali

Ireland
(☎ (01) 676 1517, fax 661 3576) Fitzwilton House, Wilton Terrace, Dublin 2

Israel
(☎ (03) 695 0450, fax 691 5223)
Beit Europa (4th Floor), 37 Saul Hamelech Boulevarde, Tel Aviv 64928

Italy
(☎ (06) 85 2721, fax 8527 2400) Via Alessandria 215, Rome 00198

Japan
(☎ (03) 5232 4111, fax 5232 4178) 2-1-14 Mita, Minato-ku, Tokyo 108
(☎ (06) 941 8601, fax 941 8602) Twin 21 MID Tower, 29th Floor, 2-1-61 Shiromi, Chuo-ku, Osaka 540

Malaysia
(☎ (03) 240 6546, fax 241 4495) 6 Jalan Yap Kwan Seng, Kuala Lumpur 50450

Mauritius
(☎ 208 1700, fax 208 8878) Rogers House, 5 Pres John Kennedy St, Port Louis

Nepal
(☎ (01) 37 1678, fax 37 1533) Bansbari, Kathmandu

Netherlands
(☎ (070) 310 8200, fax 364 3807) Carnegie-laan 4, The Hague 2517 KH

New Zealand
(☎ (04) 473 6411, fax 498 7103) 72-78 Hobson St, Thorndon, Wellington
(☎ (09) 303 2429, fax 303 2431) Union House, 32-38 Quay St, Auckland

Papua New Guinea
(☎ 325 9333, fax 325 3528) Godwit St, Waigani, Hohola, Port Moresby

Philippines
(☎ (02) 750 2840, fax 754 6269) Dona Salustiana Ty Tower, 104 Paseo de Roxas, Makati, Metro Manila

Singapore
(☎ 737 9311, fax 735 1242) 25 Napier Rd, Singapore 258507

South Africa
(☎ (012) 342 3740, fax 342 4222) 292 Orient St, Arcadia, Pretoria 0083

Sri Lanka
(☎ (01) 69 8767, fax 68 2311) 3 Cambridge Place, Colombo 7

Sweden
(☎ (08) 613 2900, fax 24 2642) Sergels Torg 12, Stockholm S-111 57

Thailand
(☎ (02) 287 2680, fax 213 1177) 37 South Sathorn Rd, Bangkok 10120

UK
(☎ (0171) 379 4334, fax 465 8218) Australia House, The Strand, London WC2B 4LA
also in Manchester

USA
(☎ (202) 797 3000, fax 797 3100) 1601 Massachusetts Ave NW, Washington DC 20036-2273 also in Los Angeles and New York

Vietnam
(☎ (04) 831 7755, fax 831 7712) Van Thuc Compound, Ba Dinh District, Hanoi
also in Ho Chi Minh City

Zimbabwe
(☎ (04) 75 7774, fax 75 7770) 4th Floor,
Karigamombe Centre, 53 Samora Machel Ave,
Harare

Foreign Embassies & Consulates
Canberra is home to most foreign embassies, but many countries maintain consulates in Brisbane as well. They include:

Denmark
(☎ 3221 8641) 180 Queen St
France
(☎ 3229 8201) 10 Market St
Germany
(☎ 3221 7819) 10 Eagle St
Japan
(☎ 3221 5188) 12 Creek St
Netherlands
(☎ 3839 9644) 101 Wickham Tce
New Zealand
(☎ 3221 9933) 288 Edward St
UK
(☎ 3236 2575) 1 Eagle St
USA
(☎ 3831 3330) 383 Wickham Tce, Spring Hill

CUSTOMS
When entering Australia you can bring most articles in free of duty provided that customs is satisfied they are for personal use and that you'll be taking them with you when you leave. There's also a duty-free per person quota of 1125ml of alcohol, 250 cigarettes and dutiable goods up to the value of A$400.

With regard to prohibited goods, there are two areas that need particular attention. Number one is, of course, drugs – Australian customs is serious about the stuff and can be extremely efficient when it comes to finding it. This particularly applies if you are arriving from South-East Asia or the Indian Subcontinent.

Problem two is animal and plant quarantine – see the boxed text 'Bin It or Declare It' for details.

Weapons and firearms are either prohibited or require a permit and safety testing. Other restricted goods include products (such as ivory) made from protected wildlife species, non-approved telecommunications devices and live animals.

There are duty-free stores at the international airports and their associated cities. Treat them with healthy suspicion: 'duty-free' is one of the world's most overworked catch phrases, and it is often just an excuse to sell things at prices you can easily beat by a little shopping around.

Bin It Or Declare It
When arriving from overseas you'll be asked to declare all goods of animal or vegetable origin – from ham sandwiches and biscuits to wooden spoons and straw hats. The lot. They'll all be examined by an official. The authorities are keen to prevent pests or diseases getting into the country and they are quite prepared to back this up with on-the-spot fines of $50 to $110 on people breaching the quarantine regulations. The fines can be heavier for serious smuggling – a recent *Courier-Mail* article reported that three undeclared 1kg tins of ham confiscated from a passenger's luggage at Cairns airport earned a $3100 fine. The same article also reported on a Kuwaiti gentleman caught smuggling food through Brisbane airport for which he received a $1500 fine.

Our advice has to be to declare everything. Searches are thorough and it is not worth the risk if you're subsequently discovered to have knowingly made a false declaration.

MONEY
Currency
Australia's currency is the decimal system of dollars and cents (100 cents to the dollar). There are $100, $50, $20, $10 and $5 notes and $2, $1, 50c, 20c, 10c and 5c coins. It's easy to confuse the new plastic $5 and $10 notes, which look much more alike than did the old paper ones. The 2c and 1c coins have been taken out of circulation, although

prices can still be set in odd cents. Shops round prices up (or down) to the nearest 5c on your *total* bill, not on individual items.

There are no notable restrictions on importing or exporting currency or travellers cheques except that you may not take out more than A$5000 in cash without prior approval.

Exchange Rates

The Australian dollar fluctuates quite markedly against the US dollar. Approximate exchange rates are as follows:

Canada	C$1	=	A$1.10
Germany	DM1	=	A$0.94
euro	€1	=	A$1.85
France	10FF	=	A$2.81
Hong Kong	HK$10	=	A$2.19
Japan	¥100	=	A$1.14
Netherlands	Dfl1	=	A$0.83
New Zealand	NZ$1	=	A$0.85
Singapore	S$1	=	A$0.95
UK	UK£1	=	A$2.72
USA	US$1	=	A$1.67

Costs

Compared with the USA, Canada and European countries, Australia is cheaper in some ways and more expensive in others. Manufactured goods tend to be more expensive – on the other hand, food is both high in quality and low in cost.

Accommodation is also very reasonably priced. In virtually every town where backpackers are likely to stay there'll be a backpackers' hostel with dorm beds for around $12 to $15 and double rooms for around $30, or a caravan park with on-site vans for around $25 for two people. Most pubs in country towns also have cheap accommodation for around $20 per person, and an average motel room will cost between $40 and $60 a night.

The biggest cost in any trip to Australia is going to be transport, simply because it's such a vast country. If there's a group of you, buying a second-hand car is probably the most economical way to go.

Changing Money

Changing foreign currency or travellers cheques is no problem at almost any bank. There are also foreign exchange booths at Brisbane and Cairns international airports which are open to meet all arriving flights. The Westpac Bank also has branches at the airports.

You will also find foreign exchange booths in the city centres of Brisbane, Cairns and some other major cities. These places are OK for emergencies – they have more convenient opening hours than the banks, but their rates generally aren't as good.

Travellers Cheques American Express, Thomas Cook and other well-known international brands of travellers cheques are all widely used in Australia. A passport will usually be adequate for identification; it would be sensible to carry a driver's licence, credit cards or a plane ticket in case of problems.

Commissions and fees for changing foreign currency travellers cheques seem to vary from bank to bank and month to month. It's worth making a few phone calls to see which bank has the lowest charges. Some charge a flat fee for each transaction, which varies from $2.50 (Commonwealth Bank) to $6.50 (ANZ Bank), while others take a percentage of the amount changed – Westpac charges 1% with a minimum charge of $10.

Major currencies like pounds sterling, US dollars and Swiss francs can be readily exchanged, but you'll be better off if you buy Australian dollar travellers cheques. These can be exchanged immediately at the bank cashier's window without being converted from a foreign currency and incurring commissions, fees and exchange rate fluctuations.

Credit Cards The most commonly accepted credit cards in Australia are Visa and MasterCard. American Express, and to a lesser extent Diners Club, are also widely accepted, although some establishments don't (or would rather not) accept them because of the higher fees they charge. The Australian-only Bankcard is also common, although less so in recent years.

Credit cards are a convenient alternative to carrying cash or large numbers of travellers cheques. With the advent of electronic banking and the proliferation of automatic teller machines (ATMs) throughout the country, a credit card, preferably linked to your savings account, is an ideal way to travel. Visa, MasterCard and American Express cards are most commonly accepted in ATMs – most machines will display the symbols of the credit cards that they accept. Cash advances are also available over the counter from all banks.

If you plan to rent cars while travelling around Australia, a credit card makes life much simpler; they're looked upon with much greater favour by rent-a-car agencies than nasty old cash, and many agencies simply won't rent you a vehicle if you don't have a card.

Bank Accounts

If you're planning to stay longer than just a month or so, it's worth considering other ways of handling money that give you more flexibility and are more economical.

Most travellers opt for an account which includes a cash card, which you can use to access your cash from ATMs all over Australia. Westpac, ANZ, National and Commonwealth bank branches are found nationwide, and in all but the most remote town there'll be at least one place where you can withdraw money from a hole in the wall.

Many businesses, such as service stations, supermarkets and convenience stores, are linked into the EFTPOS system (Electronic Funds Transfer at Point Of Sale), and here you can use your bank cash card or credit card to pay for services or purchases direct, and often withdraw cash as well.

Opening an account at an Australian bank is easy for overseas visitors if they do it within the first six weeks of arrival. After six weeks (and for Australian citi-

zens) it's much more complicated. A points system operates and you need to score a minimum of 100 points before you can have the privilege of letting the bank take your money. Passports, driver's licences, birth certificates and other 'major' IDs earn you 40 points; minor ones such as credit cards get you 20 points. Just like a game show really!

Tipping

In Australia tipping isn't 'compulsory' the way it is in the USA or Europe. A tip is more a recognition of good service than an obligation, and the amount you tip is usually weighted according to how good the service has been. It's only customary to tip in restaurants, and only then if you want to. If you do decide to leave a tip, 5% to 10% of the bill is considered reasonable. Taxi drivers don't expect tips, although if you tell them to keep the change, they're unlikely to argue with you.

POST & COMMUNICATIONS
Sending Mail

Post offices are open from 9 am to 5 pm Monday to Friday, but you can often get stamps from local post offices operated from newsagencies or from Australia Post shops, found in large cities, on Saturday morning as well.

Letters Australia's postal services are relatively efficient and reasonably cheap. It costs 45c to send a standard letter or postcard within Australia.

Internationally, aerograms cost 70c to any country, air-mail letters/postcards cost 75/70c to New Zealand, 85/80c to Singapore and Malaysia, 95/90c to Hong Kong and India, $1.05/95c to the USA and Canada, and $1.20/1 to Europe and the UK.

Parcels The rates for posting parcels are not too extortionate. By sea mail a 1/2/5kg parcel costs $11/21/33 to India, and $13/25/43 to the USA, Europe or the UK. Each kilogram over 5kg costs $4 for India, and $6 for the USA, Europe or the UK, with a maximum of 20kg for all destinations. Air-mail rates are considerably more expensive.

To New Zealand air mail is the only option. A 1/2/5kg parcel sent by 'economy air' costs $11/21/33, with a maximum of 20kg.

Receiving Mail

All post offices will hold mail for visitors and some city GPOs have very busy poste restantes. Cairns GPO poste restante, for example, can get quite hectic. You can also have mail sent to you at the American Express offices in big cities if you have an Amex card or carry Amex travellers cheques.

Telephone

The Australian telecommunications industry is deregulated and there are a number of providers offering various services. Private phones are serviced by the two main players, Telstra and Optus, but it's in the mobile phone and payphone markets that other companies such as Vodafone, One.Tel, Unidial, Global One and AAPT are also operating, and this is where you'll find the most competition.

Payphones & Phonecards

There are a number of different cards issued by the various telecommunications companies, and these can be used in any Telstra public phone which accept cards (virtually all do these days), or from a private phone by dialling a toll-free access number.

Long-distance calls made from payphones are generally considerably more expensive than calls made from private phones. If you will be using payphones to make a large number of calls it pays to look into the various cards available from providers other than Telstra.

The important thing is to know exactly how your calls are being charged, as the charges for calls vary from company to company. An explanatory booklet should be available from the card outlet – usually a newsagent or other shop.

Some public phones are set up to take only credit cards, and these too are convenient, although you need to keep an eye on how much the call is costing as it can quickly mount up. The minimum charge for a call on one of these phones is $1.20.

Local Calls

Local calls from public phones cost 40c for an unlimited amount of time. Local calls from private phones cost 30c. Calls to mobile phones attract higher rates.

Long-Distance Calls & Area Codes

It's also possible to make long-distance (sometimes known as STD – Subscriber Trunk Dialling) calls from virtually any public phone. Long-distance calls are cheaper in off-peak hours (basically outside normal business hours), and different service providers have different charges.

Australia is divided into just four STD areas – 07 covers Queensland. Confusingly, when making calls within one STD area, you still have to dial the STD area code for that area if the call is a long-distance one (ie more than about 50km). Eventually all calls within one area will be area-code free.

International Calls

From most payphones you can also make ISD (International Subscriber Dialling) calls, although calls are generally cheaper if using a provider other than Telstra.

When making overseas calls, the international dialling code varies depending on which provider you are using - 0011 is the Telstra code.

International calls from Australia are among the cheapest you'll find anywhere, and there are often specials which bring the rates down even further. Off-peak times, if available, vary depending on the destination – see the back of any *White Pages* telephone book, or call ☎ 0102 for more details. Sunday is often the cheapest day to ring.

Country Direct is a service which gives callers in Australia direct access to operators in nearly 60 countries, to make collect or credit card calls. For a full list of the countries hooked into this system, check any local *White Pages* telephone book.

Toll-Free Calls Many businesses and some government departments operate a toll-free service, so no matter where you are ringing from around the country, it's a free call. These numbers have the prefix 1800 and we've listed them wherever possible throughout this book.

Many companies, such as the airlines, have numbers beginning with 13 or 1300, and these are charged at the rate of a local call. Often these numbers are Australia-wide, or may be applicable to a specific state or STD district only. Unfortunately there's no way of telling without actually ringing the number.

Calls to these services still attract charges if you are calling from a mobile phone.

Mobile Phones As the costs come down, mobile phones have become an increasingly popular option for travellers on all budgets. They are an excellent way to keep in touch, and the costs are reasonable if you are careful about when you call and for how long. The digital mobile network covers more than 90% of the population, but this still leaves vast tracts of the country not covered, so be sure to check that the company you choose gives adequate coverage for the areas in which you want to use the phone. Basically the whole of the east coast is covered; it's when you start moving inland that it thins out. The older analogue network is less extensive and is to be wound up at the end of 1999.

Phone numbers with the prefixes 014, 015, 018, 019 or 041 are mobile phones. The three main mobile operators are the (mostly) government-owned Telstra, and the two private companies Optus and Vodafone.

Information Calls Other odd numbers you may come across are those starting with 190x. These numbers, usually recorded information services and the like, are provided by private companies, and your call is charged at anything from 35c to $5 or more per minute (more from mobile phones and payphones).

Email & Internet Access
If you want to surf the Net, even if it's only to access your email, there are service providers in the major centres. Typical costs for casual use are around $5 per half-hour.

If you actually want to open an account, on-line costs vary, but a typical price structure is a $20 registration fee (which may include a few hours of on-line time), plus $20 per month for 10 hours on-line time. A few of the current major players include:

Australia On Line
 ☎ 1800 621 258; www.ozonline.com.au
Microsoft Network
 ☎ (02) 9870 2100; www.au.msn.com
Oz Email
 ☎ 1800 805 874; www.ozemail.com.au
Telstra Big Pond
 ☎ 1800 804 282; www.onaustralia.com.au

CompuServe users who want to access the service locally should phone CompuServe (☎ 1300 307 072) to get the local log-in numbers.

BOOKS
In almost any bookshop you'll find a section devoted to Australiana, with books on every Australian subject you care to mention. If you want a souvenir of Australia, such as a photographic record, there are numerous coffee-table books available. There are also plenty of glossy picture books specifically on Queensland and its various regions – the reef, the outback, the islands, the national parks.

Apart from bookshops, it's also worth trying places like the Wilderness Society shops and Government Printing Office shops. In Brisbane, the Department of Environment's Naturally Queensland office sells a good range of books, posters and calendars with environmental themes, as does the Billabong Bookshop.

Lonely Planet
If you are travelling further afield after exploring Queensland, Lonely Planet's *Australia* is the book to take. For trips into

the outback in your own vehicle, it's worth investing in a copy of *Outback Australia*. *Islands of Australia's Great Barrier Reef* covers the reef, the islands, diving and accommodation in greater detail than the book in your hand.

Guidebooks

The RACQ publishes a comprehensive *Accommodation Guide* to Queensland which lists caravan parks, motels, resorts and hotels – it lists their facilities and prices, and rates them out of five stars. It also lists some (but not many) pubs and hostels. The guide is available from all RACQ offices.

In conjunction with the QTTC, the RACQ also publishes a series of four motoring holiday guides to Queensland. These large-format paperbacks are well produced and feature colour photos, touring maps, suggested excursions and sights and attractions, as well as some extracts from the *Accommodation Guide* and travelling tips. They are available from RACQ offices and some bookshops.

The Queensland Experience by Jan Bowen covers Queensland region by region, offering historical backgrounds, recommendations and personal anecdotes. It could be a handy primer to read before you go – it lacks hard information but is quite descriptive.

Queensland Getaways by Warwick Randall describes more than 50 interesting holiday escapes throughout Queensland, from mountain guesthouses and island resorts to outback cattle stations and five-star hotels.

There is a cornucopia of books published which deal with the Great Barrier Reef. One of the best souvenirs of the reef is the *Reader's Digest Book of the Great Barrier Reef* – it's colourful, expensive and nearly as big as the Barrier Reef itself.

Aborigines

The Australian Aborigines by Kenneth Maddock is a good cultural summary. The award-winning *Triumph of the Nomads*, by Geoffrey Blainey, chronicles the life of Australia's original inhabitants, and convincingly demolishes the myth that the Aborigines were 'primitive' people trapped on a hostile continent. They were, in fact, extremely successful in adapting to and overcoming the difficulties presented by the climate and resources (or seeming lack of them) – the book's an excellent read.

For a sympathetic historical account of what's happened to the original Australians since whites arrived, read *Aboriginal Australians* by Richard Broome. *A Change of Ownership*, by Mildred Kirk, covers similar ground, but does so more concisely, focusing on the land rights movement and its historical background.

The Other Side of the Frontier, by Henry Reynolds, uses historical records to give a vivid account of an Aboriginal view of the arrival and takeover of Australia by Europeans. His *With the White People* identifies the essential Aboriginal contributions to the survival of the early white settlers. *My Place*, Sally Morgan's prize-winning autobiography, traces her discovery of her Aboriginal heritage. *The Fringe Dwellers* by Nene Gare describes just what it's like to be an Aborigine growing up in a white-dominated society.

Don't Take Your Love to Town by Ruby Langford and *My People* by Oodgeroo Noonuccal (Kath Walker) are also recommended reading for people interested in Aborigines' experience.

The Queensland Tourist & Travel Corporation produces an excellent 30-page brochure called *A Guide to Experiencing Aboriginal and Torres Strait Islander Culture*, which covers culture and art, and lists galleries and shops, festivals and tour operators. It's free and available from QTTC.

Australian History

For a good introduction to Australian history, read *A Short History of Australia*, a most accessible and informative general history by the late Manning Clark, the much-loved Aussie historian. Robert Hughes' bestselling *The Fatal Shore* is a colourful and detailed account of the history of transportation of convicts. Geoffrey Blainey's *The Tyranny of Distance* is a captivating narrative of white settlement.

Finding Australia, by Russel Ward, traces the story of the early days from the first Aboriginal arrivals up to 1821. It's strong on Aborigines, women and the full story of foreign exploration, not just Captain Cook's role. There's lots of fascinating detail, including information about the appalling crooks who ran the early colony for long periods, and it's intended to be the first of a series.

Cooper's Creek, by Alan Moorehead, is a classic account of the ill-fated Burke and Wills expedition which dramatises the horrors and hardships faced by the early explorers.

Queensland History

If you're specifically interested in the history of Queensland, Ross Fitzgerald's *A History of Queensland* is a comprehensive, well-researched and sometimes controversial study. It was published in two volumes in the early 1980s – *From the Dreaming to 1915: A History of Queensland*, and *A History of Queensland: From 1915 to the 1980s* – and it can be difficult to find copies in bookshops, although most Australian libraries have it.

River of Gold, by Hector Holthouse, is a 'factional' account of the wild days of Cooktown and the Palmer River gold rush in the 1870s. As he explains in his author's note, Holthouse has used a little artistic licence to fill in the gaps in his research, but the result is a fascinating read and gives an impressive insight into the period.

Glenville Pike is a local writer who has produced more than 20 books based on Queensland's colourful history. They include: *Queensland Frontier*, tales of the explorers and pioneers who opened up Queensland; *The Men Who Blazed the Track*, another account of the Palmer River gold rush; and *Queen of the North*, a history of Cooktown. His books are widely available in bookshops throughout Queensland.

Queensland Politics

For an insight into the decline and fall of Queensland's National Party, pick up a copy of award-winning journalist Evan Whitton's *The Hillbilly Dictator*. Subtitled 'How Democracy and the Rule of Law in Queensland were subverted, and injustice and corruption elevated to the commonplace', Whitton's book is a fascinating study of the 1987-89 Fitzgerald Inquiry and the 250 trials for police and political corruption that followed.

NEWSPAPERS & MAGAZINES

The *Courier Mail*, Brisbane's major daily newspaper, is available almost everywhere in Queensland. It's a reasonably serious but somewhat parochial broadsheet.

The Australian, a Rupert Murdoch-owned paper and the country's only national daily, is also widely available. It makes better reading for non-Queenslanders, with good national and international news coverage, although it is definitely ultra-conservative. The *Weekend Australian* includes several excellent review sections.

Many of the larger towns and cities produce their own papers, some daily and some weekly. Major regional dailies include the *Cairns Post*, the *Townsville Bulletin* and the *Gold Coast Bulletin*. The *Sunday Mail* is a bulky but lightweight broadsheet (a somewhat oxymoronic, but accurate, description) that appears on Sunday.

Weekly magazines include an Australian edition of *Time*, and the *Bulletin*, a conservative and long-running Australian news magazine which includes a condensed version of *Newsweek*. International papers are available from larger newsagencies, particularly in the more heavily touristed areas.

RADIO & TV
Radio

The Australian Broadcasting Corporation (ABC) is government-funded, commercial-free and by far the largest broadcaster in the country. There are two main services –

Radio National, which can be heard just about everywhere (sometimes on AM and sometimes via FM relays); and the regional/metropolitan services, usually available only around major centres.

Fine Music is the ABC's classical music station, and Triple J is its national 'youth network' which can be heard in most of the larger centres in Queensland. It specialises in alternative music and young people's issues and has some interesting talk shows.

Outside Brisbane, which has more than 15 AM and FM radio stations, you'll usually be able to pick up one or more of the ABC stations, a local commercial station or two and often a local public station which will broadcast a lot of announcements about interesting local events in addition to a pretty diverse range of music and news.

TV

There are five main TV networks in Queensland: the government-funded ABC, the multicultural and multilingual SBS (Special Broadcasting Service, UHF) and the three commercial networks, channels 7, 9 and 10. All of these can be received in Brisbane. Most regional areas receive the ABC and at least one commercial network, but in the more remote areas you might only be able to pick up the ABC. SBS is only available in Brisbane, the Gold and Sunshine coasts, the Darling Downs, Townsville, Cairns, Mt Isa and Longreach.

The commercial networks have fairly similar programming formats, with the usual diet of news and current affairs, sport, soap operas and sitcoms, and an overdose of American talk shows during the day. The ABC produces some excellent current affairs shows and documentaries as well as showing lots of sport, slightly heavier news and sitcoms (mostly British).

VIDEO SYSTEMS

Australia uses the PAL system, and so pre-recorded videos purchased in Australia may be incompatible with overseas systems. Check this before you buy.

PHOTOGRAPHY & VIDEO

Australian film prices are not too far out of line with those of the rest of the western world. Including developing, 36-exposure slide film costs around $25, but with a little shopping around you can find it for around $20 – even less if you buy it in quantity.

There are plenty of camera shops in all the big cities and standards of camera service are high. Developing standards are also high, with many places offering one-hour developing of print film. While print film is available from just about anywhere (a roll of 36-exposure print film should cost under $10), slide film can be harder to find; camera shops in the larger cities are usually the best bet.

For the best results, try to take most of your photos early in the morning and late in the afternoon when the light is softer. As the sun gets higher, colours appear washed out. You must also allow for the intensity of reflected light when taking shots on the Barrier Reef or at other coastal locations – a polarising filter will help eliminate much of this glare, and also saturate colours. Remember that film can be damaged by heat, so allow for temperature extremes and do your best to keep film as cool as possible, particularly after exposure. Other film and camera hazards are dust in the outback and humidity in the tropical regions of the Far North.

Cheap disposable underwater cameras are widely available at most beach towns and resorts. These are OK for snapshots when snorkelling or shallow diving and can produce reasonable results in good conditions, but without a flash the colours will be washed out. These cameras won't work below about 5m because of the water pressure. If you're serious about underwater photography, good underwater cameras with flash unit can be hired from many of the dive shops along the coast.

As in any country, politeness goes a long way when taking photographs; ask before taking pictures of people. Note that many Aborigines do not like to have their photographs taken, even from a distance.

TIME

Australia is divided into three time zones. Queensland is on Eastern Standard Time (as are New South Wales, Victoria and Tasmania), which is 10 hours ahead of UTC (Greenwich Mean Time).

The other time zones in Australia are Central Standard Time (Northern Territory, South Australia), which is half an hour behind Eastern Standard Time; and Western Standard Time (Western Australia), which is two hours behind Eastern Standard Time.

At noon in Queensland it's 2 am in London, 3 am in Rome, 9 am in Bangkok, 2 pm in Auckland, 6 pm the previous day in Los Angeles and 9 pm the previous day in New York.

Lamentably, Queensland is on Eastern Standard Time all year, while most of the rest of Australia sensibly switches to daylight saving time over the summer months. From roughly October through March, Queensland is one hour behind NSW, Victoria and Tasmania.

ELECTRICITY

Voltage is 220-240 V and the plugs are three-pin, but not the same as British three-pin plugs. Users of electric shavers or hair dryers should note that, apart from in fancy hotels, it's difficult to find converters to take either US flat two-pin plugs or the European round two-pin plugs. Adapters for British plugs can be found in good hardware shops, chemists and travel agents.

WEIGHTS & MEASURES

Petrol and milk are sold by the litre, apples and potatoes by the kilogram, distance is measured by the metre or kilometre, and speed limits are in kilometres per hour (km/h). Nevertheless, many people still refer to the old imperial units, especially older folks and people from country areas. You're still more likely to hear someone described as six foot tall rather than 183cm, tyre pressures are given in pounds per square inch, fuel consumption is referred to as miles per gallon, and boat lengths are given in feet etc.

For those who need help with metric there's a conversion table at the back of this book.

HEALTH

Australia is a remarkably healthy country considering that such a large portion of it lies in the tropics. Tropical diseases such as malaria and yellow fever are as yet unknown, although periodic outbreaks of two mosquito-borne diseases, dengue and Ross River fevers, sometimes occur. Diseases of insanitation such as cholera and typhoid are unheard of, and even some animal diseases such as rabies and foot-and-mouth disease have yet to be recorded.

Travel health depends on your predeparture preparations, your daily health care while travelling and how you handle any medical problem that does develop. Few travellers experience anything more than an upset stomach.

Health Insurance

Make sure that you have adequate health insurance. See the Travel Insurance boxed text under Visas & Documents earlier in this chapter.

Environmental Hazards

Fungal Infections Fungal infections occur more commonly in hot weather and are usually found on the scalp, between the toes or fingers, in the groin and on the body (ringworm). You get ringworm (which is a fungal infection, not a worm) from infected animals or other people. Moisture encourages these infections.

To prevent fungal infections wear loose, comfortable clothes, avoid artificial fibres, wash frequently and dry carefully. If you do get an infection, wash the infected area at least daily with a disinfectant or medicated soap and water, and rinse and dry well. Apply an antifungal cream or powder like tolnaftate (Tinaderm). Try to expose the infected area to air or sunlight as much as possible and wash all towels and underwear in hot water, change them often and let them dry in the sun.

Medical Kit Check List

Consider taking a basic medical kit including:

☐ **Aspirin** or **paracetamol** (acetaminophen in the US) – for pain or fever.

☐ **Antihistamine** (such as Benadryl) – useful as a decongestant for colds and allergies, to ease the itch from insect bites or stings, and to help prevent motion sickness. Antihistamines may cause sedation and interact with alcohol so care should be taken when using them; take one you know and have used before, if possible.

☐ **Antibiotics** – useful if you're travelling well off the beaten track, but they must be prescribed; carry the prescription with you.

☐ **Loperamide** (eg Imodium) or Lomotil for diarrhoea; prochlorperazine (eg Stemetil) or metaclopramide (eg Maxalon) for nausea and vomiting.

☐ **Rehydration** mixture – for treatment of severe diarrhoea; particularly important for travelling with children.

☐ **Antiseptic** such as povidone-iodine (eg Betadine) – for cuts and grazes.

☐ **Multivitamins** – especially for long trips when dietary vitamin intake may be inadequate.

☐ **Calamine lotion** or **aluminium sulphate spray** (eg Stingose) – to ease irritation from bites or stings.

☐ **Bandages** and **Band-aids**

☐ **Scissors**, **tweezers** and a **thermometer** (note that mercury thermometers are prohibited by airlines).

☐ **Cold and flu tablets** and **throat lozenges**. Pseudoephedrine hydrochloride (Sudafed) may be useful if flying with a cold to avoid ear damage.

☐ **Insect repellent**, **sunscreen**, **chap stick** and **water purification tablets**.

☐ A couple of **syringes**, in case you need injections in a country with medical hygiene problems. Ask your doctor for a note explaining why they have been prescribed.

Heat Exhaustion Dehydration and salt deficiency can cause heat exhaustion. Take time to acclimatise to high temperatures, drink sufficient liquids and do not do anything too physically demanding.

Salt deficiency is characterised by fatigue, lethargy, headaches, giddiness and muscle cramps; salt tablets may help, but adding extra salt to your food is better.

Heat Stroke This serious, occasionally fatal, condition can occur if the body's heat-regulating mechanism breaks down and the body temperature rises to dangerous levels. Long, continuous periods of exposure to high temperatures and insufficient fluids can leave you vulnerable to heat stroke.

The symptoms are feeling unwell, not sweating very much (or at all) and a high body temperature (39°C to 41°C or 102°F to 106°F). Where sweating has ceased the skin becomes flushed and red. Severe, throbbing headaches and lack of coordination will also occur, and the sufferer may be confused or aggressive. Eventually the victim will become delirious or convulse. Hospitalisation is essential, but in the interim get victims out of the sun, remove their clothing, cover them with a wet sheet or towel and then fan continually. Give fluids if they are conscious.

Motion Sickness Eating lightly before and during a trip will reduce the chances of motion sickness. If you are prone to motion sickness try to find a place that minimises movement – near the wing on aircraft, close to midships on boats, near the centre on buses. Fresh air usually helps; reading and cigarette smoke don't. Commercial motion-sickness preparations, which can cause drowsiness, have to be taken before the trip commences. Ginger (available in capsule form) and peppermint (including mint-flavoured sweets) are natural preventatives.

Prickly Heat Prickly heat is an itchy rash caused by excessive perspiration trapped under the skin. It usually strikes people who

Everyday Health

Normal body temperature is up to 37°C or 98.6°F; more than 2°C (4°F) higher indicates a high fever. The normal adult pulse rate is 60 to 100 per minute (children 80 to 100, babies 100 to 140). As a general rule the pulse increases about 20 beats per minute for each °C (2°F) rise in fever.

Respiration (breathing) rate is also an indicator of illness. Count the number of breaths per minute: between 12 and 20 is normal for adults and older children (up to 30 for younger children, 40 for babies). People with a high fever or serious respiratory illness breathe more quickly than normal. More than 40 shallow breaths a minute may indicate pneumonia.

have just arrived in a hot climate. Keeping cool, bathing often, drying the skin and using a mild talcum or prickly heat powder, or resorting to air-conditioning may help.

Sunburn In the tropics or the outback you can get sunburnt surprisingly quickly, even through cloud. Use a sunscreen and hat, and barrier cream for your nose and lips. Calamine lotion or stingose are good for mild sunburn. Protect your eyes with good-quality sunglasses, particularly if you will be near water and sand.

Cuts & Scratches Wash well and treat any cut with an antiseptic such as povidone-iodine. Where possible avoid bandages and Band-Aids, which can keep wounds wet. Coral cuts are notoriously slow to heal and if they are not adequately cleaned small pieces of coral can become embedded in the wound. Clean any cut thoroughly with an antiseptic. Severe pain, throbbing, redness, fever or generally feeling unwell suggest infection and the need for antibiotics promptly, as coral cuts may result in serious infections.

Mosquito-Borne Diseases Dengue and Ross River fevers are two potentially serious diseases, transmitted by mosquitoes, that can be contracted in Queensland. Neither is normally fatal, but both can be debilitating and in areas where mosquitoes are common, remember to cover up and/or wear repellent.

Dengue Fever Small outbreaks of this viral disease have been reported from Far North Queensland, although there is a small risk to travellers of infection.

The *Aedes aegypti* mosquito which transmits the dengue virus is most active during the day, unlike the malaria mosquito, and is found mainly in urban areas.

Signs and symptoms of dengue fever include a sudden onset of high fever, headache, joint and muscle pains (hence its old name, 'breakbone fever') and nausea and vomiting. A rash of small red spots appears three to four days after the onset of fever. Dengue is commonly mistaken for other infectious diseases, including influenza. Infection can be diagnosed by a blood test.

Seek medical attention if you think you may be infected. There is no specific treatment for dengue. Aspirin should be avoided, as it increases the risk of haemorrhaging. Recovery may be prolonged, with tiredness lasting for several weeks but severe complications are currently unknown in Queensland.

There is no vaccine against dengue fever, the best prevention is to avoid mosquito bites at all times.

Ross River Fever Properly known as epidemic polyarthritis, Ross River fever occurs throughout Australia but mostly in the east. Outbreaks are most likely to occur in January and February, but the risk of infection is very low. Ross River fever is characterised by marked joint pains and muscle aches. Joints of extremities (hands and feet) are most commonly affected, but back pains are also common. Loss of appetite, headache, fever and tiredness may also occur. These symptoms are usually accompanied by a rash on the trunk and limbs. The time from the mosquito bite to the development of the illness is anywhere between three and 21 days, but generally the illness takes hold between seven and nine days.

No protective treatment is available against Ross River Fever. As with dengue, the most effective remedy is to avoid getting bitten by mosquitoes. Conventional wisdom has it that the symptoms do not last more than a few months, although there are now serious doubts about this: some people still feel the effects (mainly chronic fatigue) years after contracting the disease.

Infectious Diseases

Diarrhoea Diarrhoea is unlikely to be a major problem when travelling in Queensland. Two potential causes of diarrhoea are drinking mineralised bore water and stopping or camping at places that have been frequented by travellers with a poor understanding of hygiene.

It's always a good idea to carry plenty of safe drinking water in the car, particularly if you have small children in tow – adults can usually cope better with changes in water.

HIV & AIDS HIV, the Human Immunodeficiency Virus, develops into AIDS, Acquired Immune Deficiency Syndrome, which is a fatal disease. Any exposure to blood, blood products or body fluids may put the individual at risk. The disease is often transmitted through sexual contact or dirty needles – vaccinations, acupuncture, tattooing and body piercing can be potentially as dangerous as intravenous drug use. HIV/AIDS can also be spread through infected blood transfusions, although all blood in Australia is screened.

Worms These parasites are most common in outback animals. Meat bought from a butcher will be fine, but kangaroo or goat which has not been checked by the proper authorities can be suspect, especially if under-cooked.

Sexually Transmitted Diseases Gonorrhoea, herpes and syphilis are among these diseases; sores, blisters or rashes around the genitals, discharges or pain when urinating are common symptoms. In some STDs, such as wart virus or chlamydia, symptoms may be less marked or not observed at all especially in women. Syphilis symptoms eventually disappear completely but the disease continues and can cause severe problems in later years.

While abstinence from sexual contact is the only 100% effective prevention, using condoms is also effective. The treatment of

---

Nutrition

If your food is poor or limited in availability, if you're travelling hard and fast and therefore missing meals, or if you simply lose your appetite, you can soon start to lose weight and place your health at risk.

Make sure your diet is well balanced. Cooked eggs, tofu, beans, lentils (dhal in India) and nuts are all safe ways to get protein. Fruit you can peel (bananas, oranges or mandarins for example) is usually safe (melons can harbour bacteria in their flesh and are best avoided) and a good source of vitamins. Try to eat plenty of grains (including rice) and bread. Remember that although food is generally safer if it is cooked well, overcooked food loses much of its nutritional value. If your diet isn't well balanced or if your food intake is insufficient, it's a good idea to take vitamin and iron pills.

In hot climates make sure you drink enough – don't rely on feeling thirsty to indicate when you should drink. Not needing to urinate or small amounts of very dark yellow urine is a danger sign. Always carry a water bottle with you on long trips. Excessive sweating can lead to loss of salt and therefore muscle cramping. Salt tablets are not a good idea as a preventative, but in places where salt is not used much adding it to food can help.

gonorrhoea and syphilis is with antibiotics. The different sexually transmitted diseases each require specific antibiotics. There is no cure for herpes or AIDS.

Tetanus Tetanus occurs when a wound becomes infected by a germ which lives in soil and in the faeces of horses and other animals. It enters the body via breaks in the skin. All wounds should be cleaned promptly and adequately and an antiseptic cream or solution applied. Use antibiotics if the wound becomes hot, throbs or pus is seen. The first symptom may be discomfort in swallowing, or stiffening of the jaw and neck; this is followed by painful convulsions of the jaw and whole body. The disease can be fatal, but poses only a small risk to the traveller.

Women's Health
Gynaecological Problems Sexually transmitted diseases are a major cause of vaginal problems. Symptoms include a smelly discharge, painful intercourse and sometimes a burning sensation when urinating. Male sexual partners must also be treated. Medical attention should be sought and remember in addition to these diseases HIV or hepatitis B may also be acquired during exposure. Besides abstinence, the best thing is to practise safe sex using condoms.

Antibiotic use, synthetic underwear, sweating and contraceptive pills can lead to

Information for Disabled Travellers

A number of organisations supply information for disabled travellers visiting Queensland.

NICAN (National Information Communications Awareness Network), PO Box 407, Curtin, ACT 2605 (☎ (02) 6285 3713 or toll-free ☎ 1800 806 769), produces fact sheets on accessible accommodation and recreation facilities.

ACROD Ltd offers similar services and has an office at Highpoint Plaza, 240 Waterworks Rd, Ashgrove 4060 (☎ 3366 4366).

The Office of Disability in Brisbane offers telephone information and referral services (☎ 3224 8031 or toll-free ☎ 1800 177 120), and their Disability Information and Awareness Line (DIAL) (☎ 3224 8444, toll-free ☎ 1800 177 120; TTY 3224 8021) provides advice and referrals.

The Paraplegic and Quadriplegic Association in Brisbane (☎ 3391 2044) is another useful resource.

Getting Around

The Brisbane City Council's Disability Access & Services section, GPO Box 1434, Brisbane, Qld 4001 (☎ 3403 4268), has an excellent *Access Brisbane* brochure, with information about buildings, services, restaurants, hotels etc. They also produce a *Mobility Map* of the city centre, showing an accessible route, parking and toilets. Queensland Railways (☎ 3235 2222), at 305 Edward St in the city, has the *City Train Accessibility Guide* brochure, showing accessible stations.

The Cairns City Council has a *Cairns City Mobility Directory* – obtain a copy by writing to the Cairns Access Committee, PO Box 859, Cairns, Qld 4870.

The international wheelchair symbol for parking in allocated bays is generally recognised in Queensland. Car stickers are available from local councils.

Avis and Hertz offer hire cars with hand controls at no extra charge, which can be picked up at major airports; give 24 hours notice. Most taxi companies in the major cities and towns have modified vehicles that take wheelchairs. In Brisbane, try Black & White Taxis (☎ 3238

fungal vaginal infections when travelling in hot climates. Maintaining good personal hygiene, and wearing loose-fitting clothes and cotton underwear will help to prevent these infections.

Fungal infections, characterised by a rash, itch and discharge, can be treated with a vinegar or lemon-juice douche, or with yoghurt. Nystatin, miconazole or clotrimazole pessaries or vaginal cream are the usual treatment.

WOMEN TRAVELLERS

Queensland is generally a safe place for women travellers, although it's probably best to avoid walking alone late at night in any of the major cities. Sexual harassment is rare, although the Aussie male culture does have its sexist elements. Don't tolerate any harassment or discrimination.

Female hitchhikers should exercise care at all times. See the section on Hitching in the Getting Around chapter.

GAY & LESBIAN TRAVELLERS

Historically, Queensland had a poor reputation when it came to acceptance of gays and lesbians, but the situation has changed significantly since the fall of the right-wing National Party government in 1990. Previously repressive attitudes and laws have been relaxed, and homosexuality was decriminalised in Queensland in 1991.

Brisbane has an increasingly lively gay

1000) or Yellow Cabs (☎ 3391 0191). In Cairns, Black & White Taxis (☎ 13 1008) has vans with hydraulic lift access at the rear, and a stretch cab.

Accommodation

Accommodation in Queensland is generally good, and most of the newer places must now include facilities for people with disabilities. Contact tourist information centres for lists of accessible accommodation – see Tourist Offices earlier in this chapter.

The RACQ's *Accommodation Guide* to Queensland includes symbols indicating accommodation that is 'Independently Accessible' or 'Accessible With Assistance', but always check with the proprietors to ensure that facilities will be suitable.

A number of YHA hostels have accessible accommodation; contact the YHA Membership & Travel Centre (☎ 3236 1680), at 154 Roma St, Brisbane, Qld 4000.

An increasing number of accommodation places have wheelchair-accessible units. On the Gold Coast these include the *Labrador Holiday Units* (☎ 5537 4766) and the Teneriffe Holiday Units (☎ 5531 6575).

Attractions & Activities

Movie World, Sea World and Currumbin Sanctuary, on the Gold Coast, encourage disabled visitors.

Many tour operators can cater for people with disabilities. In Cairns, for example, Great Adventures encourages disabled people to join their trips out to the Barrier Reef by offering a discount to the wheelchair traveller's companion, and they'll take you snorkelling to see the coral. The Kuranda Scenic Railway can accommodate wheelchair passengers, and some of the tour operators to the rainforest areas of the Daintree and Cape Tribulation will take you in their vehicles, although they are not specifically accessible vehicles.

Sporting Wheelies has offices throughout Queensland, with information on accessible diving trips, sporting and recreation facilities. Contact their Brisbane office ☎ 3252 5242.

Bruce Cameron

and lesbian scene centred around the inner-city suburbs of Spring Hill and Fortitude Valley, with quite a few nightclubs, pubs and a couple of guesthouses. See the Brisbane chapter for more information on gay and lesbian culture there. There are also gay and lesbian-only accommodation places in some of the more popular tourist centres including Cairns, the Gold Coast and Noosa Heads. Elsewhere in Queensland, however, there's still a strong streak of homophobia and violence against homosexuals is not unknown.

Publications such as Brisbane's *Brother Sister* magazine list contact points, accommodation places and other gay and lesbian groups throughout Queensland. They are on the Web at www.brothersister.com.au.

The Gay & Lesbian Welfare Association of Brisbane (on the Web at glwa.queer.org.au) has information about the organisation and some listings of venues, groups and events.

TRAVEL WITH CHILDREN

Travelling with children presents few unforeseen problems.

The Barrier Reef is one of Australia's top family holiday spots so it comes as no surprise that kids are well catered for at most of the bigger places there. This is usually in the form of a Kids' Club or something similar, where the children are supervised and distracted for the greater part of the day, leaving the parents free to kick back on the beach or go diving. Most of these services are free, and are generally available between about 8 am and 6 pm, although this does of course vary from island to island.

During the evening the larger resorts can also arrange for babysitters, and this costs around $10 per hour for one or two children.

At the other end of the scale there are resorts which are resolutely child-free zones, for those who want to escape the noise and general mayhem which kids can often generate. These resorts include Bedarra and Lizard islands, while at Orpheus Island children are 'not catered

for', which basically means children are charged full price and there are no special activities.

USEFUL ORGANISATIONS
RACQ

The Royal Automobile Club of Queensland (RACQ) is the Queensland motoring association – they produce a particularly useful set of regional maps to Queensland which are free to members. Their offices also sell a wide range of travel and driving products, including good maps and travel guidebooks; book tours and accommodation; and advise on weather and road conditions.

The RACQ's head office (☎ 3361 2444) is in Brisbane at 300 St Pauls Terrace in Fortitude Valley (although their office beside the Brisbane GPO in Queen St may be more convenient). There are other offices all around the state and almost every town has a garage affiliated with the RACQ – see the information sections of the individual towns for details on these.

Department of Environment

This organisation is responsible for the management of Queensland's national parks. There are information offices and rangers' stations throughout the state, and all provide good advice and information about the respective parks. See the National Parks section in the Facts about Queensland chapter for details.

Australian Conservation Foundation

The Australian Conservation Foundation (ACF) is the largest nongovernment organisation involved in conservation. Only about 10% of its income is from the government; the rest comes from memberships and subscriptions, and from donations (72%), which are mainly from individuals.

With the growing focus on conservation issues and the increasing concern of the Australian public in regard to the environment, the conservation vote has now become increasingly important to all political parties.

The ACF's Brisbane office (☎ 3844

5011) is at 131 Melbourne St, West End, just south of the city centre across the Brisbane River.

Wilderness Society

The Tasmanian Wilderness Society was formed by conservationists who had been unsuccessful in preventing the damming of Lake Pedder in south-west Tasmania but who were determined to prevent the damming of the Franklin River in 1983. It has been a vocal lobby group ever since.

The Wilderness Society is involved in issues concerning protection of the Australian wilderness, such as forest management and logging. Like the ACF, government funding is only a small percentage of its income, the rest coming from memberships, donations, its shops and merchandising. In Brisbane, the Wilderness Society has a shop and office (☎ 3221 3695) at 97 Albert St in the city centre.

Australian Trust for Conservation Volunteers

This nonpolitical, nonprofit group organises practical conservation projects (such as tree planting, track construction and flora and fauna surveys) for volunteers to take part in. Travellers are welcome and it's an excellent way to get involved with the conservation movement and, at the same time, visit some of the more interesting areas of the country. Past volunteers have found themselves working in places such as Tasmania, Kakadu and Fraser Island.

Most projects are either for a weekend or a week and all food, transport and accommodation is supplied in return for a small contribution to help cover costs. Most travellers who take part in ATCV join a Banksia Package, which lasts six weeks and includes six different projects. The cost is $650, and further weeks can be added for $105.

Contact the head office (☎ (03) 5333 1483; users.netconnect.com.au/~atcv) at PO Box 423, Ballarat, Vic 3350, or the Queensland office (☎ 3210 0330) at Old Government House (in the grounds of the Queensland University of Technology) in George St, Brisbane.

Willing Workers on Organic Farms (WWOOF)

WWOOF is a relatively new organisation in Australia, although it is well established in other countries. The idea is that you do a few hours' work each day on a farm in return for bed and board. Some places have a minimum stay of a couple of days but many will take you for just a night. Some will let you stay for months if they like the look of you, and you can get involved with some interesting large-scale projects.

Becoming a WWOOFer is a great way to meet interesting people and to travel cheaply. There are about 200 WWOOF associates in Australia, mostly in Victoria, New South Wales and Queensland. As the name says, the farms are supposed to be organic but that isn't always so. Some places aren't even farms – you might help out at a pottery or do the books at a seed wholesaler. There are even a few commercial farms which exploit WWOOFers as cheap harvest labour, although these are quite rare. Whether they have a farm or just a vegie patch, most participants in the scheme are concerned to some extent with alternative lifestyles.

To join WWOOF send $20 to WWOOF, Mt Murrindal Coop, Buchan, Vic 3885 (☎ (03) 5155 0218; www.earthlink.com.au/wwoof), and they'll send you a membership number and a booklet which lists WWOOF places all over Australia.

National Trust

The National Trust is dedicated to preserving historic buildings in all parts of Australia. The Trust actually owns a number of buildings throughout the country which are open to the public. Many other buildings are 'classified' by the National Trust to ensure their preservation.

The National Trust also produces some excellent literature, including a fine series of walking-tour guides to Brisbane and some of Queensland's more historic towns.

These guides are often available from local tourist offices or from National Trust offices and are usually free even if you are not a member.

Membership of the trust is well worth considering, however, because it entitles you to free entry to any National Trust property for your year of membership. The National Trust's Brisbane office (☎ 3229 1788) is at Old Government House (in the grounds of the QUT) in George St.

DANGERS & ANNOYANCES
Theft
Queensland is a relatively safe place to visit, but it's better to play it safe and take reasonable precautions, especially in some of the larger centres. Unfortunately, Cairns has a bad reputation for theft, with more than a few travellers having been robbed at hostels there.

Most accommodation places have somewhere they can store your valuables, and it's always worth taking advantage of this service. Don't leave hotel rooms or cars unlocked, and don't leave your money, wallets, purses or cameras unattended or in full view through car windows, for instance.

If you are unlucky enough to have something stolen, immediately report all details to the nearest police station. If your credit cards, cash card or travellers cheques have been taken, notify your bank or the relevant company immediately.

Swimming
It seems unnecessary to mention it, but don't ever go swimming if you have been drinking alcohol. Swimming after a heavy meal is also unwise.

Surf Beaches There are surf beaches all along the coast of southern Queensland as far north as Fraser Island. Many of these, especially along the Gold Coast and Sunshine Coast, are patrolled by surf life-saving clubs, and many people need to be rescued from the surf every year. Patrolled beaches are indicated by a pair of yellow and red flags. If possible, always swim between the flags. If you get into trouble in the water, raise one arm above your head to catch the attention of the life-savers.

If you happen to get caught in a rip and are being taken out to sea, the first (and hardest) thing to do is not panic. Raise your arm until you have been spotted, and then swim parallel to the shore – *don't* try to swim back against the rip, you'll only tire yourself.

Sharks Shark attacks are extremely rare in Australia, especially along the warm waters of the Great Barrier Reef where the sharks are very well fed.

The closest you're likely to come to a shark is in the local fish and chip shop, unless you're scuba diving. Numerous small, harmless species, such as white-tipped reef sharks are common on coral reefs. Dangerous species such as tiger, hammerhead and whaler sharks are found on the reef but generally on drop-offs from the outer reef.

Box Jellyfish The potentially deadly box jellyfish, also known as the sea wasp or 'stinger', occurs in Queensland's coastal waters north of Rockhampton during the summer months. The danger period varies from year to year and place to place, but is generally from around November to April, and swimming is definitely not advisable in these places during these times. They are usually found close to the coast, especially around river mouths – they aren't often found further out on the reef or islands, although they can drift out to some of the islands that are closer to the mainland.

The sea wasp's stinging tentacles spread several metres away its body; by the time you see it you're likely to have been stung. If someone is stung, they are likely to run out of the sea screaming and collapse on the beach, with weals on their body as though they've been whipped. They may stop breathing. Douse the stings with vinegar (available on many beaches or from nearby houses), do not try to remove the tentacles from the skin, and treat as for snake bite (see Snakes & Spiders later in this section). If there's a first-aider present, they may have to apply artificial respiration until the ambulance gets there.

Some coastal resorts erect 'stinger nets' which provide small areas for safe swimming, but elsewhere, stay out of the sea when the sea wasps are around. If you're in doubt, check with a local, and if you're still in doubt, don't swim – it's not worth the risk.

Crocodiles In north Queensland, saltwater crocodiles can be a real danger and have killed a number of people (travellers and locals). They are found in river estuaries and large rivers, sometimes a long way inland, so before diving into that inviting, cool water find out from the locals whether it's croc-free. See the section on Crocodiles in the Fauna section of the Facts about Queensland chapter for more details.

Coral Cuts Coral can be extremely sharp, and you can cut yourself by merely brushing against the stuff. Even a small cut can be very painful and take a long, long time to heal. The best solution is not to get cut in the first place – avoid touching coral. Wash any coral cuts thoroughly and douse them with a good antiseptic.

Fish Poisoning Ciguatera poison is a poison which seems to accumulate in certain types of fish due to the consumption of certain types of algae by grazing fish. The poison seems to concentrate the further up the food chain it goes so it isn't the original algae-eating fish which poses the danger, it's the fish which eats the fish which eats the algae-eating fish! The danger is remote but erratic and recovery, although usually complete, is very slow. Chinaman-fish, red bass, large rock cods and moray eels have all been implicated.

Don't consider dining on pufferfish unless you're a Japanese *fugu* fan.

Other Marine Dangers There are quite a few other potential hazards lurking in the waters of the Barrier Reef, although the dangers are slight and in most cases it's simply a matter of not picking up things which are best left alone.

Butterfly cod and stonefish both have a series of poisonous spines down their back, which can inflict a serious and even fatal wound. Blue-ringed octopus and Barrier Reef cone shells can also be fatal, so don't pick them up. If someone is stung, apply a pressure bandage, monitor breathing carefully and conduct mouth-to-mouth resuscitation if breathing stops.

Also watch out for the scorpion fish, which has venomous spines; stingrays, which can inflict a nasty wound with their barbed tails; and sea snakes, which are potentially deadly, although they are more curious than aggressive.

Snakes & Spiders

The best known danger in the Australian outback, and the one that captures visitors' imaginations, is snakes. Although there are many venomous snakes there are few that are aggressive, and unless you have the bad fortune to stand on one it's unlikely that you'll be bitten. Taipans and tiger snakes, however, will attack if alarmed.

To minimise your chances of being bitten always wear boots, socks and long trousers when walking through undergrowth where snakes may be present. Don't put your hands into holes and crevices, and be careful when collecting firewood.

Snake bites do not cause instantaneous death and antivenenes are usually available. Keep the victim calm and still, wrap the bitten limb tightly, as you would for a sprained ankle, and then attach a splint to immobilise it. Then seek medical help, if possible with the dead snake for identification.

Don't attempt to catch the snake if there is even a remote possibility of being bitten again. Tourniquets and sucking out the poison are now comprehensively discredited.

Australia has a couple of nasty spiders too, including the funnel-web, the redback and the white-tail, so it's best not to play with any spider. Funnel-web spiders are mostly found in New South Wales and their bite is treated in the same way as snake bite. For redback bites apply ice and seek medical attention.

Insects

Flies In the cities the flies are not too bad; it's in the country that it starts getting out of hand, and the further 'out' you get the worse the flies seem to be.

In central Queensland the flies start to come out with the warmer spring weather (late August) and last until winter. They are such a nuisance that virtually every general store sells the Genuine Aussie Fly Net (made in Korea), which is rather like a string onion bag but is very effective. It's either that or the 'Great Australian Wave' to keep them away. Repellents such as Aerogard and Rid go some way to deterring the little bastards.

Mosquitoes 'Mozzies' can be a problem, especially in the warmer tropical and subtropical areas. Fortunately malaria is not present in Australia, although its counterpart, dengue fever, is a significant danger in the tropics (see the Health section for more information on dengue and Ross River fevers).

Mosquitoes are most active at dusk, and also at night, but there are some precautions you can take to avoid being bitten. The first is to use a good insect repellent such as Rid. Slap it on all over – during the day, at dusk and at night before you go to bed. Wearing long, loose clothing will at least reduce the amount of flesh a mozzie has to choose from. It's also worth considering investing in a mosquito net or a packet of mosquito coils, which will burn all night and keep most rooms mozzie-free. You'll rarely be bitten if you sleep under a reasonably fast ceiling fan.

Ticks & Leeches The common bush-tick (found in the forest and scrub country along the eastern coast of Australia) can be dangerous if left lodged in the skin, as the toxin

the tick excretes can cause paralysis and sometimes death. Check your body for lumps every night if you're walking in tick-infested areas. The tick should be removed by dousing it with methylated spirits or kerosene and levering it out, but make sure you remove it intact. Remember to check children and dogs for ticks after a walk in the bush.

Leeches are common, and while they will suck your blood they are not dangerous and are easily removed by the application of salt or heat.

On the Road

Cows and kangaroos can be a real hazard to the driver. A collision with one will badly damage your car and probably kill the animal. Unfortunately, other drivers are even more dangerous, particularly those who drink. Australia has its share of fatal road accidents, particularly in the countryside, so don't drink and drive. The dangers posed by stray animals and drunks are particularly enhanced at night, so it's best to avoid travelling after dark. See the Getting Around chapter for more on driving hazards.

Bushfires

Bushfires happen every year in Queensland. Don't be the mug who starts one. In hot, dry, windy weather, be extremely careful with any naked flame – don't throw live cigarette butts out of car windows. On a day of Total Fire Ban (listen to the radio, watch the billboards on country roads or front pages of daily newspapers), it is forbidden even to use a camping stove in the open. The locals will not be amused if they catch you breaking this particular law; they'll happily dob you in, and the penalties are severe.

If you're unfortunate enough to find yourself driving through a bushfire, stay inside your car and try to park off the road in an open space, away from trees, until the danger has passed. Lie on the floor under the dashboard, covering yourself with a wool blanket if possible. The front of the fire should pass quickly, and you will be much safer than if you were out in the open. It is very important to cover up with a wool blanket or wear protective clothing, as it has been proved that heat radiation is the big killer in bushfire situations.

Bushwalkers should take local advice before setting out. On a day of Total Fire Ban, don't go – delay your trip until the weather has changed. Chances are that it will be so unpleasantly hot and windy, you'll be better off anyway in an air-conditioned pub sipping a cool beer.

If you're out in the bush and you see smoke, even at a great distance, take it seriously. Go to the nearest open space, downhill if possible. A forested ridge is the most dangerous place to be. Bushfires move very quickly and change direction with the wind.

BUSINESS HOURS

Business hours are from 9 am to 5 pm, Monday to Friday. Most shops in Queensland are open on weekdays from around 8.30 or 9 am until 5 pm and on Saturday morning, and most of the larger towns and cities will have at least one night a week when the shops stay open until 9 pm – usually Thursday or Friday. In the larger centres and tourist resorts – notably Brisbane, the Gold and Sunshine Coasts and Cairns – shopping hours are more flexible. In these places, many larger stores stay open later and all day on Saturday, although on Sunday you still won't find many shops open anywhere.

Banks are open from 9.30 am to 4 pm on weekdays, and until 5 pm on Friday.

There are plenty of exceptions to these standard hours. Most of the larger cities have 24-hour convenience stores, and supermarkets are often open until quite late at night. On the other hand, in the more remote areas shopping hours are often more desultory – small-town general stores seem to set their hours according to demand, opening later during the tourist season and closing whenever they feel like it during the off season.

PUBLIC HOLIDAYS & SPECIAL EVENTS

The Christmas holiday season is part of the long summer school vacation and the time you are most likely to find accommodation booked out and long queues. Easter is also a busy holiday time, and there are three other shorter school holiday periods during the year. See the earlier When to Go section for details.

The main public holidays in Queensland are:

New Year's Day
    1 January
Australia Day
    26 January
Easter
    Good Friday and Easter Saturday, Sunday and Monday (March or April)
Anzac Day
    25 April
Labour Day
    1st Monday in May
Queen's Birthday
    2nd Monday in June
Christmas Day
    25 December
Boxing Day
    26 December

Queensland's major annual festivals and events include the following:

January to February
    Australia Day – this national holiday, commemorating the arrival of the First Fleet in 1788, is observed on 26 January.
    International Cricket – one-day internationals, Test matches and Sheffield Shield games are played at the Brisbane Cricket Ground in Woolloongabba.
    Australian Skins – this big-money golf tournament is played over two days at Laguna Quays Resort on the Whitsunday Coast.
March
    Surf Life-Saving Events – several major life-saving championships are held on the Gold Coast over the summer months, including the classic Iron Man and Iron Woman events.
April
    Anzac Day – this is a national public holiday, on 25 April, commemorating the landing of Anzac troops at Gallipoli in 1915. Memorial

marches by the returned soldiers of both world wars and the veterans of Korea and Vietnam are held all over the country.

May to June

Brisbane Biennial International Music Festival – held biennially (odd years), this festival features Australian and international musicians and styles – jazz, rock, indigenous, classical and world music.

Outback Muster Drovers Union & National Outback Performing Arts Show – this major festival is held in Longreach.

Palmer Street Festival – Townsville's major festival, featuring street theatre, among other things.

Gold Coast International Jazz & Blues Festival – two-day music event.

Cooktown Endeavour Festival – commemorating Captain Cook's landing in 1770, held over the Queen's Birthday weekend.

July

Gold Coast International Marathon – this event attracts thousands of runners from around the country. A half-marathon and 10km walk are also held.

August

Brisbane International Film Festival – the festival features films from Australia and the Asia-Pacific region.

Hervey Bay Whale Festival – held over a fortnight, celebrates the return of these magnificent creatures.

Brisbane Ekka – held at the RNA Showgrounds in Brisbane, this is Queensland's largest agricultural show. Many other towns in Queensland also have agricultural shows at this time of year.

Mt Isa Rodeo – this is one of the country's richest rodeos.

September

Birdsville Races – the tiny town of Birdsville hosts the country's premier outback horse-racing event on the first weekend in September.

Brisbane Festival – Brisbane's annual arts festival is held over two weeks in early September.

Carnival of Flowers – Toowoomba's gardens are on display for eight days, with a flower show, a parade and a Mardi Gras.

Capricana Festival – Rockhampton's major festival, held over 10 days in early September, features a street parade, a carnival and daily activities.

October

IndyCar – a four-day festival centred around the IndyCar Grand Prix car race around the barricaded streets of Surfers Paradise.

Oktoberfests – traditional beerfests with food, plenty of beer and live entertainment for all ages are held in several towns in Queensland.

Reef Festival – this is Cairns' main annual festival, and features a carnival, street parades and musical events.

November

Melbourne Cup – Australia's premier horse race is run in Melbourne on the first Tuesday in November. The whole country shuts down for three minutes or so while the race is run, and many country towns schedule race meetings to coincide with it – in Cape Tribulation, the locals race their horses along the beach.

December

Woodford Folk Festival – formerly the Maleny Fold Festival, this is one of the country's best folk festivals, featuring local and international musicians, arts and crafts markets and other entertainment and activities. It's held over five days between 28 December and New Year's Day.

These are just a few of the festivals held throughout Queensland. In addition to the events mentioned here, almost every community in Queensland has at least one annual festival of its own, and these are often unique and quirky celebrations. As you travel around Queensland, it's worth keeping your ear to the ground to find out about special events that might coincide with your visit. You might find anything from rodeos and bush race meetings to cooee championships and cockroach races – and these festivals are a great way to meet the locals.

ACTIVITIES

There are plenty of activities you can take part in while travelling around the state. You can go scuba diving and snorkelling on the Great Barrier Reef, the world's largest underwater theme park. Bushwalking is cheap and you can do it anywhere – there are many fantastic walks in the various national and state parks. If you're interested in surfing, you'll find some great beaches and surf in southern Queensland. You can go horse riding in many places – from the coastal beaches, rainforests and mountains of the hinterland to the wilds of the outback.

You can cycle all around Queensland; for the athletic there are long, challenging routes and for the not-so-masochistic there are plenty of great day trips.

Bushwalking

This is a popular activity in Queensland year-round. There are bushwalking clubs in the state and several useful guidebooks. Lonely Planet's *Bushwalking in Australia* describes 23 walks of different lengths and difficulty in various parts of the country, including three in Queensland.

50 Walks; Coffs Harbour & Gold Coast Hinterland by Tyrone Thomas is a good reference book which includes maps and walking track notes to some of the best walks in Queensland's south-east corner – places like Tamborine Mountain, Springbrook National Park, Binna Burra and O'Reilly's, and Cunningham's Gap.

Tyrone Thomas has also written *50 Walks in North Queensland*, which covers the area from Cape Hillsborough (near Mackay) up to Cape Tribulation and inland as far as Chillagoe. Most of these walks are beach walks or through the rainforest areas of the World Heritage-listed Wet Tropics areas.

100 Walks in South Queensland by Tony Groom & Trevor Gynther covers a wide range of walks around Brisbane, the Gold and Sunshine coasts and Moreton Bay. It's out of date and out of print now, but may still be available.

Bushwalks in the Toowoomba Region by N McKilligan and I Savage is a small but very comprehensive guide to the best walks in this area, and includes mud maps, track notes and notes on natural history. *Bushwalking in South-East Queensland* is a large-format paperback guide with colour photos and comprehensive walking-track notes to the south-east.

One of the best ways to find out about bushwalking areas is to contact a local bushwalking club, such as the Brisbane Bushwalkers Club (☎ 3856 4050), at 2 Alderley Ave, Alderley, or look in the *Yellow Pages* under 'Clubs – Bushwalking'. Outdoor shops such as Mountain Designs and Paddy Pallin are also good sources of information.

National parks and state forests are some of the best places for walking. Almost every national park either has walking trails or offers wilderness walking. You can get full information on walking in national parks and state forests from their respective offices. There are excellent bushwalking possibilities in many parts of the state, including on several of the larger coastal islands such as Fraser and Hinchinbrook. National parks on the mainland favoured by bushwalkers include Lamington in the McPherson Ranges, Main Range in the Darling Downs, Cooloola just north of the Sunshine Coast, the Carnarvon Gorge in central Queensland, Eungella just west of Mackay and Bellenden Ker south of Cairns, which contains Queensland's highest peak, Mt Bartle Frere (1657m). See the individual sections for details.

Diving & Snorkelling

The Great Barrier Reef provides some of the world's best diving and there's ample opportunity to learn and pursue this activity. The Queensland coast is probably the world's cheapest place to learn to scuba dive in tropical water – a five-day course leading to a recognised open-water certificate usually costs somewhere between $250 and $450 and you almost always do a good part of your learning out on the Barrier Reef itself. These courses are very popular and every major town along the coast has one or more diving schools. The three most popular places are Airlie Beach, Cairns and Townsville.

Important factors to consider when choosing a course include the school's reputation, the relative amounts of time spent on pool/classroom training and out in the ocean, and whether your open-water time is spent on the outer reef as opposed to reefs around islands or even just off the mainland. The outer reef is usually more spectacular. Normally you have to show you can tread water for 10 minutes and swim 200m before you can start a course.

Most schools also require a medical which will usually cost extra (around $50).

For certified divers, trips and equipment hire are available just about everywhere. You usually have to show evidence of qualifications. You can snorkel just about everywhere too. There are coral reefs off some mainland beaches and around several of the islands, and many day trips out to the Barrier Reef provide snorkelling gear free.

During the wet season, usually January to March, floods can wash a lot of mud out into the ocean and visibility for divers and snorkellers is sometimes affected.

Cycling

There are possibilities for some great rides in Queensland. See the Getting Around chapter for information on long-distance cycling. Available from most bookshops, *Pedalling Around Southern Queensland*, by Julia Thorn, has tour notes and mud maps for 25 bike rides in and around Brisbane, the Gold Coast and the Toowoomba region.

There are companies that offer cycling tours in various places, including Cairns, Townsville and Brisbane. It might also be worth contacting one of the local cycling clubs like the Brisbane Bicycle Touring Association (☎ 3279 3666), at PO Box 286, Jindalee, Brisbane 4074. For other areas, look under 'Clubs – Bicycle' in the *Yellow Pages*.

White-Water Rafting, Sea-Kayaking & Canoeing

The Tully and North Johnstone rivers between Townsville and Cairns are the big ones for white-water rafting. You can do day trips for about $100 to $120, or longer expeditions. See the Cairns and Mission Beach sections for details.

Sea-kayaking is also popular, and there are numerous operations along the coast that offer paddling expeditions through the calm Barrier Reef waters, often from the mainland out to offshore islands. See the Cairns, Mission Beach and Cape Tribulation sections for details.

Coastal Queensland is full of waterways and lakes so there's no shortage of canoeing territory. You can rent canoes or join canoe tours in several places – among them Noosa, Townsville and Cairns.

Surfing

From a surfer's point of view, Queensland's Great Barrier Reef is one of nature's most tragic mistakes – a 2000km-long breakwater! The reef protects almost the entire Queensland coast from ocean swells, and about the only waves you'll see along the coast are those whipped up by passing boats or strong winds. Many a surfer has driven along the coast past all those picture-perfect points and coves thinking, 'if only ...'.

Thankfully, the reef finishes down near Gladstone, and there are some great surf beaches in southern Queensland. The Gold Coast has some of the best of these, including a classic right-hand point break at Burleigh Heads, although you have to be prepared for crowds. Near Brisbane, North Stradbroke Island also has good surf beaches, as does Moreton Island.

The Sunshine Coast also has lots of good beach breaks and a few rocky points – at Noosa Heads, Tea Tree Bay in the national park is a favourite with long-board riders, especially during the cyclone swells of summer.

Further north, Fraser Island often has good surf along its east coast, although not too many people surf here due to the large numbers of sharks in the water. Queensland's most northern surf beaches are at Agnes Water and the town of Seventeen Seventy, just south of Gladstone.

You can hire second-hand boards from almost any surf shop along the coast. For beginners, though, boogie-boarding or body-surfing are probably better propositions – standing up on a surfboard is much harder than it looks, and when it's crowded things can get pretty aggressive out in the water. If you're keen, there are a couple of learn-to-surf schools in Surfers Paradise and at Noosa Heads.

Surfing Australia's East Coast by Aussie

surf star Nat Young is a slim, cheap, comprehensive guide to the best breaks from Victoria to Fraser Island. He's also written the *Surfing & Sailboard Guide to Australia* which covers the whole country. Surfing enthusiasts can also look for the expensive coffee-table book, *Atlas of Australian Surfing*, by Mark Warren.

Swimming

The very word 'Queensland' conjures up visions of magnificent beaches – endless stretches of sun-bleached sand with turquoise-blue waters lapping at the shore, backed by palm trees swaying gently in the breeze; idyllic little coves where you can shed all your clothes and worries, then swim out to explore a garden of underwater coral; fabulous surf beaches with perfectly formed waves, enticingly held erect by a light offshore breeze ...

Indeed, Queensland has all of these and more, but don't expect to find perfect (or even decent) beaches everywhere. The good surf beaches are restricted to southern Queensland, and once you get north of Gladstone, many of the mainland beaches are spoiled by mudflats and mangroves. Even the sandy beaches on the mainland are often quite shallow and less than idyllic, and in the summer months you can't swim in the coastal waters of north Queensland because of box jellyfish (see the earlier Dangers & Annoyances section). The Great Barrier Reef is undeniably one of nature's most magnificent creations, but one of the drawbacks is that it acts as a breakwater and creates thousands of kilometres of comparatively still water along the Queensland coast.

Fortunately, there are hundreds of islands dotted along the reef, ranging from tropical coral cays to continental islands. This is where you'll find all those great beaches – and half of the fun is getting out and discovering them.

Inland, there are many rivers and lakes where you can cool off, and almost every country town has its own Olympic-sized swimming pool.

Sailing & Other Water Sports

Sailing enthusiasts will also find plenty of opportunities to practise their sport and many places which hire boats, both along the coast and inland. Airlie Beach and the Whitsunday Islands are probably the biggest centres and you can find almost any type of boating or sailing you want there. Waterskiing is often available too. There are water sports hire places in all the coastal resorts and on most of the islands, from where you can hire catamarans, sailboards, jet skis, canoes, paddle boats and snorkelling gear.

Hang-Gliding, Parasailing & Gliding

Hang-gliding is popular at many places along the Queensland coast, including the Lamington National Park in the south-east corner and Eungella National Park near Mackay. You can take tandem flights, or enrol in a learn-to-fly course. Parasailing outfits can be found at many beach resorts.

There are more than a dozen gliding clubs throughout the state, many of which will take you up to experience this pure form of flying. Contact the Queensland Soaring Association on ☎ 3878 1672 to find the nearest clubs.

Bungee Jumping & Skydiving

There are plenty of opportunities for adrenaline-junkies to get a hit in Queensland. Bungee jumping is big in places like Surfers Paradise, Airlie Beach and Cairns. Tandem skydiving is also big, and for around $250 you can do a tandem jump from around 10,000 feet. Surfers Paradise, Cairns, Mission Beach, Airlie Beach and Great Keppel Island all offer tandem jumps.

Horse Riding & Trekking

Horse riding is another activity available all along the coast, from one-hour strolls to gallops along the beach to overnight (or longer) treks. Check with backpackers' hostels and tourist offices to find out what's available.

Rockclimbing & Abseiling

Believe it or not, Brisbane is a good place to learn rockclimbing. There are a couple of indoor rockclimbing centres, and you can graduate to The Cliffs, a series of 18m rock faces along the southern banks of the Brisbane River. A number of operators offer climbing and abseiling instruction in Brisbane and other popular climbing areas such as the Glass House Mountains – climbing and outdoor shops are good sources of info. Look under 'Outdoor Adventure Activities' in the *Yellow Pages*.

Fishing

As you'll soon realise, fishing in all its forms is incredibly popular in Queensland – surf fishing in places like North Stradbroke Island and Fraser Island, line fishing in the clear tropical waters of the Barrier Reef, big-game fishing at places like Hamilton, Hayman and Lizard islands, and barramundi fishing in the coastal and estuarine waters of Far North Queensland. The 'barra' is Australia's premier native sport fish, partly because of its tremendous fighting qualities and partly because it's delicious! Note that the minimum size for barra is 50cm in Queensland – there are also bag limits, and the barra season is closed from 1 November to 31 January. There are quite a few commercial operators offering sports-fishing trips in the Far North.

The waters of the Barrier Reef are teeming with colourful fish, and the coral trout is the most prized catch and makes sensational eating. Not all of the reef's fish are edible, however, so make sure you have properly identified your catch before you toss it in the pan (see the Dangers & Annoyances section earlier). The reef is also divided into different zones which impose certain restrictions on what you can and can't do in each area. Zoning maps are available from most tourist offices along the coast, or from offices of the Great Barrier Reef Marine Park Authority or the Department of Environment.

Made famous by the likes of actor Lee Marvin, Lizard Island in the Far North is Queensland's big-game fishing capital. The heavy-tackle season runs from September to December, and the annual Black Marlin

Classic on Halloween night (31 October) is a major attraction. Hamilton Island also hosts the Billfish Bonanza each December.

There are also innumerable good freshwater and estuarine fishing spots around the state.

Fossicking

There are lots of good fossicking areas in Queensland – see the *Gem Fields* brochure, published by the Queensland Government Travel Centre. It tells you the places where you have a fair chance of finding gems and the types you'll find. You'll need a 'miners right' before you set out.

Most of Queensland's gemfields are in fairly remote areas. Visits to these areas can be adventurous, great fun and maybe even profitable, and even if you don't strike it lucky you're bound to meet some fascinating characters. Queensland's main fossicking areas are the gemfields around Sapphire and Rubyvale (about 300km inland from Rockhampton), the Yowah Opalfields (deep in the southern outback, 150km west of Cunnamulla) and the gemfields around Mt Surprise and Georgetown (about 300km south-west of Cairns) – see those sections for more detailed information.

WORK

If you come to Australia on a tourist visa then strictly you shouldn't work. Many travellers on tourist visas do in fact find casual work, usually in the tourism industry. The work is not well paid and as you are not working legally you are open to being exploited.

With a working holiday visa (see the Visas section earlier), the possibilities are many. Places like Cairns and various other places along the Queensland coast are good prospects, but opportunities are usually limited to the peak holiday seasons.

Other good prospects for casual work include factory work, bar work, waiting on tables, washing dishes (kitchen hand), other domestic chores at outback roadhouses, nanny work, fruit picking, station hands (jackaroo/jillaroo) and collecting for charities. People with computing or secretarial skills should have little difficulty finding work in the major cities, and for qualified nurses agency work is often available. We even got one letter from a traveller who was employed as an ostrich babysitter!

The various backpacker magazines, newspapers and hostels are good information sources – some local employers even advertise on their notice boards. Try the classified ads in the daily papers under Situations Vacant, especially on Saturday and Wednesday. The government Centrelink offices are of virtually no help.

Workabout Australia, by Barry Drebner, gives a comprehensive state by state breakdown of the seasonal work opportunities.

Tax File Number
If you have a working holiday visa, it's important to apply for a Tax File Number (TFN) – not because it's a condition of employment, but because without it tax will be deducted from any wages you receive at the maximum rate, which is currently set at 47%! To get a TFN, contact the local branch of the Australian Taxation Office (☎ 13 2861) for a form. It's a straightforward procedure, and you will have to supply adequate identification, such as a passport, and show that you have a work visa. The issue of a TFN takes about four weeks.

Paying Tax
Yes, it's one of the certainties in life! If you have supplied your employer with a Tax File Number, tax will be deducted from your wages at the rate of 29% if your weekly income is below $397. As your income increases, so does the tax rate, with the maximum being 47% for weekly incomes over $961. For nonresident visitors, tax is payable from the first dollar you earn, unlike residents who have something like a $6000 tax-free threshold. For this reason, if you have had tax deducted at the correct rate as you earn, it is unlikely you'll be entitled to a tax refund when you leave.

If you have had tax deducted at 47% because you have not submitted a Tax File Number, chances are you will be entitled to a partial refund if your income was less than $50,000. Once you lodge a tax return (which must include a copy of the Group Certificate all employers issue to salaried workers at the end of the financial year or within seven days of leaving a job), you will be refunded the extra tax you have paid. Before you can lodge a tax return, however, you must have a Tax File Number.

Superannuation
As part of the government's compulsory superannuation scheme, employers must make contributions to a superannuation fund on your behalf. These contributions are made at the rate of 7% of your wage, and the money must remain in the fund until you reach 'preservation age' (sounds nasty!), which is currently 55.

The only escape from this is if you earn less than $900 per month, in which case you can decide to opt out of superannuation and instead receive the 7% payment as part of your regular salary or wages.

Casual Employment Seasons
The table below lists the main times where casual employment is a possibility.

Type of Work	Time	Region
Apples (picking)	Feb-Mar	Warwick
Asparagus	Aug-Dec	Warwick
Bananas	year-round	Tully
Fishing trawlers	May-Aug	Cairns
Grapes	Jan-Apr	Stanthorpe
Mangoes	Dec-Jan	Atherton
Tomatoes	Oct-Dec	Bundaberg
Tourism	Apr-Oct	Cairns
Various veg	May-Nov	Bowen

ACCOMMODATION
Queensland is very well equipped with a wide range of accommodation alternatives, with everything from backpackers' hostels and caravan parks to five-star hotels and island resorts.

A typical town of a few thousand people will have a basic motel at around $40/50 for singles/doubles, an old town centre hotel with rooms (shared bathrooms) at around $20/30, and a caravan park – probably with camp sites for around $12 ($14 powered) and on-site vans or cabins from $30 for two. If the town is on anything like a main highway or is bigger, it'll probably have several of each. If there's a group of you,

the rates for three or four people in a room are always worth checking. Often there are larger 'family' rooms or units with two bed-rooms.

The RACQ produces a comprehensive accommodation directory to Queensland – see Guidebooks in the earlier Books section for details.

Backpacking in Queensland

Backpacking in Queensland is a breeze. Once you've slotted yourself into the backpacking mainstream, you don't even have to think about where to go or what to do. There's a well-worn backpackers' circuit, which basically runs up the coast between Brisbane and Cairns, with a choice of stops that includes the Gold Coast, Noosa Heads, Hervey Bay/Fraser Island, Rockhampton/Great Keppel Island, Airlie Beach and the Whitsundays, Magnetic Island, and Mission Beach.

When you get off the bus in each place, there will be a courtesy coach waiting to take you to your hostel (which you prebooked before you left the last place). Once you've settled in, you can find out about tours on offer, and even book them through the hostel. Lots of the hostels also have their own bars and provide meals, so you don't even have to worry about going out and exploring an unfamiliar town. And after a while, you'll start seeing familiar faces and renewing acquaintances with the same people you met at the other hostels.

This system provides some tremendous advantages, and many an international visitor has marvelled at how easy this travelling caper is. Gone are the bad old days of actually having to carry your backpack around while you search for a bed, or having to deal with the locals ...

The trend in Queensland in recent times is that backpackers' hostels seem to be getting bigger and bigger. There are plenty of benefits these larger hostels can provide, and the facilities are often much better than at the smaller, old-fashioned places. There are also several hostel 'chains' along the coast. For those of us who thought backpacking was about independent travel, it's a depressingly mass-market scenario – one that threatens to cross that thin grey line between independent travel and packaged tourism.

Anyhow, for those of you who do want to get off the beaten track, Queensland offers some fantastic alternatives. While the mainstream destinations are popular precisely because they have so much to offer, there are plenty of other great areas just waiting for you to discover – and that's where this book comes in. They may be out of your way or a little harder to get to – you might even have to take a local bus service, or do some walking, or find a lift – but remember the immortal last words of Ludwig Leichhardt, one of Queensland's first independent travellers, who said, 'The effort of exploring is often rewarded by the joy of discovery'. Sadly, Leichhardt and his entire exploration party disappeared in the outback in 1848, faithfully pursuing that aphorism to the very end.

Queensland's current network of backpackers' hostels is well established and operates incredibly efficiently – it's a cheap, convenient and fun way to travel around. But if you start to get that sheeplike, anonymous feeling, it can sometimes help to find somewhere quiet, take a few deep breaths and chant to yourself, 'I am an individual. I am capable of making my own decisions. I am an individual ...'

Camping & Caravanning

Camping in the bush is for many people one of the highlights of a visit to Australia. In many state and national parks camping is free, although the more popular places charge a fee – usually $3.50 per person. In lots of places in the outback or the bush, you won't even need a tent – swags are the way to go, and nights spent around a camp-fire under the stars are unforgettable.

You can also pitch your tent in one of the hundreds of caravan parks which are scattered across Queensland. The news on these places is both good and bad. The good news is that Queensland has plenty of caravan parks and they are quite cheap, with tent sites costing around $12. The bad news is that they cater predominantly for caravanners, and usually have limited (or nonexistent) cooking facilities or communal dining areas for campers – you just get a tent site and toilet, shower and laundry facilities. There are plenty of exceptions, however, and many of the better caravan parks now have swimming pools, shops and campers' kitchens.

Caravan parks are generally on the outskirts of towns, which means they can be a long way from the centre of big towns. Brisbane is the worst city in Australia in this respect because council regulations actually forbid tents within a 22km radius of the centre. Although there are some sites in Brisbane within that radius, they're strictly for caravans – no campers allowed.

Many caravan parks also have on-site vans which you can rent for the night. These give you the comfort of a caravan without the inconvenience of actually towing one of the damned things. On-site cabins are also widely available, and these are more like a small self-contained unit. They usually have one bedroom, or at least an area which can be screened off from the rest of the unit – just the thing if you have small kids. Cabins also have the advantage of having their own bathroom and toilet, although this is sometimes an optional extra. They are also much less cramped than a caravan, and the price difference is not always that great

– say $30 for an on-site van, $40 to $50 for a cabin.

Mobile Homes

The advantages of travelling in a Kombi, campervan or station wagon are that it's cheap – you don't have to pay for a bed – and you can sleep wherever you happen to be without having to worry about booking a room. Queensland is one of the few states that allows people to sleep in roadside stops, and these can be found along many of the major highways.

The main disadvantage is trying to find a shower in the morning! One option is to head for a caravan park where it costs between $1 and $3 for a hot shower, although many parks refuse to allow nonguests to use their facilities. Other options are roadhouses, gymnasiums, squash courts and town swimming pools. Along the coast, some towns have public toilet blocks with coin-operated hot showers.

Youth Hostels

Australia has a very active Youth Hostel Association (YHA). YHA hostels provide basic accommodation, usually in small dormitories or bunk rooms, although more and more of them are providing twin rooms for couples. The nightly charges are rock bottom – usually between $14 and $18 a night in a dorm, around $30 for a single room and $35 for a twin or double.

With the increased competition from the proliferation of backpackers' hostels, almost all YHA hostels have done away with the old fetishes for curfews and doing chores, but still retain segregated dorms. They also allow non-YHA members but usually charge about $3 more per person. To become a full YHA member in Australia costs $27 a year (there's also a $17 joining fee, although if you're an overseas resident joining in Australia you don't have to pay this). You can join at a state office or at any youth hostel.

There's also the introductory membership, where you pay no initial membership, but instead pay an additional $3 at any hostel. Once you have stayed for nine nights, you get a full membership.

The YHA also has Accommodation Packs, whereby you can prepay accommodation and get healthy discounts. The '20 for $250' and '10 for $130' give you 20 and 10 nights respectively at any Australian YHA hostel.

Youth hostels are part of an international organisation, the International Youth Hostel Federation (IYHF, also known as HI, Hostelling International), so if you're already a member of the YHA in your own country, your membership entitles you to use the Australian hostels. Hostels are great places for meeting people and great travellers' centres, and in many busier hostels the foreign visitors will outnumber the Australians.

The annual *YHA Accommodation & Discounts Guide* booklet, which is available from any YHA office in Australia and from some YHA offices overseas, lists all the YHA hostels around Australia with useful little maps showing how to find them. It also lists the handy discounts on things such as car hire, activities, accommodation etc which members are entitled to.

You must have a regulation sheet sleeping bag or bed linen – for hygiene reasons a regular sleeping bag will not do. If you haven't got sheets they can be rented at many hostels (usually for $3), but it's cheaper, after a few nights' stay, to have your own. YHA offices and some larger hostels sell the official YHA sheet bag.

All hostels have cooking facilities and 24-hour access, and there's usually some communal area where you can sit and talk. There are usually laundry facilities and often excellent notice boards. Many hostels have a maximum-stay period (five to seven days).

The YHA classes its main hostels as simple, standard or superior, and rural hostels also get a gum-leaf rating, from one to three gum leaves depending on how much of a wilderness experience the visitor can expect. The hostels range from tiny places to big modern buildings, from historic convict buildings to a converted railway station. Most hostels have a manager who checks you in when you arrive and keeps the peace. Because you have so much more contact with a hostel manager than the person in charge of other styles of accommodation they can really make or break the place. Good managers are often great characters and well worth getting to know.

Accommodation can usually be booked directly with the manager or through a Membership & Travel Centre. The YHA handbook tells all.

The Queensland YHA Membership & Travel Centre (☎ 3236 1680) is at 154 Roma St, Brisbane, Qld 4000.

Backpackers' Hostels

Queensland also has plenty of backpackers' hostels. The standard of these places varies enormously: there are run-down inner-city pubs which have been 'converted' to hostels by shoving a few bunks in the bedrooms; former motels where each unit, typically with four to six beds, will have fridge, TV and bathroom, and there is often a pool; and modern, purpose-built hostels with all the mod-cons. These latter places often have the best facilities, although sometimes they can simply be too big.

In some places, backpackers are employed to do the day-to-day running of the hostel and usually it's not too long before standards start to slip. The best places are often the smaller hostels where the owner is also the manager.

Backpacker hostels also vary enormously in terms of their atmosphere – some of the bigger places along the coast are heavily party-oriented, with late-night entertainment, drinking games and trips to pubs and clubs, but there are plenty of smaller, quieter, more intimate places.

With the proliferation of hostels has also come intense competition. Hop off a bus in any town on the Queensland coast and chances are there'll be at least three or four touts from the various hostels, all trying to lure you in. To this end many have introduced inducements, and virtually all have courtesy buses. Even the YHA hostels have had to resort to this to stay in the race in some places.

Prices at backpackers' hostels are generally in line with YHA hostels – typically $14, although often $16 to $18 in the more popular places. Again, singles and doubles are often available for around $28/32, and quite a few places offer private rooms with their own bathrooms – typically around $40 a double.

There's at least one organisation (VIP) which you can join where, for a modest fee (typically $15), you'll receive a discount card (valid for 12 months) and a list of participating hostels. This is hardly a great inducement to join but you do also receive useful discounts on other services, such as bus passes, so they may be worth considering.

Nomads Backpackers (☎ (08) 8224 0919, fax 8232 2911) is one organisation which runs a number of revamped pubs and hostels around the country.

As with YHA hostels, the success of a hostel largely depends on the friendliness and willingness of the manager. Some places will only admit overseas backpackers. This happens mostly in cities and when it does it's because the hostel in question has had problems with locals treating the place more as a dosshouse – drinking too much, making too much noise, getting into fights and the like. Hostels which discourage or ban Aussies say it's only a rowdy minority that makes trouble, but they can't take the risk. If you're an Aussie and encounter this kind of reception, the best you can do is persuade the desk people that you're genuinely travelling the country, and aren't just looking for a cheap place to crash for a while.

Guesthouses & B&Bs

These are the fastest growing segment of the accommodation market. New places are opening all the time, and the network of accommodation alternatives throughout the country includes everything from restored miners' cottages, converted barns and stables, renovated and rambling old guesthouses, upmarket country homes and romantic escapes to a simple bedroom in a family home. Many of these places are listed throughout this book. Tariffs cover a wide range, but are typically in the $60 to $100 (per double) bracket.

Farm & Station Stays

Australia is a land of farms (known as 'stations' in the outback) and one of the best ways to come to grips with Australian life is to spend a few days on one. Many farms offer accommodation where you can just sit back and watch how it's done, while others like to get you more actively involved in the day-to-day activities. With commodity prices falling daily, mountainous wool stockpiles and a general rural crisis, tourism offers the hope of at least some income for farmers, at a time when many are being forced off the land.

The standard of accommodation varies enormously. Some places have just bunged a couple of dongas (transportable huts, often used in mining towns) in the yard and will charge perhaps $20 a night; at others, you can pay $150 a double to stay in a historic country homestead which has been restored to provide a luxurious taste of a bygone era. Most places fall somewhere between these two extremes.

Quite a few farmstays are included in this guidebook. The QTTC also produces a brochure called *Farm & Station Holidays*, which lists many of the places with accommodation – it's available from regional information offices or from the QTTC.

Pubs

Outside of Brisbane, Cairns and a few of the larger centres, hotel accommodation means pub accommodation. Although the grandest buildings in country towns are often the pubs, the standard of accommodation rarely lives up to the architecture. Many pubs would prefer not to offer accommodation, but in the past the licensing laws required them to do so.

Pub rooms are usually clean but pretty basic, with not much more than a bed, a wardrobe and sometimes a wash-basin. The bathrooms are almost always shared. Despite the lack of luxury, it's worth considering staying in pubs rather than motels. Apart from the saving in cost (around $20/25 a single/double is average for basic pub accommodation), staying at 'the pub' means that you have an entrée to the town's social life. Generally, the smaller the town, the friendlier the pub will be.

The two essentials in choosing a pub room are to get one which isn't directly above the noisy bar (not a problem if you plan to be in the bar until closing time), and to check that the bed is in reasonable condition.

Motels

If you want a more modern place than a pub, with your own bathroom and other facilities, then you're moving into the motel bracket. Prices vary, and in motels (unlike hotels), singles are often not much cheaper than doubles. The reason is quite simple – in the old hotels many of the rooms really are singles, relics of the days when single men travelled the country looking for work. In motels, the rooms are always doubles. Costs for budget motel rooms are usually around $50 a night, although you can sometimes find rooms for less. The more upmarket motels, and those in the busier centres, charge anywhere from $60 to $80 a night.

Hotels

As well as pubs, the other end of the hotel spectrum is well represented, in Brisbane, on the Gold Coast and in Cairns at least. There are many excellent four and five-star hotels and quite a few lesser places where standards vary widely. Outside the capitals, quality accommodation is offered by the more expensive motels or beach resorts.

Serviced Apartments

Serviced apartments are pretty much restricted to Brisbane. However, they offer hotel-style convenience with cooking facilities and a bit more room to move than a hotel room. They are increasingly popular in the upper price brackets, with the cheaper ones very attractive for families travelling on a budget.

Holiday Flats

Holiday flats, found mainly in beachside towns, are geared to family holidays, so they fill up at peak times and often have minimum rental periods of a week. Outside peak times you might be able to rent one by the night. Standards and prices vary enormously, but if you have a group they can be very affordable and might even be cheaper than hostels outside the peak season.

Resorts

As you would expect, Queensland has all sorts of holiday resorts – they range from five-star places with golf courses, pools and spas, gymnasiums, fleets of windsurfers, catamarans and jet skis, diving schools and restaurants and bars; to clusters of old-fashioned cabins on lonely islands on the reef. There are hundreds of places to choose from, and many of them are included and described in this guide.

Other Accommodation

There are lots of less conventional accommodation possibilities. You don't have to camp in caravan parks, for example. There are plenty of parks where you can camp for free, or roadside rest areas where short-term camping is permitted.

In the cities, if you want to stay longer, the first place to look for a shared flat or a room is the classified ads section of the daily newspaper. Wednesday and Saturday are the best days for these ads. Notice boards in universities, hostels, certain popular bookshops and cafes, and other contact centres are good places to look for flats and houses to share or rooms to rent.

FOOD

The culinary delights can be one of the real highlights of Australia. Time was –

like 25 years ago – when Australia's food (mighty steaks apart) had a reputation for being like England's, only worse. Well, perhaps not quite that bad, but getting on that way. Miracles happen and Australia's miracle was immigration. The Greeks, Yugoslavs, Italians, Lebanese and many others who flooded into Australia in the 50s and 60s brought their food with them. More recent arrivals include the Vietnamese, whose communities are thriving in several cities.

So in Australia today you can have excellent Greek moussaka (and a bottle of retsina to wash it down), delicious Italian saltimbocca and pastas, or good, heavy German dumplings; you can perfume the air with garlic after stumbling out of a French bistro, or try all sorts of Middle Eastern and Arab treats. The Chinese have been sweet & souring since the gold-rush days, while more recently Indian, Thai and Malaysian restaurants have been all the rage. And for cheap eats, you can't beat some of the Vietnamese places.

Australian

Although there is no real Australian cuisine there is certainly some excellent Australian food to try. In recent years there's been a great rise in popularity of exotic local and 'bush' foods, and for the adventurous these dishes offer something completely different. So in a swish Cairns restaurant or Brisbane bistro you might find braised kangaroo tail samosas, emu pâté, gum-leaf smoked venison, salt-bush lamb, native aniseed frittata, Warrigal-greens salad or wattle-seed ice cream.

All major cities also have a selection of cafes and restaurants serving food which can be termed 'modern Australian'. These are dishes which borrow heavily from a wide range of foreign cuisines, but have a definite local flavour. At these places seemingly anything goes, so you might find Asian-inspired curry-type dishes sharing a menu with Mediterranean-inspired dishes. It all adds up to exciting dining.

Australia also has a superb range of seafood: fish like John Dory and the famous

Tropical Fruits & Nuts

Queensland produces a wonderful variety of tropical fruits, all of which are widely available in supermarkets and grocery shops throughout the state. As you travel around, you'll notice that there are also plenty of roadside stalls in Queensland selling produce straight off the trees or out of the ground. The list of what's available is long and delicious, and includes mangoes, lychees, bananas, avocados, rambutans, watermelons, figs and oranges. Roadside stalls are worth looking out for – not only is the produce fresher than what you'll find anywhere else and (usually) better value, but you'll also get to meet the people who grow the stuff.

If you haven't tried macadamia nuts yet, you're in for a memorable treat. These small, circular nuts grow on macadamia trees which are native to the rainforest areas of Queensland. The nuts themselves are richly flavoured and encased within a tough protective shell. You can buy them raw in the shell, or roasted and salted in bags or jars.

Macadamia nuts are delicious roasted, chocolate-covered or in ice-cream.

barramundi, or superb lobsters and other crustaceans like the engagingly named Moreton Bay bugs! Yabbies are freshwater crayfish and very good.

Another positive aspect of Australian food is the fine ingredients. Nearly everything is grown locally so you're not eating food that has been shipped halfway around the world.

At the bottom end of the food scale is the meat pie – an awful concoction of anonymous meat and dark gravy in a soggy pastry case. You'll have to try one though; the number consumed in Australia each year is phenomenal, and they're a real part of Australian culture. A pie 'n sauce at the 'footy' on a Saturday afternoon in winter is something plenty of Aussies can relate to.

Even more a part of Australian food culture is Vegemite. This strange, dark yeast extract looks and spreads like thick tar and smells like, well, Vegemite. Australians spread Vegemite on bread and become positively addicted to the stuff.

Takeaway Food

There are plenty of choices when you're looking for food on the run. In Brisbane and the larger cities, you'll find all the major fast-food chains – McDonald's, KFC, Pizza Hut etc – all in prominent positions and blatantly signposted.

On a more local level, you'll find plenty of milk bars, and most of them sell things like meat pies, pasties, sausage rolls, sandwiches and milk shakes. Then there are the speciality sandwich bars, delis and health-food shops – all worth looking out for if you're after something fresh and tasty. Another good alternative is to look for a bakery – with fresh bread, pies, pastries and cakes – and the local fruit shop.

On a less tasty note, on the highways you'll constantly encounter roadhouses and anonymous cafes with stuff they call food sitting under hot lights waiting for unsuspecting travellers – don't eat it, you'll only encourage them. On the other hand, some of the small, remote roadhouses of the outback, the Gulf and Cape York still serve enormous, old-fashioned burgers that will keep you going all day.

Pub & Club Food

Every town in Queensland has at least one pub – in fact, there are plenty of 'one-pub towns' that are just that – a pub, and nothing else.

Eating in a pub can be a great experience, as long as you choose the right pub. While the quality of food can vary enormously, it's usually fairly basic and unimaginative, but often very good value. Pub menus all start to look fairly similar after a while – steaks, roasts, seafood and pasta dishes are the standard fare, although there are plenty of exceptions. The normal eating times are from noon to 2 pm and from 6 to 8 pm, but lots of pubs don't serve meals on Sunday.

Most pubs serve two types of meals: bistro meals are served in the lounge bar (or dining room), and are usually in the $10 to $15 range (you'll often find a self-serve salad bar with bread, condiments etc); counter meals are served in the public bar and eaten at the bar. They are usually simplified versions of the bistro meals and cost around $4 to $7.

Almost every town in Queensland also has at least one club serving meals – RSLs (Returned Servicemen's League), bowls clubs and rugby league clubs are the most common. These places usually have simple

Pub Names

Historically, Queensland's publicans were not terribly imaginative when it came to naming their establishments. A popular on-the-road game is to lay bets on the name of the first pub you'll see as you drive into a town. You can just about bet your bottom dollar that it will be called the Royal, the Commercial, the Criterion, the Railway, the Imperial, the Union or the Prince of Wales. Then again, it might have just been named after the town.

pub-style food, but because they make so much money through their poker machines, the meals are often a bit cheaper than you'll get in a pub. Visitors are welcome in most clubs – you have to sign in, and there are usually basic dress regulations.

Cafes & Restaurants

In Brisbane and the larger centres, you'll find plenty of cafes and restaurants offering a huge range of cuisines and styles, but in smaller country towns you might just find an old-fashioned cafe, a pub and a Chinese restaurant.

Most of the popular tourist destinations have at least a couple of good places to eat. Brisbane, Port Douglas, Noosa Heads and Cairns are the best restaurant centres in Queensland.

DRINKS

Tap water is clean and drinkable in most parts of Queensland, with the exception of some of the more remote outback towns. Bottled water is also widely available, as are plain and flavoured mineral waters.

Most shops stock a wide range of soft drinks, fruit juices and flavoured milk; a milk shake from a local milk bar is a bit of an Aussie institution. Cafes and delis often make smoothies (a milk shake with added fruit, yoghurt, honey, nuts etc) and squeeze fresh juices.

Most cafes and restaurants in places like Brisbane, the Gold and Sunshine coasts, Cairns and Port Douglas serve cappuccinos, espressos, caffe lattes and macchiatos that will satisfy any caffeine addict. 'Real' coffee is much harder to come by in other areas, although most of the larger towns have at least one good cafe where you can get a fix.

Queensland is also the home of Australia's most famous spirit, the distinctive Bundaberg Rum, a dark rum made from raw molasses (which is a by-product of the local sugar industry).

Beer

There's a bewildering array of beer available in bottle shops, pubs, bars and restaurants. There are local beers like XXXX (pronounced fourex) and Powers; interstate beers like VB (Victoria Bitter), Foster's, Toohey's and Coopers; boutique beers like Redback; and international beers like Steinlager and Budweiser. Local beers have an alcoholic content of around 4.9% alcohol, and popular light beers, like XXXX Light, Toohey's Blue and Foster's Special range from 2% to 3.5%. A few boutique or brewery pubs brew their own beers, and Guinness (brewed under licence by Foster's) is usually found on draught in many pubs.

Beer comes in bottles (750ml), stubbies (375ml), and cans (375ml). When ordering at the bar you ask for a 'glass' (200ml) or a 'pot' (285ml). With the increasing popularity of light beers you might be asked by the person behind the bar if you want a 'light' or a 'heavy'. If in doubt, take local advice, which will readily be offered!

Wine

If you don't fancy the beer, then turn to wines. European wine experts realise just how good Australian wines can be – exporting wine is a multimillion dollar business. Wines need not be expensive: you're entering the 'pretty good' bracket if you pay over $12 for a bottle and drinkable wines can be found for less.

Queensland's climate is generally too warm to produce good wines, although there is a small but growing wine district based around the town of Stanthorpe in the cool-temperate mountains of south-east Queensland, with more than 15 boutique wineries which can be visited (see the Darling Downs chapter for details). There are a couple of other wineries in Queensland, including in the Atherton Tablelands, the Sunshine Coast and around Kingaroy, and there's a fruit winery outside Bundaberg.

It takes a little while to become familiar with Australian wineries and their styles, but it's an effort worth making. All over Queensland, you'll find restaurants advertising that they're BYO. The initials stand for 'Bring Your Own' and it means that they're not licensed to sell alcohol but you are permitted to bring your own with you. This is a real boon to wine-loving but budget-minded travellers, because you can bring your own bottle of wine from the local bottle shop or from that winery you visited last week and not pay any mark-up. There might be a small 'corkage' charge (typically $1.50 per person) if you bring your own.

ENTERTAINMENT
Cinema
Although the cinema took a huge knock from the meteoric rise of the home-video market, it has bounced back as people rediscover the joys of the big screen.

In the big cities there are commercial cinema chains, such as Village, Hoyts and Greater Union, and their cinemas are usually found in centres which will have anything from two to six screens in the one complex. Smaller towns have just the one cinema, and many of these are almost museum pieces in themselves. Seeing a new-release mainstream film costs around $12 in the big cities, less in country areas and less on certain nights at the bigger cinema chains.

In Brisbane you'll find art-house and independent cinemas, and these places generally either screen films that aren't made for mass consumption or specialise purely in re-runs of classics and cult movies.

Drive-in cinemas used to be found all over Australia. They're a dying breed now, although there are still quite a few towns in Queensland where you can watch a movie from the comfort of your own car.

Pubs, Nightclubs & Live Music
There's certainly no shortage of pubs in Queensland, and many of them feature live music or DJs, especially on Thursday, Friday and Saturday nights and Sunday afternoon. You might see a local guitarist strumming their stuff, a local rock or jazz band trying to make a name for themselves, or a major national or international act on tour.

Some of the larger cities, including Brisbane, Cairns and Townsville, have free music and entertainment magazines which list local gigs. Otherwise, look in the local papers or inquire at information offices. Cover charges usually apply, especially for well-known bands. Pubs usually stay open until around midnight or 1 am.

Most reasonably sized towns also have at least one nightclub. These places vary enormously, from grungy pick-up joints to upmarket clubs with dress codes and cover charges. Nightclubs are generally licensed until 5 am, although they'll close earlier during the week if there's no-one around.

This book provides comprehensive information on lots of pubs, clubs and venues – look under the Entertainment section for each town.

SPECTATOR SPORT
If you're an armchair – or wooden bench – sports fan, Queensland has plenty to offer.

Football
Australians play at least four brands of football, each type being called 'football' by its aficionados. All codes are played over winter, with seasons from about March to September.

Rugby is the main game in Queensland, and it's rugby league, the 13-a-side working-class version, that attracts the crowds. The ARL's (Australian Rugby League) competition produces the world's best rugby league – fast, fit and clever.

Rugby union, the 15-a-side game for ama-teurs, is less popular but gained ground when Australia won the World Cup in 1991.

Australian Rules, a fast and spectacular indigenous game based on elements of Gaelic football, is also played throughout the state, although unlike their counterparts in Victoria, South Australia and Western Australia, most Queenslanders are pretty indifferent when it comes to Aussie Rules. The Brisbane Lions, Queensland's only side in the AFL (Australian Football League), play their home games at The Gabba (the

Brisbane Cricket Ground in Woolloongabba, a suburb of Brisbane).

Soccer is widely played on an amateur basis but the national league is only semi-professional and attracts a fairly small but growing following. It's gaining popularity thanks in part to the success of the national team, the Socceroos.

Cricket

During the other (non-football) half of the year there's cricket. International Test and one-day matches are played at The Gabba every summer. There is also an interstate competition (the Sheffield Shield) and numerous local grades.

Other Sports

Basketball is growing in popularity as a spectator sport and there is a national league. Queensland has three sides in the NBL (National Basketball League) – the Brisbane Bullets, the Townsville Suns and the Gold Coast Rollers.

Surfing competitions are held at a couple of places including North Stradbroke Island and at Burleigh Heads on the Gold Coast; there are also numerous surf life-saving carnivals which take place on the beaches of southern Queensland over the summer months.

There's also yacht racing, some tennis and motor racing. The Australian IndyCar Grand Prix is held in Surfers Paradise every October. Major golf tournaments include the Coolum Classic, held on the Sunshine Coast in December, and an international 'skins' tournament at Laguna Quays on the Whitsunday Coast each February.

Rodeos are held at dozens of places throughout the state. Some of the biggest rodeos are held at Mareeba in the Far North, Warwick in the Darling Downs, and Mt Isa and Longreach in the outback.

Queensland Cricket's Holy Grail

For Queensland's cricket followers, 1995 will be joyfully remembered as the year the drought finally broke. Queensland's failure to win the Sheffield Shield, the annual trophy awarded to the state which wins the domestic 1st-class cricket competition, was one of the longest-running droughts in the history of sport.

Queensland joined the Sheffield Shield competition back in 1926, but despite the fact that there were only four teams (nowadays there are six), they managed to remain winless for almost 70 years. In the meantime Western Australia, who joined the competition in 1947, had won 12 times. But it wasn't just Queensland's failure to win that was remarkable, it was the way they went about not winning. The 'banana-benders' made it into six Shield finals – and found a different way to lose them all.

Winning the Shield become an obsession in Queensland. So much so that they even tried to 'buy' a victory, importing a string of big-name players over the years. Ian Botham and Graeme Hick from England, Viv Richards, Wes Hall and Alvin Kallicharran from the West Indies, Majid Khan from Pakistan, and interstate players Alan Border, Jeff Thomson and Greg Chappell were all enlisted to try and help break the jinx – to no avail.

But the 1994-95 season changed all that. With a new name (the Queensland Bulls), a new coach, a new captain (Australian vice-captain Ian Healy), and cricketing legend Alan Border playing regularly after his retirement from the Australian side, the Queensland Bulls finally broke through to win their historic first Shield victory. With fitting panache they thrashed South Australia at 'The 'Gabba' in Brisbane, causing widespread celebration in the city of Brisbane.

Horse Racing

Australians love to gamble, and hardly any town of even minor import is without a horse-racing track or a Totalisator Agency Board (TAB) betting office. You can place a bet on the horses, the trots (harness racing) and the dogs (greyhound racing), and you'll also find TAB agencies inside plenty of Queensland's pubs. Poker machines can be found inside most pubs and all licensed clubs – bowling clubs, RSL clubs, rugby league clubs are everywhere.

Townsville, the Gold Coast, Brisbane and Cairns all have casinos.

SHOPPING

Aboriginal & Torres Strait Islander Art

Top of the list of real Australian purchases would have to be art and craft items produced by Aboriginal and Torres Strait Islander artists.

Aboriginal art is a traditional and symbolic art form. In ancient times, the main forms of art were body painting, cave painting and rock engraving, and it's only recently that Aboriginal artists have begun painting in more portable formats and using western art materials like canvas and acrylic paints.

These works have quickly gained wide appreciation. The paintings depict traditional Dreamtime stories and ceremonial designs, and each design has a particular spiritual significance. These works capture the essence of the Australian outback, and make a wonderful reminder of a trip to Australia.

Prices of the best works are way out of reach for the average traveller, but among the cheaper artworks on sale are hand-painted boomerangs and didjeridus, ceramics, art works on paper, bark and canvas, prints, baskets, small wood carvings, and some very beautiful screen-printed T-shirts produced by Aboriginal craft cooperatives – and a larger number of commercial rip-offs. It's worth shopping around and paying a few dollars more for the real thing.

Some places worth visiting are Queensland Aboriginal Creations and the Fire-Works Gallery in Brisbane, Barambah Emus in Murgon, Flying Arts in Milton, the Dreamtime Cultural Centre in Rockhampton, and the Tjapukai Aboriginal Cultural Park in Cairns. See the brochure *Aboriginal & Torres Strait Islander Holiday Experiences*, available from the QTTC, for more information.

Antiques

A large proportion of antiques on the Australian market are imported from Europe, especially England. Instead, look for early Australian colonial furniture made from cedar or huon pine; Australian silver jewellery; ceramics – either early factory pieces or studio pieces (especially anything by the Boyd family); glassware such as Carnival glass; and Australiana collectibles and bric-a-brac such as old signs, tins, bottles etc. Look for genuine Australian pieces – the value of antiques is in what they tell you about the country's heritage, which makes the imported stuff just about worthless.

If you're serious about buying antiques, *Carter's Price Guide to Antiques in Australia* is an excellent price reference which is updated annually.

Opals

The opal is Australia's national gemstone, and opals and opal jewellery are popular souvenirs. They are beautiful stones, but buy wisely and shop around – quality and prices can vary widely from place to place.

Australiana

The term 'Australiana' is a euphemism for souvenirs. These are the things you buy as gifts for the folks back home and to remember your visit by, and are supposedly representative of Australia and Aussie culture. Some of the more popular items are:

- Stuffed toys, especially koalas and kangaroos
- Wool products such as hand-knitted jumpers
- Sheepskin products
- Akubra bush hats and straw sunhats
- T-shirts, windcheaters and towels printed with Australian symbols or typical slogans like 'No flies on me, mate!'

- Australia-shaped egg-flippers or fly swats
- Koala keyrings
- Jewellery made from opals and pewter, often in the shape of native animals or flora
- Boomerangs (most of which are decorative rather than of the returning variety)
- Painted didjeridus
- Local glassware and ceramics
- High-kitsch items like ceramic flying pigs or koalas

The seeds of many of Australia's native plants are on sale all over the place. Try growing kangaroo paws back home, if your own country will allow them in. For those last-minute gifts, drop into a deli. Australian wines are well known overseas, but why not try honey (leatherwood honey is one of a number of powerful local varieties) or macadamia nuts? We have also heard rumours of tinned witchetty grubs, honey ants and other bush tucker.

Aussie Clothing

While you're here, fit yourself out in some local clothes – made in Australia for Australian conditions. Start off with some Bonds undies and a singlet, a pair of Holeproof Explorer socks and Blundstone or Rossi boots. Then there's anything from the RM Williams line (boots, moleskin trousers, shirts), some Yakka or King Gee workwear, a shearer's top or bush shirt, a greasy-wool jumper, a Bluey (a coarse woollen worker's coat), a Drizabone (an oilskin riding coat) – and top it off with an Akubra hat.

Or there are all sorts of sheepskin products. A high-quality sheepskin to put in a child's pushchair – or to sit on yourself! – can cost as little as $50.

Australia also produces some of the world's best surfing equipment and clothing, and clothing companies like 100% Mambo produce some mind-boggling off-the-wall designs.

Outdoor Gear

With Australians among the world's keenest travellers, Queensland's outdoor and adventure shops carry an excellent range of both Australian-made and imported gear. In many cases, the locally made products are of equivalent quality to (and cheaper than) the imports. Paddy Pallin, Mountain Designs, Kathmandu and the Snowgum shops are among the local firms.

Getting There & Away

Basically getting to Australia means flying. If you're already in Australia and heading for Queensland, you have a choice of flying, taking a bus or train, driving, or hitching a ride on a yacht.

AIR (INTERNATIONAL)

The main problem with getting to Australia is that it's a long way from anywhere. Coming from Asia, Europe or North America there are lots of competing airlines and a wide variety of airfares, but there's no way you can avoid those great distances. Australia's current international popularity adds another problem – flights are often heavily booked. If you want to fly to Australia at a particularly popular time of year (Christmas time is notoriously difficult) or on a particularly popular route (like Hong Kong-Cairns) you need to plan well ahead.

While Sydney and Melbourne are the busiest international gateways, Queensland has its own international airports in Brisbane and Cairns.

If you can't get a direct flight into Queensland, chances are you'll arrive via Sydney. Sydney's airport is stretched way beyond its capacity and flights are frequently delayed on arrival and departure. If you can organise your flights to avoid Sydney, it's a wise idea.

Tickets

Discount Tickets Buying airline tickets these days is like shopping for a car, stereo or camera – five different travel agents will quote you five different prices. Rule number one if you're looking for a cheap ticket is to go to an agent, not directly to the airline. The airline can usually only quote you the absolutely by-the-rule-book regular fare. An agent, on the other hand, can offer all sorts of special deals, particularly on competitive routes.

Ideally an airline would like to fly all its flights with every seat in use and every passenger paying the highest fare possible. Fortunately life usually isn't like that and airlines would rather have a half-price passenger than an empty seat. When faced with the problem of too many seats, they will either let agents sell them at cut prices, or occasionally make one-off special offers on particular routes – watch the travel ads in the press.

Of course what's available and what it costs depends on what time of year it is, what route you're flying and who you're flying with. If you're flying on a popular route (like Hong Kong) or one where the choice of flights is very limited (like South America or, to a lesser extent, Africa) then the fare is likely to be higher or there may be nothing available but the official fare.

Similarly the dirt cheap fares are likely to be less conveniently scheduled or go by a less convenient route.

Round-the-World Tickets Round-the-World tickets are very popular and many will take you through Australia. The airline RTW tickets are often real bargains and since Australia is pretty much at the other side of the world from Europe or North America it can work out no more expensive, or even cheaper, to keep going in the same direction right round the world rather than U-turn to return.

The official airline RTW tickets are usually put together by a combination of two airlines, and permit you to fly anywhere you want on their route systems so long as you don't backtrack. Other restrictions are that you (usually) must book the first sector in advance and cancellation penalties then apply. There may be restrictions on how many stops you are permitted and usually the tickets are valid from 90 days up to a year.

An alternative type of RTW ticket is one put together by a travel agent using a combination of discounted tickets from a number of airlines. A UK agent like Trailfinders can put together interesting London-to-London RTW combinations including Australia for between £895 and £1100.

Departure Taxes

There is a $30 departure tax when leaving Australia, but this is incorporated into the price of your air ticket and so is not paid as a separate tax.

The UK

The cheapest tickets in London are from the numerous 'bucket shops' (discount ticket agencies) which advertise in magazines and papers like *Time Out*, *Southern Cross* and *TNT*. Pick up one or two of these publications and ring round a few bucket shops to find the best deal. Most bucket shops are trustworthy and reliable but the occasional sharp operator appears – *Time Out* gives some useful advice on precautions to take.

Trailfinders (☎ (0171) 938 3366) at 46 Earls Court Rd, London W8, and STA Travel (☎ (0171) 581 4132) at 86 Old Brompton Rd, London SW7, and 117 Euston Rd, London NW1 (☎ (0171) 465 0484), are good, reliable agents for cheap tickets.

The cheapest bucket shop (not direct) tickets from London to Brisbane are about £377 one-way or £529 return. London to Cairns is around £375 one-way or £595 return. Cheap fares to Perth are around £325 one-way and £529 return. Such prices are usually only available if you leave London in the low season (March to June). In September and mid-December fares go up by about 30%, while the rest of the year they're somewhere in between.

North America

There's a variety of connections across the Pacific from Los Angeles, San Francisco and Vancouver to Australia, including direct flights, flights via New Zealand, island-hopping routes and more circuitous Pacific rim routes via Asia. Qantas, Air New Zealand and United fly USA-Australia; Qantas, Air New Zealand and Canadian Airlines International fly Canada-Australia. An interesting option from the east coast is Northwest's flight via Japan.

To find good fares to Australia check the travel ads in the Sunday travel sections of papers like the *Los Angeles Times*, *San Francisco Chronicle-Examiner*, *New York Times* or *Toronto Globe & Mail*. You can typically get a one-way/return ticket from the west coast for US$876/1200, or from the east coast for US$1190/1517. At peak seasons – particularly over the Christmas period – seats will be harder to get and prices will probably be higher. In the USA good agents for discounted tickets are the two student travel operators, Council Travel and STA Travel, both with lots of offices around the country. Canadian west-coast fares out of Vancouver will be similar to those from the US west coast. From Toronto fares go from around C$1900 return and from Vancouver C$1600 return.

If Pacific island-hopping is your aim, check out the airlines of Pacific island nations, some of which have good deals on indirect routings. Qantas can give you Fiji or Tahiti along the way, while Air New Zealand can offer both and the Cook Islands as well.

One-way/return fares available from Australia include: San Francisco A$1253/1579, New York A$1340/1790 and Vancouver A$1356/1873.

New Zealand

Air New Zealand and Qantas operate a network of trans-Tasman flights linking Auckland, Wellington and Christchurch in New Zealand with most major Australian gateway cities. You can fly directly between a lot of places in New Zealand and a lot of places in Australia.

From Auckland to Brisbane with Qantas or Air New Zealand you're looking at around NZ$600 one-way and around NZ$719 return. From Auckland to Cairns you're looking at around NZ$759 one-way and NZ$899 return.

Air Travel Glossary

Apex Apex, or 'advance purchase excursion' is a discounted ticket which must be paid for in advance. There are penalties if you wish to change it.

Baggage Allowance This will be written on your ticket: usually one 20kg item to go in the hold, plus one item of hand luggage.

Bucket Shop An unbonded travel agency specialising in discounted airline tickets.

Bumped Just because you have a confirmed seat doesn't mean you're going to get on the plane – see Overbooking.

Cancellation Penalties If you have to cancel or change an Apex ticket there are often heavy penalties involved. Insurance can sometimes be taken out against these penalties. Some airlines impose penalties on regular tickets as well, particularly against 'no show' passengers.

Check In Airlines ask you to check in a certain time ahead of the flight departure (usually 1½ hours on international flights). If you fail to check in on time and the flight is overbooked the airline can cancel your booking and give your seat to somebody else.

Confirmation Having a ticket written out with the flight and date you want doesn't mean you have a seat until the agent has checked with the airline that your status is 'OK' or confirmed. Meanwhile you could just be 'on request'.

Discounted Tickets There are two types of discounted fares – officially discounted (see Promotional Fares) and unofficially discounted. The lowest prices often impose drawbacks like flying with unpopular airlines, inconvenient schedules, or unpleasant routes and connections. A discounted ticket can save you things other than money – you may be able to pay Apex prices without the associated Apex advance booking and other requirements. Discounted tickets exist only where there is fierce competition.

Full Fares Airlines traditionally offer first class (coded F), business class (coded J) and economy class (coded Y) tickets. These days there are so many promotional and discounted fares available from the regular economy class that few passengers pay full economy fare.

Lost Tickets If you lose your airline ticket an airline will usually treat it like a travellers' cheque and, after inquiries, issue you with another one. Legally, however, an airline is entitled to treat it like cash and if you lose it then it's gone forever. Take good care of your tickets.

No Shows No shows are passengers who fail to show up for their flight, sometimes because of unexpected delays or disasters; sometimes because they simply forget; and sometimes because they made more than one booking and didn't bother to cancel the one they didn't want. Full fare passengers who fail to turn up are sometimes entitled to travel on a later flight. The rest of us are penalised (see Cancellation Penalties).

On Request An unconfirmed booking for a flight, see Confirmation.

Open Jaws A return ticket where you fly out to one place but return from another. If avail-

Asia

Ticket discounting is widespread in Asia, particularly in Singapore, Hong Kong, Bangkok and Penang. Flights to or from Bangkok, Hong Kong and Singapore are often part of the longer Europe-Australia route so they are also sometimes very full.

Plan ahead. For more information on South-East Asian travel, and travel on to Australia, see Lonely Planet's *South-East Asia on a shoestring*.

Typical one-way fares to Australia from Asia include around HK$2400 for a Hong Kong to Brisbane flight, or around S$450

able this can save you backtracking to your arrival point.

Overbooking Airlines hate to fly empty seats and since every flight has some passengers who fail to show up (see No Shows) airlines often book more passengers than they have seats. Usually the excess passengers balance those who fail to show up but occasionally somebody gets bumped. If this happens, guess who it's most likely to be? The passengers who check in late.

Promotional Fares Officially discounted fares like Apex fares which are available from travel agents or direct from the airline.

Reconfirmation At least 72 hours before the departure time of an onward or return flight you must contact the airline and 'reconfirm' that you intend to be on the flight. If you don't do this the airline can delete your name from the passenger list and you could lose your seat. You don't have to reconfirm the first flight on your itinerary or if your stopover is less than 72 hours. It doesn't hurt to reconfirm more than once.

Restrictions Discounted tickets often have various restrictions on them – advance purchase is the most usual one (see Apex). Others are restrictions on the minimum and maximum period you must be away, such as a minimum of 14 days or a maximum of one year. See Cancellation Penalties.

Stand-by A discounted ticket where you only fly if there is a seat free at the last moment. Stand-by fares are usually only available on domestic routes.

Tickets Out An entry requirement for many countries is that you have an onward or return ticket – in other words, a ticket out of the country. If you're not sure what you intend to do next, the easiest solution is to buy the cheapest onward ticket to a neighbouring country or a ticket from a reliable airline which can be refunded if you don't use it.

Transferred Tickets Airline tickets cannot be transferred from one person to another. Travellers sometimes try to sell the return half of their ticket, but officials can ask you to prove that you are the person named on the ticket. This is unlikely to happen on domestic flights. On an international flight tickets may be compared with passports.

Travel Agencies Travel agencies vary widely and you should ensure you use one that suits your needs. Some simply handle tours while full-service agencies handle everything from tours and tickets to car rental and hotel bookings. A good one will do all these things and can save you a lot of money, but if all you want is a ticket at the lowest possible price, then you really need an agency specialising in discounted tickets. However, a discounted ticket agency may not be useful for things like hotel bookings.

Travel Periods Some officially discounted fares, Apex fares in particular, vary with the time of year. There is often a low (off-peak) season and a high (peak) season. Sometimes there's an intermediate or shoulder season as well. At peak times, when everyone wants to fly, not only will the officially discounted fares be higher but so will unofficially discounted fares – or there may simply be no discounted tickets available. Usually the fare depends on your outward flight – if you depart in the high season and return in the low season, you pay the high-season fare.

for Singapore to Brisbane. Hong Kong to Cairns will cost around HK$3000 return, and Singapore to Cairns about S$600 return.

From Cairns, return fares start from around $970 to Hong Kong or Singapore, and from around $1100 to Kuala Lumpur or Bangkok.

AIR (DOMESTIC)

Australia's major domestic carriers are Ansett, which also flies a few international routes, and Qantas, which is also the international flag-carrier. Both have flights from all the Australian capital cities to all the major towns and cities in Queensland.

You don't have to reconfirm domestic flights on Ansett and Qantas, but you should phone on the day of your flight to check the details. For Ansett, call ☎ 13 1515; for Qantas, call ☎ 13 1223.

Because Qantas flies both international and domestic routes, flights leave from both the international and domestic terminals. Flights with flight numbers from QF001 to QF399 operate from international terminals, and flight numbers QF400 and above from domestic terminals.

Several smaller regional airlines fly into Queensland: Eastern Australia flies to Brisbane and Coolangatta from northern New South Wales, and Augusta Airways flies to Birdsville, Boulia and Bedourie from Port Augusta in South Australia.

All airports and domestic flights are non-smoking.

Fares

Ticket prices on all domestic flights within Australia are determined by the airlines, which means that travel agents will quote you exactly the same fare as the airlines themselves. Given this, the quickest and easiest approach is to book directly through the airlines, then pay for and collect your ticket from your travel agent. Alternatively, if you have a credit card and you book more than three days in advance, the airline can forward your ticket to you by express post. Both major domestic carriers have toll-free reservations numbers; for Ansett, call ☎ 13 1300; for Qantas, call ☎ 13 1313.

Discounted Fares Although full economy fares are quoted throughout this book, in practice very few people pay full fare on domestic travel, as the airlines offer a wide range of discounts. Discounted fares depend on various factors including your age, whether you're studying, where you're going, and how far in advance you book your ticket. It's worth noting that you only get one bite at the discount cherry – you can't qualify for an advance purchase discount *and* a student discount off the same fare, you only get one or the other.

Full-time university or other higher education students under 26 get 25% off the regular economy fare on production of student ID or an ISIC card, but fares are often discounted by more than that.

The airlines also offer substantial random discounts on selected routes (mainly the heavy-volume routes, but not always) and at quiet times of the year.

All nonresident international travellers can get up to a 30% discount on internal Qantas flights and 25% on Ansett flights simply by presenting their international ticket when booking. It seems there is no limit to the number of domestic flights you can take, it doesn't matter which airline you fly into Australia with, and it doesn't have to be on a return ticket. Note that the discount applies only to the full economy fare, and so in many cases it will be cheaper to take advantage of other discounts offered. The best advice is to ring around and explore the options before you buy.

Many of the smaller regional airlines in Queensland offer cheap deals on lesser routes and at certain times of the year, often undercutting Qantas and Ansett – see the individual chapters for more details.

Advance Purchase Fares If you're planning a return trip and you have 21 days up your sleeve, you can save around 55% by travelling 'Apex' (advance purchase excursion). You have to book and pay for your tickets 21 days in advance and you must stay away at least one Saturday night. Flight details can be changed at any time (with 21 days notice), but the tickets are nonrefundable. If you book 14 days in advance the saving is 50% off the full fare. With five days advance notice you can save 10% off the full one-way or return fares.

Air Passes

With all the discounting these days, air passes do not represent the value they once did, although pre-buying a pass does save you the hassle of hunting around for special deals. Both Ansett and Qantas offer two types of passes.

The Qantas Boomerang Pass can only be purchased overseas and involves purchasing coupons for either short-haul flights (eg Hobart to Melbourne) at $200 one-way, or for long-haul sectors (such as just about anywhere to Uluru) for $250. You must purchase a minimum of four coupons before you arrive in Australia from the USA, two if you're coming from the UK or Europe, and once here you can buy up to four more.

Also available is the Qantas Backpackers Pass, which can only be bought in Australia with identification such as a YHA membership, VIP Backpackers, Independent Backpackers, Nomads Australia or a Greyhound Pioneer Aussie or Kilometre Pass. You must purchase a minimum of three sectors and stay a minimum of two nights at each stop. The discount is quite substantial; a sample fare using this pass is Sydney to Uluru for $292 one-way, as against the full economy fare of $542.

Ansett's Kangaroo Airpass can be bought in Australia and gives you two options – 6000km with two or three stopovers for $949 ($729 for children), or 10,000km with three to seven stopovers for $1499 ($1149 for children). Restrictions include a minimum travel time (10 nights) and a maximum (45 nights). One of the stops must be at a non-capital city and be for at least four nights. All sectors must be booked when you purchase the ticket, although these can be changed without penalty unless the ticket needs rewriting, in which case there's a $50 charge. Refunds are available before travel commences but not after you start using the ticket.

LAND

Travelling overland from elsewhere in Australia to Queensland usually means a major – and sometimes boring – journey. The nearest state capital to Brisbane is Sydney, 1030km away by the shortest route. To Melbourne it's at least 1735km, to Adelaide it's at least 2130km, Perth is a mere 4390km away and the shortest road to Darwin is 3495km long.

Bus

Travelling by bus is usually the cheapest way to get around Australia, but you'll need to do a little shopping around to find the best and most suitable deal. You can book directly with the bus companies.

There are basically two types of fares for bus travel – express fares and bus passes. Students, backpackers (YHA and VIP card holders) and pensioners get discounts of at least 10% off most express fares and bus passes.

There is only one truly *national* bus network – Greyhound Pioneer (☎ 13 2030). The Queensland-based McCafferty's (☎ 13 1499) is Australia's next biggest operator. It services the east coast, and also does the loop through the centre from Townsville, across to Darwin and down through Alice Springs to Adelaide. There are quite a few smaller companies running less extensive routes.

A great many travellers see Australia by bus because it's one of the best ways to come to grips with the country's size and variety of terrain, and because the bus companies have such comprehensive route networks – far more comprehensive than the railway system. The buses all look pretty similar and are similarly equipped with air-conditioning, toilets and videos. Big city bus terminals are generally well equipped – they usually have toilets, showers and facilities.

There are also a few interesting alternatives to straightforward bus travel – see the Tours section of the Getting Around chapter for details.

Express Fares Express fares are for straight point-to-point travel. Stopover conditions on these tickets vary from company to company – some give you one free stopover or allow you to stopover wherever they have a terminal, and others charge a fee of perhaps $10 for each stopover. If you want to make multiple stopovers, you'll end up paying full fares on each separate segment – in these cases a bus pass may work out to be better value.

Several companies ply the busy Brisbane to Sydney route, including Greyhound Pioneer, McCafferty's and Kirklands (☎ 3236 444). The Pacific Hwy run along the coast takes around 16 hours; the inland New England Hwy takes a couple of hours less. The fares for both routes is around $70, although these are competitive routes: you'll usually find discounted fares and special backpacker deals if you shop around.

For direct buses to the other capital cities (except Perth), you have a choice between Greyhound Pioneer and McCafferty's.

The Newell Hwy is the most direct route between Brisbane and Melbourne. This trip takes around 25 hours and costs around $130.

To Adelaide, the shortest route (via Dubbo) takes around 31 hours and costs around $160.

It's a 48 hour trip from Brisbane to Darwin (via Longreach), and the fare is around $288.

Bus Passes Greyhound Pioneer and Mc-Cafferty's both have a wide variety of passes available, so it's a matter of deciding which best suits your needs. Their networks are fairly similar throughout eastern and central Australia, but only Greyhound Pioneer has services throughout Western Australia.

Greyhound Pioneer's Aussie Kilometre Pass gives you a specified amount of travel to be completed within 12 months, the shortest being 2000km ($176), going up in increments of 1000km to a maximum of 20,000km ($1344), with a 10% discount for YHA and VIP members. The advantages of these passes are that you can travel one route as many times as you like, and they have unlimited kilometres. The disadvantage is that you may feel obliged to travel farther than you might otherwise like to, simply because you have the kilometres free to do so. As an indication, 2000km will get you from Cairns to Brisbane, 4000km ($311) from Cairns to Melbourne, and 12,000km ($832) will get you a loop from Sydney to Melbourne, Adelaide, central Australia, Darwin, Cairns and back to Sydney.

Aussie Day Passes are like the Kilometre Pass, except that you are limited by days of travel rather than by kilometres. Passes for seven ($499), 10 ($640) and 15 ($745) days of travel are valid for 30 days; 21 day passes ($982) are valid for two months.

Aussie Explorer Passes These popular passes give you three, six or 12 months to cover a set route. You haven't got the go-anywhere flexibility of the Kilometre Pass, but if you can find a set route which suits you – and there are 25 to choose from – it generally works out cheaper than the Kilometre Pass. When a pass follows a circular route, you can start anywhere along the loop and finish at the same spot.

The main limitation is that you can't backtrack, except on 'dead-end' short sectors such as Darwin to Kakadu, Townsville to Cairns and from the Stuart Highway to Uluru.

The Greyhound Pioneer Aussie Highlights pass allows you to loop around the eastern half of Australia from Sydney, taking in Melbourne, Adelaide, Coober Pedy, Uluru, Alice Springs, Darwin (and Kakadu), Cairns, Townsville, the Whitsundays, Brisbane and Surfers Paradise for $882, including tours of Uluru – Kata Tjuta and Kakadu national parks. Or there are one-way passes: the Reef & Rock goes from Sydney to Alice Springs (and Uluru) via Cairns and Darwin (and Kakadu) for $683; the Top End Explorer takes in the Cairns to Darwin (and Kakadu) section only for $279; and the Country Road takes you from Cairns to Sydney via Alice Springs, Adelaide and Melbourne for $415. There's even an All Australia Pass that takes you right around the country, including up or down through the Centre, for $1491.

McCafferty's has eight set-route passes to choose from, including one in Tasmania. The Best of the East & Centre is equivalent to Greyhound Pioneer's Aussie Highlights, and costs $795 ($890 including Uluru and Kakadu tours). The Outback Wanderer goes from Cairns to Sydney via the centre for

$440 ($480 including tours), or there's the Sun & Centre, from Sydney to Alice Springs via Cairns and Darwin, for $585 ($695 including tours).

Other Bus Options A few companies offer transport options in various parts of the country, although only one operates in Queensland. While most of these are really organised tours, they also get you from A to B, and are a good alternative to the big bus companies. Their trips are generally aimed at budget travellers and so are good fun. The buses are generally smaller and so not necessarily as comfortable as those of the big companies, but it's a much more interesting way to travel.

Oz Experience (☎ 1300 300 028) is basically a cross between a bus line and an organised group tour. It offers frequent services along the east coast and up the centre to Darwin, with off-the-beaten-track detours to cattle stations and national parks. You buy one of its 22 passes, which range from $165 to $930 depending on the distance, and are valid for six to 12 months. Its buses travel set routes, but your pass entitles you to unlimited stops, which means you can get on and off whenever and wherever you like. The drivers act as guides, providing commentary and advice, and they can also pre-book your hostels, stop at supermarkets so you can do your shopping, and arrange discounts on most tours and activities along the way.

Train

To a degree, rail travel in Australia today is more of a luxury than a convenience. Australia's railway system is less comprehensive than the bus networks, and train services are less frequent and more expensive.

Having said that, the trains are much more comfortable than buses, and you certainly see Australia at ground level in a way no other means of travel permits. Interstate trains are as fast or faster than buses and in recent years the railways have cut their prices in an attempt to be more competitive with both bus and air fares.

The interstate railway booking system is computerised, so any station (other than those on metropolitan lines) can make a booking for any journey throughout the country. For reservations call ☎ 13 2232 from anywhere in Australia; this will connect you to the nearest booking agent.

Fares & Conditions There are three standard fare levels for interstate rail travel – economy, 1st class and sleeping berths, although sleeping berths aren't available on all trains. Depending on availability, a limited number of discounted fares are offered on all trains. These cut 10% to 40% off the standard fares, and if you book early or travel at off-peak times, you'll usually qualify for one of these cheaper fares. There are also half-price concession fares available to children under the age of 16, secondary students and Australian tertiary students, but unfortunately there are no discounts for backpackers.

On interstate journeys you can make free stopovers – you have two months to complete your trip on a one-way ticket and six months on a return ticket.

There are no discounts for return travel – a return ticket is just double the price of a one-way ticket.

Interstate Services & Fares Interstate railway services basically operate between the capital cities. That means that while there are direct services from Brisbane to Sydney, if you want to go from Brisbane to either Melbourne or Adelaide, you have to go via Sydney, and if you want to go from Brisbane to Perth, you have to go via Sydney *and* Adelaide. Fares are also calculated on each sector; for example, to go from Brisbane to Melbourne you'll pay the Brisbane to Sydney fare *plus* the Sydney to Melbourne fare.

Countrylink has a daily XTP service between Brisbane and Sydney. The northbound service runs overnight, and the south-bound service runs during the day. The trip takes 13½ hours and costs $90/125 in economy/1st class, and $215 in a sleeper.

Motorail services are also available on some interstate trains.

Rail Passes There are a number of passes available which allow unlimited rail travel either across the country or just in one state, but with the exception of Queensland's Sunshine Rail Pass (see the Getting Around chapter), these passes are only available to international visitors and must be purchased before arrival in Australia.

With the Austrail Pass you can travel in economy class anywhere on the rail network during a set period. The cost is $485 for a 14-day pass, $625 for 21 days and $755 for 30 days. A seven-day extension to any of these passes costs $250.

The Austrail Flexipass allows a set number of economy class travelling days within a six-month period. The cost is $400 for eight days of travel, $575 for 15 days, $810 for 22 days and $1045 for 29 days. The eight-day pass cannot be used for travel between Adelaide and Perth or between Adelaide and Alice Springs.

Car & Motorcycle
See the Getting Around chapter for details of road rules, driving conditions and information on buying and renting vehicles.

The main road route into Queensland from the west is the Barkly Hwy, which leaves the Stuart Hwy at Threeways (about 1000km south of Darwin and 500km north of Alice Springs) and cuts across to Mt Isa. From Mt Isa, you can continue eastward along the Flinders Hwy to Townsville on the coast, or head south-east along the Matilda Hwy towards Brisbane.

There are a couple of major routes into Queensland from the south. The Pacific Hwy is the coastal route between Sydney and Brisbane – it passes through a string of resort towns, but can be slow going and isn't a particularly fun road to drive.

The New England Hwy is a longer inland route from Sydney to Brisbane, but it's a less stressful drive and can end up taking about the same number of driving hours as the slog up the coast.

The Newell Hwy is the most direct route from Brisbane to Melbourne – it's a good road through the heart of rural NSW. The major route from Adelaide to Brisbane is the Barrier Hwy which takes you across to Dubbo via Broken Hill; from Dubbo, the Newell Hwy takes you up to Brisbane.

The other major route into southern Queensland is the Mitchell Hwy, which links Bourke in outback NSW with Charleville and Barcaldine in outback Queensland.

SEA
Crewing on Yachts
It's quite possible to make your way round the Australian coast to Queensland, or even to and from other countries like New Zealand, Papua New Guinea or Indonesia, by hitching rides or crewing on yachts. Ask around at harbours, marinas or yacht clubs. It's often worth contacting the secretaries of sailing clubs and asking whether they have a notice board where people advertise for crews – some of the major Australian clubs even run waiting lists for people wanting to crew on yachts. Look under 'Clubs – Yacht' in the *Yellow Pages* telephone directory.

It obviously helps if you're an experienced sailor, but some people are taken on as cooks (not very pleasant on a rolling yacht). Usually you have to chip in something for food, and the skipper may demand a financial bond as security. A lot of yachties head north for Queensland from south-east Australia to escape the winter, so April is a good time to look for a berth in the southern harbours.

WARNING
The information in this chapter is particularly vulnerable to change: prices for international travel are volatile, routes are introduced and cancelled, schedules change, special deals come and go and rules and visa requirements are amended. Airlines and governments seem to take a perverse pleasure in making price structures and regulations as complicated as possible.

You should check directly with the airline

or a travel agent to make sure you understand how a fare (and ticket you may buy) works. In addition, the travel industry is highly competitive and there are many lurks and perks. The upshot of this is that you should get opinions, quotes and advice from as many airlines and travel agents as possible before you part with your hard-earned cash. The details given in this chapter should be regarded as pointers and are not a substitute for your own careful, up-to-date research.

Getting Around

AIR

Queensland's major regional airlines are Sunstate (a subsidiary of Qantas, who handles bookings) and Flight West Airlines (☎ 13 2392 within Queensland or toll-free ☎ 1800 777 879 from elsewhere in Australia). Flight West is independently owned, although it's associated with Ansett and Ansett can also handle its bookings.

Sunstate and Flight West fly smaller planes on the shorter intra-state routes, working in with their larger associates. For example, if you wanted to get from Melbourne to Birdsville, you'd fly Melbourne-Brisbane with Ansett and Brisbane-Birdsville with Flight West. Similarly, if you were heading from Sydney to the Sunshine Coast you could fly Sydney-Brisbane with Qantas and Brisbane-Maroochydore with Sunstate. There is quite a bit of overlap in the four airlines' networks, although their prices are identical on shared routes.

There's also a multitude of smaller airlines operating up and down the coast, across the Cape York Peninsula and into the outback. During the wet season, such flights are often the only means of getting around the Gulf Savannah or Cape York Peninsula. See the Getting There & Away sections in the individual chapters for details of these.

BUS

Greyhound Pioneer (☎ 13 2030) and McCafferty's (☎ (07) 3236 3033) have the most comprehensive bus networks throughout Queensland. Their networks cover all of the major towns and destinations, linking up with their interstate services into the Northern Territory and New South Wales. Queensland-based McCafferty's also has services to quite a few smaller centres which aren't covered by Greyhound Pioneer.

They both offer either express bus fares or bus passes – see the Getting There & Away chapter for details of their passes,

fares and conditions. Their prices are similar, although McCafferty's express fares tend to be a dollar or two cheaper.

A company called Oz Experience offers an interesting alternative to the two main companies – see the Getting There & Away chapter for details.

There are also numerous smaller bus companies with more specialised local services – see the Getting There & Away headings under individual towns for details of these.

Express Fares & Major Routes

Express fares are for straight point-to-point travel, and if you don't have a bus pass and want to make stopovers between point A and point B, you'll either have to pay separate fares for each sector or pay a stopover fee of perhaps $10.

The busiest bus route is the coastal run up the Bruce Hwy from Brisbane to Cairns. Individual sector fares and travel times to the major destinations along the coast are: Brisbane-Hervey Bay ($32, 5½ hours); Hervey Bay-Rockhampton ($54, seven hours); Rockhampton-Mackay ($39, 4½ hours); Mackay-Airlie Beach ($25, about two hours); Airlie Beach-Townsville ($36, four hours); Townsville-Cairns ($38, six hours). The express Brisbane-Cairns fare would be $144, whereas the individual sector fares are considerably more.

Both companies have passes which cover the coastal run.

The other major bus route out of Brisbane is the McCafferty's inland service to Mt Isa, from where you can continue to either Darwin or Alice Springs in the Northern Territory. The express fare for the 22 hour trip is around $112. The individual sector fares include Brisbane-Roma ($41, five hours); Roma-Longreach ($52, 8½ hours); Longreach-Mt Isa ($59, 8½ hours).

The other major bus services are from Townsville to Mt Isa via Charters Towers

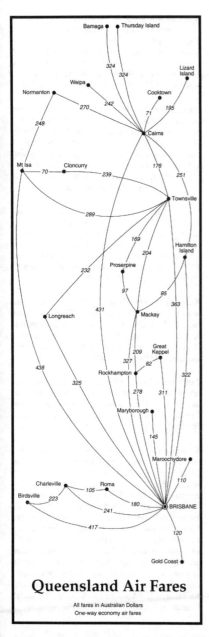

Bamaga • • Thursday Island

Weipa •

Normanton •

Mt Isa • Cloncurry

Longreach •

Charleville •   Roma

Birdsville •

Cooktown •

Lizard Island

Cairns

Townsville

Hamilton Island

Proserpine

Mackay

Great Keppel

Rockhampton

Maryborough •

Maroochydore •

• BRISBANE

Gold Coast •

324
324
242
270
248
71
195
176
251
70
239
289
169
204
232
97
95
363
431
209
327
82
322
278
311
145
110
180
105
223
241
417
438
325
120

Queensland Air Fares

All fares in Australian Dollars
One-way economy air fares

($84, 11½ hours) and from Rockhampton to Longreach via Emerald and Barcaldine (McCafferty's only, $53, 9½ hours, change buses in Emerald). McCafferty's also has a hinterland service which runs from Rockhampton to Mackay via Emerald and Clermont.

TRAIN

Rail services within Queensland are operated by Queensland Rail. There are five Queensland Rail Travel Centres throughout the state – these are basically booking offices which can advise you on all rail travel, sell you tickets and put together rail holiday packages which include transport and accommodation. There are Travel Centres based in the following cities:

Brisbane
(☎ 3235 1323) Ground floor, 305 Edward St
Cairns
(☎ 4052 6267) Cairns railway station, McLeod St
Rockhampton
(☎ 4932 0234) Rockhampton railway station, Murray St
Surfers Paradise
(☎ 5539 9088) Cavill Park Building, corner of Beach Rd & Gold Coast Hwy
Townsville
(☎ 4772 8546) Townsville railway station, Flinders St

You can also buy train tickets through travel agents. Telephone reservations can be made through one of the Travel Centres or through Queensland Rail's centralised booking service on ☎ 13 2232 from anywhere in Australia.

Rail travel within Queensland is slower and more expensive than bus travel, although some of the economy fares are comparable with bus fares. Depending on your itinerary, a rail pass might also be worth looking into (see Rail Passes later in this chapter). The trains are almost all aircon and you can get sleeping berths on most trains for $30 extra a night in economy, $50 in 1st class. You can break your journey on most services for no extra cost provided you complete the trip within 14 days (single ticket) or two months (return ticket).

Half-price concession fares are available to children under 16 years of age, Australian students, and seniors and pensioners from Queensland.

Rail Services

There are seven major rail services throughout Queensland, as well as three minor services in north Queensland which operate primarily as tourist routes:

Queenslander Promoted as a 'luxurious hotel on wheels', the *Queenslander* travels along the coast between Brisbane and Cairns once a week, leaving Brisbane on Sunday mornings and returning from Cairns on Tuesday mornings. All passengers on the *Queenslander* travel 1st class, with sleeping berths and all meals included in the fares. Brisbane to Mackay takes 15½ hours and costs $300; Brisbane to Townsville takes about 21 hours and costs $344; and Brisbane to Cairns takes about 29 hours and costs $389. The *Queenslander* is also a motorail service; for another $270 you can take you car with you from Brisbane to Cairns.

Spirit of the Outback This train travels the 1326km between Brisbane and Longreach via Rockhampton twice a week, leaving Brisbane on Tuesday and Friday evenings and returning from Longreach on Thursday and Sunday mornings. Brisbane to Rockhampton takes 10½ hours and costs $67 for an economy seat, $97 for an economy sleeper and $158 for a 1st class sleeper. Brisbane to Longreach takes 24 hours and costs $118/148/226. A connecting bus service operates between Longreach and Winton.

Spirit of Capricorn This all-economy train does the Brisbane to Rockhampton trip in just over nine hours, leaving Brisbane every morning as well as on Wednesday and Sunday evenings, and returning from Rocky every morning and on Wednesday evenings. The one-way fare is $67.

Sunlander The *Sunlander* travels between Brisbane and Cairns three times a week and the trip takes 30 hours, leaving Brisbane on Tuesday, Thursday and Saturday mornings and Cairns on Monday, Thursday and Saturday mornings. Fares are $135 for an economy seat, $165 for an economy sleeper and $253 for a 1st class sleeper.

Spirit of the Tropics The all-economy *Spirit of the Tropics* runs from Brisbane to Proserpine on Thursday afternoons, from Brisbane to Cairns on Sunday mornings, from Cairns to Brisbane on Tuesday mornings and from Proserpine to Brisbane on Friday afternoons. Brisbane to Proserpine costs $105; Brisbane to Cairns costs $135.

Westlander The *Westlander* heads inland from Brisbane to Charleville every Tuesday and Thursday evening, returning from Charleville to Brisbane on Wednesday and Friday evenings. It takes 16 hours and costs $77 for an economy seat, $107 for an economy sleeper and $172 for a 1st class sleeper. From Charleville there are connecting bus services to Cunnamulla and Quilpie.

Inlander The *Inlander* does what its name suggests from Townsville to Mt Isa twice weekly, leaving Townsville on Sunday and Wednesday afternoons and Mt Isa on Monday and Friday afternoons. Fares are $95 for an economy seat, $125 for an economy sleeper and $192 for a 1st class sleeper. The trip takes 20 hours.

Kuranda Scenic Railway This is one of the most popular tourist trips out of Cairns – a spectacular 1½ hour trip on a historic steam train to Kuranda, a market town in the mountainous rainforests west of Cairns. See the Far North Queensland chapter for details.

Gulflander The *Gulflander* is a strange, snub-nosed little train that travels once a week between the remote Gulf towns of Normanton and Croydon – it's a unique and memorable journey. See the Gulf Savannah chapter for details.

Savannahlander Queensland's newest rail service is an abbreviated version of the 'Last Great Train Ride', the old Cairns to Forsayth service which was somewhat controversially discontinued in 1995. The new service runs between Mt Surprise and Forsayth in the Gulf Savannah, leaving Mt Surprise at lunchtime on Monday and Thursday and returning from Forsayth on Tuesday and Friday mornings. The trip takes a leisurely five hours and costs $35. There are connecting bus services to/from Cairns, and in conjunction with your trip on the *Savannahlander* you can take tours to the Undara Lava Tubes and the Tallaroo Hot Springs. See the Gulf Savannah chapter for details.

Rail Passes
The Sunshine Rail Pass, available to both international and domestic visitors, gives you unlimited travel on all rail services in Queensland for 14, 21 or 30 days. Fares in economy/1st class are 14 days for \$267/388, 21 days for \$309/477 and 30 days for \$388/582. A surcharge is payable if you want to travel on the Queenslander (to cover sleeping berths and meals); the surcharge is \$260 from Brisbane to Townsville or \$293 from Brisbane to Cairns.

CAR
Queensland is a big, sprawling state where public transport is not always very comprehensive or convenient – the car is the accepted means of getting from A to B. More and more travellers are also finding it the best way to see the country – with three or four of you the costs are reasonable and the benefits many, provided of course you don't have a major mechanical problem.

In fact, if you want to get off the beaten track – and in parts of Queensland, it's a *very* beaten track – then having your own transport is the only way to go. Many of the destinations covered in this book aren't accessible by public transport, so if you want to discover the undiscovered side of Australia's most popular holiday destination, you'll need your own car or motorcycle.

Road Rules
Driving in Queensland holds few real surprises. Australians drive on the left-hand side of the road just like the UK, Japan and most countries in south and east Asia and the Pacific.

There are a few variations to the rules of the road as applied elsewhere. The main one is the 'give way to the right' rule. This means that if you approach an unmarked intersection, traffic on your right has right of way. Most places actually have signed intersections; Mt Isa doesn't!

4WD or 2WD?
You can cover most of Queensland in a standard 2WD vehicle, but there are quite a few places you *won't* be able to visit in your old Ford or Holden station wagon – places where the only access is by 4WD. The advantages of 4WDs are their high clearance, which helps cope with river crossings, minor floods and deep wheel ruts that would rip the guts out of an ordinary car; and their ability to handle different terrains like the sandy tracks of Fraser Island or the slippery bulldust-covered hills of the Bloomfield Track. Modern 4WDs also handle the endless bumps and corrugations of unsealed roads much better than conventional cars.

The following are some of the places in Queensland only accessible by 4WD vehicle: Moreton Island and the northern parts of Bribie Island (Moreton Bay), Fraser Island and the Woodgate National Park (Fraser Coast Area), Deepwater National Park (south of Agnes Water), Byfield National Park (north of Yeppoon), Cape Palmerston National Park (south of Sarina), Sundown National Park (the Darling Downs), and the Bloomfield Track (the coastal route between Cape Tribulation and Cooktown). Most of the Cape York Peninsula is also only accessible by 4WD, but you *could* drive a conventional vehicle up the main route as far as Weipa – every year a few crazies try and get all the way to the top in normal cars, but not too many make it back again. You'll also miss most of the Cape's highlights if you stick to the main road.

During the Dry, you could also tackle most of the Gulf Savannah's roads in a conventional vehicle, but again, it ain't recommended. The unsealed outback roads to Birdsville in the south-west corner fall into the same category – your Toyota Corolla might make it to Birdsville, but it will never be the same afterwards.

The general speed limit in towns and built-up areas is 60km/h, sometimes rising to 80km/h on the outskirts and dropping to 40km/h in residential areas and school zones. Out on the open highway it's usually 100 or 110km/h depending on where you are.

The police have radar speed traps and speed cameras and are very fond of using them in carefully hidden locations in order to raise easy revenue. When you're far from the cities and traffic is light, you'll see many vehicles moving a lot faster than 100km/h. Oncoming drivers who flash their lights at you may be giving you a friendly indication of a speed trap ahead.

Wearing seat belts is compulsory, and small children must be belted into an approved safety seat.

Driving standards in Australia aren't exactly the highest in the world – you'll probably encounter inconsiderate and aggressive drivers. Drunk driving is a real problem, especially in country areas. Serious attempts have been made in recent years to reduce the road toll – random breath tests are not uncommon in built-up areas. If you're caught with a blood-alcohol level of more than 0.05 then be prepared for a hefty fine, a court appearance and the loss of your licence.

Road Conditions

Australia is not crisscrossed by multi-lane highways; there simply isn't enough traffic, and the distances are too great to justify them. You'll certainly find stretches of divided road, particularly on busy roads out of the major cites – the Surfers Paradise-Brisbane road, for example. Elsewhere Queensland's main roads have only two lanes and are well-surfaced (though a long way from the billiard-table surfaces the Poms are used to driving on) on all the main routes.

However, you don't have to get very far off the beaten track to find yourself on dirt roads, and anybody who sets out to see Queensland in reasonable detail will have to expect to do some dirt-road travelling. A

few useful spare parts are worth carrying – a broken fan belt can be a damn nuisance if the next service station is 200km away.

Between cities, signposting on the main highways is generally OK, but once you hit the backroads, you'll need a good map – see Maps in the Facts for the Visitor chapter for suggestions.

Cows, sheep and kangaroos are common hazards on country roads, and a collision is likely to kill the animal and seriously damage your vehicle. Kangaroos are most active around dawn and dusk, and usually travel in groups. If one hops across the road in front of you, slow right down – its friends are probably just behind it. Many Australians try to avoid travelling altogether between 5 pm and 8 am, because of the hazards posed by animals. Finally, if one hops out right in front of you, hit the brakes and only swerve to avoid the animal if it is safe to do so. Many people have been killed in accidents caused by swerving to miss an animal – better to damage your car and probably kill the animal than kill yourself and others with you.

Flooding can occur with little warning, especially in outback areas and the tropical north. Roads are sometimes cut off for days during floods, and floodwaters sometimes wash away whole sections of road.

Fuel

Service stations generally stock diesel, super and unleaded fuel, although some of the more remote places may not stock unleaded. Liquid petroleum gas (LPG, Autogas) is usually available at larger service stations along the main highways.

Fuel is generally cheaper in Queensland than in the southern states, although prices vary from place to place and from price war to price war. Some of the service stations in the more remote outback are not above exploiting their monopolies. Distances between fill-ups can be long in the outback.

Outback Travel

You can drive all the way round Australia on Hwy 1 or through the middle all the way from Adelaide in the south to Darwin in the north without ever leaving sealed road. But if you really want to see outback Australia there are still lots of roads where the official recommendation is that you report to the police before you leave one end, and again when you arrive at the other. That way if you fail to turn up at the other end they can send out search parties. Nevertheless many of these tracks are now much better kept than in years past and you don't need 4WD or fancy expedition equipment to tackle them. You do need to be carefully prepared and to carry important spare parts, however. Backtracking 500km to pick up a replacement for some minor malfunctioning component or, much worse, to arrange a tow, is unlikely to be easy or cheap.

When travelling to really remote areas it's advisable to travel with a high frequency outpost radio transmitter which is equipped to pick up the Royal Flying Doctor Service bases in the area.

You will of course need to carry a fair amount of water in case of disaster – around 20L a person is sensible – stored in more than one container. Food is less important – the space might be better allocated to an extra spare tyre.

The RACQ (Queensland's automobile association) can advise on preparation and supply maps and track notes. See the section on Travel Guides in the Facts for the Visitor chapter for recommended books that cover preparation for outback travel.

Most tracks have an ideal time of year – in central Australia it's not wise to attempt the tough tracks during the heat of summer (November-March), when the dust can be severe, the chances of mechanical trouble much greater and when water will be scarce and hence a breakdown more dangerous. Similarly in the north travelling in the wet season may be impossible because of flooding and mud. You should always seek advice on road conditions when you're travelling into unfamiliar territory. The local police will be able to advise you whether roads are open and whether your vehicle is suitable for a particular track. The RACQ

has a telephone service with a pre-recorded report on road conditions throughout the state – dial ☎ 11 655, 24 hours a day. For more specific local info, you can call into the nearest RACQ office – they're listed in the information sections throughout this book.

If you do run into trouble in the back of beyond, stay with your car. It's easier to spot a car than a human being from the air, and you wouldn't be able to carry your 20L of water very far anyway.

Car Rental

If you've got the cash there are plenty of car rental companies ready and willing to put you behind the wheel. Competition is pretty fierce so rates tend to be variable and lots of special deals pop up and disappear again. Whatever your mode of travel on the long stretches, it can be very useful to have a car for some local travel. Between a group it can even be reasonably economical. There are some places where if you haven't got your own transport you really have to choose between a tour and a rented vehicle, since there is no public transport and the distances are too great for walking or even bicycles.

The three major companies are Budget, Hertz and Avis, with offices in almost every town that has more than one pub and a general store. A second-string company which is also represented almost everywhere in the country is Thrifty. Then there are a vast number of local firms, or firms with outlets in a limited number of locations. The big operators will generally have higher rates than the local firms but it ain't necessarily so, so don't jump to conclusions.

The big firms have a number of big advantages. First of all they're the ones at the airports – Avis, Budget, Hertz and, quite often, Thrifty, are represented at most. If you want to pick up or leave a car at the airport then they're the best ones to deal with. Other companies will also arrange to pick up or leave cars at some (but not all) airports – it depends on how convenient the airport is.

The second advantage is if you want to do a one-way rental – pick up a car in Sydney and leave it in Brisbane, for example. There are variety of restrictions on these. Usually it's a minimum-hire period rather than repositioning charges. Only certain cars may be eligible for one-ways. Check the small print on one-way charges before deciding on one company over another. One-way rentals are generally not available into or out of the Northern Territory or Western Australia.

The major companies offer a choice of deals, either unlimited kilometres or a flat charge plus so many cents per kilometre. On straightforward off-the-card city rentals they're all pretty much the same price. It's on special deals, odd rentals or longer periods that you find the differences. Weekend specials – usually three days for the price of two – are usually good value. If you just need a car for three days around Brisbane make it the weekend rather than midweek. Budget offers 'stand-by' rates and you may see other special deals available.

Daily rates are typically about $50 a day for a small car (Holden Barina, Ford Festiva, Daihatsu Charade, Suzuki Swift), about $75 a day for a medium car (Mitsubishi Magna, Toyota Camry, Nissan Pulsar) or about $100 a day for a big car (Holden Commodore, Ford Falcon), all including insurance. You must be at least 21 years old to hire from most firms.

There is a whole collection of other factors to bear in mind about this rent-a-car business. For a start, if you're going to want it for a week, a month or longer then they all have significantly lower rates.

OK, that's the big hire companies – what about all the rest of them? Well, some of them are still pretty big and have plenty of shiny new cars. In many cases local companies are markedly cheaper than the big boys, but in others what looks like a cheaper rate can end up quite the opposite if you're not careful.

And don't forget the 'rent-a-wreck' companies. They specialise in renting older cars and have a variety of rates, typically around $35 a day. If you just want to travel around the city, or not too far out, they can be worth considering.

Be aware when renting a car in Australia that if you are travelling on dirt roads you are generally not covered by insurance. So if you have an accident, you'll be liable for all the costs involved. This applies to all companies, although they don't always point this out. This does not apply to 4WDs.

4WD Rental Having 4WD enables you to get right off the beaten track and out to some of the great wilderness and outback places, to see some of the natural wonders that most travellers don't see.

Renting a 4WD is within a reasonable budget range if a few people get together. Something small like a Suzuki or similar costs around $100 per day; for a Toyota Land Cruiser you're looking at around $150, which should include insurance and some free kilometres (typically 100km per day). Check the insurance conditions, especially the excess, as they can be onerous – in the Queensland $4000 is typical, although this can often be reduced to around $1000 on payment of an additional daily charge (around $20). Even in a 4WD the insurance of most companies does not cover damage caused when travelling 'off-road', which basically means anything that is not a maintained bitumen or dirt road.

Hertz and Avis have 4WD rentals, with one-way rentals possible between the eastern states and the Northern Territory. Budget also rents 4WDs from Darwin and Alice Springs. Brits:Australia (☎ 1800 331 454) is a company which hires fully equipped 4WDs fitted out as campervans. These have proved extremely popular in recent years, and cost around $130 per day for unlimited kilometres, plus insurance ($20 per day, or $40 to cover everything, including windscreen and tyres). Brits: Australia has offices in all the mainland capitals, as well as in Cairns and Alice Springs, so it's one of the few companies offering one-way interstate rentals, especially involving the Northern Territory.

Renting Other Vehicles There are lots of vehicles you can rent apart from cars and motorcycles. In many places you can rent campervans – they're particularly popular in Tasmania. Motorscooters are also available in a number of locations – they're popular on Magnetic Island and in Cairns for example – and you only need a car licence to ride one. Best of all, in many places you can rent bicycles.

Buying a Car
Australian cars are not cheap – a result of the small population. Locally manufactured cars are made in small, uneconomic numbers and imported cars are heavily taxed so they won't undercut the local products. If you're buying a second-hand vehicle reliability is all important. Mechanical breakdowns way out in the outback can be very inconvenient (not to mention dangerous) – the nearest mechanic can be a hell of a long way down the road.

Shopping around for a used car involves much the same rules as anywhere in the Western world but with a few local variations. First of all, used-car dealers in Australia are just like used-car dealers from Los Angeles to London – they'd sell their mother into slavery if it turned a dollar. You'll probably get any car cheaper by buying privately through newspaper small ads rather than through a car dealer. In most states (with the notable exception of Queensland) buying through a dealer does have the advantage of some sort of warranty, but a warranty is not much use if you're buying a car in Sydney and intend setting off for Cairns next week. Used-car warranty requirements vary from state to state – but, as stated, a dealer is not required to give you any warranty whatsoever when you buy a car in Queensland, regardless of cost.

There's a great deal of discussion among travellers about the best place to buy used cars. It's quite possible that prices vary but don't count on turning it to your advantage. Cairns is a popular spot for travellers buying and selling cars.

What is rather more certain is that the further you get from civilisation, the better it is to be in a locally-manufactured vehicle, such as a Holden or Ford. New cars can be a whole different ball game of course, but if you're in an older vehicle that's likely to have the odd hiccup, life is much simpler if it's a car for which you can get spare parts anywhere from Bourke to Bulamakanka.

In Australia third-party personal injury insurance is always included in the vehicle registration cost. This ensures that every vehicle (as long as it's currently registered) carries at least minimum insurance. You'd be wise to extend that minimum to at least third-party property insurance as well – minor collisions with other cars can be amazingly expensive.

When you come to buy or sell a car there are usually some local regulations. In Queensland the vehicle needs to be re-registered locally at the time of sale. For the seller this simply means handing in the old number plates and getting a refund on the unused portion of the registration; for the buyer it means getting a certificate of roadworthiness (RWC) for the vehicle. In New South Wales and the Northern Territory roadworthy checks are compulsory every year when you come to renew the registration. Stamp duty has to be paid when you buy a car and, as this is based on the purchase price, it's not unknown for buyer and seller to agree privately to understate the price. It's much easier to sell a car in the same state that it's registered in, otherwise you (or the buyer) must re-register it in the new state, and that's a hassle.

Buy-Back Deals One way of getting around the hassles of buying and selling a vehicle privately is to enter into a buy-back arrangement with a car or motorcycle dealer. However, dealers will often find ways of knocking down the price when you return the vehicle, even if a price has been agreed in writing – often by pointing out expensive repairs – that allegedly will be required to gain the dreaded RWC needed to transfer the registration. The cars on offer have often been driven around Australia a number of times, often with haphazard or minimal servicing, and are generally pretty tired. The main advantage of these schemes is that you don't have to worry about being able to sell the vehicle quickly at the end of your trip, and can usually arrange insurance which short-term visitors may otherwise find hard to get.

A company that specialises in buy-back arrangements on cars and motorcycles, with fixed rates and no hidden extras, is Car Connection Australia (☎ (03) 5473 4469, fax (03) 5473 4520). Here a second-hand Ford Falcon or Holden Kingswood station wagon or Yamaha XT600 trail bike will set you back a fixed sum of $1950 for any period up to six months; a Toyota Land Cruiser Troopcarrier, suitable for serious outback exploration, is $3500 ($4500 for an air-con station wagon), also for up to six months. Information and bookings are handled by its European agent: Travel Action GmbH (☎ (0276) 47824, fax 7938), Einsiedeleiweg 16, 57399 Kirchhundem, Germany.

Finally, make use of automobile organisations. They can advise you on local regulations you should be aware of, give general guidelines about buying a car and, most importantly, for a fee (around $70) will check over a used car and report on its condition before you agree to purchase it. They also offer car insurance to their members.

MOTORCYCLE

Motorcycles are a very popular way of getting around. Between April and November, the climate is just about ideal for biking around Queensland, and the many small trails from the road into the bush often lead to perfect spots to spend the night in the world's largest camping ground.

The long, open roads are really made for large-capacity machines above 750cc, which Australians prefer once they outgrow their 250cc learner restrictions. But that doesn't stop enterprising individuals – many of them Japanese – from tackling the

length and breadth of the continent on 250cc trail bikes. Doing it on a small bike is not impossible, just tedious at times.

If you want to bring your own motorcycle into Australia you'll need a *carnet de passage*, and when you try to sell it you'll get less than the market price because of restrictive registration requirements. Shipping from just about anywhere is expensive.

However, with a little bit of time up your sleeve, getting mobile on two wheels in Australia is quite feasible, thanks largely to the chronically depressed motorcycle market. The beginning of the southern winter is a good time to strike. Australian newspapers and the lively local bike press have extensive classified advertisement sections where $2500 gets you something that will easily take you around the country if you know a bit about bikes. The main drawback is that you'll have to try and sell it again afterwards.

An easier option is a buy-back arrangement with a large motorcycle dealer in a major city. They're keen to do business, and basic negotiating skills allied with a wad of cash (say, $4000) should secure an excellent second-hand bike with a written guarantee that they'll buy it back in good condition minus $1500 or $2000 after your four-month, round-Australia trip. Popular brands for this sort of thing are BMWs, large-capacity, shaft-driven Japanese bikes and possibly Harley-Davidsons (very popular in Australia). The percentage drop on a trail bike will be much greater (though the actual amount you lose should be similar), but very few dealers are interested in buy-back schemes on trail bikes.

You'll need a rider's licence and a helmet. A fuel range of 350km will cover most fuel stops. Beware of dehydration in the dry, hot air – force yourself to drink plenty of water, even if you don't feel thirsty. The 'roo bars' (outsize bumpers) on interstate trucks and many outback cars tell you never to ride at night, or in the early morning and evening. Marsupials are nocturnal, sleeping in the shade during the day and feeding at night, and roadside ditches often provide lush grass for them to eat. Cows and sheep also stray onto the roads at night. It's wise to stop riding by around 5 pm.

Many roadhouses offer showers free of charge or for a nominal fee. They're meant for truck drivers, but other people often use them too.

It's worth carrying some spares and tools even if you don't know how to use them, because someone else often does. If you do know, you'll probably have a fair idea of what to take. The basics include: a spare tyre tube (front wheel size, which will fit on the rear but usually not vice versa); puncture repair kit with levers and a pump (or tubeless tyre repair kit with at least three carbon dioxide cartridges); a spare tyre valve, and a valve cap that can unscrew same; the bike's standard tool kit for what it's worth; spare throttle, clutch and brake cables; tie wire, cloth tape ('gaffer' tape) and nylon 'zip-ties'; a handful of bolts and nuts in the usual emergency sizes (M6 and M8), along with a few self-tapping screws; one or two fuses in your bike's ratings; a bar of soap for fixing tank leaks (knead to a putty with water and squeeze into the leak); and, most important of all, a workshop manual for your bike (even if you can't make sense of it, the local motorcycle mechanic can). You'll never have enough elastic straps (octopus or 'ocky' straps) to tie down your gear.

Make sure you carry water – at least two litres on major roads in central Australia, more off the beaten track. And finally, if something does go hopelessly wrong in the back of beyond, park your bike where it's clearly visible and observe the cardinal rule: *don't leave your vehicle.*

BICYCLE

Queensland can be a good place for cycling, although you need to choose your areas. There are bike tracks in most cities, but in the country it's variable. Roads such as the long haul along the Bruce Highway from Brisbane to Cairns can be long, hot and not particularly safe as there are limited verges and heavy traffic. The humid weather can

be draining too if you're not used to it, and once away from the coast distances between towns can be uncomfortably long. The Gold Coast Highway is terrible for cyclists. Having said all that, there are areas well suited to cycle touring: the Gold Coast hinterland, the Sunshine Coast secondary roads and the area north of Cairns.

Bicycle helmets are compulsory, as are front and rear lights for night riding.

Cycling has always been popular in Australia, and not only as a sport: some shearers would ride for huge distances between jobs, rather than use less reliable horses. It's rare to find a reasonably sized town that doesn't have a shop stocking at least basic bike parts.

If you're coming specifically to cycle, it makes sense to bring your own bike. Check your airline for costs and the degree of dismantling/packing required. Within Australia you can load your bike onto a bus or train to skip the boring bits. Note that bus companies require you to dismantle your bike, and some don't guarantee that it will travel on the same bus as you. Trains are easier, but you should supervise the loading and if possible tie your bike upright, otherwise you may find that the guard has stacked crates of Holden spares on your fragile alloy wheels.

You can buy a good steel-framed touring bike in Australia for about $400 (plus panniers). It may be possible to rent touring bikes and equipment from a few of the commercial touring organisations. You can also rent mountain bikes from bike shops in many cities, although these are usually for short-term hire (around $20 a day).

Much of eastern Australia seems to have been settled on the principle of not having more than a day's horse ride between pubs, so it's possible to plan even ultra-long routes and still get a shower at the end of the day. Most people carry camping equipment, but, on the east coast at least, it's feasible to travel from town to town staying in hotels or on-site vans.

You can get by with standard road maps, but as you'll probably want to avoid both the highways and the low-grade unsealed roads, the government series is best. The 1:250,000 scale is the most suitable, but you'll need a lot of maps if you're covering much territory. The next scale up, 1:1,000,000, is adequate. They're available in capital cities and elsewhere.

Until you get fit you should be careful to eat enough to keep you going – remember that exercise is an appetite suppressant. It's surprisingly easy to be so depleted of energy that you end up camping under a gum tree just 10km short of a shower and a steak.

No matter how fit you are, water is still vital. Dehydration is no joke and can be life-threatening. Summer in Queensland isn't a great time for cycling – it can get very hot and incredibly humid, and it's no fun at all trying to ride through the torrential downpours which are commonplace during the Wet. At any time of year, you should wear plenty of sunscreen and drink *lots* of water.

Of course, you don't have to follow the larger roads and visit towns. It's possible to fill your mountain bike's panniers with muesli, head out into the mulga, and not see anyone for weeks; or ever again – outback travel is very risky if not properly planned. Water is the main problem in the outback, and you can't rely on it where there aren't settlements. That tank marked on your map may be dry or the water from it unfit for humans, and those station buildings probably blew away years ago. That little creek marked with a dotted blue line? Forget it – the only time it has water is when the country's flooded for hundreds of kilometres around.

Always check with locals if you're heading into remote areas, and notify the police if you're about to do something particularly adventurous. That said, you can't rely too much on local knowledge of road conditions – most people have no idea of what a heavily loaded touring bike needs. What they think of as a great road may be pedal-deep in sand or bull dust, and cyclists have happily ridden along roads that were officially flooded out.

The Bicycle Institute of Queensland (☎ 3844 1144), at 493 Stanley St, Mater Hill, Brisbane (or write to PO Box 8321, Woolloongabba, Brisbane, Qld 4101), is worth contacting for more information on cycling in Queensland. Some of the better bike shops can also be good sources of info on routes, suggested rides, tours and cycling events.

HITCHING

Hitching is never entirely safe in any country in the world, and we don't recommend it. Travellers who decide to hitch should understand that they are taking a small but potentially serious risk. Queensland is not exempt from danger, and even people hitching in pairs are not entirely safe. Before deciding to hitch, talk to local people about the dangers, and it's a good idea to let someone know where you are planning to hitch to before you set off. If you do choose to hitch, the advice that follows should help to make your journey as fast and safe as possible.

Successful hitching depends on several factors, all of them just plain good sense. Factor one for safety and speed is numbers. More than two people hitching together will make things very difficult, and solo hitching is unwise for men as well as women. Two women hitching together may be vulnerable, and two men hitching together can expect long waits. The best option is for a woman and a man to hitch together.

Factor two is position – look for a place where vehicles will be going slowly and where they can stop easily. A junction or freeway slip road is a good place if there is stopping room. Position goes beyond just where you stand. The ideal location is on the outskirts of a town – hitching from way out in the country is as hopeless as from the centre of a city. Take a bus out to the edge of town.

Factor three is appearance. The ideal appearance for hitching is a sort of genteel poverty – threadbare but clean. Looking too good can be as much of a bummer as looking too bad! Don't carry too much gear

– if it looks like it's going to take half an hour to pack your bags aboard you'll be left on the roadside.

Factor four is knowing when to say no. Saying no to a car-load of drunks is pretty obvious, but you should also be prepared to abandon a ride if you begin to feel uneasy for any reason. Don't sit there hoping for the best: make an excuse and get out at the first opportunity.

It can be time-saving to say no to a short ride that might take you from a good hitching point to a lousy one. Wait for the right, long ride to come along. On a long haul, it's pointless to start walking as it's not likely to increase the likelihood of your getting a lift and it's often an awfully long way to the next town.

Trucks are often the best lifts but they will only stop if they are going slowly and can get started easily again. Thus, the ideal place is at the top of a hill where they have a downhill run. Truckies often say they are going to the next town and if they don't like you, will drop you anywhere. As they often pick up hitchers for company, the quickest way to create a bad impression is to jump in and fall asleep. It's also worth remembering that while you're in someone else's vehicle, you are their guest and should act accordingly – many drivers no longer pick up people because they have suffered from thoughtless hikers in the past. It's the hitcher's duty to provide entertainment!

Of course people do get stuck in outlandish places but that's the name of the game. If you're visiting from abroad a nice prominent flag on your pack will help, and a sign announcing your destination can also be useful. Uni and hostel notice boards are good places to look for hitching partners.

Just as hitchers should be wary when accepting lifts, drivers who pick up fellow travellers to share the costs should also be aware of the possible risks involved.

BOAT

At any time of the year, there are thousands of yachts and boats travelling up and down the Queensland coast. From time to time the owners of these vessels need to take on extra crew, and if you ask around at marinas and yacht clubs, it may be possible to make your way along the coast by hitching rides or crewing on yachts. Moreton Bay near Brisbane, Rainbow Beach and Tin Can Bay, Hervey Bay, Gladstone, Airlie Beach, Townsville, Cairns and Port Douglas are all good places to try. See the Sea section in the Getting There & Away chapter for more information.

LOCAL TRANSPORT

Brisbane has a comprehensive public transport system with buses, trains and river ferries. The larger cities like Surfers Paradise, Toowoomba, Mt Isa, Bundaberg, Rockhampton, Mackay, Townsville and Cairns all have local bus services.

At the major tourist centres, most of the backpackers' hostels, and some resorts and hotels, have courtesy coaches which will pick you up from train or bus stations or the airport. Most tour operators include courtesy coach transport to/from your accommodation in their prices. Elsewhere, all of the larger towns and cities have at least one taxi service.

ORGANISED TOURS

There are all sorts of tours around Queensland, although few that cover much of the state. Most are connected with a particular activity (eg bushwalking or horse riding tours) or area (eg 4WD tours to Cape York). See the Activities section of the Facts for the Visitor chapter and the various chapters of this book for some suggestions.

If you're on the lookout for tours, hostel notice boards can be good sources of information.

Up in the Far North, there are plenty of operators offering 4WD tours of the Cape York Peninsula, often with the option of driving one way and flying or boating the other. See Organised Tours in the Cape York Peninsula chapter for details.

There are all sorts of trips from the mainland out to the Great Barrier Reef. You can fly in a seaplane out to a deserted coral cay;

take a fast catamaran to the outer reef and spend the day snorkelling; join a dive boat and scuba dive in a coral garden; or take a day trip to one of the many islands.

There are hundreds of tours operating out of Cairns and Port Douglas – as well as trips to the reef and islands, you can take the Kuranda Scenic Railway up to the Kuranda markets; tour the Atherton Tablelands; visit Cape Tribulation on a 4WD tour; cruise along the Daintree River; go white-water rafting; and visit Aboriginal rock-art galleries in Cape York ...

Tours to Fraser Island, organised by the backpackers' hostels in Noosa Heads and Hervey Bay, are a convenient way of seeing one of Queensland's natural wonders for those who don't have their own 4WD.

Dozens of operators in the Whitsundays offer cruises around the islands, or if you want to do your own thing you could get a group together and charter a yacht.

From the Gold Coast, there are tours to Lamington and Springbrook national parks and to South Stradbroke Island.

Oz Experience offers an interesting alternative to travelling up the coast with one of the national bus companies. See the Bus section in the Getting There & Away chapter for details.

Brisbane

Brisbane has long been viewed by the larger, southern capitals as something of a hicksville, an overblown country town. But if there was ever any truth to that, there certainly isn't today. Since playing host to a string of major international events in the 1980s, including the 1982 Commonwealth Games and Expo '88, Brisbane has developed into a lively, cosmopolitan city with several interesting districts, a good street cafe scene, a great riverside park, a busy cultural calendar and a decent nightlife – though you'll need to do some work to find it.

The city's origins date back to 1824, when a penal colony was established at Redcliffe Point on Moreton Bay to house Sydney's more recalcitrant convicts. After a difficult first couple of months struggling with inadequate water supplies and hostile Aborigines, the colony was relocated south and inland to the banks of the Brisbane River, the site of the city centre today. As a penal colony, Brisbane was never the success it was intended to be – it only ever accommodated about 1100 convicts, and was abandoned in 1839. The Moreton Bay area was thrown open to free settlers in 1842, and by the time of Queensland's separation in 1859 Brisbane had a population of around 6000 residents. As Queensland's huge agricultural potential and then its mineral riches were developed, so Brisbane grew. Today it is the third-largest city in Australia with a population rapidly approaching 1.5 million.

Queensland's growing tourism industry has brought an influx of visitors to the capital, and with its near-perfect climate year-round Brisbane comes as a pleasant surprise to most visitors. The city is also surrounded by some of the state's major tourist destinations and there are plenty of options for day trips just an hour or two's drive away, including the Gold and Sunshine coasts and their mountainous hinterlands, and the islands of Moreton Bay.

HIGHLIGHTS

PACIFIC OCEAN

Brisbane River & Inner Suburbs p128

North Stradbroke Island p170

Central Brisbane p132
City Cat p137
Spring Hill, Petrie Terrace & Paddington p139
Fortitude Valley, New Farm & Kangaroo Point p140
Southern Inner Suburbs p142

- If you're short on time then the best way to cram everything in is to spend a day hopping on and off the City Sights bus.
- Buy an off-peak pass and spend the day exploring the city from the river on the City Cat.
- Laze about the South Bank Parklands – and take your swimming togs for a splash in the lagoon.
- Hit the Castlemaine XXXX brewery for a tour followed by a sampling session.
- Take a bus up to Mt Coot-tha lookout for a great Brisbane panorama.
- Sign on for a highly recommended day trip to the Springbrook Plateau or the Glass House Mountains with Rob's Rainforest Tours.
- Take in a gig at The Zoo, one of Australia's best small concert venues.
- Feed the wild dolphins at the Tangalooma Resort on Moreton Island.
- Sign up for a free Wednesday afternoon's yachting on Moreton Bay.

BRISBANE

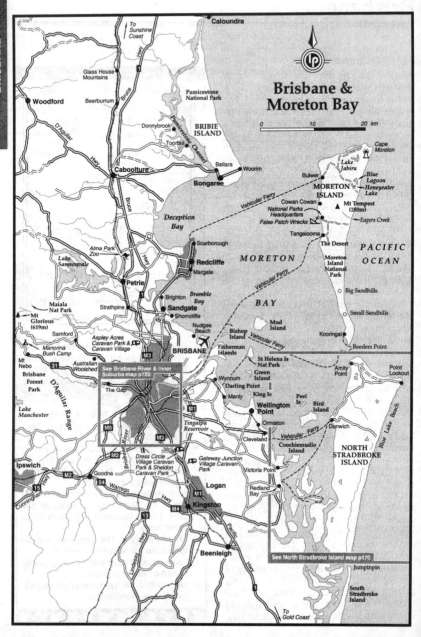

Brisbane & Moreton Bay

Caloundra

To Sunshine Coast

Glass House Mountains

Woodford

Beerburrum

Donnybrook

Pumicestone National Park

Toorbul

BRIBIE ISLAND

Bellara

Woorim

Caboolture

Bongaree

Deception Bay

Alma Park Zoo

Lake Samsonvale

Scarborough

Redcliffe

Margate

MORETON

Petrie

Brighton

Bramble Bay

Maiala Nat Park

Strathpine

Sandgate

Mt Glorious (619m)

Shorncliffe

Samford

Nudgee Beach

BAY

Manorina Bush Camp

Aspley Acres Caravan Park & Caravan Village

Australian Woolshed

BRISBANE

Bishop Island

Mud Island

Mt Nebo

Brisbane Forest Park

See Brisbane River & Inner Suburbs map p128

Fisherman Islands

St Helena Is Nat Park

Lake Manchester

The Gap

Wynnum

Darling Point

Green Island

Amity Point

Point Lookout

Manly

King Is

Wellington Point

Peel Is

Bird Island

Tingalpa Reservoir

Ormiston

Cleveland

Dunwich

NORTH STRADBROKE ISLAND

Ipswich

Goodna

Dress Circle Village Caravan Park & Sheldon Caravan Park

Gateway Junction Village Caravan Park

Coochiemudlo Island

Victoria Point

Logan

Redland Bay

Kingston

See North Stradbroke Island map p170

Beenleigh

Jumpinpin

To Gold Coast

South Stradbroke Island

Pumicestone Channel

Bruce Hwy

D'Aguilar Hwy

D'Aguilar Range

Brisbane River

Warrego Hwy

Cunningham Hwy

Lindsay Hwy

Pacific Hwy

Cape Moreton

Lake Jabiru

Bulwer

Blue Lagoon

Honeyeater Lake

MORETON ISLAND

Cowan Cowan

National Parks Headquarters

False Patch Wrecks

Mt Tempest (280m)

Eagers Creek

Tangalooma

The Desert

PACIFIC OCEAN

Moreton Island National Park

Big Sandhills

Small Sandhills

Kooringal

Reeders Point

Vehicular Ferry

Blue Lake Beach

0   10   20 km

ORIENTATION

Looking at a map of Queensland or Australia, most travellers see Brisbane's location on the coast and assume it to be a beach city. It isn't; it's the Brisbane River which plays the defining role in the city's persona.

City Centre

Brisbane's city centre is enclosed within a U-shaped loop of the Brisbane River. The centre is compact, laid out in a grid of streets measuring a little over 1km by 1km.

The Transit Centre, where you'll arrive if you're coming by bus, train or airport shuttle, is on Roma St about 500m west of the city centre. Head left as you leave the Transit Centre's main entrance and you'll come to King George Square, the large open area in front of City Hall. One block further south-east is the Queen St Mall, the city's main commercial thoroughfare.

At the eastern end of Queen St is the central business district (CBD) as well as the Riverside Centre and Eagle St Pier complexes, which house bars, cafes and restaurants. At the western end of the Queen St Mall is Victoria Bridge, which connects the centre to South Brisbane and the South Bank. The south-eastern part of the city centre – the bottom of the U – is occupied by the City Botanic Gardens.

Inner Suburbs

Most of Brisbane's accommodation and eating options are in the suburbs surrounding the city. Immediately north of the city is Spring Hill, which blends residential with commercial buildings and has a good range of accommodation. Just west of the centre is Paddington, an attractive residential suburb with good cafes and restaurants.

Across the Victoria Bridge, South Brisbane is the site of the Queensland Cultural Centre and the South Bank Parklands. Further south again are the suburbs of Highgate Hill and the trendy West End.

Heading north-east along Ann St from the city leads to Fortitude Valley (usually just referred to as the Valley) – a cosmopolitan suburb with lots of nightclubs and restaurants and a large ethnic population. To the east of the Valley is New Farm, which also has quite a few eating and accommodation options. East across the river from the city is Kangaroo Point.

Maps

Globetrotter, Sunmap and UBD all publish city and suburban maps which are available from most bookshops and newsagencies for around $5 to $7. For clarity and compact size we'd go with the Globetrotter Pocket Map *Brisbane & the Gold Coast*.

The definitive guide to Brisbane's streets is UBD's *Brisbane Street Directory* (known locally as '*Refidex'*), available in either small paperback (around $17) or telephone directory size ($30).

INFORMATION

Tourist Offices

On the 3rd level of the Transit Centre, the privately-run Brisbane Visitors Accommodation Service desk (☎ 3236 2020) offers a booking and information service for backpackers. It operates weekdays from 7 am to 6 pm and weekends from 8 am to 5 pm. There's also an information desk on the 2nd level.

The other good place is the Queen St Mall information centre (☎ 3229 5918), a kiosk on the corner of Queen and Albert Sts, which is particularly useful on things to see and do in the city. It's open Monday to Thursday from 9 am to 5.30 pm, Friday from 9 am to 9 pm, Saturday from 9 am to 4 pm and Sunday from 10 am to 4 pm.

The Tourism Brisbane information desk (☎ 3221 8411) in the foyer of City Hall on King George Square is less useful and is really just somewhere to pick up brochures and a free map. It's open weekdays from 9 am to 4.30 pm and Saturday from 10 am to 1 pm.

The Queensland Travel & Tourism Corporation (☎ 13 1801) on the corner of Adelaide and Edward Sts is more a booking office than an information centre but may be able to answer some queries. It's open weekdays from 8.30 am to 5.30 pm and Saturday from 9.30 am to 12.30 pm.

Free Publications

There are a number of free information and listings guides circulated in Brisbane. Ones to look out for include *Time Off*, *Rave* and *Scene*, all local weekly listings papers – the first two are strong on music, gigs and cinema, the third is mainly devoted to clubbing. Pick these up at Rocking Horse Records on Adelaide St near the corner with Albert St, or at almost any of the cafes in the Valley or West End.

Brisbane News is a weekly lifestyle magazine, a little gushing, but useful for picking up on Brisbane's preoccupations of the moment; it can be found at the Queen St Mall information kiosk – as can *This Week in Brisbane*, a small, glossy booklet with far too many pages of ads but a useful map of central Brisbane and the Citytrain network.

Money

There are exchange bureaus at Brisbane airport which are open for all arriving flights.

Thomas Cook has three foreign exchange offices in the city centre. Their main branch is on level E of the Myer Centre; it's open

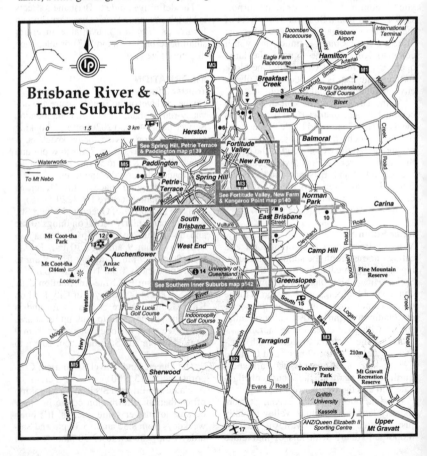

weekdays from 8.45 am to 5.15 pm and on Saturday from 9.30 am to 1 pm. The other branches are at 276 Edward St and on the 1st floor at 241 Adelaide St (opposite Qantas' international office).

American Express (☎ 3229 2022) has its office at 131 Elizabeth St, near the Albert St corner. Opening hours are from 9 am to 5.30 pm Monday to Friday and from 9 am to noon Saturday. There's also a Western Union international money transfer/currency exchange office towards the south-west end of the Queen St Mall.

Left Luggage
In the Transit Centre on Roma St there are deep, backpack-sized lockers on the 3rd level which cost $4 for 24 hours. If you need to leave luggage for longer there is also a cloak room on the same level, beside bays 24-26, which can store most items; backpacks, surfboards, golf clubs etc are $2 a day, bikes are $3 a day. It's open daily from 7.30 am to 6 pm.

Post & Communications
Brisbane's GPO is in an imposing Victorian building on Queen St, between Edward and Creek Sts. It's open weekdays only from 7 am to 6 pm. A Post Shop on the 2nd level of the Myer Centre performs the func-

1	Newmarket Gardens Caravan Park
2	Breakfast Creek Hotel
3	Bretts Wharf
4	Newstead House & Gardens
5	Breakfast Creek Wharf
6	RNA Exhibition Grounds
7	Waverley B&B
8	Paddington Antique Centre
9	Courtney Place Backpackers
10	Earlystreet Historical Village
11	Classic Cinema
12	Planetarium
13	Botanic Gardens
14	University Information Office
15	Amaroo Gardens Caravan Park
16	Lone Pine Koala Sanctuary
17	Archerfield Aerodrome

tions of a post office on Saturday and Sunday; it is open from 10 am to 4 pm.

If you have an American Express card or travellers cheques, you can receive mail sent c/o American Express Client Mail, 131 Elizabeth St, Brisbane, Qld 4000. The office will hold standard mail for up to a month before returning it (unless it receives notification of a forwarding address).

The STD telephone area code for Brisbane is ☎ 07.

Email & Internet Access
There are two Internet cafes in Brisbane. The more central of the two is The Hub Cafe (% 3229 1119) at 125 Margaret St in the city centre. It has 16 terminals for use at $6 per half-hour or $6 per hour after 10 pm or after 6 pm on Sunday. It's open seven days a week from 7 am to midnight (10 pm Sunday). Cafe Scene (% 3216 0624), at the corner of Brunswick and Ann Sts in the Valley, charges $3 per half-hour or $5 per hour. It's open 24 hours a day but has only three terminals.

The Central City Library in the basement of the City Plaza complex behind City Hall also has a couple of email terminals for public use at $4 per hour. It's open from 10 am to 6 pm Monday to Friday and from 10 am to 3 pm at weekends. Palace Backpackers hostel (see Places to Stay) has an online computer for the use of guests and charges $5 per half-hour.

Travel Agencies
STA Travel has several branches in Brisbane. Its city office (☎ 3221 3722) is at 111-117 Adelaide St, and is open on weekdays from 9 am to 5 pm and Saturday from 9 am to 3 pm. Other branches are at the University of Queensland (☎ 3371 2433) and the Queensland University of Technology (☎ 3229 0655). Trailfinders (☎ 3229 0887), 91 Elizabeth St, is open seven days a week.

There are a number of other agents worth trying if you're looking for discounted fares, including Flight Centres (☎ 3229 6600) and Brisbane Discount Travel (☎ 3221 9211).

The YHA's Membership & Travel office (☎ 3236 1680) is at 154 Roma St, opposite the Transit Centre; it's open from 8.30 am to 5 pm weekdays and 9 am to 1.30 pm Saturday.

Useful Organisations

Queensland's motoring association, the Royal Automobile Club of Queensland (RACQ) (☎ 3361 2444), has its head office beside the GPO on Queen St. It has good maps and an accommodation booking service, and can do while-you-wait passport photos.

The Department of Environment runs an excellent information centre called Naturally Queensland (☎ 3227 8186) at 160 Ann St; it is open on weekdays from 8.30 am to 5 pm. You can get maps, brochures and books on national parks and state forests, as well as camping information and Fraser Island permits.

Disabled Travellers

Brisbane City Council (BCC) produces a series of brochures including *Access Brisbane, Accessible Brisbane Parks* and the *Brisbane Mobility Map*. These should be available from the BCC Customer Services Centre at City Plaza behind the City Hall or call the Disability Services Unit on ☎ 3403 5769. It may also be worth contacting the Disability Information Awareness Line (DIAL) on ☎ 3403 4268 or toll-free ☎ 1800 177 120.

See the section on Disabled Travellers in the Facts for the Visitor chapter for more information.

Bookshops

The city's best is the Mary Ryan Bookshop on Queen St Mall, one of a small family-run chain (others are in Paddington and on Brunswick St in New Farm). Angus & Robertson Bookworld has branches on Post Office Square in Adelaide St and at the south-west end of the Queen St Mall. The largest range of travel guides and maps is to be found at World Wide Maps & Guides at 187 George St (100m south of the Queen St Mall).

For second-hand titles try Archives Fine Books, spread over three shops at 40-42 Charlotte St in the city centre, or Emma's Bookshop and Bent Books, both small but densely crammed places on the junction of Vulture and Boundary Sts in West End.

Laundry

Most accommodation provides laundry facilities. If yours doesn't, self-service laundrettes close to the centre include the New Farm Laundromat on the corner of Brunswick and Harcourt Sts in New Farm, and one on Hardgrave Rd in West End.

Film & Photography

Anderson Camera Repair Service (☎ 3221 3133) at the Adelaide St end of the Brisbane Arcade specialises in repairs to Bronica, Canon, Mamiya, Nikon and Olympus. Most repairs can be handled in two to three days, depending on what parts are needed.

Camera Tech (☎ 3229 5406), 270 Adelaide St, is a repair agent for Canon and Konica, but can handle other brands as well.

Medical Services

The Travellers' Medical & Vaccination Centre (☎ 3221 9066) on the 6th floor of the Qantas building at 247 Adelaide St can handle all vaccinations and medical advice for travellers. Consultation fees depend on the length of visit and range from $18 for four minutes to $89 for 45 minutes. The centre is open on weekdays from 8.30 am to 5 pm (Tuesday until 7 pm, Wednesday until 9 pm) and on Saturday from 8.30 am to 2.30 pm.

The 24-hour Travellers' Medical Service (☎ 3211 3611) on the 1st floor at 245 Albert St (above McDonald's) also offers travel vaccinations, women's health care and first aid kits.

The T&G Corner Pharmacy, 141 Queen St on the Mall, is open Monday to Saturday until 9 pm and Sunday from 10 am to 5 pm.

Emergency

Dial ☎ 000 for emergency help from the police, ambulance or fire brigade. There's a police post in the centre of the city – part of the Queen St Mall information kiosk – which is staffed 24 hours a day.

CITY CENTRE

Surrounded on three sides by the Brisbane River, the city centre is a pleasant and orderly precinct that combines a scattering of historic Victorian buildings with snazzy, hitech, high-rise office blocks and some pleasant parks and squares. A few of the more interesting old buildings are mentioned in the Walking Tour boxed text and following, but for more information pick up a copy of the city council's *Heritage Trail Brisbane City Centre* brochure, available from the information desk in the City Hall. (There are also walking tour brochures for the riverfront, South Brisbane, Fortitude Valley and Paddington, among others.)

City Hall

Brisbane's City Hall, on King George Square between Adelaide and Ann Sts, is surrounded by skyscrapers, but the observation platform up in the bell tower still provides one of the best views across the city. There's a free lift up which runs weekdays from 8.30 am to 4.30 pm and on Saturday from 10 am to 4.30 pm. The views up here are great, but a word of warning – beware the bells. It's truly a terrifying, deafening experience if you are up here and the bells start tolling unexpectedly.

The **City Hall Art Gallery & Museum** has a small, permanent museum collection and regularly exhibits local art; it's open daily from 10 am to 5 pm, except on public holidays, and admission is free.

One-hour **guided tours** of City Hall are conducted on weekdays at 10 am, noon and 2 pm. The cost is $4 ($3 children, free for under 13s). Phone ☎ 3403 6586 for inquiries.

Treasury Casino to Parliament

At the western end of the Queen St Mall, overlooking the river, is Brisbane's magnificent Italian Renaissance-style **Treasury Building**. Before its construction in 1885 this was the site of the penal colony's military barracks. In 1995 the Treasury was converted to use as a casino with accompanying bars and restaurants – see the Entertainment section.

The block south-east of the casino – and its architectural sibling – is the former **Land Administration Building**, now taken over by the Conrad hotel group. Just south-west of the hotel, over on the river side of William St, is the **Commissariat Stores Building**, one of only two convict-era structures still standing in the city centre (the other being the old windmill). Built in 1829 it was used as a government store right up until 1962. Today it houses the Royal Historical Society of Queensland's library and museum, and can be visited Tuesday to Friday from 11 am to 2 pm, and Sunday from 11 am to 4 pm; entry is $1.

Crossing back onto George St and continuing south, on the right immediately after the junction with Margaret St is **The Mansions**, a beautiful and unusual three-storey terrace built in 1890. Look out for the cats on top of the parapet at each end of the building.

One block south of The Mansions is **Parliament House**, overlooking the Botanic Gardens from the corner of Alice and George Sts. It dates from 1868 and was built in French Renaissance style with a roof clad in Mt Isa copper. Free tours are given five times a day on weekdays (except when parliament is sitting – in this case you can sit and observe from the public balcony).

City Botanic Gardens

While there are plenty of varieties of trees including Moreton Bay figs, bunya pines, macadamias and mangroves fringing the river's edge, what Brisbane's Botanic Gardens has most of is great expanses of grass. Anywhere else this would be called a park. The place is popular with strollers, joggers, picnickers and lunching office workers. It's also a great spot for in-line skating and bike riding. There's a pleasant cafe inside the former curator's cottage at the southern end. The gardens are open 24

BRISBANE

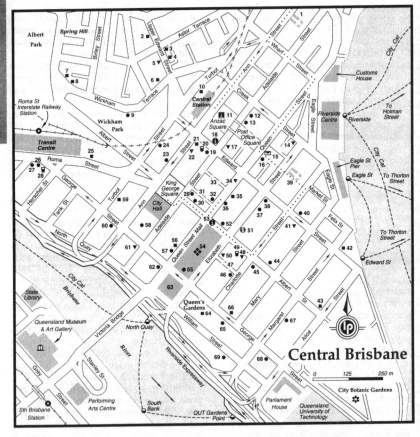

Central Brisbane

0   125   250 m

City Botanic Gardens

hours a day (and lit at night) and free guided tours leave from the rotunda just south of the Albert St entrance every day except Monday at 11 am and 1 pm; ring ☎ 3221 4528 for inquiries.

Riverfront

The riverside area north-east of the CBD is one of the most attractive and lively areas in the city centre, as well as one of the most historically significant. Last century this area was lined with timber wharves onto which steamships disgorged their passen-

gers and cargo. The only testimony to former maritime commerce is the greenish copper-domed **Customs House** (1886-89) where all ships were at one time required to pay their duties. These days the historic building is owned and has been restored by the University of Queensland. It contains a good brasserie as well as a gallery which houses a small private collection of early Australian paintings. It's open daily from 10 am to 4 pm.

Further south, the **Riverside Centre** and the **Eagle St Pier** wine and dine complex-

PLACES TO STAY	OTHER	38	Nite Owl 24 Hour
2 Dorchester Self-Contained Units	1 St John's Cathedral		Convenience Store
3 Yale Inner-City Inn	9 Old Windmill & Observatory	39	St Stephen's Cathedral
4 Annie's Shandon Inn	11 Cenotaph	40	Metro Cinema, Zane's Caffe & Pasta Bar
6 Astor Motel	12 Qantas; Travellers' Medical & Vaccination	43	Edward St Pier
7 Gazebo Hotel	Centre	45	Skatebiz & Brisbane Bicycle Sales
8 Soho Club Motel	13 Angus & Robertson Bookworld	46	Archives Fine Books
10 Sheraton Brisbane	15 GPO	47	Elizabeth Arcade
21 Palace Backpackers	16 RACQ Head Office	49	Gilhooley's
25 Brisbane City Travelodge	18 Queensland Travel & Tourism Corporation	51	American Express
35 Brisbane Hilton	19 Thomas Cook	52	Greater Union Cinemas
42 Beaufort Heritage Hotel	20 Down Under Bar & Grill	53	Information Kiosk
44 Parkroyal Brisbane	23 Naturally Queensland	54	Myer Centre
56 Lennon's Hotel	24 Suncorp Theatre	55	World Wide Maps & Guides
59 Explorers Inn	26 Secondhand Bookshop	57	Angus & Robertson Bookworld
64 Conrad International	27 YHA Travel Office	58	City Plaza; Central City Library
66 Bellevue Hotel	28 The Transcontinental	60	Dendy Cinema
PLACES TO EAT	29 Rocking Horse Records	62	Tasmania & NSW Travel Centres
5 Oriental Bangkok	30 Travellers' Medical Service	63	Treasury Casino
14 Indochine	31 Brisbane Arcade	65	Sciencentre
17 Mekong Chinese Restaurant	32 Mary Ryan Bookshop	67	The Hub Cafe
22 Palace Cafe	33 Broadway Centre	68	The Mansions
34 Jimmy's On The Mall	36 Hoyt's Regent Cinema	69	Commissariat Stores Building
41 Hungry Heart Bistro	37 Queensland Aboriginal Creations		
48 Pané e Vino			
50 Govinda's			
61 McDonald's			

es cater to hordes of lunching office workers. Despite some awful plastic kit architecture they have an attractive riverside site, overlooking boardwalks and busy ferry terminals. A good time to come here is on Sunday morning, when the area is host to a busy craft market.

MUSEUMS

Brisbane's major museum, the Queensland Museum, is part of the Queensland Cultural Centre – see that section for details. The other good museum is the **Sciencentre**, a hands-on science museum with interactive displays, optical illusions, a perception tunnel and regular film shows. This is a great place to visit with kids, but try not to come before 2 pm on school days as it is usually very crowded with groups. The Sci-

encentre is at 110 George St in the city centre and it's open from 10 am to 5 pm daily. Entry costs $7 ($5 for children and students, $24 family).

The **Queensland Maritime Museum** (☎ 3844 5361) on Sidon St in South Brisbane (just south of South Bank) has a wide range of displays for boat buffs, including a dry dock dating from 1881, an impressive collection of model ships and relics from old wrecks. Among the numerous boats to be seen here is the coal-fired tug SS *Forceful* which still gets steam up for pleasure cruises along the river (phone for sailing dates). It's open from 9.30 am to 5 pm daily; admission is $5 ($2.50 children).

Away from the centre, out in St Lucia on Sir Fred Schonell Drive, the **University of Queensland** has anthropology, antiquities

Walking Tour of Central Brisbane

As good a place as any to start is the classical-style **City Hall**, where you should take the lift up to the top of the bell tower for the **view**. This will give you a good idea of the layout of the central part of the city.

On leaving turn right, cross Adelaide St and head straight down Albert St to the **Queen St Mall**. This is the city's main shopping mall and it's nothing you're going to be writing home about, but swing right and look up to the left at some of the facades – the former Carlton Hotel, the former Telegraph Building, the former York Hotel – solid evidence of Brisbane's turn-of-the-century prosperity. Turn around and head down the mall to **Hoyts Regent Theatre**, which will be on your right, and pass through the foyer into the former booking hall, built in the days when movie houses were designed as temples to the glamour of the screen.

Retrace your steps back along the mall to the junction with Albert St and head downhill, past the information kiosk. This time keep your eyes on the ground and look for the bronze plaques set in the paving; these form part of a **literary trail** down Albert St, each plaque featuring a quote about Brisbane extracted from the work of one of the 32 featured writers. Albert St has a couple of good cafes and one of the better city centre pubs in Gilhooley's.

Take a left after Gilhooley's onto Charlotte St and continue across Edward St (notice the pattern in the street names: east-west are all queens, north-south kings and princes). After about 150m there's an entrance into the grounds of **St Stephen's Cathedral** (1874). While the cathedral isn't particularly noteworthy, beside it is the smaller **St Stephen's Church** (1850), Brisbane's oldest church, which is attributed to the English architect Augustus Pugin, builder of London's Houses of Parliament. Pass around the cathedral and out onto Elizabeth St, then turn around for a great photo opportunity of the twin Gothic spires against a background of mirrored-glass office blocks.

Opposite the cathedral on the north side of Elizabeth St is an arched opening; follow it through. This runs alongside the **post office**, built in the 1870s, with a beautiful frontage

and art museums – see the section on the university for details.

About 4km east of the centre, on McIlwraith Ave, and off Bennetts Rd in Norman Park, the **Earlystreet Historical Village** offers a re-creation of Queensland colonial life through a collection of restored old buildings, including a slab timber hut, two homesteads and a pub. It's open daily from 9 am to 4.30 pm. You can get there on bus Nos 125, 145, 155 or 255 from Ann St near King George Square, or by train to Norman Park.

The **Archerfield Warbirds Museum** at Archerfield Aerodrome, about 12km south of the centre, has a collection of fighter planes all in flying order. It's open daily from 10 am to 4 pm, while beside the airport freeway, opposite the new terminal

complex, is the **Sir Charles Kingsford Smith Memorial**. This is a hangar holding the famous *Southern Cross*, in which Sir Charles made the first Trans-Pacific flight in 1928.

QUEENSLAND CULTURAL CENTRE

This extensive cultural complex, just across Victoria Bridge from the city centre, includes the city's main art gallery, museum and theatre complex, as well as the State Library and a huge exhibition and convention centre.

The **Queensland Museum** (☎ 3840 7555) contains a fairly lively and diverse set of collections which are all relevant to the history of the state; these include a dinosaur garden, exhibitions on whales and the history of photography, and an extensive

onto Queen St, which is where you emerge. (The newsagency you pass in the alleyway has Brisbane's best selection of interstate and overseas newspapers.) Next door and to the left of the post office (as seen from Queen St) is an imposing building, complete with carved gargoyles, that looks like it was lifted from a movie set for Gotham City – it only lacks Batman perched on top. During WWII this building, now known as **MacArthur Chambers**, was used as the headquarters of the commander-in-chief of the South-West Pacific area, General Douglas MacArthur.

Walk past the chambers, crossing Creek St and on into the heart of the central business district (CBD). At the junction with Wharf St, turning right would take you to the upmarket dining and entertainment complexes of the **Riverside Centre** and **Eagle St Pier** but, instead, turn left and walk two blocks up to Ann St.

There are two choices here: a left will take you past the Victorian **Central Station** and, opposite it, to your left, the Greek Revivalist **Cenotaph** where an eternal flame burns in remembrance of Australian soldiers who died in WWI. Beneath the Cenotaph is the **Shrine of Memories**, a sombre underground war memorial with wall plaques and artistic tributes to the war dead. It is open on weekdays from 10 am to 2.30 pm. From the Cenotaph it's 300m back to City Hall, straight along Ann St.

Alternatively, back in the opposite direction Ann St runs straight to Fortitude Valley, just over 500m away. Before the Valley you'll first pass the Gothic-styled **St John's Cathedral**, which is still under construction. Elsewhere in the world Gothic had its last fling during the reign of Queen Victoria, but work began on this in 1901 and continues at a cost of $1 million a year. Guided tours are conducted between 10 am and 4 pm by appointment only (☎ 3835 2231) and you can ask them yourselves why the building is taking so damn long to finish. About 100m past the cathedral is the **Orient Hotel**, one of the city's oldest pubs and still a popular gig venue. Five minutes walk further and you're into the Valley – see the Fortitude Valley & New Farm section.

collection of Melanesian artefacts. There's also a small aviation section plane containing the *Avian Cirrus*, in which Queensland's Bert Hinkler made the first England to Australia solo flight in 1928. There are always several temporary exhibits, with related talks, workshops, films and other activities. The museum is open daily from 9 am to 5 pm. Admission is free.

The **Queensland Art Gallery** has an impressive permanent collection and also features visiting exhibitions. Australian artists in the collection include Sir Sidney Nolan, William Dobell, Charles Blackman, Margaret Preston and Fred Williams. There's a small collection of European art, including paintings by Rubens, Tintoretto, Pissarro and Degas. The gallery is open daily from 10 am to 5 pm and admission is

free. There are free guided tours during the week at 11 am and 1 and 2 pm, and on weekends at 11 am and 2 and 3 pm.

The Cultural Centre is within easy walking distance of the city centre. You can also get there by City Cat (see the Brisbane By Cat boxed text) or by train from the Transit Centre or Central Station.

SOUTH BANK PARKLANDS

Brisbane's South Bank, formerly the site of Expo '88, has been extensively redeveloped into a landscaped riverside park with streams, canals, grassy knolls, a weekend market, shops and restaurants, and a fantastic open-air **swimming pool** designed to resemble a lagoon, complete with a crescent of white sandy beach. This is the best place in Brisbane to kick back, stretch out and catch some sun.

Brisbane by Cat

Easily the best way to view Brisbane is from the river and the best way of getting about the river is on a high-speed City Cat. These large blue catamaran ferries glide upstream and downstream regularly throughout the day and provide an extremely convenient and relaxing way of sightseeing. And they're cheap – for $4 you can ride for as long as you want. For details of sailing times and fares see the Getting Around section later in this chapter.

GADI FARFOUR

To cruise the whole 19km route of the City Cat and back again takes about two hours. Although the Riverside landing stage is at the midpoint of the route, for most visitors its CBD location, at the east end of Elizabeth St, makes it the most convenient place to board the boat.

Upriver from Riverside Leaving the Riverside wharf and heading upriver, the cliffs of Kangaroo Point are off to the left. Most times of the day and night you should be able to spot a few abseilers suspended off the rock face. Across on the right-hand bank the river is fringed by the mangroves of the City Botanic Gardens. As the City Cat passes under the Captain Cook Bridge, over to the left is the Maritime Museum.

The first stop is the **QUT Gardens Point** which is the place to get off for the parliament building and the botanic gardens, after which there's a zigzag sprint across the river to **South Bank** for the parklands, a former busy industrial zone before its makeover for Expo '88, and back across to **North Quay** for the Treasury Casino and the Queen St Mall.

After North Quay comes the longest uninterrupted stretch of the City Cat route, passing under three bridges and then cruising alongside the riverside suburbs of Auchenflower and Milton on the right, and the grassy banks of South Brisbane on the left. Fronting the river in Milton is the Regatta, one of Brisbane's most famous pubs. Unfortunately the City Cat stops nowhere near it. The lighthouse-like structure passed on the left is a scriving tower for the local gasworks. South Brisbane gives way to fashionable Orleigh Park.

The next stop, **Guyatt Park**, services the university dormitory area of St Lucia, so-named because of the sizeable sugar plantations that were once here (St Lucia is a Caribbean sugar island). The **West End** landing stage is also in a residential area and there's nothing to get off for, but on the next bend is the City Cats' upstream terminus, **University of Queensland**, a place well worth spending a few hours – see the relevant section later in this chapter.

Downriver from Riverside Heading downstream, the City Cat immediately passes under the Story Bridge, built in 1934-40 and sharing the same design engineer as the Sydney Harbour Bridge. Beneath the bridge on the tip of Kangaroo Point is Captain John Burke Park, named after a local resident. After rounding the peninsula, on the right, partly hidden in the trees, you can make out a two-storey house with wrought-iron balconies; this was built in 1887 as an immigrant holding centre and still serves this purpose. Kangaroo Point itself was a former shipbuilding area, but it's now the site of a major upmarket residential development.

Across the river from the Point, on the left, is the suburb of New Farm serviced by **Sydney St**. The City Cat then shuttles over to **Mowbray Park**, the stop for East Brisbane.

As the boat leaves Mowbray Park keep a look out on the right for the grand Southern States mansion with the colonnaded facade – all it lacks is Scarlett O'Hara out on the lawn. Across the water from the mansion is the landing stage for **New Farm Park** – this is a good place to get off and walk (see the Fortitude Valley & New Farm section).

When the Cat pulls out from the park you'll see a large brick building bearing the words 'City of Brisbane Powerhouse'. A derelict power station at the time of writing, this place is due to be reborn as an Aboriginal arts centre. Further along from the powerhouse is an old wharf area with huge brick warehouses, some of which are now being converted to apartments. The two stops on this stretch, **Hawthorne** and **Bulimba**, are for residential districts.

After leaving Bulimba you can see over on the far bank a small wooded park headland; hidden within the trees is Newstead House, built in 1846 and one of Brisbane's oldest residences. It's a stately mansion beautifully fitted out with Victorian furnishings and antiques, clothing and period displays, and the house and its gardens are open to the public from 10 am to 4 pm on weekdays and from 2 to 5 pm on Sunday. There's a small admission fee.

Across the creek from Newstead is the Breakfast Creek Hotel, an excellent place for lunch (see Places to Eat).

The downriver terminus for the City Cats is **Bretts Wharf** which services the suburb of Hamilton – home of Brisbane's 'old' money. As you approach look up to the left, where on the hillside you'll see the white-painted verandahs of what is perhaps Brisbane's most beautiful Queenslander. From Bretts Wharf it's just a short walk east to trendy, cafe-ridden Racecourse Rd, or 1km back to Breakfast Creek.

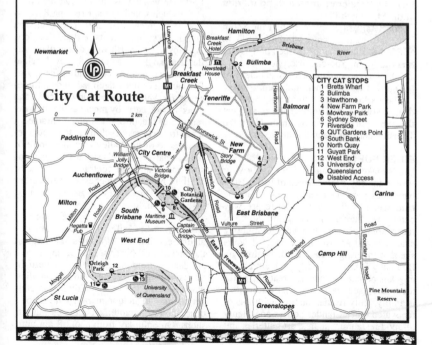

City Cat Route

CITY CAT STOPS
1 Bretts Wharf
2 Bulimba
3 Hawthorne
4 New Farm Park
5 Mowbray Park
6 Sydney Street
7 Riverside
8 QUT Gardens Point
9 South Bank
10 North Quay
11 Guyatt Park
12 West End
13 University of Queensland
● Disabled Access

On Stanley St Plaza, which is the souvenir store-fringed mall in the middle of the parkland, there's a good **Butterfly & Insect House** – a glasshouse in which hundreds of colourful butterflies are housed; there's also a large collection of other spectacular insects and spiders. It's open daily from 8.30 am to 5 pm and entry costs $7.50 ($4.50 children).

Between late October and the end of March, a mobile **alfresco cinema** screens movies in the parkland on Wednesday nights at 7.30 pm; and the **Suncorp Piazza**, an outdoor entertainment venue, has regular concerts and performances, many of which are free. It's always worth wandering down here at weekends during summer as there's usually something going on, such as a fair, food festival or music performance. Also at weekends (Friday evening and all day Saturday and Sunday) there's a large **craft and clothing market** at the Stanley St Plaza.

For details of events call in at the South Bank information centre (☎ 3867 2051), in Stanley St Plaza, which is open daily from 8 am to 8 pm. You can also phone ☎ 3867 2020 for a recorded message with details of the current entertainment program.

The parklands are within easy walking distance of the city centre. You can also get there by City Cat or by train from the Transit Centre or Central Station.

INNER SUBURBS

Don't make the mistake of confining your visit to the city centre. Much of life in Brisbane goes on in the inner suburbs, where the cafe scene, dining and nightlife are way better than they are in the centre. Some of these areas also have a very distinctive character and are worth a couple of hours spent wandering. **West End**, centred on Boundary Rd, is fairly arty with a high immigrant population and is great for pavement cafes (see Places to Eat). **Paddington** is a hilly, leafy residential area with lots of renovated Queenslander houses and plenty of good restaurants, cafes, art galleries and antique shops.

Spring Hill

Spring Hill, rising gently to the north of the city, is part residential and part commercial, with old Queenslander buildings nestling alongside clusters of modern office blocks. There's nothing much here to see or do, but there are pleasant views over the city from the green belt of King Edward, Wickham and Albert parks.

The **Old Windmill & Observatory** on Wickham Terrace, just north-east of the Transit Centre, is one of Brisbane's earliest buildings and dates from 1828. It was intended to grind grain for the convict colony, but owing to a fundamental design error (the sails were too heavy for the wind to turn them) it never worked properly. The building was converted to a signal post and later a meteorological observatory.

Fortitude Valley & New Farm

Fortitude Valley was named after the *Fortitude*, which sailed up the Brisbane River in 1849 with more than 250 immigrants on board. These immigrants settled in the low, swampy valley north-west of the main settlement and the area gradually developed to become the commercial trading centre of Brisbane. Fortunes declined and until recently the Valley was run-down, seedy and given a wide berth by most people. Its lowrent status meant that the place attracted a lot of fringe types, resulting in the recent re-emergence of the Valley as a hip centre of the alternative. There's still a smattering of strip joints and the central Brunswick St Mall is home to bunches of belligerent drunks, but the Valley is Brisbane's best place for a night out.

During the day the action focuses on **Brunswick St Mall** with a cluster of cafes at one end and **McWhirter's Markets** at the other. McWhirter's, has an impressive art deco corner facade, and was built in stages between 1912 and 1930 as a retailing emporium. In 1989 the building was converted into an indoor market with a food court and lots of clothing boutiques and gift shops. On Saturday from about 8 am until mid-afternoon the mall is taken over by an

BRISBANE

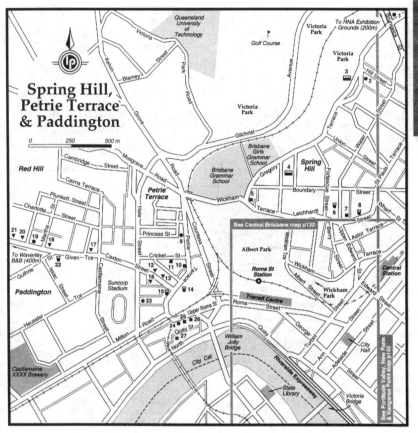

Spring Hill, Petrie Terrace & Paddington

0   250   500 m

PLACES TO STAY
2 Gregory Terrace Motor Inn
5 Albert Park Inn Hotel
7 Metropolitan Motor Inn
10 Banana Benders Backpackers
11 Aussie Way Back-packers
24 Brisbane City YHA
25 Roma St Hostel
26 City Backpackers' Hostel
27 Yellow Submarine Backpackers

PLACES TO EAT
12 Romeo's
13 The Irish Connection
16 Caxton Hotel
17 Sultan's Kitchen
18 Jakarta Indonesian Restaurant
20 King Tut's Wa Wa Hut
21 Le Scoops

OTHER
1 Old Museum Building
3 Centenary Pool
4 Spring Hill Baths
6 Options Nightclub
8 Sportman's Hotel
9 Brisbane Arts Theatre
14 The Underground
15 Casablanca
19 The Book Exchange
22 Paddo Tavern
23 La Boite Theatre

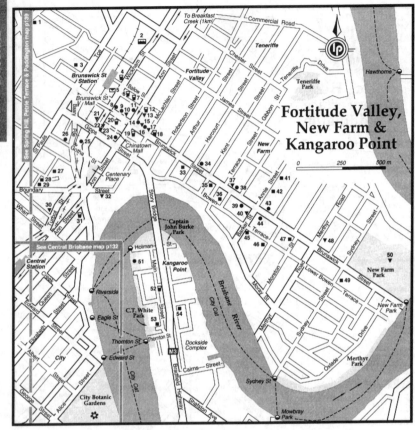

artsy-craftsy, hippyshit **market** complete with street entertainers and musicians.

The Valley is also home to Brisbane's small Chinatown centred on the uninspiring **Chinatown Mall** in Duncan St.

New Farm, the next suburb along as you travel east of the Valley down Brunswick St, also used to be fairly run-down but in recent years it's been almost completely yuppified. It now contains some very chichi restaurants and bars, as well as cheap accommodation including several backpackers' hostels. At the eastern end of

Brunswick St, **New Farm Park** is a large open parkland with playgrounds, picnic areas with gas barbecues, playing ovals, jacaranda trees and beautiful rose gardens.

A good half-day outing is to take the City Cat to New Farm Park, spend a little time there then walk up Brunswick St into the Valley. Time it so you arrive for lunch or dinner (the walk only takes about 45 minutes). If you don't feel like walking on from the Valley back into the city centre you can pick up any westbound bus on Ann St outside the Institute of Modern Art.

PLACES TO STAY
1 Tourist Guest House
3 Balmoral House
27 Thornbury House B&B
28 Dahrl Court Apartments
29 Kookaburra Inn
33 Pete's Palace
35 Red Hot Chilli Packers
    (Brunswick Hotel)
36 Globe Trekkers Hostel
41 Atoa House Travellers'
    Hostel
42 The Homestead
45 The Bowen Terrace
46 South Pacific Motel
47 Allender Apartments
49 Edward Lodge
53 Ryan's On The River
54 Il Mondo

PLACES TO EAT
10 Mellino's
13 Lucky's Trattoria
15 Cafe Europe & Bitch
17 California
21 Vietnamese Restaurant
22 Enjoy Inn
23 Universal Noodle
    Restaurant
30 Little Tokyo
32 E'cco
37 Baan Thai
40 Continental Cafe
48 New Farm Deli & Cafe
50 New Farm Kiosk

OTHER
2 The Valley Pool
4 Wickham Hotel
5 Post Office
6 The Chelsea
7 The Healer
8 McWhirter's Markets
9 24 Hour Convenience
   Store
11 Fire-works Aboriginal
    Gallery
12 The Zoo
14 Cafe Scene
16 Red Bookshop
18 Dooley's
19 The Empire
20 Ric's Cafe-Bar
24 Institute of Modern Art
25 Outdoor Gear Shops
26 CES Job Centre
31 Orient Hotel
34 New Farm Laundromat
38 24 Hour Convenience
    Store
39 New Farm Mountain
    Bikes
43 Mary Ryan Bookshop
44 Village Twin Cinemas
51 Brisbane Jazz Club
52 Story Bridge Hotel

UNIVERSITY OF QUEENSLAND

The University of Queensland occupies a 110-hectare site in a loop of the Brisbane River, 7km south of the city. You could easily spend a few hours or even a day here – it's an attractive and interesting place to visit with several museums, good sporting facilities, an excellent bookshop and a cinema. You can ride a bike all the way here from the city along the Bicentennial Bikeway, which follows the west bank of the Brisbane River out of the centre.

The helpful **information office**, in a small building beside the main entrance, has a map of the grounds and information about the facilities.

The university is centred around the lovely Great Court, a spacious area of lawns and trees surrounded by a semicircle of impressive, cloistered sandstone buildings. There are several museums open (and free) to the general public including an **Anthropology Museum**, open during semesters on Monday and Wednesday from 10 am to noon and from 1 to 4 pm, and an **Antiquities Museum** (☎ 3365 2643), **Geology**

Museum (☎ 3365 2668) and **Zoology Museum** (☎ 3365 2474), all open by appointment only.

The best way to get to there is by City Cat – see the Brisbane by Cat boxed text.

MT COOT-THA FOREST PARK

This large park has a lookout and an excellent botanic garden, and is just 8km west of the city centre. On a clear day the view from the lookout is superb. At your feet is Brisbane with the river winding through, and beyond is the sweep of Moreton Bay and its islands. If you want to linger, there's a good restaurant open daily for lunch and dinner, as well as morning and afternoon teas, and a cafe serving Devonshire teas, buffet-style lunches and sandwiches, filled croissants, cakes and coffee.

There are some good walks around Mt Coot-tha and its foothills, like the one north from the lookout (it starts below the restaurant) to JC Slaughter Falls. Off the JC Slaughter Falls track is also an **Aboriginal Art Trail**, a 1.5km walking trail which takes you past eight art sites with work by local

BRISBANE

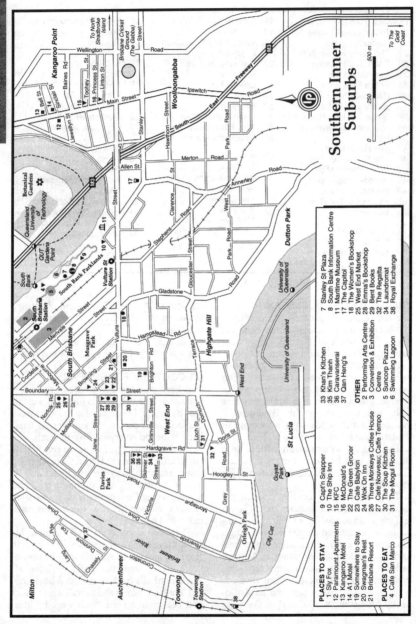

Southern Inner Suburbs

0   250   500 m

PLACES TO STAY
1 Sly Fox
12 Paramount Apartments
13 Kangaroo Motel
14 A1 Motel
19 Somewhere to Stay
20 Swagman's Rest
21 Brisbane Resort

PLACES TO EAT
4 Cafe San Marco

9 Capt'n Snapper
10 The Ship Inn
15 KFC
16 McDonald's
22 The Green Grocer
23 Cafe Babylon
24 Wok On Inn
26 Three Monkeys Coffee House
27 Cafe Nouveau; Caffe Tempo
30 The Soup Kitchen
31 The Mogul Room

33 Khan's Kitchen
35 Kim Thanh
36 Caravanserai
37 Qan Heng's

OTHER
2 Performing Arts Centre
3 Convention & Exhibition
  Centre
5 Suncorp Piazza
6 Swimming Lagoon

7 Stanley St Plaza
8 South Bank Information Centre
11 Maritime Museum
17 The Capitol
18 The Women's Bookshop
25 West End Market
28 Emma's Bookshop
29 Bent Books
32 The Regatta
34 Laundromat
38 Royal Exchange

Aboriginal artists, including tree carvings, rock paintings and a dance pit.

The very beautiful **Mt Coot-tha Botanic Gardens** at the foot of the mountain cover 52 hectares and include over 20,000 species of plants, an enclosed tropical dome, an arid zone, rainforests and a Japanese garden, plus a library and a teahouse. It is open daily from 8.30 am to 5.30 pm. There are free guided walks through the gardens at 11 am and 1 pm daily except Sunday.

Also within the gardens is the **Sir Thomas Brisbane Planetarium** (also known as the Cosmic Skydome), the largest planetarium in Australia. There are 45-minute shows at 3.30 and 7.30 pm Wednesday to Friday; 1.30, 3.30 and 7.30 pm on Saturday; and 1.30 and 3.30 pm on Sunday. Admission is $8 ($4.50 children).

To get to the botanic gardens take bus No 37A ($2) which departs at 13 minutes past each hour from Adelaide St opposite King George Square. The ride takes about 15 minutes and the bus drops you off in the car park. The lookout is a strenuous 3km walk from the botanic gardens – turn left out of the car park and start climbing. There is a bus directly to the lookout, No 10C from Adelaide St, but it departs only twice a day – at 8.50 am and 2.10 pm.

WILDLIFE SANCTUARIES
Alma Park Zoo
Alma Park Zoo at Kallangur, 28km north of the city centre off the Bruce Hwy, is set in eight hectares of subtropical gardens, with palm trees, ferns and native flora, and naturalistic enclosures. It has a large collection of Australian native birds and mammals, including koalas, kangaroos, emus and dingoes, and exotic wildlife including Malaysian sun bears, camels, leopards and lots of cute South American monkeys. You can touch and feed many of the animals – feeding times are all between 11.30 am and 3 pm.

There's a cafe, or if you want to cater for yourself there are good picnic areas with barbecues. The zoo is open daily from 9 am to 5 pm, with last entries at 4 pm; admission costs $15 ($8 children).

A special zoo train runs every day on the Caboolture line, departing from the Transit Centre at 9 am, and passing through Central Station a few minutes later. If you get off at Dakabin (a 50 minute ride from Central Brisbane) the zoo's courtesy bus will meet you.

Lone Pine Koala Sanctuary
Just a 35-minute, $2.60 bus ride south from the city centre, the Lone Pine Koala Sanctuary is an easy half-day trip. The sanctuary is set in attractive parklands beside the river (you can get there by boat) and is home to a wide variety of Australian wildlife, including kangaroos, possums, wombats, emus and lyrebirds. The star attractions though are the 130 or so koalas. They're undeniably cute and most visitors readily cough up the $8 to have their picture taken hugging one. Hand-feeding the tame kangaroos is cheaper – 20c for a bag of pellets. You can bring your own food and picnic among the marsupials in their large, paddock-like enclosure. Talks are given on the animals at set times throughout the day.

Lone Pine is open from 8 am to 5 pm daily and entry costs $12.50 ($6.50 children, $28 family). A VIP or YHA card gets you in for $9. Cityxpress bus No 581 leaves at 35 minutes past the hour from the Koala platform at the Queen St Mall bus station (see the Getting There & Away section). Alternatively, the MV *Mirimar* (π 3221 0300) cruises up the Brisbane River to the sanctuary, costing $15 return ($8 children), not including admission. It departs daily at 10 am from North Quay, next to Victoria Bridge, at the end of the Queen St Mall.

ACTIVITIES
Cycling
See the Brisbane Getting Around section later in this chapter.

Galleries
Beside the QAG (see the earlier section on the Queensland Cultural Centre) Brisbane has a number of smaller art galleries and exhibition spaces, many of which are in the

Valley and New Farm. Seventeen galleries in this area are linked by the No 555 hail and ride bus; buy an off-peak saver for $4 and you can jump on and off wherever you like. The galleries and route are described in a brochure entitled *The Art Circuit*, available from the Queen St Mall information kiosk or the galleries themselves. You can pick up the No 555 from the stop opposite Fire-Works aboriginal gallery at 678 Ann St.

Golf
The most central public course is the Victoria Park Golf Course (☎ 3854 1406) on Herston Rd in Herston, immediately north of Spring Hill; 18 holes costs $15 during the week and $18 on weekends, and club hire is another $16.

Other courses include the St Lucia Golf Links (☎ 3403 2556), about 8km south of the city centre, and the Indooroopilly Golf Club (☎ 3870 2556), which has two courses, one for members and one open to the public every day except Saturday.

Horse Riding
There are a few horse riding schools on the outskirts of Brisbane, including Silverado (☎ 3890 2280), about 10km east of the city in Hemmant, and the Samford Valley Riding Centre (☎ 3289 1046) in Samford about 14km north-west of the city. Both charge around $15 an hour for trail rides.

In-Line Skating
Skatebiz (☎ 3220 0157), 101 Albert St, hires out in-line skates and the necessary protective equipment for $10 for two hours. Some of the best skating areas are the City Botanic Gardens nearby, and the bike paths which follow the Brisbane River.

Kayaking
Kayak Escapes (☎ 13 1801) runs kayaking trips up the Upper Brisbane River. Its one-day discovery trip is a 22km paddle that departs from the Transit Centre every Thursday and costs $75 per person; another possibility is a two-day expedition, with camping gear and meals supplied, which

leaves from the Transit Centre every Tuesday ($175 per person) and Saturday ($225 per person).

Jane Clarkson's Outdoor Adventures (☎ 0411 554 079) also does day trips on the Brisbane River for $65, all gear and pick-ups included.

Rockclimbing
The Cliffs on the south banks of the Brisbane River at Kangaroo Point is a decent rockclimbing venue that is floodlit until midnight or later. Several operators offer climbing and abseiling instruction here, including Jane Clarkson's Outdoor Adventures (☎ 0411 554 079). For beginners, there are Saturday morning abseiling sessions (three to four hours; $30) and introductory rockclimbing on Wednesday nights ($10 per person). Jane also organises abseiling and climbing trips out of Brisbane.

The precipitous cliffs near the Story Bridge are a popular site for rockclimbing.

Swimming

Aside from the artificial lagoon at the South Bank Parklands, Brisbane has plenty of more conventional pools. The Valley Pool on the corner of Wickham and East Sts in Fortitude Valley is heated and open all year round.

The Spring Hill Baths in Torrington St, Spring Hill, are among the oldest in the southern hemisphere. The pool is surrounded by colourful, painted, old-style changing cubicles and is open daily.

The Centenary Pool (☎ 3831 2665) on Gregory Terrace in Spring Hill has an Olympic-sized pool, a kid's pool and a diving pool with a high tower, and is also open daily.

Tennis

Tennis Queensland (☎ 3369 5288) at 315 Milton Rd, Milton, about 2km west of the city centre, has some of the closest courts to the city. It has 25 day and night courts costing from $9 to $14 an hour.

Walking

The city council runs a Walking for Pleasure program in which heritage, cultural and environmental walks around the city and environs are led every day of the week except Friday. Pick up the WFP booklet from the Council Services office at City Plaza behind City Hall or call ☎ 3403 4521 for more information.

At the time of going to press the council was also scheduled to release a *Brisbane Walking Atlas* with maps, descriptions and illustrations of 45 walks around the city. Look in local bookshops or call ☎ 3403 6199 to check on availability.

Also worth looking out for is *Family Walks In Brisbane* by Julia Thorn which has details of 20 walks. More than half the walks described follow the Brisbane River or are near to it. You can pick up this publication at World Wide Maps & Guides at 187 George St.

For information about bushwalking near Brisbane contact the Brisbane Bushwalkers Club ☎ 3856 4050.

ORGANISED TOURS

There are all sorts of organised tours of Brisbane and the surrounding areas on offer – ask at any of the information centres for brochures and details.

City Tours

The open-sided City Sights trambus shuttles around 18 of the city's major landmarks, departing every 40 minutes between 9 am and 4.20 pm from Post Office Square in Queen St. One-day tickets that allow you to get off and on whenever and wherever you want cost $15 ($10 children). The tickets also allow unlimited use of other city bus and ferry services. They can be bought on the bus, at the City Hall information desk or at the tourist information kiosk in the Queen St Mall.

Brewery Tours

Every Monday to Wednesday at 11 am, and 1.30, 4.30 and 7 pm there are guided tours of the Castlemaine XXXX brewery (☎ 3361 7597) on Milton Rd. Most hostels organise trips or you can go along on your own, but you must book. The brewery is a 20-minute walk west from the Transit Centre. The tour lasts about an hour and costs $5 which includes four 'sample' beers.

The Carlton Brewhouse (☎ 3826 5858), brewers of Foster's and VB among others, also conducts tours of its premises south of the city centre. A bus departs the Transit Centre at 9.15 and 11.15 am and 1.15 pm daily; the cost is $10 including beer, lunch and transfers.

River Cruises

The *Kookaburra Queen* and *Kookaburra Queen II* (☎ 3221 1300) are restored wooden paddle-steamers that make 1½-hour cruises of the Brisbane River departing daily at 10 am and 12.45 pm ($20), with an additional Sunday afternoon cruise at 3.30 pm ($20). There's also a 2½-hour daily dinner cruise at 7.30 pm (Sunday at 6.30 pm) costing $40 with buffet. The cruises depart from Eagle St Pier.

Every Sunday afternoon the *Brisbane*

Star (☎ 018 190 604) makes a four-hour cruise from the city to the mouth of the Brisbane River and back. It departs at 1 pm from the Edward St Pier and the cost per person is $10.

See also the Brisbane By Cat boxed text.

Hinterland Tours

Run by a former backpacking globetrotter, Rob's Rainforest Tours (☎ 019 496 607) offers several different day trips out of Brisbane taking travellers to the rainforests at Mount Glorious, Kondalilla Falls and the Glass House Mountains, and Lamington National Park. Several readers have written with high praise for the tours. The price per person is $35 which includes morning tea, a barbecue lunch and pick-up and return to your hostel.

Araucaria Ecotours (☎ 5544 1283, ecotoura@eisnet.au), based at Running Creek Rd, 18km east of Rathdowney in the Gold Coast hinterland, offers three-day wilderness tours in the Mt Barney National Park area. The tour picks up in Brisbane every Wednesday morning (usually at South Brisbane station but also at the Transit Centre by arrangement) and calls in at the Daisy Hill Koala Information Centre and the Karawatha Wetlands on the way down to the accommodation at Mt Barney. The tour involves trekking through various forest types with halts to examine flora and fauna, including a creek where a platypus often puts in an appearance. There are also possibilities to swim and snorkel in a creek, and maybe boat too. The accent is firmly on the educational and the tours are led by Ronda Green, a qualified research wildlife ecologist who really knows her stuff. The cost is $160 including accommodation but not meals – there are a couple of evening pizza stops, but mostly you'll be taken to local supermarkets to shops and cooking facilities are provided.

Allstate Scenic Tours (☎ 3285 1777) has day trips from Brisbane to O'Reilly's Guesthouse and Lamington National Park, leaving every day (except Saturday) at 9.30 am. The return fare is $35.

For a day trip to the Gold Coast, the High Roller bus (☎ 3222 4067) to Conrad Jupiters Casino is good value. It leaves from the Transit Centre daily at 9 am and costs $10 return, which includes a $5 meal voucher and a $5 gaming voucher.

SPECIAL EVENTS

Summer

The week before Christmas is celebrated with a Christmas Festival at South Bank Parklands.

As with the rest of the country, Brisbane celebrates Australia Day each 26 January, with the cockroach races at the Story Bridge Hotel in Kangaroo Point being one of the more unusual (and popular) events.

The Chinese New Year celebrations – centred on Chinatown in the Valley – run for five days, starting in early February, and feature fireworks, banquets and a temple dragon.

The cricket season kicks off over summer, and regular interstate and international matches are played at the Brisbane Cricket Ground (The Gabba) in Woolloongabba.

Car enthusiasts flood into the RNA Exhibition Grounds in Fortitude Valley in mid-February for Brisbane's International Motor Show.

Autumn

If you're in Brisbane for St Patrick's Day (17 March) head for one of the Irish pubs listed in the Entertainment section. There's also a parade through the city.

The National Trust runs the Heritage Week Festival for two weeks in mid-April to celebrate Brisbane's architectural heritage. There's also an international comedy festival each April, and the Brisbane Travel Show is held at the Convention & Exhibition Centre on the South Bank.

The Brisbane Marathon and the Brissie to the Bay Bike Tour are held at the end of May. Also in late May, the Paniyiri Festival is a Greek cultural festival with dancing, food and music.

The Brisbane Biennial, an international

music festival held every second year (odd numbers), is an outstanding celebration of the world of music. Kicking off with a fireworks display over the South Bank Parklands, the Biennial lasts for 10 days from late May to early June, featuring everything from classical, opera, military bands, world music, jazz and blues to rock. A food and wine festival is held in conjunction with the Biennial.

Winter
The Winter Racing Carnival stretches from 1 May to 30 June, with major horse-race meetings each weekend at both Doomben and Eagle Farm racetracks, including the Brisbane Cup in mid-May.

Winter is also the football season in Brisbane: see the Spectator Sports section for details of rugby and Aussie Rules matches. A Festival of Winter is held at the South Bank Parklands over two weeks in mid-July. Fortitude Valley holds its own festival, the Valley Fiesta, over a weekend in early to mid-July.

Brisbane's annual agricultural show, the Royal National Exhibition (known as the Ekka) is held at the RNA Exhibition Grounds just north of Spring Hill for a week in early August. The Ekka features agricultural and industrial displays, a carnival, and various ring events.

The Brisbane International Film Festival runs for 12 days every August, with a diverse range of Australian and foreign films. Special features include films from the South Pacific region and by indigenous film makers.

Spring
The arrival of spring is celebrated with a number of festivals. Held over two weeks from late August/early September, the outdoor Brisbane Festival is the city's major festival of the arts; buskers fill the streets and there are concerts and performances every day. Also in early September is the Brisbane Writers' Festival. Held over three days, this brings an international gathering of authors, essayists and poets to Queensland to participate in panels, readings, debates and literary lunches. Livid, an independent rock festival that attracts international bands as well as local talent, takes place over a weekend in October.

WORK
Several of the backpackers' hostels in Brisbane have job boards on which notices of available employment are stuck up, while Red Hot Chilli Packers in New Farm and Palace Backpackers in the city centre both have job clubs which aim to find work for guests. Telemarketing, door to door sales, au pair work, labouring on building sites and table waiting are the most common jobs.

Some hostels employ travellers to drive buses, work on the desk or clean, often in exchange for free accommodation – ask at the place in which you're staying. If you are happy with bar work or waiting on tables the best advice may be to go knocking on doors. The Fortitude Valley/New Farm area is the best place to try because of its high density of drinking and eating venues and relaxed attitude. A lot of places, particularly in the city centre, are averse to taking on backpackers because they consider them unreliable.

The *Courier-Mail* has a daily Situations Vacant listing – Wednesday and Saturday are the best days to look.

PLACES TO STAY
Most of the places listed here are in the inner suburbs, generally within a couple of kilometres of the city centre. The main accommodation clusters are the city centre itself (which mainly has the more expensive options); Spring Hill, immediately north of the city; Petrie Terrace and Paddington, on the west side of the city; Fortitude Valley and New Farm, north-east of the city; and the southern inner suburbs, which include South Brisbane, West End and Highgate Hill.

If you decide to stay longer, there are places advertised under the Share Accommodation and Flats, Houses To Let/Wanted sections in the *Courier-Mail* – Wednesday and Saturday are the best days to look. It's also worth checking the notice boards in the hostels, where travellers often place ads looking for other travellers to share accommodation. If you want to share with students, try the notice boards at the universities. Many places like cafes and bookshops in the inner suburbs also have notice boards advertising rooms to rent. A possible advantage with these notice boards is that you can often get a feel for the people you'll be sharing with by the type of place they advertise in.

Caravan Parks & Camping

The closest park to the city centre is *Newmarket Gardens Caravan Park* (☎ 3356 1458), 4km to the north at 199 Ashgrove Ave, in Ashgrove. Several bus routes connect it with town and there's a railway station nearby. Powered sites for two cost $16, and on-site vans go for $29 for a double or $34 for three people. Otherwise try the following:

Aspley Acres Caravan Park (☎ 3263 2668), 1420 Gympie Rd, Aspley (13km north of the centre); tent sites from $10, on-site vans from $32, cabins at $40
Caravan Village (☎ 3263 4040), 763 Zillmere Rd, Aspley; tent sites from $16, cabins starting at $58 per double
Dress Circle Village (☎ 3341 6133), 10 Holmead Rd, Eight Mile Plain (14km south); tent sites from $10, on-site cabins from $50
Gateway Junction Village (☎ 3341 6333) & *Sheldon Caravan Park* (☎ 3341 6166), both in School Rd, Roachdale (19km south)

Alternatively, Atoa House and Globe Trekkers hostels will allow travellers to camp in their backyards – see the following Hostels section.

Hostels

The Brisbane Visitors Accommodation Service (☎ 3236 2020) on the 3rd level of the Transit Centre is a free booking service which is open on weekdays from 7 am to 6 pm and weekends from 8 am to 5 pm. This place has brochures and information on all the hostels and other budget options, and once you have decided where to stay it will ring the hostel for you and arrange for someone to pick you up.

City Centre There's only one hostel in the city centre, *Palace Backpackers* (☎ 3211 2433 or toll-free ☎ 1800 676 340), but it's probably Brisbane's best. On the corner of Ann and Edward Sts it's as central as you can get and just five minutes walk from the Transit Centre. It occupies four floors of the People's Palace, a former Salvation Army headquarters which has been extensively modernised. Facilities include a huge self-cook kitchen, TV lounges, laundries, a tour desk, a job club and a rooftop sundeck. Downstairs is the city's most popular backpackers' bar, Down Under (see under Entertainment). The only drawback is that the partying has a tendency to overspill into the hostel corridors and nights at the Palace can be far from quiet. Dorm beds cost from $15 (five to seven per room) to $17 (three or four per room), singles without/with air-con cost $22/25, doubles cost $34/38.

Fortitude Valley & New Farm The YHA-associated *Balmoral House* (☎ 3252 1397) at 33 Amelia St in the Valley has good facilities and is close to the cafes, restaurants and nightlife. That said it's a very quiet, private place with little in the way of partying going on. A bed in a three or four-bed dorm costs $13, singles/doubles with shared bathrooms cost $30/32.

The rest of the hostels are out in New Farm, most of them a 10-minute walk from the Valley. The area is very suburban, but it has plenty of eateries and shops (including a 24-hour convenience store), a cinema, and two regular bus services running along Brunswick St into the city centre.

Pete's Palace (☎ 3254 1984), 515 Brunswick St, is a modest-sized, old, three-storey timber house popular with long-termers. It feels very much like a student house. Dorm beds (four to a room) cost from $11 and a very basic double goes for $30.

One block further east, the *Red Hot Chilli Packers* (☎ 3392 0137), 569 Brunswick St, is above the Brunswick Hotel. It's a bit grubby but, again, it's popular with semi-settled travellers and has a job club to help newcomers find work. Dorm beds cost $12 (or $70 per week), doubles are $30 ($180 a week).

A block further, then right into Balfour St, *Globe Trekkers Hostel* (☎ 3358 1251) is a renovated 100-year-old timber house. It's small and tranquil and very friendly. A bed in a five-bunk dorm costs $12 (there's also a women's dorm), twins are $28 and doubles are $30. This place also allows travellers with campervans to park out the back and use the hostel facilities for $5 a night.

The Bowen Terrace (☎ 3254 1575), 365 Bowen Terrace, like the Globe Trekkers is family run and is well maintained, orderly and quiet. Singles cost from $18 to $23, while a large, well-furnished double with fridge and TV goes for $35.

The Homestead (☎ 3358 3538) at 57 Annie St is a large, lively and modern place. It has reasonable facilities, including a TV room, communal kitchen, small pool and games room. It has a free pick-up service from the airport and offers free use of bikes and free trips to Mt Coot-tha lookout. A bed in a six or eight-bed dorm costs $12 while doubles and twins with shared facilities cost $32.

Further down Annie St, at No 95, the long-running *Atoa House Travellers' Hostel* (☎ 3358 4507) occupies three adjacent Queenslander-style houses. It has several TV lounges and living areas, and various types of rooms. Dorm beds cost $14 a night, singles/doubles are $25/32. The hostel has a spacious backyard with plenty of grass and shady trees and if you have your own tent you can camp for $7 a night. However, it's a bit of trek from here up to Brunswick St and the bus stop.

Petrie Terrace & Paddington Petrie Terrace isn't the most exciting of areas, but it is close to the Transit Centre, and neighbouring Caxton St has plenty of good cafes, restaurants and bars.

There are three adjacent hostels on Upper Roma St, the first of which is the pink-painted *City Backpackers' Hostel* (☎ 3211 3221), at No 380, a newish and fairly charmless two-storey, 76-bed hostel. A bed in a four to six-bunk dorm costs $13, twins and doubles cost $32. The *Roma St Hostel*, right next door, is not recommended.

A little further along at 392 Upper Roma St is the *Brisbane City YHA* (☎ 3236 1004) with excellent facilities including a good cafe, a tour booking desk and provision for the disabled. The cost for non-YHA members is $19 per person in a four to six-bed dorm (no mixed dorms) or $42 for a twin room. There are also twins, doubles and triples with air-con and en suite for a little more.

One block south of Upper Roma is *Yellow Submarine Backpackers* (☎ 3211 3424), 66 Quay St, which occupies a brightly painted – yellow, naturally – old house. It's very homely and friendly with a pool, small garden terraces and barbecue grills. They'll also help you find work here. Dorms (three or six beds to a room) cost $13 per night, twins and singles $30.

Banana Benders Backpackers (☎ 3367 1157) on the corner of Petrie Terrace and Jessie St is painted bright yellow and blue on the outside, so you can't miss it. It's a small place with the usual facilities and it has good views over to the west. The dorms are mostly four-share and cost $14 a night; doubles are $32. The only hassle here is that Petrie Terrace can get noisy during peak hours.

Down the side street past Banana Benders is the small *Aussie Way Backpackers* (☎ 3369 0711) at 34 Cricket St. It's a recently renovated, beautiful two-storey timber house with a front balcony. This place is very clean and quiet, although the kitchen is quite small and can get crowded at meal times. A bed in one of the three to five-bunk dorms costs $14 a night; there are also two single rooms at $27 and one double at $32.

South Brisbane, East Brisbane & West End

The *Sly Fox* (☎ 3844 0022) on the corner of Melbourne and Hope Sts, South Brisbane, occupies the top three storeys of an old pub. The location is good – it's a short walk to the South Bank Parklands and the city – but the place is shabby, the kitchen is tiny and the pub has live music so it tends to be noisy. Dorm beds cost $11 and $12, twins and doubles $35.

A further 10 minutes walk south of the Sly Fox is the *Brisbane Resort* (☎ 3844 9956) at 110 Vulture St, West End, a purpose-built backpackers' complex. On the plus side, the rooms have a TV, fridge and en suite bathrooms, and there are five kitchens, a games room, a pool, a bar, a cafe serving cheap food and a tour booking desk. However, the place has a very authoritarian air and it's soulless. Dorms cost $12 or $15 depending on the number of beds in the room, while singles go for $30 and doubles $45.

The *Swagman's Rest*, over the road at 145 Vulture St, is run by the same people as the Resort and shares the same reception. It's an older place in a Queenslander house but it has been renovated and guests have access to all the Resort's facilities.

Somewhere to Stay (☎ 3846 2858), 45 Brighton Rd, is 100m south of Vulture Rd and the Resort. It's a huge, rambling, wooden house with a small pool, and a nice tree-shaded deck adjacent to a cheap cafe open for breakfast, lunch and evening meals. Drawbacks are that the place is not very well cared for. Dorm beds cost from $12 to $15, with the newer rooms having a TV, fridge, private bathroom and balcony. Single rooms cost $20 to $25, doubles and twins $30 to $45.

Over in East Brisbane, *Courtney Place Backpackers* (☎ 3891 5166), 50 Geelong St, is a very clean, comfortable and quiet, non-partying place. A bed in an eight-bed dorm costs $14, singles are $25 and good doubles are $30. Although Courtney Place is some way from the centre by road, the Mowbray Park City Cat stop is only three minutes walk away.

Spring Hill The *Kookaburra Inn* (☎/fax 3832 1303), 41 Phillips St (see the Fortitude Valley, New Farm & Kangaroo Point map), is an old Queenslander converted into a backpackers' hostel, with communal bathrooms, kitchens and laundry facilities. It's well located in a quiet, leafy street, not too far out of the city centre and is especially popular with Japanese travellers. There are no dorms; singles/doubles cost $30/40.

Budget Hotels, B&Bs & Guesthouses

Moving up a level from the backpackers' hostels, there is a wide variety of budget options around the city centre which variously advertise themselves as B&Bs, hotels or guesthouses. There are also several apartment hotels which work out to be fairly good value, especially if you're in a group.

Spring Hill On the fringe of the city, Spring Hill has a good range of budget options, including three places in Upper Edward St which are only a 10-minute (uphill) walk from the Transit Centre.

If you can stomach the kewpie dolls and cuteness, *Annie's Shandon Inn* (☎ 3831 8684), 405 Upper Edward St, is a friendly guesthouse with immaculate singles/doubles at $40/50 ($50/60 for rooms with en suites) including a light breakfast and free tea and coffee throughout the day.

The *Yale Inner-City Inn* (☎ 3832 1663), next to Annie's at 413 Upper Edward St, has singles/doubles at $35/45 and a few rooms with private bathrooms at $55. The tariff also includes a light breakfast. Both these places have small car parks at the rear.

The *Dorchester Self-Contained Units* (☎ 3831 2967), 484 Upper Edward St, is a two-storey block of renovated one-bedroom units, each with a kitchenette, air-con, phone and TV. There are also laundry facilities and off-street parking here. The units cost $60/70/80 for singles/doubles/triples.

About 500m further north-east, the *Dahrl Court Apartments* (☎ 3832 3458) at 45 Phillips St (see the Fortitude Valley, New Farm & Kangaroo Point map) has been recommended to LP by several travellers. The one-bedroom apartments have a separate kitchen, a small breakfast room, an en suite with a full-sized bath, phones and TVs – one apartment even has its own piano. There's also a pool and a small gym. The apartments cost $65/75 for singles/doubles and $100 for four people. There's also a large basement apartment that sleeps groups of up to 12 people at $25 a head.

Over the street to the north is the friendly *Thornbury House B&B* (☎ 3832 5985) at 1 Thornbury St (see the Fortitude Valley, New Farm & Kangaroo Point map). It's a charming, two-storey Queenslander built in 1886 and attractively renovated in heritage style. There are four excellent double rooms for $90 and five smaller, attic-style single rooms for $55. There's also a very pleasant breakfast courtyard.

At 555 Gregory Terrace, opposite the old museum, the *Tourist Guest House* (☎ 3252 4171) is a beautiful little place, recently refurbished with singles/doubles/triples at $35/45/55, with shared bathrooms, or $45/60/70 with en suite. It's some distance from the city (see the Fortitude Valley, New Farm & Kangaroo Point map), but offers free pick-up from the Transit Centre, and the No 7 bus stops nearby.

New Farm On the corner of Brunswick and Moreton Sts, the *Allender Apartments* (☎ 3358 5832) is a two-storey block of old cream-brick flats that have recently been refurbished. The studio units are beautiful, large and sumptuously furnished with a generous king-size bed and offer excellent value at $55 for a standard or $75 for deluxe. It's a little far to walk from here to the centre so you need to be prepared to take buses or, better still, have your own transport.

Paddington Another good B&B is the very attractive *Waverley B&B* (☎ 3369 8973), 5 Latrobe Terrace, about 2km west of the city centre. It's a renovated two-storey Queenslander with a family home upstairs and, at the rear with their own en-

trance, two guest rooms and two excellent guest units with well equipped kitchen. All rooms have en suite bathrooms and access to decks overlooking a garden with mango trees and possums. Singles/doubles are $65/90.

Hotels & Motels – Mid-Range
Most of the hotels in this range cater predominantly for corporate clients and on weekends they usually find themselves with lots of empty beds. You'll find that most offer good weekend deals which can cut the cost of accommodation dramatically.

City Centre One of the best accommodation deals in Brisbane is the *Explorers Inn* (☎ 3211 3488). It's a modern, three-star hotel in an old building at 63 Turbot St on the edge of the city centre and just a few minutes walk from the Transit Centre. The facilities are good (restaurant, bar, laundry, library) and the rooms, though a little tight and cabin-like, are immaculate and well equipped with air-con, fridge, kettle, tea and coffee, and en suite. They are excellent value at just $64 for a double or twin and $84 for a four-person family room.

The *Brisbane City Travelodge* (☎ 3238 2222, fax 3238 2288), right beside the Transit Centre in Roma St, is a four-star hotel with 191 rooms starting from $125, or $105 at the weekend.

The *Parkroyal Brisbane* (☎ 3221 3411), opposite the City Botanic Gardens on the corner of Alice and Albert Sts, is another four-star hotel, with 150 rooms, a pool, spa, gym, parking and two restaurants. Rooms start from $180, and weekend packages start from $115 for room only or $150 with breakfast included.

The *Bellevue Hotel*, 103 George St, (☎ 3221 6044) has 100 rooms, a pool, spa, restaurant and underground parking. The rooms are smallish but have been pleasantly refurbished; they start at $128 for a standard room and $180 for a suite. Weekend deals are good value.

Lennon's Hotel (☎ 3222 3222), in the heart of the city at 66 Queen St, is a four-star joint and part of the nationwide Country Comfort hotel chain. The 150 rooms have recently been refurbished, and facilities include several bars and restaurants, pool, spa and sauna, and undercover parking. Standard rooms cost $149 a night Monday to Thursday, dropping to $110 at weekends.

Spring Hill   There are plenty of motels just north of the centre. They vary greatly in quality but as a rule you get what you pay for. Out on the edge of Spring Hill at 397 Gregory Terrace, the four-star *Gregory Terrace Motor Inn* (☎ 3832 1769) overlooks Victoria Park and is just across from the Centenary Pool. Motel units cost $88 a double, and there are a couple of two-bedroom apartments that sleep up to eight people and cost $120 for two plus $10 for each extra person.

There's a string of motels along busy Wickham Terrace, most of which overlook Albert Park or Wickham Park. Closest to the city is the very attractive *Astor Motel* (☎ 3831 9522), near the junction with Upper Edward St. It charges $89/95 for comfortable singles/doubles; deluxe rooms and suites are a little more. A few minutes walk west at 333 Wickham Terrace, the *Soho Club Motel* (☎ 3831 7722) charges $49/58 for far more basic singles/doubles.

The *Gazebo Hotel* (☎ 3831 6177), 345 Wickham Terrace, offers various packages including buffet breakfasts and chilled champagne upon arrival, while the *Albert Park Inn Hotel* (☎ 3831 3111, fax 3832 1290), overlooking Albert Park from 551 Wickham Terrace, has extremely comfortable and well furnished rooms. Both hotels offer basic tariffs of $95 for a standard double room.

The *Metropolitan Motor Inn* (☎ 3831 6000) at 106 Leichhardt St is a well-run, modern motel with units from $89, and a piano bar and restaurant downstairs.

New Farm   The *South Pacific Motel* (☎ 3358 2366), on the corner of Bowen Terrace and Langshaw St, has good self-

contained motel units at $59/66 for singles/doubles. Each unit can accommodate a group of four for $80.

Kangaroo Point   North Kangaroo Point (see the Fortitude Valley, New Farm & Kangaroo Point map) is a nice place to be; it's quiet and leafy and there are frequent ferries that take just five minutes to shuttle across to the city centre. South Kangaroo Point (see the Southern Inner Suburbs map) is awful – its most distinctive features are a roaring six-lane highway and a scattering of half-built high-rises.

In north Kangaroo Point, *Ryan's On The River* (☎ 3391 1011) at 269 Main St is close to the landing stage for the city ferry. All rooms have some sort of river view and most go for $99; those directly facing the river are $119. *Il Mondo* (☎ 3392 0111), 25 Rotherham St, is in a quirky, postmodern building with a very attractive, semi-open-air cafe/restaurant on the ground floor. It has no river views but is still only a few minutes walk from the river ferries. Singles range from $59 to $70 and doubles are from $59 to $79.

In south Kangaroo Point there's a cluster of cheaper options, all within 1km of each other on Main St and all pretty similar (see the Southern Inner Suburbs map). The *Kangaroo Motel* (☎ 3391 1145), 624 Main St, has singles/doubles at $48/53, while the *Paramount Apartments* (☎ 3393 1444), 649 Main St, and the *A1 Motel* (☎ 3391 6222), at No 646, both charge $60 for self-contained units.

Hotels – Top End
Brisbane has only a handful of five-star hotels, and they generally quote prices of over $200 a night for rooms. In practice, you'll find these prices are fairly negotiable – you can often get better package deals through travel agents which might combine airfares with accommodation. Like the mid-range hotels, most of the five-stars offer good weekend deals. These vary from time to time, so ring around to see who's offering what.

The *Beaufort Heritage Hotel* (☎ 3221 1999), on the corner of Edward and Margaret Sts in the city centre, successfully manages to combine a feeling of understated luxury with excellent facilities. Among these are a pool, spa and sauna, gymnasium, several bars and good eateries, including one of the city's best Japanese restaurants. Rooms overlook the Brisbane River and start from $185; suites range from $290 to $1500.

The luxurious, 21-storey *Sheraton Brisbane* (☎ 3835 3535), 249 Turbot St, dominates the north side of town. There are 420 rooms and a standard double costs $333.

The *Brisbane Hilton* (☎ 3234 2000), in the heart of the city at 190 Elizabeth St, has standard rooms from $215/245 for singles/doubles. The Hilton also has a good range of weekend packages, including a deluxe double and buffet breakfast for $129 per night.

The classiest hotel in town is the *Conrad International* (☎ 3306 8888), on the corner of George and Charlotte Sts. It is part of the Conrad Treasury Casino complex and housed in one of Brisbane's grandest buildings, the beautifully restored former Land Administration Building. The hotel has 96 rooms and suites, no two of which are the same. Standard room rates are from $280 to $400 a night, with suites from $675 to $975 a night. However, at the time of our research the hotel was offering special $80 'leisure packages'.

PLACES TO EAT

The local restaurant and cafe scene has blossomed in recent years and there's no shortage of good eateries in the city and surrounding areas. This was confirmed in 1997 when the Brisbane restaurant *E'cco* received the best Australian restaurant award.

Chefs and cooks have ready access to a wealth of wonderful local produce, such as beef and lamb from the state's rich pastoral areas, tropical fruits from north Queensland, stone fruits and fresh vegetables from the state's cooler regions, and sensational

seafood from the abundant waters around Queensland – wonderful fish like barramundi and coral trout, prawns direct from the Gulf of Carpentaria, and delicacies like mud crabs and Moreton Bay bugs from the mangrove-lined bays and estuaries.

Most of Brisbane's restaurants and cafes are either licensed to sell alcohol on the premises or BYO (meaning you can 'Bring Your Own' booze). Some places have both. Note that most BYO restaurants charge a small fee for corkage.

There are some great areas where you can wander and check out a whole lot of different places before deciding where to eat – places like the Riverside Centre and Eagle St Pier on the riverfront north of the city; Chinatown and around Brunswick St in the Valley; the South Bank Parklands; Caxton St, Given and Latrobe Terraces in Paddington; and Boundary St and Hardgrave Rd in West End.

Brisbane's perfect winter climate makes a significant contribution to the pleasures of eating out and many places take advantage of the weather with open-air courtyards, or tables out on the street.

Self-Catering

If you're self-catering, there's a good produce market inside *McWhirter's* on the corner of Brunswick and Wickham Sts in the Valley. It has fruit and vegetable, seafood, poultry and meat sections. There's also a small enclosed market in West End, just north of the junction of Boundary and Melbourne Sts.

Cafes & Budget Dining

City Centre For breakfast, the best deal for the hungry is at *Pané e Vino* on the corner of Albert and Charlotte Sts. The breakfast special is an enormous plate of sausage, bacon, mushrooms, toast and two eggs (easily enough for two) plus coffee and juice for $7.50. Otherwise, there's the *Palace Cafe* on Ann St which offers a variety of breakfasts for $5 and under.

There's an abundance of cheap lunchtime eateries in the city centre catering for the hordes of office workers and shoppers. Probably the best variety and value is offered in the food courts found in the shopping malls – try *Eatz* in the basement of the Broadway Centre and *The Eatery* in the basement of the Myer Centre, both off the Queen St Mall.

Another office favourite, the *Hungry Heart Bistro* has a variety of pastas, rice casseroles, noodles and the like served in generous portions for under \$5. It's open – weekdays only – from 7 am to 4 pm and is at 102-104 Edward St opposite the Metro cinema.

For a big Oriental-style feed, the *Mekong Chinese Restaurant* on Adelaide St just north of Edward St, does an all-you-can-eat lunch and dinner for \$6.90, while the Hare Krishna-run *Govinda's*, upstairs at 99 Elizabeth St, offers all-you-can-eat vegetarian meals for \$5. It's open Monday to Saturday for lunch and Friday and Sunday for dinner.

The *Down Under Bar & Grill*, under the Palace Backpackers (on the corner of Edward and Ann Sts), also has cheap lunches and evening meals served from 6 pm onwards – see the Entertainment section.

Fortitude Valley Of the many Asian joints around, an excellent budget option is the *Universal Noodle Restaurant* at 145 Wickham St. It's a cheap 'n' cheerful cafeteria-style eatery with a huge range of dishes in the \$5.50 to \$6.80 range; it's open daily from 11 am until late.

There's a cluster of eateries at the east end of the Brunswick St Mall, most of which have pavement seating. Of these *Mellino's*, at No 330, a casual cafe that's open 24 hours a day, is the most reasonably priced – you can get a cooked breakfast for \$4, pastas for \$9 and a pizza for two for under \$10.

The Valley's best breakfast deal is the *California* on the corner of Brunswick and McLachlan Sts, a cafe that opened in 1951 and has the appearance of having maintained many of the original fittings. The breakfasts are good and huge – order one to share.

New Farm There are few really cheap places to eat in New Farm, it's way too fashionable to accommodate anything that might be termed budget. If you stick to salads and light snacks though, there are a few places where you can lunch for under \$10. *New Farm Deli & Cafe* at the junction of Merthyr Rd and Brunswick St is said to do the best Mediterranean salads in town, while the *Continental Cafe* just off Brunswick St at 21 Barker St is a friendly little gem of a place, very popular with locals. Pastas and risottos are around \$10, gourmet pizzas are \$6 to \$9, and open sandwiches are \$5.50.

In New Farm Park the *New Farm Kiosk* is a little timber teahouse which is open daily from 10 am to 4 pm (5 pm on weekends). It serves affordable breakfasts, sandwiches and salads, Devonshire teas, cakes and gourmet burgers. It's a very pleasant spot, with outdoor tables overlooking a croquet lawn on one side and a rose garden on the other.

Petrie Terrace & Paddington Probably the best place for a decent, reasonably priced meal round here is the *City YHA hostel cafe* at the Brisbane City YHA. You don't have to be staying at the hostel to eat there. Alternatively, the *Paddo Tavern* on Given Terrace, about 1km west of Petrie Terrace, does \$1.95 lunches during the week.

The *Irish Connection*, at 28 Caxton St, is a bar/restaurant with a good but fairly limited menu. Soups start at \$4, while the Guinness and beef pie at \$10 comes in a serving sufficient for two people. It's open for lunch and dinner. The *Caxton Hotel* at 38 Caxton St also does excellent lunches, such as focaccias, salads, pasta, kebabs, burgers and a variety of pizzas, all reasonably priced. On our visit we had a great veal pie for \$6.50.

South Bank On the southern edge of the parklands, *The Ship Inn* is an original pub dating back to the time, not too long ago, when the South Bank was a busy riverside industrial zone. The pub has since been done up and now does a good trade in reasonably priced bistro meals like fettuccine carbonara ($7), ploughman's platters ($8) and T-bone steaks ($9.90).

The other good South Bank eatery is the simple *Riverfront Cafe* at the State Library (see the Central Brisbane map). It has great rolls and sandwiches, coffee and snacks, and the tables in the outdoor courtyard overlook the river.

West End Like the Valley, West End has a fairly cosmopolitan range of cafes and restaurants, including quite a few budget places.

Three Monkeys Coffee House, at 58 Mollison St, just west of the roundabout, is a relaxed place with seductive pseudo-Moroccan decor, good coffee and cakes, and a wide range of food in the $6 to $10 range. It is open daily from 10.30 am until midnight.

South on Boundary St are at least half a dozen trendy cafes, all of which do food of some sort. They include *Caffe Tempo* at No 181, a hip little street front eatery; *Cafe Nouveau*, two doors south at No 185, an attractive Italian-style place with an outrageously pretentious menu featuring items such as 'Ming Dynasty fillet of pork' and 'Rebirth of Venus salad'; and, across the road at No 142, *Cafe Babylon* which is very New Age, with ethnic decor, astrology evenings and tarot readers. Its notice board is the place to consult should you find yourself in need of a psychic or some brushing up on your African dance techniques. One door up, *The Green Grocer* is a good healthfood shop with a wide range of organic fruit and vegies, juices, wheat and gluten-free breads etc.

For something more down-to-earth, *Qan Heng's* at 151 Boundary St offers good Chinese and Vietnamese meals from $5.50 to $9, and has an all-you-can-eat lunch for $6.50. The *Wok On Inn* at No 94 is a good noodle bar at which you choose the noodle type, cooking style (Chinese, Malay or Thai) and the ingredients. Servings are large

and cost from $7.50 to $10.50. It's open from 11.30 am to 2 pm and again from 5.30 pm until late.

Over on Hardgrave Rd, the small *Khan's Kitchen* serves cheap traditional Pakistani dishes. The most expensive dish here is $9 and there's much on the menu that's cheaper. *Kim Thanh*, at No 93, is a large and noisy Chinese and Vietnamese BYO with main courses from $7 to $9 and a good-value Vietnamese banquet menu.

Restaurants
City Centre There are surprisingly few restaurants in the city as it tends to empty out at night with the homeward migration of office and shop workers.

Gilhooley's, the Irish pub on Albert St, serves very good basic fare like stews, and beef and Guinness pie for around $8, plus other more pricey dishes like steaks for about $16. *Zane's Caffe & Pasta Bar*, underneath the Metro cinema on Edward St, has artful pasta creations in the $9 to $12 range; it's open from noon to 9 pm Tuesday and Wednesday and until 11 pm Thursday and Friday.

The city's premier dining spot is the Eagle St Pier complex and adjacent Riverside Centre. Both are home to several up-market, credit-card crimping establishments of the kind best visited when somebody else is footing the bill. The two that are constantly talked about and always seem busy are *Il Centro*, an impressive Italian joint, and *Pier Nine*, a sophisticated oyster bar and seafood restaurant – see the boxed text entitled The Critics Recommend ...

Fortitude Valley The Valley is one of the best eating areas to explore, especially on Friday evening and Saturday when it's bustling with people wandering the streets, eating at outdoor tables and spilling out of the various pubs and bars.

Duncan St, between Ann and Wickham Sts, is Brisbane's Chinatown and home to a large number of Asian restaurants. The *Enjoy Inn* on the corner of Wickham and Duncan Sts is widely regarded as serving

---

The Critics Recommend ...

It's just not possible to visit every restaurant in town, especially those at the top end of the scale. To fill the gap, we took advice from a variety of Brisbane critics and foodies to come up with the following list of the city's top places to dine. Bookings are advised at all of the following.

The place that absolutely everybody is talking about is *E'cco* (☎ 3831 8344) at 100 Boundary St (at the corner with Adelaide St at the north end of the CBD). As well as being judged Australia's best restaurant in 1997, it was also the winner of the 1997 *Courier-Mail* best restaurant award. What the judges said: 'Brilliant, up-to-the-minute, laid back Queensland version of the traditional bistro.' You'll have to take their words for it as, with a three-week waiting list for a table, we couldn't get in. Prices are supposed to be reasonable, with mains starting at $18.50.

Two more names that constantly crop up in people's must-eat-at lists are *Pier Nine* (☎ 3229 2194) and *Il Centro* (☎ 3221 6090), both on the ground level of the Eagle St Pier complex with great views over the river. Pier Nine is a stylish and sophisticated oyster bar and seafood restaurant with a hip, modern ambience. Dishes range from $22 to $30 for main courses. Il Centro is probably Brisbane's best and most impressive Italian restaurant. The stylish dining area is set around a large open kitchen, with a covered courtyard at the front. Imaginative pastas are in the $20 to $24 range and there is an interesting variety of alternatives priced from $22 upwards.

Michael's (☎ 3832 5522) at the Riverside Centre, 100m north of the Eagle St Pier, claims to be Brisbane's most awarded restaurant. It specialises in classical cuisine with an emphasis on seafood and game. Main courses here are in the $22 to $35 range. Michael's opens for weekday lunches, and dinner from Monday to Saturday.

Other highly regarded places include *Indochine* (☎ 3229 4033), on the corner of Elizabeth and Creek Sts in the CBD, *Romeo's* (☎ 3367 0955), at 216 Petrie Tce, and *The Grape Wine & Food Bar* at the Brunswick Hotel on Brunswick St, New Farm. All three were runners-up in 1997's *Courier-Mail* best restaurant award.

---

the best Cantonese food in town. During the week it's a little quiet and formal but at weekends it gets really lively. Main courses are in the $8 to $16 range, and it's open daily from noon to 3 pm and from 5 pm to midnight.

Over the road at 194 Wickham St, the licensed *Vietnamese Restaurant* is also highly recommended. It's smart but casual, with a menu that offers some interesting variations on standard Asian cuisine. The food is excellent and very reasonably priced (main dishes cost $8 to $12). Consequently the place is busy most evenings.

If you want really good Italian cooking we highly recommend *Lucky's Trattoria*, a BYO at 683 Ann St. The pasta dishes here are fantastic – some of the best we've ever

had, anywhere, Italy included. It gets busy at weekends and you may have to wait for a table; no reservations are taken. Mains start at around $9.

At 360 Brunswick St, the hip and arty *Cafe Europe* BYO is extremely popular. As the name suggests, it has a very European feel, with timber booths topped with butcher's paper inside and a row of tables out on the footpath. The home-made pastas ($10 to $13) are good and other mains hover around the $15 mark.

Dooley's, the big Irish pub on the corner of Brunswick and McLachlan Sts, also has a couple of eating options.

New Farm In the past few years New Farm has become an extremely fashionable place to eat. In particular, the area around the junction of Annie and Brunswick Sts is becoming something of a foodies' mecca. There are several interesting places here, none of which unfortunately we got to try. However, a bit further west at 630 Brunswick St, *Baan Thai* is a great BYO Thai restaurant, with mains between $10 and $16.

Spring Hill Spring Hill has one of Brisbane's best Thai restaurants in the *Oriental Bangkok*, 454 Upper Edward St, which has authentic Thai food made without MSG or preservatives. The chilli factor is toned down, but if you like it hot let them know when you order. Vegetarian dishes are $12.50 and other mains range from $15 to $30. This place is licensed.

Tucked away in narrow Bowen St, off Turbot St on the north edge of the city (see the Fortitude Valley map), *Little Tokyo* is an atmospheric Japanese restaurant – with Japanese cooks – which opens nightly from 5.30 pm to midnight. It is licensed and very reasonably priced, and has good banquet menus at $30 per person. Don't let the brick facade and yellow flashing lights put you off, the interior is a lot more attractive.

South Bank There are about a dozen restaurants and cafes in the South Bank Parklands. However, having something of a captive audience they don't have to try too hard. As a consequence a lot of the food available here is second rate and overpriced.

A popular exception would seem to be *Capt'n Snapper*, a large seafood and steak restaurant that is constantly crowded. The food here is unadventurous but wholesome and the prices are reasonable.

The other good one is the *Cafe San Marco*. It has a great location overlooking the city waterfront and you can sit out on the boardwalk to catch the breeze or dine in a secluded courtyard. The food is adventurous Mediterranean and very good. Prices are $7 to $12 for starters and $10 to $20 for mains. It's open from 9 am to midnight daily.

Petrie Terrace & Paddington There are two main clusters of eating places here: on Caxton St immediately west of the junction with Petrie Terrace, and the other a little over 500m further west, where Caxton Terrace becomes Given Terrace and then Latrobe Terrace.

Sultan's Kitchen (☎ 3368 2194), 163 Given Terrace, is an excellent BYO Indian restaurant with great curries. It's open for lunch and dinner daily (except Saturday lunch), but it's pretty popular so book on weekends. The lunchtime smorgasbord is $12.95 and at dinner mains are around $14.

The *Jakarta Indonesian Restaurant*, 215 Given Terrace, is reasonably priced and has an evocative all-bamboo decor. Rice, noodle and vegetarian dishes are $7 to $12 and seafood and meat dishes cost from $10 to $13. It's open from 6 pm Tuesday to Sunday.

A little further is the very popular *King Tut's Wa Wa Hut* at 283 Given Terrace. It's an outdoor cafe with good salads, pastas, burgers, juices and sandwiches, all in the $4 to $12 price range. Just up from King Tut's, *Le Scoops* has an outdoor crêperie serving up sweet and savoury crêpes and pancakes. It opens for breakfast, lunch and dinner – the Sunday brunch comes highly recommended by a very nice woman at the Queensland tourism office.

Don't be put off by the name – the Moreton Bay bug is a delicious part of any seafood meal.

West End On Hardgrave Rd, 400m west of Boundary St, there's a strip of more than 10 cafes and restaurants next to each other. The northernmost cluster is in the former Rialto theatre and includes the excellent *The Mogul Room*. It has an extensive menu but on weekday lunchtimes go for the smorgasbord: rice, naan, papadums, raita, daal, three curries, pickles and a sweet for $11. The restaurant opens at 11.30 am for lunch and then again at 6 pm for dinner; it's closed Monday.

A few blocks further south at 166 Hardgrave Rd is *The Soup Kitchen,* a trendy eatery fronted by an open-air courtyard. It's a cafe by day and a restaurant by night. It specialises in soups ($6 to $8) and pastas ($9.50 to $13.50), and also has interesting daily specials ($11.50 to $13.50). Around the corner on Dornoch Terrace is *Caravanserai*, a former pawnbroker's shop converted into an attractive Turkish restaurant with an open kitchen in the centre. Main dishes range from $9.50 to $11. The place features belly dancing on Saturday night.

Breakfast Creek On the north side of a bend in the Brisbane River, the famous *Breakfast Creek Hotel*, a great rambling building dating from 1889, is a Brisbane institution. It's long been an ALP and trade union hang-out. In the public bar the beer is still drawn from a wooden keg. The pub's open-air Spanish Garden Steak House is renowned for its steaks and spare ribs, and a huge beef feed will set you back between $12 and $18; there are daily specials for about $6. It's open daily from noon to 3 pm and from 5 to 9 pm. To get there take bus No 117 from Queen St (between the post office and Edward St) or a City Cat to Bretts Wharf and then walk back along the river for about 1km.

ENTERTAINMENT

The *Courier-Mail* has daily arts and entertainment listings and a comprehensive What's On In Town section each Thursday. Many of the free entertainment papers – see

---

Late-Night Eating

People tend to turn in early in Brisbane and getting something to eat after about 10 pm is not easy. Even the fast food joints have mostly shut up shop. The city centre exceptions are the *McDonald's* outlets on George St, where it meets Adelaide St, and at the corner of Albert and Elizabeth Sts; both operate until midnight.

For alcohol-countering coffee, *Jimmy's on the Mall* on the Queen St Mall is open 24 hours. The sandwiches there are good, though by midnight you'll be lucky if they have any left. If you do have the post-club munchies, *Cafe 21* at the Treasury Casino is another 24-hour place.

Over in the Valley, where most of the nightlife action takes place, there are a few more options. Both *Mellino's* on the mall and the *Cafe Scene* on the corner of Ann and Brunswick Sts are open for refuelling 24 hours.

---

the Information section earlier in this chapter – also carry listings of gigs, pubs, clubs and theatre.

Ticketworld (☎ 13 1931) is a centralised phone booking agency which handles bookings for many major events, sports and performances. The Queensland Cultural Centre also has its own phone line handling bookings for the Performing Arts Centre theatres; call ☎ 3846 4646 for bookings and ☎ 3846 4444 for inquiries.

Backpacker Bars

The backpacker bar scene in Brisbane is extremely limited – to the extent that there's really only one contender. Luckily it's a good one: the *Down Under*, near the top of Edward St in the city (underneath the Palace Backpackers), is full seven nights a week, with cheap beer, promotions most nights, and loud, loud music. Dancing on the tables is encouraged and things keep going until the early hours.

On Monday nights there's an alternative in the form of the long-running 'Monday Madness' at the *Bomb Shelter*, part of the Story Bridge Hotel in Kangaroo Point. It's a good party night, with the various hostels putting up teams to compete in beer races etc.

Pubs

Since the early 1990s cafes have very much taken over as the places to drink at, especially in the more fashionable parts of town like the Valley and West End. This has resulted in the appearance of some curious hybrid bar-cafes like the Valley's *Bitch* on Brunswick St and *Ric's Cafe-Bar*, 100m down the road in the mall. The latter is well worth visiting for its retro-chic lounge decor. More conventionally, *Dooley's*, also on Brunswick St in the Valley, is a large and excellent Irish pub with a great number of pool tables in the upstairs bar.

Dooley's is just one of a growing number of Irish bars, which includes *Kelly's*, at 521 Stanley St, South Brisbane, and the very popular *Gilhooley's* on Albert St, which is just about the best place for a drink in the city centre. Most of the other city centre pubs tend to have unwelcoming door policies and patrons that tend towards violence when mixed with alcohol; enter some of these places at your own risk.

There are a few pubs away from the centre that, depending on how much of a fan of pub culture you are, may be worth travelling to. A big favourite with us is the *Breakfast Creek Hotel* – see under Restaurants – City Centre in the Places to Eat section. Most head there for steak brunches and dinners but the Spanish Garden is a fine place to sit and drink. The *Royal Exchange* (or 'RE' as it's more commonly known) in Toowong has always been hugely popular with students and office workers alike and if you fancy drinking in loud but benevolent company this is the place. It's 150m south of Toowong station (see the Southern Inner Suburbs map), which is just two stops from the Transit Centre and three from Central Station.

Live Music

Plenty of pubs, bars and clubs feature live music. According to our source at *Time Off* listings magazine the best gig venues in town are *The Zoo* (☎ 3854 1381) at 711 Ann St in the Valley (more than one band, apparently, has rated this place as the best small venue in Australia), *The Chelsea* (☎ 3257 0619) at 25 Warner St, also in the Valley, *The Capitol* (☎ 3255 1091) at 588 Stanley St in South Brisbane, and the *Orient Hotel* at the top of Ann and Queen Sts in the city centre. All of these places host different kinds of music on different nights of the week; check the free press for details.

Jazz & Blues

The *Jazz & Blues Club* on the ground floor of the Travelodge (next to the Transit Centre) is the city's major venue for this kind of music, with good local and international acts on stage Tuesday to Saturday.

The *Brisbane Jazz Club* down by the riverside at 1 Annie St, Kangaroo Point, is where the jazz purists head on Saturday (trad and Dixie) and Sunday (big band) nights. For a Sunday afternoon jazz fix check out the *Story Bridge Hotel* in Kangaroo Point. For nightly R&B, visit *The Healer* at 27 Warner St in the Valley, a small venue in a converted church.

Nightclubs

Brisbane has a lively nightclub scene, especially if you know where to look. Mainstream clubs are mostly based in and around the city centre, while the alternative scene is centred in the Valley.

The city centre nightclubs attract a sort of hair-down-once-a-week office crowd and play a lot of soul and dance music; they include *The Gig* at 22 Market St, *City Rowers* at the Eagle St Pier and *Friday's* at 123 Eagle St. Probably the best of the mainstream clubs is *The Underground* at 61 Petrie Terrace.

Over in the Valley, a great night out is the indie music-driven *Superdeluxe*, upstairs at the Empire on the corner of Brunswick and Ann Sts, which takes place every Friday

Gay & Lesbian Brisbane

The key to Brisbane's gay and lesbian scene is *BrotherSister*, a fortnightly free newspaper that you can pick up at any of the venues listed here, or at Zane's Caffe Bar underneath the Metro cinema on Edward St in the CBD. Another free paper, *Queensland Pride*, appears monthly.

The Gay & Lesbian Welfare Association of Brisbane (GLWA) operates a gayline (☎ 3891 7377) and lesbianline (☎ 3891 7388) seven nights a week from 7 to 10 pm. They can offer information on groups and venues and also counselling. There's also a Gay and Lesbian Health Service (☎ 3844 6806) at 38 Gladstone Rd in Highgate Hill, southern Brisbane; it's open Monday to Thursday from 8 am to 8 pm, Friday from 8 am to 6 pm and Saturday from 9 am to noon.

For gay and lesbian fiction visit Red Books at 350A Brunswick St in the Valley (open daily except Monday). The Women's Bookshop (☎ 3844 6650) at 15 Gladstone Rd in Highgate Hill also has a lot of lesbian fiction and non-fiction, and specialises in books for, by and about women.

Both *BrotherSister* and the GLWA have good Web sites – for the addresses see the Web sites section in the Facts for the Visitor chapter.

Places to Stay There are a couple of good places to stay in Brisbane catering specifically for gay and lesbian travellers. Check also *BrotherSister*, which has an accommodation listing on its back pages.

The *Sportsman's Hotel* (☎ 3831 2892) at 130 Leichhardt St, Spring Hill, has simple pub-style rooms upstairs exclusively for gay men, costing $25/40 for singles/doubles including a continental breakfast.

Edward Lodge (☎ 3254 1078), at 75 Sydney St, New Farm, is an excellent two-storey guesthouse catering exclusively for gays and lesbians. Eight immaculate double rooms each have their own en suite, there's an attractive breakfast courtyard and a spa pool, and the tariff is $65/75 for singles/doubles including breakfast.

Entertainment Brisbane's gay and lesbian scene is centred on Spring Hill and the Valley. The *Sportsman's Hotel* at 130 Leichhardt St, Spring Hill, is one of the busiest gay venues. It's a pub with a different theme or show for each night of the week: gay bingo on Monday; Tuesday is party night; there's a pool competition on Wednesday; the Super Quiz on Thursday; drag shows on Friday and Saturday; and an open-to-all-comers talent quest on Sunday.

Around the corner from the Sportsman's, *Options Nightclub* at 18 Little Edward St is predominantly gay and lesbian but also attracts some straights. There's a cafe and dance room downstairs and a live show every night upstairs, with a $5 cover charge on weekends. It's open until around 5 am.

The *Wickham Hotel* on the corner of Wickham and Alden Sts in the Valley is an attractively renovated Victorian pub with good dance music, drag shows, male dancers and Mardi Gras parties. There are also two restaurants here, and a food and wine bar upstairs.

At 185 Brunswick St in the Valley, *Signal* is a dimly lit club exclusively for gay men. It has various sections including saunas, video and dark rooms, pool tables and bars. It opens until 4 am and there's a cover charge of $5 to $10. Nearby in the basement of 249 Brunswick St, *Terminus* is another gay venue and dance club with drag shows on Friday and Saturday nights.

The Sandpit is an occasional women-only night held at the Melbourne Hotel in West End; for information on dates call ☎ 0411 724 897.

Top: Kodak Beach, South Bank Parklands, Brisbane.
Middle Left: Sculptures in King George Square, Brisbane.
Middle Right: The fountain in King George Square, Brisbane, is a popular lunchtime hangout.
Bottom: A view along Moreton Island's cliffs and beaches.

Top Left: McWhirters Markets, Fortitude Valley, Brisbane.
Top Right: Markets at Southbank Parklands, Brisbane.
Bottom: Although modern and functional, Brisbane's city centre has a picturesque setting along the Brisbane River.

and Saturday night from 9 pm to 5 am. *Monkey Business*, Thursday and Saturday at the Brunswick Hotel in the Valley, is another good one, and *The Tube* at 210 Wickham St in the Valley has some good nights too. Again, check the free press for details.

For something a little different, *Casablanca* on the corner of Petrie Terrace and Caxton St is a Latin American-style bar, restaurant and club that opens Monday to Thursday until 2 am and Friday and Saturday until 5 am. There are several sections, including a dance club featuring lambada and flamenco. There's no cover charge but dress standards are fairly strict.

Cinema

Brisbane has some quaint old cinemas. Monday and/or Tuesday are discounted ticket days with half-price admission at most cinemas. For details of what's showing see the daily *Courier-Mail*.

Central and inner-suburban cinemas include:

The Classic (☎ 3393 1066), on the corner of Stanley and Withington Sts, East Brisbane. Screens art-house and foreign films. All day Tuesday and Wednesday tickets are $6 only.

Dendy Cinema (☎ 3211 3244), 346 George St. An art-house cinema showing first-release and classic movies. Shows a lot of home-grown films.

Greater Union Cinemas (☎ 3211 2345), 183 Albert St and diagonally opposite, on the corner of Elizabeth and Albert Sts. Cheap day Tuesday with all tickets at $6.

Hoyts Myer Centre (☎ 3229 2133). A grubby, unpleasant multiscreen complex in the basement of the Myer Centre.

Hoyts Regent Theatre (☎ 3229 5544), 107 Queen St (on the mall). Worth visiting for the building alone. It screens mainly mainstream first releases.

Metro (☎ 3221 3505), 109 Edward St. Screens art-house movies. On Sunday nights it has two films for $6.

Village Twin (☎ 3358 2021), 701 Brunswick St in New Farm. Screens a combination of art-house and mainstream releases. Tickets here are discounted on Tuesday, Wednesday and Thursday nights.

There are also free open-air movies screened several nights each week in the South Bank Parklands from late October until the end of March.

Theatre

The Performing Arts Centre (☎ 3846 4444) at the Queensland Cultural Centre on the South Bank features concerts, plays, dance performances and film screenings in its three venues.

Brisbane's other main theatre spaces include the Suncorp Theatre (☎ 3221 5177) at 179 Turbot St (performances by the Queensland Ballet and Queensland Theatre companies); the Brisbane Arts Theatre (☎ 3369 2344) at 210 Petrie Terrace (amateur theatre); and La Boite Repertory Theatre (☎ 3369 1622) at 57 Hale St, off Petrie Terrace.

Gambling

The pokies (poker machines) are everywhere in Brisbane's pubs and clubs. The new Treasury Casino also has plenty of pokies in addition to over 100 gaming tables, with blackjack, roulette, craps, two-up and mini baccarat. There are also cafes, bars and restaurants in the complex, including a 24-hour restaurant, as well as a VIP gaming room for those with lots to lose. The casino is open 24 hours a day and has a smart-casual dress code. Shorts, T-shirts or singlets, sandals and work boots aren't allowed. You also have to be over 18 years of age to enter.

Brisbane's two major horse-racing venues are the Doomben and Eagle Farm racecourses, which are adjacent to each other and north-east of the city, two-thirds of the way to the airport.

The main venue for trotting (harness racing) is the Albion Park Raceway, just north of Breakfast Creek.

Spectator Sports

Like the rest of Australia, Brisbane is sports-mad. And as the old saying goes, those who can, play, while those who can't, watch.

Football Rugby league is Queensland's premier winter spectator sport. Local heroes Brisbane Broncos, a Superleague team, play their home games at the ANZ/Queen Elizabeth II Stadium in Upper Mt Gravatt.

Australian Rules football is mainly played in the southern states, but the Brisbane Bears was established in Queensland in the mid-1980s when the former Victorian footy league decided to go national. In 1997 the team merged with the former Melbourne Fitzroy Lions and became the Brisbane Lions. They play their home games at the Brisbane Cricket Ground (universally known as The Gabba) in Woolloongabba, south-east of the city, and attract a smallish but passionate following.

Cricket Each summer you can see interstate Sheffield Shield cricket matches and international Test and one-day cricket matches at The Gabba in Woolloongabba, just south of Kangaroo Point.

Yachting All of the yacht clubs in Moreton Bay have weekend and mid-week races, and numerous major races such as the Brisbane to Gladstone race (every April) depart from the bay – see the Moreton Bay section later in this chapter for details.

Basketball Australia has a National Basketball League, which is based on American pro basketball. It's the fastest growing spectator sport in the country, and the NBL games are of a high standard and draw large crowds. Brisbane's NBL side, the Brisbane Bullets, is based at the Sports & Entertainment Complex in Boondall, about 15km north-east of the city.

SHOPPING
The Queen St Mall is the city's major shopping precinct. It's flanked by arcades and shopping complexes, the biggest of which, the Myer Centre, occupies most of the block bordered by Queen, Elizabeth and Albert Sts.

The Elizabeth Arcade, which runs between Elizabeth and Charlotte Sts, is an alternative shopping arcade with some of the hippest and most interesting shops in town. They include young designer boutiques, music stores and bookshops, craft shops and a body-piercing specialist.

Aboriginal Art
Queensland Aboriginal Creations at 199 Elizabeth St is a retail shop run by the Department of Aboriginal and Torres Strait Islander Affairs. It stocks a good range of art, crafts and souvenirs including woollen jumpers, paintings and prints, socks and ties, didjeridus, boomerangs, jewellery, clapsticks, bullroarers, woomeras and clothing. You might also want to check Fire-Works Aboriginal Gallery at 678 Ann St in the Valley.

Australiana
Arts and crafts, T-shirts, bush gear and the like are sold in dozens of places in the centre. Currans is one of the biggest souvenir outlets in the city, with shops at 66 Queen St, 136 Queen St and on the corner of Adelaide and Edward Sts. Alternatively, The Wilderness Society Shop at 99 Albert St has environmentally relevant and friendly gear including books, clothing, toys, posters, mugs and wind chimes. Profits help protect Australia's wilderness areas.

Aussie Clothing
RM Williams has a shop in the Wintergarden complex off the Queen St Mall. It is one of the best known makers of Aussie gear and stocks an excellent (and expensive) range of boots, oilskins, moleskins, belts, jumpers and flannelette shirts.

Greg Grant Country Clothing at shop 133 in the Myer Centre also stocks a wide range of bush gear, including Akubra hats, Drizabone oilskin coats and RM Williams boots. Hats by the Hundred, a speciality hat shop in the Wintergarden complex, also stocks Akubra hats.

Outdoor Gear
The best area in Brisbane for outdoor gear is along Wickham St in Fortitude Valley,

just south of the intersection with Gipps St. There are four specialist outdoor shops side by side all with different specialities. If you can't find what you're looking for at one of these places, it probably doesn't exist.

There are also some good shops in the city centre. Mountain Designs at 105 Albert St is a specialist outdoor shop with gear for skiers, rockclimbers and bushwalkers. Direct Camping & Outdoors, at 142 Albert St, stocks a wide range of camping, outdoor and backpacking gear. At 33 Adelaide St, Sherry's Disposals is a discount camping and outdoor shop with a reasonably extensive range.

Galleries & Antiques
Fortitude Valley is Brisbane's major centre for contemporary art – see the Activities section earlier in this chapter. Paddington has a small cluster of antique shops along Latrobe Terrace (the continuation of Given Terrace), near where it intersects with Prince St. Inside the Paddington Plaza at 167 Latrobe Terrace is the huge Paddington Antique Centre, a warehouse crammed with antiques and collectibles, bric-a-brac and furniture. There are another half-dozen antique shops in the immediate area.

Duty-Free
Duty-free shops abound in the city centre, the Valley and at the airport. Remember that a duty-free item might not have much duty on it in the first place and could be available cheaper in an ordinary shop, so shop around.

Markets
The popular Crafts Village markets at South Bank have a great range of clothing, crafts, arts, handmade goods and interesting souvenirs. Stalls are set up in the Stanley St Plaza in rows of colourful tents which are erected every weekend. Opening hours for the markets are Friday night from 5 to 10.30 pm (known as the Lantern markets), Saturday from 10 am to 6 pm and Sunday from 9 am to 5 pm.

Every Sunday, the carnival-style River-

side Centre and Eagle St Pier markets have over 150 stalls, including glass blowing, weaving, leather work and children's activities. On Saturday, the Fortitude Valley market, with a diverse collection of crafts, clothes and junk, is held in the Brunswick St Mall.

Popular permanent markets include McWhirter's, on the corner of Brunswick and Wickham Sts in Fortitude Valley, which has art and craft galleries, clothing boutiques, a food court and a produce market; and West End market, at the intersection of Melbourne and Boundary Sts, West End, which is predominantly a produce market.

GETTING THERE & AWAY
Brisbane's Transit Centre on Roma St, about 500m west of the city centre, is the main terminus and booking point for all long-distance buses and trains, as well as the airport bus.

The easiest way to book all domestic flights and bus tickets is to use the Backpackers' Travel Centre (☎ 3221 2225), on the upper floor of the Brisbane Arcade off the Queen St Mall. Debbie has manned the desk for more than 10 years and is well up on the cheapest ways to get from A to B and back again.

Air
Brisbane's main airport, Eagle Farm airport, is about 16km north-east of the city centre. (There are separate international and domestic terminals about 2km apart.) It's a busy international arrival and departure point with frequent flights to Asia, Europe, the Pacific islands, North America, New Zealand and Papua New Guinea.

Qantas has its travel centre (☎ 13 1313 for domestic flights, 13 1211 for international) at 247 Adelaide St in the city. Ansett (☎ 13 1300) has an office on the corner of Queen and George Sts. Both have frequent flights to the southern capitals and to the main Queensland centres.

Standard one-way fares from Brisbane include Sydney ($303), Melbourne ($441), Adelaide ($535) and Perth ($730). Within

Queensland, one-way fares include Townsville ($363), Rockhampton ($278), Mackay ($327), Proserpine ($329), Cairns ($431) and Mt Isa ($438, Ansett only).

The little outback airline Flight West (☎ 13 2392) goes to Roma ($180 one way), Charleville ($241), Blackall ($280), Longreach ($326), Winton and Windorah ($187) and Birdsville ($417).

See the Getting There & Away and the Getting Around chapters earlier in this book for more details on flying to and from Brisbane and around Queensland.

Bus

The main bus terminal is the Transit Centre on Roma St and all the bus companies have booking desks on the 3rd level. If you're shopping around for fare deals see the Backpackers' Travel Centre mentioned at the beginning of this section.

Greyhound Pioneer and McCafferty's both run from Sydney to Brisbane. The coastal run along the Pacific Hwy takes about 17 hours; the inland New England Hwy trip takes a couple of hours less because there's usually less traffic. The usual fare is between $69 and $75 but Premier Pioneer Motor Services (☎ 1300 368 100) often has cheaper deals.

Between Brisbane and Melbourne, the most direct route is the Newell Highway, which takes about 24 hours. Again, Greyhound Pioneer and McCafferty's travel this route daily. The fare is about $108.

To Adelaide, the shortest route (via Dubbo) takes about 31 hours and costs about $148.

North to Cairns, Greyhound Pioneer and McCafferty's run five buses a day. The approximate fares and journey times to places along the coast are as follows:

Destination	Time	Cost
Noosa Heads	2 hours	$14
Hervey Bay	4½ hours	$32-$38
Rockhampton	10½ hours	$67
Mackay	15 hours	$91
Airlie Beach	18 hours	$103
Townsville	20 hours	$119
Cairns	27 hours	$148

McCafferty's and Greyhound Pioneer also run daily services to the Northern Territory; it's a 46-hour trip to Darwin ($246) via Longreach (17 hours, $83) and Mt Isa (24 hours, $112).

Train

Brisbane's main station for long-distance trains is the Transit Centre. For reservations and information, telephone ☎ 13 2232 or call into the Railway Travel Centre at Central Station, on the corner of Ann and Edward Sts in the city.

For details of interstate and intrastate train services to/from Brisbane, see the Getting There & Away and Getting Around chapters.

Car & Motorcycle

There are five major routes into and out of the Brisbane metropolitan area, numbered from M1 to M5.

The major north-south route is the M1, which starts from the Pacific Hwy on the Gold Coast. The Pacific Hwy leads into the South East Freeway and then the Gateway Arterial Rd, which bypasses the city centre to the east and crosses the Brisbane River at the Gateway Bridge (toll payable). There's a turn-off to the Brisbane airport, then the Gateway leads into the Gympie Arterial Rd, which continues north to Pine Rivers. At Pine Rivers, the Bruce Hwy starts – this is the major coastal route from Brisbane to Cairns.

Confused yet? To put all that in simpler terms, if you're passing through Brisbane from south to north or vice versa just follow the M1.

Route M2, the Ipswich Motorway, starts south of the centre at the Gateway Motorway, heading westward to Ipswich and the Darling Downs. Route M3 is an alternative to the M1 city bypass – the South East Freeway takes you into the heart of the city. Route M4, the Logan Motorway, is a tollway which links the Pacific Hwy to the Ipswich Motorway. Route M5 bypasses the city on its west, linking the M2 with the M3.

Car Rental

All of the major companies – Hertz (☎ 3221 6665), Avis (☎ 3221 2900) and Budget (☎ 13 2727) – have offices at the Brisbane airport terminals and throughout the city. Thrifty (☎ 3252 5994), a smaller national operator, also has offices at the airport. Its deals are competitive and well worth checking out.

There are also several local firms which advertise cars from around $30 a day, with free airport pick-ups included. These include Ace Car Rentals (☎ 3252 1088), Ideal (☎ 3260 2307), Shoe String Rentals (☎ 3268 3334) and Roadway Rent-a-Car (☎ 3868 1500).

Other smaller local operators include Can Do Car Rentals (☎ 3832 3338), Car-azy Rentals (☎ 3257 1104), Compass (☎ 3891 2614), Integra (☎ 3252 5752) and National (☎ 3854 1499). Some companies do one-way rentals to Cairns and southern capitals, depending on availability, the season, and the hire period – it's best to ring around and haggle.

GETTING AROUND

Queensland Rail runs Brisbane's Citytrain services, and Brisbane Transport runs local bus and ferry services. For bus, train and ferry transport information, ring the Trans-Info Service on ☎ 13 1230; it operates daily from 6 am to 10 pm. The operators can tell you the shortest, cheapest and easiest way to get to wherever you're going. There's also a train information office at Central Station.

Bus and ferry information is available at the Queen St Mall information point, and in the Queen St bus terminal beneath the Myer Centre.

Fares & Saver Cards

Fares on buses, trains and ferries operate on a zone system. The city centre and most of the inner-city suburbs fall within zone one, which translates to a single fare of $1.40. There are various fare deals available that can cut the cost of public transport. A Day Rover card ($6) allows unlimited travel on bus, ferry and City Cat services for the day. The Off-Peak Saver ($4) allows similar travel but restricts weekday use to between 9 am and 3.30 pm and after 7 pm.

Roverlink tickets ($8) allow unlimited travel on buses, ferries and city trains. There's also an off-peak version which costs $6. There are also weekly and monthly ticket deals.

Saver cards can be bought on public transport or at shops displaying a yellow and white flag.

To/From the Airport

Coachtrans runs the Skytrans (☎ 3236 1000) shuttle bus between the Transit Centre and the airport, with services about every half-hour between 5 am and 8.30 pm. The fare is $6.50. There are other services to cover any departures and arrivals after 9 pm.

A taxi into the centre from either terminal will cost $20 to $25.

Airport to the Gold Coast & Beyond

Coachtrans also operates the Airporter (☎ 5588 8777) direct services from Brisbane airport to the Gold Coast ($29). Services leave the airport daily from 4.40 am, then every 45 minutes until 11.20 pm. The buses will drop you anywhere on the Gold Coast between Sanctuary Cove and Palm Beach.

Baxway Coaches (☎ 3844 0666) has daily buses from Brisbane airport and the Transit Centre to Ballina and Byron Bay, via Coolangatta.

Airport to the Sunshine Coast

Suncoast Pacific (☎ 3236 1901) has a direct service from Brisbane airport to the Sunshine Coast.

Bus

The red City Circle bus No 333 does a clockwise loop round the area along George, Adelaide, Wharf, Eagle, Mary, Albert and Alice Sts every five minutes on weekdays between 8 am and 5.45 pm.

Useful buses from the city centre include Nos 177 and 178 to Fortitude Valley and

New Farm (from the brown stops on Adelaide St between King George Square and Edward St). Bardon bus No 144 to Paddington leaves from the red stops opposite the Transit Centre or from outside the Coles store on Adelaide St.

Buses to Fortitude Valley (Nos 160, 180, 190), Newstead House and Breakfast Creek leave from the yellow stops on Edward St between Adelaide and Queen Sts. Bus No 177 to West End leaves from the brown stop on Edward St, opposite Anzac Square.

Buses run every 10 to 20 minutes Monday to Friday till about 6 pm, and on Saturday mornings. Services are less frequent on weekday evenings, Saturday afternoons and evenings, and Sunday. Bus services stop at 7 pm on Sunday, around midnight on Friday and Saturday and on other days at 11 pm.

In addition to the normal city buses, there are Cityxpress buses which run between the suburbs and the city centre, and Rockets, which are fast peak-hour commuter buses. The bus terminal beneath the Myer Centre is used mainly by Cityxpresses and buses to/from the south of the city.

Train

The fast Citytrain network has seven lines, out to Ipswich, Beenleigh and Cleveland in the south and Pinkenba, Shorncliffe, Caboolture and Ferny Grove in the north. All trains go through Roma St (Transit Centre) and Central Station in the city, and Brunswick St station in Fortitude Valley.

Trains run from around 4.30 am, with the last train to each line leaving Central Station between 11.30 pm and midnight. On Sunday the last trains run at around 10 pm.

The frequency of trains varies; you can expect a train every 10 minutes on weekdays from 7 to 9.30 am and from 3 to 6 pm; once an hour on weekends and after 10 pm during the week; and half-hourly at other times.

Car Parking spaces in the city centre are extremely limited but there are plenty of commercial car parks around. Quite a few places to stay have off-street parking facilities, many of which are mentioned in the Places to Stay section. Drivers need to beware of the two-hour parking limit in the city and inner suburbs – there are no signs, and the parking inspectors are merciless.

See the earlier Getting There & Away section for details of car-rental companies.

Taxi

There are usually plenty of taxis around the city centre, and there are taxi ranks at the Transit Centre and top end of Edward St, by the junction with Adelaide St.

You can also book a taxi by phone. The major taxi companies are Yellow Cabs (☎ 3391 0191), Brisbane Cabs (☎ 3360 0000), Black & White (☎ 3238 1000) and Q Cabs (☎ 3213 1222).

River Transport

Brisbane has an excellent fast and efficient ferry service along and across the Brisbane River in the form of the City Cats. These are large blue catamarans that zip along the river between Queensland University in the south and Bretts Wharf in the west, stopping en route at North Quay (for the Queen St Mall), South Bank, Riverside (for the CBD) and New Farm Park. They run every 20 minutes from 6 am until around 10.30 pm weekdays, and until midnight on Friday and Saturday, and 8.30 pm on Sunday.

The City Cats are wheelchair accessible at University of Queensland, Guyatt Park, North Quay, South Bank and Hawthorne.

In addition to the City Cats, there are three cross-river ferries, the most useful being between Eagle St and Kangaroo Point, and Riverside and Kangaroo Point.

Fares depend on the number of 'sectors' crossed: a short hop across the river is $1.40; a ride of two or three stops will be $2 or $2.60, while you can go from one end of the route to the other for $3. However, buying single tickets means if you step off you'll have to buy a new one. If you're using the Cats for sightseeing get a saver card, which means that for as little as $4 you can hop on and off wherever you like.

For more information on routes see the Brisbane By Cat boxed text.

Bicycle

Brisbane has some excellent bike tracks, particularly around the Brisbane River. Pick up a copy of the city council's *Safe Bikeways* brochure from information centres, which includes good maps of the city's bike routes, or there's also *Brisbane Bicycle Maps*, available from the Council Customer Service Centre at City Plaza behind City Hall.

A good way to spend a day is to ride the riverside bicycle track from the City Botanic Gardens out to the University of Queensland. It's about 7km one way and you can stop off for a drink en route at the riverside Regatta pub in Toowong.

There are several places that hire out bikes. Backpackers Mountain Bike Hire (toll-free ☎ 1800 635 286) charges $16 a day, including free helmet, maps, and delivery and pick-up. Brisbane Bicycle Sales (☎ 3229 2433) at 87 Albert St in the city hires out mountain bikes for $9 an hour or $20 a day. New Farm Mountain Bikes (☎ 3254 0544) at 697 Brunswick St, New Farm, charges $7 an hour, $25 a day or $70 a week.

Bicycles are allowed on city trains, except on weekdays during peak hours (7 to 9 am and 3 to 6.30 pm). Bikes must go into the first carriage of the train. You can also take bikes on City Cats and ferries for free.

Around Brisbane

AUSTRALIAN WOOLSHED

The Australian Woolshed (☎ 3351 5366) is an impressive set-up celebrating the 'outback experience'. Beyond a large souvenir shop specialising in Australiana, the Woolshed is a spacious and attractive park with free picnic and barbecue facilities, a small fauna park with koalas (available for hugging) and kangaroos (up for feeding),

and attractions such as sheep shearing and wool spinning demonstrations. There's also a one-hour 'ram show', starring eight trained rams and several sheepdogs. Shows are held daily at 10 and 11 am and 2 pm; entry costs $12 for adults, $8 for concessions and $5.50 for children.

The Woolshed is at 148 Samford Rd in Ferny Hills, 15km north-west of the centre. If you don't have a car, you can get here by train – it's an 800m walk from Ferny Grove station to the Woolshed. Some of the commercial bus tour operators also have day trips here.

BRISBANE FOREST PARK

The Brisbane Forest Park is a 28,500-hectare natural bushland reserve in the D'Aguilar Range. The park starts on the outskirts of Brisbane and stretches for more than 50km to the north-west. It's a great area for bushwalks, cycling, horse riding, camping and scenic drives.

At the entrance to the park, at 60 Mt Nebo Rd (10km from the city centre) in an area called The Gap, is the Brisbane Forest Park information centre (☎ 3300 4855). This is a good place to find out about the facilities in the park, including walking trails and picnic areas. It's open on weekdays from 8.30 am to 4.30 pm and on weekends from 10 am to 5 pm. The rangers also run regular guided bushwalks and tours – call for details.

Beside the information centre is **Walk-About Creek**, a freshwater study centre where you can see fish, lizards, pythons and turtles at close quarters. It's open daily from 9 am to 4.30 pm (weekends from 10 am); entry costs $3.50 ($2 children, $9 family). Upstairs, there's the excellent open-sided *Walk-About Creek Restaurant* which serves snacks, lunches and dinners.

There are a number of good walking trails throughout the park, including the 6km Morelia Track at the Manorina Bush Camp and the 5km Greene's Falls Track at Maiala National Park. Bushwalkers can also bush camp overnight in the park, although you need a permit to do so. These cost $3.50 per person per night and are available through the information centre. Unfortunately, only one short walking trail starts from the information centre, so bushwalkers will need their own transport to get to the others.

Mt Nebo

Mt Nebo Rd continues into the park from The Gap, winding its way through the mountains. It's an attractive and popular scenic drive with a number of good lookout points signposted along the way. A further 21km on is Mt Nebo, a small hilltop village with a scattered handful of houses. Mt Nebo has some unusual accommodation in the *Railway Carriage* (☎ /fax 3289 8120), a beautifully restored piece of rolling stock in a landscaped garden setting with a bedroom, tiny bathroom and a kitchen. It is good value at $85 a double including breakfast. On the same property is a small self-contained cottage which goes for $80 a night.

Manorina Bush Camp

This campground beside the Mt Nebo Rd, midway between Mt Nebo and Mt Glorious, has a lovely forest setting with water and toilets. Several walking trails start from here. Camping permits cost $5 per site for up to six people, and can be booked through the Brisbane Forest Park information centre.

Mt Glorious

This small and serene mountain village has a great setting atop a heavily forested mountain, with views back down to Brisbane and Moreton Bay. For motorcyclists, the ride from Samford up to Mt Glorious and down the other side to Lake Wivenhoe is rated as one of the top 10 rides in Australia. It isn't quite as much fun in a car, but still rates pretty highly as a scenic drive.

Mt Glorious has a couple of eateries and craft shops. It's quite a popular little place on weekends, although during the week it's still sleepy and laid-back.

About 1km north of the town is the entrance to **Maiala National Park**, which has some very pleasant picnic areas with barbecues and several good walking trails.

About 6km past Mt Glorious you come to **Wivenhoe Outlook**, a spectacular lookout platform with panoramic views down to Lake Wivenhoe. There's also a good picnic area here.

Places to Stay *Mt Glorious Getaways* (☎ 3289 0172), signposted down Browns Rd just past the village, is an attractive bush property with three stylish timber cottages, each with kitchen, bathroom and one bedroom. The cottages sleep up to four people and cost $100 a night ($110 on weekends). There's also a three-bedroom cottage which sleeps up to six.

Getting There & Away

To get to the park from the city, follow Musgrave, Waterworks and Mt Nebo Rds. By public transport, you can take a No 506 express bus from the corner of Albert and Adelaide Sts in the city to The Gap. This service runs every day, and it's about a 700m walk from the bus stop to the info centre and Walk-About Creek.

MORETON BAY

Moreton Bay, at the mouth of the Brisbane River, is reckoned to have some 365 islands. Of these, the two that most people head for are Moreton Island, in particular to participate in the dolphin feeding at the Tangalooma Resort, and North Stradbroke for its great beaches and surfing.

The bayside suburbs are predominantly residential areas and their beaches are mostly shallow and often muddy. On the bay 35km north of the state capital, the **Redcliffe Peninsula** is the site of the first white settlement in Queensland. The Aborigines called the place Humpybong or 'Dead Houses' and the name is still applied to the peninsula. The peninsula is linked to Brisbane by a long bridge across Bramble Bay.

South of Redcliffe, **Brighton** and **Sandgate** are long-established seaside resorts which are now more like outer suburbs of Brisbane. About 25km south-east of the city, **Cleveland** is the main access point for North Stradbroke Island. **Cleveland Point**, a narrow peninsula jutting into Moreton Bay, is one of Brisbane's most historic sites, where numerous buildings survive from colonial days.

Wynnum & Manly

Lying just a few kilometres south of the Brisbane River mouth these are two of the more attractive bayside suburbs. Yachting and fishing are big here and Manly has the largest marina in the southern hemisphere after Fremantle.

Yachting The Royal Queensland Yacht Squadron (☎ 3396 8666) has yacht races every Wednesday and Saturday afternoon. The Wednesday races are social events and many of the captains are happy to take visitors on board for the ride. Contact the club secretary for more information or ask at the Moreton Bay Lodge (see Places to Stay & Eat following).

Manly marina is also a good place to look for yacht rides along the coast. The club has a notice board where people advertise for crew and if you contact the secretary you may be placed on its crew list. It might also be worth contacting the Wynnum-Manly Yacht Club (☎ 3393 5708) or the Moreton Bay Trailer Boat Club (☎ 3396 8161).

Places to Stay & Eat

Cleveland *Glentrace* (☎ 3207 4442), at 3 Whitehall Ave in Birkdale, is a good little B&B close to Cleveland and 17km south of Brisbane. It's set in half an acre of gardens and has a nice guest lounge and comfortable verandah. Singles/doubles cost $39/50. Phone for directions.

Wynnum & Manly *Nomad's Moreton Bay Lodge* (☎ 3396 3020) has an excellent location among cafes and restaurants on Manly Village high street (Cambridge Pde) about 300m away from the marina. The rooms are spacious and clean and there's a choice of en suite or shared facilities. Dorm beds start at $14, doubles from $35. The hostel can also arrange sailing trips and tours to Moreton Island, and can help you find work in the area.

The best-value eating in Manly is probably across the road from the Lodge at the *Manly Hotel*, which does good-value pub lunches and dinners from $4.50. The *Bay Window* adjacent to the Lodge is also good but a bit pricey.

There are several fish and chip and seafood places along the Esplanade. One that comes highly recommended is *Lucky Strike*, about 10 minutes walk south along the Esplanade from Cambridge Pde, where garlic calamari, salads with blue cheese dressing and croutons and Cajun fish all feature regularly on the menu.

NORTH STRADBROKE ISLAND
pop 2300

The two Stradbroke Islands (for South Stradbroke see the Gold Coast chapter) used to be one but in 1896 a storm cut the sand spit. The division was uneven and North Stradbroke – or 'Straddie' – is by far the larger island of the two. It's a sand island and, despite some heavy sand-mining operations, there's plenty of vegetation and beautiful scenery, especially in the north. Although it is a popular escape from Brisbane it's still relatively unspoilt (that said, the Christmas and Easter holidays can get pretty hectic).

Dunwich, Amity Point and Point Lookout, the three small centres on the island, are all in the north and connected by sealed roads. Most of the southern part of the island is closed to visitors because of mining and the only road into this swampier, more remote area is a private mining company road.

The Stradbroke Island visitor information centre (☎ 3409 9555) is near the ferry terminal in Dunwich; it's open from 8.45 am to 4 pm weekdays and until 3 pm at weekends.

There are post offices in Dunwich and Point Lookout and an ANZ Bank in

BRISBANE

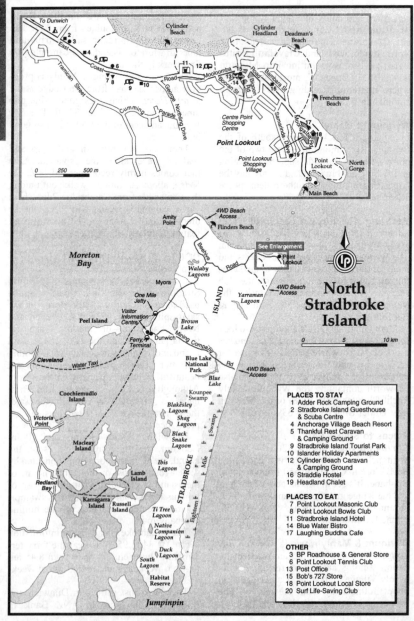

PLACES TO STAY
1 Adder Rock Camping Ground
2 Stradbroke Island Guesthouse
  & Scuba Centre
4 Anchorage Village Beach Resort
5 Thankful Rest Caravan
  & Camping Ground
9 Stradbroke Island Tourist Park
10 Islander Holiday Apartments
12 Cylinder Beach Caravan
  & Camping Ground
16 Straddie Hostel
19 Headland Chalet

PLACES TO EAT
7 Point Lookout Masonic Club
8 Point Lookout Bowls Club
11 Stradbroke Island Hotel
14 Blue Water Bistro
17 Laughing Buddha Cafe

OTHER
3 BP Roadhouse & General Store
6 Point Lookout Tennis Club
13 Post Office
15 Bob's 727 Store
18 Point Lookout Local Store
20 Surf Life-Saving Club

North Stradbroke Island

Dunwich. There are no banks in Point Lookout apart from the Commonwealth Bank agency at the post office in Endeavour St. The BP Roadhouse, Point Lookout Bowls Club, Stradbroke Island Hotel bottle shop and Bob's 727 store at the Centre Point shopping centre all have EFTPOS facilities.

Things to See
Most people come to Straddie for the **beaches**, the best of which are around Point Lookout, where there's a series of points and bays around the headland and endless stretches of white sand.

There's a good walk around the **North Gorge** on the headland, and porpoises, dolphins and manta rays are often spotted from up here. Sightings of humpback whales can also occur during migration season (see the Whales of Hervey Bay boxed text in the Fraser Coast chapter).

Apart from the beach there's the island to explore. A sealed road runs across from Dunwich to **Blue Lake** in the centre of the island; a 2.7km walking track leads from the road to the lake. You can swim in the freshwater lake or nearby **Tortoise Lagoon**, or walk along the track and watch for snakes, goannas, wallabies and birds. **Brown Lake**, about 3km along the Blue Lake road from Dunwich, also offers deep freshwater swimming and is more easily accessible.

If you want to hike the 20km across the island from Dunwich to Point Lookout, a number of dirt-track loops break the monotony of the bitumen road. A pleasant diversion is to **Myora Springs**, which is surrounded by lush vegetation and walking tracks, near the coast about 4km north of Dunwich.

Activities
Beaches & Water Sports There are some excellent surfing breaks at Point Lookout, and you can hire surfboards and boogie boards from various places. You can also sandboard – surf down the dunes just behind Main Beach. It's great fun and costs

$25 for two hours; phone ☎ 3409 8082 or ☎ 3409 8696 for information and booking. The same outfit that does the sandboarding also offers sea kayaking trips at $35 for three hours.

The island is famous for its fishing, and the annual Straddie Classic, held in August (call the tourist office for exact dates), is one of Australia's richest and best-known fishing competitions.

Diving & Snorkelling The Scuba Centre (☎ 3409 8715) adjacent to the Stradbroke Island Guesthouse offers snorkelling for $39 inclusive of a two-hour boat trip and all the gear. The same people also run diving courses ($395), and for certified divers there are all-inclusive single dives and double dives for $63/98.

Tours
Stradbroke Island Tours (☎ 3409 8051) based in Point Lookout runs good 4WD half-day tours of the island for $28. It also organises fishing trips. Stradbroke Island Coaches (☎ 3211 2501) runs day tours from Brisbane departing the Transit Centre at 8 am Monday, Wednesday and Friday; the cost is $65 inclusive of ferries and lunch.

Places to Stay
Almost all the island's accommodation is in Point Lookout, strung out along 3km of coastline.

Camping & Cabins There are seven council-run campgrounds on the island. Those in Point Lookout include the *Adder Rock Camping Ground*, a good campsite among shady eucalypts; the *Cylinder Beach Caravan & Camping Ground*, close to a rocky headland and a good surf beach with picnic tables and barbecues on the foreshore; and the *Thankful Rest Caravan & Camping Park* off East Coast Rd. Rates for all the council-run grounds are $10 for a tent site ($13 for two people plus an extra $4 for each additional person) plus $5 for power. Sites can be booked through the council's office on ☎ 3409 9025.

The *Stradbroke Island Tourist Park* (☎ 3409 8127), on East Coast Rd, has tent sites from $10 to $15, backpacker twin cabins at $15 a bed (or $10 each for three people), and self-contained cabins from $48 to $53 (or $60 for four people).

Budget Accommodation The *Stradbroke Island Guesthouse* (☎ 3409 8888) is the first place on the left as you come into Point Lookout. It's a purpose-built 64-bed hostel with modern facilities, clean and well kept. A bed in a four-bed dorm costs $16, while singles/doubles are $38. Guests get free use of a surf ski and sandsailer. The guesthouse runs a pick-up bus from Brisbane, which leaves from opposite the Transit Centre every Monday, Wednesday and Friday at 2.30 pm and also stops at hostels; you need to book and there's a water transport charge of $8.

The *Straddie Hostel* (☎ 3409 8679) is also on the main road about 2km further into Point Lookout after the guesthouse. It's a two-storey beach-house, looking a bit worse for wear when we visited but the new management is redecorating and improving facilities. The large dorms each have their own kitchen and bathroom, and beds cost $12 or $15 while doubles are $28 and $30.

A little further along the access road into Point Lookout, on the right-hand side, there's *Headland Chalet* (☎ 3409 8252). This is a cluster of 11 cabins on a hillside overlooking Main Beach. It doesn't look much from the outside but the cabins (doubles and twins only) are attractive inside and the views are great. Each has a fridge, and tea and coffee-making facilities. The cost is $20 per person which goes up to $25 at weekends. There's a pool, a games and TV room, free washing machines and a small kitchen.

On a headland above Cylinder Beach, the *Stradbroke Island Hotel* (☎ 3409 8188), the only pub on the island, has motel-style rooms with singles/doubles for $40/65 during the week; all rooms cost $80 on Friday and Saturday nights.

Holiday Units & Resorts If you're thinking of staying a while, a holiday flat or house can be good value, especially outside the holiday seasons. There are several real estate agents on the island including the *Accommodation Centre* (☎ 3409 8255) which is behind the Laughing Buddha Cafe in the Point Lookout Shopping Village.

Islander Holiday Apartments (☎ 3409 8388) on the inland side of East Coast Rd is quite good value, with studio units from $60 a night and one and two-bedroom units starting from $70 a double or $250 a week. The complex has its own pool and tennis court, and a minimum two-night stay applies during the holiday season.

The Anchorage Village Beach Resort (☎ 3409 8266) on East Coast Rd is a three-storey mid-range resort with a pool, laundry and restaurant. It has its own wooden walkway through the palms down to the beach. Prices change with the seasons – motel-style units are $145 for two nights (the minimum stay); one-bedroom units are $165 for two nights; and two-bedroom units, which sleep up to six, start at $245 for two people for two nights.

Places to Eat
There are a couple of general stores selling groceries in Point Lookout but it's worth bringing basic supplies as the price mark-up on the island is significant. The cheapest eating out is at the *Point Lookout Masonic Club*, on East Coast Rd, which does good-value lunches and dinners Wednesday to Sunday; the *Point Lookout Bowls Club* next door also does meals, including a $5 roast on Tuesday evening.

Otherwise, the two best dining options are the *Stradbroke Island Hotel* and the *Laughing Buddha Cafe*. The hotel has a bistro, open for lunch and dinner, with a fairly extensive range of food and prices in the $6 to $15 range. There's a pleasant beer terrace out the back overlooking Cylinder Beach. The Laughing Buddha, part of the Point Lookout Shopping Village complex, is a good place for breakfast and snack lunches, with plenty of filled focaccia and similar light eats. It's also open for dinner from 6 to 8 pm.

For more classy dining the *Blue Water Bistro* in the Centre Point shopping centre is reputed to be one of Queensland's best restaurants; mains start at around $15.

Getting There & Away
To get to Straddie you need to take a bus or train to Cleveland to connect with the ferry. Stradbroke Island Coaches (☎ 3807 4205) departs from bay 24 of Brisbane's Transit Centre at 8 and 9.15 am and 12.30, 4 and 5 pm Monday to Friday. The fare to Cleveland is $4 ($8 return). Alternatively, you can catch a Citylink train from any of Brisbane's central stations to Cleveland (a one-hour journey with departures about every half-hour from 5 am onwards) for $3.10. A courtesy bus departs from Cleveland railway station to the ferry terminal 15 minutes before every sailing.

At Cleveland, two water-taxi companies shuttle across to Dunwich: Stradbroke Ferries (☎ 3286 2666) and the *Stradbroke Flyer* (☎ 3286 1964). Both companies have sailings roughly every hour between 5 am and 6 pm, seven days a week (first sailings start later on Sunday). Fares are $6 one way, $10 return. It's preferable to take the Stradbroke Ferries boat as this is met on the island by a connecting bus to Point Lookout. The Stradbroke Flyer docks at One Mile Jetty, 1.5km north of central Dunwich and it's difficult to pick up public transport from here.

Stradbroke Ferries also runs a vehicle ferry from Cleveland to Dunwich about 12 times a day. It costs $63 return for a vehicle plus passengers.

People staying at the Stradbroke Island Guesthouse can take advantage of its courtesy bus – see the Places to Stay section.

Getting Around
Stradbroke Island Coaches (☎ 3807 4205) runs 10 services a day between the three main centres; Dunwich to Point Lookout costs $4 ($7 return). The Stradbroke Island Guesthouse (see Places to Stay) hires out bicycles at $25 per day or $15 per half-day.

MORETON ISLAND
pop 200
North of Stradbroke, Moreton Island is less visited and still almost a wilderness. Apart from a few rocky headlands, it's all sand, with **Mt Tempest**, towering to 280m, the highest coastal sandhill in the world. It's a strange landscape, alternating between bare sand, forest, lakes and swamps, with a 30km surf beach along the eastern side. The island's birdlife is prolific, and at its northern tip is a **lighthouse**, built in 1857. Sand-mining leases on the island have been cancelled and 96% of the island is now a national park. There are several shipwrecks off the west coast.

Moreton Island has no paved roads but 4WD vehicles can travel along beaches and a few cross-island tracks – seek local advice about tides and creek crossings. The Department of Environment publishes a map of the island, which you can get from the office at False Patch Wrecks (☎ 3408 2710). Vehicle permits for the island cost $15 and are available through the barge operators or Department of Environment offices.

Tangalooma, halfway down the western side of the island, is a popular tourist resort sited at an old whaling station. The main attraction is the wild dolphin feeding which takes place each evening around sundown. Usually about eight or nine dolphins swim in from the ocean and take fish from the hands of volunteer feeders. The feeding is carefully regulated and accompanied by commentary. Participation is free but you must be an overnight guest of the resort – there is nothing to stop campers coming to watch. Call the Dolphin Education Centre (☎ 3408 2666) between 1 and 5 pm for more details.

The only other settlements, all on the west coast, are **Bulwer** near the northwestern tip, **Cowan Cowan** between Bulwer and Tangalooma, and **Kooringal** near the southern tip. The shops at Kooringal and Bulwer are expensive, so bring what you can from the mainland.

Without your own vehicle, walking is the only way to get around the island, and you'll need several days to explore it. There are some trails around the resort area, and there are quite a few decommissioned 4WD roads which make good walks. It's about 14km from Tangalooma or the Ben-Ewa campground on the western side to Eagers Creek campground on the east, then 7km up the beach to Blue Lagoon and a further 6km to Cape Moreton at the north-eastern tip. There's a strenuous track to the summit of Mt Tempest, about 3km inland from Eagers Creek; the views from the top are worth the effort.

About 3km south and inland from Tangalooma is an area of bare sand known as the **Desert**, while the **Big Sandhills** and the **Little Sandhills** are towards the narrow southern end of the island. The biggest lakes and some swamps are in the north-east, and the west coast from Cowan Cowan past Bulwer is also swampy.

Organised Tours

Sunrover Expeditions (☎ 3203 4241) has good 4WD day tours ($100 with lunch) departing Brisbane Transit Centre at 6.45 am Monday and Friday, and 7.45 am on Sunday. Sunrover also offers three-day camping trips ($300 all-inclusive) which go once or twice a month, or four times a month January through March.

Tangalooma Resort runs day cruises from Brisbane – see Getting There & Away later in this section.

Places to Stay

There are Department of Environment *campsites*, with water, toilets and cold showers at Ben-Ewa and False Patch Wrecks, both between Cowan Cowan and Tangalooma, and at Eagers Creek and Blue Lagoon on the island's east coast. Sites cost $3.50 per person per night. For information and camping permits contact the Department of Environment (☎ 3227 8186) at 160 Ann St in Brisbane or the ranger at False Patch Wrecks (☎ 3408 2710).

There are a few holiday flats or houses for rent at Kooringal, Cowan Cowan and Bulwer. A twin room at the *Tangalooma* *Resort* (☎ 3268 6333) costs from $160 per twin/double per night.

Getting There & Away

The *Tangalooma Flyer*, a fast catamaran operated by the Tangalooma Resort (☎ 3268 6333), sails to Moreton daily at 10 am from a dock at Holt St, off Kingsford-Smith Drive. (A courtesy bus departs the Brisbane Transit Centre, bay 26 at 9.15 am.) You can use it for a day trip (it returns at 3.30 pm, which is before dolphin feeding time) or for camping drop-offs. The fare is $30 and it's advisable to book in advance, especially at weekends and on holidays.

The *Moreton Venture* (☎ 3895 1000) is a vehicular ferry that runs every day except Tuesday from Whyte Island (at the southern side of the Brisbane River mouth) to Tangalooma or to Reeders Point. The return fare is $125 for a 4WD (including a vehicle permit for the island); pedestrians are charged $20 return. The *Combie Trader* (☎ 3203 6399) also runs daily except Tuesday, sailing between Scarborough and Bulwer. Fares are as for the *Moreton Venture*.

ST HELENA ISLAND

Now a national park, little St Helena Island, which is only 6km from the mouth of the Brisbane River, was until 1932 a high-security prison. There are the remains of several prison buildings, plus the first passenger tramway in Brisbane which, when built in 1884, had horse-drawn cars. Sandy beaches and mangroves alternate around the coast.

St Helena Island Guided Tours (☎ 3260 7944) runs day trips ($35 including lunch or $28 without) from the BP Marina on Kingsford-Smith Drive, Breakfast Creek, every Sunday and two or three other days a week, leaving at 9 am and returning at 5 pm. St Helena Ferries (☎ 3396 3994) runs two to three trips a week on its *Cat o' Nine Tails* catamaran, leaving from Manly Harbour. The $30 return fare includes a one-hour tour and entry to the national park. You can reach Manly from central Brisbane in about 35 minutes by train on the Cleveland line.

COOCHIEMUDLO ISLAND

Coochiemudlo (or Coochie) Island is a 10-minute ferry ride from Victoria Point on the southern bay side. It's a popular outing from the mainland, with good beaches, although it's more built-up than most other Moreton Bay islands you can visit. You can rent bicycles, boats, catamarans and surf skis on the island. The *Coochie Ville Holiday Units* (☎ 3207 7521) has one and two-bedroom units starting from $45 a night.

Combined Ferry Services (☎ 3207 8960) runs between Victoria Point jetty and the island at 20-minute intervals throughout the day. The same company runs the MV *Island Link*, a vehicle ferry on which bookings are essential.

BRIBIE ISLAND

Bribie Island, at the northern end of Moreton Bay, is 31km long but apart from the southern end, where there are three small towns, the island is largely untouched. The island is separated from the mainland by the narrow Pumicestone Channel; there's a bridge across to the small township of Bellara on the south-west coast.

Both Bellara and Bongaree, just to the south, are predominantly residential. Woorim, on the east coast, is probably the best place from a traveller's point of view. It's an old-fashioned holiday township with good, sandy ocean beaches and a range of accommodation.

The north-west coast of the island is protected as the Pumicestone National Park, which is only accessible to 4WD vehicles.

As you cross the bridge onto the island, you'll see the Bribie Island information centre (☎ 3408 9026) in the middle of the Benabrow Ave median strip. It is open Monday to Saturday from 9 am to 4 pm and Sunday from 9 am to 12.30 pm.

Places to Stay & Eat

Accommodation options include the *Bribie Island Caravan Park* (☎ 3408 1134) in Jacana Ave, Woorim, one block back from the beach; the *Koolamara Beach Resort* (☎ 3408 1277) on the beachfront in Woorim, which is a good mid-range modern resort built around a swimming pool in a landscaped garden setting; and the *Blue Pacific Hotel-Motel* on North St, with budget motel-style units.

The small shopping centre on Jacana Ave has a good bakery, a couple of takeaway places and a pizza shop. The *Panorama Coffee Shop* at 71 Welsby Pde has pavement seating to take advantage of its great location on the foreshore. It does snacks like sandwiches and burgers, cakes and coffee and a good cooked breakfast for $5.

Getting There & Away

There are frequent train services between Brisbane and Caboolture; Bribie Island Bus & Coaches (☎ 3408 2562) runs bus services from the Caboolture railway station to Bribie Island.

Gold Coast

The Gold Coast is little more than a life-support system for a 35km strip of beach running north from the New South Wales/Queensland border. The coastline is one continuous landfill of holiday apartments and cheap motels, punctuated by clusters of convenience stores and cheap restaurants.

This has been a holiday spot since the 1880s, but developers only started taking serious notice after WWII. These days more than two million visitors a year roll in. The major draw is still the sand and sea, but this is now backed up by a glitzy nightlife and a slew of artificial 'attractions' and theme parks.

Away from the beaches, the Gold Coast possesses a little visited but beautiful hinterland which is well worth exploring – although you'll need a car.

Orientation

While the whole coast from Tweed Heads in NSW up to Main Beach north of Surfers Paradise is developed, most of the action is around Surfers itself. Tweed Heads and Coolangatta at the southern end are older, quieter and cheaper resorts. Moving north from there, you pass through Kirra, Bilinga, Tugun, Currumbin, Palm Beach, Burleigh Heads, Miami, Nobby Beach, Mermaid Beach and Broadbeach – all lower key places popular with holidaying families.

Southport, the oldest town in the area, is north and just inland from Surfers, behind the sheltered expanse of the Broadwater which is fed by the Nerang and Coomera rivers. The Gold Coast Hwy runs right along the coastal strip, leaving the Pacific Hwy just north of Tugun and rejoining it inland from Southport.

The local airport servicing the Gold Coast is at Bilinga, about 2km north of Coolangatta and 20km south of Surfers Paradise. Most buses to the Gold Coast travel the full length of the strip.

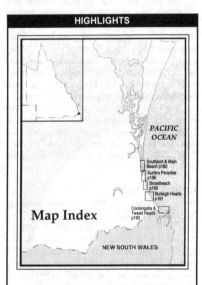

HIGHLIGHTS

PACIFIC OCEAN

Southport & Main Beach p182
Surfers Paradise p186
Broadbeach p190
Burleigh Heads p191
Coolangatta & Tweed Heads p193

Map Index

NEW SOUTH WALES

- Take in the nightclubs and bars of Surfers Paradise. Surfers is a love it or hate it place – and if you're going to love it, be prepared to party hard.
- Head for Lamington National Park, for a walk among beautiful gorges, caves, waterfalls and plentiful wildlife in a sub-tropical rainforest setting.
- Stay at the Summer House Eco Resort, a collection of small themed lodges – including the Pharaoh Lodge, a 5m-high pyramid decorated inside to resemble an Ancient Egyptian bedchamber.

Information

There are tourist information centres in Surfers Paradise and Coolangatta, and at Canungra and Tamborine Mountain in the hinterland – see those sections for details.

There are plenty of free glossy booklets available, including *Wot's On*, *Destination*

Surfers Paradise, *Today Tonight on the Gold Coast* and *Point Out*; some have street plans and a bit of useful information, but their main purpose would seem to be to rake in the cash from advertising.

Activities

Water Sports & Surfing Aussie Bob's (☎ 5591 7577) at the Marina Mirage in Main Beach, Budd's Beach Water Sportz (☎ 5592 0644) on River Drive at Surfers, and Surfers Beach Hut Beach Hire, at the beach end of the Cavill Mall, rent a wide range of gear including jet skis, fishing boats and sailboards, and can take you parasailing, water-skiing and more. Prices for jet skiing are about $50 to $60 per half hour (jet skis normally take two) and for parasailing $50 per person, and you're usually up for about 10 to 15 minutes.

XTSea Charters (☎ 5532 4299) at Fisherman's Wharf offers all the above plus speed boat canal tours, jet boats and Oz Ducks, which are like motorised inflated tyres.

You can also sea kayak from the north end of The Spit to South Stradbroke Island,

Gold Coast & Hinterland

possibly encountering dolphins en route. Trips depart at 8.30 am and last about three hours, and the price of $29 includes pick-ups. Contact ☎ 5527 5785 for bookings.

Bungee Jumping At Bungee Down Under (☎ 5531 1103) on The Spit, just north of Mariner's Cove in Main Beach, first-time jumpers pay $69, while for experienced jumpers the cost is $50; backpackers pay $49 on Monday. In Surfers, a former car park just off Ferny Ave is home to a rocket bungee ($68), which is basically a giant catapult in which you are the projectile ($25 per person), and something called a fly-coaster in which you swing like a pendulum after being released from a hoist 20m up ($29).

Horse Riding Numinbah Valley Adventure Trails (☎ 5533 4137) has three hour horse riding treks through beautiful rainforest and river scenery in the Numinbah Valley 30km south of Nerang, costing $40 per person or $45 with pick-ups from the coast.

Gum Nuts Horse Riding Resort (☎ 5543 0191) on Nerang-Broadbeach Rd in Carrara, also has half-day riding for $35 ($40 in the afternoon) and a full day with lunch for $60. The price includes Gold Coast pick-ups.

Other Activities Off The Edge (☎ 5592 6406) offers downhill mountain biking out in the hinterland forests. There are a variety of routes from those for the timid to slopes for those with a death wish – and to cut out the tiresome bit a van takes you back uphill each time. Cost is $30 for backpackers, including pick-ups. The same company also offers a 'triple challenge', which consists of some trail biking, after which you get straight into a powerboat before peaking with your choice of a bungee jump, jet ski or parasail. The all-in coast is $130, plus a free meal and a beer.

Clifftop Adventures Co (☎ 018 752 510) offers forward abseiling from $40, or you can rap jump (☎ 5526 9986) from the top of a 20 floor building for $55.

Organised Tours & Cruises

See the Surfers Paradise section for some local tours.

Hinterland Trips We've had plenty of good feedback on Off The Edge (☎ 5592 6406), which does an excellent day trip out to the Springbrook Plateau and takes in some hiking, walks behind waterfalls, swimming and a barbecue lunch with wine – the price, including pick-ups, is excellent value at $29 for backpackers.

Doug Robbins' Off The Beaten Track tours (☎ 5533 5366) offers overnight trips from the Gold Coast to Springbrook which are also great value at $40 per person, including return transport, accommodation, a meal and a half to full-day bushwalk. Doug will pick you up in the morning and drop you back on the coast the following morning.

Cruises During the summer months, cruises on offer from Surfers include two hour harbour and canal trips (about $22) and cruises to South Stradbroke Island (about $45 including lunch). Boats depart from the Marina Mirage or Fisherman's Wharf on The Spit, or from the Tiki Village Wharf at the river end of Cavill Ave. Operators change from season to season, so ask at your accommodation what's available and what has had good reports.

Festivals

There are a number of major events on the coast. The Magic Millions Summer Carnival held at the Gold Coast Turf Club, on Racecourse Drive in Bundall (3km west of Surfers), early each January is a 10 day carnival of horse-racing, glamorous social events and thoroughbred sales.

Various life-saving carnivals, and ironman and ironwoman events, are held on the coast during summer and there's also the Surfers Paradise International Triathlon each April.

June sees the Gold Coast International Jazz & Blues Festival held over two days at the Gold Coast International Hotel, and the

Gold Coast International Marathon is run in July. Each October, the Tropicarnival Festival is a week of street parades, concerts, sporting events and other activities, and then in mid-October the whole town comes to a standstill for the IndyCar – see the boxed text below.

Getting There & Away

Air Ansett and Qantas fly direct from major cities including Sydney ($306), Melbourne ($441), Adelaide ($471) and Perth ($730).

Bus Long-distance buses stop at the bus transit centres in Southport, Surfers Paradise and Coolangatta. Most companies will let you stop off on the Gold Coast if you have a through ticket.

From Surfers, McCafferty's, Greyhound Pioneer and Coachtrans all have frequent services to Brisbane ($12 to $14), Byron Bay ($18 to $19) and Sydney ($66 to $79); Greyhound also has one service a day to Noosa ($28, change at Brisbane). Kirklands (☎ 5531 7145) and Premier Pioneer Motor Service (☎ 1300 368 100) undercut the bigger operators on some of the Gold Coast routes; it has booking offices at the Surfers and Coolangatta transit centres.

From Brisbane the bus takes about 1½ hours to Surfers and just over two hours to Coolangatta.

Train The Gold Coast is served by Helensvale and the newly opened Nerang station, both of which have direct links to Brisbane's Roma St and Central stations. Neither Helensvale nor Nerang is particularly close to any of the main Gold Coast centres, but Surfside Buses runs regular shuttles from the railway stations down to Surfers and beyond and to the theme parks.

GOLD COAST

IndyCar

Since 1991 Surfers Paradise has been annual host to what has been dubbed Queensland's biggest party – the Australian leg of the IndyCar series (the US equivalent of Formula One motor racing). The main streets of central Surfers are transformed into a temporary race circuit, around which hurtle some of the world's fastest cars, whose drivers push them up to speeds of more than 300km/h.

In 1998 some quarter of a million spectators were expected for the race and the three day carnival that precedes it. It's a chance for Surfers to go even more over the top than usual, indulging in an orgy of soap opera glamour and hormonal rushes.

Hotel rooms overlooking the track are booked up 12 months in advance and owners of fortuitously sited apartments can retire to a desert island for four months on the proceeds of the rental for just these four days. Budget motor racing fans might be interested to know that the cars roar right by the deck of the *Surf & Sun* hostel (beds from $13 a night); however, anyone staying in on-track accommodation has to purchase an accommodation pass which will set them back around $170.

INDYCAR AUSTRALIA

Fast and furious IndyCar racing.

GOLD COAST

THEME PARKS

There are several major theme parks on the Gold Coast. While they're generally quite expensive, the ticket prices usually cover all rides and shows, so for a full day's entertainment they can be worthwhile and good fun.

Note that the theme parks define 'children' as anyone between four and 13 years of age. Anyone three or younger gets in for free, but anyone 14 or older pays the adult price.

If you don't have your own transport, there are plenty of tour operators and bus companies offering transfers. Coachtrans (☎ 5588 8788) picks up from Surfers all the way down to Tweed Heads for $12 return; Surfside Buslines (☎ 5536 7666) picks up from the Helensvale train station; and there are also numerous services from Brisbane.

Sea World

On The Spit in Main Beach, Sea World started out in 1971 as a water-ski show on the Nerang River, and has grown into a major tourist attraction. The main draws are the animal performances, which include twice daily dolphin (10.45 am, 2.30 pm) and sea lion (1.45 and 3.15 pm) shows, and shark-feeding. The water-ski spectacular with which the centre first made its name is still on the menu and also takes place twice a day (12.30 and 4 pm).

Besides that are the rides, including a corkscrew rollercoaster, a monorail, a pirate ship, and a water park with slides, including a freefall slide. There's also tamer stuff like swimming pools and aquariums.

Additional attractions not covered in the admission include the Sea World Helicopters (☎ 5588 2224) which offer four different tours, ranging from a 7km flight over South Stradbroke Island ($30 per person) to a 60km flight to the Springbrook Plateau in the hinterland ($150 per person). It's not necessary to enter Sea World to go up in a helicopter – there's a ticket office outside the complex at the edge of the Broadwater. There's also a water sports section at Sea World where, for a price, you can go parasailing, hire jet skis, ride the 'blue banana', and learn to water-ski.

There are plenty of snack bars, cafes and restaurants here, and souvenir shops galore. Bring lots of spendooly – Sea World might be great fun, but bargain city it ain't. There's an ATM and currency exchange bureau in the main building.

Costs & Times Sea World (☎ 5588 2222, or ☎ 5588 2205 for show times) is open every day from 9.30 am to 5 pm except Christmas Day and the morning of Anzac Day. Admission is $41 ($26 children).

Getting There & Away Bus No 9 from Scarborough St in Southport and bus No 2 from Ferny Ave in Surfers Paradise both stop off at the Sea World car park. Alternatively, a special Gold Coast shuttle bus picks up at all five-star hotels at 30 minute intervals from 9 am.

Movie World

Otherwise known as 'Hollywood on the Gold Coast', Movie World is next to the Warner-Roadshow film production studios on the Pacific Hwy at Oxenford, about 16km north-west of Surfers. It claims to be Australia's number one tourist attraction, pulling in somewhere in the region of 1.4 million visitors annually. That said, it's the least fun of the parks.

Movie World relies heavily on the appeal of oversized Warner Bros cartoon characters (Daffy Duck, Bugs Bunny etc) wandering round waving and beaming – it's a limited appeal to say the least. The one 'real life' resident Hollywood superstar is Beethoven the dog.

For the slightly older crowd the main draw is the Lethal Weapon ride, an inverted, suspended rollercoaster which has you spending most of the 105 second ride upside down – a bit like a ski-lift gone haywire. There's also Batman – The Ride, a simulator which has you in the seat of the Batmobile and rattles you up and shakes you about a bit – it's got to be more fun than the films. These two are the only thrill rides. The rest of the park is taken up with recreations of sets like the

Daily Planet building and the Riddler's Lair, China Town alley and a Bonnie & Clyde bank with ATM facilities so you can cash up before hitting the dubiously themed eateries like the Gotham City Cafe ('Batman's favourite hangout') and the Willy Wonka and the Chocolate Factory Candy Store.

Costs & Times Movie World (☎ 5573 8485) is open every day from 9.30 am to 5.30 pm except Christmas Day. Admission is $39 ($24 children).

Wet 'n' Wild

This too, along with Movie World and Sea World, is owned by Warner Bros and Village Road-show. It's a fun water sports park – probably the country's best. It has a couple of great raft slides, a twister (in which you pelt down a water-sprayed, tightly spiralled tube), a speed slide on which people have clocked up 70km/h and a 1m-wave pool. There are more sedate water activities too, like Calypso Beach – an artificial tropical island around which flows a slow moving river on which visitors languidly float in rubber tubes. For the younger kids there's something called Buccaneer Bay, where they can clamber around a pirate galleon and enjoy supervised rides in shallow water.

Wet 'n' Wild also screens 'Dive-In Movies' every Saturday night from September to April (and every night during January) – you get to watch a film while floating on a rubber tube in the wave pool.

Costs & Times Wet 'n' Wild (☎ 5573 2255) is open every day from 10 am to 4 pm in winter, 5 pm in summer and 9 pm in late December and January. It's closed Christmas Day and Anzac Day. Admission is $21 ($15 children).

Dreamworld

Dreamworld, at Coomera on the Pacific Hwy 17km north of Surfers, is a Disneyland-style creation of 10 areas with different themes including a wildlife sanctuary of Australian animals and birds, the Blue Lagoon aquatic playground, a re-creation of a gold-rush-era town, and a Bavarian village.

Rides include the Thunderbolt (a double-loop rollercoaster), a Gravitron, a raft ride through rapids, Wipeout (likened to windsurfing in a washing machine on spin cycle) and, the latest addition, the Tower of Terror, a twist on the rollercoaster on which paying victims freefall from a height equivalent to 38 storeys and reach speeds of up to 160km/h.

There are also water slides, a 3km-long railway, a giant-screen Imax Theatre which screens films throughout the day, some nicely kept gardens and a small koala park. Of all the theme parks Dreamworld is the one that probably caters best for a variety of age groups.

Costs & Times Dreamworld (☎ 5588 1111) is open daily from 10 am to 5 pm and costs $34 ($21 children).

Cableski World

Cableski World is 12km north of Surfers on Pine Ridge Rd in Runaway Bay, near Sanctuary Cove. There you can water-ski without a speedboat by being towed around a large network of lakes by overhead cables.

It also has windsurfers, jetskis and paddle boats for hire. You can also bungee jump ($68) and go-kart.

Costs & Times Water-skiing costs $30 ($18 for students) for a full-day pass or $18 for a night pass (from 5 to 10 pm), and wetsuit hire is another $8. Cableski World (☎ 5537 6300) is open daily from 11 am to 5 pm in the winter and 10 am to 9 pm in the summer. General admission is free but you pay for the activities.

Getting There & Away To get there take Surfside bus No 10, the Sanctuary Cove service.

The one-way Brisbane-Helensvale (65 minutes) fare is $7.20, while the Surfside shuttle to/from Surfers Paradise is $3.30.

There's a Queensland Rail booking office (☎ 5539 9088) in the Cavill Park Building on Beach Rd in Surfers, opposite the transit centre.

Getting Around

To/From the Airport Coachtrans (☎ 5588 8747) meets every flight into Coolangatta airport, with transfers to Coolangatta ($7 one-way), Burleigh Heads ($8), Surfers ($9) and Main Beach ($10).

Coachtrans also operate the Airporter (☎ 5588 8777) direct bus link between Brisbane airport and the Gold Coast for $29 one-way ($18 for children).

Bus Surfside Buslines (☎ 5536 7666) runs a frequent service 24 hours a day up and down the Gold Coast Hwy between Southport and Tweed Heads and beyond. You can buy individual fares, get a Day Rover ticket for $8, or a weekly one for $26.

Car & Moped Rental There are stacks of car-rental firms along the Gold Coast, particularly in Surfers – pick up any of the free Gold Coast guides, scan the *Yellow Pages* and see Getting Around in the Surfers Paradise section.

Taxi Ring Regent Taxis (☎ 13 1008) to book a taxi.

SOUTHPORT & MAIN BEACH

Sheltered from the ocean by The Spit, Southport was the original town on the Gold Coast. It's now modern, residential and rather nondescript. There is little to see or do here, but Southport makes a pleasant, quiet base from which to explore the immediate area. Buses No 1 and 1A run about every 15 minutes from outside the Australia Fair shopping centre on the main street down to Surfers ($1; 10 minutes). The service continues on an hourly schedule throughout the night.

Between Southport and Surfers is Main

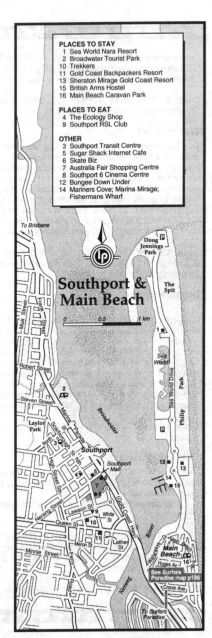

PLACES TO STAY
1 Sea World Nara Resort
2 Broadwater Tourist Park
10 Trekkers
11 Gold Coast Backpackers Resort
13 Sheraton Mirage Gold Coast Resort
15 British Arms Hostel
16 Main Beach Caravan Park

PLACES TO EAT
4 The Ecology Shop
9 Southport RSL Club

OTHER
3 Southport Transit Centre
5 Sugar Shack Internet Cafe
6 Skate Biz
7 Australia Fair Shopping Centre
8 Southport 6 Cinema Centre
12 Bungee Down Under
14 Mariners Cove; Marina Mirage;
   Fishermans Wharf

Southport & Main Beach

Beach and north of that The Spit, a narrow, 3km long tongue of sand dividing the ocean from the Broadwater. On the Broadwater side of The Spit, **Fisherman's Wharf** is the departure point for most pleasure cruises. It has a pub, restaurant, swimming pool and shops.

Immediately south of Fisherman's Wharf are the **Marina Mirage**, an upmarket shopping and dining complex, and **Mariner's Cove**, a collection of cheaper eating places. Across the road on the ocean side of The Spit is the Sheraton Mirage Gold Coast Resort, while up from Fisherman's Wharf is **Sea World** (see the Theme Parks box earlier).

The beach at the northern end of The Spit is not developed and is good for relatively secluded sunbathing.

Information

The post office and an American Express office are in the large Australia Fair shopping centre either side of Scarborough St in the centre of Southport. Up on the 1st floor of the centre, in front of the cinema, is Internet Express (☎ 5527 0335); there are several terminals charged at $2 per 10 minutes or $8 per hour. There's also the Sugar Shack Internet Cafe (☎ 5532 4495), in the Southport Mall, which is open daily from 9 am to 9 pm.

Activities

Skate Biz (☎ 5527 0066), in the Southport Mall near the corner of Marine Parade, hires out in-line skates with pads and all the gear for $10 for two hours or $20 for 24 hours. For other activities, see the relevant section at the start of this chapter.

Places to Stay

Camping The *Broadwater Tourist Park* (☎ 5581 7733), off the Gold Coast Hwy in Southport, is a very neat council-run park with good facilities on the banks of the Broadwater River. Tent sites are from $15. The *Main Beach Caravan Park* (☎ 5581 7722), on Main Beach Pde, is also council-run and has tent sites from $16.

Hostels *Trekkers* (☎ 5591 5616) at 22 White St, about 1km south of Southport's transit centre, is a strong candidate for south-east Queensland's best hostel. It's in an old house which has been well renovated and furnished. Facilities are standard – TV and games room, a couple of kitchens, a beautiful pool – but everything is very well maintained and the place has a comfortable, homely feel. Accommodation is in three or four-bed dorms, or twins with their own TV. The staff organise trips to nightclubs in Surfers every evening. The nightly cost for a dorm bed is $15 while twins are $32.

The *Gold Coast Backpackers Resort* (☎ 5531 2004), 44 Queen St, is a modern, purpose-built hostel but it's very impersonal and very scruffy; dorm beds are $13.

Over on Main Beach in the Mariner's Cove complex, the YHA-affiliated *British Arms Hostel* (☎ 5571 1776) is a fairly new place right on the wharfside. It's a little bit spartan, but the management are working hard to liven things up with free beers on check-in, twice weekly barbecues and various other activities. Dorms go for $14 while singles/doubles are $32.

Resorts The *Sheraton Mirage Gold Coast Resort*, on Sea World Drive on The Spit in Main Beach, is a five-star place with over 300 rooms and suites overlooking either the surf beach or the Broadwater River. Standard rooms start from $420 a night, suites from $800.

Further up The Spit, the *Sea World Nara Resort* (☎ 5591 1000 or toll-free 1800 074 448) is very popular with families and has 400 rooms ranging from $195 to $225 a double, which includes entry to Sea World. The resort is linked to Sea World by a monorail.

Places to Eat

Southport The cheapest place to eat is in the Australia Fair shopping centre. There's a decent *food court* which, besides a McDonald's and KFC, has counters serving pasta, Chinese and roasts. In the centre's

Fig Tree Garden *Christou's Cafe* has Greek dishes plus all-day breakfasts, roasts and sea-food served in huge portions for around $5.

Southport's *RSL Club*, near Trekkers hostel on the corner of Scarborough and White Sts, has good roasts and casseroles for $6 to $8. About 1km north, *The Ecology Shop* at 116 Scarborough St is a health food place with salads, sandwiches and juices.

Main Beach At Mariner's Cove, the *British Arms* is an English-style tavern with Guinness, Newcastle Brown and Bass beer on tap, and meals like steak and kidney pie with chips, shepherds pie, and Yorkshire pudding and roast beef all at $9.80. Opposite, across the wharf, *Frenchy's* does some cheap basic dishes like fish and chips for about $8 but most of the rest of the menu is pretty pricey.

If you are prepared to splash out, the best place to go is the Marina Mirage, the shopping complex immediately north of Mariner's Cove. *Saks* and *Cafe Roma* on the marina are two extremely popular and lively bar-restaurants with great views across the Broadwater. Food is in the $18 to $24 price range.

Further north, the Fisherman's Wharf complex is more casual and downmarket, with the emphasis on alcohol rather than food; there is a family-style *bistro* and a cafeteria-style *seafood restaurant*.

Entertainment
There's live music at the *British Arms* pub at Mariner's Cove every Friday and Saturday and also at *Saks* at the Marina Mirage. Fisherman's Wharf is also popular on Sunday afternoon, with live bands in the outdoor area.

The Southport 6 Cinema Centre on the 1st floor of the Australia Fair shopping centre in Scarborough St is a multi-screen complex showing latest releases.

Getting There & Away
Long-distance buses stop at the transit centre at the northern end of Scarborough St. Travel time from Brisbane is 1¼ hours and the one-way fare is $12.

SOUTH STRADBROKE ISLAND
This narrow, 20km-long sandy island is separated from the northern end of The Spit by a 200m wide channel. The island is an undeveloped environmental park, with a handful of holiday houses, a yacht club, four council-run camping grounds and several low-key resorts.

There are no developed walking trails, but you can explore the island on foot and there are some great beaches which are popular with surfers. There are good breaks all the way up the east coast and a bit more swell than the southern breaks. Experienced surfers can paddle across to the island from the northern end of The Spit, but there's a sign here warning of the dangers of doing so. The rip is strong, and it's often hard for passing boats to see or avoid paddlers – never try this alone and make sure you allow for the rip. If you haven't done the paddle before, it's worth waiting until someone who has comes along. Watch what they do, or better still, paddle across with them.

Contact the Department of Environment (☎ 5577 3555) if you want more information on the island.

Places to Stay
Two-thirds of the way up the island on the west coast, the *South Stradbroke Island Resort* (☎ 5577 3311) has two restaurants, tennis courts, a pool and spa, and 40 South Sea island-style cabins starting from $70 a double.

Getting There & Away
The South Stradbroke Island Resort ferry leaves from Runaway Bay Marina at the north end of the Gold Coast every day at 10.30 am and 4.30 pm; the return fare is $20.

Several tour operators also offer cruises up the Broadwater to the island.

SURFERS PARADISE
If the Gold Coast with its mix of sun, beaches, theme parks and colourful local

fauna is Australia's Florida, then Surfers is its wannabe Miami. From the gold lamé bikini-clad Meter Maids to the replica of Michelangelo's David in the Raptis Plaza shopping mall, Surfers is razzle-dazzle and glitz, and all in the most dubious of taste.

The place has come a long way since 1936 when there was just the brand-new Surfers Paradise Hotel, a little beachfront hideaway 9km from Southport. The popularity of Surfers these days rests not so much on the sand and surf (which is better down the coast) but on the shopping, nightlife and its proximity to attractions like the Gold Coast theme parks.

For backpackers it's probably the most partying place in Queensland and hostel staff here work hard to whip guests up into a good time groove every night of the week. Yet, despite all this, at most times of the year you may not have to go very far north or south to find a relatively open, blissful stretch of white sand.

Orientation

The town is extremely small and really consists of just two or three streets: Cavill Ave,

with a pedestrian mall at its beach end, is the main thoroughfare, while Orchid Ave, one block in from the Esplanade, is the nightclub and bar strip. The Gold Coast Hwy runs through Surfers just one block back from Orchid Ave. It takes the southbound traffic while Ferny Ave, another block inland, takes the northbound traffic. Another block back is the looping Nerang River.

Information

The Gold Coast Tourism Bureau (☎ 5538 4419) on Cavill Ave Mall is open from 8 am to 5 pm Monday to Friday, from 9 am to 5 pm Saturday and from 9 am to 3.30 pm Sunday. For help with finding somewhere to stay, there's the In Transit (☎ 5592 2911) backpackers' accommodation booking desk at the transit centre. There are also left-luggage lockers here for $4 a day.

The post office is in the Paradise Centre off the Cavill Ave Mall. American Express (☎ 5538 7588) has an office at 21 Cavill Ave which is open on weekdays from 8.30 am to 5.30 pm and on Saturday from 9 am to noon. Thomas Cook (☎ 5531 7770) has a foreign currency exchange office in Cavill

---

Maids In Paradise

Amid the all-you-can-eat for $5 restaurants, strip joints and entertainment centres, Surfers Paradise has a museum. Take a few guesses. A museum of art? Nope. Natural history? Nope. Science? Nope. It's a museum devoted to girls in golden bikinis.

The creation of an astutely PR-minded mayor, the Meter Maids were introduced to Surfers Paradise 30 years ago. The bikini-clad girls strolled the streets feeding parking meters with coins to prevent motorists from being booked. At the time they caused an outrage – the bikinis showed the girls' navels – but it put the small beach resort of Surfers on the map.

And the Maids are still going strong; sponsored by local businesses, they insert some $200 to $300 a week in 10c pieces into meters. They also act as shapely ambassadors for the town, giving welcoming speeches and making personal appearances. But the scandal continues, now in the form of a rival, splinter group of Maids (denounced as 'unofficial') who have stolen the limelight with some full frontal coverage in *Penthouse*.

The museum – actually, little more than an exhibition stand – contains lots of memorabilia from the 1960s to 90s and is on level 1 of the Paradise Centre, off Cavill Ave Mall. If you want to catch the Maids at work, meter feeding time is between 10 and 3 pm along the Esplanade.

GOLD COAST

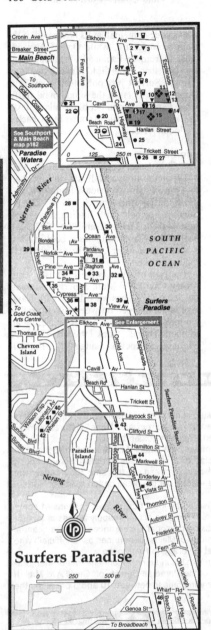

Surfers Paradise

PLACES TO STAY
19 Ramada
27 Trickett Gardens Holiday Inn
28 Marriot Resort
30 Surf & Sun Backpackers
31 Gold Coast International Hotel
32 International Beach Resort
34 Cheers Backpackers
35 Spectrum Apartments
36 Delilah Motel
38 Quarterdeck Apartments
39 Olympus
40 Surfers Central Backpackers
41 Sleeping Inn Surfers
42 Couple O'Days Accommodation
44 Silver Sands Motel
45 Admiral Motor Inn
46 Surfers Paradise Backpackers Resort

PLACES TO EAT
2 The Latin Quarter
3 Beachside Cafe
4 Costa Dora; Happy House
5 New Seoul
10 Gold Star
12 Sumo
13 McDonald's; KFC
18 Hard Rock Cafe
24 Bunga Raya

OTHER
1 Paddy Og's
6 American Express Exchange Bureau
7 Cocktails & Dreams; The Party
8 Shooters
9 Bourbon Bar
11 Raptis Plaza
14 Surfers Beach Hut Beach Hire
15 Paradise Centre
16 Gold Coast Tourism Bureau
17 Thomas Cook
20 Ansett; Queensland Rail Booking Office
21 Tiki Village Wharf
22 Bus Stop For Southport
23 Transit Centre
25 24 Hour Convenience Store
26 Qantas
29 Budd's Beach Water Sportz
33 Bungee, Bungee Rocket & Flycoaster
37 Police
43 Hoyts Cinema Centre

Ave, near the Gold Coast Hwy corner, which is open weekdays from 8.30 am to 9 pm and weekends from 9 am to 9 pm.

Organised Tours & Activities
Surfers Paradise Walking Tours (☎ toll-free 1800 654 622) leads a 1½ hour trail around central Surfers each Tuesday and Thursday at 10 am and 1.30 pm, departing from the Paradise Centre off Cavill Ave Mall. The cost is $15 per person.

The Aquabus (☎ 5539 0222) is good; it's a semi-aquatic vehicle that departs five times daily from Cavill Ave in Surfers and makes a 75 minute tour up Main Beach and the Spit then sails back on the Broadwater. The fare is $22 and you can book from the kiosk on Cavill Ave.

Places to Stay
Hostels Surfers has several decent hostel options. The best is the 100-bed *Cheers Backpackers* (☎ 5531 6539) at 8 Pine Ave. It's well set up, with a decent pool, an excellent bar area and large barbecue courtyard. Beds in dorms of either two, four or six beds cost $12 or $14. Cheers is party-oriented, with video nights, karaoke evenings and vouchers for the nightclubs, many of which are within staggering distance.

Another partying place, *Surf & Sun* (☎ 5592 2363) just north of the centre at 3323 Gold Coast Hwy, scores by being just 100m from the beach (it's a bit of a way from the transit centre but you can call to be picked up). It looks very barrack-like from outside but inside it's comfortable and all rooms have TV and en suite. It's $13 a night in a four-bed dorm or $18 each in a double.

For facilities the *Surfers Paradise Backpackers Resort* (☎ 5592 4677) at 2835 Gold Coast Hwy is unbeatable; these include a decent-sized pool, a small gym and sauna, a pool room, tennis court and basement parking. There's also a free laundry. There are two sections, one with four-bed dorms, and the other with excellent self-contained apartments, mostly accommodating four or five people in two bedrooms. A dorm or unit bed costs $14, doubles $36. The only

drawback is that the hostel is over 1km south of the centre and you can tire of the walk pretty quickly – there is, however, a courtesy bus and the hostel runs guests to the nightclubs on Orchid Ave each evening.

Just south of the transit centre on Whelan St there's a string of three hostels. Closest to the centre at No 40 is *Surfers Central Backpackers* (☎ 5538 4344) which is badly in need of renovation. Scruffy doubles are seriously overpriced at $40; dorm beds are $15, four to a room. Down the street at No 26 is *Sleeping Inn Surfers* (☎ 5592 4455), a recent conversion of two neighbouring apartment buildings. It's very modern, well-furnished and clean, and the layout is such that staying here feels very much like being a guest in someone's house. It's good for anyone who wants privacy and comfort. Dorms are $15, doubles $40.

At 18 Whelan St, *Couple O' Days Accommodation* (☎ 5592 4200) is another converted old apartment block. Dave, the guy who runs it, is friendly and an excellent source of information but the rooms badly need some money spending on them – take a look and make sure you're satisfied before paying as there are no refunds. Dorm beds are $14.

Motels If you're after a motel, the *Silver Sands Motel* (☎ 5538 6041), 2985 Gold Coast Hwy, is a good option. The rooms have been attractively refurbished and there's a small pool, a barbecue and parking. Singles/doubles start from $45/55. Close by, at No 2965, the *Admiral Motor Inn* (☎ 5539 8759) has rooms from $50.

The *Delilah Motel* (☎ 5538 1722), on the corner of Ferny and Cypress Aves, badly needs some redecorating and has rooms from $50/65.

Holiday Apartments There are hundreds of holiday apartments and flats to choose from. The Gold Coast Tourism Bureau recommends the following three. *Spectrum Apartments* (☎ 5570 2499, fax 5538 6228) at 3 River Drive overlooks the Nerang River and is a five minute walk from the

GOLD COAST

main beach. We were quoted $70 per night for a double here, based on a three-night stay. *Olympus* (☎ 5538 7288, fax 5592 0769), 60 The Esplanade, just 200m north of central Orchid and Elkhorn Aves and opposite the beach, is a mid-rise block of one and two bedroom holiday apartments with nightly tariffs of $99. A further 200m north, the *International Beach Resort* (toll-free ☎ 1800 657 471, fax 5538 9613) at 84 The Esplanade, is a high-rise with 80 one-bedroom self-contained units from $90 a double.

The Australian Gay & Lesbian Tourism Association recommends *Quarterdeck Apartments* (toll-free ☎ 1800 635 235) on Ferny Ave, just south of the junction with Cypress Ave, a high-rise a few minutes from the beach with comfortable one-bedroom apartments from $70 to $100 a night.

We've also had good word on the *Trickett Gardens Holiday Inn* (☎ 5539 0988), 24-30 Trickett St, a low-rise block of 33 refurbished apartments well located in a (relatively) quiet street but still close to the action. One-bedroom apartments range from $92 to $116 a night, and two-bedroom apartments which will sleep four adults are from $132 to $178.

In all the preceding cases rates are less the longer you stay. Some have a two-night minimum stay and a seven night minimum in the peak holiday seasons.

Hotels The *Marriott Resort* (☎ 5592 9800, fax 5592 9888), at 158 Ferny Ave just north of the centre, is ridiculously sumptuous, from the sandstone floored foyer with punkah-style fans to the lagoon-like pool complete with artificial white sand beaches and waterfall. Standard double room rates (in-season) start at $235, or $255 with ocean view.

The *Gold Coast International Hotel* (☎ 5592 1200), on the corner of the Gold Coast Hwy and Staghorn Ave, has standard rooms from $195 a night, or $215 with ocean views. Various special packages, when available, can bring that down to as little as $135.

Right in the centre of Surfers, the *Ramada* (☎ 1800 074 317), at the corner of Gold Coast Hwy and Hanlan St, has standard rooms from $220 but has a special B&B deal, subject to availability, for $125.

Places to Eat

There are plenty of choices in and around the Cavill Ave Mall. If you just want to fill up cheaply then there are a couple of all-you-can-eat Chinese places including the *Gold Star*, just east of the junction with Orchid Ave, which charges $5.90 at lunch and dinner. There are more good budget eateries in the Raptis Plaza shopping mall including Thai and Vietnamese, a carvery and bakery, and an excellent Japanese place, *Sumo*, which does cheap takeaways.

At the northern end of Orchid Ave, *Costa Dora* and *Happy House* are neighbouring pavement restaurants serving low-priced Italian and Chinese – you can eat well at either for under $10 and both are licensed.

Around the corner in Elkhorn Ave, *The Latin Quarter* is a great little BYO Italian bistro with pasta from $10 and other mains from $15 – good for a splurge. Further along toward the promenade, the *Beachside Cafe* is open 24 hours daily and has breakfast deals at $5.50 for orange juice, cereal, bacon and eggs, tea or coffee.

A particular favourite of ours is the *New Seoul*, a Korean place at the Gold Coast Hwy end of the Centre Arcade. It does a lunchtime special of a main meal, rice and kimchi for $8. Otherwise, dishes are around $10 to $12. The place gets very busy in the evenings. *Bunga Raya Malaysian Restaurant*, 3310 Gold Coast Hwy, is another good non-glitzy place. The dishes are offered in mild, medium and hot versions with entrees from $5 to $8 and mains in the $9 to $15 range. It's licensed and BYO.

Entertainment

Bars, Nightclubs & Live Music Orchid Ave is Surfers' main bar and nightclub strip. Many of the backpackers' hostels organise nights out at the clubs, usually with free admission and cheap drinks and food. The starting place most nights is *Bourbon Bar*, a fairly gloomy basement bar popular for its cut-price beer. It gets especially busy on Thursday, which is karaoke night. *Shooters* is an American-style saloon with pool tables, big-screen videos and occasional live entertainment. On Sunday night it gets busy here – groups from hostels are offered a free meal and free pool. Otherwise it's $5 to get in.

The other two big backpacker-friendly places are *Cocktails & Dreams* and *The Party* – two nightclubs, one above the other, linked by an internal staircase. They have different themes most week nights.

Paddy Og's on Elkhorn Ave is a large Irish bar which attracts an older, more sedate crowd.

Cinemas Hoyts Cinema Centre on the corner of the Gold Coast Hwy and Clifford St has three screens showing mainstream movies.

Cultural Centres The *Gold Coast Arts Centre* (☎ 5581 6900), beside the Nerang River at 135 Bundall Rd, has a 1200 seat theatre which hosts live productions and screens art-house movies. There's also a restaurant and bar, and it incorporates the Gold Coast Art Gallery, which is open on weekdays from 10 am to 5 pm and weekends from 1 to 5 pm.

Getting There & Away
The transit centre on the corner of Beach and Cambridge Rds is where you'll arrive if you're coming by bus. Inside the terminal are the bus company desks.

For more information on buses and trains see the Getting There & Away section at the start of this chapter.

Getting Around
There are dozens of car rental firms around with fliers in every hostel, motel and hotel. A few of the cheaper ones are Red Back Rentals (☎ 5592 1655) and Costless (☎ 5592 4499), both in the transit centre at Surfers, and Rent-A-Bomb (☎ 5538 8222) at 8 Beach Rd.

South Pacific Rentals (☎ 5592 5878) at 102 Ferny Ave, across from the bungee jumping, hires mopeds at $35 for two hours or $60 a day.

Red Back Rentals also has bikes for $15 a day, Surfers Beach Hut Beach Hire, at the beach end of the Cavill Mall charges $15 for a half day or $20 for a full day, while Green Bicycle Rentals (☎ 018 766 880) has good mountain bikes for $18 a day – it delivers and collects.

BROADBEACH
Broadbeach is one of those non-places that come into being in the highway limbo between two neighbouring towns. It's marked out by the huge Pacific Fair shopping centre, a casino/hotel complex and a heavy density of holiday apartments. Families are attracted here by beaches as good as those at Surfers but less crowded, and by the casino, which pulls them in by the thousands.

Conrad Jupiters Casino
On the inland side of the Gold Coast Hwy at Broadbeach, the Conrad Jupiters Casino is a Gold Coast landmark; it was Queensland's first legal casino.

The casino is open 24 hours a day and has more than 100 gaming tables, including blackjack, roulette, two-up and craps, as well as hundreds of poker machines.

Admission is free but you have to be over 18 years of age, and dress codes of 'neat casual' before 6 pm and 'smart casual' after 6 pm apply – basically, long socks if you're wearing shorts, no sleeveless T-shirts, no ripped or torn jeans and definitely no thongs. In other words, try to look like you've got money to lose.

Places to Stay
Motels & Holiday Apartments Cheap motels in Mermaid Beach along the Gold Coast Hwy include the *Red Emu Motel* (☎ 5575 2748), at No 2583, with doubles from $35 (low season); and the *Mermaid Beach Motel* (☎ 5575 1577), at No 2395 – good value, with clean units from $25.

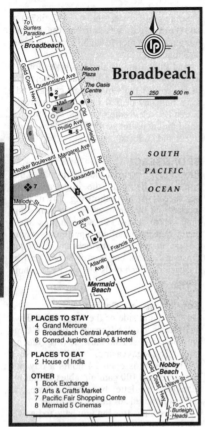

Broadbeach

0   250   500 m

SOUTH
PACIFIC
OCEAN

Mermaid
Beach

Nobby
Beach

Wave St

To
Burleigh
Heads

PLACES TO STAY
4 Grand Mercure
5 Broadbeach Central Apartments
6 Conrad Jupiers Casino & Hotel

PLACES TO EAT
2 House of India

OTHER
1 Book Exchange
3 Arts & Crafts Market
7 Pacific Fair Shopping Centre
8 Mermaid 5 Cinemas

The *Broadbeach Central Apartments* (☎ 5592 6322), 18 Phillip Ave, is a small and cheerful block of self-contained apartments with a good pool. One-bedroom units start at $70 per night, two-bedroom units $90.

Hotels If you want to stay at the casino, *Conrad Jupiters* (☎ 5592 8130 or toll-free ☎ 1800 074 344) is a 609 room hotel operated by Hilton Hotels. This upmarket place offers standard rooms from $230. The hotel's facilities include six restaurants, four tennis courts, three pools, two spas and

a gym. No mention of partridges in a pear tree.

Broadbeach's other big five-star is the *Grand Mercure* (☎ 5592 2250, fax 5592 3747) on the other side of the highway at 81 Surf Parade. A monorail runs from the third floor of the hotel across to the casino. Standard rooms start from $220.

Places to Eat
Broadbeach has a cluster of eateries along the mall and inside the adjacent Oasis and Niecon Plaza shopping centres. The Niecon Plaza also has a small international food court. For more upmarket dining, *House of India* on the Broadbeach Mall has excellent tandoori dishes and spicy North Indian curries in the $12 to $16 range. It's open daily for lunch and dinner.

There are also plenty of junky options at the Pacific Fair shopping centre.

Entertainment
You have to head north into Surfers for evening fun unless you're happy to settle for the cinema, in which case there's the Mermaid 5, 2514 Gold Coast Hwy, and also a new six screen complex buried in the Pacific Fair shopping centre.

BURLEIGH HEADS
For non-surfers, Burleigh Heads is just a set of traffic lights on the Gold Coast Hwy – a very small town with little going on. To the guys with the boards though, Burleigh is the site of one of Australia's legendary surfing breaks. In surfie-speak, it's a classic right-hand point break, famous for its fast and deep barrel rides. This definitely isn't a break for beginners – the shore is lined with vicious black rocks and there is often a strong rip, and if you make it out the back you'll find that most of the locals have a definite attitude problem.

Non-surfwise, there's the **Burleigh Heads National Park** on the northern side of the mouth of Tallebudgera Creek, a small but diverse forest reserve with walking trails around the rocky headland, a lookout and picnic area. There are also three wildlife sanctuaries in the vicinity of Burleigh Heads. If you fancy visiting just one then we recommend making it the **Currumbin Sanctuary**. It's a large bushland park mobbed by technicoloured lorikeets and other birds, with tree kangaroos, koalas, emus and lots more Australian fauna. The sanctuary is off the Gold Coast Hwy, 500m south of Currumbin Creek. It's open daily from 8 am to 5 pm and entry costs $16. If you're travelling by the Surfside bus, get off at stop No 20.

Fleay's Fauna Reserve, 2km inland along Tallebudgera Creek in West Burleigh, also has a fine collection of native wildlife and 4km of walking tracks through mangroves and rainforest. The platypus was first bred in captivity here. It's open daily from 9 am to 5 pm and costs $9.50, children $4.50. **Olson's Bird Gardens** is less interesting – it's an attractive subtropical garden with a collection of over 1000 exotic birds in enclosures. The gardens are open every day from 9 am to 5 pm and cost $9. It's on Currumbin Creek Rd – take the first right after crossing Currumbin Creek.

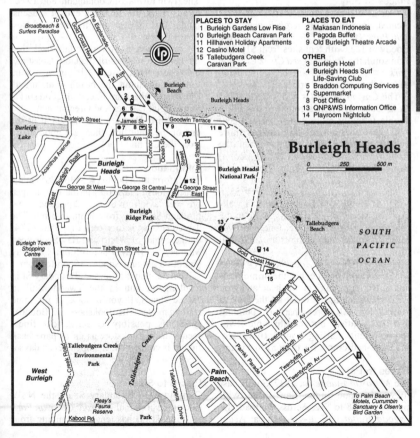

Burleigh Heads

PLACES TO STAY
1 Burleigh Gardens Low Rise
10 Burleigh Beach Caravan Park
11 Hillhaven Holiday Apartments
12 Casino Motel
15 Tallebudgera Creek Caravan Park

PLACES TO EAT
2 Makasan Indonesia
6 Pagoda Buffet
9 Old Burleigh Theatre Arcade

OTHER
3 Burleigh Hotel
4 Burleigh Heads Surf Life-Saving Club
5 Braddon Computing Services
7 Supermarket
8 Post Office
13 QNP&WS Information Office
14 Playroom Nightclub

Information

You can get more information on all natural aspects of the area from the Department of Environment information centre (☎ 5535 3032) by the Burleigh Heads National Park entrance on the Gold Coast Hwy. It's open from 9 am to 4 pm daily.

Braddon Computing Services (☎ 5535 2055), 1720 Gold Coast Hwy, offers public internet access for $10 per hour. It's open from 6 am to 6 pm Monday to Friday, from 10 am to 4 pm Saturday and from 11 am to 2 pm Sunday.

Places to Stay

As far as camping goes, there's the well-located, council-run *Burleigh Beach Caravan Park* (☎ 5581 7755), set back from Goodwin Tce, with tent sites from $16; and 1km south the *Tallebudgera Creek Caravan Park* (☎ 5581 7700), another council-run park with comparable prices.

The *Casino Motel* (☎ 5535 7133), 1761 Gold Coast Hwy, has rooms from $40 a double (slightly more expensive at weekends); otherwise there are dozens more budget motels (some cheaper than the Casino – try the *Cheshire Cat* and *Moana*) along the highway in Palm Beach, just south of the creek.

The *Burleigh Gardens Low Rise* (☎ 5576 3955) at 1849 Gold Coast Hwy is a well-kept two storey block of units, close to the beach and the town centre. One and two-bedroom self-contained units are $190/260 for three nights.

Hillhaven Holiday Apartments (☎ 5535 1055), 2 Goodwin Tce, has the prime position in Burleigh, high on the headland with great views along the coast all the way to Surfers. It's a 10 storey apartment building that has oldish but comfortable two-bedroom units starting from $110 a night, and three-bedroom units from $150 a night.

Places to Eat

The *Masakan Indonesia*, 1837 Gold Coast Hwy, has good Indonesian dishes with mains from $8 to $12. Across the road, the *Pagoda Buffet* has all-you-can-eat Asian buffets at $6.50 for lunch and $8.50 for dinner.

The Old Burleigh Theatre Arcade on Goodwin Tce is home to a couple of OK restaurants. *Tim's Malaysian Hut*, a BYO in the upstairs section, has good hawker-style noodles, vegetables, seafood and meat dishes in the $7 to $12 range. It opens nightly for dinner and for yum-cha-style lunches from Friday to Sunday. There are also a couple of good *pavement cafes* fronting the arcade.

COOLANGATTA

The 'twin towns' of Coolangatta and Tweed Heads mark the southern end of Queensland's Gold Coast and the start of New South Wales.

Coolangatta is a bit more laid-back than the northern reaches of the Gold Coast and is a good place to come if you just want time lazing about the beach undisturbed. The beaches here are fine, with good surf at Kirra, Point Danger and Greenmount.

At **Point Danger**, the headland at the end of the state line, there are good views from the Captain Cook memorial.

Information

The information booth (☎ 5536 7765) at the Beach House Plaza on Marine Pde is open on weekdays from 8 am to 2 pm and 3 to 4 pm, and Saturday from 8 am to 3 pm. The Tweed Heads visitors' centre (☎ 5536 4244) on the corner of Wharf and Bay Sts is open Monday to Friday 9 am to 5 pm, Saturday 9 am to 3 pm and Sunday 10 am to 3 pm.

There are post offices on Boundary St in Coolangatta and in the Tweed Mall in Tweed Heads. If you're looking for some reading matter, The Bookshop, 133 Boundary St, is possibly Queensland's finest second-hand bookstore as far as paperback fiction is concerned. It's open seven days a week.

Places to Stay

Camping On Boundary St on the NSW side of the border, the *Border Caravan Park* (☎ 5536 3134) has tent sites ranging from

Love it or loathe it, few people leave Surfers Paradise without an opinion of the place. Despite the tasteless high-rises and glitzy arcades, lovers of sun, sand and fun visit Surfers in droves every year. Apart from the beaches, attractions include a casino, boating and theme parks.

Top: Beaches along the Sunshine Coast attract surfers from all over Australia.
Top Middle: The Glass House Mountains rise out of the Sunshine Coast hinterland.
Bottom Middle: A colourful orchard near Stanthorpe, Darling Downs.
Bottom: Fertile farming land, Darling Downs, with an outback icon – the wind pump.

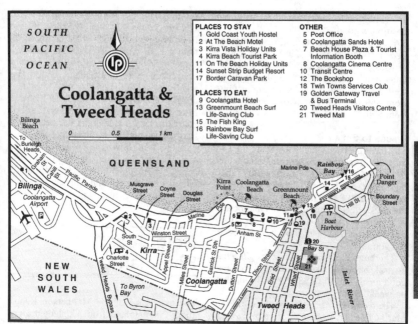

SOUTH
PACIFIC
OCEAN

**Coolangatta &
Tweed Heads**

Bilinga
Beach

0   0.5   1 km

PLACES TO STAY
1 Gold Coast Youth Hostel
2 At The Beach Motel
3 Kirra Vista Holiday Units
4 Kirra Beach Tourist Park
11 On The Beach Holiday Units
14 Sunset Strip Budget Resort
17 Border Caravan Park

PLACES TO EAT
9 Coolangatta Hotel
13 Greenmount Beach Surf
    Life-Saving Club
15 The Fish King
16 Rainbow Bay Surf
    Life-Saving Club

OTHER
5 Post Office
6 Coolangatta Sands Hotel
7 Beach House Plaza & Tourist
    Information Booth
8 Coolangatta Cinema Centre
10 Transit Centre
12 The Bookshop
18 Twin Towns Services Club
19 Golden Gateway Travel
    & Bus Terminal
20 Tweed Heads Visitors Centre
21 Tweed Mall

QUEENSLAND

GOLD COAST

\$11 to \$18, powered sites from \$13 to \$21, and on-site vans from \$27 to \$60. Tent sites aren't available in winter or at Christmas.

Kirra Beach Tourist Park (☎ 5581 7744), 200m back from the beach on Charlotte St, has unpowered sites from \$15 to \$17 and powered sites from \$16 to \$19 year round.

Budget Accommodation Best value in town is the *Sunset Strip Budget Resort* (☎ 5599 5517), 199-203 Boundary St, which has motel-style singles/doubles for \$30/40 with shared bathrooms. There's a TV lounge, kitchen and dining area and a large pool. Guests also have free use of surf and boogie boards.

The *Coolangatta YHA* (☎ 5536 7644, fax 5599 5436) is at 230 Coolangatta Rd, Bilinga, just north of the airport and about 3km from central Coolangatta. For members, a bed in a six or eight-bed dorm costs \$12 and doubles are \$32; non-members pay an extra

\$2. It's a newish building, with good facilities including a pool, but it's not convenient for anything except planespotting.

The *Coolangatta Sands Hotel* (☎ 5536 3066), on the corner of Griffith and McLean Sts, is a pub with very basic dorm accommodation in two, three or four-bed rooms for \$17/16/15.

Motels & Holiday Units *On the Beach Holiday Units* (☎ 5536 3624), 118 Marine Pde, is a complex of older-style units on the foreshore. The place is a little shabby but some of the units are extremely roomy and the location, across from the beach, is excellent. Beach view doubles are \$60, those at the back \$50.

In Kirra, the *Kirra Vista Holiday Units* (☎ 5536 7375), 12-14 Musgrave St, is a block of budget holiday units, with one-bedroom units from \$65 and two-bedroom units from \$85, plus \$10 for extras. They are quite comfortable, and the beachfront position is good.

Further north, the straightforward *At the Beach Motel* (☎ 5536 3599) on the corner of Musgrave St and Winston St has motel units ranging from $45 to $80 a night, as well as self-contained one-bedroom units from $60 to $120 and two-bedroom units from $90.

Places to Eat

The most pleasant places to eat are the two *Surf Life-Saving Clubs*, one at Greenmount Beach and the other at Rainbow Bay. They both serve lunch from 12 to 2 pm and dinner from 6 to 8 pm, and you can eat out on the deck overlooking the beach and ocean. At lunch expect to pay about $6.50, at dinner about $10. The food is fairly basic but good.

The huge *Twin Towns Services Club* has a snack bar on the second floor which has good meals for $6 to $8 and $4.50 lunches on weekdays.

The *Coolangatta Hotel*, on the corner of Marine Pde and Warner St, has a bistro with all-you-can-eat soup, salad and pasta deals, and reasonably cheap main courses. There's also an inexpensive food court at the *Tweed Mall*, open seven days.

In a higher price bracket, *The Fish King*, next door to the Rainbow Bay Surf Life-Saving Club, is an excellent BYO seafood restaurant. Entrees are all in the $12 to $15 bracket while mains all top the $20 mark, but the food is unpretentious, substantial and superb. What's more, there's a good atmosphere and a very pleasant beachside setting. It's open for lunch Tuesday to Friday and for dinner Tuesday to Saturday. Bookings are advised.

Entertainment

Out on the deck at either of the two Surf Life-Saving Clubs is the place to spend an evening. Alternatively, the *Coolangatta Sands Hotel* has live bands several nights a week.

The Coolangatta Cinema Centre, on level two in the Beach House Plaza, has four screens showing the latest releases.

Getting There & Away

Golden Gateway Travel (☎ 5536 1700) on Boundary St, just south of the border, is the terminal for McCafferty's, Kirklands and Coachtrans buses. McCafferty's has regular buses from here to Brisbane, Byron Bay and Sydney. Kirklands also runs to Sydney and Byron Bay, as well as Ballina, Lismore, Murwillumbah and other towns on the north coast of NSW. Coachtrans has services to Brisbane and Brisbane airport.

A block north on the corner of Griffith and Warner Sts, the Coolangatta transit centre (☎ 5536 6600) is the terminal for Greyhound Pioneer and Lindsay Coaches. Coachtrans buses also stop here.

Gold Coast Hinterland

The mountains of the McPherson Range, about 20km inland from Coolangatta and stretching about 60km back along the NSW border to meet the Great Dividing Range, are a paradise for walkers. The great views and beautiful natural features are easily accessible by car and there are plenty of wonderfully scenic drives. Otherwise, there are several places offering tours and day trips from the coast (see the Organised Tours & Cruises section at the start of this chapter). Expect a lot of rain in the mountains from December to March, and in winter the nights can be cold.

TAMBORINE MOUNTAIN

Just 45km north-west of the Gold Coast, this 600m-high plateau is on a northern spur of the McPherson Range. Patches of the area's original forests remain in nine small national parks. There are gorges, spectacular cascades like Witches Falls and Cedar Creek Falls, great views over the coast, and walking tracks. Because of its proximity to the coast this area is more developed and quite commercialised compared to the ranges further south. The main access roads to this area are from Oxenford on the Pacific Hwy or via Nerang if you're coming from the coast.

The adjoining townships of North Tamborine and Eagle Heights are popular destinations for day trippers and bus tours from the coast, and both have a collection of art and craft galleries, Devonshire teahouses, cafes and restaurants. There's a visitor information centre (☎ 5545 1171) at Doughty Park, North Tamborine.

Some of the best lookouts are in **Witches Falls National Park**, south-west of North Tamborine, and at **Cameron Falls**, north-west of North Tamborine. **Macrozamia Grove National Park** has some extremely old macrozamia palms.

Accommodation in the area includes the *Tall Trees Motel* (☎ 5545 1242) in Tamborine Mountain, a small and friendly motel with five units from $42; and in Tamborine (confusingly 13km north of North Tamborine) *St Bernards Hotel* (☎ 5545 1177), 101 Alpine Tce, a rustic old mountain pub (1911) with cosy pub-style rooms with shared bathrooms at $35/50 for singles/doubles including breakfast, and newer motel units next door at $45/70.

SPRINGBROOK PLATEAU

This forested 900m-high plateau, like the rest of the McPherson Range, is a remnant of the huge volcano which used to be centred on Mt Warning in NSW. It's an excellent winding drive up from the Gold Coast and can be reached by paved road via Mudgeeraba.

Springbrook National Park has three sections: Springbrook, Mt Cougal and Natural Bridge. The vegetation is temperate rainforest and eucalypt forest, with gorges, cliffs, forests, waterfalls, an extensive network of walking tracks and several picnic areas.

There are rangers' offices and information centres at Natural Bridge and Springbrook (☎ 5533 5147) where you can pick up a copy of the National Parks walking tracks leaflet.

Places to Stay

A great place if you want a base for exploring the national park area while staying close to the bright lights of the Gold Coast is the *Summer House Eco Resort* (☎ 5530 4151) in Upper Mudgeeraba. Summer House offers some of the best and most unusual accommodation in Queensland. The Resort is a collection of small themed lodges – Aboriginal, American Indian, Colonial and, most amazing of all, the Pharaoh Lodge. The Pharaoh Lodge is a 5m-high pyramid, decorated inside to resemble an Ancient Egyptian bedchamber (with the addition of some choice 20th century items such as a TV, CD player and spa). The pyramid's apex is glass so that lying on your back on the pharaoh's bed you have a clear view of the moon and stars. Rates are a very reasonable $150 per night twin-share for the pyramid and $120 for the other lodges. There are also special midweek deals that bring the prices down.

To get there take the Springbrook Rd turning off the Pacific Hwy – the Summer House is about 5km along on the right.

Springbrook

Springbrook is a scattering of guesthouses, farmlets and teahouses stretched along the plateau – there's a general store, English tea rooms (rumoured to soon undergo transformation into a Buddhist temple) and craft shops, as well as some great picnic areas and a camping ground.

At the **Gwongorella Picnic Area** just off the Springbrook road, the lovely Purling Brook Falls drop 109m into rainforest. Beside the car park there's a grassy area with picnic tables and barbecues; walking trails include a short stroll to the falls lookout, a 4km circuit walk to the falls, and a 6km-return walk to Waringa Pool, a beautiful summer swimming hole. There's a good campground beside the picnic area.

Two good walking trails start from the **Canyon Lookout**: a 4km circuit walk to **Twin Falls** and the 17km **Warrie Circuit**.

At the end of the road, the **Goomoolahra Picnic Area** is another pleasant picnic area with barbecues beside a small creek. A little further on there's a great lookout point beside the falls with views across the plateau and all the way back to the coast, with Surfers and its high-rises dotting the coastline like Lego blocks.

The **Best of All Lookout** is fairly spectacular, with views from the southern edge of the plateau to the flats below. There's a 350m trail from the car park to the lookout which takes you past a clump of unusual Antarctic beech trees.

Places to Stay & Eat You can camp at the national park *Gwongorella Camping Ground* for $5 a night per site. There's a self-registration booth at the site, and camping permits can be booked through the ranger at Springbrook (☎ 5533 5147, between 3 and 4 pm weekdays only).

Most guesthouses are along or signposted off Springbrook Rd. The first place you come to, just before you reach Springbrook, is the *Springbrook Mountain Chalets* (☎ 5533 5205, fax 5533 5156). These stylish and unusual cathedral-like chalets are in a lovely bush setting, are fully self-contained, and range from $95 a double (applicable Sunday to Thursday, off peak) to $135 a double for the deluxe chalet with a spa. The chalets actually accommodate six; it's $25 for each additional person. Rates are $10 higher during peak season and on Friday and Saturday.

The *Mouses House* (☎/fax 5533 5192) consists of 10 impressive alpine-style timber chalets, all self-contained with a loft bedroom and wood stove. Facilities here include half-court tennis, a spa and sauna, and bikes. The tariffs are $230 a double for two nights, with a minimum two-night stay.

The *Springbrook Mountain Lodge* (☎ 5533 5366), 3km off the Springbrook Rd on the Best of All Lookout road, has a lodge and cabins. The lodge is a large, timber-lined building reminiscent of a ski lodge, and has five bedrooms with en suites, a large communal kitchen and lounge, a recreation room and great views. It's popular with groups but also welcomes individuals, and costs $80 a double plus $20 for each extra person. There are also three good self-contained cabins at $120 a double. The owner of this place takes guests on bushwalking tours, and also runs good overnight tours from the Gold Coast – see Off The Beaten Track tours in the Organised Tours and Cruises section at the start of this chapter.

The *Canyon Lookout Guesthouse* (☎ 5533 5120), beside the lookout of the same name, is an attractive timber restaurant which opens for lunch Saturday and Sunday and dinner from Wednesday to Sunday. A three-course dinner will cost around $25 per person. Downstairs behind the restaurant are two simple, comfortable guest rooms with en suites that cost $76 a double.

The *Tulip Cottage Guesthouse* (☎ 5533 5125) is an attractive timber guesthouse with four doubles sharing two bathrooms charged at $60 each, breakfast included. There's also one deluxe suite at $90, breakfast included. Lunch and dinners can be provided on request.

The *Springbrook Homestead Bar & Eatery* is a modern pub-like tavern which opens for lunch and dinner from Wednesday to Sunday. For lunch it does things like ploughman's lunches or gourmet pies and salads ($6 to $10), and the dinner menu has an assortment of main courses at $10.90.

Natural Bridge

The Natural Bridge section of the national park is just a couple of kilometres west of Springbrook as the crow flies. But to get between the two by road you have to drive back up to Numinbah and then down the Murwillumbah road – a total trip of about 35km. There are picnic areas beside the car park, and a steep 1km walking circuit leads to a rock arch spanning a water-formed cave, which is home to a huge colony of glow-worms, and a small waterfall tumbling into a swimming hole.

About 1km north of the turn-off to Natural Bridge, the *Two Pines Cafe* sells fuel and has takeaway meals and Devonshire teas.

CANUNGRA

This small town 25km west of Nerang is at the junction of the northern approach roads to the Green Mountains and Binna Burra sections of the Lamington National Park. It has a tourist information office (☎ 5543 5156), on the corner of Kidston St and Lawton Lane, which is open Sunday to Friday from 10 am to 4 pm and Saturday from 9.30 am to 12 pm.

The *Canungra Hotel* (☎ 5543 5233), a white timber pub on Kidston St, has rooms upstairs at $35/40 for singles/doubles and one room with its own bathroom at $45. It also does good cheap lunches and dinners. The *Canungra Motel* (☎ 5543 5155) on Kidston St has budget units at $35/45. There's a *cafe* and a seafood and Italian *bistro* in the centre of town.

LAMINGTON NATIONAL PARK

West of Springbrook, this 200 sq km park covers much of the McPherson Range and adjoins the Border Ranges National Park in NSW. It includes thickly wooded valleys, 1100m high ranges, plus most of the Lamington Plateau. Much of the vegetation is subtropical rainforest. There are beautiful gorges, caves, superb views, a great many waterfalls and pools, and lots of wildlife. Satin and regent bowerbirds are quite common and pademelons, a type of small wallaby, can be seen on the grassy forest verges in late afternoon. The area across from the Department of Environment office at Green Mountains is frequented by gaudy lorikeets and other parrots that will happily land on the palms, shoulders and head of anyone who offers them birdseed (which is sold on site).

The two most popular and accessible sections of the park are **Binna Burra** and **Green Mountains**, both reached via paved roads from Canungra, or in the case of Binna Burra also from Nerang. The 24km Border Trail walk links the two.

The park has 160km of walking tracks ranging from a 'senses trail' for the blind at Binna Burra to an excellent tree-top canopy walk along a series of rope and plank sus-

pension bridges at Green Mountains. Walking trail guides are available from Department of Environment offices. There are ranger stations at both Binna Burra (☎ 5533 3584) and Green Mountains (☎ 5544 0634), both open weekdays only from 1 to 3.30 pm.

Places to Stay & Eat

Binna Burra The *Binna Burra Mountain Lodge* (☎ 5533 3622 or toll-free ☎ 1800 644 150) is a good mountain retreat with three types of rustic log cabins which cost from $99 to $149 per person per night. This includes all meals, free hiking and climbing gear, and activities like guided walks, bus trips and abseiling. The lodge has an attractive restaurant with good views and very good smorgasbord-style meals.

The *Binna Burra Camp Ground* (☎ 5533 3758) has a great setting with a laundry, hot showers, shelters with coin-operated barbecues and hotplates. Tent sites and van sites cost $9 per person, plus another $3 per site for power. On-site tents with lights and mattressed beds cost $36 a night for two people or $54 for four people. The camping ground is very popular, so remember you'll need to book on weekends and especially during holidays.

Binna Burra Kiosk next to the camping ground does good breakfasts as well as sandwiches, rolls, hot dogs, burgers etc. It's open daily from 8 am to 7.30 pm.

Green Mountains The famous *O'Reilly's Guesthouse* (☎ 5544 0644, fax 5544 0638) at Green Mountains has three levels of accommodation. The original guesthouse units built back in the 1930s have twin single beds and communal bathrooms and cost $114 per person per night; motel-style units cost $150 per person per night; and larger balcony units cost $165 per person per night. Tariffs include all meals and activities including bushwalks, spotlighting walks and 4WD bus trips. The restaurant here is also open to the public ($20 for lunch, $25 for dinner), but you'll need to book during holiday seasons.

There's also a kiosk and a camping ground, about 600m away, with sites for $3.50 per person per night.

You can bush camp in Lamington ($3.50 per night or $14 per family), but only a limited number of permits are issued. You can get information from the Department of Environment offices at Burleigh Heads or Brisbane, but camping permits must be obtained from the ranger at Green Mountains.

Getting There & Away
The Binna Burra bus service (☎ 5533 3622) operates daily between Surfers and Binna Burra. The trip takes one hour and costs $16. The bus departs from Surfers transit centre at 1.15 pm; departures from Binna Burra are at 10.30 am daily. Bookings are essential.

Allstate Scenic Tours (☎ 3285 1777) runs a bus service six times a week between Brisbane and O'Reilly's. Trips depart from the Transit Centre at 9.30 am Sunday to Friday, take about three hours and cost $20 one-way or $35 return for a day trip.

Mountain Coach Company (☎ 5524 4249) has a daily service from the Gold Coast to Green Mountains via Tamborine Mountain, costing $30 return or $16 one-way. It will do a pick-up from your accommodation.

MT LINDESAY HIGHWAY
This road runs south from Brisbane, across the Great Dividing Range west of Laming-ton National Park, and into NSW at Wood-enbong. **Beaudesert**, in cattle country 66km from Brisbane, is just 20km south-west of Tamborine Mountain. There's nothing much to do here – it's a small commercial centre with several motels (the *Kerry Motel* ☎ 5541 1593 is clean and good value) and hotels, and a pioneer museum. The tourist information centre (☎ 5541 1284) on the corner of Brisbane and McKee Sts is open from 9 am to 4 pm Tuesday, Thursday, Saturday and Sunday, and from 12.30 to 4 pm Wednesday and Friday.

West of Beaudesert is the stretch of the Great Dividing Range known as the **Scenic Rim** (see the Darling Downs section). Further south, **Mt Barney National Park** is undeveloped but popular with bushwalkers and climbers. It's in the Great Dividing Range, just north of the state border, and reached from the Rathdowney to Boonah road. There's a camping ground in the park as well as the *Mt Barney Lodge* (☎ 5544 3233) which offers B&B in the main building for $95 per couple; hire of one of two rustic huts for either $60 or $75 for up to five people, then $12 or $15 for each extra person.

There's a tourist information office (☎ 5544 1222) on the highway at Rath-downey. It's open Wednesday to Sunday. Araucaria Ecotours runs a three day tour of the region using the Mt Barney Lodge as a base – see Organised Tours in the Brisbane chapter.

Sunshine Coast

The stretch of coast north of Brisbane from the top of Bribie Island to just north of Noosa is known as the Sunshine Coast. It's a popular holiday area, renowned for fine beaches, good surfing and fishing. Although it doesn't have the high-rise jungle and neon-lit strips of the Gold Coast, the coast is still quite commercial and has been heavily developed, especially in the last decade.

Noosa is the most fashionable and exclusive town on the coast; it has a good range of accommodation and restaurants, an excellent national park and great beaches. North of Noosa is the Coolloola National Park and Rainbow Beach, an access point for Fraser Island.

Activities
There are separate Activities sections in the Maroochydore, Alexandra Headland & Mooloolaba, and Noosa sections, covering things like surfing, canoeing, cycling, camel trekking, sky diving, abseiling, tennis and water sports.

Climbing & Walking The Glass House Mountains have some good bushwalks and are very popular with rock climbers. There are several small national parks in the hinterland with good bushwalks, and the Noosa National Park also has some great short walking tracks.

North of Noosa, the Coolloola National Park is another good walking area; the 46km Coolloola Wilderness Trail takes you through the park all the way up to Rainbow Beach, with camp sites along the route.

Canoeing The Noosa River is excellent for canoeing; it's possible to follow its course up through Lakes Cooroibah and Cootharaba, and through the Coolloola National Park to a point just south of Rainbow Beach Rd, where you can arrange to be picked up – see Noosa and Gagaju in the Coolloola Coast section for details.

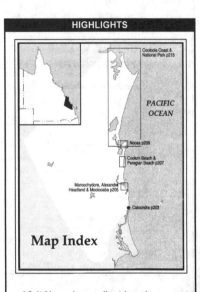

HIGHLIGHTS

Cooloola Coast & National Park p215

PACIFIC OCEAN

Noosa p209

Coolum Beach & Peregian Beach p207

Maroochydore, Alexandra Headland & Moolooaba p205

Caloundra p203

Map Index

- Visit Noosa's excellent beaches, great national park, and lively wining and dining scene.
- Hone your survival instincts at Gagaju, a rough-arse, back-to-basics camp where you not only cook your own food – you've got to catch it too.
- Admire the Blackall region's beautiful scenery, using Maleny as a base to explore the area.
- See *The Son of the Sheik* with Rudolph Valentino on a Thursday night at Pomona's Majestic Theatre – a unique evening's entertainment from another era.

Surfing The Sunshine Coast is renowned for its great beaches. There are surf beaches all along the coast, ranging from endless stretches of sandy beach breaks to the rocky point-breaks at Alexandra Headland. The

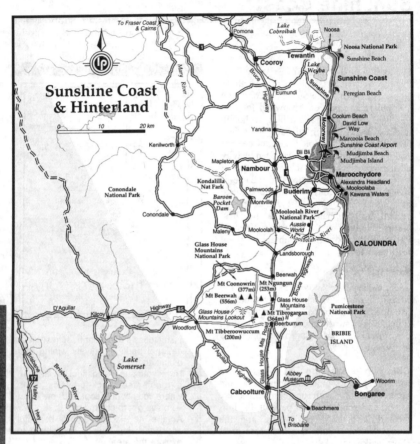

Sunshine Coast & Hinterland

most famous (and, unfortunately, most popular) breaks are the series of classic right-hand points around the Noosa National Park.

Getting There & Away

Air The Sunshine Coast airport is on the coast road at Mudjimba, 10km north of Maroochydore and 26km south of Noosa.

Sunstate has daily flights between Brisbane and the Sunshine Coast ($94 one way). Ansett and Qantas also fly to the Sunshine Coast from all major capitals – some flights are direct, others go via Brisbane. The one-

way fare from Melbourne is $390; from Sydney it's $269.

Bus Both Greyhound Pioneer and McCafferty's travel along the Bruce Hwy but not across to the coast (although Greyhound Pioneer has one service a day that detours across to Maroochydore and Noosa).

Suncoast Pacific (Brisbane office ☎ 3236 1901) is the major company servicing the coast from Brisbane, with nine to 10 services a day between Brisbane and Noosa via Caloundra and Maroochydore. Six of these run via Brisbane airport. The one-way fares from Brisbane include Maroochydore $14 and Noosa $17.

There are a couple of other companies offering local services: Tewantin Bus Services (☎ 5449 7422) has 10 services a day (six on Sunday) up and down the coast between Maroochydore, Noosa and Tewantin. It also has services linking Noosa with Cooroy and Nambour on the Bruce Hwy.

Sunshine Coast Coaches (☎ 5443 4555) has about 15 services on weekdays and nine on weekends south from Maroochydore to Caloundra and inland across to Landsborough. It also goes north from Maroochydore as far as Mt Coolum, and across to Nambour on the Bruce Hwy.

See the following Getting Around section for details of bus services to and from the airport.

Train The main coastal railway line runs roughly alongside the Bruce Hwy inland from the coast; there are daily services along here on the Brisbane to Rockhampton run. The most convenient stations for the Sunshine Coast are Nambour and Cooroy – there are bus services linking both of these places with the coast.

Car & Motorcycle The Bruce Hwy runs parallel with the coast, 20 to 30km inland. There are half a dozen roads linking the highway with the coast.

The major coastal road between Maroochydore and Noosa is David Low Way, which is scenic but can be slow going. If you are in a hurry, the newer Sunshine Motorway will whiz you north from Maroochydore. A toll is payable.

The Sunshine Coast hinterland offers some outstanding scenic drives – see that section for details.

Getting Around
To/From Mudjimba Airport There are two local bus services that meet every flight into the airport. Henry's (☎ 5449 1440) has buses going north from the airport and will drop you at the door of wherever you're

staying. One-way fares are $6 to Coolum and $12 to Noosa. Airport Bus Service (☎ 5444 7288) has airport-to-your-door bus services to the towns south of the airport, including Maroochydore ($6 one-way) and Caloundra ($12).

CABOOLTURE
This region, 49km north of Brisbane, once had a large Aboriginal population. Nowadays it's a prosperous dairy centre, famous for its yoghurt, and serves as a dormitory town for Brisbane commuters. The Community Information Centre (☎ 5495 3122) in the centre of town at 43 King St is staffed by helpful volunteers and has information on the surrounding area.

The **Caboolture Historical Village**, on Beerburrum Rd 2km north of the town, has more than 50 early Australian buildings in a bush setting and a huge range of memorabilia ranging from the fascinating to the kitsch. There's an impressive maritime museum with model ships depicting the First Fleet, and a car museum. It is open daily from 9.30 am to 3.30 pm. Entry costs $5 ($3 children).

About 7km east of Caboolture, the **Abbey Museum** is a world social history museum with a 4500-item collection including ancient artefacts, weaponry, pottery and costumes. This collection had previously been housed in London, Cyprus, Egypt and Sri Lanka before finding its home in Australia. It's open on Tuesday, Thursday, Friday and Saturday from 10 am to 4 pm, and entry is $4. The Abbey is on Old Toorbul Point Rd, signposted off the road to Bribie Island (see the Sunshine Coast map).

GLASS HOUSE MOUNTAINS
About 20km north of Caboolture, the Glass House Mountains are a dramatic visual starting point for the Sunshine Coast. They're a bizarre series of 13 volcanic crags rising abruptly out of the plain to 300m or more. They were named by Captain Cook and, depending on whose story you believe, he either noted the reflections on the

glass-smooth sides of the rocky mountains or thought they looked like the glass furnaces in his native Yorkshire.

This is a great area for scenic drives, bushwalking and rock climbing, with four small national parks around Mts Coonowrin, Ngungun, Beerwah and Tibrogargan. There are various picnic grounds, walking trails, climbs and lookouts within the parks, but no camping grounds. The main access is via Forest Drive, a 22km-long series of sealed and unsealed roads which runs off the Glass House Mountains Rd (also known as the Old Bruce Hwy). It winds through the ranges from Beerburrum to the Glass House Mountains township, with several spectacular lookout points en route.

The mountains are particularly popular with rock climbers. Col Smithies' good reference book *A Guidebook to Rockclimbing on the Glass House Mountains* should be available locally.

Mt Coonowrin is a tall and pointy shaft of rock only suitable for experienced rock climbers, with climbs up to grade 21. **Mt Ngungun** (pronounced *gun-gun*) has an easy one to two-hour return walk to the summit as well as several rock face climbs. The trails to the summits of **Mts Beerwah** and **Tibrogargan** are steep and difficult three hour return climbs.

The Department of Environment has a rangers office (☎ 5494 6630) at Beerwah, 1km east of Glass House Mountains Rd, where you'll find information on the area.

Wildhorse Mountain Lookout

There are great views from this lookout tower on Wildhorse Mountain, which is about 15km north of Caboolture beside the (new) Bruce Hwy. You can drive to the car park and walk up to the lookout – it's a steep 700m walk – but don't leave any valuables in your car as people are quite often ripped off here. A safer and less strenuous way of getting to the lookout is to park at one of the Mobil roadhouses on either side of the highway and take their free courtesy bus up to the summit. The bus runs every hour on the hour between 9 am and 2 pm on weekdays and 9 am and 4 pm on weekends. It's about a 35 minute round trip, and you get a commentary on the legend of the mountains on the way up.

Organised Tours

The Glass House Mountains are included in a three day/two night tour (incorporating the Bunya Mountains – see the Darling Downs chapter) run by Why Not Tours (☎ 4128 0774 or toll-free ☎ 1800 353 717). The trip departs from Hervey Bay or from the Sunshine Coast, but only five times a year from each place.

Places to Stay

Mt Tibrogargan Relaxapark (☎ 5496 0151) 1.5km north of Beerburrum is a good camping park with a shop and pool, and a neat landscaped setting with lots of trees and mountain views. Tent sites are $11 ($14 powered), on-site vans $21 and self-contained units that sleep up to six are $34 for a double plus $4 for extras.

The *Log Cabin Caravan Park* (☎ 5496 9338) is nestled among the trees at the Glass House Mountains and convenient for all the peaks. Facilities include a coffee shop, barbecue pits, tennis court and swimming pool. Tent sites are $11 ($13 powered). There are also two on-site vans at $22 and $24 for two, and self-contained, air-con log cabins at $45 for a double. The people at the caravan park will pick you up from the Glass House Mountain railway station and can also organise abseiling and rock climbing tours.

CALOUNDRA

At the southern end of the Sunshine Coast strip, Caloundra is no longer in vogue as a resort. The money has abandoned it and moved further north up the coast – which is good news for anyone looking for somewhere that little bit quieter. Caloundra also benefits from being a proper small seaside town (as opposed to a hastily developed bit of beachfront highway) and it has an attractive and busy main street and decent uncrowded beaches.

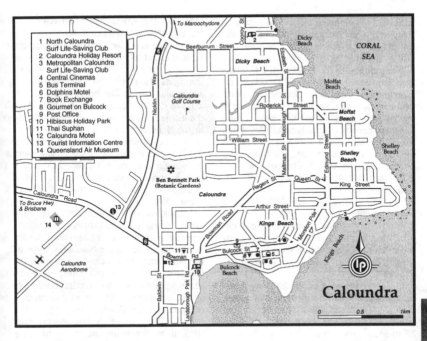

Caloundra

0   0.5   1km

Orientation & Information

The town is located on a low headland opposite the northern end of Bribie Island and at the northern entrance to the Pumicestone Passage. The town centre is along Bulcock St, which is where you'll find the post office, major banks and quite a few places to eat.

The Caloundra tourist information centre (☎ 5491 0202) is out at 7 Caloundra Rd, a couple of kilometres west of the town centre. It's open weekdays from 8.15 am to 4.55 pm and weekends from 9 am to 5 pm.

Things to See & Do

Caloundra's **beaches** are its major attraction, and they range from long, sandy surf beaches to small rocky coves and sheltered bays. Spread along the headland and separated by a series of coves and points, most of the beaches are backed by bunya pines and attractive foreshore parks. Bulcock Beach, good for windsurfing, is just down

from the main street, overlooking the northern end of Bribie Island.

Other possible points of interest include the **Queensland Air Museum** at Caloundra aerodrome, which is open Wednesday, Saturday and Sunday from 10 am to 4 pm and costs $4 (children $2), and **Aussie World & the Ettamogah Pub** on the Bruce Hwy just north of the Caloundra turn-off (see the Sunshine Coast map). This is a kind of Aussie theme park with camel and pony rides, a snake collection, some craft displays and beer and tucker. General admission is free but some of the attractions have fees; it's open daily from 9 am.

Places to Stay

Caloundra has six caravan parks, of which the *Hibiscus Holiday Park* (☎ 5491 1564) on the corner of Bowman Rd and Landsborough Park Rd is the closest to both the beach and the city centre. Tent sites start from $12 ($14 powered), on-site vans cost from $22 to $27 and cabins from $40. These are the out of season prices; in season they rise by about 30%.

Next closest to the beach is the *Caloundra Holiday Resort* (☎ 5491 3342) on Beerburrum St at Dicky Beach, 2km north of the town centre. Prices are comparable to the Hibiscus but there are no on-site vans.

Of the numerous motels or holiday units, the *Dolphins Motel* (☎ 5491 2511), 6 Cooma Terrace, has a good location opposite the bus terminal. Units range seasonally from $42/48 to $65/75 for singles/doubles.

The *Caloundra Motel* (☎ 5491 1411) at 30 Bowman Rd is one of the cheapest options, with basic units ranging from $35/40 to $45/55. It's less than 1km out of the town centre and 400m from the beach.

Places to Eat

The *Metropolitan Caloundra Surf Life-Saving Club* at the northern end of Kings Beach has a casual upstairs bistro serving breakfast, lunch and dinner, ranging from $8 to $12.

At lunch time, head for *Gourmet on Bulcock*, a small deli and cafe with good burgers, sangers and cheap meals such as chicken and chips for $5.

At night, *Thai Suphan* on the corner of Bowman Rd and First Ave has good MSG-free Thai food with beef and lamb dishes (mostly $9.50), seafood (around $14) and a good vegetarian selection ($5.50 to $7.50). It's open from 5.30 pm every night except Monday.

Entertainment

Central Cinemas is a multi-screen complex on the upper floor of an arcade on the corner of Knox and Bulcock Sts. Budget days are Tuesday and Thursday.

Getting There & Away

Long-distance buses stop at the bus terminal (☎ 5491 2555) on Cooma Terrace. See the Getting There & Away section at the start of this chapter for details of bus services.

MAROOCHYDORE, ALEXANDRA HEADLAND & MOOLOOLABA

Not so long ago Maroochydore, Alexandra Headland and Mooloolaba were idyllic little coastal centres with fine beaches, backed by the waterways of the Maroochy and Mooloolah rivers. The beaches and waterways haven't changed much, but nowadays these three centres are adjoining 'suburbs' in the Sunshine Coast's biggest and most heavily developed urban conglomeration.

It's not an attractive grouping and there isn't much to do here. The beaches, which are why most people come, are much better and less crowded elsewhere on the Sunshine Coast.

Maroochydore – the largest of the three centres – has a soulless main street (Aerodrome Rd) lined with car hire lots, while the streets neighbouring the beaches are suburban and drab. Maroochydore is also the location of the enormous Sunshine Plaza shopping centre, which incorporates a couple of hundred stores, a food court and cinema.

Alexandra Headland, immediately to the south, is little more than a coastal road flanked by beach on one side and more holiday accommodation on the other.

Mooloolaba at the south-eastern end of Alexandra Parade has the brightest atmosphere, with a long, sandy (and often overcrowded) beach, a seafront strip of shops, cafes, restaurants and nightspots, and more of the same at The Wharf, a plastic entertainment and dining complex on the Mooloolah River.

Information

The Maroochy tourist information centre (☎ 5479 1566) is near the corner of Aerodrome Rd and Sixth Ave. It's open from 9 am to 5 pm weekdays and from 9 am to 4 pm weekends. There's also a smaller information centre at The Wharf, opposite the Pier One restaurant.

Things to See & Do

Maroochydore's **Underwater World** at The Wharf is the largest oceanarium in the southern hemisphere. It's a bit pricey but it

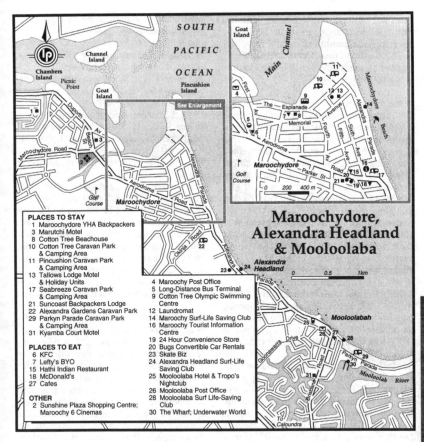

Maroochydore, Alexandra Headland & Mooloolaba

PLACES TO STAY
1 Maroochydore YHA Backpackers
3 Marutchi Motel
8 Cotton Tree Beachouse
10 Cotton Tree Caravan Park & Camping Area
11 Pincushion Caravan Park & Camping Area
13 Tallows Lodge Motel & Holiday Units
17 Seabreeze Caravan Park & Camping Area
21 Suncoast Backpackers Lodge
22 Alexandra Gardens Caravan Park
29 Parkyn Parade Caravan Park & Camping Area
31 Kyamba Court Motel

PLACES TO EAT
6 KFC
7 Lefty's BYO
15 Hathi Indian Restaurant
18 McDonald's
27 Cafes

OTHER
2 Sunshine Plaza Shopping Centre; Maroochy 6 Cinemas
4 Maroochy Post Office
5 Long-Distance Bus Terminal
9 Cotton Tree Olympic Swimming Centre
12 Laundromat
14 Maroochy Surf-Life Saving Club
16 Maroochy Tourist Information Centre
19 24 Hour Convenience Store
20 Bugs Convertible Car Rentals
23 Skate Biz
24 Alexandra Headland Surf-Life Saving Club
25 Mooloolaba Hotel & Tropo's Nightclub
26 Mooloolaba Post Office
28 Mooloolaba Surf Life-Saving Club
30 The Wharf; Underwater World

is good and worth a visit, especially if you take children along. There's a transparent tunnel underneath the oceanarium which puts you in among the sharks and stingrays. There are also touch tanks and interactive displays and a good performing seal show five times a day. It's open from 9 am to 6 pm daily; entry costs $16.90 ($11 students, $9.50 children, $47 family).

Boats depart The Wharf three times a day for an hour's **cruise** up the Mooloolah River and along some of the canals off it. Fares are $9 ($3.50 children).

Activities
Half a dozen or more surf shops along the beachfront hire out surfboards and boogie boards, and a couple of the hostels also have them free for guests.

Bugs Convertible Car Rentals (☎ 5443 7555), on Aerodrome Rd opposite Sizzlers restaurant, has bikes for $10 a day or $50 per week.

Skate Biz (☎ 5443 6111) on Alexandra Parade, Alexandra Headland, hires out in-line skates with all the gear for $7 an hour or $20 a day. It also has mountain bikes for the same rates. There are good **walking and cycling trails** all along the Maroochy River and the beachfront.

The **Cotton Tree Olympic Swimming Centre** on the Esplanade in Maroochydore is a great pool.

Places to Stay

Camping The best caravan and camping parks are the foreshore parks run by the local council. They include the *Cotton Tree Caravan Park & Camping Area* (☎ 5443 1253) and the *Pincushion Caravan Park & Camping Area* (☎ 5443 7917), both on Cotton Tree Parade beside the river in Maroochydore; the *Seabreeze Caravan Park & Camping Area* (☎ 5443 1167) behind the Maroochydore tourist office (powered sites only); and the *Parkyn Parade Caravan Park & Camping Area* (☎ 5444 1201), opposite The Wharf in Mooloolaba. These places have tent sites from $12 ($14 powered) but no vans or cabins.

The *Alexandra Gardens Caravan Park* (☎ 5443 2356), on Okinja Rd, Alexandra Headland, is 200m back from the beach and has powered sites from $14 to $17 plus on-site cabins and villas ranging from $30 to $67.

Hostels There are three hostels in Maroochydore – they'll all pick you up from the bus terminal if you phone. The *Cotton Tree Beachouse* (☎ 5443 1755) is a comfortable, rambling old timber guesthouse overlooking the river. It has free surfboards and boogie boards, and free jet skiing sessions twice a week. Dorm beds are $14, singles $30 and doubles and twins $32. It's at 15 The Esplanade, five minutes walk from the bus terminal.

One block south of Aerodrome Rd, the *Suncoast Backpackers Lodge* (☎ 5443 7544), at 50 Parker St, is a modern, purpose-built hostel with free bikes, surfboards and boogie boards; dorms cost $14 and doubles $34.

Maroochydore YHA Backpackers (☎ 5443 3151) is at 24 Schirmann Drive, buried in a residential estate a couple of turns off Bradman Ave. It's a bit institutional and has

mainly six to eight-bed dorms from $16 a night, with a few doubles at $36.

Motels & Holiday Apartments There are plenty of motels and hundreds of holiday apartments available for rent here but few bargains. Most of the apartments have a two night minimum stay.

At the cheaper end of the scale, *Tallows Lodge Motel & Holiday Units* (☎ 5443 2981) is located one block back from the beach at 10 Memorial Ave, Maroochydore, and has self-contained units ranging from $45 to $70.

Although the *Marutchi Motel* (☎ 5443 1245), at 8 Beach Rd, is close to the Sunshine Plaza shopping centre, is a bit far from the beaches (though its large rooms can sleep four and cost only $50). At the other end of town there's the small *Kyamba Court Motel* (☎ 5444 0202) at 94 Brisbane Rd, Mooloolaba, is one of the cheapest motels with doubles from $40. There are also a couple of other cheapies further south on this road.

Places to Eat

For cheap eating the best option is the *food court* at the Sunshine Plaza shopping centre, where about 20 outlets offer a huge variety of foods at reasonable prices.

Over at The Wharf, *Friday's* is a popular tavern/bar and eatery which has a great deal on T-bone steaks – from $8. There's also a branch of the *Hog's Breath Cafe* at The Wharf. For a decent salad, pasta or coffee, try the *cafes* lining the extension of Alexandra Parade, east of the junction of Brisbane Rd.

Back in Maroochydore, *Hathi Indian Restaurant*, 25 Aerodrome Rd, has all-you-can-eat Indian smorgasbords for $14 a head and main courses in the $8 to $10 range. *Lefty's BYO* is an intimate BYO that specialises in very good Greek, Italian and Mexican food; mains are $14 to $18. It's open Tuesday to Saturday for dinner.

Entertainment

At The Wharf in Mooloolaba, *Friday's* has live bands on Friday and Saturday nights and Sunday afternoons; if you prefer dance music there's a nightclub upstairs that's open Wednesday to Sunday.

The *Mooloolaba Hotel*, on the corner of Mooloolaba Esplanade and Venning St, has live bands in the small bar downstairs while upstairs is *Tropo's* nightclub. However, last time we were here the building was up for sale so by the time you read this it may be the Mooloolaba Hotel no more.

The Maroochydore 6 Cinemas at the Sunshine Plaza shopping centre on Aerodrome Rd screens mainstream films.

Getting There & Away
Long-distance buses stop at the Suncoast Pacific bus terminal (☎ 5443 1011) on First Ave in Maroochydore, just off Aerodrome Rd (near KFC). See the start of this chapter for details of bus services to and from Maroochydore.

COOLUM BEACH & PEREGIAN BEACH
Coolum Beach and Peregian Beach are far less developed than most other parts of the coast. Both are laid-back, low-rise residential areas, with long stretches of sandy beaches.

The main shopping and eating area is at Coolum, with a post office, mall and a couple of banks. Stretching along the foreshore between Coolum and Peregian, the **Peregian Beach Environmental Park** is a large reserve of coastal heathland with several walking trails leading from a car park off David Low Way through to the beach.

Places to Stay
Camping On the foreshore at Coolum Beach, the *Coolseas Caravan Park & Camping Area* (☎ 5446 1474) is a good council-run park with tent sites for $10.50 ($12.50 powered). Across the road, the *Coolum Gardens Caravan Park* (☎ 5446 1177) has caravan sites for $12, on-site vans from $22 and cabins from $25.

Motels & Units *Coolum Beach Budget Accommodation* (☎ 5471 6666) at the corner of David Low Way and Ann St offers ex-

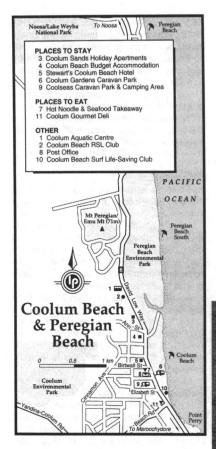

PLACES TO STAY
3 Coolum Sands Holiday Apartments
4 Coolum Beach Budget Accommodation
5 Stewart's Coolum Beach Hotel
6 Coolum Gardens Caravan Park
9 Coolseas Caravan Park & Camping Area

PLACES TO EAT
7 Hot Noodle & Seafood Takeaway
11 Coolum Gourmet Deli

OTHER
1 Coolum Aquatic Centre
2 Coolum Beach RSL Club
8 Post Office
10 Coolum Beach Surf Life-Saving Club

Coolum Beach & Peregian Beach

SUNSHINE COAST

cellent value. Formerly a backpackers', this place is in the process of being upgraded to family-style accommodation. The rooms are spotlessly clean and there are doubles, twins and four-bed dorms all charged at $14 per person per night. Amenities include a kitchen, TV room, games room and pool.

There are more budget beds at *Stewart's Coolum Beach Hotel* (☎ 5446 1899), a big modern pub at 1822 David Low Way with motel units starting from $35/45.

A little way north, the *Coolum Sands Holiday Apartments* (☎ 5446 4523), at

34 First Ave, has upmarket Mediterranean-style apartments with a pool and spa, games room and underground parking. One-bedroom units range from $85 to $130 a night, two-bedroom units from $95 to $140.

Sails Lifestyle Resort (☎ 5448 1011), 43 Oriole Ave in Peregian Beach (off the map), is a stylish modern complex of 21 two and three bedroom timber houses, in a residential area two blocks back from the beach. The houses are all self-contained and cost from $70 a double or $80 for four people.

Places to Eat
Most of the eating options are around the Coolum Beach area. Just beside the petrol station on David Low Way is the *Hot Noodle*, a noodle and sushi bar that does mainly takeaway but has some seating on the pavement outside. Large noodles are $8.50 and it also does laksa and satays. It's open daily from 12 pm until late. Next door is a great *seafood takeaway*.

A little way south, between Elizabeth St and Beach Rd, is Coolum's small shopping centre with a bakery and a couple of cafes – the best is the glass-fronted *Coolum Gourmet Deli* with its good ocean views. It does basic fare: sandwiches, salads, muffins, cakes and good coffee.

Getting There & Away
All the local bus services between Noosa and Maroochydore stop at Coolum Beach at a halt beside the Coolseas Caravan Park, opposite the main stretch of shops and cafes.

NOOSA
Despite being a surfers' Mecca since the early 1960s, Noosa has so far managed to avoid the blitzkrieg development that has afflicted the Gold Coast. It remains a low-key resort for the fashionable, as well as a popular stop-off for travellers moving up or down the coast. It has good beaches, some fine cafes and restaurants, a very accessible national park nestling next door and, just a little to the north, the walks, waterways and beaches of the Cooloola National Park.

Orientation
Noosa is actually a string of small, linked centres stretching back from the mouth of the Noosa River and along its maze of tributary creeks and lakes. The most popular resort area and the liveliest part of town is Noosa Heads, centred on the trendy shopping and dining zone of Hastings St. About 3km west and inland along the Noosa River is Noosaville, which is where river tours depart. The river at this point is seawater with a sandy shoreline. Gympie Terrace, which runs along the river shore, has a string of eating and drinking places and is quite lively most evenings.

About 1km south of Noosa Heads, up the hill, is Noosa Junction, another shopping and eating area, from where a main road leads east to Sunshine Beach, the quietest and most residential of the four main areas, but also the place with the best beaches and surf.

Information
The tourist information centre (☎ 5447 4988) in Hastings St is open daily from 9 am to 5 pm. There are also several less useful, privately run tourist information offices which double as booking agents for accommodation, trips and tours. The post office is 100m south of Noosa Junction, down Noosa Drive.

The best bookshop in the area is Written Dimensions, next to the cinema on Sunshine Beach Rd in Noosa Junction. A few doors away at the back of a small arcade is the Book Exchange, a secondhand place. Down on Hastings St in Noosa Heads there's a Dwyer's Bookstore in the Laguna Arcade and a Mary Ryan Bookshop in the Bay Village Mall.

Noosa National Park
This small but lovely national park extends for about 2km south-west from the headland that marks the end of the Sunshine Coast. It has fine walks, great coastal scenery and a string of bays on the northern side with waves which draw surfers from all over the country. Alexandria Bay on the eastern side has the best sandy beach.

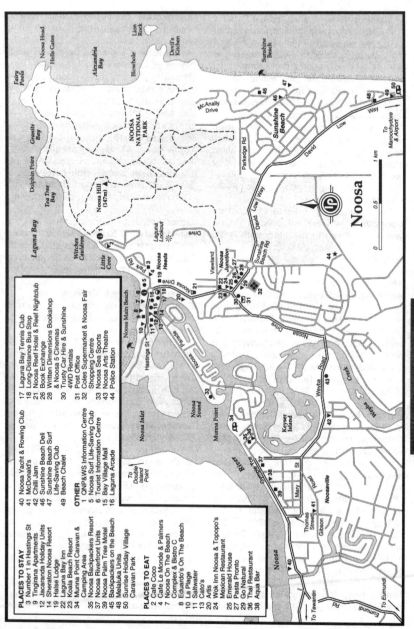

PLACES TO STAY
3 Number 1 in Hastings St
9 Tingirana Apartments
12 Jacaranda Holiday Units
14 Sheraton Noosa Resort
19 Halse Lodge
22 Laguna Bay Inn
23 Koala Beach Resort
34 Munna Point Caravan &
    Camping Area
35 Noosa Backpackers Resort
37 Noosa Riverfront Units
39 Noosa Palm Tree Motel
45 Backpackers on the Beach
48 Melaluka Units
50 Sunrise Holiday Village
    Caravan Park

PLACES TO EAT
2 Cafe Coco
4 Cafe Le Monde & Palmers
7 Noosa On The Beach
   Complex & Bistro C
8 Eduardo's On The Beach
10 La Plage
11 Saltwater
13 Catto's
20 Artis
24 Wok Inn Noosa & Topopo's
    Mexican Restaurant
25 Emerald House
27 Pasta Pronto
29 Go Natural
36 Thai Restaurant
38 Aqua Bar

40 Noosa Yacht & Rowing Club
41 McDonald's
42 Chilli Jam
46 Sunshine Beach Deli
47 Sunshine Beach Surf
    Life-Saving Club
49 Beach Chalet

OTHER
1 QNP&WS Information Centre
5 Noosa Surf Life-Saving Club
6 Tourist Information Centre
15 Bay Village Mall
16 Laguna Arcade
17 Laguna Bay Tennis Club
18 Long-Distance Bus Stop
21 Noosa Reef Hotel & Reef Nightclub
26 Book Exchange
28 Written Dimensions Bookshop
    & Noosa 5 Cinemas
30 Trusty Car Hire & Sunshine
    4WD Rentals
31 Post Office
32 Coles Supermarket & Noosa Fair
    Shopping Centre
33 Noosa Sea Sports
43 Noosa Arts Theatre
44 Police Station

SUNSHINE COAST

The main entrance at the end of Park Rd (the eastern continuation of Hastings St) has a car park, picnic areas and a Department of Environment information centre where you can obtain a walking track map, a bird list (there are reportedly 200 species in the park) and other literature.

There are five great **walking tracks**, starting at the Department of Environment information centre, which range from 1km to 7km in length. There's always a chance of spotting koalas in the park's eucalypts, especially in the late after-noon when they come down to the lower branches to feed. Tea Tree Bay is apparently the place where they're most often seen.

You can also drive up to the **Laguna Lookout** from Viewland Drive in Noosa Junction, or walk into the park from McAnally Drive or Parkedge Rd in Sunshine Beach.

Activities

Adventure Activities Total Adventures (☎ 5474 0177 or 018 148 609) is based at the Noosa Leisure Centre on Wallace Drive in Noosaville. It runs a good range of adventure activities including abseiling and rock-climbing trips, mountain bike tours and canoeing trips up the Noosa River. Sea-kayaking trips are offered from September to June.

Surfing, Boating & Water Sports Noosa Sea Sports (☎ 5447 3426) in Noosa Sound shopping centre rents surfboards, boogie boards and fishing and snorkelling gear.

Catamarans and surf skis can be hired from the Noosa Main Beach. Most of the surf shops rent boards, including Ozmosis (☎ 5447 3300) in Hastings St, which has mini-malibus for hire for $30 a day.

There are also several different places along the Noosa River in Gympie Terrace, Noosaville, that rent out fishing dinghies, barbecue pontoons, catamarans, jet skis, canoes and surf skis.

Tennis Just off Hastings St, the Laguna Bay Tennis Club (☎ 5447 4020) has good mod-grass courts costing around $20 an hour; it is open daily from 7 am to 10 pm.

Horse Riding & Camel Safaris South of Noosa at Lake Weyba, Clip Clop Treks (☎ 5449 1254) offers two hour rides ($30), half-day rides with lunch ($60), and full-day rides for experienced riders ($95). It also has six-day camping and horse riding trips to Fraser Island leaving once a month ($780 per person).

The Camel Company Australia (☎ 5442 4402), based at the Lake Cooroibah Holiday Park about 10km north-west of Noosa, offers horse riding and camel safaris – see the Cooloola Coast section for details.

Other Activities Other activities on offer include paraflying (☎ 5449 9630), tandem skydiving (☎ 5491 5415), joy flights in the Red Baron biplane (☎ 5474 1200) and hot-air ballooning (☎ 5495 6714).

Organised Tours & Cruises

Fraser Island A number of operators offer trips from Noosa up to Fraser Island via the Cooloola Coast.

Fraser Explorer Tours (☎ 5449 8647) has daily trips to Fraser departing Noosa Heads at 6.45 am. You get five to six hours on the island including at least an hour at Lake McKenzie; cost per person is $90 (children $70) including morning tea and lunch at Eurong Beach Resort. It's possible (and recommended) to extend your stay on Fraser to two days for $145.

Adventure Tours (☎ 5447 6957) and Sunlover Holidays (☎ 5474 0777) both also operate daily Fraser tours for $115 and $105 respectively ($75 for children in both cases). All three of the above companies make pick-ups from anywhere on the Sunshine Coast.

For the more adventurous, Trailblazer Tours (☎ 5449 8151) offers good value with three day camping safaris to Fraser Island costing $165 per person, which covers everything including your driver and guide, all meals and camping gear. The tours depart twice a week.

For more information on the island and alternative ways of visiting it see the Fraser Coast chapter.

Everglades Tours Several companies run boats up the Noosa River into the 'Everglades' area: the Everglades Water Bus Co (☎ 5447 1838) has a four hour cruise departing daily at 12.30 pm from $43 per person; Noosa River Tours (☎ 5449 7362) has a daily 10 am departure, returning at 3 pm for $50; Everglades Express (☎ 5449 9422) offers a 3½ hour cruise, departing twice daily for $38.

Places to Stay
Although it has a reputation as a resort for the rich and fashionable, Noosa has a huge range of accommodation covering everything from caravan parks and backpackers' hostels to resort hotels and apartments. See also Gagaju in the Cooloola Coast section for a great bush camp.

With the exception of backpackers' hostels, accommodation prices can rise by 50% in busy times and 100% in the December to January peak season. In the off season, some estate agents rent private holiday homes at bargain rates, or advertise for caretakers – look on Sunshine Beach Rd in Noosa Junction or Hastings St in Noosa Heads for estate agents, or ask at the information office.

Camping One of the best sited caravan parks here is the *Sunrise Holiday Village* (☎ 5447 3294), on David Low Way overlooking Sunshine Beach. In the off-season, tent sites range from $12 to $15, on-site vans from $30 to $45, and cabins that sleep up to five from $30 to $55 a double, plus $3 to $5 for extra people.

Another good option is the *Munna Point Caravan & Camping Area* (☎ 5449 7050) in Russell St, Noosaville. It has a good setting beside the river with lots of grass and shady trees, with tent sites from $11 ($13 powered).

Hostels All of Noosa's hostels have courtesy buses and do pick-ups from the bus

stop – all, that is, except the *Halse Lodge* (☎ 5447 3377 or toll-free ☎ 1800 24 2567) which is only 100m away. The location is tremendous: not only is it close to the bus stop but it's just a couple of minutes walk from Hastings St and the beach, and the national park is literally out the back garden gate. The lodge itself is a beautiful 100 year old heritage-listed building with polished wooden floors, a colonial-type dining room and big verandahs. The only drawback is that the place is a little austere – no partying here. Dorms go for $16 (six-bed) and $18 (four-bed), but the spartan doubles are way overpriced at $44.

A 10 minute walk uphill from the beach, *Koala Beach Resort* (☎ 5447 3355) at Noosa Junction is the place to go for noise and beery evenings. It's a converted motel with good facilities including a pool and bar. A place in a six-bed dorm costs $14, doubles are $30 and motel units go for $50 for a double plus $7.50 for extras (they'll sleep five or six).

The *Noosa Backpackers Resort* (☎ 5449 8151), 9 William St, over in Noosaville is a pleasantly relaxed place with a good seated courtyard area, a pool and a small bar. Like the above two places there are cheap meals available (it's also next door to a Thai restaurant – see Places to Eat) and free boogie boards and surfboards, and a variety of trips and tours on offer. Dorm beds are $15, doubles $32.

Over in Sunshine Beach, *Backpackers on the Beach* (☎ 5447 4739), 26 Stevens St, is a little remote – but it is almost on top of Noosa's best stretch of beach. Beds cost $14 a night, and bikes, surfboards, boogie boards and laundry are free.

Also at Sunshine Beach, right by the beach, is the *Melaluka Units* (☎ 5447 3663) at 7 Selene St. It has two and three bedroom holiday units with beds costing $16 per person, plus a one-bedroom unit for $40.

Motels & Units The prime location in Noosa would have to be on the Main Beach side of Hastings St. You can literally step out of your room onto the beach and there

SUNSHINE COAST

are dozens of restaurants, cafes and bars just the toss of a credit card away. You have to pay for the privilege, of course.

Considering the location *Tingirana* (☎ 5447 3274, fax 5447 4781) on the beachfront at 25 Hastings St is excellent value, with motel units ranging from $65 to $95 and one-bedroom apartments for four from $95 to $130, depending on the season.

The *Jacaranda Holiday Units* (☎ 5447 4011) on the south side of Hastings St is also good value with motel-style units that sleep up to three ranging from $70 to $105 a night, and self-contained one-bedroom units sleeping up to five costing from $90 to $150. The back units have river views and there's a pool.

Just under 1km back from Hastings St, the *Laguna Bay Inn* (☎ 5449 2873) at 2 Viewland Drive in Noosa Junction has four excellent self-contained units in an attractive and shady garden setting, with a good pool and barbecue area. These comfortable one and two-bedroom units sleep up to six people and range from $60 to $100 a night.

One of the best areas for cheaper accommodation is along Gympie Terrace, the riverside main road through Noosaville. The *Noosa Riverfront Units* (☎ 5449 7595), 277 Gympie Terrace, is a small two storey block of good budget holiday units starting from $40 for a studio unit or $80 for a two bedroom unit.

Further west at No 233, the *Noosa Palm Tree Motel* (☎ 5449 7311) has eight motel-style units and eight self-contained units that range from $50/55 to $55/90 for singles/doubles in the low/high season.

Top End The *Sheraton Noosa Resort* (☎ 5449 4888) between Hastings St and the Noosa Sound is, surprisingly, Noosa's only five star hotel. It's an impressive but relaxed low-rise hotel with 140 rooms and 30 suites, four bars, three restaurants, a gym, pool, sauna, spa etc. Rooms start from $350 a night (jumping to $400 in high season), although there are various packages and supersaver rates that can bring them down as low as $193.

Number 1 in Hastings St (☎ 5449 2211) is an exclusive complex of 20 apartments and four penthouses, all with great views over Laguna Bay, with a gym, pool, spa and barbecue area. Nightly tariffs for the apartments start from $150 for one bedroom, $185 for two bedrooms, and $220 for the penthouses and three bedroom apartments.

Places to Eat

Budget For a cheap lunch on Hastings St, the *food court* at the Bay Village Mall has a pizza and pasta bar, a bakery, a Chinese kitchen, a fish bar and a deli. You can eat well here for around $6.

In the Noosa On The Beach complex, just west of the tourist information centre, *The Appetizer*, a greasy, stand-up type place, does an Aussie brekky for $4.90, and snacks like burgers and fish and chips from around $4. It's open from 7 am to 8 pm.

In the same complex but on the beachfront, the *Beach Cafe* is a good spot for breakfast with a menu including muesli with fresh fruit ($5.70) or bacon and eggs ($6.50). It also does pastas, salads and other meals from $8.50.

At Noosa Junction, a few doors past KFC, the *Emerald House* is a cheap Chinese restaurant with most dishes at about $7. It's open daily from 11.30 am to 2 pm for lunch (Monday excepted) and from 5 to 9 pm for dinner.

Hastings St Hastings St is lined with sun-shaded cafes and chic restaurants catering to the caffe latte and focaccia crowd, who by night wield their Amex gold cards by candlelight. Of the cafes, the flavour of the moment is the elegant *Cato's*; the cool, sophisticated interior design belies some very down-to-earth prices for coffee and sweets and, in fact, this place is far better value than many of its less-designer neighbours. Unfortunately, both pretensions and prices run high in the restaurant section at the rear.

Possibly the best value restaurant on Hastings St remains the ever-popular *Cafe Le Monde*, east of the roundabout. Dining is out front in a large covered courtyard with

SUNSHINE COAST

a large (quite literally) menu that attempts to please everyone – and pretty much manages it, too. We tried Thai, Italian and Aussie dishes and all were excellent, served in enormous portions and at pretty good prices – $12 to $16 for mains. Upstairs, *Palmers* is one of Noosa's most up-market restaurants.

Eduardo's on the Beach at the end of an arcade at 25 Hastings St has about the best setting in town. It's a relaxed BYO with a beachy decor and a small beachfront deck, and opens every day for breakfast, lunch and dinner. For lunch, meals such as pastas, seafood curries or reef fish with lime and ginger sauce range from $12 to $14. The dinner menu mains are around $18. Eduardo's is very popular and it's a good idea to book ahead – ask for a table on the deck.

Noosa Junction *Pasta Pronto* at 2/25 Sunshine Beach Rd, down toward the cinema, has excellent homemade pastas ranging from bolognaise at $10.50 to marinara at $16.90. At lunch time (11.30 am to 2.30 pm) it has daily specials for $7.50. It's open for dinner from 5.30 to 9 pm Monday to Saturday.

Back on the roundabout at the junction *Wok Inn Noosa* offers a variety of noodle dishes with large portions going for $9.50. It's open from 11 am until late. A couple of doors away up the hill *Topopo's Mexican Restaurant* is a colourful cantina with main courses for around $10 and combo dishes for around $13, as well as margaritas and sangria by the glass or by the jug – drinks prices tend to be kept pretty low to attract the crowds from Koala over the road.

Back on Sunshine Rd, *Go Natural* is a health-food shop with plenty of sandwich and salad lunch options.

Noosaville In front of the Noosa Backpackers Resort in William St, the *Thai Restaurant* is very good, with competitive prices to appeal to the budget conscious lodged in the dorms behind. It's BYO and opens nightly for dinner.

Fine Dining: Noosa vs Paris

Shortly after spending a year living in Paris, Lonely Planet founders and sometime authors, Tony and Maureen Wheeler, spent a week at Noosa. They decided to put to the test the town's claim to be 'the epicurean capital of Queensland'. Tony and Maureen ate at six top-end restaurants and, on average, rated them higher than the Paris competition.

Of the six, *Artis* (☎ 5447 2300), 8 Noosa Drive, was the most expensive – at $100 for two – but also the best. Dishes ordered included olive-braised octopus and swordfish steak, then tapioca pudding, lychees and coconut ice cream. The verdict: terrific.

Also getting top marks was the innovative Thai food at *Chilli Jam* (☎ 5449 9755), on the corner of Weyba Rd and Swan St, Noosaville, which Tony described as 'knockout'. *La Plage* (☎ 5473 308), 5 Hastings St, was praised for its resolutely French cuisine and *Saltwater* (☎ 5447 2234), just over the road at No 8, for its award-winning seafood – the grilled sardines on quenelles of aubergine 'caviar' and wok-fried blue fin tuna with ravioli went down particularly well.

The other two restaurants that won the approval of Tony and Maureen were *Bistro C*, on the beachfront off Hastings St, and *Cafe Coco* at 62 Park Rd, beside the entrance to Noosa National Park.

And while Tony and Maureen would point out that none of the above is particularly cheap (a meal for two will cost from $65, minimum), they are all far less pricey than the Parisian restaurants. Better weather outside, too.

There are two clusters of cafes and restaurants along Gympie Terrace; the first bunch by Pelican Beach and the second further west around the junction with Thomas St. Between them they cover most cuisines. The best is the *Aqua Bar*, which is about the first place you come to if walking from the Backpackers Resort hostel.

Further along Gympie Terrace, just before you cross the river, the *Noosa Yacht & Rowing Club* is a newish two storey riverfront building which opens every day for lunch and dinner and on Sunday for breakfast. The food here is cheap and hearty.

Sunshine Beach If you're staying in Sunshine Beach, there's a general store, a fruit and vegie shop, and a couple of eateries in the small shopping centre in Duke St – of these the *Sunshine Beach Deli* is a decent gourmet deli with vegetarian dishes, home-made pastries and burgers and hot sandwiches. Down at the beach, the *Sunshine Beach Surf Life-Saving Club* serves bistro meals and has a courtyard overlooking the ocean.

Further south at 1 Tingira Crescent, the *Beach Chalet* (☎ 5447 3944) is a fun and funky cafe above a general store with an open-air balcony overlooking the ocean.

Entertainment
Bars, Nightclubs & Live Music The bar and club scene in Noosa is not particularly great. If you are staying at the *Koala Beach Resort* you're sorted, as that's pretty much the liveliest place most evenings. Alternatively, downstairs at the Noosa Reef Hotel on Noosa Drive, the *Reef Nightclub* opens from Thursday to Sunday nights till late, while the pub also has occasional live bands and Sunday afternoon sessions. Otherwise most folks tend to sip in cafe/bars like *Cato's* on Hastings.

Noosa's main nightclub is the *Rolling Rock* upstairs in the Bay Village Plaza off Hastings St. It's open every night until around 3 am, with a 'smart casual' dress code and cover charges between $5 and $7. Nearby and run by the same operator, the

New York Bar is a quieter, more sophisticated cocktail bar with an outdoor courtyard.

The *Beach Chalet* (see Places to Eat) is a good live music venue, bar and eatery that features everything from world music, reggae and African soul music to jazz and rock 'n' roll. Phone for details of what's on.

Cinema The *Noosa 5 Cinemas* at Noosa Junction is a plush, comfortable cinema screening the latest flicks. Tickets are cheaper before 6 pm and Tuesday is budget day. The cinema also has a special 'movie mania' deal on Sunday evenings with three current release films for $10 (and there's a choice of three programs of three).

Getting There & Around
Bus Long-distance buses stop at the bus stop (there's no bus terminal in Noosa) near the corner of Noosa Drive and Noosa Parade, just back from Hastings St. Advance tickets are bought from the booking desk inside the Avis office across the road. See Getting There & Away at the start of this chapter for more information on long-distance bus services.

Tewantin Bus Services (☎ 5449 7422) runs frequent daily services up and down the coast between Noosa and Maroochydore, and has local services linking Noosa Heads, Noosaville, Noosa Junction etc. It also runs a special service on Saturday to the Eumundi Markets – see the Eumundi section for times.

Car Rental Most of the car rental agencies, including Thrifty (☎ 5447 2299) and Budget (☎ 5447 4588), are on or around Hastings St. Avis and Henry's (☎ 5447 3777) are opposite the bus stop on Noosa Drive, and Virgin (☎ 5474 5777) is on Sunshine Beach Rd. Trusty Car Hire (☎ 5447 4777) shares an office beside the Noosa Junction post office with Sunshine 4WD Rentals.

If you want to drive up the Cooloola Coast beach to Rainbow Beach or Fraser Island, Sunshine 4WD Rentals (☎ 5447 3702) rents four seater Suzuki Sierras from

$80 a day and seven seater Nissan Patrols from $135 a day. It has a two day minimum hire for trips to Fraser Island.

Bicycle Hire Bikes can be hired from a number of places, including Sierra Mountain Bike Hire (☎ 5474 8277) based in the Budget car rental offices in Bay Village on Hastings St, which charges $12 per day. Koala Bike Hire (☎ 5474 2733) has mountain bikes from $10 a day, and delivers and picks up. Both companies provide the obligatory headgear.

COOLOOLA COAST

Stretching for 50km between Noosa and Rainbow Beach, the Cooloola Coast is a remote strip of long sandy beaches backed by the Cooloola National Park. Although this stretch is undeveloped it is so popular with campers that you may at times be excused for thinking otherwise.

From Tewantin the Noosa River ferry operates continuously every day from 6 am to 10 pm (until midnight on Friday and Saturday); cars cost $4 and motorcycles and horses $3.

Up the Beach

If you have a 4WD you can drive right up the beach to Rainbow Beach (and on up to Inskip Bay, from where you can take a ferry across to Fraser Island), but check the tide times before setting out – in 1997, something like 50 vehicles misjudged the tides and ended up in a watery grave (see the 'Beach Hogs' boxed text in the Fraser Coast chapter).

On the way up the beach you'll pass the Teewah coloured sand cliffs, estimated to be about 40,000 years old, and the rusting *Cherry Venture*, a 3000 tonne freighter swept ashore by a cyclone in 1973.

Lake Cooroibah

A couple of kilometres north of Tewantin, the Noosa River widens out into Lake Cooroibah. If you take the ferry across the Noosa River, you can drive up to the shore of the lake in a conventional vehicle; there

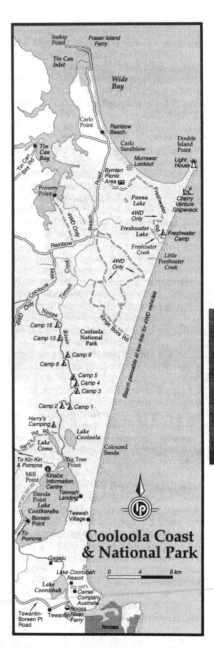

Cooloola Coast & National Park

SUNSHINE COAST

are a couple of good camping grounds between the east side of the lake and the coast.

Camel Company Australia (5442 4402), based at the Lake Cooroibah Resort, offers camel rides and safaris ranging from one hour in the bush ($20) and half-day beach rides ($45) to overnight safaris ($125), and six day safaris to Fraser Island ($720 adults, $475 children).

Places to Stay *Gagaju* (☎ 5474 3522) is an unconventional and totally laid-back riverside wilderness camp midway between lakes Cooroibah and Cootharaba in forest bordering the Cooloola National Park. It's run by two former travellers who have built the place – furniture and bunks included – from scavenged timber. Possible activities here include free canoeing and mountain biking, bush walking and, in season, cane toad golf – cruel it may sound but we were assured that it's totally environmentally friendly. There's just one communal dorm, with beds at $10 a night, or you can pitch your own tent for $6. Shower and toilet facilities are basic and bring your own food.

The *Lake Cooroibah Resort* (☎ 5447 1225) is a low-key resort on the east shore of the lake with a bunch of facilities including a pub and restaurant, store, tennis and squash courts and horse riding. It has camp sites, powered sites, on-site tents for four costing $25 a night and cabins (shared amenities, bring your own linen) starting from $40. There are also self-contained cottages, units and apartments from $100 a night.

Lake Cootharaba & Boreen Point

Cootharaba is the Cooloola National Park's biggest lake, measuring some 5km across and 10km in length. On the western shores of the lake and at the southern edge of the national park, Boreen Point is a good place to explore the area from. It's a relaxed, laid-back little town on a promontory of land with water on three sides. Unsurprisingly, it's a major boating centre with a big boat club; it also has a couple of places to stay, a pub and a good lakeside restaurant.

There are two roads up to Boreen Point – one from Tewantin, one from Pomona, both sealed and accessible in a conventional vehicle (Noosa is only a 20 minute drive away). From Boreen Point, an unsealed road leads another 5km up to Elanda Point, where there's a ranger station (☎ 5449 7364 from 9 am to 3 pm) and a lakeside campground.

Places to Stay & Eat The cheapest option is to pitch a tent at the *Boreen Point Camp Grounds* on the foreshore of the lake, just south of Laguna St, for $10 a night. At 64 Laguna St, the *Lake Cootharaba Holiday Units* (☎ 5485 3153) are two units attached to an art gallery that are both self-contained and sleep up to four people. There's a minimum two night stay for which rates are $60 per double, getting cheaper the more nights you stay.

There's also accommodation (10 double rooms with shared bathrooms from $35 a double) at the historic *Apollonian Hotel* (☎ 5485 3100). Originally erected in Gympie during the gold rush and later transported here, this is a really attractive timber pub with broad, shady verandahs. It's worth coming just for the good lunches and dinners.

The Jetty (☎ 5485 3167), with a lovely setting on the edge of Lake Cootharaba, is a stylish licensed restaurant with an excellent reputation. It is open every day for lunch and on Friday and Saturday for dinner. You can drive up, come by boat up the Noosa River, or the restaurant runs a free courtesy bus from Noosa every day if you book in advance.

Cooloola National Park

The Cooloola National Park, or the Great Sandy National Park as it's also known, covers over 54,000 hectares from Lake Cootharaba north up to Rainbow Beach. It's a varied wilderness area with long sandy beaches, mangrove-lined waterways, forest, heath and lakes, all of it featuring plentiful birdlife – including rarities such as red goshawk and grass owl – and lots of wildflowers in spring.

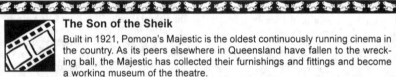

The Son of the Sheik

Built in 1921, Pomona's Majestic is the oldest continuously running cinema in the country. As its peers elsewhere in Queensland have fallen to the wrecking ball, the Majestic has collected their furnishings and fittings and become a working museum of the theatre.

At one time the cinema ran first-run releases, but in June 1986 that stopped and every week since the Majestic has screened Rudolph Valentino's last film *The Son of the Sheik* every Thursday at 8.30 pm.

Why *The Son of the Sheik*? For no better reason than the theatre's owner Ron West happened to have a copy. Ron accompanies the film on a genuine Wurlitzer pipe organ, installed in 1923. The $8 admission price includes sandwiches, cake, coffee and wine.

Ron also has an extensive collection of other great old films and comedy shorts from the 1920s, which he screens by arrangement for parties of 10 or more ($5.50 per person) and at the Majestic's annual silent movie festival each November. Give him a call and find out what's on: ☎ 5485 2330 or ☎ 019 496 358.

The Cooloola Way, a gravel road which runs from Tewantin through the western catchment area of the national park all the way up to Rainbow Beach, is open to 4WD vehicles unless there's been heavy rain – check with the rangers before setting out.

Although there are many 4WD tracks running to lookout points and picnic grounds, the best way to see Cooloola is from a boat up the Noosa River, which runs through the centre of the park. Boats can be hired from Tewantin and Noosa (along Gympie Terrace), Boreen Point and Elanda Point – see also Gagaju in the Lake Cooroibah section.

Several walking trails start from Elanda Point on the shore of Lake Cootharaba, including the 46km Cooloola Wilderness Trail and a 7km trail to the Department of Environment information centre (☎ 5449 7364) at Kinaba Island.

Camping There are around 15 campgrounds in the park, many of them alongside the river. The main ones are *Fig Tree Point* at the north of Lake Cootharaba; *Harry's Hut* about 4km upstream; and *Freshwater*, on the coast 6km south of Double Island Point. These three campsites all have fairly good facilities, but the rest are far more basic. Harry's Hut and Freshwater are accessible by 4WD, and all the others are by hiking or river only. Camping fees are $3.50 per person per night or $14 per family. For site bookings and information, contact the ranger's offices at Elanda Point, Kinaba information centre or Rainbow Beach.

POMONA

Pomona is a small but attractive rural centre in the shadows of looming Mt Cooroora (440m), which stands several kilometres to the east. A gruelling King of the Mountain foot race up to the top is held every July.

The town has a small **historical museum** open Sunday and Thursday afternoon, but the main draw is the wonderful **Majestic Theatre** – see the boxed story The Son of the Sheik.

EUMUNDI

Just off the east side of the Bruce Hwy, Eumundi is a charming little rural township famous for its **Saturday market** which draws in thousands of visitors from all over the region. From roughly 6.30 am to 12.30 pm the main street and areas just off it are crowded with more than 200 artsy-craftsy stalls, selling everything from Spice Girls rings to home made strawberry jam. The market has a good laid-back feel, and the fact that the buskers are some of the world's worst seems to bother no-one.

Buses depart from the Noosa Heads bus stand for Eumundi roughly every half hour from 7.25 am until 11.10 am. It's an $8.33 return trip.

Eumundi also has another weekly market, the **Country Fair**, held every Wednesday from 8 am to 2 pm.

After the markets a second, less widely recognised claim to fame is the local boutique beer, **Eumundi Lager**. This magnificent beer was originally brewed in the Imperial Hotel but nowadays it's made down at Yatala on the Gold Coast. You can still sample it on tap in the Imperial Hotel, while the former brewing room is now an art gallery with glass-blowing displays.

On Memorial Drive, the **Eumundi Historical Museum** (☎ 5442 8762) opens Tuesday, Wednesday and Saturday mornings, or at other times by arrangement.

Places to Stay & Eat

The *Imperial Hotel* (☎ 5442 8303), a charismatic old pub in the centre of town, has basic budget accommodation upstairs for $30 a room. On Saturday mornings it serves cooked brekkies on the verandah for $6.95 with all the trimmings. The *Eumundi Motel* (☎ 5442 8215) about 2km south of town has units from $40.

A good place to eat is *Bartu Jimba*, 100m on past the Imperial. This is a beautiful little BYO cafe in a renovated timber building with an open-air courtyard/garden. It does breakfasts on weekends (from $3 to $8) and opens for lunch and dinner daily except Monday.

YANDINA

On the Bruce Hwy 10km south of Eumundi, Yandina's biggest attraction is **The Ginger Factory** on Pioneer Rd. This place is very popular with tourists and has train rides, tours of the factory and plantations, audiovisual shows, a car museum, a bistro restaurant and a huge range of ginger prod-

ucts and souvenirs on sale. Entry is free, but the train ride costs $4 for big kids and $2.50 for little kids. Within the factory grounds is also the **Bunya Park Sanctuary**, a small landscaped zoo with koalas, wombats, kangaroos and crocodiles; admission is $6 for adults, $3 for children. The factory and park are open from 9 am to 5 pm daily.

On the highway 600m south of the centre, the riverside *Yandina Caravan Park* (☎ 5446 7332) has tent and powered sites.

Sunshine Coast Hinterland

The Blackall Range rises just in from the coast, and this scenic hinterland area has mountain villages, guesthouses and B&Bs, national parks with rainforests and waterfalls, and some great restaurants. There are also numerous art, craft, pottery and antique shops and galleries to visit, as well as a few other interesting tourist attractions. It's a great area for scenic drives, bushwalks or leisurely exploring and, if you don't have your own, it's definitely worth hiring a car for a day or two's exploration.

The short drive from Maleny to Mapleton is one of southern Queensland's outstanding scenic routes. The road follows a ridge across the Blackall Mountains that runs parallel with the coast, with great views across the Sunshine Coast lowlands to the ocean beyond.

NAMBOUR

Nambour is the main commercial centre for the hinterland. Set among hills and surrounded by cane farms and pineapple plantations, it's an attractive town with a wide range of services and facilities, but holds little of interest for travellers unless you need a bank, shops or some such thing.

The **Big Pineapple**, one of Queensland's less-than-impressive 'big things', is just off the Bruce Hwy about 6km south of

Nambour. Aside from the 15m-high fibre-glass fruit there's a train ride through a plantation, a macadamia orchard tour and a themed boat ride which together cost $13.50 ($10 children). Then of course, there are lots of things to buy, buy, buy. Alternatively, you could just put your foot down and skip the whole thing. It's open from 9 am to 5 pm daily.

MALENY

In the heart of the hinterland, Maleny is a laid-back rural township with an attractive mountain setting. It's something of an alternative centre, with lots of artists and craftspeople living in the area. Maleny has a couple of good restaurants and cafes as well as craft and antique shops and several interesting accommodation options.

There's a small information centre (☎ 5499 9033) at the Maleny Community Centre, which is open every day from 9 am to 3 pm. The centre, a yellow timber building in the centre of town, screens art-house movies on Saturday nights.

Lake Baroon, signposted 9km north of Maleny, is the main water supply for the coast as well as a popular swimming, boating, fishing and picnicking venue. You can hire boats, canoes and aqua bikes at the lake and there are free barbecues and a small kiosk.

Woodford Folk Festival

The famous Woodford (formerly Maleny) Folk Festival, which is held on a property near the town of Woodford, runs annually over the five days leading up to New Year's Day. The festival program features a huge diversity of music including folk, traditional Irish, indigenous and world music, as well as buskers, belly dancers, craft markets, visual arts performances and lots more. If you want to settle in for the festival, camping grounds are set up on the property with toilets, showers etc.

You can buy tickets at the gate or in advance through the festival office (☎ 5476 0600).

Places to Stay

Maleny Palms Home Park (☎ 5494 2933) at 23 Macadamia Drive, 1km north of the centre, is an upmarket caravan park with self-contained cabins from $52 for a double and villas from $72. It also has tent sites for $15, but these aren't always available because of the often wet weather.

The *Hotel Maleny* (☎ 5494 2013), on Bunya St in the centre of town, is a stylishly restored old timber pub with renovated rooms for $30/34 for singles/doubles, plus another $6 for a continental breakfast.

The *Maleny Lodge Guest House* (☎ 5494 2370) right in the centre of town at 58 Maple St is a beautifully restored 1894 timber guesthouse furnished in period style with

Everything you wanted to know about pineapples can be learned at the big one near Nambour.

antiques. B&B costs $76/100 for singles/doubles; it also has dinner and weekend packages. It's highly recommended.

South of Maleny at Mt Mellum, *Rowan House* (☎ 5494 1042) is a grand old timber mountain home with spectacular views across to the coast and Brisbane. There are four comfortable guest rooms, two with en suites, with doubles ranging from $100 to $160 a night for B&B. There's also a tennis court and pool. Rowan House is signposted off the Maleny-Landsborough road.

Places to Eat

On Maple St in the centre, the *Up Front Club* is a licensed club and co-op that has vegetarian and meat meals in the $6 to $9 range, as well as herbal teas, smoothies and juices. It's a casual, earthy place with healthy and wholesome food. It is open every day for lunch and dinner and on Sunday for breakfast. Nearby, the *Food Gallery* is an upmarket gourmet deli and cafe with good, if somewhat over-priced, food.

Malcolm's, 2km south of town, is set on a hillside with magnificent views of the bizarre Glass House Mountains to the south. It's an attractive licensed restaurant which opens from Wednesday to Sunday for lunch and on Friday and Saturday for dinner.

MONTVILLE

On a ridge midway between Mapleton and Maleny, Montville is an historic mountain village that has developed into a major tourist attraction. Sadly, somewhere in the transformation, Montville lost much of its original charm and character and became a commercialised version of the quaint 'Olde English' village – many of the 'historic' buildings are relatively new. Still, the setting is beautiful and there are some lovely original cottages and houses that have been restored.

There are half a dozen upmarket guesthouses and resorts on the mountain, and the village has quite a few restaurants, tea rooms, art and craft and pottery galleries,

herb gardens, gift and souvenir shops. A heritage trail guides you around the village.

Kondalilla Falls National Park

About 3km north of Montville, on the road to Mapleton, is the turn-off to the lovely Kondalilla Falls National Park, where the falls drop 80m into a rainforested valley. From the car park there's a 4.8km round-trip walk to the bottom of the falls; the less energetic can content themselves with reaching a mid-falls plunge pool and lookout just 20 minutes walk from the car park.

It's possible to visit Kondalilla on a day visit from Brisbane with Rob's Rainforest Tours – see the Brisbane chapter.

Places to Stay & Eat

In the centre of the village, the *Montville Mountain Inn* (☎ 5442 9499) has modern motel-style rooms from $70 during the week, and dinner and B&B packages on weekends from $160 a double.

On Western Ave, about 4km west of Montville, the *Genfield Boutique Guesthouse* (☎ 5442 9366) is an elegant and luxurious guesthouse on an eight-hectare property overlooking Lake Baroon, with landscaped gardens, a pool and tennis court. B&B costs $175 a double.

The food is superb at *Mirabelle*, a cafe/bar/restaurant at 96 Main St at the north end of the village. We were told that the cook used to work for Aristotle Onassis, though it's a rumour we weren't able to confirm. You can dine out on the deck or in the conservatory area and the views are excellent. It's open for lunch Wednesday to Sunday and dinner Wednesday to Saturday.

MAPLETON

Mapleton is a laid-back little township 8km north of Montville. It has a couple of caravan parks, a couple of craft and pottery galleries, and a good pub which has fine views from the verandah and does decent meals.

Continuing westwards from Mapleton, the unsealed **Obi Obi Rd** is a rough but very scenic drive through state forests to the small town of **Kenilworth** (20km). Along the route is the **Mapleton Falls National Park** where Pencil Creek plunges 120m down into Obi Obi Valley. There's a lookout point just a couple of hundred metres from the car park. This is also a great place for exploring, with lots of birdlife and several walking tracks.

There are two caravan parks at Mapleton. The better of the two is the *Lilyponds Caravan Park* (☎ 5445 7238) in Warruga St, about 400m north of the pub, which overlooks the Mapleton Lily Ponds. It has tent sites from $12 ($14 powered) and self-contained cabins that sleep up to six and cost from $40 for two people.

SUNSHINE COAST

Darling Downs

West of the mountains of the Great Dividing Range stretch the rolling plains of the Darling Downs, some of the most fertile and productive agricultural land in Australia. Setting out from Sydney, English botanist Allan Cunningham first explored this region in 1827. After six weeks his party arrived in a large valley which he described as the best piece of country he had ever seen. It was Cunningham who named the Downs, after the then governor of New South Wales.

The Downs was the first part of Queensland to be settled after the establishment of the Moreton Bay penal colony, and towns like Warwick and Toowoomba are among the state's oldest. There are also some interesting attractions scattered through the region, including the scenic Granite Belt region (near Stanthorpe) with Queensland's only wine-growing district and some fine national parks; the historic Jondaryan Woolshed complex west of Toowoomba; and the excellent historical village at Miles.

To the north and west of Brisbane is the South Burnett region with the popular Bunya Mountains National Park and a string of small rural centres along Hwy 17.

GETTING THERE & AWAY
Air
Flight West have daily flights between Brisbane and Roma.

Bus
McCafferty's has two major bus services that pass through the Darling Downs. Their Brisbane-Longreach service runs along the Warrego Hwy via Toowoomba, Dalby, Miles and Roma, while their inland Brisbane to Melbourne service along the Newell Hwy goes via Toowoomba and Goondiwindi. Greyhound Pioneer also does the Brisbane-Melbourne run.

See Getting There & Away in the Toowoomba section for more details of

---

HIGHLIGHTS

Map Index

PACIFIC OCEAN

- Roma p238
- Toowoomba p233
- Warwick p225
- Goondiwindi p231
- Stanthorpe p228

NEW SOUTH WALES

- There's no better way to experience the Downs than by staying at a traditional homestead like Talgai, Argyle or Valden House.
- Wake up with wallabies: the Bunya Mountains National Park is a great place to camp among friendly furry and feathered wildlife.
- Visit Miles Historical Village, an accurate recreation of a turn-of-the-19th century high street.

McCafferty's services, as well as those of smaller bus companies that service the region.

Brisbane Bus Lines has daily services from Brisbane into the South Burnett region.

Train
The air-con *Westlander* runs twice weekly from Brisbane to Charleville, via Ipswich,

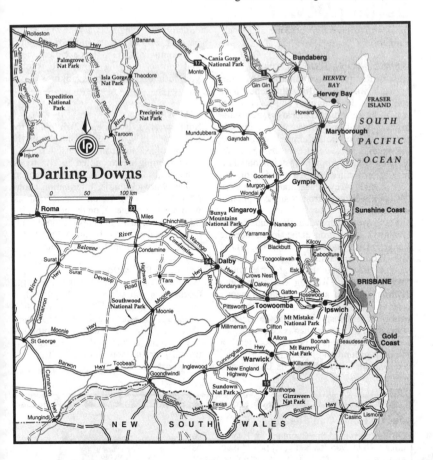

Toowoomba and Roma. The 777km journey from Brisbane to Charleville takes about 17 hours; there are connecting bus services from Charleville to Quilpie and Cunnamulla.

Car & Motorcycle

The major route through the Darling Downs is the Warrego Hwy, which runs west from Ipswich to Charleville. There's also the Cunningham Hwy, which runs south-west from Ipswich to Warwick and Goondiwindi.

The two main north-south routes in the Downs are the Leichhardt Hwy, which runs north from Goondiwindi to Rockhampton via Miles, and the Carnarvon Hwy which runs north from Mungindi on the NSW border to Roma.

The most scenic drives in this region pass through the Great Dividing Range, particularly around Stanthorpe and Killarney, and the Bunya Mountains. West of the mountains most of the highways are pretty dull.

The South Burnett section of this chapter follows Hwy 17, which is an alternative inland route between Brisbane and Rock-hampton.

IPSWICH TO WARWICK (120km)

Now virtually an outer suburb of Brisbane, Ipswich was originally established as a convict settlement as early as 1827, and was one of the most important early Queensland towns. It still possesses many fine old houses and public buildings, described in the excellent *Ipswich City Heritage Trails* leaflet available from the Ipswich tourist information centre (☎ 3281 0555) on the corner of D'Arcy Place and Brisbane St. It's open weekdays from 9 am to 5 pm and weekends from 10 am to 4 pm.

South-west of Ipswich, the Cunningham Hwy to Warwick crosses the Great Dividing Range at **Cunningham's Gap**, with 1100m high mountains rising either side of the road. **Main Range National Park**, which covers the Great Dividing Range for about 20km north and south of Cunningham's Gap, is great walking country; there are a variety of walks starting from the car park at the crest of Cunningham's Gap. Much of the range is covered in rainforest. There's a camping ground and information office by the road on the western side of the gap:

contact the ranger (☎ 4666 1133) for permits. **Spicer's Gap**, in the range south of Cunningham's Gap, has excellent views and another camping ground. To reach it you turn off the highway 5km west of Aratula, back towards Ipswich.

WARWICK

South-west of Brisbane, 162km inland and near the NSW border, Warwick is the second-oldest town in Queensland. It's a busy farming centre noted for its roses, dairy produce, historic buildings and rodeo.

The Warwick tourist information centre (☎ 4661 3122), 49 Albion St, is a good one with plenty of material on the neighbouring South Downs towns; it's open from 9 am to 5 pm weekdays, from 10 am to 3 pm Saturday, and from 10 am to 2 pm Sunday.

Things to See & Do

Warwick's major attraction is the **Pringle Cottage & Museum** on Dragon St, a cottage dating from 1863, stuffed with a collection of old telephones, costumes, photos and assorted historical contraptions. The museum is open daily except Tuesday from 10 am to noon and from 2 to 4 pm; entry costs \$3.50.

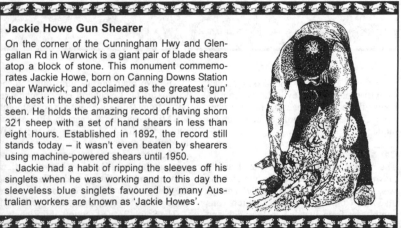

Jackie Howe Gun Shearer

On the corner of the Cunningham Hwy and Glen-gallan Rd in Warwick is a giant pair of blade shears atop a block of stone. This monument commemorates Jackie Howe, born on Canning Downs Station near Warwick, and acclaimed as the greatest 'gun' (the best in the shed) shearer the country has ever seen. He holds the amazing record of having shorn 321 sheep with a set of hand shears in less than eight hours. Established in 1892, the record still stands today – it wasn't even beaten by shearers using machine-powered shears until 1950.

Jackie had a habit of ripping the sleeves off his singlets when he was working and to this day the sleeveless blue singlets favoured by many Australian workers are known as 'Jackie Howes'.

Warwick has plenty of impressive old buildings, many built from locally quarried sandstone. They include the **post office** on the corner of Palmerin and Grafton Sts, a solid structure with unusual keyhole arches and topped with a copper-domed tower; **St Mary's Catholic Church** on the corner of Palmerin and Wood Sts; the **Masonic Temple** on Guy St; and the magnificent **Sophia College** (1891) on Locke St, two blocks behind the museum. The tourist office has a good heritage trail brochure.

Next to the tourist office, the **Warwick**

Regional Art Gallery houses regular exhibitions and is open from 10 am to 4 pm Tuesday to Saturday, and from 1 to 4 pm Sunday.

Festivals

Warwick's major annual event is the Warwick Rodeo & Campdraft. The rodeo and its accompanying festival and street parade are held on the last weekend in October.

Other festivals and special events include the Warwick Show, held in March; the

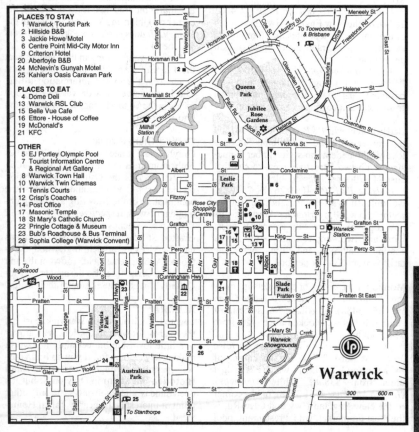

PLACES TO STAY
1 Warwick Tourist Park
2 Hillside B&B
3 Jackie Howe Motel
6 Centre Point Mid-City Motor Inn
9 Criterion Hotel
20 Aberfoyle B&B
24 McNevin's Gunyah Motel
25 Kahler's Oasis Caravan Park

PLACES TO EAT
4 Dome Deli
13 Warwick RSL Club
15 Belle Vue Cafe
16 Ettore - House of Coffee
19 McDonald's
21 KFC

OTHER
5 EJ Portley Olympic Pool
7 Tourist Information Centre
  & Regional Art Gallery
8 Warwick Town Hall
10 Warwick Twin Cinemas
11 Tennis Courts
12 Crisp's Coaches
14 Post Office
17 Masonic Temple
18 St Mary's Catholic Church
22 Pringle Cottage & Museum
23 Bub's Roadhouse & Bus Terminal
26 Sophia College (Warwick Convent)

Warwick

Warwick Country & Western Singers Competition in September; and the Facetors' Guild Meeting, said to be the country's biggest swap-meet for collectors of precious and semiprecious stones. The meet is held at the Warwick Showgrounds every year over Easter.

Places to Stay
Camping & Budget The *Warwick Tourist Park* (☎ 4661 8335), at 18 Palmer Ave off the New England Hwy on the northern outskirts of town, has sites at $10 ($13 powered) and dormitory accommodation at $10 per person.

Kahler's Oasis Caravan Park (☎ 4661 2874), on the New England Hwy 1km south of the centre, has tent sites for $6 or on-site vans at $12 per person and cabins at $17.50 per person.

The *Criterion Hotel* (☎ 4661 1042) 84 Palmerin St, is a huge old country pub with basic but clean rooms opening onto a broad front verandah costing $25 per person.

B&Bs *Aberfoyle B&B* (☎ 4661 8334), on the corner of Wood and Albion Sts, is a lovely old Federation-style timber homestead with two attractive guest rooms that cost $45/70 for singles/doubles.

Hillside B&B (☎ 4661 2671), 25 Weewondilla Rd, is an elegant sandstone former rectory on a hill overlooking Warwick. It's now a private house with a separate guest wing and two simple, family-style rooms sharing a bathroom and sitting room. The tariff is from $35 per person.

Motels Of the dozen or so motels in town, the *Centre Point Mid-City Motor Inn* (☎ 4661 3488), 32 Albion St, is the most central. It has well looked after units from $54 a double.

The cheapest place is the *Jackie Howe Motel* (☎ 4661 2111), on the corner of Palmerin and Victoria Sts, which has budget units from $38/48, while *McNevin's Gunyah Motel* (☎ 4661 5588), on the corner of the New England Hwy and Glen Rd, is the most up-market, with a restaurant, pool

and spa, and singles/doubles ranging from $54/63 to $75/85.

Places to Eat
At 119 Palmerin Ave, the *Belle Vue Cafe* is a classic country town cafe/milk bar with a Laminex and vinyl decor straight out of the 1950s. They serve up a good range of meals and snacks, including great milk shakes in the old aluminium containers. Around the corner at 19 Grafton St, the coffee's good at *Ettore – House of Coffee,* which also has cakes and pastries, filled croissants and sandwiches.

For something more substantial try under the multicoloured geodesic dome on the corner of Albion and Victoria Sts, where the *Dome Deli* does cooked breakfasts, burgers and the like.

The best value dining in the evening is at the *Warwick RSL Club* on Albion St, just along from the tourist information office. The bistro serves a wide variety of good meals in the $6 to $12 range; dinner is from 6 to 8 pm only.

Getting There & Away
Greyhound Pioneer and Border Coaches both stop at Bub's Roadhouse (☎ 4661 7539), which is the Caltex service station on the corner of Wallace and Wood Sts (the continuation of the New England and Cunningham Hwys, respectively).

Crisp's Coaches (☎ 4661 2566), 72 Grafton St near the Albion St corner, has daily services to Ipswich, Inglewood, Stanthorpe, Allora, Tenterfield, Toowoomba and Brisbane. Crisp's are also the agents for McCafferty's, whose buses stop at their office.

ALLORA
Located 26km north of Warwick, just off the road to Toowoomba, Allora is an attractive little township but certainly not worth making any detours for. If you do find yourself passing through, there's a small **Historical Museum** in Drayton St but it's open Sunday afternoon only. The only other point of interest is the nearby Talgai Homestead.

Talgai Homestead

About 8km west of Allora, along Dalrymple Creek Rd, is one of Queensland's most impressive guesthouses. *Talgai Homestead* (☎ 4666 3444, fax 4666 3780) is a magnificent sandstone homestead of palatial proportions that has been heritage listed.

Formerly the centrepiece of a large cattle stud, the homestead has been superbly transformed into an elegant restaurant and guesthouse. The broad verandahs are prowled by peacocks and herds of camels graze the pastures (Why camels? Because the owner happens to like them). The enormous honeymoon suite, with a bathroom bigger than most bedrooms, costs $260 a night, and there are five smaller suites with their own bathrooms that cost $220 a double. Breakfast is included, as is a tour of the farm in a horse-drawn carriage. Lunch and dinner are also available. If you just want a sample of Talgai, the restaurant is open to the public but you need to book.

KILLARNEY

Killarney, 35km south-east of Warwick near the NSW border, is a fairly nondescript town in an area of fine mountain scenery. There are several attractive waterfalls nearby, the best of which is possibly the **Queen Mary Falls**, tumbling 40m into a rainforested gorge 10km east of town. If you want to stay around here there's the *Queen Mary Falls Caravan Park* (☎ 4664 7151) on the road near the falls, which has tent sites for $8 and on-site vans from $20.

Alternatively, *Adjinbilly* (☎ 4664 1599), a forested property 12km north of Killarney in the Condamine River Gorge, has three secluded, self-contained cabins (with pot belly stoves) that sleep up to five people; the tariffs are $110 a double plus $30 for each extra person, with a minimum two night stay. Adjinbilly is signposted from opposite the Westpac bank in Killarney.

WARWICK TO STANTHORPE (59km)
Vecchio's Fruit Barn
The area around Stanthorpe is known as Brisbane's orchard, and as you drive around

here you'll see numerous roadside stalls selling fruit and vegies straight off the farms. So how come this one gets its own listing? Well, apart from having a great selection of lovingly presented fruit and vegies, it's the only fruit barn we've ever visited that has its own cappuccino machine. We pulled up here early one morning planning to buy a mixed bag of fruit for breakfast, next thing we're enjoying an excellent coffee served with almond macaroons.

The Vecchio fruit barn is beside the New England Hwy, 17km north of Stanthorpe. Call in and say hi, but be warned – Mrs Vecchio is a ferocious saleswoman and you'll be lucky to get away with only a coffee.

STANTHORPE
At an altitude of 915m, Stanthorpe is the coolest town in the state. This is one of the few places in Queensland where you might need a jumper – and in winter a coat, hat and gloves might also come in handy.

Stanthorpe celebrates its winters every July with its Brass Monkey Festival, and the region's four seasons climate provides the basis for a flourishing fruit and vegetable industry. The town is also at the centre of Queensland's only wine-making region, with more than 20 boutique wineries which open to the public. Stanthorpe is a popular base for people visiting the wineries and has a good range of accommodation – pick up a list at the tourist information office (☎ 4681 2057) in the civic centre on the corner of Marsh and Lock Sts, open on weekdays from 8.45 am to 5 pm and from 10 am to 1 pm on Saturday.

Things to See & Do
The **Stanthorpe Historical Museum** on the northern outskirts on High St has a slab-timber jail (1876), an old shire council building (1914), a former school residence (1891), plus a meticulously presented collection of local memorabilia. It's open from 10 am to 4 pm Tuesday to Friday, from 1 to 4 pm Saturday, and from 9 am to noon Sunday.

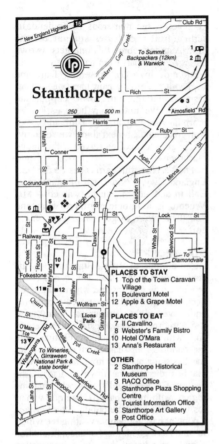

Stanthorpe

0   250   500 m

PLACES TO STAY
1 Top of the Town Caravan
   Village
11 Boulevard Motel
12 Apple & Grape Motel

PLACES TO EAT
7 Il Cavalino
8 Webster's Family Bistro
10 Hotel O'Mara
13 Anna's Restaurant

OTHER
2 Stanthorpe Historical
   Museum
3 RACQ Office
4 Stanthorpe Plaza Shopping
   Centre
5 Tourist Information Office
6 Stanthorpe Art Gallery
9 Post Office

The **Stanthorpe Art Gallery** in Lock St has exhibitions of works by local artists. It's open on weekdays from 10 am to 4 pm and weekends from 1 to 4 pm.

Red Gum Ridge Trail Rides (☎ 4683 7169) offers various horse rides ranging from a one-hour trot to a tour of the wineries or overnight pub rides – ring for details.

Places to Stay

Caravan Parks The *Top of the Town Caravan Village* (☎ 4681 4888), 10 High St, on the northern edge of town, has tent sites

for $10 ($13 powered), on-site vans from $26 and self-contained units from $60 – however, we've received bad word on the vans here so check things carefully.

Hostels *Summit Lodge Backpackers* (☎ 4683 2599) on the New England Hwy 12km north of Stanthorpe at Thulimbah, specialises in finding fruit and vegetable-picking work for travellers. Be warned: the place is extremely remote and very basic, being little more than a glorified shack – and a badly looked after one at that – but you can make good money here picking apples, tomatoes, pears, capsicums, cabbages etc. The hostel often has a waiting list for work, so you need to ring ahead rather than just turn up. The main harvesting season starts in October and runs through to mid-June, although work is sometimes available in the winter months. Dorm beds costs $12.50 a night or $80 a week. Buses running between Brisbane and Stanthorpe can drop you at the door – otherwise the owners will pick you up from Stanthorpe.

Motels There are half a dozen motels in town to choose from. One of the best and most central is the *Apple & Grape Motel* (☎ 4681 1288), 63 Maryland St, with units from $50/57. Across the road, the *Boulevard Motel* (☎ 4681 1777) is part of the Budget chain and has rooms overlooking a small park from $38/42. Half a kilometre south of the centre, the *Granite Court Motel* (☎ 4681 1811) at 34 Wallangarra Rd has tidy units at $55/60.

B&Bs, Cabins & Cottages The tourist information centre has an extensive list of this kind of accommodation and it's best to tell them exactly what you are looking for and get their recommendations. Rates per night begin at about $80 for two.

The *Happy Valley Vineyard Retreat* (☎ 4681 3250), an impressive resort complex 4km west of Stanthorpe (signposted off the Texas road), is great value. It stands on a bush property studded with granite outcrops, with a good range of cabins and units, a tennis court and a restaurant. You have a choice between modern homestead units or more secluded timber cabins, all with their own bathrooms and wood fires. Tariffs include breakfast and dinner and range from $89 per person per night. The resort also runs daily winery tours in their minibuses.

Places to Eat

Il Cavallino, 136 High St, is a straightforward little Italian eatery which, despite appearances, has better than average Italian food for around $10. It opens for lunch and dinner every day except Monday. A few doors along is the popular and attractive *Webster's Family Bistro* inside the Central Hotel, with lunches from $5 to $9 and dinners from $9 to $12. The *Hotel O'Mara* in Maryland St also does good pub meals.

Anna's Restaurant, on the corner of Wallangarra Rd and O'Mara Terrace, is a family-run BYO Italian restaurant set in a cosy Queenslander. They serve good, hearty tucker, with pastas from $9 to $13 and other main courses from $10 to $15.

SOUTH OF STANTHORPE
Granite Belt Wineries
The Granite Belt is an elevated plateau of the Great Dividing Range and ranges from 800m to 950m above sea level. It's the only part of the Sunshine state with a climate suitable for viticulture; set among some spectacular scenery is a cluster of vineyards constituting Queensland's only true winery district.

Grapes were first grown in the district in the mid-19th century and an influx of Italian immigrants after WWI led to the establishment of the region as a producer of bulk wine. There are now some 16 wineries dotted around the area. None of these are large producers; all are boutique wineries selling the majority of their wines through their 'cellar doors', which range from small tin sheds draped in vines to impressive stone chalets. The region produces everything from sparkling wines and vermouth to the more traditional styles. It's better known

for its reds, but that said, the Ballendean winery picked up a lot of plaudits at the 1997 Australian Small Winemakers Show for its whites.

All of the wineries are open weekends for cellar-door sales, and most also open during the week. Finding these places isn't hard – most are spread along either side of the 17km stretch of the New England Hwy between Stanthorpe and Ballendean to the south.

Wineries south of Stanthorpe include **Kominos Wines** (☎ 4683 4311) at Severnlea, with its famous grape-eating dog; **Granite Cellars** at Glen Aplin; **Felsberg Winery** (☎ 4683 4332), an impressive stone building high on a hill on the east side of the highway; **Rumbalara Vineyards** (☎ 4684 1206), with a wide variety of styles including a sweet vermouth and a cider; and the scenic **Bald Mountain Winery** near Wallangarra.

There are also a couple of wineries north of Stanthorpe, including **Heritage Wines** (☎ 4685 2197) at Cottonvale, 16km north, which has a craft shop and gallery and accommodation in a small heritage-style timber cottage; **Mt Magnus Winery**, 7km west of the highway at Pozieres (turn off at Thulimbah, 13km north of Stanthorpe); and the **Old Caves Winery** (☎ 4681 1494) just 1km north of Stanthorpe.

Tours Stanthorpe Winery Tours (toll-free ☎ 1800 657 009) operate full day guided tours at 10 am daily. The trips take in five or so different wineries with commentary and tasting, and include lunch. The cost is $40 per person.

Rob's Rainforest Tours (☎ 019 496 607) runs a weekend wine tasting tour out of Brisbane. It departs every Saturday morning during August through October (returning Sunday) and the cost of $99 includes transport, a night's accommodation, breakfast and a barbecue lunch and, of course, wine tasting in as many wineries as possible.

Places to Stay & Eat The most popular base for visits to the wineries is Stanthorpe

– see that section earlier – or there are a few options around Girraween National Park. One interesting place worth mentioning here is the *Vineyard Cottages & Cafe* (☎ 4684 1270) on the northern outskirts of Ballendean, 17km south of Stanthorpe. It has four comfortable and attractive heritage-style brick cottages with their own en suites and spas costing from $130 to $145 a double or $220 for up to four people. The cafe is a tiny cream-coloured church which has been converted into a licensed restaurant with a garden courtyard; it's open for lunch from Friday to Sunday and for dinner on Saturday night.

Another great place to eat is *The Picnic Basket* (☎ 4683 4324) at Glen Aplin, 10km south of town. It's a small, plain-looking cottage tucked behind the Granite Cellars winery, but the owner/chef Una produces an outstanding range of home made breakfasts, lunches and snacks using fresh local produce. It's open from 8 am to 5 pm every Friday, Saturday and Sunday.

Girraween National Park

From the New England Hwy 26km south of Stanthorpe, a paved road leads 9km east to Girraween National Park, an area of 1000m high hills, valleys and huge granite outcrops. The park has a visitors centre (☎ 4684 5157) which is (usually) open Monday to Saturday between 8 am and 4 pm (but staffed only from 2 pm) and two good camping grounds with hot showers and several walking tracks – the visitors' centre has a park guide with a map and walks description.

Girraween adjoins Bald Rock National Park over the border in NSW. It can fall below freezing on winter nights here, but summer days are hot. Call the visitors centre to book camp sites.

Places to Stay

Apart from the two camping grounds in the national park, there are a couple of accommodation options close to the park. Around 2km west of the visitors' centre, *Wisteria Cottages* (☎ 4684 5121) is a modern two bedroom timber cottage on a cleared property behind a craft and pottery gallery. The cottage, which sleeps six, is self-contained and costs $50 per person per night ($30 for children), including breakfast. On the same road nearby is also the *Wybera Host Farm* (☎ 4684 5115) which offers B&B for $30 per person.

The *Girraween Country Inn* (☎ 4683 7109), on the northern edge of the park, is a two-storey chalet-style guesthouse with nine en suite rooms upstairs and a restaurant downstairs. Dinner and B&B costs $90 per person per night. To get there, turn off the New England Hwy at Ballendean and follow the Eukey Rd for 9km.

Sundown National Park

On the Queensland/NSW border, about 80km south-west of Stanthorpe, the Sundown National Park is a rugged and rocky landscape dominated by the steep, spectacular gorges of the Severn River. The park is largely undeveloped and offers good fishing and swimming, with an abundance of birdlife. The Broadwater camping ground can be reached in a conventional vehicle along a 4km gravel road. The northern section of the park is only accessible by 4WD vehicles from Ballendean south of Stanthorpe.

For information and to book camping permits, contact the park rangers on ☎ (02) 6737 5235.

TEXAS

A sleepy border town 55km south of Inglewood, Texas falls way short of the romantic images conjured up by its name. The name apparently has its origins with two brothers who settled some property here then left to try their luck on a goldfield. By the time they returned someone else had claimed their land. An ownership dispute ensued. Around this time the war of independence between Mexico and Texas was raging, inspiring the brothers to call their territory the Texas station.

Should you need to spend the night here the options are the *Yellow Rose Guesthouse* (☎ 4653 1592) behind the Chinese restaurant on High St, which is a simple – if a bit eccentric – guesthouse in a private home or, also on High St, the *Texas Motel* (☎ 4653 1300). Both places cost about $50 for a double.

GOONDIWINDI

West of Warwick, Goondiwindi (pronounced 'gun' not 'goon') is on the NSW border and the MacIntyre River. It's a small but attractive town and a popular stop for travellers on the Newell Hwy between Melbourne and Brisbane.

Perhaps Goondiwindi's greatest claim to fame is as the home of the great 'Gunsynd', a particularly successful racehorse also known as 'The Goondiwindi Grey'. There's a memorial statue of the beast in MacIntyre St, beside the bridge across the MacIntyre River. There's also a Gunsynd memorial lounge in the **Victoria Hotel**, a beautiful old country pub with broad verandahs and an eccentric tower; it's on the corner of Marshall and Herbert Sts.

Near the Gunsynd monument, the **Customs House Museum** houses an interesting collection put together by the local historical society. It's open daily (except

Tuesday) from 10 am to 4 pm. There are also a couple of other interesting historical buildings in town; round the corner on Bowen St, the **Holy Trinity Church** has fine stained glass windows, while 200m east, **Martha's Cottage** is a 100-plus year-old dwelling constructed of bush timber.

For further information the municipal tourist office (☎ 4671 2653) is in the base of a concrete water tower on McLean St, 50m north of the junction with Marshall St, the town's main drag. It's open from 9 am to 5 pm Monday to Friday.

Places to Stay & Eat

Goondiwindi has three caravan parks, seven motels and quite a few pubs with accommodation. The most central of the caravan parks, and the one with the most attractive site, is *Devon's Caravan Park* (☎ 4671 1383), at 3 Delacy St just east of the MacIntyre bridge. Tent sites go for $11 ($13 powered), on-site vans for $28 and cabins for $34. The *Goondiwindi Mobile Village* (☎ 4671 2566) is slightly cheaper but it's a couple of kilometres north of the centre on Hungerford St.

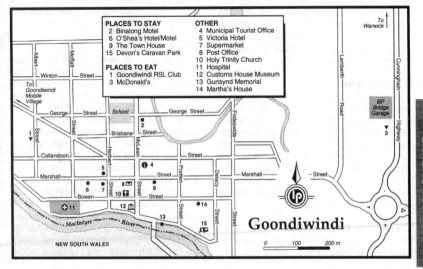

PLACES TO STAY
2 Binalong Motel
6 O'Shea's Hotel/Motel
9 The Town House
15 Devon's Caravan Park

PLACES TO EAT
1 Goondiwindi RSL Club
3 McDonald's

OTHER
4 Municipal Tourist Office
5 Victoria Hotel
7 Supermarket
8 Post Office
10 Holy Trinity Church
11 Hospital
12 Customs House Museum
13 Gunsynd Memorial
14 Martha's House

Goondiwindi

NEW SOUTH WALES

0   100   200 m

DARLING DOWNS

Most of the pubs and motels are spread along Marshall St. About the best value is *O'Shea's Royal Hotel-Motel* (☎ 4671 1877, fax 4671 3110) which has motel-style rooms at $39/46 for singles/doubles; hotel rooms with shared showers are $28/39. The next cheapest option is the *Binalong Motel* (☎ 4671 1777), 30 McLean St, 100m north of the tourist information office. Its singles/doubles start at $44/50.

The top place in town is *The Town House* (☎ 4671 1855), 110 Marshall St, just east of the junction with McLean. Rates are $79/81, and the motel has a pool and an extremely good restaurant.

For cheaper but good and substantial eating try the bistro at *O'Shea's Hotel* or the *Goondiwindi RSL Club*.

Getting There & Away
Brisbane-Melbourne buses stop at the BP Bridge Garage petrol station, 1km east of town on the Cunningham Hwy.

WEST OF GOONDIWINDI
At the junction of the Carnarvon, Moonie and Balonne Hwys, **St George** is 200km west of Goondiwindi. It's at the centre of a major cotton-growing district, and has two motels and a caravan park. From here it's another long and lonely 290km westwards to Cunnamulla, which is well and truly in the outback – see the Outback Queensland chapter for details of this area.

TOOWOOMBA
On the edge of the Great Dividing Range and the Darling Downs and 138km inland from Brisbane, Toowoomba is the largest town in the region. It has a commanding location, perched 700m above sea level on the crest of the Great Dividing Range, and there are great views from the parks and gardens that fringe the east side of town. The centre is graced by some stately old Queenslanders and other early buildings.

Orientation & Information
The heart of town is loosely centred on Ruthven St (part of the north-south New England Hwy) 1km north of its junction with James St (part of the east-west Warrego Hwy).

The very efficient Toowoomba tourist information centre (☎ 4639 3797) is inconveniently located (unless you are driving in from Brisbane) on James St, at the junction with Kitchener St, about 1.5km south-east of the centre. It's open weekdays from 8.30 am to 5 pm and weekends from 9.30 am to 3 pm.

Bookshops There's a Mary Ryan Bookshop at 55 Russell St with a cafe upstairs; a few doors down at 69 Russell St is Maie's Book Exchange, which has a good range of second-hand (mostly pulp) fiction.

Email & Internet Access Coffee On Line (☎ 4639 4686), 148 Margaret St, has around eight terminals for use at $6 per half hour ($4 for students). It's open 9 am to 9 pm daily.

Bicycle Hire If you don't have a car it may be worth renting a bike, especially if you want to visit the Japanese Gardens or escarpment parks; Bikeline (☎ 4638 2242) at 16 Bell St near the coach station rents them out at $18 a day. They're open weekdays from 8.30 am, Saturday from 9 am.

Things to See & Do
Toowoomba's **Botanic Gardens** occupy the northern section of Queens Park. The gardens have lawns, rose gardens and flower beds shaded by old bunya pines and other trees. Immediately north of the gardens is the **Cobb & Co Museum** at 27 Lindsay St, which has a large collection of old horse-drawn carriages and buggies, Cobb & Co mail coaches, bullock wagons and sulkies. It's open from 9 am to 4 pm daily and admission costs $4 ($2 children).

The **Toowoomba Regional Art Gallery**, 531 Ruthven St, is a small but beautifully designed modern gallery housing three permanent micro collections (including examples of colonial Australian paintings, ceramics, European and Asian paintings

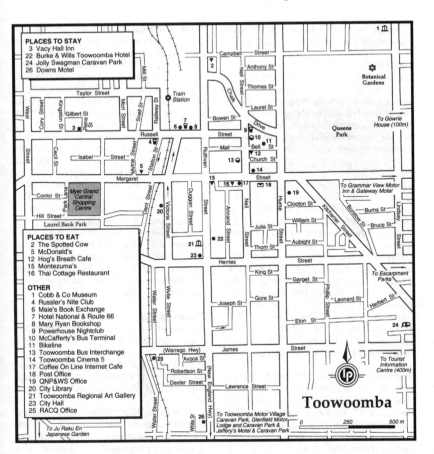

PLACES TO STAY
3 Vacy Hall Inn
22 Burke & Wills Toowoomba Hotel
24 Jolly Swagman Caravan Park
26 Downs Motel

PLACES TO EAT
2 The Spotted Cow
5 McDonald's
12 Hog's Breath Cafe
15 Montezuma's
16 Thai Cottage Restaurant

OTHER
1 Cobb & Co Museum
4 Russler's Nite Club
6 Maie's Book Exchange
7 Hotel National & Route 66
8 Mary Ryan Bookshop
9 Powerhouse Nightclub
10 McCafferty's Bus Terminal
11 Bikeline
13 Toowoomba Bus Interchange
14 Toowoomba Cinema 5
17 Coffee On Line Internet Cafe
18 Post Office
19 QNP&WS Office
20 City Library
21 Toowoomba Regional Art Gallery
23 City Hall
25 RACQ Office

Toowoomba

and prints, and some porcelain, furniture, gold and silverware) plus frequently changing temporary exhibitions. Entry is free and it's open from 10 am to 4 pm Tuesday to Saturday and from 1 to 4 pm Sunday.

The **Ju Raku En Japanese Garden** is a beautiful spot for picnicking and strolling with 3km of walking trails around a lake, waterfalls and streams. It's several kilometres south of the centre at the University of Southern Queensland in West St, and you need a car or bike to get there. The garden is open daily from 7 am to 7 pm.

The other great places for walking are the series of **escarpment parks** along the eastern edge of town. There are no less than seven separate small bushland parks all with great views and signposted trails. The biggest two are the most northerly, Jubilee and Redwood parks, while next down Picnic Point, just south of the Warrego Hwy, is possibly the most scenic. Table Top, which occupies the easternmost promontory and is reached by 2km of dirt track, offers the best views of all. The parks can be reached by following Margaret, Herries or James Sts to their eastern ends – again, it's preferable to have a bike or car.

Festivals
Toowoomba's Carnival of Flowers is a colourful celebration of spring that is held over the last week in September, and includes floral displays, a grand parade and exhibition gardens. In early September, the Ag Show is a three-day agricultural and horticultural festival.

Places to Stay
Caravan Parks The modern *Toowoomba Motor Village Caravan Park* (☎ 4635 8186), 821 Ruthven St, is the best of the caravan parks here, with tent sites at $12 ($15 powered), on-site vans at $24 and cabins and units from $30 to $42.

Closer to the centre, the small *Jolly Swagman Caravan Park* (☎ 4632 8735), 47 Kitchener St, has tent and powered sites and on-site vans for slightly less. There are also four other caravan parks, including the *Glenfield Motor Lodge Caravan Park* (☎ 4635 4466) on the corner of Ruthven and Stenner Sts, and *Jeffrey's Motel-Caravan Park* – see the next section.

Guesthouses Probably the best budget accommodation in town is offered by *Gowrie House* (☎ 4632 2642, fax 4632 5433), 112 Mary St, just 100m east of Queens Park and a 10 minute walk from the centre. It's a beautiful single-storey, old place offering singles, twins and doubles at $20 per person. Toilets and bathrooms are shared but the price includes breakfast.

The *Vacy Hall Inn* (☎ 4639 2055), a couple of blocks uphill from the town centre at 135 Russell St, is a magnificent 1880s mansion which offers heritage-style accommodation of the highest standard – it's like stepping back into another era. There are 12 guest rooms; those in the side wing share bathrooms, while the rooms in the main house have an en suite and open fire, and open onto the verandah. Doubles range from $114 to $189 a night with breakfast.

Motels & Hotels There are at least two dozen accommodation options in this category. At the cheaper end of the range are the *Downs Motel* (☎ 4639 3811), 669 Ruthven St, with budget units from $42/48 and *Jeffery's Rainforest Motel-Caravan Park* (☎ 4635 5999), 864 Ruthven St, which has excellent, modern self-contained units from $41/43.

Closer to the centre, opposite historic Toowoomba Grammar School on the eastern outskirts of town, the *Grammar View Motor Inn* (☎ 4638 3366), 39 Margaret St, has modern units from $79/89, while the *Gateway Motel* (☎ 4632 2088) next door has budget units from $42/48.

The *Burke & Wills Toowoomba Hotel* (☎ 4632 2433, fax 4639 2002), in the centre of town at 554 Ruthven St, is a good five-storey hotel with 90 recently renovated rooms ranging from $100 to $140 a night. The hotel has several bars and an upmarket conservatory restaurant.

Places to Eat
For a town of its size Toowoomba offers fairly limited options when it comes to eating.

For budget eating there's a food court on the first floor of Myers Grand Central shopping centre at the western end of Margaret St.

Otherwise, Margaret St has the greatest concentration of restaurants and cafes; there's a *Montezuma's*, part of a Mexican restaurant chain, near the junction with Ruthven St, while 100m east at 160 Margaret St is the *Thai Cottage Restaurant*, a BYO that has mains for around $10. On Neil St, just north of the cinema, is a *Hog's Breath Cafe*, one of the chain of popular American-style bar and grills.

On the corner of Ruthven and Campbell Sts, the popular *Spotted Cow* hotel has been renovated in the style of an English country pub. It's a relaxed, elegant place with three small bars including the Udder Bar, a covered courtyard and a restaurant which serves upmarket pub food: light meals cost around $8 and main courses are $9 to $15.

For something a bit special try the *Atrium Brasserie*, part of a dining complex at Picnic Point, one of the escarpment parks east of the town centre. The views are magnificent and the food's not bad either. The menu is huge and quite sophisticated, while the desserts are exquisite. Prices are reasonable (mains $15 to $20) and it's open daily for lunch and dinner.

Entertainment

The Toowoomba Cinema 5 on the corner of Margaret and Neil Sts screens mainstream releases, as well as art-house films on Sunday and Monday nights.

The Powerhouse is a live band venue on Neil St beside the McCafferty's terminal; *Russler's Nite Club* in the Canberra Hotel, on the corner of Russell and Station Sts, has country and western bands on Friday and Saturday nights.

Getting There & Away

Air There are daily flights between Toowoomba and Brisbane and twice weekly services from Toowoomba to St George, Cunnamulla and Thargomindah.

Bus McCafferty's has a terminal (☎ 4690 9888) at 28-30 Neil St. McCafferty's has about 20 services a day from Toowoomba to Brisbane and the Gold Coast. It also has regular services west along the Warrego Hwy to Dalby, Chinchilla, Roma and Charleville. McCafferty's also acts as the local agent for Polley's Coaches, who has services to Gympie and Kingaroy.

Crisp's Coaches runs to Stanthorpe, Warwick and Moree. Graham's Coaches runs to St George, Cunnamulla and Lightning Ridge. Suncoast Pacific runs to the Sunshine Coast. All of these services leave from the McCafferty's terminal and tickets can be booked through them.

Train You can get here on the *Westlander*, which runs between Brisbane and Charleville twice weekly. The railway station is close to the town centre, just north of Russell St.

Getting Around

Local bus services depart from the Toowoomba bus interchange on Neil St. There's an information booth in the terminal where you can find out which bus will take you where.

TOOWOOMBA TO NANANGO (141km)

The route north along the New England Hwy travels along the ridges of the Great Dividing Range, passing through a series of small villages.

About 15 minutes drive north of Toowoomba just off the highway is the **Spring Bluff Historic Railway Station & Gardens**, a non-operational heritage-listed station dating from 1867. There isn't much here, just a landscaped, flowerbedded site with a small museum and a railway carriage converted into a refreshment van. The one time it would be worth visiting is during the local Carnival of Flowers in the last week of September when the place comes back to life and a steam train rattles the line between Spring Bluff and Toowoomba.

Back on the New England Hwy at Highfield there's the **Highfield Orchid Park**, in bloom from April through to September. A little further north, at Cabarlah, **Black Forest Hill**, a kitsch cuckoo-clock cabin in the worst possible south Germanic taste. Put your foot down until **Crow's Nest**, a pretty little township centred around a well-tended village green. It's well worth breaking your journey here for a coffee or something to eat. While you're here, take a look at **Salt's Antiques**, an amazing antique store in a barn half a kilometre north of town.

About 6km east of town is the **Crow's Nest Falls National Park**, an area of eucalypt forest punctuated by craggy granite outcrops. There's a ranger station at the park entrance from where a 500m trail leads to some cascades. A further 1km on are the Crow's Nest falls. There are also two scenic storage lakes, **Lake Perseverance** and **Lake Cressbrook**, that are about 8km and 15km, respectively, south-east of Crow's Nest. They're good places for picnicking

DARLING DOWNS

and at Cressbrook there's a 3km walking trail along the lakeshore.

Beyond Crow's Nest the road continues 96km north to Nanango, entering the region of South Burnett – see later in this chapter for details.

Places to Stay

Built in 1884, the *Argyle Homestead* (☎ 4696 6301) is permeated with a sense of history, aided by the current owners' attention to period detail: iron bedsteads, lacy valances etc. It has large bedrooms downstairs that open out onto wide verandahs or smaller attic rooms with good views over the extensive grounds. The tariff of $65/98 a single/double includes breakfast, afternoon tea and evening port and chocolates. The Argyle is at Geham, approximately midway between Toowoomba and Crows Nest. A further 10km north at Hampton is the *Valden House* (☎ 4697 9277), a cosy B&B where the breakfasts are especially good; singles/doubles are $50/70.

Accommodation is also available at the *Crows Nest Caravan Park* or **Crows Nest Motel** (☎ 4698 1399), a couple of kilometres south of town.

TOOWOOMBA TO MILES (211km)
Jondaryan Woolshed Complex

Built in 1859, this enormous woolshed, 45km north-west of Toowoomba, holds a significant place in Queensland's history books – it was here in 1890 that the first of the great shearers' strikes began, when maritime workers refused to handle Jondaryan wool because it had been shorn by non-union labour.

Today the woolshed is the centrepiece of a large tourist complex with an interesting collection of rustic old buildings, daily blacksmithing and shearing demonstrations, period displays and antique farm machinery. The complex is open daily from 8.30 am to 5 pm. Entry costs $10 ($5 children), which includes a tour with demonstrations. Tours are given daily at 1 pm, as well as at 10.30 am on weekends and during school holidays.

There's also a YHA-affiliated youth hostel and camping ground here. The hostel has been set up in authentically spartan shearers' quarters, with old mattresses on old iron beds in old tin sheds. There's an open-sided, sawdust-floored communal cooking and dining shelter, as well as hot showers and toilets. You need to bring your own linen. Beds cost $9 a night in four-bed dorms, tent sites cost $8 and caravan sites cost $10.

Jondaryan hosts a number of annual events, including an Australian Heritage Festival over nine days in late August and early September, a New Year's Eve bushdance, an Australia Day celebration, and a Working Draft Horse Expo in June.

Dalby

Dalby is a dusty rural town in the centre of Queensland's richest grain-growing region. What little there is here of interest to travellers is well sketched out by the ladies at the tourist office (☎ 4662 1066) in front of Thomas Jack Park on the corner of Drayton St and Condamine St. It's open Monday to Saturday from 9 am to 4.30 pm and Sunday 9.30 am to 2 pm.

Highlights – if they can be called such – include the **Pioneer Park Museum**, signposted off the Warrego Hwy a couple of kilometres west of the centre, which has a collection of old buildings and farm machinery, and is open daily from 10 am to 3 pm (entry costs $4, $1 for children) and the **Cactoblastis Cairn**, beside Myall Creek in Marble St, possibly the only monument ever erected in honour of an insect. *Cactoblastis cactorum*, an Argentine caterpillar/moth, saved much of rural Queensland when it was recruited into the country in 1925 to combat the dreaded prickly pear cactus which had overrun huge tracts of farming land.

The **Dalby Saleyards** are among the largest in Queensland – if you're interested in attending, sheep and lamb sales are held on Monday, cattle and pig sales on Wednesday.

Places to Stay If you decide to stop over, the *Pioneer Caravan Village* (☎ 4662

1811), on the western outskirts, has sites, cabins and on-site vans, and there are at least eight motels. The *Dalby Parkview Motel* (☎ 4662 3222) at 31 Drayton St, opposite the tourist office, has budget units at $50/57, or there's the modern *Manor Motor Inn* (☎ 4662 1011) on the corner of Drayton and Pratten Sts, with units at $57/70.

MILES

This small rural centre at the intersection of the Warrego and Leichhardt Hwys is known as 'The Crossroads of the Golden West' and was named by the eccentric Prussian explorer Ludwig Leichhardt, who stopped here on his 31st birthday on 23 October 1844.

Most people passing through stop off at the excellent **Miles Historical Village** (☎ 4627 1492) on the main road on the east side of town. This is one of the best historical villages in the state and, if you like this sort of thing, it is definitely worth a visit. The main building houses a collection of glass cabinets crammed with all sorts of bits and pieces, from rocks and gems to tie stretchers and silk-screen printers. There are also numerous historic shop settings, including a bootmaker, a saddlery, a general store, a bakery and a bank, as well as a war museum and displays on the Artesian Basin and Aboriginal heritage. The village is open daily from 8 am to 5 pm and costs $9 ($3 children, $18 family). There's an information centre at the village with the same opening hours.

Places to Stay

There are two caravan parks in town: the *Miles Caravan Park* (☎ 4627 1640), beside the Ampol service station on Murilla St, with tent sites at $8 ($10 powered) and on-site vans at $22, and the *Crossroads Caravan Park* (☎ 4627 1211), opposite the Historical Village, with similar prices.

There's also a pub, the *Hotel Australia* (☎ 4627 1106), offering cheap accommodation in the centre of town at 55 Murilla St, and four motels, the most central of which is the *Golden West Motor Inn* (☎ 4627

1688), 50 Murilla St, with singles/doubles from $54/64.

NORTH FROM MILES

The Leichhardt Hwy runs north from Miles all the way to Rockhampton. If you're heading this way, see the Banana to Miles – the Leichhardt Hwy section in the Capricorn Coast chapter.

ROMA

An early Queensland settlement, and now the centre of a sheep and cattle-raising district, Roma also has some curious small industries. There's enough oil in the area to support a small refinery, which produces just enough petroleum for local use. Gas deposits are rather larger, and Roma supplies Brisbane through a 450km pipeline.

While there isn't a lot here, Roma is a good place to break a journey if you're heading up to Carnarvon.

The local information centre (☎ 4622 4355) sits in the shadow of the Historic Oil Rig, an authentic drilling rig from the 1920s, at the eastern entrance to town. It's open from 9 am to 5 pm daily.

Things to See & Do

The town centre (focused on McDowall St, one block north of the main Warrego Hwy) has some fine turn-of-the-century buildings – the **School of Arts Hotel** and the **Hotel Royal**, on opposite corners of McDowall and Hawthorne Sts, are two good examples.

Heroes' Avenue is a plantation of bottle trees, stretching along Station, Wyndham and Bungil Sts, planted to honour the young men from the district who were killed in WWI. Each of the 90-plus trees originally bore a brass plaque with the name of the soldier whom it honoured.

There are cattle sales at the **Roma Saleyards** on the eastern outskirts of town every Tuesday (from 11 am) and Thursday (from 8 am).

Festivals

Roma's major festival is Easter in the Country, which includes a rodeo, markets,

DARLING DOWNS

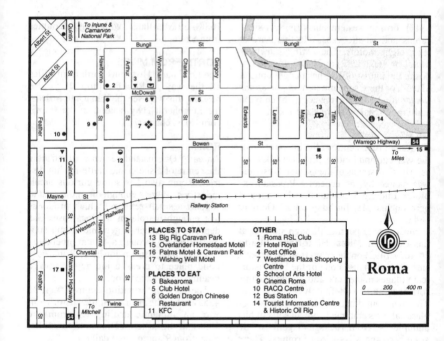

PLACES TO STAY
13 Big Rig Caravan Park
15 Overlander Homestead Motel
16 Palms Motel & Caravan Park
17 Wishing Well Motel

PLACES TO EAT
3 Bakearoma
5 Club Hotel
6 Golden Dragon Chinese
  Restaurant
11 KFC

OTHER
1 Roma RSL Club
2 Hotel Royal
4 Post Office
7 Westlands Plaza Shopping
  Centre
8 School of Arts Hotel
9 Cinema Roma
10 RACQ Centre
12 Bus Station
14 Tourist Information Centre
  & Historic Oil Rig

Roma

0   200   400 m

horse races, bush dances and country music, a street parade and an art show.

Places to Stay
The *Big Rig Caravan Park* (☎ 4622 2538) on McDowall St has tent sites from $9 ($12 powered) and on-site vans from $25. If it's busy try the *Palms Motel & Caravan Park* (☎ 4622 6464) across the highway at 6 Bowen St or the *Villa Caravan Park* (☎ 4622 1309) on the Carnarvon road.

At the cheaper end of the motel range are the *Palms Motel & Caravan Park* which charges $34/42 for single/double units and the very friendly *Wishing Well Motel* (☎ 4622 2566), 77 Quinton St, which charges $35 to $42 for singles and $45 to $50 for doubles.

The best motel in town is the colonial-style *Overlander Homestead Motel* (☎ 4622 3555), on the highway on the eastern outskirts of town. Singles/doubles start from $65/75 and the motel has its own licensed steak and seafood restaurant.

Places to Eat
The *Club Hotel* on the corner of McDowall and Charles Sts has a good bistro open every night of the week. The licensed *Golden Dragon Restaurant* opposite the post office on McDowall St is also quite good. It has an extensive menu with most mains around $8, or there's an all-you-can-eat deal for $8.50. It's open daily for lunch (Sunday excepted) and dinner from 5 to 9 pm (10 pm on Friday and Saturday).

For breakfast try *Bakearoma*, across the road 50m west of the Chinese restaurant, which has good pastries, sandwiches and cakes; there's a seated area so you can eat in.

Entertainment
Cinema Roma at 37 Hawthorne St has six screenings a day (like we said, not much to

do in Roma) swapping between three different films. Budget day is Wednesday with the first show of the day (10.30 am) preceded by morning tea.

Getting There & Away
Flight West has regular flights between Roma and Brisbane. McCafferty's has daily buses through Roma on the Brisbane to Mt Isa run. The *Westlander* train passes through twice weekly on the Brisbane-Charleville run.

ROMA TO CHARLEVILLE (265km)
Muckadilla
About 40km past Roma, Muckadilla is just a pub, a service station, a railway station and a couple of houses. If you're looking for a beer, a meal or a bed, there's the friendly *Muckadilla Hotel-Motel* (☎ 4626 8318), a modern colonial-style pub where good value rooms have their own bathroom, TV and fan. There's also a pool and barbecue area out the back.

Mitchell
On the Maranoa River, Mitchell was named after the Surveyor-General of NSW, Major Thomas Mitchell, who passed this way in 1845. It's a relaxed commercial centre with a couple of pubs and supermarkets, a butcher, a baker and a newsagent. The local library, beside the huge windmill in the centre of town, has a small tourist information section with brochures on the local area.

A road heads north from Mitchell to the Mt Moffat section of the Carnarvon National Park. It's a remote 200km trip, and the road is mostly unsealed after the first 50km – see the section on the Carnarvon Gorge in the Capricorn Coast chapter for more details.

Accommodation-wise, there's a straightforward council-run caravan park beside the river on the east side of town, while closer to the centre there's the *Bridge Service Station & Caravan Park* (☎ 4623 1125). The blue and white *Devonshire Arms Hotel* (☎ 4623 1321) on the corner of Cambridge

and Alice Sts also has very basic pub rooms, or the *Berkeley Lodge Motel* (☎ 4623 1666) at 20 Cambridge St has standard units at around $50/60 for singles/doubles.

Morven
Continuing west from Mitchell, it's another 89km to the small highway town of Morven. Originally called Saddler's Waterhole, nowadays Morven is something of a driver's water hole with two pubs, a motel (the *Morven Hotel-Motel*; ☎ 4654 8101), a cafe and a general store.

Both pubs have bistro meals, while the *Duck Inn Cafe* has a good range of takeaway tucker and also sells fuel – it's open every day from 7 am to 8 pm. There's also a Mobil Roadhouse a couple of hundred metres east of town which is open daily from 7 am to 3 am.

The junction of the Warrego and Landsborough Hwys is 3km west of Morven. From here, you can continue west to Charleville (90km) or take the Landsborough Hwy north-west to Augathella (90km) – see the Outback Queensland chapter for details of these places.

South Burnett Region

Stretching north-west from Brisbane, the South Burnett is centred around the Burnett River and its various tributaries. Highway 17, which is made up of sections of the Brisbane Valley, D'Aguilar and Burnett Hwys, starts near Ipswich and runs north for almost 600km to Rockhampton. Highway 17 is a popular alternative inland route for travellers between Brisbane and Rockhampton who want to avoid the much more hectic Bruce Hwy. It's a slower, more laid-back route which takes you through a string of small rural centres which service the surrounding cattle and dairy properties, peanut farms and citrus orchards.

There are several natural attractions in the region, including the Bunya Mountains

National Park and the Cania Gorge National Park.

Getting There & Away
Brisbane Bus Lines (☎ 3355 0034 in Brisbane) has two services a day (one on Saturday) north from Brisbane to Murgon via Caboolture and Kingaroy. On Tuesday, Thursday, Friday and Saturday, these services continue up the Burnett Hwy to Gayndah and Biloela. They also have services from Brisbane to Bundaberg via the Burnett on Wednesday only.

BUNYA MOUNTAINS NATIONAL PARK
The Bunya Mountains are the place to go for guaranteed wallaby sightings and to be mobbed by brightly hued crimson rosellas and king parrots.

Outliers of the Great Dividing Range, the Bunyas rise abruptly to over 1000m from country south-west of Kingaroy. This is the second-oldest national park in Queensland (first declared in 1908) and one of the most popular – so much so that it's best avoided at weekends and on public holidays. Vegetation ranges from rainforest and eucalypt forest to heath, and there's an abundance of birds and other wildlife. An extensive network of walking tracks leads to numerous waterfalls and lookouts; walks range from a 500m discovery walk to a 10km trail to the Big Falls Lookout.

The park takes its name from the native bunya pine trees that grow here. Every three years or so these trees produce a crop of edible nuts, each of which grows to about the size of a pineapple. Before European settlers came and started logging these forests in the 1860s, Aboriginal tribes used to gather for feasts and ceremonies whenever the bunya nuts were ripe. Falling bunya nuts can be a serious hazard.

The Department of the Environment has an information centre (☎ 4668 3127) at Dandabah near the southern entrance to the park, which is open daily from 7.30 am to 4 pm but staffed by rangers only between 2 and 4 pm. Also at Dandabah are a general store including an accommodation booking

desk, a small museum, a snack bar and the excellent *Rosella's Restaurant* (☎ 4668 3131), which opens daily for lunch and dinner with meals from $8.

The main access route from the south is via Dalby or Jondaryan on the Warrego Hwy; if you're coming from the north, the park is 56km south from Kingaroy by sealed road.

Horse Riding
Bushland Park (☎ 4663 4717) offers guided rides for beginners and experienced riders alike lasting 1½ to two hours for $30 per person. Accommodation is also available – see the next section.

Places to Stay
Camping There are national park camping grounds at Dandabah, Westcott and Burton's Well. All have toilets, water and picnic areas; Dandabah also has hot showers and wild wallabies bounding around the site. Camping costs $3.50 per person per night. The sites are popular and you'll need to book in advance through the Department of the Environment office (seethe previous section) especially during holiday periods.

Bushland Park (☎ 4663 4717), 10km south of Dandabah on the road to Dalby, also offers camping at $10 ($15 powered). There are hot showers and toilets.

Other Accommodation There's plenty of accommodation available, most of it around Dandabah where there's a helpful central accommodation booking desk (☎/fax 4668 3131).

The cheapest Dandabah options are *Rice's Bunya Mountain Retreat* which has five self-contained log cabins costing from $45 a double plus $8 to $10 for extra people, and the *Dandabah Holiday Units* (☎ 4668 3131), self-contained motel-style cabin units which sleep up to five people and start from $55 a double plus $8 for extras. Both are booked through the accommodation desk. There are also numerous chalets ranging in price from $65 to $170 for a double but sleeping as many as seven – again, make inquiries at the accommodation desk.

Away from Dandabah, on the road south to Dalby, is *Munro Camp Cabins* (☎ 4668 3150), which we highly recommend to anyone looking for some peace and solitude – peace that is if you don't count the incessant chattering of the birdlife and solitude if you discount the crowds of wallabies out front. There are only two cabins, both large and self-contained, and each costing $35. The price is for two people but the cabins will sleep six with each additional person costing $7. *Bushland Park* (see Camping) also has cabins

KINGAROY

Kingaroy, at the junction of the Bunya Mountains and D'Aguilar Hwys, is the prosperous little capital of the South Burnett region and the centre of Australia's most important peanut growing area. The tourist office (☎ 4162 3199) at 128 Haly St just north of the centre can tell you all about it – you can't miss the place, it's opposite a cluster of enormous white peanut silos. It's open weekdays from 9 am to 5 pm and weekends from 10 am to 2 pm.

Next to the tourist office, the **Heritage Museum & Peanut Exhibition** has displays with photos and machinery associated with the early days of the peanut industry. Its opening hours are the same as the tourist office.

Other than peanuts (and the fact that Queensland's notorious ex-premier, Joh Bjelke-Petersen comes from here), Kingaroy's other main point of note is that it's the northern access point for the Bunya Mountains National Park. However, there's plenty of accommodation up in the park and it's not necessary to stay in Kingaroy.

Places to Stay & Eat

There are a couple of caravan parks around town; on the Brisbane Hwy 1km south of the centre is the *Fairfield Caravan Park* (☎ 4162 1808), while the *Kingaroy Caravan Park and Cabins* (☎ 4162 1808) at 48

Walter Rd is 1.5km out of the centre just off the Brisbane-Nanango Hwy.

The best place we found was the *Kingaroy Hotel-Motel* (☎ 4162 1677) right at the centre of town on the corner of Haly and Youngman Sts. It's very modern and clean motel units go for $48 a double; the hotel rooms are cheaper. The hotel also has a very good restaurant serving reasonably priced lunches and evening meals.

There are also a couple of more pricey motels in the centre of town, in the form of the *Pioneer Lodge Motel* (☎ 4162 3999) at 100 Kingaroy St, which charges $58/63, and across the road the *Burke & Wills Motor Inn* (☎ 4162 2933) where doubles go for $60.

MURGON

Murgon is the main town of the region north of Kingaroy and a centre for the surrounding cattle industry. On the northern outskirts, opposite the saleyards, the **Queensland Dairy Industry Museum** is open weekdays from 1 to 4 pm or by appointment – contact the local council on ☎ 4168 1499.

About 6km south of Murgon the Cherbourg Aboriginal community runs the **Barambah Emu Farm** (☎ 4168 2655), open to visitors daily from 8 am to 3 pm.

There's a caravan park in town on Krebs St and the *Murgon Motor Inn* (☎ 4168 1400) on the Bunya Hwy 500m north of the centre with units from $40/48.

GAYNDAH

Officially gazetted back in 1852, Gayndah is an attractive little township famous for its oranges and mandarins. The town's **Orange Festival**, held every second year (odd-numbered years) on the Queen's Birthday weekend in June, includes a parade, the crowning of the Orange Queen, and demonstrations of old machinery at the town's museum.

The **Gayndah & District Historical Museum** has an interesting local history collection spanning three buildings, including a one-teacher school display, war memorabilia and an 1864 slab-timber hut. It's open daily from 9 am to 4 pm and there's a small entry fee.

For accommodation there's the *Riverview Caravan Park* (☎ 4161 1280) with an attractive setting by the river and good tent sites for $9 ($12 powered) and on-site vans from $20, or the *Colonial Motel* (☎ 4161 1999), 58 Capper St, with good units from $48/55.

MUNDUBBERA

Situated 25km west of Gayndah, Mundubbera is on the banks of the Burnett River. It's at the centre of another citrus-growing area, and you can buy local crafts and products from the **Big Mandarin** inside the *Citrus Country Caravan Village* (☎ 4165 4549), which has on-site vans from $25, cabins from $30 and tent sites at $10. There are two motels in town; the better is the *Billabong Motor Inn* (☎ 4165 4410), on Durong Rd, with a licensed restaurant, a pool and singles/doubles from $52/58.

Based at Mundubbera, BJ's Packhorse Tours (☎ 4165 4713) offers a good range of one to five day guided tours on horse back. Tours cost $85 per person per day, and they provide tents and sleeping bags, fishing gear, all meals – and the horses.

EIDSVOLD

The Eidsvold district was settled in 1848 by two brothers with Norwegian backgrounds – hence the name. Gold was discovered here in 1887, and in the ensuing rush a town sprang up from nowhere with some 15 pubs catering to several thousand hopeful diggers. The rush didn't last, and nowadays Eidsvold relies on the cattle industry for its existence.

The **Eidsvold Historical Complex** comprises seven heritage buildings housing an extensive and quirky range of displays, including the Schultz Duncan collection of several thousand bottles (no two the same) and the George Schafer collection of rocks, gems, more bottles and other bits and pieces. The complex is open daily from 9.30 am to 3 pm.

The *Eidsvold Motel & General Store* (☎ 4165 1209) in the centre of town at 51 Morton St is a general store, tourist information centre, cafe, service station and motel (six battered old motel-style units with shared facilities costing $25/35) all rolled into one. It's open daily from 6 am to 9.30 pm. There's also the *Eidsvold Caravan Park* (☎ 4165 1168) on the Esplanade one block back from the main road.

MONTO

Monto is near the junction of the Burnett River and Three Moon Creek. According to local legend, the creek was named by a swagman who was boiling his billy on the banks of the creek one night when he saw three moons – one in the sky, one reflected in the creek and another reflected in his billy.

The centre of town is just north-east of the railway line where it's bridged by the Burnett Hwy. The main drag, Newton St has three big old pubs with cheap accommodation and meals.

Just west of town on the highway are the *Monto Caravan Park* (☎ (4166 1492) and the *Monto Three Moon Motel* (☎ 4166 1777), a drab, Willy Loman type of place with singles/doubles at $45/52. We recommend spending a couple of bucks more and checking in at the *Colonial Motor Inn & Restaurant* (☎ 4166 1377) at 6 Thomson St, on the right, off the highway, as you approach town from the south. It's fronted by a 100-year-old timber building which houses an atmospheric, colonial-style restaurant, while at the back are modern motel units costing $46/54. The restaurant is licensed and is open from Monday to Saturday for dinner. Alternatively, there's a pretty good Chinese place in town on Lister St, parallel to the rail line.

CANIA GORGE NATIONAL PARK

This small national park 26km north of Monto is well worth visiting if you're anywhere in the region. It features some spectacular scenery, with strange rock formations, rugged sandstone escarpments, rainforests and bushland, and there's an abundance of birds and wildlife. Several walking trails of varying lengths start from the main picnic area and take in many of the more interesting formations.

About 7km beyond the picnic area is the *Cania Gorge Tourist Park* (☎ 4167 8188) with a shop, a pool, campers' kitchens and a playground, as well as hot showers, laundries etc. Tent sites are $12, a bed in the backpackers' bunkhouse $11, and cabins range from $35 to $60, the difference being shared or en suite facilities.

MONTO TO ROCKHAMPTON

The Burnett Hwy continues north from Monto to Rockhampton via Biloela and Mt Morgan. See the Capricorn Coast chapter for details of this area.

DARLING DOWNS

Fraser Coast

The main attraction of the Fraser Coast is majestic Fraser Island, the world's largest sand island. It offers great bushwalking and camping among some absolutely stunning scenery. Hervey Bay is the major access point for the island; seasonal whale-watching has turned it into a fairly busy little tourist centre with a wide range of accommodation. The other access point for Fraser is Rainbow Beach, a sleepy and attractive seaside town near the southern tip of the island.

Bundaberg, the largest city in the area, is famous throughout Australia as the home of the distinctive Bundaberg Rum. For travellers 'Bundy' offers access to the Southern Reef Islands, turtle-watching at Mon Repos beach and seasonal fruit-picking work.

Getting There & Around

Flight West and Sunstate have daily flights to Hervey Bay and Bundaberg from all major centres. The major bus companies have regular services along the Bruce Hwy, with detours to Bundaberg and across to Hervey Bay. There are local bus services from Gympie to Rainbow Beach and Tin Can Bay. Gympie, Maryborough and Bundaberg are also all on the main coastal train route between Brisbane and Rockhampton.

GYMPIE

Gympie came into existence in 1867, the result of a gold rush triggered by a solo prospector who hit pay dirt in a small gully off the Mary River. Gold fever struck and more than 15,000 diggers rushed in. The town that sprung up was initially called Nashville, after James Nash, the man who first struck gold, but was soon renamed Gympie after *gimpi gimpi*, the Aboriginal name for a local tree.

The Gympie of today is a pleasant – if uninspiring – town with many reminders of its glory days, including a town centre with dozens of old buildings, a gold-mining museum, and a timber and forestry museum.

HIGHLIGHTS

Map Index

PACIFIC
OCEAN

Fraser Island p259

Bundaberg p266

Hervey Bay pp252-3

Maryborough p249

Gympie p246

- Don't miss Fraser Island; when there, swim in the beautiful waters of Lake Wabby and Lake MacKenzie.
- Whale-watch off the coast of Fraser Island – but only if you're there between July and October.
- Sample Australia's most famous rum at the distillery in Bundaberg.
- Walk to the coloured sand cliffs at Rainbow Beach.

The *Discover Gympie* map and brochure, available from the Cooloola Regional Information Centre (☎ 5482 5444), beside the Bruce Hwy on the southern outskirts of town, outlines a heritage walk and a driving tour. The centre is open daily from 8.30 am to 3.30 pm. It also incorporates a Department of Environment office, where you can get permits and information for Fraser Island and Cooloola National Park.

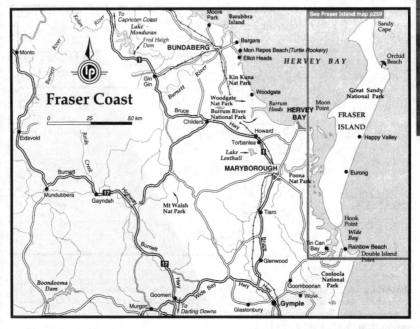

See Fraser Island map p259

Things to See & Do

The **Gympie & District Historical & Mining Museum**, just north of the tourist office on the southern outskirts of town, has a large and diverse collection of old buildings, artefacts and displays. Among the treasures there's a military museum, an old steam locomotive and assorted rolling stock, and an impressive collection of restored steam-driven equipment. It's open daily from 9 am to 5 pm; entry is $6 ($2 children).

A few kilometres north of Gympie on Fraser Rd (which runs off the Bruce Hwy on the north side of the golf course) is a second museum devoted to another source of Queensland's early wealth, the timber industry. The **Woodworks Forestry & Timber Museum** is open Monday to Friday from 9 am to 4 pm; entry costs $2.50 ($1.20 students). You can get information here on camping in nearby state forests.

Festivals

Gympie's Country Music Muster is one of Australia's major country music festivals, and held every year over a weekend in August. A week-long Gold Rush Festival is held in Gympie every October.

Places to Stay & Eat

The small *Gympie Caravan Park* (☎ 5483 6800), 1 Jane St, has an attractive setting, with tent sites at $12 ($15 powered), on-site vans from $25 and cabins from $35 to $45 a double.

On the southern outskirts of town, the *Great Eastern Motor Inn* (☎ 5482 7288) is a modern motel with units from $60. The motel, across the highway from the Cooloola Regional Information Centre, has its own licensed restaurant, *Geordie's,* and a swimming pool.

Another good motel is the *Gympie Muster Inn Motel* (☎ 5482 8666), closer to

FRASER COAST

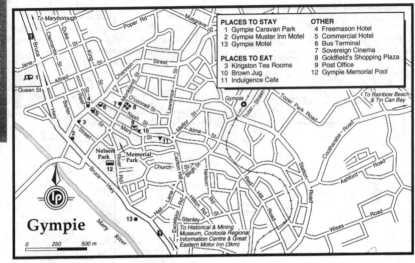

Map of Gympie

PLACES TO STAY
1 Gympie Caravan Park
2 Gympie Muster Inn Motel
13 Gympie Motel

PLACES TO EAT
3 Kingston Tea Rooms
10 Brown Jug
11 Indulgence Cafe

OTHER
4 Freemason Hotel
5 Commercial Hotel
6 Bus Terminal
7 Sovereign Cinema
8 Goldfield's Shopping Plaza
9 Post Office
12 Gympie Memorial Pool

Gympie

0   250   500 m

the centre at 21 Wickham St, with units from \$70. The *Gympie Motel* (☎ 5482 2722), 83 River Rd, is quite a good budget option with rooms from \$38/44.

An excellent place for lunch is the *Kingston Tea Rooms*, a ye-olde-worlde type place in an old Queenslander with broad verandahs. It has sandwiches and rolls, vegetarian meals, lasagnas and quiches, salads etc, in the \$4 to \$6 range. It's on the corner of Channon Rd and Barter St, and opens from 10 am to 11 pm daily except Monday.

There are more eateries along Mary St, including the *Brown Jug* near the post office at No 79, a straightforward coffee lounge, and the *Indulgence Cafe,* at No 46, a tiny gourmet cafe with a good range of sandwiches, salads and filled croissants.

Getting There & Away
Gympie is on the major train and bus routes between Brisbane and Rockhampton. Long-distance buses stop at the Polley's Coaches (☎ 5482 2700) terminal in the centre of town, on the corner of Channon and Mary St, while the main railway station is 1km east of the post office on Tozer St.

See the Rainbow Beach section for details of bus services between Gympie and Rainbow Beach.

RAINBOW BEACH
This little settlement on Wide Bay, 70km north-east of Gympie, is the southern access point for Fraser Island and the northern access point for Cooloola National Park. The 'town', which started life in the 1970s as a base for sand-mining operations, is little more than a cluster of shops, a post office and a caravan park perched on cliffs above an expansive sweep of good beach.

About 1km south-east of town is the 120m-high **Carlo Sandblow**, (named for one of Captain Cook's deckhands), best reached by taking the first right (Double Island Drive) as you enter town and then the second left to Rainbow Heights Lookout, from where it's an easy 600m walk. Beyond the sandblow are the coloured sand cliffs which gave the town its name – you can walk to them along the beach. The privately run Rainbow Beach tourist information centre (☎ 5486 3227) at 8 Rainbow Beach Rd has a list of other walks in the area.

From Rainbow Beach it's a 13km drive north along the beach to Inskip Point, where ferries leave for Fraser Island (see the Fraser Island section for details of services). In a 4WD it's also possible to drive south to Noosa along the beach – see the Cooloola Coast section in the Sunshine Coast chapter for more details.

The place for information on Fraser Island and Cooloola National Park is the Rainbow Beach information centre, actually the Department of Environment office (☎ 5486 3160), to the right of the main road as you enter town. This is also the place to get vehicle and camping permits. It's open daily from 7 am to 4 pm.

Organised Tours

Rainbow Beach Backpackers runs a free trip south down the beach every morning for guests. It also organises day trips to Fraser Island for about $95 per head.

Surf & Sand Safaris (☎ 5486 3131) runs four-hour 4WD trips south down the beach, taking in Double Island Point, the *Cherry Venture* wreck and the Coloured Sands with an optional Lake Poona walk. The cost is $40 ($20 for children).

Sun Safari Tours (☎ 5486 3154) offers day trips to Fraser Island costing $60 ($33 for children), which includes morning tea and lunch. The tour follows the coastline north as far as Eurong, and then heads

inland to explore the island and its lakes. Sun Safari Tours also offers a half-day tour south from Rainbow Beach to Double Island Point, the wreck of the *Cherry Venture*, and Cooloola National Park; the cost is $30 ($20 children) and includes morning tea.

Places to Stay & Eat

Rainbow Beach Backpackers (☎ 5486 3288) at 66 Rainbow Beach Rd (it's the first place on the left as you enter town) charges from $12 per person in a dorm or $30 for a double. Camping sites out back are $12 for two people. Rooms are sparse and facilities are poor – a small cramped kitchenette and just one shower and two toilets for use of all.

The *Rainbow Beach Holiday Village & Caravan Park* (☎ 5486 3222), on Rainbow Beach Rd, is a good foreshore camping and caravan park. It has a backpackers' section with three-bed cabin-tents for $10 per person, tent sites costing from $12 ($14 powered), on-site vans from $25 and cabins from $45 to $60. There's also the *Rainbow Waters Holiday Park* (☎ 5486 3200), on Carlo Rd just north of the centre, which has similar facilities and prices.

The *Rainbow Beach Hotel-Motel* (☎ 5486 3125) is as near as you can get to the beachfront, but it's also a little decrepit. Motel-style units go for $38/45. More expensive but more comfortable alternatives

Beach Hogs

Ever heard of a 4WD Rolls Royce? There is such a thing, and you can see it at Rainbow Beach. It's a 1975 Rolls Royce Silver Shadow, elevated two feet off the ground on enormous off-road tyres. It's a conversion carried out for a client by the guy who runs the Rainbow Beach RACQ depot; he drives a 4WD Cadillac himself.

Most Saturday mornings these two bizarre vehicles can be seen thundering along the sands amid a pack of other 4WDs. It's a local sport that draws a regular crowd of spectators – the drivers dare each other to race through the ebbing tide, pitting tens of thousands of dollars' worth of vehicle against shifting sands and hidden rocks. The risk is very real and the vehicular fatality count is high – the Rainbow Beach pub carries a scoreboard with accompanying pictures. If you're planning on driving the beach yourself you might want to check it out; you'll be amazed what salt water and waves can do to a car.

The *Cherry Venture* was a cargo vessel blown ashore during wild winds and high seas in 1973. Its rusting hulk lies on North Teewah Beach, where it is a popular tourist sight.

include the *Rainbow Sands* (☎ 5486 3400), 42-46 Rainbow Beach Rd, about 500m back from the beachfront, with modern apartments from $69 a double; the *Gazebo Gardens Motel* (☎ 5486 3255) with units ranging from $50 to $70 a double; and the *Mikado Motor Inn* (☎ 5486 3211), up on the hill south-east of the centre, which offers good value for classy motel suites with balconies costing $55 to $65.

There are a couple of cafes and takeaways in the main shopping arcade on Rainbow Beach Rd. *Archie's* is a small takeaway/bistro, while round the back is *KoKo's*, a restaurant serving good meals in the $12 to $15 range.

Getting There & Away

Polley's Coaches (☎ 5482 2700) in Gympie runs bus services between Gympie and Rainbow Beach every weekday. Buses leave Gympie at 6 am and 2 pm, returning from Rainbow Beach at 7.45 am and 4 pm.

TIN CAN BAY

Tin Can Bay is a narrow inlet at the southern reaches of the Sandy Straits, the body of water separating Fraser Island from the mainland. The township has in recent years

begun to change from a sleepy fishing village and retirement centre into a popular destination as more people are attracted by the area's excellent boating and fishing. The biggest draw with day visitors is the dolphins which most mornings swim into the harbour and right up to the boat ramp.

Tin Can Bay township has three caravan parks and a couple of reasonably priced motels.

Getting There & Away

The Gympie-Rainbow Beach bus services runs via Tin Can Bay – see the earlier Rainbow Beach section for details.

MARYBOROUGH

A working town and service centre for the local timber and sugar industries, Maryborough's major claim to fame is as the turn-off point for Hervey Bay. However, the town's early importance as a major port on the Mary River, through which 21,000 Europeans entered Australia in the second half of the 19th century, led to the construction of a series of imposing Victorian buildings, many of which have been beautifully restored. The local tourist office has an excellent *Walk & Drive Tours* brochure.

It's worth visiting on Thursday for the **heritage market**, held between 8 am and 2 pm along Kent and Adelaide Sts, or on Friday evening for the **lamplight bazaar**, (from 5 pm onwards) on Wharf St.

Information

The Maryborough & District Tourist Information Centre (☎ 4121 4111) is on Ferry St about 1km south of Kent St (the main street). It's extremely well provisioned with leaflets, brochures and booklets on the whole Fraser Coast region and is open weekdays from 8.30 am to 5 pm and weekends from 10 am to 4 pm.

Things to See & Do

The greatest concentration of **old buildings** is on and around Wharf St, the original port area. The Wharf St precinct includes early hotels, a couple of warehouses (now converted into a restaurant and an art

gallery), a bond store (now a museum) and customs houses. There's a grand Italianate post office (1865), the oldest surviving post office in Queensland. A former bank on the corner of Wharf and Richmond Sts is now the **Maryborough Heritage Centre**, open from 9 am to 4 pm Monday to Friday and also from 7 to 9 pm on Thursday evening.

One block south, on the corner of Kent St and Richmond St, is the pastiche classical **former Union Bank**. PL Travers, the author of *Mary Poppins*, was born in this building.

Maryborough's best attraction is the National Trust-classified **Brennan & Geraghty's Store** at 64 Lennox St. This historic general store opened for business in 1871 and was run by the same family for 100 years. It has been preserved intact as a museum with its original stock, shelving, trading records and other fascinating remnants. It's open daily from 10 am to 3 pm; entry costs $3 ($2 children, $7 family).

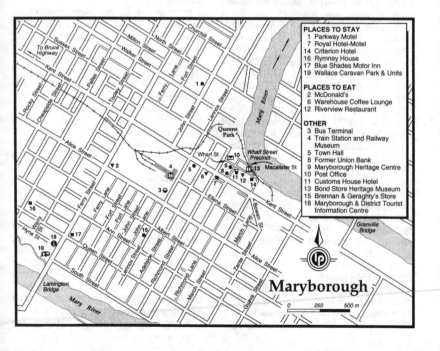

PLACES TO STAY
1 Parkway Motel
7 Royal Hotel-Motel
14 Criterion Hotel
16 Rymney House
17 Blue Shades Motor Inn
19 Wallace Caravan Park & Units

PLACES TO EAT
2 McDonald's
6 Warehouse Coffee Lounge
12 Riverview Restaurant

OTHER
3 Bus Terminal
4 Train Station and Railway Museum
5 Town Hall
8 Former Union Bank
9 Maryborough Heritage Centre
10 Post Office
11 Customs House Hotel
13 Bond Store Heritage Museum
15 Brennan & Geraghty's Store
18 Maryborough & District Tourist Information Centre

Maryborough

Queens Park, immediately north of the centre between Lennox St and the Mary River, is an attractive open parkland with two ferneries, a band rotunda and a miniature railway which runs on the last Sunday of each month. Maryborough also has a **railway museum** in the railway station on Lennox St.

Places to Stay & Eat

At 98 Wharf St, the old *Criterion Hotel* (☎ 4121 3043) has pub-style rooms at $15/25 for singles/doubles. They're not terribly flash, but they are cheap and you get to enjoy great views from the pub's front balcony. Another old pub with budget rooms is the *Royal Hotel-Motel* (☎ 4121 2241) on the corner of Kent and Bazaar Sts, with simple rooms with shared bathrooms from $20/28 or motel-style units from $35/40.

Next to the tourist office in Ferry St, the *Wallace Caravan Park & Units* (☎ 4121 3970) has motel-style units with limited cooking facilities from $37/45, tent sites at $10 and on-site cabins at $26 for a double or $38 with a bathroom and kitchenette. Nearby, on the corner of Ferry and Queen Sts, the *Blue Shades Motor Inn* (☎ 4122 2777) has better units from $58/63.

The *Parkway Motel* (☎ 4122 2888) at 188 John St is an excellent modern motel with three types of units ranging from $50/58 to $68/78 for singles/doubles. The rooms have all the mod cons and there's a licensed restaurant, a pool, sauna and spa.

For something a bit different, *Rhymney House* (☎ 4123 2080) is a beautiful old Queenslander with wide, palm-shaded verandahs set in landscaped gardens. It has two elegant guest suites: one double with en suite for $130, and one twin with shared bathroom for $100. It's at 47 Pallas St, which is off Queen St 400m west of the tourist office.

For a light snack, the *Warehouse Coffee Lounge* at 374 Kent St isn't a bad place. The women at the tourist office recommend the *Riverview Restaurant*, which occupies a warehouse on Wharf St dating back to 1879.

Getting There & Away

Maryborough's railway station is on Lennox St just west of the centre. Long-distance buses stop at the bus terminal beside the railway station.

Maryborough-Hervey Bay Coaches (☎ 4121 3719) has nine bus services every weekday and three services on Saturday between Maryborough and Hervey Bay. Buses depart Maryborough from outside the Town Hall in Kent St.

HERVEY BAY

Hervey (pronounced 'Harvey') Bay is actually a string of five small linked settlements (from west to east: Point Vernon, Pialba, Scarness, Torquay and Urangan) strung along a 10km, north-facing stretch of coast. There's no central district – the town's real focal point is the bay and Fraser Island. Most of the accommodation is on or just off the Esplanade, concentrated in Scarness and Torquay.

In response to the large number of tourists and weekenders descending on the place – as a stopoff en route to Fraser or, during the season, to go out whale-watching – Hervey Bay is busy developing other attractions to get visitors to spend a few more nights in town. It's possible to go on Aboriginal tours, dive coral reefs or use Hervey Bay as a base for organised trips to neighbouring places like Maryborough. Although there's no surf here, the beaches are good and underused, with the best being in Torquay.

Information

There are numerous privately run information centres and tour booking offices, the most helpful of which is the Hervey Bay Tourist & Visitors Centre (toll-free ☎ 1800 649 926; email: bookitere@cyberlink.com.au) at 63 Old Maryborough Rd in Pialba. It's open daily from 7.30 am to 5 pm. The owner, Pete, organises various Aboriginal activities and tours (see later in this section) and this is also the best place to come if you need help with accommodation.

For bookings there's also the Hervey Bay

The Whales of Hervey Bay

Up to 3000 humpback whales *(Megaptera novaeangliae)* enter the waters of Hervey Bay every year, starting in the last days of July and continuing through until the last week of October. They arrive in clusters of two or three (known as pods) and numbers usually peak in early September. The whales are all stopping off in the Bay on the return leg of their annual migration. Every year these massive creatures (they can grow up to 15m in length and weigh 40 tonnes) swim some 5000km from Antarctic waters up to the warmer waters off eastern Australia, where they mate and give birth.

No one is quite sure why the whales make the diversion from their homeward leg into Hervey Bay; one theory is that it is a kind of pitstop that gives them a chance to rest up after a stressful period of birthing and mating. A few weeks in the calm, warm waters may also give the new calves more time to develop the protective layers of blubber necessary for survival in the icy Antarctic waters.

The R&R theory seems borne out by the behaviour of the whales, which are positively playful some days. It's not uncommon for the animals to swim up to boats and cruise alongside within touching distance of the excited camera-wielding whale-spotters aboard. Often one eye will be clear of the water, raising the question of who's actually watching whom.

Central Booking Office (☎ 4124 1300) at 363 Charlton Esplanade. It also offers use of its online computer terminal for $12 an hour.

Cyberlink Technologies (☎ 4124 7722), 143 Old Maryborough Rd, offers email and Internet access at $6 for 30 minutes or $10 an hour.

The main post office is at 3 Bryant St,

Pialba, with branch post offices at 426 Charlton Esplanade, Torquay and 546 Esplanade, Urangan.

Things to See
Near the corner of the Maryborough Rd and Fairway Drive in Pialba, **Hervey Bay Natureworld** has native fauna including wedge-tailed eagles and koalas, as well as

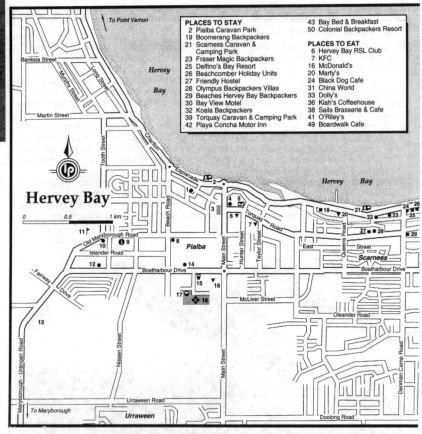

PLACES TO STAY
2 Pialba Caravan Park
19 Boomerang Backpackers
21 Scarness Caravan & Camping Park
23 Fraser Magic Backpackers
25 Delfino's Bay Resort
26 Beachcomber Holiday Units
27 Friendly Hostel
28 Olympus Backpackers Villas
29 Beaches Hervey Bay Backpackers
30 Bay View Motel
32 Koala Backpackers
39 Torquay Caravan & Camping Park
42 Playa Concha Motor Inn
43 Bay Bed & Breakfast
50 Colonial Backpackers Resort

PLACES TO EAT
6 Hervey Bay RSL Club
7 KFC
16 McDonald's
20 Marty's
24 Black Dog Cafe
31 China World
33 Dolly's
36 Kiah's Coffeehouse
38 Sails Brasserie & Cafe
41 O'Riley's
49 Boardwalk Cafe

introduced species such as camels and water buffaloes. Crocodiles are fed at 11.30 am and lorikeets at 3.30 pm. Snakes are handled at 12.30 pm. Natureworld is open daily from 9 am to 5.30 pm; entry costs $7.

Vic Hislop's Great White Shark Expo (☎ 4128 9137), on the corner of Charlton Esplanade and Elizabeth St in Urangan, has a collection of photos, newspaper articles, jaw bones, and three great white sharks kept in a freezer with viewing portals. It also continuously screens a couple of shark documentaries. The displays, facts and fig-

ures presented here are pretty gruesome and sensational but Hislop, a well-known renegade shark catcher, claims the main aim of the exhibition is to be educational. The centre is open daily from 8.30 am to 6 pm; entry costs $10 ($8 for students and backpackers, $4 for children, $24 for a family). If you just want to visit the shark display and skip the movies, tickets cost $6.

About 1km east of 1.4km-long Urangan pier, at Dayman Point, is **Neptune's Reef World**, a small and old-fashioned aquarium with coral displays, fish, seals, turtles and a

OTHER
1 Caprice Twin Cinemas
3 Former Pialba Station
4 Book Exchange
5 Main Post Office
8 Cyberlink Technologies
9 Hervey Bay Tourist & Visitors Centre
10 Safari 4X4 Hire
11 Hervey Bay Golf & Country Club
12 Bay 4WD Centre & Aussie Trax
13 Hervey Bay Nature World
14 Cinema Six
15 Stockman's Bar & Grill
17 Bay Central Bus Station
18 Bay Plaza Shopping Centre
22 Central Booking Office & Laundromat
34 Torquay Beach Hire
35 Torquay Hotel
37 Torquay Post Office
40 Hervey Bay Life-Saving Club
44 Vic Hislop's Great White Shark Expo
45 Urangan Post Office
46 Neptune's Reef World
47 Matthew Flinders & Z Force Memorials
48 Urangan Marina
51 Swimming Pool

shark. There are touch tanks where turtles and stingrays can be petted and there are seal displays at 10.30 am and 3 pm. It is open every day from 9.30 am and costs $8 ($5 for children). From the point itself, there are good views over to Woody and Fraser islands, and there are monuments to Matthew Flinders, the first man to circumnavigate Australia, and the Z Force, WWII commandos who sailed in a converted fishing boat to sink 40,000 tonnes of Japanese shipping in Singapore Harbour in 1943. Much of their training was done on Fraser Island.

Whale-Watching

Boat tours to watch the majestic humpback whales on their annual migration operate out of Hervey Bay every day, weather permitting, between mid-July and late October. There are 17 licensed operators out of Hervey Bay and which boat you go with depends on what kind of experience you want.

The whales are most often found in Platypus Bay, some 50km out of Urangan marina. Some days there may be as many as 20 pods in the area but on other days it may be as few as four or five. A small boat can get out to Platypus Bay within an hour and can then zip around from pod to pod to find the most active whales. The small boats take between 32 and 50 passengers and tend to go out twice a day for four hours each time, once in the early morning and once in the afternoon. Whale-wise the time of the day doesn't matter but the sea tends to be calmer in the earlier part of the day. Prices for half-day tours are $55 to $60, with substantial reductions for children. We can recommend the MV *Seaspray* (☎ 4125 3586), the smallest and fastest of all the whale-watching boats operating out of the marina.

The larger boats run full-day trips. This doesn't necessarily mean more time spent with the whales as some of these boats can take two hours or more to cruise out to Platypus Bay. However, amenities are better, with most boats including a lunch of some kind and all having a licensed bar. The MV *Bay Runner* (☎ 4125 3188) is highly recommended by locals, and charges $58 for a seven-hour trip. At the top end of the range is the MV *Discovery One* (☎ 4124 7247), owned by Mimi Macpherson, sister of Elle Macpherson. The $75 per head cost on this boat includes morning and afternoon tea, a full-cooked lunch, live music, and the name-dropping potential of having spent a day on a boat owned by the sister of a supermodel. Wow! The MV *Eclipse* is wheelchair accessible – some of the other boats may be too.

Seeing whales is as good as guaranteed (in eight years of seasonal daily sailings one captain we spoke with had experienced only four no-whale days). The exception is during the last days of the season, 20 to 25 October, when most of the pods have departed. At this time most boat owners will offer passengers credit for a repeat voyage if no whales are sighted.

Bookings for boats can be made through your accommodation or one of the information centres. Take a hat, sunglasses and sunscreen and don't forget your camera – the whales can make spectacular breaches.

Other Activities

Coral Viewing & Snorkelling The glass-bottomed MV *Krystal Klear* (☎ 4128 9537) spends a day cruising above the bay's coral reefs, and has snorkelling gear available. There are usually turtles around and quite often schools of dolphins too. A barbecue lunch on Round Island, midway between Hervey Bay and Fraser Island, is included. The cost per person is $46.

Fishing Numerous vessels such as the MV *Snapper I* (☎ 4124 3788), MV *Princess II* (☎ 4128 9087) and MV *Reel Easy* (☎ 4124 1300) are available for charter for big game fishing (shark and marlin), fly fishing off Fraser Island and reef fishing. Contact the Hervey Bay Tourist & Visitors Centre (see Information in this section) or call by at the fishing shop on Torquay Esplanade, just west of the Torquay Hotel.

Horse Riding You can go horse riding at the Susan River Homestead (☎ 4121 6846), on Hervey Bay Rd, which offers two-hour rides through bushland for $30.

Skydiving For $240 you can launch yourself out of an aeroplane 3000m above Hervey Bay in a tandem parachute jump. Contact Skydive Hervey Bay (☎ 4124 8248) or book through one of the town's information offices.

Water Sports There are a couple of places along the waterfront where you can hire water sports gear. Torquay Beach Hire, a beach shed on the foreshore, has catamarans ($20 an hour), windsurfers ($15 an hour), fishing dinghies ($60 a day) and will take you water-skiing ($20 for 10 minutes); it also has canoes, deck chairs and other beach essentials.

Shelley Beach Jet Ski Hire (☎ 018 36 366 897) hires out jet-skis at $25 for 15 minutes or $40 for 30 minutes.

Weather permitting, the Hervey High Flyer (☎ 018 36 6897) charges $38 for six minutes parasailing, towed behind a vessel as it speeds along the bay. It departs from the Urangan Harbour or does pick-ups from Torquay Beach Hire.

Organised Tours
Pete Reeve of the Hervey Bay Tourist & Visitors Centre (see Information in this section) can organise two-hour walks in the Hervey Bay area led by an Aboriginal guide, highlighting the collection of naturally occurring foods and medicines. The walk also includes a demonstration of spear and boomerang throwing.

Festivals
The Hervey Bay Whale Festival, held over a fortnight each year in August, celebrates the return of these magnificent creatures.

The Gladstone to Hervey Bay Yacht Race finishes in Hervey Bay in April and participating yachts are on display for two days afterwards. The Bay to Bay yacht race from Hervey Bay to Tin Can Bay is held in May every year.

Places to Stay
Camping & Caravan Parks There are at least a dozen caravan parks in Hervey Bay. Some of the best are the council-run parks along Charlton Esplanade – you'll need to book ahead during the holiday seasons. The *Pialba Caravan Park* (☎ 4128 1399) is the largest and perhaps the best, with plenty of grass and big old trees, a camper's kitchen and barbecues. The *Scarness Caravan & Camping Park* (☎ 4128 1274) occupies a narrower strip along the foreshore, as does the *Torquay Caravan & Camping Park* (☎ 4125 1578). All three charge the same rates, which go up in the holiday seasons – tent sites start from $12 ($14 powered), and on-site vans from $30 a double.

Hostels Hervey Bay has a growing number of backpackers' hostels, spread between Scarness and Urangan. All do pick-ups from the main bus stop, and most organise trips to Fraser Island as well as booking whale-watching tours and other activities.

The best organised is *Koala Backpackers* (☎ 4125 3601), at 408 Charlton Esplanade,

Torquay, across the road from the beach. The set up is attractive, with a central palm-shaded pool, a TV room and a large bar with a deck overlooking the pool. Cheap evening meals are available. It's got a party atmosphere, with games and entertainment most nights. Rooms are on the sparse side – six-bed dorms at $14 per person or doubles and twins at $30. Showers and toilets are communal but clean.

Beaches Hervey Bay Backpackers (☎ 4124 1322), at 195 Torquay Terrace, is run along similar lines to Koala but isn't half as appealing. Accommodation is in flimsy four-berth cabins with communal toilet/shower blocks and a charmless bar/restaurant block in the middle. It feels like a 1950s holiday camp. More objectionable is that sheets and blankets have to be paid for separately at $1 each item – this is also the case at Koala. Beds at Beaches are $15, plus surcharges.

Linen comes free at the *Friendly Hostel* (☎ 4124 4107, fax 4124 4619) at 182 Torquay Rd, Scarness. It's a small, quiet place with three separate units, each with three bedrooms (two or three beds), a TV lounge, kitchen and bathroom. The place is immaculately clean and, in the form of owners Doug and Margaret, lives up to its name – it's like staying over with a favourite aunt and uncle. Beds are $12 per person.

The other place we'd recommend is *Boomerang Backpackers* (☎ 4124 3970) at 335 Charlton Esplanade, Scarness. It specialises in doubles and twins with two bedrooms to a unit, and each unit has its own kitchen, bathroom and lounge. Rates are $26 per double, or there are some private units where you get the whole thing to yourself for $35 a double. Boomerang also has about 20 dorm beds from $11 a night.

For anyone who prefers untamed nature to ranks of other backpackers the *Colonial Backpackers Resort* (☎ 4125 1844, fax 4125 3161), on the corner of Boatharbour Drive and Pulgul St, is the place to go. The Colonial is set in 4.5 hectares of bushland, near the marina from where the whale-watching and Fraser Island boats depart. As a change from German cyclists, Kiwi drifters and British round-the-worlders, your neighbours are possums, frogmouths and a cockatoo named Freddy. Accommodation is in wooden cabins: dorms contain three beds for $13 per person, twins are $14 per person (both shared facilities), while doubles have an en suite and kitchen and go for $32. There are also self-contained cabins which will take up to six people for $45. Facilities include a restaurant/bar, two tennis courts, a volleyball court and one of Queensland's few hostel pools large enough to actually swim in.

Other options include *Fraser Magic Backpackers* (☎ 4124 3488), 369 Charlton Esplanade, which despite being relatively new is fairly rundown and has a very gloomy atmosphere (dorms $14, doubles $30); and *Olympus Backpackers Villas* (☎ 4124 5331), 184 Torquay Rd, Scarness, a purpose-built hostel with eight separate two-storey apartments, each with bathroom, kitchen and TV lounge (dorms $13, twins and doubles $28).

Motels & Holiday Flats Some of these places offer fantastic value and can work out much cheaper than a hostel, particularly if there's a group. *Beachcomber Holiday Units* (☎ 4124 2152) at 384 Charlton Esplanade has comfortable self-contained units with a double bedroom, bathroom, kitchen and living room with fold-out double bed for $40. The nearby *Bay View Motel* (☎ 4128 1134), 399 Charlton Esplanade, offers similar for the same price but is a little less homely.

Move up into a slightly higher price bracket of $60 or more for a self-contained unit, and you'll find dozens of options. Two of the best are the *Playa Concha Motor Inn* (☎ 4125 1544), on the corner of Charlton Esplanade and Ann St, Torquay, which has modern motel units at $85, a licensed restaurant, and a pool and spa; and *Delfino's Bay Resort* (☎ 4124 1666), 383 Charlton Esplanade, Torquay, with modern motel units starting at $70 a night.

B&Bs *Bay Bed & Breakfast* (☎ 4125 6919), 180 Cypress St, Urangan is a beautifully kept private house with four extra rooms for guests charged at $60 per double or $80 for the deluxe, both with breakfast included. There's also a self-contained cottage which sleeps six to eight people at $20 per night (minimum four people). There's a pool and deck dining area.

Places to Eat

Colonial, Koala and *Beaches* hostels have their own cheap restaurants, and in the case of the latter at least, non-residents are welcome to eat there.

Otherwise, Charlton Esplanade in Torquay is the food focus in Hervey Bay. Cheapest deal has to be *Marty's*, on the corner of the Esplanade and Queens Rd, which does a T-bone steak, fries and salad, plus a pot of beer for $6.50. There's no skimping on the servings either. Other meals are in the $6.50 to $8.50 range.

China World, 402 Charlton Esplanade on the corner of Tavistock St, has an all-you-can-eat deal for $7 at lunch and $9 in the evening. Dishes on the standard menu are also very good, and most are in the $8 to $10 range. Be on time – it closes at 9 pm.

O'Riley's, on the corner of the Esplanade and Macks Rd, is a relaxed BYO pancake, pizza and pasta joint with savoury crepes and pasta under $9, pizzas in the $10 to $12 range (enough for two) and a range of dessert pancakes from $4 to $6. It's open from 5 to 9.30 pm daily, and until 10.30 pm on Friday and Saturday.

More upmarket, *Sails Brasserie & Cafe* on the corner of Charlton Esplanade and Fraser St is a chic Mediterranean-style eatery with main courses in the $14 to $16 range. It's licensed and open Monday to Saturday nights and Thursday and Friday for lunch.

The *Black Dog Cafe* at the corner of Denman Camp Rd also has some interesting dishes centred on sushi ($4 to $5), teriyaki and noodles ($7 to $8). It's open daily from 9.30 am to 10 pm, closed Tuesday.

For atmosphere try the *Boardwalk Cafe*

Top Left: Crystal clear Lake McKenzie, one of many freshwater lakes on Fraser Island.
Top Right: Tall rainforests grow in the sands of Fraser Island and support many bird species.
Middle: Indian Head, on the north-east coast of Fraser island.
Bottom: Coloured sands glow on Fraser Island.

QUEENSLAND TOURIST AND TRAVEL CORPORATION

MARK ARMSTRONG

ROBERT CHARLTON

MARK ARMSTRONG

Top Left: A waterfall in the beautiful Blackdown Tableland National Park, near Dingo.
Top Right: The historic Mt Morgan train station and a local character.
Middle: Lady Musgrave Island, near Bundaberg, a popular stopover for yachts.
Bottom: Budget accommodation is a short walk from Fisherman's Beach, Great Keppel Island.

overlooking the Urangan marina. It does good pasta, quiche and filled pastry lunches for \$5.50 to \$7 and dinners in the \$12 to \$15 range. It's open from 6.30 am till late Tuesday to Saturday and from 6.30 am to 6.30 pm Sunday and Monday.

For late night dining, *Dolly's* on Charlton Esplanade serves until 1.30 am, while for good breakfasts try *Kiah's Coffeehouse* on the corner of Bideford and Truro Sts. It also has plenty of vegetarian options for lunch.

Entertainment
Bars Koala and Beaches hostels both have their own bars at which staff work hard to induce some kind of party atmosphere. Far better though is the back bar at *Marty's* on the Esplanade at the corner with Queens St. This is a popular local bar with four pool tables, live music Thursday through Sunday and a small dance floor. The *Torquay Hotel* on Charlton Esplanade, Torquay also sometimes has live bands at weekends. *Stockman's Bar & Grill* on Boatharbour Drive has live rock bands on Friday and Saturday nights; there's no cover charge and it is open till midnight.

Cinema Up by Bay Central bus station at 128 Boat Harbour Drive is Hervey Bay's six screen cinema (☎ 4124 8200). Budget days are Tuesday and Thursday, when all tickets are \$6. Some of the hostels run courtesy buses up to evening screenings.

Getting There & Away
Air Sunstate and Flight West have daily flights between Brisbane and Hervey Bay. The one-way fare is \$124. Hervey Bay airport is off Booral Rd, Urangan.

Bus Hervey Bay is on the main coastal bus route and Greyhound Pioneer, McCafferty's and Suncoast Pacific each has three or four services passing through every day. It's about 4½ hours from Brisbane (\$32 to \$38 depending on the carrier) and about 5½ hours from Rockhampton (\$55).

Maryborough-Hervey Bay Coaches (☎ 4121 3719) runs a service between the two centres, with nine trips every weekday and three on Saturday.

Getting Around
Getting around Hervey Bay is a major problem. Distances from the main accommodation areas to the Bay Central bus station and the marina are prohibitive for walking and there's no decent bus service – Maryborough-Hervey Bay Coaches (☎ 4121 3719) does run local services every weekday and on Saturday morning, but the buses on each route run at intervals of up to two hours or more. Taxis are expensive and have to be ordered. If you're staying in a hostel you'll probably be reliant on its courtesy buses; otherwise hire a bike.

Car Rental Hervey Bay Rental Cars (☎ 7124 5589), at the Ambassador Motor Lodge on the Esplanade at Scarness, has cars at \$39 per day including 200km mileage. It's advisable to book in advance as there are only four cars. A slightly more expensive alternative is Thrifty (☎ 4128 4866) at Geldards Travel, Central Ave, off Boatharbour Drive in Pialba.

4WD Rental The Bay 4WD Centre (☎ 4128 2981), 54 Boatharbour Drive, Pialba, and Safari 4X4 Hire (toll-free ☎ 1800 689 819) at 55 Old Maryborough Rd have good, reliable vehicles ranging from about \$90 a day for a Suzuki Sierra to \$125 for a Toyota Landcruiser, usually with a two day minimum.

Aussie Trax (toll-free ☎ 1800 062 275), 56 Boatharbour Drive, Pialba, has old exarmy jeeps from \$85 a day, as well as Suzuki Sierras and Landrover Defender Wagons at \$130 a day.

A \$500 deposit is generally required – this can be made on a credit card if you have one – and drivers must be over 21. All the preceding operators give 4WD instruction to first time drivers.

You can also hire 4WD from several places on Fraser island – see that section for details.

Bicycles & Scooters Some of the hostels, including the Colonial, the Friendly and

Koala, have bikes available for guests. Otherwise, you can hire bikes from the Hervey Bay Central Booking Office, 363 Charlton Esplanade, for $10 for a half-day, $15 for a full day. Hervey Bay Scooter Hire (☎ 015 628 359) charges $15 for the first hour then $10 per hour, or $35 per day.

FRASER ISLAND

The thing to keep in mind about Fraser Island is that it's all sand. There's no soil, no clay and only two or three small rocky outcrops. It's one gigantic, 120km by 15km vegetated sand bar – the world's largest. It was inscribed as such on the World Heritage List in 1993 and the northern half of the island is protected as the Great Sandy National Park.

Fraser Island is a delight for those who love fishing, walking, exploring by 4WD or simply enjoy nature. Some of the sand blows (large drifting dunes) are magnificent, while much of the island is densely forested with an amazing variety of trees and plants, many of which are only to be found on Fraser. There are also about 200 lakes, some of them superb for swimming. This is just as well, as the sea is a definite no-go: there are lethal undertows as well as the odd man-eating shark or ten. Other wildlife is in abundance, including 40 different mammal species and more insects and reptiles than you want to know.

The island is sparsely populated and although more than 20,000 vehicles a year pile on to it, it remains wild. A network of sandy tracks criss-crosses the island and you can drive along great stretches of beach – but it's 4WD only; there are no paved roads. You can camp on Fraser or stay in accommodation.

History

The island takes its name from the captain of a ship which was wrecked further north in 1836. Making their way south to look for help, a group from the ship fell in with Aborigines on the island. Some of the group died during their two month wait for rescue but others, including Fraser, survived with Aboriginal help.

To the Butchulla Aborigines, the island was known as K'gari (which translates as 'Paradise') after a spirit who helped the great god Beeral create the earth and other worlds. K'gari loved earth so much she asked Beeral to let her live there and so he changed her into a beautiful island, with trees and animals for company, and limpid lakes for eyes through which she could gaze up at the heavens, her former home. The Aborigines were driven off K'gari onto missions when timber cutters moved onto the island in the 1860s. The cutters were after satinay, a rainforest tree highly resistant to the marine life which normally rots timber and which grows only on Fraser. Satinay was used to line the Suez Canal. It was not until 1991 that logging on the island ceased.

In the mid-1970s Fraser Island was the subject of a bitter struggle between conservationists and industry – in this case a sand-mining company. The decision went to the conservationists.

Information

There's a visitor centre on the east coast of the island at Eurong (☎ 4127 9128), and ranger offices at Dundubara and Waddy Point. These places all have plenty of leaflets detailing walking trails and the flora and fauna found on the island.

At Central Station (the old forestry depot) there's a small display on the history of exploration and logging on the island.

General supplies are available from stores at Eurong, Happy Valley and Cathedral Beach but, as you might expect, prices are high. There are also public telephones at these sites.

Permits You'll need a permit to take a vehicle onto the island and to camp. The most convenient place to get permits is the River Heads general store, just 500m from the ferry to Wanggoolba Creek (also called Woongoolber Creek). Vehicles cost $30, or $40 if the permit is purchased on the island. Camping costs $3.50 per person per night – you don't need to pay this if you're staying

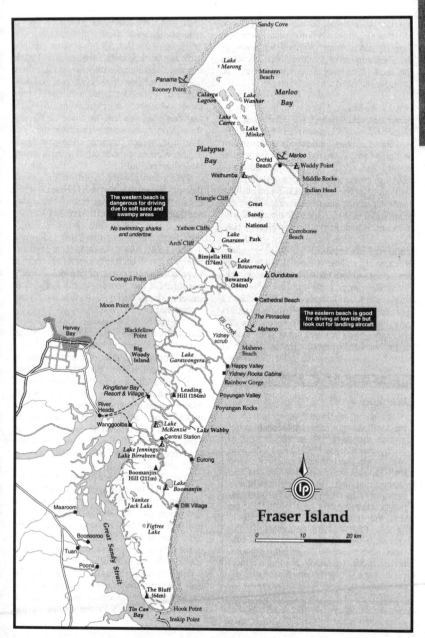

Sandy Cove

Lake Marong

Panama

Rooney Point

Calanga Lagoon

Lake Wanhar

Manann Beach

Marloo Bay

Lake Carree

Lake Minker

Platypus Bay

Orchid Beach

Marloo

Waddy Point

Wathumba

Middle Rocks

Indian Head

The western beach is dangerous for driving due to soft sand and swampy areas

Triangle Cliff

Great Sandy National Park

No swimming: sharks and undertow

Yathon Cliffs

Corroboree Beach

Arch Cliff

Lake Gnarann

Bimjella Hill (174m)

Lake Bowarrady

Bowarrady (244m)

Dundubara

Coongul Point

Cathedral Beach

Moon Point

Eli Creek

The Pinnacles

The eastern beach is good for driving at low tide but look out for landing aircraft

Hervey Bay

Blackfellow Point

Yidney scrub

Maheno

Big Woody Island

Lake Garawongera

Maheno Beach

Kingfisher Bay Resort & Village

Happy Valley

Yidney Rocks Cabins

Rainbow Gorge

River Heads

Leading Hill (184m)

Poyungan Valley

Poyungan Rocks

Wanggoolba

Lake McKenzie

Lake Wabby

Central Station

Lake Jennings

Lake Birrabeen

Eurong

Boomanjin Hill (211m)

Lake Boomanjin

Maaroom

Yankee Jack Lake

Dilli Village

Figtree Lake

Fraser Island

Boonooroo

Tuan

Poona

Great Sandy Strait

0   10   20 km

The Bluff (64m)

Tin Can Bay

Hook Point

Inskip Point

in cabin accommodation or camping in one of the island's private campgrounds. Permits can also be obtained from any of the Department of Environment offices in the area (Rainbow Bay, Maryborough & Gympie included).

Books & Maps The excellent, 250-page paperback *Bushpeople's Visitor Guide to Fraser Island & Cooloola* ($16) is worth investing in as both a guidebook and souvenir of the island. It includes notes on natural history and advice on camping and bushwalking, canoeing and whale-watching.

A good map is essential if you will be spending a few days exploring. The Sunmap 1:140,000 provides all the detail you need and is widely available in Hervey Bay.

Visiting Fraser Island

Backpacker Tours Self-drive tours to Fraser Island organised by the backpackers' hostels are popular and cost around $95 per person for a three day trip. This doesn't include food or fuel but all the gear is organised for you. These trips are an affordable and (usually) fun way to see the island but you'll probably be in a group of

---

Warning

When hiring 4WDs and equipment for a trip to Fraser the cheapest option is not always the best. We've had reports of dodgy operators in Hervey Bay who offer what seem like attractive rates, but send travellers out with unreliable vehicles and faulty equipment. In some cases these operators have then refused to return deposits, claiming that wear on the vehicle was the result of the travellers' negligence. Check the reputation of the company before handing any money over (and most of Hervey Bay's hire operators are perfectly reputable), and make a thorough check yourself of any equipment you take out.

---

eight and, like relatives, you can't choose who you go with.

Independent Travel Some of the hostels tell travellers that the only way to get there is on one of their trips. Not true. If you'd rather do your own thing, you could quite easily get a group together yourself. 4WDs and camping gear can be hired in Hervey Bay, permits are readily available and you have a choice of catching a ferry or flying to the island (see Getting There & Away later this section).

4WDs can also be hired on the island through Kingfisher Bay 4WD Hire (☎ 4120 3366), with Lada Nivas from $120 a day and Landrover Defenders from $150 a day; Happy Valley 4WD Hire (☎ 4127 9260), with Suzuki Sierras from $100 a day and Toyota Landcruisers from $160 a day; and Shorty's Off Road Rentals (☎ 4127 9122) at Eurong, with a couple of Suzukis for $90 per day. On the island you can get fuel at Eurong, Happy Valley, Cathedral Beach and Kingfisher Bay.

Organised Tours While the freedom that comes with crunching your own 4WD over tree stumps and thundering along beaches at low tide is extremely satisfying, a large part of Fraser's allure is in the whole load of geology that's going on there, and in the island's plantlife and the things that flap, pad and crawl about in it. It takes someone who knows their stuff to bring it to life. Several operators offer one, two or three-day tours led by astoundingly well-informed guides.

Prices for day tours to Fraser Island begin at $65 ($35 for children) with Top Tours (toll-free ☎ 1800 063 933) or Fraser Venture Day Tours (☎ 4125 4444). Kingfisher Bay (toll-free ☎ 1800 072 555) is slightly more expensive at $75 ($40 for children). Each outfit follows a different route but a typical tour, conducted in a hulking 4WD bus with a ranger guide, might take in a trip up the east coast to the *Maheno* wreck and the Cathedrals, plus Central Station and a couple of the lakes in the centre of the island. Most day tours to Fraser Island allow you to split the trip and stay a few days on the island before coming back.

Air Fraser Island (☎ 4125 3600) flies out of Hervey Bay airport and lands on the island's east coast beach. You can do a day trip for $35 per person (once down you're left to amuse yourself for the day until it's time to fly back), or for $85 per person a day's hire of a 4WD is included; it also has two-day tours for around $150 per person which includes return flights, a tent and one day's 4WD hire.

Top Tours has a two day trip for $150 including a night's accommodation at Happy Valley, while Fraser Venture Tours offer similar with an overnight at the Eurong Beach Resort for $145. In both cases accommodation is quad share and a sleeping bag is required.

Kingfisher Bay also has a three day 'Wilderness Adventure'. This is the one we tried and can wholeheartedly recommend. It takes in all the island's major sites and includes opportunities for bushwalking, swimming and snorkelling. The $225 package also includes three meals a day (the breakfast is fantastic), twin or quad accommodation and use of all facilities at the luxurious Kingfisher Bay Resort.

For more Fraser Island packages see the Noosa and Rainbow Beach sections.

Driving on the Island

The only thing stopping you taking a conventional (non-4WD) vehicle onto the island is the fact that you probably won't get more than 500m before you get bogged in sand. Small 4WD sedans are OK, but you may have ground clearance problems on some of the inland tracks – a 'proper' 4WD gives maximum mobility.

Driving on the island requires a good deal of care, to protect not only yourself but the fragile environment. When planning your trip reckon on covering roughly 20km an hour on the inland tracks and 50km an hour on the eastern beach.

Note: during the time we were in southeast Queensland researching this book no

fewer than five serious accidents were reported in the local press involving inexperienced drivers rolling 4WDs on Fraser. In two cases injured passengers had to be airlifted off the island. If you've never driven a 4WD before and are going to be doing so on Fraser then the following are a few pointers:

- Don't rush. Braking can be unpredictable in soft sand. The best way to cope with uneven surfaces and obstacles is to maintain a slow but steady speed.
- When driving on the island's tracks you should have 4WD engaged at all times, not so much because of the danger of getting stuck, but because your wheels are less likely to spin and damage the sandy tracks.
- Apart from the beaches, where you are free to drive at will, all tracks are obvious and you must stick to them.
- The tracks are only wide enough to accommodate one vehicle. When meeting an oncoming vehicle the IBTY (I'm Bigger Than You) rule applies – pull over to allow buses and trucks to pass.
- When driving on the beaches the speed limit is 80km/h. Keep an eye out for washouts at the many creek outlets, especially after heavy rain – cross creeks as close to the ocean as possible and never stop in a creek as the sand under your wheels will be washed away.
- Driving on the eastern beach, the island's 'main highway' is fairly straightforward but the western beach is treacherous and has swamps and holes – avoid it.
- Make sure you know the tide times. Two hours either side of low tide is the best time to travel as large expanses of smooth, hard sand are exposed. At high tide it is much more difficult and quite slow going.
- Do not drive at speed through shallow salt water – it causes rust and the sand could be quickly washed from under your wheels, bogging down the vehicle.
- Use your indicators to show oncoming vehicles which side you intend passing on.
- Drive slowly when passing walkers and people fishing, as they probably won't hear you coming above the roar of the surf.

Duncan's Off Road 4WD Driver Training (toll-free ☎ 1800 357 475) runs one day courses ($95) at Kingfisher Bay in 4WD handling and the specifics of driving on Fraser Island. The course is great fun, involving several 'obstacle courses' meant to reproduce the worst conditions any driver could expect to encounter.

Around the Island

Starting from the south at Hook Point, you cross a number of creeks and get to Dilli Village, the former sand-mining centre. A little further on is the settlement of Eurong.

About 4km beyond Eurong is a signposted walking trail to the beautiful **Lake Wabby**, possibly the highlight of the island. The deepest of Fraser's lakes, it's surrounded on three sides by eucalypt forest, while on the fourth is a massive sandblow whose steep bow crashes into the lake. The sand blow is advancing at a rate of about 3m a year, threatening to fill in the lake. Wabby is a 45 minute walk from the beach (rewarded by a swim in the lake), or you can drive a further 2.6km north along the beach to take a scenic route up to a lookout on the inland side of the lake – this is well worth doing as the lake seen from the lookout is spectacular. *Don't* dive into the lake after running down the steep sand dunes – in the last few years, five people have suffered spinal injuries from doing just that. Take a look in the far eastern corner under the trees, where you'll find large catfish and small turtles.

A popular inland area for visitors is the south-central lake and rainforest country around Central Station and McKenzie, Jennings, Birrabeen and Boomanjin lakes. **Lake McKenzie** is unbelievably clear. Known as a 'window' lake, the water here is actually part of the water table, and so has not flowed anywhere over land. It's a wildly disorienting experience to look down through a face mask where the bottom drops precipitously away to a visible depth of 15m.

After Eurong and Happy Valley, you cross **Eli Creek**, the largest stream on the east coast. Wooden boardwalks go 400m back up the creek and it's pleasant to enter the water up here and drift back down to the

beach. About 2km from Eli Creek are the remains of the *Maheno*, a former passenger liner which was blown ashore by a typhoon in 1935 as it was being towed to a Japanese scrapyard.

Two signposted vehicle tracks lead inland from Happy Valley: one goes to **Lake Garawongera**, then south to the beach again at Poyungan Valley (15km); the other heads to **Yidney Scrub** and a number of lakes before returning to the ocean beach north of the *Maheno* (45km). The latter route will take you to some fine lakes and good lookout points among the highest dunes on the island.

Not far north of Happy Valley you enter the national park, and pass the *Maheno* and the **Cathedrals** – 25km of coloured sand cliffs. Dundubara has a rangers' hut, and probably the best camping ground on the island. Then there's a 20km stretch of beach before you come to the rock outcrop of **Indian Head**, the best vantage point on the island. Climb up onto the headland and scan the waters below for sharks, manta rays, dolphins and, further out, whales if they're in season.

Beyond Indian Head are Middle Rocks and Waddy Point and then **Orchid Beach**, and it's a further 30km of beach up to **Sandy Cape**, the northern tip, with its lighthouse a few more kilometres to the west.

Places to Stay & Eat

Come well equipped since supplies on the island are limited and only available in a few places. And be prepared for mosquitoes and March flies.

Camping The Departments of Environment and Forestry operate 11 camping grounds on the island, some accessible only by boat or on foot. Those in the north at Dundubara, Waddy Point and Wathumba, and in the south at Central Station, Lake Boomanjin and Lake McKenzie have toilets and showers. You can also camp on some stretches of beach. To camp in any of these public areas you need a permit.

There's also the privately run *Cathedral Beach Resort & Camping Park* (☎ 4127 9177) 34km north of Eurong. Tent sites cost $14 and cabins cost $75 for up to four people – note that they don't take backpacker groups here.

Other Accommodation The *Dilli Village Recreation Camp* (☎ 4127 9130) is 200m from the east coast, 24km from Hook Point and 9km from Eurong. A four-bed cabin with shower and kitchen costs $45 per night for up to four people or there are cabins without kitchens or bathrooms at $10 per person. You can also camp here for $4 per person.

The *Eurong Beach Resort* (☎ 4127 9122) 35km north of Hook Point on the east coast has several sections. The cheapest are cabins, each containing four bunks charged at $12 per bed. Linen is supplied. A-frame cottages are $90 for four people plus $5 per extra person, with a maximum of eight. Motel units with double and a fold-out bed go for $70 and $80, while two-bedroom apartments sleeping six to eight people are $90 per night. The resort also has a general store, bar and bistro.

Just south of Happy Valley, the low-key *Yidney Rocks Cabins* (☎ 4127 9167) are right on the edge of the beach. They're old but comfortable; the nightly rate is $65 for up to six people or $80 for up to eight.

The *Fraser Island Retreat Happy Valley Resort* (☎ 4127 9144, fax 4127 9131) has good self-contained timber lodges for $160/175 a night for doubles/triples, and larger lodges for $195 a night for up to four people. The resort also has a bar, bistro and shop.

The impressive and luxurious *Kingfisher Bay Resort* (toll-free ☎ 1800 072 555, fax 4120 3326) on the west coast has what are called 'Wilderness Cabins' which contain a kitchen, dining area, bathrooms and two four-bed dorms plus two twins all charged at $30 per person. There are also hotel rooms from $220 per double, two-bedroom villas suitable for four/five people from $690 for three nights, and three-bedroom

villas suitable for six from $960 for three nights. The resort has restaurants, bars and shops, and, architecturally, it's worth a look even if you're not staying here. There's also a day trippers' section near the jetty, with the *Sandbar* bar and brasserie.

Getting There & Away

Air Air Fraser Island (☎ 4125 3600) charge $35 for a return flight to the island's east coast beach, departing Hervey Bay airport.

Ferry Vehicle ferries (known locally as barges) operate to the southern end of Fraser Island from Inskip Point, and to the west coast of the island from River Heads, south of Urangan. The *Rainbow Venture* (☎ 5486 3154) operates the 10 minute crossing from Inskip Point (near Rainbow Beach) to Hook Point on Fraser Island. It makes this crossing regularly from about 7 am to 4.30 pm daily. The price is $45 return for a vehicle and passengers, and you can get tickets on board the ferry. Walk-on passengers pay $5.

The *Fraser Venture* (☎ 4125 4444) makes the 30 minute crossing from River Heads to Wanggoolba Creek (also called Woongoolber Creek) on the west coast of Fraser Island. It departs daily from River Heads at 9 and 10.15 am and 3.30 pm, and returns from the island at 9.30 am, 2.30 and 4 pm. On Saturday there is also a 7 am service from River Heads, which returns at 7.30 am from the island. The barge takes 27 vehicles but it's still advisable to book. The return fare for vehicle and driver is $55, plus $3 for each extra passenger. Walk-on passengers pay $10 return.

The Kingfisher Bay Resort (☎ 4125 5155) also operates two boats. The *Fraser II* does the 45 minute crossing from River Heads to Kingfisher Bay daily. Departures from River Heads are at 7 and 11 am and 2 pm, and from the island at 9.45 am, and 12.45 and 4.30 pm. The return fare is $60 for a vehicle and driver, plus $4 for extras. The *Kingfisher 3* is a passenger catamaran that crosses from the Urangan Boat Harbour to Kingfisher Bay five times a day (first departure 8.30 am) for a return fare of $30 ($15 children).

There's also a ferry, the *Fraser Dawn*, from Urangan to Moon Point on the island, but this is an inconvenient place to land as it's a long drive across to the other side.

CHILDERS
On the Bruce Hwy 60km north-west of Maryborough is the historic township of Childers. The town centre features numerous turn-of-the-century buildings, and most of the main street has been classified as a heritage area. If you are passing through by car it's definitely worth stopping for an hour or two. Childers is also a good place for backpackers to find fruit picking work.

Information
The Pharmaceutical Museum (see the next section) also serves as an information centre. Childers Internet Shop (☎ 4126 3555) at the north end of the main street offers use of its terminal to access the Web or send email for $5 per half-hour.

Things to See & Do
At the **Childers Pharmaceutical Museum & Art Gallery** (☎ 4126 1994), opposite the post office at 90 Churchill St, all of the old bottles, instruments, potions and prescription books that were used by the town's first pharmacist are on display in their beautiful original cedar cabinets. Up a set of narrow stairs a large hall is used for the display of local craft and art work. The place is open from 8.45 am to 4.30 pm weekdays and from 8.30 am to noon on Saturday.

Other interesting old buildings along the main street include the **Federal Hotel** on the corner of North St, which still has its original swinging doors leading into the corner bar; **Ye Olde Boutique** on the corner of Ashby Lane, which was built as the Queensland Bank; and the **Palace Hotel**, which is now a backpackers' hostel (see Places to Stay). There's a small **historical complex** in Taylor St off the main road just south of the centre, but it's open by

appointment only. Check with the information centre.

During the cane-crushing season (July to November) you can take a tour through the **Isis Sugar Mill** at 2 pm on weekdays; ring ☎ 4126 6166 to book.

Places to Stay
Workers' Hostels The *Palace Backpackers Hostel* (☎ 4126 2244), right in the centre of Childers at 72 Churchill St, is a conversion of the historic two-storey Palace Hotel. It's a workers' hostel completely geared to fruit picking and catering to long term stays. The facilities are very good, with a big communal kitchen with walk-in fridge, a big TV room, games and clean showers. Although there are a few doubles and triples most dorms have four or six beds and there's a giant dorm which sleeps a couple of dozen. All beds cost $14 per night or $90 per week, including transport to and from work. Priority on the doubles goes to those who've been at the hostel longest.

Other Accommodation The *Sugarbowl Caravan Park* (☎ 4126 1521) is a neat and well-kept park on the north side of town with good valley views from a hillside. Tent sites cost $10, on-site vans $25 and there are cabins from $30 a double. For anyone interested in staying around fruit picking for a while, the site owners offer deals of a van from $70 to $110 a week, and will help find work and provide transport.

The *Federal Hotel* (☎ 4126 1438), on the corner of Churchill and North Sts, has basic rooms at $16/26 for singles/doubles.

The *Avocado Motor Inn* (☎ 4126 1608), on the highway 1km north of the centre, has budget units from $38, or there's the *Motel Childers* (☎ 4126 1177), at the northern end of the high street, at 136 Churchill St, with doubles at $50.

Places to Eat
Try the *Federal Hotel* on the corner of Churchill and North Sts for a pub feed. It's a relaxed, big old pub with bistro meals in the $6 to $10 range and kid's meals for

$3.50. Otherwise, there's the *Laurel Tree Cottage* on the highway just north of town at No 89, which specialises in lunch, afternoon teas and snacks. It's open daily from 8.30 am to 4 pm and for dinner from 6 pm on Friday and Saturday.

Getting There & Away
Childers is on the main bus run up the Bruce Hwy; long-distance buses stop at the Shell service station just north of the town centre.

WOODGATE
Woodgate, 37km east of Childers, is basically a string of holiday houses stretching for about 4km along the coast. It's a very quiet and laid-back town with pleasant beaches, a pub, a bowling club and a general store. Just north of the entrance to Woodgate on Frizzel's Rd is the Woodgate Central Plaza, a small shopping centre which contains an information office.

Most of the accommodation is along The Esplanade south of the point where the road into Woodgate meets the coast, while 3km north is the broad estuary of Theodolite Creek, where there's a picnic area, a good calm-water swimming spot and a boat ramp. The creek reputedly offers excellent fishing and mud-crabbing.

Places to Stay & Eat
The *Barkala Caravan Park* (☎ 4126 8802) in the centre of The Esplanade, is a good park with a shop, tent sites at $10, on-site vans at $22 and self-contained cabins from $25 to $40 a double. You need to supply your own bedding for the cabins.

The *Beach Hotel-Motel* (☎ 4126 8988) on the Esplanade 1km north of the main road into Woodgate, is a modern, brick beer barn with motel units next door at $50 a double in the low season and $60 in the high season.

There are quite a few holiday units along the beachfront. The *Hibiscus Holiday Units* (☎ 4126 8709) next to the general store at 139 The Esplanade, is a renovated block of oldish one and two-bedroom units that

range from $40 to $60 a night. At the other end of the scale, you could rent *Barcoo* (☎ 4126 8816), an ultra-modern split-level timber and iron beach-house designed by the architects responsible for the Kingfisher Bay Resort on Fraser Island.

The house has four bedrooms and all the mod cons, and goes for $400 a week in the low season and $600 a week in the high season. It's at the southern end of The Esplanade.

The *Beach Hotel-Motel* has a large bistro with a pleasant courtyard area at the front, and the *Woodgate General Store* has pretty good burgers.

WOODGATE NATIONAL PARK
A couple of kilometres south of Woodgate is the Woodgate National Park, at the mouth of the Burrum River. The park has good beaches and is popular with anglers, and you'll probably need to book camp sites during holiday periods. The road down to the park is sealed and you can drive part way into the park in a conventional vehicle, but to get to the camping ground and the Burrum River you'll need a 4WD.

A 400m boardwalk through a melaleuca swamp and a 5km circuit walk are in the northern corner of the park; both start from Acacia St, which runs parallel with The Esplanade one block back from the beachfront. There are several other walking tracks starting from near the camping ground. Contact the rangers at the park (☎ 4126 8810) to book camping permits or for more information.

BUNDABERG
At the northern end of Hervey Bay and on the southern edge of the Capricorn Coast, Bundaberg is a very attractive small town 50km off the Bruce Hwy and 15km inland from the coast on the Burnett River. It's a major sugar-growing, processing and exporting centre and some of the sugar ends up in the famous Bundaberg Rum. A visit to the distillery is probably the town's biggest attraction. Bundaberg is also the southernmost access point for the Great Barrier Reef

and the departure point for Lady Elliot and Lady Musgrave islands.

The town attracts a steady stream of travellers looking for harvest work picking everything from avocados to zucchinis. The hostels here can often help you find work, but be wary of promises of work that doesn't exist. It's worth ringing a few of the hostel managers and inquiring before you come. There's usually some sort of harvest going on throughout the year – the main harvest season runs from mid-March until Christmas.

Information

The Bundaberg tourist information centre (toll-free ☎ 1800 060 499) is on the corner of the Isis Hwy, the main road as you enter the town from the south, and Bourbong St. It's open daily from 9 am to 5 pm, and can supply information on things to do in the area and where to look for a place to stay. The Department of Environment (☎ 4153 8620) has an office in Quay St.

The post office is the grand building with the clock tower on the corner of Bourbong and Barolin Sts.

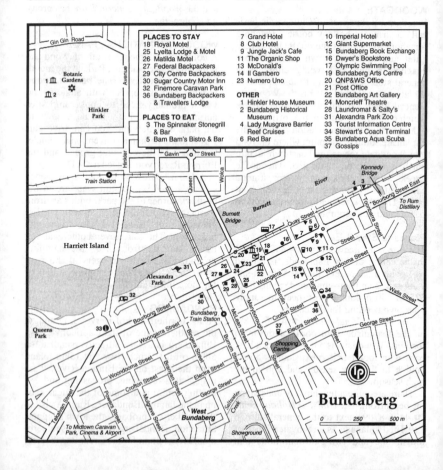

PLACES TO STAY
18 Royal Motel
25 Lyelta Lodge & Motel
26 Matilda Motel
27 Federal Backpackers
29 City Centre Backpackers
30 Sugar Country Motor Inn
32 Finemore Caravan Park
36 Bundaberg Backpackers
   & Travellers Lodge

PLACES TO EAT
3 The Spinnaker Stonegrill
   & Bar
5 Bam Bam's Bistro & Bar
7 Grand Hotel
8 Club Hotel
9 Jungle Jack's Cafe
11 The Organic Shop
13 McDonald's
14 Il Gambero
23 Numero Uno

OTHER
1 Hinkler House Museum
2 Bundaberg Historical
   Museum
4 Lady Musgrave Barrier
   Reef Cruises
6 Red Bar
10 Imperial Hotel
12 Giant Supermarket
15 Bundaberg Book Exchange
16 Dwyer's Bookstore
17 Olympic Swimming Pool
19 Bundaberg Arts Centre
20 QNP&WS Office
21 Post Office
22 Bundaberg Art Gallery
24 Moncrieff Theatre
28 Laundromat & Salty's
31 Alexandra Park Zoo
33 Tourist Information Centre
34 Stewart's Coach Terminal
35 Bundaberg Aqua Scuba
37 Gossips

Bundaberg

Things to See
Aficionados of Bundy rum can tour the **Bundaberg Rum Distillery** on Avenue St in East Bundaberg, about 2km east from the centre of town. Tours start with an introductory video before visiting the fermentation house, distillery, bottling plant and store. At the end of the tour you visit Spring Hill House which has a museum, souvenir shop and a bar where you can do a taste test. Tours are run weekdays between 10 am and 3 pm, and Saturday and Sunday between 10 am and 2 pm; the cost is $5 (which includes a sample of the product) and $2 for anyone under 18 years of age. While you're here it's worth visiting **Schmeider's Cooperage & Craft Centre** nearby on Alexandra St, where you can watch the coopers handmaking timber barrels and other craft products, all of which are for sale. Schmeider's is open weekdays from 9 am to 5 pm and weekends from 9 am to 3 pm; entry is free.

Bundaberg's attractive **Botanic Gardens** are 2km north of the centre on Gin Gin Rd. Within the reserve are rose gardens, walking paths, a historical museum, and the **Hinkler House Museum**, dedicated to the life and times of the aviator Bert Hinkler. Hinkler was born in Bundaberg, and in 1928 made the first solo flight between England and Australia. Hinkler's former home was transported here from Southampton, England, and rebuilt to house a collection of memorabilia and information on the aviation pioneer. Nearby is the **Bundaberg & District Historical Museum**. Both museums are open daily from 10 am to 4 pm, and both charge $2.50 ($1 children).

The **Bundaberg Art Gallery** is in the historic School of Arts building beside the civic centre in Bourbong St. It is open weekdays from 10 am to 3 pm and Sunday from 12.30 to 3 pm; entry is free. The gallery houses a small permanent collection and features regular travelling exhibitions. The **Bundaberg Arts Centre** (☎ 4152 3700), 1 Barolin St, also has changing exhibits of local and national art. It's open from 10 am to 5 pm weekdays, and from 11 am to 4 pm on weekends.

On Gin Gin Rd 1km west of the Botanic Gardens, Bundaberg's **Tropical Winery** at 78 Mt Perry Rd makes an interesting range of wines and soft drinks from tropical fruits. It's open Monday to Saturday for tastings and sales.

The strange **Mystery Craters** – 35 small craters, said to be at least 25 million years old – are 17km along the Bundaberg road from Gin Gin. Entry to the craters costs $3.50 ($1.50 children).

Island Trips
Lady Musgrave Barrier Reef Cruises (toll-free ☎ 1800 072 110), based on the riverfront at 1 Quay St, has day trips to Lady Musgrave Island every Monday to Thursday, and on Saturday (more frequent during school holidays). The cruises depart from Port Bundaberg, 17km north-east of Bundaberg, at 8.30 am and return at 5.45 pm. The cost is $105 ($53 children, plus another $8 for the return bus trip to Port Bundaberg), which includes lunch, snorkelling gear and rides in a semi-submersible, glass-bottomed boat.

Alternatively, you can fly to Lady Musgrave Island with Bundaberg Seaplane Tours (☎ 4155 2068). A day trip costs $165 per person for between two and four people, including lunch and snorkelling gear. You get around five hours on the island.

You can also fly to Lady Elliot Island with Lady Elliot Island Resort (toll-free ☎ 1800 072 200). Day trippers pay $135 ($68 children) for a deluxe trip which includes the return flight, lunch, snorkelling gear and a guided reef walk.

Whale-Watching
From mid-August to mid-October, Lady Musgrave Barrier Reef Cruises (toll-free ☎ 1800 072 110) runs whale-watching trips out of Port Bundaberg, 20 minutes drive out of town (return coach transfers from town cost $7). The trip departs at 9.15 am and returns at 3.30 pm; it costs $68 ($35 children) including lunch. See the Hervey

Bay section for more details on whale-watching.

Diving

Salty's (☎ 4151 6422), 200 Bourbong St, and Bundaberg Aqua Scuba (☎ 4153 5761), on Targo St next to the bus station, both offer what must be the cheapest PADI open courses in Queensland – great value at i$149, which includes a dive off Lady Musgrave Island.

Festivals

Bundy's major festivals include the Country Music Festival at Easter; Bundy in Bloom, a spring floral festival held in the second week of September and featuring fashion parades, garden competitions and garden parties; and a week-long Arts Festival each October featuring film, music and theatre.

Places to Stay

Caravan Parks The *Finemore Caravan Park* (☎ 4151 3663) on the riverfront at the west end of Quay St, has tent sites for $8 ($14 powered) and two and four-bed 'Camp-o-tels' – permanent tents with beds and lighting – for $10 per person.

The *Midtown Caravan Park* (☎ 4152 2768), 61 Takalvan St, is a good park about 2km south-west of the post office, with a pool, shop and campers' kitchen. Tent sites are $9 ($12 powered), cabins start at $30 and self-contained villas start at $40.

Hostels All three hostels given here specialise in finding harvesting work for travellers.

The *Bundaberg Backpackers & Travellers Lodge* (☎ 4152 2080) is diagonally opposite the bus terminal on the corner of Targo and Crofton Sts. It's a clean and modern workers' hostel with a friendly atmosphere; a bed in a four-bed dorms costs $15 a night, which includes transport to and from work.

The well set up *City Centre Backpackers* (☎ 4151 3501), in the former Grosvenor Hotel at 216 Bourbong St, has two sections: two to eight-bed bunkrooms upstairs, and

six-bed motel units out the back. Bunk beds cost $13 and a bed in one of the motel units costs $15. It also has three doubles at $30.

Across the road is *Federal Backpackers* (☎ 4153 3711) at 221 Bourbong St. It's in a big old wooden building leased from the pub downstairs and has plenty of character, but it's also extremely dirty and badly kept. Facilities are poor. Dorms in a room with 10 beds are $14 or in a room with four beds $15.

Motels The *Royal Motel* (☎ 4151 2201), on the corner of Barolin and Bourbong Sts, has good budget motel units from $32/42 for singles/doubles. The motel is upstairs with an entrance in Barolin St – if there's no-one at reception, the coffee shop downstairs handles bookings.

Another cheaper motel option is the *Lyelta Lodge & Motel* (☎ 4151 3344), 8 Maryborough St, which has motel-style rooms at $34 and a guesthouse section with singles/doubles with shared bathrooms for $25/30. This place is quite old and fairly basic though.

The *Matilda Motel* (☎ 4151 4717) at 209 Bourbong St is far more modern and impressive; the en suite rooms have an iron and ironing board, a hairdryer, kettle and tea/coffee. It represents extremely good value at $54 for a double.

The *Sugar Country Motor Inn* (☎ 4153 1166), 220 Bourbong St, is also very modern and smart; units here are $70. There's also a pool and a licensed restaurant.

Places to Eat

For a cheap pub feed, head for the *Grand Hotel*, on the corner of Bourbong and Targo Sts, or the *Club Hotel*, on the corner of Bourbong and Tanotitha Sts, which has a small garden dining area round the side entered off Tanotitha.

Jungle Jack's Cafe on Bourbong St just east of the junction with Tanotitha St, has pastas and chicken and fish lunches at $4.50, roasts with chips and salad at $5.50, and other changing daily lunch specials at $6.50.

The Organic Shop, 21 Woongarra St, is a small health food shop with tasty sandwiches, smoothies and juices, vegetarian pies and rolls, and organic fruits and vegies.

Numero Uno at 163 Bourbong St is a popular Italian bistro with good pastas under $12, pizzas under $10 and mains from $12 to $15. It's open nightly for dinner and on weekdays for lunches, and is licensed.

Il Gambero, 57 Targo St, is run by an Italian family and has pastas, pizzas, seafood and steak dishes for between $12 and $18. This place is also licensed, and has a strangely comforting decor straight out of the 1970s – dim lighting, brick arches and all.

Down at the riverfront off Quay St, *The Spinnaker Stonegrill & Bar* specialises in meals cooked at your table on a white-hot volcanic stone. Their lunches range from $6 to $8 for open sandwiches to $12 for pastas and $18 for a steak; at dinner, mains are in the $14 to $18 range. This place enjoys a great setting, and has an outdoor decking area overlooking the river.

Also recommended is *Bam Bam's Bistro & Bar*, part of the Bundy Tavern complex on Quay St. The food is inventive and good, with main courses priced between $10 and $15. There's an early bird deal where if you dine between 6 and 7 pm you get a three course dinner for $10; or you could tackle the Big Bamma – three courses and a beer for $17, but it's free if you manage to polish off the lot.

Entertainment

Bars & Nightclubs The *Imperial Hotel* on Targo St has backpacker nights two or three times a week, while the *Grand Hotel*, a bikies' bar on the corner of Targo and Bourbong Sts, has live bands Thursday through Saturday. The *Red Bar*, a few doors east, is a pool hall. The *Federal* at 221 Bourbong St has a beer garden popular with backpackers. It is reached down the side alley.

The *Spinnaker Stonegrill & Bar* on Quay St, has jazz bands downstairs on Friday and Saturday nights, and Sunday afternoon sessions with live music out on their riverfront decking area – well worth checking out.

There are a couple of discos around town. *Krystals*, 2km out of the centre on Princess St, East Bundaberg, is very popular with backpackers; alternatively, there's the slightly more upmarket *Gossips* is in Electra St.

Cinema & Theatre The Moncrieff Theatre (☎ 4153 1985), 177 Bourbong St, alternates between being a theatre, a cinema and a music venue.

Bundaberg's Boulevard 4 cinema complex (☎ 4151 1511) is out towards the airport on Takalvan St. Budget days are Tuesday and Thursday when all tickets are $6. The only way to get there is by car or taxi (the fare will cost about $6).

Getting There & Away

Air Bundaberg's Hinkler Airport is about 4km south-west of the centre on Takalvan St.

Air services are by Sunstate (from Brisbane, Gladstone, Rockhampton, Mackay and Townsville daily) and Flight West (daily from Brisbane and Gladstone). The one-way fare from Brisbane (50 minutes) is $186.

Bus All the main bus companies serve Bundaberg on the north-south route. The main stop is Stewart's Coach Terminal (☎ 4153 2646) at 66 Targo St. One-way bus fares from Bundaberg include Brisbane ($46), Hervey Bay ($22), Rockhampton ($42) and Gladstone ($38).

Local bus services are handled by Duffy's Coaches (☎ 4151 4226). It has four services every weekday to the local beaches and Port Bundaberg; buses depart from the Shire Office bus stop in Barolin St, north of the post office, and the one-way fare is around $2.

Train Bundaberg is a stop for trains between Brisbane and Rockhampton or Cairns. There are daily trains heading both north and south. The one-way fare to Brisbane

(5½ hours) is $43 for an economy seat or $73 for an economy sleeper.

BUNDABERG BEACHES

The beaches of **Moore Park**, 20km north of Bundaberg, and **Bargara**, 13km east, are popular with families. Bargara is a small township with plenty of places to stay, and Moore Park is a 16km stretch of beach with a neighbouring environmental park that's good for birdwatching. Local buses connect both places with Bundaberg post office.

Australia's most accessible mainland **turtle rookery** is at Mon Repos Beach, 15km north-east of Bundaberg. Four types of turtle – loggerhead, green, flatback and leatherback – have been known to nest here from late November to January, but it's predominantly the loggerhead which lays its eggs here. The rookery is unusual, since turtles generally prefer sandy islands off the coast. The young emerge and quickly make their way to the sea from mid-January to March. Access to the beach is controlled by staff from the Department of Environment information centre (☎ 4159 2628) between 6 pm and 6 am, the time when turtles generally put in an appearance. The centre is open between 7 pm and 6 am every day during the turtle season, with informative displays, lighting and boardwalk access to the beach. Entry costs $4 ($2 children, $1 students). The centre is also open to visitors during the day, when entry is free.

The *Turtle Sands Caravan Park* (☎ 4159 2340), on the beachfront at Mon Repos Beach, has tent sites from $13 ($14 powered), on-site vans from $20 and cabins from $35. The park also has catamarans, windsurfers and surfboards for hire.

Capricorn Coast

This central coastal area of Queensland takes its name from its position straddling the Tropic of Capricorn. Rockhampton is the major population centre in the area, and just off the coast lies the popular Great Keppel Island and the other islands of the Keppel Bay group.

South of Rockhampton is the city of Gladstone, one of Queensland's major industrial and shipping centres. Offshore from Gladstone is the Capricornia Marine Park and the Southern Reef Islands, the southernmost part of the Great Barrier Reef. Lady Elliot Island and Heron Island both have resorts that are popular with divers, and you can take day trips to and camp on Lady Musgrave Island and several other islands in the group.

On the coast south of Gladstone are the laid-back holiday towns of Seventeen Seventy and Agnes Water, the focus of a small stretch of coastline known as the Discovery Coast.

Inland, the Capricorn Hinterland has the fascinating Gemfields region and the spectacular Carnarvon and Blackdown Tableland national parks, both of which are well worth a visit.

GEOGRAPHY

The Tropic of Capricorn passes through the centre of this region, just south of Rockhampton and just north of Emerald. Geographically, the Capricorn Hinterland is dominated by the broad, flattened plateaus of the Great Dividing Range with numerous spectacular outcrops of sandstone escarpments, most notably around the Carnarvon and Blackdown Tableland national parks.

This Central Highlands region is one of Queensland's richest natural resources: the fertile soils support major pastoral and agricultural industries, and the area's vast coal deposits supply the majority of the state's coal exports. Between the mountains and the coast are the flatter coastal plains.

HIGHLIGHTS

Map Index

PACIFIC OCEAN

Rockhampton p285
Central Rockhampton p288 ●   ● Great Keppel Island p296

Gladstone p277 ●

Carnarvon National Park p305

- It's tough getting there, but for some of Queensland's most dramatic scenery try to make it to Carnarvon National Park.
- The township of Seventeen Seventy – the sort of place that the word 'idyllic' was coined to describe.
- Dive the reef at one of the coast's premier dive islands – Heron Island.
- Wash some dirt – and maybe strike it lucky – on the gemfields.

ACTIVITIES

The Southern Reef Islands offer some of the best diving and snorkelling on the entire Barrier Reef. The Gemfields region in the Capricorn Hinterland is the best area in Queensland to go fossicking for gemstones, particularly sapphires. And for bushwalkers, the Carnarvon and Blackdown Tableland national parks offer a wide range of walking trails and climbs.

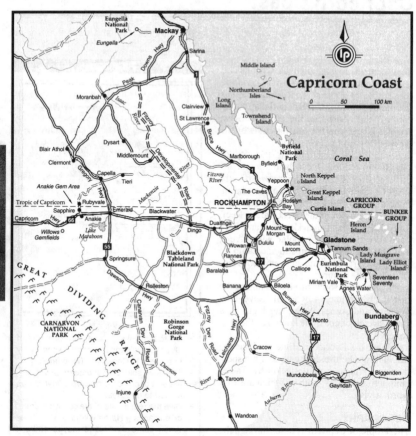

GETTING THERE & AROUND
Air
Rockhampton and Gladstone both have major regional airports from where you can also fly out to Lady Elliot, Heron and Great Keppel islands – see the relevant sections for details.

Sunstate and Flight West both have flights linking Brisbane with Emerald.

Bus
The major bus lines, Greyhound Pioneer and McCafferty's, both have frequent ser-vices up and down the Bruce Hwy and from Rockhampton inland to Emerald, Long-reach and Mt Isa.

McCafferty's also has a number of re-gional runs, including a daily inland service from Rockhampton to Mackay via Emerald and Clermont.

Train
The major coastal railway line follows the Bruce Hwy up the coast. Twice weekly, the *Spirit of the Outback* train does the inland run from Rockhampton to Longreach.

Car & Motorcycle

The Bruce Hwy runs all the way up the Capricorn Coast, although it runs a long way inland and only touches the coast briefly at the township of Clairview. The major inland route is the Capricorn Hwy, which takes you west from Rockhampton through Emerald and the Gemfields. From Gladstone, the Dawson Hwy takes you west towards the Carnarvon National Park and the town of Springsure.

The Burnett Hwy, which starts at Rockhampton and heads south through the old gold-mining town of Mt Morgan, is an interesting and popular alternative route to Brisbane – see the Darling Downs chapter for details of the Burnett Hwy south of Biloela.

Gladstone Area

MIRIAM VALE

Miriam Vale, 70km south of Gladstone, is no more than a tiny cluster of buildings either side of the Bruce Hwy. Nevertheless, it's the administration centre of the surrounding shire. It's also the main turn-off point for the coastal towns of Agnes Water and Seventeen Seventy.

Miriam Vale has one of Queensland's less convincing 'big things' – a sickly-looking giant red crab atop the roof of the Shell Roadhouse in the centre of town. The roadhouse specialises in mudcrab sandwiches.

The Discovery Coast information centre (☎ 4974 5428) is across the highway from the roadhouse.

Places to Stay & Eat

The *Caltex Roadhouse Caravan Park* (☎ 4974 5249) is on the highway on the north side of town.

The *Miriam Vale Motel* (☎ 4974 5233), 100m south of the information centre, has motel rooms at $40/45 for singles/doubles and $55 for family rooms for four. Behind

the motel, the *Miriam Vale Cafe* is open early for breakfast and until 9 pm each night.

AGNES WATER & SEVENTEEN SEVENTY

These two coastal towns are among the state's less commercialised seaside destinations, with Seventeen Seventy being perhaps the most beautiful and tranquil spot on the whole south-east Queensland coast. Part of the reason it has stayed that way is that the 57km sole access road from Miriam Vale is unsealed for a good third of its length, making for a rough ride. This is due to change in the near future, meaning the area may well see increased numbers of visitors and rapid development.

Seventeen Seventy, on a narrow and hilly peninsula on the south side of the estuary of Round Hill Creek, was named in 1970 in honour of Captain Cook's landing here on Bustard Beach on 24 May 1770 – the second place he landed in Australia, and the first in Queensland.

Things get fairly hectic around here at Christmas and Easter time – you'll need to book ahead to secure accommodation at these times – but, for the time being, for the rest of the year this area is a peaceful and unhurried getaway.

Information

The office of 1770 Environmental Tours (☎ 4974 9422) at the marina on Captain Cook Drive serves as an information centre for the immediate area and can help with booking activities and finding accommodation. It's open from 9 am to 5 pm Monday to Saturday, and from 1 to 5 pm Sunday.

At the time of writing there were no banks here and only a couple of shops and one pub, but a small shopping complex was under construction beside the Shell service station at the entrance to the two hamlets. The service station is open daily from 7 am to 6 pm and sells super, unleaded and diesel fuel, has EFTPOS facilities and takes all major credit cards.

1770 Foods & Liquors (see Places to Eat)

also has EFTPOS facilities and sells super and unleaded fuel.

Things to See & Do

The creek at Seventeen Seventy provides a calm anchorage for **boats**, there's good **fishing** and **mudcrabbing** upstream, and the southern end of the Great Barrier Reef is easily accessible from here, with Lady Musgrave Island about two hours offshore.

Agnes Water is Queensland's northernmost **surf beach**. A surf life-saving club patrols the main beach and there are often good beach breaks along the coast. The surf beaches south of Agnes Water are only accessible by 4WD.

The **Agnes Water Historical Museum** has a small collection of artefacts, rocks and minerals, as well as assorted flotsam and jetsam, as well as extracts from Cook's journal. It is open on weekends from 10 am to noon.

See the following Local National Parks section for details of parks in the area.

Boating & Water Sports Hire

You can hire paddle boats and catamarans from beside the boat ramp at Seventeen Seventy. 1770 Marine Services (☎ 4974 9227) hires out 3.6m aluminium dinghies for exploring Round Hill Creek at $25 for two hours or $60 a day.

Charter Boats

There are a number of charter boats available for fishing trips, including the MV *Spirit of 1770* (see the following Organised Tours section) and the MV *James Cook* (☎ 4974 9241) which sleeps up to nine people. Mad Jack Sailing Charters (☎ 4974 9539) run a 10m catamaran, the *Island Cat*, available for half, full-day and overnight cruises.

Organised Tours

The LARC *Sir Joseph Banks* (☎ 4974 9422), a large amphibious vehicle, does full-day environmental tours of Round Hill Creek, Bustard Head and Eurimbula National Park. Tours operate on Wednesday and Saturday (more often during the peak season), and cost $70 (children $35 or $45 depending on age) which includes morning tea and lunch. It also operates a one-hour sunset cruise for $15 per person.

The MV *Spirit of 1770* (☎ 4974 9077) has day trips to Lady Musgrave Island (85 minutes to get there, six hours on the island) costing $105 ($53 for children), with lunch, snorkelling and fishing gear included. Cruises depart from Seventeen Seventy at 8 am on Tuesday, Thursday and Sunday – more often during holiday periods. Island camping transfers and reef fishing charters are also available.

Places to Stay

Agnes Water The *Agnes Water Caravan Park* (☎ 4974 9193) on the foreshore in Jeffery Court has tent sites from $8 and cabins from $30. Nearby, the *Mango Tree Motel* (☎ 4974 9132) is a good budget motel with singles/doubles from $45/54.

About 4km inland from Agnes Water just off the main access road, *Hoban's Hideaway* (☎ 4974 9144) is a friendly, well-run B&B in an attractive, colonial-style timber homestead. The guests' section contains three immaculately presented double bedrooms with en suites, a lounge room and dining room, an outdoor patio and a barbecue area. The tariff for singles/doubles is $70/86 including breakfast. (Children aren't catered for here.)

About 7km west of Agnes Water, the *1770 Holiday Cabin Retreat* (☎ 4974 9270) is a 15-hectare bushland property with six timber cabins that sleep from four to 10 people. The cabins are simple, clean and well equipped with cooking facilities, bathroom, linen etc. Tariffs are $45/55 for singles/doubles plus $10 for additional adults and $5 for additional kids.

Seventeen Seventy The *Seventeen Seventy Camping Ground* (☎ 4974 9286) is a spacious camping ground right beside the mouth of Round Hill Creek. Tent sites cost $10 ($12 powered), and there are four on-site vans at $30 a double.

About 1km south, the *Captain Cook Holiday Village* (☎ 4974 9219) is an excellent camping and caravan park in a great bush setting 300m from the beach. Nightly rates are $10 for tent sites ($12 powered) and $15 per person for a bed in a twin-share backpackers' bungalow. There are also self-contained timber bungalows and cabins that sleep up to seven people; the bungalows cost $45 a double plus $5 for extras (BYO linen), and the cabins are $60 a double plus $10 for extras (linen supplied).

The *Beach Shack* (☎ 4974 9463) on the creekside Captain Cook Drive right next to the 1770 store, is something really special. It's a beautiful two-storey thatched cabin with an Oriental-styled interior with woven bamboo-ply walls. Each self-contained level sleeps six (a double and two sets of bunks) and is let complete at $120 a night.

Close by, up the hill, the *Sovereign Lodge* (☎ 4974 9257) on Elliot Drive is a large blue-painted house with five bedrooms to let. There's a pool (although the beach is only 200m away) and the views over the bay are fantastic.

Places to Eat

At the Shell service station, the *Hard Rock Cafe* sells takeaway meals and a limited range of groceries. At the time of our last visit a *Chinese restaurant* was also just about to open in the shopping complex next door. The food at the *Captain's Table Restaurant* at the Agnes Water Tavern, a modern timber pub on the outskirts of town, is said to be excellent, especially the seafood.

1770 Foods & Liquors on Captain Cook Drive just south of the camping ground, is a great little general store with a bottle shop and an outdoor courtyard with good home-made meals. The menu changes daily.

At the Captain Cook Holiday Village, *The Deck* is a very pleasant licensed bistro with great views. Light lunches like burgers, chicken pie or reef fish and salad range from $6 to $11, and at dinner mains range from $12 to $14. Downstairs, there's a garden patio with a self-serve char-grill where for $6 to $10 you can cook yourself fish, chicken or steak.

Getting There & Away

There are no bus or train services into the area, so you'll need your own transport. From Miriam Vale, on the Bruce Hwy, it's 57km eastwards to Agnes Water, about 19km of which is presently unsealed. Alternatively, it's 123km north from Bundaberg to Agnes Water via Rosedale with the last half of the trip over unsealed roads. These dirt roads are in reasonably good condition, although less so after heavy rains.

EURIMBULA & DEEPWATER NATIONAL PARKS

There are several coastal national parks around Agnes Water and Seventeen Seventy. For information or to book camping permits, contact the Department of Environment in Gladstone or Bundaberg. If you do turn up at the parks without a camping permit you can obtain one from a self-registration stand.

The 7830-hectare **Eurimbula National Park** is on the north side of Round Hill Creek, and has a varied landscape of dunes, mangroves and eucalypt forest. There's a basic campground at Bustard Beach with toilets but no drinking water . The main access road to the park is about 11km south-west of Agnes Water. From the entrance, it's another 11km along a sandy track to the campground – conventional vehicles can make it, although you'll need a 4WD after rain. Alternatively you could hire a dinghy from Seventeen Seventy and cross Round Hill Creek to the park.

South of Agnes Water, **Deepwater National Park** is only accessible by 4WD vehicles. The park has an unspoilt coastal landscape with long sandy beaches, fresh-water creeks, good fishing spots and a camping ground. It's also a major breeding ground for **loggerhead turtles** which build their nests and lay eggs on the beaches here between November and February. Visitors to the park can watch the turtles laying eggs and see hatchlings emerging at night, but you need to observe various precautions to protect the turtles and their environment. The Department of Environment brochure on the park (obtainable at the Miriam Vale tourist information centre) outlines these precautions, which include not driving onto the beaches and minimising noise and light on the beaches in summer. You can use torches to watch the turtles lay their eggs, but once the nest is covered and the turtle is returning to the sea, all lights should be turned off or they could become disoriented. The hatchlings emerge at night between January and April, and shouldn't be handled. You also need to avoid standing on the nests, which could collapse.

The park entrance is about 8km south of Agnes Water, then it's another 7km from the entrance to the Wreck Rock camping (one shower and self-composting toilets) and picnic areas.

GLADSTONE

About 20km off the Bruce Hwy, Gladstone is one of the busiest ports in Australia, handling agricultural, mineral and coal exports from central Queensland. From a visitor's point of view though, it's a pretty dull place and the town's otherwise attractive estuary setting is marred by a scattering of scenically challenged industrial plants.

Gladstone's marina is the main departure point for boats to Heron, Masthead and Wilson islands on the Barrier Reef.

Information

The Gladstone visitor information centre (☎ 4972 9922) at the marina is open on weekdays from 8.30 am to 5 pm and on weekends from 9 am to 5 pm. The staff work hard to push their region and can supply visitors with mounds of brochures and ideas on things to do.

The Department of Environment (☎ 4972 6055) has an office at 136 Goondoon St, which is open on weekdays from 9 am to 5 pm. You can get information on all the Southern Reef Islands here, as well as the mainland parks in the area.

Things to See

Housed in the old town hall, on the corner of Goondoon and Bramston Sts, the **Glad-stone Art Gallery & Museum** has a small permanent collection of contemporary Australian paintings and ceramics, and regularly features theme exhibitions of art and craft. It is open from 10 am to 5 pm weekdays and from 10 am to 4 pm Saturday.

The **Auckland Point Lookout** has good views over the harbour, port facilities and shipping terminals. A brass tablet on the lookout maps the harbour and its many islands.

Barney Point Beach, 2km east of the centre, is a small rocky cove which doesn't have much of a beach, although it's backed by a good foreshore reserve with lawns and shady trees.

If you have a bicycle or car the **Tondoon Botanic Gardens** on Glenlyon Rd, about 7km south of the town centre, is a 55-hectare area of rainforest and Australian native plants, with walking trails. There's a visitors' centre and free guided tours are given daily starting at 10 am. It's open daily from 9 am to 6 pm in winter, and from 8.30 am to 5.30 pm in summer.

Diving

Central Queensland Dive (☎ 4972 7126) on the corner of Lord and Glenlyon Sts offers one day scuba introductory dive courses, diving day trips and overnight dives. All gear is available for hire.

Organised Tours

The MV *Aristocat III* (☎ 0418 790 528) operates day trips to the reef for snorkelling and reef walking. The cost of $130 ($65 for children) includes lunch and snorkelling equipment. The boat departs from the marina ferry terminal next to the information centre and bookings are necessary.

Festivals

The Gladstone Harbour Festival is held every year from the Monday before Easter until Easter Monday. The festival coincides with the Brisbane to Gladstone yacht race, and features different activities each day, including street parties, an Easter parade, a

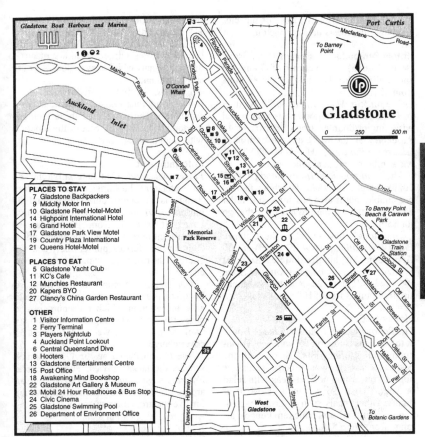

Gladstone Boat Harbour and Marina

Port Curtis

Macfarlane

Road

To Barney Point

O'Connell Wharf

Auckland Inlet

Gladstone

0   250   500 m

Drain

To Barney Point Beach & Caravan Park

Gladstone Train Station

Memorial Park Reserve

West Gladstone

To Botanic Gardens

CAPRICORN COAST

PLACES TO STAY
7 Gladstone Backpackers
9 Midcity Motor Inn
10 Gladstone Reef Hotel-Motel
14 Highpoint International Hotel
16 Grand Hotel
17 Gladstone Park View Motel
19 Country Plaza International
21 Queens Hotel-Motel

PLACES TO EAT
5 Gladstone Yacht Club
11 KC's Cafe
12 Munchies Restaurant
20 Kapers BYO
27 Clancy's China Garden Restaurant

OTHER
1 Visitor Information Centre
2 Ferry Terminal
3 Players Nightclub
4 Auckland Point Lookout
6 Central Queensland Dive
8 Hooters
13 Gladstone Entertainment Centre
15 Post Office
18 Awakening Mind Bookshop
22 Gladstone Art Gallery & Museum
23 Mobil 24 Hour Roadhouse & Bus Stop
24 Civic Cinema
25 Gladstone Swimming Pool
26 Department of Environment Office

birdman rally, mudcrab races and a prawn-peeling competition.

Places to Stay

Caravan Parks There are two good caravan parks at Barney Point Beach, about 2km east of the centre. Take your pick of the *Sea Breeze Caravan Park* (☎ 4972 1736) or the *Barney Beach Caravan Park* (☎ 4972 1366); both are well-established parks near the foreshore with tent sites from $10 ($12 powered) and on-site vans from $25. The Barney Beach Caravan Park also has on-site cabins from $35, or $40 with an en suite.

See Getting Around for details of bus services from the centre.

Hostels *Gladstone Backpackers* (☎ 4972 5744), 12 Rollo St, is a small, extremely friendly place close to both the marina and the town's main street. The owner, Bob, is the local parks and commissions snake catcher and he usually has a reptile or two in the garage. Dorms have three or four beds which go for $15 a night; doubles are

$32. The hostel offers free use of bicycles and will pick guests up from the bus.

Hotels & Motels The *Queens Hotel-Motel* (☎ 4972 6615) on the corner of Goondoon and William Sts has budget motel units from $27/37.

The *Midcity Motor Inn* (☎ 4972 3000) at 26 Goondoon St is a good mid-range motel with singles/doubles from $45/50. At 42 Roseberry St, the white and pink-trimmed *Gladstone Park View Motel* (☎ 4972 3344) has similar rooms at similar prices.

The *Gladstone Reef Hotel-Motel* (☎ 4972 1000) charges $80 ($85 if harbour facing) per double, but it also has some fine older en suite rooms on the ground floor that go for $59.

Gladstone's best motel is the *Country Plaza International* (☎ 4972 4499) at 100 Goondoon St; singles/doubles start at $79/89. The *Highpoint International Hotel* (☎ 4972 4711) at 22 Roseberry St has singles/doubles from $100/115.

Places to Eat

The *Bellowing Bull Char Grill Steak House* at the Queens Hotel, on the corner of Goondoon and William Sts, is one of the best-value eateries you'll come across. A huge T-bone, rump or fillet steak with salad or vegies costs $6 at lunch or $8.50 at dinner. Other meals such as lasagne, pork chops, reef fish and chicken kebabs all range from $6 to $10.

Kapers BYO, nearby at 124 Goondoon St, is a bright, beachy, quirky cafe with sky-blue walls and hand-painted tables. The food is interesting, with good seafood, vegetarian and other dishes; mains are around $18. Kapers is open for dinner from Wednesday to Monday.

Upstairs at the *Gladstone Yacht Club*, at the north end of Goondoon St, good cheap lunches (served between noon and 2.30 pm) and dinner are available in the bar area. You can eat on the deck overlooking the harbour.

Munchies Restaurant, 42 Goondoon St, specialises in Mexican food but also does steaks and seafood with mains in the $13 to $18 range. The food is variable in quality. *KC's Cafe*, next door to Munchies at 40 Goondoon St, is a decent breakfast place (it opens at 7 am) which stays open 24 hours at the weekend.

Flinders, on Flinders Parade by the waterfront, is another restaurant with a good reputation. There are also three Chinese restaurants on Tank St, east of the junction with Goondoon St.

Entertainment

Players Nightclub, in an unusually renovated waterfront building up on Flinders Parade, is a spacious club with a good atmosphere, DJ music and, occasionally, live bands. It is open from Wednesday to Sunday until around 3 am; on weekends a courtesy bus ferries punters between the club and the centre of town. There's a cover charge.

Hooters, on Goondoon St near the Lord St corner, is a party bar with pool tables and an eating section which sells burgers and chips. It is open every night except Monday until around 3 am; on weekends there's a $3 cover charge.

The *Civic Cinema* at 165 Goondoon St screens the latest movies. The *Gladstone Entertainment Centre* (☎ 4972 2822), in an arcade off Goondoon St, is the main venue for live theatre, concerts and performances – ring to find out what's on.

Getting There & Away

Air Sunstate and Flight West have daily flights between Brisbane and Gladstone ($248), a couple of them via Bundaberg. Sunstate also flies north to Cairns every day, via Rockhampton, Mackay and Townsville. The airport is 7km from town and $9 by taxi.

Bus Most of Greyhound Pioneer's and McCafferty's coastal services stop at Gladstone; the terminal for long-distance buses is at the Mobil 24 Hour Roadhouse, on the Dawson Hwy about 200m south-west of the centre.

Train Gladstone is on the main Brisbane-Rockhampton rail route. The *Spirit of Capricorn*, the *Spirit of the Outback*, the *Queenslander* and the *Sunlander* all stop in Gladstone.

Getting Around
Gladstone Bus & Coach (☎ 4972 1670) runs local bus services on weekdays only, including a service along Goondoon St to Barney Point and the beach which stops out the front of the two caravan parks there.

To book a taxi, call Blue & White Taxis on ☎ 4972 1800.

GLADSTONE HARBOUR ISLANDS
There are numerous islands scattered throughout Gladstone Harbour. The largest of these, the 40km-long **Curtis Island**, is predominantly used for grazing cattle but there's a small settlement at the southern end with a general store, camping ground and lodge. The *Curtis Trader* ferry runs over to the island twice every Friday, Sunday and every second Wednesday, as well as once on a Saturday morning. The return fare is $16. It departs from O'Connell Wharf; call ☎ 4972 5842 for further information.

The long and narrow **Facing Island** also has picnic and camping grounds.

AROUND GLADSTONE
Calliope, on the Calliope River 26km south of Gladstone, has the **Calliope Historical Village** with 10 restored, heritage-style buildings including an old pub, a railway station and a slab hut. The village is open daily from 8 am to 4 pm and admission is $1. A good craft and food market is held here about six times a year.

Lake Awoonga, created by the construction of the Awoonga Dam in 1984, is a popular recreational area south of Gladstone, with good swimming, fishing, sailing and water-skiing facilities. The main access road to the lake is from Benaraby on the Bruce Hwy about 22km south of Gladstone; it's another 8km to the lake from the turn-off. Backed by the rugged **Mt Castletower**

National Park, the lake has a scenic setting with landscaped picnic areas, barbecues, walking trails and an abundance of birdlife. There's also a caravan park (☎ 4975 0155) and a hilltop restaurant here.

SOUTHERN REEF ISLANDS
The Capricornia section of the Great Barrier Reef, which includes the Southern Reef Islands, begins 80km north-east of Bundaberg around Lady Elliot Island. The coral reefs and cays in this group dot the ocean for about 140km up to Tryon Island east of Rockhampton.

Several cays in this part of the reef are excellent for snorkelling, diving and just getting back to nature – though reaching them is generally more expensive than reaching islands nearer the coast. Access is from Bundaberg, Gladstone or Rosslyn Bay near Yeppoon. A few of the islands are important breeding grounds for turtles and seabirds, and visitors to the islands should be aware of the precautionary measures necessary to ensure the protection of the wildlife – precautions are outlined in the Department of Environment brochures on the islands.

Camping is allowed on the Lady Musgrave, Masthead, Tryon and North West national park islands, and campers must be totally self-sufficient. Numbers of campers are limited so it's advisable to apply well ahead for a camping permit. You can book up to 12 months ahead for these islands instead of the usual six to 12 weeks for other Queensland national parks. Contact the Department of Environment in Gladstone. If you get a permit you'll also receive information on any rules, such as restrictions on the use of generators, and on how to avoid harming the wildlife.

Lady Elliot Island
About 80km north-east of Bundaberg, Lady Elliot is a 0.4 sq km vegetated coral cay at the southern end of the Great Barrier Reef. The island has a simple, no-frills resort and its own airstrip. It is very popular with divers and snorkellers, and has the advan-

tages of superb diving straight off the beach, as well as numerous shipwrecks, coral gardens, bommies and blowholes to explore.

Lady Elliot Island is not a national park, and camping is not allowed.

Places to Stay The *Lady Elliot Island Resort* (☎ 4156 4444) was updated in 1985 but it's still a very straightforward place with a couple of different styles of accommodation. There are tent-cabins and timber lodges which cost $115 per person for two or three people or $99 per person for four; motel-style units cost $150 per person for up to four adults. There's a $60 supplement to take a tent as a single.

The 'Reef Units' are simple motel-type rooms with a common verandah area out the front and attached bathrooms. Nightly costs are $150 per person for up to four adults, and again, there's a $60 supplement for single occupancy.

One and two bedroom suites come with a separate lounge and kitchen, and cost $170 per person. All rates include dinner and breakfast.

The resort has good diving facilities and you can take certificate courses there.

Getting There & Away Lady Elliot is the only cay on the Great Barrier Reef with its own airstrip. You can fly there from Bundaberg or Hervey Bay with Whitaker Air Charters – phone the Sunstate Travel Centre (☎ 4151 6077 or toll-free ☎ 1800 072 200) for bookings. Resort guests pay $130 for return transfers.

Lady Musgrave Island

This 0.15 sq km cay in the Bunker Group is an uninhabited national park about 100km north-east of Bundaberg. The island sits at the western end of a huge lagoon which is one of the few places along the entire Barrier Reef where ships can safely enter, and is a popular stopover for passing yachties.

Lady Musgrave offers some excellent diving opportunities, and the day trip boats can supply you with snorkelling and diving gear. The lagoon offers some excellent snorkelling and some good shallower dives for beginners, and there are good reef dives of up to 20m off the northern side of the lagoon.

The island itself is covered with a dense canopy of pisonia forest. You can walk right around the island in half an hour and there is a trail across the middle from the usual landing place to the camping ground. Shearwaters, terns and white-capped noddies nest here from October to April, and green turtles nest here from November to February.

Places to Stay There's a national park camping ground on the western side of the island, but there are no facilities apart from bush toilets. Campers – a maximum of 50 at any one time – must be totally self-sufficient. You'll need to bring your own drinking water and a gas or fuel stove – open fires are not permitted, and the island's timber and driftwood cannot be burned.

Getting There & Away The MV *Lady Musgrave* (☎ 4152 9011) operates day trips from Bundaberg, leaving from Port Bundaberg on Tuesday, Thursday, Saturday and Sunday at 8.30 am. The cost is $105 ($53 children) which includes lunch, snorkel gear and a glass-bottom boat ride. The trip takes 2½ hours and you have about four hours on the island. The connecting bus service from Bundaberg to the port costs another $8. You can use this service for camping drop-offs for $200 return.

There are also day trips to Lady Musgrave from Seventeen Seventy – see Organised Tours in the earlier Agnes Water & Seventeen Seventy section for details.

Heron Island

Only 1km long and 0.17 sq km in area, Heron Island is 72km east of Gladstone. This fascinating island is a true coral cay, densely vegetated with pisonia trees and surrounded by 24 sq km of reef. There's a resort and research station on the north-eastern third of the island – the rest is national park.

Heron, famed for superb scuba diving, is something of a mecca for divers. There's good snorkelling over the shallow reef, and the resort's dive boat runs excursions to the many good diving sites. The dive shop has a full range of diving equipment available for hire – you can do a day trip for $38 including diving equipment and one dive – and six-day certificate courses are available for $395.

The only place to stay on the island is the *Heron Island Resort* (☎ 4978 1488). The only way to get there is by helicopter or via the resort's catamaran, which sails out of Gladstone and is for guest transfers only – there are no day trips to Heron.

GREAT BARRIER REEF
Facts & Figures
The Great Barrier Reef stretches 2000km from just south of the Tropic of Capricorn, somewhere out from Bundaberg or Gladstone, to the Torres Strait, just south of New Guinea. It is the most extensive reef system in the world and the biggest structure made by living organisms. At its southern end the reef is up to 300km from the mainland, while at the northern end it runs nearer the coast, is much less broken and can be up to 80km wide. In the 'lagoon' between the outer reef and the coast, the waters are dotted with smaller reefs, cays and islands. Drilling has indicated that the coral can be more than 500m thick. Most of the reef is around two million years old, but there are sections dating back 18 million years.

What is It?
Coral is formed by a small, primitive animal, a marine polyp of the phylum Coelenterata. Some polyps, known as hard corals, form a hard surface by excreting lime. When they die, the hard 'skeletons' remain and gradually build up the reef. New polyps grow on their dead predecessors and continually add to the reef. The skeletons of hard corals are white and the colours of reefs come from living polyps.

Coral needs a number of preconditions for healthy growth. First, the water temperature must not drop below 17.5°C; the water must also be clear to allow sunlight to penetrate, and it must be salty. Coral will not grow below depths of 30m because sufficient sunlight does not penetrate. Nor does it grow around river mouths – the Barrier Reef ends near Papua New Guinea because the Fly River's enormous water flow is both fresh and muddy.

One of the most spectacular sights of the Barrier Reef occurs for a few nights after a full moon in late spring or early summer each year, when vast numbers of corals spawn at the same time. The tiny bundles of sperm and eggs are visible to the naked eye and the event has been likened to a gigantic underwater snowstorm.

Reef Types
What's known as the Great Barrier Reef is not one reef but about 2600 separate ones. Basically, reefs are either fringing or barrier. Fringing reefs develop off the sloping sides of islands or the mainland coast. Barrier reefs are further out to sea: the 'real' Great Barrier Reef, or outer reef, is at the edge of the Australian continental shelf, and the channel between the reef and the coast can be 60m deep. In places, the reef rises straight up from that depth. This raises the question of how the reef built up from that depth when coral cannot survive below 30m. One theory is that the reef gradually grew as the sea bed subsided, implying that the reef was able to keep pace with the rate of subsidence. Another theory is that the sea level gradually rose, and again the coral growth was able to keep pace.

Reef Inhabitants

There are about 400 different types of coral on the Great Barrier Reef. Equally colourful are the many clams which appear to be embedded in the coral. Other reef inhabitants include about 1500 species of fish, 4000 types of mollusc (clams, snails etc), 350 echinoderms (sea urchins, starfish, sea cucumbers and so on, all with a five-arm body plan), and countless thousands of species of crustaceans (crabs, shrimps and their relatives), sponges and worms.

Reef waters are also home to dugong (the sea cows which gave rise to the mermaid myth) and are breeding grounds for humpback whales, which migrate every winter from Antarctica. The reef's islands form important nesting colonies for many types of seabird, and six of the world's seven species of sea turtle lay eggs on the islands' sandy beaches in spring or summer.

Crown-of-Thorns Starfish One reef inhabitant which has received enormous publicity is the crown-of-thorns starfish – notorious because it appeared to be chewing through large areas of the Great Barrier Reef. It's thought that the crown-of-thorns develops a taste for coral when the reef ecology is upset – as, for example, when the supply of bivalves (oysters, clams), which comprise its normal diet, is diminished.

Dangerous Creatures Hungry sharks are the usual idea of an aquatic nasty but the Barrier Reef's most unpleasant creatures are generally less dramatic. For a start, there are scorpion fish with highly venomous spines. The butterfly cod is a very beautiful scorpion fish and relies on its colourful, slow-moving appearance to warn off possible enemies. In contrast, the stonefish lies hidden on the bottom, looking just like a rock, and is very dangerous to step on. Although they're rather rare, it's a good idea to wear shoes when walking on the reef – this is sensible anyway to protect yourself against sharp coral and rocks.

Stinging jellyfish are a danger only in coastal waters and only in certain seasons. The deadly 'sea wasp' is in fact a box jellyfish (see Dangers & Annoyances in the Facts for the Visitor chapter). As for sharks, there has been no recorded case of a visitor to the reef islands meeting a hungry one.

Viewing the Reef

By far the best way of seeing the reef is by diving or snorkelling in it – this allows close up views of small marine life and a chance to interact with larger creatures, such as fish and turtles. Otherwise you can walk on it, view it through the floor of glass-bottom boats or the windows of semi-submersibles, or descend below the ocean surface inside 'underwater observatories'. You can also see a living coral reef and its accompanying life forms without leaving dry land, at the Great Barrier Reef Wonderland aquarium in Townsville.

Innumerable tour operators run day trips to the outer reef and to coral-fringed islands from towns on the Queensland coast. The cost depends on how much reef-viewing paraphernalia is used, how far the reef is from the coast, how luxurious a vessel takes you there and whether lunch is included. Usually, free use of snorkelling gear is part of the package. Some islands have good reefs too; they're usually cheaper to reach and you can stay on quite a few of them.

The Great Barrier Reef Marine Park Authority (☎ 4781 8811) is the body looking after the welfare of most of the reef. Its address is PO Box 1379, Townsville, Queensland 4810. It has an office in Great Barrier Reef Wonderland in Townsville.

Islands

There are three types of island off the Queensland coast. In the south, before you reach the Barrier Reef, are several large vegetated sand islands like North Stradbroke, Moreton and Fraser islands. These are interesting to visit for a variety of reasons but not for coral. Strung along the whole coast, mostly close inshore, are continental islands like Great Keppel, most of the Whitsundays, Hinchinbrook and Dunk. At one time, these would have been the peaks of coastal ranges, but rising sea levels submerged the mountains. The islands' vegetation is similar to that of the adjacent mainland.

The true coral islands, or cays, may be on the outer reef, or may be isolated between it and the mainland. Green Island near Cairns, the Low Isles near Port Douglas and Heron Island off Gladstone are all cays. Cays are formed when a reef is above sea level, even at high tide. Dead coral is ground down by water action to form sand and, in some cases, eventually vegetation takes root. Coral cays are low-lying, unlike the often hilly islands closer to the coast. There are about 300 cays on the reef, 69 of them vegetated.

The Queensland islands are extremely variable so don't let the catchword 'reef island' suck you in. Most of the popular resort islands are actually continental islands and some are well south of the Great Barrier Reef. Being a reef island is not necessarily important, since many continental islands will still have fringing reefs as well as other attractions that a tiny dot-on-the-map coral cay is simply too small for – like hills to climb, bushwalks, and secluded beaches where you can get away from other island lovers.

The islands also vary considerably in their accessibility – Lady Elliot for instance is a $130 return flight, while others are just a few dollars by ferry. If you want to stay on an island rather than make a day trip from the mainland, this too can vary widely in cost. Accommodation is generally in the form of expensive resorts, where most visitors will be on an all-inclusive package holiday. But there are a few exceptions to this rule and on some islands it's possible to camp. A few islands have proper camping areas with toilets and fresh water on tap; at the other extreme, on some islands you'll even have to bring drinking water with you.

For more information on individual islands, see the Whitsunday Coast, North Coast and Far North Queensland chapters of this book. Also good is Lonely Planet's *Islands of Australia's Great Barrier Reef*.

The cheapest accommodation is $158 per person a night in 'Turtle Cabins' – simple three to four-bed bunkrooms with shared bathroom facilities. There are also modern motel-style suites which start at $224 per person. Tariffs include all meals.

Stand-by rates are often available from travel agents in Gladstone – contact the tourist information office there for details.

Masthead & Erskine Islands

Masthead Island is an uninhabited coral cay slightly south-west of Heron Island. The entire island is protected as a national park, and is an important nesting ground for log-gerhead turtles, as well as for shearwaters, black noddies and other birds. The main turtle-nesting season is from November to January; for seabirds the nesting season is from October to April.

Camping is permitted, with limits of 30 people in the summer birdwatching season and 60 people at other times, but there are no facilities and campers have to be totally self-sufficient.

Erskine Island is just north of Masthead and only day visits are permitted.

Wilson Island

North of Heron, Wilson Island is a national park and a popular day trip for Heron guests looking for a break from diving. The resort operates day trips to the island which cost $45 including a barbecue lunch. You can swim at the island's excellent beaches and there's superb snorkelling around the island.

However, not everyone enjoys the visitors. Apparently 300 nesting pairs of endangered roseate terns temporarily abandoned the island when regular visitors began turning up – it's important to avoid disturbing them.

North West Island

At 0.9 sq km, North West Island is the second biggest cay on the Barrier Reef. Guano was mined on the island from 1894 to 1900, and a turtle-soup factory operated here up until 1928. Nowadays the entire island is a national park, and it's one of the major nesting sites for green turtles, with nesting occurring between November and February.

North West Island is a popular destination for campers and day trippers. There's a limit of 150 campers – again, you need to be fully self-sufficient and facilities are limited to pit toilets.

Getting There & Away There are no scheduled services to North West, so without your own boat it's a matter of finding a charter from Gladstone or Rosslyn Bay near Rockhampton.

Tryon Island

Immediately north of North West Island, this tiny, beautiful, 11 hectare national park cay is another important nesting area for seabirds and green turtles. There is a camping ground on the island, but there are no regular boat services from the mainland.

Rockhampton Area

ROCKHAMPTON
pop 64,500

Rockhampton, which sits astride the Tropic of Capricorn, is the administrative and commercial centre of central Queensland. Its fortunes are closely linked to the cattle industry, and the city proclaims itself the 'beef capital' of Australia. It's said that there are more than two million cattle within a 250km radius of the city, and it could be said that Rocky has something of an obsession with beef – large statues of Brahman, Braford and Santa Gertrudis bulls mark the northern and southern approaches to the city. Not surprisingly, this is a great place to tuck into a steak.

Queensland's largest river, the Fitzroy, flows through the heart of the city. The city centre occupies the southern side of the river and many of its numerous historic buildings are classified by the National

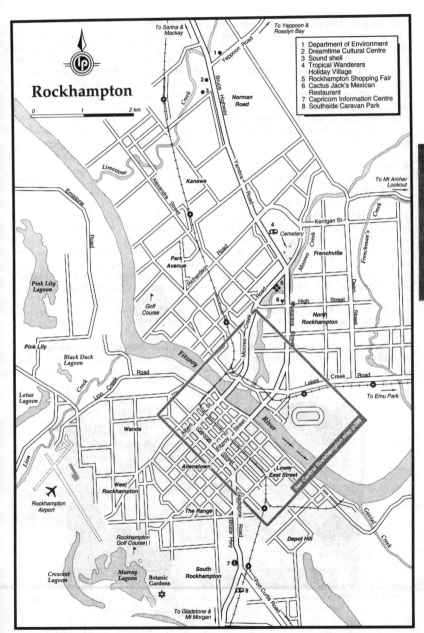

CAPRICORN COAST

Rockhampton

1 Department of Environment
2 Dreamtime Cultural Centre
3 Sound shell
4 Tropical Wanderers
  Holiday Village
5 Rockhampton Shopping Fair
6 Cactus Jack's Mexican
  Restaurant
7 Capricorn Information Centre
8 Southside Caravan Park

To Sarina &
Mackay

To Yeppoon &
Rosslyn Bay

Yeppoon Road

Bruce Highway

Norman Road

Yamba Road

Creek

Limestone

Kanawa

To Mt Archer
Lookout

Emstone

Alexandra Street

Road

Kerrigan St

Cemetery

Frenchville

Frenchman's Creek

Moores Creek

Dean Street

Park Avenue

Richardson Road

Musgrave Street

High Street

North Rockhampton

Pink Lily Lagoon

Golf Course

Pink Lily

Black Duck Lagoon

Fitzroy

Moores Creek

Lakes Creek Road

Road

To Emu Park

Lotus Lagoon

Lion Creek

Road

Creek

Wanda

Albert St

George St

Fitzroy Street

River

See Central Rockhampton map p288

Lion

Rockhampton Airport

West Rockhampton

Allenstown

Lower East Street

The Range

Gladstone Road

Bruce Hwy

Depot Hill

Ganial Creek

Rockhampton Golf Course

South Rockhampton

Port Curtis Road

Crescent Lagoon

Murray Lagoon

Botanic Gardens

To Gladstone &
Mt Morgan

0   1   2 km

Trust. This compact centre is surrounded by a progressive city of attractive gardens, huge shopping plazas and modern housing estates.

Rocky has a few tourist attractions of its own, including a good art gallery, an Aboriginal cultural centre and some excellent gardens and parklands. It's also the access point for Great Keppel and other islands, with boats leaving from Rosslyn Bay, about 40km away near Yeppoon.

History
Rockhampton was established as a river trading port in 1853 by the Archer brothers, the first settlers to establish a property in the area. The port's growth was boosted by a minor gold rush at Canoona in 1858, but the real development began with the discovery of the rich gold and copper deposits at Mt Morgan in 1882. Rockhampton quickly developed into the major trading centre for the surrounding region, and its turn-of-the-century prosperity is evident in the many fine Victorian-era buildings around the older parts of the city.

This century, mining was gradually replaced by sheep, and later cattle farming, as the region's major source of income.

Orientation
Rockhampton is about 40km from the coast. The Fitzroy River flows through the heart of the city, with the small city centre, the oldest part of Rocky, on the southern bank of the river. The long Fitzroy Bridge connects the city centre with the newer suburbs to the north.

Coming in from the south, the Bruce Hwy skirts the town centre and crosses the river via the Neville Hewitt Bridge.

Information
Tourist Information The Capricorn Information Centre (☎ 4927 2055) is on the highway beside the Tropic of Capricorn marker, 3km south of the town centre. It's open daily from 9 am to 5 pm.

The more central Riverside Information Centre (☎ 4922 5339) is in a riverfront rotunda, on Quay St, and is open weekdays from 8.30 am to 4.30 pm and weekends from 9 am to 4 pm. The staff here can suggest various tours and ways of getting to attractions in the surrounding area even if you don't have your own transport.

Post & Communications Rockhampton's post office, in the centre of the East St Mall

Rockhampton has a love affair with cattle – some two million live within a few hours' drive of the city centre, and statues of various breeds guard the approaches to town.

and on the corner of Denham St, is certainly one of the city's most impressive historic buildings. It's open weekdays from 8.30 am to 5 pm.

Useful Organisations The RACQ (☎ 4927 2255) is at 134 William St. The Department of Environment district office (☎ 4936 0511) is on Yeppoon Rd, about 7km north-west of central Rocky. Head out on the Bruce Hwy and take the Yeppoon turn-off – you'll see it on your left, about 200m after the turn-off.

Bookshops Angus & Robertson Bookworld has a large outlet inside the City Centre Plaza shopping centre (locally known as the Target centre), on the corner of Fitzroy and Bolsover Sts.

Things to See
There are many fine old buildings in the town, particularly on **Quay St**, which has a number of grand Victorian-era buildings dating back to the gold-rush days. You can pick up tourist leaflets and magazines which map out walking trails around the town.

The **City Heart Markets**, with arts and crafts, plants, clothing and food on sale, are held in the East St Mall every Saturday morning.

The **Rockhampton City Art Gallery**, on Victoria Parade, is open on weekdays and public holidays from 10 am to 4 pm, and on weekends from 1.30 to 4.30 pm; admission is free. The gallery houses a small but impressive collection of Australian paintings.

On the Bruce Hwy, 7km north of the centre, is the **Dreamtime Cultural Centre**, an Aboriginal and Torres Straits Islander heritage display centre. It's open daily from 10 am to 3.30 pm, and tours are run daily at 11 am and 2 pm; admission is $11 ($5 for children).

The **Botanic Gardens**, at the end of Spencer St in the south of the city, were established in 1869. These large and very beautiful gardens include a children's playground, a lovely picnic area, a formal Japanese garden, a wetlands area with prolific birdlife, a walk-through aviary, a kiosk which serves Devonshire teas and a rather nasty zoo. There's also a grove of pine trees grown from seeds from the Gallipoli Peninsula, which were a gift from the Turkish government to commemorate the Australian troops who fought and died there in WWI, and a German Howitzer which was captured by the Australian Light Horse Regiment in Palestine in WWI.

North of the city centre, just across the Fitzroy River, the **Cliff Kershaw Gardens** is an excellent botanical park devoted to Australian native plants. Within the park are numerous walking trails, a slab timber cottage which serves Devonshire teas, picnic and barbecue areas, a monorail and a children's playground, and an impressive artificial waterfall. To get to the gardens, cross the Fitzroy Bridge and take a left into Charles St, which runs off Musgrave St.

Mt Archer, on the city's northern outskirts, is an environmental park with lots of walking trails, wildlife including some colourful birds and several swimming holes. An 11km trail leads from the summit to the lower entrance, and there are also shorter walks to several lookout points. The Department of Environment publishes a brochure to the park which is available from the information centres.

Organised Tours
Fitzroy River Historic Cruises (☎ 4921 1811) offers a two-hour river cruise with an accompanying commentary on Rockhampton's history. The tour costs $19.50 ($8.50 children). Departure times vary according to the season – check with the Riverside Information Centre for times.

Festivals
Rocky's main annual festival is the Capricana Festival, held over 10 days in early September. It features a street parade, a carnival and daily activities. The Bauhinia Arts Festival, held in early August, features a range of stage productions, art exhibitions and musical performances.

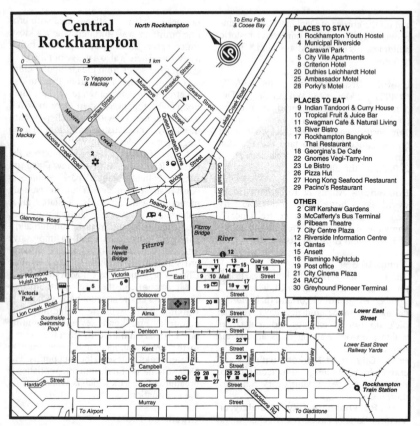

Central Rockhampton

North Rockhampton

To Emu Park & Cooee Bay

To Yeppoon & Mackay

To Mackay

Musgrave Street
Charles Street
Palmwick Street
Edward Street
Queen Elizabeth Drive
Lakes Creek Road
Goodsall Street
Bridge Street

Moores Creek Road
Moores Creek

Glenmore Road

Reaney St

Fitzroy Bridge

Fitzroy River

Neville Hewitt Bridge

Sir Raymond Huish Drive
Victoria Park
Lion Creek Road
Southside Swimming Pool

Victoria Parade
Bolsover Street
Alma Street
Denison Street
Kent Street
Campbell Street
George Street
Murray Street
Hardacre Street

North Street
Albert Street
Cambridge Street
Archer Street
Fitzroy Street
Denham Street
William Street
Derby Street
Stanley Street
South St

Quay Street
Mall
East Street

Lower East Street
Lower East Street Railway Yards

Rockhampton Train Station

To Airport
To Gladstone
Gladstone Rd

PLACES TO STAY
1 Rockhampton Youth Hostel
4 Municipal Riverside Caravan Park
5 City Ville Apartments
8 Criterion Hotel
20 Duthies Leichhardt Hotel
25 Ambassador Motel
28 Porky's Motel

PLACES TO EAT
9 Indian Tandoori & Curry House
10 Tropical Fruit & Juice Bar
11 Swagman Cafe & Natural Living
13 River Bistro
17 Rockhampton Bangkok Thai Restaurant
18 Georgina's De Cafe
22 Gnomes Vegi-Tarry-Inn
23 Le Bistro
26 Pizza Hut
27 Hong Kong Seafood Restaurant
29 Pacino's Restaurant

OTHER
2 Cliff Kershaw Gardens
3 McCafferty's Bus Terminal
6 Pilbeam Theatre
7 City Centre Plaza
12 Riverside Information Centre
14 Qantas
15 Ansett
16 Flamingo Nightclub
19 Post office
21 City Cinema Plaza
24 RACQ
30 Greyhound Pioneer Terminal

Places to Stay

Camping & Caravan Parks There are half a dozen caravan parks in Rocky. The most central place is the pleasantly situated *Municipal Riverside Caravan Park* (☎ 4922 3779), in Reaney St, just across the bridge to the north of the city centre. It has tent sites for $9 ($12 powered), but no on-site vans or cabins.

The *Southside Holiday Village* (☎ 4927 3013) is on the Bruce Hwy 3km south of the centre, near the Capricorn Information Centre. It's a well set up park with a shop, swimming pool, half-court tennis court and a courtesy coach that runs into the centre three times a day (except Sunday). Tent sites cost $13 ($16 powered), and fully self-contained cabins cost from $36 for two.

On the Bruce Hwy, about 3km north of the centre, the *Tropical Wanderer Holiday Village* (☎ 4926 3822) is another good camping and caravan park with similar facilities; tent sites cost $14 ($18 powered) and on-site cabins and villas go from $37.

Hostels The *Rockhampton Youth Hostel* (☎ 4927 5288), over the river at 60 MacFarlane St, has dorms at $15, twin rooms at

Top: Jetty at South Molle Island, Whitsundays – the start and finish of many a pleasure cruise.
Middle Left: Racing is one of the few good points associated with the introduced cane toad.
Middle Right: Whitehaven Beach is the longest and finest beach on Whitsunday Island.
Bottom: Ferries shuttle between the various islands of the Whitsundays.

Top: Yachting is a popular pastime in the Whitsundays.
Middle Left: Sugar cane is harvested mechanically all along the Queensland coast.
Bottom Left: Sugar processing is one of Queensland's biggest industries.
Bottom Right: A rather grand freemasons' lodge in Mackay.

$34 and family rooms for $44; non-members pay $3 extra per night. They also have evening meals for $5. The hostel is five minutes walk from the McCafferty's terminal and a 20-minute walk north of the centre. Greyhound Pioneer will drop you nearby on request, or if you ring the hostel they can pick you up. This is a good place to organise trips to Great Keppel Island, and to make bookings for the popular YHA hostel there.

Duthies Leichhardt Hotel (☎ 4927 6733), on the corner of Denham and Bolsover Sts, has recently refurbished two and three-bed motel-type rooms at $15 per person, which is good value, although these may not be available if the hotel is close to full.

Pubs On Quay St, overlooking the river from beside the Fitzroy Bridge, the *Criterion Hotel* (☎ 4922 1225) is one of Rockhampton's most magnificent old buildings. It's a good place to stay, with the feel of a friendly country pub. The meals are good, and the small Newsroom Bar has live music most nights. Upstairs, there are budget rooms with shared bathrooms which can be had for $20/30 (singles/twins), and a few rooms with their own shower for $25/30. There are also motel-style units and attractive hotel suites renovated in period-style, which are good value from $45/50 with air-con.

Motels The newly renovated *Duthies Leichhardt Hotel* (☎ 4927 6733), on the corner of Denham and Bolsover Sts, is a six-storey hotel with 120 motel-style rooms, a bistro, shops, a bar and restaurant. Motel units are $50/60 for singles/doubles; units in the north wing are $70/75 and suites start from $94.

Porky's Motel (☎ 4927 8100), at 141 George St, is quite central and affordable, and despite the dodgy name has respectable rooms at $39/44 for singles/doubles. Next door at No 131 the *Centre Point Motor Inn* (☎ 4927 8844) is a little more upmarket and has a licensed restaurant, a pool and rooms from $72/82.

The *Ambassador on the Park* (☎ 4927 5855), at 161-167 George St, is a modern six-storey motel with a pool, restaurant, and units from $79/84. You'll find lots of other motels on the Bruce Hwy as you come into Rockhampton from both the north and south.

Self-Contained Apartments If you're looking for somewhere self-contained, the *City Ville Luxury Apartments* (☎ 4922 8322), at 21 Bolsover St, can be highly recommended. These modern apartments are stylish and well equipped, and there's a small pool. Costs start from $68 for a studio-style unit and from $180 for a three-bedroom unit. The larger units have a separate lounge, laundry and full kitchen, and upstairs bedrooms.

Places to Eat
Cafes & Takeaways The *Swagman Cafe*, at 8 Denham St, has cooked breakfasts from $5 as well as the usual burgers, sangers and pies. Two shops north, *Natural Living* is a good health-food shop with delicious lunches and salads. The *Tropical Fruit & Juice Bar*, on the mall across from the post office, has good fruit salads and smoothies.

Georgina's De Cafe, at 171 Bolsover St, is a trendy cafe-eatery open daily from 9.30 am till around 10 pm. Evening meals, such as Cajun chicken, cost $14 to $16, and there are also pastas, salads $7.50, and they have sangers, focaccias, filled croissants, great coffee and a sensational array of cakes and pastries.

Pubs The *Criterion Hotel*, on Quay St, has excellent public bar meals ranging from $7.50 to $9. The pub also has the *Bush Inn Steakhouse* with steak and seafood from $8 to $10.

Restaurants On the corner of William St and Denison Lane, *Gnomes Vegi-Tarry-Inn* is an excellent vegetarian restaurant and coffee shop. Housed in a charmingly renovated Victorian-era building, it has an open-sided courtyard and garden section. Interesting mains such as pumpkin pie, mushroom and avocado quiche and spinach cheesecake are all $8 with salad, and they also have great desserts and cakes, smoothies, juices and a huge range of herbal teas. Gnomes is open from Tuesday to Saturday for lunch and dinner.

The *Indian Tandoori & Curry House*, at 39 East St, has good-value Indian food. This BYO place is open for dinner only, and has main courses from $11 to $13.

The *Rockhampton Bangkok Thai Restaurant*, on the corner of Bolsover and William Sts, is a large and popular Thai restaurant with main meals from $9 to $13 and vegetarian dishes from $6 to $7. It is closed on Monday lunchtime; but open for dinner seven days.

Pacino's, on the corner of Fitzroy and George Sts, about 1km south of the Fitzroy Bridge, is a good Italian restaurant if you're in the mood for a minor splash. It is open nightly for dinner and has pastas from $12 to $14, pizzas for $12.50 and main courses from $17 to $19.

The *River Bistro* on Quay St is a smart and snappy eatery, with excellent light lunches – such as chicken and bacon mignon for $8 – and evening main courses from $16. The cosy *Le Bistro* on William St specialises in Modern Australian cuisine, and has modern Australian prices – $18 to $24 for a main course.

On Denham St the *Hong Kong Seafood Restaurant* has Chinese food with main meals around $10. *Cactus Jack's Mexican Restaurant*, a couple of kilometres north of the centre, on the corner of Musgrave and High Sts, is a popular licensed Mexican restaurant chain.

Pilbeam's (☎ 4927 4001), upstairs above the River Bistro, is a stylish cafe-bar-bistro open for dinner only; it's a good idea to book.

Entertainment
Pubs & Live Music The Criterion Hotel has a busy but relaxed scene in its small *Newsroom Bar* where local musicians and groups play from Wednesday to Saturday nights. Jazz, blues, folk, pop and rock all feature, and they also have an open-to-all-comers jam session on Monday nights. There is no cover charge.

Nightclubs The largest and most popular place is the *Flamingo*, on Quay St between William and Derby Sts, open from Wednesday to Sunday until late. It has a large dance floor and DJ music, a section with live bands on weekends and a pool room. There's a small cover charge.

Theatre & Cinema The *Pilbeam Theatre* (☎ 4927 4111) at the Rockhampton Performing Arts Complex (ROKPAC) on Victoria Parade is the main venue for theatre and music, and the *City Cinema Plaza* is on Denham St. There's also a huge open-air *Sound Shell*, off the Bruce Hwy about 7km north-west of the centre, which is the venue for large rock concerts and the annual carols by candlelight.

Getting There & Away
Air You can fly to Rocky with Ansett or Qantas from all the major centres along the coast. Sunstate does a daily coastal hop from Brisbane to Rockhampton ($278), Rockhampton to Mackay ($209), and back.

Qantas and Sunstate are on the mall at 107 East St and Ansett is nearby at 137 East St.

Bus McCafferty's and Greyhound Pioneer buses all pass through Rockhampton on the coastal route. Destinations include Mackay (four hours, $43), Cairns (16 hours, $98) and Brisbane (10½ hours, $67). McCafferty's also runs to Emerald ($28) twice daily, and has services to Longreach ($51) three times a week.

The McCafferty's terminal (☎ 4927 2844) is just north of the bridge off Queen Elizabeth Drive; the Greyhound Pioneer terminal is at the Mobil roadhouse in George St, near the corner of Fitzroy St, although they also stop at the Mobil station close to McCafferty's north of the river.

Young's Coaches (☎ 4922 3813) and Rothery's Coaches (☎ 4922 4320) both operate loop services around the Capricorn Coast to Yeppoon and Rosslyn Bay ($6.30

one way), Emu Park and back, leaving from outside Duthies Leichhardt Hotel. Young's also has buses to Mt Morgan ($6.30) daily except Sunday.

Train The Rockhampton railway station is about 1km south-east of the centre. Three rail services – the *Sunlander* (three times a week), the *Queenslander* (once a week) and the *Spirit of the Tropics* (twice a week) – all travel between Brisbane and Cairns, and stop at Rockhampton. The *Spirit of Capricorn* travels between Rockhampton and Brisbane daily. Twice weekly, the *Spirit of the Outback* runs between Brisbane, Rockhampton, Emerald and Longreach. For more information, contact the Queensland Rail Travel Centre at the railway station (☎ 4932 0453), 1km south-east of the centre.

Getting Around
Rockhampton airport is about 5km south of the centre. There are no bus services from the airport into the centre – a taxi costs about $9. To book a taxi, call Rocky Cabs on ☎ 4922 7111.

There's a reasonably comprehensive city bus network which operates from Monday to Friday.

AROUND ROCKHAMPTON
The rugged Berserker Range, to the north of Rockhampton, is noted for its spectacular limestone caves and passages. There are a couple of places where you can take tours through the caves region, both of which are within a couple of kilometres of **The Caves** township, 23km north of Rocky.

Olsen's Capricorn Caves (☎ 4934 2883) is the more impressive of the two operations here. The main entrance to these caves is via a collapsed cave framed by a canopy of remnant vegetation. Tours include a visit to the impressive Cathedral cave, complete with church pews, where songs such as *Amazing Grace* are played to demonstrate the cave's great acoustics. The caves are open daily from 8.30 am, with the first tour at 9 am and the last at 4 pm. There

are six different tours you can take, including a one-hour Cathedral tour ($10), an adventure tour where you don overalls and helmets ($30) and do some serious exploring through the cave system, including some narrow spots with names such as Fat Man's Misery. You need to book in advance for the adventure and night tours. Children pay half price. There are barbecue areas, a swimming pool and walking trails on the property, and by now there should be self-contained *holiday cabins*.

The **Camoo Caves** is a smaller operation. Half-hour tours here are self-guided, with six audio stations providing commentary on the various formations. These caves are open daily from 8.30 am to 4.30 pm. There are no set tour times, and entry costs $7 ($6 for students, $3 for children).

Nearby, the **Mt Etna National Park** is the habitat of the endangered ghost bat. There are no facilities here and access to the park is restricted, but the park rangers run tours of the bat caves from mid-November until mid-February. Tours depart from The Caves township, and cost $6.40 ($3.20 children); bookings are essential (☎ 4936 0511).

BOULDERCOMBE
If you're looking for somewhere to get away from it all, *Belgamba Cottage* (☎ 4938 1818) is a three-bedroom cottage on a 500-hectare property about 40km from Rocky on the way to Mt Morgan. The property is a reserve for native plants. The landscape is predominantly dry but quite interesting, and there are plenty of walking trails to explore. The owners offer free guided walks through the property and the adjacent Bouldercombe Gorge Reserve.

The timber cottage is bright, spacious and sleeps up to six people, and nightly costs are $55 a double or $80 for up to six people (cheaper rates for longer stays), with everything supplied except food. Belgamba is 22km south-west of Rockhampton and 16km north-east of Mt Morgan – phone for driving directions, or to arrange a pick-up from the turn-off if you're coming by bus.

MT MORGAN
pop 3200

The historic gold and copper-mining town of Mt Morgan is 38km south-west of Rockhampton on the Burnett Hwy. Gold was first discovered here in 1880 by William Mackinlay, a stockman.

Two years later the Morgan brothers, Thomas, Frederick and Edwin, arrived and started mining, and within a couple of years had made their fortunes.

Thinking the mine's future prospects were limited, the Morgan brothers then sold out to a mining syndicate for £90,000 – a huge sum of money at the time, but nothing compared to what would later come out of the ground. In its first 10 years of operations from 1886, the Mt Morgan Gold Mining Company returned massive dividends on the initial capital, making its major investors into some of the richest and most powerful men in Australia. Gold yields fell dramatically by the turn of the century, but in 1903 the company began extracting the rich copper deposits that were found deeper in the mine. Open-cut operations continued until 1981.

Mt Morgan has a well-preserved collection of turn-of-the-19th century buildings, and is registered as a heritage town. There's an interesting historic museum and you can take a tour of the former mine site.

Information

The Golden Mount Tourist Information Centre (☎ 4938 2312), in the old railway station, is open daily from 9 am to 4 pm.

Things to See & Do

The **Mt Morgan Historical Museum**, on the corner of Morgan and East Sts, is very well set up with displays including an old kitchen, a 1921 black Buick hearse, and collections of sewing machines, cameras, musical instruments, riding and farming gear, as well as old photos tracing the history of the mine. The museum is open Monday to Saturday from 10 am to 1 pm and Sunday from 10 am to 4 pm; there's a small admission charge.

Mt Morgan Mine Tours (☎ 4938 1081), with an office next to the Golden Nugget Hotel at 38 Central St, runs two-hour tours that take in the town's sights, the open-cut mine, and a large cave which has dinosaur footprints on the roof and is home to a colony of bats. Tours depart from their office and the museum every day at 9.30 am and 1 pm and cost $18.50 ($10 children, $45 families); Devonshire tea is included in the cost.

Mt Morgan's lovely old **railway station** is something of a focal point for the town. It houses the tourist office, and a **market** is held at the station on the first Saturday of each month from 2 pm. On Saturday afternoons from 2 pm you can take a historic 3.5km **train tour** which costs $5 ($2.50 for children, $15 for families).

The **Running the Cutter** monument on the corner of Morgan and Central Sts, opposite the post office, commemorates the old custom of serving 'cutters' (two-quart billy cans) of beer to the mine workers in Cutter Lane behind the hotels.

Festivals

Mt Morgan's major festival is the Golden Mount Festival held every May. It features a 'Running the Cutter' event.

Places to Stay

The *Silver Wattle Caravan & Tourist Park* (☎ 4938 1550), on the southern outskirts of town, is a good camping ground with an attractive bush setting and tent sites from $10 ($12 powered), on-site vans from $18 and cabins from $30.

The old two-storey *Leichhardt Hotel* (☎ 4938 1851) on the corner of Morgan and East Sts, opposite the museum, has basic but clean timber-lined pub rooms upstairs at $20/25 for singles/doubles.

The *Miners' Rest Motel Units* (☎ 4938 2350), 1km south of the centre on the outskirts of town, is a set of three small Victorian-style cottages, each with its own en suite, kitchenette, spa, TV and air-con. Tariffs range from $40 a double, which includes breakfast.

Getting There & Away

Young's Bus Service (☎ 4922 3813) operates a regular bus from Rockhampton to Mt Morgan three times daily on weekdays, twice on Saturday. The one-way fare is $6.30 and buses leave from outside Duthies Hotel, on the corner of East and William Sts in Rocky.

You can also get to Mt Morgan every day with McCafferty's – buses pass through several times a day on the inland route between Rocky and Brisbane.

ROCKHAMPTON TO BARALABA

Myella Farm Stay (☎ 4998 1290) is a 1050-hectare Brahman-cross cattle property 125km south-west of Rockhampton and about 22km east of Baralaba, the nearest town. Guests stay in a renovated timber farmhouse which has three bedrooms, nine beds, a central living area and a broad, shady verandah. You join the family for home-cooked meals in their house nearby. You can join in the cattle mustering or fence building, ride horses, climb the local mountain, or just lounge around on the verandah. Costs for a single/double are $120/220 for two days, which includes all meals and activities.

Getting There & Away

If you're driving, take the Leichhardt Hwy and turn-off towards Baralaba, midway between Wowan and Banana. The farm is signposted off the Baralaba Rd, 18km west of the Leichhardt Hwy.

If you're travelling by bus, take a McCafferty's bus to Dululu at the junction of the Burnett and Leichhardt Hwys – if you ring in advance, the owners will pick you up from there.

YEPPOON
pop 7350

Yeppoon is a relaxed little seaside township 43km north-east of Rockhampton. It's the main centre on the coast, and although Great Keppel Island is the area's main attraction, Yeppoon has quite good beaches and is a reasonably popular holiday town with a pleasant hinterland (see the following Yeppoon to Byfield section). Boats to Great Keppel leave from Rosslyn Bay, 7km south.

Information

The Capricorn Coast Information Centre (☎ 1800 675 785 or ☎ 4939 4888), beside the Ross Creek Roundabout at the entrance to the town, has a good range of info on the Capricorn Coast and Great Keppel Island, and is open daily from 9 am to 5 pm.

Places to Stay

About 1km north from the centre of town, the *Beachside Caravan Park* (☎ 4939 3798) is a neat beachfront caravan park with tent sites from $9 ($18 powered).

Up on the hill behind the town, *Barrier Reef Backpackers* (☎ 4939 4702), at 30 Queen St, is a relaxed place in a comfortable old timber house. It has all the usual facilities, a large backyard and good views of the town. Four-bed dorms cost $15 ($1 less for YHA or VIP members), doubles $33. It offers a free pick-up service from Rocky and will drop you at the Rosslyn Bay harbour if you're going to Great Keppel.

There's a string of motels and holiday units along Anzac Parade, opposite the beachfront. At No 32 the *Como Holiday Units* (☎ 4939 1594) is a two-storey block of good one and two-bedroom self-contained units which start from $50 a double, plus $8 for each extra person. Further along the beachfront, on the corner of Normanby and Adelaide Sts, is the *Bayview Tower Motel* (☎ 4939 4500), a tall, modern high-rise motel. All the rooms have good ocean views, and prices range from $68 a double on the 2nd floor to $96 a double on the 8th floor.

On the coast 8km north of Yeppoon, the *Capricorn International Resort* (☎ 4939 5111 or toll-free ☎ 1800 075 902) is a large four-star resort hotel. This hotel is very 1980s with its pastel-pink colour scheme; it has a huge swimming pool, tennis courts, a gym, and several cafes and eateries including an authentic Japanese restaurant. This place has several different types of accom-

CAPRICORN COAST

modation, with rates from $175 to $220 a night for a hotel room and around $320 a night for a suite or self-contained apartment.

The resort also has a great golf course which is open to the public. The $60-a-round fee includes lunch and a motorised buggy – to hire clubs costs another $30.

Places to Eat
In the Seaview Arcade on the waterfront there's the cheap *Thai Take-Away & Dine-In*, which is pretty self-explanatory, and also *Seagulls Seafood* for good fish and chips.

Close by is *Pass da Pasta*, a good licensed bistro with dishes from $8 to $15. It's open for dinner from Tuesday to Sunday, also for Sunday lunch.

Entertainment
The *Strand Hotel*, on the corner of Anzac Parade and Normanby St, is a popular pub with live bands on weekends. Back on Hill St is the flashier *Bonkers* disco/nightspot, open from Wednesday to Saturday until around 5 am. It sometimes has live bands on weekends.

Getting There & Away
If you're heading for Great Keppel or the reef, some of the ferry operators will transport you between your accommodation and Rosslyn Bay Harbour. Otherwise, Young's Bus Service (☎ 4922 3813) and Rothery's (☎ 4922 4320) both run buses from Rockhampton to Yeppoon ($6.30 one way) and the rest of the Capricorn Coast, departing from Duthies Hotel in Rocky.

If you're driving to Rosslyn Bay there's a free day carpark at the harbour, and the Kempsea lock-up carpark (on the main road near the harbour turn-off) charges $4.50 a day ($6 under cover), $3 for motorcycles) and runs a free bus to and from the harbour.

YEPPOON TO BYFIELD
The coastal hinterland north of Yeppoon is largely undeveloped, and there are a number of state forest parks and one national park in the area. You can't get across

to the coast without a 4WD, but there are some good picnic and camping grounds in the state forests, and you can visit a pottery and a historic homestead near the small township of Byfield, 40km from Yeppoon. There is also an excellent bush retreat and restaurant nearby.

Heading out of Yeppoon, the drive north takes you through the pine plantations of the Byfield State Forest, with turn-offs along the way to various other state forest parks and the Upper Stoney Dam. After about 30km the sealed road ends, and the last section alternates between sealed and unsealed (but well maintained) roads.

Just south of Byfield, there are turn-offs to the **Nob Creek Pottery** (2km west), where you can visit the workshop and gallery, and to the **Waterpark Creek Forest Park**. It's 2km east from the main road to the creek crossing, beyond which are an attractive picnic area, with tables and gas barbecues, and a self-registration camping ground. From here, a dirt road continues through the pine plantations to the **Byfield National Park**, which is an undeveloped area of mostly low coastal scrub. If you have a 4WD, you can continue through the park to the coast – the beach along here is very popular with anglers.

The town of **Byfield** consists of a general store (which sells delicious fruit and coconut slices), a school and a handful of houses. About 1km north of the town is the historic **Raspberry Creek Homestead**, which houses the local library and a small collection of local history items, documents and photos. It's open on Sunday from 1 to 4 pm, on Tuesday from 3 to 5.30 pm and on Friday from 9.30 to 11.30 am.

Places to Stay & Eat
Signposted off the road a couple of kilometres north of Byfield is the *Ferns Hideaway* (☎ 4935 1235), a wonderful bush retreat on a 40-hectare property beside the Waterpark Creek. There are five self-contained cabins and a three bedroom house here, all in secluded settings. The cabins sleep up to six people and cost from $100

to $120 a night; the house costs $25 for each adult and $12 for each child. There are also some good camp sites down near the creek which cost $10 per person; firewood and hot showers are provided. This place is very well set up – there are marked walking trails through the property, and you can play tennis, swim in the pool, paddle canoes down the creek and go horse riding. There's also a licensed restaurant which is open for lunches on Saturday and Sunday, and for dinner on Saturday night. Main courses are from $12 to $15 and you'll need to book.

YEPPOON TO EMU PARK

There are beaches dotted all along the 19km coast running south from Yeppoon to Emu Park. At **Cooee Bay**, a couple of kilometres from Yeppoon, the annual Australian 'Cooee' Championships are held each August.

Reached by a short side road about 7km south of Yeppoon, **Rosslyn Bay Harbour** is the departure point for trips to Great Keppel and other Keppel Bay islands.

South of Rosslyn Bay are three fine headlands with good views – **Double Head**, **Bluff Point** and **Pinnacle Point**. After Pinnacle Point the road crosses **Causeway Lake**, a saltwater inlet where you can rent canoes and sailboards. Further south at **Emu Park** there are more good views and the 'Singing Ship' memorial to Captain Cook – a series of drilled tubes and pipes which emit whistling or moaning sounds when there's a breeze blowing.

The **Koorana Crocodile Farm** is 5km off the Emu Park to Rockhampton road. The turn-off is 15km from Emu Park. The farm has hundreds of crocs; it is open daily from 11.30 am and has a 1½-hour tour every day at 1 pm for $10 ($5).

Most towns along this stretch of coast have caravan and camping parks, and there are numerous motels and holiday flats.

GREAT KEPPEL ISLAND

Although it's not actually on the reef, Great Keppel is the equal of most islands up the coast. It's 13km offshore, and big enough to take a few days to explore. It covers 14 sq km and boasts 18km of very fine beaches.

The Great! Keppel Resort, owned by Qantas Airlines, is a very popular resort, especially among young families and couples. Keppel is promoted as the 'active island', with a wide range of activities and entertainment to keep guests busy – 'Forget the Rest', as they say.

The good news about Great Keppel is that, unlike many of the resort islands, there are some good budget accommodation alternatives, and it's also one of the cheapest and easiest Queensland islands to reach. Great Keppel is a popular destination for day trips; the resort has a separate section for day trippers, with a small pool, bar, outdoor tables and umbrellas, a restaurant and a cafe – and all sorts of water sports gear for hire.

Things to See & Do

Great Keppel's beaches are among the best on any of the resort islands. It only takes a short stroll from the main resort area to find your own deserted stretch of white, sandy beach. The water is clear, warm and beautiful, and there is good coral at many points around the island, especially between Great Keppel and Humpy Island to the south. A 30-minute walk around the headland south of the resort brings you to **Monkey Beach**, where there's good snorkelling. Another walking trail from the southern end of the airfield takes you to **Long Beach**, perhaps the best of the island's beaches.

There are a number of bushwalking tracks from **Fishermans Beach**, the main beach. The longest, and one of the more difficult, goes across to the lighthouse near **Bald Rock Point** on the far side of the island (2½ hours one way). Some beaches, like **Red Beach** near the lighthouse, are only accessible by boat.

There's an **underwater observatory** by Middle Island, close to Great Keppel. A confiscated Taiwanese fishing junk was sunk next to the observatory to provide a haven for fish.

There are two places where you can hire

CAPRICORN COAST

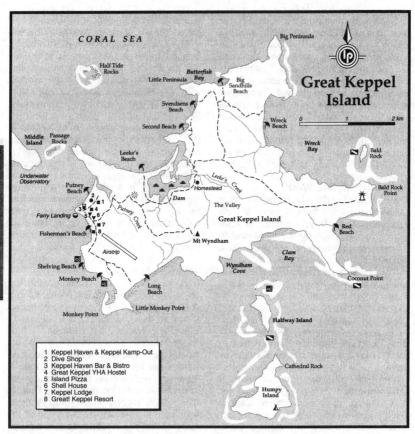

CORAL SEA

Big Peninsula

Great Keppel Island

Half Tide Rocks

Little Peninsula

Butterfish Bay

Big Sandhills Beach

Svendsens Beach

Wreck Beach

0   1   2 km

Second Beach

Middle Island

Passage Rocks

Wreck Bay

Bald Rock

Leeke's Beach

Underwater Observatory

Putney Beach

Homestead

Leeke's Creek

Bald Rock Point

Ferry Landing

Dam

The Valley

Putney Creek

Great Keppel Island

Fisherman's Beach

Red Beach

Airstrip

Mt Wyndham

Clam Bay

Shelving Beach

Monkey Beach

Wyndham Cove

Coconut Point

Long Beach

Little Monkey Point

Monkey Point

Halfway Island

Cathedral Rock

Humpy Island

1 Keppel Haven & Keppel Kamp-Out
2 Dive Shop
3 Keppel Haven Bar & Bistro
4 Great Keppel YHA Hostel
5 Island Pizza
6 Shell House
7 Keppel Lodge
8 Great! Keppel Resort

water sports equipment – use of all non-powered water sports gear is free for resort guests. The Beach Shed on Putney Beach and Keppel Watersports on Fisherman's Beach both have sailboards, catamarans, motorboats, fishing tackle and snorkelling gear, and they can also take you paragliding or water-skiing. Keppel Reef Scuba Adventures (☎ 4939 5022) on Putney Beach offers introductory dives for $80, or, if you're qualified, two dives with all gear supplied for $100. You can also do a five-day diving course for $420.

Organised Cruises

Keppel Tourist Services (☎ 4933 6744) runs various cruises, mainly in the *Reefcat*. Its island cruise departs daily from Rosslyn Bay at 9.15 am and from Fisherman's Beach at 9.50 am, and continues on a three-hour cruise to its large floating pontoon moored 50m off the northern tip of the island. The cruise includes boom-netting and snorkelling, and a visit to the underwater observatory. It returns to the mainland at 4.30 pm; the cruise costs $70 from Rosslyn Bay or $33 if you're already on the island.

Several vessels are available for longer diving, fishing or cruising trips – ask at Rockhampton tourist office or Rosslyn Bay harbour.

Places to Stay

Camping, Hostels & Motels *Keppel Haven* (☎ 4939 1907) has semi-permanent safari tents that sleep up to four people and cost $25 per person. The tents come complete with mattresses, and communal facilities in the tent village include fridges, barbecues and basic kitchen equipment. There are also a number of somewhat rundown cabins at $110 for two people plus $30 for each extra person; the cabins sleep up to six people, and have bedding, kitchen and laundry facilities and shared bathrooms. Maintenance is certainly not what it might be at this place.

Next door to Keppel Haven is *Keppel Kamp Out* (☎ 4939 2131), which is geared to the 18 to 35 age bracket, and has organised activities. The cost of $69 per person per day includes twin-share tents, three meals and activities such as water sports, parties and video nights. A stand-by rate of $49 is usually available.

The *Great Keppel YHA Hostel* (☎ 4939 4341) is quite old and very straightforward, but it's still very popular and is often booked out well in advance. There are two 16-bed dorms at $16, and two eight-bed cabins with their own bathrooms at $17; non-members pay $3 extra. The hostel rents snorkelling gear and organises bushwalks and other activities. Book through the Rockhampton Youth Hostel or the YHA head office in Brisbane (☎ 3236 1680). Its $79 deal ($89 non-members) is good value – you get one night in Rocky, two nights on the island and bus and boat transfers.

Keppel Lodge (☎ 4939 4251) is a pleasant and modern little place with four spacious motel-style units, a large communal lounge and kitchen, and an outdoor barbecue area. Each room sleeps up to five people, and the nightly costs are $90 a double plus $30 for each adult or $15 for each child under 12 years old.

Resorts The popular Qantas-owned *Great! Keppel Resort* (☎ 4939 5044) is stylish and comfortable without being sophisticated. The facilities include squash and tennis courts, a couple of swimming pools, a six-hole golf course, and water sports gear including catamarans and windsurfers; the use of these, plus volleyball, archery and aerobics facilities, is included in the tariffs.

There are over 190 units, ranging from the older motel-style Garden and Beachfront Units to the impressively upmarket Hillside Villas. Daily costs are $270 in the Garden Units, $300 in the Beachfront Units and $380 in the Ocean View Villas. Rates are cheaper for five nights or more, and cheaper stand-by rates are available (typically around 50% discount if you book three days in advance). The standard rates include breakfast and include quite a few activities, and you have the option of taking a lunch and dinner package for another $38.

Qantas also has a variety of package deals available which include return airfare and accommodation – contact Qantas Australian Holidays (☎ 13 1415) for details.

Places to Eat

If you want to cook it's best to bring supplies with you, although the kiosk at *Keppel Haven* has a few basics. Next door, the *Keppel Haven Bar & Bistro* is a bit pricey with burgers for $6 to $7, sandwiches at $4, grills at $15 and breakfast for $6 to $9.

Between Keppel Haven and the resort is *Island Pizza*, open Wednesday to Sunday for lunch and dinner. This place is run by a friendly young couple and has hot dogs for $2.70, subs for $4.20, pastas from $3.50 and good pizzas ranging from $10 to $26.

There's a couple of possibilities in the resort area. The *Keppel Cafe* has burgers from $4, meat pies, sandwiches etc, and nearby the *Anchorage Char Grill* serves lunches and dinners with grilled steak or fish with salad and chips for $12.

Entertainment

Neptune's Bar at the resort is open to all comers every night until 2 am, with live bands from Monday to Saturday and on Sunday afternoon from 1 to 4 pm. The *Keppel Haven Bar* also has live entertainment on Wednesday and Saturday nights.

Getting There & Away
Air Sunstate (Qantas) flies at least twice daily between Rockhampton and Great Keppel; the one-way fare is $82.

Boat Ferries for Great Keppel leave from Rosslyn Bay Harbour on the Capricorn Coast. You can book the ferries through your accommodation or agents in Rockhampton and on the Capricorn Coast. If you're staying at the YHA hostel in Rocky, they have a special deal of $35 for the bus trip, the ferry across and a three-hour island cruise.

Keppel Tourist Services (☎ 4933 6744) operates two boats, *Reefcat* and *Spirit of Keppel*. *Reefcat* leaves Rosslyn Bay at 9.15 am, returns from Great Keppel at 4.30 pm and costs $25 return. *Spirit of Keppel* leaves Rosslyn Bay at 11.30 am and 3.30 pm, and returns from Great Keppel at 8.15 am and 2 pm. *Reefcat* also goes on to a pontoon on the north side of the island, or you can buy a $39 package to the island which includes lunch at the resort and a 10% discount on water sports.

OTHER KEPPEL BAY ISLANDS
Great Keppel is only the biggest of the 18 continental islands which are dotted around Keppel Bay, all within 20km of the coast. It's possible to visit **Middle Island**, with its underwater observatory, or **Halfway** and **Humpy islands** if you're staying on Great Keppel.

Some of the islands are national parks where you can maroon yourself for a few days of self-sufficient camping. Most have clean, white beaches and several, notably Halfway, have good fringing coral reefs which are excellent for snorkelling or diving.

Places to Stay
To camp on a national park island, you need to take all your own supplies including

water. The number of campers allowed on each island is restricted – for example, eight on Middle and six on Miall. You can get information and permits from the Department of Environment regional office in Rockhampton (☎ 4936 0511) or the QNPW rangers' office at Rosslyn Bay Harbour (☎ 4933 6595).

The second largest of the group and one of the most northerly is **North Keppel Island**. It covers 6 sq km and is a national park. The most popular camping spot is Considine Beach on the north-west coast, which has well water for washing, and toilets. Take insect repellent.

Other islands with camping grounds include Humpy, Halfway, Miall and Middle.

Just south of North Keppel, privately owned **Pumpkin Island** has five cabins (☎ 4939 2431) which accommodate five or six people at a cost of $130 per night per cabin. There's water and solar electricity, and each cabin has a gas stove and fridge, a barbecue and a bathroom with shower. All you need to bring is food and linen. You can also camp on this tiny island for $12 per person – the camping ground has tank water, a shower and toilet, and a fireplace.

Getting There & Away
The Keppel Bay Marina (☎ 4933 6244) can organise a water taxi for camping drop-off services from Rosslyn Bay to the islands; prices start from $300 return for up to four people, plus $40 for each extra person.

ROCKHAMPTON TO SARINA
It's almost 300km from Rockhampton to Sarina, with only a handful of small towns and roadhouses, and a couple of points of interest, between the two. This stretch of highway passes through cattle country and low hills covered with eucalypt forests, and after a while the monotony of the landscape makes it hard to resist the temptation to tread a little more firmly on the accelerator.

Marlborough
Marlborough, 102km north-west of Rockhampton, is a quiet little one-pub town just

east of the highway. It has a railway station, lots of cattle yards, a takeaway food shop, a garage and a small public pool, as well as the interesting **Marlborough Historical Museum**. The museum is open weekdays from 9 am to 5 pm.

Places to Stay & Eat The old *Marlborough Hotel* (☎ 4935 6103) is a straightforward little timber pub. Back in 1907, if you wanted a drink here you had a choice of rum, or rum and milk, and the menu offered a selection of roast goat or roast goat. Nowadays the selection is a little more varied. The pub also has a couple of clean and simple rooms which open onto the front verandah – singles/twins cost $25/35.

On the west side of the highway, the *Marlborough Caravan Park* (☎ 4935 6112) has tent sites for $12, on-site vans for $22.50 a double and motel units from $48/52.

Marlborough to Sarina

At **Clairview**, about 100km north of Marlborough, the highway meets the coast and you get a brief but tantalising glimpse of blue ocean waters. Clairview itself is just a string of old houses along the foreshore, but the beach is quite good for swimming (outside the stinger season) at high tide.

The **Cape Palmerston National Park**, a small coastal park, unsignposted off the Bruce Hwy about 32km south of Sarina, is only accessible to 4WD vehicles. There are basic camping facilities only, and the park features long sandy beaches, inland lagoons and melaleuca forests.

Capricorn Hinterland

The Capricorn Hwy runs inland from Rockhampton, virtually along the Tropic and across the central Queensland highlands to Barcaldine, from where you can continue west and north-west along the Landsborough Hwy to meet the Townsville to Mt Isa road.

The area was first opened up by miners chasing gold and copper around Emerald, and sapphires around Anakie, but cattle, grain crops and coal are its lifeblood today. Carnarvon, south of Emerald, and the Blackdown Tableland, south-east of Blackwater, are two of Queensland's most spectacular and interesting national parks.

The Gemfields region, around the towns of Sapphire and Rubyvale, is a fascinating area to visit and explore, and you can fossick for valuable gemstones here.

Several of the massive open-cut coal mines in the area give free tours lasting about 1½ hours; you generally need to book ahead.

ROCKHAMPTON TO EMERALD

It's 270km from Rockhampton to Emerald. On the way, you can take an interesting detour to the spectacular Blackdown Tableland National Park, and visit the coal mining centre of Blackwater.

Blackdown Tableland National Park

The Blackdown Tableland is a spectacular sandstone plateau which rises suddenly out of the flat plains of central Queensland to a height of 600m. Blackdown is definitely worth a visit, and features stunning panoramas, great bushwalks to waterfalls and lookout points, Aboriginal rock art, eucalypt forests, creeks and waterfalls. There's also a good campground here.

The turn-off to the park is signposted from the Capricorn Hwy, 11km west of Dingo and 40km east of Blackwater. A reasonably good dirt and gravel road takes you south for about 15km to the base of the tableland. For the next 7km the road is a very steep, winding climb, and the red gravel surface can be incredibly slippery. The access road can be unsafe in wet weather and is not suitable for caravans at any time.

At the top of the climb you come to the spectacular **Horseshoe Lookout**, with picnic tables, barbecues and toilets beside the carpark. Walking trails also start from here to **Two Mile Falls** (2.2km), **Sunset**

Lookout (500m) and **Peregrine Lookout** (1.3km).

Further on is the spacious camping ground at **South Mimosa Creek**, with toilets, water and fireplaces. Bring a gas stove for cooking and to boil drinking water. The camping ground is sometimes booked out during school holidays – sites can be booked in advance through the rangers at Dingo (☎ 4986 1964). Several other walking trails start from the camping ground.

Blackwater (pop 6900)

Blackwater is one of Queensland's major coal mining centres, with half a dozen large mines in the vicinity of the town. Rail yards and coal-shipping facilities line the southern side of the highway, while motels, roadhouses and eateries line its northern side.

The **Frank Tutungi Memorial Park**, on the highway west of the centre, flies a collection of 37 flags representing the different nationalities of people who have worked in local mines. The park is dominated by a huge Olympic-torch-shaped water tower, and has picnic facilities. Beside the park, the **Blackwater Community Pool** is a good place for a refreshing dip.

You can take a guided tour of the huge **Blackwater Open-cut Mine** (☎ 4986 0666), 20km south of the town, on Wednesday at 10 am. Tours leave from the mine site and you need to ring in advance to book.

Blackwater also has a caravan park and a motel.

EMERALD
pop 6800

At the junction of the Gregory and Capricorn Hwys, Emerald is the gateway town of the Capricorn Hinterland region. Established back in 1879 as a railway siding, Emerald has grown into a major centre for the surrounding mining and agricultural industries.

Most of the town's older buildings were destroyed in a series of disastrous fires in 1936, 1940, 1954 and 1968. One notable exception is the fine old **Emerald Railway Station**, on Clermont St in the centre of town, built in 1900 and restored in 1987.

The Central Highlands Tourist Information Centre (☎ 4982 4142), at the western end of Clermont St, is open daily from 9 am to 5 pm.

Things to See & Do

The **Emerald Pioneer Cottage & Museum**, in Centenary Drive, has a collection of historic buildings including the town's first church and gaol. It is open Saturday from 9 am to noon and other days from 2 to 4 pm. Entry costs $2 for adults.

The very pleasant **Botanic Gardens** are on Clermont St, beside the Nogoa River, and have walking trails and picnic and barbecue facilities.

Places to Stay & Eat

There's not much reason to linger, but the town has the usual options: a couple of caravan parks and pubs and a rash of motels. The food scene is equally straightforward, with cafes on the main street and counter meals at the pubs. Top of the range is the *Steakhouse Restaurant* at the Emerald Meteor Motel, on the corner of Opal and Egerton Sts.

Getting There & Away

McCafferty's has a terminal at 115 Clermont St. Their buses pass through daily on the Rockhampton to Longreach run. You can also get here on the twice-weekly *Spirit of the Outback* train, which runs from Rocky to Longreach.

AROUND EMERALD

There are free tours of the **Gregory Coal Mine** (☎ 4982 8282), 50km north-east of Emerald, every Tuesday and Thursday at 1 pm.

Queensland's second-largest artificial lake, **Lake Maraboon**, is 18km south-west of Emerald. There's a boat ramp and attractive picnic areas at the lake, and the *Sunrover Resort Caravan Park* (☎ 4982 3677).

CAPELLA
pop 900
Midway between Emerald and Clermont, the township of Capella has the **Capella Pioneer Village**, set in a historic 1869 homestead building with an interesting collection of memorabilia and machinery. The village is open on Tuesday and Sunday from 10 am to 4 pm or by appointment (☎ 4984 9311). Entry costs $1.

Based in Capella, Leichhardt Tours (☎ 4984 9224) offers trail rides and overnight horse riding tours to the Peak Range area for groups of four to 10 people. Its overnight tours cost from $80 per person for one day, or $110 per day for two or more days; all meals and camping gear are included in the price. Leichhardt Tours also does 4WD tours of the Central Highlands for four to six people, costing $80 per person per day.

CLERMONT
pop 2900
Just over 100km north of Emerald is Clermont and the huge Blair Athol open-cut coal mine – Australia's largest exporter of steaming coal, which produces 11 million tonnes a year. Clermont is Queensland's oldest tropical inland town, founded on wealth from copper, gold, sheep and cattle. It was the scene of goldfield race riots in the 1880s, and a military takeover of the town occurred in 1891 after a confrontation between striking sheep shearers and non-union labour.

In December 1916 a flood virtually destroyed the town and claimed 65 lives. The **Flood Memorial**, a concrete 'tree stump' in Drummond St, has an indicator showing the high water mark during the flood.

The **Clermont Museum**, near the junction of the Gregory and Peak Downs Hwys about 3km north of the centre, has an interesting collection of relics and memorabilia, a historic slab timber hut and old machinery.

Free tours of the **Blair Athol Mine** depart from the mine office at 38 Jellico St every Tuesday at 9 am. You need to ring in advance to book (☎ 4983 1866).

Places to Stay
At 1 Haig St the *Clermont Caravan Park* (☎ 4983 1927) has tent sites from $10 ($12 powered) and on-site vans from $25. The *Clermont Motor Inn* (☎ 4983 3133), on the corner of Box and Capella Sts, has singles/doubles from $60/68.

CLERMONT TO MACKAY
The 274km-long Peak Downs Hwy runs north-east from Clermont to Mackay. There isn't much of interest for travellers along this route – most people use it to cut across to or from the coast.

The only towns along this route with shops and fuel are **Coppabella**, 133km north-east of Clermont, and **Nebo**, 92km south-west of Mackay. Nebo also has an RACQ depot, the B&S Service Centre (☎ 4950 5150).

The landscape along the first section of the route, from Clermont to Moranbah, is dominated by the rugged volcanic outcrops of the **Peak Range Mountains**.

Purpose-built as a coal mining centre in 1971, **Moranbah** (pop 6700) services three large coal mines – Peak Downs, Goonyella and Riverside. Bus tours of the Peak Downs mine (☎ 4941 6233) depart from Moranbah's town square at 10 am on Thursday. There are a couple of caravan parks in town, and the *Black Nugget Hotel* (☎ 4941 7185), in Griffin St, has motel-style units. Moranbah is 13km north-west of the highway; the turn-off is 97km north-east of Clermont.

GEMFIELDS
West of Emerald, about 270km inland from Rockhampton, the gemfields around Anakie, Sapphire, Rubyvale and Willows Gemfield are known for their sapphires, zircons, amethysts, rubies, topaz, jasper, and even diamonds and gold.

The gemfields are the world's richest sapphire deposits, and it is still possible to find valuable gems in the area. In 1993 a couple from Mt Isa found a sapphire worth $300,000, and in 1979 a 14-year-old boy found the 2000-carat Centenary Sapphire here, which is worth more than $1 million.

If you're just passing through, there are a number of fossicking parks in the area which sell buckets of dirt which you can wash and sieve by hand – 'doing a bucket' is great fun and a good way to learn how to identify raw sapphires. Every bucket of dirt contains at least a few sapphire chips, and you might even find something worthwhile. There are also several tourist mines that will take you on underground or surface tours. If you do strike it lucky, there are a number of professional cutters around who can cut your stones for around $20 per carat.

If you catch the bug and decide to go fossicking you need a fossicking licence, which can be obtained from the Emerald Courthouse or from one of the general stores and post offices on the gemfields. You can buy permits for bush camping from the same places; these cost $2 per night and allow you to pitch a tent anywhere in the fields. Basic fossicking equipment includes sieves, a pick and shovel, water and a container. You can bring this with you, or hire it when you arrive.

The gemfields attract a fascinating diversity of characters – adventurers, alternative lifestylers, battlers and travellers, all hoping to strike it lucky. The most popular times to visit are the drier, cooler months from April to September – when the population swells from around 3000 to close to 7000 – but you can come here at any time of year.

Festivals

Two major annual festivals are held in the area – the Gemfields Ironman Wheelbarrow Derby every June and the Gemfest Festival of Gems held in August. The latter features exhibitions of gems, jewellery, mining and fossicking equipment, art and craft markets, and a variety of entertainment.

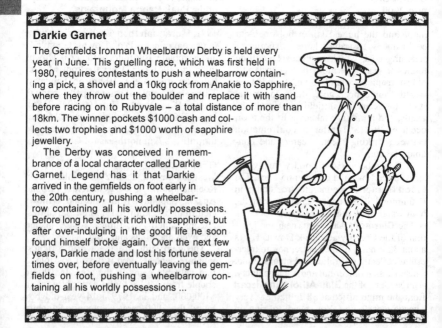

Darkie Garnet

The Gemfields Ironman Wheelbarrow Derby is held every year in June. This gruelling race, which was first held in 1980, requires contestants to push a wheelbarrow containing a pick, a shovel and a 10kg rock from Anakie to Sapphire, where they throw out the boulder and replace it with sand before racing on to Rubyvale – a total distance of more than 18km. The winner pockets $1000 cash and collects two trophies and $1000 worth of sapphire jewellery.

The Derby was conceived in remembrance of a local character called Darkie Garnet. Legend has it that Darkie arrived in the gemfields on foot early in the 20th century, pushing a wheelbarrow containing all his worldly possessions. Before long he struck it rich with sapphires, but after over-indulging in the good life he soon found himself broke again. Over the next few years, Darkie made and lost his fortune several times over, before eventually leaving the gemfields on foot, pushing a wheelbarrow containing all his worldly possessions ...

Getting There & Away

You can get to Anakie on a McCafferty's bus or on the *Spirit of the Outback* train. From there you'd need to get a lift up to Sapphire or Rubyvale, although a couple of the places to stay might pick you up if you ring and book in advance.

Vaughan's Bus Service (☎ 4982 1275) has school buses from Emerald to Rubyvale on weekdays at 3.10 pm, returning from Rubyvale at 7.30 am ($5 one way).

Rubyvale
pop 720

Rubyvale is the main centre for the gemfields, but don't expect any bright lights or hustle and bustle. It's a small, ramshackle place with a scattered collection of dwellings, a pub, a few gem shops and galleries, a general store and a service station.

Rubyvale is 18km north of Anakie. From here, it's another 62km of often slippery dirt road to Capella on the Gregory Hwy.

Mine Tours & Gem Galleries There are a couple of commercial mines and galleries around Rubyvale which open up to tourists. One of the best of these is the **Silk 'n' Sapphire Mine**, on Heritage Rd, 1.5km north of town.

This place offers hands-on adventure tours down a 17m vertical shaft to a working mine. You get to work the mine face with an electric jackhammer, shovel and barrow before taking your diggings up to the surface for a mechanical wash. This tour isn't for the faint-hearted and the work can be strenuous, but it's great fun and a realistic experience of life underground. The minimum age is 16 and tours cost $30 for two hours or $60 for a half day. You can also do a bucketful of wash for $5, or a skipful for $20. There's also a small shopfront here selling gems, jewellery and hand-painted silks.

Also on Heritage Rd is the very friendly and informative **Miners' Heritage Walk-in Mine**. Half-hour tours of the mine tunnels here cost $5 ($2 for children). There's also an underground showroom with gems and jewellery on sale and gem-cutting services. Up on the surface, you can buy a bucket of wash for $4, or rest in the well set up picnic area. The mine is open every day from 9 am to 5 pm.

The **Miners Cottage** is a small timber cottage with a collection of crafts, jewellery and gems on sale, and you can do a three-hour surface tour which involves filling a barrow with dirt from the creek bed and learning how to sieve, wash and sort it. Tours cost $30 per barrow, and up to three people can work one barrow. The cottage is open daily from 8 am to 4 pm (closed Thursday afternoon), and is signposted off Goanna Flat Rd about 500m from the centre.

The **Bobby Dazzler Mine**, just south of the centre, with 20-minute underground mine tours costing $3 ($1.50 children), is also open daily from 9 am to 5 pm. There's also a jumbled little museum and jewellery shop here.

The **Rubyvale Gem Gallery** (☎ 4985 4388) does good half-day 4WD tours of the gemfields for $35.

Places to Stay & Eat The *Rubyvale Caravan Park* (☎ 4985 4118), on Goanna Flat Rd, has tent sites from $8, on-site vans from $20 and cabins from $40.

The *Gemfields Motel* (☎ 4985 4150), in Keilambete Rd just up from the post office, has cramped accommodation in transportable cabins at $30/38 for singles/doubles, which includes a light breakfast. There's also an old-fashioned dining room and bar serving cheap meals.

Bedford Gardens Caravan Park & Holiday Units (☎ 4985 4175), in Vane Tempest Rd one block back from the post office, has self-contained cabins which sleep up to eight people and cost $50 for a double plus $5 for each extra person. You can also camp here – there are showers, a barbecue area and a campers' kitchen with a fridge and stove.

The *New Royal Hotel* has counter meals for $5, or there's *Rainbow's End* for good casual meals.

Sapphire
pop 700

About 10km north of Anakie, Sapphire has a petrol station, a post office, and a few houses scattered around the hillside. It also has one of the best accommodation places in the area, and a couple of fossicking parks.

Fossicking Parks At **Pat's Gems**, 1km north of Sapphire, buckets of dirt cost $5 each or you can have six for $20. They also have fossicking gear available for hire.

The **Forever Mine**, on the northern outskirts of Sapphire, has a kiosk, a cutting room and jewellery on sale. You can buy a bucket of dirt for $5 and wash it by hand, or a tractor-scoop of dirt for $30 and put it through the mechanical pulsator before hand washing it.

Places to Stay & Eat About 1km out of Sapphire, on the road to Rubyvale, *Sunrise Cabins & Camping* (☎ 4985 4281) has simple timber and stone cabins that sleep from one to six people, with communal toilets, shower blocks, and a cooking and dining cabin. The nightly cost of the cabins is $12/26 for singles/doubles plus $2 for each extra person. You need to bring your own linen. If you have a tent, camp sites cost $10. You can get information, licences and maps, and hire fossicking gear here.

There's also a caravan park, where *Kesorn's Food & Gift House* is an unexpected find – it offers Thai food, with mains from $8 to $10.

Anakie
pop 400

About 1km south of the highway, Anakie consists of not much more than a pub, a railway station and a caravan park.

Between the town and the highway is the **Gemfields Information Centre** (☎ 4985 4525), which sells fossicking licences and has mud maps of the gemfields.

The *Gemfields Caravan Park* (☎ 4985 4142) has tent sites for $8, on-site vans for $20 and cabins for $25.

The *Anakie Hotel* (☎ 4985 4100) has cheap motel-style units, some with air-con, and serves bistro meals at nights. *Ramboda Homestead* (☎ 4985 4154) offers dinner, B&B for $35/80.

SPRINGSURE

Springsure, 66km south of Emerald, has an attractive setting with a backdrop of granite mountains and surrounding sunflower fields (the sunflowers are used to produce oil and seed). There's a small **historical museum** by the windmill as you enter town from the south. The **Virgin Rock**, an outcrop of Mt Zamia on the northern outskirts, was named after early settlers claimed to have seen the image of the Virgin Mary in the rock face.

About 10km south-west at Burnside is the **Old Rainworth Fort**, built following the Wills Massacre of 1861 when Aborigines killed 19 whites on Cullin-La-Ringo Station north-west of Springsure.

Places to Stay

The *Springsure Roadhouse & Caravan Park* (☎ 4984 1418) on the south side of town has tent sites for $8 and on-site vans for $25. The *Springsure Zamia Motel* (☎ 4984 1455) on Charles St has units from $48/58 for singles/doubles.

ROLLESTON

Rolleston, on the Dawson Hwy 70km south-east of Springsure, is the northern turn-off for Carnarvon National Park. The town has a couple of service stations, and Rolleston Motors (☎ 4984 3102) is the local RACQ depot. There's a basic caravan park and the *Rolleston Hotel* (☎ 4984 3288) has motel-style units at about $50 for a double.

CARNARVON NATIONAL PARK

Rugged Carnarvon National Park, in the middle of the Great Dividing Range, features dramatic gorge scenery and many Aboriginal rock paintings and carvings. The national park has several sections but most are virtually inaccessible; most people see the impressive Carnarvon Gorge (the other

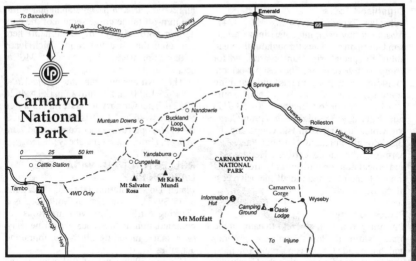

sections are Mt Moffat, Ka Ka Mundi and Salvator Rosa).

There are no buses from anywhere to Carnarvon National Park so you need your own transport to get there. The other option is to join one of the organised tours described further on in this section.

Carnarvon Gorge

The Gorge is stunning, partly because it's an oasis surrounded by drier plains and partly because of its scenic variety, which includes sandstone cliffs, moss gardens, deep pools and rare palms and ferns. There's also lots of wildlife. Aboriginal art can be viewed at three main sites – **Balloon Cave**, the **Art Gallery** and **Cathedral Cave**.

About 3km into the Carnarvon Gorge section there's an information centre and a scenic camping ground. The main walking track starts beside the information centre and follows the Carnarvon Creek through the gorge. Detours lead to various points of interest, such as the Moss Garden (3.6km from the camping ground), Ward's Canyon (4.8km), the Art Gallery (5.6km) and Cathedral Cave (9.3km). You should allow

at least half a day for a visit here and you must bring lunch and water with you as there are no shops.

Getting There & Away From Rolleston to Carnarvon Gorge the road is bitumen for 20km and unsealed for 75km. From Roma via Injune and Wyseby, the road is good bitumen for about 200km then unsealed and fairly rough for the last 45km. After rain, both roads become impassable.

Mt Moffat

To get into the more westerly and rugged Mt Moffatt section of Carnarvon National Park there are two unsealed roads from Injune: one through Womblebank Station, the other via Westgrove Station. There are no through roads from Mt Moffatt to Carnarvon Gorge or to the other remote sections of the park. Mt Moffatt has some beautiful scenery, diverse vegetation and fauna, and **Kenniff Cave**, an important Aboriginal archaeological site with stencil paintings on the rock walls. It's believed Aborigines lived here as long as 19,000 years ago.

Organised Tours

Sunrover Expeditions (☎/fax 3203 4241) runs a six day camping safari into Carnarvon Gorge on set dates throughout the year, although special trips can be arranged for groups of five or more. The cost per person, including transport, meals and camping equipment, is $770. Why Not Tours (☎ 4128 0774 or toll-free ☎ 1800 353 717) runs a six-day/five-night Carnarvon Gorge trip which also takes in Isla Gorge and the Blackdown Tableland National Park. Departures (alternating between Hervey Bay and Rockhampton) are weekly from April to mid-December and the all-inclusive cost of the trip is $480.

Places to Stay

Camping You need a permit to camp at the main National Parks camping ground, which is beside Carnarvon Creek. You must book well ahead by phoning the Carnarvon Gorge rangers (☎ 4984 4505). Camping permits cost $3.50 per person per night. Wood for cooking is scarce, so bring your own gas cooking equipment.

You can also camp at Big Ben camping area, 500m upstream from Cathedral Cave – a 10km walk up the gorge – and walkers can bush camp anywhere in the park beyond Big Ben. Again, permits are required.

In the Mt Moffatt section camping with a permit is allowed at six sites, but you need to be completely self-sufficient and a 4WD is advisable. You also need to book several weeks in advance – phone the Mt Moffatt rangers for details (☎ 4626 3581).

Lodges The *Oasis Lodge* (toll-free ☎ 1800 644 150, fax 4984 4500), near the entrance to the Carnarvon Gorge section of the park, offers safari cabins from $150 a night per person, including all meals and organised activities. From January to March, the cost is $96 per person, not including activities. There's a general store with fuel.

INJUNE

Injune is the southern gateway to the Carnarvon National Park. You can continue along the Carnarvon Developmental Rd to the turn-off to the gorge section of the park 110km north at Wyseby, or turn off here and take the unsealed road which leads 140km north-west into the Mt Moffat section of the park.

The town has one pub, the *Injune Motel* (☎ 4626 1328) and a caravan park (☎ 4626 1222). The Carnarvon Gateway Service Station (☎ 4626 1279) is the local RACQ depot and open every day from around 7 am to 7 pm (from 8 am on Sunday).

ROLLESTON TO BANANA – THE DAWSON HWY

Planet Downs Station (☎ 3265 5022, fax 3265 3978), 30km east of Rolleston, is a working cattle station with luxurious accommodation at $530 per person per day, twin share, including all meals, tours and activities.

About 150km east of Rolleston is the coal mining centre of **Moura**. The town holds an infamous place in Queensland's mining history, being the site of three of Queensland's most tragic mining disasters. In September 1975 13 miners were killed; in July 1986 12 miners were killed; and in the most recent accident, in August 1994, 11 miners were killed. A simple brass memorial, with a statue of a mine worker, stands on the main road opposite the post office. Moura has a couple of motels, a pub and a caravan park. It's another 19km from Moura to Banana.

BANANA TO MILES – THE LEICHHARDT HWY

It's a fairly uneventful 280km south along the Leichhardt Hwy from Banana to Miles.

Banana (the town is named after Banana Gully which, in turn, is named after a bullock buried there) has a caravan park and a service station. *Cooper Downs Cattle Station* (☎ 4996 5276), 37km north-east of Banana, is a working cattle property with upmarket accommodation at $180/300 for singles/doubles. The price includes all meals, and activities such as horse riding and 4WD tours. For similar accommodation see Myella Farm Stay under Baralaba earlier in this chapter.

It's 59km from Banana to **Theodore**, a neat and unexceptional town 1km east of the highway on the banks of the Dawson River. It was built during the 1930s to house workers from the local irrigation projects and has the appearance of being a planned town, with wide streets and central plantations. The **Dawson Folk Museum** in Second Ave has an impressive collection of memorabilia and local history items. It opens by appointment – phone ☎ 4993 1686 or inquire at the nearby pub. The *Hotel Theodore* (☎ 4993 1244), a simple two-storey white pub on The Boulevard, has rooms upstairs with shared bathrooms costing $30/40 for singles/doubles, budget motel units at $40/50 and newer units at $45/60. You can also stay in the former workers' barracks across the road – a bunk bed costs $15 with shared amenities. There's also a caravan park beside the town's small swimming pool.

About 40km south of Theodore is the **Isla Gorge National Park** – a 1.5km gravel road leads off the highway to the **Isla Gorge Lookout** where there is a small self-registration camping ground and a picnic area. The lookout has 180° views over a somewhat eerie landscape of eroded gorges and escarpments. A rough walking track leads from the carpark across a narrow saddle of rock for about 500m with gorges dropping away on either side of the track.

Taroom is 95km south of Theodore on the banks of the Dawson River. Ludwig Leichhardt passed this way on his expedition of 1844, carving his initials into a coolabah tree which still stands in the centre of town. There's a sandstone memorial to Leichhardt in the small park opposite the Ford dealer on the main street and a small **historical society museum** in Kelman St. The *Cattle Camp Motel* (☎ 4627 3412) on Taroom St has units from $46/57 for singles/doubles. There are slightly cheaper units at the *Leichhardt Hotel-Motel* (☎ 4627 3137), a modern timber pub which also serves lunch and dinner daily (no meals

Sunday nights). There's also a small caravan park 1km north of the centre.

Wandoan, a small township just off the highway 59km north of Miles, is dominated by a cluster of huge concrete grain silos. The town has a cafe, a caravan park and a pub.

About 45km south of Wandoan (and 20km north of Miles) and off the Leichhardt Hwy, is *Possum Park* (☎/fax 4627 1651), a 280-hectare bushland property that was an RAAF base and ammunition store during WWII. About 10 years ago, David and Julie Hinds converted the old underground bunkers and admin buildings into a unique accommodation complex. It's a friendly and peaceful place to stay, with a good range of accommodation, walking trails, games rooms, a campers' kitchen, amenities blocks, laundry facilities etc. The bunkers are now simple, self-contained guest units which cost $45 a double and $10 for extras, or there are three former troop-train carriages which also cost $45 a double. Tent sites cost $5 per person per night and caravan sites are $12 a double.

See the Darling Downs chapter for details of Miles and surrounds.

BILOELA

At the junction of the Dawson and Burnett Hwys, Biloela is a modern commercial centre for the surrounding agricultural, pastoral and coal mining industries.

The town centre is on the north side of Gladstone Rd (the Dawson Hwy) with most of the banks, shops and the post office along Kariboe and Callide Sts, parallel to and on the east side of the railway line. The small tourist information centre (☎ 4992 2405), beside the Shell service station on the corner of the two main highways, is open from 9 am to 5 pm on weekdays and from 9 am to noon on Saturday.

Things to See & Do

Biloela has just two distractions but between them they speak volumes on the development of life in Australia. The **Grey-cliffe Homestead**, on the highway on the east side of town, is a National Trust listed building knocked together from slab timber around 1870. The huge **Callide B Power Station** (☎ 4992 9427), 18km east of town, was built slightly more than 100 years later and is a major supplier of electricity to Queensland. There are free tours of the plant departing from the station entrance at 1.30 pm Tuesday to Friday. Visit them both and then spend an evening in deep contemplation.

Places to Stay

Biloela's accommodation options include half a dozen motels and two caravan parks.

The *Boomerang Caravan Park* (☎ 4992 1815) is on Dunn St, just across the railway line from the town centre, and has tent sites from $10 and five on-site cabins from $25 a double; the *Biloela Caravan Park* (☎ 4992 1211) is on the Dawson Hwy just west of the centre and has tent sites from $10 ($12 powered), on-site caravans from $24 and air-con cabins from $32 a double.

The *Apollo Motor Inn* (☎ 4992 1122), on the corner of Gladstone Rd and Rainbow St, is a good modern motel with a pool, bar and restaurant, and singles/doubles from $48/54. It's the one with the cute little windmill out front.

Whitsunday Coast

This chapter covers the coastal strip from Sarina to Bowen and the corresponding hinterland. Mackay is the major town in the region, while the Whitsunday Islands are the major point of interest for travellers.

Accordingly, the chapter is split into two sections: the area around Mackay, which includes the wonderful Eungella National Park and numerous offshore islands such as Brampton, Carlisle, Newry and Rabbit; and the Whitsunday area, which includes the islands themselves as well as the mainland towns and access points for the Whitsundays.

ACTIVITIES

There are trips to the outer Barrier Reef from Mackay, as well as a huge range of boat trips on offer in the Whitsundays. For bushwalkers, the Eungella National Park is a highlight; Cape Hillsborough National Park and Brampton Island also have some excellent walks.

There are a few good golf courses in this area, including those at Mackay and the Laguna Quays Resort. Lindeman Island, South Molle Island and Brampton Island also have courses.

GETTING THERE & AWAY
Air

Mackay has a major domestic airport, and Ansett and Qantas both have regular flights to all the major centres. Brampton Island also has its own airport, and Sunstate (Qantas) flies between Mackay and Brampton.

If you're heading for the Whitsundays, Ansett has frequent flights to Hamilton Island, from where there are transfers to all the other islands. Qantas flies into Proserpine on the mainland – from there you can take a charter flight to the islands or a bus to Airlie Beach or Shute Harbour, just south of Airlie Beach.

There's also the Whitsunday airport, a small airfield near Airlie Beach with regular

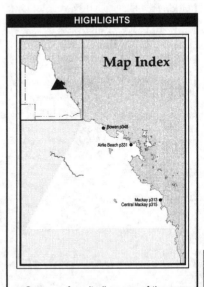

- Get away from it all on one of the many spectacular Whitsunday Islands.
- Try to spot the elusive platypus in the superb Eungella National Park.
- Hire a boat and cruise the Whitsundays at your leisure.

services to the islands. Lindeman Island has its own airstrip.

Bus

The major bus companies have regular services along the Bruce Hwy with stops at all the major towns. They also detour off the highway from Proserpine to Airlie Beach.

Train

The only passenger-carrying railway line in the region is the main coastal line from Brisbane to Cairns; trains on this run stop at Sarina, Mackay, Proserpine and Bowen.

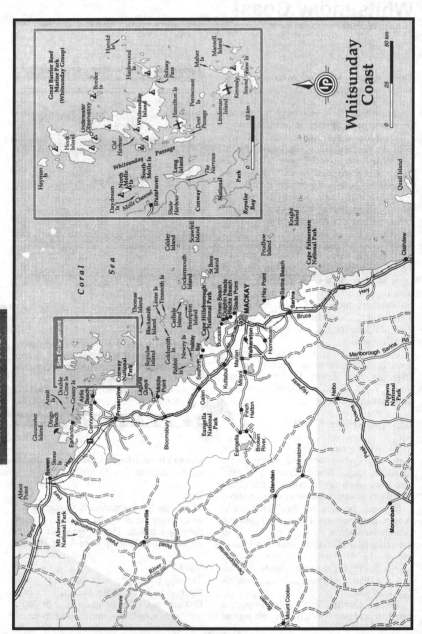

Sea

There are regular ferry services from Mackay to Brampton Island.

Airlie Beach and Shute Harbour are the main launching pads for boat trips to the Whitsundays – see that section for details.

Mackay Area

SARINA
pop 3200

In the foothills of the Connors Range, Sarina is a service centre for the hundreds of surrounding sugar cane farms. On the town's southern outskirts are the huge Plane Creek sugar mill and CSR's ethanol distillery, which produces about 43,000kL of alcohol each year.

There are several roads leading across to the coast from Sarina, and a choice of good beaches includes Armstrong's, Sarina and Campwin.

Places to Stay

The *Sarina Caravan Park* (☎ 4956 1480) on the outskirts of town along Clermont Rd, has tent sites and on-site vans.

The *Tramway Motel* (☎ 4956 2244) on the highway north of the centre has good motel units with singles/doubles at $42/48, and a small pool. In the centre of town, the *Sarina Motor Inn* (☎ 4943 1431) has singles/doubles from $45/50.

Places to Eat

Sarina has one of the quaintest and most enduring eateries in Queensland. Known just as *The Diner*, it's a tiny roadside timber shack with tilt-up wooden panels and bench seats. It is open on weekdays from 4 am to 6 pm and on Saturday from 4 am to 10 am, so if you're driving through you can stop and have an early breakfast with the truckies and cane farmers who've been frequenting the place for the last 70-odd years. Burgers, sangers, pies and kebabs are all available. To find it, take the turn-off to

Clermont and Moranbah in the centre of town – you'll see it on your left, just before the railway crossing.

The *Colonial Corner Takeaway*, on the corner of the highway and Anzac St, just north of the town centre, has sandwiches, pies, drinks and roast chicken. There's also a small but very good fruit and vegie market next door, and *Alcorn's Hot Bread Shop* next to that.

SARINA BEACH

Set on the shores of Sarina Inlet, Sarina Beach is a laid-back little coastal community with good fishing and a long, pleasant beach. There are a couple of motels, a general store and a service station, as well as a surf life-saving club on the beachfront and a boat ramp at the inlet. The town is 13km east of the Bruce Hwy.

At the north end of The Esplanade, the friendly *Sarina Beach Motel* (☎ 4956 6266) on the beachfront has a tennis court, a licensed restaurant and a good swimming pool. Motel units cost from $50/58.

At the south end of The Esplanade, the *Sarina Beach Caravan Park* (☎ 4956 6130) is basically a grassy field with a row of pine trees and an amenities block. Tent sites cost $10.50 ($14.50 powered).

SARINA TO MACKAY

It's 36km from Sarina to Mackay via the Bruce Hwy, but if you have a little time a longer alternative route takes you past a few local points of interest. The brochure *Discover the Homebush Connection*, available from the Mackay information centre, is a guide to the route. Five different attractions are covered by the brochure, but you'll have to do a bit of doubling back if you want to visit them all.

Heading along the Bruce Hwy, take the turn-off to Homebush 2km north of Sarina. This section of the road is quite narrow, and takes you through the cane fields with regular cane-train crossings (July to November) – so drive carefully.

The first stop, **Orchidways**, is an attractively landscaped orchid garden with a kiosk and Devonshire teas; entry costs $8 ($3 for children). Further on is the **Homebush Store**, a craft and pottery gallery (Thursday to Tuesday). The **General Gordon Hotel** is an old country pub surrounded by sugar cane farms. It's a friendly place and a good spot for a cold drink or a counter meal.

About 3km south of the town of Walkerston is **Greenmount Homestead**, a house built by the Cook family in 1915 on the property where Mackay's founder, John Mackay, first settled in 1862. It houses a collection of memorabilia, personal effects and old farm equipment. It's open to the public on weekdays from 9.30 am to 12.30 pm and on Sunday from 10 am to 3.30 pm; entry costs $6 ($2 for children).

If you've always wanted to visit a working sugar cane farm, Merv Harris offers good tours of his **Polstone Sugar Cane Farm**. The two-hour tours start at 1.30 pm on Monday, Wednesday and Friday between May and November, and also at 1.30 pm on Sunday during July and August. The cost is $12 ($6 for children, $30 per family), which includes an educational video, a wagon ride and afternoon tea.

MACKAY
pop 61,000

Mackay is surrounded by sugar cane – a crop which has been farmed here since 1865. One-third of Australia's sugar crop is processed here and loaded onto carriers at one of the world's biggest sugar-loading terminals, at Port Mackay.

Mackay is nothing special, although its town centre is quite attractive and has a number of historic buildings, and there are some good beaches a bus ride away. It's also an access point for the national parks at Cape Hillsborough and Eungella, and for the Great Barrier Reef; there are some interesting islands just an hour or two away, including the popular resort at Brampton Island.

Orientation

Mackay is split into two halves by the broad Pioneer River. The city centre is a compact area, with the main streets laid out in a simple grid on the southern side of the river. Victoria St, the main street, is an attractive thoroughfare with a central plantation, lots of trees and other greenery, paved and decorated footpaths and quite a few historic buildings. The bus terminal is a few hundred metres west of the centre on Milton St. Heading east from the centre, Gordon St, which runs parallel to Victoria St, takes you past Queens Park to Town Beach.

The railway station, the airport and the tourist information centre are all about 3km south of the city centre.

Sydney St takes you across Forgan Bridge to North Mackay and the city's newer suburbs. Mackay Harbour, 6km north of the centre, is predominantly an industrial area, dominated by a massive bulk sugar terminal. The jetty here is the departure point for Roylen's Cruises to the islands and the reef. There's a good beach just south of the harbour.

Mackay's best swimming spots are at the Northern Beaches, about 15km north of the centre.

Information

Mackay's tourist information centre (☎ 4952 2677) is about 3km south of the centre on Nebo Rd (the Bruce Hwy). It is open from 8.30 am to 5 pm weekdays and from 9 am to 4 pm on weekends. The building is a replica of the old Richmond Sugar Mill, and there's a kiosk and souvenir shop inside. While you're here, pick up a copy of the very handy *Things to See & Do in Mackay* brochure.

Mackay's post office is in Sydney St, near the corner with Gordon St and next to Billy Baxter's Cafe. The Globe cafe on Sydney St has Internet and email access.

The Department of Environment office (☎ 4951 8788) is on the corner of Wood and River Sts.

Things to See & Do

Despite the effects of several severe cyclones, particularly one that devastated the city in 1918, Mackay still has a number of

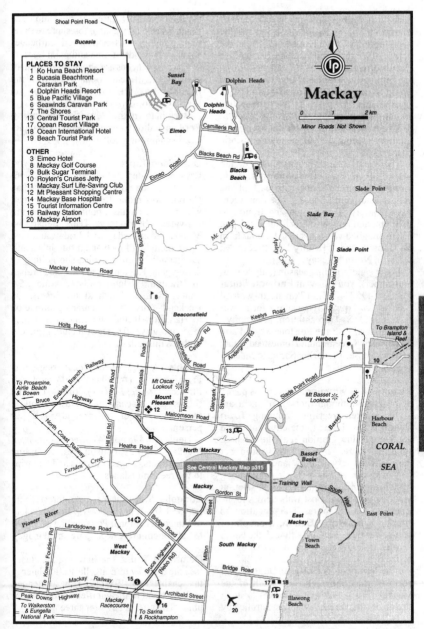

historic buildings around the city centre. The most impressive of these include the neo-Georgian **Court House** (1938), on the corner of Victoria and Brisbane Sts, and the **Commonwealth Bank** (1880) next door, the impressive **Masonic Lodge** (1925) in Wood St, and the **Old Courthouse** (1885) in Brisbane St, which is now the police station. The brochure *A Heritage Walk in Mackay*, available from the tourist centre, guides you around 21 of the town's historic sites.

There are botanic gardens and an orchid house in the attractive **Queen's Park**, along Gordon St about 1km east of the centre. The orchid house is open on weekdays from 10.30 to 11 am and from 2 to 2.30 pm, and on weekends from 2 to 5 pm. There are good views over the harbour from **Mt Basset**, and at **Rotary Lookout** on Mt Oscar in North Mackay.

In the cane-crushing season (July to mid-November), you can visit **Farleigh Sugar Mill** (☎ 4957 4727), 12km north-west of Mackay, at 1 pm on weekdays for a two-hour tour for $10 ($5 children, $25 family). You can also visit the Polstone Sugar Farm and historic Greenmount Homestead, south of Mackay. See the earlier Sarina to Mackay section for details.

Beaches & Swimming Mackay has plenty of beaches, although not all of them are idyllic or even great for swimming. **Town Beach** is the closest to the city centre – to get there, follow Gordon St all the way east from the centre. There is a sandy strip, but the water is very shallow and subsides a long way out at low tides, leaving a long stretch of sand and mud flats – in fact, at low tide you can almost walk across to the islands 4km offshore. The situation is similar at **Illawong Beach**, a couple of kilometres further south, although the beach here is probably the more attractive of the two.

A better option is **Harbour Beach**, 6km north of the centre and just south of the Mackay Boat Harbour. There's a long stretch of sandy beach which is patrolled by

the Mackay Surf Life-Saving Club. The beach is backed by a large foreshore reserve, with picnic tables and wood barbecues among tall stands of pine and palm trees.

The best beaches are about 16km north of Mackay at Blacks Beach, Eimeo and Bucasia. See the following section on Mackay's Northern Beaches for details.

Back in town, the **Memorial Swimming Pool** on Milton St is an excellent Olympic-sized swimming pool.

Organised Tours

Cruises Roylen's Cruises (☎ 4955 3066) runs fast catamaran trips from Mackay Harbour to Credlin Reef on the outer reef, where Roylen's has a pontoon with an underwater observatory. Trips depart on Monday, Wednesday and Friday and cost $100, including lunch and a ride in a semi-submersible; you can hire snorkelling or diving gear. Roylen's also has good cruises to Brampton Island daily, costing $50, which includes lunch at the resort. On weekends only, its catamarans continue on to Hamilton Island and Lindeman Island ($35 one-way, $95 return including lunch) in the Whitsundays.

Flights A couple of local operators, Fredrickson's (☎ 4942 3161) and Air Pioneer (☎ 4957 6661), offer seaplane flights from Mackay out to Bushy Atoll on the Barrier Reef for around $150 per person.

Helijet (☎ 4957 3574) offers flights from Mackay to the Whitsundays, including scenic flights, island transfers and day trips to the reef and islands.

Eungella National Park Reeforest Tours (☎ 4953 1000) has a day trip from Mackay to Eungella National Park costing $45 ($20 to $30 for children, depending on their age).

Gemfields Tours The Illawong Sanctuary (see the Mackay to Eungella section later in this chapter) (☎ 4959 1777) has extended outback tours to the gemfields around Sapphire. The cost is $275 for three days.

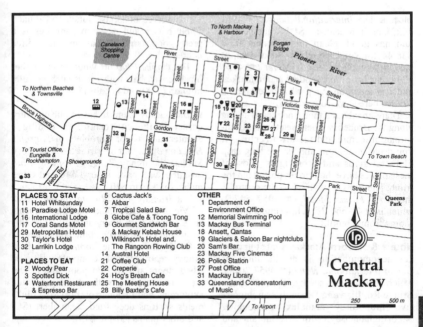

PLACES TO STAY
11 Hotel Whitsunday
15 Paradise Lodge Motel
16 International Lodge
17 Coral Sands Motel
29 Metropolitan Hotel
30 Taylor's Hotel
32 Larrikin Lodge

PLACES TO EAT
2 Woody Pear
3 Spotted Dick
4 Waterfront Restaurant
& Espresso Bar

5 Cactus Jack's
6 Akbar
7 Tropical Salad Bar
8 Globe Cafe & Toong Tong
9 Gourmet Sandwich Bar
& Mackay Kebab House
10 Wilkinson's Hotel and.
The Rangoon Rowing Club
14 Austral Hotel
21 Coffee Club
22 Creperie
24 Hog's Breath Cafe
25 The Meeting House
28 Billy Baxter's Cafe

OTHER
1 Department of
Environment Office
12 Memorial Swimming Pool
13 Mackay Bus Terminal
18 Ansett, Qantas
19 Glaciers & Saloon Bar nightclubs
20 Sam's Bar
23 Mackay Five Cinemas
26 Police Station
27 Post Office
31 Mackay Library
33 Queensland Conservatorium
of Music

Central Mackay

0   250   500 m

Places to Stay

Camping The *Beach Tourist Park* (☎ 4957 4021), on Petrie St at Illawong Beach, about 4km south of the centre, is a large and modern beachfront caravan park with a shop, a good pool, a campers' kitchen and a barbecue area. Tent sites are $13, camp-o-tels are $18 a double and cabins cost from $40.

Across the river and about 2km north of the centre, the *Central Tourist Park* (☎ 4957 6141), at 15 Malcomson St in North Mackay, is another good camping option. It also has a shop and a pool. Tent sites cost $10 a double and self-contained cabins cost from $25 a double.

There are other caravan parks along the Bruce Hwy south of the centre, and at the Northern Beaches – see that section.

Hostels *Larrikin Lodge* (☎ 4951 3728), at 32 Peel St, is a small YHA-associate hostel in an airy timber house. The hostel itself is pretty straightforward, but it's well run and has a friendly atmosphere – it's one of those places where you always seem to meet everyone else. There's a small pool in the backyard. Dorm beds cost $14 and doubles $30; there's also a family room at $40 and units in the backyard with twins for $30.

Pubs *Taylor's Hotel* (☎ 4957 2500), on the corner of Wood and Alfred Sts, has clean single rooms (only) for $15, and the *Metropolitan Hotel* (☎ 4957 2802) on the corner of Gordon and Carlyle Sts has en suite singles/doubles for $40/50 including a light breakfast.

On the corner of Victoria and Macalister Sts, the *Hotel Whitsunday* (☎ 4957 2811) is sort of a cross between a pub and a motel. It's an oldish, three- storey building with a bar and nightclub downstairs, and motel-style rooms from $49.

Motels The *International Lodge* (☎ 4951 1022), at 40 Macalister St, is quite central, and has good, clean motel rooms from $38/44 for singles/doubles. Next door, at No 44, the *Coral Sands Motel* (☎ 4951 1244) is a little more modern and upmarket, and has a swimming pool and restaurant. Rooms here start from $52/57.

There are about a thousand motels strung along the Bruce Hwy between the tourist information centre and the town centre – if you drive in at night, this is one long strip of motel signs and neon lights. Most of these places have their prices posted out the front. The closest of these to the centre is the *Cool Palms Motel* (☎ 4957 5477), which is at 4 Nebo Rd. It has simple budget rooms from $38/40.

Hotels & Resorts Mackay's most upmarket accommodation is at the four-star *Ocean International Hotel* (☎ 4957 2044), which is about 2km south of the centre, at 1 Bridge Rd, Illawong Beach. It's an impressive four-storey complex overlooking Sandringham Bay, with a restaurant and cocktail bar, a pool and a spa. Tariffs start at $221/280.

Right next door, at 5 Bridge Rd, the *Ocean Resort Village* (☎ 4951 3200) is a good mid-range resort with a pool, a barbecue area and half-court tennis courts. There are 34 self-contained apartments in the complex, with prices starting at $68 for two people and $8 for each extra adult.

Places to Eat
Cafes, Delis & Takeaways The *Tropical Salad Bar*, on the corner of Victoria and Sydney Sts, has freshly crushed fruit and vegie juices, smoothies, and good sandwiches and salads.

At 23 Wood St, the narrow and popular *Gourmet Sandwich Bar* is a lunch time bargain, with fresh rolls and sandwiches, and cheap salads and cakes. Nearby, the *Mackay Kebab House* has chicken and lamb kebabs and felafels.

Billy Baxter's Cafe, on the corner of Sydney and Gordon Sts, is a stylish cafe

which serves breakfast, lunch and dinner. Their bacon and eggs on pancakes is a pretty good start to the day, and their coffee is great.

The *Coffee Club* on Wood St is another hip licensed bar, with meals such as fillet mignon ($18) and kebabs ($8).

Pubs Mackay seems to have a pub on every corner in the city centre, so finding a counter meal is not a problem. *Wilkinson's Hotel* on the corner of Victoria and Gregory Sts has the trendy *Rangoon Rowing Club* upstairs, with pasta around $10 and other mains for $18 to $20.

The friendly *Austral Hotel* on the corner of Victoria and Peel Sts has the tropical-style *Coco's* with mains in the $10 to $16 range and cheap meals in the corner bar.

On Sydney St, the *Spotted Dick* is a groovy renovated pub, complete with polished floors and red-felt pool tables. The menu is interesting without being too adventurous, and includes pizzas ($10), light meals such as deep-fried camembert ($8) and other mains ($10 to $13).

Restaurants Mackay's most fashionable restaurant, by a country mile, is the *Waterfront Restaurant and Espresso Bar* (☎ 4957 8131), at 8 River St, amid the warehouses along the river front. The restaurant is licensed and is open for lunch on weekdays and for dinner Monday to Saturday; it's wise to book. The menu has light meals like Greek octopus salad, seafood antipasto and gourmet-style focaccias for $8 to $10, or main courses like fish and chips, baked whole barramundi and roast lamb cutlets for $16 to $25.

At 10 Sydney St, *Toong Tong* is a cosy wood-panelled Thai restaurant with great tom kah gai soup, a wide range of curries and other mains from $10 to $14. For Indian food, try *Akbar* across the road, at No 27. It has seafood dishes from $11 to $13, other mains around $9.50, and vegetable dishes from $5 to $7.50. It also has a small lunch menu with mains from $6 to $7. Both of these places are BYO.

The *Woody Pear* on Wood St is a cosy little BYO restaurant, open for dinner Tuesday to Saturday. The menu is solid but unadventurous, with mains from $18 to $20.

The *Creperie* on Gregory St serves excellent savoury pancakes for around $10, and dessert crêpes with strawberries, apples, blueberries and liqueurs. The *Hog's Breath Cafe* on Wood St, just south of Victoria St, is a saloon-style bar and grill with burgers and snacks for around $10 and steaks and grills for around $18.

The lively *Cactus Jack's* on Victoria St has Mexican meals from $10 to $13 and is licensed. *The Meeting House* on Sydney St, near the Victoria St corner, has a lunch menu with soups, crêpes, quiches and curries from $5 to $7, and interesting dinner mains like Nonya chicken, home-made pastas and fish of the day from $10 to $14. It's a warm and friendly little BYO.

Entertainment

Pubs & Live Music The *Austral Hotel* has live entertainment every Friday and Saturday night, and a great jazz night on the first Thursday of each month.

Sam's Bar, upstairs in the former pub on the corner of Wood and Victoria Sts, is a laid-back meeting place with pool tables, a couple of balconies looking over Wood St and occasional live music.

The Mackay campus of the Queensland Conservatorium of Music, at 418 Shakespeare St, has regular jazz and classical performances throughout the year at lunch time and in the evenings. Call ☎ 4957 3727 for details.

Nightclubs Mackay has a couple of nightclubs along Victoria St in the heart of the city: the *Saloon Bar* at No 99 and *Glaciers* upstairs at No 85. Both have a cover charge on weekends.

Theatre & Cinema The *Mackay Entertainment Centre* on Gordon St is the city's main venue for theatre, ballet, musicals and other live productions. Phone the box office

on ☎ 4957 2255 to find out what's on during your visit.

The *Mackay Five Cinemas* (☎ 4957 3515) at 30 Gordon St screen all the latest flicks.

Things to Buy

Camping World, in Alfred St next to Taylor's Hotel, is well stocked with just about everything for the happy camper.

Getting There & Away

Air Ansett and Qantas have direct flights most days between Mackay and Brisbane ($327), Cairns ($253), Rockhampton ($209) and Townsville ($204), and you can get to most other cities along the coast with Flight West and Sunstate. Ansett also flies from here to Hamilton Island; Qantas flies to Brampton Island and Proserpine.

Ansett's offices are on the corner of Victoria and Macalister Sts; Qantas and Sunstate (☎ 4957 1411) are at 105 Victoria St.

Helijet (☎ 4957 7400) has helicopter and seaplane flights from here to the Whitsunday Islands.

Bus Greyhound Pioneer and McCafferty's buses doing the coastal run all stop at the Mackay Bus Terminal (☎ 4951 3088) on Milton St, about a 10 minute walk west of the town centre. The terminal is open 24 hours, but the booking office's hours are from 7.30 am to 8.30 pm every day.

Average journey times and typical fares are: Cairns, 11 hours ($72); Townsville, eight hours ($47); Airlie Beach, two hours ($24); and Brisbane, 15 hours ($91).

Train The *Sunlander* and *Queenslander* (both from Brisbane to Cairns) stop at Mackay. A sleeper to/from Brisbane on the Sunlander costs $130/199 in economy/1st class; to/from Cairns it's $102/172. The *Queenslander* has only 1st class at $300 to/from Brisbane. The railway station is at Paget, about 3km south of the centre.

Train bookings are handled by any travel agent, including the Mackay Bus Terminal (☎ 4951 3088).

Getting Around

For a taxi, call Mackay Taxis on ☎ 4951 4999. Count on about $10 for a taxi from either the railway station or the airport to the city centre. Thrifty, Avis, Budget and Hertz have counters at the airport. For a cheaper, slightly older car, try Cut Rate Rentals (☎ 4953 1616).

Local bus services are operated by Mackay Transit Coaches (☎ 4957 3330). The Taxi Transit Service (☎ 1800 815 559) takes people to the northern beaches for $3.60 one way.

MACKAY'S NORTHERN BEACHES

The coastline north of Mackay is made up of a series of headlands and bays. The small residential communities strung along here are virtually outer suburbs of Mackay, although they are all about 15km from the centre of town. If you're prepared to do a bit of exploring, there are some reasonably good beaches at these places. There are also a few beachfront caravan parks, holiday flats and resorts in the various centres.

To get to the other northern beaches, turn right at the 'Northern Beaches' sign 4km north of town on the Bruce Hwy.

Black's Beach

At Black's Beach the *Seawinds Caravan Park* (☎ 4954 9334), on Bourke St, is a rambling beachfront park with lots of shade and plenty of grass. It has tent sites and on-site vans. In the same street, the *Blue Pacific Village* (☎ 4954 9090) is a well-kept set of holiday units, with a restaurant, swimming pool and tennis court. Tariffs range from $66 for a studio unit to $120 for a beachfront unit. *The Shores* (☎ 4954 8322), at 9 Pacific Drive, is a set of modern two-bedroom apartments which start from $85 a double plus $12 for each extra person.

Dolphin Heads

At Dolphin Heads, the *Dolphin Heads Resort* (☎ 4954 9666) is the most impressive of the northern beaches resorts. It's a modern resort in a garden setting, overlooking an attractive (but rocky) bay. The

beach isn't much but the pool and spa more than make up for it. The 84 motel-style units cost from $105 to $140, depending on the season. There's also a good restaurant and a courtesy coach.

Eimeo

Beside Dolphin Heads is Eimeo. The *Eimeo Hotel* is a fairly straightforward old pub, but its wonderful location atop a headland makes it a great spot to come to for a meal or just a drink.

Bucasia

Bucasia is just across Sunset Bay from Eimeo and Dolphin Heads, but you have to head all the way back to the main road to get up there. The *Bucasia Beachfront Caravan Park* (☎ 4954 6375) doesn't have much going for it apart from being on the beachfront.

Seemingly in the middle of a residential development, the *Ko Huna Beach Resort* (☎ 4954 8555), on Griffin Ave, is actually a very pleasant resort with a cluster of timber cabins in a tropical garden setting. The resort has catamarans for hire, an excellent swimming pool, a bar, a casual bistro, an à la carte restaurant and a courtesy bus. There are 60 self-contained cabins, with costs ranging from $99 a double to $126 for a family unit.

BRAMPTON ISLAND

About 32km north-east of Mackay, Brampton Island has a popular mid-range resort which was taken over and upgraded by Qantas in 1985, before being sold to P&O Resorts in 1998. Brampton is also the access point for adjacent Carlisle Island, which has a couple of national park campsites.

This is an excellent island to visit if you're considering making a day trip, with quick access from Mackay, good beaches and walking trails and a range of water sports equipment available for hire.

Mountainous Brampton Island is part of the Cumberland Islands group which, together with the Sir James Smith Group further north, is sometimes referred to as the southern Whitsundays. These forested continental islands are very similar in appearance to those of the Whitsundays.

Brampton is a national park and wildlife sanctuary with lush forests surrounded by coral reefs. It is connected to nearby Carlisle Island by a sand bar which you can walk across at low tide. Last century, the island was used by the Queensland government as a nursery for palm trees, and there are still plenty of these fine trees on the island. The Busuttin family, who moved to the island in 1916 to raise goats and horses, established the first resort here in 1933.

Activities
The resort has two swimming pools, tennis courts, a small golf course and a games room. There's a water sports shed on the main beach where day trippers can hire snorkelling gear, catamarans, windsurfers and paddle skis – this equipment is free for resort guests.

The **main beach** at Sandy Point is very pleasant. There's good snorkelling over the coral in the channel between Brampton and Carlisle islands, and at low tide you can wade from one to the other.

There are two excellent **walking trails** on the island. The 7km walk circumnavigates the central section of the island, and side tracks lead down to Dinghy Bay and Oak Bay. The 2km steady climb to the top of 219m Brampton Peak takes about two hours, and is rewarded with fine views along the way and from several lookout points.

Organised Tours
Roylen's *Spirit of Roylen* (☎ 4955 3066) cruises to Credlin Reef every Monday, Wednesday and Friday, costing $100 from Mackay or $85 from Brampton, including lunch. At the reef there's a pontoon with underwater observatory and a semi-submersible. Diving ($65) and snorkelling ($5) facilities are offered on these trips.

Places to Stay
The *Brampton Island Resort* (☎ 4951 4499; for reservations contact P&O Resorts ☎ 13

2469) is popular with couples, families and honeymooners – in fact, just about everyone except the 'young singles' crowd. It's definitely not a party island.

The resort is at Sandy Point in the north of the island, and consists of a cluster of attractive two-storey motel-style units with their own balcony or verandah. Daily costs are $280 for singles/doubles in the older and smaller Carlisle Units. Costs in the newer Blue Lagoon Units are $300 for a garden-view room, and $350 for an ocean-view room.

All rates include breakfast and use of all non-powered equipment for activities including golf, tennis, windsurfing and catamarans. Lunch and dinner costs $48 ($25 for children). Rates are cheaper for five or more nights, and discounted standby rates are available (starting at around $70 per person twin share not including meals).

Places to Eat
Resort guests have the option of paying an additional $48 a day for a package, or paying for meals separately. Day trippers can also eat at the resort.

The main dining room, the *Carlisle Restaurant*, serves buffet-style lunches ($15); dinner is $35 for four courses and à la carte main dishes are around $21 to $24.

For guests not on the meals package or for day visitors, there's also the somewhat gloomy *Rocks Sandwich Bar* downstairs in the main resort complex. It does drinks and ice creams as well as good sandwiches ($5), salads and light meals ($10 to $13), and is open all day.

Getting There & Away
Air Sunstate does the 10 minute flight from Mackay to Brampton for $80 one way.

Sea Roylen's Cruises (☎ 4955 3066) has two fast cats, *Sunbird* and *Spirit of Roylen*, which take turns to make the 55-minute run to Brampton. They leave Mackay Harbour every day at 9 am, and the return fares are $35 or $50 including lunch. A bone-shaking

WHITSUNDAY COAST

mini-railway transports visitors from the wharf to the resort.

CARLISLE ISLAND

Carlisle Island is connected to Brampton Island by a narrow sand bar, and at low tide you can walk or wade from one island to the other. Carlisle is covered in dense eucalypt forests, and there are no walking trails. The wreck of the iron steamship SS *Geelong* lies just off the north-west coast. It ran ashore during a storm in 1888 and two crew members were drowned.

There's a national park campground at Southern Bay, which is directly across from the Brampton resort, and another site further north at Maryport Bay. Both sites are undeveloped and have no facilities, so you must be totally self-sufficient; you could always pop across to the resort at low tide for a meal or a cold beer.

The Southern Bay camp site has a limit of 15 people. Nightly site fees are $3.50 per person. Bookings and permits are handled by the Department of Environment office in Mackay (☎ 4951 8788).

You can get to Carlisle Island by private boat, although you could also go via Brampton – simply wait for low tide and walk across.

OTHER CUMBERLAND ISLANDS

If you fancy a spot of Robinson Crusoeing and have your own boat, or can afford to charter a boat or seaplane, most other islands in the Cumberland Group and the Sir James Smith Group to the north are also national parks.

Scawfell Island, 12km east of Brampton, is the largest island in the group. Refuge Bay on its northern side has a safe anchorage, a beach and a basic campground, but no facilities or water.

About 3km east of Brampton, **Cockermouth Island** also has a good anchorage and beach on its west side, and a basic campground.

In the Sir James Smith group, just northwest of Brampton, **Goldsmith Island** has a safe anchorage on its north-western side,

good beaches and a camp site with toilets, tables and fireplaces.

Contact the Department of Environment office in Mackay (☎ 4951 8788) for all camping permits and information.

CAPE HILLSBOROUGH NATIONAL PARK

This small coastal park, 54km north of Mackay, takes in the rocky, 300m-high Cape Hillsborough and nearby Andrews Point and Wedge Island, which are joined by a causeway at low tide. The scenery ranges from cliffs, a rocky coastline, sand dunes and scrub, to rainforest and woodland. Kangaroos, wallabies, sugar gliders and turtles are quite common in the park.

There's a ranger's office and visitors' information centre (☎ 4959 0410) on the foreshore here, and a good picnic and barbecue area nearby.

There are also some good short walking trails through the park. From near the Cape Hillsborough Resort a trail leads via several lookout points to Andrews Point, and at low tide you can walk across the causeway to Wedge Island. South of the resort is the Hidden Valley rainforest walk, a 1.5km circuit. And from the western end of the foreshore reserve, there's a 1.6km trail to Beachcombers Cove.

Places to Stay

At the end of Cape Hillsborough Rd is the *Cape Hillsborough Resort* (☎ 4959 0152) has tent sites for $10 a double, cabins from $30, and motel-type rooms from $49. Facilities include a swimming pool, a laundry, bar and restaurant.

There's a small national parks campground ($8 per site) at Smalleys Beach, in the western part of the park; you'll need a permit, which can be booked through the ranger's office.

NEWRY ISLAND GROUP

The Newry Island Group is a cluster of small, little-known islands just off the coast from the town of Seaforth, about 40km north-west of Mackay. They are rocky, wild-looking continental islands with grassy open forests and small patches of rainforest. Five of the islands are national parks.

Newry Island
In the centre of the group, 1km-long Newry Island has a small and very low-key resort (☎ 4959 0214) which accommodates only 40 people and has a licensed bar. There are eight basic cabins, all with showers, toilets and tea/coffee-making equipment. These cost $20 per person per night (maximum $60). There are also 20 camping sites at the resort which cost $7 per tent (two people). Camping is only allowed on Newry at the resort site. Meals are also available at the resort – breakfast costs around $5 and dinner around $12.

Most of the visitors to Newry are locals, here for the good fishing and oystering – the beaches aren't great.

Getting There & Away The resort picks up guests from Victor Creek, 4km west of Seaforth, for $15 return.

Other Newry Group Islands
At 4.5 sq km, **Rabbit Island** is the largest island of the Newry Island Group. It has a national parks campground with toilets and a rainwater tank which can be empty in dry times. It also has the only sandy beaches in the group along its eastern side, although because of its proximity to the mainland box jellyfish may be present in summer. From November to January green turtles nest on the beaches here.

There's also a campground with toilets and picnic tables on **Outer Newry Island**. Camping permits for the national park sites are obtained from the Department of Environment office (☎ 4951 8788) in Mackay.

MACKAY TO EUNGELLA
The main access road to the Eungella National Park takes you through the centre of the long and narrow **Pioneer Valley**, which is framed by low mountains on three sides. The first sugar cane was planted here in

1867, and today almost the entire valley is planted with the stuff.

The road takes you through a string of small townships: **Marian** is mainly notable for its enormous sugar mill. At **Mirani**, there's a local history museum in Victoria St behind the library. There's an interesting collection of local history relics, including a tribute to Dame Nellie Melba, whose husband used to manage the Marian sugar mill. The museum is open from Sunday to Friday from 10 am to 4 pm; entry costs $3.

Illawong Fauna Sanctuary (☎ 4959 1777), is an excellent private fauna park at Mirani. Among its attractions are kangaroos, birds, crocodiles (fed at 2.30 pm) and koalas (3.30 pm); it's open daily and costs $10 ($5 children). There's also a children's playground, a swimming pool and homestay accommodation. A day tour from Mackay is $40 ($20).

In the township of **Finch Hatton**, the Cedar Gallery houses an amazing collection of timber sculptures, carvings and furniture by Jack Wilms – it's open every day except Monday. The *Finch Hatton Caravan Park* (☎ 4958 3222) is a well-established park with a swimming pool; tent sites cost $10, on-site vans are $27.

Eungella
From Finch Hatton, it's another 28km to the township of Eungella. The last section of this road climbs suddenly and steeply, with several incredibly sharp corners – trying to tow a caravan up here is not recommended. At the top of the climb, Eungella is a quiet and old-fashioned mountain village with a general store, a chalet and a couple of tea rooms/galleries.

Places to Stay & Eat In Eungella township there's the *Eungella Chalet* (☎ 4958 4509), an old-fashioned guesthouse perched on the edge of the mountain, with views all the way back down the Pioneer Valley. There are clean and simple guest rooms upstairs with shared bathrooms, costing $30/45 for singles/doubles or $15 per person for backpackers. Motel-style units are $65 a double. Up on the hill behind the chalet are modern one and two-bedroom timber cabins which cost $80 a double or $99 for a family. The chalet has a cosy bar and a dining room which serves straightforward meals.

There are also several tea rooms in Eungella. The *Rainforest Cafe-Gallery* is a simple little place with a balcony and lovely valley views. Nearby is the *Coach House Gallery*, a stylish Queenslander with broad verandahs, Devonshire teas, lunches and a collection of local arts and crafts. Both are closed on Monday.

EUNGELLA NATIONAL PARK

Eungella (pronounced *young*-gulla, meaning Land of Clouds) covers nearly 500 sq km of the Clarke Range, climbing to 1280m at Mt Dalrymple. The area has been cut off from other rainforest areas for probably 30,000 years and has at least six life forms which exist nowhere else: the Eungella honeyeater (a bird), the orange-sided skink (a lizard), the Mackay tulip oak (a tall, buttressed rainforest tree) and three species of frog, one of which – the Eungella gastric brooding frog – has a highly unusual habit of incubating its eggs in its stomach and then giving birth by spitting out the tadpoles!

Most days of the year you can be pretty sure of seeing platypuses in the pools near the Broken River bridge and campground, 84km west of Mackay. The best times to see the creatures are the hours immediately after dawn and before dark; you must remain patiently silent and still.

Finch Hatton Gorge

About 27km west of Mirani, just before the town of Finch Hatton, is the turn-off for the Finch Hatton Gorge section of the park. The last 2 or 3km of the 12km drive from the main road are quite rough and involve several creek crossings. At the car park, there's a good picnic area with push-button gas barbecues, and a couple of small swimming holes where the creek tumbles over huge boulders. A 1.6km walking trail leads

from the picnic area to Araluen Falls, with its spectacular waterfalls and swimming holes. There's a kiosk 1km south of the gorge, and a bush retreat 2km south (see Places to Stay & Eat).

Broken River

There's an information office, campground, picnic area and kiosk near the bridge over **Broken River**, 5km south of the Eungella township. There's a platypus viewing platform near the bridge, and a short walk downstream there's a good swimming hole. Near the bridge colourful birds are prolific. Park rangers sometimes lead wildlife-watching sessions, or spotlighting trips to pick out nocturnal animals.

There are some excellent walking tracks which start from either the Broken River picnic ground, or along the road between Broken River and Eungella. They include a rainforest discovery circuit (2.1km), the Sky Window circuit (2.5km) and the Palm Walk (8km). The staff at the information office are friendly and helpful, and can advise you on the various walks and provide you with maps. The office, which has displays on the park's wildlife, is staffed daily between 7 and 8 am, 11 am and noon, and 3 and 3.30 pm.

Places to Stay & Eat

Finch Hatton Gorge Just a couple of kilometres from the Finch Hatton Gorge is the *Platypus Bush Camp* (☎ 4958 3204). It's a bush retreat in a beautiful forest setting beside a creek. You can camp here for $5 per person, or there are three slab-timber huts which are basically roofed-over sleeping platforms, sleeping up to three people and costing $45 a night. There are communal cooking shelters, hot showers and toilets, and you need to bring your own food and linen. If you phone from Finch Hatton township someone will pick you up.

Broken River The national park campground is beside Broken River, about 500m past the information centre and kiosk. You'll need to get camping permits ($3.50 per person per night) from the information office at Broken River (☎ 4958 4552). It's advisable to book during school holiday periods.

On the other side of Broken River, the *Broken River Mountain Retreat* (☎ 4958 4528) has modern timber cabins set in landscaped grounds. Motel-style rooms are from $55 and one and two-bedroom self-contained cabins sleep up to six people and cost from $75 a double, plus $10 for extras. The retreat has its own restaurant and organises various tours for its guests.

Getting There & Away

There are no buses to Eungella, but hitching is quite possible. Reeforest Adventure Tours (☎ 4953 1000) runs day trips from Mackay costing $45 ($20 to $30 for children depending on age).

Whitsundays Area

The 74 Whitsunday Islands are probably the best known of Queensland's islands. The group was named by Captain Cook, who sailed through here on 3 July 1770. They're scattered on both sides of the Whitsunday Passage and are all within 50km of Shute Harbour. The Whitsundays are mostly continental islands, the tips of underwater mountains, but many of them have fringing coral reefs. The actual Barrier Reef is at least 60km out from Shute Harbour; Hook Reef is the nearest part of it.

The islands – mostly hilly and wooded – and the passages between them are simply beautiful, and while seven of the islands are developed with tourist resorts, most are uninhabited and several offer the chance of some back-to-nature beach camping and bushwalking. All but four of the Whitsundays are predominantly or completely national park. The exceptions are Dent Island, and the resort islands of Hamilton, Daydream and Hayman. The other main resorts are on South Molle, Lindeman, Long and Hook islands.

Information

Airlie Beach is the mainland centre for the Whitsundays and there are plenty of travel agents and tour operators based here.

The Whitsunday District office of the Department of Environment (☎ 4946 7022) is 2km past Airlie Beach on the road to Shute Harbour. This office deals with camping permits for the islands, and the staff here are generally very helpful and good sources of information on a wide range of topics. This is a good place to visit when you first arrive, particularly for travellers interested in exploring the islands independently rather than joining a packaged tour.

Books & Maps *100 Magic Miles of the Great Barrier Reef – The Whitsunday Islands* by David Colfelt is sometimes referred to as the bible to the Whitsundays. Now in its 5th edition, this large format paperback guide has great colour photos, articles on the islands and resorts, features on diving, sailing, fishing, camping and natural history, and an exhaustive collection of charts with descriptions of all boat anchorages around the islands. Colfelt's book costs around $50 and is widely available.

Two of the best maps to this area are the Travelog *Great Barrier Reef* map, which has a *Whitsunday Passage* map on the back, and Sunmap's *Australia's Whitsundays*.

Zoning The Great Barrier Reef Marine Park Authority's zoning system divides the waters around the Whitsundays into five different zones, each with certain restrictions on what you can and can't do. The widely-available brochure *Boating in the Whitsundays* contains a colour-coded map which clearly shows the different zones, with an accompanying chart explaining the restrictions which apply to each.

Briefly, most of the waters around the Whitsundays are zoned General Use A and B, with some important exceptions around the islands. In those areas Marine National Park A and B zoning applies. For the visitor, the main difference is that although both zones are 'look but don't take', Zone A permits limited fishing whereas Zone B permits no fishing at all.

Activities

Diving & Snorkelling There are at least five companies offering learn-to-dive courses in Airlie Beach, and most of the island resorts also have their own dive schools.

For certified divers, there's a huge range of boats offering diving trips to the islands, or further out to the outer reef areas.

Fishing Trips Numerous charter boats offer fishing trips out of Shute Harbour. They include the following:

GFV *Invader* (☎ 4946 6848 or ☎ 018 186 900) – reef and gamefishing trips, $155 all inclusive
MV *Jane II* (☎ 4946 6224) – all inclusive day trips, $64 ($32 for children)
MV *Moruya* (☎ 4946 6665 or ☎ 018 185 653) – day trips, $64 all inclusive

You could also hire your own boat. There are quite a few operators hiring boats with fishing gear, including Quinns Boat House (☎ 0418 182 584) at Shingley Beach. They have dinghies for $40 a day plus fuel.

Sail Yourself/Bareboat Charters Sailing through the Whitsunday Passage in 1770, Cook wrote that 'the whole passage is one continued safe harbour'. In fact, stiff breezes and fast flowing tides can produce some tricky conditions for small craft but, with a little care, the Whitsundays offer superb sailing and bareboat charters have become enormously popular. 'Bareboat' doesn't refer to what you wear on board – it simply means you rent the boat without skipper, crew or provisions.

While the charter companies don't actually require potential renters to have any previous sailing experience, it is definitely advisable. As mentioned, conditions can become tricky, especially if the weather turns a bit nasty – chartered boats are run aground on a regular basis. If you lack ex-perience, it's a good idea to hire an experienced skipper at least for the first day, although even then it's difficult to absorb the amount of instruction you are given in such a short time.

The operators usually require a $500 bond, payable on arrival and refunded after the boat is returned undamaged. Bedding is usually supplied and provisions can also be provided if you wish. Most companies have a minimum hire period of five days.

Most of the charter companies have a wide range of yachts and cruisers available. You'll pay around $240 a day in the high season for a Holland 25 yacht which sleeps two people; around $380 a day for a Robertson 950 yacht which sleeps up to four; around $530 a day for a Hunter 376 which sleeps up to six people; and around $400 a day for a Flybridge 35 cruiser which sleeps up to eight people.

There are a number of bareboat charter companies at Airlie Beach, including:

Mandalay Boat Charters
   (☎ 4946 6298 or ☎ 1800 075 123), PO Box 273, Airlie Beach, Qld 4802
Prosail Whitsunday
   (☎ 4946 7533), Shute Harbour
Sail Whitsunday
   (☎ 4946 7070 or ☎ 1800 075 045), PO Box 929, Airlie Beach, Qld 4802
Whitsunday Escape
   (☎ 4946 7367 or ☎ 1800 075 145), PO Box 719, Airlie Beach, Qld 4802

Organised Tours

Island & Reef Cruises All boat trips to the Whitsundays depart from either Shute Harbour or the Abel Point Marina near Airlie Beach. There's a bamboozling array of trips on offer, and all the places to stay and agencies have dozens of brochures. Most of the cruise operators do coach pick-ups from Airlie Beach and Cannonvale. You can take a bus to Shute Harbour, or you can leave your car in the Shute Harbour car park for $7 for 24 hours. There's a lock-up car park a few hundred metres back along the road by the Shell service station, costing $5 from 8 am to 5 pm or $8 for 24 hours.

All of the boats and trips are different, so it's worth speaking to a couple of booking agents to find out what trip will suit you. There are leisurely sailing cruises to uninhabited islands, high-speed diving trips to the outer reefs, and cruises that take in several different destinations. Most day trips include activities like snorkelling and boom netting, with scuba diving as an optional extra. Children generally pay half fare.

The following are some of the day trips on offer:

Apollo
(Phone ☎ 1800 635 334 for details) This famous 80-foot veteran Sydney-to-Hobart racer does day trips to Langford Reef or Whitehaven Beach for $49 each or $80 for the two.

Fantasea
(Phone ☎ 4946 5111 for bookings) Outer Great Barrier Reef cruises on the high-speed catamaran *Fantasea 2000* cost $117, including smorgasbord lunch, snorkelling and rides in a semi-submersible.

Jade
(Phone ☎ 4946 6848) A popular 46-foot sailing cat that does cruises to South Molle, Sunlovers Reef and Daydream Island for $55, or to Langford Reef, also for $55, or $85 for the two trips.

Nari
(Phone ☎ 4946 6224 for details) The twin-keeled *Nari* operates sailing cruises to Nari Beach in Cid Harbour, costing $49 including lunch and snorkelling gear ($59 for divers).

Providence V
(Phone ☎ 1800 655 346 for bookings) This modern replica of an old gaff-rigged Gloucester schooner sails around the islands for three days; the cost is $250, which includes all meals and snorkelling gear.

There are also dozens of overnight or longer trips around the islands on offer. Meals and snorkelling gear are usually included, and you either sleep on board or in tents on an island. These include:

Anaconda II
(Phone ☎ 4946 6032 or toll-free ☎ 1800 075 035) This nine-cabin maxi-yacht has three-day/three-night cruises to Bait, Black and/or Fairey Reefs for up to 20 passengers. Cruises cost $325 for snorkellers, $365 for divers with their own gear or $410 for divers with gear supplied.

Prosail
(Call ☎ 4946 5433 to book) Prosail runs adventure sailing cruises for the 18-to-35s market on a range of modern sailing yachts, costing from $295 per person for three days.

Flights Air Whitsundays Seaplanes (☎ 4946 9130), based at the Whitsunday airport, has the only day trip to exclusive Hayman Island. For $150 per person you can fly in one of its seaplanes to the island, where you have use of all the resort facilities for the day and get a $30 credit towards your lunch. It also does three-hour trips to Hardy Reef ($175) and 1½ hour trips to beautiful Whitehaven Beach ($120), or you can combine the two in one day for $225.

Also based at the Whitsunday airport, Helireef (☎ 4946 9102) has helicopter flights out to Fantasea's huge Reef World pontoon on the outer reef. The fare is $195, which includes snorkelling gear, rides in the glass-bottomed boat and semi-submersible, lunch and the Fantasea fast cat back to Shute. To fly both ways it's $295.

Places to Stay

Camping Although accommodation at the island resorts is mostly expensive, it's possible to camp on several islands at national parks campsites. In addition, Hook Island has a privately run campground. You must be self-sufficient to camp in these national parks sites; some have toilets, but only a few have drinking water, and then not always year-round. You're advised to take 5L of water per person per day, plus three days' extra supply in case you get stuck. You should also have a fuel stove – wood fires are banned on all islands. There's a national parks leaflet which describes the various sites, and provides detailed information on what to take and do.

Camping permits are available from the Department of Environment office (see the information section earlier) and cost just

Sailing – The Basics

Picture this: the sun's already risen to another beautiful day in the Whitsundays. After an al fresco breakfast on deck with your companions you hoist the mainsail and head for Whitsunday Island, where you spend a lazy day on the white-crystal sand of Whitehaven Beach.

Sounds ideal, doesn't it? And the best thing about this picture is you can be in it, even if you don't know how to sail.

You don't have to be Dennis Connor to hire a yacht on the Whitsundays. A lot of the people who hire yachts here have little or no sailing experience when they start. The bareboat charter companies can teach you all you need to know before you set sail.

Getting the basics of sailing is not so difficult – we're not talking about entering the America's Cup here – and the following will give you insight into what to expect:

Wind One thing you'll learn quickly about sailing is that the wind is rarely constant and from the same direction. It requires constant attention. Take note of where the wind is coming from. Look up to the top of the mast, there should be a flag or some other wind indicator up there. Good sailors don't need to look, they can feel it on their face – practise that, but look up to make sure.

Also, look for wind changes on the water's surface: a darkening of the water indicates an increase in wind strength.

Terminology If this is going to be your only sailing experience then you're not going to need to know all the terminology. The US Navy uses left (port) and right (starboard), so you can do the same. Windward (the side the wind is coming from) and leeward (opposite) are important to know, and you should know what a mainsail and headsail are. After a few hours with an experienced yachtie you'll learn a sheet is a line (or rope), a shroud is a wire line holding the rigging in place, trimming (the sails) has nothing to do with your waistline, and luff (forward edge of the sail) may have four letters but the kids can safely say it without offending anybody.

Sails The boat will come with a basic rig of a mainsail and headsail, and there won't be any need to change these. Usually, the headsail will be self-furling, which means that it doesn't need to be pulled down when not it use (it simply rolls up like a blind).

Safety Most of the charter companies require you to report in by radio twice daily. This provides plenty of opportunity to get answers to any sailing questions and also report any problems – one company we spoke to said, typically, they had only one boat sustain hull damage a year. There is also an emergency service based at Airlie Beach that you can reach by radio 24 hours a day. When you hire the boat ensure it has appropriate emergency gear and you are familiar with where it is and how to use it.

If somebody falls overboard shout out 'MAN OVERBOARD' straightaway to get all crew on deck. Somebody other than the helmsman (the person steering) should point to the person in the water all the time, never losing sight of them. If you feel confident handling the boat you'll need to tack back around; otherwise drop your sail and turn the engine on to pick the person up.

Steering Usually, the smaller/older boats have a tiller (a steering arm attached to the rudder), although the bigger boats will likely have a steering wheel. When steering with a tiller the boat will move in the opposite direction to the way you move it: move it to the right and the boat will move left, move it to the left and it'll go right. However, with a steering wheel it works just like your car, steer right and you go right, etc. The best way to ensure you steer a straight line is to pick an object off in the distance (most of the time you'll be surrounded by islands on the Whitsundays) and aim for it.

The object of sailing is to harness the wind, not sail straight into it. Turn into the wind if you're in danger of capsizing, but while steering normally you should avoid the 45° either side of true wind. If you're sailing at about 45° then you're sailing 'close to the wind' (on the fastest course).

On each of the sails there are several tell-tales (pieces of wool, hanging off it like loose threads) that should, ideally, be streaming aft (to the back). If they aren't, you're pointing the boat too close to the wind or too far off it and you'll need to make a course correction.

Keeping Balance The keel under the boat helps keep it balanced when the sails are full of wind and prevent it from capsizing. If there is a lot of wind it will be necessary to position the crew on the windward side of the boat to help with the counterbalance. If you don't want so much wind you can steer slightly towards the wind (called luffing) until the gust eases, or you can limit its effect by easing the mainsail.

Navigation No, you won't need to break out the sextant, but you will have to know how to read a map (which will be provided with the boat). The degree of navigational skills you'll need will depend on your objective. Most of the time you'll be able to navigate visually – you'll be amazed how much the 'skyscrapers' on Hamilton Island stand out.

Trimming Getting a sail properly trimmed is important for efficiency and can be a com-

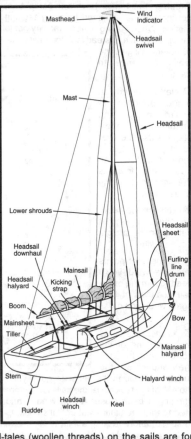

plicated business to get right. Not all the tell-tales (woollen threads) on the sails are for checking the boat's course – the precise tell-tales we're talking about here should be pointed out to you during your training on the boat – some are for checking the sail's trim (tightness). A sail can be too tight and too loose; getting it right will improve your boat speed. Generally, you should trim the headsail first and adjust the mainsail's trim (possibly by also adjusting the mainsheet – the rope holding down the boom, at the back) to match it.

Anchoring After the tension of sailing 'solo' for the first time you shouldn't relax completely when you reach your mooring and simply drop anchor. Anchoring needs to be handled well, both because of the damage you can do to the boat if it slips during the night and because of the potential damage you can do to the environment on the sea floor. You'll be given detailed advice on how to do this tricky procedure when you hire the boat.

WHITSUNDAY COAST

Tacking Tacking is how you get a boat upwind, and is achieved by a zig-zagging motion. When setting up for a tack try not to tack into a wave, instead look for a flat piece of water – it'll give the least resistance to the turn.

❶ Alert everybody on board about what you're doing and ensure they understand. Push the tiller (slowly at first and more firmly as the boat turns) towards the sails, or turn the wheel away.

❷ Release the headsail sheets (lines) just before turning straight into the wind.

❸ As the boat points into the wind you'll need to trim the mainsail, and then let it out again when you cross the wind.

❹ As the sails cross the centreline of the boat, begin to ease the angle of the rudder – although it's better to go beyond the 45° of the tack to get the sails full, before bringing it back closer to the wind – and start to trim the sails. Wait until it's back up to speed before tacking again.

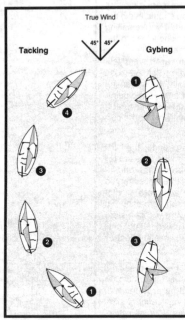

True Wind

Tacking

Gybing

45° 45°

Gybing A gybe is essentially the reverse of a tack, although it's a slightly trickier manoeuvre. If you find yourself heading in the wrong direction on a downwind leg you gybe to bring the wind in from the other side.

❶ Alert everybody on board about what you're doing and ensure they understand. Pull the tiller (slowly at first and more firmly as the boat turns) away from the sails, or turn the wheel towards the sails. At the same time start to recover the mainsail, pulling in about half of the mainsheet (mainsail line).

❷ Look out for the boom (and control it) as the sails cross the centre of the boat.

❸ The tiller needs to be centralised – if this is done late it might be necessary to check the boat with some opposite rudder for a second or two. As the wind hits the mainsail, ease the mainsheet out to take some of its force – it's easy to sustain rigging damage if you simply let the mainsail go. Trim the sails.

$3.50 per person per night; numbers are limited for each camping area.

Get to your island with a day cruise boat (use the sail-around ones rather than the resort boats) or with Whitsunday Allover Water Taxis. Island Camping Connection (☎ 4946 5255) can drop you at Long, North or South Molle, Planton or Tancred islands for $35 return (minimum of two people).

If you've got camping gear give it a try – Robinson Crusoeing on your very own island can be a lot of fun. The booking offices in Airlie Beach are helpful and can advise which boats are best to go where.

The possibilities for camping in national parks in the Whitsundays are summarised in the table. Note that some sites are subject to seasonal closures because of bird nesting.

Whitsunday Islands Campgrounds

Island	Location	People	Drinking water
Tancred	northern end	4	no**
North Molle	Cockatoo Beach	36	seasonal
Whitsunday	Dugong Beach	30	yes, but may be seasonal
	Sawmill Beach	15	seasonal
	Joe's Beach	6	no
Thomas	Sea Eagle Beach	4	no**
Shaw	Neck Bay Beach	12	no**
South Repulse	western beach	18	no**
Gloucester*	Bona Bay	15	yes
Armit*	western beach	5	no
Saddleback*	western side	6	no**
	Olden*	4	no**
Lindeman	Boat Port	6	no
	Planton	4	no**
Henning	Northern Spit	20	no
Long	Sandy Bay	6	no
South Molle	Sandy Bay	15	no
Hook	Maureens Cove	20	no
	Denman	4	no**

* Northern islands like Armit, Gloucester, Olden and Saddleback are harder to reach since the water taxi and cruises from Shute Harbour don't usually go there. Glouces- ter and Saddleback are best reached from Earlando, Dingo Beach or Bowen.
** Bush camping site. No facilities.

Resorts There are resorts on seven of the Whitsunday Islands. Most were built or re- vamped during the tourism boom of the 1980s, and with the exception of the Hook Island resort they are reasonably expensive. All the resorts are quite different, ranging from the five-star luxury of the Hayman Island resort to the simple little beachfront huts of the eco-friendly Long Island Wilderness Lodge, and from the high-rise development of Hamilton Island to the simple cabins of Hook Island.

The rates quoted in this chapter are the standard rates, but hardly anyone pays these. Most travel agents can put together a range of discounted package deals which combine air fares and/or transfers to the resort with accommodation and, in some cases, meals.

It's also worth noting that, unless they're full, almost all of the resorts offer heavily discounted stand-by rates. The amount of discount depends on the time of year, but they can be significant. The limiting factor is that you usually have to book less than five days in advance. All the tourist agents in Airlie Beach have brochures.

Getting There & Around

Air The two main airports for the Whitsun- days are Hamilton Island and Proserpine. Only Ansett flies into Hamilton Island, whereas both Ansett and Qantas fly into Proserpine. See those sections for more details.

The Whitsunday airport also has regular flights from the mainland to the island – light planes, seaplanes and helicopters. See

Getting There & Away in the Airlie Beach section for details. Lindeman Island also has its own airstrip.

Bus Greyhound Pioneer and McCafferty's both have bus services that detour off the Bruce Hwy to Airlie Beach. Local bus services operate between Proserpine, Airlie Beach and Shute Harbour.

Boat The Whitsunday Sailing Club is at the end of Airlie Beach Esplanade. Check the notice boards at the Abel Point Marina for possible rides or crewing opportunities on passing yachts.

The services to the islands all operate out of Shute Harbour or the Abel Point Marina near Airlie Beach. Fantasea Cruises, Whitsunday Allover and Seatrek are the major operators for transfers to the islands – see the Getting There & Away sections for the individual islands for details of water taxis and ferries.

LAGUNA QUAYS

Two-thirds of the way from Mackay to Proserpine, there are two turn-offs from the Bruce Hwy leading to Midge Point and Laguna Quays on the coast.

A couple of kilometres north, Laguna Quays is an elaborate and upmarket tourism resort and residential development, centred around a marina and a golf course. The resort's **Turtle Point golf course** is one of the best resort courses in Australia. It's the home of the rich Australian Skins Tournament, held every year in February; it's open to the general public, and 18 holes costs $55 (hire of clubs is another $20).

The *Laguna Quays Resort* (☎ 4947 7777) is very impressive. There are several restaurants and cocktail bars, a 'beach club' with a lagoon and a range of water sports equipment, a huge swimming pool, tennis courts, a 'kid's club' which organises all sorts of games and activities for children, and the great golf course. Daily tariffs start at $360 for a room and $270 for a one-bedroom villa.

Despite all this, it's hard to figure out why you would stay here unless you're an absolute golf nut. It's a scenic and isolated setting, but the beaches aren't great and if you want to take a boat to the Whitsundays, you have to drive to Airlie Beach or Shute Harbour first. For these prices, you could be out on one of the island resorts.

PROSERPINE
pop 3000
The turn-off point for Airlie Beach and the Whitsundays, Proserpine is pretty typical of the numerous sugar-mill towns that are strung along the Bruce Hwy in north Queensland. A tourist information centre (☎ 4945 3711) on the highway on the Mackay side of town provides information about the Whitsundays and the surrounding region. It's open daily from 10 am to 6 pm. The **Proserpine Cultural Hall** is a theatre complex which also acts as the local cinema, screening a different movie each week. At the end of Main St, before the railway crossing, the **Proserpine Historical Museum** is open on Tuesday and Thursday from 9.30 am to 4 pm.

During the processing season, from June to November, there are tours of the **Proserpine Sugar Mill** every weekday at 10 am and 2 pm. Bookings can be made through the information centre.

Places to Stay
There are three or four motels along the Bruce Hwy south of Proserpine; most people head for the coast.

Getting There & Away
Air Sunstate (Qantas) has direct flights between Proserpine and Brisbane ($346), Mackay ($86), Townsville ($170) and Cairns ($240). The airport is 14km south of town.

Bus Sampsons (☎ 4945 2377) has around 20 services daily from Proserpine to Airlie Beach ($6.50) and Shute Harbour between 6 am and about 6 pm.

Train Proserpine is on the Brisbane-Cairns line; the *Sunlander*, *Spirit of the Tropics* and *Queenslander* trains all stop here.

AIRLIE BEACH
pop 3100

Airlie Beach, 25km north-west of Proserpine, is the gateway to the Whitsunday Islands. It's a small but lively centre which has grown phenomenally over the past 10 years or so, a pattern which seems set to continue for some years to come. The whole town revolves around tourism and pleasure boating, and it attracts a diverse bunch of boaties, backpackers, tourists, and divers, all of whom are here for a good time. Apart from being the main access point for the Whitsundays, Airlie's attributes include a good range of accommodation – from backpackers' hostels to resorts – plenty of good eateries and restaurants, a broad range of activities on offer, and a lively nightlife.

Airlie Beach also has a reputation as a centre for learning to scuba dive. Whale-watching boat trips, between July and September, are another attraction. Despite all the recent development, it's still a small place which has managed to retain something of its relaxed air.

Orientation

Airlie Beach itself stretches for less than 1km from end to end. Shute Harbour Rd runs through the centre of town, and you'll find just about everything of importance along here.

The town is backed by low hills and set back from Airlie Bay, which has two small crescent-shaped beaches separated by a creek. There's plenty of sand for sunbakers, but these aren't great beaches for swimming, especially at low tide when the water subsides to leave a shallow and muddy strip.

Long-distance buses stop in the car park in the centre, between Shute Harbour Rd and the bay. Boats to the Whitsundays leave from either Shute Harbour, 8km east of

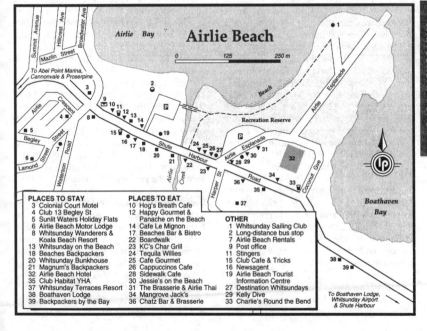

PLACES TO STAY	PLACES TO EAT
3 Colonial Court Motel	10 Hog's Breath Cafe
4 Club 13 Begley St	12 Happy Gourmet &
5 Sunlit Waters Holiday Flats	Panache on the Beach
6 Airlie Beach Motor Lodge	14 Cafe Le Mignon
8 Whitsunday Wanderers &	17 Beaches Bar & Bistro
Koala Beach Resort	22 Boardwalk
13 Whitsunday on the Beach	23 KC's Char Grill
18 Beaches Backpackers	24 Tequila Willies
20 Whitsunday Bunkhouse	25 Cafe Gourmet
21 Magnum's Backpackers	26 Cappuccinos Cafe
32 Airlie Beach Hotel	28 Sidewalk Cafe
35 Club Habitat YHA	30 Jessie's on the Beach
37 Whitsunday Terraces Resort	31 The Brasserie & Airlie Thai
38 Boathaven Lodge	34 Mangrove Jack's
39 Backpackers by the Bay	36 Chatz Bar & Brasserie

OTHER
1 Whitsunday Sailing Club
2 Long-distance bus stop
7 Airlie Beach Rentals
9 Post office
11 Stingers
15 Club Cafe & Tricks
16 Newsagent
19 Airlie Beach Tourist
   Information Centre
27 Destination Whitsundays
29 Kelly Dive
33 Charlie's Round the Bend

Airlie Beach, or from the Abel Point Marina, 1km west.

Before you arrive in Airlie Beach, you pass through Cannonvale, which is virtually a newer (and bigger) satellite suburb of Airlie Beach. Cannonvale sprawls along the Proserpine-Shute Harbour road for about 4km and is growing quickly, with several housing and industrial developments on its outskirts. Cannonvale has a good golf course, several shopping centres, a handful of resorts and restaurants and a beach with a stinger enclosure.

Information

Tourist Information While every second shopfront in Airlie Beach claims to be a 'tourist information centre', these places are all privately run tour-booking and ticket agencies. They include the Airlie Beach Tourist Information Centre (☎ 4946 6665) on Shute Harbour Rd, near the bus stop, and Destination Whitsundays (☎ 4946 6846), upstairs on the corner of Shute Harbour Rd and Airlie Esplanade. All of the places to stay can also give advice and book tours, boat trips and transport to the islands.

The Department of Environment office (☎ 4946 7022), on the corner of Shute Harbour Rd and Mandalay Rd, about 3km past Airlie Beach towards Shute Harbour, is open from 8 am to 5 pm Monday to Friday and at varying weekend hours. It deals with camping bookings and permits for Conway and the Whitsunday Islands national parks. The staff here are very helpful and can advise you on which islands to camp on, how to get there, what to take etc.

Bookshops The newsagency on Shute Harbour Rd has a large selection of holiday reading and beach literature, as well as a small travel section with a range of books on the Whitsundays. It also stocks a wide range of interstate and overseas newspapers.

Laundry The Airlie Beach Coin Laundromat is in the Beach Plaza shopping arcade, and is open daily from 7 am to 9 pm.

Things to See & Do

Wildlife Park The Wildlife Park has a large collection of Australian mammals, birds and reptiles, with various shows each day such as crocodile-feeding, koala-feeding and snake handling. The park is open daily from 8.30 am to 5 pm and entry costs $15 ($7 children). It's 8km west of Airlie Beach, and a courtesy bus does pick-ups and drop-offs from wherever you're staying.

Diving This is one of the best and most popular places to learn to dive, and four outfits in Airlie Beach offer scuba-diving certificate courses. Costs for open-water courses vary from $250 to $500, but note that with the cheaper courses you spend most of your time in the pool and classroom and you might do only four or five dives. For another couple of hundred dollars, you get to enjoy what you've learned and, more importantly, build up invaluable experience with 10 or more dives. Generally, courses involve two or three days' tuition on the mainland with the rest of the time diving on the Great Barrier Reef – ask whether meals and accommodation are included in the price. Book where you are staying, or at one of the agencies on the main road in Airlie Beach.

The companies are: Oceania Dive (☎ 1800 075 035), Pro-Dive (☎ 1800 075 035), True Blue (☎ 1800 635 889) and Kelly Dive (☎ 1800 063 454), all with office/shops in the centre of Airlie Beach.

The same companies also offer a good range of diving trips for certified divers, from day trips to overnighters which combine the reef with the islands.

Swimming & Water Sports There are reasonable beaches at Airlie Beach and Cannonvale, although at low tide you'll have a long walk before you get more than your knees wet, and the presence of marine stingers means that swimming isn't advisable between October and May. There is a swimming enclosure at the Cannonvale beach.

There are two (seasonal) operators down at Airlie Bay who hire out a range of water sports equipment, including jetskis, cata-marans, windsurfers and paddle skis.

As an alternative to the beaches, there's an excellent 25m freshwater pool at the Coral Sea Resort, on Ocean View Ave; it's open to the public daily from 7 am to 6.30 pm and costs $5 per person.

Horse Riding You can take horseback trail rides with Brandy Creek Trail Rides (☎ 4946 6665), 12km from Airlie Beach back towards Proserpine. They can pick you up from your accommodation. The three-hour rides cost $37 and depart twice daily.

Other Activities Other action possibilities include tandem skydiving ($239), paintball wars ($49), sea kayaking ($58) and para-sailing ($40) – you can book these through your accommodation or one of the agents in Airlie Beach.

Organised Tours

Cruises and Fishing Trips A huge range of cruisers, yachts and boats offer trips out to the Whitsundays from the Abel Point Marina and Shute Harbour. See the intro-duction to the Whitsunday Area section for details of some of these.

Rainforest Tours There are a couple of op-erators offering tours of the rainforest areas of the Conway National Park. Whitsunday 4WD Tours has a half-day tour which leaves at 9 am daily and costs $38 ($20 for chil-dren), including a stop for billy tea and damper. Fawlty's 4WD Tropical Tours leaves at 10.30 am daily and costs $38 ($20 for children), including a barbecue lunch.

Both of these can be booked through your accommodation or one of the agencies in Airlie Beach.

Festivals

Airlie Beach is the centre of activities during the annual Whitsunday Fun Race Festival (for cruising yachts) each Septem-ber. The festivities include a Miss Figurehead competition where the contes-tants traditionally compete topless.

Places to Stay

Camping There are no caravan parks in Airlie Beach itself, but there are plenty of choices within a couple of kilometres of the centre. Most of these places get busy during the school holidays.

There are four good caravan parks along the road between Airlie Beach and Shute Harbour. The closest of these, the *Island Gateway Holiday Resort* (☎ 4946 6228), is about 1.5km east of Airlie Beach. It has good facilities including a campers' kitchen, a pool, a shop and half-court tennis. Further along are the *Shute Harbour Gardens Caravan Park* (☎ 4946 6483), 2.5km east; the *Airlie Cove Resort Van Park* (☎ 4946 6727), 2.5km east; and the *Flame Tree Tourist Village* (☎ 4946 9388), 6km east. All of these have comparably good fa-cilities, and tent sites for around $12, on-site vans for around $30 and on-site cabins for around $40.

You can also camp at the central *Koala Beach Resort* (see Hostels) for $8/12 for one/two people, but only if you don't have a car.

Hostels Airlie Beach has become one of the main stopovers on the backpackers' circuit and has a good range of hostels, so there should be something to suit most tastes, whether you're after a big party place or somewhere small and quiet.

There is fierce competition to get bodies on beds, with a couple of places offering bunks for $8 in the quiet times, but as with most things, you generally get what you pay for. The standard price for a dorm bed is usually around $14. At the main bus stop there's a row of booths where the hostel reps tout for trade when the buses arrive. All the places out of the centre run courtesy buses to and from Airlie Beach.

Right in the centre, *Magnum's Backpack-ers* (☎ 4946 6266) is a huge place, set out in a very pleasant tropical garden with two pools. The emphasis here is on partying – there's a bar/eatery next door with activities each night. The cheapest dorms are the eight-share units at $12 a night; four-share is $14.

Also in the centre is *Beaches Backpackers* (☎ 4946 6244), another big place with a party attitude and its own bar and restaurant. The rooms and facilities in this converted motel are good, with five-bed (not bunk) units with their own bathroom and balcony, TV and air-con, a pool and a good kitchen. Beds cost $14 a night ($13 VIP).

Sandwiched between Magnum's and Beaches is *Whitsunday Bunkhouse* (☎ 1800 683 566), another converted motel. This place isn't particularly flash, and lacks a pool and other outdoor areas. The eight-bed units have basic cooking facilities, but it's a cheap option with dorms at $10 and doubles at $30.

A little further along Shute Harbour Rd is *Club Habitat YHA* (☎ 4946 6312), yet another motel converted to backpackers' accommodation. A night in a four to six-bed unit with bathroom costs $15, and twin rooms cost $35; non-members pay an extra $6. There's a pool, good communal kitchen and lounge, and the atmosphere is friendly.

Also in the centre is the *Koala Beach Resort* (☎ 4946 6001), part of the Whitsunday Wanderers Resort. Dormitory accommodation (up to six beds) is $14 ($13 VIP), or there are twins and doubles for $36. The units sleep up to six people, have air-con and are fully self-contained. The best thing about this place is that there is plenty of open space, with coconut palms and a good-sized swimming pool.

Club 13 Begley St (☎ 4946 7376) overlooks the bay from the hill just above the centre. This is a multilevel complex of five three-bedroom apartments, with each apartment sharing two bathrooms (some with spa), a kitchen and laundry. There's a pool and spa, undercover parking and great views from the balconies. A bed in a four or six-share room costs $14 ($13 VIP, YHA), including breakfast.

A short walk out of town towards Shute Harbour is *Backpackers by the Bay* (☎ 4946 7267), at Lot 5, Hermitage Drive. It's a small, relaxed hostel with a good atmosphere, and is generally quieter than those in the centre. It's recently been thoroughly renovated and so boasts excellent facilities. The nightly cost in a small four-bed dorm is $13 and doubles are $30.

Further along towards Cannonvale, about 1.5km west from Airlie Beach, is the *Bush Village Backpackers Resort* (☎ 4946 6177) in St Martin's Lane (just off Shute Harbour Rd). This place has clean and simple four-bed cabins in a pleasant garden setting. Dorms range from $10 to $16, twins are $34 and doubles are $34 to $44; prices include breakfast. Each cabin has cooking facilities, fridge, bathroom and TV. There's also a pool and a spa, bikes and mopeds for hire, and a courtesy bus which makes frequent runs into the centre.

The *Reef Oceania Village* (☎ 4946 6137), at 141 Shute Harbour Rd in Cannonvale, is about 3km west of Airlie Beach. This is a good resort complex (see the Resorts section for details) and has a small section for backpackers, with beds in the six to eight-share bunk room at $14 including breakfast.

Motels There are a couple of budget motels in central Airlie Beach. The *Airlie Beach Motor Lodge* (☎ 4946 6418), on Lamond St, has rooms from $56/62 for singles/doubles and two-bedroom self-contained units from $80. On the corner of Shute Harbour Rd and Broadwater Ave, the *Colonial Court Motel* (☎ 4946 6180), has motel units with kitchenettes from $46.

Holiday Flats & Apartments There are quite a few blocks of older-style holiday flats and apartments in and around Airlie Beach which can be good value, especially for a group of friends travelling together or a family. Generally, these places have cooking facilities and supply bed linen.

Right in the centre of town, at 26 Shute Harbour Rd, *Whitsunday on the Beach* (☎ 4946 6359) is a two-storey block of brightly renovated studio apartments from $75 to $85. Each has air-con, TV and full cooking facilities.

On the rise above Airlie Beach, *Sunlit Waters* (☎ 4946 6352), on the corner of Begley St and Airlie Crescent, has a pool and five small, basic studio-style flats with great views. The flats can sleep up to four people (at a squeeze) and cost around $40 a double plus $8 for each extra person.

Boathaven Lodge (☎ 4946 6421), about 200m east of the town centre, at 440 Shute Harbour Rd, is a small strip of neat, renovated studio units on a hill overlooking Boathaven Bay. The units sleep two or three people and cost $50 a double plus $10 for extra adults.

On the beachfront in Cannonvale, the *Whitsunday Apartments* (☎ 4946 6860), at 48 Coral Esplanade, has one and two-bedroom self-contained units starting from $65 for a double.

Resorts Most of the resorts here have package deals and stand-by rates which are much cheaper than their regular rates.

In Cannonvale, *Club Crocodile* (☎ 4946 7155 or toll-free ☎ 1800 075 151), is 1.5km west of Airlie Beach on Shute Harbour Rd. It is a popular and modern mid-range resort with 160 motel-style units built around an attractive central courtyard featuring landscaped gardens, fountains, a pool, spa, tennis court, and a courtyard bar. There's a casual bistro with pub-style meals and a more expensive restaurant. The rate is a very reasonable $55 per person including breakfast.

The *Coral Sea Resort* (☎ 4946 6458), 25 Ocean View Ave, sits at the end of a low headland overlooking the ocean and the Abel Point Marina. The resort has a large and excellent pool, a poolside cocktail bar and a good restaurant. Standard motel units range from $130 a double to $165 for a room with ocean views.

Set on eight hectares in central Airlie Beach, *Whitsunday Wanderers* (☎ 4946 6446) on Shute Harbour Rd is another large resort. There are four pools, tennis courts, landscaped gardens, a bar, restaurant and nightly live entertainment, plus modern Melanesian-style units for $38 to $54 per person, depending on the season.

The *Reef Oceania Village* (☎ 4946 6137), mentioned earlier in the hostels section, is in Cannonvale about 3km east of Airlie Beach. It has a pleasant garden setting, a large pool, a bar with a covered courtyard, a restaurant and communal cooking and laundry facilities. Modern timber cabins cost $55 for a double or $75 for a family, including breakfast. A courtesy bus runs a shuttle service into Airlie Beach.

The huge *Whitsunday Terraces Resort* (☎ 4946 6788), up on Golden Orchid Drive overlooking Airlie Beach and the ocean, has modern studio-style and one-bedroom apartments with cooking facilities and all mod cons costing from $90 to $125 a night.

Places to Eat
If you're preparing your own food, there's a small supermarket on the main street (near the carpark entrance) which has a good range of groceries, fruit and vegies.

Cafes, Delis & Takeaways Airlie Beach may be small, but it has some great eateries, including a good selection of delis, cafes and sandwich bars.

The *Happy Gourmet*, at 263 Shute Harbour Rd, is a great place for lunch, and you can eat in or takeaway. They make delicious filled rolls and sandwiches. Further along Shute Harbour Rd, beside the main car park, is the small and popular *Cafe Le Mignon*. It does good breakfasts, including croissants, muesli with fresh fruit and continentals. They also have good coffee, filled croissants and sandwiches, pancakes and omelettes.

At another good gourmet sandwich bar, *Cafe Gourmet* at 289 Shute Harbour Rd, you can invent your own or order from their suggestion menus. It has good rolls and sandwiches plus smoothies and juices.

If you're after a good cooked breakfast, head for the *Sidewalk Cafe*, on Airlie Esplanade. This friendly place looks like a basic takeaway, but has good food with everything from toasted sandwiches to cooked meals. It's open for breakfast, lunch and early dinners.

Cappuccino's Cafe, both indoors and outdoors in a breezy arcade, has focaccias ($6), pasta ($10 to $12) and serious coffee. *Jessie's on the Beach* does good breakfast deals for $3.65.

The *Club Cafe* is a modern licensed place open all day, with an Asian inspired menu – laksa ($9), tempura ($9) and noodle dishes ($9 to $12). It's just a pity there isn't more outside seating.

The open-air *Boardwalk* next to Magnum's is popular in the evenings, and its pizzas ($10 to $13) are good value. *Panache on the Beach* is a very pleasant open-air place with pasta from $12 to $14 and other mains from $18 to $22.

Bars & Bistros *Beaches Bar & Bistro* in the Beaches Backpackers complex is popular with both travellers and locals, and serves lunches and dinners. The dining area, a large covered courtyard with long timber tables, always seems to be pretty crowded, and the bar has various happy hours and plays good music. Meals are unexciting but of reasonable quality, and range from salads, pastas and burgers from $5 to $6; roasts, chicken, calamari and fish dishes from $6 to $8; and steaks from $12.

Magnum's Bar & Grill is almost as popular and equally lively, but mainly attracts the backpackers. It's only open for dinner and you get a free beer with your meal. In the recently redeveloped Airlie Beach Hotel there's *Mangrove Jack's*.

Restaurants At 261 Shute Harbour Rd is the *Hog's Breath Cafe*, one of a chain of bar and grill places. It has burgers, salads, sandwiches, steaks, seafood and prime ribs, with lunches from $8 to $12 and dinners from $14 to $20.

Further along, *KC's Char Grill* is a bit more upmarket, and good for a splurge. It has a rustic, lively atmosphere and excellent food, with char-grilled steaks and seafood in the $16 to $22 range. It's licensed, is open for lunch and dinner, and has live music most nights.

Further along Shute Harbour Rd is *Chatz Bar & Brasserie*. At the front is a lively little bar, with an eatery out the back offering burgers, salads, vegetarian meals, seafood and Italian-style main courses, all in the $10 to $15 range.

On the corner of Shute Harbour Rd and Coconut Grove, *Charlie's Round the Bend* is a fairly trendy bar/eatery with a small courtyard on the streetfront. This place has an interesting and diverse menu, with gourmet pizzas around $13 and other main courses from $14 to $18. The bar here features live acoustic music every night.

Airlie Beach's most upmarket restaurant is *The Brasserie*, a sophisticated licensed restaurant upstairs in the Beach Plaza shopping arcade. The dining room is quite romantic, or there are tables out on the balcony. Main meals, which include some interesting seafood dishes, beef medallions, coral trout, and honey-roasted spatchcock, range from $16 to $22, or you can choose any two/three courses for $16/20.

In the same complex is *Airlie Thai*, an economical place with a pleasant balcony. This BYO place is open for dinner Tuesday through Sunday, and the varied menu features main courses in the $8 to $14 range.

If you must have Mexican, *Tequila Willie's* is open for lunch and dinner and is good value at $9 for main courses, and $13 to $18 for grills.

Entertainment

Airlie Beach has a reputation for partying hard, and has a small but lively nightlife scene. The bars at *Magnum's* and *Beaches*, the two big backpackers' resorts in the centre of town, are usually pretty crowded, and good places to meet other travellers. Drinks also tend to be cheaper here than elsewhere.

At the time of writing, the *Airlie Beach Hotel* was undergoing a refurbishment. It should have reopened by now and may have some interesting entertainment options.

Several of the bar/restaurants along Shute Harbour Rd also have regular live music. *Charlie's Round the Bend* has live acoustic music every night and stays open until 2 am; *KC's Char Grill* also has live music most nights.

There are a couple of nightclubs on Shute Harbour Rd: *Tricks*, upstairs next to the newsagent, and *Stingers*, upstairs in an arcade near the post office. Both stay open until 5 am. Tricks seems to be popular with the locals and the boaties, whereas Stingers attracts the backpackers.

Getting There & Away
Air The Whitsunday airport, a small airfield midway between Airlie Beach and Shute Harbour, is 6km west of Airlie Beach. Half a dozen different operators are based here, and you can take a helicopter, a light plane or a seaplane out to the islands or the reef.

Island Air Taxis (☎ 4946 9933) flies to Hamilton ($45) and Lindeman ($55) islands. Helireef (☎ 4946 9102), Coral Air Whitsunday (☎ 4946 9111) and Island Air Taxis all do joy flights out over the reef.

Bus Most McCafferty's and Greyhound Pioneer buses along the Bruce Hwy detour to Airlie Beach. (If you're reading this while sitting on a bus that doesn't make the detour, you'll have to get off in Proserpine and catch a local bus from there.)

There are buses between Airlie Beach and all the major centres along the coast, including Brisbane (18 hours, $103), Mackay (two hours, $24), Townsville (4½ hours, $35) and Cairns (11 hours, $59).

Long-distance buses all stop in the car park behind the shops, about halfway along Shute Harbour Rd. Any of the booking agencies along Shute Harbour Rd can make reservations or sell bus tickets.

Sampson's (☎ 4945 2377) runs local bus services from Proserpine to Airlie Beach ($6.50) and Shute Harbour ($8.40); buses operate daily from 6 am to 7 pm. Sampson's meets all flights at Proserpine airport, and goes to Airlie Beach ($11) and Shute Harbour ($13).

Sea The Whitsunday Sailing Club is at the end of Airlie Esplanade. There are notice boards at the Abel Point Marina showing when rides or crewing are available. Ask around Airlie Beach or Shute Harbour.

Getting Around
Airlie Beach is small enough to cover by foot, and all of the cruise boats have courtesy buses that will pick you up from wherever you're staying and take you to either Shute Harbour or the Abel Point Marina.

Several car-rental agencies operate locally; Avis, Budget and National all have agencies on Shute Harbour Rd. Airlie Beach Rentals (☎ 4946 6110) one block back from the main street on the corner of Begley St and Waterson Rd, has cars from $45 a day and scooters from $30 a day.

There's a taxi rank in Shute Harbour Rd, opposite Magnum's. To book a taxi, call Whitsunday Taxis on ☎ 1800 811 388.

CONWAY NATIONAL PARK
This national park is the mainland equivalent of the Whitsunday Islands. These mountains and the islands were once part of the same coastal mountain range, but rising sea levels after the last Ice Age flooded the lower valleys and cut off the coastal peaks from the mainland.

Most of the park is composed of rugged ranges and valleys covered in rainforest, although there are also areas of mangroves and open forest. Only a small area of the park is accessible by road.

The road from Airlie Beach passes through the northern section of the park. Several walking trails start from near the picnic and day use area, including a 1km circuit track to a mangrove creek. About 1km past the day use area and on the north side of the road, there's a 2.4km walk up to the Mt Rooper lookout, which provides good views of the Whitsunday Passage and islands.

There's bush camping on the coast at Swamp Bay and access is only on foot.

CEDAR CREEK FALLS & CONWAY BEACH
To reach the beautiful **Cedar Creek Falls**, turn off the Proserpine to Airlie Beach road on to Conway Rd, 8km north of Proserpine. It's then about 15km to the falls – the roads

WHITSUNDAY COAST

are well signposted. This is a popular picnic and swimming spot.

At the end of Conway Rd, 20km from the turn-off, is **Conway Beach**. A small coastal community on the shores of Repulse Bay and at the southern end of the Conway National Park, it consists of a few old houses and pleasant picnic areas along the foreshore. The *Black Stump Caravan Park* (☎ 4947 3147) has a bar, pool, tent sites and on-site vans.

LONG ISLAND

The closest of the resort islands to the coast, Long Island has two active resorts and one small eco-lodge, and is nearly all national park. The island is about 11km long but no more than 1.5km wide anywhere, and a channel only 0.5km wide separates it from the mainland. The 16.5 sq km island has lots of rainforest, 13km of walking tracks and some fine lookouts. Day trippers to the island have use of the facilities at the Club Croc resort, which is where boats arrive.

Activities

The beaches on Long Island are quite attractive, but severe tidal variations mean that low tide at Happy Bay is time to head for the swimming pool. The walking trails include a 2km trail between the two northern resorts, a 3km loop from Happy Bay to the north of the island, and a 4km walk from Palm Bay south to Sandy Bay.

The two northern resorts have a range of water sports equipment. *Club Croc* has a wider range, and hires out dinghies ($80 a day) and jetskis ($50 a half hour), and you can go water-skiing ($20) or parasailing ($49). Day trippers and guests at Palm Bay can also avail themselves of these facilities.

Sea kayaking is a featured activity at the Whitsunday Wilderness Lodge on the southern side of the island.

Places to Stay & Eat

Camping There's a national parks camp site at Sandy Bay, midway along the western side of the island. There is space here for just six people, and there are no facilities. For permits check with the Department of Environment office in Airlie Beach.

Club Croc At Happy Bay in the north of the island, *Club Croc* (☎ 4946 9400 or toll-free ☎ 1800 075 125) is operated by Club Crocodile Holdings, which runs a similarly styled resort in Airlie Beach. It's a modern mid-range resort with three levels of affordable accommodation, and is popular with families and couples, with plenty of activities to keep children and adults busy.

The Beachfront Units, modern motel-style units overlooking Happy Bay, cost $190 per person per night. The Garden Rooms, which are of a similar standard but look out on the garden, are $160 per person. The Lodge Units are more basic rooms with shared bathrooms and no air-con, and go for $25 per person (including transfers). A meal package is available for $47, or you can pay as you go. The resort has two swimming pools, tennis courts, a gym, a games room, windsurfers and catamarans, and use of all of these is included in the tariffs.

There are two eating options here: *The Palms* is the more formal of the two, a large and stylish restaurant with white linen tablecloths. It's open in the mornings with a choice between a continental breakfast ($10.50) and a full buffet breakfast ($16.50). Lunch is a set $12, while at night a three-course set meal costs $24, or à la carte dishes cost from $14 to $20. The more casual *Cafe Paradiso* has both outdoor and indoor tables and opens from 10 am to 9 pm.

Palm Bay About 2km south, the *Palm Bay Hideaway Resort* (☎ 4946 9233 or toll-free ☎ 1800 334 009) is a low-key, old-fashioned retreat with just 14 individual cabins and bures (Melanesian-style bungalows) set around the sandy sweep of Palm Bay. They all have a double bed and four bunks, a kitchenette, a bathroom and their own little verandah, complete with a hammock for lazing the days away. There are no TVs or telephones. In the centre of the resort is a large island-style building which serves as the main dining area, bar, lounge and meeting place.

This is a good place to visit if you want to see what the island resorts used to be like before all the developers and hoteliers moved into the Whitsundays. The only catch is that the prices are certainly no reminder of days gone by – you're paying a premium for the individuality and smallness of the resort. Nightly costs in the cabins are $146/224 for singles/doubles, and in the bures $194/328. Both sleep up to six people; extra adults cost another $35 ($38 in the bures), extra children $20 ($25).

At Palm Bay you have a choice of fixing your own food or an additional $61 per person per day ($38 for children) covers breakfast, lunch and dinner – they're straightforward 'home-style' meals. You can also buy meals individually: breakfast costs $10 for continental, $15 for cooked, lunch is $17 and dinner $29. If you opt to fix your own meals there are cooking facilities, crockery and cutlery in each of the cabins.

Whitsunday Wilderness Lodge The isolated lodge on the very small Paradise Bay consists of just eight spacious but basic cabins, each with a double and single bed, and en suite bath. There is no fan or air-con, but the cabins are positioned to make the most of the sea breezes. The solar powered lodge is staffed by a friendly crew of just three, and so informality is the name of the game. Meals are buffet style, and most are cooked in camp-ovens over a campfire. The food is simple but filling, and vegetarians are well catered for.

Accommodation is only offered in six-night packages, which run from Monday to Sunday. The cost is $1290 per person, which includes everything except drinks, and you arrive by helicopter from Hamilton Island.

Getting There & Away
Whitsunday Allover's boats operate to Long Island from Shute Harbour for $15 return. It's a quick trip, just 20 minutes or

so. It's only 2km between the Happy Bay and Palm Bay resorts and you can walk between them in just 15 or 20 minutes. Departures are from Shute at 7.15 and 9.15 am, and 1.30, 4 and 5.15 pm. From Club Croc they are at 7.45 and 9.45 am, and 1.50, 4.30 and 5.30 pm. From Palm Bay Hideaway departures are at 8 and 9.30 am, and 4.15 and 5.45 pm.

Fantasea has one service from Hamilton to Long Island at 5 pm, which then leaves Long Island (Club Croc) at 5.55 pm for Shute Harbour.

HOOK ISLAND
Second largest of the Whitsundays, Hook Island is 53 sq km and rises to 450m at Hook Peak. There are a number of good beaches dotted around the island, and Hook has some of the best diving and snorkelling locations in the Whitsundays, mostly at the northern end of the island.

The southern end of the island is indented by two very long and narrow fjord-like bays. Beautiful Nara Inlet is a very popular deep-water anchorage for visiting yachts, and Aboriginal wall paintings have been found in the inlet.

There's an **underwater observatory** at the southern tip of the island, although its coral displays aren't particularly impressive and it isn't worth the $5 entry fee.

Hook also has a small and low-key resort and campground. Facilities include a swimming pool, a volleyball net and a couple of paddle skis. There's also a dive shop based here, offering a five-day certificate course for $277 including accommodation and transfers – one of the cheapest deals around.

Places to Stay
Camping There's a national park campground at Maureen Cove on the north side of the island.

Resort The *Hook Island Wilderness Lodge* (☎ 4946 9380) is the only true budget resort in the Whitsundays. It's a simple and basic lodge with 12 adjoining units, each with either eight bunks or a double bed and four bunks. The lodge is fairly old and basic, but it's clean, comfortable and cheap at $14 per person per night. Two people can have a unit to themselves for $55 a night. There are also good camping areas at both ends of the resort and the cost is $9 per person. Facilities such as toilets and showers are shared by cabins and campers, but there is no laundry.

Places to Eat

The resort has a very casual restaurant with lunches like sandwiches, burgers and fish and chips from $3 to $6. Dinner costs $10 for something simple like pasta, chicken, baked fish or a barbecue. You can also use the barbecues or kitchen area to prepare your own food.

Getting There & Away

Seatrek (☎ 4946 5255) runs a daily boat service to and from Hook Island. Services leave Shute Harbour at 8.45 am, returning from the island at 2 pm. The return fare is $25.

DAYDREAM ISLAND

Daydream, the closest of the resort islands to Shute Harbour, is just over 1km long and only a couple of hundred metres across at its widest point. The island has a large and modern resort, the main part of which is at the northern end.

Daydream is a popular island for day trips. Catamarans, windsurfers, paddle boards, dinghies, jetskis and snorkelling equipment are available for hire (free for resort guests), and you can also go water-skiing here.

A nature walk links the southern and northern ends of the island. It's a steep and rocky path which climbs over the centre of the island, and takes about 20 minutes. Just before the main resort building at the northern end, a short path branches off to the tiny but lovely Sunlovers Beach. There's also a concrete path around the east side of the island. And once you've done these walks, you've just about covered this little island from head to foot.

Places to Stay

The *Daydream Island Resort* (☎ 4948 8488 or toll-free ☎ 1800 075 040) is a stylish and modern family resort. Built in 1990, it's a three-storey complex with over 300 rooms, surrounded by impressively landscaped tropical gardens. The resort caters for children particularly well and offers plenty of activities, but with such a large resort on such a small island it's not the place to come to if you're looking for isolation. You certainly won't be lost or lonely on Daydream.

The rooms are comfortable motel-style units which sleep up to four people. There are two types of rooms, with daily tariffs at $175 per adult in a Garden View room, $195 per adult in a Daydream room with ocean view. Children are charged $25 a night.

Included in the room rates are the use of tennis courts, a gym, sauna and spa, two swimming pools, aerobics classes, snorkelling gear, catamarans, windsurfers and more. The free Kids Only club keeps children entertained day and night with a diverse range of activities.

Places to Eat

The resort has a few different eateries. The *Waterfall Cafe* specialises in buffet-style breakfasts, lunches and dinners. *Langford's Lounge* in the centre of the atrium area serves light snacks and sandwiches, and the *North Pool Bar* has various snacks and meals if you want to eat poolside. *Sunlovers*, a more formal à la carte restaurant, opens for dinners with main courses around $20 to $25.

Down at the southern end of the island, *Skip's Cafe & Bakery* has a great selection of pies, sandwiches, rolls and cakes, and the *South Pool Bar* sells hot dogs.

Getting There & Away

Whitsunday Allover has six daily transfers to Shute Harbour between 7.30 am and 10.30 pm ($24 return), four of them via South Molle Island and Hamilton Island airport ($44 return).

Seatrek also has five services to Shute and South Molle, while Fantasea has two services to Shute Harbour ($16 return), five to South Molle ($16 return) and on to Hamilton ($36 return), and one to Abel Point Marina ($16 return).

SOUTH MOLLE ISLAND

Largest of the Molle group of islands at 4 sq km, South Molle is virtually joined to Mid Molle and North Molle islands – you can actually walk across a causeway to Mid Molle. Apart from the resort area and golf course at Bauer Bay in the north, the island is all national park. There is some forest cover around the resort, but because of overgrazing in the years before it was declared a national park the rest of the island is mainly rolling grasslands. The island is crisscrossed by numerous walking tracks, and has some superb lookout points. The highest point is 198m Mt Jeffreys, but the climb up Spion Kop is also worthwhile.

The island is known for its prolific birdlife. The most noticeable birds are the dozens of tame, colourful lorikeets that will eat out of your hand at feeding time (3 pm). Currawongs and the endangered stone curlews are also common.

The beaches are reasonably good at high tide, but because of severe tidal shifts in the Whitsundays low tides tend to reveal unattractive mud flats. The resort has a big pool, a nine-hole golf course, a gym, and tennis and squash courts. There is also a wide range of water sports gear available for day trippers to hire (nonpowered water sports equipment is free for resort guests).

Places to Stay

The *South Molle Island Resort* (☎ 4946 9433 or ☎ 1300 363 300) is one of the older resorts in the Whitsundays. It's not particularly sophisticated, but it's a good family resort as children are well catered for. Most activities and all meals are included in the tariffs, which makes it a little more affordable than most other resorts.

Accommodation is in straightforward motel-style units. There are six different ac-commodation blocks, some looking out over Bauer Bay, some overlooking the golf course. Daily costs are $155 per person in the Golf units, $170 per person in the Reef and Polynesian units, and $185 in the Beachcomber and Whitsunday units.

Places to Eat

The resort's main restaurant, the *Island Restaurant*, serves plain buffet-style breakfasts and lunches. The dinner menu offers bistro-style mains – steak, chicken and seafood dishes. Most nights there is the alternative of a barbecue beside the pool, and Friday is Island Feast Night, with an extensive spread and live entertainment.

There's also the smaller *Coral's* restaurant. Starters are $12, mains $20 to $24 and desserts from the trolley $3.

Getting There & Away

Hamilton serves as the main arrival port for South Molle. Whitsundays Allover has four daily boat transfers ($44 return).

Seatrek also has regular services to and from Shute Harbour, leaving Shute Harbour at 9 am and 12.30 and 4 pm, and returning from South Molle at 7.45 and 10.30 am, and 3.10 and 4.45 pm. The fare is $18 return.

Fantasea has three trips a day to Shute Harbour ($16 return), all via Daydream Island (also $16 return), and five services to Hamilton Island ($36 return).

HAMILTON ISLAND

The most heavily developed resort island in the Whitsundays, Hamilton is more like a town than a resort, with its own airport, a 200-boat marina, shops, restaurants and bars, and accommodation for more than 2000, including three high-rise tower blocks.

Hamilton was originally the creation of Gold Coast entrepreneur Keith Williams, who somehow managed to convince the Bjelke-Petersen state government to convert his 'deer farming' lease into a tourism one in the early 1980s. Williams' bulldozer-driven transformation of the island was not only ambitious but somewhat controversial, but by the end of 1986 the resort was up and running.

However, after the success of the early years various adverse circumstances led to Hamilton Island being placed in receivership in 1992. Keith Williams returned to live on the Gold Coast, only to reappear as the star player in a another controversial development proposal in 1994 (see the Cardwell section in the North Coast chapter). In 1994 Hamilton Island was successfully floated on the Australian Stock Exchange, and the international hotel chain Holiday Inns took over the management.

Hamilton Island still attracts plenty of tourists. It isn't everyone's cup of tea, but it does have an extensive range of accommodation, restaurants, bars and shops, plus plenty of entertainment possibilities including helicopter joy rides, gamefishing, paragliding, cruising, scuba diving and a hilltop fauna reserve. It can make an interesting day trip from Shute Harbour and you can use all the resort facilities.

Things to See & Do

The **fauna park**, at the northern end of the island, has koalas, kangaroos, deer and other wildlife. Crocodile-feeding at 10.15 am and cockatoo capers at 10.30 am are the most popular shows; entry costs $10 for adults, $5 for kids.

The resort has tennis courts, squash courts, a gym, a golf-driving range and a mini-golf course. From **Catseye Beach**, in front of the resort, you can hire windsurfers, catamarans, jetskis and other equipment, and go paragliding or water-skiing. **Wire Flyer**, a cross between a hang-glider and a flying fox, costs $25 a ride.

A **dive shop** by the harbour organises dives and open-water certificate courses; you can take a variety of cruises to other islands and the outer reef. **Dinghies** are available for hire at $55 a half day or $80 a full day, with fishing gear supplied.

There are a few **walking trails** on the island, the best being the walk from Catseye Bay up to 230m Passage Peak on the northeast corner of the island.

A variety of cruises operate from the island, including sunset and adventure trips.

Hamilton also has a Day Care centre and a free Fun Club, with activities for kids from 5 to 18 years old.

Places to Stay

Hamilton has a range of accommodation, with hotel rooms, self-contained apartments, penthouses and private villas. All the accommodation is modern and of a good standard. Rates here are for room only, but all rooms have air-conditioning and ceiling fan, TV, an iron and ironing board, tea and coffee-making facilities, hairdryer and minibar.

Flanking the main resort complex with its reception area, restaurants, bars, shops and pools are 60 five-star rooms in the *Beach Club*. Behind the resort complex are 51 individual *Coconut Palm Bungalows*, which cost $235. These have a double and a single bed, air-con and fan, minibar, phone, TV and a small patio.

The large 20-storey *Reef View Hotel* has 386 large rooms and suites. They range from 18 'junior' rooms at $200 a night, 350 'premier' rooms at $350 a night and 18 suites from $745 a night up to $1700 for the two 'Presidential' suites, complete with private pool. The premier rooms have two double beds, air-con, fan, TV, phone, minibar, en suite with separate bath and shower, and superb views from the balcony.

Lastly there are the *Whitsunday Holiday Apartments*, in the two 13-storey and adjoining lower blocks. The 168 one-bedroom apartments take four people at $335 a night, while the two-bedroom apartments take five people and cost $465 a night. The apartments are modern, comfortable and equipped with complete kitchens with cooking utensils, crockery, cutlery and so on.

Much cheaper local rates are often available if the resort is not full. It's worth inquiring if you're on the mainland as these reduced rates also include transfers between Shute Harbour and Hamilton Island.

If you really need a room and cost is no obstacle then the *Yacht Harbour Towers* has self-contained penthouses accommodating eight people at $2000 a night. Each four-bedroom apartment occupies a whole floor. Or you could rent one of the private houses, such as *Illalangi*, costing around $1250 a night, although $600 is more typical. You can even buy your own Hamilton condo and rent it out when you're not in residence – Hamilton Island has a real estate agency.

Places to Eat
Accommodation on Hamilton Island is all room-only but meal packages are available at $80 for three meals or $60 for breakfast and dinner. The restaurants participating in the package are: *Toucan Tango Bar & Cafe*, *Beach House* and the *Outrigger Restaurant* at the resort itself, and at harbourside the *Manta Ray Cafe*, *Tang Dynasty*, *Mariners* and *Romano's* restaurants.

Resortside The bright, airy and thoroughly modern *Toucan Tango Cafe & Bar* in the main resort complex serves breakfast and dinner indoors or outside beside the pool. Live entertainment features here most nights.

Another breakfast option is the *Coral Lounge & Breakfast Room* on the ground floor of the Whitsunday Holiday Apartments building.

You can also get drinks, lunch or an early dinner at the pleasant *Beach House* where you can sit inside or outside on the verandah overlooking the swimming pool and beach. Main dishes go for $24 to $30.

There's also a bar (with swim-up facilities of course) on the pool island.

The final option in the main resort area is the *Outrigger Restaurant*, a seafood specialist. Main meals range from $19 to $25.

Harbourside The restaurants and shops at Harbourside are independently run although you can still charge all meals at island restaurants to your room and settle the total bill on departure.

There's also a supermarket for those in the apartments preparing their own meals.

Working your way round the harbourside from the ferry jetty, the first place you come

across is the *Ice Cream Parlour*. Next along is *Turtles*, a snack bar and cafe with expensive gourmet pies ($3), lasagne ($5) and sandwiches ($3 to $5). Upstairs here is *Mariners Seafood Restaurant* with a great verandah overlooking the harbour. Obviously seafood is the focus (main dishes are $22 to $27), but you can also get grills (from $20 to $23). It's open in the evenings only Monday to Saturday, and is licensed and BYO.

Next along is the *Barefoot Bar*, with lunchtime pub meals for $5 to $8, and next door again is *Spinnakers Bar & Grill*, upstairs above the General Store supermarket. It's an evening place with a pleasant verandah. The menu is fairly unambitious, with steaks from $16, pasta from $15 to $18 and seafood for $18 to $20.

Across the road is the formal Italian restaurant, *Romano's*, with a deck built right out over the water. Main dishes are $13 to $18, up to $28 for seafood specialities. On the same side of the road is the *Manta Ray Cafe*, open for breakfast ($6 to $9), lunch and dinner (mains $15 to $20). If you come to Hamilton on a day trip which includes lunch, this is one of the places you can eat at (the other is the *Yacht Club*, see later in this section).

Turn the marina corner, by the picnic tables in a 'sailing craft' creation, and back across the road you come to the *Tang Dynasty Chinese Restaurant* with a typical Chinese menu upstairs and a takeaway counter, also upstairs but at the end of the building. It's open for lunch Monday to Thursday and dinner every night.

Next along is the *Harbourside Eatery*, which is a basic fish and chip and burger place with tables outside on the footpath. The *Bakery* next door turns out good fresh bread and other baked products and good-value sandwiches.

Last in the line is the new and decidedly un-nautical *Yacht Club*, which has a self-cook barbecue buffet with steaks at $12 and kebabs at $8. It is elevated and has plenty of open-air space and so is breezy and has great views.

WHITSUNDAY COAST

Entertainment

In the evening there are the bars in the resort and harbourside. The *Toucan Tango* has a pianist in the evenings or you can head to *Boheme's Bar* at harbourside which opens from 9 pm with a disco from 11 pm till late.

Getting There & Away

Air The Hamilton Island airport is the main arrival centre for the Whitsundays and takes both domestic flights and international charter flights. Until recently Ansett had exclusive rights to the trunk routes to and from Hamilton.

Ansett flies non-stop to Hamilton from Brisbane ($322 one way), Cairns ($251), Melbourne ($540) and Sydney ($457), though advance purchase fares are much cheaper. There are also shorter flights with Helijet between Hamilton and Mackay ($95), Shute Harbour ($45) or Lindeman Island ($45).

Boat Fantasea's Hamilton Island catamaran or other launch takes 35 minutes to cross to or from Shute Harbour on the mainland ($39, children half-fare) with at least five departures daily.

With regular daily flights to and from the major capital cities, Hamilton is also the main arrival point for Long, South Molle, Daydream, Hamilton and Lindeman islands. Whitsunday Allover (☎ 4946 9499) has services to these islands that meet all incoming and outgoing flights. Boat transfers to South Molle, Daydream and Long islands all cost $41 one way. Transfers to Lindeman Island are usually included in accommodation packages; otherwise it's $44.

Getting Around

On arrival and departure there's a free bus service for guests between the airport or marina and the resort.

Hamilton is big, no question about it, but there are a few alternatives to walking. One is the island shuttle, which connects all points around the island on an hourly (or better) basis between 8 am and 10 pm. The cost is $5 for a 24-hour pass, although this is usually included in package deals.

Next are the taxis, which also shuttle around the island and charge a flat $5 per person regardless of distance.

The other, and much more expensive, alternative is the rent-a-buggies. They're small golf-course buggies which can be rented for $15 an hour, $40 per day or $55 for 24 hours. Buggies can be rented from the office near reception or from the Charter Base at harbourside.

HAYMAN ISLAND

The most northern of the Whitsunday Group, Hayman has an area of 4 sq km, and rises to 250m above sea level. It has forested hills, valleys and beaches. It also has one of the most luxurious resorts on the Barrier Reef, owned by Ansett Airlines. The resort is fronted by a wide, shallow reef which emerges from the water at low tide.

Hayman is closer to the outer reef than the other islands, and there is good diving around its northern end and at nearby Hook Island. There are several small, uninhabited islands close to Hayman. You can walk out to Arkhurst Island at low tide. Langford Island, a couple of kilometres south-west, has some good coral around it, as do Black and Bird islands nearby.

Activities

Resort guests have free use of catamarans, windsurfers and paddle skis, but you must pay for just about everything else, including parasailing, water-skiing, tennis and squash. There's also a golf-driving range, putting green and a well-equipped gym.

Hayman has a free Kidz Club which keeps children entertained, and a crèche. The resort has its own dive shop, and the *Reef Goddess* does a range of diving and snorkelling trips to the Barrier Reef. Dinghies can be hired for $95 a day, including fishing and snorkelling gear.

Bushwalks include an 8km island circuit, a 4.5km walk to Dolphin Point at the northern tip of the island, and a 1.5km climb up to the Whitsunday Passage lookout.

Organised Tours

Coral Air Whitsunday (☎ 4946 9130) offers a variety of seaplane tours for resort guests. They'll fly you to Whitehaven Beach for 1½ hours for $165 or to Blue Lagoon at Hardy Reef for two hours of snorkelling for $240.

Places to Stay

Hayman Island Resort (☎ 4940 1234 or toll-free ☎ 1800 075 175) is a member of the exclusive 'Leading Hotels of the World' group. It's the most luxurious big resort on the Great Barrier Reef, and if you're looking for a five-star hotel dripping with style and sophistication, look no further.

An avenue of stately 9m-high date palms leads to the main entrance, and with its 214 rooms, six restaurants, five bars, a hectare of swimming pools, landscaped gardens and grounds, an impressive collection of antiques and arts, and exclusive boutiques, Hayman is certainly impressive. And, in keeping with the island setting, it manages to combine all this style with a reasonably laid-back atmosphere and friendly, informal staff.

The rooms have all the usual five-star facilities, and tariffs include breakfast. Nightly costs start from $490 for the Palm Garden rooms, climb to $690 to $750 for the newer Beachfront, West and East Wing rooms, and the West and East Wing suites go for over $1000 a night. There are also 11 individually styled penthouses if you really feel the need to spend up big.

If you don't have to plan ahead, keep an eye out for stand-by rates, as these can start as low as $150 per person including transfers and breakfast.

Places to Eat

Breakfast, which is included in the room rates, is served buffet-style in the *Coffee House*, a relaxed indoor/outdoor cafe with a great outlook over the beach. At lunch time head down to the *Beach Pavilion*, a casual open-air eatery where you have a choice of grills, salads, sandwiches and desserts for $20 to $25.

La Fontaine is the most formal of the restaurants, with a Louis XIV-style dining room and French cuisine. It is open in the evenings and 'a jacket is preferred'. Main courses are around $38.

The other restaurants are the *Oriental Seafood Restaurant*, with Japanese food in a Japanese garden setting (main courses $38); *La Trattoria*, a casual Italian bistro with an alfresco dining area (mains around $35); and *Planters Restaurant*, with an Australian tropical theme (mains $32 to $36).

The Hayman wine cellar numbers over 20,000 bottles of Australian and European wine, and *La Fontaine* has an additional 400 vintages.

Getting There & Away

Air Helijet (☎ 4946 8249) has seaplane transfers to Hayman from Hamilton Island and the mainland.

Coral Air Whitsundays has the only day trip to Hayman Island, by seaplane from the mainland – see the earlier Organised Tours section for details.

Sea The resort's luxury cruisers, *Sun Goddess* and *Sun Paradise*, transfer guests to the resort from Hamilton Island or Shute Harbour. There are twice daily services which cost $80 return if your package does not include transfers (most do).

LINDEMAN ISLAND

One of the most southerly of the Whitsundays, Lindeman covers 8 sq km, most of which is national park. In 1992, Lindeman Island became the site of Australia's first Club Med resort.

The island has 20km of walking trails and the highest point is 210m Mt Oldfield. With plenty of little beaches and secluded bays on Lindeman it's no hassle at all to find one to yourself. There are also a lot of small islands dotted around, some of which are easy to get across to.

Activities

The resort's daily activities sheet lists an array of things to do, although nothing is compulsory or too regimented. There's a good golf course here, as well as tennis courts, an archery range, a gym, beach volleyball, bingo, basketball etc. You can even take lessons on the resort's impressive flying trapeze set up.

The usual range of water sports equipment is available, and a diving school offers various dive courses and snorkelling trips. Children are also kept busy with all sorts of organised activities.

Walking trails include a 4km climb to the top of Mt Oldfield, with a trail branching off to Gap Beach; a 6km loop walk from the airstrip down to Boat Port and Coconut Beach; and a trail around the south-eastern side of the island to Plantation Beach, via Hempel's Lookout.

Places to Stay
The *Club Med Resort* (☎ 4946 9333 or toll-free ☎ 1800 807 973) opened in 1992. The internationally famous Club Med style is very evident here. There are plenty of activities, nightly entertainment and young, friendly staff to help you enjoy yourself and get the most out of your stay.

The main resort complex, with its pool, dining and entertainment areas, is flanked by three-storey accommodation blocks looking out over the water, and all the motel-style rooms have their own balcony.

Nightly rates range from $199 to $255, depending on the time of year you visit. Rates include all meals and most activities. There are also five-night packages available from major cities, which include airfares and transfers, and one and two-night deals from Mackay and Airlie Beach – phone the resort for details.

Places to Eat
All meals and beer, wine and juices are included in the tariffs. The *Main Restaurant* serves buffet-style breakfasts, lunches and dinners; the casual *Top Restaurant*, by the pool and tennis courts, has barbecued steaks and chicken, salads and fruit; and *Nicholson's*, a smaller à la carte restaurant, opens nightly for dinner.

Entertainment
Every night at 9.30 pm there's a live show in the main theatre, and you're just as likely to find yourself up on stage at some time. Later in the evening *Silhouettes* nightclub opens up.

Getting There & Away
Air Island Air Taxis (☎ 4946 9933) has flights to Lindeman from Shute Harbour ($60 one way; $75 day return) and Mackay ($105 one way).

Sea Whitsunday Allover (☎ 4946 6900) has an early morning (5 am!) day trip from Shute Harbour to Lindeman, which costs $108 including lunch and use of all of the resort's facilities, but it's a *very* long day.

Club Med has its own launch which connects with flights from the airport at Hamilton Island.

WHITSUNDAY ISLAND
The largest of the Whitsunday Group, this island covers 109 sq km and rises to 438m at Whitsunday Peak. There's no resort, but it is possible to do some fine bushwalking; 6km-long **Whitehaven Beach** on the south-east coast is the longest and best beach in the group (some say in the country), with good snorkelling off its southern end. Many of the day-trip boats visit Whitehaven Beach

There are national parks campgrounds at Dugong and Sawmill beaches on the west, and at Joe's Beach.

NORTHERN WHITSUNDAY ISLANDS
The northern islands of the Whitsundays group are undeveloped and seldom visited by cruise boats or water taxis. Several of these – Gloucester, Saddleback, Olden and Armit islands – have national park campgrounds, and the Department of Environment office in Airlie Beach (☎ 4946 7022) can issue camping permits and advise you on which islands to visit and how to get there. The northern islands are best reached from Dingo Beach, Bowen or Earlando on the mainland.

Dingo Beach

This secluded coastal township is north of Proserpine and Airlie Beach. To get there turn off the Bruce Hwy 12km north of Proserpine. You can also cut across to this road from the Proserpine-Airlie Beach road.

Dingo Beach is a quiet little place set on a long sandy bay backed by low, forested mountains. Nothing much happens here, but it's a popular spot with the fishing fraternity and there's a pleasant foreshore reserve with shady trees, picnic tables and barbecues.

The only facilities are at the Dingo Beach General Store on the foreshore, which sells fuel, booze, takeaway meals, a small range of groceries and bait. Adjoining the store is the *Dingo Beach Resort* (☎ 4945 7153), a two-storey block of holiday flats. Costs are $65 a night for up to four people and $6 for each additional person.

There are two islands a little way off both ends of the bay, both with small national park campgrounds: **Gloucester Island** is to the north-west and **Saddleback Island** sits to the north-east. If you don't have your own boat, you could hire a dinghy from Dingo Beach Watersports (☎ 4945 7215) for around $60 a day.

Earlando

About 15km south of Dingo Beach, there's a turn-off to the *Earlando Tourist Resort* (☎ 4945 7133), a budget resort set on an attractive bay. There's a bar with a shady beer garden and a casual restaurant. The resort has campsites and on-site vans, and a few old fibro cabins along the beachfront, which are clean, simple and self-contained. These cost $60 a double.

There's a small jetty and boat ramp near the resort, and you can hire dinghies here for fishing or getting to the islands for $50 a day.

OTHER WHITSUNDAY ISLANDS

There's a campground on **North Molle Island** at Cockatoo Beach, on the island's southern end, with tables, toilets and water. **Henning Island**, just off the west side of Whitsunday Island, also has a campground at Northern Spit.

Between Cid and Whitsunday islands, **Cid Harbour** was the anchorage for part of the US Navy before the Battle of the Coral Sea, the turning point in the Pacific theatre of WWII. Today, visiting cruise liners anchor here.

BOWEN
pop 13,200

Bowen, founded in 1861, was the first coastal settlement to be established north of Rockhampton. Although soon overshadowed by Mackay to the south and Townsville to the north, Bowen survived, and today it's a thriving fruit and vegetable-growing centre which attracts hundreds of people for seasonal picking work. The main picking season stretches from April to November, with the major crops being tomatoes, beans, corn, rock melons and pumpkin. There's also a short mango-picking season in December.

Although it's fairly laid-back and has some pleasant beaches a couple of kilometres north of the centre, Bowen is much more a working and fishing town than a scenic seaside resort.

Bowen's Gem of the Coral Coast festival is held each October.

History

On his 1770 voyage up the Australian coast, Captain Cook named Cape Gloucester east of Bowen, which he thought was part of the mainland. It was actually the island now known as Gloucester Island which forms the eastern flank of Edgecumbe Bay.

In 1859 Captain Henry Sinclair sailed into Edgecumbe Bay, returning two years later with George Elphinstone Dalrymple. Dalrymple was a dynamic Scot who also pioneered a route inland from near present-day Cardwell to the Valley of Lagoons in the upper Burdekin Valley.

Together, Sinclair and Dalrymple founded Bowen, naming it after the first governor of the new colony of Queensland, which had just separated from New South Wales.

WHITSUNDAY COAST

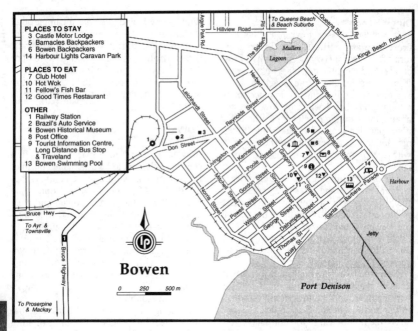

PLACES TO STAY
3 Castle Motor Lodge
5 Barnacles Backpackers
6 Bowen Backpackers
14 Harbour Lights Caravan Park

PLACES TO EAT
7 Club Hotel
10 Hot Wok
11 Fellow's Fish Bar
12 Good Times Restaurant

OTHER
1 Railway Station
2 Brazil's Auto Service
4 Bowen Historical Museum
8 Post Office
9 Tourist Information Centre,
    Long Distance Bus Stop
    & Traveland
13 Bowen Swimming Pool

Bowen

Port Denison

Information

There's a tourist office (☎ 4786 4494) at 34 Williams St.

The local RACQ depot is Brazil's Auto Service (☎ 4786 1412) at 28 Don St.

Things to See & Do

The **Bowen Historical Museum**, at 22 Gordon St, has displays relating to the town's early history. It's open on weekdays from 10.30 am to 4 pm and Sunday mornings during the tourist season; entry costs $2.

Bowen has an interesting collection of **murals** painted on various buildings around the centre. There are 11 of these large murals depicting different phases in the town's history, on buildings in Powell, Herbert, Williams and George Sts.

Herbert St, the main street, leads down to Port Denison. It's worth a visit to the harbour to see all the fishing boats and

yachts down here, and there's a seafood co-op where you can buy fresh seafood.

A couple of kilometres north from the centre of town are Bowen's **beaches**. Queens Beach is a long crescent-shaped stretch of sandy beach. Driving west around Queens Bay, you come to a series of secluded coves and bays.

Places to Stay

Camping The *Harbour Lights Caravan Park* (☎ 4786 1565) is close to the centre of town, opposite the harbour at 40 Santa Barbara Parade. It has tent sites from $12 a double and on-site vans from $28.

Hostels There are three 'workers hostels' in Bowen that specialise in finding seasonal picking (mainly tomatoes) work for travellers. All three are fairly basic, and have buses that do pick-ups and run workers to and from work (sometimes free

– Barnacles is $4). It's a competitive scene, so it's worth ringing around before you come to find out what's available.

Barnacles Backpackers (☎ 4786 4400), at 16 Gordon St, has two sections, with dorm beds at $12 and doubles $28. It can get quite crowded, however, as the kitchen facilities are woefully inadequate. As it is essentially a workers' hostel, you may not feel comfortable here if you are just passing through.

The long-running *Bowen Backpackers* (☎ 4786 3433) is nearby at 56 Herbert St (the main road). It has a good reputation for finding fruit-picking work, although the owners may get very annoyed if, after finding you work, you move elsewhere. The nightly cost is $13 in four to eight-bed dorms.

The latest hostel to open here is *Trinity's Backpackers* (☎ 4786 4199), at 93 Horseshoe Bay Rd. It has five or 10-share self-contained units at $11 per person. Once again, help is given to find work.

Motels On the main road into town from the highway, the *Castle Motor Lodge* (☎ 4786 1322), at 6 Don St, is one of the better motels here, with good units from $55/60 a single/double, a pool and a licensed restaurant.

There's also a string of motels and caravan parks along the Bruce Hwy south of Bowen, catering for the more transient traffic.

Beach Suburbs There are also quite a few accommodation possibilities in the beach suburbs to the north of Bowen.

Out on the headland of Cape Edgecumbe, the *Whitsunday Sands Resort* (☎ 4786 3333) is quite a good mid-range resort in a pleasant setting, with gardens and palm trees and access to several coves and beaches. The complex has a bar, a kiosk and a restaurant. There are motel units from $55 for singles/doubles. There is also a caravan park and another budget resort out on the cape, overlooking Horseshoe Bay.

Around at Queens Beach, there are several caravan parks along the foreshore

including *Coral Coast Caravan Park* (☎ 4785 1262), on Horseshoe Bay Rd, which has powered tent sites from $14 and on-site vans from $30, and the *Tropical Beach Caravan Park* (☎ 4785 1490), in Argyle St, which has tent sites from $14, on-site vans from $28 and cabins from $35.

Between these two caravan parks, the *Palm View Holiday Units* (☎ 4785 1415), on the corner of Soldiers Rd and Howard St, is a set of four basic holiday units, starting from $43 a night for two plus $7 for each extra adult.

Places to Eat

The *Club Hotel*, on the corner of Herbert and Powell Sts, is close to both the hostels and is the most popular watering hole for pickers, packers and backpackers. It also has reasonably good bistro meals.

On Gregory St, parallel to Herbert St, *Fellows Fish Bar* is a popular little takeaway fish and chip place, and nearby the *Hot Wok* has cheap Chinese takeaways. Next to the long-distance bus stop in Williams St is the *Bluebird Cafe*, a typical country town cafe.

At 37 Herbert St, *Good Times* is a bright and interesting licensed restaurant in a restored old building with pressed-metal ceilings. The food is 'international cuisine', with mains like grilled coral trout, Bowen pork medallions, spaghetti marinara and eye fillet steak priced from $14 to $17.

Getting There & Away

Bus Long-distance buses stop outside the Traveland travel agency (☎ 4786 2835), in Williams St, between Herbert and Gregory Sts.

Greyhound Pioneer and McCafferty's both have frequent bus services to and from Rockhampton (7½ hours, $74), Airlie Beach (one hour, $21) and Townsville (2½ hours, $31).

Train The *Sunlander* and *Queenslander* trains both stop here, but note that they stop at Bootooloo Siding 3km south of the centre, *not* at the Bowen railway station.

The fare from Brisbane is $139 for an economy sleeper .

Getting Around
Bowen Bus Services (☎ 4786 4414) runs local buses on weekdays from near the post office to Queens Beach and Horseshoe Bay. They also have a service out to the coal-mining centre of Collinsville.

COLLINSVILLE
pop 2700
It's 85km south-west from Bowen to the coal-mining town of Collinsville. Coal was first discovered here in the 1860s, but the coalfield wasn't fully developed until the rail link to Bowen was completed in 1917.

Coal is sent from here to Abbott Point north of Bowen, where it is loaded onto container ships and transported around the world. You might like to take a three-hour tour of the Abbot Point Coal Loading Facility; it runs on Wednesday mornings and bookings can be made on ☎ 4786 4414.

The town itself has few tourist attractions, although the surrounding area is popular with fossickers looking for agate and amethyst. For advice on where to hunt for which gems, you can contact the Bowen Lapidary Club on ☎ 4786 1346.

North Coast

This chapter covers Queensland's North Coast – an area that stretches from the Cape Upstart National Park to the Mission Beach area, and inland as far as the Gregory Developmental Rd.

At the centre of the North Coast is Townsville, the largest city in north Queensland. Townsville has a fine aquarium, good dive courses and trips to the outer Barrier Reef, and Magnetic Island is just a short boat ride offshore.

Inland from Townsville you can visit the former gold-mining centres of Charters Towers and Ravenswood. From Charters Towers, the Flinders Hwy continues its run clear across outback Queensland.

There are some wonderful national parks along this stretch of the coast. The majestic Hinchinbrook Island is one of Queensland's great natural wonders; pack your tent and walking boots and tackle the 32km Thorsborne Trail. South of Hinchinbrook is Orpheus Island, with an exclusive resort and excellent diving off its fringing reefs.

Further north is Mission Beach, a cluster of settlements scattered along a scenic strip of coastline. This area is an increasingly popular destination, with rainforests running right down to the coast, good beaches, and the resort islands of Dunk and Bedarra just offshore.

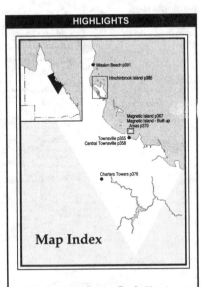

HIGHLIGHTS

Mission Beach p391

Hinchinbrook Island p385

Magnetic Island p367
Magnetic Island - Built up Areas p370

Townsville p355
Central Townsville p358

Charters Towers p376

Map Index

- Check out the Barrier Reef without even getting wet at the Great Barrier Reef Wonderland in Townsville.
- Take a trip back in time to the living ghost town of Ravenswood.
- Walk the Thorsborne Trail on Hinchinbrook Island, one of Queensland's best wilderness experiences.

GEOGRAPHY & CLIMATE

The south-west corner of this region is dominated by the valleys of the Burdekin River and the massive Burdekin Falls Dam. The Burdekin areas are some of the richest farmlands in the state, with sugar cane and rice being the major crops.

The mountain ranges of the Great Dividing Range run parallel with the coast, and become higher and move closer to the coast the further north you go. Largely covered in thick rainforests, these mountains are part of the Wet Tropics World Heritage Area, which starts just north of Townsville and stretches along the Queensland coast almost as far as Cooktown.

Like the rest of the north, this region has a tropical climate. Summer (December to March) is hot, wet and humid; the rest of the year you can expect predominantly warm, sunny weather with no great extremes. The northern section of this coast, from Ingham to Innisfail, is the wettest part of Queensland – and Tully is the wettest place in Australia, receiving over 4000mm of rain annually.

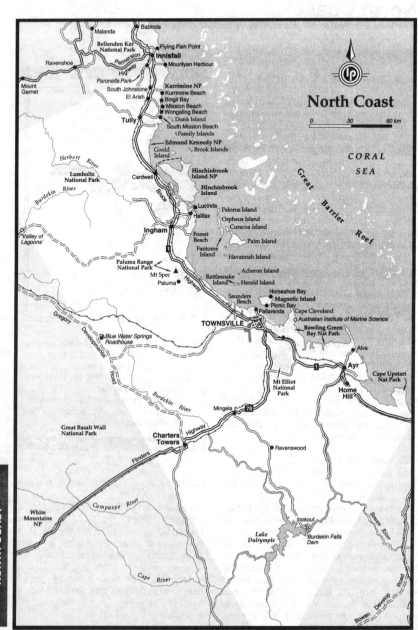

ACTIVITIES
White-water rafting trips on the Tully River operate out of Mission Beach. You can also take trips to the outer Barrier Reef from Mission Beach, Magnetic Island and Townsville, and dive courses are offered at the same three places.

Highlights for bushwalkers in this area include Hinchinbrook Island, Magnetic Island, the Mission Beach area, Jourama Falls and Mt Spec in the Paluma Range National Park (south of Ingham), and the Bowling Green Bay National Park (south of Townsville).

GETTING THERE & AWAY
Air
Townsville is the major airport for the North Coast, with flights to/from all major centres and capital cities.

Dunk Island has its own airport, with regular flights to/from Townsville and Cairns.

Bus
Bus services in this area are almost identical to the routes covered by the trains. Greyhound Pioneer and McCafferty's both have frequent services up the Bruce Hwy on the Brisbane-Cairns run, with detours off the highway to the Mission Beach area. Brisbane to Townsville takes 20 hours and costs $119.

Both companies also have inland services from Townsville to Mt Isa, via Charters Towers, continuing onto Threeways in the Northern Territory (from where you can either head north to Darwin or south to the Alice).

Train
The main Brisbane-Cairns railway line runs alongside the Bruce Hwy, with stops at all the major centres including Ayr, Townsville, Ingham, Cardwell and Tully. The Brisbane-Townsville trip takes around 22 hours and the one-way fare is $148 for an economy sleeper or $226 for a 1st-class sleeper.

The *Inlander* operates twice a week between Townsville and Mt Isa. The trip

from Townsville to Charters Towers takes three hours and costs $20.

Car & Motorcycle
The Bruce Hwy is the major route up the coast, while the Flinders Hwy from Townsville is the major inland route. If you have a little time, the detour off the Bruce Hwy to the mountain village of Paluma is one of the most spectacular scenic drives along this section of the coast.

The Gregory Developmental Rd runs parallel with the coast, on the inland side of the Great Dividing Range, passing through Charters Towers to the Lynd Junction. From here, the Kennedy Hwy continues north to the Atherton Tableland.

Sea
If you're heading offshore, the major ferry services out to the islands along this coast are from Townsville to Magnetic Island, from Cardwell to Hinchinbrook Island, and from Mission Beach to Dunk Island.

Ayr to Townsville

HOME HILL
pop 3200
At Home Hill, a small highway town 9km south of Ayr, a faded sign modestly announces **Ashworth's Fantastic Tourist Attraction**. This is one of the largest souvenir shops you'll ever see, with a wild collection of tea-towels, T-shirts, watches, place mats, jewellery and teaspoons. There's also a large pottery gallery at the front and, down a couple of stairs from the shop, the 'Treasures of the Earth' exhibition. It costs $2 to see this very impressive collection of fossils, gemstones and rocks.

AYR
pop 8800
Ayr is a fairly busy country town, but it seems to pop up out of nowhere: one minute you're driving along through cane fields,

the next you're surrounded by car dealers, fast food outlets and a bustling shopping centre ... and a couple of minutes later you're back in the cane fields.

Ayr is on the delta of one of the biggest rivers in Queensland, the Burdekin, and is the major commercial centre for the rich farmlands of the Burdekin Valley. Sugar cane and rice are the major crops grown in the area.

There's a tourist office on the southern edge of town. The town's cultural centre is an impressive complex which includes the **Burdekin Theatre** (☎ 4783 3455), a modern theatre which alternates as a venue for live performances and cinema.

The **Ayr Nature Display**, in a section of a private house in Wilmington St (signposted off the main roads), has a collection of thousands of butterflies preserved under glass, as well as moths, beetles and sea shells. The display is open daily from 8 am to 5 pm and entry costs $2.50 ($1 children).

Places to Stay

The *Ayr Caravan Park* (☎ 4783 1429) is next to the swimming pool on Queen St, just south of the centre. Across the road is the *Country Ayr Motel* (☎ 4783 1700), at 197 Queen St, which has modern motel units from $58/64 for singles/doubles.

The *Parkside Motel* (☎ 4783 1244), just off the highway on the west side of the centre at 74 Graham St, is another good motel with units from $52/55. This place also has a good restaurant (see Places to Eat).

Places to Eat

There are quite a few eateries along Queen St in the centre of town. The best of these is *Chrissie's Place*, 95 Queen St. It has a takeaway section at the front and a comfortable air-con coffee lounge out the back.

The *Country Kettle*, 148 Queen St, is a typical country town coffee shop. For a counter meal, you could try the *Queens Hotel* in the centre of town.

Ivories Restaurant at the Parkside Motel in Graham St is stylish and licensed, with dishes in the $16 to $22 range.

AUSTRALIAN INSTITUTE OF MARINE SCIENCE (AIMS)

If you're interested in marine biology, you can visit the Australian Institute of Marine Science (☎ 4778 9211), a marine research facility at Cape Ferguson between Ayr and Townsville. It's open to the public every weekday between 8 am and 4 pm, although visitors are restricted to the 'blue carpet' area which means you only get to see the reference library and a collection of photo display boards. The best time to visit is on a Friday between March and November, when free two hour guided tours are conducted at 10 am. A video show and a visit to the touch tanks and wharves are included, and you can have lunch in the canteen afterwards.

The turn-off to AIMS is on the Bruce Hwy about 53km north-west of Ayr or 35km south-east of Townsville.

BOWLING GREEN BAY NATIONAL PARK

At Alligator Creek, 28km south of Townsville or 72km north-west of Ayr, there's a turn-off from the Bruce Hwy to this national park. Alligator Creek tumbles down between two rugged ranges which rise steeply from the coastal plains. The taller range peaks at Mt Elliot (1234m), whose higher slopes harbour some of Queensland's most southerly tropical rainforest.

A sealed road heads 6km inland from the highway to the park entrance, from where a good gravel road leads to some pleasant picnic areas with tables and barbecues. Further on there's a good camping ground with lawns, shady trees, toilets, showers and barbecues. There are 20 self-registration sites, which can be booked through the ranger (☎ 4778 8203).

About 300m beyond the camping ground, there are good swimming holes in Alligator Creek. Two walking trails start from the camping ground. One follows Alligator Creek through a forest to Hidden Valley and the Alligator Falls – it's a 17km, five hour return walk. The other trail (8km) follows Cockatoo Creek south, taking about six hours return.

The park gates are closed from sundown to 6.30 am, so if you're planning to arrive or leave at night, you'll need to make arrangements with the ranger. There's no public transport to the park.

TOWNSVILLE
pop 122,600
The third largest centre in Queensland and the main centre in the north of the state, Townsville is the port city for the agricul-

tural and mining production of the vast inland region of northern Queensland.

Townsville is a working city, a major armed forces base, and the site of James Cook University. It's also the start of the main route from Queensland to the Northern Territory. It's the only departure point for Magnetic Island (20 minutes away by ferry), while the Barrier Reef is about 1¾ hours away by fast catamaran.

Despite concerted efforts to get visitors to stop in Townsville rather than going straight through to Cairns, and a boom in budget ac-

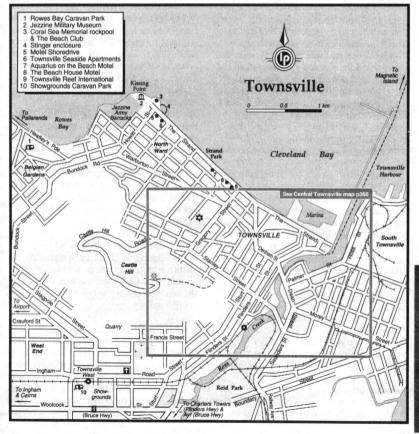

1 Rowes Bay Caravan Park
2 Jezzine Military Museum
3 Coral Sea Memorial rockpool & The Beach Club
4 Stinger enclosure
5 Motel Shoredrive
6 Townsville Seaside Apartments
7 Aquarius on the Beach Motel
8 The Beach House Motel
9 Townsville Reef International
10 Showgrounds Caravan Park

Townsville

See Central Townsville map p358

NORTH COAST

commodation and in the eating and entertainment scene, visitors are still staying away in droves. Apart from a few attractions, such as the excellent Great Barrier Reef Wonderland, and its role as an access point for Magnetic Island and the reef itself, Townsville still hasn't really got a lot going for it from a traveller's point of view.

History

Townsville was founded in 1864 by the work of a Scot, John Melton Black, and the money of Robert Towns, a Sydney-based sea captain and financier. Together these two owned pastoral lands in the high country inland which had already been pioneered. Their sheep and cattle farms couldn't survive without a boiling-down works on the coast for animal carcasses. Towns aimed to build this at Bowen, but Bowen residents objected and instead the pair set up the works on Cleveland Bay to the north of Bowen. Towns wanted it to be a private depot for his stations but Black saw the chance to make his fortune by founding a settlement and persuaded Towns to part with £10,000 for the project.

Despite a cyclone in 1867, Black persisted and was elected Townsville's first mayor the same year. The town developed mainly due to Chinese and Kanaka labour. European attitudes at the time were such that there was more alarm when a horse rather than a Kanaka was snatched from the banks of the creek by a crocodile. The horse was considered to be of more value! Eventually a road was forged up to Towns' stations inland, contributing to both their survival and Townsville's.

By the start of WWII, Townsville was a busy port town with a population of around 30,000, but with the outbreak of the war Townsville became one of the major bases for the Australian and US armed forces, boosting the population overnight to more than 100,000.

Orientation

Townsville's sprawl is extensive, but the centre, which is the only real area of inter-est to travellers, is a fairly compact area that you can easily get around on foot. The Bruce Hwy bypasses the city centre.

The city centre is flanked by Ross Creek to the south-east and Cleveland Bay to the north-east, with 290m Castle Hill towering over the centre to the west. The Great Barrier Reef Wonderland is at the northeast end of Flinders St East. The Sheraton Breakwater Hotel/Casino and the Entertainment Centre are on the breakwater close to the city centre, and there's a boat marina on the west side. There are two terminals on Ross Creek for the ferries to Magnetic Island: one on Flinders St East and one on the breakwater.

The transit centre, the arrival and departure point for long-distance buses, is on the corner of Palmer and Plume Sts, on the south side of Ross Creek. The train station is south of the centre near the corner of Flinders and Blackwood Sts.

Information

Tourist Information Townsville Enterprises' main tourist information office (☎ 4778 3555) is on the Bruce Hwy, 8km south of the city centre. It is open every day from 9 am to 5 pm. There's also a more convenient information centre (☎ 4721 3660) in the middle of Flinders St Mall, between Stokes and Denham Sts. It's open Monday to Friday from 9 am to 5 pm, and Saturday and Sunday from 9 am to 12.30 pm.

Post The main post office is on the corner of the Flinders St Mall and Denham St. The poste restante section is a small window around the back. There's also a post office shop in the Barrier Reef Wonderland which is open daily.

Useful Organisations The Department of Environment has an information office (☎ 4721 2399) at the Great Barrier Reef Wonderland which is open weekdays from 9 am to 5 pm and Saturday from 1 to 5 pm.

The RACQ (☎ 4775 3999) is at 202 Ross River Rd, in the suburb of Aitkenvale, about 7km south of the centre.

Bookshops The Mary Who Bookshop, 155 Stanley St, is a small bookshop with a good range of literature, travel and environmental books, children's books and classical music. The shop also has Internet/email access, at $5 per half hour.

QBD's Bumble Bee Bookshop on the Flinders St Mall is a larger mainstream bookshop which includes a large travel section.

The Ancient Wisdom Bookshop, in Shaw's Arcade off the Flinders St Mall, has a more esoteric collection of New Age books. Also in Shaw's Arcade is Jim's Book Exchange, which has a pretty wide selection of second-hand books.

Great Barrier Reef Wonderland
Townsville's top attraction is at the end of Flinders St East beside Ross Creek. While its impressive aquarium is the highlight, other sections include a theatre, a museum, shops, a good national parks information office and the Great Barrier Reef Marine Park Authority office.

Aquarium The aquarium's huge main tank has a living coral reef and hundreds of reef fish, sharks, rays and other life, and you can walk beneath the tank through a transparent tunnel. To maintain the natural conditions needed to keep this community alive, a wave machine simulates the ebb and flow of the ocean, circular currents keep the water in motion and marine algae are used in the purification system. The aquarium also has several smaller tanks, extensive displays on the history and life of the reef, and a theatrette where slide shows on the reef are shown. There are guided tours every day at 11.20 am and 2.30 pm, as well as daily diver shows, turtle-feeding and various other activities. It is open daily from 9 am to 5 pm and admission is $13 ($11 students, $6.50 children, $33 family).

Omnimax Theatre This cinema has angled seating and a dome-shaped screen to create a 3D effect. Hour-long films on the reef and various other topics, such as outer space, alternate through the day from 9.30 am till 4.30 pm. Omnimax film is a unique large format film which is projected through a fish-eye lens four times faster than normal 35mm film. You can read these and other fascinating facts here, or, perhaps more interestingly, you can see the huge film reels in operation in a small glass room beside the entrance. Admission to one film is $11.50 ($10 students, $6 children).

Museum of Tropical Queensland This small museum has two sections: one display focusing on the Age of Reptiles, with a collection of fossils found throughout Queensland and several reconstructions of dinosaurs; and the other devoted to the natural history of north Queensland, including wetland birds and other fauna, rainforests, ocean wrecks and Aboriginal artefacts. The museum is open every day from 9 am to 5 pm and admission is $4 ($2 children, $10.50 family).

Other Museums & Galleries
The **Townsville Museum** on the corner of Sturt and Stokes Sts has a permanent display on early Townsville and the north Queensland independence campaigns, as well as temporary exhibitions. It's open daily from 10 am to 3 pm (to 1 pm on weekends); entry is by gold coin donation.

The **Jezzine Military Museum** is in an 1890s fort and command post atop Kissing Point, in the grounds of the Jezzine Army Barracks beyond the northern end of The Strand. The museum has a collection of military paraphernalia dating back to the 1880s, and is open on Monday, Wednesday and Friday from 9.30 am to 12.30 pm.

There's also a **Maritime Museum** on Palmer St, beside Ross Creek in South Townsville. Housed in two heritage-style buildings, one section has an exhibition which focuses on north Queensland's maritime history, while the Gallery section exhibits old black and white photos of Port Townsville's golden olden days. The museum opens up on weekdays from 10 am to 4 pm and on weekends from 1 to 4 pm; entry costs $3 ($2 children).

NORTH COAST

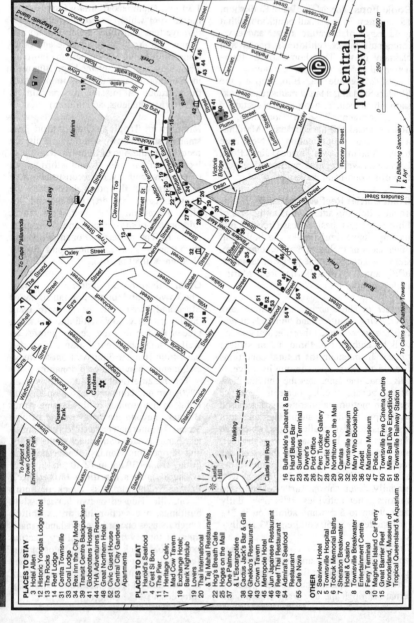

PLACES TO STAY
3 Hotel Allen
12 Historic Yongala Lodge Motel
13 The Rocks
14 Reef Lodge
31 Centra Townsville
33 Coral Lodge
34 Rex Inn the City Motel
39 Transit Centre Backpackers
41 Globetrotters Hostel
44 YHA Adventurers Resort
48 Great Northern Hotel
52 Civic Guest House
53 Central City Gardens
Apartments

PLACES TO EAT
1 Harold's Seafood
4 C'est Si Bon
11 The Pier
17 Heritage Cafe;
Mad Cow Tavern
18 Exchange Hotel;
Bank Nightclub
19 Lovers
20 Thai International
& Taj Mahal Restaurants
22 Hog's Breath Cafe
25 Hogs on the Mall
37 One Palmer
& L'Escargolière
38 Cactus Jack's Bar & Grill
40 Ghekko's Restaurant
43 Crown Tavern
45 Metropole Hotel
46 Jun Japanese Restaurant
49 Reef Thai Restaurant
54 Admiral's Seafood
Restaurant
55 Cafe Nova

OTHER
2 Seaview Hotel
5 Townsville Hospital
6 Tobruk Memorial Baths
7 Sheraton Breakwater
Hotel & Casino
8 Townsville Breakwater
Entertainment Centre
9 Ferry Terminal
10 Magnetic Island Car Ferry
15 Great Barrier Reef
Wonderland, Museum of
Tropical Queensland & Aquarium
16 Bulwinkie's Cabaret & Bar
21 Hard Blues Bar
23 Sunferries Terminal
24 Dwyer's
26 Post Office
27 Perc Tucker Gallery
29 Northtown on the Mall
30 Qantas
32 Townsville Museum
35 Mary Who Bookshop
36 Ansett
42 Maritime Museum
47 Police
50 Townsville Five Cinema Centre
51 Mike Ball Dive Expeditions
56 Townsville Railway Station

The **Perc Tucker Regional Gallery** at the Denham St end of the Flinders St Mall is a good regional art gallery and admission is free. It's open varying hours daily except Monday.

Parks & Gardens

The **Queens Gardens** on Gregory St, 1km north-west from the town centre, contain sports playing fields, tennis courts and Townsville's original Botanic Gardens, dating from 1878. The entrance to these lovely gardens is on Paxton St. The new botanic gardens, **Anderson Park**, were established in 1932. These gardens cover a 27-hectare site and feature mostly rainforest plants and palms from north Queensland and Cape York Peninsula. A conservatory houses almost 500 species of tropical plants. The gardens are 6km south-west of the centre on Gulliver St, Mundingburra. The **Kokoda Swimming Pool** is in the south-west corner of the gardens.

The **Palmetum**, about 15km south-west of the centre, off University Rd, is a 25-hectare botanic garden devoted to native palms in their natural environments, ranging from desert to rainforest species.

For a chance to see some birdlife, make your way out to the **Town Common Environmental Park**, 5km north of the centre, just off Cape Pallarenda Rd. A 7km road leads through this 32-sq km area, which ranges from mangrove swamps and salt marsh to dry grassland and pockets of woodland and forest. It's not a terribly attractive park, but the common is known for water birds such as magpie geese, which herald the start of the wet season, and stately brolgas, which gather in the Dry. There's an observation tower overlooking the wetlands area – early morning is the best time to see the birds.

Pallarenda is a fairly quiet little residential area on the waterfront about 8km north from the centre of Townsville. There isn't much incentive to drive out this way unless you live here, but if you do, you'll find the **Cape Pallarenda Environmental Park** on the headland at the end of the road.

There are picnic tables and walking tracks in the park, which is centred around a historic quarantine station.

Wildlife Sanctuary

The Billabong Sanctuary, 17km south on the Bruce Hwy, is a 10-hectare wildlife park of Australian native animals and birds. There are barbecue areas, a swimming pool and a kiosk in the park, and various shows throughout the day (including crocodile, koala and giant eel feeding). Admission costs $18 ($9 children). It's open daily from 8 am to 5 pm.

There is no public transport to the sanctuary, although daily tours come here – see the Organised Tours section later.

Other Attractions

The **Flinders St Mall** is the retail heart of the city. Every Sunday morning, the busy **Cotters Market** is held in the mall, with a wide range of crafts and local produce on offer.

East of the mall you can stroll along **Flinders St East** beside the creek. Many of the best 19th-century buildings are in this part of town, while further out on a breakwater at the mouth of Ross Creek the casino, entertainment centre and an upmarket seafood restaurant are located on the waterfront.

A more pleasant walk is north along **The Strand**, a long beachfront drive with a marina, gardens, some awesome banyan trees, the Tobruk Memorial Baths swimming pool and a big artificial waterfall.

The road up to the top of **Castle Hill** is very popular with joggers and power-walkers, especially at dawn and sunset. If you're feeling more adventurous, there's also a steeper but shorter walking track to the top from the end of Hillside Crescent on the city side of the hill. If you're feeling less energetic, you can drive up. Regardless of how you do it, it's worth coming up here as there are great 360° views from several lookout points.

The **Tobruk Memorial Baths** on The Strand is an Olympic-sized swimming pool

NORTH COAST

with good grassed areas and umbrella-shaded tables on either side of the pool.

Up the top end of The Strand is the **Coral Sea Memorial Rockpool**, a huge artificial swimming pool on the edge of the ocean. There's a pontoon out in the middle, and lawns and sandy beaches around the shore, and a huge filtration system keeps it clean and stinger-free. There is no admission fee. During the summer months when stingers are a problem on the beaches, there's a **Stinger Enclosure** on the beach at the north end of The Strand, about 100m south of the rockpool.

Activities

Dive Courses Townsville has four or five diving schools, and you can get cheap or free accommodation at some hostels if you book a dive course from that hostel.

Mike Ball Dive Expeditions (☎ 4772 3022), 252 Walker St, has two versions of its five day certificate course, both of which include free accommodation. The basic course starts every Saturday and costs $395, with three days training in Townsville and two day trips out to the reef. The more expensive course is better value – it starts every Wednesday and costs $480, with three days training in Townsville and two days/three nights spent out on the reef, staying on board its boat *Watersport*. You have to take a $50 medical before you start the course.

Pro-Dive, another well-regarded diving school, also runs courses in Townsville. Its office (☎ 4721 1760) is in the Great Barrier Reef Wonderland. Pro-Dive's weekly five-day certificate course costs $480 that includes two nights and three days on the reef, with a total of eight dives.

Diving Trips For experienced divers, there are diving trips from Townsville out to the wreck of the *Yongala*, one of the best dives in Australia.

The *Yongala* was a passenger liner which sank off Cape Bowling Green during a cyclone in 1911. She went down with all 122 of her crew and passengers and for years her disappearance was a complete mystery.

During WWII the ship's location was discovered and the first diver went down to the *Yongala* in 1947. The 90m-long wreck lies intact on the sea bottom in 30m of water and has become a haven for a huge variety of marine life.

Mike Ball and Pro-Dive both run trips out to the *Yongala* (from $165).

The wreck of the *Yongala* is more of an attraction than the John Brewer Reef, the destination for many day trips. John Brewer Reef has been damaged by cyclones and the crown-of-thorns starfish, and parts of the reef have little live coral.

Fishing Charters A number of charter boats operate fishing trips out of Townsville. Operators include Coral Sea Fishing Charters (☎ 018 778 524), True Blue Charters (☎ 4771 5474) and Challenger Charters (☎ 4725 1165).

The tourist information centre has a full list of fishing and yacht charter operators.

Other Activities Risky Business (☎ 4725 4571) has abseiling ($54) and skyseiling (like a huge flying fox, $79), and Coral Sea Skydivers (☎ 4725 6780) will let you throw yourself out of a plane for $197 (tandem dive); freefall courses cost $390.

Tour de Townsville Bicycle Tours (☎ 4721 2026) has a variety of cycling tours ($25 to $29) as well as bikes for hire.

Organised Tours

Reef Trips Pure Pleasure Cruises (☎ 4721 3555) has day trips on its 30m Wavepiercer catamaran to Kelso Reef, east of the Palm Island group, where it has a large floating pontoon. The cost is $130 ($65 children), which includes lunch, viewing from a glass-bottomed boat and snorkelling equipment. You can also do scuba dives as an optional extra.

Cruises The *Coral Princess* (☎ 4721 1673) does a four day cruise between Townsville and Cairns every week – see Cruises in the

Cairns section of the Far North Queensland chapter for more details.

Day Tours Detour Coaches (☎ 4721 5977) offers a variety of tours in and around Townsville, including a weekday city sights tour ($22, children $8), bus trips to the Billabong Sanctuary (daily, $29/15 including entry fee) and a tour to Charters Towers (Monday and Wednesday, $67/27). Detour also has day trips to Mt Spec from Townsville, with visits to Paluma, a rainforest walk and more (see the later Paluma Range section for details on this national park). The cost is $145.

Cycling Tours Tour de Townsville (☎ 4721 2026) runs a cycling tour around the sights of the city, including the marina, the rockpool, the botanic gardens and Rowes Bay. The 3½-hour tour is fully guided and costs $28 per person which includes bike hire.

Tours to Cairns If you're heading for Cairns, Pop Sullivan's Side Track Tours (☎ 4778 5925) does a two day trip to Cairns via the inland route, with stops at Mt Fox (an extinct volcano), the Burdekin River, the Undara lava tubes (where you stay overnight) and the Atherton Tableland. The trip costs $245 ($165 children) which includes accommodation, a tour at Undara and all your meals.

Festivals
Townsville's major annual event is the Palmer St Festival. Held each year in May, it features street theatre and other activities.

Places to Stay
Camping There are two caravan parks which are only about 3km from the centre of town. The *Rowes Bay Caravan Park* (☎ 4771 3576), opposite the beach on Heatley's Parade in Rowes Bay, has good facilities including a pool and a shop. Tent sites are $12 a double, and the on-site cabins start from $34 a double, rising to $38 with air-con and $46 with en suites. It also has self-contained villas from $49 a double.

The *Showground Caravan Park* (☎ 4772 1487), 16 Kings Rd, West End, has tent sites for $10 and on-site vans for $25.

If you don't need to be close to the centre, there are quite a few caravan parks strung along the Bruce Hwy to the north and south of Townsville.

Hostels With two huge backpackers hostels and a number of smaller ones, Townsville has more budget accommodation than it will ever need.

There are three hostels on or near Palmer St, on the southern side of Ross Creek. These places are close to the bus transit centre and convenient if you're just passing through, although this area can feel a little isolated and you'll find that most of Townsville's eateries, attractions and nightclubs are on the other side of the river.

The *YHA Adventurers Resort* (☎ 4721 1522), at 79 Palmer St, is a modern multi-level complex with over 300 beds, a shop, a car parking area and a swimming pool. The facilities are quite good, although because the place is so large it can feel a bit anonymous. Its courtesy bus does regular runs to the city centre and the ferry terminals. Accommodation in a four-bunk dorm costs $14 for YHA members, singles/doubles cost $24/32 and non-members pay $3 extra.

Townsville's other large offering is *Transit Centre Backpackers* (☎ 1800 628 836), which is upstairs on top of the transit centre. Although convenient for bus departures, the place lacks atmosphere. Dorm beds are $14 and singles/doubles are $25/32. Included in the price is a sunset tour of the city, and it also has a courtesy bus which runs to the ferry terminals and the beach.

Between these two places is the smaller *Globetrotters Hostel* (☎ 4771 3242), behind a house at 45 Palmer St. This relaxed hostel has all the usual facilities – kitchen area, lounge, pool, laundry – and it's clean and well run. Six-bed dorms cost $13 per night, singles cost $26 and a twin room is $32.

Townsville's other hostels are on the north side of Ross Creek, in and around the city centre. The pick of this bunch is probably *Civic Guest House* (☎ 4771 5381), at 262 Walker St. This clean and easy-going hostel has three or four-bed dorms for $14 or six-bed dorms with bathroom and aircon for $16. It also has very pleasant singles/doubles from $28/33, and doubles with a private bathroom and air-con for $48. A courtesy bus does pick-ups and drop-offs to the transit centre, and on Friday night there's a free barbecue for guests.

The *Reef Lodge* (☎ 4721 1112), at 4 Wickham St, is close to the Great Barrier Reef Wonderland and the ferry terminals. It's another small, old-fashioned but fairly clean place with various types of rooms spread over several buildings. There seem to be different prices for every room, but dorm beds are around $12, singles/doubles start at $28/32, and twin rooms are from $26. Most rooms have coin-in-the-slot air-con ($1). This place also has a courtesy bus.

Guesthouses At 32 Hale St, the *Coral Lodge* (☎ 4771 5512) is a recently renovated Queenslander which has two self-contained air-con units upstairs and eight guest rooms with shared bathroom and cooking facilities downstairs. The guesthouse rooms cost $38/48 for singles/doubles; the self-contained units are $48/58. Breakfast is included in the tariffs.

The Rocks (☎ 4771 5700) at 20 Cleveland Terrace is a superb, renovated historic home with bags of atmosphere and great views over the bay. It was originally built in the 1880s for a prominent local banker, and was used by the US navy command during WWII – and even has a concrete bunker in the back yard to prove it! All the rooms have period furnishings and are great value at $78/88 including breakfast. Evening meals are available on request, and these are excellent, reflecting the owner's Sri Lankan family background.

Pubs A number of Townsville's pubs offer accommodation. Generally, these pub rooms are fairly basic, with shared bathroom facilities.

The *Great Northern Hotel* (☎ 4771 6191), across the road from the train station at 500 Flinders St, is a good old-fashioned pub with clean, simple rooms, most of which open out onto a broad verandah. Nightly costs are $20/30; some doubles have private bathrooms for an extra $10. The food downstairs is good.

The *Hotel Allen* (☎ 4771 5656), on the corner of Eyre and Gregory Sts, has motel-style rooms with air-con which start from $45/55.

Motels There are plenty of motels in Townsville. One of the better areas to stay is along The Strand, which runs along the waterfront from the centre to the north.

The *Beach House Motel* (☎ 4721 1333), at 66 The Strand, is a neat, renovated budget motel with good units from $57/63 for singles/doubles. The *Regatta* restaurant at the front of the motel is quite good and overlooks a small pool.

The *Motel Shoredrive* (☎ 4771 6048) at 117 The Strand is across the road from the Coral Sea Memorial Rockpool and the swimming enclosure. Units here start from $59/65.

If you can afford a little more, the *Historic Yongala Lodge Motel* (☎ 4072 4633), at 11 Fryer St, has modern motel units and self-contained rooms starting from $69 a single/double, and period-style units from $79/89. At the front of the motel is a lovely 19th-century building which houses a Greek restaurant (see Places to Eat).

The *Townsville Reef International* (☎ 4721 1777), overlooking the waterfront from 63-64 The Strand, is a modern four-star, three-storey motel with a restaurant and a pool. Rooms here start from $108.

Closer to the centre of town, *Rex Inn the City* (☎ 4771 6048), at 143 Wills St, is a bright, renovated motel with a good pool, a barbecue area and a guest laundry. Standard units start from $65, there are units with kitchenettes from $70 and family units which sleep up to six people cost from $110.

If you're passing through Townsville, you'll find plenty of other motels strung along the Bruce Hwy on either side of the city.

Holiday Flats The *Townsville Seaside Apartments* (☎ 4721 3155), at 105 The Strand, is a long, two-storey strip of renovated 1960s apartments. The units don't win any interior design prizes, but they're comfortable enough and fully equipped with good kitchens and air-con. Prices vary according to the season and the number of people, but the one-bedroom units start from $55 and the two-bedroom units from $90.

If you want to be closer to the centre, the *Central City Gardens Apartments* (☎ 4772 2655), at 270 Walker St, is a four-storey complex of reasonably modern apartments with a good pool area and underground parking. All the units have a separate kitchen and lounge. One-bedroom units are from $86 a double, two-bedroom units from $110 for up to four people, and three-bedroom units are from $134 for up to six people.

Hotels & Apartment Hotels *Aquarius on the Beach* (☎ 4772 4255), at 75 The Strand, is an excellent all-suite hotel. At 14 storeys this is the tallest building on the waterfront, with more than 130 self-contained units, all of which have great views, air-con, kitchenettes and all the other mod-cons. There's a pool and a restaurant on the 14th floor. Rooms here range from $110 a double and from $130 for four people.

You can't miss the *Centra Townsville* (☎ 4772 2477) – it's the prominent 20-storey circular building in the centre of the Flinders St Mall. The Centra is a four-star hotel and has 159 rooms, two gyms, a rooftop pool, a piano bar and a restaurant. Rooms, all with air-con, fridge and minibar start from $160 a night single or double. Suites are $20 extra.

Another four-star offering is the *Sheraton Breakwater Casino/Hotel* (☎ 4722 2333), perched on the breakwater at the end of Sir Leslie Thiess Drive. Rooms here range from $220 to $240, depending on your views. For the high rollers, suites range from $300 to $850.

Places to Eat
Cafes, Delis & Takeaways Flinders St East is the main area for eateries, and it offers plenty of choice. The *Heritage Cafe & Bar* is a modern, cosy place with light meals (pasta etc) from $8 to $10; other mains are slightly more.

On the same street is *Lovers*, a trendy cafe/restaurant with a downstairs licensed cafe section (main courses $12 to $15) and a slightly more formal upstairs section ($17 to $20).

There are quite a few cafes and other eateries along the Flinders St Mall, although most of them are hidden in arcades and shopping centres off the mall. Northtown on the Mall, an arcade opposite the tourist information centre, has a couple of good places including *Le Cafe de France*, a sit-down cafe which serves sandwiches and cakes. *Strollers Cafe*, in Shaw's Arcade up near the Stanley St end, is another popular sit-down lunch place with sandwiches, burgers, filled croissants and quiches.

There's also a cluster of eateries further up The Strand around the Gregory St corner. On the corner itself, *Harold's Seafood* is a takeaway fish and chippery with good burgers, and the coral trout is especially good. There's a kebab place next door on The Strand.

If you're waiting for a bus, *Andy's* in the transit centre on Palmer St serves quite substantial meals and is open from 5 am to 11.30 pm.

C'est Si Bon, about 1km north of the centre on Eyre St near the Gregory St corner, is an excellent little gourmet deli and takeaway which has good salads, sandwiches, marinated chicken pieces, pork pies, home-made cakes and other goodies.

Pubs Many of the pubs do decent counter meals. The Great Northern Hotel, on the corner of Flinders and Blackwood Sts, has the excellent *Blarney Bar Bistro* with mains from $12 to $15 and good bar meals from $5 to $7; the steaks are the size of dinner plates.

The Exchange Hotel, at 151 Flinders St East, has the casual *Portraits Wine Bar* downstairs with bistro meals and the more expensive *Thai Exchange* upstairs on the balcony, with mains from $9 to $14.

There are a few good pubs over the creek along Palmer St. The *Metropole Hotel*, next to the YHA Adventurers Resort, has a covered garden bistro out the back with pastas, seafood and steaks from $10 to $15, and a good range of cheaper 'chef's specials'. Also in the pub is a good little à la carte restaurant, *La Met*, with main meals around $18.

On the other side of the YHA, the *Crown Tavern* has a beer garden and bistro meals from $6 to $10.

Behind the Coral Sea Memorial Rockpool at the northern end of The Strand is the *Beach Club*, which is a pleasant alternative to the pubs. This place has a bar, poker machines and tables overlooking the rockpool and the ocean. Bistro meals are mostly $9 to $12. This is a licensed club – non-members are welcome but must sign in first.

Finally, the *casino* has amazingly cheap (and low glam) pub-style meals for the punters – $6 gets you a roast and vegies.

Restaurants Flinders St East is one of the main areas for eateries, and offers plenty of choices. The *Hog's Breath Cafe*, one of a chain of American saloon-style bar and grills, is near the Denham St corner. It has burgers from $8 to $9, salads from $9 to $12, and steak, chicken and fish grills for around $16 to $18. Its speciality is the prime ribs, which cost around $18.

Moving along the street, the *Thai International Restaurant*, upstairs at No 235, has fine soups for $6, a good range of vegetarian dishes from $6 to $9, and imaginative main courses for $10 to $14. Downstairs is the *Taj Mahal*, an Indian and Persian restaurant with vegetarian dishes from $11 to $14; others are $15 to $18. Both of these places are BYO.

Still in Flinders St, but on the Mall, is *Hoges on the Mall*, a family restaurant with main meals at $13 to $16, and breakfast from $6.

Past the southern end of the mall, is the small *Jun Japanese Restaurant*, which is

nothing special but has lunchtime main courses from $11 and a range of set five-course menus from $24 to $28 per person.

The *Reef Thai Restaurant* on Flinders St, near Blackwood St, is a spacious Thai restaurant which is open weekdays for lunch and every night for dinner. Main courses are in the $9 to $14 range.

Cafe Nova, on Blackwood St, near the Flinders St corner, is an interesting little BYO cafe which is open from 10.30 am till late. It has good coffee, milk shakes and a great range of cakes and desserts, as well as snacks $3 to $8. There's also a few mains like lasagne, crepes or tortillas from $5 to $7. On the corner of Blackwood and Sturt Sts, *Admiral's Seafood Restaurant* serves seafood in a nautical-style setting.

The Pier (☎ 4721 2567) is an up-market, licensed seafood restaurant perched out on the breakwater on Sir Leslie Thiess Drive, surrounded by water on three sides. It's a cosy, stylish restaurant with a vaguely nautical feel. At lunch time main courses are from $18, while the dinner menu has mains in the $20 to $25 range.

The *Historic Yongala Lodge*, at 11 Fryer St, has a Greek restaurant in a lovely old building, with displays of period furniture, memorabilia, and finds from the *Yongala* wreck. Main meals are in the $18 to $25 range, or there's a banquet menu at $35 a head. There's live Greek music here on Friday and Saturday nights.

Palmer St also has a handful of good restaurants. *One Palmer*, on the corner of Palmer and Dean Sts, is a modern licensed cafe (mains $14 to $18), while next door is *L'Escargotiére*, a simple BYO French restaurant with a small courtyard out the back and mains around $18.

At No 21 is *Cactus Jack's Bar & Grill* (☎ 4721 1478), a lively licensed Mexican place with main courses in the $10 to $14 range. It's pretty popular, and the sangria and margaritas tend to flow fast and furious; you'll need to book on weekends.

Further along, in front of the transit centre, is *Ghekko's*, a training restaurant staffed by catering students. The full works here, including silver service and starched linen, costs just $9 for main courses. It's open for lunch Wednesday to Friday and dinner Wednesday to Sunday.

Entertainment

Townsville's nightlife is almost as lively as Cairns' and ranges from pub bands to flashy clubs and, of course, the casino. The main nightlife area is along Flinders St East, with a couple of other places along The Strand.

Pubs & Live Music The *Hard Blues Bar*, in the James Cook Tavern at 237 Flinders St East, is one of the main venues for live music in Townsville. It has a different theme each night; Monday is musos' night, with jam sessions and try-outs. There's a cover charge on the weekend, which ranges from $5 for local bands to $30 or more for major international acts.

The *Mad Cow Tavern* is a new bar on Flinders St East, and close by is *Dwyer's*, an Irish bar with live music Wednesday to Saturday.

Most of the other pubs along Flinders St East have live bands or DJs on weekends. *Tattersalls Hotel,* on the corner of Flinders St East and Wickham St, has a nightclub which is open from Wednesday to Sunday nights until 3 or 4 am. There's no cover charge, and there are usually drinks specials here to lure thirsty punters.

Along The Strand, the popular *Seaview Hotel*, on the corner of Gregory St, has the live music in the *beer garden*, as well as the *Arizona Bar* and *Breezes* upstairs (an over-28s nightclub) with occasional rock and roll bands.

The *Australian Hotel*, south of the creek on Palmer St, is a relaxed, old-fashioned pub with live music sessions on Sunday afternoon.

Nightclubs *The Bank*, in a former bank building at 169 Flinders St East, is the city's most up-market nightclub. It's open nightly until around 5 am, with a $5 cover charge and dress regulations. *Bullwinkle's Cabaret & Bar,* on the corner of Flinders St East and Wickham St, has a nightclub section which

stays open nightly until 3 am, and a coffee shop and eating area upstairs.

Casino Townsville's *Sheraton Breakwater Casino* is at the end of Sir Leslie Thiess Drive in the Sheraton Hotel complex. You can try your luck at roulette, blackjack, two-up, keno or various other games from 9 am to 3 am daily (until 4 am on Friday and Saturday). There's no admission fee, although dress regulations specify neat casual wear, which means no T-shirts, runners, thongs or bare feet.

Theatre & Cinema The *Townsville Five Cinema Centre* (☎ 4771 4101), on the corner of Sturt and Blackwood Sts, shows mainstream current releases.

The impressive 5000 seat *Townsville Breakwater Entertainment Centre* (☎ 4771 4000) is now the main venue for concerts, the performing arts and other major events.

The *Civic Theatre* (☎ 4772 2677), on Boundary St South Townsville, is a smaller venue for performing arts and other varied cultural pursuits.

Things to Buy

John Melick & Co, 481 Flinders St, sells a good range of camping and bushwalking gear, Drizabone oilskins, Akubra hats, work boots and walking boots, tents, sleeping bags and work wear. Another place to try for this type of stuff is Askern's Army Disposals, further down at 525 Flinders St, which sells tarps, jerry cans, stoves and various camping and walking gear.

Getting There & Away

Air Ansett and Qantas have regular flights between Townsville and the major destinations in Australia. Regular one-way fares include Cairns $176 and Brisbane $363. Both airlines have offices in the mall, with Qantas at 320 Flinders St and Ansett at 350 Flinders St.

Sunstate (Qantas) has services between Townsville and Dunk Island ($129), Mackay ($204), Proserpine ($169), Rockhampton ($291), Gladstone and Bundaberg.

Flight West has flights to Mt Isa ($289) at least once a day, often with stops at smaller places on the way. It also flies direct to Mackay ($204) and Rockhampton ($291).

Bus Townsville is on the main Brisbane to Cairns coastal run, and both Greyhound Pioneer (☎ 13 2030) and McCafferty's (☎ 13 2499) have frequent daily services to and from here. All the long-distance buses operate from the Townsville transit centre on Palmer St. Average fares and times from Townsville include Brisbane (20 hours, $119), Rockhampton (nine hours, $73), Mackay (4½ hours, $47), Airlie Beach (four hours, $35), Mission Beach (3½ hours, $33) and Cairns (six hours, $37).

Townsville is also the start of the main inland route from Queensland across to Darwin and Alice Springs. If you're heading west, the trip to Charters Towers takes 1¾ hours and costs $14; to Mt Isa the trip takes 12 hours and costs $81.

Train The Brisbane-Cairns *Sunlander* travels through Townsville three times a week. The trip from Brisbane to Townsville takes 22 hours ($148 for an economy sleeper, $226 for a 1st class sleeper). From Townsville, Proserpine ($36/57 economy/1st class seat) is a four-hour journey, Rockhampton ($77/122) is 11 hours and Cairns ($41/65) 7½ hours.

The *Queenslander* does the Brisbane-Cairns run once a week (leaving Brisbane on Sunday morning and Cairns on Tuesday morning). It's a bit faster than the *Sunlander*, as well as being a lot more luxurious and more expensive – the fare from Brisbane to Townsville is $344 which includes all meals and a sleeping compartment.

The *Inlander* operates twice weekly from Townsville to Mt Isa (18 hours; $125/192 an economy/1st class sleeper). Townsville to Charters Towers takes three hours ($20/32 economy/1st class seat).

Getting Around
To/From the Airport Townsville airport is 5km west of the city centre at Garbutt; a

taxi to the centre costs $11. Acacia Luxury Transport runs the Airport Shuttle (☎ 4775 5544), servicing all main arrivals and departures. The cost is $5 one way or $8 for two people travelling together, and it will drop off or pick up almost anywhere fairly central.

Bus Sunbus runs local bus services around Townsville. Route maps and timetables are available in the Transit Mall (near the Flinders St Mall tourist office).

Taxi There's a taxi rank at the Transit Mall on the corner of Stokes St and the Flinders St Mall. To book a taxi, call Standard White Cabs (☎ 13 1008).

Car Rental The larger car-rental agencies are all represented in Townsville. Thrifty (☎ 4772 4600), Avis (☎ 4721 2688), Budget (☎ 4713 2727) and Hertz (☎ 4771 6003) all have rental desks at the airport.

Smaller operators include Rent-a-Rocket (☎ 4772 1442) at 14 Dean St, South Townsville; Sunrunner Moke Hire (☎ 4721 5038), 11 Anthony St, South Townsville; and Townsville Car Rentals (☎ 4772 1093) at 12 Palmer St, South Townsville. All of these places are close to the bus transit centre.

Four Wheel Drive Hire Service (☎ 1800 803 420), 711 Flinders St, has a wide range of 4WDs available for rent.

MAGNETIC ISLAND
pop 2100
Magnetic Island is one of Queensland's oldest resort islands, with the first tourists arriving from the mainland more than 100 years ago. It's a large (52 sq km) and scenic continental island, and today it remains a popular if somewhat old-fashioned resort island, with the main attractions being its fine beaches, excellent bushwalks, an abundance of wildlife and its laid-back nature.

Only 8km offshore, the island is almost an outer suburb of Townsville, with many people commuting to the mainland daily by ferry which are frequent, affordable and fast.

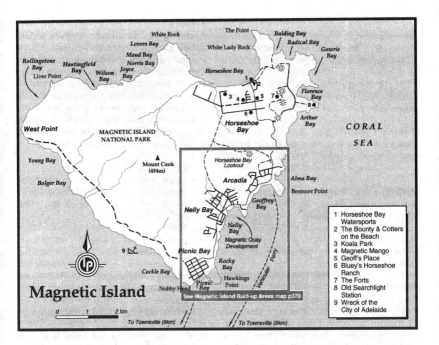

Magnetic Island

1 Horseshoe Bay
  Watersports
2 The Bounty & Cotters
  on the Beach
3 Koala Park
4 Magnetic Mango
5 Geoff's Place
6 Bluey's Horseshoe
  Ranch
7 The Forts
8 Old Searchlight
  Station
9 Wreck of the
  City of Adelaide

0   1   2 km

To Townsville (8km)   To Townsville (8km)

See Magnetic Island Built-up Areas map p370

There are four small townships spread around the east coast, with a wide range of budget to mid-range accommodation and a good range of restaurants and cafes. About 70% of the island is national park, with the 500m Mt Cook in the centre of the island being the dominant point.

History
The island was named by Captain Cook, who thought his ship's compass went funny when he sailed by in 1770.

Aborigines were frequent visitors to the island, which they could easily reach from the mainland. The first European settlement was established by timber cutters in the early 1870s. In 1887 Harry Butler and his family settled at Picnic Bay and started putting up visitors from the mainland in thatched huts, and thus the Magnetic Island tourist business was born. In 1899, Robert Hayles saw the potential of the island as a

holiday destination for the booming gold-mining centre of Charters Towers. The Hayles family built a hotel and dance hall and started up the first ferry service, and remained involved in the Magnetic Island tourist industry for the next 90 years.

Orientation & Information
Magnetic Island is roughly triangular in shape, with Picnic Bay, the main town and ferry destination, at the southern corner. The main road runs up the eastern side of the island through a string of small towns to Horseshoe Bay, with a turn-off to Radical Bay. There's also a rough track along the uninteresting west coast. Along the north coast it's walking only.

The Island Travel Centre (☎ 4778 5155) has an information centre and booking office between the end of the pier and the Picnic Bay Mall. You can book local tours and accommodation here, and it can also handle domestic and international travel arrangements.

The Department of Environment (☎ 4778 5378) has an office on Hurst St in Picnic Bay.

There are no banks or ATMs on the island, although most of the supermarkets on the island have EFTPOS facilities.

Zoning Geoffrey Bay, Arcadia and Five Beach Bay on the north coast of the island are all zoned Marine Park B – in other words fishing is not permitted.

Warning Box jellyfish are found in the waters around Magnetic Island between October and April. There is a netted swimming enclosure at Picnic Bay and Alma Bay is usually safe for swimming, but in other areas swimming is not recommended during the danger months.

Picnic Bay

The main settlement on the island, and the first stop for ferries, is Picnic Bay. The mall along the waterfront has a selection of shops and eateries, and you can hire bikes, mokes and scooters here. Picnic Bay also has quite a few places to stay, and the main beach has a stinger-free enclosure and is patrolled by a life-saving club.

There's a lookout above the town and just to the west of Picnic Bay is **Cockle Bay**, where you can see the wreck of the *City of Adelaide*. Heading around the coast in the other direction is **Rocky Bay** where you can take a short but steep walk down to a beautiful sheltered beach (don't forget about the sea wasps).

Nelly Bay

Next around the east coast is Nelly Bay, which has a good beach with shade, and a reef at low tide. At the far end of the bay there are some pioneer graves.

The north end of Nelly Bay is enclosed by a half-finished rocky marina. The developers of this project went broke and disappeared some years ago, and the site has been abandoned.

Arcadia

Round the next headland you come to **Geoffrey Bay**, a marine park which has an interesting 400m low-tide walk over the fringing coral reef from the southern end of the beach; a board indicates the start of the trail. The vehicle ferry stops at the jetty on Geoffrey Bay. Overlooking the bay is the town of Arcadia, with shops and more places to stay. Just around the next headland is the very pleasant **Alma Bay beach**.

Radical Bay & The Forts

The main road runs back from the coast between Arcadia and Horseshoe Bay, with a turn-off mid-way to Radical Bay. This narrow, winding and hilly road is private, and if you're in a rental vehicle your insurance doesn't cover you on this section. On the way to Radical Bay, there are walking tracks leading off to the old **Searchlight Station** on a headland between **Arthur** and **Florence bays**. There are fine views from up here, and the bays are secluded.

Radical Bay has a very attractive beach, although a resort that closed down here is now private property and there is limited access to the beach. From the car park here a walking trail leads across the headland to Horseshoe Bay, with a turn-off halfway to the beautiful and secluded **Balding Bay**, which is an unofficial nude-bathing beach.

Back at the junction of the road to Radical Bay, there's also a 1.4km walking track leading to **The Forts**, an old WWII command post and signal station with gun sites and an ammunition store.

Horseshoe Bay

Horseshoe Bay, on the north coast, is the longest and most sheltered, although not necessarily the best, beach on the island. This quiet town has a few shops and a couple of dated tourist attractions. **Magnetic Mango**, a working mango plantation, has an outdoor eatery which serves Devonshire teas and lunches. There's also a desultory **Koala Park**, but there are so many koalas on the island that you'll be better off skipping this place and just looking up a tree.

At the beach there are boats and sailboards for hire. From the beach you can walk to Maud Bay, around to the west, or back east to Radical Bay.

Activities
Bushwalking The National Parks service produces a leaflet for Magnetic Island's excellent bushwalking tracks. Possible walks, with distances and one-way travel times, include:

Nelly Bay – Arcadia	6km	2 hrs
Picnic Bay – West Point	8km	2½ hrs
Horseshoe Bay road to		
– Arthur Bay	2km	½ hr
– Florence Bay	2.5km	1 hr
– The Forts	2km	¾ hr
Horseshoe Bay to		
– Balding Bay	3km	¾ hr
– Radical Bay	3km	¾ hr

All times and distances are one way.

Diving Magnetic Island Pleasure Divers (☎ 4778 5788) at the Arcadia Resort Hotel offers a basic five-day dive course for $199, or a more comprehensive course for $295. The Townsville-based dive operators also do dives to the reef.

Water Sports On the beach at Horseshoe Bay, Horseshoe Bay Water Sports has a range of water-sports gear for hire, including dinghies ($70 a day), aquabikes, canoes and surf skis (all $8 a half hour). You can also go water-skiing here ($25 for 15 minutes).

Horse Riding Bluey's Horseshoe Ranch (☎ 4778 5109), at Horseshoe Bay, offers horse rides at $18 an hour, $40 for two hours or $45 for a half-day ride.

Organised Tours
Reef Trips Pure Pleasure Cruises (☎ 4721 3555) does a day trip out to Kelso Reef on the outer Barrier Reef, usually stopping at Magnetic on its way out from Townsville. See Townsville's Organised Tours section for details.

Cruises & Fishing Trips Barnacle Bill (☎ 4758 1237) takes up to three people out on fishing expeditions, with all gear and bait supplied. Two hours costs $40, four hours $70. It also has dinghies for hire.

Motorcycle Tours You can also take a tour of the island on the back of a Harley-Davidson. Based at the end of the jetty in Picnic Bay, the tours cost $35 for an hour or $25 for half an hour. Call ☎ 018 767 377 for details.

Places to Stay
Camping Camping facilities on the island are somewhat limited, and camping isn't allowed anywhere in the national park. Two of the backpackers' hostels, *Geoff's Place* and *Coconuts at the Beach*, have areas set aside for campers – Geoff's Place is probably the better set up. See the Hostels section following for more details.

Hostels There's a good selection of backpackers' hostels on the island and it's a competitive scene, with several hostels sending vehicles to meet the ferries at Picnic Bay. Most places have cheaper rates during the quiet times and for longer stays, and there are also package deals on accommodation and transport (see Getting There & Away).

Picnic Bay Only a minute's walk from the Picnic Bay ferry pier, the small *Hideaway Budget Resort* (☎ 4778 5110), 32 Picnic St, is a clean, renovated place with a kitchen, TV room with a video library, a good pool and laundry facilities. It's well located and good value, with a bed in a twin or double room (no dorms) costing $14, and there are self-contained cabins at $45.

Nelly Bay As you round the corner into Nelly Bay, you'll notice the blue-and-white-striped 'Camp-O-Tel' accommodation (a cross between a cabin and a tent with beds or bunks) at *Coconuts on the Beach* (toll-free ☎ 1800 065 696). It costs $8 per person to camp in your own tent (no shade),

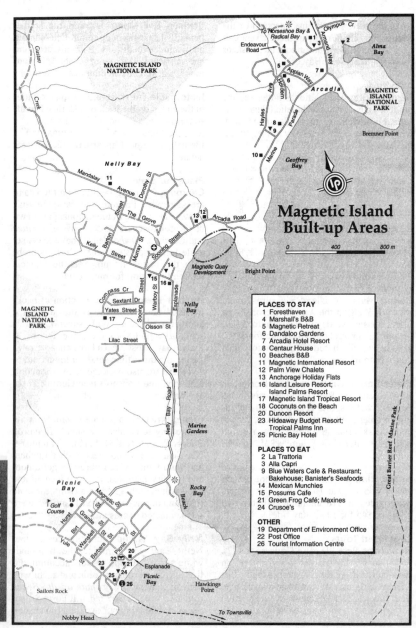

Magnetic Island Built-up Areas

0   400   800 m

PLACES TO STAY
1 Foresthaven
4 Marshall's B&B
5 Magnetic Retreat
6 Dandaloo Gardens
7 Arcadia Hotel Resort
8 Centaur House
10 Beaches B&B
11 Magnetic International Resort
12 Palm View Chalets
13 Anchorage Holiday Flats
16 Island Leisure Resort;
    Island Palms Resort
17 Magnetic Island Tropical Resort
18 Coconuts on the Beach
20 Dunoon Resort
23 Hideaway Budget Resort;
    Tropical Palms Inn
25 Picnic Bay Hotel

PLACES TO EAT
2 La Trattoria
3 Alla Capri
9 Blue Waters Cafe & Restaurant;
   Bakehouse; Banister's Seafoods
14 Mexican Munchies
15 Possums Cafe
21 Green Frog Café; Maxines
24 Crusoe's

OTHER
19 Department of Environment Office
22 Post Office
26 Tourist Information Centre

NORTH COAST

$16 per head in an eight-bed dorm or the camp-o-tels (which apparently get unbearably hot in summer). Coconuts promotes itself as a party hard place, which is fine if that's what you're after.

The *Magnetic Island Tropical Resort* (☎ 4778 5955), on Yates St, just off the main road, is a very good budget resort with a good swimming pool, an inexpensive restaurant and a pleasant garden setting. Backpackers can stay in a four to six-bed A-frame cabin with its own bathroom for $16. Alternatively, you can rent a whole cabin, which costs $45 a double for the standard model, $65 a double for the deluxe model with TV, fridge and tea and coffee-making facilities, or $79 a double with self-contained facilities and air-con. It's another $10 for each extra adult, or $5 per child. This place is good if you're after somewhere quiet.

Arcadia *Centaur House* (☎ 4778 5668), 27 Marine Parade, is a small, rambling, old-style hostel opposite the beach. The atmosphere is relaxed, and there's a pleasant garden out the back with hammocks and a barbecue. A bed in the large downstairs dorm costs $15; double rooms upstairs are $35. This place is quiet and friendly.

Also in Arcadia, at 11 Cook Rd, is *Foresthaven* (☎ 4778 5153). This hostel has seen better days, and the buildings and facilities are pretty old and basic, although the peaceful bush setting is nice. Accommodation is spread across several buildings, with units with two or three-bed rooms sharing one kitchen and eating area. Dorm beds cost $14, twins and doubles are $34, or there are self-contained rooms from $25 per person. Barbecues are held in the large courtyard, and you can rent mountain bikes. The owners speak German and French.

Horseshoe Bay *Geoff's Place* (☎ 4778 5577), on Horseshoe Bay Rd, is one of the island's most popular places for travellers with its party atmosphere and nightly activities, although maintenance and service are suffering these days. There are extensive

grounds, and you can camp for $6 per person, or share a four or eight-bed A-frame cedar cabin for $14. (The eight-bed cabins have their own bathroom.) There's a communal kitchen, a popular pool, a bar and a cheap restaurant. You can hire mountain bikes here, and the courtesy bus shuttles between here and Picnic Bay to meet the ferries.

Hotels, Motels, Holiday Flats & Resorts
There are lots of other accommodation options on the island. There are a couple of pubs and motels, and a few fairly new resorts, but by far the most common type of accommodation is in self-contained holiday flats. Many of these are quite old-fashioned, some are downright ancient, although there are a handful of newer places on the island.

Rates for all of these places vary with the seasons and demand, and most have cheaper 'stand-by' rates. They're also cheaper if you rent by the week. When you book, check whether linen, towels, etc are included in the tariff – you may have to BYO.

Picnic Bay The *Picnic Bay Hotel* (☎ 4778 5166), on the Esplanade in Picnic Bay, has motel rooms from $50 for twin rooms. In Picnic St next to the Hideaway hostel, the *Tropical Palms Inn* (☎ 4778 5076) has good motel units from $63, and self-contained cottages from $325 a week.

The *Dunoon Resort* (☎ 4778 5161), on the corner of Granite St and the Esplanade, is an older place that has been renovated and is set in good landscaped gardens, with two pools and laundry facilities. The one and two-bedroom self-contained units sleep four to six people and cost from $76 a double, plus $10 for extra adults and $6 for extra children.

Nelly Bay The *Island Leisure Resort* (☎ 4778 5511), close to the waterfront at 4 Kelly St, is an impressive resort with good facilities including a pool in a garden setting, a floodlit tennis court, a gym and a games room. All the units have a double bed and three bunks and cost $94 a double – children are free. Around the corner at 13 the Esplanade, the *Island Palms Resort* (☎ 4778 5571) is also good and has 12 self-contained two-bedroom units that cost from $89 a double.

The *Palm View Chalets* (☎ 4778 5596), 114 Sooning St, is a collection of stylish A-frame timber chalets which sleep up to six people, and are self-contained. They are excellent value from $50 a double. Also on Sooning St, the *Anchorage Holiday Flats* (☎ 4778 5596) is a complex of two-bedroom units starting from $75 a night. The waterfront aspect of both places is spoilt by the unfinished Magnetic Quay Development.

The *Magnetic Island Tropical Resort* also has a good range of cabins – see the Hostels section earlier.

The *Magnetic International Resort* (☎ 4778 5200) is on Mandalay Ave and is the biggest resort on the island. There are 80 units and 16 suites, all with air-con, fans, telephone, TV, radio, tea/coffee-making equipment and refrigerator. There's a swimming pool, tennis court and laundry facilities. Room costs are from $140 to $170.

Arcadia The *Arcadia Hotel Resort* (☎ 4778 5177) has motel-style units which range from $60 to $80, depending on the time of year and how close you are to the pool.

There are a number of budget holiday flats along Hayles Ave. Starting from the Alma Bay end of the street, *Magnetic Retreat* (☎ 4778 5357), with its entrance a little way up Rheuben Terrace, has one and two-bedroom units from $50 to $80. The *Magnetic North Holiday Units* (☎ 4778 5647), on the corner of Hayles Ave and Endeavour Rd, has two-bedroom units for up to six people from $65 a night, and a weekly rate of $390.

The *Dandaloo Gardens* (☎ 4778 5174), 40 Hayles Ave, has eight one-bedroom units that sleep up to five and start at $60 a night.

B&Bs There are also a couple of B&Bs on the island. The friendly *Marshall's B&B* (☎ 4778 5112), 3 Endeavour Rd, is a

relaxed place with singles/doubles from $35/50.

On the Arcadia waterfront, *Beaches B&B* (☎ 4778 5303), 39 Marine Parade, is a modern timber cottage that has a separate B&B section with two bedrooms. There's a good pool out the back and a front verandah overlooking the bay, and the rates here are good value at $60 a double, including breakfast.

Places to Eat
Picnic Bay The Esplanade at Picnic Bay, along the waterfront, has a selection of eating places. The *Picnic Bay Hotel* has counter meals from $6 to $12, and there are cheaper snacks.

Further along, *Crusoe's* is a casual little BYO restaurant with a takeaway section and a few outdoor tables. It does breakfast, lunch, dinner and takeaways including good pies. Further along again, the *Green Frog Cafe* is nice little lunchtime place with good sandwiches and cakes. It also does breakfasts and Devonshire teas.

At the far end of the mall is *Maxine's*, a stylish bar and restaurant which is open nightly for dinner. Main courses range from $10 to $17, and the speciality here is oysters.

Nelly Bay *Mexican Munchies,* 31 Warboy St, runs the gamut from enchiladas to tacos, and is open daily from 6 pm. Main courses are in the $12 to $14 range. There's a black-board outside where you can chalk up your reservation during the day.

Nearby, in the small shopping centre on the main road, is *Possums*, good for snacks and takeaways. Also here is a *bakery*, which does a good full breakfast for $5.

Arcadia The *Arcadia Hotel Resort* has a number of eating possibilities; bistro meals range from $10 to $14, and you can eat outdoors by the pool. *Gatsby's Restaurant* is open on weekends and has more expensive meals.

Alla Capri, on Hayles Ave, is a licensed place with a pleasant outdoor eating area. It specialises in steaks and Italian food. Main course dishes cost around $11 to $15, pizzas are $15 for a medium or $18 for a large and there's house wine. Tuesday is all-you-can-eat pasta night for $7.50. It's open Tuesday to Sunday from 6 pm.

La Trattoria, at Alma Beach with a great setting overlooking this pretty little bay, does the pizza, pasta and seafood thing for lunches and dinner (closed Tuesday).

In the small Arcadia shopping centre on the corner of Hayles Ave and Bright St, the *Blue Waters Cafe & Restaurant*, which looks deceptively like a basic takeaway joint, actually has some of the best food on the island. There's a pleasant courtyard out the back and an interesting selection of mains ranging from $14 to $17, or a three-course set menu for $15. It's open for dinner from Tuesday to Saturday.

On the Hayles Ave side of the junction, the *Bakehouse* is open early and is a good place for a coffee and croissant breakfast. Next door is *Banister's Seafood*, which is basically a fish and chips place with an open-air BYO dining area. It's open daily from 8 am to 8 pm.

Horseshoe Bay On the waterfront at the bay you can get takeaways or snacks at *The Bounty*, and the general store next door has a small supermarket section where you can buy groceries and supplies if you're cooking for yourself.

On the other side of The Bounty is *Cotters on the Beach*, a licensed indoor/outdoor restaurant that opens for lunch and dinner. There's a small brunch menu with light meals around $5 to $9, and the dinner menu offers steaks, chicken and seafood dishes from $10 to $17.

Getting There & Away
Two companies operate passenger ferries between Townsville and Magnetic.

Sunferries (☎ 4771 3855) operates about 10 services a day between 6.20 am and 7.15 pm from the terminal on Flinders St East. The trip takes about 20 minutes and costs $7/13 one-way/return. The only inconve-nience is that there is not much in the way of car parking in the Flinders St area.

Magnetic Island Ferries (☎ 4772 7122) runs a similar service from its terminal at the breakwater on Sir Leslie Thiess Drive near the casino. The first ferry leaves Townsville daily at 6 am; the last to the island is at 6.15, 7, 10.30 or 11.30 pm, de-pending on the day of the week. The trip takes about 15 minutes and the return fare is $14 ($11 for students).

You can also buy package deals that include return ferry tickets and accommoda-tion; one-night packages start at $29. Check with the hostels in Townsville for deals.

The Capricorn Barge Company (☎ 4772 5422) runs a vehicular ferry to Arcadia from the south side of Ross Creek four times a day during the week and twice a day on weekends. It's $96 return for a car and up to six passengers, $31 return for a motorbike and $12 return for walk-on passengers.

Bicycles are carried free on all ferries.

Getting Around
Bus The Magnetic Island Bus Service (☎ 4778 5130) operates up and down the island between Picnic Bay and Horseshoe Bay from 11 to 20 times a day, meeting all ferries and dropping off at all accommoda-tion places. If you've got a ferry to catch it takes about 45 minutes all the way from Horseshoe Bay to Picnic Bay, 30 minutes from Arcadia to Picnic Bay.

You can either get individual tickets ($1.50 to $3.50) or a full-day pass ($9).

Taxi Taxis meet arriving ferries at Picnic Bay. Call ☎ 13 1008 to book a taxi.

Motorcycle Hire Road Runner (☎ 4778 5222) is at Shop 2, Picnic Bay Arcade on the Picnic Bay waterfront. Scooter hire, in-cluding insurance and a crash helmet, costs $19 for a half-day, $25 for a full day (from 9 am to 5 pm) and $30 for 24 hours. No mo-torcycle licence is required for these small 50cc scooters, just a valid car drivers licence. You certainly don't need anything larger to explore Magnetic.

NORTH COAST

Moke & Car Rental Moke Magnetic (☎ 4778 5377), in an arcade of the Picnic Bay Mall, and Holiday Moke Hire (☎ 4778 5703), based in the Jetty Cafe in the Picnic Bay Mall, have Mokes from $33 a day ($30 if you're over 25) plus 30c per kilometre. Both companies also have Suzuki Sierras, Mazda 121s and other vehicles.

Bicycle Magnetic Island is ideal for cycling, and mountain bikes are available for rent at several places, including the Esplanade in Picnic Bay, Foresthaven in Arcadia and on the waterfront in Horseshoe Bay. Bikes cost $10 for a day, and $6 for half a day.

Hitching You could also hitch around, observing the precautions in the Getting There & Away chapter. Plenty of people do hitch – just start walking, and if you don't get a lift you will end up in the next town before long.

Townsville to Charters Towers

The Flinders Hwy heads inland from Townsville and runs virtually due west for its entire length – almost 800km from Townsville to Cloncurry. The first section of the highway takes you 135km south-west from Townsville to the gold-mining town of Charters Towers, with a turn-off at the halfway mark to Ravenswood, another gold-mining centre.

Refer to the Charters Towers to Camooweal section in the Outback chapter for details of the Flinders Hwy west of Charters Towers.

RAVENSWOOD
At Mingela, 88km from Townsville, a paved road leads 40km south to Ravenswood, a former ghost town from the gold rush days which has returned to life in

recent years. The town is spread across a series of hills of rough red earth, and although most of the buildings were demolished or fell down years ago, two pubs, a church, a school and a couple of hundred people linger on amid the old mines.

Ravenswood is an interesting and friendly little town, almost a living museum, and is well worth the detour off the main highway.

History
Gold was first discovered in this area in 1868. In October 1869 a rich deposit of alluvial gold was found at Top Camp, north of Ravenswood, and the first rush was on. The first crushings in 1870 were incredibly rich, and the field prospered for two years, but by 1872 the 'brownstone' (surface ore that had been oxidised and was easily crushed) was exhausted. The deeper ore proved almost impossible to work, and the field suffered a steady decline over the next 20 years.

In 1893 mine manager Laurence Wilson travelled to London and convinced a number of British investors to invest in the mines. Using new crushing and processing techniques, the mines again proved to be viable and people began to return to the area.

During Ravenswood's boom years, from 1900 to 1912, the area produced an incredible 12,500kg of gold, and the population peaked at around 4000. But by 1912 the ore bodies appeared exhausted, and operations ceased in 1917.

Ravenswood became a virtual ghost town. Then in 1987 the Carpentaria Gold company established a new open-cut mine here which successfully extracted gold using the heap leaching process. In 1994 another new mine opened, bringing another couple of hundred people back to the area and breathing new life into Ravenswood.

Things to See
The **old post office** (1878) is a lovely timber building which now houses a general store. The **old court house, police**

station and lock-up, up on the hill between the two pubs, have been restored and house a **mining and historical museum**. It is open from 10 am to 3 pm daily except Sunday, and the gregarious Woody, the keeper of the keys, will show you around.

A series of **old photos** mounted in steel boxes along the main street show Ravenswood in its boom years. A visit to the town **cemetery**, which is signposted from Macrossan St, is somewhat sobering. Graves date back to the 1880s, and it soon becomes evident that they died young around here.

Places to Stay & Eat

There's a basic council *campground* under big shady tress and close to the swimming pool. There's showers and toilets, and the there is no charge for camping for one or two nights, unless you want power in which case it's $2. For more than two nights it's $3/4 per night. The *Top Camp Resort* (☎ 4770 2188), 2km north of town, has a caravan park with sites from $14 and motel units from $38.

The *Imperial Hotel* (☎ 4770 2131) is an absolute gem of a pub. This two-storey Victorian-era hotel is virtually unchanged from 100 years ago and is built in the extravagant style known as 'goldfields brash' – it has an ornate, solid red-brick facade and the verandah is trimmed with iron lace. The public bar features a magnificent old red cedar bar with leadlight inserts. There are 16 timber-lined bedrooms upstairs, some with old brass beds and opening out onto the verandah. They are clean and well presented, and B&B costs $35/45 for singles/doubles. The dining room serves simple, hearty tucker at around $12 for a three-course meal.

The *Railway Hotel* (☎ 4770 2144) is another solid old red-brick pub that was built in 1871. It also has pub rooms upstairs, although they are often booked out during the week. When they're available, they cost $26/43 with a cooked breakfast. The pub also serves evening meals.

CHARTERS TOWERS
pop 9000

This busy town, 130km inland from Townsville, was Queensland's fabulously rich second city in the gold-rush days. Many old houses, with classic verandahs and lace work, and imposing public buildings and mining structures remain. It's possible to make a day trip here from Townsville and get a glimpse of outback Queensland on the way.

At 336m above sea level, the dry air of Charters Towers makes a welcome change from the humid coast.

The town is very proud of its history, gold heritage and historic buildings, and even the local police station was renovated in heritage style following lobbying by concerned residents.

History

The gleam of gold was first spotted in 1871, in a creek bed at the foot of Towers Hill, by an Aboriginal boy called Jupiter Mosman. Within a few years, the surrounding area was peppered with diggings and a large town had grown. In its heyday (around the turn of the century) Charters Towers had a population of 30,000, nearly 100 mines, and even its own stock exchange. Mosman St, the main street in those days, had 25 pubs.

When the gold ran out in the 1920s, the city shrank, but survived as a centre for the beef industry. Since the mid-1980s, Charters Towers has seen a bit of a gold revival as modern processes have enabled companies to work deposits in previously uneconomical areas. It is now a prosperous, lively country town with a growing population. There are now three gold mines being worked in the area.

Orientation & Information

Gill St, which runs from the train station to Mosman St, is Charters Towers' main street. Towers Hill stands over the town to the south. Lissner Park, a couple of blocks north of the centre, is the town's best park and the swimming pool is at its north end.

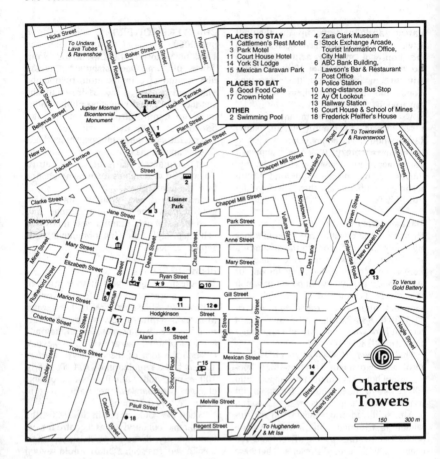

PLACES TO STAY
1 Cattlemen's Rest Motel
3 Park Motel
11 Court House Hotel
14 York St Lodge
15 Mexican Caravan Park

PLACES TO EAT
8 Good Food Cafe
17 Crown Hotel

OTHER
2 Swimming Pool
4 Zara Clark Museum
5 Stock Exchange Arcade,
   Tourist Information Office,
   City Hall
6 ABC Bank Building,
   Lawson's Bar & Restaurant
7 Post Office
9 Police Station
10 Long-distance Bus Stop
12 Ay Ot Lookout
13 Railway Station
16 Court House & School of Mines
18 Frederick Pfeiffer's House

Charters Towers

0   150   300 m

The helpful tourist office (☎ 4752 0314), between the historic City Hall and Stock Exchange buildings, is open daily from 9 am to 5 pm. Pick up the free *Guide to Charters Towers* booklet and a copy of the National Trust's walking tour leaflet.

The National Trust of Queensland (☎ 4787 2374) office is in the Stock Exchange Arcade on Mosman St.

Things to See & Do

On Mosman St a few metres up the hill from the corner of Gill St is the picturesque **Stock Exchange Arcade**, built in 1887 and restored in 1972. Today it houses the National Trust office and several shops, and there is an art gallery upstairs. At the end of the arcade, opposite the information office, the **Assay Room & Mining Museum** is a former metallurgical laboratory for smelting gold and silver and determining the content of ore and minerals. It's open daily from 9 am to 5 pm; entry is $1.

At 62 Mosman St, the **Zara Clark Museum** is well worth a visit, with an interesting collection which includes old photos of Charters Towers, farming equipment, a great collection of Royal Doulton toby jugs, and period costumes. It also includes the small **Charles Wallis military museum**, dedicated to a local hero who was killed in WWI. The museum is open everyday from 10 am to 3 pm; entry costs $3 ($1 children).

The former **ABC Bank Building** (1891) on Mosman St, just up from the Stock Exchange, was recently renovated and now houses the World Theatre. The facade is a magnificent mixture of Doric and Corinthian styles.

Probably the finest of the town's old houses is **Frederick Pfeiffer's** on Paull St. It's now a Mormon chapel, but you can walk around the outside. Pfeiffer was a gold-miner who became Queensland's first millionaire.

Another fine old mansion is **Ay Ot Lookout**, a restored house now owned by Leyshon Mining, one of the gold mining companies in the area. Leyshon uses it for VIP accommodation, but the ground floor is open to the public. The timber building is one of many around town (and, in fact, throughout north Queensland) built using a method known as 'balloon framing', where the walls lack external cladding, and so do not have a cavity which can lead to vermin (rat) problems.

About 5km from town is the **Venus Gold Battery**, where gold-bearing ore was crushed and processed from 1872 until as recently as 1972. The battery has been restored to working order and is open daily from 9 am to 3 pm, with guided tours at 10 am and 2 pm; entry is $3.

Organised Tours

Gold Nugget Scenic Tours (☎ 4787 1568) runs half-day city tours ($15) four days a week. Ian at York St Lodge runs informative daily walking tours from the tourist office (1 pm, $5) and weekly three-hour surface mine tours (Thursday, $12) and underground tours.

You can stay on or visit a number of cattle stations in the area, including: *Bluff*

Downs (☎ 4770 4084), 1½ hours drive away, $70 double including dinner and breakfast; *Powlathanga* (☎ 4787 4957), 34km to the west; *Wambiana* (☎ 4787 6689), dorm accommodation, 69km; and *Virginia Park* (☎ 4770 3125), between Charters and Townsville.

Festivals

During the Australia Day weekend in late January, more than 100 cricket teams and their supporters converge on Charters Towers for a competition known as the Goldfield Ashes.

Charters Towers holds a major rodeo every Easter. The town also hosts one of Australia's biggest annual country music festivals on the May Day weekend each year.

Places to Stay

Camping There are three caravan parks in town. The most central is the *Mexican Caravan Park* (☎ 4787 1161), 75 Church St. It has tent sites at $9 and on-site cabins for $43, plus a swimming pool and store.

Pubs The next cheapest beds in town are in the old *Court House Hotel* (☎ 4787 1187), 120 Gill St, which has very basic pub rooms at $20/30 a single/double.

Hostels The excellent *York St Lodge* (formerly Scotty's) (☎ 4787 1028), 58 York St, is 1.4km south of the town centre. The owners will pick you up from the bus stop if you ring. It's a renovated timber house built in the 1880s, with pleasant breezy verandahs and sitting areas, and a swimming pool. Four-share dorms cost $15, or the aircon doubles are a bargain at $38. You can hire bikes, and the enthusiastic owners run good day trips (see Things to See earlier).

Motels The *Park Motel* (☎ 4787 1022), 1 Mosman St, has pleasant grounds, a pool and a good restaurant. Standard motel units go for $60/68, and there are two excellent heritage-style 'honeymoon suites' upstairs which go for $70/85.

NORTH COAST

The *Cattleman's Rest Motor Inn* (☎ 4787 3555), on the corner of Bridge and Plant Sts, has good modern motel units from $62/69.

Places to Eat
There are a few pubs in town serving counter meals. The *Crown Hotel* in Mosman St has an all-you-can-eat Chinese smorgasbord for lunch/dinner which is great value at $5.90/6.40. For a bit of local outback atmosphere, try the *Court House Hotel* on Gill St.

The *Good Food Cafe*, on Gill St, opposite the library, is a good gourmet cafe with great sandwiches, smoothies, burgers and other snacks.

Lawson's Bar & Restaurant, in a recently restored heritage building next to the ABC Bank building on Mosman St, is an attractive, casual eatery with burgers at $8 and mains at $14 to $18.

Entertainment
There are a couple of nightclubs in town. The *Regent's Club 69 Bar*, on Gill St, is open from Wednesday to Saturday (and some Sundays) until 3 am. *Pegasus*, the nightclub at the Whitehorse Tavern, on the corner of Gill and Deane Sts, also opens until 3 am Friday to Sunday.

There's no cinema here, but the Tors Drive-In (☎ 4787 1086) on the west side of town screens latest releases.

The Charters Players stage regular plays throughout the year. They are based at the St Pauls Playhouse, a restored timber church at the south end of Mosman St.

Getting There & Away
McCafferty's has daily buses from Townsville to Charters Towers (1¾ hours, $14) and on to Mt Isa (10 hours, $79). Buses arrive and depart at the Caltex service station at 105 Gill St. Greyhound Pioneer buses don't stop in Charters Towers.

The twice-weekly *Inlander* service takes three hours from Charters Towers to Townsville and costs $20/32 in economy/1st class.

The *Inlander* continues on to Mt Isa, taking another 17 hours and costing $115/177 in an economy/1st class sleeper. The train station is on Enterprise Rd, 1.5km east of the centre.

Townsville to Mission Beach

PALUMA RANGE NATIONAL PARK
Mt Spec – Big Crystal Creek Section
About 60km north-west of Townsville is the large (7200 hectares) Mt Spec – Big Crystal Creek section of the national park. It straddles the 1000m-plus high Paluma Range on the inland side of the Bruce Hwy. There are quite a few creeks running throughout this national park, and the landscape varies from open eucalypt forests on the lower slopes to the rainforests of the upper, wetter areas. Bower birds are relatively common here.

There are two main access roads into the park, which both lead off a bypassed section of the Bruce Hwy. To get to these, turn off the new highway either 62km north of Townsville or 47km south of Ingham.

The southern access route, known as the Mt Spec Road, was built by relief labour during the depression years from 1931 to 1935. It's a narrow and spectacular road which twists its way up the mountains to the village of Paluma. After 7km you come to **Little Crystal Creek**, where a pretty stone bridge arches across the creek. (Although it looks surprisingly like a Roman relic, the bridge was actually built by the road crew in 1932.) This is a great swimming spot with waterfalls and a couple of deep rockpools, and there's a small picnic area opposite the car park. From here it's another 11km up to Paluma (see the following section).

The northern access route is a 4km dirt road into **Big Crystal Creek**, which has a good self-registration camping ground with toilets, hot showers, firewood and water.

Sites cost $3.50 per person per night – to book (compulsory as the key must be collected and a deposit paid), contact the Department of Environment's Ingham office (☎ 4776 1700). Beyond the camping ground is **Paradise Waterhole**, a good swimming and picnic area.

Jourama Falls section

The Jourama Falls section of the park is 6km (unpaved) off the highway, 91km north of Townsville. Centred around Waterview Creek, this small but beautiful park has good swimming holes, several lookouts, a picnic area and a camping ground with toilets and barbecues. Sites cost $3.50 per person per night, and you can self-register or book with the Jourama Falls ranger at ☎ 4777 3112. About 1km past the camping ground is the start of a walking trail to the waterfalls (600m) and the falls lookout (1.2km).

PALUMA

The Mt Spec Rd, which follows the southern boundary of the Paluma Range National Park up to the mountain village of Paluma, leaves the Bruce Hwy 61km north of Townsville. It's a scenic and winding 18km drive, with panoramic views down to the floodplains of the Big Crystal Creek and the ocean beyond. Just before Paluma is **McClelland's Lookout**, which is the start of walking trails to **Benham's Lookout** (600m), **Witt's Lookout** (1.5km) and last but not least **Cloudy Creek** (2km).

Paluma is a sleepy little top-of-the-mountain place with a handful of old holiday shacks, a couple of craft shops and a tea room. The town was founded in 1875 when tin was discovered in the area. If you decide to stay here overnight, the old *Misthaven Units* (☎ 4770 8620) have self-contained holiday flats which sleep up to six people and cost $50 a double plus $5 per extra person; or there's the *Mt Spec Cottage* (☎ 4770 8520), a tiny and simple timber shack.

About 4km beyond Paluma is the turn-off to **Paluma Dam**, a popular boating and water-skiing spot. Another 20km past this turn-off you come to Hidden Valley. The *Hidden Valley Cabins* (☎ 4770 8088) are a group of six log cabins which sleep up to four people each and cost $80 a night for the cabin. The cabins complex includes a licensed restaurant, a pool and spa.

INGHAM
pop 5300

Ingham is the centre of a large sugar-cane growing district. The first sugar cane farms were established in this area in the 1880s, and from early in its history the region attracted a large number of Italian immigrants. The town's Italian heritage is celebrated with the Australian-Italian Festival in May.

Ingham is a busy commercial centre and a pleasant enough town with all the usual services, although it has few pretensions to being a tourism hotspot. The **Memorial Gardens**, signposted off the main highway from the centre of town, are the town's botanical gardens and a good place for a stroll or a picnic lunch.

Information

There's a good tourist information centre (☎ 4776 5211) on the corner of Lannercost St and Townsville Rd. It's open on weekdays from 8 am to 5 pm and on weekends from 9 am to 2 pm.

The Department of Environment office (☎ 4776 1700), at the end of an arcade at 11 Lannercost St, deals with information for the Paluma Range and Lumholtz (Wallaman Falls) national parks. It is open on weekdays from 9 am to 5 pm.

Places to Stay & Eat

The cheapest place to stay is the *Royal Hotel* (☎ 4776 2024) on Lannercost St, across from the intersection with Townsville Rd. The upstairs rooms here are about as spartan as they come, and a bed costs $15. The *Hotel Hinchinbrook* (☎ 4776 2227), down the road at 83 Lannercost St, is a much nicer pub and has backpacker beds for $15, or $25 for a twin

NORTH COAST

room. The Hinchinbrook is also a good place to eat, with meals in the *Garden Court* bistro from $6 to $9 and a restaurant with mains around $16.

If you're after a motel, the *Herbert Valley Motel* (☎ 4776 1777), on the Bruce Hwy just south of the centre, has singles/doubles from $46/50.

Getting There & Away
McCafferty's and Greyhound Pioneer Australia both stop in Ingham on the main coastal run. Long-distance buses stop in the centre of town on Townsville Rd, close to the corner of Lannercost St (and the information centre). Ingham is also on the main Brisbane to Cairns railway line.

AROUND INGHAM
There are a number of places worth visiting around Ingham, including **Wallaman Falls** in Lumholtz National Park. The falls are 50km west of Ingham, where a tributary of the Herbert River cascades 305m and creates the longest permanent single-drop falls in Australia. The falls are much more spectacular in the wet season, after good rains. You can normally reach them by conventional vehicle along an unpaved road; there's a camping ground with a swimming hole nearby.

Only 7km east of Ingham is the **Victoria Mill** (☎ 4776 1722), the largest sugar mill in the southern hemisphere. Free tours are given in the crushing season (about July to December).

About 25km north-east of Ingham is **Lucinda**, a port town at the southern entrance to the Hinchinbrook Channel. Most visitors to Lucinda come for the fishing, or to have a look at the town's amazing 6km-long jetty which is used for shipping the huge amount of sugar produced in the area. Lucinda is also the access point for the southern end of Hinchinbrook Island. The *Wanderer's Holiday Village* (☎ 4777 8213) has tent sites ($10) and on-site units ($30), or the *Lucinda Point Hotel-Motel* (☎ 4777 8103) has air-con motel units from $40/45 for singles/doubles.

ORPHEUS ISLAND
Lying about 20km off the coast east of Ingham, Orpheus is a long (about 11km from end to end) and narrow (less than 1km wide) continental island, with some fine beaches and some of the best fringing reef to be found on any of the Great Barrier Reef islands. The second largest of the Palm Islands Group, it's a quiet, secluded island which is good for camping, snorkelling and diving. Orpheus is mostly national park and is heavily forested, with lots of birdlife; turtles also nest here.

There is a fairly expensive resort on the island, as well as three national park camping grounds and a giant clam research station.

During the 1800s goats were released on the island as part of a madcap scheme to provide food for possible shipwreck survivors. There obviously weren't enough Robinson Crusoes washed ashore here – the goats thrived to the extent that at one stage they numbered over 4000. A 'control program' initiated by national parks personnel in 1991 has proved largely successful in culling the goats, and nowadays there are less than a dozen left on the island.

Zoning
Most of the water around the island is zoned Marine Park B – 'look but don't touch'. From the top of Hazard Bay to the southern tip is zoned 'A' which allows limited line fishing. Collecting shells or coral is not permitted.

Things to See & Do
With its fine fringing reefs, Orpheus is a great island for snorkelling. It also has some pleasant sandy beaches, including those at Mangrove Bay and Yank's Bay, south of the resort, and at Pioneer Bay north of the resort. Some of the beaches are quite shallow, which rules out swimming at low tide.

The island also has a great reputation as a diving resort. The dive centre caters exclusively to resort guests, and conducts dive courses and a range of diving and snorkelling trips.

At Little Pioneer Bay, north of the resort, the James Cook University **Marine Research Station** specialises in breeding and raising giant clams and other Barrier Reef clams. Clams raised here are being transplanted to Pacific island reefs where overgathering has wiped them out. In the station you can see the clams in the large water tanks (including the 'stud clams' used for breeding) while other clams are raised out in the shallow waters of the bay. Call ☎ 4777 7336 to inquire about visiting the station.

While you're at the station, ask about the **Aboriginal shell midden** nearby.

Places to Stay

Camping There are bush camping sites at Yank's Jetty, South Beach and Little Pioneer Bay. All sites have toilet facilities and a picnic area but there is no regular fresh water supply and a fuel stove should be used. Yank's Bay offers the best low-tide swimming and snorkelling

Applications to camp on Orpheus should be made to the Department of Environment office (☎ 4066 8115) at Cardwell.

Resorts The *Orpheus Island Resort* (☎ 4777 7377 or toll-free ☎ 1800 077 167) was established here in the 1940s. In 1981 it was completely rebuilt as an up-market Mediterranean-style resort. There are 15 Studio Units and eight slightly smaller Terrace Suites along the beach and two larger bungalows. The rooms are stylish and very comfortable, with wood panelling, en suites, air-con and ceiling fans, and there is no TV or telephone in the rooms. The Terrace Suites are $525/840 and the Studio Units $625/1012 per night. The bungalows are only available as doubles at $570 per person. Tariffs include all meals and use of all the resort's facilities, which include a tennis court, swimming pool, catamarans, windsurfers and dinghies. A snorkelling trip is organised each afternoon.

Up the hill from the resort there are also six very impressive two-bedroom villas, which cost $590 per person per night for a minimum of two people, $405 per person for four people.

The resort doesn't cater for anyone under 15 years of age.

Places to Eat

The resort's restaurant is only open to house guests, so if you're camping you'll have to be totally self-sufficient.

If you're staying at the resort, all meals are included in the tariffs. Orpheus has a great reputation for its food – breakfasts are buffet-style while for lunch and dinner you choose from the couple of options. The restaurant is licensed and there's a small bar. The resort will also pack picnic hampers for guests who are taking a dinghy out for the day.

Getting There & Away

Air Most resort guests fly into either Cairns or Townsville; the resort has a seaplane which handles transfers from these airports to Orpheus. One-way fares are $145 from Townsville or $230 from Cairns.

Sea There are no regular boat services to Orpheus, but if you want to camp you can get out to the island from Dungeness, near Lucinda, by water taxi. Count on about $120 per person return – contact the MV *Scuba Doo* (☎ 4777 8220) for details.

OTHER PALM ISLANDS

Orpheus is part of the Palm Island group, which consists of 10 main islands. Apart from Orpheus, which is predominantly national park, and nearby Pelorus, which is crown land, all of the islands are Aboriginal reserves and permission must be obtained from the Aboriginal & Islander Affairs office in Townsville before you can land on them. You'll need to declare the purpose of your visit, and when and how long you're planning to stay.

The main islands of the group (and their Aboriginal names) are Orpheus (Goolboddi), Pelorus (Yanooa), Brisk (Culgarool), Curacao (Inoogoo), Eclipse (Garoogubbee), Esk (Soopun), Falcon (Carbooroo), Fantome

NORTH COAST

(Eumilli), Havannah and Great Palm (Bukaman) islands.

CARDWELL
pop 1400

South of Cardwell, the Bruce Hwy climbs high above the coast with tremendous views down across the winding, mangrove-lined waterways known as the Mangroves, which separate Hinchinbrook Island from the coast.

Cardwell's main claim to tourism fame is as the access point for Hinchinbrook Island, but it is also a popular fishing spot and there are quite a few interesting sights in the immediate area. It's also become prominent recently as the battle ground between conservationists and a developer building a marina just to the south of town.

Cardwell itself is a fairly old-fashioned holiday town, sprawled along a 3km length of the Bruce Hwy between the mountains and the ocean. It's the only town on the highway between Brisbane and Cairns which is actually right on the coast.

History

Cardwell is one of north Queensland's very earliest towns, dating from 1864, though there's little evidence of its origins now. It predates Townsville and was intended as a port and supply centre for pioneer cattle stations inland in the Valley of Lagoons on the upper Burdekin River, but it had a shaky start since finding a decent route over the forested ranges proved very difficult and the early settlement suffered from constant Aboriginal harassment. It was the determination of Cardwell's founder George Elphinstone Dalrymple, who also established Bowen, that saw the establishment of a rough track, after many attempts even in the rainy season, through to the Valley of the Lagoons. Unfortunately for Cardwell, it was

---

Development vs Conservation – the Oyster Point Experience

In 1994 a proposal by a Queensland developer, Keith Williams, to build a 500-bed tourist resort at Oyster Point, just south of Cardwell, sparked a major controversy – which is far from over.

On one side are the environmental activists and protesters, who claim the development destroys mangrove areas vital to the coastal ecosystem and bring unsustainable numbers of tourists to Hinchinbrook Island. Keith Williams' previous record also worked against him from the conservationists' point of view – after starting the Sea World theme park and playing a major role in developing the Gold Coast, in the 1980s he transformed Hamilton Island from an untouched continental island into a concrete jungle of high-rise hotels and apartments. Pro-development lobbyists argue that the resort will be the economic life-blood that will save a dying town, create employment and finance badly needed development in Cardwell.

The controversy divides the town – although it doesn't quite verge on the 'civil war' portrayed in the media.

The Cardwell dispute typifies the dilemmas that Queensland faces as its tourism industry grows and provides an increasing proportion of the state's income. The questions being asked – such as whether the Gold Coast-style develop-at-all-costs mentality should be allowed to spread along the coast, and to what extent Queensland's natural resources should be exploited to take advantage of the current boom in ecotourism – are as relevant in the rest of Queensland as they are in Cardwell.

At the time of writing, the Oyster Point development is well under way, although the issue is far from dead and conservationists still maintain a strong presence at the site.

out-developed by Townsville from where an easier route was found to the high country.

Orientation & Information

The Bruce Hwy passes through the centre of Cardwell and is the town's main street, and almost all of the facilities and services are found along the highway.

Cardwell has the Department of Environment Rainforest & Reef Information Centre (☎ 4066 8601), beside the main jetty in the middle of town. The office handles camping permits and bookings for Hinchinbrook Island and the other national parks in the area, and is open weekdays from 8 am to 5 pm.

Cardwell has a post office, Westpac and National banks and two supermarkets.

If you are travelling south, there is a papaya fruit fly inspection post south of town where you have to deposit basically all fruit and vegetables – eat them before you leave Cardwell.

Boating & Fishing

A couple of operators have boats available for hire. U-Drive Cardwell (☎ 4066 8671) has fishing dinghies for $60 a day or $35 a half-day – plus fuel costs. Hinchinbrook Rent-A-Yacht (☎ 4066 8007) has yachts, motor cruisers and houseboats for cruising around Hinchinbrook, Dunk and Brook islands. The cost is around $800 per day for up to six people

Cardwell Fishing Safaris (☎ 4066 8176) takes small groups (up to four people) on fishing trips and supply all tackle and bait. They depart daily and cost $50 per person.

Places to Stay

Camping & Caravan Parks The *Kookaburra Holiday Park* (☎ 4066 8648), 800m north of the centre at 175 Bruce Hwy, is the best set-up of the three caravan parks here. It has tent sites from $12 for two, on-site vans from $28, on-site cabins from $36 and self-contained units and cabins from $50 a double. There's also a youth hostel within the park (see below).

Further north at 43 Marine Parade is the *Cardwell Sunrise Village* (☎ 4766 8550), a large accommodation complex with a motel and restaurant, as well as tent sites from $11 and on-site cabins and self-contained cottages from $35 a double.

Hostels The YHA *Hinchinbrook Hostel* (☎ 4066 8648), within the grounds of the *Kookaburra Holiday Park*, 175 Bruce Hwy, is about a 10-minute walk north from the town centre and the bus stop. The small hostel has dorm beds at $14 and doubles at $30; members pay $1 less. Backpackers can also camp beside the hostel, and use the facilities, for $7 each. This place has good facilities and is a good source of information about Hinchinbrook Island and other attractions in the area. It also has camping gear for hire, and can store your luggage while you're on the island.

The *Cardwell Backpackers Hostel* (☎ 4066 8014), at 178 Bowen St just over 1km north of the centre in the street behind the 'big crab', is basically a workers hostel, and is somewhat seedy.

Motels & Holiday Units The previously mentioned *Sunrise Village & Leisure Park* (☎ 4066 8550), 43 Marine Parade, has motel units from $45/60 for singles/doubles. The *Lyndoch Motor Inn* (☎ 4066 8500) on the highway at the north end of town has oldish motel units from $35/50.

Cardwell Beachfront Holiday Units (☎ 4066 8776), opposite the waterfront at 1 Scott St, is a small 1960s-style complex of two-bedroom holiday units. The units are fairly basic, costing around $45 a double or $70 for up to five people.

Places to Eat

Cardwell has about half a dozen cafes and eateries. If you're after a quick snack around lunchtime, there are usually two pie vans parked on the foreshore beside the highway at the southern end of town.

Annie's is a cafe on the main street with seriously good fish and chips for $4. The *Seaview Cafe*, next to the BP service station, is where buses pull in for a meal break and serves the usual takeaway fare.

NORTH COAST

The *Marine Hotel* has passable pub meals. There's a casual bistro out the back or the concrete beer garden.

Cardwell Muddies is a licensed seafood cafe with excellent food at reasonable prices. Main meals range from $11 to $16, and it also has cheaper snacks for lunch. You can eat inside or out on the balcony, and it also does great takeaway fish and chips. Muddies is on the highway about 1km north of the centre – it's the place with a giant crab-on-a-stick out the front.

The *Edmund Kennedy Restaurant*, at the Sunrise Village Leisure Park, also has a good reputation. Its Thursday night seafood smorgasbord for $8.50 is popular with the locals.

Getting There & Away

All Greyhound Pioneer and McCafferty's buses between Townsville and Cairns stop at Cardwell. The fare is around $20 from either place. Cardwell is also on the main Brisbane to Cairns railway.

Buses stop by the BP station and the Seaview Cafe, which has a travel agency.

AROUND CARDWELL

The **Cardwell Forest Drive** starts from the centre of town and is a 26km round trip, taking you to some excellent lookouts, swimming holes, walking tracks and picnic areas. Turn off the highway beside the BP service station in the centre of town – the drive is signposted from the other side of the train station.

Most of the coastal forest north of Cardwell is protected as the **Edmund Kennedy National Park**, named after the ill-fated explorer who was killed by Aborigines at Cape York. At the southern end of the park, there's an interesting boardwalk through the mangroves – turn off the highway 4km north of Cardwell to reach them. Don't swim or cross any of the creeks in the park – the mangroves here are home to estuarine crocodiles.

The **Murray Falls** have fine rockpools for swimming, a walking track, camping ground and a barbecue area. They're 22km west of the highway, signposted about 27km north of Cardwell. Take care when swimming, as the rocks are incredibly slippery – there have been several drownings here.

Just off the Bruce Hwy, 7km south of Cardwell, the **Five Mile Swimming Hole** is another good swimming spot with picnic facilities.

The **Dalrymple Gap Walking Track**, originally an Aboriginal trail which was upgraded by George Dalrymple in the 1860s as a stock route to the Valley of Lagoons, passes through the **Lumholtz National Park**. The track is 9km long and takes eight hours return, although you have the option of a two-hour 3km walk to an old stone bridge which is registered by the National Trust. The turn-off to the track is off the highway 15km south of Cardwell.

HINCHINBROOK ISLAND

Hinchinbrook Island is a spectacular and unspoiled wilderness area, with granite mountains rising dramatically from the sea and a varied terrain – lush tropical forest on the mainland side, thick mangroves lining the shores, towering mountains in the middle and long sandy beaches and secluded bays on the eastern side. All 635 sq km of the island is a national park and rugged Mt Bowen, at 1121m, is the highest peak. There's plenty of wildlife, especially prettyface wallabies and the iridescent blue Ulysses butterfly.

Hinchinbrook Island is very popular with bushwalkers and naturalists and has some excellent walking tracks. The highlight is the **Thorsborne Trail**, a 32km walking track from Ramsay Bay to Zoe Bay and on to George Point at the southern tip. You need to allow three to five days for the whole walk, although individual sections can be walked if you don't have that much time. There is a limit of 40 people allowed on the trail at any one time, so it's worth booking, especially if you're planning to visit during the school holidays.

Walkers are warned to take plenty of insect repellent – the sandflies and mossies

The regal angelfish, just one of the hundreds of colourful fish species that can be seen by snorkelling or diving on the Great Barrier Reef.

Top Left: Colourful and bizarre fungi grow in the forests on Hinchinbrook Island.
Top Right: Abandoned mining equipment, Ravenswood
Middle: Picturesque Arthur Bay, Magnetic Island – one of several secluded coves on the island.
Bottom: The *Inlander* train runs between Townsville and Mt Isa twice weekly.

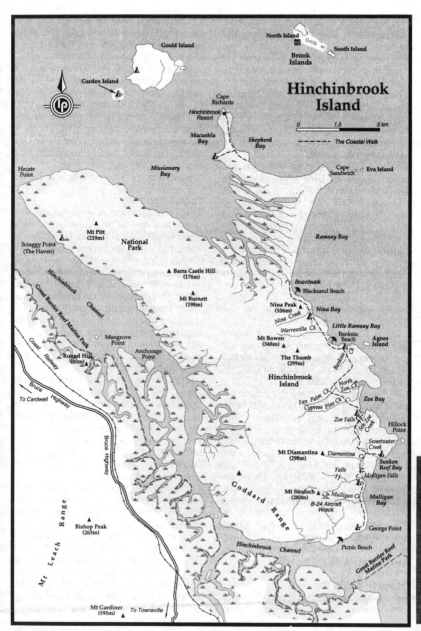

on Hinchinbrook can be a real pest – and if you react badly, some sort of treatment like antihistamine tablets. You'll also have to learn how to protect your food from the native bush rats, and there are estuarine crocodiles in the mangroves.

Apart from the national park camping grounds, the only accommodation is at an excellent and unobtrusive resort at Cape Richards, the northernmost tip of the island.

Information & Permits

The Department of Environment has two useful leaflets on Hinchinbrook and the islands to the north. Those planning to walk the coastal track from Ramsay Bay to George Point on Hinchinbrook should get a copy of the *Thorsborne Trail* leaflet. The *Hinchinbrook to Dunk Island* park guide is a small brochure full of fascinating information about Hinchinbrook Island, Goold Island, the Brook Islands, the Family Islands and Dunk Island.

You can make bookings for camping permits and the Thorsborne Trail through the Reef & Rainforest Centre (☎ 4066 8601) in Cardwell. Don't leave arranging your permit until the last minute: try and ring in advance to make sure there is a vacancy, and arrive at the office well before the ferry departure time.

Before a permit is issued to them, all potential walkers must view the Department's 15-minute *Without a Trace* video, which gives guidance on minimal impact bushwalking. It is available for viewing at the Reef & Rainforest Centre in Cardwell and at other Department offices in Queensland and various centres interstate. Phone the Cardwell office for details.

Hinchinbrook Island with text by Arthur and Margaret Thorsborne and photos by Cliff and Dawn Frith is a coffee-table book on the wonders of Hinchinbrook with some superb photos and an engrossing text revealing a real love for the island.

Things to See & Do

There are some fine beaches on Hinchinbrook Island. The resort's main beach,

Orchid Beach, is an idyllic little stretch of sand framed by granite boulders at either end. Also near the resort is **Turtle Bay**, a rocky inlet further west.

It's worth noting that Hinchinbrook is close enough to the mainland for you to be cautious about box jellyfish during the November to March summer season.

There are several **walking trails** starting from the resort, including short strolls to the top of Cape Richards or to Turtle Bay, and a 2km walking trail through the rainforest to North Shepherd Beach, with a continuation on to South Shepherd Beach.

Thorsborne Trail

This 32km coastal track from Ramsay Bay to Zoe Bay and on to George Point is the finest island walk along the Great Barrier Reef. The walk *can* be completed in two hard days but allowing at least three nights camping on the island is a much better idea.

The walk includes long sandy beaches, mountain streams, humid rainforests and magnificent mountain scenery. The trail is ungraded and includes some often challenging creek crossings. The maximum elevation along the trail is 260m, reached between Upper South Zoe Creek and Sweetwater Creek.

The *Thorsborne Trail* brochure, published by and available from the Department of Environment offices, is an essential guide for those intending to walk the trail. It gives you advice on how to plan your trip, book permits and how to conserve the delicate island environment. It divides the walk into stages giving pertinent advice for each section.

The trail is recommended for moderately experienced bushwalkers who should be adequately prepared and carry a map, compass and drinking water. Water is reliably available year-round only at **Nina Bay**, **Little Ramsay Bay** and at the southern end of **Zoe Bay**. During the dry season, from July to December, water may be very scarce and adequate supplies should be carried. If you find a dry creek or the water is salty it's often possible to find freshwater further upstream.

During the wet season, from December to March, too much water can pose problems at the opposite extreme. The trail may be very slippery, creek crossings can be difficult and you should be prepared for heavy rainfall. In tropical conditions walking in a raincoat or poncho is likely to be very uncomfortable – better to simply get wet and have dry clothes to change into later.

At any time of the year it can be hot and humid during the daytime but from May to September the nights can be cold enough to require a sleeping bag. A good tent is necessary if there is heavy rain at night.

Insects like mosquitoes, sandflies and march flies can be a nuisance so bring a good insect repellent. As with anywhere along the Great Barrier Reef, a good sunscreen and a shady hat are also vitally important.

Protecting your food supplies from the native bush rats is another of Hinchinbrook's challenges. These ever-hungry critters will eat anything and can chew their way through just about any type of food container, including metal ones. Rat-proof food boxes are provided at some camp sites. Check with the national park rangers for advice on ways of protecting your food. One of the most effective methods is to hang your food container from a length of nylon fishing line strung between two trees.

Open camp fires and cooking fires are not allowed; you must carry your own fuel stove. A hand trowel is also handy for digging toilet holes.

See Getting There & Away at the end of this section for information on drop-offs at the beginning and end of the coastal walk.

Places to Stay

Camping There are six national parks camping grounds along the Thorsborne Trail, plus ones at Macushla Bay and Scraggy Point in the north.

The Thorsborne Trail camping grounds are at Little Ramsay Bay, Zoe Bay, Sunken Reef Bay, Mulligan Falls, Mulligan Bay and George Point. Numbers for each camping ground are limited and depend on the total number of walkers on the island. For camping permits and detailed trail information, contact the Cardwell Department of Environment office. Permits should be applied for at least six weeks in advance.

Resort The Hinchinbrook Island Resort (☎ 4066 8585) was established in 1975 when 15 simple cabins were built at Cape Richards. In 1989 the resort received a major upgrade when another 15 architect-designed 'treehouses' were built. These impressive timber cottages are built into the steep hillside behind Orchid Beach and linked by a series of timber boardwalks. Each cottage is timber lined and has its own bathroom and separate lounge area, ceiling fans, fridge, and tea and coffee-making facilities. There is no radio, TV or phone in the rooms. The one-bedroom treehouses cost from $315/590 for singles/doubles; the two-bedroom prices are $355/640, plus $120 for children.

Seven of the older cabins are still in use. These are fairly basic and straightforward, but comfortable enough with two bedrooms, a bathroom and ceiling fans. These cabins cost $225/430 for singles/doubles, plus $95 for children. These rates include all meals and use of most equipment.

The resort's facilities include a bar, restaurant, an excellent swimming pool, canoes, snorkelling gear, surf skis and fishing equipment.

Places to Eat

The resort's restaurant is in a very pleasant open-sided building beside the pool, and has a small bar. Breakfast is buffet-style, lunch can be in the restaurant or a packed lunch if you're heading out for the day, and dinner is a more elaborate four-course affair. Hinchinbrook has an excellent reputation for its food. The restaurant is only open to resort guests.

Getting There & Away

Ferry Services There are ferry services and day trips from Cardwell, at the northern end of the island, and from Lucinda at the southern end. You can easily arrange to be picked up and dropped off from either end of the island, and your surplus gear can be stored or transported as well.

Hinchinbrook Island Ferries (☎ 1800 682 702) at 131 Bruce Hwy has a ferry departing at 9 am returning around 4.30 pm (return fare $69). This service operates daily from June through November, and three times a week December through May. If you want to walk the Thorsborne Trail the one-way cost from Cardwell to the northern end is $45 with Hinchinbrook Island Ferries. You also need to arrange your southern boat pick-up with Hinchinbrook Wilderness Safaris (☎ 4777 8307). The cost is also $45 which includes transport back to Cardwell.

The resort transfers its guests between Cardwell and Hinchinbrook for $80 return.

ISLANDS NEAR HINCHINBROOK
There are two small island groups just north of Hinchinbrook Island. Both are national parks, and both are accessible by ferry from Cardwell. **Goold Island** is just 4.5km north-west of Cape Richards and 17km north-east of Cardwell. The whole 8.3-sq km island is a national park. The granite island is covered in eucalyptus forest with smaller patches of rainforest in the gullies, and there is a wide arc of sandy beach on the western side with a national park camp site nearby. There are toilets, picnic tables and fireplaces at the camping ground, but you'll need to bring your own drinking water. There is a limit of 50 campers, and permits are available from the Department of Environment office in Cardwell.

Just south of Goold Island is tiny **Garden Island** with a recreation reserve controlled by the local council. Unlike the national park restrictions which apply to Goold, there are no restrictions on camping here and the island has a good sandy beach but, as usual, no freshwater is available.

Hinchinbrook Island Ferries in Cardwell can drop campers at Goold Island on request.

About 8km north-east of Cape Richards are the four small islands of the **Brook** Islands group. South Island has a Commonwealth lighthouse but the other three islands – Middle Island, Tween Island and North Island – are all national parks and covered in thick vegetation. The fringing reef around the three northern islands offers fine snorkelling and North Island's beach is a good picnic spot, but there are no facilities on the island and camping is not permitted.

TULLY
pop 2800
Tully, a small township wedged between the Bruce Hwy and Mt Tyson (678m), is the wettest place in Australia with a drenching average of over 4000mm of rain a year. The town is almost completely ringed by mountains and, as you would expect, the surrounding areas are green and fertile.

Tully is the cheapest place to start from if you're doing a white-water rafting trip on the Tully River, although nearby Mission Beach is a much more appealing place to stay, and the rafting operators will pick you up from there.

The Tully Information Centre (☎ 4068 2288) on the highway just south of the Tully turn-off is open on weekdays from 8.45 am to 5 pm and during the tourist season on weekends from 9 am to 1 pm.

The **Tully Sugar Mill** has informative 1½ hour tours at 10 am on weekdays during the crushing season (mid-June through November). The cost is $7 ($18 family).

About 8km north of Tully is **Alligator's Nest**, a great swimming spot with picnic tables, barbecues and lawns. To get there, follow Murray St north from the town centre.

Places to Stay
Tully has a caravan park and a couple of pubs with cheap accommodation. There's also the *Tully Backpackers Hostel* (☎ 4068 2820), at 19 Richardson St, one block north of the main street. It's a small and fairly basic worker's hostel – most people staying here are picking bananas, watermelons or lychees or working on the sugar cane

Imperial Pigeons

The Brook Islands are a nesting place for thousands of pigeons that migrate from New Guinea every summer to breed in Australia. Known by various names, including nutmeg pigeon, Torresian imperial-pigeon and pied imperial-pigeon, they are large, striking birds – pure white with black tail and wing tips.

The pigeons arrive each September, establish large nesting colonies on the islands and depart with their offspring in February. They fly to the mainland each day to feed on fruit trees before returning to the islands each afternoon. Farmers on the mainland used to consider the birds pests, and regularly shot them on the islands in their thousands.

Margaret and Arthur Thorsborne (authors of the book *Hinchinbrook Island*) first saw the pigeons arriving here in 1964. The following year they decided to return and try to count the birds, and in December 1965 they sat back to back on North Island and counted 3342 birds arriving. They returned in 1967 only to find that thousands of birds had been shot by farmers. Outraged by the slaughter, they made moves to stop the shooting and protect the birds. Their efforts were gradually successful and by 1975 the bird count had been formalised by the Queensland national parks service.

Since then, the number of pigeons arriving on the islands has continued to rise dramatically each year, and by 1994 the count was in excess of 30,000.

The Brook Islands are also a breeding place for black-naped terns over summer. If you're visiting the islands, you should be extremely careful not to disturb the birds or their nests. Nesting areas are indicated by signs on the beach. Visits are actually prohibited from October through February.

harvest. Dorm beds cost $11 a night or $60 a week.

On the highway, the *Tully Motel* (☎ 4068 2233) has singles/doubles from $46/52.

Getting There & Away

Tully is on the main Brisbane to Cairns train line. Greyhound Pioneer and McCafferty's buses also stop here on demand.

MISSION BEACH
pop 1050

This small stretch of coast has become an increasingly popular tourist destination in recent years. The name Mission Beach actually covers a string of small settlements along a 14km coastal strip east of Tully.

Mission Beach, where the long-distance buses stop, is in the centre; Wongaling Beach and South Mission Beach are to the south, and Bingil Bay Beach and Garners Beach are to the north.

The coastal strip is surrounded by large areas of dense rainforest, which comes right down to the beach in places. The area has a wide range of accommodation, from beachfront camping grounds and backpackers' hostels to exclusive and expensive resorts. These places are spread up and down the coast between Bingil Bay and South Mission Beach, with most of the developments being fairly low-key and low-rise. There are also some great restaurants along here.

NORTH COAST

The area is a good base for a number of activities, including visits to Dunk Island and boat trips out to the reef, white-water rafting trips on the Tully River and walks through the rainforest.

It's a great drive north from Mission Beach to **Bingil Bay**. Beyond the Clump Point jetty, the road hugs the coastline and winds past a series of bays and beaches. Bingil Bay, 5km north of Mission Beach, is one of the best beaches in the area, backed by a cluster of shady trees.

History

On 21 May 1848 the barque *Rattlesnake* landed on the southern side of Tam O'Shanter Point, south of South Mission Beach, dropping the 30-year-old explorer Edmund Kennedy and his companions at the start of their ill-fated overland expedition towards Cape York. All but three of the party's 13 members died, and Kennedy himself was speared to death by Aborigines a little way south of Cape York. There's a memorial to the expedition at Tam O'Shanter Point.

The first White settlement in the area was by a group of pioneers who gradually established a series of crops, planting mangoes, bananas, coconuts and tea and coffee. A timber mill was also built to process the locally cut cedar.

In 1914 the Queensland government established an Aboriginal mission to house the remainder of the local Aboriginal population. The site of the old mission, from which the area takes its name, can still be seen at South Mission Beach.

One of Queensland's worst ever cyclones struck this stretch of coast in 1918, with winds of over 150km/h, floods and tidal waves destroying the mission and many other buildings and claiming a number of lives.

Information

The Mission Beach Tourist Information Centre (☎ 4068 7099) is on Porters Promenade at the north end of Mission Beach. It's well set up with good displays and a small library with books on the environment and local history. It's open daily from 9 am to 5 pm (Sunday to 4 pm).

Right next door is the Wet Tropics Visitors Centre (☎ 4068 7179), an environmental interpretative centre which focuses on the cassowary conservation, and has videos and displays plus a range of environmental-style gifts on sale (open 10 am to 4 pm daily).

Mission Beach proper is a compact little holiday village with a good selection of restaurants and cafes, a butcher, a supermarket, a chemist and an ANZ Bank. Wongaling Beach to the south has its own shopping centre, with a supermarket, an Ampol service station and a National Bank.

Zola's Books in the cluster of shops at Mission Beach has expensive email facilities in addition to new and secondhand books.

Activities

Walks & Walking Tours The rainforest around Mission Beach is a haunt of cassowaries but unfortunately the population has been depleted by road accidents and the destruction of rainforest by logging and cyclones. There are some impressive walks including the **Licuala Walking Track** (two hours), **Laceys Creek Walk** (half hour), the **Bicton Hill Lookout** (1½ hours) and the **Edmund Kennedy Walking Track** (three hours). The local tourist information centre produces an excellent *Walking Track Guide*, a brochure and map which details these and other walks.

Mission Beach Rainforest Treks (☎ 4068 7152) takes guided walks through the forests – the four hour morning walk costs $28 and the 2½ hour night walk is $18.

The Girramay Walkabout (☎ 4068 8676) combines a walking trek guided by people from the local Girramay tribe with a barbecue lunch, a rainforest tour, boomerang and spear-throwing demonstrations and bush tucker. The trek costs $50 per person (minimum age 12).

White-Water Rafting & Sea Kayaking Raging Thunder (☎ 4031 1466) and R'n'R (toll-free ☎ 1800 079 039) charge $118 from

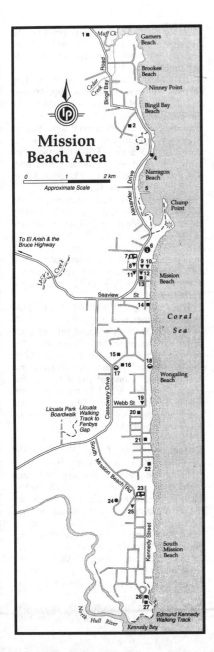

Mission
Beach Area

PLACES TO STAY
1   The Treehouse
2   Bingil Bay Resort Motel
4   Clump Point Ecovillage
7   Hideaway Caravan Park
13 Ceud Mile Failte
14 Castaways
15 Mission Beach Backpacker's Lodge
16 Mission Beach Resort Hotel
20 Scotty's Mission Beach House
21 The Wongalinga
22 Beaches
23 Beachcomber Coconut Village
26 Lugger Bay Rainforest Apartments
27 The Point Resort

PLACES TO EAT
8   On the Bite & Beach Terraces Cafe
9   Friends & Food Restaurant
10 Piccolo Paradiso
11 Port 'o Call Cafe & McCafferty's Bus
    Stop
12 Butterflies
19 Hungry Hound Cafe
25 Blarney's

OTHER
3   Clump Mountain National Park
5   Clump Point Jetty
6   Tourist Information Centre & Wet
    Tropics Visitors Centre
17 Greyhound Pioneer Bus stop
18 Dowd's Water Taxi
24 Old Mission Site

Mission Beach for trips on the Tully River. These are the same as the trips on offer in Cairns, but you'll save about $10 and several hours travel by doing them from here.

Raging Thunder also offers sea-kayaking day trips to the Family Islands for $90. Sunbird Adventures (☎ 4068 8229) has morning sea kayaking and snorkelling trips for $32.

Other Activities Jump the Beach (☎ 4050 0671) offers dual skydives for $228, or there's watersports gear for hire on the beach at Castaways.

The Jumbun Horseride Adventure (☎ 4068 7877) is a day's ride through the rainforest to a swimming hole, guided by locals from the Girramay tribe. The trips operate on Monday, Wednesday and Friday, and the $70 cost includes lunch and morning and afternoon tea.

Organised Cruises

There are three cruise companies based at the Clump Point jetty just north of Mission Beach. Friendship Cruises (☎ 4068 7262) takes day trips out to the reef, with snorkelling and a ride in a glass-bottomed boat, for $59, and you can do a resort dive for another $50. Certified divers can do one dive for $35 or two dives for $50.

The *Quick Cat* (☎ 4068 7289) is a fast catamaran which does the trip to Dunk Island in 20 minutes for $22 ($11 children). You can also combine this trip to Dunk with a cruise to the outer Barrier Reef for $122 ($61 children), which includes lunch and snorkelling gear.

Dunk Island Ferry & Cruises (☎ 4068 7211) operates the MV *Lawrence Kavanagh*, an old passenger ferry that does a day trip to Dunk for $22. For another $22 you can also do the 1½-hour cruise around Bedarra and the Family Islands, and a barbecue lunch is available for $8.

Places to Stay

Camping The *Hideaway Holiday Village* (☎ 4068 7104), right in the centre of Mission Beach, is an excellent camping village with tent sites from $16 ($18 powered) for two people and on-site cabins from $49. Right across the road on the beachfront is the council-run *Mission Beach Caravan Park*, with good grassy areas and tent sites for $8 ($11 powered).

There's also a very good council-run camping ground set among trees on the foreshore, just north of the Clump Point jetty. Sites here cost $8 a night.

At South Mission Beach, the *Beachcomber Coconut Village* (☎ 4068 8129) is another good camping ground with tent sites from $15.50 ($17.50 powered), camp-o-tels from $24 for two and a range of on-site cabins from $43.

Hostels There are three very good hostels in the area, all of which have courtesy buses and do pick-ups from the bus stop in Mission Beach proper.

Two of the hostels are at Wongaling Beach, 5km south of the bus stop. *Mission Beach Backpackers Lodge* (☎ 4068 8317), 28 Wongaling Beach Rd, is a modern, well-equipped place with a pool and garden. There are two buildings, one with spacious dorms at $15 a bed ($14 VIP), the other with very good double rooms priced from $32 to $38. This easy-going hostel is a five-minute walk from the beach.

Scotty's Mission Beach House (☎ 4068 8676) is at 167 Reid Rd, also at Wongaling Beach. This friendly and fun-oriented place is right opposite the beach. Dorm beds are $15 ($14 VIP) and twins are $35 or $40, with the more expensive rooms having their own bathrooms and air-con. There's a pool, evening meals from $5 to $20, and regular barbecues.

The *Treehouse* (☎ 4068 7137), an YHA-associate hostel, is at Bingil Bay, 6km north of Mission Beach. It's a quiet, relaxed place in an impressive timber stilt house with a pool and good views over the surrounding rainforest and the coast. This secluded and earthy place is one of the most popular along the coast. A bed in a six-bed dorm costs $16, doubles cost $40, or you can camp here on the grass for $10. There are bikes for hire for $12 a day.

Motels The *Bingil Bay Resort Motel* (☎ 4068 7208), overlooking Bingil Bay from high on a hillside, is a good mid-range motel with rooms ranging from $55 to $80 for a double. The upstairs front rooms are the most expensive, but it's worth paying a bit extra for these great views. The motel has lovely gardens and a good swimming pool, plus its own restaurant.

The *Mission Beach Village Motel* (☎ 4068 7212), at 7 Porter Promenade in Mission Beach, has rooms from $55.

Holiday Units Just south of the bus stop in Mission Beach, *Ceud Mile Failte* (☎ 4068

7444) is a bright yellow block of 1960s holiday flats. They're pretty basic and light on for glam, but reasonably cheap at $60 a double plus $12 for extra people.

Beaches (☎ 4068 8467), at 82 Reid Rd in Wongaling Beach, has good self-contained holiday units on the waterfront. There's also a saltwater pool. The two and three-bedroom flats sleep up to nine and cost from $100 to $150 a day.

There are plenty of other holiday units scattered along the length of Reid Rd. If you're after somewhere a little more up-market, *The Wongalinga* (☎ 4068 8221), at 64 Reid Rd, Wongaling Beach, is a waterfront complex of nine luxurious self-contained apartments. The one-bedroom units start at $120 a night, two-bedrooms at $160 and three-bedrooms from $200.

Resorts The *Clump Point Ecovillage* (☎ 4068 7534), which is on the foreshore at Clump Point, is a resort with good, modern self-contained timber bungalows. The units sleep up to five people and cost $98 a night. The resort is close to the beach, and has a great pool and lush gardens.

With 54 units, two bars, two restaurants and a great pool, *Castaways* (☎ 4068 7444 or toll-free ☎ 1800 079 002) is an impressive big resort on the beachfront in central Mission Beach. There are four styles of accommodation here, ranging from motel-style units from $110/122 a single/double room, one and two-bedroom units from $145 to $175 and a penthouse unit from $225. The resort has a good range of water sports gear available for its guests.

The *Point Resort* (☎ 4068 8154 or toll-free ☎ 1800 079 090), at South Mission Beach, is very stylish with rooms from $160 a double.

If you're after somewhere self-contained, secluded and a little out of the ordinary, the *Lugger Bay Rainforest Apartments* (☎ 4068 8400), right next to the Point Resort, is about the best of this area's offerings. It's a set of nine wonderful timber cabins built on timber poles on a rainforest-covered hillside, and most have great ocean views.

They sleep up to six people and start at $250 a double plus $45 for extra people, but are cheaper by the week.

The *Mission Beach Resort Hotel* (☎ 4068 8288 or toll-free ☎ 1800 079 024), in Wongaling Beach, is a large resort complex with a pub attached. There are four pools, spacious grounds and tennis courts, and motel-style units start at $80/90 a single/double, or $100 for a self-contained unit. All rooms have three or four beds and children are free.

Places to Eat
Mission Beach Mission Beach proper has a good selection of eateries. The tiny *Port 'o Call Cafe*, beside the bus stop, has breakfasts, home-made meals, pancakes, great pies and good coffee. In the arcade just across Campbell St is *On the Bite*, a casual seafood cafe with excellent takeaway fish and chips, burgers, pizzas and sandwiches. Close by is the *Beach Terraces Cafe*, a modern cafe with an interesting and varied menu, main courses around $15 and some vegetarian dishes.

Across the road is *Butterflies*, a friendly and laid-back little Mexican place with vegetarian and seafood dishes. Entrees are from $8 and main courses from $11. Next door is *Food*, a trendy brasserie with mains around $15 and vegetarian dishes, such as lasagne, at $12.

The cosy *Friends* is a popular open-air BYO with some exotic mains, such as bugs and bacon with chilli plum sauce, for about $17. Further down David St is an Italian bistro called *Piccolo Paradiso*, with pizzas and pasta from $7 to $10, and other mains at $14 to $16. This friendly place is licensed and open seven days a week.

Other Areas The *Mission Beach Hotel* in Wongaling Beach has a bistro with standard main meals in the $10 to $12 range. It also has the more up-market *Rainforest Restaurant* for intimate wining and dining, with main meals from $15 to $20. If you're preparing your own food, there are supermarkets at Mission Beach and Wongaling Beach.

Close to Scotty's is the *Hungry Hound Cafe*, a lively, licensed, open-air place with a varied menu and occasional live music.

At South Mission Beach there's *Blarney's* (☎ 4068 8472), a popular little BYO with a great open-sided dining area upstairs. It's a soft-lights-and-music type of restaurant, with main courses such as grilled coral trout and roast rack of lamb from $13 to $17.

Getting There & Away
A number of McCafferty's and Greyhound Pioneer buses on the coastal run make the detour into Mission Beach. McCafferty's buses stop outside the Port 'o Call Cafe in Mission Beach, while Greyhound Pioneer stops at the Mission Beach Resort in Wongaling Beach. The average fare is $15 from Cairns and $39 from Townsville.

Australia Coach (☎ 4031 3555) does five runs a day between Mission Beach and Cairns (town and airport) for $25 ($15 to or from Innisfail). Advance bookings are required.

Getting Around
Bus Mission Beach Bus Service does regular runs from Bingil Bay to South Mission between 8.30 am and 5 pm, with limited evening services. The bus stops anywhere on demand and the maximum fare is $4.

Most of the tour and cruise companies, and accommodation houses, have courtesy buses.

Car Rental Moke & Moped Hire (☎ 4068 7783) has mokes for $40 per day and scooters for $30.

Bike Hire Most of the hostels hire out bicycles; the typical cost is $12 per day for mountain bikes.

Taxi Phone ☎ 4068 8155 if you need a taxi.

DUNK ISLAND
The Family Group of islands, a little way offshore from Mission Beach, consists of Dunk Island and seven smaller islands. The islands of the group (and their Aboriginal names) are Dunk (Coonanglebah), Thorpe (Timana), Richards (Bedarra), Wheeler (Toolghar), Coombe (Coomboo), Smith (Kurrumbah), Bowden (Budjoo) and Hudson (Coolah). Dunk is about three-quarters national park, and of the other islands five – Wheeler, Coombe, Smith, Bowden and Hudson islands – are national parks. Two – Timana and Bedarra – are privately owned and now known by their Aboriginal names.

There is a large resort and an area with day trippers' facilities on Dunk, a small and very exclusive resort on Bedarra, and you can camp on Dunk, Wheeler or Coombe islands. Because of the heavy rainfall in this area all of the islands are cloaked in dense rainforest, and most have excellent beaches.

The islands were named by Captain Cook, who sailed through the group on 8 June 1770. Lord Montague Dunk was at that time the First Lord of the Admiralty.

Just 4.5km off the coast, Dunk is a lush rainforest island with steep hills, some fine walking trails and good sandy beaches. The island has a large resort owned by P&O Resorts, a good camping ground and a separate day trippers' section with a kiosk, showers, toilets and a water sports shop with windsurfers, catamarans, paddle skis and snorkelling gear for hire.

From 1897 to 1923 EJ Banfield lived on Dunk and wrote *The Confessions of a Beachcomber* and several other books describing life on Dunk; the island is remarkably little changed from his early descriptions. Dunk is noted for its prolific birdlife (nearly 150 species) and many butterflies. There are superb views over the entrances to the Hinchinbrook Channel from the top of 271m Mt Kootaloo. Around 13km of **walking tracks** lead from the camping ground area to headlands and beaches, including a 10km circuit walk around the north and western half of the island.

There is a small **artists' colony** at the southern end of the circuit walk, centred around Bruce Arthur, a tapestry maker and former Olympic wrestler. The colony is open to visitors on Monday and Friday from 10 am to 3 pm – a charge of $4 gives you a brief introduction to the island and the artists' activities. The artwork is for sale, and includes pottery, ceramics, jewellery and Bruce Arthur's tapestries.

Dunk is an easy and affordable day trip from the mainland, with regular water taxis running between Mission Beach and the island.

Places to Stay

Camping There's a national parks camping ground next to the day trippers' area. There are toilets, showers, fireplaces and picnic tables, and drinking water is available. There is a limit of 30 campers and a maximum stay of three days here. Camping permits are booked through reception at the resort (☎ 4068 8199).

Resorts The *Dunk Island Resort* (☎ 4068 8199; reservations through P&O Resorts on ☎ 13 2469), at Brammo Bay, on the northern end of the island, has accommodation for up to 400 guests, although it has managed to avoid being too 'mass market'. Architecturally the rooms are straight out of the 1960s bland-box school, but inside they are quite comfortable and the lush Dunk greenery certainly helps to hide them.

The resort has 141 rooms in four different styles. The older Banfield and Garden Cabana rooms are mostly set back from the bayfront while the Beachfront units face the water. The Bayview Villas, with their ultra-modern white and blue decor, also have impressive views over Brammo Bay. All the rooms have en suite, air-con and ceiling fan, a verandah, TV and telephone, a fridge and tea and coffee-making facilities.

Daily rates for one or two people are $340 in the Banfield units, $410 in the Garden Cabanas, $480 in the Beachfront units and $520 in the Bayview Villas. The tariff is room-only, but includes most activities. Children aged three to 14 years are charged at $30. Two/three meal packages are $57/75 ($30/38 for children).

The resort's facilities include squash and tennis courts, a small golf course, two swimming pools, and laundry facilities. The activities desk can arrange horse riding, clay-target shooting, and diving and snorkelling trips to the Barrier Reef.

Places to Eat

The main restaurant is the large, tropical-style *Beachcomber* restaurant. Breakfast and lunch are fairly elaborate buffets, with a good range of fresh fruit, cereals, hot foods, salads, cold meat and seafood. At dinner entrees are $8 to $14 and main courses $23.

EJ's on the Deck is a casual, open-air lunchtime cafe with an interesting menu. Inevitable focaccias ($10) are supplemented by dishes such as laksa ($10) and gulf prawn wontons ($15).

The resort also has the smaller *Cascades*, which is open for dinner with more exotic and inspired food; main courses range from $25 to $30.

Even if you're not staying in the resort, you can eat in the Beachcomber restaurant by buying a resort pass for $10, or $25 including lunch.

The *Tavern by the Jetty*, in the day trippers' area, is a fast-food cafe with burgers, sandwiches, salads and fish and chips.

Getting There & Away

Air Sunstate (Qantas) has regular flights to and from Townsville (45 minutes, $135) or Cairns (40 minutes, $134).

Boat It's a 10-minute trip from the mainland to the island. Dowd's Water Taxis (☎ 4768 8310) has seven daily services from Wongaling Beach to Dunk and back. The fare is $22 return. Surprisingly, there is no jetty at Wongaling and the water taxi doesn't use the jetty at Dunk, so at both ends passengers have to wade out into at least knee-deep water to board.

There are also several cruise companies based at the Clump Point jetty just north of Mission Beach. Day trips to the island with the *Quick Cat* (☎ 4068 7289) cost $22, or you can do a day trip out to the reef, which offers snorkelling and a ride in a glass-bottomed boat, for $122.

The MV *Lawrence Kavanagh* (☎ 4068 7211) does Dunk Island trips from $18, and for another $22 you can also join its 1½-hour cruise around Bedarra. Lunch is available for $8.

BEDARRA ISLAND

Bedarra Island is just 6km south of Dunk and about 5km offshore. The island is rocky, hilly and cloaked in rainforest, and fringed with some fine, sandy beaches, a short stretch of mangroves and wildly tumbled collections of giant boulders.

The island is home to one of Australia's best island resorts, which is operated by P&O Resorts. The resort is very exclusive and expensive, with a maximum number of 32 people and costs starting at $1000/1290 a day for a single/double. If you can afford that sort of money, Bedarra is about the best resort island on the Great Barrier Reef, perhaps only matched by Lizard Island.

Places to Stay & Eat

For bookings, phone the resort on ☎ 4068 8233 or P&O Resorts on ☎ 132469. You could also write to Bedarra Bay Resort, Bedarra Island, via Townsville, Qld 4810.

The accommodation here is stylish without being over the top or at all glitzy. The resort has 16 architect-designed timber cottages, each with a two-level room with a sleeping area above and a lounge area below. The cottages are almost hidden from each other by the rainforest, and have their own private verandah.

There is a central restaurant, bar and lounge area, as well as swimming pools, spas, tennis courts, catamarans, windsurfers, paddle skis and dinghies for the guests.

The tariff includes all meals, drinks, activities and equipment – in fact just about everything your heart may desire. The resort hangs its hat on its reputation for great food. You can order from the menu, or just eat oysters and lobster and drink champagne all day if that's what you feel like. It's up to you.

Getting There & Away

Bedarra is reached from Dunk, a 20-minute boat ride away. The resort's boat connects with Dunk flights or the water taxis between the mainland and Dunk.

OTHER FAMILY ISLANDS

The other five small national park islands of the Family group are Wheeler, Coombe, Smith, Bowden and Hudson islands. With a permit from the Department of Environment's Reef & Rainforest Centre at Cardwell, you can camp on Wheeler or Coombe islands. There are picnic tables at the camp sites, but no toilet facilities. Wheeler Island has fresh water during the cooler months. The maximum number of campers is limited to 20 on Wheeler Island, to 10 on Coombe Island.

Charter boats operate from the Clump Point jetty at Mission Beach or from Cardwell to the islands.

MISSION BEACH TO INNISFAIL

The small township of **El Arish** just off the highway 17km north of Tully, is the main turn-off point to Mission Beach. In the town is the El Arish Tavern, a historic timber pub draped in hanging baskets and assorted greenery – it's a popular watering hole.

About 8km north of El Arish there's a turn-off to **Kurrimine Beach**, another quiet little beachfront community 10km from the highway. From the beach here you can sometimes wade through knee-deep water all the way out to **King Reef**, which is about 1km offshore. The walk takes about 45 minutes and can *only* be done on low tides during winter – check local advice before attempting the walk, as people have been stranded out here in the past.

The *Kurramine Beach Camping Area*, a council-run camping ground right on the foreshore, has good, shady tent sites for $7, or $8 with hot showers. The *King Reef Hotel* (☎ 4065 6144) has a camping ground here, and a few motel rooms and holiday units.

At **Mourilyan**, 7km south of Innisfail, you could drop into the Australian Sugar

Industry Museum. It has a collection of old tractors, harvesters, steam-driven crushing engines and backlit displays depicting the sugar production process. The museum is open from 9 am to 4.30 pm daily and costs $4. The museum complex also houses the Innisfail Tourist Office (☎ 4063 2306).

Old Bruce Hwy

An interesting alternative route to Innisfail is to turn off the Bruce Hwy and take the Old Bruce Hwy north through Silkwood, Mena Creek and South Johnstone. This route leaves the highway 8km north of El Arish, meeting up with the main highway again at the southern outskirts of Innisfail. It's a slower but much more scenic drive, taking you through banana plantations and cane fields surrounded by densely forested mountains on either side. It also takes you to the fascinating Paronella Park, one of the weirdest and most interesting attractions in this area.

After turning off, you drive through the small and old-fashioned sugar cane township of Silkwood. The *Silkwood Hotel* has budget accommodation. From here the road follows and frequently crosses the cane railways, so take care if you're here during the harvesting season (June to December).

It's 22km to Mena Creek, where the very pleasant *Mena Creek Hotel* (☎ 4065 3201) has good pub-style rooms at $20/30 for singles/doubles. The pub does bistro meals, and has a shady verandah and a good beer garden out the back.

Paronella Park This unusual place was the dream-child of José Paronella, a Spaniard who came to Australia from Catalonia in 1913. After working as a cane cutter and farmer for 10 years, he returned to Spain, and brought his new wife Margarita back to Australia. Together they bought a block of land and started building a house in 1929. Next they built a castle, the Grand Staircase down to the river, a Lovers' Tunnel and a hall, all out of poured concrete reinforced with old railway tracks. They also planted thousands of trees and commissioned a hydroelectric plant to supply power.

Paronella Park was opened to the public in 1935, and was an instant success and became one of the most popular tourist attractions in north Queensland. José died in 1948, but his family continued running the park until 1977, when it was sold.

Today its still a fascinating and quite bizarre place to visit. Many of the buildings are in ruins, but large parts remain and you can walk through the remains of the castle, down the grand staircase to the river and stroll through Lovers' Tunnel. You can swim in the river or feed the ducks, walk the suspension bridge across the falls, and trails lead through several hectares of lovely gardens. The park is open every day from 9 am to 5 pm; entry costs $7 ($3 children).

There is also a camping and caravan park (☎ 4065 3225) with tent sites and on-site cabins. Campers also pay the entry fee for the park, but you then have 24-hour access for the duration of your stay.

Far North Queensland

Although the region covered by this chapter is geographically small it is packed with natural assets. The strength of the region's tourist industry is based on this unique combination.

Cairns and Port Douglas are the main tourist centres, and both offer a huge range of possibilities. An armada of tourist boats operates out of both places to the numerous islands, reefs and coral cays of the Great Barrier Reef.

Inland from Cairns is the high plateau of the Atherton Tableland, which offers a cool respite from the heat of the coast. There are some interesting places to visit and things to do – waterfalls and lakes, old mountain villages, bushwalks through the forests, birdwatching – and great places like old pubs, guesthouses and farms to stay in.

North of Port Douglas is the majestic Daintree River. A cruise along this river is a wonderful experience. North of the Daintree are the rainforested mountains of Cape Tribulation National Park, the place where the rainforest meets the reef.

Further north again is the remote town of Cooktown, which is refreshingly unaffected by the hype of tourism – just getting there is an adventure in itself.

An hour or two's drive inland from the coast the great Australian outback begins, stretching clear across to the other side of the continent. You can get a taste of the outback by visiting Chillagoe, an interesting former mining centre 2½ hours drive west of Cairns.

HISTORY

The gold discoveries of the 1870s were primarily responsible for opening up this area to European settlers. Cooktown was established as a port for the fabulously rich Palmer River goldfield in 1873, and became the first major township in the Far North, virtually overnight. Cairns (in 1876) and Port Douglas (in 1877) were both estab-

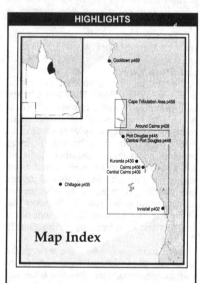

HIGHLIGHTS

Cooktown p469

Cape Tribulation Area p456

Around Cairns p428

Port Douglas p445
Central Port Douglas p448

Kuranda p430
Cairns p406
Central Cairns p409

Chillagoe p435

Innisfail p402

Map Index

- Get the adrenaline pumping with white-water rafting on the North Johnstone River.
- Cut loose and sample some of Cairns' legendary nightlife.
- Explore the scenic Atherton Tableland.
- Visit the World Heritage Listed rainforests at Cape Tribulation.
- Escape to Cooktown and see a corner of Queensland without tourists.
- Dive at Lizard Island, arguably the best diving island on the entire Great Barrier Reef.

lished as ports for the Hodgkinson River goldfields; Cairns gained the upper hand when it was later chosen as the terminal for the railway line from the rich tin-mining township of Herberton, in the Atherton Tableland.

Many of the area's mines had short life spans, and the diggers drifted from one rush

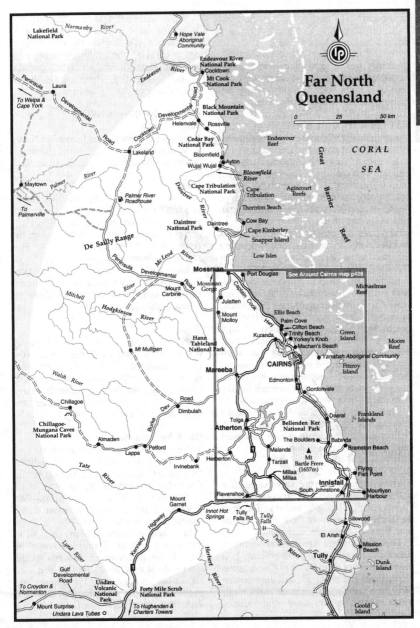

Far North Queensland

0   25   50 km

See Around Cairns map p428

to the next. The port towns, on the other hand, prospered and soon became the main centres for life in the Far North.

As the initial flurry of mining activity gradually waned, agriculture and pastoral activities became the mainstays of the region, with the sugar industry quickly becoming the major source of income.

GEOGRAPHY & CLIMATE

Geographically, the Far North is a microcosm of the entire state of Queensland. The mountains of the Great Dividing Range run parallel with the coast, dividing the region into two distinct zones: a green and fertile coastal strip; and a harsher, outback-type region which stretches from the western side of the mountains.

The coastal mountain ranges are densely forested; large areas of these rainforests are protected as national parks and included in the Wet Tropics World Heritage Area.

Climatically, the Far North has two distinct seasons – summer, and the rest of the year. This is something of a simplification, of course, but the summer months (December to March) are characterised by high temperatures and humidity; tropical downpours are a regular feature, and when cyclones approach the coast rain depressions can set in for days on end. The rest of the year tends to be what summer is like elsewhere – plenty of sunshine and warm weather. It seldom gets cold here – with the exception of the Atherton Tableland, which is one of the few areas where you may require a jumper or a jacket.

ACTIVITIES

There are many adventure activities on offer in the Far North. There are diving courses in Cairns and Port Douglas, and if you want to go snorkelling or diving there are dozens of boat trips out to the reef and islands.

There are some spectacular national parks in the area, and bushwalking is a popular activity here. South of Cairns is the Bartle Frere National Park, and the Daintree and Cape Tribulation National Parks north of Mossman also have some great walks.

White-water rafting trips on the Tully and North Johnstone rivers are among the most popular activities, or you can try canoeing or sea-kayaking. Paragliding, bungee jumping and hang-gliding are other popular adventure activities. There are also a few horse riding ranches in this area.

GETTING THERE & AWAY
Air

Cairns is the major airport for the Far North, with international flights and domestic flights to all the major cities in Australia.

Bus

The two major bus companies, McCafferty's and Greyhound Pioneer, ply the coastal route up the Bruce Hwy as far as Cairns.

Coral Coaches continues the run up the coast from Cairns, with services to Port Douglas, Mossman, Daintree, Cape Tribulation and Cooktown. There are also local bus services from Cairns to the Northern Beaches, up to the Atherton Tableland, and across to the Gulf Savannah.

Train

Cairns is the end of the main coastal railway link from Brisbane. Three trains (the *Queenslander*, the *Sunlander* and the *Spirit of the Tropics*) run up and down the coast. From Cairns, the popular Kuranda Scenic Railway climbs spectacularly through the mountains to the market town of Kuranda.

Car & Motorcycle

The Bruce Hwy, which runs all the way up the Queensland coastline from Brisbane, finishes in Cairns. From Cairns, the Captain Cook Hwy continues along the coast as far as the town of Daintree – the Cairns-Port Douglas stretch is one of the most scenic coastal drives in Queensland.

Just south of Daintree is the turn-off to the ferry across the Daintree River. The Cape Tribulation road which starts on the other side is now mostly sealed and well maintained, making Cape Trib an easy and popular day trip destination. Beyond Cape Trib, the unsealed Bloomfield Track is

4WD territory all the way to Cooktown. There's also an inland route from Cairns to Cooktown, via Mareeba and Mt Molloy. This road can be tackled by conventional vehicles, although the second half is over unsealed, rough and bumpy roads.

There are two major routes heading inland to the Atherton Tableland from Cairns. Leaving the Captain Cook Hwy at Smithfield, north of Cairns, the Kennedy Hwy climbs up to Kuranda and across to Mareeba. From Mareeba you can head north up the inland route to Cooktown and beyond; continue west to the old mining township of Chillagoe; or head south and into the heart of the Atherton Tableland. The second route, the Gillies Hwy, leaves the Bruce Hwy at Gordonvale, south of Cairns, and climbs up to the Tableland via Yungaburra and Atherton.

Innisfail to Cairns

INNISFAIL
pop 8700

Innisfail is a solid and prosperous country town at the confluence of the North and South Johnstone rivers. The North Johnstone, flowing down from the Atherton Tableland, is popular for white-water rafting and canoeing.

Innisfail has been a sugar city for over a century. It's a busy place, with a large Italian population. The Italians first arrived early this century to work the cane fields – some became plantation owners themselves and in the 1930s there was even a local branch of the Mafia, called the Black Hand!

Despite being in the centre of a popular tourism area, Innisfail is a largely unaffected working town. Perhaps more than anything else, it offers a chance to get a feel for what life was like in the Far North pre-tourism.

Orientation & Information

Innisfail sprawls around the banks of the Johnstone Rivers, with the town centre just

west of where the two rivers meet. The Bruce Hwy passes through the centre of town.

There's an information centre at Mourilyan south of town.

The Department of Environment has an office (☎ 4061 4291) in the Rising Sun shopping complex on Owen St.

The Shell Johnstone Driveway (☎ 4061 1941), on the corner of Ernest and Lily Sts, is the local RACQ depot.

Things to See & Do

Innisfail is something of a fishing centre, and from the town centre you can wander down to the banks of the North Johnstone and have a look at the colourful trawlers moored alongside. The Innisfail Fish Depot sells fresh fish and excellent prawns.

On Owen St there's a **Chinese Joss House**, a small temple that was built in the 1940s. The original Joss House, built in 1900, was destroyed in a cyclone.

Warrina Lakes, at the north end of Charles St, is a pleasant park with gardens, walking paths, a lake, a kid's playground, barbecues and picnic areas, and a pool with a large spa. The gardens are open from 9 am (10 am weekends) to 6.30 pm.

The town's **Historical Society Museum** is upstairs in the old School of Arts building, at 11 Edith St. It is open on weekdays from 10 am to 12 noon and 1 to 3 pm ($2).

Places to Stay

There are three caravan parks in Innisfail. The best is the *River Drive Van Park* (☎ 4061 2515), on the Bruce Hwy 1km south of the centre, on the banks of the South Johnstone. Tent sites cost $12 and on-site cabins start at $35.

Backpackers Innisfail (☎ 4061 2284), at 73 Rankin St, is an old timber house with the usual hostel facilities. Quite a few workers stay here – picking bananas is the most common job. Dorm beds cost $15.

The *Codge Lodge*, also on Rankin St is a new hostel in a renovated house. It is very well equipped, with facilities such as washing machines and dryers. There's also

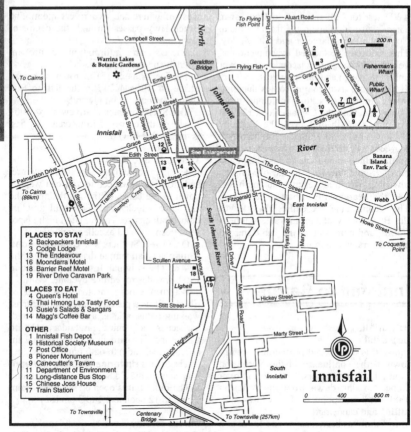

PLACES TO STAY
2 Backpackers Innisfail
3 Codge Lodge
13 The Endeavour
16 Moondarra Motel
18 Barrier Reef Motel
19 River Drive Caravan Park

PLACES TO EAT
4 Queen's Hotel
5 Thai Hmong Lao Tasty Food
10 Susie's Salads & Sangars
14 Magg's Coffee Bar

OTHER
1 Innisfail Fish Depot
6 Historical Society Museum
7 Post Office
8 Pioneer Monument
9 Canecutter's Tavern
11 Department of Environment
12 Long-distance Bus Stop
15 Chinese Joss House
17 Train Station

Innisfail

a pool, and views of the river from the back balcony. Dorm beds are $15, or singles/double are $17/34. The owner may be able to help with finding banana-picking work.

The Endeavour (☎ 4061 6610), at 31 Gladys St, is another workers' hostel in a more comfortable two-storey Queenslander. Dorm beds here cost $15 and singles/doubles cost $30/40.

The *Moondarra Motel* (☎ 4061 7077), at 21 Ernest St, is a friendly little budget motel with singles/doubles from $38/48. There are many other motels in and around town.

Places to Eat

There are plenty of cafes and takeaways in town and along the highway, including all the big-name chains.

Susie's Salads & Sangars, at 49 Edith St, is a little sandwich bar with better-than-average takeaway tucker. If you need a decent coffee, try *Magg's Coffee Bar*, at 88 Edith St.

The *Queen's Hotel*, at 74 Rankin St, has budget bistro meals from $6.

At *Thai Hmong Lao Tasty Food* the name says is it all. This is a cheap and cheerful

Asian place on Rankin St with dishes around $6 to $7.

Entertainment
The *Tropic Rock* nightclub at the Canecutters Tavern on Edith St is open from 9 pm to 3 am and has live bands on weekends. It can sometimes get a bit rough as the night wears on.

Getting There & Away
Innisfail is on the main north-south railway line. Long-distance buses stop opposite King George V Park on Edith St.

AROUND INNISFAIL
The sleepy community of **Flying Fish Point**, 7km east of Innisfail on the northern side of the Johnstone River mouth, has a caravan park one block back from the beach.

Halfway along the road to Flying Fish Point is the **Johnstone River Crocodile Farm**, which has a large collection of breeding crocs and is open daily from 9 am to 5 pm; entry costs $10 ($5 children).

Heading north along the Bruce Hwy from Innisfail, there's a turn-off after about 1km to the *Garadung Hotel*, a rambling 1888 pub sitting alone in the middle of the cane fields. The pub has cheap rooms, and the counter meals here are excellent.

WEST FROM INNISFAIL
The Palmerston Hwy leaves the Bruce Hwy 5km north of Innisfail and winds westwards up to the Atherton Tableland. It follows the original route taken by the famous bushman Christie Palmerston. In 1882 Palmerston and his Aboriginal companions set out from the tin-mining town of Herberton, walked about 100km through thick jungle in search of a useable route to the coast and finally arrived at Innisfail after 12 days.

The highway passes through the rainforests of the **Palmerston (Wooroonooran) National Park**. There are some great walking trails through the park, leading to waterfalls and creeks and linking the picnic and camping grounds. They include Craw-

ford's Lookout to Tchupala Falls (5km, two to three hours), Tchupala Falls to Goolagan's picnic area (3km, one to two hours) and the Nandroya Falls Circuit (7.2km, three to four hours). There's a rangers' station (☎ 4064 5115) at the eastern entrance to the park, 33km from Innisfail, where you can pick up a copy of the self-guided trail brochure. There are also picnic areas throughout the park, and a camping ground at Henrietta Creek, just off the highway, with toilets, picnic tables and coin-operated barbecues.

The Palmerston Hwy continues to Millaa Millaa, passing the entrance to the 'waterfalls circuit' just before the town. See the Atherton Tableland section for details of this area.

JOSEPHINE FALLS
About 22km north of Innisfail there's a turn-off to Josephine Falls, a popular picnic spot 8km inland from the highway. It's a 10-minute walk from the car park to the falls, which offers great swimming in a number of natural pools. The smooth rocks connecting the pools are slippery and can be treacherous, and the flow can be powerful after rain. Observe the signs advising where it's safe to swim – people have drowned here.

The falls are at the foot of the Bellenden Ker Range, which includes Queensland's highest peak, **Mt Bartle Frere** (1657m). The **Mt Bartle Frere Hiking Track** leads from the falls car park to the Bartle Frere summit. Don't underestimate this walk: the ascent is for fit and experienced walkers only – it's a 15km, two-day return trip, and rain and cloud can close in suddenly. There's an alternative 10km return walk to Broken Nose. You can self-register at the start of the walk, but it's also a good idea to speak to the rangers at the Department of Environment office in Innisfail (☎ 4061 4291).

Close to the falls car park is *Bartle Frere Homestay* (☎ 4067 6309) with camping ($3 per person) and B&B accommodation ($70 double).

BRAMSTON BEACH
pop 320
A couple of kilometres further on is the turn-off to Bramston Beach. It's 17km from the highway through cane fields to this small beachfront community. There's a general store and a stinger net on the beach here, plus a couple of accommodation options.

The council runs a basic campground on the foreshore. The *Bramston Beach Holiday Motel* (☎ 4067 4139) has basic motel units, costing $40/48 for singles/doubles.

About 1km further south, the *Plantation Village Resort* (☎ 4067 4133) is a somewhat run-down budget resort fronting the beach. It offers camping ($12), motel-style units ($39) and self-contained units ($49 to $59). The resort has two bars, a restaurant, a pool, tennis courts and a nine-hole golf course.

BABINDA
pop 1300
Hidden behind a huge sugar mill, which fronts the Bruce Hwy, Babinda is a small town of verandah-fronted buildings and old timber pubs. You can take a trip back in time by taking in a movie at the **Munro Theatre**, a quaint cinema that dates back to the 1940s. It still has old hessian-slung seats and a hessian-covered ceiling.

The *Babinda Hotel* (☎ 4067 1202) is an old two storey timber pub. Its bars were once regularly flooded with cane cutters at the end of their shifts, and locals can remember it being so crowded that drinkers would spill out onto the streets. The pub has simple but clean rooms upstairs, and reasonable meals downstairs.

BABINDA BOULDERS
Babinda Boulders, where a creek rushes between enormous rocks, is 7km inland from Babinda. This is truly a lovely (and therefore popular) spot, with lawns, gardens, great picnic areas with push-button barbecues. There's a huge swimming hole with clear water, and walking trails lead to Devil's Lookout (470m) and the Boulders Gorge Lookout (600m).

A suspension bridge takes you across the river to an 850m circuit walk through the rainforest.

There's also a small, basic camping ground 100m back from the main car park. The caretaker comes around to collect the $8 site fee.

Just before the entrance to the Boulders' car park is *Bowenia Lodge* (☎ 4067 1631), a timber homestead which offers B&B accommodation. There are two guest bedrooms with their own en suites, a guest kitchen and a lounge area, and it's good value at $30 per person including breakfast. Meals are available if you don't want to cook for yourself.

From the Boulders you can walk the **Goldfield Track** – first opened up in the 1930s when there was a minor gold rush. It leads 10km to the Goldsborough Valley, across a saddle in the Bellenden Ker Range. The track ends at a causeway on the Mulgrave River, from where a forestry road leads 8km to a camping ground in the **Goldsborough Valley State Forest**. From there it's 15km on to the Gillies Hwy between Gordonvale and Atherton.

GORDONVALE
pop 2800
Back on the Bruce Hwy, Gordonvale is another town with a huge sugar mill. The town sits at the base of **Walsh's Pyramid** (922m), which is at the northern tip of the Bellenden Ker National Park. On the highway north of the town are two Sikh *gurdwaras* (places of worship).

During the cutting season (July through October), you can take a tour of the **Mulgrave Sugar Mill** (☎ 4056 3300). Tours depart each weekday during the season at 10 am, 1.30 and 3 pm; the tour lasts 1½ hours and costs $6 ($3 children and students). Close by is a small **Settlers' Museum**.

GORDONVALE TO YUNGABURRA
The winding Gillies Hwy leads from here up onto the Atherton Tableland. It's 43km from here to Yungaburra. The first section

twists and climbs steeply as you head up into the mountains, and you can feel the temperature drop as you climb higher.

About 13km from Gordonvale is the turn-off to **Orchid Valley**, a lovely orchid garden in the Little Mulgrave Valley. The best time to visit is from April to November. It's open daily from 9 to 5 pm and costs $8 ($4 children).

Just near this turn-off is the *Mountain View Hotel*, which is a great spot for a meal or a cool drink.

YARRABAH ABORIGINAL COMMUNITY
pop 1800
Midway between Gordonvale and Edmonton is a turn-off to the Yarrabah Aboriginal community. It's a scenic 37km drive through cane fields and mountains to Yarrabah. Unlike many Aboriginal communities, you don't need permission to visit.

About 3km after you leave the highway there's another turn-off to the **Cairns Crocodile Farm**, a further 5km. This place is very different to most croc farms – it's not here to entertain tourists, it's a commercial breeding and hatching farm with over 3000 crocs housed in spacious enclosures. You can buy croc meat and leather products from a shop. The farm is open daily from 9 am to 4.30 pm, and feeding time is at 1.45 pm. Entry costs $10 ($5 for children).

The Yarrabah community is set on Mission Bay, a pretty cove backed by palm trees and decorated with the rusting hulls of two ships which were dumped here some years ago. In the town you can visit the **Menmuny Museum**, which has a collection of Aboriginal artefacts and cultural exhibits from a number of different communities. There is also a commercial section with locally made T-shirts, spears, pottery and crafts on sale. Traditional dances are also performed at various times. Behind the museum there's a boardwalk through the rainforest, with signboards pointing out the traditional uses of various native plants. The museum is open on weekdays from 8.30 am to 4.30 pm; entry costs $6 ($3 children).

Cairns

pop 106,600
The 'capital' of the Far North and perhaps the best known city on the Queensland coast, Cairns is now firmly established as one of Australia's top travellers' destinations.

Not so long ago, Cairns was a laid-back country town, all but languishing in the tropics. Today, it's a modern, vivacious city that lives and breathes tourism. Cairns' airport is one of the busiest in Australia, and international arrivals have been growing at a rapid rate.

On the other hand, Cairns' rapid growth has destroyed much of its laid-back tropical atmosphere. It also comes as a surprise to many travellers that Cairns doesn't have a beach, although there are some good ones not far north. And you can always head out to the islands.

Cairns is primarily a base for getting to the many attractions that surround it. Top of the list is the Great Barrier Reef, and dozens of operators run trips out to the reef and islands. The Atherton Tableland, Port Douglas, Chillagoe and Mission Beach are all within a couple of hours' drive of Cairns.

Cairns is also a centre for a host of other activities – not just scuba diving but also white-water rafting, canoeing, horse riding and, of course, crazes like bungee jumping and sky diving. It also has some excellent restaurants and a more than lively nightlife. Lots of international travellers start or finish their Australian odyssey in Cairns, and either way, wild celebrations seem to be in order.

HISTORY
Trinity Bay was named by Captain Cook, who sighted the bay on Trinity Sunday in 1770.

The town came into existence in 1876 as a beachhead in the mangroves, intended as a port for the Hodgkinson River goldfield 100km inland. Initially it struggled under

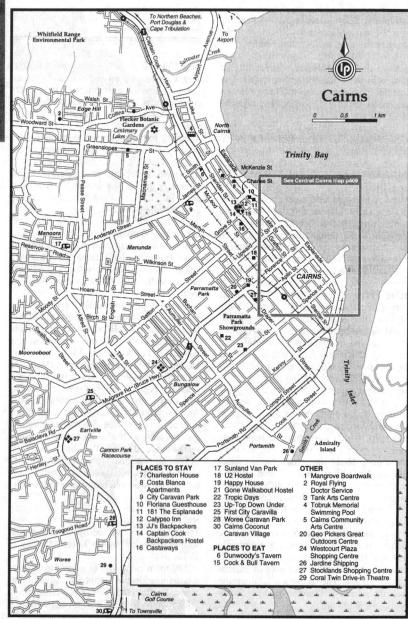

Cairns

0   0.5   1 km

See Central Cairns map p409

PLACES TO STAY
7 Charleston House
8 Costa Blanca
   Apartments
9 City Caravan Park
10 Floriana Guesthouse
11 181 The Esplanade
12 Calypso Inn
13 JJ's Backpackers
14 Captain Cook
   Backpackers Hostel
16 Castaways

PLACES TO EAT
6 Dunwoody's Tavern
15 Cock & Bull Tavern

17 Sunland Van Park
18 U2 Hostel
19 Happy House
21 Gone Walkabout Hostel
22 Tropic Days
23 Up-Top Down Under
25 First City Caravilla
28 Woree Caravan Park
30 Cairns Coconut
   Caravan Village

OTHER
1 Mangrove Boardwalk
2 Royal Flying
   Doctor Service
3 Tank Arts Centre
4 Tobruk Memorial
   Swimming Pool
5 Cairns Community
   Arts Centre
20 Geo Pickers Great
   Outdoors Centre
24 Westcourt Plaza
   Shopping Centre
26 Jardine Shipping
27 Stocklands Shopping Centre
29 Coral Twin Drive-in Theatre

rivalry from Smithfield and Port Douglas. The former was a rowdy frontier town 12km to the north that was washed away by a flood in 1879 (it's now an outer Cairns suburb); and Port Douglas was founded in 1877 after the famous bushman Christie Palmerston discovered an easier route from there to the goldfield. The Atherton Tableland 'tin rush' from 1880 saved Cairns. Cairns became the starting point of the railway to the Tableland, built a few years later in 1886; its supremacy was consolidated as the Tableland was opened up for agriculture and timber, and sugar-growing started in the lowlands.

Despite being the regional capital, Cairns settled into its role as a sleepy and remote northern outpost, with both progress and life moving along in the slow lane. Most of the mining activity in the surrounding regions had dried up by the end of WWI, and the rail link with Brisbane wasn't completed until 1924. Economically, the town was mainly dependent on the sugar industry, with some support coming from pastoral activities, the timber industry and the Tableland's agriculture.

By 1947 Cairns had a population of just 16,000, but fuelled by a booming sugar industry, it grew rapidly through the 1950s and 60s. The first tourists started arriving around this time, and a trickle of visitors throughout the 1970s suddenly became a flood with the opening of Cairns International Airport in 1984.

ORIENTATION

Cairns is ringed on three sides by green and forested hills – probably the most noticeable feature when you first arrive. On the fourth side is the V-shaped Trinity Bay. At the southern end of the bay Trinity Inlet and Smith's Creek form a loop around Admiralty Island; north of the bay is the Barron River estuary.

The urban area is predominantly flat, and sprawls back from the bay to the foot of the hills. The Bruce Hwy leads into Cairns from the south. After it enters the city it becomes Mulgrave Rd, which takes you east towards the city centre, before turning north and heading out of town, with another change of name – to the Captain Cook Hwy.

The city centre is relatively compact, roughly bordered by the Esplanade, Wharf St, McLeod St and Aplin St. Off Wharf St (the southern continuation of the Esplanade), you'll find Marlin Jetty, the Great Adventures Wharf and the Pier – the main departure points for reef trips. Further south is Trinity Wharf (a cruise-liner dock with shops and cafes) and the Transit Centre, where long-distance buses arrive and depart. The airport is about 6km north of the city centre, just south of the Barron River estuary.

INFORMATION
Tourist Information

There's no shortage of tourist information in Cairns. The Wet Tropics Information Centre, on the Esplanade across from the Shields St corner, combines information with displays on the environment and rainforests of the far north. It's open daily from 9.30 am to 5.30 pm. For phone queries, call Tourism Tropical North Queensland (☎ 4051 3588).

There are dozens of privately run 'information centres' in Cairns, and these places are basically tour-booking commission agencies. Most of the backpackers hostels also have helpful tour-booking desks. Note that each booking agent will be pushing different tours, depending on the commission deal it has with the tour companies, so shop around.

The Community Information Service (☎ 4051 4953) in Tropical Arcade off Shields St, half a block back from the Esplanade, is good for some tourist information plus more offbeat things like where you can play croquet or do t'ai chi. It also has details on foreign consulates in Cairns and health services.

Money

All of the major banks have branches throughout central Cairns, and most of these have foreign exchange sections.

Thomas Cook has a Bureau de Change on Lake St.

Post

The main post office, on the corner of Grafton and Hartley Sts, is open on weekdays from 8.30 am to 5 pm. The poste restante service prints a daily alphabetical list of all mail that has arrived. For general business (stamps etc), there's an Australia Post Shop in the Orchid Plaza on Lake St.

American Express (☎ 4051 8811) is at Shop 29, 79-87 Abbott St.

There's email/Internet access at Virtual Reality on the Abbott St entrance to the Night Markets centre. Access costs $6/10 per half-hour/hour. The Call Station, upstairs in The Pier by the food stalls charges $4 for the first 15 minutes and $3.50 for each extra 15 minutes. It also has competitive international telephone rates.

Useful Organisations

The RACQ office (☎ 4051 4788), at 112 Sheridan St, is a good place to get maps and information on road conditions, especially if you're heading bush.

The Department of Environment office (☎ 4052 3096), at 10 McLeod St, is open on weekdays from 8.30 am to 4.30 pm and deals with camping permits for the region's national parks, including islands.

Medical & Emergencies

The Cairns Base Hospital (☎ 4050 6205) is on the Esplanade just north of the centre, and has a casualty ward and a free STD (sexually transmitted diseases) clinic.

Bookshops

Proudmans, in The Pier, and Walker's Bookshop, at 96 Lake St, both have a good range of travel books, local history, literature and children's books.

Cairns Book & Gift Centre, 27 Shields St, has a range of books on ecology, the New Age, crystals, happiness, bush medicine and astronomy, among other subjects.

The Bookshelf, 65 Grafton St, has a good range of second-hand books and magazines.

Laundry

Most places to stay have laundry facilities, but if you need a laundrette, try the Central Laundromat, at 145 Lake St, or Laundry Express, at 49 Grafton St.

THINGS TO SEE

Cairns' main attraction for tourists is as a base for heading to the places that surround it; the town itself has a relatively small number of attractions.

A walk around the town centre turns up a few points of historical interest, although with the recent spate of development, the older buildings are now few and far between. The oldest part of town is the **Trinity Wharf** area, but even this has been redeveloped. There are still some imposing neoclassical buildings from the 1920s on Abbott St, and the frontages around the corner of Spence and Lake Sts date from 1909 to 1926.

The **Esplanade Walking Trail** follows the foreshore for almost 3km north from the centre of town. It makes for an agreeable stroll, with views over to rainforested mountains across the estuary and cool evening breezes.

The **Pier Marketplace** is an up-market shopping plaza with a good range of speciality shops and boutiques selling books, music, clothes, art, jewellery, gifts, souvenirs and lots more. There are also some good eateries here (see Places to Eat), plus a collection of stalls selling local crafts and art (see the Things to Buy section). Also here is the impressive **Undersea World** aquarium, which is open daily from 8 am to 8 pm; entry is steep at $10, but 20% discount vouchers are often available from various hostels. The best time to visit is when the sharks are being fed (four times daily).

Right in the centre of town, on the corner of Lake and Shields Sts, the **Cairns Museum** is housed in the 1907 School of Arts building, an excellent example of early Cairns architecture. The museum has Aboriginal artefacts, a display on the construction of the Cairns to Kuranda

PLACES TO STAY
2 Castle Holiday Flats
3 Bel-Air Hostel
4 Rosie's Backpackers
5 Silver Palm Guesthouse
6 Caravella's 149
8 Inn the Tropics
9 Tracks Hostel
10 Cascade Gardens Apartments
11 Poinsettia Motel
12 Parkview Backpackers
13 Holiday Inn
14 Outrigger Inn
17 Lake Central
18 Lyons Motor Inn
19 YHA on the Esplanade
   & Chapel Bar
22 Il Palazzo
23 Hostel 89
24 Bellview
25 Jimmy's on the Esplanade
26 Caravella's Hostel 77
28 International Hostel
31 Radisson Plaza Hotel

33 Pacific International Hotel
51 Leo's
53 Hides Hotel/Motel
60 Cairns Hilton Hotel
64 Cairns International Hotel
68 Aussie II Hostel
80 Rydges Plaza Cairns
88 Billabong Backpackers
92 Macleod St Youth Hostel
94 Dreamtime Travellers Rest
95 Ryan's Rest

PLACES TO EAT
20 The Meeting Place
27 Night Markets & Rattle n Hum
29 Kani's & Barnacle Bill's
34 Taste of China
40 Galloping Gourmet
41 George's Greek Taverna
42 Old Ambulance Cafe Bistro
45 Silver Dragon Chinese
   Restaurant& Willie's Seaside Cafe
69 Cafe ZuZu
70 Paris Croissant
71 Sawasdee
72 La Fettucine & Gypsy Dee's
73 Red Ochre Grill
74 Victory Cafe
76 John & Diana's Breakfast
   & Burger House
79 Mozart Pastry
81 Yama Japanese Restaurant
82 Turkish Michael's
83 Tiny's Juice Bar
89 Taj & Bombay Palace Restaurants
90 Bangkok Room Thai Restaurant
   & Hog's Breath Cafe

OTHER
1 Cairns Base Hospital
7 Cheap Car Rentals
15 Jolly Frog Car Rentals
16 Cairns Civic Theatre
21 Beach Nightclub
30 Wet Tropics Information Centre
32 Pro Dive
35 Cairns Regional Gallery
36 Johno's Blues Bar
37 Air Niugini
38 Cairns Dive Centre
39 Taka II Dive
43 Cairns 5 Cinemas
44 Cairns Library
46 Walker's Bookshop
47 Wool Shed & Cairns Curry House
48 Qantas & Sunstate Airlines
49 City Place Amphitheatre
50 Cairns Museum
52 Cairns Book & Gift Centre
54 Lake St Transit Centre
55 Orchid Plaza, Australia
   Post Shop & American Express
56 Thomas Cook
57 Reef Teach
58 Ansett
59 Reef Hotel Casino
61 Cairns Yacht Club
62 Great Adventures Booking Office
63 Transit Centre & Trinity Wharf
65 Sports Bar & Rock Cafe, Dundee's
   & Redback Pancake & Steak House
66 Central Arcade & Tropo's Nightclub
67 STA Travel
75 Harris Bros
77 Rusty's Bazaar
78 Rusty's Pub
84 Samuel's Saloon, Court Jester
   & Playpen International
85 Tourism Tropical North Queensland
86 Post Office
87 Police
91 Department of Environment
93 Railway Station

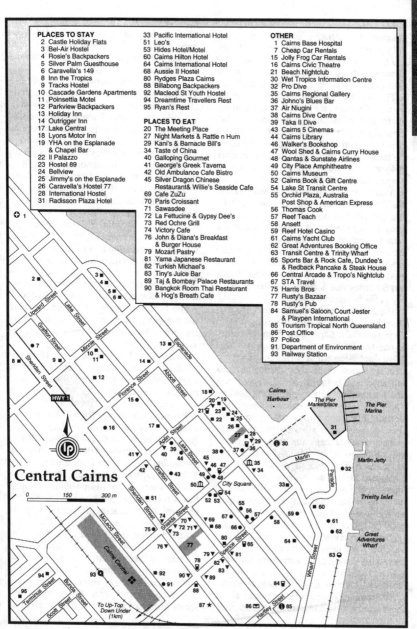

Central Cairns

0   150   300 m

Cairns Harbour

The Pier Marketplace

The Pier Marina

Martin Jetty

Trinity Inlet

City Square

Great Adventures Wharf

To Up-Top Down Under (1km)

railway, the contents of a now demolished Grafton St joss house, exhibits on the old Palmer River and Hodgkinson goldfields, and material on the early timber industry. It is open Monday to Saturday from 10 am to 4pm and entry costs $3 ($1 children).

The **Cairns Regional Gallery**, on the corner of Abbott and Shields Sts, is another of the city's few remaining historic buildings, although the modern cafe which has been tacked on to the front has utterly spoilt the facade. The collection features the work of local artists and is well worth a look. It is open daily from 10 am to 6 pm.

A colourful part of town on weekends is the **Rusty's Bazaar** area – bounded by Grafton, Spence, Sheridan and Shields Sts. The bustling weekend markets held here are great for people-watching and for browsing among the dozens of stalls, which sell produce, arts and crafts, clothes and lots of food. The markets are held on Friday nights and Saturday and Sunday mornings; Saturday is the busiest and best.

The **Flecker Botanic Gardens** are bordered by Collins Ave and Greenslopes St, in Edge Hill, 3km north-west from the centre of Cairns. The gardens have various sections, including an Aboriginal plant use area, a palmetum, bamboos, tropical fruits and a formal botanic garden. There is a small restaurant in the centre of the gardens where you can get a meal or a snack, and the administration office nearby supplies visitors with tapes (in English, German, French or Japanese) for the self-guided walks through the rainforest. The tapes cost $4 to hire plus a $20 deposit for the Walkman. The gardens are open from 7.30 am on weekdays and 8.30 am on weekends, but unfortunately close at 5.30 pm. There are free guided walks through the gardens every weekday at 1 pm.

Over the road from the gardens, a boardwalk leads through a patch of rainforest to **Saltwater Creek** and **Centenary Lakes**.

Near the gardens is the entrance to the **Whitfield Range Environmental Park**, the last remnant of rainforest around Cairns. There are two walking tracks, a one-hour walk (marked in red) and a 3½-hour walk (marked in blue) which give good views over the city and coast. You can get to the gardens or the park with Cairns Sunbuses from the Lake St Transit Centre.

The **Tank Arts Centre**, which is at 46 Collins Ave, Edge Hill, just north of the Botanic Gardens, is one of Cairns' most interesting art spaces. These circular cement and iron WWII naval supply tanks were recently transformed into an exhibition and function centre, and they now host a variety of art exhibitions throughout the year. Ring the centre on ☎ 4032 2349 to see what's on.

Also in Edge Hill, the **Royal Flying Doctor Service** regional office, at 1 Junction St, is open to visitors on weekdays from 8.30 am to 5 pm, and 9 am to 4.30 pm on weekends; entry is $5. You'll find out all about the service and its origins, and there are pedal radios and other items on display.

Heading out of Cairns towards the airport, you'll find an interesting and informative elevated **mangrove boardwalk** off Airport Ave, about 200m before the airport. Signs explain the ecological complexities of mangrove forests, and there's a small observation platform.

Kamerunga Rd, off the Cook Hwy just north of the airport turn-off, leads inland to **Freshwater Connection**, which is a railway museum complex where you can also catch the Kuranda Scenic Railway. It's 10km from the centre of town. Just beyond Freshwater is the turn-off south along Redlynch Intake Rd to **Crystal Cascades**, a popular destination with waterfalls and swimming holes 22km from Cairns.

The **Tjapukai Dance Theatre**, an award-winning Aboriginal dance troupe, has a theatre complex beside the Skyrail terminal at Smithfield, just off the Captain Cook Highway, about 15km north of the centre. This multimillion dollar complex incorporates four sections – a cultural village, a 'creation theatre', an audio-visual show, and a traditional dance theatre. Performances include a re-enactment of a traditional corroboree, boomerang and spear-throwing, and the telling of Dreamtime stories. The gift shop here has a selection of books, didjeridus, tapes and CDs, and other handicrafts. The complex is open daily from 9 am to 5 pm; entry costs $24 ($12 children), or $36 ($18) with return bus transfers from Cairns. Allow at least two hours.

ACTIVITIES

There is a huge range of activities on offer in Cairns. Bookings can be made through your accommodation or any of the booking agencies here – see the earlier Information section.

Dive Courses

Cairns is the scuba-diving capital of the Barrier Reef and the reef is closer to the coast here than it is further south.

Most people look for a course which takes them to the outer Barrier Reef rather than the reefs around Green or Fitzroy islands. Some places give you more time on the reef than others – but you may prefer an extra day in the pool and classroom before venturing out. A chat with people who have already done a course can tell you some of the pros and cons. A good teacher can make all the difference to your confidence and the amount of fun you have. Another factor is how big the groups are – the smaller the better if you want personal attention.

The main schools include: Deep Sea Divers Den (☎ 4031 2223), 319 Draper St; Pro-Dive (☎ 4031 5255), Marlin Jetty; Down Under Dive (☎ 4031 1288), 155 Sheridan St; Cairns Dive Centre (☎ 1800 642 591), 135 Abbott St; Tusa Dive (☎ 4031 1248), 93 The Esplanade; and Taka II Dive (☎ 4051 8722), 131 Lake St. Most of these places can be booked through the hostels.

Prices differ quite a bit between schools, but usually one or other has a discount going. Expect to pay from $350 to $450 for the standard five day course, with two days in the pool and classroom, one day trip to the reef and back, and two more days on the reef with an overnight stay on board. There are cheaper short courses, but the longer courses make sense if you have the time –

they give you more pleasure dives and a chance to reward yourself for all the work it takes to get certified.

If you want to learn about the reef before you dive, Reef Teach offers an entertaining and educational lecture at Boland's Centre, 14 Spence St, every night (except Sunday) from 6.15 to 8.30 pm. The lectures are well worth attending and get good reports from travellers. The cost is $10 – for more details phone ☎ 4051 6882.

White-Water Rafting, Sea Kayaking & Canoeing

Three of the rivers flowing down from the Atherton Tableland make for excellent white-water rafting. Most popular is a day in the rainforested gorges of the Tully River, 150km south of Cairns. So many people do this trip that there can be 20 or more craft on the river at once, meaning you may have to queue up to shoot each section of rapids – despite this, most people are exhilarated at the end of the day. The Tully day trips leave daily year-round. Two companies running them from Cairns are Raging Thunder (☎ 4030 7990), at 111 Spence St, and R 'n' R (☎ 4051 7777 or toll-free ☎ 1800 079 039), at 74 Abbott St. Day trips on the Tully cost around $128 from Cairns. There are cheaper half-day trips on the Barron River ($66), not far inland from Cairns, or you can make two day ($350) or five day ($770) expeditions on the remote North Johnstone River which rises near Malanda and enters the sea at Innisfail.

Foaming Fury (☎ 4032 1460), at 13 Moody St, offers white-water rafting for $118 on the Russell River south of Bellenden Ker National Park; half-day trips on the Barron River for $66; and two-day trips on the North Johnstone River for $123.

The Adventure Company (☎ 4051 4777) has one day wilderness canoe paddles on the Musgrave River ($89) and three-day sea-kayaking tours out of Mission Beach ($498).

Beaches & Swimming

Cairns doesn't have a beach of its own – Trinity Bay is quite shallow and muddy. If you want to go swimming you'll have to head out to the islands, or up to the Northern Beaches – see the later Cairns to Port Douglas section.

Alternatively, you could head for one of the swimming pools in town. The Tobruk Memorial Swimming Pool, on Sheridan St, is an excellent 50m swimming pool.

Horse Riding

There are a couple of options if you want to go horse riding around Cairns. Check with the information centres for full details.

Blazing Saddles and Springmount Station (☎ 4093 4493) both offer half-day horse trail rides for about $65, including pick-ups from Cairns.

Scenic Flights & Helicopters

Northern Air Adventures (☎ 4035 9156) has half hour flights out over Green Island and Arlington and Upton Reefs ($50), or one hour flights which also include Batt Reef ($90).

Other Activities

There are two AJ Hackett (☎ 4057 7188) bungee jumping sites near Cairns. The closest is 15km north on the Cook Hwy, just past the Kuranda turn-off, where for $95 you can take the plunge from a steel tower with sensational views. A courtesy bus does pick-ups from hostels. There's another in the markets at Kuranda – see the Atherton Tableland section.

Dan's Tours (☎ 4033 0128) has full day ($95) mountain bike tours to the Daintree. The Adventure Company (☎ 4051 4777) has two-day tours of the Atherton Tableland for $275.

Skydive Cairns (☎ 4035 9667) has tandem skydiving, or for air travel at a more leisurely pace, there are three ballooning outfits with half hour ($105) and one hour flights ($170), including transfers and breakfast. Contact Raging Thunder (☎ 4030 7990), Hot Air (☎ 1800 800 829) or Champagne Balloon Flights (☎ 1800 677 444).

Tropical Jet (☎ 4031 1949) operates jet boat trips from The Pier. A ride is $55, or

you can have a ride and a parasail for $99. Cairns Parasail & Jet Ski (☎ 4031 7888) also do parasailing for $60.

At Smithfield there's an indoor rock climbing centre (☎ 4057 8677) where you pay $10 with no time limit.

ORGANISED TOURS

As you'd expect, there are hundreds of tours available from Cairns. Some are specially aimed at backpackers and many of these are pretty good value. You can make bookings through your accommodation or at travel agencies which specialise in this type of trip – see the Information section earlier.

Cairns

Half-day trips around the city sights, or two-hour cruises from Marlin Jetty along Trinity Inlet and around Admiralty Island, cost from $20.

Atherton Tableland

Day trips to the Atherton Tableland with the 'conventional' tour companies, which usually include the waterfalls and lakes circuit and a trip on the Kuranda Scenic Railway to the Kuranda markets, will cost anywhere from $66 to $85. The smaller companies which specialise in tours for backpackers, such as Jungle Tours (☎ 1800 817 234), offer similar but much more enjoyable trips for $45 to $50. Uncle Brian's quirky tours (☎ 4050 0615) have received good reports from travellers and a day trip is $55. Again, tours can be booked through your accommodation or one of the booking agencies.

The *On the Wallaby* hostel in Yungaburra offers an overnight trip to the Tableland for $55 including meals and activities – see Yungaburra in the Atherton Tableland section for details.

Daintree & Cape Tribulation

Cape Trib is one of the most popular day-trip destinations from Cairns, and there are literally dozens of companies offering trips up here. Don't be fooled by those '4WD adventure' brochures: the tour companies all use 4WD vehicles, but almost the whole route is now over sealed roads and, with the daily flood of tourists, the adventure has gone out of it a little. Most day trips range from $75 to $100.

Jungle Tours (☎ 1800 817 234) offers fun-oriented trips up to Cape Trib, usually with a cruise on the Daintree River thrown in, for $82 (no lunch). If you have time, you'd be better off taking one of its overnight or longer packages, which cost $78 for two days and $89 for three days, including accommodation at Crocodylus Village and/or PK's Jungle Village. Dan's Tours has mountain bike trips to Cape Trib – see Other Activities earlier in this section.

Cooktown

Strikie's Safaris (☎ 1800 809 999) runs good 4WD trips to Cooktown from Cairns & Port Douglas, visiting places like Black Mountain and the Lion's Den Hotel along the way. Day trips costs $85, two-day trips $220 (meals and accommodation not included).

Wild Trek Adventure Safaris (☎ 4055 2247) offers a two-day trip to Cooktown, going up via the coast road and back via the inland route, for $199. It also has one day trips where you fly up and drive back, or vice versa, which cost $229 via the coastal road or $179 via the inland road.

Barrier Reef & Islands

There are dozens of options for day trips to the reef. It's worth asking a few questions before you book, such as how many passengers the boat takes; what's included in the price and how much the 'extras' (such as wetsuit hire and introductory dives) cost; and exactly where the boat is going. Some companies have a dubious definition of 'outer reef'; as a general rule, the further out you go, the better the diving.

Great Adventures (☎ 1800 079 080) is the major operator. It has the biggest boats and a wide range of trips, and it's worth picking up one of its brochures to see what's on offer. Apart from trips to Green

and Fitzroy islands (see the Islands off Cairns section for details), it has various combination trips including a nine-hour, $130 ($65 children) outer reef trip. You get three hours on the reef itself, lunch, snorkelling gear, and a semi-submersible boat ride thrown in. Great Adventures has its own wharf on Trinity Inlet near the Transit Centre.

Compass (☎ 1800 815 811) and Noah's Ark Cruises (☎ 4051 5666) have popular day trips to Hastings Reef and Michaelmas Cay for $55, including boom netting, snorkelling gear and lunch. Certified divers can take two dives for an extra $45.

Falla (☎ 4031 3488), Seahorse (☎ 4031 4692) and Passions of Paradise (☎ 4050 0676) are all ocean-going yachts that sail to Upolo Cay, Green Island and Paradise Reef daily for about $50, which includes lunch and snorkelling gear.

The majority of cruise boats depart from Trinity Wharf, Marlin Jetty or The Pier Marina in Trinity Inlet – check with the agent when you book.

There are many, many other boats and operators, so shop around. See the Islands off Cairns section for details of trips to Green, Fitzroy and the Frankland islands.

Diving Trips

Apart from the popular day trips to Hastings, Moore and Norman Reefs and Michaelmas Cay, quite a few operators offer longer trips for certified divers who want to dive on the outer Barrier Reef. They include the following: Pro Dive, which has three day trips to the famous Cod Hole for $600; the Deep Sea Divers Den, which charges $390 for three days; Tusa Dive, which has day trips for $130; and Taka Dive, which does the Cod Hole on a four day trip for $600 or five days for $700.

Cruises

The Coral Princess (☎ 4031 1041) does four-day cruises between Cairns and Townsville, via Hinchinbrook, Dunk, Pelorus and Orpheus islands and Sudbury Reef. You can board at either end, and the four days starts from $922 per person, including all meals and activities except diving.

There is also a cruise ship which leaves from Cairns for the Cape York Peninsula – see the Organised Tours section at the start of that chapter for details.

Chillagoe & Mt Mulligan
Chillagoe is a fascinating place to get to and to visit. A couple of companies offer tours out of Cairns, or you can make your own way there.

Jungle Tours (☎ 4032 2111) has six day guided walking expeditions to the Chillagoe area, following the path of the 1848 Edmund Kennedy expedition through the Walsh River gorges. Trips leave from Cairns on Monday (April to October) and cost $688 per person, which includes meals and camping equipment. Ring them to find out when the next trip departs as there's a minimum of four required.

There are also off-the-beaten-track tours to a cattle station around Mt Mulligan – see Mareeba to Chillagoe in the Atherton Tableland section for details.

Gulf Savannah & Undara Lava Tubes
Several companies run tours to various places in the Gulf Savannah, including the Undara Lava Tubes, the Tallaroo Hot Springs, and Karumba. You can also link up with the *Gulflander* and the *Savannahlander*.

Australian Pacific (☎ 13 1304) and Undara Experience (☎ 4031 7933) have two-day trips out to the Undara Lava Tubes for $297, which includes accommodation, meals and the tour of the remarkable lava tubes.

Cape York
For something completely different, Cape York Air Services (☎ 4035 9399), the local mail contractor, does mail runs to remote outback stations on weekdays. Space permitting, you can go along on these runs, but it's not cheap at $195 to $390, depending on the length of the trip. Flights depart from Cairns airport.

See the Cape York chapter for details of other organised tours from Cairns to Cape York.

FESTIVALS
Cairns' major annual festival is the Reef Festival, held for a week in the second week of October. The festival includes live entertainment and activities around the town centre, a fireworks display, a parade, and a beach party at Palm Cove.

Cairns Amateur Race Weekend, dubbed the Melbourne Cup of the Far North, is a horse race held in early September.

PLACES TO STAY
As you would expect, Cairns has a wide range of tourist accommodation catering for everybody from budget-conscious backpackers to deep-pocketed package tourists. The city still attracts huge numbers of backpackers, and there are plenty of hostels and guesthouses to choose from. There are also a couple of caravan parks in town, although none very close to the centre. The next level up are the motels and holiday apartments, and at the top of the price scale there are a few five-star hotels and resorts.

The accommodation business is extremely competitive here and prices go up and down with the seasons. Lower weekly rates are par for the course. Prices given here for the more expensive places can rise 30% or 40% in the peak season, and some of the hostels will charge $1 or $2 less in quiet times.

Camping
There are about a dozen caravan parks in and around Cairns, though none is really central. Almost without exception they take campers as well as caravans. The closest to the centre is the *City Caravan Park* (☎ 4051 1467), about 2km north-west of the city centre on the corner of Little and James Sts. It's quite well set up (if somewhat cramped), with plenty of shady trees and a sheltered barbecue area; tent sites cost from $14 and on-site vans from $44.

The *First City Caravilla* (☎ 4054 1403) is the next closest option, 1km further west at Kelly St, Earlville, just off the Bruce Hwy. It has tent sites at $18.50 and on-site cabins from $51. There's a good shaded pool and barbecue area.

Out on the Bruce Hwy, about 8km south of the centre, is the *Cairns Coconut Caravan Village* (☎ 4054 6644), a huge and modern caravanning and camping village with camp sites from $18.50 ($21 powered), on-site cabins from $49 and self-contained units from $75. This place has excellent facilities but is often booked out during school holidays. Bus No 1B from the Lake St Transit Centre in the city stops right outside the gate, and runs 24 hours a day.

If you want to camp by the beach, the nearest option is at Yorkey's Knob, about 20km north from the centre of Cairns. A little further north, Palm Cove and Ellis Beach also have very good beachfront camping grounds – see the Cairns to Port Douglas section for details of all of these.

Hostels

The Cairns hostel scene is constantly changing as new places open up, old ones change hands and others rise and fall in quality and popularity. The type of accommodation is pretty standard – fan-cooled bunk rooms with shared kitchen and bathroom, and usually sitting areas, laundry facilities and a swimming pool or spa. Theft is a problem in some places – use lock-up rooms and safes if they're available.

The Esplanade has the greatest concentration of hostels, and is a lively place. The hostels here tend to pack them in, and have very little outside space – any outdoor area is usually cramped with a swimming pool – but you can always lounge on the waterfront across the road. On the plus side, they are ideally located. Those away from the centre offer much more breathing space and are generally quieter; any inconvenience is minimal because courtesy buses make regular runs into town.

Esplanade Starting from the corner of Shields St and heading along the Esplanade, the *International Hostel* (☎ 4031 1424), at

No 67, is a big multilevel place with about 200 beds. The accommodation is fairly basic, with fan-cooled four, six and eight-bed dorms for $12 or twin rooms for $28. There are also doubles from $28 to $36, with either air-con and TV or a private bathroom.

Caravella's Hostel 77 (☎ 4051 2159), at 77 The Esplanade, is another big rambling place. It's one of the longest established Cairns hostels and has old-fashioned but clean rooms, all with air-con. The cost in four to six-bunk dorms is $16, and singles/doubles range from $22/30 to $26/34, or $40 with private bathroom. All these prices include an evening meal and there's free luggage storage.

Jimmy's on the Esplanade (☎ 4031 6884), at No 83, is a reasonably modern smaller place. Accommodation is in six-bed units with their own bathroom and a fridge, and there's a pool and kitchen. Dorms cost $15, and there are also double rooms with shared bathrooms for $36, or with en suites for $50. The front rooms have sea views and are popular, and all rooms have air-con. It's a popular place.

The *Bellview* (☎ 4031 4377), at No 85, is a good, quiet hostel with clean and comfortable four-bed dorms at $16 per person, singles at $27 and twin rooms at $36, and all rooms are air-conditioned. There are also motel-style units from $49. The kitchen facilities are good, and there's a small pool, a laundry and an excellent breakfast cafe. This place has good security, and is also popular.

Hostel 89 (☎ 1800 061 712), at No 89, is one of the best kept hostels on the Esplanade. It's a smallish and helpful place, with twin and double rooms and a few three ($18) or four-bed ($17) dorms, all air-conditioned. Singles/doubles are from $36/44. Security is good, with a locked grille at the street entrance.

At No 93 is *YHA on the Esplanade* (☎ 4031 1919). There are two blocks: one has spacious, airy five-bed dorms with their own bathroom, the other with small twins and doubles. Some rooms have air-con.

Dorm beds cost $17 and doubles $38, and non-members pay an extra $3.

Three blocks further along the Esplanade there's another cluster of backpackers' hostels, and being away from the very centre of town are much quieter. At No 149 is another bigger hostel, *Caravella's 149* (☎ 4031 5680). Its popularity means that even the big cooking/sitting/TV/pool/ games area at the back can get pretty busy. You pay $16 in a six-share dorm, $15 in a four-share room with fan. Doubles and twins cost $30, or $32 with air-con. All prices include an evening meal.

The popular *Rosie's Backpackers* (☎ 4051 0235), at No 155, has several buildings with both spacious dorms in the main building and six-bed flats; dorms are $15 and there are a couple of doubles at $35. This place is helpful, well-run and has a small pool.

Next door, at No 157, the *Bel-Air Hostel* (☎ 4031 4790) is a two-storey Queenslander, with hellishly hot, poorly ventilated doubles and twins downstairs for $30, and four-bunk dorms upstairs for $16. All rooms have fan or air-con, and there's a spa, kiosk and pool table here. The price includes breakfast at the hostel and dinner at one of the backpacker nightclubs (see Entertainment).

Around Town Three blocks back from the Esplanade, *Parkview Backpackers* (☎ 4051 3700) is at 174 Grafton St. This is a very laid-back place where you can relax by the pool and listen to music. It's in a rambling old timber building with a large, verdant tropical garden. Four to eight-bed dorms cost $14 per person, and twin rooms cost $30.

Tracks Hostel (☎ 4031 1474), on the corner of Grafton and Minnie Sts, spans three old timber houses and has a number of kitchens and other facilities. Costs are $14 per person in four-bed dorms, or $28 a double, and you get a voucher for a free evening meal at one of the backpackers' nightclubs.

At 72 Grafton St, the *Aussie II Hostel* (☎ 4051 7620) is a bit of a crash pad, with

space for about 60 people. It's cheap, though – dorm beds are $10 and doubles are $20 for the first three nights, subsequent nights cost $13 and $26 respectively. The hostel has two kitchens and a TV room. There's no pool but you can use the pools at the two Caravella hostels.

Close to the railway station, the YHA *McLeod St Youth Hostel* (☎ 4051 0772), at 20-24 McLeod St, has dorm beds for $16 and singles/doubles for $26/36. Non-members pay $3 extra. The facilities are good and the hostel has car parking spaces.

On the corner of Spence and Sheridan Sts, the *Billabong Backpackers* (☎ 4051 6946) has dorm beds for $14 ($16 air-con), twin rooms and doubles at $30. It's a clean, simple place in an old timber house, with a nice garden and a pool, and the price includes a free evening meal.

Two blocks west of the railway station, at 274 Draper St, *Gone Walkabout Hostel* (☎ 4051 6160) is a small, simple and well-run place with a friendly atmosphere. Rooms are mostly twins and doubles, with a few four-bed dorms, and there's a tiny pool. You pay $12 in a dorm and $25 for a twin or double. It's not a place for late partying however.

The *Up-Top Down Under* (☎ 4051 3636), at 164-170 Spence St, is a spacious backpackers' complex 1.5km from the town centre. Facilities include a well-equipped kitchen, two TV lounges and a pool. Dorm beds are $15 and there are good single/ double rooms for $28/32, all with shared bathrooms.

The *U2 Hostel* (☎ 4031 4077), at 77 McLeod St, is a two-storey Queenslander divided into five flats, with a pool and a communal kitchen and lounge. It's clean and basic, although most of the rooms are internal and windowless. Dorm beds cost $13; singles/doubles are $26/30.

JJ's Backpackers (☎ 4051 7642), at 11 Charles St, is a small block of apartments converted into a hostel. There are dorm beds for $14 and doubles for $32, and there's a small pool, a pool table and a TV room here.

MARK ARMSTRONG

MARK ARMSTRONG

DAVID SHERMAN

Top: Mangrove roots and coral rubble exposed at low tide at Cape Tribulation.
Middle: The Daintree River empties into the Coral Sea after passing through magnificent lowland
    rainforest – home to unique life forms that are protected in the Daintree National Park.
Bottom: Buttress roots and mangrove seedlings in the Daintree River basin.

DAVID SHERMAN

The Mossman Gorge is an easy day trip from Cairns or Port Douglas. This popular destination features clear swimming holes, picnic tables and bushwalking to suit all ages and experience.

Captain Cook Backpackers Hostel (☎ 4051 6811), at 204 Sheridan St, is a huge place with over 300 beds in two sections. It's a converted former motel which has been recently renovated and offers modern facilities and good value for money. Dorm beds for $15 and doubles $48. The facilities include two pools, a bar and a restaurant with cheap evening meals (free if you buy a jug of beer or wine). You can't miss this place – there's a giant statue of Captain Cook out the front.

At 207 Sheridan St is *Castaways* (☎ 4051 1238), a quiet and smallish place with mostly double and twin rooms costing $32. There are also five singles at $27, plus a few three-bed dorms at $15 per bed. All rooms are fan-cooled and have a fridge, and there's a communal kitchen, a pool, bikes for hire and a courtesy bus.

The *Calypso Inn* (☎ 1800 815 628), on Digger St behind the Cock & Bull tavern, is a friendly, low-key hostel in a renovated Queenslander. The downstairs area has a pool, bar and restaurant in a tropical garden. Dorm beds are $14 and singles/doubles $25/30.

Inn The Tropics (☎ 4031 1088), at 141 Sheridan St, has a good pool and a small guests' kitchen. Dorm beds are $15, motel-style rooms are $28/36 with shared bathroom or $38/46 with en suite.

Guesthouses

A couple of places in this bracket cater for budget travellers, the difference being that their emphasis is on rooms rather than dorms. These places are generally quieter, smaller and a bit more personalised than the hostels.

Dreamtime Travellers Rest (☎ 4031 6753), at 4 Terminus St, is a small guesthouse run by a friendly and enthusiastic young couple. It's in a brightly renovated Queenslander and has a good pool, double rooms from $35 and three or four-bed (no bunks) rooms at $15 per person.

Another good guesthouse with a similar set-up is *Ryan's Rest* (☎ 4051 4734), down the road at 18 Terminus St. It's a cosy and quiet family-run place with three very good double rooms upstairs at $35, twins/doubles at $25 and a four-bed dorm at $15 per person. Cheap cooked and tropical breakfasts are available.

The *Floriana Guesthouse* (☎ 4051 7886), at 183 the Esplanade, is a 1920s-era guesthouse with two sections. The reception area might remind you of your grandmother's house, with its dark wood-panelling, Art Deco furniture and memorabilia. There are four self-contained units above the reception area, all clean and simple, with polished timber floors, ceiling fans, TV, en suites and kitchenettes. These sleep up to four and are excellent value at $55 to $70 a night. In the old building next door, there are 24 simple rooms, with a communal laundry, kitchen, pool and TV lounge. The upstairs rooms with ocean views are great value at $48, and the rest of the rooms go for $28 a single or from $42 for doubles.

At 8 McKenzie St, *Charleston House* (☎ 4051 6317) is an old Queenslander renovated in Art Deco style. It's generally for people staying weekly, although it also takes overnighters. There are eight rooms with two or three beds in each, with singles/doubles/triples costing $112/150/225 a week; and a self-contained flat which sleeps four and costs $225 per week. The communal lounge and living areas are very comfortable, and there's a spa, kitchens and laundry, and a decking area out the back.

The *Happy House* (☎ 4031 5898), at 25 Maranoa St in Parramatta Park, is an old Queenslander that has been restored with tender loving care and a bit of artistic flair. It's a bright, cheerful place divided up into seven one to three-bedroom flats, each with its own kitchen, bathroom and living area. There's a spa, laundry and barbecue area out the back. The weekly rate is $75 per person and there's a two-week minimum stay.

At 153 the Esplanade, the *Silver Palms Guesthouse* (☎ 4031 6099) is a clean, quiet little place with singles/doubles from $33/38 with shared bathrooms, or $48 with an en suite. There's also a self-contained six-bed flat here, with a kitchen and lounge room, which costs $57 a double or $90 for four people. Guests here have use of a kitchen, laundry, pool and TV room.

Leo's (☎ 1800 636 626), at 100 Sheridan St, is a recently renovated place where bright single/double rooms with fridge and share bathroom cost $35/40, or with sink and air-con cost $45/48.

Tropic Days (☎ 4041 1521) at 28 Bunting St has also been recommended by a number of our readers.

18-24 James (☎ 1800 621 824) at, funnily enough, 18-24 James St, is an exclusively gay and lesbian hotel with four-share rooms at $50 per person or singles/doubles at $95/109, all including a tropical breakfast.

Motels

The *Poinsettia Motel* (☎ 4051 2144), at 169 Lake St, is one of the cheapest central motels. It has clean budget rooms at $46/50, although the pool is in a gloomy brick enclosure and there's no outdoor area to speak of.

The high-rise *Lyons Motor Inn* (☎ 4051 2311), on the corner of the Esplanade and Aplin Sts, is also in the thick of things, and has budget rooms from $65 or rooms with a view from $70/82.

Hides Hotel/Motel (☎ 4051 1266), a big pub in the heart of town on the corner of Lake and Shields Sts, has old pub-style rooms with shared bathrooms from $65 ($85 with en suite) and motel-style units from $110.

Top of the motel range would have to be the *Outrigger Inn* (☎ 4051 6188), on the corner of Abbott and Florence Sts, where rooms go for $109 for singles/doubles, or $124 with an ocean view.

Holiday Flats & Apartments

Holiday flats are well worth considering, especially for a group of three or four people who are staying a few days or more. Expect pools, air-con, cooking and laundry facilities in this category. Holiday flats generally supply all bedding, cooking utensils etc.

At 209 Lake St, the *Castle Holiday Flats* (☎ 4031 2229) is an oldish red-brick place with clean, well-kept flats and units. There are one-bedroom flats from $50, two-bedroom flats that sleep up to four and cost $80, and singles/doubles with shared bathroom and kitchen facilities for $20/30. There's a small pool.

The *Costa Blanca Apartments* (☎ 4051 3114), at 241 the Esplanade, is one of the few affordable places along the waterfront. There are seven one-bedroom units, plus one two-bedroom unit, and rates start at $45 a double plus $5 per extra person. They aren't flashy, but they're all clean and comfortable, sleep four people, and have kitchens and ceiling fans. The upstairs units have good views, and there's a guest laundry and a big old pool here.

Lake Central (☎ 4051 4933), at 137 Lake St, is a modern complex of motel-style units around a central courtyard. All the rooms have air-con, en suite and kitchenette, and doubles range from $80 to $115 depending on the season. The family units sleep up to five and cost $135 a night.

At 175 Lake St, the *Cascade Gardens Apartments* (☎ 4051 8000) has a similar setup – modern self-contained apartments with full kitchens. Studio apartments range from $89 to $118; one-bedroom apartments sleep up to four and range from $100 to $134 a double, plus $10 for extra adults.

181 The Esplanade (☎ 4052 6888), obviously at 181 the Esplanade, is a 10-storey complex of modern, up-market one, two and three-bedroom apartments which range from $180 to $280 a night – they're cheaper by the week.

Hotels

A new hotel right in the heart of city centre is *Il Palazzo* (☎ 1800 813 222) at 62 Abbott St. All 38 units have cooking facilities, balcony, air-con, separate en suite and bedroom, and cost $175 for two. This modern place also has off-street undercover parking.

The *Pacific International Hotel* (☎ 4051 7888), on the corner of the Esplanade and

Spence St, is one of Cairns' original hotels. It's a bit smaller and more laid-back than some of the newer places, and has 176 rooms starting from $225.

The *Holiday Inn* (☎ 4031 3757), on the corner of the Esplanade and Florence Sts, is a modern four-star hotel with rooms from $240, although it's worth paying another $25 for a room with ocean views.

The *Rydges Plaza Cairns* (☎ 4041 1022), on the corner of Grafton and Spence Sts, is a modern four-star hotel with 98 rooms from $165.

The most impressive of Cairns' five-star hotels is the *Cairns International Hotel* (☎ 4031 1300), at 17 Abbott St. It has a cavernous marble foyer and the rooms are tastefully furnished in tropical decor. Rooms range from $265 to $375, and suites from $540 to $1400.

The *Radisson Plaza Hotel* (☎ 4031 1411), in The Pier Marketplace complex, is another good five-star hotel with a rainforest recreation in the foyer and 197 rooms ranging from $275 to $320, depending on the view. Suites range from $430 to $900.

The new *Reef Hotel Casino* (☎ 4030 8888), part of the casino complex on Abbott St, is the latest addition to the five-star scene, and has rooms from $340 to $470 and suites at $680 to $2500.

The *Cairns Hilton Hotel* (☎ 4052 1599), beside Trinity Inlet, is another five-star with 265 rooms from $230 and suites from $750 to $1250.

PLACES TO EAT

Cairns is certainly well stocked with eateries of all types, and you shouldn't have too much trouble finding something to satisfy your gastronomic cravings. A lot of backpackers end up eating in bars and nightclubs, lured by free or heavily discounted meal vouchers which are handed out by the hostels.

The Esplanade, between Shields and Aplin Sts, is virtually wall-to-wall eateries, and you'll find Italian and Chinese food, seafood restaurants, burgers, kebabs, pizzas, seafood and ice cream – at all hours.

Quite a few places take advantage of the climate by providing open-air dining.

Cafes & Delis

Mozart Pastry, near the corner of Grafton and Spence Sts, is a popular spot to browse through the morning papers over coffee and a pastry. The coffee is good, there are outdoor tables and it serves a range of pastries, cakes and sandwiches. The staff are friendly and most of them speak German, if that helps. *Paris Croissant* is another good breakfast bet, with croissants from $2.

The *Galloping Gourmet*, a casual little place on Aplin St near the Lake St corner, offers a cooked breakfast deal for $5. Over at 35 Sheridan St, *John & Diana's Breakfast & Burger House* is fairly down market, but offers virtually every combination of cooked breakfast imaginable for $5 or less.

Tiny's Juice Bar, on Grafton St near the Spence St corner, is a good little lunch spot. It has a great range of freshly squeezed fruit and vegetable juices, milk and tofu smoothies as well as healthy filled rolls, and lentil and tofu burgers at good prices.

On the corner of Grafton and Aplin Sts, the *Old Ambulance Cafe Bistro* is a chic new place in, as the name suggests, the old ambulance station. It's a popular place and has great coffee and filled croissants.

The *Victory Cafe*, at 62 Shields St, is a narrow and atmospheric BYO cafe with timber booths, and blues, jazz and soul music. It serves food with vegetarian, seafood, Thai and Indian influences and is open for dinner only; dishes range from $15 to $20.

Willie's Seaside Cafe is a bright and airy (if misnamed) cafe right by City Square – it's a good place to catch lunchtime performances in the amphitheatre. A focaccia and cafe latte lunch costs $6.50.

Nightclubs, Bars & Pubs

Most of the hostels supply vouchers for cheap or free meals at various nightclubs, pubs and bars around town, often with free or discounted drinks thrown in. *Samuel's Saloon*, near the corner of Hartley and Lake

Sts, is one of the most popular places, with burgers, roasts, pastas and chillies from $4 to $6. It even has a bus that picks hungry travellers up from the hostels.

The *Beach* nightclub on the corner of Abbott and Aplin Sts has very basic food, but it's cheap and a lot of people eat here, again with hostel meal vouchers.

Wool Shed, on Shields St in the mall, is another very popular backpackers' bar and restaurant. Meals include pastas, stews, steaks, and schnitzels, and range from $5 to $10. On Sunday there's a 50c barbecue. It is open daily from 5 pm until 2 am.

The *Pier Tavern*, on the north-west side of The Pier Marketplace, is a popular pub with several bars and an outdoor deck overlooking Trinity Bay and the Esplanade. Bistro meals in the Boatbar range from $6 to $10.

The *Cock & Bull Tavern*, on the corner of Digger and Grove Sts, is an excellent and popular English-style tavern. The atmosphere at this place is lots of fun, and it has a good range of beer, a darts bar, friendly staff and even a snorkelling boar on the wall! The meals are of the hearty, stodgy English variety – roasts, curries, shepherd's pie, veal steaks – and all cost from $8 to $10. It's just the spot for homesick Poms, and far enough from the touristy centre of town to have the atmosphere of a 'local'.

Restaurants & Food Halls

If you're doing a spot of shopping at The Pier Marketplace, there are plenty of eateries up on the 1st level. The *Food Court* offers a good choice, including Thai or Mongolian food, Chinese noodles, sushi, pizzas, gourmet sandwiches, seafood and fresh juices, to name but a few. Nearby is the *Beach Hut*, a seafood and Aussie-style buffet with all-you-can-eat deals – $6.45 for breakfast, $8 for lunch and $18 for dinner. Then there's *Johnny Rocket's*, a 1950s-American burger joint complete with red vinyl booths and personal juke boxes. Burgers start at $5, sandwiches at $4, and yep, you can finish off with a slice of good ol' apple pie ($3.50).

Also on the first level is *Donnini's* (☎ 4051 1133), which is a smart but casual licensed restaurant with some of the best Italian food in town. Gourmet pizzas range from $9 to $16, pastas from $12 to $16, salads and antipasto from $8.50 to $13 and Italian mains around $17. It is open daily for lunch and dinner.

Over on the east side of The Pier complex, next to the Radisson Plaza Hotel, *Pesci's* is a trendy bar and eatery with a good outdoor deck overlooking Trinity Inlet and the marina. It serves modern Australian lunches and dinners from $18.

Also overlooking Trinity Inlet, from between The Pier and the Cairns Hilton Hotel, is *Tawny's* (☎ 4051 1722), which is reputed to be Cairns' best seafood restaurant. It has an elegant dining area with full-length windows, is licensed and opens nightly and on Friday for lunch. Main courses like crocodile with Kakadu plums are around $25.

There are two seafood restaurants side-by-side on the Esplanade, both open-fronted with tables spilling out onto the footpath: *Barnacle Bill's* is the more casual of the two, with most mains in the $23 to $30 range and kid's meals for $11. If you order by 5.45 pm and leave by 7 pm a discount of 30% is offered. *Kanis* is a little more up-market, with mains from $25. Both places are licensed and open nightly for dinner.

The Meeting Place, on Aplin St near the Abbott St corner, is a good international food hall with a number of different stalls. You can choose between Japanese, Thai, Chinese, Italian, and steak and seafood meals in the $8 to $20 range. There's also a small bar in the complex.

The *Night Markets* is a modern but somewhat stark and soulless hawker-style food court with plenty of choices; there's a bar here too.

Sawasdee (☎ 4031 7993), at 89 Grafton St, is a BYO Thai restaurant with lunch specials for $7.50 and dinner mains ranging from $11 to $16. It's a very friendly place with wonderfully fresh food – it has only half a dozen tables, so it's a good idea to book. Across the road at 74 Grafton St is *Phuket Thai*, which is much the same. Almost next door is *Cafe ZuZu*, a groovy little place with hip music and friendly staff. Pastas range from $8 and other mains from $8 to $12.

Close by, on the corner of Grafton and Spence Sts, *Turkish Michael's* is great value at lunchtime, with dishes for $7. In the evening mains are in the $10 to $13 range, which is pretty cheap by Cairns standards.

There are quite a few Japanese restaurants in Cairns. One of the best is *Yama*, on the corner of Spence and Grafton Sts. It's a fairly casual place with a good range of lunch specials from $7; the dinner menu has mains for around $17. Yama is licensed.

Just along Spence St is *Dundee's*, a modern Australian place open for dinner nightly. It features what I like to call novelty meats – kangaroo, emu, crocodile and buffalo – with main courses from $18 to $25. Next door is the *Redback Pancake & Steak House*, a carnivore's delight with main courses from $15. It's open for dinner only.

The stylish *Taste of China*, at 36 Abbott St, serves 'fresh, light and healthy' yum chas and dinners, with mains from $14 to $20. The *Silver Dragon*, a straightforward Chinese restaurant at 102 Lake St, has a great lunchtime buffet for $5. It also opens nightly for dinner, with mains in the $10 to $15 range.

The *Bangkok Room Thai Restaurant*, at 62 Spence St, has a pleasant setting and friendly service; tasty Thai dishes are around $13 to $18. Next door is the popular *Hog's Breath Cafe*, a saloon-style bar and grill. Lunch time offerings like burgers, sandwiches and salads will set you back $7 to $10, and in the evening main courses like prime ribs, grilled fish and steaks are in the $16 to $18 range. It also has a kid's menu at $6.

Across the road at 61 Spence St, the *Taj* serves pretty good Indian food, with main meals around $14 to $18. It's BYO (no beer) and open in the evening only. The *Bombay Palace* in the same block is a bit cheaper, with mains from $12 to $15.

If you've always wanted to try emu paté or eucalyptus salmon, head for the *Red Ochre Grill*, at 43 Shields St. It's a bush tucker restaurant which uses indigenous seeds, plants, leaves, flowers and animals in the cooking. The decor is very smart – ochre with raw timber and Aboriginal artwork. Main meals range from $17 to $25 (less at lunch time), and it has good mixed platters ($32 for two) so you can try a bit of everything. Some great Australian wines are available by the glass.

La Fettucine, at 43 Shields St, is an atmospheric little BYO with excellent home-made pastas for $12 and Italian mains for around $16 to $18. It is open nightly for dinner. Next door at No 41 is *Gypsy Dee's* (☎ 4051 5530), a dim and rather exotic place with a bar, a stage and live acoustic music every night. The menu is also fairly exotic – kangaroo sirloin, linguini, chargrilled oysters – and mains range from $12 to $18. You'll probably need to book.

George's Greek Taverna, on the corner of Grafton and Aplin Sts, is a fairly up-market place with Greek and seafood mains around $18. It's open in the evenings only.

Another place popular with locals and backpackers is *Dunwoody's Tavern*, about 2km north of the centre on the corner of Sheridan and Smith Sts. It's a modern, barn-sized tavern that's open for lunch and dinner daily, and has a bar, lounge area and a restaurant. You can get just about anything here, with lunches in the $8 to $12 range and dinners from $10 to $18.

ENTERTAINMENT

The best guide to what's on is the free entertainment rag, *Son of Barfly*, which covers music gigs and reviews, movies, pubs and clubs, restaurants etc. It appears weekly and is available all over town in cafes and shops, and is usually pretty entertaining reading in itself.

Pubs & Live Music

Free lunch time concerts are held every day at the City Place Amphitheatre, in the mall at the intersection of Lake and Shields Sts.

The *Pier Tavern*, at The Pier Marketplace complex, has live bands from Wednesday to Sunday. It's a popular pub at anytime, and *the* place to be on a Sunday afternoon – a blues band usually kicks off the Sunday sessions at around 2.30 pm. It has an outdoor deck area which overlooks Trinity Bay. Next door is *Gilhooley's*, an Irish bar serving guess what? Upstairs is the *Memphis Rock Cafe* and no prizes are given for guessing who's featured here!

Gypsy Dee's, an exotic bar and restaurant at 41 Shields St, has live acoustic music. There's no cover charge, and you can dine here cabaret-style (see Places to Eat) or just drink and listen at the bar. It is open every night until 2 am. *Dunwoody's Tavern* (see Places to Eat) also has live acoustic music.

Johno's Blues Bar, above McDonald's on the corner of Shields St and the Esplanade, is Cairns institution. It's a big, lively place with blues, rock and R&B bands every night until at least 4 am. There's a cover charge of $5 to $10, depending on the night and who's playing.

Quite a few pubs in Cairns have regular live bands, including the *Fox & Firkin*, on the corner of Spence and Lake Sts, *Rusty's Pub* on the corner of Spence and Sheridan Sts, and the *Crown Hotel* on the corner of Shields and Grafton Sts. Check with *Son of Barfly* to see who's on where.

Bars

Wool Shed on Shields St in the mall has an incredibly popular backpackers' bar. It has pool tables, a quiet cocktail bar downstairs, meals and regular party games – toga parties, drinking competitions and bare-it-all events – it's usually pretty lively.

Rattle n Hum on the Esplanade next to Caravella's 77 Hostel is a popular new bar, although it's a bit gloomy and cramped. Further along is *Chapel*, upstairs by the YHA hostel entrance. This is a relaxed little place which often has live acoustic music.

The *Sports Bar & Rock Cafe* on Spence St is very lively and loony behaviour seems to be the go – there's even a ceiling harness so you can dance upside down on the bar,

and hopefully retain your stomach contents at the same time.

For a quieter, more relaxed drink, head for the casual *Cairns Yacht Club* on the Esplanade. It's one of the few surviving bits of old Cairns and is sandwiched uncomfortably between the Hilton and the Great Adventures Wharf. Grab a beer and sit out on the shady verandah.

Nightclubs

Cairns' nightclub scene is notoriously wild, especially in the early hours of the morning. The complex on the corner of Lake and Hartley Sts houses three places: *Samuel's Saloon*, a backpackers' bar and eatery; the *Playpen International*, a huge nightclub which often has big-name bands, stays open until sunrise and charges from $5 entry; and the more up-market *Court Jester* bar.

Beach nightclub, on the corner of Abbott and Aplin Sts, is another popular place for a drink and a bop, with huge video screens, a party-sized dance floor, pool tables, loud music and cheap meals deals. It runs various 'theme' nights – free kegs, karaoke, Mr Backpacker competitions – and has a cover charge of around $5, although backpackers with hostel vouchers get in free. It closes at around 5 am.

Tropos, upstairs in Central Arcade near the Fox & Firkin, is a lively dance club with good music, pool tables, a wide outdoor balcony area and a $5 cover charge on weekends. It closes at 5 am.

Casino

The Reef Hotel Casino is a gaudy and tasteless affair with wall to wall poker machines and a few gaming tables. Since opening it has failed to pull in the punters and is reportedly in financial difficulty. Worth a visit if you can't think of a better way to relieve yourself of some hard-earned cash (oh yes, credit cards will also do nicely, thank you).

Gay Venues

Rusty's Pub, on the corner of Spence and Sheridan Sts, has a gay night with a floor show every Saturday night.

Theatre, Cinema & Drive-In
If you want to catch a movie, there's the Cairns 5 Cinemas (☎ 4031 1077), at 108 Grafton St, or the Coral Twin Drive-in, on the Bruce Hwy on the southern edge of town.

The Cairns Civic Theatre (☎ 4051 3211), a modern theatre complex near the corner of Florence and Grafton Sts, is the city's main theatre venue and hosts regular performances throughout the year.

SHOPPING
Many artists live in the Cairns region, so there's a wide range of local handicrafts available – pottery, clothing, stained glass, jewellery, leather work and so on. Aboriginal art is also for sale in a few places, as are crafts from Papua New Guinea and places further afield in the Pacific.

Apart from the many souvenir shops dotted around the town centre, there are a couple of good markets in town. The previously mentioned Rusty's Bazaar is mainly a food market, but also has a few craft stalls. The recently redeveloped Night Markets, in the centre of the Esplanade between Shields and Aplin Sts, has a good collection of stalls.

The Mud Markets, held in The Pier Marketplace every Saturday and Sunday, feature the best collection of stalls selling everything from souvenirs, clothes, beachwear, jewellery, leatherwork, hats, boomerangs, handpainted T-shirts and woodwork. The Mud Markets are always busy and, with live musicians to keep shoppers entertained, they're well worth a visit. It's also a convenient alternative to going up to Kuranda.

Camping & Outdoor Gear
City Place Disposals, on the corner of Grafton and Shields Sts, is one of several disposal-type shops in town, and sells a range of cheaper camping and outdoor gear.

Another good place for camping gear is the huge Geo Pickers Great Outdoors Centre, at 108 Mulgrave Rd. It sells camping gear, tents, backpacks, tarps, outdoor cooking gear and yacht chandlery. It also rents out camping gear, which is handy if you're heading to Cape York or the islands.

If you're in the market for an Akubra hat, Harris Bros, a 'gentlemen's outfitter' on the corner of Shields and Sheridan Sts, has the best selection in town.

GETTING THERE & AWAY
Air
Qantas and Sunstate Airlines (☎ 13 1313) are on the corner of Shields and Lake Sts, and Ansett (☎ 13 1300) are at 13 Spence St.

Domestic Flights Airlines serving Cairns include Ansett, Qantas, Sunstate and Flight West. See the Getting There & Away chapter for details of interstate and international flights.

Flights within Queensland are shared among a number of smaller airlines. Sunstate flies to Bamaga ($280), Lizard Island ($195) and Thursday Island ($324). Ansett flies to Weipa ($242) and Mt Isa ($237). Flight West flies to Cooktown ($75) and operates a service through the Gulf, the Cape York Peninsula and to Bamaga and the Torres Strait Islands. Hinterland Aviation (☎ 4035 9323) has flights to Cow Bay, south of Cape Tribulation, for $83.

International Flights Qantas and Air Niugini are currently the only airlines with direct flights into Cairns. See the Getting There & Away chapter for details.

Bus
All the bus companies operate from the Transit Centre at Trinity Wharf. Most of the backpackers' hostels have courtesy buses which meet the arriving buses to ferry you off to your waiting bed.

Greyhound Pioneer (☎ 13 2030) and McCafferty's (☎ 13 1499) both run at least five buses a day up the coast from Brisbane and Townsville to Cairns. Journey times and average fares are: Brisbane, 27 hours, $148; Rockhampton, 15 hours, $98; Mackay, 11 hours, $78; and Townsville, six hours, $42.

Coral Coaches (☎ 4031 7577), also based at the Transit Centre, runs regular daily services from Cairns to Port Douglas ($16 one way) and on to Cape Tribulation ($28), and Cooktown via either the inland road ($47) or the coastal road ($52). See those sections later in this chapter for more details. There's also a weekly service to and from Weipa ($125).

White Car Coaches (☎ 4091 1855) has bus services from Cairns to Kuranda and around the Atherton Tableland, with connections on to Chillagoe. See the Atherton Tableland section later in this chapter for details.

Cairns-Karumba Coachline (☎ 4031 5448) has a service three times a week between Cairns and Karumba ($122) on the Gulf of Carpentaria, via Undara Lava Tubes ($42). See the Gulf Savannah chapter for details.

Train
Three trains run between Brisbane and Cairns; the *Queenslander*, which runs weekly and has a motorail service; the *Sunlander*, which runs three times a week; and the *Spirit of the Tropics*, which also runs weekly.

The 1631km trip from Brisbane takes about 32 hours. The 1st class Brisbane-Cairns fare on the *Queenslander* costs $389 (including sleeping berth and all meals). The 1st class/economy fare for a sleeper on the *Sunlander* or *Spirit of the Tropics* is $253/165. Call Queensland Rail in Cairns for bookings (☎ 13 2232) or information (☎ 4052 6249). See the Getting Around chapter for more details.

Car, 4WD & Motorcycle Rental
It's well worth considering renting a vehicle. There's plenty to see and do on land around Cairns, whether it's making the beach crawl up to Port Douglas or exploring the Atherton Tableland. Mokes are about the cheapest cars to rent and ideal for relaxed, open-air sightseeing.

While the major firms are along Lake St, local firms have mushroomed all over Cairns and some of them offer good deals, particularly for weekly rental. However, don't be taken in by advertising for cut-rates – once you add in all the hidden costs, prices are fairly similar everywhere. Shop around and find the deal that suits. Generally, small cars are about $45 per day with 300km free.

Note that most Cairns rental firms specifically prohibit you from taking their cars on the road to Cooktown, to Chillagoe or up the Cape Tribulation road. If you ignore this prohibition and get caught, you'll lose your deposit and/or be up for a hefty fine, so if you're planning to tackle one of these routes you'll need to hire a 4WD. These are widely available, but they cost about $95 a day with up to 300km free. See the Cape York chapter for details of some operators who rent 4WDs for Cape York trips.

Car Rentals In addition to the big companies, there's others such as Gem (☎ 4031 6655) at 55 Spence St, with small cars from $55; Minicar Rentals at 150 Sheridan St, with cars from $39 with unlimited kilometres; and Sheridan Rent a Car (☎ 4051 3942) at 36 Water St, where prices start at $52 with unlimited kilometres.

4WD Rentals Cairns 4WD Hire (☎ 4051 0822) has Suzukis from $95 and Landcruisers from $129 including 250km free. These are for local (ie not Cape York) use only.

Brits:Australia (☎ 1800 331 454) has Landcruisers for $115 with unlimited kilometres, and you can take these to cape York.

Hertz (☎ 4053 1344) at 436 Sheridan St has 4WD campers for $122.

Motorcycle Rentals Jolly Frog Rentals at 149 Lake St rents off-road motorbikes from $65 a day (200km free) and road bikes up to 1100cc from $120. It also has mopeds (motorcycle license not required) for $29.

Boat
The daily *Quicksilver* (☎ 4099 5500) fast catamaran service links Cairns with Port

Douglas. The trip takes 1½ hours, departing from the pier Marina in Cairns at 8 am and from Port Douglas at 5.30 pm. Adult fares are $20/30 one-way/return, children's fares are $10/15.

GETTING AROUND
To/From the Airport
The airport in Cairns has two sections, both off the Captain Cook Hwy north of town. The main domestic and international airlines use the new section, officially called Cairns International airport. This is reached by an approach road that turns off the highway about 3.5km from central Cairns. The other part of the airport, which some people still call Cairns airport, is reached from a second turning off the highway, 1.5km north of the main one.

The Australia Coach shuttle bus (☎ 4031 3555) meets all incoming flights and runs a regular pick-up and drop-off service between the airport and town; the one-way fare is $4.50. A taxi is about $11.

Bus
There are a number of local bus services in and around Cairns, operated by Sunbus. Schedules for most of them are posted at the main city stop (known as the Lake St Transit Centre) in City Place. Buses on the main routes operate 24 hours a day.

The routes most likely to be of use are:

No 1C – 24-hour service to Holloway' Beach and Yorkey's Knob
No 1, 1A, 1Z – 24-hour service to Trinity and Clifton beaches and Palm Cove
No 1B – 24-hour service to Woree and Cairns Coconut Caravan Village on Bruce Hwy

The Cairns Explorer (☎ 4055 1240) is an air-con service that plies a circular route around the city, and you can get on or off at any of the eight stops. It departs daily every hour from 9 am to 4 pm (Monday to Saturday from October through April) from the Lake St Transit Centre, and a day ticket costs $25. Stops include The Pier Marketplace, the mangrove boardwalk near the airport, the botanic gardens and the Royal Flying Doctor Service complex.

Bicycle
Most of the hostels and car-rental firms, plus quite a few other places, have bikes for hire so you'll have no trouble tracking one down. Expect to pay $10 to $15 a day.

Islands off Cairns

Off the coast from Cairns are Green Island – a coral cay – and Fitzroy Island, a continental island. Both of these very pretty islands attract hordes of day trippers, and both have resorts operated by the cruise company Great Adventures, which in turn is owned by the Japanese corporation Daikyo.

South of Cairns, the Frankland Islands group is a cluster of undeveloped national park islands. You can do day trips to these islands or camp overnight or longer.

GREEN ISLAND
Green Island, 27km north-east of Cairns, is a true coral cay, 660m long by 260m wide. The beautiful island and its surrounding reef are all national park, although the luxurious five-star resort which opened in 1994 takes up a substantial proportion of the island. The resort has good day trippers' facilities, which were extensively upgraded as part of the same development.

Green is a tiny island which you can walk around in about 15 minutes. It was named by Captain Cook after the chief astronomer on the *Endeavour*. The island was home to a be-mer boom, and from the 1870s most of the trees were cut down for fires to boil the be-mer.

Things to See & Do
The island's most interesting attraction is the long-running **Marineland Melanesia**. It houses a gallery, museum and aquarium, with a bizarre collection of Melanesian artefacts and crafts, plus a wide variety of fish,

turtles, stingrays and crocodiles in ponds and tanks. Admission costs $7 ($3 children).

Glass-bottom boats ($8) and semi-submersibles ($12) operate short trips from the pier. If you are a house guest or come to Green Island on one of the day-out trips (rather than the transport-only trips), admission to these wonders is included.

The new day trippers' facilities are very impressive, and include a swimming pool, a bar and several eateries. There's a dive shop which rents out snorkelling and diving gear, and offers introductory dives.

Places to Stay & Eat
The five-star *Green Island Reef Resort* (☎ 4031 3300) has luxury accommodation for up to 92 guests. There are two types of units, both very impressive and linked by timber boardwalks. The Island Rooms cost $500 single or double and the Reef Suites are $600. Children under 15 stay free of charge, unless an extra bed is needed, in which case a charge of $60 is made. The rates include use of water-sports equipment and most activities.

There's a variety of eating options, from the *Canopy Grill*, with snacks and light meals from $3 to $12, to the more formal *Emeralds Restaurant*, with lunchtime mains at $17 to $21 and evening three/five-course meals at $45/75.

Getting There & Away
Green Island is 27km from Cairns, about halfway to the outer reef. Great Adventures (toll-free ☎ 1800 079 080) is the main operator to Green Island and will take you there and back for $50 by fast catamaran. The return trip plus the various island activities will cost you $65, or $90 with lunch. Finally, for $125 you can have three hours on Green Island plus a visit to Michaelmas Cay.

There are other operators to Green Island. The *Big Cat* (☎ 4051 0444) does a return trip, taking 80 minutes, for $42. This includes either snorkelling or a glass-bottom boat trip, and another $8 gets you a barbecue lunch.

FITZROY ISLAND
About 6km off the coast and 26km east of Cairns, Fitzroy is a large continental island which is incredibly popular with day trippers. It also has a resort run by Great Adventures with camping grounds, a bunkhouse and villa units. Day trippers can use the resort facilities, which include a good swimming pool, a bar and a restaurant.

Fitzroy's coral-covered beaches are good for snorkelling, and there's good coral only 50m off the beach in the resort area. The beaches are not ideal for swimming and sunbaking, although Nudey Beach is quite pleasant. There are some fine walks, including one to the island's highest point.

The island was named by Captain Cook after the Duke of Grafton, a noted politician of the era who put more effort into wine, women and horse racing than government. In 1877 the island was made a quarantine station for Chinese immigrants bound for the north Queensland goldfields, and a number of Chinese graves remain from that period. Fitzroy also had a be-mer business for a time.

Things to See & Do
The giant clam breeding centre and pearl oyster hatchery, **Reefarm**, which conducts research into giant clams, can be visited. A half-hour educational program is held daily at 10 and 10.45 am and 1 pm, and costs $8 ($4 children).

The resort has water-sports equipment for hire, including catamarans, windsurfers, paddle-skis and canoes. The resort's dive shop conducts diving courses and hires out snorkelling and diving gear.

There are two good walking trails on the island: the 20 minute **Secret Garden Walk**, and the two-hour **Lighthouse & Peak Walk**.

Places to Stay & Eat
The *Fitzroy Island Resort* (☎ 4051 9588) has a variety of accommodation. Bunks in hostel-style units sleeping four people with shared kitchen and bathroom cost $28 each or $112 if you take the whole room.

The 'villa units' cost $240/340 for singles/doubles, including activities and breakfast and dinner. If all that's beyond your budget, you can camp at the council-run camping ground (permits and bookings through Department of Environment in Cairns). Sites cost $3.50 per person, and campers can use most of the resort's facilities.

The resort has a kiosk with fish and chips, pizzas, pies and sandwiches, and the *Flare Grill* does pub food like steak and chips, fish and salad, and so on. The *Mango Bar* is open from 10 am until late for drinks.

Getting There & Away

Great Adventures (☎ 1800 079 080) has a variety of excursions to Fitzroy. A return trip costs $30 for transport only, or $46 for a half-day trip (10.30 am to 3.30 pm) with lunch and snorkelling gear thrown in. The trip takes about 45 minutes each way. Coach pick-up from your accommodation in Cairns is $5.

Sunlover Cruises (☎ 1800 810 512) has day trips to the outer reef (Moore Reef), with a one-hour stop at Fitzroy Island ($130). Transfers-only to Fitzroy Island cost $30 return.

FRANKLAND ISLANDS

The Frankland Islands make up a relatively untouched national park south of Fitzroy Island and about 12km off the coast. They were named by Captain Cook after Admiral Sir Thomas Frankland. The islands consist of High Island to the north and four smaller islands – Normanby, Mabel, Round and Russell islands – to the south. They're continental islands with good beaches and some fine snorkelling. On the day trips from Cairns the island time is usually spent on Normanby Island while divers go to Round Island.

Camping

Campers can be dropped off on High or Russell islands, but there are no facilities on either so you must come totally equipped. Usually campers go to Russell Island; High Island drop-offs are only made at peak

periods (like Christmas) when Russell is full. A maximum of 15 campers is allowed on each island and permits are available from the Department of Environment office in Cairns.

Getting There & Away

There's an $89 day trip to the islands operated by Frankland Islands Cruise & Dive (☎ 4031 6300). You're taken by bus from Cairns to Deeral, on the Mulgrave River, from where you go out through the mangroves to the islands. A barbecue lunch is included in the cost of $125. Certified divers pay another $50 for one dive, while the campers' drop-off cost is $140 return from Cairns.

Atherton Tableland

Inland from the coast between Innisfail and Cairns, the land rises sharply then rolls gently across the lush Atherton Tableland towards the Great Dividing Range. The Tableland's altitude, more than 900m in places, tempers the tropical heat, and the abundant rainfall and rich volcanic soil combine to make this one of the greenest places in Queensland. In the south are Queensland's two highest mountains – Bartle Frere (1657m) and Bellenden Ker (1591m).

Little more than a century ago, this peaceful, pastoral region was still wild jungle. The first pioneers came in the 1870s, looking for a repeat of the Palmer River gold rush further north. As elsewhere in Queensland, the Aboriginal population was violently opposed to this intrusion but was soon overrun. Some gold was found and rather more tin, but although mining spurred the development of roads and railways through the rugged, difficult land of the plateau, farming and timber soon became the chief activities.

The Tableland is a great contrast to the hustle and bustle down on the coast. It's a

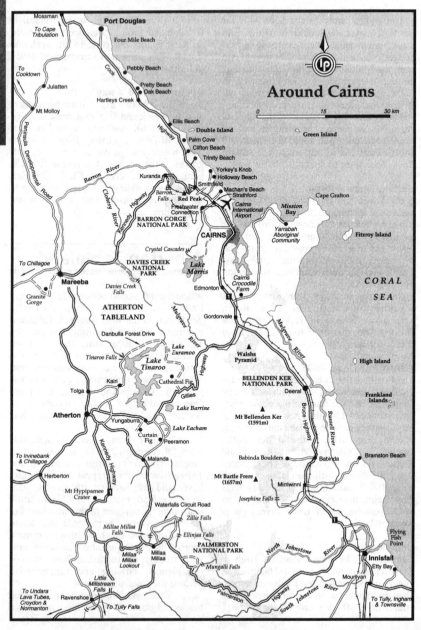

Around Cairns

region of beautiful scenery, with lakes and waterfalls, national parks and state forests, small villages and busy rural centres. There are some excellent accommodation options, including old pubs, timber guesthouses, farmstays and B&Bs, and you can visit some of the farms, go bushwalking, check out the Kuranda markets or just relax.

West of the Tableland are some fascinating old mining areas, including the historic tin-mining centre of Herberton and edge-of-the-outback Chillagoe, with its limestone caves and mining relics.

Getting There & Around

The historic train ride and the Skyrail cableway from Cairns to Kuranda are both Tableland attractions; there are bus services to the main towns from Cairns, but your own vehicle is the best way to get around.

From south to north, the three major roads from the coast are the Palmerston Hwy from Innisfail to Millaa Millaa and Ravenshoe; the Gillies Hwy from Gordonvale past Lakes Tinaroo, Barrine and Eacham to Yungaburra and Atherton; and the Kennedy Hwy from Cairns to Kuranda and Mareeba. Heading north from Mareeba, the Peninsula Developmental Road runs through Mt Molloy to Mossman.

White Car Coaches (☎ 4091 1855) has regular bus services connecting Cairns with the main towns on the Tableland. There are three services on weekdays, two on Saturday and one on Sunday leaving from outside Tropical Paradise Travel, at 25 Spence St in Cairns. The buses travel one way from Cairns to Mareeba ($12), Atherton ($16), Yungaburra ($20), Malanda ($22), Herberton ($19) and Ravenshoe ($23), as well as Kuranda ($7) and Chillagoe ($39). See the Kuranda and Chillagoe sections for more details.

Organised Tours

There are plenty of companies offering day trips and tours from Cairns. Day tours to Kuranda cost from around $65, and usually include a combination of Skyrail and train travel. See the Cairns section for details.

On the Wallaby backpackers' hostel in Yungaburra runs overnight trips to the Tableland from Cairns for $55; the price includes accommodation, transport, all meals, and activities such as rainforest walks, canoeing and platypus spotting.

There are also interesting tours to Chillagoe and Mt Mulligan – see the Mareeba to Chillagoe and Chillagoe sections.

KURANDA
pop 1000

Famed for its markets, this beautiful mountain village is surrounded by spectacular scenery. Unfortunately, Kuranda's charms have long been known to the masses, and the place is flooded with busloads and trainloads of tourists on market days.

Kuranda can still be a pleasant place to stay overnight. While it's no longer the sleepy, old-fashioned hippy village it once was, in the afternoons and evenings, and on non-market days, it reverts to the laid-back atmosphere it was once renowned for.

Seventh Day Adventists founded the Mona Mona Mission near Kuranda around the turn of the 20th century. At the time the government's policy was to collect north Queensland Aborigines into missions and reserves. Mona Mona was one of the more successful missions, becoming almost self-sufficient and housing about 350 people at its peak. It was closed in 1962, and many of the people and their descendants now live in or near Kuranda.

Things to See & Do

The **Kuranda markets** are held every Wednesday, Thursday, Friday and Sunday, although things quieten after about 2 pm. There's a huge range of stalls here, and if you can ignore the tea-towels, plastic boomerangs and 'I'm with stupid' T-shirts, there are some excellent hand-made arts and crafts on sale – leather belts, wooden puzzles, painted T-shirts, bush saxophones, jewellery, essential oil burners, sarongs, hats, pottery and didjeridus.

At the market, **Birdworld** ($7) is a large canopied garden with a lake, waterfalls and

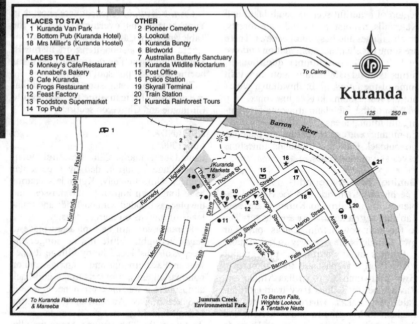

PLACES TO STAY
1 Kuranda Van Park
17 Bottom Pub (Kuranda Hotel)
18 Mrs Miller's (Kuranda Hostel)

PLACES TO EAT
5 Monkey's Cafe/Restaurant
8 Annabel's Bakery
9 Cafe Kuranda
10 Frogs Restaurant
12 Feast Factory
13 Foodstore Supermarket
14 Top Pub

OTHER
2 Pioneer Cemetery
3 Lookout
4 Kuranda Bungy
6 Birdworld
7 Australian Butterfly Sanctuary
11 Kuranda Wildlife Noctarium
15 Post Office
16 Police Station
19 Skyrail Terminal
20 Train Station
21 Kuranda Rainforest Tours

Kuranda

To Cairns

over 30 species of birds; it's open daily from 9 am to 4 pm. A jump at **Kuranda Bungy** costs $60.

Near the market area, the **Australian Butterfly Sanctuary** ($10) is open daily from 10 am to 3 pm and has regular guided tours. On Coondoo St, the **Kuranda Wildlife Noctarium** ($9 for adults, $4.50 for children), where you can see nocturnal rainforest animals like gliders, fruit bats and echidnas, is open from 10 am to 4 pm daily. Feeding times, which are the best times to visit, are at 10.30 and 11.30 am, and 1.15 and 2.30 pm.

Over the footbridge behind the railway station you'll find **Kuranda Rainforest Tours**, where you can hire a canoe to paddle along the Barron River. It also runs four riverboat cruises each day which cost $10 ($5 children), and a guided one hour walk through the rainforest at 11.45 am daily which costs $10/5.

There are several picturesque walks starting with short, signed tracks down through the market. **Jumrum Creek Environmental Park**, off Barron Falls Rd, 700m from the bottom of Thongon St, has a short walking track and a big population of fruit bats. Further down, Barron Falls Rd divides: the left fork takes you to a lookout over the falls, while a further 1.5km along the right fork brings you to Wrights Lookout, where you can see back down the Barron Gorge to Cairns.

Places to Stay

Kuranda Van Park (☎ 4093 7316) is in a quiet setting a few kilometres out of town, up the road directly opposite the Kuranda turn-off on the Kennedy Hwy. It's a bushy, well-established camping ground close to the Barron River, with a good saltwater pool and a courtesy bus. Campsites cost $8 ($10 powered), on-site cabins are $30 and twin share backpacker accommodation is $12.

The agreeably rustic *Kuranda Hostel* (☎ 4093 7355), also known as *Mrs Miller's*, is at 6 Arara St, near the railway station. It's a big, rambling old timber building with a huge garden, a small saltwater pool, a sitting/video room, an enlightening graffiti room and a separate TV room. It's a quiet, relaxing place to stay, especially if you've got a good book or two, although the mosquitoes are annoyingly friendly. Dorm beds cost $13 and there are double rooms for $32 (VIP, YHA $1 less).

Tentative Nests (☎ 4093 9555), at 26 Barron Falls Rd about 2km from town, offers unusual accommodation in tented platforms in the rainforest. The cost is $50 per person, or $60 with breakfast and $88 with full board. Transfers to or from Cairns cost $5.

The *Bottom Pub/Kuranda Hotel* (☎ 4093 7206), on the corner of Coondoo and Arara Sts, remains doggedly down-market. It has a pool and 12 basic motel-style rooms with ceiling fans at $39/49.

A couple of kilometres south-west of town, back on the Kennedy Hwy towards Mareeba, the up-market *Kuranda Rainforest Resort* (☎ 4093 7555) has excellent facilities, including a bar, a tropical-style restaurant, a great swimming pool and tennis courts. The two-bedroom timber cabins (some with cooking facilities) cost from $120/138 plus $30 for each extra adult. The resort has a free courtesy bus which makes pick-ups three times daily from Trinity Wharf in Cairns and also does airport transfers.

Places to Eat
Some of the best food is found in the *food stalls* scattered around the markets – you can get a freshly squeezed juice, a sandwich, satays, a Thai stir-fry, an Indian curry – just follow your nose! There are also quite a few *cafes*, *bakeries* and *coffee shops* in the village.

Both pubs do counter meals. The *Garden Bar & Grill*, out in the backyard of the Bottom Pub, is a surprisingly pretty spot, with a swimming pool, shady lawns and palm trees. There's a thatched barbecue bar where you can get burgers for $5 or grills for around $8 – and have a swim while you're there. The Top Pub has a bistro called *Troppo's Lounge*, which serves mixed grills, fish and chips, ham steak and pineapple, and the like for $7 to $9.

Monkey's Cafe/Restaurant, at the bottom end of Therwine St near the markets, is a good, earthy BYO cafe with an outdoor deck. It serves good breakfasts and lunches – bacon and eggs, croissants, salads and fruit salads, sandwiches and bagels – and is also open for dinner, when main courses cost from $18.

Frogs Restaurant on Coondoo St is another good local, which also has live music on Sunday nights. The *Feast Factory* is a large, popular place with balconies looking right into the rainforest and buffet meals for $11.

Cafe Kuranda, on the corner of Coondoo and Therwine Sts, does sandwiches, snacks and takeaways. Just a few doors along, the excellent *Annabel's Bakery* has a large range of pastries.

Getting There & Away
Bus White Car Coaches (☎ 4091 1855) has five buses from Cairns to Kuranda on weekdays and two to three on weekends. They leave from outside Tropical Paradise Travel, 25 Spence St, Cairns, and the fare is $7 each way.

Train The appropriately named Kuranda Scenic Railway winds 34km from Cairns to Kuranda. This line, which took five years to build, was opened in 1891 and goes through 15 tunnels, climbing more than 300m in the last 21km. Kuranda's railway station, decked out in tropical flowers and ferns, is justly famous.

The historic steam trains operate daily and the trip takes 1½ hours. The one-way/return fares are $25/40 ($13/21 children). You also get a booklet on the line's history and a photo stop at the 260m

Barron Falls. The train has its own ticket office at Cairns train station (☎ 4052 6249) – or you can board at Freshwater Connection (☎ 4055 2222), 10km north of Cairns. Trains leave Cairns at 8.30 and 9.15 am, returning from Kuranda at 2 and 3.30 pm.

Cable Car A 7.5km gondola cableway runs from Smithfield, a northern suburb of Cairns, to Kuranda in about 30 minutes. There are two stops along the way, at Red Peak and at Barron Falls. The cableway runs daily between 8 am and 3.30 pm, with the last departure from Kuranda at 2.30 pm. One-way/return fares are $27/45 ($13.50/22.50 children).

KURANDA TO MAREEBA
It's 37km from Kuranda to the town of Mareeba, along the Kennedy Hwy. The first section of the drive continues to twist and climb through the green mountains, but the road soon levels out as you enter the flatter, drier farmlands to the west of the Tableland.

There's a rather intriguing accommodation possibility along this route. About 14km from Kuranda is the turn-off to the *Cedar Park Rainforest Resort* (☎ 4093 7022) – it's another 6km of dirt road from the turn-off to the resort. This place is in the middle of nowhere, on 240 hectares. The resort building can only be described as different – a quirky blend of raw timber poles, medieval brick arches, second-hand materials and tacky 1970s architecture. There are nine units that sleep up to four, a bar and a restaurant, but the best parts are the forest environment, the lovely gardens and the small stream running through the property. Rooms go for $70/130 a double plus $30 for each extra person, and this includes breakfast. Children under 14 are only accommodated by special arrangement.

About 23km south-west of Kuranda is the turn-off to **Davies Creek National Park**. It's another 7km of gravel road to this small but pretty park of eucalypt forest. The park is a great spot for bushwalks, picnics or camping. There's a self-registration campground with toilets, fireplaces and picnic tables, and several walking tracks lead to the creek, a waterfall and a lookout point.

MAREEBA
pop 18,300
Mareeba is in the far corner of the Tableland, in the centre of a rich farming area. The main crops are tobacco, macadamia nuts, coffee, sugar and cattle. The cattle saleyards, on the northern outskirts of town, are an interesting place to visit when the sales are on – you'll see more Akubra hats and bowed legs than I've had hot steaks. Cattle sales are held every Tuesday morning.

Mareeba itself is a busy commercial centre, and the Mareeba Rodeo held each July is one of Australia's biggest rodeos, but most tourists just pass through here on their way to somewhere else.

Granite Gorge, 10km south-west of Mareeba, is famous for its large population of rock wallabies. It's a very scenic spot and a popular day-trip destination, with walking trails, huge granite formations and waterfalls. There is also a camping ground here.

The new **Information Centre & Museum** (☎ 4092 5674) near the Kuranda turn-off is open daily from 8 am to 4 pm. The $4 admission to the museum is a bit steep.

Places to Stay
The *Riverside Caravan Park* (☎ 4092 2309), on Egan St, has tent sites for $10 and on-site vans from $25. There are two motels in town.

The renovated *Ant Hill Hotel* (☎ 4092 1011), in the centre of town at 79 Byrnes St, has classic pub-style rooms upstairs at $25/32 for singles/doubles; and the *Highlander Hotel* (☎ 4092 1032), also in the main street, has backpacker rooms at $13 per person.

Places to Eat
There are plenty of cafes and takeaways along the main street, and the previously mentioned *Ant Hill Hotel* is a good place for a counter meal.

MAREEBA TO CHILLAGOE

The Burke Developmental Rd leaves the Kennedy Hwy at Mareeba and heads west all the way across to Karumba and Normanton on the Gulf of Carpentaria. Most of the route is unsealed and passes through some of the most remote and inhospitable parts of the state. It is only suitable for well-equipped and experienced 4WD adventurers, preferably travelling in a convoy with extra water and spare parts.

However, the first section of the route, the road to Chillagoe, is well within the reach of the average day tripper. It's less than 150km from Mareeba to Chillagoe, a fascinating old mining town where you can get a brief taste of life in the outback, visit impressive limestone caves and rock pinnacles, Aboriginal rock-art galleries, ruins of smelters from early this century, a working mine and a museum. All but the last 34km of the route is along sealed roads, and while these last 34km are pretty bumpy, they won't present a problem for conventional vehicles during the dry season.

Mt Mulligan Station

Mt Mulligan was the site of Queensland's worst mining disaster; the mountain itself is an eerie and spectacular formation. There isn't much left of the old mining township but it's an interesting area if you have time to explore.

The town's former hospital, a big old Queenslander, is now used as the homestead for *Mt Mulligan Station* (☎ 4094 8360). The owner of this large cattle station runs good 'bush experience' tours from Cairns, costing $95 per person for two nights and three days here. If you have your own vehicle, you can stay here overnight for $40 per person, which includes breakfast and dinner. Mt Mulligan is 50km north of the Burke Developmental Rd. The unsealed road is rough in patches; 4WDs are recommended, although you *can* make it in a conventional vehicle during the Dry.

Irvinebank

At Petford, 79km south-west of Mareeba, there's a turn-off which leads south and

The Mt Mulligan Mining Disaster

Mt Mulligan became infamous in 1921 as the site of the Queensland's worst mining disaster. Rich coal deposits were discovered here in 1910, and a town was established and named after James Venture Mulligan, the famous prospector who discovered the Palmer River goldfields and opened up much of Cape York in the 1870s. By 1914 a train line had been constructed to link Mt Mulligan to Dimbulah, and it became one of Queensland's most productive coal mines.

On the morning of 19 September 1921, 75 men went to work down the mine. At 9.25 am an explosion ripped through the mine and a ball of fire flashed out of the tunnel entrance. Reports at the time claim the explosion was heard 60km away. Rescue teams and medical staff rushed to the scene, but it was to no avail. Everyone who went down the mine that morning was killed in the blast. The last casualty was Thomas Evans, the mine's underground manager, who died a few days later in the Mareeba hospital.

A commission of inquiry attributed the explosion to the fact that the mine had been poorly ventilated, dusty and that explosives were '... stored underground in a careless manner, without regard to the regulations'. It was suspected that the disaster was triggered by the accidental firing of explosives.

The mine was reopened for work five months later and operations continued until it closed in 1957.

then west across to Herberton, via the old mining township of Irvinebank. This road is dirt all the way, but it's reasonable and you can attempt it in a conventional vehicle if it hasn't been raining.

There are still a few people living out at Irvinebank, in an interesting collection of restored old houses and cottages. Tin, copper and silver were the main targets here, and the old privately run mill still crushes tin a few days a week.

The **Loudoun House Museum** is set in the former home of John Moffat, one of Queensland's most successful mining pioneers. Built in 1884, it's said to be the oldest erect two-storey timber and iron building in north Queensland. It's open daily (except Thursday) from 10 am to noon and from 1 to 4 pm; entry is free, although donations are accepted gratefully.

If you decide to stop overnight, you can camp in the back yard of the *Irvinebank Tavern* (☎ 4096 4176); it also has beds in a double and two single rooms at $20 a head.

Petford to Chillagoe

Back on the road to Chillagoe, it's another 7km west from Petford to the **Lappa Junction Hotel**, a ramshackle cluster of tin and timber buildings that are gradually being restored. There's a small museum here.

Some 25km on is **Almaden**, a nondescript little place with an interesting old pub and a very general store. Beyond Almaden the gravel sections of the road begin; the landscape starts to look like the outback, with distinctive red earth showing among scattered trees, jagged outcrops and rocky hills.

CHILLAGOE
pop 450

A visit to the old mining village of Chillagoe offers a fascinating glimpse into life in the outback. There are plenty of relics from the not-so-good old days when gold, silver, copper, lead, and wolfram were mined in the surrounding area. Although Chillagoe's ore deposits were extensively explored by a number of major companies, the Red Dome

gold mine which started here as recently as the 1980s has been one of the area's few profitable ventures. Marble is also still being quarried in the area.

Apart from the mining relics and the old town itself, Chillagoe is famous for its spectacular limestone caves, and there are a number of significant Aboriginal rock-art sites around the town.

It may only be a couple of hours drive from the coast, but it's a long, long way from the commercialisation of Cairns or the glamour of Port Douglas. If you're feeling a little jaded by bright lights and tourist traps, Chillagoe is definitely worth a day trip, and there's a range of options if you feel like staying longer.

Things to See & Do

There are extensive cave systems within the limestone pinnacles that surround Chillagoe. The **Chillagoe-Mungana Caves National Park** which protects the cave areas is in nine separate sections. The main caves are the Donna, Royal Arch and Trezkinn, and rangers run daily guided tours of the Donna Cave at 9 am (one hour, $5), the Trezkinn Cave at 11 am (half hour, $5) and the Royal Cave at 1.30 pm ($7.50). The Donna and Trezkinn Caves are both electrically lit, with steep steps taking you through their delicate formations. The Royal Cave is a larger, more open cave system with daylight chambers.

It's worth contacting the Department of Environment office (☎ 4094 7163) on Queen St when you arrive, because the tours can be booked out, especially in the tourist season, and times can vary at other times of year. The rangers are very helpful and can also tell you about other caves with self-guiding trails, for which you'll need a torch (flashlight).

A 3.5km walking trail links the Royal Arch Cave section with the Donna and Trezkinn Caves car park, taking you through a harsh, craggy landscape via the interesting **Balancing Rock** formation. It's a great walk, but make sure you wear a hat and bring drinking water.

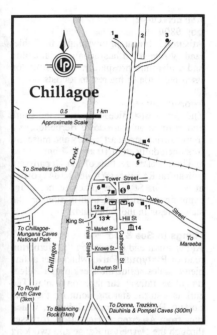

Chillagoe

0   0.5   1 km
Approximate Scale

To Smelters (2km)

Tower Street

To Chillagoe-
Mungana Caves
National Park

King St

Market St

Hill St

Knowe St

Atherton St

To Royal
Arch Cave
(3km)

To Balancing
Rock (1km)

To Donna, Trezkinn,
Dauhinia & Pompei Caves (300m)

To
Mareeba

Creek

Chillagoe

Frew Street

Cathedral St

The Chillagoe Museum, otherwise known as the **Chillagoe Historical Centre**, is an interesting place on Hill St. It contains a diverse collection of odds and sods that includes rocks, minerals and gemstones; bottled snakes and pinned butterflies; copies of old mining leases; sepia-tinted photos and old cinema projectors; and even tribal artefacts from the island of Papua New Guinea. The museum is open daily from 8.30 am to 4.30 pm, and entry costs $3.

About 2km north-west of town are the ruins of the **Chillagoe Smelters**, which were built at the turn of the century and operated until 1943. All that remains are some crumbling stone and brick walls, three massive brick chimneys and a jumble of rusting tanks and machinery. The Department of Environment office has a brochure which details the background of the smelters.

Places to Stay

There's a small national parks camping ground at the Royal Arch Cave section of the national park.

In Queen St, the *Chillagoe Caravan Park* (☎ 4094 7177) has tent sites for $10 and on-site cabins at $40. There are four modern and comfortable units with kitchen, air-con, TV and en suite, costing $50 a double and $5 per extra person. There is also a pool.

The *Post Office Hotel* (☎ 4094 7119), at 37 Queen St, is a classic old country pub with quaint but simple rooms upstairs costing $15/30 – these iron beds are about the narrowest thing I've slept in, at least in this lifetime. The *Black Cockatoo Hotel* (☎ 4094 7168), in Tower St, has basic motel-style rooms at $30/40.

At the *Chillagoe Caves Lodge Motel* (☎ 4094 7106), at 7 King St, you can camp in the yard for $8; there are budget rooms with shared bathrooms at $20/25; or the motel-style units (which sleep up to six) cost $40/45 plus $5 for extras. The motel has a pool and a restaurant.

About 1km from the centre of town, near the railway station, the *Chillagoe Bush Camp* (☎ 4094 7155) is a former miners' village with accommodation in dongas and transportables. There are singles/twins for

$20/30, doubles for $45 or family units (up to four people) for $45. It's a friendly place to stay, and reasonably priced meals are available.

A kilometre further out of town is the *Chillagoe Creek Homestead* (☎ 4094 7160), which has three guest rooms which cost $85 a double for B&B. You can also camp in the yard here for $10. The owner does walking tours around the town and local area, depending on what people are interested in seeing. To get to the homestead, follow the signs to the airstrip, then turn left. You'll see two houses – it's the one on the right.

Places to Eat
The *Black Cockatoo Hotel* has basic pub food. The *Chillagoe Caves Lodge* has its own restaurant, and you can also eat out at the *Chillagoe Bush Camp* even if you're not staying there.

Getting There & Away
White Car Coaches (☎ 4091 1855) runs a return service between Cairns and Chillagoe twice a week. The full trip takes about 3½ hours and costs $39 each way.

A couple of companies run tours to Chillagoe from Cairns – see Organised Tours in the Cairns section for details.

TOLGA
pop 850
Tolga, a small township 5km north of Atherton, has some interesting craft shops including the Tolga Woodworks, which sells beautiful crafted wood.

You can turn east at Tolga to reach the **Danbulla Forest Drive**, which technically starts at Tinaroo Falls 13km north-east of here (see the Lake Tinaroo section for details).

Just south of town is a turn-off to the *Homestead Tourist Park* (☎ 4095 4266), a modern tourist complex in an 80-hectare avocado farm. You can visit the packing shed, and there's an art gallery, a colonial-style restaurant and four motel units which cost $60/70 a single/double. This place is a popular stop for the tourist buses.

ATHERTON
pop 5200
Atherton is the major township in the Tableland. While it's a busy commercial centre and a pleasant, prosperous town, Atherton itself has little of interest to tourists.

Information
The Old Post Office Gallery, at the south end of town on the road to Herberton, is a tourist office, small art gallery and museum; it is open daily from 10 am to 4 pm.

The Forestry section of the Department of Natural Resources' (☎ 4091 1844) office at 83 Main St is the place to come for camping permits and information on the state forests in the Tableland.

Things to See & Do
At the south end of town on the Herberton road is **Platypus Park**, which has a few picnic tables beside the creek plus a collection of old railway carriages on display. The park is also the starting point for the **Herberton Range Historic Railway**, which runs from Atherton to Herberton. It passes through the Herberton Range and two long tunnels, and climbs a grade of one in 33 over 7km, making it the steepest railway in Queensland. The train is run by volunteers, and trips to Herberton run from Wednesday to Sunday. The trip takes 1½ hours each way and costs $25 return.

Places to Stay
The *Woodlands Tourist Park* (☎ 4091 1407), on the Herberton road at the southern entrance to town, is a pleasant little camping ground with tent sites for $12 and on-site cabins from $40 a double.

Atherton Backpackers (☎ 4091 3552), at 37 Alice St near the town centre, is a quiet, friendly family-run hostel with dorm beds from $12 to $14 and doubles for $29. It's signposted off the main road into town from Yungaburra, just before it meets the Kennedy Hwy.

There are three motels in town, all of a fairly similar standard, with rooms from $45.

LAKE TINAROO

From Atherton, Tolga or Yungaburra it's a short drive to this large lake created for the Barron River hydroelectric power scheme. It's now a popular water sports and fishing spot – it's open for barramundi fishing year-round.

Danbulla Forest Drive

The Department of Natural Resources publishes a good map/brochure called the *Danbulla Forest Drive*, which highlights the main camping grounds and sights on the circuit drive around the lake.

The drive starts at **Tinaroo Falls**, a sleepy village at the north-western corner of the lake, with a caravan park and a motel.

Just out of town there's a lookout over the huge **Tinaroo Falls Dam**, where *Cafe Pensini's Deckbar & Bistro* is a fairly mod bar and bistro with great views. It is open for lunch daily, with meals from $9 to $12.

Once you're past the dam, the road turns to dirt and the Danbulla Forest Drive officially starts. The drive is a 31km circuit of the lake, finally emerging on the Gillies Hwy at Boar Pocket Rd, 4km north of Lake Barrine. It passes several free lakeside camping grounds (with showers and toilets) run by the Department of Natural Resources (☎ 4091 1844).

One of the most pleasant of these is the first place you come to, **Platypus Rocks Lookout**. There's a great camping ground with grass and shady pine trees and a boat ramp. Further on, just after the **Kauri Creek camping area**, you pass a 4WD track which leads north through the hills all the way to Mareeba. It's a spectacular drive with some great views along the way, but you need a permit from the Department of Natural Resources (☎ 4091 1844) in Atherton to do the drive.

Lake Euramoo, about halfway around the circuit, is in a double volcanic crater; there's a short botanic walk around the lake. There is another crater at **Mobo Creek**, a short walk off the drive. Then, 25km from the dam it's a short walk to the **Cathedral Fig**, a gigantic strangler fig tree.

YUNGABURRA
pop 820

This pretty village is 13km east of Atherton along the Gillies Hwy. It's right in the centre of the Tableland, and if you have transport it's a good base from which to explore the lakes, waterfalls and national parks nearby. There are a couple of craft shops and galleries here, some good restaurants, and the central streets of the town have been classified by the National Trust and are quite atmospheric.

About 3km south of Yungaburra is the **Curtain Fig**, a strangler fig whose aerial roots form a 15m-high hanging screen.

Places to Stay

The excellent *On the Wallaby* (☎ 4095 2031), at 37 Eacham Rd, is a small and comfortable backpackers' hostel. There's a free pick-up bus from Cairns and the nightly cost is $15 per person, $35 for a double, or you can camp in the backyard for $8 per tent. It has a good $55 package which includes return bus from Cairns, accommodation and canoe trips.

The *Lake Eacham Hotel* (☎ 4095 3515), is a fine old village pub with a magnificent timber dining room and comfy rooms upstairs at $30/35. The (non-smoking) *Kookaburra Lodge* (☎ 4095 3222), on the corner of Oak St and Eacham Rd, is a small, friendly and peaceful place with bright modern units from $65 a double. There's a pool and tiny dining room with three-course meals for $20.

Gumtree Getaway (☎ 4095 3105) is a B&B farm just outside town on the Atherton road, with accommodation at $88 for a double.

The *Yungaburra Park Motel* (☎ 4095 3211), on the Atherton road, has modern motel units with air-con and TV from $52.

Places to Eat

There are three good restaurants in Yungaburra, which just about certifies the town as the eating capital of the Tableland.

The *Burra Inn* is a charming little BYO gourmet restaurant opposite the pub. The country-style food is excellent, with main meals for around $18.

On the Gillies Hwy (the main road through Yungaburra), *Nick's Swiss-Italian Restaurant* is a modern chalet-style building with occasional live music. The lunch menu here covers sandwiches, salads and pastas, with mains mostly from $9 to $12; at night the pastas range from $11 to $15 and other mains $16 to $23. It's closed on Wednesday.

Also on the Gillies Hwy is *Snibbles BYO*, which is open daily except Monday. It's set in a restored Queenslander, and you can eat inside or out on the verandah. It serves light lunches like sandwiches, crepes and filled croissants from $6 to $8, and at night main courses are in the $15 to $18 range. From Wednesday to Saturday a two course dinner is available for $15, and there's a Sunday barbecue lunch from 10 am to 12 noon.

LAKES EACHAM & BARRINE

These two lovely crater lakes are off the Gillies Hwy just east of Yungaburra. Both are reached by paved roads and are great swimming spots. There are rainforest walking tracks around their perimeters – 6km around Lake Barrine, 4km around Lake Eacham.

At Lake Barrine the *Lake Barrine Tea House* (☎ 4095 3847) serves Devonshire teas, snacks and light lunches daily from 9 am to 5 pm. From the teahouse, you can take a 45 minute cruise (at 10.15 am, 12 noon or 3.15 pm) which costs $7 ($4.50 children). Lake Eacham is quieter and more beautiful – an excellent place for a picnic, or a swim in clear water, and there's a small kids' pool.

Both lakes are national parks and camping is not allowed. However, there are camp sites at *Lake Eacham Tourist Park* (☎ 4095 3730), 2km down the Malanda road from Lake Eacham. The secluded *Chambers Wildlife Rainforest Apartments* (☎ 4095 3754) has self-contained one-bedroom apartments sleeping one to four people at $80 for two. It also supplies binoculars and bird books.

PEERAMON

This tiny village is tucked into the hills midway between Malanda and Yungaburra. The *Peeramon Hotel* (☎ 4096 5873) is a wonderful old country pub with a great atmosphere. Old-fashioned but comfortable accommodation upstairs costs $30 a double. There's also a restaurant serving good pub tucker with an exotic twist, and a beer garden.

MALANDA
pop 950

About 15km south of Lake Eacham, Malanda is one of the most pleasant spots to stay on the Tableland. It is a small town with some old buildings in its centre, a couple of pubs and some good places to eat and stay. Malanda also has a huge dairy.

Things to See & Do

On the outskirts of town, beside the Johnstone River crossing, the **Malanda Falls** drop into a big pool which is surrounded by lawns and forest. It's a popular swimming spot, and there are picnic tables and a 1km walking trail through the forest nearby.

If you're staying in town, the **Majestic Theatre**, on Eacham Place, is a great old-fashioned cinema which screens the latest releases.

A couple of kilometres west of Malanda is the **Bromfield Swamp**, where a viewing platform beside the road overlooks an eroded volcanic crater. This wetland is an important sanctuary for waterbirds, although you can't see a lot from the lookout without binoculars. At certain times of year flocks of cranes fly to roost in the crater at sunset.

Places to Stay & Eat

Malanda Next to the Malanda Falls, the *Malanda Falls Caravan Park* (☎ 4096 5314), at 38 Park Ave, has tent sites at $11 and on-site cabins from $30.

The *Malanda Hotel* (☎ 4096 5101) is in the centre of town on the corner of James and English Sts. It's a huge old timber pub with a great dining room that has a good reputation. Pub-style rooms cost $16/32. *Muppee's BYO*, at 22 James St, is a casual pizza and pasta joint. Next door, *Grannie's Country Kitchen* has tempting cakes and other treats.

The *Malanda Lodge Motel* (☎ 4096 5555), on the edge of town on the Millaa Millaa road, has good modern units from $65/68.

There are also a couple of good places to stay in the hills around Malanda – see the following section.

Around Malanda The *Honeyflow Country Guesthouse* (☎ 4096 8173), signposted off the road heading north to Gordonvale, is an old heri-tage homestead set in lovely gardens. There are four guest suites, each with its own bathroom and living area, TV, ceiling fan and heater, and tea and coffee-making facilities. Dinner, B&B costs $160 a double.

Fairdale Farmstay (☎ 4096 6599) is on Hillcrest Rd, 3km south of Malanda; take the turn-off near the Malanda Lodge Motel on the Millaa Millaa road – it's signposted from there. This is a 120-hectare dairy farm in a scenic setting, and guests can get in-volved in the farm activities. Accommo-dation consists of a charming Federation-style cottage that sleeps up to six and has great valley views. The cottage costs $100 a night for a family of four, plus $20 for each extra person. There is also a renovat-ed farmhouse with B&B rooms at $65/85 for singles/doubles.

The *Travellers Rest* (☎ 4096 6077) is a newly-established B&B about five minutes drive from Malanda on the Millaa Millaa road. The rate is $60 for a double including breakfast.

MILLAA MILLAA
pop 350
Set in the heart of dairy country 24km south of Malanda is the tiny township of Millaa Millaa. The **Eacham Historical Society Museum**, on the main street, has a collec-tion of tools, equipment and historical items relating to the area's timber and dairy in-dustries. It is open daily in the mornings (except Tuesday and Saturday).

A few kilometres west of Millaa Millaa, the East Evelyn road passes the **Millaa Millaa Lookout** with its superb panoramic view.

Waterfalls Circuit
The start of this 16km circuit is a little way east of Millaa Millaa, and passes some of the most picturesque falls on the Tableland. You enter the circuit by taking Theresa Creek Rd, 1km east of Millaa Millaa on the Palmerston Hwy. **Millaa Millaa Falls**, the first you reach, are the most spectacular; they have the best swimming hole, and the grassy area in front of the falls is ideal for a picnic.

Continuing around the circuit, you reach **Zillie Falls**, where a short walking trail leads to a lookout point beside the falls. Further on you come to **Ellinjaa Falls**, with a 200m walking trail down to a swimming hole at the base of the falls, before return-ing to the Palmerston Hwy just 2.5km out of Millaa Millaa.

A further 5.5km down the Palmerston Hwy there's a turn-off to **Mungalli Falls**, 5km off the highway, where the *Mungalli Falls Outpost* (☎ 4031 1144) has a tea-house/restaurant and offers horse-trail rides. Accommodation is in modern self-con-tained cabins with communal cooking facilities for $40 a double plus $5 for extra bodies.

The Palmerston Hwy continues through Palmerston National Park to Innisfail.

MT HYPIPAMEE NATIONAL PARK
The Kennedy Hwy between Atherton and Ravenshoe passes the eerie Mt Hypipamee crater. There's good birdwatching in this little rainforested park – watch out for the golden bowerbird as you walk the trails. It's a scenic 800m (return) walk from the car park, past **Dinner Falls**, to the narrow, 138m-deep crater with its spooky, evil-looking lake far below. The surface of the lake is covered in a green crust of duck-weed. Back at Dinner Falls there's a good

swimming area, and there is a picnic area beside the car park.

HERBERTON
pop 1500

On a slightly longer alternative route between Atherton and Ravenshoe, this old tin-mining town holds a colourful Tin Festival each September. The town is basically a collection of old timber buildings scattered across a cluster of hills, and there are three pubs and a couple of cafes on the main street. On Holdcroft Drive is the **Herberton Historical Village**, made up of about 30 old buildings which have been transported here from around the Tableland.

Herberton is also one of the departure points for the **Herberton Range Historic Railway** – see the Atherton section for details.

If you're feeling adventurous, you can also head west from Herberton through the old mining township of **Irvinebank**, eventually linking up with the road to Chillagoe – see the Mareeba to Chillagoe section.

Places to Stay

Herberton has a *caravan park* with tent sites and cabins; the *Royal Hotel* (☎ 4096 2231) on Grace St, in the centre of town, has average pub-style rooms at \$15/25.

Signposted off the highway 9km south of Herberton, *Banyula Homestay* (☎ 4096 2668) is a modern, comfortable home in a peaceful bush setting. It has two guest rooms costing \$80/120 for B&B, and for another \$20 you can enjoy a three-course home-cooked dinner.

RAVENSHOE
pop 900

At an altitude of 915m, Ravenshoe is a forestry centre on the western edge of the Tableland. It was once a thriving timber town, and while there are still a couple of mills operating here, most of the logging has stopped and things are pretty quiet around here nowadays.

From Ravenshoe you can take a ride on the **Millstream Express**, an historic steam

train which runs north along a 7km track to Tumoulin. The train runs every Saturday and Sunday at 2.30 pm except during February or March. The cost is \$10 (\$5 children), and light refreshments are available.

Little Millstream Falls are 2km south of Ravenshoe on the Tully Gorge road, and the **Tully Falls** are 24km south.

About 6km past Ravenshoe and 1km off the road are the **Millstream Falls**. The falls are the widest in Australia, although only 13m high, and have some great swimming areas.

Places to Stay

The *Tall Timbers Caravan Park* (☎ 4097 6325), on the Kennedy Hwy, has tent sites at \$10 and four cabins at \$30. The *Club Hotel/Motel* (☎ 4097 6109), at 47 Grigg St, has motel rooms at \$30/40.

The *Kool Moon Motel* (☎ 4097 6325), at 6 Moore St, has units for \$38/48.

RAVENSHOE TO UNDARA OR CHARTERS TOWERS

The Kennedy Hwy (part of Australia's Highway 1 at this point) continues southwest from Ravenshoe for 114km, where it forks. The road south goes to Charters Towers and is paved road all the way; to the west is the Gulf Developmental Rd to Croydon and Normanton via Undara Lava Tubes.

About 32km west of Ravenshoe are the **Innot Hot Springs**, where you can lie in one of the sandy bath-like springs beside the highway and watch the traffic go by – a bizarre experience, really.

The small mining town of **Mt Garnet**, 15km west of Innot Hot Springs, comes alive one weekend every May when it hosts one of Queensland's top outback race meetings. If heading west there is a staffed papaya fruit fly quarantine inspection station about 4km west of town, and you are required to deposit virtually all fruit and vegetables here.

About 60km south of Mt Garnet the road passes through **Forty Mile Scrub National Park**, where the semi-evergreen vine thicket is a descendant of the vegetation that covered much of the Gondwanaland supercontinent 300 million years ago.

A little further on is the turn-off to Undara Lava Tubes and the Gulf country (see the Gulf Savannah chapter for details) or you can head straight on along good gravel for Hughenden on the Flinders Hwy (see the Outback Queensland chapter).

Cairns to Port Douglas

The Bruce Hwy, which runs nearly 2000km north from Brisbane, ends in Cairns, but the surfaced coastal road continues for another 110km north through Mossman to Daintree, with a turn-off to Port Douglas. This final stretch, the Captain Cook Hwy, is one of Queensland's most scenic coastal drives, along what is known as the Marlin Coast. The middle section, from Ellis Beach to Port Douglas, runs right along the coastline past a string of pretty coves and superb beaches.

NORTHERN BEACHES
North along the Captain Cook Hwy are Cairns' northern beaches, which are really a string of coastal suburbs. In order, these are Machan's Beach, Holloway's Beach, Yorkey's Knob, Trinity Beach, Kewarra Beach, Clifton Beach and Palm Cove. Holloway's, Trinity and Palm Cove are the best for a short beach trip from Cairns. See Getting Around in the Cairns section for details of buses to these places.

Machan's Beach & Holloway's Beach
Machan's Beach is a quiet little residential community. It doesn't really have much of a beach – the sandy strip starts a little further north at Holloway's Beach, which has a life-saving club and a netted swimming enclosure. The peace is disturbed only by the constant roar of low-flying jets as they approach Cairns airport.

The beachfront *Garden Cafe* is a very popular place for an alfresco Sunday morning coffee. *Tides* next door is also popular, especially on Sunday afternoon when it has live music. Meals range from $6 to $10 at lunchtime and $10 to $14 in the evening.

Yorkey's Knob
Yorkey's Knob also has sandy beaches, and the *Yorkey's Knob Beachfront Van Park* (☎ 4055 7201) has the closest beachfront camping to Cairns. It's a well-established park with plenty of trees, and tent sites from $14 and on-site vans from $30 a double.

Trinity Beach
Trinity is one of the best of Cairns' northern beach suburbs. It's also a suburb which is going rapidly upmarket, with a number of new fancy apartment developments. It has a long stretch of sand sheltered by a high headland at the southern end, and there's a life-saving club and a stinger net here over summer. There's water sports equipment for hire at the beach.

Places to Stay The *Trinity Beach Motel & Backpackers* (☎ 4055 7466), on the corner of the main road and the Esplanade, has six motel-style units. They don't look much from the outside, but they are clean and neat and good value. Dorm beds are $18, or a whole unit is $55.

At 47 Vasey Esplanade, the rather unusual *Casablanca Domes* (☎ 4055 6339) is a set of nine concrete domes which each house a self-contained, comfortable holiday unit with air-con and full kitchen. The one bedroom domes sleep up to four and cost around $60 a double; the two-bedroom models sleep up to six and cost around $70 a double; each extra person costs another $5. The complex has its own pool and restaurant.

Trinity Beach is being developed at a fierce pace. There are a couple of big, upmarket apartment complexes along the beachfront – including the *Roydon Beachfront Apartments* (☎ 4057 6512), at 85

Vasey Esplanade, with two and three-bedroom apartments from $160 a night for two people.

Places to Eat Trinity Beach has a couple of good places to eat on the beachfront. *Trinity Pizza* is a tiny place which serves a great range of salads at lunch time, as well as pastas and mini-pizzas. At night it serves up delicious gourmet pizzas, pastas and salads.

Also opposite the beach, on the other side of the main road, is the *Bar Luna* – a glossy, trendy brasserie. It's open daily from 8 am to midnight, and has an eclectic menu on which seafood is prominent, and dishes cost around $8 to $12 at lunchtime, $13 to $18 in the evening.

The *Boatshed Cafe* is open in the evening only.

Up on the hill overlooking the waterfront is the old *Trinity Beach Hotel*. It's a popular spot for a cool drink, and has a covered beer garden with a bistro section.

Clifton Beach

Another 3km north of the Trinity Beach turn-off is Clifton Beach, a laid-back residential community which is a lot less developed than its neighbours Palm Cove and Trinity Beach.

Places to Stay There are two caravan parks at Clifton Beach. The *Paradise Gardens Caravan Resort* (☎ 4055 3712), on the corner of the highway and Clifton Rd, has tent sites from $14 and on-site vans.

There are a couple of holiday apartments along the beachfront: *Agincourt Holiday Apartments* (☎ 4055 3500), 69 Arlington Esplanade, has one-bedroom units from $98, and *Argosy* (☎ 4055 3333), 119 Arlington Esplanade, has units starting at $105.

Dolce Vita B&B (☎ 4055 3889), at 133 Arlington Esplanade, is one of the few B&Bs in this area. It's a modern and comfortable home, and has two guest rooms which cost $40/70 for singles/doubles, including a tropical breakfast.

Palm Cove

Since the mid-1980s, Palm Cove has developed from a sleepy little beach community into an exclusive resort town. It's still quite small and a very pretty spot despite all the development, and has a good patrolled beach, plenty of shady melaleuca trees, some excellent restaurants and a collection of expensive shops and boutiques. Most of the accommodation is of the upmarket resort/hotel variety, and you'll see as many Rolex watches and gold-embossed T-shirts around here as you would in Port Douglas.

Palm Cove has its own jetty, and many of the cruise boats call in for pick-ups on their way out to the reef and islands. There are no banks here, but the shopping village in the centre of Williams Esplanade has a post office, clothes boutiques, a tour-booking desk and several cafes and restaurants.

Places to Stay The *Palm Cove Camping Area* (☎ 4055 3824), at 149 Williams Esplanade, is a beautifully kept beachfront camping ground run by the local council. Sites cost $8 a night; dogs aren't allowed, and the showers are cold water only.

The *Coconut Lodge Motel* (☎ 4055 3734), at 95-97 Williams Esplanade, has modern motel units with kitchenettes which go for $59, more with air-con. The *Reef Retreat* (☎ 4059 1744), 100m back from the beachfront at 10-14 Harpa St, is an attractive complex of self-contained one and two-bedroom units which start at $95 a night. There's a great pool here, surrounded by towering melaleuca trees.

Marlin Waters (☎ 4055 3933), at 131 Williams Esplanade, is a four-storey complex of modern serviced apartments. There are 21 one-bedroom units, a pool and spa, and rooms start at $105 a night.

The *Melaleuca Resort* (☎ 4055 3222) is a new place at 85 Williams Esplanade. The self-contained units at this modern resort go for $145 for two plus $25 for extra adults.

The *Allamanda* (☎ 4055 3000), at 1 Vievers Rd, is an impressive 4½-star resort hotel on the beachfront, with three pools, a spa and a good bar/restaurant. The units are all self-contained and range from $195 to $460.

The *Novatel Palm Cove Resort* (☎ 4059 1234), on Coral Coast Drive a couple of hundred metres back from the beach, is a huge four-star resort with a golf course, 10 pools, squash and tennis courts and much more. Rooms range from $195 to $480 a night.

Places to Eat & Drink There are several eateries in the Paradise Village shopping complex in the centre of Williams Esplanade. *Cocky's at the Cove* is a good, casual spot for a cappuccino, sandwich or muffin. *Il Forno Pizza* is a small and stylish BYO pizza joint with pizzas from $10 to $13 and a few pasta dishes. *Colonies Cafe* is a more up-market licensed restaurant with mains in the $18 to $20 range.

The *Seabreeze Restaurant* is a seafood place with a pleasant balcony. Main courses here go for $18 to $23.

The *Palm Cove Tavern Bar* on Vievers Ave is the local pub. The bistro serves counter meals; on weekends it does barbecue lunches for $13 a head; and on Sunday night there's a three course meal deal for $16.

On the corner of the Captain Cook Hwy and Vievers Rd, the *Coach House* is a popular and cosy licensed restaurant with a good reputation. It specialises in seafood and steaks, with main courses in the $18 to $25 range.

The *Beach Bar Cafe* is a colourful little cocktail shack next to the shopping village. It's a popular spot for a drink or a casual meal and is open from 2 pm until around midnight most nights, and has live entertainment most Wednesday to Sunday nights.

Double Island
This small island is just a couple of hundred metres off shore from Palm Cove. There's an exclusive resort on the island, the *Double Island Retreat* (☎ 4057 7222), which is the former home of the business-

woman Janet Holmes a Court. The resort, which recently underwent a $5 million refurbishment, is based around a beautiful timber roundhouse. Accommodation starts at $270 for a double in a luxury, safari-style permanent tent; the room tariff is $360 a night including transfers from Palm Cove. A full meal package is available in the beautiful restaurant for around $150; otherwise you can pay for meals as you go, or Palm Cove is only a few minutes away by boat.

Ellis Beach
Round the headland past Palm Cove and Double Island, the highway meets the coast at Ellis Beach, which is a lovely spot. Its southern end is an unofficial nude-bathing beach and the central part of the beach has a good camping ground. The *Ellis Beach Caravan Park* (☎ 4055 3538) has excellent beachfront camping grounds with tent sites at $13, cabins from $38 and motel units for $50. The *Ellis Beach Resort* across the road serves sit-down meals and takeaways, and there is live music here most Sunday afternoons.

ELLIS BEACH TO PORT DOUGLAS
This section of the Captain Cook Hwy follows the coastline for much of its length. Soon after Ellis Beach and 40km north of Cairns, **Hartleys Creek Crocodile Farm** has a collection of Australian wildlife typically found in the Far North. Most of the enclosures are a bit run-down but showmanship makes it more interesting than many similar 'animal places'. The wildlife park is open daily (8 am to 5 pm); there's a park tour at 11 am and a snake show at 2 pm, but make sure you're there at crocodile-feeding time which is at 3 pm; entry is $13 ($7 children).

About 45km north of Cairns is the *Turtle Cove Resort* (☎ 4059 1800), an exclusive gay and lesbian beachfront resort. The resort has good motel-style units with aircon, TV etc, its own restaurant, access to a private beach and a great swimming pool and spa. Prices start from $105 for a double including breakfast.

Port Douglas to Cape Tribulation

PORT DOUGLAS
pop 3400

In the early days of Far North Queensland's development, Port Douglas was a rival for Cairns. When Cairns got the upper hand, Port Douglas became a sleepy little backwater. In the mid-1980s, entrepreneurs began to realise what a delightful place it is, and up went multimillion dollar resorts, a golf course and heliport, hovercraft services from Cairns, a marina and shopping complex, and an avenue of palms lining the road from the Captain Cook Hwy to Port Douglas. Today it has all the ingredients of a retreat for the rich and fashionable, but 'Port' has kept some of its original charm and there is still cheap accommodation.

The town has relaxed village feel about it, with its open-air Sunday markets, a long stretch of beach backed by palm trees and a couple of good old pubs on Macrossan St with outdoor courtyards. Of course, it also has plenty to offer in the glitz and glamour stakes, like the marina with its own shopping complex, a golf course that has played host to some of the world's great golfers and an excellent range of restaurants.

Part of Port's appeal lies in the fact that it's a great base from which to explore the rest of Far North Queensland. From here you can take a cruise out to the Great Barrier Reef or the Low Isles, visit Mossman Gorge and Cape Tribulation, or cruise the Daintree River.

History

Port Douglas was founded in 1877 as the port town for the Hodgkinson River goldfields, and went through several name changes – Island Point, Owensville and Salisbury – before it was named Port Douglas, in honour of the then Queensland premier John Douglas. The town flourished from the outset, and by 1879 had 14 hotels and a fleet of Cobb & Co coaches linking the town with the goldfields.

All this prosperity came to a grinding halt in the mid-1880s when Cairns was chosen ahead of Port Douglas as the terminal for the new rail line from Kuranda and Mareeba. A disastrous cyclone in 1911 destroyed most of the town's buildings, and Port remained a sleepy Brigadoon-like coastal village until its recent emergence from the mists of obscurity into the glare of the tourism spotlight.

Orientation

Port Douglas is spread along a long, low spit of land, with the Coral Sea on the east side and Packers Creek on the west. It's 6km from the highway along Port Douglas Rd, then Davidson St, into the town centre. About half-way in you'll pass the Sheraton Mirage resort and its golf course. There are fine views over the coastline and sea from Flagstaff Hill lookout.

The Marina Mirage, just west of the centre, is the departure point for most of the trips to the reef and Low Isles. Buses arrive at and depart from the Coral Coaches terminal, which is off Wharf St just north of the marina.

Information

Tourist Information While there isn't an independent tourist information office in Port Douglas, there are quite a few private tour booking agents, including the helpful Port Douglas Tourist Information Centre (☎ 4099 5599) at 23 Macrossan St, and the Paradise Information & Booking Centre (☎ 4099 4144) at 30 Wharf St.

Money The ANZ, National and Westpac banks all have branches with ATMs along Macrossan St, and there's a Commonwealth Bank agency inside the post office.

Post & Communications Port's post office is in Owen St. There's a cluster of public telephone booths, including a credit-card phone, on Macrossan St between Grant and Owen Sts.

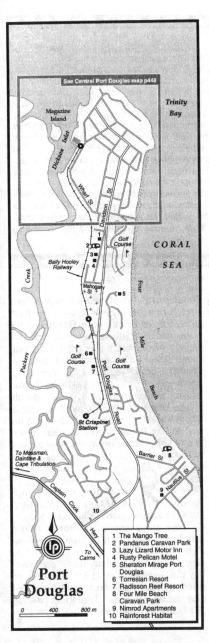

See Central Port Douglas map p448

Trinity
Bay

Magazine
Island

Dickson Inlet

Wharf St

Davidson St

CORAL

SEA

Golf
Course

Bally Hooley
Railway

Mahogany
St

Four

Mile

Beach

Creek

Golf
Course

Golf
Course

Packers

Port Douglas Road

St Crispine
Station

To Mossman,
Daintree &
Cape Tribulation

Barrier St

Nautilus St

Captain Cook

Hwy

To
Cairns

**Port
Douglas**

0   400   800 m

1 The Mango Tree
2 Pandanus Caravan Park
3 Lazy Lizard Motor Inn
4 Rusty Pelican Motel
5 Sheraton Mirage Port
   Douglas
6 Torresian Resort
7 Radisson Reef Resort
8 Four Mile Beach
   Caravan Park
9 Nimrod Apartments
10 Rainforest Habitat

Bookshop The Jungle Bookshop, at 46 Macrossan St, has a good range of novels, travel guides, books on the environment and lots more.

Things to See

On the pier off Anzac Park, Ben Cropp's **Shipwreck Museum** has an interesting collection of maritime relics and displays. There's a 'tomb' dedicated to the famous wreck of the *Yongala*, a luxury steamship which sank in the Whitsundays in 1911 with the loss of 120 people; there's also a *Titanic* display and you can watch continuous maritime films. The museum is open from 9 am to 5 pm daily; admission is $6 ($2 children).

Port's **Sunday Markets**, held every Sunday in Anzac Park (at the north end of Macrossan St), are great fun to visit. There's always a good crowd wandering around among dozens of stalls and tents selling everything from hats, sarongs, wind chimes, wood carvings and painted T-shirts to fresh tropical fruit and vegies.

The **Old Courthouse** (1879), on Wharf St just north of the Macrossan St intersection, is the oldest building in Port, and the only public building to have survived the 1911 cyclone. The courthouse was recently restored and is now an interesting little museum. It's open Tuesday to Sunday from 9 am to 12 noon.

The **Rainforest Habitat**, near where the Port Douglas road meets the main highway, is an 'eco-attraction' – a huge enclosed canopy forms an artificial rainforest environment with elevated timber boardwalks, and this is home to a large number of birds and butterflies. It would be worth a look if the entry was a bit more reasonable – $16 ($8 children) is a bit over the top. It's open daily from 8.30 am to 5 pm, and there's a kiosk.

The **Marina Mirage** is a glamorous and up-market shopping complex full of exclusive speciality shops – fashion boutiques, gift and souvenir shops, jewellery shops and the like. There are also a couple of dive companies and several cafes, restaurants and nightclubs in the complex. The marina here

Port Douglas' Prodigal Son

Port Douglas is one of the few places in Australia where people openly admire Christopher Skase, the high-flying entrepreneur of the 1980s. Skase's vision transformed Port Douglas from a sleepy seaside village into one of Australia's most prestigious tourist destinations.

Skase's media and tourism empire collapsed in 1989 with debts of $1.6 billion and he fled to the Spanish island of Mallorca, leaving his investors in the lurch. Although the Australian government persistently sought his extradition to face 32 charges over the collapse, Skase's doctors and lawyers claimed he has a terminal lung disease which prevents him from travelling. He appeared in public during the trials in a wheelchair with an oxygen mask clamped to his mouth. Back in Australia the media cartoonists had a field day.

In 1994 the Spanish courts agreed to send Skase back to Australia, but he won a last-minute appeal and was granted immunity from further prosecution. Soon after, Skase appeared in public without wheelchair or oxygen mask – a remarkable and timely recovery.

The battle to extradite Skase continues. At the time of writing he had purchased a passport for the tiny Caribbean island of Dominica. However, it's unlikely he'll ever visit his new home – Dominica has an extradition treaty with Australia. He is currently working as a 'consultant' for a proposed luxury resort in Mallorca, in spite of 'collapsing into a coma', according to his family.

---

is lined with dozens of boats of every size and shape, and this is where the trips out to the reef and the Low Isles depart from.

The Port Douglas Restoration Society has mapped out several walking trails through the town and along the waterfront. A series of brass plaques relate the history of various building sites, and maps and brochures for the walks are available from the information centres.

Activities

Diving Courses This is quite a popular place to learn to dive, although it's not particularly cheap when compared to places further south. It's worth shopping around as there is healthy competition between the companies which offer open-water courses.

The Port Douglas Dive Centre (☎ 4099 5327), with a shop near the public pier, has a four-day course at $530; Aussie Dive (☎ 1800 646 548) is the cheapest at $350 for a PADI course; and Quicksilver (☎ 4099 5050), based at the Marina, has a five-day course at $439. Most of the boats heading out to the reef offer dives for certified divers – see the following sections.

Other Activities If you are after a long stretch of sandy beach, backed by palm trees, then try **Four Mile Beach**. At the north end is a life-saving club, and this section of the beach is patrolled all year round. There's also a stinger net from November until mid-May. Windsurfers, paddle-skis, beach chairs and umbrellas can be hired from in front of the life-saving club.

The **Bally Hooley Railway** is a small steam train that shuttles daily between the marina, the Radisson Royal Palms Resort and St Crispins station (at the southern end of the golf course). It operates hourly between 9 am and 5 pm, and return tickets cost $6 ($2 children).

You can go **paragliding** with Get High Parafly (☎ 019 674 774), which departs from the marina hourly. Rides cost $55.

There are a couple of **horse riding ranches** in the area. Mowbray Valley Trail Rides (☎ 4099 3268), based south of Port Douglas on the Mowbray River, does half-day ($60) and full-day ($90) rides, and the price includes transport to and from Port Douglas. Wonga Beach Trail Rides (☎ 4098 7583) and Mt Perseverance Station (☎ 4094

1438) also have good reputations – see the Mossman to Daintree and Mossman to Mt Molloy sections later for details of their rides.

Golfers will be thrilled to hear that the **Mirage Country Club** is open to the general public. The not-so-thrilling catch is that it costs $135 a round, although if you're staying at the Mirage it's a mere $115. If you think that's a bit steep, the Mossman Golf Club is only a 15 minute drive away and a lot more reasonably priced.

Organised Tours

There's a huge range of tours operating out of Port Douglas. Options include trips to Cape Tribulation and the Daintree River, Kuranda and the Atherton Tableland, whitewater rafting trips, and 4WD safaris to places like Cooktown and the Cape York Peninsula. Almost all of the tours operating out of Cairns also do pick-ups from Port Douglas – check with one of the information centres or booking offices, and see Organised Tours in the Cairns section for more details.

Reef Trips Various operators offer trips out to the Barrier Reef in boats of all shapes, sizes and speeds. Before deciding which trip to take, it's worth checking on a few different points, such as how many passengers the boat takes, where it goes and how quickly it gets there. Everyone will have a preference for something different – for example, if you're just interested in diving, you'll prefer to be on something that gets you out to the reef quickly rather than on a leisurely yacht cruise.

Quicksilver's (☎ 4099 5500) fast cats depart daily from the marina at 10 am, travelling out to Agincourt Reef on the outer reef. The cruise costs $130, which includes snorkelling gear, a semi-submersible ride, underwater observatory viewing and lunch. Optional extras include a snorkelling expedition ($28), an introductory dive ($90), two 40 minute dives for certified divers ($90), or a helicopter flight over the reef ($85). Children pay half fare.

If you'd rather go in a smaller group, there are quite a few boats which offer similar but much more personalised reef, snorkelling and diving trips. These include the following:

Haba Queen (☎ 4099 5254)
  Snorkelling cruise $95, with resort dive $155, with a certified dive $135
MV Aristocat (☎ 4099 4727)
  Fishing and snorkelling cruise $124
Phantom (☎ 4094 1220)
  Snorkelling cruise $135, with resort dive $215
Poseidon (☎ 4099 5599)
  Snorkelling cruise $90, with resort dive $145, with two certified dives $130
Wavelength (☎ 4099 5031)
  Snorkelling cruise $80

These costs generally include lunch and transfers from your accommodation. You can book these trips through your accommodation or at one of the booking agencies.

Low Isles There are also cruises out to the Low Isles, a fine little coral cay surrounded by a lagoon and topped by an old lighthouse (1878). Several smaller boats offer good day trips: *Shaolin* (☎ 4099 4650), a refitted Chinese junk, has snorkelling cruises for $80; *Sail Away* (☎ 4099 5070), a sailing catamaran, has snorkelling cruises for $85; and *Wavelength* (☎ 4099 5031) has half-day snorkelling trips on Wednesday and Saturday for $58.

Quicksilver (☎ 4099 5500) also offers trips out to the Low Isles on *Wavedancer*, a huge sailing catamaran. The cruise costs $89 ($45 children), which includes lunch, snorkelling, a trip in a glass bottomed boat, a guided beach walk and presentations by a marine biologist. A resort dive is also available for another $75. You can also go for $49 without snorkelling or lunch.

Mossman Gorge Coral Coaches (☎ 4098 2600) has three services a day out to Mossman Gorge and back. The return fare is $18 and they'll pick you up from wherever you're staying. See the Mossman section for more information on the gorge.

River Cruises Amber Dahlberg's Eco Cruises (☎ 4099 5327) offers cruises and birdwatching tours of the mangroves and wetlands of Dickson Inlet. Cruises depart from the marina every day and cost $35 per person, with a maximum of six passengers.

Bicycle Tours Bike N Hike does mountain bike day trips to Mowbray Valley for $45.

Places to Stay

Although it's sometimes perceived as an exclusive and expensive resort town, Port also

has a pretty good range of more affordable accommodation, from caravan parks and backpackers' hostels to holiday apartments and motels.

Almost all of the accommodation places vary their prices depending on the season. During the high season (June to October), not only are prices considerably higher but you'll probably need to make your reservations well in advance.

Caravan Parks Port Douglas has three caravan parks: the *Kulau Caravan Park*

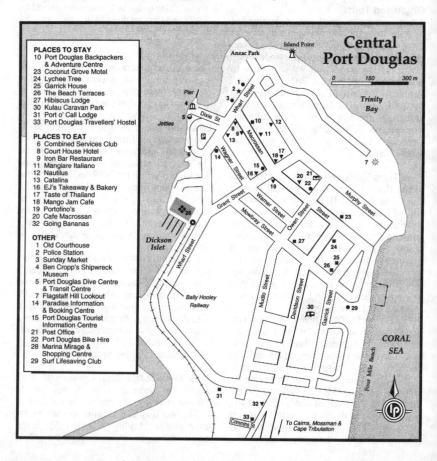

PLACES TO STAY
10 Port Douglas Backpackers
     & Adventure Centre
23 Coconut Grove Motel
24 Lychee Tree
25 Garrick House
26 The Beach Terraces
27 Hibiscus Lodge
30 Kulau Caravan Park
31 Port o' Call Lodge
33 Port Douglas Travellers' Hostel

PLACES TO EAT
6   Combined Services Club
8   Court House Hotel
9   Iron Bar Restaurant
11 Mangiare Italiano
12 Nautilus
13 Catalina
16 EJ's Takeaway & Bakery
17 Taste of Thailand
18 Mango Jam Cafe
19 Portofino's
20 Cafe Macrossan
32 Going Bananas

OTHER
1   Old Courthouse
2   Police Station
3   Sunday Market
4   Ben Cropp's Shipwreck
     Museum
5   Port Douglas Dive Centre
     & Transit Centre
7   Flagstaff Hill Lookout
14 Paradise Information
     & Booking Centre
15 Port Douglas Tourist
     Information Centre
21 Post Office
22 Port Douglas Bike Hire
28 Marina Mirage &
     Shopping Centre
29 Surf Lifesaving Club

Central Port Douglas

Island Point
Anzac Park
Trinity Bay
Pier
Dixie St
Jetties
Dickson Islet
Bally Hooley Railway
Wharf Street
Wagner Street
Grant Street
Mowbray Street
Macrossan
Warner Street
Owen Street
Street
Murphy Street
Mudlo Street
Davidson Street
Garrick Street
Four Mile Beach
CORAL SEA

Crimmins St
To Cairns, Mossman &
Cape Tribulation

(☎ 4099 5449), at 28 Davidson St, is the closest to the centre and a short walk from the beach. It has shady tent sites for $14 ($16 powered) and on-site cabins from $50.

About 1km further south, the *Pandanus Caravan Park* (☎ 4099 5944), at 111 Davidson St, has tent sites at $13 ($16 powered) and cabins from $45. This place is also well set up and has a pleasant swimming pool.

Almost 4km south of the centre is the *Four Mile Beach Caravan Park* (☎ 4098 5281). It has a beach frontage, and tent sites for $14, on-site vans for $35 and cabins for $52.

Hostels The *Port o' Call Lodge* (☎ 4099 5422) is in Port St about 1km south from the centre. It's a YHA associate and has modern four-bed units with private bathrooms at $17 per person ($18 for non-members). Private rooms are also available from about $72 a double. There's a pool, cooking facilities, a licensed restaurant and a free courtesy coach to and from Cairns every Monday, Wednesday and Saturday. You can also hook up with a couple of the tours which operate between Cairns and Cape Trib from here.

A good alternative and more central, although lacking in outdoor space and facilities, is the *Port Douglas Backpackers* (☎ 4099 4883), above the Adventure Centre at 8 Macrossan St. Dorm beds cost $15. It's a good place to stay if you are looking for work in Port.

The third hostel option is the Nomads *Port Douglas Traveller's Hostel* (☎ 4099 6200) on the corner of Davidson and Crimmins St, about 1km south of the centre. It's well kept with cooking and seating areas, garden and pool. Accommodation costs $18 ($17 VIP, YHA), while air-con doubles are $50. There's also a camping area at the rear ($11/14 for one/two people, $18 powered).

Motels Of the motels here, the *Coconut Grove Motel* (☎ 4099 5124), at 58 Macrossan St, is the among cheapest and the most central. Double rooms range from $55 to $75.

The *Central Hotel* (☎ 4099 5271), at 9 Macrossan St, also has motel units out the back, with singles/doubles at $55.

If you're after a more modern motel, try either the *Lazy Lizard Motor Inn* (☎ 4099 5900), at 121 Davidson St, or the *Rusty Pelican Motel* (☎ 4099 5266), next door at 123 Davidson St – both are very good and have rooms with all the mod-cons from around $79 to $95.

Holiday Flats & Apartments Moving up a level, Port has a huge range of apartments and holiday flats on offer. They all have a fairly similar range of features – full kitchen, laundry facilities, air-con, TV, phone and swimming pool, and some also have tennis courts. Rates for these places are generally cheaper by the week.

While most of these places are fairly expensive, there are a few affordable exceptions. *Hibiscus Lodge* (☎ 4099 5315), on the corner of Mowbray and Owen Sts, has three simple one-bedroom holiday units and three newer units. The price ranges from $60 to $120 a double, depending on the season, plus $10 for each extra person.

The well-located *Archipelago Studio Apartments* (☎ 4099 5387), at 72 Macrossan St, has small self-contained studio units which range from $75 to $145 a double (the more expensive ones with sea views).

The *Lychee Tree* (☎ 4099 5811) at 95 Davidson St has good one and two-bedroom units sleeping from one to five people at $85 to $105.

There are several good options in the area between the town centre and the beach – perhaps one of the best areas to stay in. *Garrick House* (☎ 4099 5322), at 11-13 Garrick St, has airy, modern one and two-bedroom apartments which range from $95 to $215.

The Mango Tree (☎ 4099 5677), at 91-93 Davidson St, is a friendly place with 19 bright and spacious apartments, and a tennis court. The apartments accommodate either four or six, and cost from $105 to $140, with extra adults from $6 to $15. There's a minimum stay of three nights.

The Beach Terraces (☎ 4099 5998), closer to the beach and the centre at 15 Garrick St, has recently renovated one, two and three-bedroom apartments ranging from $110 to $275.

The *Nimrod Apartments* (☎ 4099 3399), at 31 Nautilus St, in Four Mile Beach, is an impressive complex of 29 two and three-bedroom apartments. There is a tennis court for guests' use. Four Mile Beach is 4km south of the centre – good if you're after a little peace and quiet, but it's a disadvantage if you don't have your own car. The apartments range from $99 to $126.

The *Torresian Resort* (☎ 4099 5577), on Port Douglas Rd, has 180 two-storey town-house apartments, three swimming pools, tennis courts, a gymnasium, a kid's club and an hourly shuttle bus into town. There are one, two and three-bedroom apartments, and tariffs start from $175 a double plus $20 for each additional adult.

Resort Hotels At the top of the range, Port Douglas has two resort hotels. The *Radisson Reef Resort* (☎ 4099 5577) has standard hotel rooms and two-bedroom self-contained apartments. The standard rooms cost $140 a double, and the apartments are $225 for two plus $20 for each extra adult (maximum five). The family rate of $235 is good value as it covers two adults and two children, and includes breakfast.

The *Sheraton Mirage Port Douglas* (☎ 4099 5888), is in a league of its own. It rates as one of the best resort hotels in Australia, somehow managing to be over the top without being too ostentatious. It's set among tropical gardens, surrounded by its own 18 hole golf course and has an amazing, enormous saltwater swimming lagoon, complete with private beaches. (If you'd rather the real thing, it's a short stroll from the hotel to Four Mile Beach.) There are also nine tennis courts, six restaurants, a gymnasium, a sauna and freshwater swimming pools. Rooms range from $490 to $670 a night; two, three and four-bedroom villas range from $750 to $950. Even if you can't afford to stay here, at least

pop in and have a drink or a (discreet) swim and a look around.

Places to Eat
Considering the size of the place, Port Douglas has a surprisingly good array of cafes and restaurants. Although eating here isn't particularly cheap, a few places cater to budget travellers. Most of the eateries are along or near Macrossan St.

Cafes & Takeaways For breakfast, try *Cafe Macrossan* at 42 Macrossan St. It serves good cheap breakfasts, as well as lunches, snacks and dinner, when main courses range from $13 to $20.

For takeaways, there's a couple of places in Grant St near the corner of Macrossan St. *EJ's Takeaway & Bakery* does fish and chips and burgers, and the *Port Douglas Bakery* has pies, breads and pastries.

Pubs If you're after a pub meal, the *Court House Hotel* on the corner of Macrossan and Wharf Sts has an outdoor garden bistro with meals from $10; and the *Central Hotel* further up Macrossan St has reasonably good bistro meals.

An interesting alternative to the pubs is the *Combined Services Club* down on the waterfront near the marina. It's a great old tin and timber building with a balcony overlooking the water – very laid-back, and just the spot to watch the sun go down. Visitors are welcome, and the bistro meals, while pretty uninspiring, are good value at $8 to $12.

Restaurants The restaurant at the *Coconut Grove Motel*, near the intersection of Davidson and Macrossan Sts, is popular with the locals. It is good value and has live music on weekends.

The *Mango Jam Cafe*, at 24 Macrossan St is a funky, lively and very popular bar/restaurant which features live bands on Friday and Saturday nights. The menu offers gourmet pizzas from a wood-fired oven ($10), a great range of salads, pasta and a variety of other mains.

The relaxed *Mangiare Italiano* at 18 Macrossan St has pizzas ($10 to $12) and other mains from $12 to $15.

On Grant St behind the Commonwealth Bank near the Macrossan St corner, the BYO *Taste of Thailand* has a very modestly priced selection, with mains from $10 to $14. It's open in the evening only and does deliveries (☎ 4099 4384).

Portofinos, at 31 Macrossan St, is a casual and earthy licensed bistro with gourmet pizzas ($12 to $14), pastas ($10 to $12) and other mains, plus a good kid's menu. It's open for lunch and dinner.

The *Iron Bar Restaurant*, wedged between two pubs at 5 Macrossan St, has been decked out like an outback wool shed, with slab-timber furniture, bush dunnies and corrugated iron walls – it's fairly impressive and worth a visit. There's live music in the back bar most nights and it specialises in pasta and Aussie tucker, with main meals in the $15 to $22 range.

Catalina is a fairly formal, open-air restaurant on Wharf Street. It's open in the evening only, and seafood features heavily on the interesting menu. Main courses are around the $22 mark.

Port's best-known restaurant is the bizarre *Going Bananas* (☎ 4099 5400), at 87 Davidson St. The decor is almost beyond description – a sort of post-cyclone tropical forest look – and the service is often equally strange. The eclectic menu has main courses ranging from $22 to $30. There's a small bar and a good wine list, and it's open for dinner from Monday to Saturday – you'll need to book.

Nautilus (☎ 4099 5330), at 17 Murphy St (with another entrance on Macrossan St), is another local restaurant with a great reputation. It has a magical open-air setting under a canopy of tall palm trees and ferns – the perfect place if you're feeling romantic. It specialises in fresh seafood but you could also try King Island beef or spatchcock. Mains range from $24 to $30 and the wine list features good Australian wines. It opens nightly for dinner and bookings are advisable.

Entertainment

On the corner of Macrossan and Wharf Sts, the *Court House Hotel* usually has live bands appearing in the beer garden on Friday and Saturday nights and Sunday arvos (more often during the peak tourist season). Next to the pub is the *Iron Bar Restaurant*, which often has acoustic music in its back bar. Further up Macrossan St, the *Mango Jam Cafe* also features live music on weekends and is usually still firing when most other places have wound down for the night.

FJs Nightspot, upstairs at the Marina, is a disco/bar with a restored FJ Holden (a type of car) as its centrepiece. It has a pool table, pinball machines and a balcony overlooking the marina. It serves meals and has regular happy hours for cocktail drinkers. It is open daily from 11 am until 3 am.

The *Waterfront Bar & Bistro*, also in the Marina, is open every day from 10 am to 3 am, and has three bars, a disco and dance floor, and features live bands three nights a week. It also serves lunch and dinner. The small bar out on the balcony is a good place to sit and watch the boats coming back from the reef.

The bar at *Going Bananas* is a popular watering hole, as is the *Combined Services Club* down on the waterfront. If you'd rather drink in more opulent surrounds, the bars at the *Sheraton Mirage Resort* are open to non-guests.

It's also worth asking at the Jungle Bookshop or one of the information centres about the Karnak Playhouse, an amphitheatre set in the Daintree rainforest north-west of Mossman. It stages regular productions and also has a sound and light show. See the Mossman to Daintree section for details.

Getting There & Away

Air It comes as a surprise to some people that Port Douglas doesn't have its own airport, or even an airstrip. It's about an hour by road to Cairns' international airport. Many places to stay provide pick-up services, and Coral Coaches (☎ 4098 2600) has around 15 daily services (between 6 am and 9.15 pm) between the airport and Port Douglas. The one-way fare is $22.

Bus Coral Coaches (☎ 4098 2600) is a Mossman-based bus company which covers the Cairns to Cooktown coastal route via Port Douglas, Mossman, Daintree, Cape Tribulation and Bloomfield. Bookings and departures in Port Douglas are from the Port Douglas Transit Centre.

Coral Coaches has about eight buses a day between Cairns and Port Douglas (1½ hours, $16); about 13 buses a day from Port Douglas to Mossman ($6); twice daily buses to Daintree village ($12) and Cape Trib (2½ hours, $20); and buses to Cooktown via the (coastal) Bloomfield Track on Tuesday, Thursday and Saturday (about six hours, $45). Every Wednesday, Friday and Sunday, they go from Cairns to Cooktown via the inland road (about 5½ hours, $47), and on Friday to Weipa (12½ hours, $220).

Boat There's a daily *Quicksilver* fast catamaran service from Port Douglas to Cairns and back. The trip takes 1½ hours, departing from Cairns at 8 am and from Port Douglas at 5.30 pm, and the fare is $20/30 one-way/return. The *Quicksilver* booking office (☎ 4099 5500) in Port Douglas is in the Marina Mirage complex.

Getting Around

Bus The Port Douglas Bus Service runs in a continuous loop from the Rainforest Habitat (near the Captain Cook Hwy turn-off) to the Marina, stopping at all the major places to stay. It operates daily from 7.30 am until midnight, and you can either wait at a designated stop or flag the driver down. One-way fares cost from $1.50 to $2, or you can buy a weekly ticket for $12.

Train The Bally Hooley railway is a small steam train that shuttles between the marina, the Radisson Reef Hotel and St Crispins station (at the southern end of the golf course). It operates daily, roughly every hour between 9 am and 5 pm, and return tickets cost $6 ($2 children).

Car Rental Avis (☎ 4099 4331), National (☎ 4099 4652) and Budget (☎ 4099 4690) all have offices in Port Douglas, and all have a wide range of cars and 4WDs available. Cheaper local operators include Network (☎ 4099 5111) and Crocodile Car Rentals (☎ 4099 555), who specialise in 4WD hire. Both have Suzuki Sierra soft-tops at $69 a day on sealed roads or $99 a day on unsealed roads, and Suzuki Vitara hard-tops at $79 a day on sealed roads or $109 a day on unsealed roads.

Bicycle Port is very compact, and the best way to get around is by bike. Port Douglas Bike Hire, at 40 Macrossan St, and Aussie Bike Hire (☎ 4099 4444), at 79 Davidson St, both hire good bikes for $10 a day, with helmets and locks provided.

For scooter hire contact Port Scooter Hire on ☎ 4099 3077.

Taxi To book a taxi call Port Douglas Taxis on ☎ 4099 5345.

MOSSMAN
pop 1800

Mossman is at the centre of Queensland's most northerly sugar-growing district, and is also a centre for tropical fruit growing. It's an unpretentious working town, largely unaffected by the frenzied tourist activity which surrounds and passes through it.

Although it's a fairly pleasant little place, it is of little interest in its own right; the main attraction here is the beautiful Mossman Gorge, 5km west of the town centre.

Mossman Gorge

The Mossman Gorge is one of this area's most popular day trip destinations and, while it's a lovely spot, it can get pretty crowded here at the height of the tourist season.

From the main car park, there are walking trails leading to various points of interest. Bring your togs – there are some great swimming holes here, with crystal clear water tumbling over giant boulders, all shaded by the rainforest. Beyond the swimming spots, a suspension bridge takes you across the river to a 2.4km circuit trail through the rainforest. Back at the car park, there are toilets and picnic facilities.

The Gorge is in the southern section of the Daintree National Park. The upper reaches of the park are also accessible, but this area is only suitable for fit and experienced bushwalkers, and you need to be self-sufficient if you want to camp overnight.

There's a ranger's office (☎ 4098 2188) in the Mt Demi plaza on the corner of Front and Johnston Sts, Mossman (near the main turn-off to the Gorge). Here permits are issued for overnight bush camping in the national park ($3.50 per person), and a pamphlet and map are available to guide you through the park.

Coral Coaches (☎ 4098 2600) runs regular bus services from Mossman and Port Douglas out to the Gorge and back, and can pick you up from wherever you're staying. The return fare is $6 from Mossman or $14 from Port Douglas.

Other Attractions

Mossman has a good swimming pool behind the caravan park. The **Mossman Golf Club**, alongside the turn-off to Newell Beach 4km north of town, is quite a good country course and welcomes visitors.

As you drive through Mossman, keep your eyes open for a house on the southern approach to the centre. The front fence is lined with a colourful collection of handmade wooden wind-toys.

Nature Guide Safari Tours (☎ 4098 2206) is an Aboriginal tour company doing informative tours of the local area.

Places to Stay

There are no designated camping grounds at the Gorge.

The *Mossman Bicentennial Caravan Park* (☎ 4098 1922), on Foxton Ave at the northern end of Mossman, has tent sites for $10 and on-site vans for $25 a double. The town swimming pool and the Mossman River are right beside the park.

The old *Exchange Hotel* (☎ 4098 1410), at 2 Front St, in the centre of town, is a classic Aussie pub with the usual basic accommodation.

If you can afford a little more, the best place to stay is at the *White Cockatoo Cabins* (☎ 4098 2222), at 9 Alchera Drive (the main road), 1km south of the centre. The timber cabins are straightforward but spacious, with their own bathroom, fully equipped kitchen, air-con, TV and a phone. Prices vary seasonally, ranging from $60 to $75, plus another $10 for each extra person.

Another option is the *Demi View Motel* (☎ 4098 1277), at 41 Front St, an oldish budget motel with clean rooms at $50/60.

Places to Eat

Temptations, a coffee lounge and takeaway on Front St opposite the Royal Hotel, has a good range of sandwiches, hot dogs, cakes and ice-cream sundaes.

The Exchange Hotel on the corner of Front and Mill Sts has the large *Martin's Bar & Chargrill* where you can get a decent pub meal for around $9 to $12.

About 1.5km south of the centre is *Lynne's Restaurant*, a laid-back little pizza and pasta joint with dine-in and takeaway sections. It's a friendly place and reasonably priced, and opens nightly for dinner.

Getting There & Away

Coral Coaches (☎ 4098 2600), based at 37 Front St, runs regular daily bus services to and from Port Douglas ($6), Cairns ($18), Newell Beach ($8) and Wonga Beach ($8), Daintree ($10), Cape Tribulation ($19) and Cooktown ($44), among other places.

MOSSMAN TO MT MOLLOY

Just south of Mossman is the turn-off to Mt Molloy, which links up with the inland route to Cooktown. For 33km this road climbs and winds through some very pretty and productive farmlands (mainly tropical fruit and cattle farms). Along the early sections of the route are two sensational lookout points – on a clear day it's worth pulling over to take advantage of this panoramic photo opportunity of the Mossman valley, with the deep blue sea laid out in the distance.

At Julatten, about 20km from the turn-off, *Kingfisher Park* (☎ 4094 1263), is a birdwatchers' lodge and private sanctuary. The lodge has a very serene garden setting, and a good range of accommodation. There are modern self-contained villas costing $90 a double plus $20 for each extra person (up to six); self-contained units at $75/85; a bunkhouse (two beds per room) costing $20 per person; and camp sites at $17 ($19 powered). Campers and bunkers share communal kitchen facilities.

MOSSMAN TO DAINTREE

It's another 36km north from Mossman to the village of Daintree. The road passes through the cane fields and farms, with turn-offs en route to Newell Beach, Wonga Beach and Cape Tribulation. If you have a little time, there are a few potentially interesting detours along here – exotic fruit farms, a spectacular open-air theatre and some accommodation possibilities.

A couple of kilometres north of Mossman you'll see the turn-off to *Silky Oaks Lodge* (☎ 4098 1666, reservations ☎ 13 2469). Owned by P&O Resorts, it's one of the area's most upmarket nature retreats. Set in the thick of the rainforest, beside the Mossman River, the lodge has 60 individual timber chalets, restaurant and bar, a pool, a tennis court, a boutique and full conference facilities. The daily activities program includes cruises along the Daintree River, guided walks along nature trails, canoe trips and slide shows. The chalets are very comfortably set up, with bathroom, a mini-bar, air-con and ceiling fan. To help city slickers resist techno-temptation, there are no phones or TVs in the rooms. The chalets cost $375 a night, which includes transfers from Port Douglas.

The lodge's *Treehouse Restaurant*, an all-timber open-sided affair, has a great outlook over the Mossman River. Main meals cost around $15 at lunch time and from $20 to $25 at dinner.

At Miallo, about 8km north-west of Mossman, is the **Karnak Playhouse** (☎ 4098 8111) (it's signposted off the main highway). This amphitheatre has a magical setting – the open-air seats look down onto a timber stage set beside a small lake, and the whole set-up is surrounded by a backdrop of rainforest-covered hills. The main attraction here is the high-tech Creations laser show, which features whiz-bang effects and includes a performance by Aboriginal children.

The shows are on Wednesday and Saturday and cost $25 ($12.50 children), or $75 ($40) including dinner and transfer from Port Douglas. Another novelty and great fun are the regular theme dinners held during the full moon, where guests dress according to the theme, and the menu is also matched. The cost is $75. Karnak is open from April/May to November, and bookings are essential.

The turn-off to **Wonga Beach** is 22km north of Mossman. About 1km after this road is the turn-off to the *Pinnacle Village Holiday Park* (☎ 4098 7566), one of the best caravan and camping parks in the area. It has a great setting – it's well-grassed with huge old trees providing plenty of shade, and fronts a long, sandy beach. It has all the usual facilities including a kiosk, pool and the charming *Joy Bell Restaurant* in old, converted railway carriages. Tent sites cost $10, cabins are $38, en suite units are $48 and self-contained villas with air-con are $65. All these prices are for two people; each extra adult costs $5.

Just north of the Wonga Beach turn-off is **Wonga Beach Trail Rides** (☎ 4098 7583). Every day at 3 pm, 2½-hour horse rides are organised through the surrounding cane fields, rainforest and beaches. No more than eight people can participate, so it's worth booking. Trail rides cost $45 per person, or $55 with return transport from Port Douglas.

Further on is the turn-off to the Daintree River ferry crossing and Cape Tribulation; continue straight on for another 11km to get to Daintree village.

DAINTREE

Daintree is a small village on the banks of the Daintree River that marks the end of the sealed highway to the north. Originally established as a logging town, where timber cutters concentrated on the prized red cedar trees that were once common in the area, it is now a centre for cruises along the mighty Daintree River.

A recent influx of tourists has livened up this backwater somewhat, and several B&Bs and a stylish resort have opened in recent years to cater for the added demand.

Things to See & Do

In the centre of the village, the **Timber Museum, Gallery & Shop** is worth a visit. Out the back there's a timber workshop where you can watch local craftsmen at work; the museum houses a large collection of old woodworking tools; and if you're in buying mode, there's a gallery with some expensive but beautifully crafted pieces on sale.

Fine Feather Tours (☎ 4098 3103) specialises in birdwatching and takes people out on bird-banding expeditions. It runs birdwatching tours of the rainforests every

Wet Tropics World Heritage Area

Most of Australia was covered in rainforest 50 million years ago, but by the time Europeans arrived only about 1% was left. Today, logging and clearing for farms have reduced that figure to less than 0.3% – about 20,000 sq km. More than half of this, and nearly all the tropical rainforest, is in Queensland.

The biggest area of virgin rainforest is called the Greater Daintree and covers the ranges from south of Mossman up to Cooktown.

Throughout the 1980s a series of battles over the future of the forests was waged between conservationists on one side, and the timber industry and the Queensland government on the other. Conservationists argued that, apart from its value as natural habitat, this region has special value as a storehouse of genetic diversity. The timber industry's case, aside from job losses, was that only a small percentage of the rainforest was used for timber; that extraction is selective and therefore not destructive; and that time is left for the forest to regenerate before being logged again.

In 1983 the controversial Bloomfield Track, which was bulldozed through pristine forest from Cape Tribulation to the Bloomfield River, attracted international attention to the fight to save the Daintree rainforests. The greenies lost that battle, but the publicity generated by the blockade indirectly led to the Federal government's moves in 1987 to nominate Queensland's wet tropical rainforests for World Heritage listing. Despite strenuous resistance by the Queensland timber industry and state government, the area was listed in 1988; one of the key outcomes was a total ban on commercial logging in the area.

Stretching from Townsville to Cooktown, the Wet Tropics World Heritage Area covers 900,000 hectares of the coast and hinterland and includes the Atherton Tableland, Mission Beach, Mossman Gorge, Jourama Falls, Mt Spec and the Daintree-Cape Tribulation area. The scenery is diverse and spectacular, ranging from coastal mangroves and eucalypt forests to some of the oldest rainforests in the world.

Despite the past discord, a survey in 1993 found that 80% of north Queenslanders support the Wet Tropics designation. The turnaround can be partially attributed to the buzzword of the 1990s, and north Queensland's green gold mine – ecotourism. With reef and rainforest-related tourism now easily eclipsing sugar production as the Far North's biggest industry, the rainforests have become a vital part of the area's livelihood. The challenge now is to learn how to manage and minimise the environmental impact of the enormous growth in tourism and population.

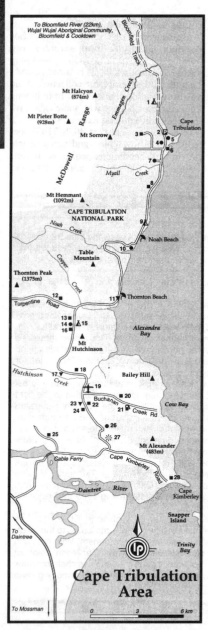

Cape Tribulation Area

PLACES TO STAY
1 Pilgrim Sands Holiday Park
3 Cape Trib Retreat
6 PK's Jungle Village
8 Coconut Beach Rainforest Resort
9 Noah Beach Camping Area
12 Heritage Lodge
13 Deep Forest Lodge
14 Lync-Haven
15 Rainforest Camp
17 Crocodylus Village
18 Daintree Wilderness Camp
19 Cow Bay Hotel
24 Rainforest Retreat
25 Daintree Manor B&B
28 Club Daintree

PLACES TO EAT
11 Cafe on Sea Kiosk
23 Latitudes 16.12°

OTHER
2 Cape Tribulation Parking Area
4 Bat House
5 Ranger station
7 Cape Trib Store
10 Marrdja Botanical Walk
14 Wundu Trailrides
17 Daintree Ice-Cream Company
19 Cow Bay Airstrip
21 Matt Lock's Service Station & General Store
26 Daintree Rainforest Environmental Centre
27 Alexandra Range Lookout

day except Saturday, departing at 7 am and returning at 1 pm, costing $95 per person, which includes brunch and pick-up from your accommodation.

Organised Tours

There are a number of river tour operators spread along the Daintree between the village and the ferry crossing. You can book a cruise direct with the operators, or through booking agents everywhere – there are at least four agents in Daintree village. It's certainly a worthwhile activity: birdlife is prolific, particularly early in the morning, and in the cooler months (April to September) croc sightings are common, especially on sunny days when the tide is low, as they love to sun themselves on the exposed banks.

There are a number of larger commercial operators, such as Daintree Rainforest River Trains (☎ 4090 7676) (based beside the ferry crossing to Cape Trib). The low-key Daintree River Cruise Centre (☎ 4098 6115), 4km north-west of the ferry turn-off on the Mossman to Daintree road, has three boats taking from 30 to 52 passengers. The trips take one hour, cost $10 and depart six times daily. A longer tour (1½ hours) departs daily at 11.10 am and costs $15.

Several operators offer tours for smaller groups. Chris Dahlberg's Specialised River Tours (☎ 4098 6233), based at the Red Mill B&B in Daintree village, takes groups of up to 12 people; Chris is an enthusiastic bird-watcher and knowledgeable guide. His two-hour trips depart at 6.30 am in winter and 6 am in summer, and cost $25.

Electric Boat Cruises (☎ 1800 686 103) take groups of 12 people in very quiet elec-tric-powered boats for 1½-hour cruises at $25 including breakfast, or one-hour cruises throughout the day ($15).

Far North River Safaris (☎ 4098 6120) takes only four passengers, as does On the Daintree (☎ 4090 7638). The latter does 2½-hour early morning cruises from the crossing for $25, and at other times on demand.

Places to Stay

Caravan Park The *Daintree Riverview Caravan Park* (☎ 4098 6119) is well located in the heart of the village, and close to the river and jetty. Grassy tent sites are $12, although there isn't much shade around. On-site cabins are $32 a double, or $34 with air-con.

B&Bs There are a few B&Bs in Daintree. The excellent *Red Mill House* (☎ 4098 6233) in the centre of town has three com-fortable rooms with shared bathroom facilities. The house is a breezy two-storey Queenslander, set in lovely gardens which are great for birdwatching; there is also a pool. The tariff is $25/55 for singles/

doubles, and includes a delicious breakfast on the balcony. The owners of this place also run Chris Dahlberg's Specialised River Tours – see the earlier Daintree River Tours section for details.

Views of the Daintree (☎ 4098 6118), on Stewart Creek Rd, is a modern homestead with great views over the big river. There are two double rooms, one in the main house and one in a separate section. Both have en suites, and there's a timber deck where you can enjoy the sensational views. The cost is $75 a double, including breakfast.

Billirene B&B (☎ 4098 6199), in the centre beside the information centre, is a cosy family home with two guest rooms with private bathrooms. It has an attractive garden with a swimming pool, a huge fish pond and a variety of wildlife wandering round. The cost is $65 a double.

Weroona B&B (☎ 4098 6198), 2 Douglas St, is a small cabin, set behind the main house, with air-con, its own bathroom, fridge and microwave. Doubles cost $65. There's also a small pool. Next door, *Dain-tree Cottage* is self-contained and fully furnished, and can accommodate five people at $75 for the whole cottage.

Resorts Set in the thick of the rainforest 3km south of the village is the impressive *Daintree Eco Lodge* (☎ 4098 6100). The resort has 15 very stylish timber cabins, all built on stilts so they look out onto the rain-forest canopy. Inside, the cabins have all the mod-cons like air-con, TV, phone and a minibar. The resort has a swimming pool, a bar and an excellent restaurant – see Places to Eat below. The tariff is $308/330 for singles/doubles, which includes breakfast and transfers from Cairns or Port Douglas. It doesn't cater for children under 10 years of age.

Places to Eat

There are a couple of eateries in the centre of the village. *Jacanas Restaurant*, a casual cafe and takeaway with an open-air section, serves sandwiches, burgers and snacks, and main meals.

Cassowaries – the Vital Link

The cassowary, an enormous flightless bird, was once common in the rainforests of north Queensland. Adult cassowaries probably have no natural enemies, but their eggs and chicks are vulnerable to predation by dogs and wild pigs. Cassowaries are also frequently hit by cars – drive slowly and keep your eyes peeled when driving through rainforest.

In 1993 a scientific report estimated that only 54 adult cassowaries remained in the area north of the Daintree River. The most pressing threat to the birds' survival is habitat destruction, and cassowary numbers appear to be in decline. The report emphasised the vital role played by the cassowary in rainforest ecology. It is perhaps the only 'dispersal agent' for some 70 species of plants in the rainforest, as well as the main dispersal agent for another 30 species. Cassowaries carry out this crucial role by swallowing fruits and berries whole – the seeds are later deposited in their dung elsewhere in the forest.

Mission Beach, south of Cairns, also has a dwindling population of cassowaries. Mission Beach is now the home of C4 (the Consultative Committee for Cassowary Conservation), which is dedicated to gathering information on the birds and proposing a management plan. It has an office beside the Mission Beach Information Centre – drop in and pay them a visit when you're in town.

If you are lucky enough to see a cassowary in the forest, take care – people are sometimes chased and attacked by these birds.

Nearby is the *Daintree Village Coffee Shop*, where you can get anything from barra and chips ($10) to prawn and avocado salad ($13).

Across the road, the *Big Barramundi*, beside a Timber Museum, has an outdoor eating area and serves sandwiches, hot dogs and barra-burgers. The barbecued barramundi with a tropical salad ($12) is delicious.

The *Daintree Tea House*, at Barratt Creek, 3km south of Daintree, is an old-fashioned timber tea room in a peaceful setting which serves open sandwiches, morning and after-noon teas, seafood dishes and salads. It is open from 10 am to 6.30 pm.

Baaru House (☎ 4098 6100), the restaurant at the Eco Lodge 3km south of Daintree, is open to guests and the public for breakfast, lunch and dinner. It serves lunches like barramundi or burgers from $6 to $11; and at night you have a choice of entrées and mains ($17 to $21). Vegetarian meals are also available.

Getting There & Away

Coral Coaches (☎ 4098 2600) has a twice-daily bus service from Cairns to Cape Tribulation which will detour to Daintree on request. The one-way fare is $22 – ring to check times and make reservations.

Many of the river cruise operators can pick you up from your accommodation.

CAPE TRIBULATION AREA

Cape Tribulation is famed for its superb scenery, with long beaches stretching north and south and a backdrop of rugged, forest-covered mountains. It's an incredibly beautiful stretch of coast, and is one of the few places in Australia where tropical rainforest meets the sea.

It has long held a reputation as one of the Far North's best spots for those who want to get away from it all, although things have changed somewhat in the last decade. With the booming tourism industry and continuing improvements to the access roads, Cape Trib has become one of the most popular day trips from Port Douglas and Cairns. Whereas once you'd pass the occasional 4WD or battered old station wagon, nowadays there's a steady stream of tour operators and independent visitors heading up to the area.

Most of this region is national park – there aren't any towns, just a scattering of places to stay, general stores, camping grounds and the like.

After crossing the Daintree River by ferry, it's another 34km of mostly paved road, with a few hills and creek crossings, to Cape Tribulation. Most of the road is sealed and, unless there has been exceptionally heavy rain, conventional vehicles can easily make it to Cape Trib.

Remember that this is rainforest – you'll need mosquito repellent and wet weather gear may come in very handy. Approaching Cape Trib from the south, the last bank is at Mossman. You can get fuel at two or three places between Mossman and Cooktown by this coastal route.

History

Cape Tribulation was named by Captain Cook, since it was a little north of here that his barque, the *Endeavour*, struck an offshore reef. Mt Sorrow was also named by Cook.

Because of its mountainous terrain, the area north of the Daintree is one of the few areas in Queensland that was never cleared for agriculture. The first European to settle permanently was Andrew Mason, father of the present owner of the Cape Trib Store, who started building a house beside Myall Creek 1928. During WWII a number of land army women came to the area to help grow food for the war effort. After the war, sawmilling and then cattle grazing became the area's main sources of income.

The first ferry service across the Daintree River began in 1956. By the 1970s, a trickle of visitors had started to arrive, and Cape Trib started to gain a reputation for its remote beauty. The area became something of a hippie outpost, with settlements like the alternative Cedar Bay community in the rainforests north of Cape Trib. By the 1980s the trickle had developed into a steady stream.

In 1981 recognition of the unique natural values of this area led to the declaration of the Cape Tribulation National Park. The park stretches from the Daintree River to the Bloomfield River, with the mountains of the McDowell Range providing the western boundary. As part of the Wet Tropics area, Cape Trib was also granted World Heritage listing in 1988.

Cape Trib's rainforests, dry woodlands and coastal mangroves are home to a host of unique flora and fauna, including rare and threatened species such as Bennett's tree kangaroo. Birdlife is abundant, especially along rainforest edges.

Information

There isn't an official information centre here, although the Bat House and the Daintree Rainforest Environmental Centre are both good sources of info on the rainforests – see the Things to See & Do section.

There's a ranger station (☎ 4098 0052), on the main road just before the turn-off to Cape Trib beach. It's staffed only between 9 and 11 am; for information at other times, contact the Department of Environment office at Mossman on ☎ 4098 2188.

Most of the places to stay are also very helpful, and can book tours and give general advice.

Money The Cow Bay Hotel has EFTPOS facilities, but apart from that there are no banking facilities here. The closest banks are in Mossman.

Fuel & Supplies Matt Lock's Cow Bay Service Station and general store (☎ 4098 9127) is halfway along Buchanan Creek Rd (the road to Cow Bay). It is open daily from 7.30 am to 6 pm, and sells fuel (diesel, super and unleaded), fishing tackle, bait and general groceries.

The Rainforest Camp (☎ 4098 9015), 5km north of the Cow Bay turn-off, sells fuel (diesel, unleaded, super and outboard) and has a small general store.

The Cape Trib Store (☎ 4098 0070), just off the main road about 1.5km south of the Cape, is open every day from 8.30 am to 5 pm. It sells a reasonably good range of groceries, takeaway meals, film and booze, and also sells fuel (diesel, unleaded and super). There are some interesting photos and tidbits of information up on the walls inside this place, and a swimming hole near the store is open to the general public during daylight hours.

Things to See & Do

About 3km past the Daintree River crossing, Cape Kimberley Rd turns off the main road and heads east down to **Cape Kimberley beach**, near the estuary of the Daintree River. There are boat trip and sea kayaking expeditions out to **Snapper Island**, which is just off shore from the Cape. The island has a national parks camp site at West Point.

About 9km from the ferry, just after you cross the spectacular **Heights of Alexandra Range**, is the **Alexandra Range Lookout**, with panoramic views out over the Daintree River estuary and the national park.

Further on is the **Daintree Rainforest Environmental Centre**. This is a great place to learn more about rainforests. There's a self-guided boardwalk with informative signboards, an information centre with rainforest displays, and a small theatre that screens a choice of six videos. It's open daily from 9 am to 5 pm; entry is $8 ($6 children).

About 12km from the ferry you reach Buchanan Creek Rd, which is the turn-off

for **Cow Bay** (5.5km) and the Crocodylus Village hostel.

After crossing Hutchinson Creek the road swings sharply inland, and on the left here is the **Daintree Ice-Cream Company**, which sells sensational home-made ice creams made from exotic fruits grown locally – try the chocolate pudding fruit flavour! The farm is open Sunday to Friday from 12 noon to 5 pm.

Further on, the road strikes the shore at **Thornton Beach**. The **Marrdja Botanical Walk**, across Noah Creek, is an interesting 800m boardwalk which follows the creek through the rainforest. The walk is suitable for the disabled, there are information signboards along the way, and the final section is through mangroves. At the north end of Noah Beach there's a very pleasant **picnic ground** with tables.

The **Bat House**, opposite PK's Jungle Village, is a small rainforest information and education centre, open daily from 11.30 am to 3.30 pm. This place is run by volunteers from AUSTROP, a local conservation organisation which operates a research station, and your $2 donation goes towards the running of the station. As the name suggests, it's also a nursery for fruit bats.

The car park at **Cape Tribulation** is usually fairly crowded with tour buses and 4WDs. The beach on the north side of the cape is a beautiful stretch of white sand, although dramatic tidal changes mean it's a long walk out to the water at low tide. Near the car park is a **Wet Tropics information board** which describes many of the plants and animals in the area, and a 350m **walking trail** follows the Cape south to a timber boardwalk and lookout point (suitable for disabled). There's also a picnic area here with toilets and water.

The road heading north becomes progressively rougher after Cape Tribulation itself. With care, conventional vehicles can make it another 5km to the Emmagen Creek crossing – despite a sign saying '4WD Vehicles Only Past This Point' about 3km past the Cape. Just before you reach Emmagen Creek, the road passes a huge strangler fig.

From beside the tree, a walking path leads down to a pretty crescent-shaped beach.

The creek crossing is 100m further on. If you feel like a swim, park here and follow the creek upstream for about 400m, and you'll come to two deep swimming holes and a sandy 'beach'. Don't go downstream; there may be crocs.

Activities
If you want to do more than relax on the beach, there's a good range of activities on offer up here including reef trips, fishing, horse riding and guided bushwalks.

Swimming If you are heading for the beach, remember that deadly sea wasps are a hazard between October and April. Seek local advice before swimming.

Saltwater crocodiles also inhabit the mangroves, creeks and estuaries, so avoid swimming or wading where creeks or rivers meet the sea.

Guided Walks Paul Mason's Cape Trib Guided Rainforest Walks (☎ 4098 0070), based at the Cape Trib Store, takes people on informative guided walks along private trails through the forest. Its day walk takes about four hours and covers 4 to 5km, and the night walk takes 2½ hours and covers around 2km. Either walk costs $20 per person. Paul advises booking ahead if you want to do the night walk during the busy season (July to October). You can book at the store or wherever you're staying.

Reef Trips At least three Cairns boat operators offering trips out to the Great Barrier Reef depart from Cape Trib Beach.

Jungle Dive (☎ 4031 0030) departs daily and the cost is $68 which includes lunch and snorkelling gear. Certified divers can do one/two dives for $30/45.

The *Taipan Lady* (☎ 4031 1588) is a large sailing catamaran. It departs every day and costs $59 ($49 children). Again, lunch and snorkelling gear are included and introductory ($45) and one/two certified dives ($35/50) are available.

The third operator is *Rum Runner* (☎ 1800 686 444), which offers day trips for $65, and as with the other boats, introductory ($50) and certified dives ($35/60) are available.

River Cruises Cooper Creek Wilderness (☎ 4098 9126), based at the Thornton Beach Kiosk, takes groups of up to 20 on a one-hour morning cruise up the Cooper Creek, which meets the ocean a little way south of the kiosk. The cruise costs $10 ($6 children), or $20/12 with lunch. Departure times depend on the tides – ring the kiosk to check. It also does 1½-hour night cruises at 6.30 pm three times a week.

Horse Riding Wundu Trailrides (☎ 4098 9156), on the main road about 5km north of the Cow Bay turn-off, has three-hour horse-trail rides departing from here twice daily. You ride through local plantations to a water hole, have a swim and finish up with a cuppa at Lync-Haven. The rides cost $39 per person.

You can also go horse riding with PK's Jungle Village – see Places to Stay.

Joy Flights Cow Bay Air Services (☎ 4098 9153), based at the airstrip just north of the Cow Bay turn-off, offers joy flights in a light plane over Cape Trib and the reef from $40 per person.

Places to Stay – Daintree River to Cape Trib
Camping & Cabins At Cape Kimberley beach, *Club Daintree* (☎ 4090 7500) is a beachfront camping park with camp sites for $8 per person and four-share cabins for $198 a night. The resort has a casual and inexpensive restaurant, a small pool and a pool table, and offers boat trips to Snapper Island, day trips to Cooktown and guided walks. Cape Kimberley is on the lowlands of the Daintree River estuary, so mosquitoes are sometimes a problem here.

There are also *national parks camp sites* on Snapper Island, just offshore from Cape Kimberley. There are toilets, showers and

Things That Go 'Munch' in the Night

Crocodylus Village is one of the most popular backpackers' hostels on the Queensland coast. Accommodation is in large, airy canvas cabins where you really feel you're in the heart of the rainforest – complete with bird calls and visits from insects and other small animals. Bandicoots are frequent visitors to the dining area at night, hopping from table to table and feasting on crumbs underneath.

Small, friendly native bush rats called melomys are also common visitors. Melomys aren't disease-carrying, but have an acute sense of smell and sharp teeth – and therefore pose another threat to the unsuspecting backpacker. If you leave *any* food in your luggage, no matter how well wrapped up or sealed it is, chances are a melomys will pay you a visit and chew its way through to the food. This can be an expensive experience – one unlucky traveller wrote to tell how her new Gore-Tex jacket was ruined by hungry melomys. It can also make you unpopular with everyone else in the dorm, as these chewing machines aren't very discriminating once they sniff out a meal. The only answer is to stick to Crocodylus' golden rule – no food anywhere in the dorms. Unless, that is, you prefer your luggage ventilated.

water on the island, but wood fires are banned so you'll need a fuel stove. Sites for up to six people are $3.50 per person per night. You can either get a permit from the Department of Environment office in Mossman (☎ 4098 2188) or self-register when you arrive.

About 5km north of the Cow Bay turn-off is *Lync-Haven* (☎ 4098 9155), a 16-hectare property with walking trails and plenty of wildlife. There are tent sites at $5 person and a self-contained six-berth cabin which costs $85 a double plus $10 for each

extra person. There is a kiosk and cafe here (see Places to Eat).

A little way north, on the opposite side of the road, is the *Rainforest Camp* (☎ 4098 9015), a budget camping ground on cleared land behind a general store and petrol station. There isn't much shade for campers and the facilities are fairly basic. Camping here costs $5 per person, and there are on-site vans for $40.

Further north at Noah Beach there's the national parks *Noah Beach Camping Area*, with 16 good, shady sites set 100m back from the beach. There are toilets and water is available. It's a self-registration site, with sites costing $3.50 per person per night for up to six people. Permits can be booked through the rangers at Cape Trib (☎ 4098 0052).

Hostels *Crocodylus Village* (☎ 4098 9166) is a YHA-associate hostel 2.5km off the main Cape Trib road, down Buchanan Creek Rd. It is set in the rainforest and has spacious, elevated canvas cabins. Nightly costs in the 16 to 20-bed dorms are $15 ($16 for non-members). There are also cabins with a double bed, six bunks and bathrooms – these cost $50 a double plus $10 for each extra person. There's a swimming pool, a bar and a small cafe that serves good breakfasts, lunches and dinners. The meals are cheap, healthy and hearty, and vegetarians are well catered for. You can hire bikes and the hostel vehicle runs guests to and from Cow Bay beach. The hostel also organises quite a few activities, including informative guided walks through the forests each morning and evening, half-day horse rides ($39), a three-hour sunrise paddletrek ($35), and a two-day sea-kayak trip to Snapper Island ($159 with everything supplied).

Hotels & Motels Back on the Cape Trib road, just south of the Cow Bay turn-off, is the modern *Cow Bay Hotel* (☎ 4098 9011), which has modern motel units with air-con at $60/65 for singles/doubles.

Across the road is the *Rainforest Retreat* (☎ 4098 9101), with spacious motel-style units with cooking facilities are from $70 or $90 for a family unit. This is a relaxed little place with a swimming pool.

Self-Contained Units About 5km north of the Cow Bay turn-off, the *Deep Forest Lodge* (☎ 4098 9162) has two motel-style units with kitchen facilities which can sleep up to four people (although they're better for two). The units cost $100 a night.

Lodges & B&Bs About 1km north of the ferry crossing is the *Daintree Manor B&B* (☎ 4090 7041) on Forest Creek Rd. En suite rooms in this elevated Queenslander go for $65/85.

About 1km north of the Cow Bay turn-off is the *Daintree Wilderness Lodge* (☎ 4098 9105), a small and quiet resort built in the heart of the rainforest. There are 10 timber bungalows, all linked by timber boardwalks. The bungalows are bright and modern, with ceiling fans and their own bathroom, and the tariff is $160 a double plus $30 for each extra person, which includes breakfast.

Turpentine Rd runs inland near Thornton Beach. About 2km along is the secluded *Heritage Lodge* (☎ 4098 9138), a small, low-key resort with comfortable timber cabins, a pool and a wonderful swimming hole on Cooper Creek. The restaurant has a small but varied menu, with Thai curries, vegetarian dishes, fresh fish and steaks ranging from $17 to $20. The nightly tariff is $155 a double including breakfast. Ask about the two-hour hike up to Alexandra Falls from here.

Places to Stay – Cape Trib
Camping & Cabins About 2km north of Cape Trib is the *Pilgrim Sands Holiday Park* (☎ 4098 0030). This camping ground has a great setting in the thick of the forest, and a short path leads down to a lovely secluded beach. The tent sites are well shaded and close to the beach, and cost $13. It also has self-contained two-bedroom units that sleep up to five and cost $72 a double plus $12 for each extra adult; and a smaller cabin

that sleeps up to four people and costs $53 a double plus $9.50 for extras (this cabin doesn't have its own bathroom). Bed linen is included in the price, and there is a minimum two-night stay in the units and cabin. Note that Pilgrim Sands closes for the Wet, from November until Easter.

Hostels *PK's Jungle Village* (☎ 4098 0040) is a very well set up backpackers' hostel, with comfortable log cabins, a pool, bar and a restaurant with breakfasts, lunches and dinners (see Places to Eat). The nightly cost in an eight-bed cabin is $17 per person. There are also four-share rooms which cost $50 for a double, or $54/74 for triples/quads, or you can camp in the grounds for $8 per person. PK's is fun-oriented with a party atmosphere, so if you're looking for peace and quiet you'll be better off down at Crocodylus Village. It has a half-day paddle trek (departing twice daily) for $36 and three-hour horse rides for $49. It also hires out mountain bikes ($15 a day) and 4WDs ($120 for a day including a full tank of petrol).

B&Bs At 19 Nicola Drive, signposted from PK's, is the *Cape Trib Retreat* (☎ 4098 0037), a casual B&B with rainforest literally in the backyard. The elevated timber home has cathedral ceilings and features rainforest timbers. The cost is $45/65, or $85 for an en suite double.

Resorts About 3km south of the cape is Cape Trib's most up-market accommodation, the *Coconut Beach Rainforest Resort* (☎ 4098 0033). The resort has 27 hillside units and 40 rainforest villas, built predominantly with black wattle and cypress pine, respectively. All rooms have their own bathrooms and there is no phone or TV in the rooms. The resort has two pools, two restaurants and its own shop, and can arrange a wide range of activities – fishing, guided walks, 4WD expeditions, reef trips and scenic flights. The units cost $215 a night for one or two people plus $45 for extra adults. The villas, which are freestanding and offer a bit more privacy, cost $315 a night for one or two people or $360 for three people. The prices include breakfast.

Closer to the Cape and just off the main road is the *Ferntree Rainforest Resort* (☎ 4098 0000), which has two sections. One section has four-star accommodation with 20 impressive timber cabins in a landscaped garden setting, plus eight suites overlooking the pool. The cabins are linked by timber boardwalks, and each has its own bathroom, a double bed downstairs and two single beds in a loft. Air-con, ceiling fans, phones, a mini-bar and all the other mod cons are included. The nightly cost is $185/210 per person in the cabins including breakfast; suites are $215/240. The other section of the resort, on an adjacent property, has renovated bungalow-style accommodation at $160/185, also including breakfast. The resort also has its own bar and restaurant (see the Places to Eat section).

Places to Eat
If you're doing your own cooking you should bring supplies, although there are several general stores where you can get basics like meat, fruit, vegies and booze. There are also a few good restaurants, cafes and kiosks along the coast.

Just south of the Cow Bay turn-off, *Latitudes 16.12°* (☎ 4098 9133) is a relaxed open-sided place serving simple, tasty and reasonably cheap meals (around $8). It's licensed, and open for lunch and dinner daily.

The *Cow Bay Hotel* has a pleasant bistro which serves lunch and dinner seven days a week; main meals are in the $10 to $14 range and a cheap barbecue is $5. Nearby, the *Floravilla Tea Garden* is an open-air tea room, with a shop and art gallery, that serves meals and snacks.

Lync Haven, about 5km north of the Cow Bay turn-off, is a kiosk and licensed cafe which is open from 8 am to 9 pm. You can get takeaway burgers, sandwiches and snacks, and cheap lunches and dinners.

At Thornton Beach, the *Cafe on Sea Kiosk* is a laid-back beachfront cafe and takeaway. The takeaway section makes great sandwiches and rolls, and sells pies,

drinks etc. The open-sided cafe has a small bar and serves in the $5 to $12 range, as well as good cappuccinos. The kiosk is open daily from 7.30 am until around 5 pm.

PK's Jungle Village has a casual restaurant which serves simple, cheap meals; you can eat here even if you're not staying here.

Opposite PK's, the *Boardwalk Takeaway* is open from 7.30 am to 7 pm and serves good breakfasts, burgers and sandwiches at very reasonable prices. It also sells a limited range of groceries, film and other essentials.

The *Long House* (☎ 4098 0033) restaurant at the Coconut Beach Rainforest Resort is open to the public for lunch and dinner. The Long House is quite a spectacular Melanesian-style building with its own turtle pond and a bar overlooking the pool, and is well worth a visit. Lunch mains cost around $12, but at dinner you're looking at $22.

The restaurant at the *Ferntree Rainforest Resort* is also open to the public for lunch and dinner. It's a breezy timber building with alfresco dining. The lunch menu is light and simple, with dishes ranging from $8 to $20; dinner mains are $20 to $25.

Getting There & Away
Air Hinterland Aviation (☎ 4035 9323) has flights most days between the Cow Bay airstrip and Cairns. The one-way fare is $65.

Bus Coral Coaches (☎ 4098 2600) has a daily bus service from Cairns and Port Douglas to Cooktown, via Cape Trib. See Getting There & Away in the Port Douglas section for details, times and fares.

The Rainforest Coach Express (☎ 4042 7444) has daily return trips from Cairns departing at 8.15, returning from Cape Trib at 5.30 pm. The one-way/return fare is $35/52.

Tours Dozens of operators run tours to Cape Trib from Port Douglas and Cairns, and some excellent deals combine tours and transport to Cape Tribulation with hostel accommodation – for instance $79 including one night's accommodation or $89 including two nights. See Organised Tours in the Cairns section for details.

Resort Transfers Most of the resorts in this area can arrange transfers from Cairns or Port Douglas (for a price) – ask for details when you're booking your accommodation.

Ferry The cable ferry across the Daintree River operates every few minutes from 6 am to midnight and costs $6 for a car, $3 for a motorcycle, $1 for a bicycle and $1 for a pedestrian.

Car & Motorcycle The roads to Cape Trib are quite good and shouldn't present any problems for conventional vehicles or bikes at any time of year.

Note that despite the relatively good roads most car hire companies still won't allow you to take a 2WD hire car to Cape Trib – they'd much rather hire you a (more expensive) 4WD. According to the bush telegraph, some car hire companies pay people a commission to ring them with the rego numbers of any hire cars that go across the ferry, so you'll be up for a hefty fine if you break this condition.

Hitching It's reasonably easy to hitch, since beyond the Daintree ferry all vehicles must head to Cape Trib – there's nowhere else to go!

Getting Around

Apart from Coral Coaches passing through, there are no scheduled public transport services here. Both of the backpackers' hostels, and a few of the other places to stay, have mountain bikes for hire and PK's also has 4WDs for hire.

North to Cooktown

There are two routes to Cooktown from the south: the Bloomfield Track from Cape Tribulation (known as the 'coast road') and the Peninsula Developmental Rd (known as the 'inland route').

CAPE TRIBULATION TO COOKTOWN – THE COAST ROAD

The controversial Bloomfield Track, also known as the 'coast road', starts at Cape Tribulation and carves its way through mountains and rainforest for almost 80km before linking up with the 'inland route' 28km south of Cooktown.

The Track was built back in 1983, when the local Douglas Shire Council decided to bulldoze a gravel road through the forest from just north of Cape Tribulation to the Bloomfield River. The proposal was vigorously opposed by local conservationists who were concerned about the impact the track would have on the local environment, and Cape Trib became the scene of a classic 'greenies vs bulldozers' blockade. Several months and numerous arrests later, the road builders won and the Bloomfield Track was opened, despite serious concerns that soil run off from the track would wash into the ocean and damage the Great Barrier Reef.

The scenery along this route is quite spectacular, although while the coast is never too far away, you don't get to see much of it because of the dense jungle that all but encloses the road in parts. The road is generally well maintained, although some sections are seriously steep and perilously slippery with bull dust, and this road is only recommended for 4WD vehicles. While it is *possible* for a conventional 2WD vehicle to drive the track in the Dry, you do so at your own risk, and if you get stuck you'll probably have trouble finding help or sympathy. During the Wet this road can be closed – check with the RACQ in Cairns (☎ 4033 6433) before heading off.

Cape Tribulation to the Bloomfield River

It's 5km from Cape Trib to Emmagen Creek, which is the actual start of the Bloomfield Track. A little way beyond this crossing, the road begins to climb a series of hills. With a combination of very steep climbs and descents, sharp corners, and fine, slippery bull dust, this is the most challenging section of the drive – in fact,

Stinging Plant & Wait-a-While

As you're wandering through the rainforest, beware of a couple of sinister plants laying in wait for you. The more dangerous of the two is the gympie-gympie, also known as the stinging plant, which can cause severe and long-lasting pain if you so much as brush against it. Stinging plants have large hairy, heart-shaped leaves with serrated edges and can grow up to 6m high.

Another of nature's terrors is the lawyer vine, a barbed creeper which trails from rainforest ferns. Once you're hooked by one you have to wait patiently until you finish unhooking yourself; appropriately enough, the plant has been nicknamed 'wait-a-while'. Despite the charming name, the vine's barbs can be very painful on bare skin, and they'll do a pretty good job of ruining your favourite T-shirt.

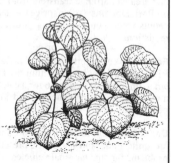

Watch out for the stinging Gympie Gympie plant, found in rainforests.

especially after rain, this climb can even be difficult for 4WD vehicles. There are some great views of the offshore reefs and surrounding rainforest along here.

The road then follows the broad **Bloomfield River**, before crossing it 30km north of Cape Trib. The **Wujal Wujal Aboriginal Community** is on the northern bank of the river. If you stick to the main road heading north to Ayton and Cooktown, (ie turn right at the T-intersection), you won't need a permit.

About 5km beyond Wujal Wujal is the *Bloomfield River Inn* (☎ 4060 8174), which sells fuel (super, unleaded and diesel) as well as takeaway food, drinks and limited grocery supplies. From here it's another 5km to the hamlet of **Ayton**.

Just north of Ayton is *Bloomfield Beach Camping* (☎ 4060 8207). It has a great setting and is well grassed with plenty of tall, shady gum trees, and the beach is only 400m away. There's a bar and casual restaurant. Reef trips, river cruises, scenic flights and bushwalks can be arranged. Tent sites cost $6 per person per night, or if you don't have your own camping gear there are on-site tents here which cost $15 with bedding supplied.

The *Bloomfield Wilderness Lodge* (☎ 4035 9166), close to the mouth of the Bloomfield River, is set back from the beach on Weary Bay and is surrounded by the Cape Tribulation National Park. This remote resort is only accessible from the sea, and the tariff includes scenic air transfer, all meals, and accommodation in luxury suites. The lodge offers river cruises, guided rainforest walks, local fishing, reef trips and 4WD safaris. Packages start at $658 per person twin-share for three nights, including air transfers, meals and activities.

Bloomfield River to Cooktown

North of Bloomfield, the road passes through the **Cedar Bay National Park**, which stretches inland a short distance. There are no facilities here, and access into the park is either by boat or by walking along the numerous small tracks through the bush.

The turn-off to the *Home Rule Rainforest Lodge* (☎ 4060 3925) is signposted from Rossville, 33km north of the Bloomfield River crossing. At the end of a very long and bumpy driveway, this place has a lovely and peaceful setting, with a bar, good cooking facilities and/or cheap meals. It has bunk rooms at $15 per person and camping at $6 per person. There's a two-hour walk to a nearby waterfall, and horse riding is available. Ring from Rossville for a pick-up.

At Helenvale, 9km further north, the famous *Lion's Den Hotel* (☎ 4060 3911) is a colourful bush pub that dates back to 1875. With its corrugated, graffiti-covered tin walls and slab-timber bar, it attracts a steady stream of travellers and local characters. The pub is open daily from 10 am until 10 pm. It has cheap meals and you can camp out the back by the river ($4) or – if the boss thinks you're up to scratch – stay in the spartan rooms for $18/25.

A little further on is *Wilma's Country Kitchen*, which is sort of a cafe/kiosk in an open-sided shed. Wilma sells drinks, burgers and sandwiches, fruit and vegies, and a few other bits and pieces.

Across the road from Wilma's place is the entrance to *Mungumby Lodge* (☎ 4060 3972), a verdant little oasis of lawns and mango trees, with 10 timber cabins scattered around. The cabins are straightforward and comfortable, with a bathroom, a double bed and a single bed. The nightly tariff is $65 a double – less for stays of three or more nights. There's also a spacious, open-sided lodge overlooking the pool where meals are served. Various guided tours are offered, such as walks to local waterfalls, day trips to Cape Trib and the Bloomfield River or tours of the Split Rock Aboriginal rock-art galleries at Laura.

Around 4km further on the road meets the Cooktown Developmental Rd (the inland route), from where it's another 28km to Cooktown.

CAIRNS TO COOKTOWN – THE INLAND ROAD

The 'inland route', the main route between Cairns and Cooktown, is 332km long; you need to allow 4½ to five hours for the trip. The road is open to conventional 2WD vehicles and shouldn't present any major problems, although the second half is over unsealed roads which tend to be rough, cor-

rugated and mighty dusty – it can be slow going, but it's all part of the challenge of getting to Cooktown! The scenery is in dramatic contrast to the lush rainforests which surround the coastal road. This route is more like an outback trip, passing through dry eucalypt forests.

As with the coast road, this route may be closed during the Wet – check with the RACQ in Cairns (☎ 4033 6433) before heading off.

Cairns to the Palmer River Roadhouse

After heading north out of Cairns, take the turn-off to Kuranda and climb over the Atherton Tableland. At Mareeba you meet the Peninsula Developmental Rd, which takes you north, and about 40km further on the small township of **Mt Molloy**.

James Venture Mulligan, the man who started both the Palmer River and Hodgkinson River gold rushes, is buried in the Mt Molloy cemetery. *Mt Molloy Trail Rides* (☎ 4094 1382) offers trail rides to the ruins of an old copper smelter and to Rifle Creek. It can arrange pick-ups from Port Douglas and you can camp out or stay overnight at the pub in town. The *National Hotel* (☎ 4094 1133) has cheap accommodation and is a pleasant place for a cool refreshment.

The former wolfram-mining town of **Mt Carbine**, 30km north-west of Mt Molloy, consists of a pub, a roadhouse and a handful of houses. Just south of the town is the *Mt Carbine Village & Caravan Park* (☎ 4094 3160), a former mining village which has been transformed into a scenic, if somewhat secluded, holiday park. You can camp there for $10 or stay in a self-contained units for $42 a double.

The **McLeod River** crossing, 14km west of Mt Carbine, is one of the best spots to camp along this section of road and it is popular with travellers. Further north the road climbs through the DeSailly Range and there are panoramic views from **Bob's Lookout** that are worthy of a quick photo stop.

At the **Palmer River** crossing, 85km north-west of Mt Carbine, is the *Palmer*

River Roadhouse (☎ 4060 2152), a solitary stone and timber building which sits on a rise. It has fuel, a bar, and a cafe/restaurant. There's an interesting collection of paintings inside, including James Baines' *River of Gold*, a huge mural which depicts the times and characters of the Palmer River gold rush. The roadhouse is open daily from 10 am to midnight, and it accepts only BP fuel cards or cash. There is a caravan and camping park behind the roadhouse. Camping costs $7 per person and on-site vans cost $32 a double.

The bitumen finishes a couple of kilometres beyond the roadhouse. There are a couple of sealed sections further on, but the majority of the trip from here to Cooktown is along unsealed roads of varying standards.

Palmerville & Maytown

The 1873 to 1883 gold rush, for which the Palmer River is famous, happened in very remote country about 70km west of the Palmer River Roadhouse. Its main towns were Palmerville and Maytown, of which very little is left today, but the area is protected as a historic site and if you have a 4WD and a little time, a visit to the former goldfields can make for an interesting side trip.

The turn-off from the Peninsula Developmental Rd is about 17km south of the Palmer River Roadhouse, near the White's Creek crossing – it isn't signposted, but there's usually a tree with white plastic tied around it to mark the road. There are other roads leading into this area from the Burke Developmental Rd north of Chillagoe and from the Peninsula Developmental Rd north of Laura. These roads are all 4WD-only, and some of them pass through private property so you'll need to ask the property owners' permission beforehand. Before heading west, bear in mind that this is wild, remote country – the roads are very rough and you are unlikely to encounter any other traffic. Good maps, a companion vehicle, local advice and proper preparation are essential.

Contact the ranger at Chillagoe (☎ 4094 7163) for information, a camping permit,

maps and current track details. There are no facilities at Maytown or Palmerville. The road from Maytown to Laura is *not* recommended – if you want to continue north, cut across to Palmerville and then head north. This road meets the Peninsula Developmental Rd about 20km north-west of Laura.

Lakeland to Cooktown

It's another 30km from the Palmer River Roadhouse to **Lakeland**, a hamlet at the junction of the Peninsula Developmental Rd and the Cooktown Developmental Rd. Turn left (west) and you're on your way to Laura and Cape York; continue straight on (north-east) and you've got another 82 unsealed and bumpy kilometres to Cooktown. Lakeland has a roadhouse, a hotel/motel and a caravan park.

The *Lakeland Cash Store* (☎ 4060 2133) is a general store and service station, as well as the local RACQ Service Depot. It is open seven days a week, and accepts major credit cards and cold hard cash. Attached is the *Gateway to the Peninsula Caravan Park*, which has tent sites at $8 ($10 powered). The owner of this place also runs Wobbly Bob's Wallaby Walk, a free 20 minute stroll along a 'nature trail' taking in local birdlife, roos and a few other things.

The *Lakeland Downs Hotel-Motel* (☎ 4060 2142) serves lunch and dinner seven days a week and has basic motel-style rooms at $37/47 for singles/doubles.

The next major point of interest to watch out for is the **Annan River Gorge**, which is about 52km past Lakeland. It's well worth stopping here and walking downstream a little way – the river has carved an impressive gorge through solid rock, and you'll soon come to a waterfall which is equally impressive, especially during the rains.

A little further down the road is the turn-off to **Helenvale** and the famous Lion's Den Hotel, which is just about an essential visit – see the previous section for details.

Continuing to Cooktown, the road soon passes **Black Mountain**, a pile of thousands of oddly stacked granite boulders. It's said there are ways between the huge rocks which will take you under the hill from one side to the other, but people have died trying to find them. Black Mountain is known to Aboriginal people as Kalcajagga – 'place of the spears'. The colour comes not from the rocks themselves, but from lichen which grow on them. From here, it's only another 28km to Cooktown itself.

COOKTOWN
pop 1350
Cooktown is just far enough away from Cairns, and just hard enough to get to, to

have remained relatively untouched by mass tourism. It's a fascinating, no-frills place to visit, pretty rough around the edges but at least it's authentic. The fishing is great, the three pubs are full of interesting characters, and there's an excellent historical museum housed in an old convent.

Cooktown is something of a 'last-frontier' town – for 2WD travellers, anyway. Beyond the town stretches the wilds of the Cape York Peninsula. The task of getting here is rewarded not just by the relaxed atmosphere but by some fascinating remin-

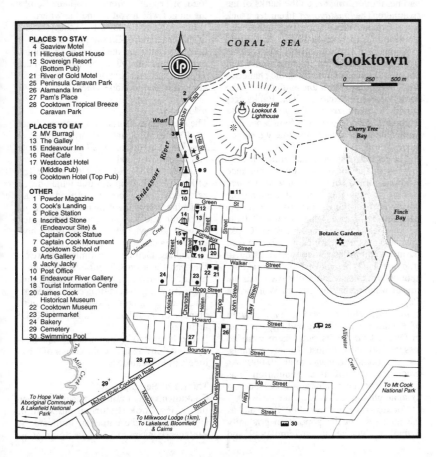

PLACES TO STAY
4 Seaview Motel
11 Hillcrest Guest House
12 Sovereign Resort (Bottom Pub)
21 River of Gold Motel
25 Peninsula Caravan Park
26 Alamanda Inn
27 Pam's Place
28 Cooktown Tropical Breeze Caravan Park

PLACES TO EAT
2 MV Burragi
13 The Galley
15 Endeavour Inn
16 Reef Cafe
17 Westcoast Hotel (Middle Pub)
19 Cooktown Hotel (Top Pub)

OTHER
1 Powder Magazine
3 Cook's Landing
5 Police Station
6 Inscribed Stone (Endeavour Site) & Captain Cook Statue
7 Captain Cook Monument
8 Cooktown School of Arts Gallery
9 Jacky Jacky
10 Post Office
14 Endeavour River Gallery
18 Tourist Information Centre
20 James Cook Historical Museum
22 Cooktown Museum
23 Supermarket
24 Bakery
29 Cemetery
30 Swimming Pool

CORAL SEA

Cooktown

0   250   500 m

Grassy Hill Lookout & Lighthouse

Cherry Tree Bay

Finch Bay

Botanic Gardens

Wharf

Endeavour River

Chinaman Creek

Green St

Furneaux Street

Walker Street

Hogg Street

Adelaide Street

Charlotte Street

Helen Street

Hope Street

John Street

May Street

Howard Street

Boundary Street

Ida Street

To Mt Cook National Park

Alligator Creek

To Hope Vale Aboriginal Community & Lakefield National Park

Two Mile Creek

McIvor River–Cooktown Road

Mason Street

Cooktown Developmental Rd

To Milkwood Lodge (1km), To Lakeland, Bloomfield & Cairns

ders of the area's past. You can use the town as a base for visiting the Quinkan rock art near Laura or even Lakefield National Park.

For details on the area north of Cooktown, including the Hope Vale Aboriginal Community, the Lakefield National Park and Laura see the Cape York Peninsula chapter.

History

On 17 June 1770, Cooktown became the site of Australia's first White settlement when Captain James Cook beached his barque, the *Endeavour*, on the banks of the river here. The *Endeavour* had earlier struck a reef offshore from Cape Tribulation, and Cook and his crew spent 48 days here while they patched up the damage. During this time, Joseph Banks the chief naturalist, and botanist Daniel Solander took the chance to study Australian flora and fauna along the banks of the Endeavour River. Banks collected 186 plant species and wrote the first European description of a kangaroo. The north side of the river has scarcely changed since then.

The region's explorers had amicable contacts with the local Aborigines, but race relations turned sour a century later when Cooktown was founded and became the unruly port for the Palmer River gold rush between 1873 and 1883. Hell's Gate, a narrow pass on the track between Cooktown and the Palmer River, was the scene of frequent ambushes as Aborigines tried to stop their lands being overrun. Battle Camp, about 60km inland from Cooktown, was the site of a major battle between Whites and Cape York Aborigines.

In 1874, before Cairns was even thought of, Cooktown was the second biggest town in Queensland. At its peak there were no less than 94 pubs, almost as many brothels, and the population was over 30,000! As much as half of this population was Chinese, and their industrious presence led to some wild race riots.

Cooktown's glory was short-lived and as the gold ran out the population gradually dwindled. Cyclones in 1907 and 1949, and an evacuation in WWII came close to killing the place off. It wasn't until the James Cook Historical Museum opened in 1970 that visitors started arriving and Cooktown's steady decline was halted.

Orientation

Cooktown sits at the mouth of the Endeavour River on a north-pointing headland which separates the river from the Coral Sea. Along Charlotte St, the main street, is the post office, a bank, a handful of shops and three pubs. At it's northern end Charlotte St becomes Webber Esplanade, near the end of which you'll find the wharf.

Overlooking the town from the north end of the headland is Grassy Hill, and east of the town centre are the beaches, the botanic gardens and the Mt Cook National Park. The airfield is 10km west of the centre, along the road to Hope Vale.

Information

The Cooktown Tourist Information Centre (☎ 4069 6100) is in O'Connor Arcade on Charlotte St, between the Cooktown Hotel and Westcoast Hotel.

In front of the post office stands the Tree of Knowledge, a big old tree which serves as a local notice board, with notices announcing everything from rooms to rent and items for sale to when the dentist is next coming to town. There are public phone booths beside the post office.

Banking facilities are limited: there's a Westpac Bank on Charlotte St (housed in one of the town's most impressive buildings, featuring a beautiful cedar interior). There are no hole-in-the-wall banks but a number of local businesses have EFTPOS facilities.

The local RACQ depot is at Cape York Tyres (☎ 4069 5233), on the corner of Charlotte and Furneaux Sts.

Things to See & Do

Cooktown's major attraction is the wonderful **James Cook Historical Museum** on Helen St, near the corner of Furneaux St. Built as a convent in 1889, the museum has a fascinating collection of displays relating to all aspects of Cooktown's past – Aboriginal artefacts, Cook's life and voyages, the Palmer River gold rush and the Chinese community, and a particularly gruesome dental room. The museum is open daily from 9.30 am to 4 pm. Admission costs $5 ($1.50 children).

Nearby, on the corner of Helen and Walker Sts, is the rather strange **Cooktown Museum** – it's more of a souvenir shop than a museum and isn't really worth the $5 admission, especially when compared to its more illustrious neighbour.

Charlotte St has a number of interesting **monuments** starting with one to the tragic Mary Watson (see the Lizard Island section) opposite the Sovereign Hotel. She is buried in the Cooktown cemetery. A little further towards the wharf are **memorials** to the explorer Edmund Kennedy and to Captain Cook. Behind these stands a **cannon**, which was sent from Brisbane in 1885 along with three cannonballs, two rifles and one officer in response to Cooktown's plea for defences against a feared Russian invasion! Further on there's an impressive and much-photographed **bronze statue** of Cook, and right by the waterside, a **stone** with an inscription marks the spot where the *Endeavour* was careened.

The **Gungarde Aboriginal Centre**, south of the Cooktown Hotel, has on sale a small selection of work by local Aboriginal artists. The **Cooktown School of Arts Gallery** beside the post office houses a varied collection of local art works, and on the opposite side of the road is the **Jacky Jacky**, a small timber building with a window display of interesting historical photos.

A short walk along Webber Esplanade past the wharf brings you to the old **powder magazine**. It dates back to 1874, making it one of the first brick buildings to be constructed in far north Queensland, and probably the oldest still standing. It has recently been saved from oblivion by some National Trust restoration work and is worth a look around.

The **Grassy Hill Lookout** has sensational 360° views of the town, river and ocean. Captain Cook climbed this hill looking for a passage out through the reefs – there's a signboard with extracts from his journal, as well as an old lighthouse. A **walking trail** leads from the summit down to the beach at Cherry Tree Bay. East of the town is the **Mt Cook National Park**, where there's another walking trail leading to the 430m summit of Mt Cook. It's a great half-day climb, although the views from the top are mostly obscured by trees.

The **Cooktown Cemetery** on McIvor River-Cooktown Rd is worth a visit. There are many graves dating back to the 1870s, including those of Mary Watson and the 'Normanby Woman' – thought to have been a European who survived a shipwreck as a child and lived with Aboriginal people for years until 'rescued' by White people. She died soon after.

The very pleasant **Botanic Gardens**, off Walker St, were first planted in 1886 and restored in 1984. This is a great spot for a picnic, with shady lawns and colourful flower beds, and two walking trails lead from the gardens to the beaches at Cherry Tree Bay and Finch Bay.

Warning If you're visiting any of the local beaches, remember that deadly box jellyfish are present in these waters, particularly from around October to April – if in doubt, seek local advice *before* swimming. Saltwater crocodiles, another potential hazard, can be found in the open sea and in tidal creeks and rivers – don't even think about swimming or dangling your toes in the Endeavour River, and take care when walking along its banks.

Activities
River Cruises Cooktown Cruises (☎ 4069 5712) runs an interesting two-hour commentary cruise up to the head of the Endeavour River, then back down to a mangrove creek. The boat departs from the Cook's Landing jetty daily at 2 pm (and some days at 9 am); the cost is $18 ($8 children).

Fishing Charters & Cruises Reel River Sportsfishing (☎ 4069 5346) offers lure-fishing trips on weekends and during school holidays (from $60/100 per person for a half/full day).

The *Coral Vista*, an 8m fast cat, is available for fishing charters for groups of up to six people. A full day costs from $130 per person, which includes all fishing tackle, snorkelling gear and bait. Ring ☎ 4069 5519 for more info.

Organised Tours
Cooktown Tours (☎ 4069 5125) offers 1½-hour town tours ($16) and full-day 4WD trips to Black Mountain and the Lion's Den Hotel ($99); both depart daily at 9 am.

Munbah Aboriginal Cultural Tours has day trips to various sights around town, including the Coloured Sands and Cape Bedford ($99 including lunch), and you can take an interesting trip on the local bus out to the Hope Vale Aboriginal Community ($20 return, departures on weekdays at 7.30 am and 3 pm). For bookings contact the Tourist Information Centre.

There are various tours and day trips to Cooktown from Port Douglas and Cairns – see the Getting There & Away section for details.

Festivals
The Cooktown Endeavour Festival, commemorating Captain Cook's landing in 1770, is held over the Queen's Birthday weekend every June. Highlights of the three-day event include a re-enactment of Cook's landing, a gala ball, a parade, various sporting events and a fishing competition.

The Cooktown Amateur Turf Club holds two-day race meetings twice a year (usually June and August). These are popular events and the town is crowded with people from the stations as far away as Weipa for the sport and socialising.

Places to Stay
Camping & Caravan Parks Cooktown has two caravan parks. The *Cooktown Tropi-*

cal Breeze Caravan Park (☎ 4069 5417), on the McIvor River-Cooktown Rd, has very good facilities including a small shop and two swimming pools. Tent sites cost $12, on-site vans are $29 a double, and motel-style cabins and self-contained units start from $35/49.

On the outskirts of the town at the eastern end of Howard St, the *Peninsula Caravan Park* (☎ 4069 5107) has a lovely bush setting, with stands of big old paperbark and gum trees. Tent sites here cost $12, on-site vans are from $30 and self-contained units from $50.

Hostels *Pam's Place* (☎ 4069 5166), on the corner of Charlotte and Boundary Sts, is a comfortable, associate YHA hostel. There's a good kitchen, dining area, pool, garden and TV lounge. A bunk is $15 and singles/doubles cost $20 per person (non-members pay $1 extra).

Guesthouses There are two old-fashioned guesthouses in town, both offering clean and simple private accommodation. The *Hillcrest Guest House* (☎ 4069 5305), in Hope St, is a friendly place with 12 guest rooms, all with shared bathroom facilities. There's a spacious lounge, a pool, a butterfly enclosure, and a two-room display of fish tanks and sea shells. Singles/doubles cost $30/45 including breakfast.

The *Alamanda Inn* (☎ 4069 5203), also in Hope St, has 10 bright rooms all with air-con and TV. Singles/doubles cost $24/32 with shared bathrooms or $32/40 with private bathrooms. There's a small kitchen for guests' use.

The new *Milkwood Lodge* (☎ 4069 5007) is about 1.5km south of town at Annan Rd (signposted just off the Development Rd), and offers good value accommodation in a rainforest setting at $75 for a double. It also has 4WD vehicles for hire and can arrange tag-along trips.

Hotels & Motels The impressive *Sovereign Resort* (☎ 4069 5400) is in the middle of town on the corner of Charlotte and Green

Sts. Previously known as the Bottom Pub, it has a superb pool and a range of accommodation, with well-appointed single/double rooms at $95/105, one-bedroom resort apartments at $105/116 and two-bedroom apartments at $135. It also has a pretty good restaurant – see the Places to Eat section.

The *Seaview Motel* (☎ 4069 5377), on Charlotte St, is a pleasant little motel overlooking the Endeavour River, with a small pool and guest barbecue area. Room costs are from $60/70. The more modern *River of Gold Motel* (☎ 4069 5222), on the corner of Hope and Walker Sts, has singles/doubles from $60/68.

Places to Eat

If you're planning to do your own cooking, you'll find a supermarket in town, as well as a butcher and a bakery.

If you're after a decent takeaway meal, there are a few cafes and takeaways, although they're nothing to write home about. The *Reef Cafe* in Charlotte St makes good toasted sandwiches and also has a wide range of takeaway or eat-in meals like fish and chips, chicken and burgers.

The *China Dina Cafe*, hidden in the arcade between the Cooktown and Westcoast hotels, is the spot for pizzas and vaguely Chinese food.

The *Cook's Landing Kiosk*, just south of the wharf, has outdoor tables overlooking the river and is a pleasant spot for a drink, a cuppa or a snack. Next to the Sovereign Resort is *The Galley*, which has pizzas and burgers.

The *Cooktown Hotel*, also known as the Top Pub, serves excellent bistro meals and also has a great beer garden. Main meals range from $8 to $12 and it serves lunch and dinner every day except Sunday.

The *Sovereign Resort* has an excellent balcony restaurant upstairs with tables overlooking the river. Mains are about $14 at lunchtime and from $19 to $23 at dinner.

The *Endeavour Inn* (☎ 4069 5384), on the corner of Charlotte and Furneaux Sts, opens nightly for dinner and specialises in seafood and steaks. It's a relaxed, colonial-style place with a small bar and a courtyard dining area. The menu features delicacies such as paperbark baked barramundi and kangaroo fillets, with mains from $17 to $19; it has a good selection of Australian wines.

For something different, eat aboard the MV *Burragi*, a small, refurbished former Sydney Harbour ferry now permanently moored near the jetty. It's both licensed and BYO, and mains, such as coral trout, cost around $18.

Getting There & Away

Air Cooktown's airfield is 10km west of town, along McIvor River-Cooktown Rd.

Flight West (☎ 13 2392) operates daily flights between Cairns and Cooktown costing $71 each way. The booking agent in Cooktown is the Seaview Motel (☎ 4069 5377). Endeavour Air (☎ 4069 5860) has charter flights from here to Lizard Island – see the Lizard Island section following.

Bus Coral Coaches (☎ 4098 2600) operates two regular services between Cairns and Cooktown, one via the coast road and the other via the inland route. The coast road service (8½ hours, $52) via Port Douglas and Cape Tribulation, departs from Cairns at 7 am (and from Port Douglas at 8.30 am) every Tuesday, Thursday and Saturday; from Cooktown the departures are at 11 am on the same days. The inland route service (6½ hours, $47) departs Cairns at 7 am every Wednesday, Friday and Sunday, with departures from Cooktown at 2.30 pm on the same days.

For details and bookings contact the agent in Cooktown, the Endeavour Farm Trading Post (☎ 4069 5723) on Charlotte St.

Car & Motorcycle If you're driving up here, there are two main roads from the south – the coastal road (4WD only) and the inland road. Both routes present something of a challenge, and both offer great scenery and some fascinating places to stop along the way. If you have a 4WD, it's worth heading up one way and coming back the other. For more info, read the relevant sections earlier in this chapter.

Tours There are numerous operators offering tours to Cooktown from Cairns and Port Douglas – see Organised Tours in the Cairns section for details.

Getting Around

Cooktown is small enough to cover on foot, if you have the time and energy.

The Hire Shop (☎ 4069 5601), on Charlotte St just south of the Sovereign Hotel, rents out boats ($50 for a half day, $80 for a full day with fuel supplied).

Endeavour Tours (☎ 4069 6100) is the only vehicle rental agency in town. It has 4WD Suzukis for $90 per day including insurance and 300 free kilometres.

LIZARD ISLAND

Lizard Island, the furthest north of the Barrier Reef resort islands, is about 100km from Cooktown and 240km from Cairns. Lizard is a continental island with a dry, rocky and mountainous terrain – a far cry from the tropical paradise of swaying palm trees that some people seem to expect. Nevertheless, the island has superb beaches, probably the best on any of the Barrier Reef islands. It's a great island for swimming, snorkelling and diving, and has some good bushwalks and great views from Cook's Look – at 368m, the highest point on the island.

The accommodation here covers both ends of the spectrum – with nothing in between. You can either stay in an exclusive (and expensive) resort frequented by millionaires and those into big-game fishing, or pitch a tent in the national park camping ground. Campers aren't exactly welcomed or encouraged by the resort, so if you choose the latter you'll have to be totally self-sufficient for the period of your stay. Almost all of the island is national park, which means it's open to anyone who makes the effort to get here.

Lizard is accessible by air or boat from either Cairns or Cooktown, although because of the distances involved it's a pricey place to get to. However, the expense is justified if you stay a few days or more.

History

Captain Cook and his crew were the first Europeans to visit Lizard Island, in 1770. Having successfully patched up the *Endeavour* in Cooktown, they sailed north and stopped on Lizard Island, where Cook and the botanist Joseph Banks climbed to the top of Cook's Look to look for a way out through the Barrier Reef to the open sea. Banks named the island after the large lizards that were its only apparent occupants. Meanwhile, other crew members had found a safe route out to deeper water, and the *Endeavour* continued its journey.

Zoning

The waters immediately around Lizard Island are all zoned as Marine National Park where shell and coral collecting and spear fishing are not permitted. Around the northern part of the island it's Zone A, which permits limited line fishing. The southern part, including all of Blue Lagoon and the waters around Palfrey and South islands and Seabird Islet, as well as Watson's Bay and Turtle Beach north of the resort, are all Zone B, where all fishing is prohibited.

Things to See & Do

Lizard Island's **beaches** are nothing short of sensational, and range from long stretches of white sand to idyllic little rocky bays. The water is crystal clear, and the island is surrounded by magnificent coral. Snorkelling here is superb.

Immediately south of the resort are three postcard beaches – Sunset Beach, Pebbly Beach and Hibiscus Beach. Watson's Bay to the north of the resort is a wonderful stretch of sand with great snorkelling at both ends and a clam field in the middle, and there are plenty of other choices right around the island.

The island is noted for its **diving**. There are good dives right off the island, and the

A Queensland Tragedy

During Cook's visit Banks had noticed that 'the Indians had been here in their poor embarkations' and later visits also noted that Aborigines had visited the island; these visits were to lead to a Queensland tragedy. In 1881 Robert and Mary Watson settled on the island in order to collect be-mer, or sea slugs, a noted Chinese delicacy. They built a small stone cottage overlooking what is now Watson's Bay. In September of that year, Robert Watson and his partner left the island to search for new fishing grounds, leaving Mary Watson with her baby, Ferrier, and their two Chinese servants Ah Sam and Ah Leong. On 29 September a party of Aborigines arrived on the island and attacked the group, killing Ah Leong and wounding Ah Sam. The next day Mary Watson decided to leave the island, and with a few supplies, her baby and her wounded houseboy, paddled away in an iron tank used for boiling up the be-mer. For 10 days they drifted from sandbank to island to reef to man-grove swamp, narrowly missing passing steamers or signalling unsuccessfully to them until eventually all died of thirst. Their bodies weren't found until January the next year. During this ordeal Mary kept a diary, which is now held by the Queensland Museum in Brisbane.

The ruined walls of the Watsons' cottage can still be seen on the island. Near the top of Cook's Look there are also traces of stones marking an Aboriginal ceremonial area and it's possible that Mary Watson's unhappy end may have come about because they had un-wittingly strayed into an area sacred to Aborigines.

---

outer Barrier Reef is less than 20km away, including what is probably Australia's best known dive, the Cod Hole. The resort offers a full range of diving facilities to its guests, although this isn't a particularly cheap place to dive.

Lizard is also famed for its fishing, par-ticularly **heavy tackle fishing** for which the annual competition over Halloween night (31 October) is a big attraction. Sep-tember through December is the heavy tackle season. The Marlin Centre, at the north end of the resort bay caters for the many game-fishing boats that use Lizard as a base at the height of the season. Its bar is renowned for extremely tall fishing tales. The resort's MV *Gamefisher* is available for charter during the marlin season, or if

you'd rather tackle something a bit smaller you can take out one of its dinghies.

The climb to the top of **Cook's Look** is undoubtedly the most popular walk on the island. The trail, which starts from the northern end of the beach near the camp site, is clearly signposted and, although it can be steep and a bit of a clamber at times, is easy to follow all the way with regular white or blue painted arrows. The views from the top are sensational, and on a clear day you can see the opening in the reef where Cook made his thankful escape. The climb can take anywhere from 45 minutes to 1½ hours.

The privately funded **Lizard Island Re-search Station** researches topics as diverse as examining marine organisms for cancer research; trying to explain the deaths of giant clams; coral reproductive processes; sea bird ecology; and life patterns of reef fish during their larval stage. Tours of the station are conducted at 9.30 am each Monday and Friday.

Lizard has plenty of **wildlife**. There are 11 different species of lizards, including large sand goannas which can be up to 1m long. More than 40 species of birds have also been recorded on the island and a dozen or so actually nest there, including the beautiful little sunbirds with their long, hanging nests. They even build them inside the small, open airstrip terminal! Bar-shouldered doves, crested terns, Caspian terns and a variety of other terns, oyster-catchers and the large sea eagles are other resident species. Seabird Islet in the Blue Lagoon is a popular nesting site for terns and visitors should keep away from the islet during the summer months.

Places to Stay
Camping The national parks camp site is at the north end of the Watson's Bay beach. The site has toilets, barbecues, tables and benches, and fresh water is available from a pump about 250m from the site. Campers must be totally self sufficient. You also need take your garbage with you when you leave, and bring charcoal for the barbecues as all timber on the island (including driftwood) is protected, and fuel stoves aren't allowed on aircraft. Sites cost $3.50 per person per night, and permits are available from the Department of Environment office (☎ 4053 4533) in Cairns.

Resorts The *Lizard Island Resort* (☎ 4060 3999), run by Qantas, is one of the most exclusive and expensive resorts on the Great Barrier Reef. The resort is modern but quite straightforward – you're paying for the isolation and great location, less than 20km from the outer edge of the reef, rather than five-star luxury.

The 30 double rooms have air-con and ceiling fan, fridge, tea and coffee-making equipment, bathrobes and toiletries, and

telephone. There is no TV or radio in the rooms. The tariffs are $860/1040 per night for singles/doubles. These rates include all meals and general equipment use and activities. The resort's facilities, which are exclusively for the use of house guests, include a floodlit tennis court, swimming pool, windsurfers, catamarans, outboard dinghies and water-skiing.

Boat trips cost extra and these are put on every day, either for fishing, diving and snorkelling, picnic and barbecue excursions to neighbouring islands, or various combinations of these activities.

Children between six and 14 pay half price, and children under six are banned. For bookings, write to the Lizard Island Resort, Private Mail Bag 40, Cairns, Qld 4870.

Places to Eat
The restaurant at the resort is open only to house guests, so if you're camping here you'll have to bring all supplies from the mainland.

The resort's cuisine has an excellent reputation and the main dining area is an open-air deck with a great outlook across lawns to the sea. The kitchen will pack picnic hampers if you're heading out for the day.

Getting There & Away
Air Sunstate Airlines (☎ 13 1313) has daily flights from Cairns and the hour-long flight costs $388 return.

Aussie Airways (☎ 4053 3980) has a day trip from Cairns to Lizard Island daily depending on demand, which costs $290 per person including lunch and snorkelling gear.

Boat There is no regular shipping or ferry service to Lizard Island. The *Reef Endeavour*, operated by Captain Cook Cruises (☎ 1800 221 080), does a four-night cruise from Cairns to Lizard Island and back, leaving Cairns every Monday at 2 pm. The ship calls in at Fitzroy Island on day one, Cooktown on day two then continues to

Lizard Island, where you spend two days – snorkelling, diving, walking or just lazing around. Fares range from $1010 per person in a three-berth cabin to $1460 per person in a deluxe twin stateroom, which includes all meals, entertainment and activities.

Alternatively, the Cairns to Thursday Island cruise ship, the *Kangaroo Explorer* (☎ 4032 4000), spends a day at Lizard on its way north and south. A four-day trip from Cairns costs from $1134 in a four-berth lower-deck cabin to $1659 for an upper deck double, including airfare back to Cairns. To do the full seven-day trip to or from Thursday Island costs from $1753 to $2628.

ISLANDS AROUND LIZARD ISLAND

There are four other smaller islands in the Lizard group. **Osprey Island**, with its nesting birds, is right in front of the resort and can be waded to. Around the edge of Blue Lagoon, south of the main island, are **Seabird Islet**, **South Island** and **Palfrey Island** with an automatic lighthouse.

There are a number of continental islands and small cays dotted around Lizard Island and south towards Cooktown. Camping is permitted on a number of the islands with a Department of Environment permit. The sites are all very basic and the permits cost just $3.50 per person a night.

Immediately south of Lizard Island is **Rocky Islet**, wooded and with good beaches, and two adjoining islets, one covered in scrub, one bare rock. Day trips are sometimes made to the islets from Lizard Island and there is good snorkelling and diving there. Camping is permitted on the north side of the main island between February and September.

Just north of the Rocky Islets, **South Direction Island** is scrub-covered but without beaches. Yachts sometimes anchor here although it's not easy to get inside the reef. **North Direction Island** is another popular destination for day trips from Lizard Island. There's a good beach and sand spit and some fine coral for divers or snorkellers. Aboriginal rock paintings can be seen on the island.

Eagle Islet, a small cay at the northern end of Eyrie Reef, is only about 8km from Lizard. The islet is noted for its three eagle nests. From December to March it harbours a huge number of sea birds, particularly nesting terns.

About 25km west of Lizard Island is **Nymph Island**, a good picnic spot with good snorkelling around the reef. Reportedly there have even been crocodiles in the island's inner lagoon. It's a good island for walking and camping is permitted from April through September. Slightly southwest of Nymph Island are the islands of the Turtle Group, small sand and vegetated cays. Camping is permitted on three of the islands in the group.

Cape York Peninsula

Cape York is one of the last great frontiers of Australia. It is a vast patchwork of tropical savannah cut by numerous rivers and streams, while along its eastern flank is the northern section of the Great Dividing Range.

In among the Range's rugged peaks and deep valleys are some of the best and most significant rainforests in Australia. Streams tumble down the rocky mountains to the sea, where just offshore the coral ramparts of the Great Barrier Reef stretch over thousands of square kilometres. The reef is protected in a marine park, and much of the land mass of the Cape is protected in a number of spectacular, rarely visited and wild national parks.

Giving access to that vast natural wonderland is the route to the Cape. Initially the corrugated road you follow is the Peninsula Developmental Rd, but once that heads away to the mining town of Weipa, you follow the Telegraph Track to the 'Tip', and the real adventure begins.

North of the Weipa turn-off a 4WD vehicle is definitely required and, as you head further north, the creek crossings become more common and more challenging. By the time you get back from a trip to the Tip, you'll be an expert in water crossings.

From Cairns to the top of Cape York is 952km via the shortest and most challenging route. Most travellers will want to visit Cooktown, Weipa and a few other places off the main route, and those diversions will add considerably to the total distance covered.

There are a number of alternative routes. Down south you can choose between the inland route, or the coastal route via Daintree and Cape Tribulation. From Lakeland you can travel straight up the heart of the Cape or go via Cooktown and Battle Camp to Laura or Musgrave.

From the Archer River you can head north via Weipa and Stones Crossing, or via

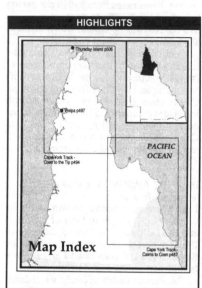

HIGHLIGHTS

Thursday Island p506

Weipa p497

PACIFIC
OCEAN

Cape York Track -
Coen to the Tip p494

Map Index

Cape York Track -
Cairns to Coen p487

- Take a 4WD on one of Australia's great wilderness adventures to the tip of Cape York.
- See superb Aboriginal rock art at the Lakefield National Park galleries.
- Soak up the casual Torres Strait Island atmosphere of Thursday Island.

the Telegraph Track. Further north you have the choice of continuing on the Telegraph Track or taking the newer bypass roads.

Covering an area totalling around 207,000 sq km, which is about the same size as the state of Victoria, Cape York has a population of around 15,000 people. The largest towns in the region are Cooktown, on the south-east coast, and Weipa, a large mining community on the central-west coast. A handful of smaller towns make up the remainder of the communities throughout the Cape.

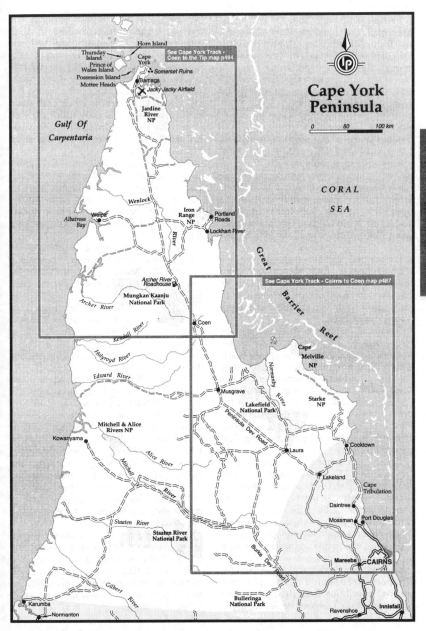

Vast areas of Cape York are designated Aboriginal land, and the rich Aboriginal and Torres Strait heritage is alive and well. Travellers will see much of it on their way through the Cape. Of special importance is one of the world's most significant collections of prehistoric art in the escarpment country surrounding Laura.

HISTORY

Before the arrival of Europeans there were a large number of different Aboriginal tribal groups spread throughout the Cape. A unique group of people inhabited the islands dotted across the reef-strewn Torres Strait that separates mainland Australia from New Guinea. The Torres Strait Islanders came from Melanesia and Polynesia about 2000 years ago and are culturally distinct from the Aborigines.

For the most part, the tribes of the Cape were aggressive, fighting between themselves and attacking the early European explorers. In fact, there are few accounts of early explorers that do not relate attacks by Aborigines or Islanders.

European history in Australia can be traced back to the early Dutch navigators who from 1606 explored much of the coastline. Willem Jansz and Abel Tasman were the first Europeans to report seeing the Great South Land. (It is unclear whether the Spanish navigator Torres, after whom the strait is named, actually sighted the land.) Their exploits are remembered in the names of bluffs and bays dotted down the Gulf side of the Cape.

James Cook mapped the east coast of Australia in 1770, and claimed the continent for England while on Possession Island, just off the northerly tip that he named Cape York. Over the next 100 years other great English navigators, including Bligh, Flinders and King, mapped sections of the coast and bestowed their names upon it.

Ludwig Leichhardt was the first explorer to journey over a section of the Cape during his 1845 expedition from Brisbane to Port Essington on the Cobourg Peninsula in the Northern Territory. Edmund Kennedy and his party had a horrific time in 1848 heading up the east coast along the Great Dividing Range. Kennedy was fatally speared by Aborigines among the swamps and waterways of the Escape River, southeast of the Tip. Only Jacky Jacky, his Aboriginal guide, reached their destination just a few kilometres north at Albany Passage. (For more information on Kennedy see the History section in the Facts about Queensland chapter.)

Frank Jardine and his brother led a group taking cattle from Rockhampton to the new government outpost at Somerset in 1863. This was to be the start of the Jardine legend on Cape York, with Frank Jardine dominating the top of the Cape until his death in 1919.

Other explorers followed, opening up the region. The discovery of gold on the Palmer River in 1873 was the great catalyst for the development of Cooktown, Laura and, later, Cairns.

In 1887 the Overland Telegraph Line from near Somerset to Palmerville and Cooktown was finally completed, linking the northernmost outpost with Brisbane. This is the route most travellers to Cape York follow today.

During WWII, Cape York was a major staging post for the battles against the Japanese in New Guinea and the Coral Sea. Some 10,000 troops were stationed on the Cape at such places as Iron Range and Portland Roads, on the mid-east coast; Horn Island, Mutee Heads and Jacky Jacky airfield (then called Higgins Field) at the northern tip of Cape York; as well as around Cooktown. Many relics of those days can still be seen, including wrecks of some of the 160-odd aircraft that were reported lost over the region.

During the 1950s bauxite was discovered along the coast near Weipa, and by the 1980s it had grown into the world's biggest bauxite mine. With reserves stockpiled well into the next century, Weipa will continue to be a major community and a place to visit for years to come.

Top: The James Cook Historical Museum, Cooktown, is one of the state's best.
Middle Left: Kapok trees and termite mounds dot the harsh landscape of the Cape.
Middle Right: Creek crossing – one of many on the drive to the tip of Cape York Peninsula.
Bottom: Black Mountain, near Cooktown, is an unusual mound of massive boulders.

Top: The sun sets over mangroves at Karumba Point, Gulf of Carpentaria.
Middle: Rugged landscape at Jowalbinna Station, Cape York Peninsula.
Bottom: Morris Islet, Cape York Peninsula.

INFORMATION

Of course you need all the usual gear for travelling in a remote area, and you must carry water. Although you will cross a number of rivers south of the Archer River, water can be scarce along the main track north, especially late in the Dry.

It is possible to take a well-constructed off-road trailer all the way to the top, but be prepared to get bogged occasionally. Less sturdily built trailers will fall apart somewhere along the track. Caravans can make it to Cooktown if driven with care. They can even make as far north as Weipa, but it's hard going and we wouldn't recommend it.

You are also entering crocodile country, so while there are plenty of safe places to swim, be aware that any deep, dark, long stretch of water can hold a big hungry saltie.

The most common accidents on the Cape are head-on collisions in the heath country south of the Jardine River. The track is narrow here with many blind corners; people often travel too fast, and sometimes they meet head-on. Nobody has been killed yet, but that is more because by good luck than good driving. Drive slowly and keep your wits about you.

When to Go & Road Conditions

The wet season greatly restricts vehicle movement on Cape York. For that reason the best time to go is as early in the Dry as possible, generally from the beginning of June. The country is greener, there is more water around, there are less travellers and generally the roads are better than later in the season. The peak period is between August and September, with the last travellers being out of the Cape by around mid-November.

If you plan to visit early or late in the season, it pays to check with locals to see what is happening weather-wise and what the roads are like. Speaking to police in Coen, Weipa or Cooktown wouldn't go astray, nor would a phone call to the friendly people at the Archer River Roadhouse. Alternatively, you can contact the Queensland Department of Transport (☎ 1800 077

247) or the RACQ Road Reports (24 hours ☎ 4051 6711).

Occasionally people get caught out by the early rains of the Wet when they're at the very top of Cape York. They'll be looking at either an extended stay or a barge trip with their vehicle back to Cairns.

Tourist Information

There are no official tourist information centres along the route to the tip of Cape York, although travellers will find information readily available from the many helpful locals in the roadhouses and towns along the way, such as Cooktown, Coen, Weipa and Bamaga. The Seisia Camping Ground, at the very top of Australia, is also a mine of information.

Money

Banking facilities are very limited on Cape York, and full banking facilities are only available at Weipa, Cooktown and Thursday Island.

Cheques are not normally accepted, but credit cards such as Bankcard, MasterCard and Visa are accepted widely for most services, and EFTPOS is increasingly available. However, in many places cash is still the only form of currency accepted.

Police

The police can provide information to travellers on road conditions etc. Contact the following police stations: Cooktown (☎ 4069 5320), on Charlotte St; Hopevale Aboriginal Community (☎ 4060 9224), 4 Flierl St; Laura (☎ 4060 3244); Coen (☎ 4060 1150); Weipa (☎ 4069 9119) at Rocky Point; Lockhart River Aboriginal Community (☎ 4060 7120); and Bamaga (☎ 4069 3156), Sagauka St.

Medical Services

Hospitals on Cape York include: Cooktown (☎ 4069 5433) on Hope St; Coen (☎ 4060 1141); Weipa (☎ 4069 9155) at Rocky Point; and Bamaga (☎ 4069 3166). There is also a dentist (☎ 4069 9411) at Rocky Point, Weipa, and a clinic (☎ 4060 3320) in Laura.

CAPE YORK PENINSULA

Permits

Permits are not required for travelling to Cape York via the main route described.

Once you are north of the Dulhunty River, however, you will need a permit to camp on Aboriginal land, which in effect is nearly all the land north of the river. The Injinoo people are the traditional custodians of much of this land, along with other Aboriginal communities at Umagico and New Mapoon. Please respect the signs and bylaws of the community councils.

Designated campgrounds are provided in a number of areas, including Seisia, Pajinka and Punsand Bay. Camping elsewhere in the area requires a permit from the Injinoo Community Council (☎ 4069 3252) or Pajinka Wilderness Lodge. You can write to the Injinoo Community Council, PO Box 7757, Cairns, Qld 4870.

Alternatively, you can wait until you get to the Injinoo-owned and operated ferry across the Jardine River. The $80 (return) fee includes the cost of camping at a number of pleasant, isolated sites, and the permit fees.

Travelling across Aboriginal land elsewhere on the Cape may require a permit. Some are easy to obtain while others are difficult – it all depends on the community concerned. It is best to write to the relevant community council stating the reason for your visit, dates etc. Allow plenty of time for an answer.

Books & Maps

There is a wide range of books and maps on Cape York available in Cairns, Cooktown and Weipa, and from good bookshops all over Australia.

The Hema map *Cape York* and the RACQ maps *Cairns/Townsville* and *Cape York Peninsula* are the best. Ron and Viv Moon's *Cape York – An Adventurer's Guide* is the most comprehensive guidebook for the do-it-yourself camper and 4WD traveller.

The Last Frontier: Cape York Wilderness by Glenville Pike covers the history of the region well. For those interested in the Palmer River goldfields, the book *River of*

Gold by Hector Holthouse is by far the best. If you want to know about the flowers of the region, a colourful, small book, *A Wilderness in Bloom*, written and published by B & B Hinton, is a good place to start.

There are no modern books readily available that give a comprehensive look at the Aboriginal art of the area. Percy Trezise wrote *Quinkan Country* and *Last Days of a Wilderness*, as well as a report titled *Rock Art of South-East Cape York*, which was produced by the Australian Institute of Aboriginal Studies some years ago. They are difficult to get now.

Radio Frequencies

Unless you are doing something way out of the ordinary, a HF radio, while nice to have, is not a necessity for the Cape. Contact the RFDS base in Cairns for details of emergency frequencies covering the Cape.

Fuel

The distances between fuel stops aren't great and the condition of the road is fair at most times of the year. Diesel, unleaded and super are generally readily available along the route to the Cape, but there is no LPG after Cairns, except at Cooktown.

Towing

Should you need a tow to the nearest town, the following towing services will be extremely useful:

Mt Molloy Service Centre & RACQ Service Depot (24 hours ☎ 4094 1260) Brown St, Mt Molloy
Lakeland Cash Store & RACQ Service Depot (24 hours ☎ 4060 2133)
Cooktown Towing & Transport (☎ 4069 5545) McIvor Rd, Cooktown
JBSI Transport (24 hours ☎ 4069 7795) Weipa – towing and salvage anywhere on Cape York
WRAFTEC Industries (☎ 4069 7877) 1 Iraci Ave, Weipa

Camping Equipment Rental

Geo Pickers Great Outdoors Centre (☎ 4051 1944), 108 Mulgrave Rd, Parramatta Park, Cairns, has a range of camping equipment and accessories for hire.

ORGANISED TOURS

For most people travelling to the Tip, Cairns is the stepping-off point, and has everything you need to organise a trip north: rental vehicles, camping equipment rentals, guiding services, as well as a host of tour operators who can organise part, or all, of your trip to the Cape.

Tour Operators

A host of companies operates 4WD tours from Cairns to Cape York. The trips generally range from six to 16 days, and take in Laura, the Quinkan rock-art galleries, Lakefield National Park, Coen, Weipa, Indian Head Falls, Bamaga, Somerset and Cape York itself. Most trips also visit Thursday Island, as well as taking in Cape Tribulation, Cooktown and/or the Palmer River goldfields at the start or end of the odyssey.

Travel on standard tours is in 4WDs with five to 12 passengers; accommodation is in tents and all food is supplied. Some of the better known 4WD tour operators include Oz Tours Safaris (☎ 1800 079 006), Australian Outback Travel (☎ 4031 5833), Heritage 4WD Tours (☎ 4038 2186), Kamp Out Safaris (☎ 4038 2628) and Wild Track Adventure Safaris (☎ 4055 2247), the last one being among the most experienced of the operators and with an excellent reputation.

Most of the companies offer a variety of alternatives, such as to fly or sail one way and travel overland the other. Expect to pay about $1000 to $1400 for a seven-day fly/drive tour and anywhere from $1500 to $2500 for a 12 to 14-day safari.

Cape York Motorcycle Adventures (☎ 4059 0220) offers a five-day trip for $1550 ($1150 with your own bike) or a 12-day trip for $3600 ($1950). Prices include fuel, all meals and equipment.

Guide Services

One of the most popular ways to see the Cape is in the company of a tag-along op-

erator. Some companies supply a cook and all food, while others act only as guides, supplying information, permits, HF radio facilities and recovery expertise. While they do not supply a vehicle, if you need to hire one they can organise it for you. Tag-along companies include the following:

Cape York Connections
   (☎ 4098 4938) PO Box 371, Port Douglas, Qld 4871
Guides to Adventure
   (☎ 4091 1978) PO Box 908, Atherton, Qld 4883
Oz Tours
   (☎ 4055 9535) PO Box 6464, Cairns, Qld 4870

Mail Run

Based in Cairns, Cape York Air (☎ 4035 9399) operates the Peninsula Mail Run, the world's longest mail run. It flies a different route every weekday, delivering mail to remote cattle stations and towns including Laura. Space permitting, you can go along on these runs, but it's not cheap at $195 to $390, depending on the length of the trip.

Cruise Ships

Even without your own yacht, visiting the islands north from Lizard Island to Torres Strait is certainly possible. The *Kangaroo Explorer* (☎ 4032 4000, fax 4032 4050) does a variety of cruises between Cairns and Cape York, including four-day and seven-day return cruises and seven-day one-way cruises with a return flight. The ship is a 25m cruising catamaran with 15 twin cabins, each air-conditioned and with its own bathroom. Fares for the seven-day cruises range from $2068 per person for a twin cabin on the lower deck up to $2628 for a cabin on the main or upper deck. Costs include all meals and activities. Write to PO Box 7110, Cairns, Qld 4870 for details.

FESTIVALS

Cape York's major festivals include the Laura Aboriginal Dance Festival, held on the banks of the Laura River in June of odd-numbered years; the Hopevale Show & Rodeo, staged in July or August each year at Hopevale; and the Bamaga Annual Show, normally run in August or September each year in Bamaga.

GETTING THERE & AWAY
Air
Sunstate/Qantas flies daily from Cairns to Bamaga ($324), Lizard Island ($195) and Thursday Island ($324). Ansett flies to Weipa ($242). Flight West also operates a daily service through the Peninsula and to the Torres Strait Islands.

Skytrans (☎ 4035 9444), based in Cairns, has flights from Weipa to Bamaga, while from Cairns it flies to Lockhart River, Coen, Aurukun and Yorke Island.

A number of smaller airlines operate flights and charter services from Thursday Island around the islands of the Torres Strait and to Cape York. These include Northern Air Services (☎ 4069 2777), Coral Sea Airlines (☎ 4069 1500) and Uzu Air (☎ 4069 2377). Coral Sea Airlines flies from Thursday Island to Bamaga (among other places) for $80.

Bus
No bus company actually runs a service all the way to the top of Cape York, but Coral Coaches has a twice-weekly service from Cairns to Weipa – see the Weipa section for details.

Boat
A number of shipping companies cruise the coast of Cape York carrying a variety of cargo and stores. While many can transport vehicles, only a couple actually take passengers.

The weekly *Gulf Express* is a cargo boat which makes the trip at the very relaxed rate of 11 knots. It hugs the coast for the bulk of the way and although there's not much to do, there's plenty to look at – the trip through the narrow Albany Passage just off the tip is probably the highlight – and the relaxed pace is perfect. The boat is operated by Jardine Shipping (☎ 4035 1299), takes about 40 hours and costs $240/400 one way/return, including meals and ac-

commodation in a four-berth, air-con cabin. There's accommodation for eight passengers, and bookings should be made a few weeks in advance, although it's rarely full. Vehicles can also be transported, which might be handy if you have driven to the tip of Cape York and can't face driving back.

The fare is $600 from Thursday Island to Cairns ($750 in the opposite direction) and this includes barge transport between Horn Island (Thursday Island's port) and Seisia (Bamaga) on the mainland.

Gulf Freight Services (☎ 4069 8619; bookings only ☎ 1800 640 079) operates weekly barge services between Weipa and Karumba at a cost of $275 to $370 per vehicle depending on direction, and $210 per passenger. There are only three cabins and this service is very popular during the tourist season, so you should book as far in advance as possible.

4WD Rental
A number of rental companies based in Cairns and Port Douglas hire out 4WDs, but the majority will only let you take them as far as Cooktown and Laura. In Cooktown there are a couple of rental places where you can get a vehicle, but as elsewhere you'll only be able to drive it into the surrounding district, or in some instances as far as Laura.

Only a few companies will allow you to take the vehicle beyond Laura; these include:

Brits:Australia
(☎ 4032 2611), 411 Sheridan St, Cairns – 4WDs and 4WD campervans available for a minimum of seven-day hire to go to the Tip, from $155 a day plus insurance
Cairns Leisure Wheels
(☎ 4051 8988), 196A Sheridan St, Cairns – 4WDs available for hire to drivers over 26 years of age
Cairns Off-Road Accessories 4WD Hire
(☎ 4051 0088), 55 Anderson St, Maununda, Cairns

There are local car hire companies in Weipa and Seisia, near Bamaga.

4WD or not 4WD – that is the question!

It's a common perception that Cape York is only accessible for well-equipped and experienced 4WD adventurers. But when you actually go there this idea is soon challenged by the not insubstantial number of 2WD vehicles on the roads. There are also plenty of tales of people making it to the Tip in old Holdens and Fords, although not so many tales of them making it back again ...

While the roads on the Cape are all unsealed – some sections are smooth dirt, others are soft sand, and others are rocky and corrugated – the majority are reasonably well maintained. The main route to Weipa is used by mining company vehicles and is virtually a dirt highway. It is certainly *possible* to drive as far as Weipa in a conventional vehicle – whether you attempt to or not depends on how much (or how little) respect you have for your car. North of Weipa, the road conditions deteriorate rapidly and the numerous river crossings, from the Wenlock north, make it inadvisable to attempt going beyond Weipa in the family station wagon.

The other major drawback about not having a 4WD is that you'll have to stick to the main road, which means you'll miss out on the most spectacular parts of the Cape, such as the national parks.

The conditions of the roads can also vary substantially depending on a number of factors, including how recently they have been graded, the time of year and how much water is about, the effects of recent rain, and the amount of traffic using the roads.

Whatever type of vehicle you take, the important thing with a Cape trip is to be well prepared. Before heading off, seek expert advice on road conditions and routes (see the introductory Information section in this chapter). It's also vital to make sure your vehicle is in good condition for the trip, and to carry plenty of water plus all the spares, tools and equipment that you might need. If you do break down or get stuck it's a long way between mechanics, and even if you find one repairs will probably be costly.

Motorcycle Rental

It is very difficult to hire a motorcycle to take up to the top of Cape York, although there are a couple of motorcycle tour operators running trips up there – see the Organised Tours section earlier.

The Route

CAPE YORK SAMPLER

For those who don't have time to travel to the very top of Cape York, but still want to sample the delights of the region away from the glitz and glamour of Cairns and Port Douglas, an interesting loop to do is from Cairns to Cooktown and on to Musgrave via Battle Camp and Lakefield National Park, returning to Cairns via Laura and the Peninsula Developmental Rd. Even if you are travelling to the top, this is an enjoyable alternative to the main route.

The first sector of this route – Cairns to Cooktown – is covered in the earlier Far North Queensland chapter. The sections from Cooktown to Musgrave via Lakefield National Park, and from Musgrave back to Lakeland are covered in the following sections.

COOKTOWN TO MUSGRAVE VIA LAKEFIELD NATIONAL PARK (275km)

This route is a great alternative to the main road north, taking you on a short sidetrack to Hopevale, through the Lakefield National Park via Battle Camp. Battle Camp was the site of a major battle during the Palmer River gold rush when, in 1873, a group of 500 Aborigines attacked a party of diggers and police.

This route is very isolated, without any facilities or fuel stops along the way. For those doing it the hard way – walking or pedalling – the distances between water, especially towards the end of the Dry, can be a fair way and other travellers few and far between. You must be prepared to carry enough water to get between the permanent water points.

Cooktown to Hopevale

The McIvor River Rd heads west out of Cooktown, taking you past the cemetery and racecourse. The bitumen soon ends, and 10km west of town you cross the **Endeavour River** before passing the Cooktown airfield. The *Endeavour Falls Tourist Park* (☎ 4069 5431) is 33km north-west of Cooktown and offers camping and a kiosk for basic supplies.

At the 36km mark is the turn-off for Battle Camp and Lakefield. Continue straight on (north) to get to the **Hopevale Aboriginal Community**. The community has a number of shops including a hardware shop, butcher and a general store selling a variety of goods, including Aboriginal artefacts. Fuel (super, unleaded and diesel) is available at the service station. The Hopevale Show & Rodeo is staged in July or August each year. For further information, contact the Administration Clerk (☎ 4060 9185), Hopevale Community Council.

Munbah Cultural Tours (☎ 4060 9173 or write to Pleasant View, Cooktown Rd, Hopevale, Qld 4871) is operated by the local Aboriginal community. The program costs $100 per person per day. Visitors are shown many aspects of traditional life and enjoy a river cruise or bushwalking. Accommodation is provided in bush-timber huts on the beachfront, and all meals are included in the tour. Pick-up from Cooktown can be arranged for another $40. Photography is permitted on the tour.

Hopevale to Musgrave

The turn-off to Battle Camp and Lakefield is back along the Cooktown-Hopevale Rd, 36km north-west of Cooktown. Turn to the north-west, and about 5km further on there is a stony river crossing; just downstream is **Isabella Falls**. This is a magic spot – it's worth a stop and even a swim.

Keep left at the next junction 2.5km up the road. From here the road begins to climb the range and patches of rainforest begin.

The **Normanby River** is crossed 66km from Cooktown. Early in the Dry this river will have water in it, but by the end of the season it is just a sandy bed. There are pools upstream and downstream. About 1km before the river is the turn-off to *Melsonby Station* (☎ 4060 2259), which offers camping.

Keep on the main track heading west across undulating country with numerous gates, and 18km from the river crossing you pass the turn-off to **Battle Camp Homestead**. The mountains to the south are the rugged Battle Camp Range. Less than 3km further on you enter **Lakefield National Park**.

There is a large number of campgrounds spread along the rivers and billabongs of the park. You will often see tracks leading to these as you travel along the main track. If you want to camp here, you'll need to get a permit. The ranger will let you know the best spot to camp. The ranger station is at New Laura Homestead, 51km from the park boundary.

The **Laura River** is crossed 25km from the park boundary (112km from Cooktown). This crossing can be a little tricky early in the Dry, but by the end of the season it is generally no problem. The **Old Laura Homestead** on the far bank is worth a good look around. Pioneers lived here and in places like this right through the Cape, and after they had built such a place they thought they were on easy street. Most of us could not handle this sort of luxury for too long before we'd be running back to modern civilisation! The homestead was restored with the help of Operation Raleigh in 1986.

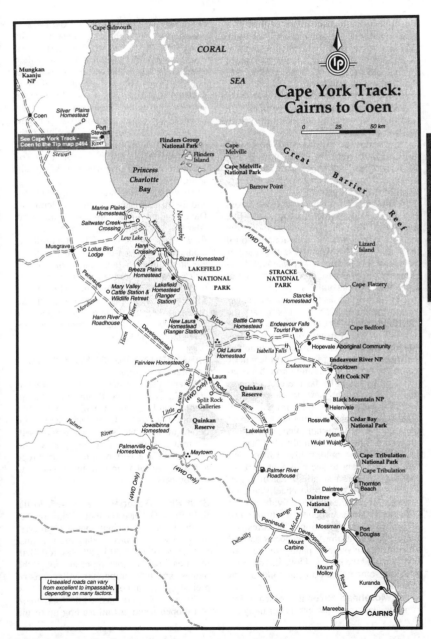

Cape York Track: Cairns to Coen

0   25   50 km

CORAL

SEA

Great Barrier Reef

Mungkan Kaanju NP

Coen

Silver Plains Homestead

Port Stewart

Stewart River

See Cape York Track - Coen to the Tip map p494

Cape Sidmouth

Flinders Group National Park

Flinders Island

Cape Melville

Cape Melville National Park

Barrow Point

Princess Charlotte Bay

Marina Plains Homestead

Saltwater Creek Crossing

Low Lake

Musgrave

Lotus Bird Lodge

Hann Crossing

Bizant Homestead

Breeza Plains Homestead

Kennedy River

Normanby River

LAKEFIELD NATIONAL PARK

STRACKE NATIONAL PARK

Lizard Island

Cape Flattery

Peninsula

Morehead

Mary Valley Cattle Station & Wildlife Retreat

Lakefield Homestead (Ranger Station)

Starcke Homestead

Hann River Roadhouse

Hann River

Developmental

New Laura Homestead (Ranger Station)

Laura River

Battle Camp Homestead

Endeavour Falls Tourist Park

Cape Bedford

Fairview Homestead

Old Laura Homestead

Isabella Falls

Hopevale Aboriginal Community

Endeavour R

Endeavour River NP

Cooktown

Mt Cook NP

Laura

Quinkan Reserve

Split Rock Galleries

Quinkan Reserve

Jowalbinna Homestead

Little Laura River

Laura River

Lakeland

Black Mountain NP

Helenvale

Rossville

Cedar Bay National Park

Ayton

Wujal Wujal

Palmer River

Palmerville Homestead

Maytown

Palmer River Roadhouse

Cape Tribulation National Park

Cape Tribulation

Thornton Beach

Daintree

Daintree National Park

DeSailly

Mount Carbine

Peninsula Developmental

McLeod R

Range

Mossman

Port Douglas

Mount Molloy

Kuranda

Mareeba

CAIRNS

Unsealed roads can vary from excellent to impassable, depending on many factors.

CAPE YORK PENINSULA

Just past the homestead and within 1km of the river crossing, you reach a T-junction. Turning left here will take you south to Laura, 28km away. This is the nearest place for fuel and supplies if you have decided to stay in the park for longer.

During the Dry there is a papaya fruit fly inspection post here where vehicles are searched and virtually all fruit and vegies must be deposited.

To continue to Musgrave and deeper into the Lakefield National Park, turn right at the T-junction. The **ranger station** (☎ 4060 3260) at New Laura Homestead is 25km north of the junction.

Heading north from here, you pass across vast grass plains, bordered by trees that line the rivers. Termite hills tower above the gold of drying grass and occasionally you'll see a shy wallaby skip across the road, or the occasional mob of wild pigs. After travelling 33km, you pass the ranger station at **Lakefield Homestead**.

The turn-off to **Bizant**, another ranger station (☎ 4060 3258), is 15km past the Lakefield ranger station, with yet another turn-off 10km further on. Just a few hundred metres past this track junction is the **Hann crossing** of the North Kennedy River. For travellers passing through the national park, this is by far the best place to stop. The crossing itself demands a little care as it has potholes and is rough.

Just downstream from the crossing there are a couple of waterfalls that drop into a large pool. The river is tidal to the base of the falls and we wouldn't advise swimming here. If you want to see how many crocodiles can inhabit a small stretch of water, take a spotlight down and check the pool one night. Count the eyes and divide by two!

There is some excellent camping upstream from the crossing. The sites are numbered and at times the place is booked out. It's safe to swim or paddle in the shallows here and the kids will love it. There are turtles in some of the pools that like a feed of bread.

The **Morehead River** is crossed 13km from the Hann crossing and is normally an easy crossing. The turn-off to **Low Lake**, a spectacular bird habitat, especially at the end of the Dry, is found 15km further on. Continue straight ahead and in less than 2km you'll reach **Saltwater Creek** crossing; it is sandy but generally no problem in a 4WD. You can camp around here, but it isn't as good as the Hann crossing.

The road swings south-west as it begins to head towards Musgrave. Keep left at the next few track junctions, as the tracks on the right lead to Marina Plains Station. You leave the national park 16km west of Saltwater Creek.

Stick to the main track heading westward and 34km later you will hit the Peninsula Developmental Rd, opposite Musgrave. About 15km before Musgrave is the *Lotus Bird Lodge* (☎ 4059 0773, lotusbird@iig .com.au), a new set-up with 10 individual elevated timber cabins, each with fridge, fans and small verandah. Meals are served in the central dining building. The tariff is $165 per person per night including all meals, or there are fly-in packages available from Cairns. The lodge cannot accommodate children under 16.

LAKELAND TO MUSGRAVE (200km)
Lakeland to Laura
Lakeland, the 'inland road' to Cooktown, is at the junction of the Peninsula Developmental and Cooktown Developmental Rds. See the Far North Queensland chapter for details of that route, and of Lakeland itself.

From Lakeland you're on your way to Laura and Cape York on a formed dirt road and this is about as good as the run north to the top gets.

Split Rock Galleries The turn-off to the Split Rock Galleries is about 52km further north. These Aboriginal rock-art galleries are well worth a look as they are the most accessible of the 1200 galleries found in this area. Together they represent one of the biggest and most important collections of prehistoric art in the world.

From the car park, just off the road, there is a looped walking trail leading up to the

Lakefield National Park

Lakefield National Park is the second-largest national park in Queensland and covers more than 537,000 hectares. It encompasses a wide variety of country around the flood plains of the Normanby, Kennedy, Bizant, Morehead and Hann rivers.

During the wet season these rivers flood the plains, at times forming a mini inland sea. Access during this time is limited or nonexistent. As the dry season begins, the rivers gradually retreat to form a chain of deep waterholes and billabongs. Along these rivers, rainforest patches are in stark contrast to the surrounding grass plains and eucalypt woodland.

Flora & Fauna In the north of the park, around Princess Charlotte Bay, mud flats and mangroves line the coast and the estuaries of the rivers. It might be an area full of sandflies, mosquitos and crocodiles, but it's also the nursery for the rich fish and marine life for which the area is so well known.

As the Dry progresses birdlife begins to congregate around permanent water, and at times thousands of ducks and geese create an unholy noise but a spectacular sight. Groups of brolgas dance on the open plain, and tall stately jabirus stalk their way through the grass. Birds of prey soar on the thermals looking for a meal, while in the deepest, darkest patches of the rainforest, pheasant coucals and Torres Strait pigeons can be found. In all, over 180 species of birds have been identified in the park. At times like these a small pair of binoculars comes in handy.

Agile wallabies are probably the most commonly seen mammal in the park, but feral pigs are prevalent and a problem for park staff. Bats make up the largest group of mammals found here. The large flying foxes are an impressive sight as they burst from their roosting spots in their thousands, on their evening search for nectar and fruit. You won't forget the sight, smell or damage they can do to the trees in which they roost.

Crocodiles Both the freshwater and saltwater (estuarine) crocodile are found in Lakefield National Park. The park is one of five areas in the state designated as important for the conservation of the estuarine crocodile in Queensland, and for many people it offers the best chance of seeing one of these animals in the wild.

Fishing Lakefield is one of the few national parks in Queensland where you are allowed to fish, and barramundi is the prize catch. The season is closed between 1 November and 31 January; at other times there's a bag limit of two fish per day, and no more than five fish may be taken out of the park. Line fishing is the only permitted method of catching these magnificent fish.

Canoeing & Boating Many of the big waterholes make for excellent canoeing or boating, and you can spend many enjoyable hours paddling a quiet stretch of water, watching birds or mammals as they come down to drink.

Camping Camping is allowed in a number of places, with a permit. A camping fee is payable for each night spent in the park, with a maximum of 21 nights allowed. Permits are available from the rangers at New Laura (☎ 4060 3260) or Lakefield (☎ 4060 3271). Bookings can be made six to 12 weeks in advance by writing to the ranger, Lakefield National Park, PMB 29, Cairns Mail Centre, Qld 4870. Explain what you are interested in and the vehicle you have, and the ranger will let you know the best spots to camp. If you have the time, try a couple of different locations.

Ron & Viv Moon

escarpment and across the plateau to the various galleries.

Laura

About 12km on from the Split Rock Galleries is Laura, a good little town in which to enjoy a beer at the pub, or to use as a base to explore the surrounding area. From here, you can easily visit the Lakefield National Park, the Aboriginal rock-art galleries at Split Rock, and the Jowalbinna Bush Camp, a wilderness reserve 40km west of Laura.

The Laura Store (☎ 4060 3238), next to the pub, sells a good range of groceries including fresh fruit and vegies, gas refills for camping bottles and fuel (super, unleaded and diesel). It accepts major credit cards,

Ampol cards and Australian travellers cheques. The store opens daily from 7 am to 6 pm.

Organised Tours At Jowalbinna Bush Camp (☎ 4060 3236), 40km west of Laura by 4WD, the Trezise Bush Guide Service (☎ 4055 1865) offers excellent guided day walks to some of the magnificent rock-art sites in the area ($60 per adult). Visitors can stay overnight at the bush camp ($5 per person to camp or $30 in a cabin). You can also get to the camp using the Coral Coaches (☎ 4098 2600) weekly Cairns to Weipa bus service. It has a package for $355, which includes return bus travel from Cairns, two nights at Jowalbinna, meals and

---

Quinkan Art

Quinkan is one of the great art styles of northern Australia. Vastly different to the X-ray art of Arnhem Land in the Northern Territory, or the Wandjina art of the Kimberley in Western Australia, Quinkan art gets its name from the human-shaped spirit figures with unusually shaped heads, called Quinkans, that appear often in the art of the region.

Over 1200 galleries have been discovered around the settlement of Laura, in the escarpment country that surrounds the lowlands along the great rivers of Lakefield National Park.

This great body of art is testimony to the Aborigines who once lived here. When the Palmer River gold rush began in 1873, the Aborigines fought to defend their land against the new invaders. Those who survived the bullets succumbed to disease, and the few remaining became fringe dwellers on the outskirts of towns and missions.

The rock-art galleries contain many fine paintings of kangaroos, wallabies, emus, brolgas, jabirus, crocodiles, snakes and flying foxes – wildlife still seen along the rivers and plains.

Spiritual figures and ancestral beings also point to a lifestyle that was rich in culture and religious beliefs. Among the paintings there are 'good' and 'bad' spiritual figures, the 'good' being heroes of old and figures depicting fertility, while the 'bad' are depicted by spirit figures such as the Quinkans.

Other paintings depict tools such as boomerangs and axes, while in some galleries stencils of hands and implements can be seen. Rock engravings are also found in small numbers, and in a couple of galleries images of horses echo the European invasion.

Only the Split Rock and Guguyalangi galleries are open to the public. South of Laura and close to the main road, they are readily accessible and joined by a walking track.

There are a number of overhangs in the Split Rock group of galleries, and while Split Rock itself is the most visually stunning, within 100m there are smaller galleries containing flying foxes, tall Quinkans and hand stencils.

The Guguyalangi group of galleries consists of over a dozen overhangs adorned with a vast array of figures, animals and implements and are possibly the best of the lot.

guide services. The bus drops you in Laura, from where you are picked up.

Festivals The Laura Aboriginal Dance Festival is held near Laura, on the banks of the Laura River. It brings together Aborigines from all over Cape York for three excellent days. The festival is held in June of odd-numbered years. Contact the Ang-Gnarra Aboriginal Corporation (☎ 4060 3214) for up-to-date information on festival dates and activities.

The Laura horse races and rodeo are held on the first weekend in July. It is an entertaining weekend where the locals from the surrounding cattle stations show their skills and let down their hair. It has become a tra-dition on the Cape with people coming from far afield.

Places to Stay & Eat Apart from camping near the Laura River, you have a choice of staying at the *pub* or in the *caravan park*. There is also accommodation at Jowalbinna (see Organised Tours earlier).

The *Quinkan Hotel* (☎ 4060 3255) has clean and simple singles/doubles with shared bathrooms for $35/45. You can also camp for $10 per site.

On the main north-south road is the *Laura Cafe*, which sells fuel, a few groceries and takeaways. It opens from 7 am to 10 pm, and accepts major credit cards and good old cash.

A walking trail leads from the car park at Split Rock, past the galleries in this group and then up onto the plateau to a lookout at Turtle Rock. The view from here is stunning. From this point the trail wanders through the open forest of the plateau for 1km to the Guguyalangi group. The views here are, once again, spectacular. If you're going to do this walk, save it for the late afternoon or early morning – it can get quite warm wandering across the plateau at midday. Take some water and food and enjoy the art and solitude of this place.

The Giant Horse galleries, across the road from the Split Rock and Guguyalangi sites, are a little harder to see and consist of five shelters depicting many animals, including a number of horses. These galleries can only be visited with a guide from the local community, and pre-arrangement with the ranger is essential.

Much study on the sites has been done since 1960 by Percy Trezise, a pilot, artist and amateur archaeologist. Trezise and his sons, Steve and Matt, have established a wilderness reserve at Jowalbinna. The Jowalbinna Bush Camp is open to travellers and Steve runs the Trezise Bush Guide Service, specialising in guided walking trips to the many superb galleries in the nearby area.

The Magnificent Gallery, deep in the ranges behind Jowalbinna Bush Camp, stands out from the rest. Along a rock shelter 50m or more in length a profusion of colourful spirit figures, animals and Quinkans adorns every available space.

For more information on Quinkan art around Laura, contact the Ang-Gnarra Aboriginal Corporation (☎ 4060 3214, fax 4060 3231). Maps, brochures and information for self-guided walks around the art sites are obtainable from the ranger station, which is beside the caravan park.

It may also be possible to organise a tour of the art sites with a ranger, if one is available. There is a ranger station, which is usually staffed, at the Split Rock Gallery car park. Although there is no fee to visit the art sites, visitors are requested to make a donation of $3 per adult.

If you want to visit Jowalbinna phone ☎ 4060 3236. Alternatively, contact the Trezise Bush Guide Service (see Organised Tours in the Laura section).

Ron & Viv Moon

Laura to Musgrave

The road continues to be well-formed dirt as it heads north from Laura. Most of the creek crossings are dry, but early in the dry season some may have water in them. Some of these creek and river crossings provide a welcome spot to camp. The Little Laura River, 12km north of Laura, and the Kennedy River, 32km north, are two such spots.

On the banks of the Hann River, 75km north of Laura, is the *Hann River Roadhouse* (☎ 4060 3242). This is another pleasant place to stop. The roadhouse sells fuel and does minor repairs, has limited food supplies, takeaways, a bar and a restaurant. The combination of a campground with all amenities, including powered sites, and the nearby permanent water and fishing make it a pleasant spot to camp. Campsites cost $5 per person.

From here to Musgrave it is 62km of corrugated dirt road that in sections winds through some hilly country. A few bad creek crossings and nasty dips will keep your speed down. About the only spot worth camping at is the **Morehead River**, 29km north of the Hann River.

Musgrave

There is only one main building in Musgrave – the historic *Musgrave Telegraph Station* (☎ 4060 3229), built in 1887. It sells fuel, a few groceries, meals, takeaway food and cold beer. Accommodation is available for $20/30 a single/double. It is also possible to camp ($5).

From near here, tracks run east to the Lakefield National Park or west to Edward River and the Pormpuraaw Aboriginal Community.

MUSGRAVE TO COEN (107km)

The road to Coen is little different to what you have experienced before. There may be a few more bull dust patches which can play hell with a motorcycle rider or a low-slung conventional car, but if you've got this far you'll probably make it to Weipa.

About 80km north of Musgrave you meet a road junction. The better, newer road leads left to Coen, while the older, rougher road swings right, crossing the **Stewart River** twice before reaching Coen. With little traffic, the first crossing of the Stewart River makes a fine campsite.

The old road gives access to the road to **Port Stewart** on the east coast of the Cape (reasonable camping and good fishing).

Coen

Coen is the 'capital' of the Cape, and unless you take the turn-off into Weipa, it is the biggest town you'll see north of Cooktown. People have some entertaining times in this place, all of course in and around the pub, the social heart of any country town.

There is a choice of places to buy food and fuel and even a couple of places offering accommodation, not including the police station lock-up or the hospital.

Facilities *Clark's General Store & Garage* (☎ 4060 1144) has groceries, fuel, gas refills for camping bottles, mechanical repairs and welding. The store is open daily but the workshop is not usually open on Sunday. Major credit cards are accepted.

Ambrust & Co General Store (☎ 4060 1134) also has a good range of groceries, and doubles as the post office with a Commonwealth Bank agency. Fuel and camping gas are available. It also is open daily. The store runs a campground for $10 ($12 powered).

The national parks ranger's office (☎ 4060 1137) is worth visiting if you require any information about Cape York's national parks.

Places to Stay & Eat The *Exchange Hotel* (☎ 4060 1133) has basic air-con pub rooms with shared bathrooms costing $25/35 for singles/doubles, or motel rooms for $35/45. The pub's bistro serves lunches and dinners.

Just down from the pub is the *Homestead Guest House* (☎ 4060 1157). The guesthouse has simple, comfortable rooms with ceiling fans and shared bathroom facilities. Singles/doubles cost $30/50. Home-cooked meals are also available.

COEN TO ARCHER RIVER (66km)

About 3km north of Coen, the main road north parallels the **Coen River** for a short distance. There is some good camping along the river, and while it is a popular spot, there is generally no problem in finding a place to throw down the swag or erect a tent. Toilet facilities are provided.

For the first 23km north of Coen the road is very well maintained, but once you have passed the Coen airfield the road quickly returns to its former standard. About 2km past the airfield you reach the main access track to **Mungkan Kaanju National Park**. This park consists of two large sections and straddles much of the Archer River and its tributaries. The Rokeby section takes in much of the country from the western edge of the Great Dividing Range almost to the boundary of the Archer Bend section of the same park. The Rokeby section has excellent camping on a number of lagoons and along the banks of the Archer River.

Access to the more remote **Archer Bend section** is only by rarely given permit. No facilities are provided. The ranger station (☎ 4060 3256) is about 70km west from the Peninsula Developmental Rd at **Rokeby Homestead**, or see the district ranger based in Coen.

Further north, the main road continues as before, until about 50km north of Coen where the road becomes more like a roller coaster.

Archer River

Just down the hill from the roadhouse is the magnificent Archer River. During the Dry this river is normally just a pleasant stream bordered by a wide, tree-lined sandy bed. It is an ideal spot to camp, although at times space is at a premium. As with many of the permanent streams on the Cape, the banks are lined with varieties of paperbarks, or melaleucas. Growing to more than 40m tall, these often stout, flaky-barked trees offer shade for passing travellers; and when in flower they attract hordes of birds and fruit bats that love the heavy, sweet-smelling nectar.

The Archer River crossing used to be a real terror, but now, with its concrete causeway, is quite easy. However, any heavy rain in the catchment will quickly send the water over the bridge, cutting access to Weipa and places further north.

Places to Stay & Eat The *Archer River Roadhouse* (☎ 4060 3266) is a great place to stop and enjoy a cold beer and the famous Archer Burger with friendly company. General food supplies, takeaway food, snacks, books, maps and fuel can be purchased. Limited repairs can also be carried out. It is open from 7 am to 10 pm. Campers can pitch a tent in the campground for $5 per person per night. There are also good, clean units with share facilities that sleep up to four people and cost $30/40.

ARCHER RIVER TO IRON RANGE NATIONAL PARK (128km)

The **Iron Range National Park** is probably the greatest tropical rainforest park in Australia. Forget what you've heard about the Daintree; this place is better and wilder, with more endemic animals and plants. There is a rich variety of vegetation, from heathland to dense rainforest.

Birds in the area include the vivid eclectus parrot; the large and vocal palm cockatoo; the shy fawn-breasted bowerbird; the stunning, migratory red-bellied pitta; and that giant of the rainforest, the southern cassowary.

The spotted and the grey cuscus and the rufous spiny bandicoot are three of the mammals found in the park, and are also found in the forests of Papua New Guinea. One animal that is commonly seen here is the northern quoll (also – erroneously – called native cat). This striking marsupial is a small predator that sometimes wanders into camps and houses looking for something to eat. If you're lucky enough to see one you won't forget the encounter.

Some 10% of Australia's butterfly species also reside in this park; of these, 25 species are found no further south and the park is their stronghold.

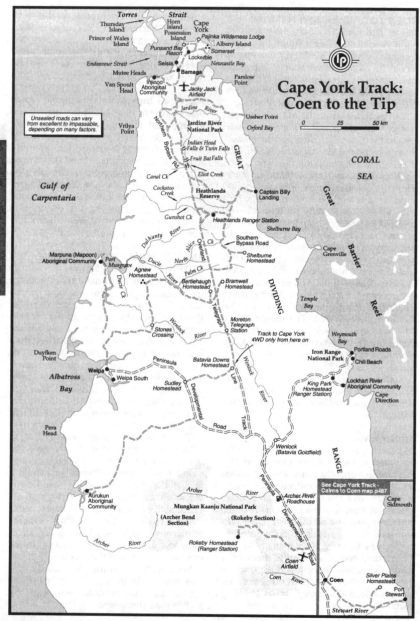

CAPE YORK PENINSULA

Torres   Strait

Thursday Island
Prince of Wales Island
Horn Island
Possession Island
Cape York
Pajinka Wilderness Lodge
Albany Island
Somerset
Punsand Bay Resort
Lockerbie
Seisia
Bamaga
Newcastle Bay
Parslow Point
Mutee Heads
Ihinoo Aboriginal Community
Van Spoult Head
Jacky Jack Airfield
Endeavour Strait

Jardine River
Jardine River National Park
Ussher Point
Orford Bay
Northern Bypass Rd
Vrilya Point

Indian Head Falls & Twin Falls
Fruit Bat Falls
GREAT

CORAL
SEA

Canal Ck
Eliot Creek

Gulf of Carpentaria

Cockatoo Creek
Heathlands Reserve
Captain Billy Landing

Great

Gunshot Ck
Heathlands Ranger Station

Shelburne Bay

Dalhunty River
Alice Ck
Southern Bypass Road
Shelburne Homestead

Barrier

Overland
North
Palm Ck
Ducie River
Marpuna (Mapoon) Aboriginal Community
Port Musgrave
Agnew Homestead
Bertiehaugh Homestead
Bramwell Homestead
Cape Grenville

Ducie Ck
DIVIDING

Temple Bay

Telegraph

Stones Crossing
Wenlock River
Moreton Telegraph Station
Track to Cape York 4WD only from here on

Reef

Duyfken Point
Peninsula
Batavia Downs Homestead
Weymouth Bay
Iron Range National Park
Portland Roads
Chili Beach

Wenlock

Developmental
Weipa
Weipa South
Sudley Homestead
Albatross Bay

Line
King Park Homestead (Ranger Station)
Lockhart River Aboriginal Community
Cape Direction

River
Road
Track

Pera Head

Wenlock (Batavia Goldfield)

RANGE

Archer   River
Archer River Roadhouse

Aurukun Aboriginal Community
Mungkan Kaanju National Park
(Archer Bend Section)
(Rokeby Section)

Peninsula
Developmental
Cape Sidmouth

See Cape York Track - Cairns to Coen map p487

Archer   River
Rokeby Homestead (Ranger Station)

Coen Airfield

Silver Plains Homestead
Port Stewart

Coen   River
Coen
Road

Stewart River

> **Cape York Track:
> Coen to the Tip**
>
> 0   25   50 km

Unsealed roads can vary from excellent to impassable, depending on many factors.

There are only a couple of campgrounds in this park. Near the East Claudie River and Gordon Creek is the Rainforest campground. The other is at Chili Beach, but this is hardly in the rainforest. Other small campsites are dotted on or near streams along the road. The ranger (☎ 4060 7170) is based at King Park Homestead.

Portland Roads, 135km east of the track, is a small fishing port with no facilities for the traveller, except a telephone. The fishing offshore, if you have a small boat, is excellent.

Chili Beach is just a few kilometres south of Portland Roads and is where all the travellers camp. Pit toilets are provided. It is part of the Iron Range National Park and a camping permit is required, available from the ranger based at King Park Homestead or the Department of Environment office in Cairns. While it's a nice spot, it would be even better if the wind would stop blowing – which it does occasionally late in the season.

Visitors to the **Lockhart River Aboriginal Community**, 40km south of Portland Roads, are welcome to stop for fuel and supplies, but are asked to respect the community's privacy. Use of cameras and videos is not permitted. There are also a police station and a hospital. A permit is not required to enter the community. You can contact the Lockhart River Community Council on ☎ 4060 7144.

The *General Store* (☎ 4060 7192) can supply most food items as well as fuel (which is expensive). It also has a post office with a Commonwealth Bank agency.

There are no camping facilities, but accommodation is available at the *guesthouse* (☎ 4060 7139) and it is best to book ahead. The house is self- contained, but you need to supply your own linen. It costs $40 per person per day.

ARCHER RIVER TO WEIPA

The road north of the Archer is good all the way to Weipa. There are two main routes leading into Weipa, known respectively as the Southern Access Route and the North-

ern Access Route. Both routes are described below.

Weipa via the Southern Access Route (145km)

The most direct route to Weipa is the continuation of the Peninsula Developmental Rd, which leaves the Overland Telegraph Line 47km north of the Archer.

Just over halfway, at the 74km mark, a track which leaves the Telegraph Track at Batavia Downs, south of the Wenlock River, joins up with the Peninsula Developmental Rd at the Sudley Homestead, 71km east of Weipa. This track is often chopped up and a couple of the creek crossings are muddy early in the Dry. This route gives people another option to leave or join the route to the Tip.

As you get closer to Weipa, the mining activities increase and the road improves. Heed all the warning signs, especially where the road crosses the mine haulage ways.

Weipa via the Northern Access Route (169km)

Heading north out of Weipa, this route goes via Stones Crossing, over the Wenlock River, to the Agnew Homestead and eastward to the Telegraph Track, south of the Bertiehaugh Homestead.

This track crosses private land and, depending on the owner, access across Bertiehaugh is sometimes open, sometimes closed! This is a good run and well worth the effort, so ask other travellers at each end of the route for the latest advice.

Stones Crossing is 57km north-east of Weipa. First, take the Old Mapoon Rd and at the 28km mark veer right at the major Y-junction. The road swings east for 20km before turning north for the last 9km to the crossing of the Wenlock River. This is a magic spot to camp, but remember that the river is tidal as far as the crossing itself and is inhabited by estuarine crocodiles.

From the river, the track deteriorates and heads north for 31km before turning east. **Agnew** was once a wartime airstrip that is

CAPE YORK PENINSULA

Be Sure and Tell 'Em Toots Sent You

In the car park in front of the Archer River Roadhouse is a memorial stone to 'Toots' Holzheimer, a truckie who drove her way into the Cape York history books. Toots, one of the Cape's transport pioneers, was killed in a loading accident in February 1992. She is fondly remembered by locals as one of the legends of Cape York, someone who frequently battled flooded roads, cyclones and other hazards to deliver her loads. One of her fellow truckies tells of the time he drove past and saw a very pregnant-looking Toots rolling 40-gallon barrels onto her truck – a couple of days later, he heard she'd given birth to her second daughter.

Reading about Toots, it's hard not to notice some uncanny parallels between her story and a sequence out of Pee Wee Herman's weird first film *Pee Wee's Big Adventure*. Lost on a dark and foggy night, Pee Wee is picked up by a female truckie who appears out of nowhere. When she drops him at a roadhouse, she utters the immortal words: 'Be sure and tell 'em Large Marge sent you'. Pee Wee does just that, but is horrified when the locals tell him that Large Marge was killed in a traffic accident 10 years earlier, on that very night. Large Marge may have died in the crash, but her spirit lived on, driving her enormous rig up and down the highway and watching over lost and lonely travellers ...

now dominated by tall termite mounds. You drive down the edge of the old airstrip before turning eastward. From here you continue on a sandy, rough track for 50km before coming to a track junction. Keep to the right and after 11km you will meet the Telegraph Track, 26km north of the Wenlock River.

WEIPA
pop 2500

Weipa is a modern mining town which works the world's largest deposits of bauxite (the ore from which aluminium is processed). It offers an interesting glimpse of what life is like in a remote mining community. The mining company, Comalco, runs tours of its operations, and the town has a wide range of facilities including a hotel/motel and a campground. In the vicinity there's interesting country to explore, good fishing and some pleasant campsites in a little-visited corner of Australia.

History

Aborigines lived in this area for thousands of years and beside many of the rivers around Weipa are enormous midden heaps, consisting mainly of cockle shells – these sites are protected under the Aboriginal Relics Preservation Act.

The first European to sight this coast was the Dutch explorer Willem Jansz, who sailed into the Gulf in 1606. In 1802, during his historic circumnavigation of the Australian coastline, Matthew Flinders sailed the *Investigator* into Albatross Bay, naming Duyfken Point in honour of Jansz's ship.

In 1955 a geologist, Harry Evans, led an expedition to Cape York in search of oil. Almost by chance, he discovered a large outcrop of bauxite near Weipa. He collected a number of ore samples which were later analysed and found to be high-grade, and within a few years Comalco commenced mining operations. Its first trial shipment of bauxite was sent to Japan in 1961.

Information

Weipa is the largest town on the Cape, and because it is a mining town, all facilities are available. These include a Commonwealth Bank (with full banking facilities), a post office, a chemist, a hospital, a large super-market in the suburb of Nanum, and numerous mechanical service centres.

Things to See & Do

Around Weipa itself and the areas north there are some excellent fishing places. Full/half-day fishing safaris costing $140/

70 can be booked from the Pax Haven Caravan & Camping Ground (☎ 4069 7871), or you can hire a boat yourself from the Weipa Snack Shack & Boat Hire Service (☎ 4069 7495), at the Evans Landing wharf. It has 4m tinnies, and it's best to ring and book a boat during the tourist season. Cost is $70/50 per day/half-day.

Campbell's Coach Tours (☎ 4069 7871) runs 2½-hour tours of Comalco's mining operations every day (at 9 am and 1 pm) during the tourist season. The tours cost $15

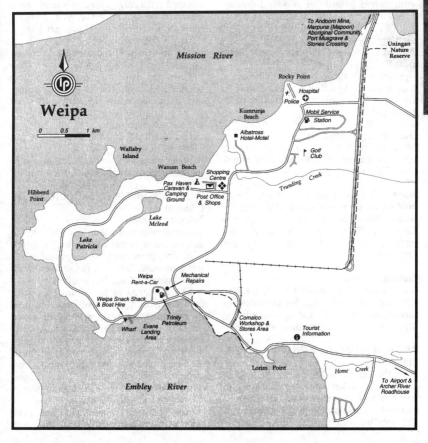

($6 children), and pick-ups and bookings (advisable) can be made at the campground.

Weipa even has its own golf course. The Carpentaria Golf Club (☎ 4069 7332) is open to the public.

Places to Stay & Eat

The only camping area is the *Pax Haven Caravan & Camping Ground* (☎ 4069 7871) which has tent sites for $14 ($16 powered).

The *Albatross Hotel-Motel* (☎ 4069 7314) has motel rooms from $90/120 for singles/doubles, or it has basic bungalows with shared bathrooms at $80 a double. Meals are served in the restaurant or bistro.

Getting There & Away

Air Ansett (☎ 13 1300) has a daily flight from Cairns to Weipa ($242).

Skytrans (☎ 4069 7248), based in Cairns, has twice-weekly flights from Weipa to Bamaga ($152 one way) and Thursday Island ($170).

Bus From April to October Coral Coaches (☎ 4098 2600) operates a weekly service between Cairns and Weipa (13½ hours, $125/235 one way/return).

Boat Gulf Freight Services (☎ 4069 8619; bookings only ☎ 1800 640 079) operates weekly barge services between Weipa and Karumba ($275 to $370 per vehicle depending on direction, and $210 per passenger).

Getting Around

Weipa Rent-A-Car (☎ 4069 7311), at Evans Landing, has 4WD vehicles available for touring around Weipa and for going to the Tip, from $140 to $180 a day.

ARCHER RIVER TO WENLOCK RIVER (117km)

After the turn-off to Weipa, which is 47km north of the Archer River, the road heading north quickly deteriorates and becomes more of a track, although it's still reasonably well maintained.

On the left of the road is **Batavia Downs Homestead**, which marks the second major turn-off to Weipa, 48km north of the first, southernmost one. The final 22km to the Wenlock River is along a road that is sandy and rough in places.

The **Wenlock River** is the first major water challenge you meet on your way north to the Cape. It looks surprisingly easy, but it is astonishing how many people come to grief here. Early or late in the dry season, the river may be running high because of rains in the ranges to the east.

A base of rocks has been placed in the riverbed at the crossing and, if it hasn't been washed away in the last Wet, you shouldn't have too much trouble. If you get bogged don't despair, you're not the first.

The north bank of the Wenlock River is a popular spot to camp and at times it does get crowded. Toilets are provided, as is a telephone. A small store is open sometimes and sells drinks, souvenirs and the like, and provides information and minor mechanical and welding repairs.

Just north of the Wenlock is the old *Moreton Telegraph Station*, which now provides homestead accommodation, camping and very limited stores.

WENLOCK RIVER TO JARDINE RIVER (155km)
Telegraph Track

The 155km from the Wenlock River to the Jardine River is the best part of the trip, with some great creek crossings and excellent campsites. Take your time and enjoy all the delights the Cape has to offer.

The challenge of following the rough track along the historic Overland Telegraph Line means that the trip will take at least a very long day, even if all goes well. A newer and easier route, known as the DCS road or the 'main' Cairns road, bypasses much of the Telegraph Track and avoids most of the creeks and rivers between the Wenlock and Jardine rivers. This route is covered later in the section on Bypass Roads.

Most of the major creek crossings have water in them; however, it's not the water that is the problem but the banks on each side. Take care.

Among the scattered timber and blanket of grass you can see zamia, or cycad palms. In places they form quite dense stands, and they come in male and female forms. Aborigines once used the palm nuts as a food source. The nuts are poisonous when raw and need special preparation and cooking before they are safe to eat.

The track is reasonable for the first 40km north of the Wenlock, until the first of the bypass roads leaves the old track.

The turn-offs to **Bramwell Homestead** and **Bertiehaugh Homestead** are 26km north of the Wenlock River. *Bramwell Homestead* (☎ 4060 3237) is on the east side of the road and offers very pleasant and reasonably priced accommodation and camping.

The route westward through Bertiehaugh leads to Stones Crossing and then onwards to Weipa (see the Weipa via the Northern Access Route section earlier).

The first of the major bypass roads, the **Southern Bypass Rd**, turns off the Telegraph Track 40km north of the Wenlock. This route keeps to the high country, staying well away from the many creek crossings the Telegraph Track makes. See the section on Bypass Roads that follows for more details.

Palm Creek, 43km north of the Wenlock, is followed by Ducie Creek, South Alice Creek and North Alice Creek, before you reach the **Dulhunty River**, 70km north of the Wenlock. This is a popular spot to camp. There are also some lovely places to swim, and the falls beside the road make a pleasant natural spa.

After crossing another major stream, a road leaves the Telegraph Track 2km north of the Dulhunty and heads for **Heathlands Ranger Station**, the base for the Jardine River National Park ranger. This road also bypasses the **Gunshot Creek** crossing. This crossing, just 15km past the track junction, requires care but is otherwise straightforward.

About 2km north of the Gunshot crossing, a track heads east to Heathlands Station. The vegetation changes again. No longer is it dominated by straggly eucalypts such as ironbarks and bloodwoods, but instead the country is covered in tall heathland.

One of the plants that observant nature lovers will find around here is the pitcher plant. These are found along the banks of the narrow creeks, Gunshot Creek being a prime spot for them. These plants trap insects in the liquid at the bottom of the 'pitcher', where their nutrients are absorbed by the plant.

After Gunshot Creek the track is sandy until you come to the **Cockatoo Creek** crossing, 94km north of the Wenlock River. Once again the actual riverbed is no drama, although it is rocky and rough; it's the banks that are the problem. In this case it is the north bank which often has a long haul of soft sand. The Injinoo people have a permanent camp set up at Cockatoo Creek.

For the next 24km the road improves slightly. A couple more creek crossings follow and 14km past Cockatoo Creek the Southern Bypass Rd joins up with the Telegraph Track.

Just 9km further on, the second major bypass, the **Northern Bypass Rd**, heads west away from the Telegraph Track to the ferry that crosses the Jardine River. Stick to the Telegraph Track at this point and keep heading north, even though the track north does deteriorate a little. There are other tracks that lead back to the Northern Bypass Rd and the ferry, if you don't want to drive across the Jardine River.

Within 200m a track heads off to the east, taking travellers to **Fruit Bat Falls**. Camping is not allowed here but it is a good spot to stop, have lunch and enjoy the waters of **Eliot Creek**.

The turn-off to **Indian Head Falls** and **Twin Falls** is 6.5km north of the previous track junction to Fruit Bat Falls. The track leads less than 2km to an excellent campground. On one side is Canal Creek and the delightful Twin Falls, while on the other is the wider Eliot Creek and Indian Head Falls which drop into a small, sheer-sided ravine.

CAPE YORK PENINSULA

Pit toilets and showers are set up within the campground and the ranger from Heathlands keeps the place in good condition, with your help. This is the most popular camping spot on the trip north, and although it gets crowded, it is still very enjoyable. A camping permit is required and a small camping fee payable.

Back on the Telegraph Track, over the next 10km there are Canal, Sam, Mistake, Cannibal and Cypress creeks to cross. All offer their own sweet challenge. Just south of **Mistake Creek** a track heads west to join up with the Northern Bypass Rd, which in turn leads to the ferry across the Jardine River.

From Cypress Creek it is a 7.5km run to **Logan Creek**. From here the road is badly chopped up and often flooded in places. You are now passing through the heart of an area the early pioneers called the 'Wet Desert' because of the abundance of water but lack of feed for their stock.

About 5.5km further on is **Bridge Creek**, or Nolan's Brook, which once had a bridge, and when you get to it you'll know why. It is an interesting crossing, and though it is short it does demand a lot of care. Less than 2km north of here the last track to the ferry heads west, while just 4km past this junction the main track veers away from the original telegraph line route to the right and winds for 2km through tall open forest to the Jardine River.

Jardine River

The Jardine River has some magical camping sites along its southern bank, west of the vehicle ford. There are no facilities here, and because you are in a national park, a camping permit is required from the ranger at Heathlands Station.

The river is wide and sandy. If you want to swim, stick to the shallows where the sandbars are wide. Crocs don't like such open territory but may be lurking in the deep, dark, lily-covered holes that line sections of the river.

Fishing upstream of the crossing is not allowed as you are in a national park.

Downstream from this point there is no problem and at times the fishing can be good, although closer to the mouth is better again.

Jardine River Vehicle Ford The vehicle ford leads out across the wide, sandy bed of the fast-flowing Jardine River. Midway across the river is a steep-sided tongue of sand that constantly changes its position. This tongue of soft sand often causes vehicles to bog in the middle of the stream. The water slowly gets deeper and is at its deepest (generally over 1m) within a few metres of the trees on the northern bank. The shallow exit point runs between a corridor of trees. There are some old timbers in this dark water between the trees which can easily stub a toe or hang up a vehicle, so be careful.

Never underestimate this crossing, even if it looks shallow. The 170m between entrance and exit is a long way – certainly most winch cables can't reach you if you stop mid-stream!

Remember, the Jardine River is inhabited by estuarine crocodiles, and although you might not be able to see them they are definitely there. In December 1993 a man was killed by a crocodile while he was swimming to the ferry at the ferry crossing, not far downstream from the vehicle ford.

In recent times the Department of Environment and the Injinoo Aboriginal Community have asked that all travellers use the ferry crossing and do not drive across the river at the vehicle ford. See the following Northern Bypass section for more information on the ferry.

Bypass Roads

As an alternative to sticking to the old Telegraph Track, there are several bypass roads which avoid most of the creeks and rivers between the Wenlock and Jardine rivers. This route is also called the DCS road or the 'main' Cairns road.

Both sections of this road are corrugated and people travel too fast on them. Each year a number of head-on accidents occur in the first two months of the Dry, most on the Southern Bypass Rd – be careful!

Southern Bypass Rd This road leaves the Telegraph Track 40km north of the Wenlock River crossing and heads east and then north. The turn-off east to Shelburne Homestead is 24km north of the junction, while another 35km will find you at the junction to Heathlands Ranger Station, 14km to the west.

When you reach a large patch of rainforest, 11km north of the Heathlands turn-off, the bypass road swings north-west, while a track to Captain Billy Landing, on the east coast, continues straight ahead. Keep on the bypass road for the next 45km to rejoin the Telegraph Track 14km north of Cockatoo Creek.

Northern Bypass Rd This road leaves the Telegraph Track 9km north of where the Southern Bypass Rd rejoins the Telegraph Track, north of Cockatoo Creek.

This route heads west away from the Telegraph Track and for 50km winds through tropical savannah woodland to the ferry across the Jardine River. At the 18km and 30km marks, tracks head east to the Telegraph Track.

The Jardine River ferry (☎ 4069 1369) normally operates seven days a week during the Dry from 8 am to 5 pm. A fee (currently it costs $80 return) is charged to use the ferry, but the money gets you a permit and allows you to camp in the area north of the Jardine River, including at Pajinka.

The *Jardine River Roadhouse*, on the south bank of the river, opens only sporadically, but it sells fuel and basic provisions, and has a basic campground. Contact the Injinoo Community Council (☎ 4069 3252) for further details.

JARDINE RIVER TO CAPE YORK (69km)

From the ferry crossing to the Tip it is less than 70km and for most of the way the track is in good condition. Once you have crossed the Jardine, the track swings to the east,

joining up with the old Telegraph Track, before heading north to the Tip.

The track, once out of the trees bordering the Jardine River, swings to the west and rejoins the Telegraph Track. Turning right, or northward, will lead to the main road to the north, while turning left will take you back to the river and the ferry point.

A number of minor tracks in this area lead back down to the river and some reasonable campsites. The best campsite is on the northern bank where the telegraph line crosses the river; an old linesman's hut marks the spot. The sandy beach here is a pleasant swimming place – but keep to the shallows.

Following the old line north brings you to a major crossroad, less than 2km from the exit point on the Jardine. Ignore the Telegraph Track that leads away directly north – this is unused and leads into the heart of the swamp. The main road heading off to the west leads to the ferry crossing of the river. Turning right, or eastward, will take you to Bamaga.

At the next T-junction, 22km north of where you came onto this major dirt road, turn right. Left will lead to the coast at the old wartime port of **Mutee Heads**, just north of the Jardine River.

Just 7km further on there is a small car park beside a fenced area that encloses the remains of an **aeroplane wreck**. Dating back to WWII, these remains are of a DC-3 which ploughed in on its return from New Guinea. This is the easiest aeroplane wreck to see in the area but there are a few more scattered around the main airfield, which is just a stone's throw away.

A couple of hundred metres past the car park there is a second T-junction. Right will lead to the main airfield, while left will lead to Bamaga.

Less than 5km from the second T-junction, a signposted road heads off to the right leading to Cape York, Somerset and places close to the Tip. This is the road you will require, but most travellers will need fuel and other supplies, and will continue straight ahead to Bamaga.

Bamaga

Bamaga is the largest Islander community on the northern Cape and is a spread-out town with all the facilities most travellers need. There are a hospital, police station, general store and service station. There is no campground at Bamaga, these being located at Seisia (Red Island Point), Umagico and Pajinka Wilderness Lodge at the Tip. The Bamaga Annual Show is run in August or September each year and features rodeo events, horse races, carnival stalls and an amusement fair.

Facilities The *Bamaga Service Centre* (☎ 4069 3275) has fuel available and can provide mechanical repairs, along with ice and camping-gas refills. It is open from Monday to Friday, and Saturday and Sunday mornings, and accepts major credit cards.

A reasonably well-stocked *supermarket* is open seven days a week during the tourist season, with limited trading hours on the weekend. There is also a National Australia Bank agency within the store (passbook only). The post office is also the Commonwealth Bank agency (again, passbook only).

Beer and wine can be purchased from the *Bamaga Canteen*, fresh bread from the bakery, and ice from the ice works. There are also a snack bar and newsagency.

Seisia

The Islander settlement of Seisia, 5km north-west of Bamaga, is an idyllic spot for the weary traveller to relax after the long journey to the Tip. There is an excellent foreshore campground, a kiosk and service station, and the nearby jetty is a great place for fishing.

Information The Seisia Camping Ground (see Places to Stay & Eat) is definitely the place to learn about what is happening in and around the top end of Cape York. It's the booking agent for all tours, the ferry service, taxi service, and anything else available. You can get up-to-date fishing information and maps, along with general tourist information.

Facilities Seisia Marine Engineering (☎ 4069 3321) is the place for all major repairs. Major credit cards are accepted. Top End Motors (☎ 4069 3182), Tradesmans Way, is the place to go for all mechanical and welding repairs to your vehicle.

The Seisia Palms Service Station (☎ 4069 3172) is Australia's northernmost service station and can supply all fuels.

Places to Stay & Eat The *Seisia Camping Ground* (☎ 4069 3243) overlooks the islands of Torres Strait and features palm-thatched picnic shelters, hot showers, washing machines and calm-water boating. Camping fees are $7 per person per night. During the tourist season the Seisia Island Dancers give regular performances. Also in the campground is the *Seisia Seaview Lodge*, with units for $65/96 a single/double.

The *Seisia Kiosk*, next to the campground, is open seven days a week and has meals and takeaways.

Getting There & Away Peddell's Ferry Services runs regular ferries between Seisia and Thursday Island – see the Thursday Island section later in this chapter for details.

Getting Around A taxi service (☎ 4069 3400) operates out of Seisia.

Injinoo Aboriginal Community

The small township of Injinoo is 8km south-west of Bamaga. It has a general store, Commonwealth Bank agency, fuel and mechanical repair facilities. For information, phone the Injinoo Community Council (☎ 4069 3252).

Umagico

Limited facilities, including a general food store and canteen, are available from this small community. A pleasant beachside *campground* costs $7 per person. For more details, contact the Umagico Community Council (☎ 4069 3251).

Bamaga to Cape York

From Bamaga, turn north towards the Tip along a well-formed dirt road. The ruins of Jardine's outstation, **Lockerbie**, are 16km north. The galvanised iron and timber building is a more recent residence, built by the Holland family in 1946. Nearby are mango trees and paths established by Jardine. There is usually a small store at the Lockerbie site and visitors are welcome to stop for refreshments, souvenirs and information.

Just north of Lockerbie a track heads west to **Punsand Bay**, about 11 bumpy, sandy kilometres away. A few kilometres later the main track north begins to pass through an area of rainforest called the **Lockerbie Scrub**. This small patch of rainforest, only 25km long and between 1 and 5km wide, is the northernmost rainforest in Australia.

About 7km from Lockerbie a Y-junction in the middle of the jungle gives you a choice of veering right for Somerset or left for the top of Australia. Less than 3km from this point on the way to the Tip, a track on the left will lead you 7km to the **Punsand Bay Private Reserve**, with tents, cabins and camping.

A further 7km brings you to the **Pajinka Wilderness Lodge** and the campground. There is a small kiosk to service the campground. From near the kiosk, a walking track leads through the forest bordering the campground at Pajinka to the beach near the boat ramp. From the beach you can head overland on the marked trail, or when the tide is low you can head around the coast to the northern tip. Both routes are relatively easy walks of an hour or so.

The islands of Torres Strait are just a stone's throw away and dot the turquoise sea all the way to New Guinea, just over the horizon. Swimming is not recommended here as the tidal stream never seems to stop running one way or the other. The fishing, though, can be pretty good.

Pajinka Wilderness Lodge

The *Pajinka Wilderness Lodge* (☎ 4031 3988 or ☎ 1800 802 968) is run by the Injinoo Aboriginal Community and is only 400m from the northernmost tip of Australia. This is a great place to reward yourself with a little luxury for making it to the top. There are cabin-style rooms in groups of four, a swimming pool, an open-sided restaurant and a bar. The rooms are simple and airy with a tropical feel, with their own bathroom and a little verandah. The standard nightly tariff is $230 per person which includes all meals. The lodge also has its own *campground*, with unpowered sites costing $8 per person. A licensed kiosk supplies limited stores, takeaway food and ice.

There is a regular ferry service from Pajinka to Thursday Island – see the Thursday Island section for details.

Punsand Bay

Punsand Bay, on a north-facing beach just a few kilometres west from the tip of Cape York, is one of the best and most scenic spots on the Cape. The *Punsand Bay Resort* (☎ 4069 1722) is very well set up, with a campground ($8 per person), on-site tents ($95 including meals), cabins ($135), a kiosk and dining room, hot showers and a laundry. Activities include night walks and tours to Cape York and the surrounding area. There is also a resident fishing guide.

Thursday Island & Torres Strait

There are a number of islands scattered across the reef-strewn waters of Torres Strait, running like stepping stones from the top of Cape York to the south coast of Papua New Guinea, about 150km north of the Australian mainland. The islands are politically part of Australia, although some of them are only a few kilometres from Papua New Guinea.

The islands of the Torres Strait exhibit a surprising variety in form and function.

CAPE YORK PENINSULA

There are three main types: the rocky, mountain-top extension of the Great Dividing Range makes up the western group that includes Thursday Island and Prince of Wales Island; the central group of islands that dot the waters east of the Great Barrier Reef are little more than coral cays; while the third type of islands are volcanic in origin and are in the far east of the strait, at the very northern end of the Great Barrier Reef. These Murray Islands are some of the most spectacular and picturesque in the area.

While Thursday Island (or 'TI' as it's usually known) is the 'capital' of Torres Strait, there are 17 inhabited islands, the northernmost being Saibai and Boigu islands, a couple of kilometres from the New Guinea coast. The population of the islands is about 9000 and the people are Melanesians, racially related to the peoples of Papua New Guinea.

History

Despite the islands being likened to a stepping stone between Papua New Guinea and Australia, there seems to have been remarkably little movement across the straits and the dramatic differences between development in Papua New Guinea and among the Aboriginals of Australia is of great scientific interest.

In 1606 two explorers became the first Europeans to pass through Torres Strait, although they were unaware of each other's presence at the time. Jansz sighted the west coast of Cape York from his ship the *Duyfken*. He led a party ashore and could have claimed the honour of being the first European to set foot on Australia, except that he thought he was still on Papua New Guinea. Meanwhile Spanish explorer Luiz Vaez de Torres was approaching the strait from the eastern side with his ship the *San Pedrico*. He had set out from Peru as part of an expedition to search for *Terra Australis Incognita*, the Great South Land, but the two ships were separated. Torres continued east and was swept through the straits by the prevailing winds and current. He landed on several islands before continuing around

Papua New Guinea, eventually reaching the Philippines.

The Spanish, however, did not reveal Torres' historic discovery and for the next two centuries the straits remained a rumour until Captain Cook confirmed their existence in 1770. After his involuntary halt at Cooktown to repair his damaged vessel Cook continued north and then, like Torres, was carried through the straits by the prevailing winds and current. He paused long enough at Possession Island to claim the whole east coast of Australia for King George III.

In 1802 Matthew Flinders, during his epic circumnavigation of Australia, made the most systematic survey yet of the islands and channels of the straits and also named the straits after Torres.

In 1868 rich oyster beds were discovered in the strait, and within months a pearling rush had begun. Around the same time missionaries arrived. They were obviously successful, as the Islanders are still one of the most church-going populations in Australia.

In WWII Torres Strait and the islands were part of Australia's front line in the battle against the Japanese. Horn Island, in essence TI's airport, was bombed a number of times in 1942, but TI never had a bomb dropped on it. Some say that was due to the legend that a Japanese princess was buried on the island, but it was more likely the fact that there was a large population of Japanese living on TI.

THURSDAY ISLAND
pop 2300

No visit to the top of the Cape would be complete without a visit to TI. The island can be a fascinating place to visit, although it's a long way removed from the resort islands down along the Queensland coast. It's a working island, and life here can be somewhat tough and uncompromising.

The island is little more than 3 sq km in area, with the town of TI on its southern shore.

There are a few stores, including a

The World's Your Oyster

Discovery of pearl shell in the waters of the Torres Strait during the 1860s led to an invasion of boats and crews in search of this new form of wealth. It was a wild and savage industry with murder and blackbirding – a form of kidnapping for sale into slavery – common. Many pearlers made a regular practice of raiding Islander and Aboriginal camps, to kidnap men to dive for pearls and women to entertain their crews. The strait was on the frontier, and all those who plundered its resources were beyond the reach of the law.

During the first half of the 20th century the pearling industry was still the lifeblood of the area. It was dangerous work, as there was little knowledge of the physiological aspects of deep diving, and death from the 'bends', or decompression sickness, was common. Poor equipment and the odd storm or cyclone were also perils divers and crews faced – a cyclone in March 1899 devastated the industry and killed several people.

While a number of nationalities made up the working population, the Japanese were considered by many to make the best divers. A wander round the Thursday Island cemetery will show the price they paid for their expertise: over 500 are buried there, most of whom died while diving for pearls.

After WWII plastics took over where pearl shell left off. A number of cultured pearl bases still operate around the waters of TI, but the 100 or more boats that once worked the beds have long since disappeared.

Today much of the wealth of the area still comes from the sea in the form of prawns from the Gulf, for which TI is a major port, and crayfish from the reefs of the strait.

---

general store, chemist, takeaways, a post office and a branch of the National Bank. There are also four hotels, three with accommodation (as well as cold beer). TI also has a police station (☎ 4069 1520) and a hospital (☎ 4069 1109).

Things to See

The **Quetta Memorial Church** was built in 1893 in memory of the *Quetta*, wrecked three years earlier with 133 lives lost. The TI **cemetery**, with its Japanese graves and the more recent Japanese Pearl Memorial for those who lost their lives diving for shell, is a poignant place. **Green Hill Fort**, on the west side of town, was built in 1891 when the Russians were thought to be coming.

While there are some other historic buildings and places of interest around Thursday Island, it is the atmosphere of the island and the people that set it apart from the rest of Australia.

Places to Stay

The *Jumula Dubbins Hostel* (☎ 4069 2122), on Victoria Parade, is a modern hostel which mainly caters for Aboriginals and Islanders, but also takes in travellers. Accommodation is in basic twin-share rooms costing $19 per person per night, which includes three basic meals. There's another hostel, the *Mura Mudh Hostel* (☎ 4069 1708), in Douglas St, which operates on a similar basis and is only a couple of dollars more.

The old *Federal Hotel* (☎ 4069 1569), also on Victoria Parade, has air-con motel rooms with attached bathrooms at $55/75 for singles/doubles and hotel rooms for $45/65. The *Torres Hotel* (☎ 4069 1141), on the corner of Douglas and Normanby Sts, costs $40/50 for singles/doubles.

The *Rainbow Motel* (☎ 4069 2460), easily missed on the main street opposite the shire building, has comfortable air-con rooms for $60/90.

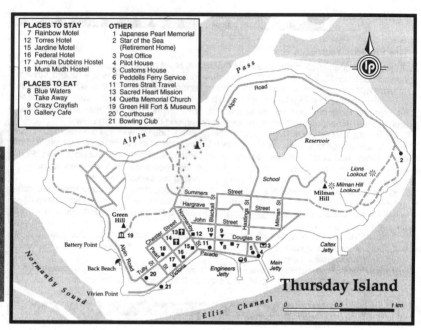

Thursday Island

Key:

PLACES TO STAY
7 Rainbow Motel
12 Torres Hotel
15 Jardine Motel
16 Federal Hotel
17 Jumula Dubbins Hostel
18 Mura Mudh Hostel

PLACES TO EAT
8 Blue Waters Take Away
9 Crazy Crayfish
10 Gallery Cafe

OTHER
1 Japanese Pearl Memorial
2 Star of the Sea (Retirement Home)
3 Post Office
4 Pilot House
5 Customs House
6 Peddells Ferry Service
11 Torres Strait Travel
13 Sacred Heart Mission
14 Quetta Memorial Church
19 Green Hill Fort & Museum
20 Courthouse
21 Bowling Club

The *Jardine Motel* (☎ 4069 1555) has a pool, bar and restaurant, and air-con motel rooms cost $130/160.

At Wasaga on Horn Island, just a short ferry ride across the bay, there are a couple of options. The *Gateway Torres Strait Resort* (☎ 4069 2222), one block back from the jetty, has rooms and a separate camping area with cabins (weekly rates only). The motel-type rooms have a fan, TV and limited cooking facilities, and cost $109/135 including a full breakfast.

Places to Eat

There's a number of snack/takeaway joints on the main street. Best is the *Burger Bar* at the rear of the Rainbow Motel which is open only at lunchtime. The *Blue Waters Take Away* and the *Crazy Crayfish* are also on the main street.

Offering something a bit different is the *Gallery Cafe* on the corner of Douglas and Blackall Sts. Here you can while away a pleasant hour or so on the verandah of an old timber home and choose from the limited but interesting menu. There are also paintings and craft works to look at while you wait.

The *Federal Hotel* is a bit rough around the edges but is the better of the two pub options (the rebuilt *Grand* being the other). Meals (lunch and dinner) can be eaten in the beer garden, and cost from $9 to $14.

The *Somerset Restaurant* at the Jardine Motel specialises in seafood and beef dishes and is TI's top eating spot.

Getting There & Away

Air The TI airport is actually on neighbouring Horn Island. Sunstate (Qantas) Airlines has regular flights between Cairns and Thursday Island. The one-way fare is $254 and the flight takes two hours. On TI the Sunstate office is at Torres Strait Travel

(☎ 4069 1264) on the corner of Victoria Parade and Blackall St, and this is also where you complete check-in for outgoing flights. The airfare includes a shuttle across the harbour between Horn and TI.

A number of smaller airlines operate flights and charter services around the islands of the Torres Strait and to Cape York. These include Northern Air Services (☎ 4069 2777), Coral Sea Airlines (☎ 4069 1500) and Uzu Air (☎ 4069 2377). Coral Sea Airlines flies to Bamaga (among other places) for $80.

Boat The cheapest and most interesting way to travel between TI and Cairns is on the weekly *Gulf Express* cargo boat. See the Getting There & Away section at the beginning of this chapter.

There are regular ferry services between Seisia (Bamaga) and Thursday Island. Phone Peddells Ferry Services (☎ 4069 1551) on TI for details. From November to May it has morning and afternoon services on Monday, Wednesday and Friday, and from June to October it has two services every day except Sunday. The fare is $60 same-day return or $35 one way. In the high season it also has connections between Pajinka Wilderness Lodge (Red Island Point) and TI ($40 one way). These are basically day trips, leaving Pajinka in the morning and returning from TI in the afternoon.

Intrepid travellers have, in the past, continued on from the Torres Strait Islands to Papua New Guinea by finding a fishing boat across the straits to Daru, from where you can fly or take a ship to Port Moresby. These days you will probably run into severe visa problems if you try this since Papua New Guinea officials frown on this unconventional entry method.

Getting Around
NETS (☎ 4069 2132) operates a regular ferry service between Thursday Island and Horn Island, where the TI airport is, daily except Sunday. The ferries run roughly hourly between 6.30 am and 5 pm, the trip takes about 15 minutes and costs $4.50 one way.

Around TI there are plenty of taxis, and Peddell's also runs bus tours on demand ($14 including the museum), usually when a day trip group comes across from Pajinka.

TI is small enough to walk around quite easily in a couple of hours.

OTHER ISLANDS
The other inhabited islands of the strait are isolated communities wresting a living from the surrounding reef-strewn sea. The Islanders who inhabit them are fiercely proud of their heritage, with a separate identity to the Aborigines.

Outside of TI the largest group of people is found on Boigu, close to the New Guinea coast, where the population numbers less than 400. Most of the inhabited islands have populations of between 100 and 200 people, while Booby Island in the far west of the strait is home to just a couple of families who look after the lighthouse.

Getting around and staying on the other islands of Torres Strait is really for the adventurous traveller. To visit any of the islands other than TI or Horn Island, you usually need a permit or permission from the island's council; however, these may not be easy to get. Contact the Torres Strait Regional Authority (☎ 4069 1247), at the office on Victoria Parade, Thursday Island.

Places to Stay & Eat
Accommodation on these islands is very limited. The community on Yorke Island, 110km north-east of TI, runs a small, self-contained *guesthouse*. Intending visitors should first write to the community council stating details of their visit. It will then be put before the chairperson for approval. For further details, contact the Yorke Island Community Council (☎ 4069 4128).

Getting There & Away
Once you have a permit you have a choice of flying or chartering a boat. Flying may be quicker and easier, but the essence of Torres Strait is somehow lost. See the Thursday Island Getting There & Away section for details of operators.

Gulf Savannah

The Gulf Savannah is a vast, flat and empty landscape of bushland, saltpans and savannah grasslands, all cut by a huge number of tidal creeks and rivers which feed into the Gulf of Carpentaria. It's a remote, hot, tough region with excellent fishing and a large crocodile population.

The coastline of the Gulf is mainly mangrove forests, which is why there is so little habitation – only a few thousand people live in the area, scattered among a handful of small towns, lonely pubs and roadhouses, isolated cattle stations, and Aboriginal communities.

The Gulf's two major natural attractions are at opposite ends of the region: the Lawn Hill National Park is a virtual oasis in the midst of the arid north-west, a stunning river gorge which harbours a verdant remnant of rainforest and the superb Riversleigh fossil field; and the spectacular Undara Lava Tubes, a collection of ancient and enormous volcanic lava tubes, which are near the east end of the Gulf Developmental Rd.

The Gulf's main towns – Burketown, Normanton and Karumba – still have the feel of frontier settlements. There are plenty of interesting fossicking areas in the area, including the rich gemfields and old mining towns around Croydon, Georgetown and Mt Surprise.

HISTORY

The coastline of the Gulf of Carpentaria was charted by Dutch explorers long before Cook's visit to Australia. Willem Jansz sailed the *Duyfken* into the Gulf in 1606; in 1644 Abel Tasman named it the Gulf of Carpentaria after the then-governor of Batavia.

In 1802 Matthew Flinders sailed into the Gulf during his historic circumnavigation of the Australian continent, stopping at Sweers Island (among other places) where he is said to have dug a well.

HIGHLIGHTS

- The Undara Lava Tubes offer an unusual underground experience.
- Make the effort to visit the Riversleigh fossil field, one of two World Heritage Listed fields in Australia.
- Take a ride on the *Gulflander*, Australia's quirkiest railway journey.

The first European to pass through this area was Ludwig Leichhardt, the eccentric Prussian explorer who skirted the Gulf on his 1844 trek from Brisbane to the newly settled Port Essington (near Darwin). After Leichhardt came the ill-fated Burke and Wills expedition. Burke, Wills, King and Gray camped a little way west of Normanton in February 1861. Because of the thick mangroves which line the coast here they didn't actually reach the sea, but knew they were close to it because of the tidal movement of the rivers.

After their disappearance a number of other explorers came looking for them, including the intrepid William Landsborough, who was responsible for opening up much of the Gulf region. Landsborough's enthusiastic reports of the Gulf's potential as fine pastoral land motivated many settlers to come to the area in the 1860s with herds of sheep and cattle.

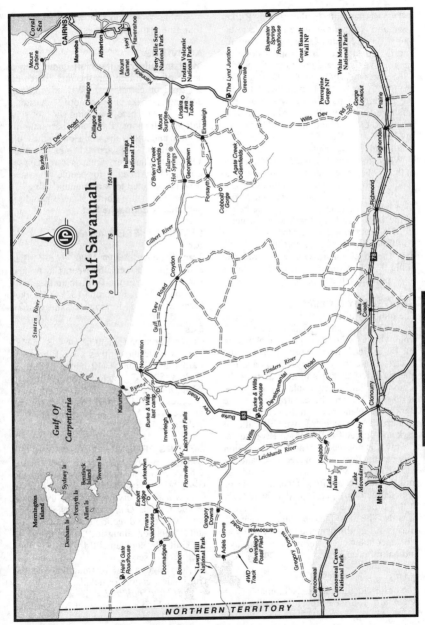

Two settlements in the region, Burketown and Normanton, were founded in the 1860s, before better-known places on the Pacific coast like Cairns and Cooktown came into existence. Burketown, founded in 1865, was nearly wiped out by a fever brought by a ship from Java a year later, and the remaining population was evacuated offshore to Sweers Island. Many of them moved to the new settlement of Normanton in 1867 and Burketown has been the smaller place ever since.

When gold was discovered near Croydon in the 1880s, the ensuing rush brought thousands of hopefuls into the region. Croydon developed into a major town, and at one time had more than 30 pubs. At the height of the rush, a railway line was constructed from Normanton to Croydon to link the goldfields to the nearest port town. Nowadays the anachronistic *Gulflander* train trip along this short route is one of the region's most popular attractions.

GEOGRAPHY & CLIMATE

The majority of the Gulf Savannah is made up of the vast, empty plains and saltpans from which it takes its name. The plains are cut by an intricate network of creeks and rivers; during the Wet these fill up and frequently flood, at times turning parts of the region into an immense inland lake. In the north-west region, the escarpments of the Barkly Tableland rise – in the centre of this area are the spectacular Lawn Hill National Park and unique fossil fields of Riversleigh.

Travel is not recommended in the region between the beginning of December and the end of March, when extreme heat and humidity make conditions uncomfortable or even dangerous. Apart from that, heavy rain at this time can close the roads for lengthy periods. The most pleasant time to visit the Gulf is during the winter months, when you will encounter cool mornings, warm days and balmy evenings.

MAPS

The best road guide to use is Sunmap's *Gulf Savannah* Tourist Map (1:750,000). It is available from most newsagencies and tourist information centres.

ACTIVITIES

Most travellers to the Gulf come with a sense of adventure; prospectors searching for gold or gemstones, 4WD adventurers and anglers make up the majority of visitors.

The fishing here is nothing short of sensational. Inshore, there are barramundi, salmon and mudcrabs, while out in the Gulf mackerel, tuna, cod and red emperor are all abundant. A number of places have been set up especially to cater for people who have become addicted to barramundi fishing.

The Gulf is also a birdwatcher's paradise, particularly during the Wet.

GETTING THERE & AWAY
Air

Trans State Airlines (☎ 1800 677 566) flies a few times a week between Cairns and various places in the Gulf, including Normanton ($270), Karumba ($294), Burketown ($356) and Mornington Island ($367).

Bus

Cairns-Karumba Coachline (☎ 4031 5448) has a service three times a week between Cairns and Karumba (12 hours, $122) via Undara ($42), Georgetown ($64), Croydon ($87) and Normanton ($110). Campbell's Coaches (☎ 4743 2006) has a weekly bus service from Mt Isa to Normanton ($69) and Karumba ($75).

GETTING AROUND
Train

While there are no direct rail services *into* the Gulf, there are two short services *within* the Gulf which are very popular with travellers.

The famous *Gulflander* runs just once weekly in each direction between Croydon and Normanton, alongside the last stretch of the Gulf Developmental Rd. There are connecting bus services from Cairns and Mt Isa to Croydon and Normanton. See the Gulflander section for details.

The *Savannahlander* is a new train service which runs between Mt Surprise and Forsayth twice weekly. Again, there are connecting bus services and packaged tours from Cairns. See the Mt Surprise section for details.

Car & Motorcycle
This chapter is divided into sections which basically follow the routes of the major roads through the Gulf.

From Queensland's east coast, the Gulf Developmental Rd takes you from the Kennedy Hwy, south of the Atherton Tableland, across to Normanton and Karumba.

If you're coming from the Northern Territory, the unsealed Gulf Track takes you across the top of the Gulf country to Burketown and on to Normanton. From Burketown you have two options if you're heading south: the unsealed road to Camooweal, via Gregory Downs and the Lawn Hill National Park; or the Nardoo-Burketown Rd, which cuts across to meet the Burke Developmental Rd at the Burke & Wills Roadhouse.

The other major route is the Burke Developmental Rd, a good sealed highway which takes you south from Normanton to the Burke & Wills Roadhouse. From here, you can continue south to Cloncurry, or head south-east to Julia Creek.

There aren't too many options apart from these major routes, particularly if you don't have a 4WD. Even if you do, remember that this is remote country and the going can be rough once you get off the beaten track. If you're thinking of attempting other routes, such as the continuation of the Burke Developmental Rd, which takes you east from between Normanton and Karumba to Mareeba via Chillagoe, you'll need to be well prepared and carry good maps, plenty of water and preferably a radio.

Eastern Gulf Region

The Gulf Developmental Rd is the main route into the Gulf from the east. It leaves the Kennedy Hwy 66km south of Mt Garnet, passing through the towns of Georgetown and Croydon en route to Normanton. The first section of the highway is paved and in reasonably good condition. About 110km past Georgetown the surface changes to unsealed dirt, and the rest of the route alternates between sections of sealed and unsealed highway. This section of the route is sometimes impassable during the Wet – check on road conditions before heading out.

The region crossed by this road has many ruined gold mines and settlements, and still attracts some gem fossickers.

UNDARA VOLCANIC NATIONAL PARK
Just 17km past the start of the Gulf Developmental Rd is the turn off to the Undara Lava Tubes, one of inland Queensland's most fascinating natural attractions. An impressive tourist complex has been built here to cater for visitors. Guided tours of the tubes and the surrounding countryside are offered, and you can camp or stay overnight in restored railway carriages.

These massive lava tubes were formed around 190,000 years ago following the eruption of a single shield volcano. The eruption continued for three months. The huge lava flows drained towards the sea, following the routes of ancient river beds, and as the lava cooled it formed a surface crust – just like skin on a cooling custard. The hot lava continued to flow through the centre of the tubes, eventually leaving huge hollow basalt chambers.

Organised Tours
You can only visit the tubes as part of a guided tour. The Undara Lava Lodge runs three different tours of the lava tubes: full-day tours depart daily at 9 am and cost $85 including lunch; half-day tours depart at 9.30 am and at 1 pm and cost $66 including lunch, $55 without; and there's also 1½-hour tours, which depart at various times throughout the day and cost $21. Out of the tourist season tours are less frequent and it's worth ringing ahead to book and check times.

GULF SAVANNAH

Undara Lava Tubes are an unusual and fascinating relic of ancient volcanic activity.

Places to Stay & Eat

The *Undara Lava Lodge* (☎ 4097 1411) is a unique tourist complex with three levels of guest accommodation. There are plenty of camping or caravan sites costing $16 per person, with good facilities including barbecues, hot showers and laundries. Then there are the 'camp-o-tels', semi-permanent tents with beds and lights which cost $18 per person, or $58 with breakfast and dinner included. Top of the range is the collection of charmingly restored old railway carriages, which make rather quaint and comfortable sleeping quarters; these have shared bathroom facilities. The nightly cost is $98 per person, which includes breakfast and dinner.

The lodge has a souvenir shop, a bar and a restaurant, but there are no shops or kiosks and you can't buy groceries or takeaway meals here – so if you're self-catering stock up on supplies before you come.

Getting There & Away

The lodge and lava tubes are 15km of well-maintained dirt road off the main highway.

Cairns-Karumba Coachline (☎ 4031 5448) has services three times a week from Cairns to Undara (continuing on to Karumba). The one-way fare is $42. (See Organised Tours in the Cairns section for details of tours to Undara.)

MT SURPRISE

Back on the Gulf Developmental Rd, 39km past the Undara turn off, is the small township of Mt Surprise, which has a pub, a railway station and two roadhouses. In the centre of rich cattle country, the town was founded in 1864 by Ezra Firth, a stonemason and gold-miner turned sheep farmer. You can read his strange story in the cafe at the Shell Roadhouse.

O'Brien's Creek Gemfields, 42km north-west of town, is one of Australia's best topaz fields.

The **Old Post Office Curiosity Museum** has a small and quirky display of local history items.

The *Mobil Service Station & General Store* (☎ 4062 3115) sells groceries and takeaway meals. It does welding and most mechanical repairs, and has a towing service. It has EFTPOS facilities.

The *Shell Roadhouse & Caravan Park* (☎ 4062 3153) has tent sites at $12 and on-site vans for $30. The cafe next door serves a good range of meals, and has a couple of information books full of interesting details on what to see in the area, yarns and local history, as well as mud maps of the fossicking fields around Mt Surprise.

The *Mt Surprise Hotel* (☎ 4062 3118) has basic pub-style rooms upstairs costing $20 per person. It also serves meals any time the pub is open.

Getting There & Away

You can get to Mt Surprise from Cairns with Cairns-Karumba Coachlines (☎ 4031 5448); several of its services connect with the *Savannahlander* (see the following section).

STEVE WOMERSLEY

MARK ARMSTRONG

R & V MOON

QUEENSLAND TOURIST AND TRAVEL CORPORATION

Top: Einasleigh Gorge is a good swimming spot in the hot dusty Gulf Savannah.
Middle Top: The Birdsville Hotel – a quiet watering hole for most of the year.
Middle Bottom: Cattle on the 'Long Paddock', North of Winton.
Bottom: Lawn Hill National Park is an oasis of colourful gorges and tropical vegetation.

MARK ARMSTRONG

A massive red sandhill near Windorah, Outback Queensland. West of Windorah the roads get rougher, the dust finer, and vehicles are few and far between.

THE SAVANNAHLANDER

Mt Surprise is connected to Forsayth, 120km south-west, by the *Savannahlander*. This service is an abbreviated version of the old Cairns-Forsayth service which was discontinued (somewhat controversially) in 1995.

The *Savannahlander* runs twice weekly, departing from Mt Surprise every Monday and Thursday at 12.30 pm and returning from Forsayth every Tuesday and Friday at 7.30 am (most people stay overnight in Forsayth, returning the next day). The trip takes five hours, with several stops along the way, and the one-way fare is $35 ($18 children).

You can connect with the *Savannahlander* by bus from Cairns.

EINASLEIGH & FORSAYTH

About 32km west of Mt Surprise, you can take an interesting if somewhat slow detour off the highway through the old mining townships of Einasleigh and Forsayth. Both towns are on the old Cairns-Forsayth railway line, so you can also visit them on the *Savannahlander* train.

The turn-off to Einasleigh from the Gulf Developmental Rd is poorly marked and easy to miss. It's a 150km loop from here back to Georgetown, and the going is quite slow and bumpy. The road is unsealed and fairly rough in sections, but is passable for normal vehicles during the dry season. You can also cut across to Einasleigh from The Lynd Junction on the Kennedy Developmental Rd, via 76km of unsealed dirt road.

Einasleigh, a former copper-mining centre and railway siding, has a population of about 35. Set in a rugged landscape of low, flat-topped hills, it's a sprawling, ramshackle town with a collection of mostly derelict tin and timber buildings. The *Central Hotel* (☎ 4062 5222) on Daintree St has pub-style accommodation and snacks. Across the road from the pub, the Einasleigh Gorge is a good swimming spot. The **Kidston goldmine**, the largest opencut goldmine in the country, is 45km south of Einasleigh off the Einasleigh-Lynd Junction road.

Forsayth is 67km further west. This place isn't much bigger than Einasleigh, although it is perhaps a little more alive, and has a railway station, a post office and a phone booth. The *Goldfields Hotel* (☎ 4062 5374) has basic accommodation in dongas, with rooms with air-con and shared bathrooms costing $50 per person including breakfast and dinner. The pub also sells fuel and a few groceries.

There are a couple of operators who offer tours in the local area: Forsayth Gold Fossicking Tours (☎ 4062 1282) has a half-day tour ($45) of a mining lease 15 minutes from town, which includes a lesson on gold panning and detecting. It also has a shorter tour for $25.

You can also drive from Forsayth to the **Agate Creek Gemfields**, which are 75km south-west, although the road conditions are fairly rough and you'll need a good map (or ask at the pub for directions).

If you're driving from Forsayth on to Georgetown, be sure to turn right just *before* the pub. Believe me, it's quite easy to miss the sign to Georgetown and end up in the middle of nowhere, opening and closing cattle gates as the sun slowly sets ...

COBBOLD GORGE

The lovely Cobbold Gorge was discovered a number of years ago on a cattle station 45km south of Forsayth. It's a scenic oasis, with a swimming hole, rugged cliffs and gorges, and an abundance of wildlife. You can camp nearby and take a tour of the gorge.

The *Cobbold Camping Village* (☎ 4062 5470) has toilets, showers and barbecue facilities and sites cost $10. There are half-day tours of the gorge for $50, or three-hour tours for $25. Tours depart from the campground, although if you're travelling on the *Savannahlander* the operators will pick you up from Forsayth.

MT SURPRISE TO GEORGETOWN

Back on the Gulf Developmental Road, 40km west of Mt Surprise is the turn-off to the **Tallaroo Hot Springs**, where you can soak in one of five naturally terraced hot springs. The springs are open every day from 8 am to 5 pm between Easter and the end of September. Admission costs $8 ($4 kids), which includes a tour of the property. Meals are available from a kiosk here.

GEORGETOWN
pop 310

Georgetown has three roadhouses, a pub, a post office and two cafes. During the days of the Etheridge River gold rush, Georgetown was a bustling commercial centre, but things are much quieter nowadays and, unless you need fuel, food or sleep, there aren't too many reasons to linger here.

Places to Stay & Eat

The *Midway Caravan Park & Service Station* (☎ 4062 1219) on the highway has camp sites for $9.50 and on-site cabins for $25. It also has a cafe and takeaway section, and has EFTPOS facilities.

The *Wenaru Hotel* (☎ 4062 1208), on the corner of St George and Normanton Sts, has simple but clean pub rooms with shared bathrooms at $25/40 for singles/doubles.

The *Latara Resort Motel* (☎ 4062 1190), on the highway 1km west of Georgetown, is by far the best place to stay. It has modern motel units with air-con ($48/60), and meals are available.

The *Travellers Tavern*, at the Ampol service station, has a small supermarket and does takeaway meals. It also has EFTPOS facilities.

CROYDON
pop 220

Connected to Normanton by the curious-looking *Gulflander* train, this old goldmining town was once the biggest in the Gulf. Gold was discovered here in 1885 by JW Aldridge, and within a couple of years there were 8000 diggers living here. It's reckoned there were once 5000 gold mines in the area and reminders of them are scattered all around the countryside. The goldfields were spread over an area 36km wide and 180km long, and Croydon was surrounded by more than 30 satellite townships. Such was the prosperity of the town that it had its own aerated water factory, a foundry and coach-builders, gas street lamps, and more than 30 pubs.

The town's boom years were during the 1890s, but by the end of WWI the gold had run out and Croydon became little more than a ghost town. There is still a handful of interesting historic buildings here to remind passers-by of the days of yore: the old **Shire Hall** on Samwell St is a great old timber building topped by a clock tower – inside there are several interesting and large murals painted on hessian by Steve Johns. The **Old Courthouse**, the **Mining Warden's Office**, the **General Store**, the **old butcher shop** and the **Club Hotel** also date back to the mining days.

Facilities

The *Croydon General Store* (☎ 4745 6163) is the local RACQ depot. It sells fuel, does most repairs and has a 24-hour towing service. The general store sells takeaway meals and groceries; next door there's a small museum with a collection of photos, tools, rocks and records, all fairly well hidden under an even more impressive collection of dust and cobwebs.

Organised Tours

Chris Weirman is the local tour guide. He has lived in the town for most of his life, and knows a fair bit about local history and sights around Croydon. Chris conducts walking tours of Croydon's historic precinct according to demand – he can usually be contacted at the Shire Hall or by phoning ☎ 4745 6185.

Places to Stay & Eat

The *Golden Picdewehousma Caravan Park*, on the corner of Brown and Alldridge Sts, is a bleak little tcampground run by the local council.

The *Club Hotel* (☎ 4745 6184), on the corner of Brown and Sircom Sts, has accommodation upstairs. The rooms are pretty basic but have plenty of character, with bare timber floors and corrugated iron walls. Single beds on the enclosed verandah are $15, or it's $30/40 for singles/doubles. Next to the pub are a couple of air-con motel-style units with communal bathrooms at $35/50. The pub has an excellent swimming pool.

THE GULFLANDER

The Normanton to Croydon railway line was completed in 1891 with the aim of linking the booming gold-mining centre with the port town at Normanton.

Normanton's railway station is a lovely old Victorian-era building with well-kept gardens, a small souvenir shop and a railway museum. When it's not running, the *Gulflander*, a weird-looking, snub-nosed little train, is housed here under the arch-roofed platform.

The *Gulflander* travels the 153km from Normanton to Croydon and back once a week, leaving Normanton on Wednesday at 8.30 am and returning from Croydon on Thursday at 8.30 am. The trip takes a leisurely four hours, with a couple of stops at points of interest along the way. It's one of the Gulf's most popular attractions – if you have the time, don't miss it. Most people stay overnight in Croydon at the Club Hotel, returning to Normanton the next day. The Thursday run is more leisurely as there are no deliveries along the way (as there are on the Wednesday run) and stops are made at points of interest. The one-way/return fare is $35/70. From mid-June to mid-September, the *Gulflander* also does a two-hour 'tea and damper' trip every Saturday at 9 am. The cost is $25 (children free); on other 'non-train' days there are often short trips on which you can also tag along. For bookings, phone the station on ☎ 4745 1391.

NORMANTON
pop 1250

Normanton, the Gulf's major town, was established on the banks of the Norman River back in 1868. The town's boom years were during the 1890s, when it acted as the port town for the gold rush around the Croydon goldfields.

The *Gulflander* is a popular way of making the four-hour journey from Croydon to Normanton.

Since the heady days of gold ended, the town has existed as a major supply point for the surrounding cattle stations, and as the shire centre. Today more and more travellers pass through Normanton on their way to the Gulf or Cape York.

It's a busy little town with three pubs, a motel and a caravan park, as well as several roadhouses, fuel outlets and two supermarkets. Some of the historic buildings still in use include the **Shire Offices** and the large **Burns Philp & Co Ltd store**, down towards the river end of the town, the **Westpac Bank,** and the simple **Normanton Railway Station**.

Travellers may also be interested in the Normanton Rodeo & Gymkhana held in June, the area's biggest social and sporting event of the year. In August the Normanton Races and a ball take place.

As a base for fishing, Normanton is hard to beat, with the Norman River producing some magic-sized barramundi.

Facilities
The *Gulf Service Station* (☎ 4745 1221), on Landsborough St, is the local RACQ depot and does repairs, welding and 24-hour towing. It sells fuel and a range of auto accessories.

Carpentaria Shire Offices (☎ 4745 1166), on the corner of Haig and Landsborough Sts, has a small information section with brochures and a collection of old photos.

Normanton's post office has a Commonwealth Bank agency, and there's a Westpac Bank on the corner of Landsborough and Little Brown Sts.

Organised Tours
Len Taylor, the manager of the caravan park, runs day trips on Monday to Burke and Wills' last camp site, an old stagecoach crossing on the Norman River. The tour takes a couple of hours and costs around $10 a head including morning tea. Len also does excellent evening information chats at the caravan park on Tuesday, Friday and Sunday at 5.30 pm, although these are for caravan parks guests only. Contact Len at the park or phone ☎ 4745 1121 for details.

Places to Stay
The *Normanton Caravan Park* (☎ 4745 1121), in Brown St, has tent sites for $10 and two air-con on-site vans for $35 a double. It also has a 25m pool.

The *Albion Hotel/Motel* (☎ 4745 1218), on Haig St just off the main road, is a friendly little place with good air-con motel-style rooms for $45/50.

The *Central Hotel* (☎ 4745 1215), on the corner of Haig and Landsborough Sts, and the *National Hotel* (☎ 4745 1324), widely known as the Purple Pub, both have pub rooms.

The *Gulfland Motel* (☎ 4745 1290), the first place you see as you drive in from Croydon, is a well-kept motel with good air-con singles/doubles for $60/72. The motel has its own licensed restaurant and a good swimming pool.

Places to Eat
There are several cafes and takeaways along the main street, with the usual selection of burgers, sandwiches, fried chicken, and fish and chips.

The *Albion Hotel* serves good pub meals and there's a shady balcony next to the bar. The *Central Hotel* also has counter meals.

Getting There & Away
Flight West has regular flights from Mt Isa to Normanton ($248) and from Cairns to Normanton ($270). There are also regular bus services from Mt Isa and Cairns to Karumba, via Normanton – see the Karumba section for details.

NORMANTON TO KARUMBA (72km)
Heading out of town, the Burke Developmental Rd soon crosses the Norman River and, less than 29km up the road, a major tributary of the river, Walker Creek. At the 30km mark from the centre of town, you come to a major intersection. Veer left here, sticking to the bitumen, and the road quickly swings almost due west.

Traversing these great plains, it is not hard to imagine that during the torrential rains of the wet season, this area becomes one huge lake. At times, with king tides backing up the waters of the rivers, the floods isolate towns like Normanton for weeks at a time.

The birdlife is rich and varied – this region is the best in Australia to see the stately brolga and the very similar sarus crane – a recent natural invader from South-East Asia. Another large bird which you'll see is the magpie-coloured jabiru, certainly one of the most majestic birds of the tropics.

KARUMBA
pop 620

Karumba, 70km north of Normanton, lies at the point where the Norman River meets the Gulf of Carpentaria. The town actually has two separate sections – Karumba itself is on the banks of the Norman River, while Karumba Point is a couple of kilometres north (as the crow flies) on the shores of the Gulf.

Originally established as a telegraph station in the 1870s, it became a stopover for the flying boats of the Empire Mail Service in the 1930s. The discovery of prawns in the Gulf in the 1960s brought Karumba alive, and today the prawning and barramundi industries keep the town humming. You certainly can't miss seeing the boats as they sit beside the jetty, draped with nets, just a stone's throw from the pub and the centre of town.

Karumba has a supermarket, pub, a couple of caravan parks and a number of holiday units, all of which mainly cater for those going fishing. The pub can really be jumping when the boats come in for a short break or for resupply.

The town lives and breathes fish and fishing, prawns and prawning. If you aren't interested in these things, you won't stay long. You can get to the sea at Karumba Point, but once you've done that, looked around town and enjoyed a prawn or two at the pub, there is not much else to hold your attention. You could always fly to Mornington or Sweers islands out in the Gulf, but once again, these are favoured fishing haunts and you need to love fishing to fully appreciate these wild, remote places.

Note that while the beach at Karumba Point may look rather inviting, don't even *think* about having a swim in the Gulf – if the sharks don't get you, the crocs will.

Facilities
The Westpac Bank, in Yappar St, is open only on Tuesday and Thursday, and there is a Commonwealth Bank agency at the post office.

Boat Hire
If you don't have your own boat, there are several places where you can hire one. Karumba Boat Hire (☎ 4745 9132), at Karumba Point, has a variety of dinghies.

Cruises & Tours
A number of boating and fishing tours run from Karumba.

Air Karumba (☎ 4745 9354) has flights to Mornington and Sweers islands, as well as further afield around the Gulf.

Festivals
Festivals held during the year include the Karumba Kapers (July), the Barra Ball (November) and the Fisherman's Ball (December).

Places to Stay
The *Gulf Country Caravan Park* (☎ 4745 9148), in Yappar St, has tent sites at $11 and on-site cabins at $28/40. Also in Yappar St is *Matilda's End Holiday Units* (☎ 4745 9368). These are old and plain holiday units, some with kitchens. They sleep from two to eight people and cost $50 for doubles plus $10 for extras.

The *Karumba Lodge Hotel* (☎ 4745 9143) has motel-style units overlooking the Norman River, costing $55/65 for singles/doubles.

There are also two caravan parks and several holiday units out at Karumba Point. Among the best of these is *Ashs Holiday Units* (☎ 4745 9132), on the corner of Palmer and Ward Sts. The self-contained units sleep up to six people and cost $50 a night for two plus $10 for each extra person.

GULF SAVANNAH

There's a good pool and a kiosk selling meals, tackle and bait.

Places to Eat

The *Karumba Cafe*, in Yappar St next to the B&B Supermarket, sells fresh fish and snacks. The *Karumba Lodge Hotel* has a bistro with lunches and dinners, and a restaurant which opens most nights.

The *Karumba Recreation Club*, about 3km east of Karumba, is a good alternative to the pub if you're looking for a quieter atmosphere. It has a small bar and bistro, with meals from Wednesday to Saturday nights.

Getting There & Away

Air Flight West has regular flights from Cairns to Karumba ($294) and from Mt Isa to Karumba ($248).

Bus Cairns-Karumba Coachline (☎ 4035 5448) has services from Cairns to Karumba three times a week. Campbell's Coaches (☎ 4743 2006) has a weekly service from Mt Isa to Karumba. See Getting There & Away at the start of this chapter for details.

Boat Gulf Freight Services (☎ 4745 9333) has regular weekly barge services from Karumba to Weipa on the Cape York Peninsula, transporting freight, people and vehicles. See Getting There and Away at the start of the Cape York Peninsula chapter for more details.

Western Gulf Region

NORTHERN TERRITORY BORDER TO BURKETOWN (228km)

This route is part of the historic Gulf Track, which stretches from Roper Bar in the Northern Territory's Top End to Normanton. The entire route is along unsealed roads, although a 4WD vehicle isn't normally required during the dry season unless you plan to take the track that leads to the coast from Hell's Gate. Traffic along this route varies from none in summer to an average of about 30 vehicles a day at the height of the winter tourist season. Travel isn't recommended between the beginning of December and March, when extreme heat and humidity make conditions uncomfortable or even dangerous. Heavy rains at this time can also close the roads for lengthy periods.

This section of road is good – you can safely sit on 80km/h most of the way – unless, of course, a big Wet has destroyed the government's good work. The country has little going for it in the way of scenery, being mainly flat and covered with scrubby vegetation. In fact, apart from Hell's Gate and the Gregory River, there is little reason to linger on this section.

Hell's Gate

About 52km east of the border you arrive at the *Hell's Gate Roadhouse* (☎ 4745 8258), located among low outcrops of grey conglomerate that rise from the surrounding bush. In the droving days the police from Turn-Off Lagoon, on the Nicholson River, escorted westbound travellers as far as these rocks, after which they were on their own.

The roadhouse has four air-con, two-bed rooms costing $25 per person. It also has camp sites at $10 each, and a good licensed restaurant that serves breakfast, lunch and dinner – the Sunday night barbecue is not to be missed if you're in the area. The roadhouse is open daily from 7 am to 10 pm (or later). Bookings are recommended for accommodation.

Bill Olive, the owner of the roadhouse, runs half-day and full-day 4WD tours for groups of five or more, taking in spectacular escarpment landscapes and lagoons rich in birdlife. Bookings are preferred.

Kingfisher Camp & Bowthorn Homestead

Between Hell's Gate and Doomadgee there's a signposted turn-off to *Kingfisher Camp* (☎ 4745 8212), a good campground beside a long hole on the banks of the Nicholson River. The facilities here include hot showers, toilets and laundry, and firewood is supplied. There's a small kiosk selling basic supplies. It costs $5 per person to camp here.

From Bowthorn Homestead (no tourist facilities), 33km south of Kingfisher Camp, you can head east 72km and join up with the Gulf Track east of the Nicholson River, or head south 100km or so to Lawn Hill National Park.

Doomadgee
Other than patches of open forest along occasional creek lines, there is little break in the mallee and paperbark scrub that lines the track for the 80km between Hell's Gate and the Doomadgee turn-off. Doomadgee is an Aboriginal community of about 1300 residents. While you are welcome to shop at the store, camping on the community's land is subject to permission being obtained from the council.

The well-stocked *Doomadgee Retail Store* sells fuel, meat, groceries, limited hardware items, Aboriginal art and a good range of motoring accessories. It's open from 8.30 am to 5 pm weekdays and 8.30 to 11.30 am on Saturday.

Doomadgee to Burketown
About 4km past Doomadgee you arrive at the **Nicholson River** crossing, which is the longest and least attractive of all the track's fords. The river is about 600m across, and in the dry season its bed of solid rock presents a desolate picture.

In remarkable contrast, the **Gregory River**, 53km further on, presents a lush picture of running water crowded by tropical vegetation. Herons stalk the shallows, and the milky water holds promise of feasts of yabbies. However, motorists must exercise extreme care here, as the single-lane concrete crossing has a sharp bend in it and you can't see the other side.

On the other side is the deserted Tirranna Roadhouse, and 8km later there's a major road junction – turn right for the Gregory

Downs Hotel (90km) and left for Burketown.

Escott Lodge About 5km before you reach Burketown, there's a turn-off to *Escott Lodge* (☎ 4748 5577). It's another 13km north-west from the turn-off to the lodge. The lodge is a working cattle station on the Nicholson River, and has a range of accommodation for travellers. You can fish for barramundi here.

BURKETOWN
pop 230
For many, Burketown is 'on the Gulf', but in reality it is over 30km from the waters of the Gulf of Carpentaria. Even so, it sits precariously on the very flat plains that border the waters of the Gulf, just a few metres above the high-tide mark. Just a stone's throw from the waters of the Albert River, Burketown operated as a port – ships travelled up the muddy waters of the river to service the town and hinterland.

Founded in 1865, Burketown almost came to a premature end a year later when a fever wiped out most of the residents. In 1887 an extremely big tidal surge almost carried the town away and, while nothing so dramatic has occurred since, the township is often cut off from the rest of Australia by floods.

Once (by all accounts) the wildest township in Australia, Burketown today is much more peaceful and friendly. Not only is it the administrative centre for a vast region dotted with huge cattle properties, it is also a major supply centre for travellers heading to, from or along the Gulf.

There are a few **historic sites** to see around the place including the old wharves, the boiling-down works (where meat, hooves and hides were processed) and, not far away, the tree emblazoned by the explorer Landsborough. Like many historic sites, this one is fast decaying under the onslaught of the weather and white ants. The cemetery is also interesting.

Burketown is also home to a phenomenon known as 'Morning Glory' – weird tubular cloud formations, extending the full length of the horizon, which roll out of the Gulf in the early morning, often in lines of three or four. This only happens from September to November.

Facilities
The Burketown & Gulf Regional Tourist Information Centre (☎ 4745 5111) can supply tourist information, and make arrangements for local tours on the Albert River and elsewhere.

The Burketown General Store, on Beames St, also sells fuel and has a supermarket, a licensed restaurant and a takeaway food section. It also has EFTPOS, as does the pub.

Festivals
Burketown hosts a number of events throughout the year. A barramundi fishing competition is held over Easter, the Burketown Rodeo is held on the second week in July, and the famous Variety Club Bash car rally comes through town in May.

Places to Stay & Eat
The *Burketown Caravan Park* (☎ 4745 5101) on Sloman St has tent sites for $9.50 a double ($12 powered).

The *Burketown Pub* (☎ 4745 5104) is the heart and soul of Burketown. Originally built as the local customs house, it's the oldest building in town – all its contemporaries have been blown over or washed away! It's a well-run outback pub and definitely worth a visit. The pub has air-con pub accommodation at $50/65 for singles/doubles, and motel-type units at $65/95. The pub also has a small dining room and serves a good range of meals.

Getting There & Away
Flight West has regular flights to Burketown from Mt Isa and Cairns.

BURKETOWN TO NORMANTON (233km)
From Burketown the Track improves as it sweeps across the flat plains of the Gulf to Normanton. The road, which follows the original coach route between Darwin and Port Douglas, was known as the Great Top Rd.

This route is open to conventional vehicles throughout the dry season, and shouldn't present too many problems if you take it easy. As you head south on the Burketown road, most of the creek crossings of any note have been upgraded to a bitumen causeway-type affair. How bad the road is depends on when the graders have been out and how bad the preceding wet season has been – sometimes it can be little better than a track, while at other times it is a wide, graded road interspersed with a few corrugations, potholes and stretches of bull dust.

Heading south out of Burketown you'll pass the 100-year-old artesian bore on the right, just on the outskirts of town. At Harris Creek, 15km from the centre of town, the dirt begins. The bull dust on these vast, flat plains is finer, deeper and seemingly more enveloping than anywhere else in Australia.

Floraville Station
The turn-off to Floraville Station is found at the 73km mark, on the right. A 'Historic Site' sign indicates that this is more than a station track, and it is worth the 1.3km diversion to check the plaque and monument to Frederick Walker, who died here in 1866. He was a wild lad in his time, but a fine explorer, who had been sent out to find Burke and Wills. Although he didn't find them, he did discover their Camp 119, from which they made their final push to the Gulf.

Walker's monument is found through the gate, heading towards the station. Keep left at the first track junction, about 400m from the road, and turn left again a short time later. By now you should be able to see the monument, down the rise a little, across a narrow creek. Please respect the privacy of the station people and stay away from the nearby homestead.

Leichhardt Falls
Just 1km after the turn-off to Floraville, the road drops down the bank of the Leichhardt

River and winds its way across the rock bar that makes up the wide bed of the river here. A narrow, short bridge crosses the stream in one spot.

The best place to pull up for a short wander, and probably the best camp on the run between Burketown and Normanton, is at the small, sandy, tree-covered island on the left – about halfway across the river's rocky bed, just past the narrow bridge. From here it is only a short walk downstream to the spectacular Leichhardt Falls. There are pools of water to cool off in (don't swim in the big stretch of water above the road crossing – there are crocs), the trees offer plenty of shade and the birdlife is rich and varied. In a big flood, there is so much water coming down the river that the falls are barely a ripple. Those sorts of floods occur every 10 years or so.

The owners of Floraville, who found Walker's grave and erected the monument to him, are also responsible for the thought-provoking sign near the road crossing in the middle of the riverbed. 'God Is' is all that it says.

Leichhardt Falls to Normanton

Once you have climbed the eastern bank of the Leichhardt River, the road winds a short distance and crosses a causeway before reaching a road junction, which can be easy to miss. You are less than 4km from the Floraville Station turn-off, less than 2km from the eastern bank of the Leichhardt and a total of 77km from Burketown. You need to turn left here for Normanton. Heading south on the better-looking road will take you to the Burke & Wills Roadhouse, 146km away on the Burke Developmental Rd.

Turn left at the junction, go through a gate, and 500m later you will begin crossing the rough – very rough – bed of the **Alexandra River**.

After the Alexandra, the road continues in a north-easterly direction, crossing the occasional creek (some have a causeway) and ploughing through bull dust and across corrugations. The turn-off to **Wernadinga station** is 16km from the Alexandra River

crossing, while the track into Inverleigh station is 85km from the road junction.

You cross the **Flinders River** 28km past the Inverleigh turn-off, and then 3km later the Big Bynoe River. The Little Bynoe River is crossed 2.5km further east. Just up the top of the eastern bank, 500m from the river, is a track heading south (right); it leads less than 2km to Burke and Wills' **Camp 119**. This is a good spot to have a brew, and if you want to camp, a track leads a short distance back to the edge of the **Little Bynoe**.

Camp 119 was the northernmost camp of the Burke and Wills expedition. Leaving their companions, Gray and King, to mind the camels and their equipment at Cooper Creek (near present-day Innamincka in South Australia), Burke and Wills pushed north across the wet and flooded country to try and reach the waters of the Gulf. It was 11 February 1861. While the water was salty and they observed a rise and fall in the tide, they were disappointed that the barrier of mangroves and mud kept them from seeing waves lapping on the shore.

Returning to Camp 119, they planned their dash back to Cooper Creek. No longer was it an exploratory expedition with mapping and observing a prime consideration, but a dash south for survival. In the end, only King survived.

Camp 119 is marked by a ring of trees and a centre one blazed by Burke and Wills. A couple of monuments also mark the spot.

All the rivers previously mentioned are home to estuarine crocodiles, so swimming is not advisable. A huge number of cattle use these places for drinking and cooling off, so unless the river is flowing, it's not recommended for drinking either.

Continuing eastwards you reach the bitumen at a road junction 32km east of the turn-off to Camp 119. Turn left here and 5km later you are in Normanton.

BURKETOWN TO CAMOOWEAL (334km)

The road from Burketown to Camooweal via Gregory Downs is the most direct way

GULF SAVANNAH

for people heading to the Lawn Hill National Park, although for conventional vehicles the longer route via the Burke & Wills Roadhouse provides much easier access, as it is sealed for most of the way. This road is unsealed dirt all the way, and while there are no major river crossings to negotiate, the road is quite rough in patches and a 4WD vehicle is recommended. Having said all that, it is *possible* to drive this route in a conventional vehicle, particularly if the road has been recently graded. On the other hand, conditions can quickly deteriorate after heavy rain, so either way it's important to check on local conditions before heading out here.

From Burketown it's 117km south to Gregory Downs, which is the main turn-off to Lawn Hill. Gregory Downs consists of a pub and little else. The *Gregory Downs Hotel* (☎ 4748 5566) has four motel units with air-con which cost $50/60 for singles/doubles, or you can camp behind the pub on the river bank. The pub sells meals and fuel, and can handle emergency repairs.

Every Labour Day weekend in May, the pub hosts the famous Gregory River Canoe Races – a great event, and not to be missed if you're around at this time of year.

From Gregory Downs, it's another 217km to Camooweal. About 40km south the road turns from dirt to gravel as you start to move into a series of low hills. This section gets pretty bumpy, with stony patches and sand drifts competing for your attention, and the occasional (and sudden) sharp dip to keep you on your toes. About 69km south of Gregory Downs, you pass the second turn-off to Lawn Hill – this route is only open to 4WD vehicles.

The next section of the road resembles a dirt rollercoaster, and it's a real boneshaker in sections. About 126km south of Gregory Downs the road splits in two. The left-hand branch heads south for another 58km before meeting the Barkly Hwy, and this is the route you'll take if you're heading for Mt Isa. The right-hand branch continues southwest for another 91km, meeting the Barkly Hwy 2km west of Camooweal.

LAWN HILL NATIONAL PARK

Amid arid country 100km west of Gregory Downs, the Lawn Hill Gorge is an oasis of gorges, creeks, ponds and tropical vegetation that the Aboriginal people have enjoyed for perhaps 30,000 years. Their paintings and old camping sites abound. Two rock-art sites have been made accessible to visitors. There are freshwater crocodiles – the inoffensive variety – in the creek.

In the southern part of the park is the amazing World Heritage listed **Riversleigh fossil field**. The field contains fossils ranging from 15 million to a mere 50,000 years old, making it one of the world's pre-eminent fossil sites. The fossils include everything from giant snakes to carnivorous kangaroos to small rodents. The Riversleigh Fossils Interpretive Centre in Mt Isa has fossils on display and is well worth a look if you can't get out to the park.

There are 20km of walking tracks as well as a tcampground with showers and toilets at Lawn Hill; it's very popular and sites must be booked well in advance (especially from March through September) with the park rangers (☎ 4748 5572) or the Department of Environment office in Mt Isa (☎ 4743 2055). *Adel's Grove Kiosk* (☎ 4748 5502), 10km east of the park entrance, sells fuel and basic food supplies. It also has a campground and canoes for hire.

Getting there is the problem – it's a beautiful, pristine place that's miles from anywhere or anybody, and the last 230km or so from Mt Isa is unsealed. There are a couple of different ways of getting here, and, as mentioned above, the easiest route for conventional vehicles is to come via the Burke & Wills Roadhouse. If you're coming along the Camooweal to Burketown road, 4WD vehicles are recommended, though they are not always necessary in the dry season.

CLONCURRY TO NORMANTON (375km)

The major road into the Gulf from the south is the Burke Developmental Rd, which runs from Cloncurry to Normanton. This is the last section of the route known as the Matilda Hwy, which starts way down south at Cunnamulla near the Queensland/New South Wales border. The highway is bitumen all the way and in excellent condition.

Quamby, 43km north of Cloncurry, was once a Cobb & Co coach stop and a centre for the gold mining that helped develop the region. Quamby now has nothing but the historic *Quamby Hotel* (☎ 4742 5952). The pub has fuel, simple accommodation and serves meals.

Continuing north across the rolling hills dotted with low, spindly gums, you reach the turn-off to **Kajabbi**, 29km north of Quamby. Once the focus of the area, Kajabbi has been all but forgotten. The town was once the railhead for this part of the Gulf's cattle industry and the nearby copper mines, but all that has long since disappeared. The *Kalkadoon Hotel* (☎ 4742 5979) is the focal point for locals and visitors alike. From here there is much to explore, including the Mt Cuthbert Mine site, and Battle Mountain, the site of the last stand of the local warlike Kalkadoon people, who resisted the white invasion in bloody battles during the 1880s.

Just before you get to the Burke & Wills Roadhouse along the Burke Developmental Rd, 180km north of Cloncurry, the Wills Developmental Road from Julia Creek joins the road you are on from the right.

Nearly everyone stops at the *Burke & Wills Roadhouse* (☎ 4742 5909) where there's a little shade, some greenery at any time of the year, ice creams to buy from the well-stocked store and, if you really need it, fuel. You can camp here ($4 per person, $6 powered) and there are four air-con cabins at $30/40 for singles/doubles.

From the roadhouse you can strike northwest along the Wills Developmental Rd to the fabulous Gregory River and the famous *Gregory Downs Hotel* (see the Burketown to Camooweal section). From there the reasonable dirt road leads to Burketown.

For those travelling on to Normanton, the route continues in a more northerly direction towards the Gulf. The country remains reasonably flat, but once you get to **Bang Bang Jump-up** and descend about 40m to the Gulf plains proper, you really know what 'flat' means. This near-sheer escarpment vividly marks where the high country ends, 80km north of the roadhouse.

From this point the road stretches across vast, billiard-table-flat plains covered in deep grass, which in the Dry is the colour of gold. Dotted here and there are clumps of trees, and wherever there is permanent water or shade there are cattle. In this country the cattle stand out – during the day. At night, as everywhere in outback Queensland, they can make driving on the roads very hazardous.

GULF ISLANDS

There are numerous islands scattered in the Gulf of Carpentaria north of Burketown, most of which are Aboriginal communities and are not open to visitors. There are, however, a couple of places set up specifically to cater to people wanting to fish the abundant waters of the Gulf. Reef fish such as coral trout, sweetlip, cod, and red emperor, as well as mackerel and tuna, are all plentiful.

Mornington Island

The largest of the Gulf Islands, Mornington Island has an Aboriginal community administered from Gununa, on the south-west coast.

On the north-west coast of the island is the *Birri Fishing Resort* (☎ 4745 7277), a remote lodge which caters for anglers. The lodge is open from the last week in March to the end of October; the cost is $85 per person per day for accommodation and meals only, or $240 including fishing guides and all tackle and boat hire.

There are regular flights to the island from Karumba, and you can also fly there from Burketown – see those sections for details.

Sweers Island

The smaller Sweers Island, midway between Burketown and Mornington Island, became the headquarters of the Gulf district after an outbreak of fever in Burketown in 1865, but because of its remoteness Normanton later took over as the administrative centre. Today, Sweers Island also has its own fishing resort.

The *Sweers Island Resort* (☎ 4748 5544) has cabin-style accommodation with shared bathroom facilities and caters for families and anglers. The tariff is $175 per person, which includes all meals, boat hire, fuel, bait and handlines. You'll need to book during the peak Spanish mackerel season (June to August).

There are flights to the island from Karumba and Burketown; Savannah Aviation (☎ 4745 5177) also has day trips to the resort from Burketown for $300 for up to five people.

Outback Queensland

This chapter covers Queensland's vast outback region. Stretching westward beyond the mountains of the Great Dividing Range, the legendary outback is truly, in the well-worn words of Dorothea Mackellar, 'a sunburnt country, a land of sweeping plains, of rugged mountain ranges, of droughts and flooding rains'.

The outback has some outstanding attractions, including the Australian Workers Heritage Centre in Barcaldine, the Stockman's Hall of Fame & Outback Heritage Centre in Longreach, and the Birdsville Working Museum. But the outback isn't really about attractions or sights, it's essentially about experiences – the characters you meet in pubs and roadhouses; the exhilaration of being in the middle of nowhere in the shimmering heat, surrounded by silence, spinifex and sand; the acute boredom of sitting behind the wheel watching the unchanging landscape for hour after hour …

There are plenty of reminders of the outback's history out here, from the old stone and timber buildings bleached by the sun of a hundred summers, to the fascinating tales of the early explorers and pioneers who opened up the region to white settlement.

Remember that this is harsh, unforgiving country – as the locals say, you should never underestimate the outback. No matter how safe you feel sitting in your air-con 4WD, expect the unexpected. The combination of the extreme temperatures, scarcity of water and isolation make it one of the few places in the world where your survival is in your hands. There is no substitute for good preparation.

HISTORY

Ludwig Leichhardt crossed the outback's Western Plains on his way to Port Essington in the Northern Territory in 1844. Over the next 20 years, some of Australia's greatest explorers, including Thomas Mitchell (later

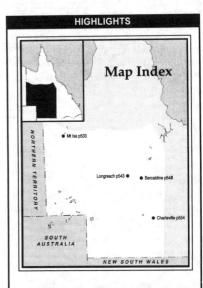

HIGHLIGHTS

Map Index

NORTHERN TERRITORY

● Mt Isa p533

Longreach p543 ●   ● Barcaldine p548

● Charleville p554

SOUTH AUSTRALIA

NEW SOUTH WALES

- A visit to the huge Mt Isa mine never fails to impress.
- The Stockman's Hall of Fame in Longreach is a must-see and worth travelling a long way for – as indeed you must.
- Head for remote Birdsville in the state's far south-west for the annual race meeting.

knighted for his achievements), the doomed Robert Burke and William Wills, William Landsborough, Augustus Gregory and John McKinlay, crisscrossed the vast plains and the low rugged ranges of outback Queensland. In the process, they opened up this land to the sheep and cattle graziers who quickly followed.

GEOGRAPHY

The area 'out back' of the Great Dividing Range is a vast, semi-arid region known as

Outback Queensland

0   100   200 km

the Western Plains. Beneath these endless grassy plains lies the Great Artesian Basin, an enormous underground water supply that supports the outback's sheep and cattle stations. The arid south-west corner of the state, known as the Channel Country, is cut by innumerable rivers and creeks that remain dry for most of the year until they are filled to overflowing by waters running from the north of the state during the Wet.

The outback isn't all flat land – there are several low mountain ranges in the region, including the ancient Selwyn Range east of Mt Isa, the Aramac Range north of Barcaldine, and the Grey Range which stretches from near Blackall down to the New South Wales border.

The outback's major river systems include the Diamantina, Thomson, Barcoo, Bulloo and Warrego.

CLIMATE

Summer isn't a great time to visit the outback. Average temperatures are over 35°C and frequently soar towards 50°C, and travelling in such heat can be hazardous. Summer is also the time of the Wet, when monsoon rains in the north of the state fill the region's hundreds of rivers and creeks, sometimes flooding vast areas of the Channel Country and cutting many outback roads.

Conditions are much more favourable in the cooler months between April and October, with generally mild to warm days and temperatures seldom topping 30°C, although it can be bitterly cold at night in winter – temperatures below freezing are not uncommon.

Rain is a rare occurrence in the outback, with the southern areas averaging around 150mm a year. Rainfall is slightly heavier north of the Tropic of Capricorn, particularly in the summer months.

GETTING THERE & AWAY
Air
The major towns of the outback are serviced by Flight West Airlines, which flies from Brisbane to Birdsville via Charleville, Quilpie and Windorah; from Brisbane and Townsville to Longreach and Winton; and from Townsville to Cloncurry and Mt Isa.

Ansett also flies to Mt Isa from Cairns and Brisbane. Augusta Airways flies from Port Augusta in South Australia; it does a weekly mail run to Birdsville, Bedourie and Boulia on Saturday, and back on Sunday.

Bus
There are three major bus routes through the outback – from Townsville to Mt Isa via Hughenden, from Rockhampton to Longreach via Emerald, and from Brisbane to Mt Isa via Roma and Longreach. McCafferty's services all three routes; Greyhound Pioneer operates only between Townsville and Mt Isa. Buses continue from Mt Isa to Threeways in the Northern Territory, from where you can head north to Darwin or south to Alice Springs.

The Art of the Drive-By Wave

Driving along the long, remote roads of the outback certainly gives you plenty of time to contemplate life, loneliness and the transient nature of contemporary existence. In the days of yore when the pace of the world was much gentler, travellers would have the time to stop and chat with those riding or walking the other way and exchange news and information, such as which inns had the softest beds, the best meals, the coldest beer etc. Nowadays all of this has been compressed into a split-second greeting as we zoom past each other on smooth black-topped highways, encased in our metal contraptions, at collective speeds of over 200km/h.

The incidence of drive-by waves rises in direct proportion to the remoteness of the road being travelled. Closer to the coast and larger cities, hardly anyone acknowledges other drivers, but as you head into the outback you'll start to notice passing drivers waving at you. At first you might think all these waves are identical, but a closer study will reveal subtle but significant variations in the wave.

The most common method is the four-finger version, in which the thumb remains hooked around the steering wheel while the four fingers of the right hand are raised in an abrupt, mini-Nazi salute. This is widely recognised as the state-of-the-art wave. Variations include the nonchalant one or two finger-wave – this is usually practised by seasoned outback travellers, although an imitation is often attempted by novices trying to be cool.

At the other extreme is the full-hand wave, where the right hand actually leaves the steering wheel. Those practising this potentially dangerous method are probably deeply lonely, insecure people, desperate for a fleeting moment of on-the-road acceptance that they can never hope to achieve back in urban society.

Train

Similarly, there are three train services from the coast to the outback, all running twice weekly: the *Spirit of the Outback* runs from Brisbane to Longreach via Rockhampton, with connecting bus services to Winton; the *Westlander* runs from Brisbane to Charleville, with connecting bus services to Cunnamulla and Quilpie; and the *Inlander* runs from Townsville to Mt Isa.

Car & Motorcycle

The outback, although sparsely settled, is well serviced by major roads – the Flinders Hwy connects northern Queensland with the Northern Territory, meeting the Barkly Hwy at Cloncurry; the Capricorn Hwy runs along the Tropic of Capricorn from Rockhampton to Longreach; and the Landsborough and Mitchell Hwys run from the New South Wales border south of Cunnamulla right up to Mt Isa.

However, once off these major arteries road conditions deteriorate rapidly, services are extremely limited and you need to be completely self-sufficient with spare parts, fuel and water. With the right preparation, it's possible to make the great outback journeys down the tracks connecting Queensland with South Australia – the Strzelecki and Birdsville tracks.

Charters Towers to Camooweal – the Flinders & Barkly Hwys

The Flinders Hwy, which stretches for almost 770km from Townsville to Cloncurry, is the major route across the top of outback Queensland. From Cloncurry, the Barkly Hwy picks up where the Flinders Hwy leaves off and takes you on to Mt Isa, Camooweal and into the Northern Territory.

As a scenic drive, this is probably the most boring route in Queensland, although there are a few minor points of interest along the way to break the monotony. Apart from the Charters Towers to Torrens Creek section, which passes through the Great Dividing Range, the terrain is flat as a pancake and features a seemingly endless landscape of dry, grassy plains. There is little visual relief until you pass Cloncurry and reach the low red hills that surround Mt Isa.

The highway is sealed all the way and is generally in good condition, although west of Mt Isa it deteriorates to a narrow, poorly engineered and dangerous single-lane strip of bitumen. The inland railway line runs beside the highway for the majority of the route.

Greyhound Pioneer and McCafferty's operate daily services along the Townsville to Mt Isa route and on to the Northern Territory. The *Inlander* train follows an almost identical route twice weekly, with stops at most towns along the way.

CHARTERS TOWERS TO HUGHENDEN

It's 243km from Charters Towers to Hughenden. This route is a former Cobb & Co stage run, and along its length is a series of tiny townships which were originally established as stopovers for the coaches. The theory is that the towns are evenly spaced – with roughly a day's run for the Cobb & Co horses between each.

The first section of the route, from Charters Towers to Torrens Creek, passes through the hills of the Great Dividing Range. Beyond Torrens Creek, the land soon starts to become flatter and drier, trees start to become a rarity and the flat grassy plains begin.

The small settlement of **Pentland**, 105km west of Charters Towers, has a small art gallery and craft store, a motel, service station, general store and caravan park.

It's another 94km to the aptly-named town of **Prairie**, which consists of a small cluster of houses around a railway station and a hotel. The *Prairie Hotel* (☎ 4741 5121) is an interesting old pub. It was first licensed in 1884, but operated for about a dozen years before that as a Cobb & Co coach stop – you can still see the old rounding yard out in the backyard. The pub has a good collection of old artefacts and even has its own ghost (you can read about him in the pub). Travellers can camp out the back of the pub, or there are basic rooms.

HUGHENDEN
pop 1650

Hughenden is on the banks of the Flinders River, in the same spot where explorer William Landsborough camped in 1862 during his fruitless search for survivors from the Burke and Wills expedition. Today Hughenden is a busy commercial centre that services the surrounding cattle, wool and grain industries.

The town bills itself as the home of beauty and the beast. The 'beauty' is the Porcupine Gorge National Park, 65km to the north; the 'beast' is imprisoned in the **Dinosaur Display Centre**, a large tin shed on Gray St.

Inside the display centre is a replica of the skeleton of *Muttaburrasaurus*, one of the largest and most complete dinosaur skeletons ever found in Australia. It was found by a grazier in 1961 in a cattle holding yard at Muttaburra, 206km south of Hughenden. The centre also has a few locally found fossils and other historic relics on display.

Information

The Hughenden Visitor Information Centre (☎ 4741 1493) is part of the Dinosaur Display Centre on Gray St.

Close Auto Sales (☎ 4741 1311), the BP service station on the Richmond side of town, is the local RACQ depot.

Places to Stay

The *Allan Terry Caravan Park* (☎ 4741 1190), on the Winton road and opposite the train station, has tent sites for $8 and on-site vans from $30. The town swimming pool is next door, although the railway yard opposite is a bit noisy.

On the corner of Gray and Stanfield Sts is the *Grand Hotel* (☎ 4741 1588), a classic old two-storey timber pub. Basic but comfortable singles/doubles cost $15/30, or $40 with air-con. There's a big old dining room downstairs that serves country-style tucker on Friday and Saturday nights.

The *Rest Easi Motel* (☎ 4741 1633), on the highway on the western outskirts, is a neat little motel with a pool and motel units at $45/55, as well as camp sites for $12 ($14 powered).

PORCUPINE GORGE NATIONAL PARK

If the weather has been dry, and you're not in a hurry and have a vehicle, take a trip out to Porcupine Gorge National Park. It's an oasis in the dry country north of Hughenden off the mostly unpaved, often corrugated Kennedy Developmental Rd.

The best spot to drive to is **Pyramid Lookout**, about 70km north of Hughenden. You can camp here and it's an easy 30-minute walk down into the gorge, with some fine rock formations and a permanently running creek. Few people come here and there's a fair bit of wildlife.

The Kennedy Developmental Rd, a well-maintained dirt road takes you to The Lynd (a remote roadhouse), on to the turn-off to the Undara Lava Tubes and eventually to Ravenshoe and the Atherton Tableland. It's a reasonably scenic road but is not recommended after heavy rain.

RICHMOND
pop 650

Like most of the towns out here, Richmond exists primarily to service the local cattle and sheep industries. The town is set on the Flinders River and was a Cobb & Co stopover. There's a restored Cobb & Co **mail coach** in a cage beside the main intersection – it's worth stopping here and considering what it would have been like travelling in one of these things over unpaved roads through the heat and dust. Makes the hours you've just spent sitting in your air-conditioned car or bus a lot less painful, doesn't it?

There's a **marine fossil museum** on the main street, with displays of fossils found in the area. It is open erratically ($3).

The area around Richmond is abundant in sandalwood, and a factory in the town processes the wood for export to Asia, where it is used for incense and joss sticks.

Information
The service station on the east side of town is open 24 hours and has EFTPOS. Richmond Panel Repairs (☎ 4741 3258) is the local RACQ depot.

Places to Stay & Eat
The *Richmond Caravan Park* (☎ 4741 2772) on the main street is a tiny council-run caravan park with tent sites at $7 ($10 powered). There are also cabins (dongas) at $15 per person twin share.

There are two pubs on Goldring St which do meals and accommodation. The friendly *Federal Palace Hotel* (☎ 4741 3463), at 64 Goldring St, has pub-style rooms, with shared bathrooms at $25/38. It also serves a good range of bistro meals but, like most pubs out here, there are no meals on Sunday.

Nearby, the *Mud Hut Hotel-Motel* (☎ 4741 3223) has a choice of cheap, pub-style rooms or motel units with air-con at $45/55. The pub was built in the 1890s from flagstones and adobe mud. Unfortunately the original walls have been covered over, but you can see some sections of the old walls inside the pub.

The *Midway Motel Roadhouse* (☎ 4741 3192) on the east side of town also has air-con motel units at $35/45.

JULIA CREEK
pop 600
It's another flat and featureless 144km from Richmond to Julia Creek, a small pastoral centre which specialises in selling and transporting cattle.

About 4km west of Julia Creek, the sealed Wills Developmental Rd leaves the highway and heads north to the Burke & Wills Roadhouse (235km). From the road-house you can continue north to Normanton and Karumba; you can also reach Burke-town this way. See the Gulf Savannah chapter for more details.

Places to Stay
The *Julia Creek Caravan Park* (☎ 4746 7305) at the end of Julia St has tent sites from $8. The town's swimming pool is nearby.

In the centre of town is *Gannons Hotel-Motel* (☎ 4746 7103) with motel-style units at $38/48 for singles/doubles. The *Julia Creek Motel* (☎ 4746 7305), on the highway on the west side of town, has rooms with air-con from $52/60.

CLONCURRY
pop 2310
The centre of a copper boom in the last century, Cloncurry (known locally as 'the Curry') was the largest copper producer in the British empire in 1916. Today it's a busy little pastoral centre with a couple of attractions for passing tourists. The Burke Developmental Rd, which takes you north from Cloncurry, is paved all the way to Normanton (375km) and Karumba (449km), near the Gulf of Carpentaria. Burketown is 443km from Cloncurry. See the Gulf Savannah chapter for details.

Information
Nev's Auto (☎ 4742 1243), on the corner of Ramsay and Sheaffe Sts, is the local RACQ agent.

Things to See & Do
The town's major claim to fame is as the birthplace of the Royal Flying Doctor Service. The **John Flynn Place Museum & Art Gallery**, on the corner of Daintree and King Sts, is a well set up museum, with interesting exhibits on the Flying Doctor Service, the School of the Air and mining. It's open from 7 am to 4 pm on weekdays and, from May to October, from 9 am to 3 pm on weekends. Entry costs $5 ($2 children). If you're feeling the heat, the town's **swimming pool** is opposite the museum.

OUTBACK QUEENSLAND

John Flynn pioneered a medical air service – the Royal Flying Doctor Service – that has saved countless lives in remote areas.

Cloncurry's **Mary Kathleen Park & Museum**, just off the highway on the eastern side of town, is partly housed in buildings transported from the former uranium-mining town of Mary Kathleen. The collection includes relics of the Burke and Wills expedition and a big collection of local rocks and minerals. It's open from 7 am to 12 noon and 1 to 4 pm on weekdays, and from 9 am to 3 pm on weekends ($5 entry).

Places to Stay & Eat

The *Cloncurry Caravan Park Oasis* (☎ 4742 1313) opposite the museum has tent sites for $10, on-site vans at $30 a double and cabins at $35. On the corner of Sheaffe and Scarr Sts, the *Central Hotel* (☎ 4742 1418) has basic pub rooms.

There are two motels here. The cheaper option, the *Wagon Wheel Motel* (☎ 4742 1866) at 54 Ramsay St, has budget singles/doubles at $35/45. The motel is fronted by a historic building which houses a restaurant and motel reception.

The best of Cloncurry's accommodation options is the new *Gidgee Inn* (☎ 4742 1599), an interesting rammed-earth motel on the eastern edge of town. It's also the most expensive, at $87 for a single or double, or $110 for a twin room. There's a good bar and restaurant here.

CLONCURRY TO MT ISA

After Cloncurry, the terrain finally starts to change as you leave the plains behind and pass into the low, rocky, scrub-scattered red hills that surround Mt Isa.

This 124km stretch of the Flinders Hwy has a number of interesting stops. Beside the **Corella River**, 41km west of Cloncurry, there's a memorial cairn to the Burke and Wills expedition, which passed here in 1861. Another 1km down the road is the **Kalkadoon & Mitakoodi Memorial**, which marks an old Aboriginal tribal boundary. The monument has unfortunately been vandalised but is still worth a stop.

After another 9km you pass the (unmarked) former site of **Mary Kathleen**, a uranium-mining town from the 1950s to 1982. It has been completely demolished.

The turn-off to **Lake Julius**, Mt Isa's reserve water supply, is 36km beyond Mary Kathleen. The lake is on the Leichhardt River – 90km of unsealed road from the highway. This is a good spot for fishing, canoeing, sailing and water-skiing, and a popular day trip from Mt Isa.

About 1km from the dam is the *Lake Julius Recreation Camp* (☎ 4742 5998). You can camp ($3 per person), or there are seven self-contained units. These have aircon and sleep five to eight people; they cost $32.60 a night for up to four people, plus $6.30 for each extra adult.

North-east of Lake Julius is the tiny town of **Kajabbi**, a former mining settlement on the banks of the Leichhardt River – see the Gulf Savannah chapter for details. South of Kajabbi is **Battle Mountain**, which was the scene of the last stand of the Kalkadoon people in 1884.

MT ISA
pop 22,400

The mining town of Mt Isa owes its existence to an immensely rich copper, silver, lead and zinc mine, and the skyline is dominated by the massive 270m exhaust stack

Last Stand of the Kalkadoons

Before the coming of the Europeans, the arid and rocky hills north-west of Mt Isa were home to the Kalkadoons, one of the fiercest and most bellicose of the Aboriginal tribes. The Kalkadoons were one of the last tribes to resist white settlement, and from the mid-1870s fought an ongoing battle against pastoralists and the Native Police.

They were a formidable and feared opponent who often used guerrilla tactics to attack settlers and troops. Warriors decorated themselves with body-paint and feathers, and used pole clubs, razor-sharp tomahawks and knives made from local stone for weapons. Hudson Fysh describes a Kalkadoon tribesman in his book *Taming the North: The Story of Alexander Kennedy and Other Queensland Pathfinders*: 'When a big member of the Kalkadoon tribe, standing over six feet high and broad in proportion, was done up ready for a ceremonial corroboree he was a fearsome object indeed. With several large emu or eaglehawk feathers decorating his head, his already tall stature is increased. His broad face, stretched wide open in a resounding yell, is banded around with minute white feathers stuck on with dried blood'.

In 1884 the authorities sent Frederic Urquhart, the Sub-Inspector of Police, to the region to take command, but the Kalkadoons continued to ambush and attack the invaders. In September of that year, Urquhart gathered his heavily armed troops and local squatters and rode to the rocky hill which came to be known as Battle Mountain.

When they saw the mounted troops, the Kalkadoons formed themselves into ranks and made a series of disciplined but suicidal charges down the hill. Armed with only spears they stood no chance against the carbines of the troopers, and were mown down in waves until they were practically wiped out. Only a handful of tribesmen survived and the massacre marked the end of Aboriginal resistance in the region.

A memorial beside the Barkly Highway, 42km west of Cloncurry, is inscribed: 'You who pass by are now entering the ancient tribal lands of the Kalkadoon/Mitakoodi, dispossessed by the European. Honour their name, be brother and sister to their descendants.'

from the lead smelter. 'The Isa', as the town is known locally, is inland Queensland's major town.

It's a rough-and-ready but prosperous town, and the job opportunities here have attracted people from about 60 different ethnic groups.

The first deposits were discovered here in 1923 by a prospector called John Campbell Miles who gave Mt Isa its name – a corruption of Mt Ida, a goldfield in Western Australia. Since the ore deposits were large and low grade, working them required the sort of investment only a company could afford. Mt Isa Mines (MIM) was founded in 1924. Life was predictably rough and tough in Mt Isa's early days and the Isa Hotel had a 'bullring' in its backyard where men could sort out their personal differences without disturbing others. It was during and after WWII that Mt Isa really took off; today it's the Western world's biggest silver and lead producer, and is in the top 10 in production of copper and zinc – the ore is railed 900km to Townsville on the coast. Virtually the whole town is run by MIM.

Information

The Riversleigh Fossils Interpretative Centre & Tourist Office (☎ 4749 1555), in Centenary Park on Marian St, is open from 8 am to 4.30 pm on weekdays, and from 9 am to 2 pm on weekends. There's also a laundromat here, as well as the Greyhound Pioneer office and depot.

QBD's Bumblebee Bookshop on Simpson St is the best between Townsville and Darwin.

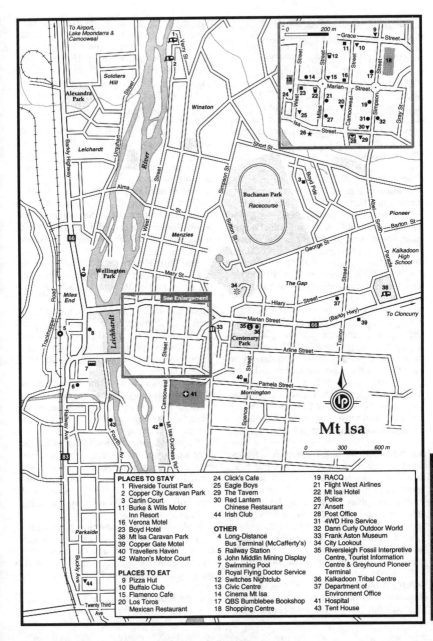

To Airport,
Lake Moondarra &
Camooweal

Soldiers
Hill

Alexandra
Park

Leichhardt

Barkly Highway

66

Wellington
Park

Miles
End

Trackhopper Road

Leichhardt

Railway Ave

83

Parkside

Buckly Ave

Twenty Third
Ave

Winston

River

Alma

St

West

Menzies

Mary St

Street

Camooweal

Fourth Av.

Soldiers St

Urquhart

Simpson St

Sutton St

Short St

Buchanan Park
Racecourse

George St

The Gap

34

Hilary   Street

Marian Street

Centenary
Park

Arline Street

Pamela Street

Mornington

Spence

See Enlargement

Mt Isa-Duchess Rd

Boyd Pde

Abel Smith Street

Kalkadoon
Parade

Trainor

Pioneer

Barton St

Kalkadoon
High
School

66

(Barkly Hwy)

To Cloncurry

Mt Isa

0   300   600 m

200 m

Grace   Street

Street

Street

West

Isa   Street

Marian   Street

Miles

Camooweal

Simpson Street

Gray St

PLACES TO STAY
1   Riverside Tourist Park
2   Copper City Caravan Park
3   Carlin Court
11 Burke & Wills Motor
     Inn Resort
16 Verona Motel
23 Boyd Hotel
38 Mt Isa Caravan Park
39 Copper Gate Motel
40 Travellers Haven
42 Walton's Motor Court

PLACES TO EAT
9   Pizza Hut
10 Buffalo Club
15 Flamenco Cafe
20 Los Toros
     Mexican Restaurant

24 Click's Cafe
25 Eagle Boys
29 The Tavern
30 Red Lantern
     Chinese Restaurant
44 Irish Club

OTHER
4   Long-Distance
     Bus Terminal (McCafferty's)
5   Railway Station
6   John Middlin Mining Display
7   Swimming Pool
8   Royal Flying Doctor Service
12 Switches Nightclub
13 Civic Centre
14 Cinema Mt Isa
17 QBS Bumblebee Bookshop
18 Shopping Centre

19 RACQ
21 Flight West Airlines
22 Mt Isa Hotel
26 Police
27 Ansett
28 Post Office
31 4WD Hire Service
32 Dann Curly Outdoor World
33 Frank Aston Museum
34 City Lookout
35 Riversleigh Fossil Interpretive
     Centre, Tourist Information
     Centre & Greyhound Pioneer
     Terminal
36 Kalkadoon Tribal Centre
37 Department of
     Environment Office
41 Hospital
43 Tent House

Dann Curly Outdoor World, on Simpson St, stocks a good range of camping and fishing gear. For equipment hire try Isa Camping Hire (☎ 4749 0535) at 9 Simpson St; it has everything from swags to portable fridges.

Power Automotive (☎ 4743 2542) at 13 Simpson St is the RACQ agent. The Department of Environment (☎ 4743 2055), on the corner of Hilary and Butler Sts, can provide information on all the national parks in the area, including Lawn Hill and Camooweal Caves.

Things to See & Do

The Mine The mine is the town's major attraction and there are two tours available.

The four-hour underground tour, for which you don a hard hat and miner's suit, takes you down into some of the 4600km of tunnels. Tours leave at 7.30 and 11.30 am on Monday, Tuesday and Thursday, and cost $35. Book ahead on ☎ 4749 1555 – there's a maximum of nine on each tour and you must be over 16 years of age.

The two-hour surface tours (by bus) are run by Campbell's Coaches (☎ 4743 2006). Drivers pick up from various places on request and the tour costs $13. It's well worth the money, especially since the bus takes you right through the major workshops and mine site, and the price includes a visit to the Riversleigh Fossils Interpretive Centre. The tours depart weekdays at 9 am (and 1 pm on demand). You must wear enclosed shoes, so no sandals or thongs (flip flops).

John Middlin Mining Display & Visitors Centre

This visitors centre, on Church St near the town centre, has various displays about the mining operations. They include informative photograph display boards, ore and mineral samples, an audio-visual program and even a 'simulated underground experience'. The centre is open weekdays from 9 am to 4 pm and weekends from 9 am to 2 pm; entry costs $4.

Other Attractions The **Frank Aston Museum** is a partially underground complex on a hill close to the town centre at the corner of Shackleton and Marian Sts. This rambling place has a diverse and interesting collection ranging from old mining gear to ageing flying doctor radios. There are also displays on the Lardil Aborigines of Mornington Island in the Gulf of Carpentaria, and the Kalkadoon people indigenous to the Mt Isa area. It is open every day from 9 am to 4 pm and costs $4.

It is possible to visit the **Royal Flying Doctor Service** base, on the Barkly Hwy, from 9 am to 5 pm on weekdays and from 10 am to 2 pm on weekends. The $2.50 admission includes a film.

The **School of the Air**, which educates children in remote places by radio, is based at the Kalkadoon High School on Abel Smith Parade. The school is open for public tours at 9 and 10 am on school days; the tours cost $2.

The **Tent House**, at 16 Fourth Ave, is one of the last surviving houses typical of the early days of Mt Isa and has been classified by the National Trust. About 200 of these half-house, half-tents constructions were built during the 1930s specifically to suit the Mt Isa climate. The interior of the house features period furniture, fittings and displays. It is open on request; inquire at the Tourist Office.

The **Kalkadoon Tribal Centre & Culture-Keeping Place**, on Marian St next to the tourist office, is open most weekdays (admission $1). It's partly a museum and houses some artefacts.

A short drive or climb off Hilary St is the **City Lookout** – coming up here certainly puts things into perspective. You can see virtually the whole town, sprawled out across a flat valley, backed by a series of low hills and watched over by the huge, dark, brooding mine.

Mt Isa has a big **swimming pool** on Isa St, just over the river and next to the tennis courts. Entry costs $1, and the pool opens daily at 7 am from May to August, and at 10 am (noon on Monday) for the rest of the year.

Lake Moondarra, 16km north of town, is a popular spot for swimming, boating, water-skiing, fishing and birdwatching. There are barbecue facilities at the lake and at Warrina Park, which is just below the dam wall.

Organised Tours

Look-About Trips (☎ 4743 9523) does day tours to Kajabbi and Lake Julius ($60), a night town tour ($10) and a half-day town tour ($15).

Between April and September, Campbell's Coaches (☎ 4743 2006) runs a three-day camping safari to Lawn Hill National Park and the Riversleigh fossil sites ($340, with all meals and equipment supplied).

Air Mt Isa (☎ 4743 2844), the local mail run operator, will take tourists on its twice-weekly flights to the more remote reaches of Queensland and the Northern Territory. Flights cost $195 per person and advance bookings are required. It also does day trips to the Riversleigh fossil sites for $315.

Festivals

Held every August, the Mt Isa Rotary Rodeo is one of the biggest in Australia, with serious prize money up for grabs. It is held at Kalkadoon Park on the Barkly Hwy. The Mt Isa Show is held each June.

Places to Stay

Camping & Caravan Parks Mt Isa has a string of caravan parks, some along the Barkly Hwy going east, others in the north of town and all about 2km from the centre.

North of the centre are two caravan parks backing onto the Leichhardt River. The *Riverside Tourist Park* (☎ 4743 3904) at 195 West St and the *Copper City Caravan Park* (☎ 4743 4676) at 185 West St both have swimming pools, tent sites for around $12 and on-site cabins from $40.

If you have transport, one of the best camping spots is the *Moondarra Caravan Park* (☎ 4743 9780). There's a good pool and shady camp sites by the river bank costing $5 per person. To get there, follow the Barkly Hwy north of town for a few kilometres and take the turn-off to Lake

Moondarra. You'll soon see the park on your left (it's another 15km to the lake).

Hostels The *Travellers Haven* (☎ 4743 0313), about 500m from the centre on the corner of Spence and Pamela Sts, is a well set up backpackers' hostel. All the rooms are twin share and have air-con, with bunk beds costing $13 and singles/doubles from $26/30. The hostel has a good pool, bikes for hire ($10 a day) and a courtesy coach.

Hotels & Motels The *Boyd Hotel* (☎ 4743 3000) on the corner of West and Marian Sts has basic pub rooms at $25/40 with shared facilities.

At 23 Camooweal St, *Walton's Motor Court* (☎ 4743 2377) is one of the cheapest central motels, with air-con singles/doubles at $45/56 and a small pool. The *Boomerang Lodge* (☎ 4743 2019) at 11 Boyd Parade has clean self-contained units with kitchenettes and air-con from $40/50 for singles/doubles – if you're staying longer, its weekly rates ($140/190) are very good value.

The *Copper Gate Motel* (☎ 4743 3233) at 97 Marian St (the Barkly Hwy) has singles/doubles from $47/56.

If you're looking for something more expensive, the three-star *Burke & Wills Motor Inn* (☎ 4743 8000) on the corner of Grace and Camooweal Sts is a modern motel with spas, waterbeds, a pool and its own licensed restaurant – rooms here range from $86 to $95 a night.

The *Verona Motel* (☎ 4743 3024) on the corner of Marian and Camooweal Sts is a four-star, three-storey motel with refurbished rooms starting from $91 and executive rooms from $105. The motel has a pool and a good licensed restaurant (see Places to Eat).

Farm Stay There are a couple of stations in the surrounding area where you can stay overnight and get a taste for life out in the sticks. *West Leichhardt Station* (☎ 4743 8947) is about half an hour's drive northeast of Mt Isa, and offers camping ($15 per vehicle, $25 powered) and accommodation at $50 per person, or $100 including meals and activities.

Malbonvale (☎ 4748 4902) about one hour south-east of Mt Isa, is another farm stay option.

Places to Eat

There are a number of centrally located pizzerias, cafes and snack bars, including *Click's*, on West St, and the *Flamenco Cafe*, on Marian St near the corner of Miles St.

Mt Isa's clubs are among the best places to eat. In the south of town, the *Irish Club*, on the corner of Buckley and Nineteenth Aves, has excellent smorgasbords at $8 for lunch and $13 for dinner, and bistro meals in the $6 to $12 range. The club specialises in big, old-fashioned servings – you won't go home hungry. On the corner of Camooweal and Grace Sts, the *Buffalo Club* also has good bistro meals (and excellent steaks!) ranging from $8 to $14. Visitors to these clubs can sign in as honorary buffaloes or Irish persons, and dress regulations apply.

The Tavern, on Isa St, has good counter meals in the public bar, and meals in the bistro range from $10.

Los Toros Mexican Restaurant, at 79 Camooweal St, is deservedly one of the most popular places in town. It's a lively cantina-style eatery with main meals in the $12 to $16 range, good sangria and incredibly spicy chorizo sausage.

For Chinese food, try the *Red Lantern* on the corner of Isa and Simpson Sts. It's a spacious place with all the usual suspects on the menu, and main meals ranging from $12 to $16. It is open for dinner seven days, and for lunch daily except Sunday.

For pizzas (takeaway or home delivery), there's *Eagle Boys* (☎ 13 14330) on West St.

There's also a very good licensed restaurant at the *Verona Motel*, on the corner of Marian and Camooweal Sts. It's an elegant dining room which specialises in Italian cuisine and seafood, with pastas from $12 and other main courses in the $20 to $30 range.

Entertainment

Switches Nightclub, on Miles St, is a huge nightclub which features both live music and DJs, and has a restaurant section upstairs. The club is open from Wednesday to Saturday nights until 3 am. There's a variable cover charge and a 'no jeans' dress code here.

There are usually live bands in the *Boyd Hotel* on weekend evenings. Also popular are the *Kave* nightclub in the Mt Isa Hotel and the *Buffalo Club* on Grace St. The *Irish Club* has a good entertainment program, with something on most nights.

Mt Isa's *Civic Centre*, on West St, which includes a theatre and a 1000 seat auditorium, is the town's major venue for live performances and hosts a variety of concerts, plays, balls and events throughout the year.

Getting There & Away

Air Ansett has an office at 8 Miles St, and Flight West Airlines (☎ 4743 9333) is at 14 Miles St.

Ansett has flights to Brisbane ($438 one way) and Cairns ($281).

Flight West also flies to Townsville ($298), Normanton ($248), Karumba ($243) and various places along the Flinders Hwy.

Air Mt Isa takes passengers along on its twice-weekly mail run – see the Organised Tours sections for details.

Bus Greyhound Pioneer has an office at the rear of the Tourist Office, and all its buses depart and arrive here. McCafferty's operates from the Campbell's Coaches terminal (☎ 4743 2006), at 27 Barkly Hwy.

Both bus companies run daily services between Townsville and Tennant Creek, passing through Mt Isa en route. Townsville to Mt Isa takes 9½ hours and costs $84, while the trip on to Tennant Creek takes another 7½ hours ($75). Both companies have connections at Tennant Creek for Alice Springs ($138 from Mt Isa) and Darwin ($158).

McCafferty's also operates daily to Brisbane ($112, about 24 hours) by the inland route through Winton ($52) and Longreach ($59).

Campbell's Coaches (☎ 4743 2006) go to Normanton (6 hours, $69) and Karumba ($75) once a week, leaving each Tuesday at 10 am and returning the next day.

Train The air-con *Inlander* operates twice weekly between Townsville and Mt Isa, via Charters Towers, Hughenden and Cloncurry. The full journey takes about 18 hours and costs $125/192 for an economy/1st class sleeper.

Getting Around

There are no local bus services. If you want a taxi, call ☎ 4743 2333.

There are several car hire firms in Isa, including Avis (☎ 4743 3752), Hertz (☎ 4743 4142) and Thrifty (☎ 4743 2911).

If you want to get to Lawn Hill and don't have a vehicle, Four Wheel Drive Hire Service (☎ 4743 6306) at 7 Simpson St has Suzukis at $110 per day or Landcruisers at $150, both with unlimited kilometres. Longer rentals are good value because they work out quite a bit cheaper.

CAMOOWEAL
pop 230

Camooweal, 13km east of the Northern Territory border, is either your first or last chance to get fuel or food in Queensland, depending on which way you're headed. Be warned that the fuel here is fiendishly expensive – up to 20c more *per litre* than in Mt Isa.

The town was established in 1884 as a service centre for the vast cattle stations of the Barkly Tablelands. It is the turn-off for the Camooweal Caves National Park. You can also turn off here for Lawn Hill National Park, Gregory Downs and Burketown (see the Gulf Savannah chapter for details). There are a couple of historic buildings – the **Shire Hall** (1922), and **Freckleton's General Store**, an old corrugated tin building which also acts as an informal tourist information centre.

The Shell Camooweal Roadhouse

(☎ 4748 2155) on the west side of town is the local RACQ depot.

Places to Stay & Eat

The *Shell Camooweal Roadhouse* (☎ 4748 2155) has a campground ($4 per person), as well as six old but cleanish motel-units with air-con and TV costing $45/50 for singles/doubles. It has a cafe that does takeaways or you can dine in – it's a cut above your average roadhouse tucker.

The *Post Office Hotel* (☎ 4748 2124) has basic pub-style rooms, and the bistro serves lunches and dinners every day except Sunday.

CAMOOWEAL CAVES NATIONAL PARK

Beneath the surface of this small national park is a network of unusual caves and caverns with sinkhole openings. The largest of these, the Great Nowranie Cave, is 70m deep and almost 300m long. The caves can be explored, but only if you're an experienced caver and have all the right equipment. For the average punter, the park can be a dangerous place to wander around and it's extremely isolated.

If you are planning to visit, check with the local police and the Department of Environment office in Mt Isa (☎ 4743 2055) first. The caves are usually flooded during the wet season, so the middle of the year is the best time to visit – at other times you can expect extremely high temperatures and the usual precautions apply.

The entrance to the national park is 8km south of Camooweal along a rough, unsealed road. There are several creek crossings and the road is usually impassable after rain. There's a self-registration campground with toilets.

CAMOOWEAL TO THREEWAYS

There's nothing much for the whole 460km from Camooweal to the Threeways junction in the Northern Territory. The next service station west is 270km along at *Barkly Homestead* (☎ (08) 8964 4549). It offers camping and motel rooms.

Cloncurry to Cunnamulla – the Matilda Hwy

The Matilda Hwy is the best and most popular north-south route through outback Queensland. This bitumen highway starts at the Queensland/New South Wales border south of Cunnamulla and runs north for over 1700km, ending in Karumba on the Gulf of Carpentaria.

The Matilda Hwy takes you through most of the outback's major towns and to some of its best tourist attractions, including the Australian Workers' Heritage Centre in Barcaldine and the Stockman's Hall of Fame in Longreach.

The Matilda Hwy is in fact the name given to a route made up of a number of roads and highways. It consists of sections of the Mitchell Hwy, the Landsborough Hwy and the Burke Developmental Rd. Only the Cloncurry to Cunnamulla section is covered in this chapter – see the Gulf Savannah chapter for details of the northern section of the route.

Books & Maps

The Queensland Tourist & Travel Corporation has produced an excellent book, *The Matilda Highway*, which is readily available in good book and map shops or from branches of the automobile clubs in each state. The Queensland State Mapping Authority has also produced a map called *The Matilda Highway*; it can be purchased from Sunmap centres or agencies, as well as from good retailers.

CLONCURRY TO WINTON

About 14km east of Cloncurry, the narrow Landsborough Hwy turns off the Flinders Hwy and heads south-east to Winton via the one-pub towns of McKinlay and Kynuna.

The first section of this route, 343km from Cloncurry to McKinlay, passes through a rugged and rocky landscape of low, craggy hills that gradually give way to the flat plains that characterise most of the outback region.

McKinlay
pop 20

McKinlay is a tiny settlement which would probably have been doomed to eternal insignificance were it not for the fact it is home to the *Walkabout Creek Hotel* (☎ 4746 8424), which featured in the amazingly successful movie *Crocodile Dundee* starring Paul Hogan. Stills from the film and other Dundee memorabilia clutter the walls of the pub.

Buses travelling between Mt Isa and Brisbane via Longreach make a refreshment stop here. If you want to hang around for a day or two, the Walkabout Creek Hotel has clean and simple rooms with air-con at $38/46 for singles/doubles; you could also try the *Crocodile Dundee Van Park* behind the pub.

Kynuna
pop 30

Kynuna, another 74km south-east, isn't much bigger than McKinlay. The 107-year-old *Blue Heeler Hotel* (☎ 4746 8650) is another renowned old outback pub, which for some reason has its own surf life-saving club! The pub serves meals and has hotel rooms from $30 and motel rooms from $50, all with air-con. There is also a caravan park.

Every year in September, the Blue Heeler hosts its own surf life-saving carnival. The nearest beach may be almost 1000km away, but in true outback tradition the locals improvise by carrying a surf boat up and down the main street. The festival also features surfboard relays, a tug of war and an evening beach party with a live band. You can't miss the pub at night – it's the place with the blue neon dog with a flashing red tongue on the roof.

The *Never Never Caravan Park* (☎ 4746 8683) has tent sites, powered van sites, one on-site van and four cabins, and a licensed restaurant.

Kynuna to Winton (165km)

The turn-off to the **Combo Water Hole**, which Banjo Paterson is said to have visited in 1895 before he wrote *Waltzing Matilda*, is signposted off the highway about 12km east of Kynuna. The water hole is on Dagworth Station.

WINTON
pop 1800

Winton is a sheep-raising centre and also the railhead from which sheep and cattle are transported after being brought from the Channel Country by road train. The road north to Cloncurry is fully paved, but still gets washed out during a really bad wet season.

On the main street, there's a Jolly Swagman statue and the Qantilda Museum, which commemorates two local claims to fame: the founding of Qantas airlines at Winton in 1920 and the regionally inspired poetry of one of Australia's most famous poets, Banjo Paterson. An annual bush-verse competition, the Bronze Swagman Award, keeps alive the Banjo Paterson tradition and celebrates its influence on Australian literature. The competition attracts entries from all over Australia.

The town isn't exactly stunning, but it's a friendly, laid-back place with some interesting attractions and characters, and is a good place for a stopover if you're not in a hurry.

The town centre is spread along Elderslie St, a broad street divided by a central plantation, with three pubs, three cafes and a couple of well-stocked general stores, as well as an open-air cinema – not to be missed!

Information

The Gift & Gem Centre (☎ 4657 1296), on Elderslie St, acts as the local information centre.

Winton Fuel & Tyre Service (☎ 4657 1305), the BP roadhouse on the corner of Elderslie and Oondooroo Sts, is the local RACQ depot.

Things to See & Do

The **Qantilda Museum**, on Elderslie St beside the post office, is well worth a look with a good collection of memorabilia, including Qantas and Waltzing Matilda displays and a number of historic cottages and buildings. It is open from 9 am to 4 pm daily; entry costs $5 (children free).

The Origins of Qantas

Qantas, the Queensland & Northern Territory Aerial Service, had humble beginnings as a joy flight and air taxi service in Queensland's outback – and at times it seems like every second town in the outback has claims to being the birthplace of Australia's major airline.

The idea to establish the airline came about when two former Flying Corps airmen, Hudson Fysh and Paul McGuinness, travelled through outback Queensland to prepare the route for the famous London to Melbourne Air Race. They saw the potential for an air service to link remote outback centres and established an airline with the financial backing of local pastoralists.

The fledgling company was registered for business at Winton on 16 November 1920, and the first official board meeting was held in the Winton Club. Soon afterwards it was decided to move the company headquarters to Longreach, where the first office was opened in Duck St.

Qantas' first regular air service, begun on 22 November 1922, was between Cloncurry and Charleville; Longreach remained the headquarters of the airline until it was moved to Brisbane in 1930.

OUTBACK QUEENSLAND

Across the road from the museum is the bronze **Jolly Swagman** statue, a tribute to Banjo Paterson and the unknown swagmen who lie in unmarked graves in the area. Behind the statue is the **Winton Swimming Pool** – just the place for a cooling dip.

The **Corfield & Fitzmaurice Building**, a former general store in the centre of town now classified by the National Trust, has been restored to house a craft co-operative centre, with art exhibitions and a dinosaur display.

The **North Gregory Hotel** is said to be the place where Banjo Paterson's song *Waltzing Matilda* was first performed on 6 April 1895. The original pub has burned down, as have several subsequent constructions, and the present pub is a solid brick building built in 1955.

The **Royal Theatre**, out the back of the Stopover Cafe on Elderslie St in the centre of town, is a wonderful open-air theatre with canvas-slung chairs, corrugated tin

---

100 Years of Waltzing our Matildas

Written in 1895 by Banjo Paterson, the 'bard of the bush', *Waltzing Matilda* is widely regarded as Australia's unofficial national anthem. While not many can sing *Advance Australia Fair*, the official national anthem, without a lyric sheet, just about every Aussie knows the words to the strange ditty about a jolly swagman who jumped into a billabong and drowned himself rather than be arrested for stealing a jumbuck (sheep). But what the hell does it mean?

The Waltzing Matilda Centenary festival, held in Winton in April 1995, created a raging controversy among local historians over the origins and meaning of the famous tune; with first Winton, then Kynuna, claiming to be the true 'birthplace' of *Waltzing Matilda*.

To understand the origins of the song, it has to be seen in the political context of the its time. The 1890s were a period of social upheaval and political change in Queensland. Along with nationalistic calls for the Australian states to amalgamate and form a federation, the decade was dominated by an economic crisis, mass unemployment and severe droughts. An ongoing battle between the pastoralists and the shearers led to a series of strikes which divided the state and led to the formation of the Australian Labor Party to represent workers' interests.

In 1895 Paterson visited his fiancée in Winton, and together they travelled to Dagworth Station south of Kynuna, where they met Christina McPherson. During their stay they went on a picnic to the Combo Waterhole, a series of billabongs on the Diamantina River, where Paterson heard stories about the violent 1894 shearers' strike on Dagworth Station. During the strike rebel shearers had burned seven woolsheds to the ground, leading the police to declare martial law and place a reward of £1000 on the head of their leader, Samuel Hofmeister. Rather than allow himself to be captured, Hofmeister drowned himself in a billabong near the Combo Waterhole.

Paterson later wrote the words to *Waltzing Matilda* to accompany a tune played by Christina McPherson on a zither. While there is no direct proof that he was writing allegorically about Hofmeister and the shearers' strikes, a number of prominent historians have supported the theory and claimed that the song was a political statement. Others maintain that it is just an innocent but catchy tune about a hungry vagrant, but the song's undeniable anti-authoritarianism and the fact that it was adopted as an anthem by the rebel shearers weigh in heavily in favour of the former argument.

One hundred years later, *Waltzing Matilda* and the events surrounding the country's unofficial anthem take on even greater significance as the calls for Australia to become a republic by the millennium grow louder.

walls and a star-studded ceiling – the outback's version of *Cinema Paradiso*. Films are screened every Saturday, and on Wednesday between April and September. Saturday nights features two mainstream films; the Wednesday features are old favourites like Abbott & Costello or Laurel & Hardy, newsreels and sing-alongs, with tea and damper served afterwards.

Organised Tours

Diamantina Outback Tours (☎ 4657 1514) offers day trips to the Lark Quarry Environmental Park, costing $75 ($35 children) with lunch included.

You can also take a day trip to Carisbrooke Station – see the South of Winton section later this chapter for details.

Festivals

Winton's major festival is the nine-day Outback Festival, held every second year (odd numbers) during the September school holidays. The festival features crayfish races, a dunny derby, iron man and woman competitions, country music, bush bands and buskers. A highlight of the festival is the presentation of the Bronze Swagman Award for bush poetry.

Another regular event, the Boulder Opal Auctions, is held in the Royal Theatre every year over weekends in May and August and attracts gem buyers from around the country.

Places to Stay

The *Matilda Country Caravan Park* (☎ 4657 1607) at 43 Chirnside St has a pool, a kiosk, tent sites from $10 ($14 powered), on-site vans from $25 and cabins from $50. The *North Gregory Hotel* (☎ 4657 1375) at 67 Elderslie St has clean budget rooms with air-con at $25 a head.

Banjo's Overnight Family Motel Cabins (☎ 4657 1213) on the corner of Manuka and Bostock Sts on the Longreach side of town, has self-contained units from $45. Across the road from the Qantilda Museum, the *Matilda Motel* (☎ 4657 1433) has units from $45/50.

The ubiquitous wind pump dots the horizon wherever you travel in outback Queensland.

Places to Eat

The *North Gregory Hotel*, at 67 Elderslie St, has good bistro meals. You can eat in the bar or the dining room next door, or there's a beer garden out the back with an outdoor char-grill and plate-sized steaks.

You can also have a meal in the Qantas Board Room Lounge at the *Winton Club*, where the first board meeting of the

OUTBACK QUEENSLAND

Queensland and Northern Territory Aerial Service was held in 1921. The club is on the corner of Oondooroo and Vindex Sts, and is open for lunch and dinner from Monday to Saturday.

Getting There & Away
Winton is on the main Brisbane to Mt Isa bus route, and you can get here with Mc-Cafferty's.

There are also connecting bus services between Winton and Longreach that meet up with the twice-weekly *Spirit of the Outback* train.

SOUTH OF WINTON
The country around Winton is rough and rugged, with much wildlife, notably brolgas. There are also Aboriginal sites with paintings, carvings and artefacts.

At **Lark Quarry Environmental Park**, 115km south-west of Winton, dinosaur footprints have been perfectly preserved in limestone for 100 million years. It takes around two hours to drive from Winton to

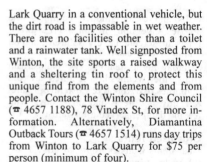

Captain Starlight
Longreach was the starting point for one of Queensland's most colourful early crimes. In 1870 Harry Redford and two accomplices stole 1000 head of cattle from Mt Cornish, north of Longreach, and drove them down the Thomson River and its continuation, Cooper Creek, to the present site of Innamincka. From there he followed the Strzelecki Creek south, finally selling his ill-gotten gains to a station owner north of Adelaide.

His exploit opened up a new stock route south, and when he was finally brought to justice in Roma in 1873, he was found not guilty by the adoring public! Rolf Boldrewood's novel *Robbery Under Arms* later immortalised Redford as 'Captain Starlight'.

Lark Quarry in a conventional vehicle, but the dirt road is impassable in wet weather. There are no facilities other than a toilet and a rainwater tank. Well signposted from Winton, the site sports a raised walkway and a sheltering tin roof to protect this unique find from the elements and from people. Contact the Winton Shire Council (☎ 4657 1188), 78 Vindex St, for more information. Alternatively, Diamantina Outback Tours (☎ 4657 1514) runs day trips from Winton to Lark Quarry for $75 per person (minimum of four).

Carisbrooke Station (☎ 4657 3885), set amid spectacular escarpment country 85km south-west of Winton. It's an interesting place that features a wildlife sanctuary, an old opal mine, Aboriginal paintings and bora rings (ceremonial grounds). The station offers day tours (with advance notice) starting from Winton ($85 per person, minimum of four), or from the homestead ($60). It also has a self-contained unit at $50, shearers' quarters at $20 per person and camping for $5.

The **Opalton Mining Field**, 115km south of Winton, is a remote gemfield where the unique boulder opals can be found. Unlike opals from places like Lightning Ridge and Coober Pedy, which are found in clay, boulder opals are attached to a host rock which has to be ground away to free the opal. The name relates more to the host rocks than to the size of the opals. There are no facilities here apart from a phone box, and the road is unsealed and slow going.

LONGREACH
pop 4420
This prosperous outback town was the home of Qantas earlier this century, but these days it's equally famous for the Australian Stockman's Hall of Fame & Outback Heritage Centre, probably the biggest attraction in outback Queensland.

Longreach's human population is vastly outnumbered by the sheep, which number over a million; there are a fair few cattle too.

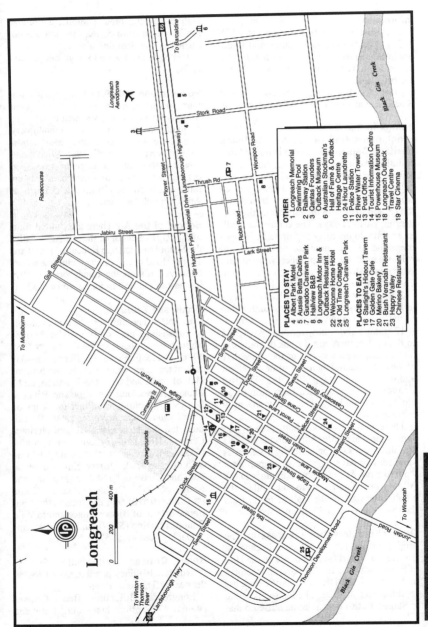

Longreach

0   200   400 m

To Muttaburra

To Winton & Thomson River

Racecourse

Showgrounds

Longreach Aerodrome

To Barcaldine

Black Gin Creek

PLACES TO STAY
4 Albert Park Motel
5 Aussie Betta Cabins
7 Gunadoo Caravan Park
8 Hallview B&B
9 Longreach Motor Inn & Longreach Restaurant
22 Welcome Home Hotel
24 Old Time Cottage
25 Longreach Caravan Park

PLACES TO EAT
16 Starlight's Hideout Tavern
17 Merino Gate Cafe
20 Merino Bakery
21 Bush Verandah Restaurant
23 Happy Valley Chinese Restaurant

OTHER
1 Longreach Memorial Swimming Pool
2 Railway Station
3 Qantas Founders Outback Museum
6 Australian Stockman's Hall of Fame & Outback Heritage Centre
10 24 Hour Laundrette
11 Police Station
12 River Water Tower
13 Post Office
14 Tourist Information Centre
15 Powerhouse Museum
18 Longreach Outback Travel Centre
19 Star Cinema

Gull Street
Currawong St
Eagle Street North
Snipe Street
Swan Street
Cassowary Street
Crane Street
Parrot Lane
Pelican Street
Galah Street
Magpie Lane
Eagle Street
Ibis Street
Swan Street

Jabiru Street
Plover Street
Stork Road
Thrush Rd
Lark Street
Robin Road
Wompoo Road

Sir Hudson Fysh Memorial Drive (Landsborough Highway)

Landsborough Hwy
Thomson Development Road

To Windorah
Jundah Road

Black Gin Creek

OUTBACK QUEENSLAND

Information

The tourist information office (☎ 4658 3555) is on the corner of Duck and Eagle Sts in the centre of town. It is open from 9 am to 5 pm daily; hours are shorter during the off season.

The local RACQ depot is Slade & Son Smash Repairs (☎ 4658 1609) on Crane St.

Things to See & Do

Stockman's Hall of Fame & Outback Heritage Centre

The centre is housed in a beautifully conceived building, 2km east of town along the road to Barcaldine. The excellent displays are divided into periods from the first white settlement through to today, and deal with all aspects of the pioneering pastoral days. The centre was built as a tribute to the early explorers and stockmen, and also commemorates the crucial roles played by the pioneer women and Aboriginal stockmen, although the section on the latter is pathetically brief.

It's well worth visiting the Hall of Fame, as it gives a fascinating insight into this side of the European development of Australia. A 12-minute slide show introduces visitors to the centre; there are dozens of static exhibits featuring the stories of the characters of the outback; and there are some excellent audio-visual displays like the **Talking Drover** – a computerised recreation of an old drover reminiscing in a stockman's bush camp at dusk.

There is a good bookshop, plus a souvenir shop and a cafe. Admission is $15 ($7 for children, $35 for a family), which is valid for two days. The centre is open from 9 am to 5 pm daily (except Christmas Day). Allow yourself half a day to take it all in. It's a half-hour walk to the Hall of Fame from the town centre; a taxi will cost about $6.

Qantas Founders Outback Museum

The original Qantas hangar, which still stands at Longreach airport (almost opposite the Hall of Fame), was also the first aircraft 'factory' in Australia – six DH-50 biplanes were assembled here in 1926. The hangar is home to Stage 1 of this new aviation museum that features, among other exhibits, a life-size replica of an Avro 504K, the first aircraft owned by the fledgling airline.

It is open from 9 am to 5 pm daily; entry is $6.

Powerhouse Museum

Longreach's former powerhouse on Swan St has been turned into a museum, and will be of interest to anyone with an interest in machinery. The huge old diesel and gas-vacuum engines were in use until 1985 when a new power station on the edge of town was opened. Entry is $3 and hard hats are supplied. It's open daily from 2 to 5 pm from April through October.

School of the Air

There are guided tours of the RFDS School of the Air (now called the School of Distance Education), at 9 and 10 am Monday to Friday (including school holidays). It's on the Landsborough Hwy just east of the Hall of Fame; entry is $2.50.

Organised Tours

Day Tours

The number of tours available is surprising, and most can be booked through the Outback Travel Centre (☎ 4658 1776) at 115 Eagle St. It offers a one-day tour of the town which includes visits to the Hall of Fame and an outback station, and a dinner cruise along the Thomson River at $49 ($25 for children). Other day trips on offer include tours to Winton ($69), Barcaldine and the Australian Workers Heritage Centre ($109), half-day tours to Ilfracombe ($38/ 25), and a combined day trip to Winton, the Lark Quarry Environmental Park and Carisbrooke Station (Monday and Friday, $109). Outback Aussie Tours (☎ 1800 810 510) does day trips to the Aboriginal art site of Blacks Palace and to Wild Winodka Station ($109), and half-day trips to Oakley Station ($25).

River Cruises

Yellowbelly Express (☎ 4658 1919) does popular river trips on the nearby Thomson River.

Longreach Billabong Boat Cruises (☎ 4658 1776) offers three-hour 'sunset and stars' dinner cruises along a water hole on the Thomson River, with live entertainment and a barbecue or camp oven meal with billy tea and damper. The cost is $25 ($15 for children).

Stations You can also make a visit to one or more of the sheep stations in the area. They include: Toobrack (☎ 4658 9158), 68km south; Longway (☎ 4658 2191), 17km north; and Avington (☎ 1800 685 099), 75km west of Blackall. Some of these places are open only for day trips while others offer accommodation and a range of activities. Avington, for example, has beds in its shearers' quarters for $15 as well as rooms in its homestead for $65/100, including B&B and dinner. Activities include horse riding, trail-bike riding, canoeing and barge cruises on the Barcoo River. Remember to phone ahead before making any visit to a station – don't just turn up unannounced.

Mustering on horseback is an exciting part of any cattle station's work.

Festivals
In May Longreach holds the Outback Muster Drovers Union & National Outback Performing Arts Show, the National Bronco Branding and the annual Show; and in July there are the Diamond Shears Shearing Championships and the Starlight Stampede Festival.

Places to Stay
Caravan Parks The *Gunnadoo Caravan Park* (☎ 4658 1781), east of town on the corner of the highway and Thrush Rd, has a shop and two pools, with tent sites at $12, on-site vans at $28 and self-contained cabins from $48.

Pubs There's a choice of at least four pubs on Eagle St. Best value are the *Royal* (☎ 4658 2118) and the *Central* (☎ 4658 2263), with basic air-con pub rooms for $20/35. The *Lyceum Hotel* (☎ 4658 1036) at 131 Eagle St has also been recommended, with air-con rooms from $15.

Cabins & B&Bs If you're looking for somewhere self-contained, the *Aussie Betta Cabins* (☎ 4658 3811), out on the highway about 300m west of the Hall of Fame, is a complex of cabins that sleep up to five people and have cooking facilities and air-con. The tariff is $50/55 for singles/doubles plus $5 for each extra person.

Hallview Lodge B&B (☎ 4658 3777) is a comfortable, renovated, air-con timber house on the corner of Wompoo and Thrush Rd. It has singles/doubles with en-suite and breakfast for $45/62 and does pick-ups from the train and bus terminals.

For a group or family, the *Old Time Cottage* (☎ 4658 3557) at 158 Crane St is a self-contained old-style cottage with an established garden. It has air-con, sleeps six and costs $55 a double, or $65 for a family.

Motels At 84 Galah St, the *Longreach Motor Inn* (☎ 4658 2322) is quite central and has a licensed restaurant (see Places to Eat), a pool and good motel rooms from $62/72, plus $10 for each extra person – the rooms sleep up to six people.

On the corner of the highway and Stork Rd, the *Albert Park Motel* (☎ 4658 2411) is a large modern motel with a good pool, a spa and a licensed restaurant. Singles/doubles are $59/69.

Places to Eat

There are several cafes and takeaways along Eagle St. The pub meals are about as dreary as you'll find – this is what Australian food used to be like everywhere! Best is perhaps *Starlight's Hideout Tavern*, also on Eagle St, with bistro meals of a sort.

The licensed *Outback Restaurant* at the Longreach Motor Inn, on Galah St, opens nightly for dinner. It's quite formal and up-market, with international cuisine in the $16 to $20 range and a few vegetarian dishes in the $8 to $10 range.

On the corner of Galah and Swan Sts, the *Bush Verandah Restaurant* is a small BYO (no liquor licence) with rustic décor and country-style cooking (mains $16 to $20, open Wednesday to Saturday).

The licensed *Happy Valley Chinese Restaurant* on Eagle St is open for dinner seven days.

Entertainment

The *Star Cinema*, at 117 Eagle St, screens latest-release movies on Friday, Saturday and Sunday, and sometimes on Wednesday.

Getting There & Away

Air Flight West has daily flights from Longreach to Brisbane ($326), and also flies twice a week to Winton ($94) and Townsville ($233).

Bus McCafferty's has daily services to Winton (two hours, $22), Mt Isa (7½ hours, $59) and Brisbane (17 hours, $83), and three times a week to Rockhampton (nine hours, $65). Buses stop at Longreach Travel World (☎ 4658 1155), at 113 Eagle St.

Train The twice-weekly *Spirit of the Outback* connects Longreach with Rockhampton (14 hours, $102/165 in an economy/1st class sleeper); there are connecting bus services between Longreach and Winton ($26).

LONGREACH TO WINDORAH – THE THOMSON DEVELOPMENTAL RD

The 310km Thomson Developmental Rd, which roughly follows the route of the Thomson River from Longreach to Windorah, is the most direct route for people wanting to cut across to Birdsville (the Diamantina Development Rd) from Longreach. The first half of the route, from Longreach to Stonehenge (150km), is over a narrow sealed road; the second leg, from Stonehenge to Windorah (160km), is over unsealed roads of dirt and gravel, and then soft red sand – this section is slower going and is often closed during the Wet.

Located 4km off the main road, **Stonehenge** is a tiny settlement in the middle of a dry, dusty and rocky landscape, with half a dozen tin houses and a pub. The *Stonehenge Hotel* (☎ 4658 5944) has rooms at $20 a head or $50 with three meals a day. The pub sells fuel – super, unleaded and diesel. Stonehenge has a bush horse race meeting every year in March and a rodeo every year in mid to late-August.

About 65km south of the Stonehenge turn-off is **Jundah**, a neat little township which acts as the administrative base for the Barcoo Shire council. The town's general store sells super, unleaded and diesel fuel; it is open daily from 8 am to 7 pm, but closes at 2 pm on Sunday in summer. The *Jundah Hotel-Motel* (☎ 4658 6166) is a low and little two- room pub; an accommodation block next door has clean, tidy rooms with shared bathrooms and air-con at $20/35 for singles/doubles. Counter meals are served every day. The council-run *caravan park* in Miles St is a small, treeless block of land with an amenities block.

It's another 95km from Jundah to Windorah. Another unsealed road which heads south out of Jundah also meets the Diamantina Development Rd, about 50km east of Windorah (see the Channel Country section later in this chapter for details of Windorah).

LONGREACH TO BARCALDINE (108km)

Ilfracombe (pop 150)

This tiny little township 28km east of Longreach modestly calls itself 'the Hub of the West', and boasts a railway station, a general store, a swimming pool, a golf course and a good pub.

The **Ilfracombe Folk Museum**, situated along the north side of the highway through the centre of town, features an impressive collection of old tractors and farm machinery, carts and buggies, and several historic buildings with period furniture and memorabilia. The museum is always open and entry is free.

Places to Stay & Eat The *Teamster's Rest Caravan Park* (☎ 4658 2295), on the highway, is a straightforward little park with tent sites ($8, or $10 powered) and a couple of on-site vans ($22).

The *Wellshot Hotel* (☎ 4658 2106) is a charming and historic little pub with a row of clean, simple rooms with shared bathroom facilities out the back. Singles/doubles cost $20/35 and meals are available. The 'Public Baa' has an aquarium and a great display of old stockmen's hats and cattle brands; the dining room features a bar made from old wool presses, walls lined with stencilled wool-packs, and a whole wall covered with a long poem called *The Wellshot & The Bush Pub's Hall of Fame* by Robert Raftery: 'She has heard the creak of wagons and the snort of tethered beasts, Fortified their flinty drivers for their prospects further east'.

BARCALDINE
pop 1850
Barcaldine lies at the junction of the Landsborough and Capricorn Hwys, 575km west of Rockhampton via Emerald, and is surrounded by sheep and cattle stations. It's known as the 'Garden City of the West', with good supplies of artesian water nourishing orchards of citrus fruits – in 1887 Barcaldine was the first town in Australia to realise its underground bounty.

Established in 1886 when the railway arrived, Barcaldine gained a place in Australian history in 1891 when it became the headquarters of the historic shearers' strike, during which over 1000 men camped in and around the town. That confrontation saw

troops called in, and the formation of the Australian Workers' Party, the forerunner of today's Australian Labor Party. The **Tree of Knowledge**, a ghost gum near the railway station, was the meeting place of the organisers, and still stands as a monument to workers and their rights.

The Australian Workers Heritage Centre is one of the outback's major attractions, and although it gets nowhere near the publicity generated by Longreach's Hall of Fame, it is equally impressive in its own way.

Beside the centre is **The Artesian Memorial**, a giant windmill dedicated to the pioneers who explored the Artesian Basin.

Note that, unless you want to get into a fight, Barcaldine is pronounced 'Bar-*call*-din' – *not* 'Barcal-*dean*' or 'Barcal-*dine*'; the locals simply call it Barky.

Information
Barcaldine's tourist information centre (☎ 4651 1724) is in a small railway carriage next to the train station on Oak St.

The local RACQ depot is Barcaldine Engineering Works (☎ 4651 1337) on Oak St.

Things to See & Do
Australian Workers Heritage Centre
This centre, built to commemorate the role played by workers in the formation of Australian social, political and industrial movements, was opened during the Labor Party's centenary celebrations in Barcaldine in 1991. Set in landscaped grounds around a central billabong, the centre includes the impressive **Australian Bicentennial Theatre**, a huge, circular big top which toured Australia in 1988 as part of the Bicentennial celebrations. A theatre inside screens the film *Celebration of a Nation* every half hour between 9 am and 4.30 pm, and there is an interesting display here tracing the history of the shearers' strike.

Another notable feature is the **One Teacher School**, the old Torrens Creek schoolhouse which takes you back in time to an old-fashioned school room with

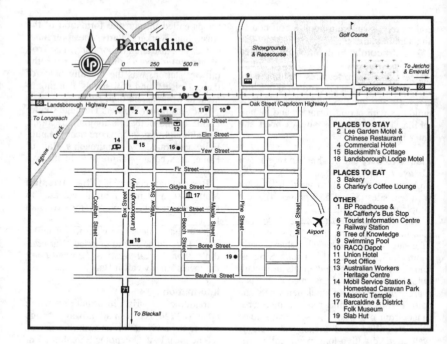

Barcaldine

0   250   500 m

Golf Course

Showgrounds & Racecourse

To Jericho & Emerald

Capricorn Highway 66

Landsborough Highway

To Longreach

Creek

Lagoon

Oak Street (Capricorn Highway)

Ash Street

Elm Street

Yew Street

Fir Street

Gidyea Street

Acacia Street

Boree Street

Bauhinia Street

Coolibah Street

Box Street (Landsborough Hwy)

Willow Street

Beech Street

Maple Street

Pine Street

Myall Street

Airport

To Blackall

71

PLACES TO STAY
2 Lee Garden Motel & Chinese Restaurant
4 Commercial Hotel
15 Blacksmith's Cottage
18 Landsborough Lodge Motel

PLACES TO EAT
3 Bakery
5 Charley's Coffee Lounge

OTHER
1 BP Roadhouse & McCafferty's Bus Stop
6 Tourist Information Centre
7 Railway Station
8 Tree of Knowledge
9 Swimming Pool
10 RACQ Depot
11 Union Hotel
12 Post Office
13 Australian Workers Heritage Centre
14 Mobil Service Station & Homestead Caravan Park
16 Masonic Temple
17 Barcaldine & District Folk Museum
19 Slab Hut

timber desks, slates, learners and an original school bell. It also has the classic 'Good Manners' poster, which instructed students to 'Be Honest, Truthful and Pure', 'Never be Rude to Anybody' and 'Do not Bully; only Cowards Do This'.

Other displays include a replica of an **Old Hospital Ward**, a **Powerhouse** contrasting the old generators that supplied Quilpie's power with the power supplies of the future, a replica of Queensland's Legislative Assembly, and the **Workers Wall**, a photographic montage of prominent members of the Labor Party.

This centre is a major achievement and offers a fascinating look into Australian history. It is open from 9 am to 5 pm Monday to Saturday, and from 10 am to 5 pm on Sunday. Entry costs $7 (children under 14 free), and the ticket is valid for seven days. The entrance gate is at the western end of the complex.

Other Attractions The **Barcaldine & District Folk Museum**, on the corner of Gidyea and Beech Sts, is an old Queenslander crammed with a fascinating collection of memorabilia. It is open every day from 7 am to 5 pm; entry costs $2.

On the corner of Pine and Bauhinia Sts is **Mad Mick's**. Also known as the **Funny Farm** or **Slab Hut**, it's a ramshackle, cluttered farmlet with a collection of historic buildings, art studios, shearers' quarters and dray sheds, and a small fauna park with emus, possums, peacocks and wallabies. The complex is open from 9 am to 1 pm daily, except Monday, between April and September; entry costs $7 ($4 for children).

Organised Tours
Barcaldine Town & Country Tours (☎ 4651 1308) (based at the Homestead Caravan Park) offers day tours: the 'Town & Country' tour visits the Tree of Knowledge,

OUTBACK QUEENSLAND

the Australian Workers Heritage Centre, Mad Mick's, an outback station and a deer farm; the cost is $90.

Places to Stay

The *Homestead Caravan Park* (☎ 4651 1308), behind the Mobil service station on Box St, has tent sites from $10, on-site vans from $25 and cabins from $35. The owners of this place are helpful with information on the area, and run tours of the town and surrounding areas (see the preceding Organised Tours section).

At 67 Oak St is the *Commercial Hotel* (☎ 4651 1242), a green and white two-storey pub built in the 1920s. It's a friendly place with good meals and clean, simple rooms upstairs opening onto a broad verandah; the beds are comfortable, but the lack of ceiling fans or air-con is a serious drawback on a hot day. Singles/doubles cost $16/32.

The *Blacksmith's Cottage* (☎ 4651 1724) at 7 Elm St is a quaint, restored cottage which dates back to the turn of the century. It sleeps up to four people and is good value at $50 for four ($60 with breakfast).

The best of the motels is perhaps the *Landsborough Lodge Motel* (☎ 4651 1100), south of the centre on the corner of Box St (the Landsborough Hwy) and Boree St. It's a modern colonial-style place with motel units at $55/68.

The *Lee Garden Motel* (☎ 4651 1488), on the corner of Oak and Box Sts, has units from $50.

Places to Eat

Head to the *Commercial Hotel* for a good pub feed – bistro meals are in the $7 to $10 range, and it also has light lunches for around $4. Next door, the friendly *Charley's Coffee Lounge* is a good cafe.

The *Witch's Kitchen*, the bistro inside the Union Hotel on the corner of Oak and Maple Sts, also has good meals. Beside the Lee Gardens Motel on Oak St, the *Lee Gardens Chinese Restaurant* is a simple little place serving eat-in or takeaway Chinese meals.

Getting There & Away

Bus Barcaldine is on the main Brisbane-Mt Isa bus route, and McCafferty's has daily services to Brisbane ($77), Longreach ($13) and Mt Isa ($74). You can also get to Rockhampton three times a week ($52). Buses stop at the BP Roadhouse which is at the intersection of the Landsborough and Capricorn Hwys.

Train The *Spirit of the Outback* between Rockhampton and Longreach stops in Barcaldine twice weekly.

BARCALDINE TO HUGHENDEN

From Barcaldine you can head through the small but interesting towns of **Aramac** and **Muttaburra** to Hughenden, 357km north of Barcaldine. The unsealed road from Muttaburra to Hughenden passes through flat country and can be a bit rough in places, but is usually quite manageable in a conventional vehicle with sufficient ground clearance if driven carefully.

BARCALDINE TO ALPHA – THE CAPRICORN HIGHWAY

The Capricorn Hwy starts in Barcaldine and runs 136km across to Rockhampton on the coast.

North Delta Station (☎ 4651 1634), 32km east of Barcaldine, is a working sheep and cattle station that is open to visitors for shearing demonstrations, property tours and lunches, and budget accommodation for up to eight people – phone to say you're coming.

Midway between Barcaldine and Alpha is the small township of **Jericho**, with a train station, pub and a cafe. There's a strange, interesting sculpture called *The Crystal Trumpeters* in the centre of town opposite the old town hall. Inspired by the trumpeters who blew down the walls of Jericho, it's an abstract work of large clay trumpets surrounded by obelisk-like boulders.

The *Jordon Valley Hotel* has budget accommodation, and you can get a bite to eat at the *Jordan Cafe*. Pearce's Garage (☎ 4651 4237) is the local RACQ depot.

ALPHA
pop 460

Alpha, 136km east of Barcaldine, has an interesting and growing collection of murals which were started by a group of local artists in 1991. The murals are on a number of public buildings along Shakespeare St, the main street, including the hardware shop, art gallery, railway station and school. There are also murals inside both pubs – there's even a great bush camping scene on the toilet block in front of the rail yards.

From Alpha you can turn off south to Tambo (163km) or north-east to Clermont (184km). Both of these routes are along unsealed roads for the majority of the way – they can be tackled in a conventional vehicle, with care, but might be impassable during the Wet.

Places to Stay & Eat

There are two caravan parks in town.

In Shakespeare St, the *Criterion Hotel* (☎ 4985 1215) is a traditional, old two-storey verandah-fronted pub with simple rooms at $20/30. The pub serves bistro meals from Monday to Saturday evenings.

Next door to the pub, the *Alpha Hotel-Motel* (☎ 4985 1311) has a set of neat motel units which cost $45/54 for singles/doubles.

ALPHA TO ROCKHAMPTON

See the Capricorn Coast chapter.

BLACKALL
pop 1830

Blackall claims to be the site of the mythical black stump – according to outback mythology, anywhere west of Blackall was considered to be 'beyond the black stump'.

Gazetted in 1868, Blackall is named after the second governor of Queensland, Samuel Blackall. The town is a pleasant spot to stop on trips north or south along the Matilda Hwy, and fuel and supplies are available from a good range of outlets.

The town prides itself on the fact that it was near here, at Alice Downs station, that the legendary shearer Jackie Howe set his world record of shearing 321 sheep in less

than eight hours, with a set of hand shears – see the boxed text in the Darling Downs chapter. After his shearing days were over, Jackie ran one of the hotels in Blackall, where he's buried.

Blackall is also famous as the site of the first artesian well to be drilled in Queensland, although the well didn't strike water at first and when it did the product was undrinkable. After you use the bore water for washing or whatever, you'll probably agree with most travellers and say it stinks a little. Locals say it's got a bit of 'body'.

Information

The Blackall Historic Woolscour & Tourist Office (☎ 4657 4637) on Short St is open from 8.30 am to 5 pm on weekdays and from 9 am to 3 pm on weekends.

Banks represented in Blackall are the Commonwealth, National and Westpac. The local RACQ depot is Wood's Mechanical Repairs (☎ 4657 4100, after hours ☎ 4657 4400) on Rose St.

Things to See & Do

The **Blackall Woolscour**, the only steam-driven scour (wool-cleaner) left in Queensland, is 4km north-east of Blackall. Built in 1908, it operated up until 1978 and all the machinery is intact and still in working order. The complex incorporates a shearing shed, a wool-washing plant and a pond fed by an artesian bore. It's open for personalised tours from 8 am to 4 pm daily; entry costs $5 ($2 children).

The bronze **Jackie Howe Memorial Statue** has pride of place in the centre of town on the corner of Short and Shamrock Sts. When Jackie retired in 1900, he bought Blackall's Universal Hotel. The original pub was demolished in the 1950s, but the facade of the **New Universal Garden Centre & Gallery**, built on the original site at 53 Shamrock St, reflects the design of the old pub. The gallery houses a great collection of Jackie Howe memorabilia and souvenirs, as well as works by local artists.

About 130km east of Blackall is **Black's Palace**, an Aboriginal site with burial caves and impressive rock paintings. It's on private property but can be visited with the permission of the warden (☎ 4657 4455, ☎ 4657 4663).

Festivals

Annual events in Blackall include the Claypan Bogie Country Music Festival (in March), the Show (in May) and the Jackie Howe Run shearing competition (in October). In September or October every even-numbered year, the Barcoo Rush Festival takes place. It's a 10-day town festival with a street parade, fireworks displays, barbecues and a ball.

Places to Stay

The *Blackall Caravan Park* (☎ 4657 4816), just off the highway east of the centre at 53 Garden St, has tent/caravan sites at $10/12, on-site vans from $22 and three cabins from $30 a double.

The three pubs along Shamrock St (the main street), all have budget accommodation: the *Barcoo Hotel* (☎ 4657 4197) is at No 95, the *Prince of Wales Hotel* (☎ 4657 4731) is at No 63 and the *Bushman's Hotel* (☎ 4657 4143) is at No 166. There's also the *Blackall Motel* (☎ 4657 4491), on the corner of Shamrock and Myrtle Sts, and the *Coolibah Motel* (☎ 4657 4380) – both with singles/doubles at around $40/55.

ISISFORD
pop 150

A small historic township 90km south of Ilfracombe and 125km west of Blackall, Isisford was established in 1877 by the Whitman brothers, two travelling hawkers who broke an axle on their wagon while crossing the Barcoo River and decided to stay. Kerry Packer's **Isis Downs Station**, with the largest shearing shed in Australia, is 20km east of Isisford.

Clancy's Overflow Hotel (☎ 4658 8210), built in 1875, has budget accommodation downstairs at $20 a room and more comfortable rooms upstairs at $30/35 for singles/doubles. The pub serves breakfast, lunch and dinner every day; and the publi-

can, Jim Kilby, runs 4WD expeditions to the Grey Ranges which cost $85 per person per day.

IDALIA NATIONAL PARK

This remote national park off the Blackall-Emmet road 112km south-east of Blackall is only accessible for 4WD vehicles. In the rugged escarpment country of the Gowan Ranges, the park includes the headwaters of the Bulloo River and its numerous tributaries, with a predominantly mulga scrub landscape.

There are no facilities here and visitors need to be totally self-sufficient. Camping permits are required in advance; contact the park office (☎ 4657 5033) or the Department of Environment in Longreach (☎ 4658 1761) for more information.

BLACKALL TO CHARLEVILLE (300km)
Barcoo River

Continuing south-east along the Landsborough Hwy, the Barcoo River is crossed 42km south of Blackall and there is an excellent spot to stop and camp on the east side of the road. You can even get back a bit off the road, away from the traffic.

The Barcoo is one of the great rivers of western Queensland and must be the only river in the world that becomes a creek in its lower reaches. The Barcoo flows northwest past Blackall, then swings south-west through Isisford and into the Channel Country of south-western Queensland, where it becomes Cooper Creek, probably the most famous of Australia's inland rivers.

While Mitchell had waxed lyrical about this river in 1846, thinking it was a route to the Gulf, it was left to his second-in-command Edmund Kennedy (later of Cape York fame) to discover the real course of the river and to name it in 1847.

Both Banjo Paterson and Henry Lawson mention the Barcoo in their writings. The name has also entered the Australian idiom, appearing in the *Macquarie Dictionary* in such terms as 'Barcoo rot' (scurvy), the

'Barcoo salute' (waving to keep flies away from the face) and the 'Barcoo spews' (vomiting caused by the heat).

Tambo

On the banks of the Barcoo River, Tambo is surrounded by perhaps the best grazing land in western Queensland, and this hamlet also has some of the earliest historic buildings in the region. In the main street are timber houses that date back to the town's earliest days in the 1860s, while the 'new' post office has been operating since 1904. The 'old' **post office**, built in 1876 and at the time the main repeating station for south-west Queensland, is now preserved as a museum.

The information centre is at the shire council chambers (☎ 4654 6133). There's a National Australia Bank branch in Arthur St. The RACQ depot is Ricks Tyre Centre (☎ 4654 6276) in Arthur St.

The town promotes itself as 'the friendly town of the west' and each year horse races are held at the local track, a tradition dating back to the formation of the Great Western Downs Jockey Club in 1865.

From Tambo you continue southwards on the Matilda Hwy but for a good excursion, there is access to the **Salvator Rosa** section of Carnarvon National Park. The Salvator Rosa park is 120km east of Tambo and is reached via the Dawson Development Rd and Cungelella station, generally a 4WD route. See the Capricorn Coast chapter for more information on the Carnarvon National Park.

Places to Stay The *Tambo Caravan Park* (☎ 4654 6463), on the highway west of the centre, caters for campers with tent sites at $10 ($12 powered).

The *Royal Carrangarra Hotel* (☎ 4654 6127) has basic pub-style rooms at $10/20 for singles/doubles and the *Club Hotel-Motel* (☎ 4654 6109) has budget rooms ($12 for a single) or motel-style units from $30/45. The very attractive *Tambo Mill Motel* (☎ 4654 6466) has a swimming pool and good rooms from $48/58.

Augathella (pop 720)

The town of Augathella is 116km south of Tambo and 5km north of the junction of the Mitchell Hwy and the south-east route to Brisbane via Morven. Travellers heading north to Mt Isa, the Gulf or the Northern Territory often join the Matilda at this point.

Surveyed in 1880, Augathella began as a bullock team camp beside the Warrego River. Today, it services the sheep properties that dot the surrounding countryside.

Tourist information can be obtained from Russell's Roadhouse (☎ 4654 5255), open from 4.30 am to 11 pm daily.

The town has one hotel and one motel/caravan park – *Augathella Motel & Caravan Park* (☎ 4654 5177), where tent sites are $10 ($12 powered) and motel units are $45/55. Fuel and supplies are available from the shops in town.

CHARLEVILLE
pop 3600

One of the largest towns in outback Queensland, Charleville is situated on the Warrego River, 760km west of Brisbane. Edmund Kennedy passed this way in 1847 and the town was gazetted in 1868, six years after the first settlers had arrived. By the turn of the century the town was an important centre for the outlying sheep stations.

Cobb & Co began building coaches here in 1893 and these coaches, especially designed for Australian conditions, continued to be produced here until 1920. Charleville is also linked to the origins of Qantas: the airline's first regular route was between Charleville and Cloncurry in 1922.

The 1990 floods devastated large areas of the Channel Country and Charleville was one of the towns hardest hit. As the Warrego River rose the floodwaters swept through Charleville at around 70km/h; houses were carried away like toys, and the streets literally opened up and swallowed cars. There are photos and books on the floods in the town's tourist office and a red line almost 2m up the wall shows the high water mark.

━━

The Meteorologist and the Drought-Buster Guns

Charleville was the site of one of the more bizarre episodes in meteorological history. In 1902, meteorologist Clement Wragge proposed importing from Germany six Stiger Vortex guns in an attempt to break the 'great drought', which since 1896 had devastated large areas of Queensland.

Wragge had seen vignerons in northern Italy firing guns at storm clouds to try and reduce hailstones into raindrops. He theorised that the guns could be used in the outback as sure-fire drought-busters.

When they arrived the conical, 5m-high guns were assembled and installed around the town. On 26 September 1902, Wragge poured gunpowder into the guns and detonated them with fuses.

Horses bolted at the deafening noise and two of the guns exploded. Fortunately, no one was injured. Rain continued not to fall and Wragge left town the next day.

You can see two of the original guns on display in front of Bicentennial Park in Sturt St.

━━

Information

Tourist Information The tourist information centre (☎ 4654 3057) is located in the Bicentenary Park on the southern side of Charleville. This helpful office can supply details of points of interest in and around Charleville and the surrounding region. Between March and September the tourist information centre is open every day from 9 am to 6 pm; during the quieter – and hotter – summer months hours vary according to demand.

The Department of Environment also has an office (☎ 4654 1255) at the end of Park St, just off the highway and across the railway line; opening hours are weekdays from 8.30 am to 4.30 pm.

Fuel & Services The Shell Roadhouse at 50 Wills St is open from 7 am to 9 pm Monday to Thursday, and to 10 pm on Friday and Saturday; it takes all credit cards and has EFTPOS facilities.

The local RACQ depot is Bert's Body Shop (☎ 4654 1733, after hours ☎ 4654 1214) on Sturt St.

Post & Money There are Westpac and National banks in Wills St, and a Commonwealth Bank in Alfred St beside the post office.

Things to See & Do

The **Historic House Museum** at 91-93 Alfred St is an old Queenslander that was originally built as the Queensland Bank, and later became a private residence, then a guesthouse. Nowadays it's a folk museum with an impressive collection of memorabilia; entry costs $3.

The Department of Environment office (see the Information section) operates a captive breeding program and has an **aviary** and a **fauna display** where you can see several endangered species – such as yellow-footed rock wallaby, bridled nail-tail wallaby and bilby (sometimes called the rabbit-eared bandicoot) – in small enclosures.

At the front of a small park in Sturt St, you can see 1½ of the **Stiger Vortex Rainmaker Guns** that were used in a futile drought-breaking attempt on 26 September 1902. The half gun exploded during testing.

The volunteer-run **Skywatch** observatory at the Meteorological Bureau (4km south of the centre off Airport Drive) has high-powered telescopes which you can gaze through in the evenings. It opens every night (unless it's cloudy) between March and October; the sessions start at 6.30 pm from May to August and at 7 pm at other times, and run for 1½ to two hours. You need to book in advance at the tourist office

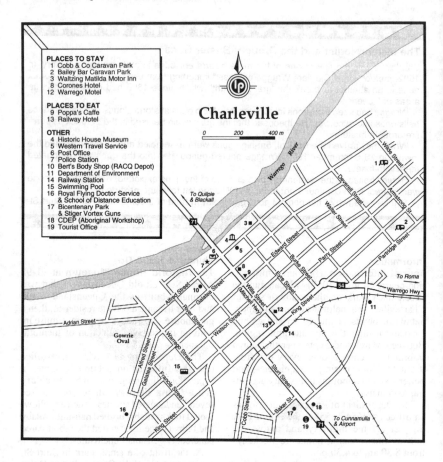

Charleville

PLACES TO STAY
1 Cobb & Co Caravan Park
2 Bailey Bar Caravan Park
3 Waltzing Matilda Motor Inn
8 Corones Hotel
12 Warrego Motel

PLACES TO EAT
9 Poppa's Caffe
13 Railway Hotel

OTHER
4 Historic House Museum
5 Western Travel Service
6 Post Office
7 Police Station
10 Bert's Body Shop (RACQ Depot)
11 Department of Environment
14 Railway Station
15 Swimming Pool
16 Royal Flying Doctor Service
     & School of Distance Education
17 Bicentenary Park
     & Stiger Vortex Guns
18 CDEP (Aboriginal Workshop)
19 Tourist Office

0   200   400 m

To Quilpie
& Blackall

To Roma

Warrego Hwy

To Cunnamulla
& Airport

or by phoning ☎ 4654 1260. The cost is $8 ($5 for children, $20 per family).

The office of the **Meteorological Bureau** also opens for free guided tours, and interested people can visit the vital facilities at the **Royal Flying Doctor Service base** (☎ 4654 1341) and the **School of the Air** (now called the School of Distance Education) – check with the information office.

Opposite the tourist office is the **CDEP Aboriginal Workshop**. It sells a few good handicrafts and can give an impromptu didjeridu demonstration.

Places to Stay

Caravan Parks The better of the two caravan parks here is the *Bailey Bar Caravan Park* (☎ 4654 1744) at 196 King St. It's a well-kept park with lots of grass and eucalypt trees; tent sites cost $10 ($12 powered), on-site vans $28 and self-contained cabins from $40.

Pubs On the corner of Wills and Galatea Sts, *Corones Hotel* (☎ 4654 1022) is one of Queensland's grand old country pubs. It doesn't look much from the outside but the interior is a monument to nostalgia, from the huge public bar with its lovely, simple leadlight windows to the honey-coloured timber lounge with its central staircase, old club lounge chairs, open fire and colonial furnishings. There are literally dozens of rooms upstairs. Simple pub-style rooms cost $10 per person twin share, or $30/40 with a private bathroom. There are also motel units out the back from $35/45.

Motels Charleville has three motels. The *Waltzing Matilda Motor Inn* (☎ 4654 1720) at 125 Alfred St is a straightforward little timber motel with a pool, spa and units around a central courtyard – singles/doubles go for $38/45. The *Warrego Motel* (☎ 4654 1299) at 75 Wills St has better units at $61/72.

Places to Eat
The *Railway Hotel* on the corner of Wills and King Sts has good-value bistro meals with barbecues on Friday nights, and a carvery on Saturday.

In the Corones Hotel on the corner of Wills and Galatea Sts, *The Carvery* is open evenings from Monday to Saturday. Beside the pub, *Poppa's Caffe* is a classy and stylish daytime cafe with excellent food – highly recommended and certainly a notch or two above your average country town cafe.

The cafe at the Shell Roadhouse on Wills St has pretty good breakfasts and takeaways.

Getting There & Away
Western Travel Service (☎ 4654 1260) at 94 Alfred St can handle all bus, train and plane reservations and ticket sales. Flight West has daily flights into Charleville from Brisbane via Roma, and twice-weekly direct flights from Brisbane.

McCafferty's buses pass through daily on the Brisbane to Mt Isa run.

The twice-weekly *Westlander* runs from Brisbane to Charleville; one-way fares are $77/107 for an economy seat/sleeper and $172 for a 1st class sleeper. There are connecting bus services to Cunnamulla and Quilpie.

CHARLEVILLE TO CUNNAMULLA
This 199km section of the Mitchell Hwy parallels the Warrego River (which is off to the west). The old railway line follows a similar route northward, and a couple of railway sidings, the odd station homestead and the small community of **Wyandra**, with the obligatory hotel and general store, make up the habitation profile of the trip to Cunnamulla. For the most part, the mainly flat country is clothed in mulga, a low tree of the wattle family.

CUNNAMULLA
pop 1670
The southernmost town in western Queensland, Cunnamulla is on the Warrego River 120km north of the Queensland/NSW border.

The town was gazetted in 1868 and in 1879 Cobb & Co established a coach station here. In the 1880s an influx of farmers opened up the country to sheep farming and today two million sheep graze the open plains around Cunnamulla. The railway arrived in 1898 and since then Cunnamulla has been a major service centre for the district; in good years it is Queensland's biggest wool-loading rail yard.

Information
Cunnamulla's tourist information centre (☎ 4655 2121) is based in the Shire Hall on Jane St.

The Commonwealth, National Australia and Westpac banks have branches in town, while the local RACQ depot is Bill's Auto (☎ 4655 1407).

Things to See
For sightseers, there's the **Historical Society Display** on John St, telling the story of the pioneers of the district, and the **Robber's Tree** at the southern end of Stockyard St, a reminder of a robbery that was bungled back in the 1880s. Another tree at the civic centre takes some importance from the fact that it is a yapunyah tree, floral emblem of the Paroo Shire – and this one was planted by royalty.

OUTBACK QUEENSLAND

Festivals

In late August the town celebrates the Cunnamulla-Eulo Festival of the Opal, a week-long festival with arts and crafts, a parade and ball. Another major event is the annual show, held in May.

Places to Stay

The *Jack Tonkin Caravan Park* (☎ 4655 1421) on Watson St has tent sites at $10 ($12 powered) and four cabins from $28 a double. The *Warrego Hotel-Motel* (☎ 4655 1737) at 9 Louise St has pub rooms at $25/35 and motel units at $45/55. The *Corella Motor Inn* (☎ 4655 1593) on the corner of Emma and Wicks Sts and the *Billabong Hotel-Motel* (☎ 4655 1225) at 5 Murray St both have units at $40/50.

Getting There & Away

There are bus services connecting Cunnamulla with the twice-weekly *Westlander* train service from Charleville to Brisbane.

The Channel Country

The remote and sparsely populated southwestern corner of Queensland, bordering the Northern Territory, South Australia and New South Wales, takes its name from the myriad channels which crisscross the area. In this inhospitable region it hardly ever rains, but water from the summer monsoons further north pours into the Channel Country along the Georgina, Hamilton and Diamantina rivers and Cooper Creek. Flooding towards the great depression of Lake Eyre in South Australia, the mass of water arrives on this huge plain, eventually drying up in water holes or salt pans.

Only on rare occasions (the early 1970s, 1989 and again in 1995) has the vast amount of water actually reached Lake Eyre and filled it. For a short period after each wet season, however, the Channel Country becomes fertile and cattle are grazed here.

Getting There & Around

Some roads from the east and north to the fringes of the Channel Country are paved, but during the October to May wet season even these can be cut – and the dirt roads become quagmires. In addition, the summer heat is unbearable, so a visit is best made in the cooler months – from May to September.

Visiting this area requires a sturdy vehicle (4WD if you want to get off the beaten track) and some experience of outback driving. If you're travelling anywhere west of Cunnamulla or Quilpie, always carry plenty of petrol and drinking water and notify the police, so that if you don't turn up at the next town, the necessary steps can be taken.

The main road through the Channel Country is the Diamantina Developmental Rd that runs south from Mt Isa through Boulia to Bedourie and then turns east through Windorah and Quilpie to Charleville. In all it's a long and lonely 1340km, a little over half of which is sealed.

The Kennedy Developmental Rd runs from Winton to Boulia and, for the most part, is surfaced with a couple of fuel and accommodation stops on the way.

MT ISA TO BOULIA

This 295km section of the Diamantina Developmental Rd is the northern access route into the Channel Country. This first section is over narrow, sealed bitumen. The only facilities along the route are at **Dajarra**, a small railway siding 150km south of Mt Isa. The *Dajarra Hotel* (☎ 4748 4955) has budget accommodation and there's a roadhouse.

BOULIA
pop 280

Boulia is the 'capital' of the Channel Country. Burke and Wills passed through here on their ill-fated trek, and there's a museum in a restored 1888 stone house in the little town. Near Boulia, the mysterious Min Min Light, a sort of earthbound UFO, is sometimes seen. It's said to resemble the headlights of a car and can hover a metre or two above the ground before vanishing and reappearing in a different place.

Boulia has the *Australian Motel/Hotel* (☎ 4746 3144), on Herbert St, with pub-style rooms at $30/35 for singles/doubles and motel units at $45/55. There's also the council-run *Boulia Caravan Park* (☎ 4746 3134), on the Winton road, with tent sites at $6.

The Shell Roadhouse (☎ 4746 3131), on Herbert St, is the local RACQ depot. If you need emergency fuel after hours, knock on the door of the house behind the roadhouse.

BOULIA TO WINTON

The Kennedy Developmental Rd links Boulia with Winton, 360km away. The only fuel stop along this route is 192km east of Boulia at **Middleton**. Middleton started out as a staging post for Cobb & Co coaches. The *Middleton Hotel* (☎ 4657 3980) sells fuel, serves meals daily and has two caravans which it rents out for $20 a night.

BEDOURIE
pop 60

Almost 200km south of Boulia is Bedourie. First settled in 1880 as a depot for Cobb & Co coaches, Bedourie is now the administrative centre for the huge Diamantina Shire council. You can get tourist information from the shire council offices (☎ 4746 1202), where there's a good rest stop with a shaded picnic and barbecue area and toilets.

The old *Royal Hotel* (☎ 4746 1201) hasn't changed much since it was built in 1880. The pub has budget accommodation at $25/30 for singles/doubles, sells fuel and acts as a post office agency. There's also a general store selling fuel, groceries and takeaway meals.

The impressive *Simpson Desert Roadhouse* (☎ 4746 1291) on the northern side of town sells super, unleaded and diesel fuel, as well as having a general store and a restaurant, and it's open from 9 am to 9 pm daily; there's a night bell for emergency fuel. The roadhouse also includes a motel with modern units from $45/57 for singles/doubles and a caravan park across the road with tent sites and powered sites.

Bedourie hosts a horse race meeting on the second weekend in September.

BIRDSVILLE
pop 100

This tiny settlement is the most remote place in Queensland and possesses one of Australia's most famous pubs – the Birdsville Hotel.

Birdsville, only 12km from the South Australian border, is at the northern end of the 481km Birdsville Track which leads down to Marree in South Australia. In the late 19th century, Birdsville was quite a busy place as cattle were driven south to South Australia and a customs charge was made on each head of cattle leaving Queensland. With Federation the charge was abolished and Birdsville almost became a ghost town. In recent years a growing tourism industry has revitalised the town; its big moment is the annual Birdsville Races, on the first weekend in September, when as many as 6000 racing and boozing enthusiasts make the trip to Birdsville.

Birdsville gets its water from a 1219m artesian well which delivers the water at over 100°C.

Information

The only banking facilities are at the Commonwealth Bank agency at the post office (☎ 4656 3263), although both service stations have EFTPOS facilities. Birdsville Auto (the Shell roadhouse) (☎ 4656 3226) is open daily from 8 am to 6 pm. This place is the local RACQ depot and can handle towing, all mechanical repairs and has a limited range of spare parts. There's also a Mobil service station opposite the pub. Both of these places sell super, unleaded and diesel (the most expensive fuel in Queensland), have EFTPOS facilities and take all major credit cards, and will also open for after-hours fuel.

Historic Brookland's Store, the ubiquitous general store, sells groceries and a bit of everything else. It is generally open from 8.30 am until 5 or 5.30 pm, and closes at lunchtime for a couple of hours.

Things to See & Do

One of Birdsville's highlights is a visit to the **Birdsville Working Museum**. From the outside it just looks like a big tin shed, but inside is one of the most impressive private museums you'll ever see. This well-presented collection includes an amazing array of ... well, stuff. Old tobacco tins and road signs, petrol bowsers and gas drums, farm machinery, drovers' gear, shearing equipment, wool presses, an art gallery, mule-driven rounding yards out the back, and lots more. Just about everything is in working order, and the owner, John Menzies, will take you on a private tour complete with demonstrations. The museum is open from 8.30 am to 8.30 pm daily; entry is good value at $5 for adults and $3 for kids.

Birdsville's **cemetery** has a grim, desolate setting among sand dunes and spinifex, with several small clusters of headstones – some marble, others just scraps of wood or tin with roughly tattooed epitaphs to those whose 'earthly race is run'. To get there, take the road towards Big Red and the Simpson Desert and turn right after 1km; a rocky, sandy track leads 1.5km to the cemetery.

Opposite the pub are two **stone memorials** to several expeditions which crossed the Simpson Desert with camels in the 1930s.

Flying To The Birdsville Races

Country race meetings are often low-key occasions on which the locals get together to bet on the horses and have a few beers. But Birdsville attracts thousands of people from all over the country. And they drink more than just a few beers.

The weekend is also notable for the hundreds of light aircraft that fly in. Normally one of the remotest runways in Australia, Birdsville aerodrome gets so busy that the Civil Aviation Safety Authority has to issue special flight rules to help control the traffic. So, being a city-based private pilot, I decided that this was an experience I ought to try.

Getting There & Away From Melbourne's Moorabbin Airport to Birdsville is about 1900km as the crow flies, and even further on the route we took in a single-engine Piper Arrow. We had planned a loop through central Queensland, but rain arrived over most of eastern Australia so we headed for Arkaroola in the Flinders Ranges instead. Amended flight plans are a fact of life for small aircraft. The manager at Arkaroola who refuelled the Arrow was surprised that we were going to the Birdsville Races. He said we seemed too intelligent.

Undeterred, we continued on the last leg, a two-hour flight that took us into a 'designated remote area'. The flat brown uniformity of the desert offers very few recognisable landmarks, so we had to trust the instruments and were quite glad when a town finally appeared ahead of us. This had to be Birdsville, if only because no other town would have so many planes at the aerodrome.

Even if you're not a pilot or the friend of one, consider getting a few people together to charter a plane; check the phone book under 'Aircraft Charter' or 'Flying Clubs'. If you prefer a commercial carrier, Flight West (an Ansett-related airline) flies from Brisbane on Monday and Thursday, while Augusta Airways flies up from Port Augusta on Saturday. You will need to book months ahead.

You can, of course, go by road, and several outback tour operators offer camping trips to the races. Buses will also take your camping gear if it's too heavy or bulky for the plane.

On Sunday morning the first engines start before dawn, waking everyone except the ter-

The **Birdsville Cup** race meet is held on the first weekend in September every year. The races are a fairly wild and woolly event with up to 6000 visitors driving or flying into town (see the boxed text Flying To The Birdsville Races) and consuming between them, according to the publican of the Birdsville Hotel, some 35 tonnes of beer, or 80,000 cans, over the weekend.

Places to Stay & Eat

The *Birdsville Caravan Park* (☎ 4656 3214) behind the Shell roadhouse, backs onto a billabong on the Diamantina River. The park has modern toilets and laundry facilities, hot showers and coin-operated barbecues, although the park is fairly barren and there isn't much shade. Powered sites cost $10 for the first person and $5 for extras, $15 for a family. There are no on-site vans or cabins here.

The *Birdsville Hotel* (☎ 4656 3244) dates from 1884 but has been tastefully and impressively renovated inside, with slate floors and whitewashed walls. The public bar has a collection of old photos, road signs and battered old bushmen's hats; and there are several other bars and a separate dining room. This is one of the great Australian pubs, full of outback history and characters – definitely not to be missed. Behind the pub is a row of modern, motel-style units with air-con and bathrooms, but no phones or TVs. Singles/doubles cost $45/70, triples/quads $78/92. Breakfast, lunch and dinner are served in the dining

minally inebriated, and from first light there is a steady stream of planes taking off. For some an early start is essential if they are to get home in daylight, even though the passengers might prefer to be sleeping off their hangovers. By midday Birdsville is just about empty again, except for the council workers who are already cleaning up.

Things to Do Getting drunk is the favourite activity, ahead of falling over and wearing tasteless T-shirts. Brawls used to be popular, but these days the crowds are fairly good-natured.

Evening entertainment is provided by Fred Brophy's boxing troupe who set up their tent in the centre of town, right across from the pub. This must be one of the last traditional travelling boxing troupes left in Australia – if not the world. Their days may be numbered since such acts are now outlawed in several other states. The bass drum booms out across the desert as the spruiker works the crowd (`Here's Mad Dingo. Who reckons he could fight Mad Dingo?'). There's always a few blokes drunk enough to try a few rounds against the professionals and no shortage of others who will pay to see them try.

Oh yes, there are horse races too, on Friday and Saturday. The bookmakers work with speed and efficiency to take your money, though you may find they move a bit slower if your horse wins.

Places to Stay & Eat Put your tent up right beside the plane, or just hang a plastic sheet over the wing. It can get cold at night and the ground is hard and stony, so bring a good sleeping bag and mat.

The Diamantina Shire Council provides temporary toilets and showers, complete with hot running water straight from the bore. Your nose will remind you that the sewage treatment pump runs 24 hours a day.

Don't count on eating at the pub – they're too busy selling beer. Hot dogs and steak sandwiches from the roadside stalls are as good as it gets, so bring your own.

Jim Hart

room – you'll need to book during the high season – or there are cheaper meals in the public bar. The pub is open from 10 am until around midnight; hours are limited on Sunday, usually from 11 am to 7 pm, and the pub closes between 1 and 5 pm on Sunday in summer.

Getting There & Away

Air Birdsville has its own sealed airstrip. Avgas, jet fuel and petrol are available through the hotel.

Two airlines have regular flights to Birdsville. Augusta Airways (☎ (086) 42 3100) has a weekly mail-run service between Port Augusta in South Australia and Birdsville, arriving in Birdsville on Saturday and leaving on Sunday. The one-way fare is $205.

Flight West Airlines (☎ 13 2392 within Queensland or toll-free ☎ 1800 777 879 from elsewhere in Australia) has a twice-weekly service between Brisbane and Birdsville via Charleville, Quilpie and Windorah; the one-way fare is $392.

Flight West Airlines also has a twice-weekly service between Mt Isa and Birdsville via Boulia and Bedourie; the one-way fare is $211.

Car & Motorcycle There are two roads into Birdsville from Queensland: the north-south Eyre Developmental Rd from Bedourie and Boulia, and the east-west Birdsville Developmental Rd from Windorah and Betoota.

Both of these routes are rough and unsealed, and while both can be tackled in a conventional vehicle you'd be much better off in a 4WD. The surfaces vary from gravel and dirt to soft red sand with frequent cattle grids and creek crossings. You need to watch out for the sudden dips at dry creek beds, particularly in a conventional vehicle – it's easy to bottom out and come to grief if you go too fast over these natural 'speed bumps'. Apart from the potholes, bull dust patches, dips and crests, another hazard are the sharp rocks; it's advisable to carry at least two spare tyres as well as plenty of drinking water and spare parts.

AROUND BIRDSVILLE

Off the Simpson Desert Rd about 40km west of Birdsville is **Big Red**, a massive wave-like sandhill which is a popular destination for 4WD travellers. Off the road to Bedourie, about 15km north of Birdsville, is a patch of rare **waddi trees** which only in central Australia.

Birdsville Track

To the south, the Birdsville Track passes between the Simpson Desert to the west and Sturt Stony Desert to the east. The first stretch from Birdsville has two alternative routes. Ask local advice about which is better. The Inner Track – marked 'not recommended' on most maps – crosses the Goyder Lagoon (the 'end' of the Diamantina River) and a big Wet will sometimes cut this route.

The longer, more easterly Outside Track crosses sandy country at the edge of the desert, where it is sometimes difficult to find the track.

While it is no longer necessary to register with the Birdsville police before tackling the track, it's a good idea to keep friends or relatives informed of your movements so they can notify the authorities should you fail to report in on time. You can contact the Birdsville police (☎ 4656 3220) for advice on road conditions.

Simpson Desert National Park

The waterless Simpson Desert occupies a massive 200,000 sq km of central Australia, and stretches across the Queensland, Northern Territory and South Australian borders. The Queensland section of the desert, in the far south-west corner of the state, is protected as the Simpson Desert National Park and adjoins South Australia's Simpson Desert Conservation Park and Simpson Desert Regional Reserve.

The park is a remote, arid region with a landscape of long, high sand dunes, and limited vegetation of spinifex, canegrass and various shrubs.

While conventional cars can tackle the Birdsville Track quite easily, the Simpson crossing requires a 4WD and far more preparation. Official advice is that crossings should only be tackled by parties of at least two 4WD vehicles and that you should have an HF radio to call for help if necessary. Temperatures are extreme, ranging from over 35°C in summer to freezing on some winter mornings. Travel in the summer months is not recommended.

There are no facilities, so you need to be totally self-sufficient and equipped with adequate supplies of water, food, fuel and spare parts. The park boundary is 80km west of Birdsville; from the boundary, it's another 70km to Poeppel Corner, the intersection of the three states.

Permits are required and you should advise the Birdsville police of your intended movements. Permits are available from the police station in Birdsville or from Department of Environment offices. For more information, contact the Department of Environment offices in Longreach (☎ 4658 1761), Emerald (☎ 4982 2246) or Charleville (☎ 4654 1255).

You also need a separate permit to travel into the South Australian sections of the park – these are available through the South Australian National Parks and Wildlife Service (☎ (086) 48 4244) in Hawker, South Australia.

BETOOTA
pop 1
The old pub which constituted the 'township' of Betoota, 164km east of Birdsville, closed its doors for good in September 1997. Simon Remienko the publican, who'd been keeping the flies company out here for 38 years, went into retirement. Although he'll still remain as Betoota's sole resident he'll no longer be offering facilities to passing motorists. This now means there are no fuel stops at all on the 395km stretch between Birdsville and Windorah. Motorists out this way should carry additional fuel.

WINDORAH
Windorah has a pub, a general store and a caravan park. *Gordon's General Store*

(☎ 4656 3145) is open from 8 am to 6 pm on weekdays, and from 8.30 am to 1.30 pm and from 4 to 6 pm on weekends, although it'll open at any time if you need fuel. It sells super, unleaded and diesel, plus a range of groceries and takeaway meals and it has EFTPOS and takes all major credit cards.

Across the road, the *Western Star Hotel* (☎ 4656 3166) is a colonial-style pub fronted by three tall eucalypts, with nine good, air-con rooms going for $25/35. It serves bistro meals on Friday nights, and can do evening meals other nights if you ring in advance and say you're coming.

The *Windorah Caravan Park* is a small fenced-in block on the west side of town, with a couple of trees and an amenities block.

QUILPIE
Quilpie is an opal-mining town and the railhead from which cattle, grazed here during the fertile wet season, are railed to the coast. The name Quilpie comes from the Aboriginal word for stone-curlew, and all but one of the town's streets are named after birds.

Information
The town has two pubs with rooms, a motel and a good swimming pool. For tourist information phone ☎ 4656 1133.

The local RACQ agent is John Crawley (☎ 4656 1344) at the Ampol service station on the corner of Chulungra and Boonkai Sts. You can also get fuel from the Mobil service station on Brolga St and from the Quilpie Cafe, which is open from 8 am to 9 pm daily.

Places to Stay
The *LR McManus Caravan Park* (☎ 4656 1371) in Chipu St, 100m off the highway, has tent sites at $10 ($12 powered).

The modern *Imperial Hotel-Motel* (☎ 4656 1300) on the corner of Brolga and Buln Buln Sts has average motel-style rooms in transportable units at $45/50 for singles/doubles, and serves bistro meals.

The *Quilpie Motor Inn* (☎ 4656 1277) on Brolga St 100m west of the centre, has good units from $45/50. If you're interested in staying on a cattle station in this area, the owner of this motel can book you in and take you out to one of five properties on his books – ring him and ask what's available.

Getting There & Away
There are bus services connecting Quilpie with the twice-weekly *Westlander* train service from Charleville to Brisbane.

QUILPIE TO CHARLEVILLE
There are a couple of small townships along this 210km section of the Diamantina Developmental Rd: **Cheepie**, 76km east of Quilpie, has a railway station and a phone booth, while **Cooladdi** 45km further east has a motel and general store that has emergency fuel. See the earlier Matilda Hwy section for information about the Charleville region.

CUNNAMULLA TO INNAMINCKA
Heading west from Cunnamulla 640km to Innamincka, the all-bitumen Bulloo Developmental Rd takes you through the small settlements of Eulo, Thargomindah and Noccundra. You can take a northern detour to the Yowah opalfields and if you have a 4WD you can continue west from Noccundra to Innamincka on the Strzelecki Track in South Australia.

Eulo
Eulo, 68km west of Cunnamulla, is on the Paroo River close to the Yowah opalfields. In late August/early September the town hosts the **World Lizard Racing Championships**. Next to the Eulo Queen Hotel is the **Destructo Cockroach Monument**, erected in memory of a racing cockroach who died when a punter stood on it. This granite plinth must be the only cockroach memorial in the world.

The *Eulo Queen Hotel* (☎ 4655 4867) has air-con pub rooms at $15/25 for singles/twins or there's the *Eulo Caravan Park* (☎ 4655 4890) with sites at $7 ($10 powered). The Eulo Store sells fuel and supplies.

Yowah
Yowah is an opal-mining settlement about 90km north-west of Eulo – the road is good bitumen most of the way with 23km of gravel at the final section. It's a popular fossicking field where boulder opals are found.

Yowah has a caravan park, a general store, a motel and a museum, and a couple of the mines open up for visitors. For tourist information call ☎ 4655 2481.

About 100km further north from Yowah are the **Duck Creek opalfields**.

Thargomindah
On the banks of the Bulloo River, Thargomindah is almost 200km south of Quilpie and almost 200km west of Cunnamulla. The road from Cunnamulla is good sealed bitumen; the majority of the route to Quilpie is unsealed. The town was gazetted back in 1874 and camel trains used to cross from here to Bourke in New South Wales.

The *Bulloo River Hotel-Motel* (☎ 4655 3125) has six air-con rooms at $30/40 for singles/doubles, and the *Thargomindah Oasis Motel* (☎ 4655 3155) has units from $40/45. There's also a council-run caravan park (☎ 4655 3133) with sites at $7 ($10 powered).

The pub serves bistro meals, and there's a cafe and restaurant at the *Oasis Motel*. Baxy's General Store sells fuel, as does the BP service station.

Contact the shire council offices (☎ 4655 3133) for further information.

Noccundra
pop 8
Noccundra, 145km further west on the Wilson River, was once a busy little community. It now has just a hotel. The *Noccundra Hotel* (☎ 4655 4317), a sandstone building which dates back to 1882, serves breakfasts and evening meals every day, and has a small guesthouse with air-con rooms at $15/25 for singles/twins and $35 for a double. The pub also sells super, unleaded and diesel fuel, and can handle some emergency repairs. It can also supply avgas with advance notice. If you're after a

meal or need a bed, it's best to ring in advance and say you're coming – you might miss out if you just blow in.

Continuing on from Noccundra, head 20km north back to the Bulloo Developmental Rd, which continues west for another 75km through the Jackson Oil Field to the Naccowlah Oil Field. The sealed road ends here but you can continue across to Innamincka on the Strzelecki Track in South Australia via the site of the **Dig Tree**, of Burke and Wills fame, on Nappa Merrie Station on the Cooper Creek, near the Queensland/South Australia border (see History in the Facts about Queensland chapter). This route is particularly rough and stony with frequent creek crossings, and is only recommended for 4WD vehicles. The road is usually closed during the Wet. If you are heading this way, check at the pub for directions – the signs tend to go missing along this route.

Glossary

Australian English

Any visitor from abroad who thinks Australian (that's 'Strine') is simply a weird variant of English/American will soon have a few surprises. For a start many Australians don't even speak Australian – they speak Italian, Lebanese, Vietnamese, Turkish or Greek.

Those who do speak the native tongue are liable to lose you in a strange collection of Australian words. Some have completely different meanings in Australia than they have in other English-speaking countries; some commonly used words have been shortened almost beyond recognition. Others are derived from Aboriginal languages or from the slang used by early convict settlers.

There is a slight regional variation in the Australian accent, while the difference between city and country speech is mainly a matter of speed. Some of the most famed Aussie words are hardly heard at all – 'mates' are more common than 'cobbers'. If you want to pass for a native try to speak slightly nasally, shorten any word of more than two syllables and add a vowel to the end of it, make anything you can into a diminutive (even the Hell's Angels can become mere 'bikies') and pepper your speech with as many expletives as possible.

Lonely Planet publishes an *Australian phrasebook*, which is an introduction to both Australian English and Aboriginal languages, and the list that follows may also help:

arvo – afternoon
avagoyermug – traditional rallying call, especially at cricket matches
award wage – minimum pay rate

back o' Bourke – back of beyond, middle of nowhere
bail out – leave
bail up – hold up, rob, earbash

banana bender – resident of Queensland
barbie – barbecue (BBQ)
barrack – cheer on team at sporting event, support (as in 'who do you barrack for?')
bastard – general form of address which can mean many things, from high praise or respect ('He's the bravest bastard I know') to dire insult ('You rotten bastard!'). Only use on males and avoid if unsure!
battler – hard trier, struggler
beaut, beauty, bewdie – great, fantastic
be-mer – sea cucumber, bêche-de-mer
big mobs – a large amount, heaps
bikies – motorcyclists
billabong – water hole in dried up riverbed, more correctly an ox-bow bend cut off in the dry season by receding waters
billy – tin container used to boil tea in the bush
bitumen – surfaced road
black stump – where the 'back o' Bourke' begins
block (ie 'to do your block') – to lose your temper
bloke – man
blow-in – stranger
blowies – blowflies
bludger – lazy person, one who won't work
blue (ie 'have a blue') – to have an argument or fight
bluey – swag, or nickname for a red-haired person
bonzer – great, ripper
boogie board – half-sized surfboard
boomer – very big, a particularly large male kangaroo
boomerang – a curved flat wooden instrument used by Aboriginal people for hunting
booze bus – police van used for random breath testing for alcohol
bot – scrounger
bottle shop – liquor shop
brekky – breakfast
Buckley's – no chance at all
bug (Moreton Bay bug) – a small edible crustacean

bull dust – fine and sometimes deep dust on outback roads; also bullshit
bunyip – mythical bush spirit
burl – have a try (as in 'give it a burl')
bush, the – country, anywhere away from the city
bushbash – to force your way through pathless bush
bushranger – Australia's equivalent of the outlaws of the Wild West (some goodies, some baddies)
bush tucker – native foods, usually in the outback

camp oven – large, cast-iron pot with lid, used for cooking on an open fire
cark it – to die
cask – boxed wine (a great Australian invention)
chain – archaic unit of measurement, still in use in Queensland
Chiko roll – vile Australian junk food
chocka – completely full, from 'chock-a-block'
chook – chicken
chuck a U-ey – do a U-turn
clobber – to hit, also clothes
clout – to hit
cobber – mate (archaic)
cocky – small-scale farmer
compo – compensation, such as workers' compensation
counter meal, countery – pub meal
cow cocky – small-scale cattle farmer
crack the shits – lose your temper, also 'crack a mental'
crook – ill, badly made, substandard
crow eater – resident of South Australia
cut lunch – sandwiches

dag, daggy – dirty lump of wool at back end of a sheep; also an affectionate or mildly abusive term for a socially inept person
daks – trousers
damper – bush loaf made from flour and water and cooked in a camp oven
dead horse – tomato sauce
dead set – fair dinkum, true
deli – milk bar in South and Western Australia, but a delicatessen elsewhere.

didjeridu – cylindrical wooden musical instrument traditionally played by Aboriginal men
dill – idiot
dinkum, fair dinkum – honest, genuine
dinky-di – the real thing
dip out – to miss out or fail
divvy van – police divisional van
dob in – to tell on someone
donk – car or boat engine
down south – the rest of Australia, according to anyone north of Brisbane
drongo – worthless or stupid person
Dry, the – dry season in northern Australia (April to October)
duco – car paint
dunny – outdoor lavatory
dunny budgies – blowies

earbash – talk nonstop
esky – insulated box for keeping beer cold

fair crack of the whip! – fair go!
fair go! – give us a break
flake – shark meat, used in fish and chips
flat out – very busy or fast
floater – meat pie floating in pea soup
flog – sell, steal
fossick – hunt for gems
from arsehole to breakfast – all over the place
furphy – a rumour or false story

galah – noisy cockatoo, thus noisy idiot
game – brave (as in 'game as Ned Kelly')
gander – look (as in 'have a gander')
garbo – person who collects your garbage
g'day – good day, traditional Australian greeting
gibber – Aboriginal word for a stone or rock, hence gibber plain or desert
give it away – give up
good on ya – well done
grazier – large-scale sheep or cattle farmer
grog – general term for alcoholic drinks
grouse – very good

haitch – aitch, the 8th letter of the alphabet
homestead – residence of a station owner or manager

hoon – idiot, hooligan, yahoo
how are ya? – standard greeting, expected answer 'good, thanks, how are *you*?'

icy-pole – frozen lolly water on a stick
iffy – dodgy, questionable

jackaroo – young male trainee on a station (farm)
jiffy – a very short time
jillaroo – young female trainee on a station
jocks – men's underpants
journo – journalist
jumped-up – full of self-importance, arrogant
jumper – sweater

kick the bucket – to die
kiwi – New Zealander
knock – criticise, deride
knocker – one who knocks
Koori – Aboriginal person (mostly south of the Murray River)

lair – layabout, ruffian
lairising – acting like a lair
lamington – square of sponge cake covered in chocolate icing and coconut
larrikin – a bit like a lair
lay-by – put a deposit on an article so the shop will hold it for you
lob in – drop in (to see someone)
lollies – sweets, candy
lurk – a scheme

mate – general term of familiarity, whether you know the person or not
Mexican – resident of Victoria (ie from south of the border)
milk bar – general store
mozzies – mosquitoes
mulga – outback tree or shrub, usually covering a large area

never-never – remote country in the outback
no hoper – hopeless case
no worries – she'll be right, that's OK
northern summer – summer in the northern hemisphere

ocker – an uncultivated or boorish Australian
off-sider – assistant or partner
OS – overseas, as in 'he's gone OS'
outback – remote part of the bush, back o' Bourke

paddock – a fenced area of land, usually intended for livestock
pastoralist – large-scale grazier
pavlova – traditional Australian meringue and cream dessert, named after the Russian ballerina Anna Pavlova
perve – to gaze with lust
piker – someone who doesn't pull their weight, or who chickens out
pinch – steal
piss – beer
piss turn – boozy party, also piss up
pissed – drunk
pissed off – annoyed
piss weak – no good, gutless
plonk – cheap wine
pokies – poker machines
Pom – English person
postie – mailman

Queenslander – traditional timber dwelling

ratbag – friendly term of abuse
ratshit (RS) – lousy
rapt – delighted, enraptured
reckon! – you bet!, absolutely!
rego – registration, as in 'car rego'
rellie – family relative
ridgy-didge – original, genuine
ring-in – a substitute or outsider
ripper – good (also 'little ripper')
road train – semitrailer-trailer-trailer
root – have sexual intercourse
rooted – tired, broken
ropable – very bad-tempered or angry
rubbish (ie to rubbish) – deride, tease

Salvo – member of the Salvation Army
sandgroper – resident of Western Australia
scallops – fried potato cakes (Queensland, New South Wales), shellfish (elsewhere)
schooner – large beer glass (New South Wales, South Australia)

scrub – bush
sealed road – bitumen road
sea wasp – deadly box jellyfish
session – lengthy period of heavy drinking
Shanks' pony – to travel on foot
shark biscuit – an inexperienced surfer
sheila – woman
shellacking – comprehensive defeat
she'll be right – no worries
shonky – unreliable
shoot through – leave in a hurry
shout – buy a round of drinks (as in 'it's your shout')
sickie – day off work ill (or malingering)
slab – carton of beer bottles or cans
smoko – tea break
snag – sausage
sparrow's fart – dawn
spunk – good-looking person
squatter – pioneer farmer who occupied land as a tenant of the government
station – large farm
sticky beak – nosy person
stinger – (deadly) box jellyfish
strides – daks
stroppy – bad tempered
stubby – 375ml bottle of beer
Stubbies – popular brand of men's work shorts
sunbake – sunbathe (well, the sun's hot in Australia)
swag – canvas-covered bed roll used in the outback; also a large quantity

tall poppies – achievers (knockers like to cut them down)
tea – evening meal
thingo – thing, whatchamacallit, doovelacki, thingamajig
thongs – flip-flops, an ocker's idea of formal footwear
tinny – 375ml can of beer; also a small, aluminium fishing dinghy

togs – swimming costume (Queensland, Victoria)
too right! – absolutely!
Top End – northern part of the Northern Territory
trucky – truck driver
true blue – dinkum
tucker – food
two-pot screamer – person unable to consume a large quantity of alcohol
two-up – traditional heads/tails gambling game

uni – university
up north – New South Wales and Queensland when viewed from Victoria
ute – utility, pick-up truck

vegie – vegetable

wag (ie to wag) – to skip school or work
wagon – station wagon, estate car
walkabout – lengthy walk away from it all
wallaby track (on the) – to wander from place to place seeking work (archaic)
weatherboard – wooden house
Wet, the – rainy season in the north
wharfie – dockworker
whinge – complain, moan
wobbly – disturbing, unpredictable behaviour (as in 'throw a wobbly')
woomera – stick used by Aborigines for throwing spears
woop-woop – outback, miles from anywhere

yabbie – freshwater crayfish
yahoo – noisy and unruly person
yakka – work (from an Aboriginal language)
yobbo – uncouth, aggressive person
yonks – ages; a long time
youse – plural of you, pronounced 'yooze'

Index

TEXT

BOXED TEXT

LONELY PLANET

Phrasebooks

L onely Planet phrasebooks are packed with essential words and phrases to help travellers communicate with the locals. With colour tabs for quick reference, an extensive vocabulary and use of script, these handy pocket-sized language guides cover day-to-day travel situations.

- handy pocket-sized books
- easy to understand Pronunciation chapter
- clear & comprehensive Grammar chapter
- romanisation alongside script to allow ease of pronunciation
- script throughout so users can point to phrases for every situation
- full of cultural information and tips for the traveller

'... vital for a real DIY spirit and attitude in language learning'
    – *Backpacker*

'the phrasebooks have good cultural backgrounders and offer solid advice for challenging situations in remote locations'
    – *San Francisco Examiner*

Arabic (Egyptian) • Arabic (Moroccan) • Australian *(Australian English, Aboriginal and Torres Strait languages)* • Baltic States *(Estonian, Latvian, Lithuanian)* • Bengali • Brazilian • Burmese • British *(English, dialects, Scottish Gaelic, Welsh)* • Cantonese • Central Asia *(Kazakh, Kyrgyz, Pashto, Tajik, Tashkorghani, Turkmen, Uyghur, Uzbek & others)* • Central Europe *(Czech, German, Hungarian, Polish, Slovak, Slovene)* • Costa Rica Spanish • Eastern Europe *(Albanian, Bulgarian, Croatian, Czech, Hungarian, Macedonian, Polish, Romanian, Serbian, Slovak, Slovene)* • East Timor *(Tetun, Portuguese)* • Egyptian Arabic • Ethiopian *(Amharic)* • Europe *(Basque, Catalan, Dutch, French, German, Greek, Irish, Italian, Maltese, Portuguese, Scottish Gaelic, Spanish, Turkish, Welsh)* • Farsi *(Persian)* • Fijian • French • German • Greek • Hebrew • Hill Tribes *(Lahu, Akha, Lisu, Mong, Mien & others)* • Hindi/Urdu • Indonesian • Italian • Japanese • Korean • Lao • Latin American Spanish • Malay • Mandarin • Mongolian • Moroccan Arabic • Nepali • Papua New Guinea • Pidgin • Pilipino (Tagalog) • Polish • Portuguese • Quechua • Russian • Scandinavian *(Danish, Faroese, Finnish, Icelandic, Norwegian, Swedish)* • South-East Asia *(Burmese, Indonesian, Khmer, Lao, Malay, Tagalog Pilipino, Thai, Vietnamese)* • South Pacific *(Fijian, Hawaiian, Kanak languages, Maori, Niuean, Rapanui, Rarotongan Maori, Samoan, Tahitian, Tongan & others)* • Spanish *(Castilian, also includes Catalan, Galician & Basque)* • Sri Lanka • Swahili • Thai • Tibetan • Turkish • Ukrainian • USA *(US English, Vernacular, Native American, Hawaiian)* • Vietnamese

Lonely Planet Journeys

JOURNEYS is a unique collection of travel writing – published by the company that understands travel better than anyone else. It is a series for anyone who has ever experienced – or dreamed of – the magical moment when they encountered a strange culture or saw a place for the first time. They are tales to read while you're planning a trip, while you're on the road or while you're in an armchair in front of a fire.

These outstanding titles explore our planet through the eyes of a diverse group of international writers. JOURNEYS books catch the spirit of a place, illuminate a culture, recount a crazy adventure or introduce a fascinating way of life. They always entertain, and always enrich the experience of travel.

IN RAJASTHAN
Royina Grewal

As she writes of her travels through Rajasthan, Indian writer Royina Grewal takes us behind the exotic facade of this fabled destination: here is an insider's perceptive account of India's most colourful state, conveying the excitement and challenges of a region in transition.

SHOPPING FOR BUDDHAS
Jeff Greenwald

In his obsessive search for the perfect Buddha statue in the backstreets of Kathmandu, Jeff Greenwald discovers more than he bargained for ... and his souvenir-hunting turns into an ironic metaphor for the clash between spiritual riches and material greed. Politics, religion and serious shopping collide in this witty account of an enlightening visit to Nepal.

BRIEF ENCOUNTERS
Stories of Love, Sex & Travel
edited by Michelle de Kretser

Love affairs on the road, passionate holiday flings, disastrous pick-ups, erotic encounters ... In this seductive collection of stories, 22 authors from around the world write about travel romances. A tourist in Peru falls for her handsome guide; a writer explores the ambiguities of his relationship with a Japanese woman; a beautiful young man on a train proposes marriage ... Combining fiction and reportage, *Brief Encounters* is must-have reading – for everyone who has dreamt of escape with that perfect stranger.

Includes stories by Pico Iyer, Mary Morris, Emily Perkins, Mona Simpson, Lisa St Aubin de Terán, Paul Theroux and Sara Wheeler.

LONELY PLANET

Lonely Planet Travel Atlases

Lonely Planet has long been famous for the number and quality of its guidebook maps. Now we've gone one step further and produced a handy companion series: Lonely Planet travel atlases – maps of a country produced in book form.

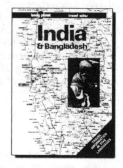

Unlike other maps, which look good but lead travellers astray, our travel atlases have been researched on the road by Lonely Planet's experienced team of writers. All details are carefully checked to ensure the atlas corresponds with the equivalent Lonely Planet guidebook.

- full-colour throughout
- maps researched and checked by Lonely Planet authors
- place names correspond with Lonely Planet guidebooks
- no confusing spelling differences
- legend and travelling information in English, French, German, Japanese and Spanish
- size: 230 x 160 mm

Available now: Chile & Easter Island ● Egypt ● India & Bangladesh ● Israel & the Palestinian Territories ● Jordan, Syria & Lebanon ● Kenya ● Laos ● Portugal ● South Africa, Lesotho & Swaziland ● Thailand ● Turkey ● Vietnam ● Zimbabwe, Botswana & Namibia

---

Lonely Planet TV Series & Videos

Lonely Planet travel guides have been brought to life on television screens around the world. Like our guides, the programs are based on the joy of independent travel, and look honestly at some of the most exciting, picturesque and frustrating places in the world. Each show is presented by one of three travellers from Australia, England or the USA and combines an innovative mixture of video, Super-8 film, atmospheric soundscapes and original music.

Videos of each episode – containing additional footage not shown on television – are available from good book and video shops, but the availability of individual videos varies with regional screening schedules.

Video destinations include: Alaska ● American Rockies ● Australia – The South-East ● Baja California & the Copper Canyon ● Brazil ● Central Asia ● Chile & Easter Island ● Corsica, Sicily & Sardinia – The Mediterranean Islands ● East Africa (Tanzania & Zanzibar) ● Ecuador & the Galapagos Islands ● Greenland & Iceland ● Indonesia ● Israel & the Sinai Desert ● Jamaica ● Japan ● La Ruta Maya ● Morocco ● New York ● North India ● Pacific Islands (Fiji, Solomon Islands & Vanuatu) ● South India ● South West China ● Turkey ● Vietnam ● West Africa ● Zimbabwe, Botswana & Namibia

The Lonely Planet TV series is produced by: Pilot Productions
The Old Studio
18 Middle Row
London W10 5AT, UK

LONELY PLANET

FREE Lonely Planet Newsletters

We love hearing from you and think you'd like to hear from us.

Planet Talk

Our FREE quarterly printed newsletter is full of tips from travellers and anecdotes from Lonely Planet guidebook authors. Every issue is packed with up-to-date travel news and advice, and includes:

- a postcard from Lonely Planet co-founder Tony Wheeler
- a swag of mail from travellers
- a look at life on the road through the eyes of a Lonely Planet author
- topical health advice
- prizes for the best travel yarn
- news about forthcoming Lonely Planet events
- a complete list of Lonely Planet books and other titles

To join our mailing list, residents of the UK, Europe and Africa can email us at go@lonelyplanet.co.uk; residents of North and South America can email us at info@lonelyplanet.com; the rest of the world can email us at talk2us@lonelyplanet.com.au, or contact any Lonely Planet office.

Comet

Our FREE monthly email newsletter brings you all the latest travel news, features, interviews, competitions, destination ideas, travellers' tips & tales, Q&As, raging debates and related links. Find out what's new on the Lonely Planet Web site and which books are about to hit the shelves.

Subscribe from your desktop: www.lonelyplanet.com/comet

Guides by Region

Lonely Planet is known worldwide for publishing practical, reliable and no-nonsense travel information in our guides and on our Web site. The Lonely Planet list covers just about every accessible part of the world. Currently there are sixteen series: Travel guides, Shoestring guides, Condensed guides, Phrasebooks, Read This First, Healthy Travel, Walking guides, Cycling guides, Watching Wildlife guides, Pisces Diving & Snorkelling guides, City Maps, Road Atlases, Out to Eat, World Food, Journeys travel literature, Traveller's Advice titles and Illustrated pictorials.

AFRICA Africa on a shoestring • Cairo • Cairo Map • Cape Town • Cape Town Map • East Africa • Egypt • Egyptian Arabic phrasebook • Ethiopia, Eritrea & Djibouti • Ethiopian (Amharic) phrasebook • The Gambia & Senegal • Healthy Travel Africa • Kenya • Malawi • Morocco • Moroccan Arabic phrasebook • Mozambique • Read This First: Africa • South Africa, Lesotho & Swaziland • Southern Africa • Southern Africa Road Atlas • Swahili phrasebook • Tanzania, Zanzibar & Pemba • Trekking in East Africa • Tunisia • Watching Wildlife East Africa • Watching Wildlife Southern Africa • West Africa • World Food Morocco • Zimbabwe, Botswana & Namibia
Travel Literature: Mali Blues: Traveling to an African Beat • The Rainbird: A Central African Journey • Songs to an African Sunset: A Zimbabwean Story

AUSTRALIA & THE PACIFIC Aboriginal Australia & Torres Strait Islands • Auckland • Australia • Australian phrasebook • Australia Road Atlas • Bushwalking in Australia • Cycling Australia • Cycling New Zealand • Fiji • Fijian phrasebook • Healthy Travel Australia, NZ and the Pacific • Islands of Australia's Great Barrier Reef • Melbourne • Melbourne Map • Micronesia • New Caledonia • New South Wales & the ACT • New Zealand • Northern Territory • Outback Australia • Out to Eat – Melbourne • Out to Eat – Sydney • Papua New Guinea • Papua New Guinea Phrasebook • Pidgin phrasebook • Queensland • Rarotonga & the Cook Islands • Samoa • Solomon Islands • South Australia • South Pacific • South Pacific phrasebook • Sydney • Sydney Map • Sydney Condensed • Tahiti & French Polynesia • Tasmania • Tonga • Tramping in New Zealand • Vanuatu • Victoria • Walking in Australia • Watching Wildlife Australia • Western Australia
Travel Literature: Islands in the Clouds: Travels in the Highlands of New Guinea • Kiwi Tracks: A New Zealand Journey • Sean & David's Long Drive

CENTRAL AMERICA & THE CARIBBEAN Bahamas, Turks & Caicos • Baja California • Bermuda • Central America on a shoestring • Costa Rica • Costa Rica Spanish phrasebook • Cuba • Dominican Republic & Haiti • Eastern Caribbean • Guatemala • Guatemala, Belize & Yucatán: La Ruta Maya • Havana • Healthy Travel Central & South America • San Diego & Tijuana • Jamaica • Mexico • Mexico City • Panama • Puerto Rico • Read This First: Central & South America • World Food Mexico • World Food Caribbean • Yucatán
Travel Literature: Green Dreams: Travels in Central America

EUROPE Amsterdam • Amsterdam Map • Amsterdam Condensed • Andalucía • Austria • Baltic States phrasebook • Barcelona • Barcelona Map • Belgium & Luxembourg • Berlin • Berlin Map • Britain • British phrasebook • Brussels, Bruges & Antwerp • Brussels Map • Budapest • Budapest Map • Canary Islands • Central Europe • Central Europe phrasebook • Copenhagen • Corfu & the Ionians • Corsica • Crete • Crete Condensed • Croatia • Cycling Britain • Cycling France • Cyprus • Czech & Slovak Republics • Denmark • Dublin • Dublin Map • Eastern Europe • Eastern Europe phrasebook • Edinburgh • England • Estonia, Latvia & Lithuania • Europe on a shoestring • Europe Phrasebook • Finland • Florence • France • Frankfurt Condensed • French phrasebook • Georgia, Armenia & Azerbaijan • Germany • German phrasebook • Greece • Greek Islands • Greek phrasebook • Hungary • Iceland, Greenland & the Faroe Islands • Ireland • Istanbul • Italian phrasebook • Italy • Krakow • Lisbon • The Loire • London • London Map • London Condensed • Madrid • Malta • Mediterranean Europe • Milan, Turin & Genoa • Moscow • Mozambique • Munich • The Netherlands • Normandy • Norway • Out to Eat – London • Paris • Paris Map • Paris Condensed • Poland • Polish Phrasebook • Portugal • Portuguese phrasebook • Prague • Prague Map • Provence & the Côte d'Azur • Read This First: Europe • Rhodes & the Dodecanese • Romania & Moldova • Rome • Rome Condensed • Rome Map • Russia, Ukraine & Belarus • Russian phrasebook • Scandinavian & Baltic Europe • Scandinavian phrasebook • Scotland • Sicily • Slovenia • South-West France • Spain • Spanish phrasebook • St Petersburg • St Petersburg Map • Sweden • Switzerland • Trekking in Spain • Tuscany • Ukrainian phrasebook • Venice • Vienna • Walking in Britain • Walking in France • Walking in Ireland • Walking in Italy • Walking in Spain • Walking in Switzerland • Western Europe • World Food France • World Food Ireland • World Food Italy • World Food Spain
Travel Literature: A Small Place in Italy • After Yugoslavia • Love and War in the Apennines • On the Shores of the Mediterranean The Olive Grove: Travels in Greece • Round Ireland in Low Gear

LONELY PLANET

Mail Order

Lonely Planet products are distributed worldwide. They are also available by mail order from Lonely Planet, so if you have difficulty finding a title please write to us. North and South American residents should write to 150 Linden St, Oakland, CA 94607, USA; European and African residents should write to 10a Spring Place, London NW5 3BH, UK; and residents of other countries to Locked Bag 1, Footscray, Victoria 3011, Australia.

INDIAN SUBCONTINENT Bangladesh • Bengali phrasebook • Bhutan • Delhi • Goa • Healthy Travel Asia & India • Hindi & Urdu phrasebook • India • Indian Himalaya • Karakoram Highway • Kerala • Mumbai (Bombay) • Nepal • Nepali phrasebook • Pakistan • Rajasthan • Read This First: Asia & India • South India • Sri Lanka • Sri Lanka phrasebook • Tibet • Tibetan phrasebook • Trekking in the Indian Himalaya • Trekking in the Karakoram & Hindukush • Trekking in the Nepal Himalaya
Travel Literature: The Age of Kali: Indian Travels and Encounters • Hello Goodnight: A Life of Goa • In Rajasthan • A Season in Heaven: True Tales from the Road to Kathmandu • Shopping for Buddhas • A Short Walk in the Hindu Kush • Slowly Down the Ganges

ISLANDS OF THE INDIAN OCEAN Madagascar & Comoros • Maldives • Mauritius, Réunion & Seychelles
Travel Literature: Maverick in Madagascar

MIDDLE EAST & CENTRAL ASIA Bahrain, Kuwait & Qatar • Central Asia • Central Asia phrasebook • Dubai • Farsi (Persian) phrasebook • Hebrew phrasebook • Iran • Israel & the Palestinian Territories • Istanbul • Istanbul Map • Istanbul to Cairo on a shoestring • Istanbul to Kathmandu • Jerusalem • Jerusalem Map • Jordan • Lebanon • Middle East • Oman & the United Arab Emirates • Syria • Turkey • Turkish phrasebook • World Food Turkey • Yemen
Travel Literature: Black on Black: Iran Revisited • The Gates of Damascus • Kingdom of the Film Stars: Journey into Jordan

NORTH AMERICA Alaska • Boston • Boston Map • Boston Condensed • British Colombia • California & Nevada • California Condensed • Canada • Chicago • Chicago Map • Deep South • Florida • Great Lakes • Hawaii • Hiking in Alaska • Hiking in the USA • Honolulu • Las Vegas • Los Angeles • Los Angeles Map • Louisiana & The Deep South • Miami • Miami Map • Montreal • New England • New Orleans • New York City • New York City Map • New York City Condensed • New York, New Jersey & Pennsylvania • Oahu • Out to Eat – San Francisco • Pacific Northwest • Puerto Rico • Rocky Mountains • San Francisco • San Francisco Map • San Diego & Tijuana • Seattle • Southwest • Texas • Toronto • USA • USA phrasebook • Vancouver • Virginia & the Capital Region • Washington DC • Washington DC Map • World Food Deep South, USA • World Food New Orleans
Travel Literature: Caught Inside: A Surfer's Year on the California Coast • Drive Thru America

NORTH-EAST ASIA Beijing • Beijing Map • Cantonese phrasebook • China • Hiking in Japan • Hong Kong • Hong Kong Map • Hong Kong Condensed • Hong Kong, Macau & Guangzhou • Japan • Japanese phrasebook • Korea • Korean phrasebook • Kyoto • Mandarin phrasebook • Mongolia • Mongolian phrasebook • Seoul • Shanghai • South-West China • Taiwan • Tokyo • World Food – Hong Kong
Travel Literature: In Xanadu: A Quest • Lost Japan

SOUTH AMERICA Argentina, Uruguay & Paraguay • Bolivia • Brazil • Brazilian phrasebook • Buenos Aires • Chile & Easter Island • Colombia • Ecuador & the Galapagos Islands • Healthy Travel Central & South America • Latin American Spanish phrasebook • Peru • Quechua phrasebook • Read This First: Central & South America • Rio de Janeiro • Rio de Janeiro Map • Santiago • South America on a shoestring • Santiago • Trekking in the Patagonian Andes • Venezuela
Travel Literature: Full Circle: A South American Journey

SOUTH-EAST ASIA Bali & Lombok • Bangkok • Bangkok Map • Burmese phrasebook • Cambodia • East Timor Phrasebook • Hanoi • Healthy Travel Asia & India • Hill Tribes phrasebook • Ho Chi Minh City • Indonesia • Indonesian phrasebook • Indonesia's Eastern Islands • Jakarta • Java • Lao phrasebook • Laos • Malay phrasebook • Malaysia, Singapore & Brunei • Myanmar (Burma) • Philippines • Pilipino (Tagalog) phrasebook • Read This First: Asia & India • Singapore • Singapore Map • South-East Asia on a shoestring • South-East Asia phrasebook • Thailand • Thailand's Islands & Beaches • Thailand, Vietnam, Laos & Cambodia Road Atlas • Thai phrasebook • Vietnam • Vietnamese phrasebook • World Food Thailand • World Food Vietnam

ALSO AVAILABLE: Antarctica • The Arctic • The Blue Man: Tales of Travel, Love and Coffee • Brief Encounters: Stories of Love, Sex & Travel • Chasing Rickshaws • The Last Grain Race • Lonely Planet Unpacked • Not the Only Planet: Science Fiction Travel Stories • Lonely Planet On the Edge • Sacred India • Travel with Children • Travel Photography: A Guide to Taking Better Pictures

The Lonely Planet Story

Lonely Planet published its first book in 1973 in response to the numerous 'How did you do it?' questions Maureen and Tony Wheeler were asked after driving, bussing, hitching, sailing and railing their way from England to Australia.

Written at a kitchen table and hand collated, trimmed and stapled, *Across Asia on the Cheap* became an instant local bestseller, inspiring thoughts of another book.

Eighteen months in South-East Asia resulted in their second guide, *South-East Asia on a shoestring*, which they put together in a backstreet Chinese hotel in Singapore in 1975. The 'yellow bible', as it quickly became known to backpackers around the world, soon became *the* guide to the region. It has sold well over half a million copies and is now in its 9th edition, still retaining its familiar yellow cover.

Today there are over 350 titles, including travel guides, walking guides, language kits & phrasebooks, travel atlases, diving guides and travel literature. The company is the largest independent travel publisher in the world. Although Lonely Planet initially specialised in guides to Asia, today there are few corners of the globe that have not been covered.

The emphasis continues to be on travel for independent travellers. Tony and Maureen still travel for several months of each year and play an active part in the writing, updating and quality control of Lonely Planet's guides.

They have been joined by over 120 authors and 280 staff at our offices in Melbourne (Australia), Oakland (USA), London (UK) and Paris (France). Travellers themselves also make a valuable contribution to the guides through the feedback we receive in thousands of letters each year and on our web site.

The people at Lonely Planet strongly believe that travellers can make a positive contribution to the countries they visit, both through their appreciation of the countries' culture, wildlife and natural features, and through the money they spend. In addition, the company makes a direct contribution to the countries and regions it covers. Since 1986 a percentage of the income from each book has been donated to ventures such as famine relief in Africa; aid projects in India; agricultural projects in Central America; Greenpeace's efforts to halt French nuclear testing in the Pacific; and Amnesty International.

LONELY PLANET OFFICES

Australia
Locked Bag 1, Footscray, Victoria 3011
☎ 03 8379 8000 fax 03 8379 8111
email: talk2us@lonelyplanet.com.au

USA
150 Linden St, Oakland, CA 94607
☎ 510 893 8555 TOLL FREE: 800 275 8555
fax 510 893 8572
email: info@lonelyplanet.com

UK
10a Spring Place, London NW5 3BH
☎ 020 7428 4800 fax 020 7428 4828
email: go@lonelyplanet.co.uk

France
1 rue du Dahomey, 75011 Paris
☎ 01 55 25 33 00 fax 01 55 25 33 01
email: bip@lonelyplanet.fr
www.lonelyplanet.fr

World Wide Web: www.lonelyplanet.com *or* AOL keyword: lp
Lonely Planet Images: lpi@lonelyplanet.com.au